BEST AMERICAN PLAYS

Fifth Series—1957-1963

by JOHN GASSNER

BEST AMERICAN PLAYS SERIES

25 BEST PLAYS OF THE MODERN AMERICAN THEATRE: *Early Series, 1916-1929*

20 BEST PLAYS OF THE MODERN AMERICAN THEATRE: *1930-1939*

BEST PLAYS OF THE MODERN AMERICAN THEATRE: *Second Series, 1939-1946*

BEST AMERICAN PLAYS: *Third Series, 1945-1951*

BEST AMERICAN PLAYS: *Fourth Series, 1951-1957*

BEST AMERICAN PLAYS: *Supplementary Volume, 1918-1958*

20 BEST EUROPEAN PLAYS ON THE AMERICAN STAGE

THEATRE AT THE CROSSROADS

FORM AND IDEA IN THE MODERN THEATRE

THE THEATRE IN OUR TIMES

HUMAN RELATIONS IN THE THEATRE

COMEDIES OF MOLIERE

ENGLISH COMEDIES

BEST FILM PLAYS OF 1945 (with Dudley Nichols)

BEST FILM PLAYS OF 1943-44 (with Dudley Nichols)

TWENTY BEST FILM PLAYS (with Dudley Nichols)

OUR HERITAGE OF WORLD LITERATURE

PRODUCING THE PLAY

MASTERS OF THE DRAMA

A TREASURY OF THE THEATRE (3 volumes)

INTRODUCING THE DRAMA (with Morris Sweetkind)

THE LIBRARY OF WORLD DRAMA (General editor, 12 volumes)

Best AMERICAN Plays

FIFTH SERIES 1957-1963

EDITED WITH AN INTRODUCTION
AND PREFACES TO THE PLAYS BY

John Gassner

Crown Publishers, Inc., NEW YORK

In Affectionate and Grateful Memory

of

LAWRENCE LANGNER

1890–1963

MAN OF MANY PARTS, DREAMER AND DOER

WHO COULD HAVE TRULY SAID

homo sum, et nihil humani a me alienum puto

TABLE OF CONTENTS

PREFACE IX

ACKNOWLEDGMENTS X

INTRODUCTION: AMERICAN CRISIS?
John Gassner XI

A TOUCH OF THE POET
Eugene O'Neill I

THE NIGHT OF THE IGUANA
Tennessee Williams 55

THE DARK AT THE TOP OF THE STAIRS
William Inge 105

WHO'S AFRAID OF VIRGINIA WOOLF?
Edward Albee 143

THE ROPE DANCERS
Morton Wishengrad 203

LOOK HOMEWARD, ANGEL
Ketti Frings 237

ALL THE WAY HOME
Tad Mosel 277

SILENT NIGHT, LONELY NIGHT
Robert Anderson 313

TWO FOR THE SEESAW
William Gibson 341

MARY, MARY
Jean Kerr 379

A THOUSAND CLOWNS
Herb Gardner 419

THE CAVE DWELLERS
William Saroyan 459

vii

OH DAD, POOR DAD, MAMMA'S HUNG YOU
IN THE CLOSET AND I'M FEELIN' SO SAD
    Arthur L. Kopit 483

ORPHEUS DESCENDING
    Tennessee Williams 509

GIDEON
    Paddy Chayefsky 553

J.B.
    Archibald MacLeish 589

THE BEST MAN
    Gore Vidal 635

OTHER AMERICAN PLAYS OF INTEREST PRODUCED ON BROADWAY................ 675

OTHER AMERICAN PLAYS OF INTEREST, PRODUCED IN THE OFF-BROADWAY THEATRE 677

PREFACE

THE PRESENT COLLECTION covers another five-year period in the professional American theatre and is concerned with the plays that went into its hopper to become successes or failures—mostly, as usual, failures. As usual, too, no sharp distinction is made here between Broadway and so-called off-Broadway items so long as they are full-length plays and were professionally performed. Nowadays, moreover, it is possible to say that a number of the off-Broadway plays would have been presented on Broadway, and more likely to its credit than discredit, if fallible but rarely reckless producers had felt they could take the risk. The most unusual aspect of this publication is that it represents a recent period in which opinions of the American theatre's performance and estimates of its prospects were exceedingly low.

It is unnecessary to dwell upon the depressing details after noting that shortly before we started going to press *The New York Times* printed a front-page report to the effect that never before had Broadway sustained greater losses than during the 1962–63 season, and the League of New York Theatre countered with a heated repudiation of the *Times* statistics. The rebuttal may be viewed with some scepticism, but it does not follow that the local jeremiads are conclusive either. The fact that it has been possible to compile the present volume and to supplement its contents with the list of plays at the end of the book may not satisfy rigorous critical standards but can be accepted as a counterweight to the direst reports of Decline and Fall.

To me the plays in this collection suggest that the course of American drama remains about par. We have merely had in the past some exceptional seasons and occasional discoveries of new plays or playwrights that boosted critical estimates and raised extravagant expectations. In his green and impulsive years, incited by having read as a professional playreader hundreds—nay, thousands!—of commonplace playscripts, the present editor once trumpeted that "The bourgeois theatre is dead." That was almost thirty years ago, in the mid-thirties, and the obit was based not solely on American drama but on plays that reached me regularly from half a dozen European countries, not excluding Soviet Russia, which had become as bourgeois as any other modern nation in its tastes and values.

I have had little reason to retract this generalization since then. But, as in the history of all art, there have been degrees of deadness, and in the case of competent stage productions the corpses have had a way of giving some lively twitches, even if these have hardly amounted to a resurrection. And it is likewise true that not all the plays of recent decades have been "bourgeois" in the sense of dealing with the concerns of petty people as observed by petty temperaments and small minds.

I do not of course expect to convince everyone that we have not been denuded of tolerable drama during the past five-year period. Scholars accustomed to dealing almost exclusively with literary masterpieces, except where their special research interests are concerned, will remain scornful toward the theatre. And the gifted young Turks of contemporary criticism, whom I find so stimulating when they are malcontent, will be properly unimpressed by the harvest offered here, and even by the harvest that could have been offered if it had been possible to obtain all desired clearances from the original publishers.* I am not sure that I am impressed myself by the over-all record of this short period, and the word "best" in the title of the volume continues to give me twinges of embarrassment; I have had them ever since this title was decided upon by the publishers a quarter of a century ago. But I trust

---

* Jack Gelber's *The Connection*, which was withheld by the publisher despite the author's interest in being represented, will be found in *Seven Plays of the Modern Theatre*, Grove Press, 1962. Lorraine Hansberry's *Raisin in the Sun* and Lillian Hellman's *Toys in the Attic*, withheld by Random House, will be found in Modern Library and Vintage collections. See *Four Contemporary American Plays*, Selected and with Biographical Notes by Bennett Cerf, Vintage Books, 1961.

it will be instructive to have a comprehensive collection of the plays of the period on the shelves.

Having collected well over a hundred American plays in the previously published volumes of the Best American Plays series (I have now passed the 130 mark), I can conclude, moreover, that the new collection contains plays not significantly inferior to the "best" in the preceding compilations. Nor less flawed, nor less perishable perhaps either, to which the only qualifying reply could be that we are dealing with a medium in which flaws become especially conspicuous, shortcomings seem to be inevitable (what alert critic has not found them even in acknowledged master-pieces), and most of the work is perishable. But that which is perishable can be briefly treasurable (which is about all we can say about our earthly life itself), and it can also possess subjective importance to those who cherish it and relative importance to those who see it in perspective. There is, for example, hardly a virtue or defect in the work of the period under review here that does not relate to the entire cen-tury's theatre in America, which it reflects or refracts—such as our addiction to surface realism, to explicitness, and to prosiness. And lest I seem too niggardly in introducing the reader to this book, let me also point out first of all, that there are scenes in the plays I have included, as well as in those I should have liked to include, that came to life vividly on the professional stage, that could conceivably come to life again, and that can be read with interest or pleasure. Moreover, I believe that even these few lean years have brought distinctive new talent to our stage as varied as the work of Edward Albee, Lorraine Hansberry, William Gibson, Gore Vidal, Jack Gelber, Arthur Kopit, and Jack Richardson. There is evidence aplenty in the individual work of these and other writers on and off Broadway that we can still find authors who are alive even if the period as a whole has been considered moribund, even if the specifically "bourgeois" theatre is "deader" than it was some thirty years ago. It is my intention, of course, to salute the quick rather than to inter the dead.

JOHN GASSNER

ACKNOWLEDGMENTS

As USUAL the compilation of a Best American Plays volume has entailed a great deal of cooperation from authors, play agents, and publishers as well as editorial help in securing clearances, increasingly difficult to obtain. There were a few in-explicable obstacles interposed by some publishers, but efforts to accommodate me as far as possible were made by Bennett Cerf, Alfred Knopf, Arthur Wang of Hill and Wang, Robert MacGregor of New Directions, Hiram Haydn of Atheneum, Paul Brooks of Houghton Mifflin Co., and Chester Kerr of the Yale University Press.

I am very grateful to them and their associates, and especially to Miss Leah Daniels of the permissions department of Random House. In several instances, too, the authors' representatives went well beyond the routine course to facilitate clearances, and I am particularly beholden to Leah Salisbury, Audrey Wood, and James Bohan for their good offices. Among the authors themselves, Messrs. Archibald MacLeish, Edward Albee, Paddy Chayefsky, William Gibson, Arthur Kopit, and Jean Kerr were also extremely helpful. I am also grateful to Lillian Hellman, Herman Shumlin, Jack Gelber, and Dore Schary for their attempts to help.

Messrs. Nat Wartels and Herbert Michelman of Crown Publishers were most assiduous and patient in helping to put together a volume that would be sufficiently representative of recent years in the theatre, and members of their staff, especially Miss Lucile Wilder, contributed their labors.

My debt to my wife, Mollie Gassner, for editorial assistance grows from year to year. For the present volume she compiled an enormous amount of research to which I helped myself generously yet without being able to utilize more than a mere fraction of it.

Introduction

AMERICAN CRISIS?

by JOHN GASSNER

I.

THE PERIOD under present review started auspiciously with a slight and well-acclaimed rise in the prestige of Broadway and off-Broadway enterprise, and presumably with improved financial status. Optimism declined, however, as the expense of theatrical productions and the cost of attendance rose, multiplying the riskiness of the enterprise. Whether there was a *direct* connection between the economics and the esthetics of the theatre (and I doubt that there was any), it did become evident that conditions were not favorable to distinguished playwriting at home, and that we had reason to be grateful for the availability of plays discovered and seasoned abroad.

Our playwrights in turn did nothing to alter the deplorable situation except in the superficial sense of providing hits encouraging to investors and to producers restored to temporary solvency. By then it was no longer possible to blame the intimidations of "McCarthyism" for the curious disengagement of most current playwriting and the lukewarm character of its infrequent engagement to social causes. At this writing the absence of social ferment in the nation as a whole is no longer an issue, although its wisdom or direction can be. Yet it would be rash to conclude that our old writers have acquired dreams and our younger writers vision, or *vice versa*. Social activity is one thing, art is another. It involves a process of transformation or some kind of transcendence of the mundane. Nor is it possible to assert that our playwrights have suddenly started taking delight in the exchange of ideas or putting any trust in their potency.

The shallowness of ordinary practitioners of theatre is a well-known fact that has its source in the need to communicate with unselective audiences, a need to which even Shakespeare ministered, and not always without penalty. Superficiality and glibness have been charged against playwrights at least since Aristophanes attacked Euripides. Shaw's published opinions of Shakespeare's intellectual equipment were no higher than the present highbrow opinion of middlebrow playwriting—which is virtually the only kind that has a chance of appearing on Broadway without previous sanction from London or Paris. Experience supports the late Irwin Edman's generalization that there is a time lag in the arts, and the theatre has undoubtedly lagged behind poetry and fiction in recent decades, as it also did during the greater part of the nineteenth century in England and the United States, when melodramas and farces were the order of the day.

But the American playwright has been susceptible to a *special* degenerative process in our time, and in what John Mason Brown has aptly called "a melodramatically altered world." The old enthusiasms for liberal, Socialist, Communist, and even simply democratic ideals have largely faded from the playwright's horizon. He cannot rely on mere qualifications and pseudo-convictions such as nowadays he possesses to give creative impetus to his writing. He has tended to fumble with ideas like a sophomore, extracting them from popularizations of Marx, Freud, cold-war speeches or discussions, and the platitudes of both liberalism and anti-liberalism. It is not surprising that they don't fill him with zest or conviction; he is fortunate if he can turn out a workmanlike job of journalism, and he is doubly fortunate if he is able to make it sparkle now and then in a context of comedy and comedic characterization, as does Gore Vidal in *The Best Man*. The playwright believes he is best off when he can resort to pungent colloquialism, environmental realism, and character creation. It is no wonder that he remains loyal to the tradition of American "realism," with which he is familiar and from which he derives support while floundering in the quicksands of contemporary uncertainties and confusions. It is true, of course, that there is an alternative available to him, for he can adopt or domesticate the scepticism and negations of the recent European avant-garde known as Theatre of the Absurd. But negativism is thin gruel on which to nourish a theatre, especially without wit—a commodity usually in short supply in American literature. And a great big No can become just as tedious when repeated as a great big Yes. Frequency of repetition, moreover, can be marked even in a single play as well as in the class of plays now categorized as absurdist. It- is with some reason that, among the highly prized absurdist pieces, very few, whether homegrown or imported, attained the dimensions of "full-length" drama; the best pieces, as a rule, have been one-acters.

Regardless of possible explanations and proffered extenuations, however, it was also altogether evident that the immediate future of American playwriting was coming to rest with a new generation whose talent still awaited crystallization no less than its values did. The old order virtually passed except for the long-delayed production of one more posthumously uncovered O'Neill manuscript, *A Touch of the Poet*. As staged by Harold Clurman in 1958, it reminded us of a striving for the momentous that had belonged to our sole giant before the flood—and for which there seemed to be no prospects in the years to come. *A Touch of the Poet* was, in fact, a historical drama concerned with the founding of a family that would work out its fate in the ensuing century of conflict between American materialism and American idealism. But for one more play by O'Neill, first staged in Sweden in 1962, and the one-act play *Hughie,* which received productions in Boston and London in 1963, O'Neill's legacy of new plays seemed exhausted, and one could only wonder how decidedly much poorer the past decade would have been but for Mrs. O'Neill's laudable decision to make *A Long Day's Journey into Night* and *A Touch of the Poet* available to American playgoers. And let us not overlook the revivals, even disappointing ones, of his older work. It was perhaps significant that the five-year period's most ambitious undertaking should have been the 1963 revival of *Strange Interlude* with which the Actors Studio Theatre headed

by Lee Strasberg started its plunge into Broadway production after an earlier effort with O'Casey's *Shadow of a Gunman*. Earlier in the 1962–63 season, a revival of O'Neill's *Desire Under the Elms* was a major exertion of the off-Broadway theatre. The American theatre continued to lean on O'Neill for self-respect and persisted in regarding him as its culture-hero—sometimes to its own embarrassment and sometimes to the discomfiture of avant-garde critics of a new generation.

From O'Neill's generation, only S. N. Behrman (born some five years after him) continued to be active in the theatre. To it he contributed, however, only adaptations of his autobiographical *Worcester Story,* and of his biography of Duveen, both originally *New Yorker* stories. Now and then an affecting genre picture, *The Cold Wind and the Warm* stubbornly resisted the effort to make it cohere as a play, and the Duveen-based comedy *Lord Pengo* earned complimentary adjectives (it was called "urbane" and "stylish and sophisticated") without developing the force and relevance of the Behrman comedies of the nineteen-thirties. Thornton Wilder, who became known as a playwright during the same decade, was evidently far from idle during the present period. But he cautiously exposed only three one-act plays to the public gaze in New York, when Circle in the Square presented them under the collective title of *Plays for Bleecker Street* in 1962. Paul Green confined his playwriting to the composition of pageant plays intended for outdoor presentation. But a recent Dramabook (Hill and Wang) publication of some of his plays of earlier decades could only inspire regret that Broadway had failed to secure the loyalty of so gifted a writer. From the generation that also produced Maxwell Anderson, Philip Barry, George Kelly, Robert E. Sherwood, Elmer Rice, Sidney Howard, George S. Kaufman and some of his collaborators, the 1957–63 period acquired nary a play of potency except for O'Neill's posthumously published dramas and *J.B.* (in 1958), a morality play in verse by Archibald MacLeish, hitherto best known as a non-dramatic poet.

The recent period was also let down by the vital generation of the nineteen-thirties associated with the theatre of so-called social consciousness. Clifford Odets, its major discovery, had withdrawn to Hollywood and had begun to transfer his allegiance to television dramatics by the time of his death on August 15, 1963. Sidney Kingsley, chiefly remembered for his naturalistic problem play *Dead End* in 1935, busied himself with the stage but with results in *Night Life* that did not measure up to his earnest intent. Robert Ardrey, best known to Broadway and London for his heartening fantasy *Thunder Rock,* written on the eve of World War II, contributed a play about the Hungarian uprising, *Shadows of Heroes,* which won a Theresa Helburn prize for its libertarian sentiments, but found scant public support. Irwin Shaw, who roused the thirties with *Bury the Dead,* provided a thoughtful and acidulous, if somewhat inert, work, *Children from their Games,* that failed to capture an audience, which it deserved at least as much as many a Broadway hit. (It would probably have been applauded if it had been the work of an unknown writer on the off-Broadway stage.) William Saroyan continued to be the maverick author of the nineteen-thirties and was as prolific as he was predictable. All but one of his dramatic ventures, *The Cave Dwellers,* an intermittently entrancing return to the Saroyan-land of fancy and *bonhomie,* did not get an airing in the Times Square district. *The Cave Dwellers* found considerable support from those of us who had welcomed his almost meteoric rise in the late thirties and still enjoyed the expected unexpectedness of his improvisatory bent. *The Cave Dwellers,* however, made considerably less impression on a more taciturn generation of critics less merciful to the author's sentiments and indulgences.

Lillian Hellman's *Toys in the Attic* alone bridged the gap between the generations, belonging as it did to character drama in general and to the moral jurisprudence of the nineteen-thirties. Characteristically, she exposed possessiveness as venal even when love engenders it and self-sacrifice masks it. Miss Hellman had put iron into the soul of the theatre of the thirties with *The Children's Hour* and *The Little Foxes.* In the season of 1959–1960 her familiar relentlessness in character-drawing brought her writing close to the temper of Tennessee Williams and Theatre of the Absurd nihilism which has looked askance at humanity and its

prospects. But it may be doubted that Miss Hellman's play, a powerful piece of dramatic writing and uniquely her own, satisfied any particular faction. Since *Toys in the Attic* contained several sympathetic characters, it must have struck literary nihilists of the new generation as too tractable and qualified, while it was evidently too unsettling for other persons such as members of the Pulitzer Prize Advisory Board who were apparently accustomed to equating art with contentment. Nevertheless, the play had considerable success at the box office and earned respect in opinion-forming circles at home and abroad, even if dramatic action was less in focus here than in some other Hellman dramas.

Finally, the period under review benefited less than could have been expected from the generation of the nineteen-forties, which had witnessed the flowering of new talent in the case of Williams, Miller, Inge, Robert Anderson, and others. To an unfriendly critic, it was certain that their work was deteriorating, and even a friendly one had reason for concern when Miller became an absentee playwright after the production of *A View from the Bridge* in 1955, when Williams produced *The Milk Train Doesn't Stop Here Anymore,* when Inge lapsed from grace with his *Loss of Roses* and *Natural Affection.* Even some unique efforts by them, apart from what strict criticism could urge against them, missed the target as far as Broadway success was concerned. Thus, Robert Anderson, avoiding contrivances that had been charged against his first successful play *Tea and Sympathy,* turned out an affecting two-character drama of cul-de-sac romance, *Silent Night, Lonely Night.* But he risked some lukewarmness and some stasis that the New York production failed to overcome sufficiently to give him a complete public success. (The economics of Broadway today tend to convert a partial success into a financial fiasco.) Thus, too, Williams endeavored to combine naturalism with symbolism in his *Orpheus Descending,* and to express a tragic sense of life (his own peculiarly romantic-naturalistic one) with more than ordinary voltage. His tragic feeling, however, became turbulent, and his technique jolted playgoers in calling for rapid transitions from a naturalistic to a symbolic plane of interest. Nevertheless such efforts as these helped to enrich the experience of playgoing in New York, as did the more successful plays of these and other playwrights already known on the Main Stem. (One thinks of Inge's *The Dark at the Top of the Stairs*, Williams' *The Night of the Iguana*, Paddy Chayefsky's *The Tenth Man* and *Gideon*, Wishengrad's *The Rope Dancers*, Ketti Frings' dramatization of *Look Homeward, Angel*, and Jean Kerr's *Mary, Mary*.) Whatever may be said of their individual merits and defects, these playwrights produced a body of work that contradicts the hasty impression that they had failed the theatre.

But it cannot be denied they needed support from the new generation—a good deal of support. Fortunately, they began to receive it with an influx of new talent into the Broadway or, more frequently, off-Broadway scene. That talent appeared in considerable diversity. It manifested itself conservatively but with compelling authenticity in Lorraine Hansberry's *Raisin in the Sun*, a Chicago Negro family drama with social overtones especially noteworthy for Miss Hansberry's convincing characterization; and less conservatively, in Ossie Davis' parodistic comedy-spoof, *Purlie Victorious*. In neither play, besides were the naturalistic play structure and speech servilely adapted to Broadway showmanship. (Unless Miss Hansberry's decision to let the young hero reject a white community's bribe is regarded as a concession to Broadway's optimism and penchant for reformation of character.) In other instances, the new arrivals in the theatre brought with them a long-brewing revolt against naturalistic art.

In *The Connection*, a drama about drug addiction, Jack Gelber combined the utmost naturalism with a play-within-a-play technique and other anti-naturalistic devices. These were supposed to place the spectator on a level with the characters on the stage as a person who, like the rest of mankind, is metaphorically speaking in need of a "fix" and dependent on a "connection" that might make life at least briefly and tentatively bearable. He startled the theatre with this very successful off-Broadway ("Living Theatre") production, and followed *The Connection* with a seriously flawed but fiercely imaginative assault on our civilization, *The Apple*, in 1962. A mordant literary bent appeared in the work of Jack Richardson, author of *The Prodigal* and *Gallows Humor*. And the note of striking bizarreness one associates with avant-gardism was well struck too. It is represented in the present collection by the work of Edward Albee, who acquired a well-deserved prominence in less time than it takes most playwrights to try their wings, and Arthur Kopit, youngest of the newcomers, who finished a draft of his first play while still an undergraduate. Their avant-garde themes were either seriously or comically conceived in a variety of ways that gave no quarter to conventional sentiment and reduced the norms of Broadway-depicted middle-class life to nightmares (Albee's *The Zoo Story* and *Who's Afraid of Virginia Woolf?*) or travesties (Albee's *The American Dream* and Kopit's *Oh Dad, Poor Dad . . .*). It is not surprising that these authors should have had to get their start in the off-Broadway theatre.

Standing among the new playwrights at the other extreme were the neophytes who found the Broadway theatre their immediate haven. They were not few in number, although their effort to please Broadway's clientele were rarely rewarded with a long enough run. A lucky exception represented in the present volume was Herb Gardner, whose comedy *A Thousand Clowns* had staying power—perhaps inevitably, since the play was so well adapted to the congenial disposition of the general public, which is normally on the side of lovable eccentrics and marrying maidens. But other Broadway playwrights were newcomers only in the sense that they had been known until recently for other accomplishments than that of providing grist for the Broadway mill. Thus Tad Mosel and Morton Wishengrad, who accounted very respectably for the Pulitzer Prize dramatization *All the Way Home* and *The Rope Dancers* respectively, had made their reputations previously in the fields of radio and television writing. The professional theatre received them with considerable cordiality. And their experience was not exactly singular. Gore Vidal certainly could not complain of lack of encouragement. He was quickly enrolled in the company of recruits to Broadway who were likely to stay there for a good long while. This successful novelist and scenarist made a genial entry with the satirical science-fiction comedy *Visit to a Small Planet* early in 1957, and next, giving a sceptical glance at politics in *The Best Man,* contributed the period's brightest topical piece. If in adapting Duerrenmatt's quasi-historical play *Romulus* the same young playwright (he was a mere thirty-five when *The Best Man* opened in 1960) engaged politics in more imaginative terms and was defeated, it was not for want of trying. It was the right kind of trying for Broadway show business if the wrong kind for dramatic art—the endeavor to make the play all things to the public by churning together philosophy and farce, history and horseplay, characterization and plot contrivance.

William Gibson, who had published a sharp criticism of Broadway in *The Seesaw Log* after great success with *Two for the Seesaw,* was apparently reconciled to the commercial theatre with the honorable success of his Helen Keller drama, *The Miracle Worker.* He failed *off* Broadway!

A considerable stir was made by Dore Schary, long outstanding in Hollywood, who, turning to Franklin Delano Roosevelt's critical early years, gave the theatre one of its most attractive biographical dramas, *Sunrise at Campobello.* He also took on the difficult task of adapting for the stage Morris L. West's novel *The Devil's Advocate,* and he made a valiant if unsuccessful effort to dramatize the moral anguish of a nuclear scientist in *The Hidden Tree.* During this same brief period, he also directed and co-produced the interracial romantic comedy *A Majority of One,* which Gertrude Berg, playing a Jewish widow, and Sir Cedric Hardwicke, playing a Japanese widower, carried to success. Its author, Leonard Spigelgass, was another visitor from the mass media, and he stayed on with another play tailored for Gertrude Berg, *Dear Me, the Sky is Falling,* in 1962. Joining Mr. Schary in a temporary transfer of loyalties, Budd Schulberg, in collaboration with the *New York Times* book reviewer Harvey Breit, dramatized his own novel based on the life of Scott Fitzgerald, *The Disenchanted,* which had a fair success on the stage. Saul Levitt, the author of a novel *The Sun is Silent* and of stories and television and film scripts, was an especially welcome arrival with the production of *The Andersonville Trial.* This play was a timely and provocative treatment of the theme of responsibility in situations where a man's military duty comes into conflict with human conscience. Jean Kerr could also be considered a newcomer with the extravagantly successful domestic comedy *Mary, Mary,* although she had arrived on Broadway somewhat earlier with a fairly successful collaboration. And an unusual talent for character revelation appeared in the work of Hugh Wheeler when he abandoned fiction temporarily and gave the period two plays, one of which—the mordant comedy *Big Fish, Little Fish*—narrowly missed the success it deserved.

Finally it may be noted that among the neophytes introduced by off-Broadway producers was to be found a considerable reservoir of playwriting talent aside from that already referred to. There were playwrights who were more or less ready, not to say extremely willing, to try their fortunes on Broadway and who could remind prophets of despair that the wellsprings of dramatic creativity were not actually drying up as predicted. It was possible to observe potentialities, for example, in Meade Roberts' *Maidens and Mistresses at the Zoo* during the 1958-59 season; Robert Hock's Civil War verse drama, *Borak;* Michael Shurtleff's incisive treatment of racial tensions, *Call Me By My Rightful Name;* William Snyder's *The Days and Nights of Beebee Fenstermaker;* Oliver Hailey's Pirandellian comedy, *Hey You, Light Man!;* Josh Greenfeld's *Clandestine on the Morning Line,* Daniel Blum's *Dumbbell People in a Barbell World,* Lorees Yerby's *Save Me a Place at Forest Lawn,* John Carlino's *Cages,* Joseph Caldwell's *Cockeyed Kite,* Murray Schisgal's double bill of bizarre one-acters, *The Tiger* and *The Typists,* William Hanley's *Whisper into My Good Ear,* and Frank D. Gilroy's ironically naturalistic drama, *Who'll Save the Plowboy?* And there is no telling who else, even among those who contributed plays to the commercial theatre's annual crop of failures, might soon come up with a Broadway success; on the verge of one were the brothers James and William Goodman, who appeared on Times Square with the unsuccessful satire-farce *Blood, Sweat and Stanley Poole,* and the musical comedy *A Family Affair,* which was superior to a number of other musicals including successful ones. It was possible to entertain hopes also for others who did not turn out freak successes and for other writers hitherto known only for adaptations and play-doctoring such as Sidney Michaels who was credited with the Broadway version of *Tchin-Tchin,* a strictly downhill and more or less existentialist romance.

Regardless of the dim view of Broadway taken by Broadway itself, not to mention some of its weekly and quarterly critics, the Main Stem continued to exert a magnetic attraction. When success did come, there was seemingly no end to the emoluments reaped by the author and the management; when success did not come, there was only one alternative in show business—failure, often abysmal, if not in fact ignominious. The day of the "in-between" production, which is neither a success nor a disaster, had disappeared with the arrival of exorbitant production and running costs. Against these costs producers had virtually no defense, except perhaps the tendency in our period to eliminate trial runs before bringing the show to Manhattan. In 1962–63, the traditional "out-of-town tryout" was omitted in the case of *Who's Afraid of Virginia Woolf?, Strange Interlude,* and *Mother Courage.* But stabilized at the level of about 70 plays on Broadway and perhaps twice as many on the off-Broadway stages (augmented by "off-off-Broadway" shows in Greenwich Village restaurants and espresso dives), professional and quasi-professional performances continued apace; and there seemed to be no slack in the writing and circulation of plays throughout the land by the competent and the incompetent, the legitimately hopeful and the foolishly trusting.

To the number of playwrights would have to be added numerous composers or tunesmiths and writers of "lyrics" or "books" ready to pool their ambitions in quest of a musical-comedy or musical-revue success. That way fortune lay in fact as well as in fancy, and no trend seemed better established than that of our growing reliance on musical production for safety and profit. Mishaps occurred, and when that was the case the losses incurred for the investors were staggering. But "musicals" scored a considerably higher percentage of success than so-called "straight" plays, since they attracted larger audiences willing to pay higher prices. And not altogether unjustifiably in terms of the marketplace since the musicals offered more "value" per dollar than straight plays—more pulchritude, more variety of entertainment (including songs and dances), more pictorial display, and more prestige for the customer in terms of conspicuous consumption, if not indeed conspicuous waste.

Standards in musical *stage production* were relatively high, although they were hardly rigorous in the composition of the book and the lyrics; the standards in the writing of the book or libretto remained as depressingly low as ever, falling indeed well below those established by Rodgers and Hammerstein in *Oklahoma!* and its immediate successors in the 1940's. New Broadway productions, from *West Side Story* with memorable choreography by Jerome Robbins, to *How to Succeed in Business without Really Trying* with the knowing Abe Burrows at the helm and the cunning "juvenile" Robert Morse at the head of the cast, made Broadway the El Dorado of the musical entertainers. And before long, in plays certainly more economical and at times more deft, off-Broadway managements discovered a strip of Gold Coast showmanship with such ventures as the bouncy travesty on old-fashioned operetta, *Little Mary Sunshine,* and the ruefully romantic and witty musical version of an early Rostand comedy, *The Fantasticks,* as well as with bright semi-topical revues such as *The Premise,* which also captivated London. If most of the period's straight plays invited and received more or less severe criticism, the musical productions received a superfluity of appreciation at home and abroad; in 1962 a traveler could satisfy himself that the one American export for which there was no cessation of demand was the American musical comedy.

2.

What sense can be made of this period from any wide critical perspective depends in part upon the bias of the historian-observer. It may be noted, for example, that as in the case of other periods of transition in modern drama there has been a distinct return to the one-act play form. If this trend has been discouraged on Broadway for practical reasons, it has received much encouragement from the off-Broadway theatre. Many discoveries of latent or actual talent have been made as a result, and there is of course no artistic reason why a short play should be considered inferior to a long one. For certain subjects and attitudes toward life and art, the one-act form is, in fact, the ideal medium. Wisdom dictates the proper proportioning of ends and means, whereas the compulsory stretching out of plays customary in playwriting for Broadway is mere opportunism.

It may also be observed that while "epic theatre" has understandably made few inroads into American playwriting (I can recall only Ardrey's *Shadow of Heroes* and Corwin's play about the Lincoln-Douglas debates, *The Rivalry*), "theatre of the absurd" has infiltrated it— and hardly to great disadvantage in the case of such plays as *Who's Afraid of Virginia Woolf?, Oh Dad . . .*, and *The Connection*. Two schools of thought—one conservative, the other liberal if not indeed radical—have deplored the trend. Both feel puritanically queasy about a variety of morbid subjects or details; and both resent in the plays they deplore an absence of concern with society and a lack of faith in progress. This is not the place to argue the matter; we are concerned here only with the dramatic results, which happen to be no lower and at times considerably higher than in the case of plays of optimistic liberalism and surface realism. The present writer questions the notion that the deplorable state of our theatre is the result of moral degeneracy, and he considers it equally fallacious to assume that if avant-garde writers were suddenly to believe in the perfectibility of man or the inevitability of progress they would become better playwrights and attract a following of true believers in divine Providence or in Dialectical Materialism who are simply palpitating for an opportunity to attend plays graced with the power of positive thinking. As a matter of fact, a large number of Broadway plays have little more to offer than just that pabulum, usually chocolate-covered with Love, without noticeable benefit to art or business.

Another school of diagnosticians of Broadway's ailments, and at present the most vocal, seems to attribute all shortcomings to the economic situation, and there is much sense to their diagnosis. When Broadway productions of simple plays begin to cost at least $120,000 and when they must gross well over $20,000 a week to break even, the character of the work selected and doctored for Broadway is bound to be affected by desperately practical considerations. The inflationary wave then hits playwriting, and plays intended for Broadway are puffed up egregiously until the original molehills of idea or experience become artificial Himalayas. This is also apparent in the blown-up productions given to these plays, since every effort is made to attract the largest possible number of customers in the shortest possible time. Affected by this tendency, the individual playgoer then heads in the direction followed by the greatest number, and follows the pack to see "hits" rather than plays. And since the managements make every effort to presell their productions and arrive in New York with huge advance sales of tickets (bought up chiefly by ticket agencies and theatre-party representatives), the hits acquire prestige value in direct proportion to the scarcity of seats available to the individual purchaser. There can be no getting around the fact that while the commercial theatre may or may not be art, it never ceases to be a business— though often a very poor one—as well as a social phenomenon.

But it is a mistake to assume that the quality of the plays is determined exclusively by economics. Talent is not on tap for every merchandiser. And in playwriting, where talent flows through the complicated channels of stage production, art is not only ordinarily in scarce supply but quickly contaminated by the tastes and values of its times, so that it is folly to assume that better financing holds the solution. I have seen young playwrights actually pampered so far as financial encouragement and opportunities to judge their work on the stage are concerned. This did not improve their taste or intelligence, or prevent them from making elementary errors of judgment in play construction. They belonged to their times, their social class, their ethnic group, their personal experience, and their boundaries of thought were narrow. The limitations and defects of recent writing have been patently related to these factors. The playwrights, more than other writers of comparable stature or promise of growth, rarely transcended philistine *Zeitgeist*.

Reflecting the period, average American playwrights have registered a generally mild reaction to the world around them and concentrated upon personal matters, which in the case of their superiors in talent have been intensely felt and quite forcefully expressed. The talented writers have entertained a vision of life largely devoid of direction and consisting of private frustrations, misunderstandings, and sexual traumas. They have understandably dwelt on defeat and reacted with anxiety or scorn, but rarely to such a degree that they present a challenge to the playgoer's mind or his manner of life; and they have rarely driven on to conclusions. Thus, they have represented the very opposite of Bertolt Brecht's reaction to the world he found unacceptable —and this perhaps because, despite their disenchantments, they do find their world, the American world, fundamentally agreeable or at least acceptable. They may be irritated, but they are not enraged by it; they may want to see their world improved but they are not particularly moved to agitate against it. And they have not been greatly stirred, as Beckett, Genet, or Ionesco have been abroad, to turn on life itself. Their disenchantments have been comparatively slight. In their relatively comfortable American milieu, they have found congenial ways of salving wounds and minimizing failure; and they have been only too prone, as have American producers and stage directors, to accept love as a panacea. The present writer is not the only one or the first to voice reservations about this ready resort to sentiment. It vitiates such outstanding plays of the period as the final drafts of *The Dark at the Top of the Stairs* and *J.B.*, presented by good producers who exerted a considerable influence on their authors in preparing the Broadway stage version. In the first-mentioned instance, a husband's return to his wife's bed is apparently going to solve his family's economic situation, the introversion of his little son, and the adolescence of his traumatized daughter; a lummox of a harness salesman when harnesses are no longer being bought stands at the top of the stairs calling to his wife and offering the children money for the movies in order to get them out of the house, and we are expected to conclude that a marriage has been repaired and all's well with the world! A bill of exceptions to the Broadway production would read somewhat like the above-given arraignment.

And concerning the resolution of *J.B.*, we have reason to doubt that we get a better answer to the question of suffering from *J.B.* than from the Old Testament. The revised Broadway conclusion drew condign castigation from a brilliant young critic, Gerald Weales, who quipped that the author "has not been able to avoid the greatest cliché of the fifties, the conviction that love cures boils." (*American Drama Since World War II*, 1962, pp. 186-189.) Our playwrights were inclined to provide a severer outlook or resolution than the mass media favor, but they have been under pressure during rehearsals and tryout runs to be attentive to the tender sensibilities of their middle-class and middle-aged public.

3.

It is perhaps only against this background that one can see the period's harvest of drama and comedy with some perspective that amounts to judgment rather than complacency, on one hand, and a severe depression on the other. That it is not incumbent upon the advocate of critical absolutes to adopt such a middle-of-the-road approach goes without saying, and that the insights of inexorable critics can be valuable, especially in the analysis of individual plays, should be obvious. There is no interdict against the rigorous critic, and he is welcome to apply his faculties to the plays in the present volume. But it is not, of course, for him primarily but for the general reader, the habitual playgoer, and theatre historian that this volume has been compiled.

For them this collection offers the variety and eclecticism of the period's professional theatre. Two plays, *Mary, Mary* and *A Thousand Clowns*, while differing in substance and style, reflect a comfortable comic attitude to minor tensions and to private problems to which the public is believed to be more attentive than the possibility of the extinction of civilization by nuclear explosion or the dangers of the population explosion. Besides, these matters have not yet ceased being abstractions for the American public, while private relations retain their momentous asexual importance as subjects for concern and conversation. Fortunately Jean Kerr, who knows her public (and rises above it with her afflatus), also knows her characters and is in control of her brittle style while dallying with marital misunderstandings. Many playgoers, whether or not they have taken *Mary, Mary* more seriously than its author does, have been amused by Mrs. Kerr's apt and well-worded observations. Those who want to read a sociological treatise into the play are, of course, free to do so—at their peril. The present editor wishes them well, but rather hopes they are in possession of an aptitude for humor rather than a taste for statistics. And those formidable few who are upset by the tremendous success of the play, despite Mrs. Kerr's blithe solving of the domestic problem with a flip of her wrist, will find no ally in me; they will need none anyway since they will have their sense of critical righteousness to keep them snug. As for *A Thousand Clowns*, there is surely no need to defend Herb Gardner's comic romance between a rebellious man and a straitlaced lass who meet for the first time under unpropitious circumstances when she enters his home as a social case worker. Since the romantic attraction operates without serious impediment and there is no need to take the hero's rebellion against entrapment in the mass entertainment industry seriously, there is no particular necessity to scrutinize the development and resolution of the plot; and to accuse the author of begging questions he has not raised is to flog a nonexistent existentialist horse. No one is likely to depend upon the author's comic protagonist to put up a desperate struggle against the commonplace world at which he thumbs his nose, or even to attempt to understand his relationship to it as simultaneously its victim and ally. One can, of course, wonder whether the author does. As for the heroine of this comedy, she thinks she is one kind of biped, the reforming and professional kind, only to discover in the course of the play that she is another kind, the *marrying* kind. And this discovery is a relief, if hardly a surprise, to the paying audience that knows only one solution in the theatre—love for the little lady and wedlock for the little rebellious man. Mr. Gardner managed these developments breezily, which is the best way to place the fodder of sentiment on the platter of entertainment. If his expertise continues to grow he is sure to become one of the most successful of Broadway playwrights in a generation. *A Thousand*

Clowns, which belongs congenially to its period and place, is a very smart salute to American mores.

Others regard our *Zeitgeist* as a *Poltergeist;* Arthur Kopit (*Oh Dad . . .*) is one of those who thinks so and he expresses his reaction to it (to Momism, nymphetism, and upper-crust vacuousness) with the improvisatory buoyancy of a bright young, if not indeed boyish, talent. The play represents the extremes of rejection or alienation, which our ablest new playwrights have been prone to use. It also happens to possess considerable piquancy and humor, and there is much that is knowing in several of the scenes. The darker vision and the morbidities one can detect in *Oh Dad . . .* make the play a true Theatre of the Absurd product; so do the lighter portions of the play. Its combination of fragments from the Absurdist world vision, or lack of vision, abroad may give it the character of collage or pastiche, but *Oh Dad . . .* is actually a fairly cohesive combination of travesty, nightmare, and serio-comic observation. Mr. Kopit's extravaganza is a model of clarity and control by comparison with some ventures into modernist sophistication that appeared on our stage after 1955.

In efforts to maintain a mature sobriety with respect to human relations, our dominant tone and structure have been characteristically realistic. Two plays in the present collection deal with love affairs that fall short of total realization. Robert Anderson's *Silent Night, Lonely Night,* an atmospheric and quietly poetic work, is muted drama; it is the one play of its kind (it is "drama" rather than comedy) that affected me and that escaped the usual flatness of the genre, no doubt because it bears the impression of a personally felt rather than fabricated emotion. It is a simple and direct recognition, too, of the presence of limitations to life's possibilities. But of course there are also limitations to this kind of drama, and these were apparent in the Broadway production. To concentrate upon the pathos of such a play is to restrict the dramatic action and to keep it running in narrow channels, though these may be as deep as they are in *Silent Night, Lonely Night* or deeper. With greater complexity and variation in tone, "realism" wins out in William Gibson's *Two for the Seesaw,* a play which also pays heed to life's impossibilities and improbabilities. This is particularly apparent when the author puts an end to the romance of his middle-class refugee from a Midwestern middle-class marriage and an overly generous bohemian girl from the Bronx. The limitation of such realism is "middle-class," too. Bernard Shaw, observing that the man returns to his wife and social class after his affair with a New York *gamine,* would have noted the resemblance to Pinero's nineteenth-century pseudo-Ibsenism and made a case of it. It is difficult to know how much of the aborted romance was primary to the author's viewpoint and how much arose from pressures exerted on the author during the rehearsal and tryout periods. It is apparent that the author was dissatisfied with the changes and compromises he found himself making in the script. But whatever the play became in production, it remained *his* play and *his* responsibility—and *our* play and *our* responsibility. A deft two-character comedy of character and sentiment, *Two for the Seesaw* was plainly the best organized and most attractive job of playwriting in the romantic-realistic vein cultivated in the popular theatre. Playgoers whom the play could not satisfy—plainly a minority—could only support the impression given by the author himself in *The Seesaw Log* that he made the best of a bad bargain. Playgoers who *were* gratified—an evident majority—could enjoy the satisfaction of their democratic sentiments by the romance of a plebeian heroine and a patrician married gentleman and at the same time feel gratified by its very proper termination.

The tempestuous course of home life, a perennial concern in popular fiction, films, and television plays, also comprised the interest of many productions trimmed and polished for Broadway. It was characteristic of the period's theatre that some of the strongest plays in our book should be eligible for this category. In Ketti Frings' competent dramatization of Thomas Wolfe's *Look Homeward, Angel,* the results were a diversified human document of provincial life culminating in the education and partial liberation of the son (Tom Wolfe himself). We were expected to understand that his experience and growing comprehension of his family would enable the future novelist to ultimately impose the partial order of art on the disorder of life. What the play lacked most conspicuously was the original author's lyrical writing and poetic expansiveness. The alternative of lyric re-creation would have required the talent of a second Thomas Wolfe, and it is doubtful that American life and literature would have room for it today. The age of expansive egotism and egolatry lay in the past, and it had become fashionable to look askance at Thomas Wolfe as the Paul Bunyan of American letters.

In *All the Way Home,* family drama was also reviewed in relationship to individual development. So far as the American theatre has been concerned, Americans are nearly always *growing up* and rarely *grown up.* The portrayal of a family group in Tad Mosel's dramatization of James Agee's novel is vivid and varied. And if the experience of death as a widowed young woman and her little son are required to comprehend and assimilate it is not the most attractive experience, it is one of the most fundamental with which a play can concern itself. But it is chiefly with character relations and confrontations calling for understanding and ending in acceptance that the adaptation was most successful. Insofar as this is conducive to stasis (the scene of waiting for news of the death of the husband in the second act was the slowest and least successful part of the play) *All the Way Home* had difficulty in sustaining itself on Broadway and would not have had the fairly good run it obtained but for strong support from the reviewers. Insofar as the play touched authentically upon human fate (the scenes of the woman's rebellion against the husband's accidental death and the little lad's bewilderment were particularly moving), the play earned the support it received.

More tension and disorientation were dramatically present in William Inge's *The Dark at the Top of the Stairs,* which contains some of the best character drawing and dialogue this sensitive but determined author has been capable of supplying. It was understandable that Brooks Atkinson, then still reviewing for the *Times,* should have applauded it as the author's best play to date, until one took a hard look at its structure and especially its resolution. One could certainly question the author's optimistic conclusion, especially with respect to two severely disturbed children. It is, in fact, difficult for the present writer to understand how Mr. Inge arrived or was persuaded to arrive at that conclusion, which could easily be parodied by an unfriendly critic; and the latter's unfriendliness would be further invited by the odd injection of a racial issue and a suicide into what would have otherwise been too slight a play for Broadway. (This was surely an instance of the inflationary play-doctoring enforced upon writers by the need for a "big" play for Broadway when purely esthetic considerations would have required a "little" play.) Still, everything unforced in *The Dark at the Top of the Stairs* was too appealing not to win clemency for the work as a whole, and some of the scenes could hardly be bettered in the tradition of American realism that makes poetry out of the commonplaces.

A more cumbersomely managed realism in Morton Wishengrad's *The Rope Dancers* naturally encountered more public resistance. But this recently deceased author brought a gnarled strength to his study of failure in marriage. Plainly there was a strong sensibility at work in *The Rope Dancers,* a play that cannot be easily fitted into recent American theatre except on grounds of its author's naturalistic directness. That the failure of the marriage of a puritanically bred but naturally sensual Irish-Catholic woman and a fun-loving, volatile husband should be associated with the birth of their six-fingered child is an odd invention. The author managed to make it almost tragic rather than merely bizarre. The guilt-ridden mother considers her child's genetic abnormality condign punishment for her sexuality and wrecks the child's life and her own. Wishengrad even managed to move out of the confines of the domestic and psychopathic action—usual in American naturalistic drama—in order to engage the larger subject of alienation and the need to cope with it.

With this play two alternatives suggest themselves. One is to take note of the imperfection of things and blithely dismiss it half in fancy and half in jest, with wishfulness serving for thought and hopefulness for helpfulness. This is the way of Saroyan in *The Cave Dwellers,* as in his earlier produced plays. The risks are obvious, especially when Saroyan meets up with a spectator or a critic who will not play his game of buoyant make-believe. Once the vivacious *enfant terrible* of the American stage, Saroyan, returning to Broadway after many years' absence, continued to play the game that most American audiences still want to play but have learned to expect to be played less openly or in musical-comedy motley. Saroyan's unmasked lightheartedness—or, if you will, histrionic lightheadedness—like his unhidden sentimentality, remained refreshingly unique for the most part, without actually being unrepresentative of the optimistic temper of show business.

The alternative to his histrionic complacencies, which Saroyan still managed to make rather affecting and even randomly poetic, is to plunge glumly into the abyss of failed lives and to draw dramatic strength from acknowledged failure. This is the alternative apparent in *A Touch of the Poet,* O'Neill's last posthumous work but one, which O'Neill intended to use as the first play of a cycle recounting the rise of an American family whose fortunes were to parallel or reflect those of American society. That this play suffers in standing isolated from plays unwritten, or written and destroyed by O'Neill, is evident. But *A Touch of the Poet,* without departing from American realism in technique and style, rose above the garden variety of realistic plays with its author's characteristic sense of passion and magnitude. Aside from the insistent tension of its obstinate characters, the play carried O'Neill's familiar concern with the theme of illusion and self-deception. And this interest widens to include the social conflict of the old and the new families of the American immigration along with the mingling of backgrounds and heritages that characterize the making of American society.

In this respect *A Touch of the Poet* is not, of course, a departure from past American drama, which expressed a lively interest in social reality, especially during the 1930's. This interest, while by no means paramount in the recent period covered here, would also be represented in the present book by Lorraine Hansberry's *A Raisin in the Sun* but for a permissions problem. It is represented by the political comedy *The Best Man,* the product of Gore Vidal's interest in politics; and it is particularly representative of political playwriting in this country which has been rarely razor-sharp but often lively and engaging. Despite a modicum of satire and moral indignation, *The*

Best Man, of course, belongs to the main current of American optimism, to which the development and resolution of the play are tributary.

As might be expected, Tennessee Williams generally took an altogether different direction. It is true that he deviated into comedy (which made *me* uncomfortable) and hopefulness (which left *me* dubious) in his comedy *Period of Adjustment,* which had a friendly if not exactly enthusiastic reception on Broadway and was still better received in London, where it seemed to have been more successfully cast. No need to begrudge its author his attempt to bring some objectivity to the subject of private bedevilment and to treat it more lightly than has been his custom, although I could not but prefer the phosphorescence of this author's "decadence" to his trying to place himself on the side of "normality" and "health." But there was no need to fear that Mr. Williams had abandoned the byways of his familiar Baudelairian demon for Main Street. This strongly driven and by now rather facile playwright started the recent period with the devastating short drama *Suddenly Last Summer,* which was part of a double bill of one-acters. He did so with his usual flair for sensational yet also lyrical naturalism and with a remarkable amount of intense writing, getting trapped only toward the end by an overworked imagination and a hard-to-credit revelation of a poet's death by cannibalism. In his reworked early play *Battle of Angels,* retitled *Orpheus Descending,* the author's comprehensive vision embraced a section of the American South that was near neighbor to Hell and its actual analogue. "Orpheus" or Williams' wandering guitar player descended into the underworld and briefly recovered a small shop-keeping "Eurydice" only to lose her permanently to Hades or Death in the person of her moribund shop-keeping husband. Williams' protagonist, the itinerant entertainer, like Orpheus torn to pieces by enraged Maenads, is mangled to death by bloodhounds. If accredited members of the Theatre of the Absurd, assuming there are any, want to go further in the direction of nihilism, they will have to exert themselves.

The distinction between them and Williams is, on the face of it, stylistic, but it is also one of viewpoint. To them he must seem incurably romantic; he uses a rich palette in depicting the world, is nostalgic for some primal innocence of male and female, and is conspicuously (if not, indeed, ostentatiously) sympathetic to the poets, dreamers, and "lovers of life." This is the veriest absence of sophistication to those who cultivate detachment rather than attachment, and prefer irony to sympathy. By comparison with their dry writing reflecting a dry view of man's fate and folly, Williams' dialogue of failure is florid, and his gestures of despair picturesquely posed. But whether or not such criticism of Williams in the role of nihilist is as devastating as I have made it appear (and I am far from certain that he fancies himself in the role at all), *Orpheus Descending* is as fascinating as well as persistent an example of negativistic protest as could be found in the period's dramatic writing, exclusive of Gelber's *The Connection,* where the protest was both less scattered and less contrived.

Orpheus Descending also represents Williams' familiar striving for imaginative and poetic playwriting, a striving which, as in *Camino Real,* has brought him less success than one could desire. In the less ambitiously plotted play, *The Night of the Iguana,* we find Williams on surer ground. His sympathies and antipathies are the same as in *Orpheus Descending,* but the focus is sharper and rests on characters who are more like people than like literary figures and abstractions. The play provided principal roles that good casting could bring to life as well as caricatures the author used to represent the world against which the frail characters he usually favors somehow always get shattered. *The Night of the Iguana* was Williams' most fairly fleshed-out work of dramatic imagination since *Cat on a Hot Tin Roof.*

Other playwrights of the period undoubtedly also heard the long fashionable clamor from the sidelines of criticism calling upon them to recover "poetry" and imagination for the contemporary theatre. Most of our playwrights were not gifted enough or intrepid enough to make the effort. Those who made it and are represented in our book, Archibald MacLeish and Paddy Chayefsky, exercised discretion in their choice of means and ends—MacLeish in his modern morality play, *J.B.,* and Chayefsky in the Biblical fantasia *Gideon* as well as in the folk comedy of *The Tenth Man,* which could not be acquired for the present anthology. These ventures in verse and in prose were in the main satisfactory as well as unique popular experiments. An acute critic —and he needn't perhaps be extraordinarily acute—will have no difficulty in taking exceptions to both pieces, especially to the resolution in each of them. The present anthologist concurs in some of the published reservations in believing that in *Gideon* the shifts in tone suggest contrivance and unsteadiness of viewpoint, and that *J.B.* as revised on the road for the Broadway opening became too much of a concession to popular sentiment. But *Gideon* and *J.B.* call for attention here not only for their intrinsic interest but in representing some reach for moral understanding that could still be made on Broadway and receive public support.

Finally, the reader will encounter in this anthology the one work without which our most recent theatre could not have been properly represented, *Who's Afraid of Virginia Woolf?* This much may well be admitted even by those who take a dim view of Mr. Albee's play. It summarizes many well-noticed trends, such as absorption in domestic conflict and private tensions, frankness of language that disconcerts playgoers while possibly attracting more than a few of them too, and a despairing view of life. In Mr. Albee's play, however, the viewpoint is not so despairing as to banish humor, compassion, and even a thread of belief that "Walpurgis night" can end, delusion vanish, and purgation (however temporary) be accomplished. That a high order of artistic achievement is present in this work and outweighs the detectable faults is the very considered opinion of the editor of this anthology. That it is not strictly a Theatre of the Absurd exercise only proves that the maturing talent that went into the play is essentially original rather than imitative. It represents an early climax in a career that started in our period with a remarkable series of one-act plays, *The Zoo Story, The Death of Bessie Smith, The American Dream,* and *The Sandbox.* Into this work also went a good deal of interest, both critical and sympathetic, in the world outside the author's ego, so that the inclinations toward morbidity with which he has been charged (and to which he is as entitled

as any other young man in the course of nature and the time spirit) have been balanced by insight and objectivity. His dissatisfactions in all the work he has made public thus far have had substance and force even when they are not totally assimilated into the dramatic action and successfully resolved (or, if you will, left significantly unresolved). His scorn for conformity and complacency, his disgust with the banalities of the mundane and the pretensions of respectability, confirm his possession of the sensibility of an alienated artist and a lean critical intelligence.

Since Mr. Albee has also been uncannily skillful as a craftsman and has manifested skill in both conventional and unconventional dramatic forms, it is apparent that the period we have tended to deplore brought to the theatre a man of rare talent, which is no small thing. Should this talent ever reach full and continuing fruition, it could by itself alone compensate for recent seasons of meager harvest and blasted hopes. That the period, which was generally as mediocre in production art as in playwriting, has not greatly deserved such exculpation is an irony of happenstance that Mr. Albee's own mordant intelligence could enjoy.

4

So far as the present anthology is concerned it would be possible to conclude here, but at the risk of giving the false impression that this is all that half a decade of theatre has amounted to, give or take a few plays listed in the APPENDIX. But, of course, there is more to the theatre of any period than its literary or quasi-literary residue. While critics of the drama grew justifiably angry and the professional mourners of the theatre found more incitements to lamentation than before, a playgoer with plenty of leisure and cash could have still managed to retain an interest in life. He could have patronized (and he usually did) Broadway and off-Broadway musical comedies and revues that had entertainment to offer in part or whole, and in one department or another. He could have agreed with Harold Clurman, surely no lowbrow in show business, when he told *New York Times* readers that "Musical comedy is nothing to argue about; it is to be enjoyed"—and then proceeded to argue about it. The theatre buff could even confess that he was by no means distressed that the proportion of musicals to straight plays was growing steadily, for, as Mr. Clurman put the case, "even the weakest musical promises at least two or three good jokes, a talented performer, a bit of rhythm, one or two pretty ladies, a tune one might hum and several nice dresses . . ."

Also available to ardent playgoers were some rewarding dramatic readings of Dickens, Shakespeare, Dylan Thomas, Sean O'Casey, Carl Sandburg, Mark Twain, and Emily Dickinson by such virtuosi as John Gielgud, Emlyn Williams, Dorothy Stickney, Hal Holbrook, and others. There were the many Shakespeare festivals to attend, especially during the summer, in New York's Central Park, in nearby Stratford on the Housatonic, and points as far west as Oregon. For the peripatetic summer playgoer there were also available during the summer not only the many revivals (often excellent) in the country, but the pageant plays of Paul Green and Kermit Hunter in the South, rich sources of folk entertainment and instruction. (In 1959 there were ten such open-air productions during the summer.) And throughout the year the theatre was teeming with productions in colleges, small communities, and cities, an increasing number of which (led by Minneapolis, where Tyrone Guthrie took over production under local sponsorship in the spring of 1963) began to favor civic enterprise. Invaluable assistance to the best little theatre groups outside New York came from the Ford Foundation program in humanities and the arts, headed by W. McNeill Lowry. In the fall of 1962, Ford Foundation grants amounted to $6,100,000. The beneficiaries included New York's Actors Studio, San Francisco's valuable Actor's Workshop, Houston's Alley Theatre, Washington's notable Arena Theatre (which opened new quarters with an effective production of Brecht's modern parable *The Caucasian Chalk Circle*, staged by Alan Schneider), and the University of California Extension's theatre group in Los Angeles, headed by John Houseman, who, with Orson Welles, had founded the brilliant Mercury Theatre in New York during the nineteen-thirties.

Besides, it was not necessary to leave New York to have one's encounters with the theatre distinctly enriched by attractive, sometimes even impressive, Broadway and off-Broadway revivals of older plays, by the repertoires of visiting companies from England and continental Europe, and notably by productions created and first presented abroad. The largest number of rewarding Broadway productions came at times from England, where the drama had finally cut adrift from parlor comedy, exhausted a brief flurry of poetic theatre under the leadership of T. S. Eliot and Christopher Fry, discovered the genre of "social drama" we had developed perhaps with more stamina and point more than two decades ago in the grim nineteen-thirties, and inaugurated the reign of Britain's so-called angry young men. New York, as the chief metropolitan theatre center of the Western hemisphere, was the beneficiary. Broadway, in particular, received plays by John Osborne (*Look Back in Anger*), Robert Bolt (*A Man for All Seasons*). Harold Pinter (*The Caretaker*), Shelagh Delaney (*A Taste of Honey*), Brendan Behan (*The Hostage*), Eugène Ionesco (*Rhinoceros*), Jean Anouilh (*The Lark*), Friedrich Duerrenmatt (*The Visit*), and others, while the off-Broadway theatres played host to successful Brecht, Beckett, Ionesco, Pinter, and Genet productions. In the present anthology, as in the previous *Best American Plays* volumes, however, we are concerned only with the residue of new *American* plays. Seventeen of the most recent are presented here with some confidence, and both individually and collectively they have something important to show us about the state and character of the recent American theatre.

BEST AMERICAN PLAYS

Fifth Series—1957-1963

A TOUCH OF THE POET

Eugene O'Neill

Presented by The Producers Theatre (Robert Whitehead production) at the Helen Hayes Theatre, October 2, 1958, with the following cast:

MICKEY MALOY Tom Clancy
JAMIE GREGAN Curt Conway
SARA MELODY Kim Stanley
NORA MELODY Helen Hayes
CORNELIUS MELODY Eric Portman

DEBORAH (*Mrs. Henry Harford*)
  Betty Field
DAN ROCHE John Call
PADDY O'DOWD Art Smith
PATCH RILEY Farrell Pelly
NICHOLAS GADSBY Ludwig van Rooten

Staged by Harold Clurman
Designed by Ben Edwards

The action takes place in the dining room of Melody's Tavern, in a village a few miles from Boston, on July 27, 1828.

ACT ONE. Morning, 9 A.M.
ACT TWO. A half hour later.
ACT THREE. Evening, 8 P.M.
ACT FOUR. Midnight.

A TOUCH OF THE POET is the last but one full-length play left in manuscript at O'Neill's death. It was released for publication by the Yale University Press and then for stage production in the United States by Mrs. O'Neill. One can but applaud Mrs. O'Neill's decision because it not only gave Broadway one of its outstanding plays in a bumbling decade, but enabled the public to form an impression of the large cycle our cyclopean chief dramatist was laboring to erect on our puny stage during the many years of his self-imposed exile from the Broadway scene. Unwilling to leave to posterity an unwieldy structure with which he was patently dissatisfied, he destroyed much of the cycle and left the remainder in a few manuscripts saved from the burning and kept at Yale University's Sterling Library.

Eugene O'Neill (1888-1953) does not, of course, require any introduction to readers of this book. The only American playwright to have won international recognition with a Nobel Prize in addition to numerous productions throughout the civilized world (he also won four Pulitzer Prizes—three while alive, for *Beyond the Horizon* in 1920, *Anna Christie* in 1922, *Strange Interlude* in 1928, and a fourth posthumously for *Long Day's Journey into Night* in 1957), he has been praised for his visionary devotion to the drama as high art. It led him to experiment in various dramatic styles and to write plays much longer than the average—such as the nine-act *Strange Interlude* and the trilogy of *Mourning Becomes Electra* (1931), his translation of classic tragedy into modern psychological drama. *A Touch of the Poet* cannot indeed be judged entirely without taking into account its author's ambitious intentions, which he might very well have realized but for a long and progressive illness.

During the period under review there were other productions of O'Neill plays. The Actors Studio initiated its producing career with a revival of *Strange Interlude* early in 1963, with Geraldine Page filling the principal role originally played by Lynn Fontanne, and with José Quintero directing the new production. And a late play, *A Moon for the Misbegotten,* which had originally been tried out by the Theatre Guild and abandoned in the Midwest, was produced for the first time in New York on May 2, 1957. (See *Best American Plays: Fourth Series, 1951-1957* for the text.) *A Touch of the Poet* had 284 performances in the Times Square area.*

Time magazine's listing of *A Touch of the Poet* (Oct. 20, 1958) is perhaps the best capsule account of the play: O'Neill's "last chance to retell the tragedy of a man who lives by dreams—and lives on after they die." Whether or not the play is really a tragedy, *Time* leaves to the pundits to decide. "One black day in the life of Con Melody, Irish-born cavalry officer turned New England housekeeper," a day that brings not only disenchantment but a renunciation that is crushing whether or not it is tragic, is the actual content of the *single* "massive and moving piece of theatre" with which we are concerned. But Harold Clurman, who staged the play in New York, protested against playgoers' regarding "each play they see as a separate entity with no antecedents and no prospects into the future." (*Playbill,* Sept. 29, 1958.)

With Mr. Clurman one may see in the play a last return of the O'Neill themes of alienation and self-deception, a sense of the flux of values, and an awareness of conflict between dream and practicality. It is also a conflict between an old world of aristocratic values or pretensions already dying and a rising new mercantile society already born. As a result of Con Melody's pretensions and extravagances we may regard the play as no less comic than tragic, and one would be well advised to consider O'Neill's subject here as not merely the renunciation of the past, but as a positive urge toward the future in the impending marriage of Melody's daughter to the momentarily mooning young son of a Yankee tycoon, and a presage of the ultimate struggle between the simultaneous forward thrust of materialism and democracy on American soil.

Like so many of O'Neill's plays, *A Touch of the Poet* reflects its author's ambition to be comprehensive and significant; only in his technique, in abiding by realistic structure and rationalistic style, was O'Neill discreet and conservative. The play, reported

* For additional treatment of O'Neill's last plays by the present editor, the reader is referred to pages 232-241 in John Gassner's *Theatre at the Crossroads* (Holt, Rinehart and Winston, 1960).

to have been written around 1939 * (when "social thinking" reached its peak in the American theatre), represents O'Neill's effort to give social drama an epic sweep without loss of personal drama; and without typical chronicle-play attenuation—if not altogether without a plethora of repetition and prosaic writing. Yet it is plainly a compliment to O'Neill's blunt-edged power to carve out characters and situations impressively that so historically oriented a scholar and journalist as Max Lerner should have been able to call *A Touch of the Poet* "a strange and moving play," and exclaim "What play on Broadway today, by a living writer, plunges so abruptly into a tragic theme and works out so brooding a philosophy as man's entanglement with his image of himself?" (New York *Post,* October 22, 1958). It is also to O'Neill's credit that this tenacious and uncompromising playwright was not sufficiently satisfied with the play to have it published in his lifetime.

* Thanks to Arthur and Barbara Gelb, O'Neill's untiring biographers, we also know the exact date when O'Neill finished giving *A Touch of the Poet* its final form—November 13, 1942. It is the only completed play of his projected cycle of eleven plays, roughly sketched out and later destroyed, covering some 175 years of American life through the family started by the love affair of Con Melody's daughter and the unseen son of an upper-class Yankee family. That O'Neill's intention was to be critical of materialistic values is indicated by the title he gave to the cycle—*A Tale of Possessors Self-Dispossessed.* Illness prevented O'Neill from realizing more than a fraction of his dream. But the effort to realize it could have made even a healthy man quail, as he himself realized when he wrote Lawrence Langner of the Theatre Guild as early as 1936, his Nobel Prize year, that "A lady bearing quintuplets is having a debonaire, carefree time of it by comparison."

ACT ONE

SCENE. *The dining room of Melody's Tavern, in a village a few miles from Boston. The tavern is over a hundred years old. It had once been prosperous, a breakfast stop for the stagecoach, but the stage line had been discontinued and for some years now the tavern has fallen upon neglected days.*

The dining room and barroom were once a single spacious room, low-ceilinged, with heavy oak beams and paneled walls—the taproom of the tavern in its prosperous days, now divided into two rooms by a flimsy partition, the barroom being off left. The partition is painted to imitate the old paneled walls but this only makes it more of an eyesore.

At left front, two steps lead up to a closed door opening on a flight of stairs to the floor above. Farther back is the door to the bar. Between these doors hangs a large mirror. Beyond the bar door a small cabinet is fastened to the wall. At rear are four windows. Between the middle two is the street door. At right front is another door, open, giving on a hallway and the main stairway to the second floor, and leading to the kitchen. Farther front at right, there is a high schoolmaster's desk with a stool.

In the foreground are two tables. One, with four chairs, at left center; a larger one, seating six, at right center. At left and right, rear, are two more tables, identical with the ones at right center. All these tables are set with white tablecloths, etc., except the small one in the foreground at left.

It is around nine in the morning of July 27, 1828. Sunlight shines in through the windows at rear.

MICKEY MALOY *sits at the table at left front, facing right. He is glancing through a newspaper.* MALOY *is twenty-six, with a sturdy physique and an amiable, cunning face, his mouth usually set in a half-leering grin.*

JAMIE CREGAN *peers around the half-open door to the bar. Seeing* MALOY, *he comes in. As obviously Irish as Maloy, he is middle-aged, tall, with a lantern-jawed face. There is a scar of a saber cut over one cheekbone. He is dressed neatly but in old, worn clothes. His eyes are bloodshot, his manner sickly, but he grins as he greets* MALOY *sardonically.*

—

CREGAN. God bless all here—even the barkeep.

MALOY (*with an answering grin*). Top o' the mornin'.

CREGAN. Top 'o me head. (*He puts his hand to his head and groans.*) Be the saints, there's a blacksmith at work on it!

MALOY. Small wonder. You'd the divil's own load when you left at two this mornin'.

CREGAN. I must have. I don't remember leaving. (*He sits at right of table.*) Faix, you're takin' it aisy.

MALOY. There's no trade this time o'day.

CREGAN. It was a great temptation, when I saw no one in the bar, to make off with a bottle. A hair av the dog is what I need, but I've divil a penny in my pantaloons.

MALOY. Have one on the house. (*He goes to the cupboard and takes out a decanter of whiskey and a glass.*)

CREGAN. Thank you kindly. Sure, the good Samaritan was a crool haythen beside you.

MALOY. (*putting the decanter and glass before him*). It's the same you was drinking last night—his private dew. He keeps it here for emergencies when he don't want to go in the bar.

CREGAN (*pours out a big drink*). Lave it to Con never to be caught dry. (*Raising his glass.*) Your health and inclinations—if they're virtuous! (*He drinks and sighs with relief.*) God bless you, Whiskey, it's you can rouse the dead! Con hasn't been down yet for his morning's morning?

MALOY. No. He won't be till later.

CREGAN. It's like a miracle, me meeting him again. I came to these parts looking for work. It's only by accident I heard talk of a Con Melody and come here to see was it him. Until last night, I'd not seen hide nor hair of him since the war with the French in Spain—after the battle of Salamanca in '12. I was a corporal in the Seventh Dragoons and he was major. (*Proudly*) I got this cut from a saber at Talavera, bad luck to it!—serving under him. He was a captain then.

MALOY. So you told me last night.

CREGAN (*with a quick glance at him*). Did I now? I must have said more than my prayers, with the lashings of whiskey in me.

MALOY (*with a grin*). More than your prayers is the truth. (CREGAN *glances at him uneasily.* MALOY *pushes the decanter toward him.*) Take another taste.

CREGAN. I don't like sponging. Sure, my credit ought to be good in this shebeen! Ain't I his cousin?

MALOY. You're forgettin' what himself told you last night as he went up to bed. You could have all the whiskey you could pour down you, but not a penny's worth of credit. This house, he axed you to remember, only gives credit to gentlemen.

CREGAN. Divil mend him!

MALOY (*with a chuckle*). You kept thinking about his insults after he'd gone out, getting madder and madder.

CREGAN. God pity him, that's like him. He hasn't changed much. (*He pours out a drink and gulps it down—with a cautious look at* MALOY.) If I was mad at Con, and me blind drunk, I must have told you a power of lies.

MALOY (*winks slyly*). Maybe they wasn't lies.

CREGAN. If I said any wrong of Con Melody—

MALOY. Arrah, are you afraid I'll gab what you said to him? I won't, you can take my oath.

CREGAN (*his face clearing*). Tell me what I said and I'll tell you if it was lies.

MALOY. You said his father wasn't of the quality of Galway like he makes out, but a thievin' shebeen keeper who got rich by moneylendin' and squeezin' tenants and every manner of trick. And when he'd enough he married, and bought an estate with a pack of hounds and set up as one of the gentry. He'd hardly got settled when his wife died givin' birth to Con.

CREGAN. There's no lie there.

MALOY. You said none of the gentry would speak to auld Melody, but he had a tough hide and didn't heed them. He made up his mind he'd bring Con up a true gentleman, so he packed him off to Dublin to school, and after that to the College with sloos of money to prove himself the equal of any gentleman's son. But Con found, while there was plenty to drink on him and borrow money, there was few didn't sneer behind his back at his pretensions.

CREGAN. That's the truth, too. But Con wiped the sneer off their mugs when he called one av thim out and put a bullet in his hip. That was his first duel. It gave his pride the taste for revenge and after that he was always lookin' for an excuse to challenge someone.

MALOY. He's done a power av boastin' about his duels, but I thought he was lyin'.

CREGAN. There's no lie in it. It was that brought disgrace on him in the end, right after he'd been promoted to major. He got caught by a Spanish noble making love to his wife, just after the battle of Salamanca, and there was a duel and Con killed him. The scandal was hushed up but Con had to resign from the army. If it wasn't for his fine record for bravery in battle, they'd have court-martialed him. (*Then guiltily*) But I'm sayin' more than my prayers again.

MALOY. It's no news about his women. You'd think, to hear him when he's drunk, there wasn't one could resist him in Portugal and Spain.

CREGAN. If you'd seen him then, you wouldn't wonder. He was as strong as an ox, and on a thoroughbred horse, in his uniform, there wasn't a handsomer man in the army. And he had the chance he wanted in Portugal and Spain where a British officer was welcome in the gentry's houses. At home, the only women he'd known was whores. (*He adds hastily*) Except Nora, I mean. (*Lowering his voice*) Tell me, has he done any rampagin' wid women here?

MALOY. He hasn't. The damned Yankee gentry won't let him come near them, and he considers the few Irish around here to be scum beneath his notice. But once in a while there'll be some Yankee stops overnight wid his wife or daughter and then you'd laugh to see Con, if he thinks she's gentry, sidlin' up to her, playin' the great gentleman and makin' compliments, and then boasting afterward he could have them in bed if he'd had a chance at it, for all their modern Yankee airs.

CREGAN. And maybe he could. If you'd known him in the auld days, you'd nivir doubt any boast he makes about fightin' and women, and gamblin' or any kind av craziness. There nivir was a madder divil.

MALOY (*lowering his voice*). Speakin' av Nora, you nivir mentioned her last night, but I know all about it without you telling me. I used to have my room here, and there's nights he's madder drunk than most when he throws it in her face he had to marry her because— Mind you, I'm not saying anything against poor Nora. A sweeter woman never lived. And I know you know all about it.

CREGAN (*reluctantly*). I do. Wasn't I raised on his estate?

MALOY. He tells her it was the priests tricked him into marrying her. He hates priests.

CREGAN. He's a liar, then. He may like to blame it on them but it's little Con Melody cared what they said. Nothing ever made him do anything, except himself. He married her because he'd fallen in love with her, but he was ashamed of her in his pride at the same time because her folks were only ignorant peasants on his estate, as poor as poor. Nora was as pretty a girl as you'd find in a year's travel, and he'd come to be bitter lonely, with no woman's company but the whores was helpin' him ruin the estate. (*He shrugs his shoulders.*) Well, anyways, he married her and then went off to the war, and left her alone in the castle to have her child, and nivir saw her again till he was sent home from Spain. Then he raised what money he still was able, and took her and Sara here to America where no one would know him.

MALOY (*thinking this over for a moment*). It's hard for me to believe he ever loved her. I've seen the way he treats her now. Well, thank you for telling me, and I take my oath I'll nivir breathe a word of it—for Nora's sake, not his.

CREGAN (*grimly*). You'd better kape quiet for fear of him, too. If he's one-half the man he was, he could bate the lights out of the two av us.

MALOY. He's strong as a bull still for all the whiskey he's drunk. (*He pushes the bottle toward* CREGAN.) Have another taste. (CREGAN *pours out a drink.*) Drink hearty.

CREGAN. Long life. (*He drinks.* MALOY *puts the decanter and glass back in the cupboard. A girl's voice is heard from the hall at right.* CREGAN *jumps up—hastily.*) That's Sara, isn't it? I'll get out. She'll likely blame me for Con getting so drunk last night. I'll be back after Con is down. (*He goes out.* MALOY *starts to go in the bar, as if he too wanted to avoid* SARA.

Then he sits down defiantly.)

MALOY. Be damned if I'll run from her. (*He takes up the paper as* SARA MELODY *comes in from the hall at right.*)

(SARA *is twenty, an exceedingly pretty girl with a mass of black hair, fair skin with rosy cheeks, and beautiful, deep-blue eyes. There is a curious blending in her of what are commonly considered aristocratic and peasant characteristics. She has a fine forehead. Her nose is thin and straight. She has small ears set close to her well-shaped head, and a slender neck. Her mouth, on the other hand, has a touch of coarseness and sensuality and her jaw is too heavy. Her figure is strong and graceful, with full, firm breasts and hips, and a slender waist. But she has large feet and broad, ugly hands with stubby fingers. Her voice is soft and musical, but her speech has at times a self-conscious, stilted quality about it, due to her restraining a tendency to lapse into brogue. Her everyday working dress is of cheap material, but she wears it in a way that gives a pleasing effect of beauty unadorned.*)

SARA (*with a glance at* MALOY, *sarcastically*). I'm sorry to interrupt you when you're so busy, but have you your bar book ready for me to look over?

MALOY (*surlily*). I have. I put it on your desk.

SARA. Thank you. (*She turns her back on him, sits at the desk, takes a small account book from it, and begins checking figures.*)

MALOY (*watches her over his paper*). If it's profits you're looking for, you won't find them—not with all the drinks himself's been treating to. (*She ignores this. He becomes resentful.*) You've got your airs of a grand lady this morning, I see. There's no talkin' to you since you've been playin' nurse to the young Yankee upstairs. (*She makes herself ignore this, too.*) Well, you've had your cap set for him ever since he came to live by the lake, and now's your chance, when he's here sick and too weak to defend himself.

SARA (*turns on him—with quiet anger*). I warn you to mind your own business, Mickey, or I'll tell my father of your impudence. He'll teach you to keep your place, and God help you.

MALOY (*doesn't believe this threat but

is frightened by the possibility). Arrah, don't try to scare me. I know you'd never carry tales to him. (*Placatingly*) Can't you take a bit of teasing, Sara?

SARA (*turns back to her figuring*). Leave Simon out of your teasing.

MALOY. Oho, he's Simon to you now, is he? Well, well.

(*He gives her a cunning glance.*) Maybe, if you'd come down from your high horse, I could tell you some news.

SARA. You're worse than an old woman for gossip. I don't want to hear it.

MALOY. When you was upstairs at the back taking him his breakfast, there was a grand carriage with a nigger coachman stopped at the corner and a Yankee lady got out and came in here. I was sweeping and Nora was scrubbing the kitchen. (SARA *has turned to him, all attention now.*) She asked me what road would take her near the lake—

SARA (*starts*). Ah.

MALOY. So I told her, but she didn't go. She kept looking around, and said she'd like a cup of tea, and where was the waitress. I knew she must be connected someway with Harford or why would she want to go to the lake, where no one's ever lived but him. She didn't want tea at all, but only an excuse to stay.

SARA (*resentfully*). So she asked for the waitress, did she? I hope you told her I'm the owner's daughter, too.

MALOY. I did. I don't like Yankee airs any more than you. I was short with her. I said you was out for a walk, and the tavern wasn't open yet, anyway. So she went out and drove off.

SARA (*worriedly now*). I hope you didn't insult her with your bad manners. What did she look like, Mickey?

MALOY. Pretty, if you like that kind. A pale, delicate wisp of a thing with big eyes.

SARA. That fits what he's said of his mother. How old was she?

MALOY. It's hard to tell, but she's too young for his mother, I'd swear. Around thirty, I'd say. Maybe it's his sister.

SARA. He hasn't a sister.

MALOY (*grinning*). Then maybe she's an old sweetheart looking for you to scratch your eyes out.

SARA. He's never had a sweetheart.

MALOY (*mockingly*). Is that what he tells you, and you believe him? Faix, you

must be in love!

SARA (*angrily*). Will you mind your own business? I'm not such a fool! (*Worried again.*) Maybe you ought to have told her he's here sick to save her the drive in the hot sun and the walk through the woods for nothing.

MALOY. Why would I tell her, when she never mentioned him?

SARA. Yes, it's her own fault. But— Well, there's no use thinking of it now— or bothering my head about her, anyway, whoever she was. (*She begins checking figures again. Her mother appears in the doorway at right.*)

(NORA MELODY *is forty, but years of overwork and worry have made her look much older. She must have been as pretty as a girl as* SARA *is now. She still has the beautiful eyes her daughter has inherited. But she has become too worn out to take care of her appearance. Her black hair, streaked with gray, straggles in untidy wisps about her face. Her body is dumpy, with sagging breasts, and her old clothes are like a bag covering it, tied around the middle. Her red hands are knotted by rheumatism. Cracked working shoes, run down at the heel, are on her bare feet. Yet in spite of her slovenly appearance there is a spirit which shines through and makes her lovable, a simple sweetness and charm, something gentle and sad and, somehow, dauntless.*)

MALOY (*jumps to his feet, his face lighting up with affection*). God bless you, Nora, you're the one I was waitin' to see. Will you keep an eye on the bar while I run to the store for a bit av 'baccy?

SARA (*sharply*). Don't do it, Mother.

NORA (*smiles—her voice is soft, with a rich brogue*). Why wouldn't I? "Don't do it, Mother."

MALOY. Thank you, Nora. (*He goes to the door at rear and opens it, burning for a parting shot at* SARA.) And the back o' my hand to you, your Ladyship! (*He goes out, closing the door.*)

SARA. You shouldn't encourage his laziness. He's always looking for excuses to shirk.

NORA. Ah, nivir mind, he's a good lad. (*She lowers herself painfully on the nearest chair at the rear of the table at center front.*) Bad cess to the rheumatism. It has me destroyed this mornin'.

SARA (*still checking figures in the book*

—gives her mother an impatient but at the same time worried glance. Her habitual manner toward her is one of mingled love and pity and exasperation). I've told you a hundred times to see the doctor.

NORA. We've no money for doctors. They're bad luck, anyway. They bring death with them. (*A pause.* NORA *sighs.*) Your father will be down soon. I've some fine fresh eggs for his breakfast.

SARA (*her face becomes hard and bitter*). He won't want them.

NORA (*defensively*). You mean he'd a drop too much taken last night? Well, small blame to him, he hasn't seen Jamie since—

SARA. *Last* night? What night hasn't he?

NORA. Ah, don't be hard on him. (*A pause—worriedly*) Neilan sent round a note to me about his bill. He says we'll have to settle by the end of the week or we'll get no more groceries. (*With a sigh.*) I can't blame him. How we'll manage, I dunno. There's the intrist on the mortgage due the first. But that I've saved, God be thanked.

SARA (*exasperatedly*). If you'd only let me take charge of the money.

NORA (*with a flare of spirit*). I won't. It'd mean you and himself would be at each other's throats from dawn to dark. It's bad enough between you as it is.

SARA. Why didn't you pay Neilan the end of last week? You told me you had the money put aside.

NORA. So I did. But Dickinson was tormentin' your father with his feed bill for the mare.

SARA (*angrily*). I might have known! The mare comes first, if she takes the bread out of our mouths! The grand gentleman must have his thoroughbred to ride out in state!

NORA (*defensively*). Where's the harm? She's his greatest pride. He'd be heartbroken if he had to sell her.

SARA. Oh yes, I know well he cares more for a horse than for us!

NORA. Don't be saying that. He has great love for you, even if you do be provokin' him all the time.

SARA. Great love for me! Arrah, God pity you, Mother!

NORA (*sharply*). Don't put on the brogue, now. You know how he hates to hear you. And I do, too. There's no excuse not to cure yourself. Didn't he send you to school so you could talk like a gentleman's daughter?

SARA (*resentfully, but more careful of her speech*). If he did, I wasn't there long.

NORA. It was you insisted on leavin'.

SARA. Because if he hadn't the pride or love for you not to live on your slaving your heart out, I had that pride and love!

NORA (*tenderly*). I know, Acushla. I know.

SARA (*with bitter scorn*). We can't afford a waitress, but he can afford to keep a thoroughbred mare to prance around on and show himself off! And he can afford a barkeep when, if he had any decency, he'd do his part and tend the bar himself.

NORA (*indignantly*). Him, a gentleman, tend bar!

SARA. A gentleman! Och, Mother, it's all right for the two of us, out of our own pride, to pretend to the world we believe that lie, but it's crazy for you to pretend to me.

NORA (*stubbornly*). It's no lie. He *is* a gentleman. Wasn't he born rich in a castle on a grand estate and educated in college, and wasn't he an officer in the Duke of Wellington's army—

SARA. All right, Mother. You can humor his craziness, but he'll never make me pretend to him I don't know the truth.

NORA. Don't talk as if you hated him. You ought to be shamed—

SARA. I do hate him for the way he treats you. I heard him again last night, raking up the past, and blaming his ruin on his having to marry you.

NORA (*protests miserably*). It was the drink talkin', not him.

SARA (*exasperated*). It's you ought to be ashamed, for not having more pride! You bear all his insults as meek as a lamb! You keep on slaving for him when it's that has made you old before your time! (*Angrily*) You can't much longer, I tell you! He's getting worse. You'll have to leave him.

NORA (*aroused*). I'll never! Howld your prate!

SARA. You'd leave him today, if you had any pride!

NORA. I've pride in my love for him! I've loved him since the day I set eyes on him, and I'll love him till the day I die! (*With a strange superior scorn.*) It's little you know of love, and you never will, for there's the same divil of pride in you that's in him, and it'll kape you from ivir givin' all of yourself, and that's what love is.

SARA. I could give all of myself if I wanted to, but—

NORA. If! Wanted to! Faix, it proves how little of love you know when you prate about if's and want-to's. It's when you don't give a thought for all the if's and want-to's in the world! It's when, if all the fires of hell was between you, you'd walk in them gladly to be with him, and sing with joy at your own burnin', if only his kiss was on your mouth! That's love, and I'm proud I've known the great sorrow and joy of it!

SARA (*cannot help being impressed—looks at her mother with wondering respect*). You're a strange woman, Mother. (*She kisses her impulsively.*) And a grand woman! (*Defiant again, with an arrogant toss of her head.*) I'll love—but I'll love where it'll gain me freedom and not put me in slavery for life.

NORA. There's no slavery in it when you love! (*Suddenly her exultant expression crumbles and she breaks down.*) For the love of God, don't take the pride of my love from me, Sara, for without it what am I at all but an ugly, fat woman gettin' old and sick!

SARA (*puts her arm around her—soothingly*). Hush, Mother. Don't mind me. (*Briskly, to distract her mother's mind*) I've got to finish the bar book. Mickey can't put two and two together without making five. (*She goes to the desk and begins checking figures again.*)

NORA (*dries her eyes—after a pause she sighs worriedly*). I'm worried about your father. Father Flynn stopped me on the road yesterday and tould me I'd better warn him not to sneer at the Irish around here and call thim scum, or he'll get in trouble. Most of thim is in a rage at him because he's come out against Jackson and the Democrats and says he'll vote with the Yankees for Quincy Adams.

SARA (*contemptuously*). Faith, they can't see a joke, then, for it's a great joke to hear him shout against mob rule, like one of the Yankee gentry, when you know what he came from. And after the way the Yanks swindled him when he came here, getting him to buy this inn by telling him a new coach line was going to stop here. (*She laughs with bitter scorn.*) Oh, he's the easiest fool ever came to America! It's

that I hold against him as much as anything, that when he came here the chance was before him to make himself all his lies pretended to be. He had education above most Yanks, and he had money enough to start him, and this is a country where you can rise as high as you like, and no one but the fools who envy you care what you rose from, once you've the money and the power goes with it. (*Passionately.*) Oh, if I was a man with the chance he had, there wouldn't be a dream I'd not make come true! (*She looks at her mother, who is staring at the floor dejectedly and hasn't been listening. She is exasperated for a second—then she smiles pityingly.*) You're a fine one to talk to, Mother. Wake up. What's worrying you now?

NORA. Father Flynn tould me again I'd be damned in hell for lettin' your father make a haythen of me and bring you up a haythen, too.

SARA (*with an arrogant toss of her head*). Let Father Flynn mind his own business, and not frighten you with fairy tales about hell.

NORA. It's true, just the same.

SARA. True, me foot! You ought to tell the good Father we aren't the ignorant shanty scum he's used to dealing with. (*She changes the subject abruptly—closing Mickey's bar book.*) There. That's done. (*She puts the book in the desk.*) I'll take a walk to the store and have a talk with Neilan. Maybe I can blarney him to let the bill go another month.

NORA (*gratefully*). Oh, you can. Sure, you can charm a bird out of a tree when you want to. But I don't like you beggin' to a Yankee. It's all right for me but I know how you hate it.

SARA (*puts her arms around her mother —tenderly*). I don't mind at all, if I can save you a bit of the worry that's killing you. (*She kisses her.*) I'll change to my Sunday dress so I can make a good impression.

NORA (*with a teasing smile*). I'm thinkin' it isn't on Neilan alone you want to make an impression. You've changed to your Sunday best a lot lately.

SARA (*coquettishly*). Aren't you the sly one! Well, maybe you're right.

NORA. How was he when you took him his breakfast?

SARA. Hungry, and that's a good sign. He had no fever last night. Oh, he's on the road to recovery now, and it won't be long before he'll be back in his cabin by the lake.

NORA. I'll never get it clear in my head what he's been doing there the past year, living like a tramp or a tinker, and him a rich gentleman's son.

SARA (*with a tender smile*). Oh, he isn't like his kind, or like anyone else at all. He's a born dreamer with a raft of great dreams, and he's very serious about them. I've told you before he wanted to get away from his father's business, where he worked for a year after he graduated from Harvard College, because he didn't like being in trade, even if it is a great company that trades with the whole world in its own ships.

NORA (*approvingly*). That's the way a true gentleman would feel—

SARA. He wanted to prove his independence by living alone in the wilds, and build his own cabin, and do all the work, and support himself simply, and feel one with Nature, and think great thoughts about what life means, and write a book about how the world can be changed so people won't be greedy to own money and land and get the best of each other but will be content with little and live in peace and freedom together, and it will be like heaven on earth. (*She laughs fondly—and a bit derisively.*) I can't remember all of it. It seems crazy to me, when I think of what people are like. He hasn't written any of it yet, anyway—only the notes for it. (*She smiles coquettishly.*) All he's written the last few months are love poems.

NORA. That's since you began to take long walks by the lake. (*She smiles.*) It's you are the sly one.

SARA (*laughing*). Well, why shouldn't I take walks on our own property? (*Her tone changes to a sneer.*) The land our great gentleman was swindled into buying when he came here with grand ideas of owning an American estate! —a bit of farm land no one would work any more, and the rest all wilderness! You couldn't give it away.

NORA (*soothingly*). Hush, now. (*Changing the subject.*) Well, it's easy to tell young Master Harford has a touch av the poet in him— (*She adds before she thinks*) the same as your father.

SARA (*scornfully*). God help you, Mother! Do you think Father's a poet be-

cause he shows off reciting Lord Byron?

NORA (*with an uneasy glance at the door at left front*). Whist, now. Himself will be down any moment. (*Changing the subject*) I can see the Harford lad is falling in love with you.

SARA (*her face lights up triumphantly*). Falling? He's fallen head over heels. He's so timid, he hasn't told me yet, but I'll get him to soon.

NORA. I know you're in love with him.

SARA (*simply*). I am, Mother. (*She adds quickly*) But not too much. I'll not let love make me any man's slave. I want to love him just enough so I can marry him without cheating him, or myself. (*Determinedly.*) For I'm going to marry him, Mother. It's my chance to rise in the world and nothing will keep me from it.

NORA (*admiringly*). Musha, but you've boastful talk! What about his fine Yankee family? His father'll likely cut him off widout a penny if he marries a girl who's poor and Irish.

SARA. He may at first, but when I've proved what a good wife I'll be— He can't keep Simon from marrying me. I know that. Simon doesn't care what his father thinks. It's only his mother I'm afraid of. I can tell she's had great influence over him. She must be a queer creature, from all he's told me. She's very strange in her ways. She never goes out at all but stays home in their mansion, reading books, or in her garden. (*She pauses.*) Did you notice a carriage stop here this morning, Mother?

NORA (*preoccupied—uneasily*). Don't count your chickens before they're hatched. Young Harford seems a dacent lad. But maybe it's not marriage he's after.

SARA (*angrily*). I won't have you wronging him, Mother. He has no thought— (*Bitterly*) I suppose you're bound to suspect— (*She bites her words back, ashamed.*) Forgive me, Mother. But it's wrong of you to think badly of Simon. (*She smiles.*) You don't know him. Faith, if it came to seducing, it'd be me that'd have to do it. He's that respectful you'd think I was a holy image. It's only in his poems, and in the diary he keeps— I had a peek in it one day I went to tidy up the cabin for him. He's terribly ashamed of his sinful inclinations and the insult they are to my purity. (*She laughs tenderly.*)

NORA (*smiling, but a bit shocked*).

Don't talk so bould. I don't know if it's right, you to be in his room so much, even if he is sick. There's a power av talk about the two av you already.

SARA. Let there be, for all I care! Or all Simon cares, either. When it comes to not letting others rule him, he's got a will of his own behind his gentleness. Just as behind his poetry and dreams I feel he has it in him to do anything he wants. So even if his father cuts him off, with me to help him we'll get on in the world. For I'm no fool, either.

NORA. Glory be to God, you have the fine opinion av yourself!

SARA (*laughing*). Haven't I, though! (*Then bitterly.*) I've had need to have, to hold my head up, slaving as a waitress and chambermaid so my father can get drunk every night like a gentleman!

(*The door at left front is slowly opened and* CORNELIUS MELODY *appears in the doorway above the two steps. He and* SARA *stare at each other. She stiffens into hostility and her mouth sets in scorn. For a second his eyes waver and he looks guilty. Then his face becomes expressionless. He descends the steps and bows—pleasantly.*)

MELODY. Good morning, Sara.

SARA (*curtly*). Good morning. (*Then, ignoring him*) I'm going up and change my dress, Mother. (*She goes out right.*)

(CORNELIUS MELODY *is forty-five, tall, broad-shouldered, deep-chested, and powerful, with long muscular arms, big feet, and large hairy hands. His heavy-boned body is still firm, erect, and soldierly. Beyond shaky nerves, it shows no effects of hard drinking. It has a bull-like, impervious strength, a tough peasant vitality. It is his face that reveals the ravages of dissipation—a ruined face, which was once extraordinarily handsome in a reckless, arrogant fashion. It is still handsome—the face of an embittered Byronic hero, with a finely chiseled nose over a domineering, sensual mouth set in disdain, pale, hollow-cheeked, framed by thick, curly iron-gray hair. There is a look of wrecked distinction about it, of brooding, humiliated pride. His bloodshot gray eyes have an insulting cold stare which anticipates insult. His manner is that of a polished gentleman. Too much so. He overdoes it and one soon feels that he is overplaying a role which has become more real than his real self to him. But in spite of this, there is something formidable and impressive about him. He is dressed with foppish elegance in old, expensive, finely tailored clothes of the style worn by English aristocracy in Peninsular War days.*)

MELODY (*advancing into the room— bows formally to his wife*). Good morning, Nora. (*His tone condescends. It addresses a person of inferior station.*)

NORA (*stumbles to her feet—timidly*). Good mornin', Con. I'll get your breakfast.

MELODY. No. Thank you. I want nothing now.

NORA (*coming toward him*). You look pale. Are you sick, Con, darlin'?

MELODY. No.

NORA (*puts a timid hand on his arm*). Come and sit down. (*He moves his arm away with instinctive revulsion and goes to the table at center front, and sits in the chair she had occupied.* NORA *hovers round him.*) I'll wet a cloth in cold water to put round your head.

MELODY. No! I desire nothing—except a little peace in which to read the news. (*He picks up the paper and holds it so it hides his face from her.*)

NORA (*meekly*). I'll lave you in peace.

(*She starts to go to the door at right but turns to stare at him worriedly again. Keeping the paper before his face with his left hand, he reaches out with his right and pours a glass of water from the carafe on the table. Although he cannot see his wife, he is nervously conscious of her. His hand trembles so violently that when he attempts to raise the glass to his lips the water sloshes over his hand and he sets the glass back on the table with a bang. He lowers the paper and explodes nervously.*)

MELODY. For God's sake, stop your staring!

NORA. I— I was only thinkin' you'd feel better if you'd a bit av food in you.

MELODY. I told you once—! (*Controlling his temper*) I am not hungry, Nora. (*He raises the paper again. She sighs, her hands fiddling with her apron. A pause.*)

NORA (*dully*). Maybe it's a hair av the dog you're needin'.

MELODY (*as if this were something he had been waiting to hear, his expression loses some of its nervous strain. But he replies virtuously*). No, damn the liquor. Upon my conscience, I've about made up my mind I'll have no more of it. Besides, it's a bit early in the day.

NORA. If it'll give you an appetite—

MELODY. To tell the truth, my stomach is out of sorts. (*He licks his lips.*) Perhaps a drop wouldn't come amiss. (NORA *gets the decanter and glass from the cupboard and sets them before him. She stands gazing at him with a resigned sadness.* MELODY, *his eyes on the paper, is again acutely conscious of her. His nerves cannot stand it. He throws his paper down and bursts out in bitter anger.*) Well? I know what you're thinking! Why haven't you the courage to say it for once? By God, I'd have more respect for you! I hate the damned meek of this earth! By the rock of Cashel, I sometimes believe you have always deliberately encouraged me to— It's the one point of superiority you can lay claim to, isn't it?

NORA (*bewilderedly—on the verge of tears*) I don't— It's only your comfort— I can't bear to see you—

MELODY (*his expression changes and a look of real affection comes into his eyes. He reaches out a shaking hand to pat her shoulder with an odd, guilty tenderness. He says quietly and with genuine contrition*). Forgive me, Nora. That was unpardonable. (*Her face lights up. Abruptly he is ashamed of being ashamed. He looks away and grabs the decanter. Despite his trembling hand he manages to pour a drink and get it to his mouth and drain it. Then he sinks back in his chair and stares at the table, waiting for the liquor to take effect. After a pause he sighs with relief.*) I confess I needed that as medicine. I begin to feel more myself. (*He pours out another big drink and this time his hand is steadier, and he downs it without much difficulty. He smacks his lips.*) By the Immortal, I may have sunk to keeping an inn but at least I've a conscience in my trade. I keep liquor a gentleman can drink. (*He starts looking over the paper again—scowls at something—disdainfully, emphasizing his misquote of the line from Byron.*) "There shall he rot —Ambition's *dis*honored fool!" The paper is full of the latest swindling lies of that idol of the riffraff, Andrew Jackson. Contemptible, drunken scoundrel! But he will be the next President, I predict, for all we others can do to prevent. There is a cursed destiny in these decadent times. Every-

where the scum rises to the top. (*His eyes fasten on the date and suddenly he strikes the table with his fist.*) Today is the 27th! By God, and I would have forgotten!

NORA. Forgot what?

MELODY. The anniversary of Talavera?

NORA (*hastily*). Oh, ain't I stupid not to remember.

MELODY (*bitterly*). I had forgotten myself and no wonder. It's a far cry from this dunghill on which I rot to that glorious day when the Duke of Wellington—Lord Wellesley, then—did me the honor before all the army to commend my bravery. (*He glances around the room with loathing.*) A far cry, indeed! It would be better to forget!

NORA (*rallying him*). No, no, you mustn't. You've never missed celebratin' it and you won't today. I'll have a special dinner for you like I've always had.

MELODY (*with a quick change of manner —eagerly*). Good, Nora. I'll invite Jamie Cregan. It's a stroke of fortune he is here. He served under me at Talavera, as you know. A brave soldier, if he isn't a gentleman. You can place him on my right hand. And we'll have Patch Riley to make music, and O'Dowd and Roche. If they are rabble, they're full of droll humor at times. But put them over there. (*He points to the table at left front.*) I may tolerate their presence out of charity, but I'll not sink to dining at the same table.

NORA. I'll get your uniform from the trunk, and you'll wear it for dinner like you've done each year.

MELODY. Yes, I must confess I still welcome an excuse to wear it. It makes me feel at least the ghost of the man I was then.

NORA. You're so handsome in it still, no woman could take her eyes off you.

MELODY (*with a pleased smile*). I'm afraid you've blarney on your tongue this morning, Nora. (*Then boastfully*) But it's true, in those days in Portugal and Spain— (*He stops a little shamefacedly, but* NORA *gives no sign of offense. He takes her hand and pats it gently—avoiding her eyes.*) You have the kindest heart in the world, Nora. And I— (*His voice breaks.*)

NORA (*instantly on the verge of grateful tears*). Ah, who wouldn't, Con darlin', when you— (*She brushes a hand across her eyes—hastily.*) I'll go to the store and get something tasty. (*Her face drops as she remembers.*) But, God help us, where's the money?

MELODY (*stiffens—haughtily*). Money? Since when has my credit not been good?

NORA (*hurriedly*). Don't fret, now. I'll manage. (*He returns to his newspaper, disdaining further interest in money matters.*)

MELODY. Ha. I see work on the railroad at Baltimore is progressing. (*Lowering his paper*) By the Eternal, if I had not been a credulous gull and let the thieving Yankees swindle me of all I had when we came here, that's how I would invest my funds now. And I'd become rich. This country, with its immense territory, cannot depend solely on creeping canal boats, as shortsighted fools would have us believe. We must have railroads. Then you will see how quickly America will become rich and great! (*His expression changes to one of bitter hatred.*) Great enough to crush England in the next war between them, which I know is inevitable! Would I could live to celebrate that victory! If I have one regret for the past—and there are few things in it that do not call for bitter regret—it is that I shed my blood for a country that thanked me with disgrace. But I will be avenged. This country—my country, now—will drive the English from the face of the earth their shameless perfidy has dishonored!

NORA. Glory be to God for that! And we'll free Ireland!

MELODY (*contemptuously*). Ireland? What benefit would freedom be to her unless she could be freed from the Irish? (*Then irritably*) But why do I discuss such things with you?

NORA (*humbly*). I know. I'm ignorant.

MELODY. Yet I tried my best to educate you, after we came to America—until I saw it was hopeless.

NORA. You did, surely. And I tried, too, but—

MELODY. You won't even cure yourself of that damned peasant's brogue. And your daughter is becoming as bad.

NORA. She only puts on the brogue to tease you. She can speak as fine as any lady in the land if she wants.

MELODY (*is not listening—sunk in bitter brooding*). But, in God's name, who am I to reproach anyone with anything? Why don't you tell me to examine my own conduct?

NORA. You know I'd never.

MELODY (*stares at her—again he is moved—quietly*). No. I know you would not, Nora. (*He looks away—after a pause.*) I owe you an apology for what happened last night.

NORA. Don't think of it.

MELODY (*with assumed casualness*). Faith, I'd a drink too many, talking over old times with Jamie Cregan.

NORA. I know.

MELODY. I am afraid I may have— The thought of old times— I become bitter. But you understand, it was the liquor talking, if I said anything to wound you.

NORA. I know it.

MELODY (*deeply moved, puts his arm around her*). You're a sweet, kind woman, Nora—too kind. (*He kisses her.*)

NORA (*with blissful happiness*). Ah, Con darlin', what do I care what you say when the black thoughts are on you? Sure, don't you know I love you?

MELODY (*a sudden revulsion of feeling convulses his face. He bursts out with disgust, pushing her away from him*). For God's sake, why don't you wash your hair? It turns my stomach with its stink of onions and stew! (*He reaches for the decanter and shakingly pours a drink.* NORA *looks as if he had struck her.*)

NORA (*dully*). I do be washin' it often to plaze you. But when you're standin' over the stove all day, you can't help—

MELODY. Forgive me, Nora. Forget I said that. My nerves are on edge. You'd better leave me alone.

NORA (*her face brightening a little*). Will you ate your breakfast now? I've fine fresh eggs—

MELODY (*grasping at this chance to get rid of her—impatiently*). Yes! In a while. Fifteen minutes, say. But leave me alone now. (*She goes out right.* MELODY *drains his drink. Then he gets up and paces back and forth, his hands clasped behind him. The third drink begins to work and his face becomes arrogantly self-assured. He catches his reflection in the mirror on the wall at left and stops before it. He brushes a sleeve fastidiously, adjusts the set of his coat, and surveys himself.*) Thank God, I still bear the unmistakable stamp of an officer and a gentleman. And so I will remain to the end, in spite of all fate can do to crush my spirit! (*He squares his shoulders defiantly. He stares into his eyes in the glass and recites from Byron's "Childe Harold," as if it were an incantation by which he summons pride to justify his life to himself.*)

"I have not loved the World, nor the
    World me;
I have not flattered its rank breath,
    nor bowed
To its idolatries a patient knee,
Nor coined my cheek to smiles,—nor
    cried aloud
In worship of an echo: in the crowd
They could not deem me one of such
    —I stood
Among them, but not of them . . ."

(*He pauses, then repeats:*) "Among them, but not of them." By the Eternal, that expresses it! Thank God for you, Lord Byron—poet and nobleman who made of his disdain immortal music! (SARA *appears in the doorway at right. She has changed to her Sunday dress, a becoming blue that brings out the color of her eyes. She draws back for a moment—then stands watching him contemptuously.* MELODY *senses her presence. He starts and turns quickly away from the mirror. For a second his expression is guilty and confused, but he immediately assumes an air of gentlemanly urbanity and bows to her.*) Ah, it's you, my dear. Are you going for a morning stroll? You've a beautiful day for it. It will bring fresh roses to your cheeks.

SARA. I don't know about roses, but it will bring a blush of shame to my cheeks. I have to beg Neilan to give us another month's credit, because you made Mother pay the feed bill for your fine thoroughbred mare! (*He gives no sign he hears this. She adds scathingly*) I hope you saw something in the mirror you could admire!

MELODY (*in a light tone*). Faith, I suppose I must have looked a vain peacock, preening himself, but you can blame the bad light in my room. One cannot make a decent toilet in that dingy hole in the wall.

SARA. You have the best room in the house, that we ought to rent to guests.

MELODY. Oh, I've no complaints. I was merely explaining my seeming vanity.

SARA. Seeming!

MELODY (*keeping his tone light*). Faith, Sara, you must have risen the wrong side of the bed this morning, but it takes two to make a quarrel and I don't feel quarrelsome. Quite the contrary. I was about to tell you how exceedingly charming and pretty you look, my dear.

SARA (*with a mocking, awkward, servant's curtsy—in broad brogue*). Oh, thank ye, yer Honor.

MELODY. Every day you resemble your mother more, as she looked when I first knew her.

SARA. Musha, but it's you have the blarneyin' tongue, God forgive you!

MELODY (*in spite of himself, this gets under his skin—angrily*). Be quiet! How dare you talk to me like a common, ignorant— You're my daughter, damn you. (*He controls himself and forces a laugh.*) A fair hit! You're a great tease, Sara. I shouldn't let you score so easily. Your mother warned me you only did it to provoke me. (*Unconsciously he reaches out for the decanter on the table—then pulls his hand back.*)

SARA (*contemptuously—without brogue now*). Go on and drink. Surely you're not ashamed before me, after all these years.

MELODY (*haughtily*). Ashamed? I don't understand you. A gentleman drinks as he pleases—provided he can hold his liquor as he should.

SARA. A gentleman!

MELODY (*pleasantly again*). I hesitated because I had made a good resolve to be abstemious today. But if you insist— (*He pours a drink—a small one—his hand quite steady now.*) To your happiness, my dear. (*She stares at him scornfully. He goes on graciously.*) Will you do me the favor to sit down? I have wanted a quiet chat with you for some time. (*He holds out a chair for her at rear of the table at center.*)

SARA (*eyes him suspiciously—then sits down*). What is it you want?

MELODY (*with a playfully paternal manner*). Your happiness, my dear, and what I wish to discuss means happiness to you, unless I have grown blind. How is our patient, young Simon Harford, this morning?

SARA (*curtly*). He's better.

MELODY. I am delighted to hear it. (*Gallantly*) How could he help but be with such a charming nurse? (*She stares at him coldly. He goes on.*) Let us be frank. Young Simon is in love with you. I can see that with half an eye—and, of course, you know it. And you return his love, I surmise.

SARA. Surmise whatever you please.

MELODY. Meaning you do love him? I am glad, Sara. (*He becomes sentimentally romantic.*) Requited love is the greatest blessing life can bestow on us poor mortals; and first love is the most blessed of all. As Lord Byron has it: (*He recites*)

"But sweeter still than this, than these, than all,
Is first and passionate Love—it stands alone,
Like Adam's recollection of his fall . . ."

SARA (*interrupts him rudely*). Was it to listen to you recite Byron—?

MELODY (*concealing discomfiture and resentment—pleasantly*). No. What I was leading up to is that you have my blessing, if that means anything to you. Young Harford is, I am convinced, an estimable youth. I have enjoyed my talks with him. It has been a privilege to be able to converse with a cultured gentleman again. True, he is a bit on the sober side for one so young, but by way of compensation, there is a romantic touch of the poet behind his Yankee phlegm.

SARA. It's fine you approve of him!

MELODY. In your interest I have had some enquiries made about his family.

SARA (*angered—with taunting brogue*). Have you, indade? Musha, that's cute av you! Was it auld Patch Riley, the Piper, made them? Or was it Dan Roche or Paddy O'Dowd, or some other drunken sponge—

MELODY (*as if he hadn't heard—condescendingly*). I find his people will pass muster.

SARA. Oh, do you? That's nice!

MELODY. Apparently, his father is a gentleman—that is, by Yankee standards, insofar as one in trade can lay claim to the title. But as I've become an American citizen myself, I suppose it would be downright snobbery to hold to old-world standards.

SARA. Yes, wouldn't it be!

MELODY. Though it is difficult at times for my pride to remember I am no longer the master of Melody Castle and an estate of three thousand acres of as fine pasture and woodlands as you'd find in the whole United Kingdom, with my stable of hunters, and—

SARA (*bitterly*). Well, you've a beautiful thoroughbred mare now, at least—to prove you're still a gentleman!

MELODY (*stung into defiant anger*). Yes, I've the mare! And by God, I'll keep her if I have to starve myself so she may eat.

SARA. You mean, make Mother slave to keep her for you, even if she has to starve!

MELODY (*controls his anger—and ignores this*). But what was I saying? Oh, yes, young Simon's family. His father will pass muster, but it's through his mother, I believe, he comes by his really good blood. My information is, she springs from generations of well-bred gentlefolk.

SARA. It would be a great pride to her, I'm sure, to know you found her suitable!

MELODY. I suppose I may expect the young man to request an interview with me as soon as he is up and about again?

SARA. To declare his honorable intentions and ask you for my hand, is that what you mean?

MELODY. Naturally. He is a man of honor. And there are certain financial arrangements Simon's father or his legal representative will wish to discuss with me. The amount of your settlement has to be agreed upon.

SARA (*stares at him as if she could not believe her ears*). My settlement! Simon's father! God pity you— !

MELODY (*firmly*). Your settlement, certainly. You did not think, I hope, that I would give you away without a penny to your name as if you were some poverty-stricken peasant's daughter? Please remember I have my own position to maintain. Of course, it is a bit difficult at present. I am temporarily hard pressed. But perhaps a mortgage on the inn—

SARA. It's mortgaged to the hilt already, as you very well know.

MELODY. If nothing else, I can always give my note at hand for whatever amount—

SARA. You can give it, sure enough! But who'll take it?

MELODY. Between gentlemen, these matters can always be arranged.

SARA. God help you, it must be a wonderful thing to live in a fairy tale where only dreams are real to you. (*Then sharply*) But you needn't waste your dreams worrying about my affairs. I'll thank you not to interfere. Attend to your drinking and leave me alone. (*He gives no indication that he has heard a word she has said. She stares at him and a look almost of fear comes into her eyes. She bursts out with a bitter exasperation in which there is a strong undercurrent of entreaty.*) Father! Will you never let yourself wake up—not even now when you're sober, or nearly? Is it stark mad you've gone, so you can't tell any more what's dead and a lie, and what's the living truth?

MELODY (*his face is convulsed by a spasm of pain as if something vital had been stabbed in him—with a cry of tortured appeal*). Sara! (*But instantly his pain is transformed into rage. He half rises from his chair threateningly.*) Be quiet, damn you! How dare you— ! (*She shrinks away and rises to her feet. He forces control on himself and sinks back in his chair, his hands gripping the arms.*)

(*The street door at rear is flung open and DAN ROCHE, PADDY O'DOWD, and PATCH RILEY attempt to pile in together and get jammed for a moment in the doorway. They all have hangovers, and ROCHE is talking boisterously. DAN ROCHE is middle-aged, squat, bowlegged, with a potbelly and short arms lumpy with muscle. His face is flat with a big mouth, protruding ears, and red-rimmed little pig's eyes. He is dressed in dirty, patched clothes. PADDY O'DOWD is thin, round-shouldered, flat-chested, with a pimply complexion, bulgy eyes, and a droopy mouth. His manner is oily and fawning, that of a born sponger and parasite. His clothes are those of a cheap sport. PATCH RILEY is an old man with a thatch of dirty white hair. His washed-out blue eyes have a wandering, half-witted expression. His skinny body is clothed in rags and there is nothing under his tattered coat but his bare skin. His mouth is sunken in, toothless. He carries an Irish bagpipe under his arm.*)

ROCHE (*his back is half turned as he harangues O'DOWD and RILEY, and he does not see MELODY and SARA*). And I says, it's Andy Jackson will put you in your place, and all the slave-drivin' Yankee skinflints like you! Take your damned job, I says, and—

O'DOWD (*warningly, his eyes on MELODY*). Whist! Whist! Hold your prate!

(*ROCHE whirls around to face MELODY, and his aggressiveness oozes from him, changing to a hangdog apprehension. For MELODY has sprung to his feet, his eyes*

blazing with an anger which is increased by the glance of contempt SARA casts from him to the three men. O'DOWD avoids MELODY's eyes, busies himself in closing the door. PATCH RILEY stands gazing at SARA with a dreamy, admiring look, lost in a world of his own fancy, oblivious to what is going on.*)

ROCHE (*placatingly*). Good mornin' to ye, Major.

O'DOWD (*fawning*). Good mornin', yer Honor.

MELODY. How dare you come tramping in here in that manner! Have you mistaken this inn for the sort of dirty shebeen you were used to in the old country where the pigs ran in and out the door?

O'DOWD. We ask pardon, yer Honor.

MELODY (*to ROCHE—an impressive menace in his tone*). You, Paddy. Didn't I forbid you ever to mention that scoundrel Jackson's name in my house or I'd horsewhip the hide off your back? (*He takes a threatening step toward him.*) Perhaps you think I cannot carry out that threat.

ROCHE (*backs away frightenedly*). No, no, Major. I forgot— Good mornin' to ye, Miss.

O'DOWD. Good mornin', Miss Sara. (*She ignores them. PATCH RILEY is still gazing at her with dreamy admiration, having heard nothing, his hat still on his head. O'DOWD officiously snatches it off for him—rebukingly*) Where's your wits, Patch? Didn't ye hear his Honor?

RILEY (*unheeding—addresses SARA*). Sure it's you, God bless you, looks like a fairy princess as beautiful as a rose in the mornin' dew. I'll raise a tune for you (*He starts to arrange his pipes.*)

SARA (*curtly*). I want none of your tunes. (*Then, seeing the look of wondering hurt in the old man's eyes, she adds kindly*) That's sweet of you, Patch. I know you'd raise a beautiful tune, but I have to go out.

(*Consoled, the old man smiles at her gratefully.*)

MELODY. Into the bar, all of you, where you belong! I told you not to use this entrance! (*With disdainful tolerance*) I suppose it's a free drink you're after. Well, no one can say of me that I turned away anyone I knew thirsty from my door.

O'DOWD. Thank ye, yer Honor. Come along, Dan. (*He takes RILEY's arm.*) Come on, Patch.

(*The three go into the bar and* O'DOWD *closes the door behind them.*)

SARA (*in derisive brogue*). Sure, it's well trained you've got the poor retainers on your American estate to respect the master! (*Then as he ignores her and casts a furtive glance at the door to the bar, running his tongue over his dry lips, she says acidly, with no trace of brogue*) Don't let me keep you from joining the gentlemen! (*She turns her back on him and goes out the street door at rear.*)

MELODY (*his face is again convulsed by a spasm of pain—pleadingly*). Sara!

(NORA *enters from the hall at right, carrying a tray with toast, eggs, bacon, and tea. She arranges his breakfast on the table at front center, bustling garrulously.*)

NORA. Have I kept you waitin'? The divil was in the toast. One lot burned black as a naygur when my back was turned. But the bacon is crisp, and the eggs not too soft, the way you like them. Come and sit down now. (MELODY *does not seem to hear her. She looks at him worriedly.*) What's up with you, Con? Don't you hear me?

O'DOWD (*pokes his head in the door from the bar*). Mickey won't believe you said we could have a drink, yer Honor, unless ye tell him.

MELODY (*licking his lips*). I'm coming. (*He goes to the bar door.*)

NORA. Con! Have this in your stomach first! It'll all get cauld.

MELODY (*without turning to her—in his condescendingly polite tone*). I find I am not the least hungry, Nora. I regret your having gone to so much trouble. (*He goes into the bar, closing the door behind him.* NORA *slumps on a chair at the rear of the table and stares at the breakfast with a pitiful helplessness. She begins to sob quietly.*)

CURTAIN

ACT TWO

SCENE. *Same as Act One. About half an hour has elapsed. The barroom door opens and* MELODY *comes in. He has had two more drinks and still no breakfast, but this has had no outward effect except that his face is paler and his manner more* disdainful. *He turns to give orders to the spongers in the bar.*

———

MELODY. Remember what I say. None of your loud brawling. And you, Riley, keep your bagpipe silent, or out you go. I wish to be alone in quiet for a while with my memories. When Corporal Cregan returns, Mickey, send him in to me. He, at least, knows Talavera is not the name of a new brand of whiskey. (*He shuts the door contemptuously on* MICKEY's "Yes, Major" *and the obedient murmur of the others. He sits at rear of the table at left front. At first, he poses to himself, striking an attitude—a Byronic hero, noble, embittered, disdainful, defying his tragic fate, brooding over past glories. But he has no audience and he cannot keep it up. His shoulders sag and he stares at the table top, hopelessness and defeat bringing a trace of real tragedy to his ruined, handsome face.*

(*The street door is opened and* SARA *enters. He does not hear the click of the latch, or notice her as she comes forward. Fresh from the humiliation of cajoling the storekeeper to extend more credit, her eyes are bitter. At sight of her father they become more so. She moves toward the door at right, determined to ignore him, but something unusual in his attitude strikes her and she stops to regard him searchingly. She starts to say something bitter—stops—finally, in spite of herself, she asks with a trace of genuine pity in her voice.*)

SARA. What's wrong with you, Father? Are you really sick or is it just—

(*He starts guiltily, ashamed of being caught in such a weak mood.*)

MELODY (*gets to his feet politely and bows*). I beg your pardon, my dear. I did not hear you come in. (*With a deprecating smile.*) Faith, I was far away in spirit, lost in memories of a glorious battle in Spain, nineteen years ago today.

SARA (*her face hardens*). Oh. It's the anniversary of Talavera, is it? Well, I know what that means—a great day for the spongers and a bad day for this inn!

MELODY (*coldly*). I don't understand you. Of course I shall honor the occasion.

SARA. You needn't tell me. I remember the other celebrations—and this year, now Jamie Cregan has appeared, you've an excuse to make it worse.

MELODY. Naturally, an old comrade in arms will be doubly welcome—

SARA. Well, I'll say this much. From the little I've seen of him, I'd rather have free whiskey go down his gullet than the others'. He's a relation, too.

MELODY (*stiffly*). Merely a distant cousin. That has no bearing. It's because Corporal Cregan fought by my side—

SARA. I suppose you've given orders to poor Mother to cook a grand feast for you, as usual, and you'll wear your beautiful uniform, and I'll have the honor of waiting on table. Well, I'd do it just this once more for Mother's sake, or she'd have to, but it'll be the last time. (*She turns her back on him and goes to the door at right.*) You'll be pleased to learn your daughter had almost to beg on her knees to Neilan before he'd let us have another month's credit. He made it plain it was to Mother he gave it because he pities her for the husband she's got. But what do you care about that, as long as you and your fine thoroughbred mare can live in style! (MELODY *is shaken for a second. He glances toward the bar as if he longed to return there to escape her. Then he gets hold of himself. His face becomes expressionless. He sits in the same chair and picks up the paper, ignoring her. She starts to go out just as her mother appears in the doorway.* NORA *is carrying a glass of milk.*)

NORA. Here's the milk the doctor ordered for the young gentleman. It's time for it, and I knew you'd be going upstairs.

SARA (*takes the milk*). Thank you, Mother. (*She nods scornfully toward her father.*) I've just been telling him I begged another month's credit from Neilan, so he needn't worry.

NORA. Ah, thank God for that. Neilan's a kind man.

MELODY (*explodes*). Damn his kindness! By the Eternal, if he'd refused, I'd have— ! (*He controls himself, meeting* SARA'S *contemptuous eyes. He goes on quietly, a bitter, sneering antagonism underneath.*) Don't let me detain you, my dear. Take his milk to our Yankee guest, as your mother suggests. Don't miss any chance to play the ministering angel. (*Vindictively*) Faith, the poor young devil hasn't a chance to escape with you two scheming peasants laying snares to trap him!

SARA. That's a lie! And leave Mother out of your insults!

MELODY. And if all other tricks fail, there's always one last trick to get him through his honor!

SARA (*tensely*). What trick do you mean?

(*Nora grabs her arm.*)

NORA. Hould your prate, now! Why can't you leave him be? It's your fault, for provoking him.

SARA (*quietly*). All right, Mother. I'll leave him to look in the mirror, like he loves to, and remember what he said, and be proud of himself.

(MELODY *winces.* SARA *goes out right.*)

MELODY (*after a pause—shakenly*). I— She mistook my meaning— It's as you said. She goads me into losing my temper, and I say things—

NORA (*sadly*). I know what made you say it. You think maybe she's like I was, and you can't help remembering my sin with you.

MELODY (*guiltily vehement*). No! No! I tell you she mistook my meaning, and now you— (*Then exasperatedly*) Damn your priests' prating about your sin! (*With a strange, scornful vanity*) To hear you tell it, you'd think it was you who seduced me! That's likely, isn't it? —remembering the man I was then!

NORA. I remember well. Sure, you was that handsome, no woman could resist you. And you are still.

MELODY (*pleased*). None of your blarney, Nora. (*With Byronic gloom*) I am but a ghost haunting a ruin. (*Then gallantly but without looking at her*) And how about you in those days? Weren't you the prettiest girl in all Ireland? (*Scornfully*) And be damned to your lying, pious shame! You had no shame then, I remember. It was love and joy and glory in you and you were proud!

NORA (*her eyes shining*). I'm still proud and will be to the day I die!

MELODY (*gives her an approving look which turns to distaste at her appearance —looks away irritably*). Why do you bring up the past? I do not wish to discuss it.

NORA (*after a pause—timidly*). All the same, you shouldn't talk to Sara as if you thought she'd be up to anything to catch young Harford.

MELODY. I did not think that! She is my daughter—

NORA. She is surely. And he's a dacent lad. (*She smiles a bit scornfully.*) Sure, from all she's told me, he's that shy he's never dared even to kiss her hand!

MELODY (*with more than a little contempt*). I can well believe it. When it comes to making love the Yankees are clumsy, fish-blooded louts. They lack savoir-faire. They have no romantic fire! They know nothing of women. (*He snorts disdainfully.*) By the Eternal, when I was his age—(*Then quickly*) Not that I don't approve of young Harford, mind you. He is a gentleman. When he asks me for Sara's hand I will gladly give my consent, provided his father and I can agree on the amount of her settlement.

NORA (*hastily*). Ah, there's no need to think of that yet. (*Then lapsing into her own dream*) Yes, she'll be happy because she loves him dearly, a lot more than she admits. And it'll give her a chance to rise in the world. We'll see the day when she'll live in a grand mansion, dressed in silks and satins, and riding in a carriage with coachman and footman.

MELODY. I desire that as much as you do, Nora. I'm done—finished—no future but the past. But my daughter has the looks, the brains—ambition, youth— She can go far. (*Then sneeringly*) That is, if she can remember she's a gentlewoman and stop acting like a bogtrotting peasant wench! (*He hears* SARA *returning downstairs.*) She's coming back. (*He gets up —bitterly*) As the sight of me seems to irritate her, I'll go in the bar a while. I've had my fill of her insults for one morning. (*He opens the bar door. There is a chorus of eager, thirsty welcome from inside. He goes in, closing the door.* SARA *enters from right. Her face is flushed and her eyes full of dreamy happiness.*)

NORA (*rebukingly*). Himself went in the bar to be out of reach of your tongue. A fine thing! Aren't you ashamed you haven't enough feeling not to torment him, when you know it's the anniversary—

SARA. All right, Mother. Let him take what joy he can out of the day. I'll even help you get his uniform out of the trunk in the attic and brush and clean it for you.

NORA. Ah, God bless you, that's the way— (*Then, astonished at this unexpected docility*) Glory be, but you've changed all of a sudden. What's happened to you?

SARA. I'm so happy now—I can't feel bitter against anyone. (*She hesitates— then shyly*) Simon kissed me. (*Having said this, she goes on triumphantly.*) He got his courage up at last, but it was me made him. I was freshening up his pillows and leaning over him, and he couldn't help it, if he was human. (*She laughs tenderly.*) And then you'd have laughed to see him. He near sank through the bed with shame at his boldness. He began apologizing as if he was afraid I'd be so insulted I'd never speak to him again.

NORA (*teasingly*). And what did you do? I'll wager you wasn't as brazen as you pretend.

SARA (*ruefully*). It's true, Mother. He made me as bashful as he was. I felt a great fool.

NORA. And was that all? Sure, kissing is easy. Didn't he ask you if you'd marry— ?

SARA. No. (*Quickly*) But it was my fault he didn't. He was trying to be brave enough. All he needed was a word of encouragement. But I stood there, dumb as a calf, and when I did speak it was to say I had to come and help you, and the end was I ran from the room, blushing as red as a beet— (*She comes to her mother.* NORA *puts her arms around her.* SARA *hides her face on her shoulder, on the verge of tears.*) Oh, Mother, ain't it crazy to be such a fool?

NORA. Well, when you're in love—

SARA (*breaking away from her—angrily*). That's just it! I'm too much in love and I don't want to be! I won't let my heart rule my head and make a slave of me! (*Suddenly she smiles confidently.*) Ah well, he loves me as much, and more, I know that, and the next time I'll keep my wits. (*She laughs happily.*) You can consider it as good as done, Mother. I'm Mrs. Simon Harford, at your pleasure. (*She makes a sweeping bow.*)

NORA (*smiling*). Arrah, none of your airs and graces with me! Help me, now, like you promised, and we'll get your father's uniform out of the trunk. It won't break your back in the attic, like it does me.

SARA (*gaily puts her arm around her mother's waist*). Come along then.

NORA (*as they go out right*). I disremember which trunk—and you'll have to help me find the key.

(*There is a pause. Then the bar door is opened and* MELODY *enters again in the same manner as he did at the beginning of the act. There is the same sound of voices from the bar but this time* MELODY *gives no parting orders but simply shuts the door behind him. He scowls with disgust.*)

MELODY. Cursed ignorant cattle. (*Then with a real, lonely yearning*) I wish Jamie Cregan would come. (*Bitterly*) Driven from pillar to post in my own home! Everywhere ignorance—or the scorn of my own daughter! (*Then defiantly*) But by the Eternal God, no power on earth, nor in hell itself, can break me! (*His eyes are drawn irresistibly to the mirror. He moves in front of it, seeking the satisfying reassurance of his reflection there. What follows is an exact repetition of his scene before the mirror in Act One. There is the same squaring of his shoulders, arrogant lifting of his head, and then the favorite quote from Byron, recited aloud to his own image.*)
"I have not loved the World, nor the
    World me;
I have not flattered its rank breath, nor
    bowed
To its idolatries a patient knee,
Nor coined my cheek to smiles,—nor
    cried aloud
In the worship of an echo: in the crowd
They could not deem me one of such—
    I stood
Among them, but not of them . . ."
(*He stands staring in the mirror and does not hear the latch of the street door click. The door opens and* DEBORAH (*Mrs. Henry Harford*), *Simon's mother, enters, closing the door quietly behind her.* MELODY *continues to be too absorbed to notice anything. For a moment, blinded by the sudden change from the bright glare of the street, she does not see him. When she does, she stares incredulously. Then she smiles with an amused and mocking relish.*

(*Deborah is forty-one, but looks to be no more than thirty. She is small, a little over five feet tall, with a fragile, youthful figure. One would never suspect that she is the middle-aged mother of two grown sons. Her face is beautiful—that is, it is beautiful from the standpoint of the artist with an eye for bone structure and unusual character. It is small, with high cheekbones, wedge-shaped, narrowing from a broad forehead to a square chin, framed by thick, wavy, red-brown hair. The nose is delicate and thin, a trifle aquiline. The mouth, with full lips and even, white teeth, is too large for her face. So are the long-lashed, green-flecked brown eyes, under heavy, angular brows. These would appear large in any face, but in hers they seem enormous and are made more startling by the pallor of her complexion. She has tiny, high-arched feet and thin, tapering hands. Her slender, fragile body is dressed in white with calculated simplicity. About her whole personality is a curious atmosphere of deliberate detachment, the studied aloofness of an ironically amused spectator. Something perversely assertive about it too, as if she consciously carried her originality to the point of whimsical eccentricity.*)

DEBORAH. I beg your pardon.

(MELODY *jumps and whirls around. For a moment his face has an absurdly startled, stupid look. He is shamed and humiliated and furious at being caught for the second time in one morning before the mirror. His revenge is to draw himself up haughtily and survey her insolently from head to toe. But at once, seeing she is attractive and a lady, his manner changes. Opportunity beckons and he is confident of himself, put upon his mettle. He bows, a gracious, gallant gentleman. There is seductive charm in his welcoming smile and in his voice.*)

MELODY. Good morning, Mademoiselle. It is an honor to welcome you to this unworthy inn. (*He draws out a chair at rear of the larger table in the foreground—bowing again.*) If I may presume. You will find it comfortable here, away from the glare of the street.

DEBORAH (*regards him for a second puzzledly. She is impressed in spite of herself by his bearing and distinguished, handsome face*) Thank you. (*She comes forward.* MELODY *makes a gallant show of holding her chair and helping her be seated. He takes in all her points with sensual appreciation. It is the same sort of pleasure a lover of horseflesh would have in the appearance of a thoroughbred horse. Meanwhile he speaks with caressing courtesy.*)

MELODY. Mademoiselle— (*He sees her wedding ring.*) Pray forgive me, I see it is Madame— Permit me to say again, how great an honor I will esteem it to be of any service. (*He manages, as he turns away, as if by accident to brush his hand against her shoulder. She is startled and caught off guard. She shrinks and looks up at him. Their eyes meet and at the nakedly physical appraisement she sees in his, a fascinated fear suddenly seizes her. But at once she is reassured as he shifts his gaze, satisfied by her re-actions to his first attack, and hastens to apologize.*) I beg your pardon, Madame. I am afraid my manners have grown clumsy with disuse. It is not often a lady comes here now. This inn, like myself, has fallen upon unlucky days.

DEBORAH (*curtly ignoring this*). I pre-sume you are the innkeeper, Melody?

MELODY (*a flash of anger in his eyes— arrogantly*). I am *Major* Cornelius Melody, one time of His Majesty's Seventh Dra-goons, at your service. (*He bows with chill formality.*)

DEBORAH (*is now an amused spectator again—apologetically*). Oh. Then it is I who owe you an apology, Major Melody.

MELODY (*encouraged—gallantly*). No, no, dear lady, the fault is mine. I should not have taken offense. (*With the air of one frankly admitting a praiseworthy weakness.*) Faith, I may as well confess my besetting weakness is that of all gen-tlemen who have known better days. I have a pride unduly sensitive to any fancied slight.

DEBORAH (*playing up to him now*). I assure you, sir, there was no intention on my part to slight you.

MELODY (*His eyes again catch hers and hold them—his tone insinuatingly ca-ressing*). You are as gracious as you are beautiful, Madame. (DEBORAH's *amuse-ment is gone. She is again confused and, in spite of herself, frightened and fas-cinated.* MELODY *proceeds with his attack, full of confidence now, the successful seducer of old. His voice takes on a cal-culated melancholy cadence. He becomes a romantic, tragic figure, appealing for a woman's understanding and loving com-passion.*) I am a poor fool, Madame. I would be both wiser and happier if I could reconcile myself to being the pro-prietor of a tawdry tavern, if I could abjure pride and forget the past. Today of all days it is hard to forget, for it is the anniversary of the battle of Talavera. The most memorable day of my life, Ma-dame. It was on that glorious field I had the honor to be commended for my bravery by the great Duke of Wellington, himself—Sir Arthur Wellesley, then. So I am sure you can find it in your heart to forgive— (*His tone more caressing*) One so beautiful must understand the hearts of men full well, since so many must have given their hearts to you. (*A coarse passion comes into his voice.*) Yes, I'll wager my all against a penny that even among the fish-blooded Yankees there's not a man whose heart doesn't catch flame from your beauty! (*He puts his hand over one of her hands on the table and stares into her eyes ardently.*) As mine does now!

DEBORAH (*feeling herself borne down weakly by the sheer force of his physical strength, struggles to release her hand. She stammers, with an attempt at light-ness*). Is this—what the Irish call blarney, sir?

MELODY (*with a fierce, lustful sincerity*). No! I take my oath by the living God, I would charge a square of Napoleon's Old Guard singlehanded for one kiss of your lips. (*He bends lower, while his eyes hold hers. For a second it seems he will kiss her and she cannot help herself. Then abruptly the smell of whiskey on his breath brings her to herself, shaken with disgust and coldly angry. She snatches her hand from his and speaks with withering contempt.*)

DEBORAH. Pah! You reek of whiskey! You are drunk, sir! You are insolent and disgusting! I do not wonder your inn en-joys such meager patronage, if you regale all your guests of my sex with this absurd performance!

(MELODY *straightens up with a jerk, taking a step back as though he had been slapped in the face.* DEBORAH *rises to her feet, ignoring him disdainfully. At this moment* SARA *and her mother enter through the doorway at right. They take in the scene at a glance.* MELODY *and* DEBORAH *do not notice their entrance.*)

NORA (*half under her breath*). Oh, God help us!

SARA (*guesses at once this must be the*

woman Mickey had told her about. She hurries toward them quickly, trying to hide her apprehension and anger and shame at what she knows must have happened). What is it, Father? What does the lady wish? (*Her arrival is a further blow for* MELODY, *seething now in a fury of humiliated pride.* DEBORAH *turns to face* SARA.)

DEBORAH (*coolly self-possessed—pleasantly*). I came here to see you, Miss Melody, hoping you might know the present whereabouts of my son, Simon. (*This is a bombshell for* MELODY.)

MELODY (*blurts out with no apology in his tone but angrily, as if she had intentionally made a fool of him*). You're his mother? In God's name, Madame, why didn't you say so!

DEBORAH (*ignoring him—to* SARA). I've been out to his hermit's cabin, only to find the hermit flown.

SARA (*stammers*). He's here, Mrs. Harford—upstairs in bed. He's been sick—

DEBORAH. Sick? You don't mean seriously?

SARA (*recovering a little from her confusion*). Oh, he's over it now, or almost. It was only a spell of chills and fever he caught from the damp of the lake. I found him there shivering and shaking and made him come here where there's a doctor handy and someone to nurse him.

DEBORAH (*pleasantly*). The someone being you, Miss Melody?

SARA. Yes, me and—my mother and I.

DEBORAH (*graciously*). I am deeply grateful to you and your mother for your kindness.

NORA (*who has remained in the background, now comes forward—with her sweet, friendly smile*). Och, don't be thankin' us, ma'am. Sure, your son is a gentle, fine lad, and we all have great fondness for him. He'd be welcome here if we never paid a penny— (*She stops embarrassedly, catching a disapproving glance from* SARA. DEBORAH *is repelled by* NORA's *slovenly appearance, but she feels her simple charm and gentleness, and returns her smile.*)

SARA (*with embarrassed stiffness*). This is my mother, Mrs. Harford.

(DEBORAH *inclines her head graciously.* NORA *instinctively bobs in a peasant's curtsy to one of the gentry.* MELODY, *snubbed and seething, glares at her.*)

NORA. I'm pleased to make your acquaintance, ma'am.

MELODY. Nora! For the love of God, stop— (*Suddenly he is able to become the polished gentleman again—considerately and even a trifle condescendingly*) I am sure Mrs. Harford is waiting to be taken to her son. Am I not right, Madame?

(DEBORAH *is so taken aback by his effrontery that for a moment she is speechless. She replies coldly, obviously doing so only because she does not wish to create further embarrassment.*)

DEBORAH. That is true, sir. (*She turns her back on him.*) If you will be so kind, Miss Melody, I've wasted so much of the morning and I have to return to the city. I have only time for a short visit—

SARA. Just come with me, Mrs. Harford. (*She goes to the door at right, and steps aside to let* DEBORAH *precede her.*) What a pleasant surprise this will be for Simon. He'd have written you he was sick, but he didn't want to worry you. (*She follows* DEBORAH *into the hall.*)

MELODY. Damned fool of a woman! If I'd known— No, be damned if I regret! Cursed Yankee upstart! (*With a sneer*) But she didn't fool me with her insulted airs! I've known too many women— (*In a rage*) "Absurd performance," was it? God damn her!

NORA (*timidly*). Don't be cursing her and tormenting yourself. She seems a kind lady. She won't hold it against you, when she stops to think, knowing you didn't know who she is.

MELODY (*tensely*). Be quiet!

NORA. Forget it now, do, for Sara's sake. Sure, you wouldn't want anything to come between her and the lad. (*He is silent. She goes on comfortingly.*) Go on up to your room now and you'll find something to take your mind off. Sara and I have your uniform brushed and laid out on the bed.

MELODY (*harshly*). Put it back in the trunk! I don't want it to remind me— (*With humiliated rage again*) By the Eternal, I'll wager she believed what I told her of Talavera and the Great Duke honoring me was a drunken liar's boast!

NORA. No, she'd never, Con. She couldn't.

MELODY (*seized by an idea*). Well, seeing would be believing, eh, my fine lady? Yes, by God, that will prove to her—

(*He turns to* NORA, *his self-confidence partly restored.*) Thank you for reminding me of my duty to Sara. You are right. I do owe it to her interests to forget my anger and make a formal apology to Simon's mother for our little misunderstanding. (*He smiles condescendingly.*) Faith, as a gentleman, I should grant it is a pretty woman's privilege to be always right even when she is wrong. (*He goes to the door at extreme left front and opens it.*) If the lady should come back, kindly keep her here on some excuse until I return. (*This is a command. He disappears, closing the door behind him.*)

NORA (*sighs*). Ah well, it's all right. He'll be on his best behavior now, and he'll feel proud again in his uniform. (*She sits at the end of center table right and relaxes wearily. A moment later* SARA *enters quickly from right and comes to her.*)

SARA. Where's Father?

NORA. I got him to go up and put on his uniform. It'll console him.

SARA (*bitterly*). Console *him*? It's me ought to be consoled for having such a great fool for a father!

NORA. Hush now! How could he know who—?

SARA (*with a sudden reversal of feeling —also vindictively*). Yes, it serves her right. I suppose she thinks she's such a great lady anyone in America would pay her respect. Well, she knows better now. And she didn't act as insulted as she might. Maybe she liked it, for all her pretenses. (*Again with an abrupt reversal of feeling*) Ah, how can I talk such craziness! Him and his drunken lovemaking! Well, he got put in his place, and aren't I glad! He won't forget in a hurry how she snubbed him, as if he was no better than dirt under her feet!

NORA. She didn't. She had the sense to see he'd been drinking and not to mind him.

SARA (*dully*). Maybe. But isn't that bad enough? What woman would want her son to marry the daughter of a man like— (*She breaks down.*) Oh, Mother, I was feeling so happy and sure of Simon, and now— Why did she have to come today? If she'd waited till tomorrow, even, I'd have got him to ask me to marry him, and once he'd done that no power on earth could change him.

NORA. If he loves you no power can change him, anyway. (*Proudly*) Don't I know! (*Reassuringly*) She's his mother, and she loves him and she'll want him to be happy, and she'll see he loves you. What makes you think she'll try to change him?

SARA. Because she hates me, Mother —for one reason.

NORA. She doesn't. She couldn't.

SARA. She does. Oh, she acted as nice as nice, but she didn't fool me. She's the kind would be polite to the hangman, and her on the scaffold. (*She lowers her voice.*) It isn't just to pay Simon a visit she came. It's because Simon's father got a letter telling him about us, and he showed it to her.

NORA. Who did a dirty trick like that?

SARA. It wasn't signed, she said. I suppose someone around here that hates Father—and who doesn't?

NORA. Bad luck to the blackguard, whoever it was!

SARA. She said she'd come to warn Simon his father is wild with anger and he's gone to see his lawyer— But that doesn't worry me. It's only her influence I'm afraid of.

NORA. How do you know about the letter?

SARA (*avoiding her eyes*). I sneaked back to listen outside the door.

NORA. Shame on you! You should have more pride!

SARA. I was ashamed, Mother, after a moment or two, and I came away. (*Then defiantly*) No, I'm not ashamed. I wanted to learn what tricks she might be up to, so I'll be able to fight them. I'm not ashamed at all. I'll do anything to keep him. (*Lowering her voice*) She started talking the second she got in the door. She had only a few minutes because she has to be home before dinner so her husband won't suspect she came here. He's forbidden her to see Simon ever since Simon came out here to live.

NORA. Well, doesn't her coming against her husband's orders show she's on Simon's side?

SARA. Yes, but it doesn't show she wants him to marry me. (*Impatiently*) Don't be so simple, Mother. Wouldn't she tell Simon that anyway, even if the truth was her husband sent her to do all she could to get him away from me?

NORA. Don't look for trouble before it comes. Wait and see, now. Maybe you'll find—

SARA. I'll find what I said, Mother—that she hates me. (*Bitterly*) Even if she came here with good intentions, she wouldn't have them now, after our great gentleman has insulted her. Thank God, if he's putting on his uniform, he'll be hours before the mirror, and she'll be gone before he can make a fool of himself again. (NORA *starts to tell her the truth—then thinks better of it.* SARA *goes on, changing her tone.*) But I'd like her to see him in his uniform, at that, if he was sober. She'd find she couldn't look down on him— (*Exasperatedly*) Och! I'm as crazy as he is. As if she hadn't the brains to see through him.

NORA (*wearily*). Leave him be, for the love of God.

SARA (*after a pause—defiantly*). Let her try whatever game she likes. I have brains too, she'll discover. (*Then uneasily*) Only, like Simon's told me, I feel she's strange and queer behind her lady's airs, and it'll be hard to tell what she's really up to. (*They both hear a sound from upstairs.*) That's her, now. She didn't waste much time. Well, I'm ready for her. Go in the kitchen, will you, Mother? I want to give her the chance to have it out with me alone. (NORA *gets up—then, remembering* MELODY's *orders, glances toward the door at left front uneasily and hesitates.* SARA *says urgently*) Don't you hear me? Hurry, Mother!

(NORA *sighs and goes out quickly, right.* SARA *sits at rear of the center table and waits, drawing herself up in an unconscious imitation of her father's grand manner.* DEBORAH *appears in the doorway at right. There is nothing in her expression to betray any emotion resulting from her interview with her son. She smiles pleasantly at* SARA, *who rises graciously from her chair.*)

DEBORAH (*coming to her*). I am glad to find you here, Miss Melody. It gives me another opportunity to express my gratitude for your kindness to my son during his illness.

SARA. Thank you, Mrs. Harford. My mother and I have been only too happy to do all we could. (*She adds defiantly*) We are very fond of Simon.

DEBORAH (*a glint of secret amusement in her eyes*). Yes, I feel you are. And he has told me how fond he is of you. (*Her manner becomes reflective. She speaks rapidly in a remote, detached way, lowering her voice unconsciously as if she were thinking aloud to herself.*) This is the first time I have seen Simon since he left home to seek self-emancipation at the breast of Nature. I find him not so greatly changed as I had been led to expect from his letters. Of course, it is some time since he has written. I had thought his implacably honest discovery that the poetry he hoped the pure freedom of Nature would inspire him to write is, after all, but a crude imitation of Lord Byron's would have more bitterly depressed his spirit. (*She smiles.*) But evidently he has found a new romantic dream by way of recompense. As I might have known he would. Simon is an inveterate dreamer— a weakness he inherited from me, I'm afraid, although I must admit the Harfords have been great dreamers, too, in their way. Even my husband has a dream —a conservative, material dream, naturally. I have just been reminding Simon that his father is rigidly unforgiving when his dream is flouted, and very practical in his methods of defending it. (*She smiles again.*) My warning was the mechanical gesture of a mother's duty, merely. I realized it would have no effect. He did not listen to what I said. For that matter, neither did I. (*She laughs a little detached laugh, as if she were secretly amused.*)

SARA (*stares at her, unable to decide what is behind all this and how she should react—with an undercurrent of resentment*). I don't think Simon imitates Lord Byron. I hate Lord Byron's poetry. And I know there's a true poet in Simon.

DEBORAH (*vaguely surprised—speaks rapidly again*). Oh, in feeling, of course. It is natural you should admire that in him—now. But I warn you it is a quality difficult for a woman to keep on admiring in a Harford, judging from what I know of the family history. Simon's great-grandfather, Jonathan Harford, had it. He was killed at Bunker Hill, but I suspect the War for Independence was merely a symbolic opportunity for him. His was a personal war, I am sure—for pure freedom. Simon's grandfather, Evan Harford, had the quality too. A fanatic in the cause of pure freedom, he became scornful of our Revolution. It made too many compromises with the ideal to free him. He went to France and became a rabid Jacobin, a worshiper of Robespierre. He would have liked to have gone to the guillotine with his incorruptible Redeemer, but he was too unimportant. They simply forgot to kill him. He came home and lived in a little temple of Liberty he had built in a corner of what is now my garden. It is still there. I remember him well. A dry, gentle, cruel, indomitable, futile old idealist who used frequently to wear his old uniform of the French Republican National Guard. He died wearing it. But the point is, you can have no idea what revengeful hate the Harford pursuit of freedom imposed upon the women who shared their lives. The three daughters-in-law of Jonathan, Evan's half-sisters, had to make a large, greedy fortune out of privateering and the Northwest trade, and finally were even driven to embrace the profits of the slave trade— as a triumphant climax, you understand, of their long battle to escape the enslavement of freedom by enslaving it. Evan's wife, of course, was drawn into this conflict, and became their tool and accomplice. They even attempted to own me, but I managed to escape because there was so little of me in the flesh that aged, greedy fingers could clutch. I am sorry they are dead and cannot know you. They would approve of you, I think. They would see that you are strong and ambitious and determined to take what you want. They would have smiled like senile, hungry serpents and welcomed you into their coils. (*She laughs.*) Evil old witches! Detestable, but I could not help admiring them— pitying them, too—in the end. We had a bond in common. They idolized Napoleon. They used to say he was the only man they would ever have married. And I used to dream I was Josephine—even after my marriage, I'm afraid. The Sisters, as everyone called them, and all of the family accompanied my husband and me on our honeymoon—to Paris to witness the Emperor's coronation. (*She pauses, smiling at her memories.*)

SARA (*against her will, has become a bit hypnotized by* DEBORAH's *rapid, low, musical flow of words, as she strains to grasp the implication for her. She speaks in a low, confidential tone herself, smiling naturally*). I've always admired him too. It's one of the things I've held against my father, that he fought against him and not for him.

DEBORAH (*starts, as if awakening—with a pleasant smile*). Well, Miss Melody, this is tiresome of me to stand here giving you a discourse on Harford family history. I don't know what you must think of me— but doubtless Simon has told you I am a bit eccentric at times. (*She glances at* SARA's *face—amusedly.*) Ah, I can see he has. Then I am sure you will make allowances. I really do not know what inspired me—except perhaps, that I wish to be fair and warn you, too.

SARA (*stiffens*). Warn me about what, Mrs. Harford?

DEBORAH. Why, that the Harfords never part with their dreams even when they deny them. They cannot. That is the family curse. For example, this book Simon plans to write to denounce the evil of greed and possessive ambition, and uphold the virtue of freeing oneself from the lust for power and saving our souls by being content with little. I cannot imagine you taking that seriously. (*She again flashes a glance at* SARA.) I see you do not. Neither do I. I do not even believe Simon will ever write this book on paper. But I warn you it is already written on his conscience and— (*She stops with a little disdaining laugh.*) I begin to resemble Cassandra with all my warnings. And I continue to stand here boring you with words. (*She holds out her hand graciously.*) Goodbye, Miss Melody.

SARA (*takes her hand mechanically*). Goodbye, Mrs. Harford. (DEBORAH *starts for the door at rear.* SARA *follows her, her expression confused, suspicious, and at the same time hopeful. Suddenly she blurts out impulsively.*) Mrs. Harford, I—

DEBORAH (*turns on her, pleasantly*). Yes, Miss Melody? (*But her eyes have become blank and expressionless and discourage any attempt at further contact.*)

SARA (*silenced—with stiff politeness*). Isn't there some sort of cooling drink I could get you before you go? You must be parched after walking from the road to Simon's cabin and back on this hot day.

DEBORAH. Nothing, thank you. (*Then talking rapidly again in her strange detached way.*) Yes, I did find my walk alone in the woods a strangely overpowering experience. Frightening—but intoxicating, too. Such a wild feeling of release and fresh enslavement. I have not ventured from my garden in many years. There, nature is tamed, constrained to obey and adorn. I had forgotten how compelling the brutal power of primitive, possessive nature can be—when suddenly one is attacked by it. (*She smiles.*) It has been a most confusing morning for a tired middle-aged matron, but I flatter myself I have preserved a philosophic poise, or should I say, pose, as well as may be. Nevertheless, it will be a relief to return to my garden and books and meditations and listen indifferently again while the footsteps of life pass and recede along the street beyond the high wall. I shall never venture forth again to do my duty. It is a noble occupation, no doubt, for those who can presume they know what their duty to others is; but I— (*She laughs.*) Mercy, here I am chattering on again. (*She turns to the door.*) Cato will be provoked at me for keeping him waiting. I've already caused his beloved horses to be half-devoured by flies. Cato is our black coachman. He also is fond of Simon, although since Simon became emancipated he has embarrassed Cato acutely by shaking his hand whenever they meet. Cato was always a self-possessed free man even when he was a slave. It astonishes him that Simon has to prove that he—I mean Simon—is free. (*She smiles.*) Goodbye again, Miss Melody. This time I really am going.

(SARA *opens the door for her. She walks past* SARA *into the street, turns left, and, passing before the two windows, disappears.* SARA *closes the door and comes back slowly to the head of the table at center. She stands thinking, her expression puzzled, apprehensive, and resentful.* NORA *appears in the doorway at right.*)

NORA. God forgive you, Sara, why did you let her go? Your father told me—

SARA. I can't make her out, Mother. You'd think she didn't care, but she does care. And she hates me. I could feel it. But you can't tell— She's crazy, I think. She talked on and on as if she couldn't stop— queer blather about Simon's ancestors, and herself, and Napoleon, and Nature, and her garden and freedom, and God knows what—but letting me know all the time she had a meaning behind it, and was

warning and threatening me. Oh, she may be daft in some ways, but she's no fool. I know she didn't let Simon guess she'd rather have him dead than married to me. Oh, no, I'm sure she told him if he was sure he loved me and I meant his happiness— But then she'd say he ought to wait and prove he's sure—anything to give her time. She'd make him promise to wait. Yes, I'll wager that's what she's done!

NORA (*who has been watching the door at left front, preoccupied by her own worry—frightenedly*). Your father'll be down any second. I'm going out in the garden. (*She grabs* SARA's *arm.*) Come along with me, and give him time to get over his rage.

SARA (*shakes off her hand—exasperatedly*). Leave me be, Mother. I've enough to worry me without bothering about him. I've got to plan the best way to act when I see Simon. I've got to be as big a liar as she was. I'll have to pretend I liked her and I'd respect whatever advice she gave him. I mustn't let him see— But I won't go to him again today, Mother. You can take up his meals and his milk, if you will. Tell him I'm too busy. I want to get him anxious and afraid maybe I'm mad at him for something, that maybe his mother said something. If he once has the idea maybe he's lost me—that ought to help, don't you think, Mother?

NORA (*sees the door at left front begin to open—in a whisper*). Oh, God help me! (*She turns in panicky flight and disappears through the doorway, right.*)

(*The door at left front slowly opens— slowly because* MELODY, *hearing voices in the room and hoping* DEBORAH *is there, is deliberately making a dramatic entrance. And in spite of its obviousness, it is effective. Wearing the brilliant scarlet full-dress uniform of a major in one of Wellington's dragoon regiments, he looks extraordinarily handsome and distinguished—a startling, colorful, romantic figure, possessing now a genuine quality he has not had before, the quality of the formidably strong, disdainfully fearless cavalry officer he really had been. The uniform has been preserved with the greatest care. Each button is shining and the cloth is spotless. Being in it has notably restored his self-confident arrogance. Also, he has done everything he can to freshen up his face and hide any effect of his morning's drinks. When he discovers* DEBORAH *is not in the room, he is mildly disappointed and, as always when he first confronts* SARA *alone, he seems to shrink back guiltily within himself.* SARA's *face hardens and she gives no sign of knowing he is there. He comes slowly around the table at left front, until he stands at the end of the center table facing her. She still refuses to notice him and he is forced to speak. He does so with the air of one who condescends to be amused by his own foibles.)*

MELODY. I happened to go to my room and found you and your mother had laid out my uniform so invitingly that I could not resist the temptation to put it on at once instead of waiting until evening.

SARA (*turns on him. In spite of herself she is so struck by his appearance that the contempt is forced back and she can only stammer a bit foolishly*). Yes, I—I see you did. (*There is a moment's pause. She stares at him fascinatedly—then blurts out with impulsive admiration*) You look grand and handsome, Father.

MELODY (*as pleased as a child*). Why, it is most kind of you to say that, my dear Sara. (*Preening himself*) I flatter myself I do not look too unworthy of the man I was when I wore this uniform with honor.

SARA (*an appeal forced out of her that is both pleading and a bitter reproach*). Oh, Father, why can't you ever be the thing you can seem to be? (*A sad scorn comes into her voice.*) The man you were. I'm sorry I never knew that soldier. I think he was the only man who wasn't just a dream.

MELODY (*his face becomes a blank disguise—coldly*). I don't understand you. (*A pause. He begins to talk in an arrogantly amused tone.*) I suspect you are still holding against me my unfortunate blunder with your future mother-in-law. I would not blame you if you did. (*He smiles.*) Faith, I did put my foot in it. (*He chuckles.*) The devil of it is, I can never get used to these Yankee ladies. I do them the honor of complimenting them with a bit of harmless flattery and, lo and behold, suddenly my lady acts as if I had insulted her. It must be their damned narrow Puritan background. They can't help seeing sin hiding under every bush, but this one need not have

been alarmed. I never had an eye for skinny, pale snips of women— (*Hastily*) But what I want to tell you is I am sorry it happened, Sara, and I will do my best, for the sake of your interests, to make honorable amends. I shall do the lady the honor of tendering her my humble apologies when she comes downstairs. (*With arrogant vanity.*) I flatter myself she will be graciously pleased to make peace. She was not as outraged by half as her conscience made her pretend, if I am any judge of feminine frailty.

SARA (*who has been staring at him with scorn until he says this last—impulsively, with a sneer of agreement*). I'll wager she wasn't for all her airs. (*Then furious at herself and him*) Ah, will you stop telling me your mad dreams! (*Controlling herself—coldly*) You'll have no chance to make bad worse by trying to fascinate her with your beautiful uniform. She's gone.

MELODY (*stunned*). Gone? (*Furiously*) You're lying, damn you!

SARA. I'm not. She left ten minutes ago, or more.

MELODY (*before he thinks*). But I told your mother to keep her here until— (*He stops abruptly.*)

SARA. So that's why Mother is so frightened. Well, it was me let her go, so don't take out your rage on poor Mother.

MELODY. Rage? My dear Sara, all I feel is relief. Surely you can't believe I could have looked forward to humbling my pride, even though it would have furthered your interests.

SARA. Furthered my interests by giving her another reason to laugh up her sleeve at your pretenses? (*With angry scorn, lapsing into broad brogue.*) Arrah, God pity you! (*She turns her back on him and goes off, right.* MELODY *stands gripping the back of the chair at the foot of the table in his big, powerful hands in an effort to control himself. There is a crack as the chair back snaps in half. He stares at the fragments in his hands with stupid surprise. The door to the bar is shoved open and* MICKEY *calls in.*)

MALOY. Here's Cregan back to see you, Major.

MELODY (*startled, repeats stupidly*). Cregan? (*Then his face suddenly lights up with pathetic eagerness and his voice is full of welcoming warmth as he calls*)

Jamie! My old comrade in arms! (*As* CREGAN *enters, he grips his hand.*) By the Powers, I'm glad you're here, Jamie. (CREGAN *is surprised and pleased by the warmth of his welcome.* MELODY *draws him into the room.*) Come. Sit down. You'll join me in a drink, I know. (*He gets* CREGAN *a glass from the cupboard. The decanter and* MELODY's *glass are already on the table.*)

CREGAN (*admiringly*). Be God, it's the old uniform, no less, and you look as fine a figure in it as ever you did in Spain. (*He sits at right of table at left front as* MELODY *sits at rear.*)

MELODY (*immensely pleased—deprecatingly*). Hardly, Jamie—but not a total ruin yet, I hope. I put it on in honor of the day. I see you've forgotten. For shame, you dog, not to remember Talavera.

CREGAN (*excitedly*). Talavera, is it? Where I got my saber cut. Be the mortal, I remember it, and you've a right to celebrate. You was worth any ten men in the army that day! (MELODY *has shoved the decanter toward him. He pours a drink.*)

MELODY (*this compliment completely restores him to his arrogant self.*) Yes, I think I may say I did acquit myself with honor. (*Patronizingly*) So, for that matter, did you. (*He pours a drink and raises his glass.*) To the day and your good health, Corporal Cregan.

CREGAN (*enthusiastically*). To the day and yourself, God bless you, Con! (*He tries to touch brims with* MELODY's *glass, but* MELODY *holds his glass away and draws himself up haughtily.*)

MELODY (*with cold rebuke*). I said, to the day and your good health, *Corporal Cregan.*

CREGAN (*for a second is angry—then he grins and mutters admiringly*). Be God, it's you can bate the world and never let it change you! (*Correcting his toast with emphasis*) To the day and yourself, *Major Melody.*

MELODY (*touches his glass to* CREGAN's—*graciously condescending*). Drink hearty, Corporal.

(*They drink.*)

CURTAIN

ACT THREE

SCENE. *The same. The door to the bar is closed. It is around eight that evening and there are candles on the center table.* MELODY *sits at the head of this table. In his brilliant uniform he presents more than ever an impressively colorful figure in the room, which appears smaller and dingier in the candlelight.* CREGAN *is in the chair on his right. The other chairs at this table are unoccupied.* RILEY, O'DOWD, *and* ROCHE *sit at the table at left front.* RILEY *is at front, but his chair is turned sideways so he faces right.* O'DOWD *has the chair against the wall, facing right, with* ROCHE *across the table from him, his back to* MELODY. *All five are drunk,* MELODY *more so than any of them, but except for the glazed glitter in his eyes and his deathly pallor, his appearance does not betray him. He is holding his liquor like a gentleman.*

Cregan is the least drunk. O'DOWD *and* ROCHE *are boisterous. The effect of the drink on* RILEY *is merely to sink him deeper in dreams. He seems oblivious to his surroundings.*

An empty and a half-empty bottle of port are on the table before MELODY *and* CREGAN, *and their glasses are full. The three at the table have a decanter of whiskey.*

SARA, *wearing her working dress and an apron, is removing dishes and the remains of the dinner. Her face is set. She is determined to ignore them, but there is angry disgust in her eyes.* MELODY *is arranging forks, knives, spoons, saltcellar, etc., in a plan of battle on the table before him.* CREGAN *watches him.* PATCH RILEY *gives a few tuning-up quavers on his pipes.*

———

MELODY. Here's the river Tagus. And here, Talavera. This would be the French position on a rise of ground with the plain between our lines and theirs. Here is our redoubt with the Fourth Division and the Guards. And here's our cavalry brigade in a valley toward our left, if you'll remember, Corporal Cregan.

CREGAN (*excitedly*). Remember? Sure I see it as clear as yesterday!

RILEY (*bursts into a rollicking song, accompanying himself on the pipes, his voice the quavering ghost of a tenor but*

still true—to the tune of "Baltiorum").
 "She'd a pig and boneens,
 She'd a bed and a dresser,
 And a nate little room
 For the father confessor;
 With a cupboard and curtains, and
 something, I'm towld,
 That his riv'rance liked when the
 weather was cowld.
 And it's hurroo, hurroo! Biddy
 O'Rafferty!"

(ROCHE *and* O'DOWD *roar after him, beating time on the table with their glasses—"Hurroo, hurroo! Biddy O'Rafferty!"—and laugh drunkenly.* CREGAN, *too, joins in this chorus.* MELODY *frowns angrily at the interruption, but at the end he smiles with lordly condescension, pleased by the irreverence of the song.*)

O'DOWD (*after a cunning glance at* MELODY's *face to see what his reaction is —derisively*). Och, lave it to the priests, divil mend thim! Ain't it so, Major?

MELODY. Ay, damn them all! A song in the right spirit, Piper. Faith, I'll have you repeat it for my wife's benefit when she joins us. She still has a secret fondness for priests. And now, less noise, you blackguards. Corporal Cregan and I cannot hear each other with your brawling.

O'DOWD (*smirkingly obedient*). Quiet it is, yer Honor. Be quiet, Patch. (*He gives the old man, who is lost in dreams, a shove that almost knocks him off his chair.* RILEY *stares at him bewilderedly.* O'DOWD *and* ROCHE *guffaw.*)

MELODY (*scowls at them, then turns to* CREGAN). Where was I, Corporal? Oh, yes, we were waiting in the valley. We heard a trumpet from the French lines and saw them forming for the attack. An aide-de-camp galloped down the hill to us—

SARA (*who has been watching him disdainfully, reaches out to take his plate—rudely in mocking brogue*). I'll have your plate, av ye plaze, Major, before your gallant dragoons charge over it and break it.

MELODY (*holds his plate on the table with one hand so she cannot take it, and raises his glass of wine with the other—ignoring her.*) Wet your lips, Corporal. Talavera was a devilish thirsty day, if you'll remember. (*He drinks.*)

CREGAN (*glances uneasily at* SARA). It was that. (*He drinks.*)

MELODY (*smacking his lips*). Good wine, Corporal. Thank God, I still have wine in my cellar fit for a gentleman.

SARA (*angrily*). Are you going to let me take your plate?

MELODY (*ignoring her*). No, I have no need to apologize for the wine. Nor for the dinner, for that matter. Nora is a good cook when she forgets her infernal parsimony and buys food that one can eat without disgust. But I do owe you an apology for the quality of the service. I have tried to teach the waitress not to snatch plates from the table as if she were feeding dogs in a kennel but she cannot learn. (*He takes his hand from the plate —to* SARA) There. Now let me see you take it properly.

(*She stares at him for a moment, speechless with anger—then snatches the plate from in front of him.*)

CREGAN (*hastily recalls* MELODY *to the battlefield*). You were where the aide-de-camp galloped up to us, Major. It was then the French artillery opened on us.

(SARA *goes out right, carrying a tray laden with plates.*)

MELODY. We charged the columns on our left—here— (*He marks the table-cloth*) that were pushing back the Guards. I'll never forget the blast of death from the French squares. And then their chasseurs and lancers were on us! By God, it's a miracle any of us came through!

CREGAN. You wasn't touched except you'd a bullet through your coat, but I had this token on my cheek to remember a French saber by.

MELODY. Brave days, those! By the Eternal, then one lived! Then one forgot! (*He stops—when he speaks again it is bitterly.*) Little did I dream then the disgrace that was to be my reward later on.

CREGAN (*consolingly*). Ah well, that's the bad luck of things. You'd have been made a colonel soon, if you'd left the Spanish woman alone and not fought that duel.

MELODY (*arrogantly threatening*). Are you presuming to question my conduct in that affair, Corporal Cregan?

CREGAN (*hastily*). Sorra a bit! Don't mind me, now.

MELODY (*stiffly*). I accept your apology. (*He drinks the rest of his wine, pours another glass, then stares moodily before him.* CREGAN *drains his glass and refills it.*)

O'DOWD (*peering past* ROCHE *to watch* MELODY, *leans across to* ROCHE—*in a sneering whisper*). Ain't he the lunatic, sittin' like a play-actor in his red coat, lyin' about his battles with the French!

ROCHE (*sullenly—but careful to keep his voice low*). He'd ought to be ashamed he ivir wore the bloody red av England, God's curse on him!

O'DOWD. Don't be wishin' him harm, for it's thirsty we'd be without him. Drink long life to him, and may he always be as big a fool as he is this night! (*He sloshes whiskey from the decanter into both their glasses.*)

ROCHE (*with a drunken leer*). Thrue for you! I'll toast him on that. (*He twists round to face* MELODY, *holds up his glass and bawls*) To the grandest gintleman ivir come from the shores av Ireland! Long life to you, Major!

O'DOWD. Hurroo! Long life, yer Honor!

RILEY (*awakened from his dream, mechanically raises his glass*). And to all that belong to ye.

MELODY (*startled from his thoughts, becomes at once the condescending squire—smiling tolerantly*). I said, less noise, you dogs. All the same, I thank you for your toast. (*They drink. A pause. Abruptly* MELODY *begins to recite from Byron. He reads the verse well, quietly, with a bitter eloquence.*)

"But midst the crowd, the hum, the shock of men,
To hear, to see, to feel, and to possess,
And roam along, the World's tired denizen,
With none who bless us, none whom we can bless;
Minions of Splendour shrinking from distress!
None that, with kindred consciousness endued,
If we were not, would seem to smile the less,
Of all that flattered—followed—sought, and sued;
This is to be alone— This, this is Solitude!"

(*He stops and glances from one face to another. Their expressions are all blank. He remarks with insulting derisiveness*) What? You do not understand, my lads? Well, all the better for you. So may you

go on fooling yourselves that I am fooled in you. (*Then with a quick change of mood, heartily*) Give us a hunting song, Patch. You've not forgotten "Modideroo," I'll be bound.

RILEY (*roused to interest immediately*). Does a duck forget wather? I'll show ye! (*He begins the preliminary quavers on his pipes.*)

O'DOWD. Modideroo!

ROCHE. Hurroo!

RILEY (*accompanying himself, sings with wailing melancholy the first verse that comes to his mind of an old hunting song*).

"And the fox set him down and looked about,
And many were feared to follow;
'Maybe I'm wrong,' says he, 'but I doubt
That you'll be as gay tomorrow.
For loud as you cry, and high as you ride,
And little you feel my sorrow,
I'll be free on the mountainside
While you'll lie low tomorrow.'
Oh, Modideroo, aroo, aroo!"

(MELODY, *excited now, beats time on the table with his glass along with* CREGAN, ROCHE, *and* O'DOWD, *and all bellow the refrain,* "Oh, Modideroo, aroo, aroo!")

MELODY (*his eyes alight, forgetting himself, a strong lilt of brogue coming into his voice*). Ah, that brings it back clear as life! Melody Castle in the days that's gone! A wind from the south, and a sky gray with clouds—good weather for the hounds. A true Irish hunter under me that knows and loves me and would raise to a jump over hell if I gave the word! To hell with men, I say! —and women, too! —with their cowardly hearts rotten and stinking with lies and greed and treachery! Give me a horse to love and I'll cry quits to men! And then away, with the hounds in full cry, and after them! Off with divil a care for your neck, over ditches and streams and stone walls and fences, the fox doubling up the mountainside through the furze and the heather— ! (SARA *has entered from right as he begins this longing invocation of old hunting days. She stands behind his chair, listening contemptuously. He suddenly feels her presence and turns his head. When he catches the sneer in her eyes, it is as if cold water were dashed in his face. He addresses her as if she were a servant.*) Well? What is it? What are you waiting for now?

SARA (*roughly, with coarse brogue*). What would I be waitin' for but for you to get through with your blather about lovin' horses, and give me a chance to finish my work? Can't you—and the other gintlemen—finish gettin' drunk in the bar and lave me clear the tables?

(O'DOWD *conceals a grin behind his hand;* ROCHE *stifles a malicious guffaw.*)

CREGAN (*with an apprehensive glance at* MELODY, *shakes his head at her admonishingly*). Now, Sara, be aisy.

(*But* MELODY *suppresses any angry reaction. He rises to his feet, a bit stiffly and carefully, and bows.*)

MELODY (*coldly*). I beg your pardon if we have interfered with your duties. (*To* O'DOWD *and his companions.*) Into the bar, you louts!

O'DOWD. The bar it is, sorr. Come, Dan. Wake up, Patch. (*He pokes the piper. He and* ROCHE *go into the bar, and* RILEY *stumbles vaguely after them.* CREGAN *waits for* MELODY.)

MELODY. Go along, Corporal. I'll join you presently. I wish to speak to my daughter.

CREGAN. All right, Major. (*He again shakes his head at* SARA, *as if to say, don't provoke him. She ignores him. He goes into the bar, closing the door behind him. She stares at her father with angry disgust.*)

SARA. You're drunk. If you think I'm to stay here and listen to—

MELODY (*his face expressionless, draws out his chair at the head of the center table for her—politely*). Sit down, my dear.

SARA. I won't. I have no time. Poor Mother is half dead on her feet. I have to help her. There's a pile of dishes to wash after your grand anniversary feast! (*With bitter anger*) Thank God it's over, and it's the last time you'll ever take satisfaction in having me wait on table for drunken scum like O'Dowd and—

MELODY (*quietly*). A daughter who takes satisfaction in letting even the scum see that she hates and despises her father! (*He shrugs his shoulders.*) But no matter. (*Indicating the chair again*) Won't you sit down, my dear?

SARA. If you ever dared face the truth, you'd hate and despise yourself! (*Passionately*) All I pray to God is that someday when you're admiring yourself in the mirror something will make you see at last what you really are! That will be revenge in full for all you've done to Mother and me! (*She waits defiantly, as if expecting him to lose his temper and curse her. But* MELODY *acts as if he had not heard her.*)

MELODY (*his face expressionless, his manner insistently bland and polite*). Sit down, my dear. I will not detain you long, and I think you will find what I have to tell you of great interest.

(*She searches his face, uneasy now, feeling a threat hidden behind his cold, quiet, gentlemanly tone. She sits down and he sits at rear of table, with an empty chair separating them.*)

SARA. You'd better think well before you speak, Father. I know the devil that's in you when you're quiet like this with your brain mad with drink.

MELODY. I don't understand you. All I wish is to relate something which happened this afternoon.

SARA (*giving way to bitterness at her humiliation again—sneeringly*). When you went riding on your beautiful thoroughbred mare while Mother and I were sweating and suffocating in the heat of the kitchen to prepare your Lordship's banquet? Sure, I hope you didn't show off and jump your beauty over a fence into somebody's garden, like you've done before, and then have to pay damages to keep out of jail!

MELODY (*roused by mention of his pet —disdainfully*). The damned Yankee yokels should feel flattered that she deigns to set her dainty hooves in their paltry gardens! She's a truer-born, well-bred lady than any of their women—than the one who paid us a visit this morning, for example.

SARA. Mrs. Harford was enough of a lady to put you in your place and make a fool of you.

MELODY (*seemingly unmoved by this taunt—calmly*). You are very simple-minded, my dear, to let yourself be taken in by such an obvious bit of clever acting. Naturally, the lady was a bit discomposed when she heard you and your mother coming, after she had just allowed me to kiss her. She had to pretend—

SARA (*eagerly*). She let you kiss her? (*Then disgustedly*) It's a lie, but I don't doubt you've made yourself think it's the truth by now. (*Angrily*) I'm going. I don't want to listen to the whiskey in you boasting of what never happened—as usual! (*She puts her hands on the table and starts to rise.*)

MELODY (*with a quick movement pins hers down with one of his*). Wait! (*A look of vindictive cruelty comes into his eyes—quietly*) Why are you so jealous of the mare, I wonder? Is it because she has such slender ankles and dainty feet? (*He takes his hand away and stares at her hands—with disgust, commandingly*) Keep your thick wrists and ugly, peasant paws off the table in my presence, if you please! They turn my stomach! I advise you never to let Simon get a good look at them—

SARA (*instinctively jerks her hands back under the table guiltily. She stammers*). You—you cruel devil! I knew you'd—

MELODY (*for a second is ashamed and really contrite*). Forgive me, Sara. I didn't mean—the whiskey talking—as you said. (*He adds in a forced tone, a trace of mockery in it*) An absurd taunt, when you really have such pretty hands and feet, my dear. (*She jumps to her feet, so hurt and full of hatred her lips tremble and she cannot speak. He speaks quietly.*) Are you going? I was about to tell you of the talk I had this afternoon with young Harford. (*She stares at him in dismay. He goes on easily.*) It was after I returned from my ride. I cantered the mare by the river and she pulled up lame. So I dismounted and led her back to the barn. No one noticed my return and when I went upstairs it occurred to me I would not find again such an opportunity to have a frank chat with Harford —free from interruptions. (*He pauses, as if he expects her to be furious, but she remains tensely silent, determined not to let him know her reaction.*) I did not beat about the bush. I told him he must appreciate, as a gentleman, it was my duty as your father to demand he lay his cards on the table. I said he must realize that even before you began nursing him here and going alone to his bedroom, there was a deal of gossip about

your visits to his cabin, and your walks in the woods with him. I put it to him that such an intimacy could not continue without gravely compromising your reputation.

SARA (*stunned—weakly*). God forgive you! And what did he say?

MELODY. What could he say? He is a man of honor. He looked damn embarrassed and guilty for a moment, but when he found his tongue, he agreed with me most heartily. He said his mother had told him the same thing.

SARA. Oh, she did, did she? I suppose she did it to find out by watching him how far—

MELODY (*coldly*). Well, why not? Naturally, it was her duty as his mother to discover all she could about you. She is a woman of the world. She would be bound to suspect that you might be his mistress.

SARA (*tensely*). Oh, would she!

MELODY. But that's beside the point. The point is, my bashful young gentleman finally blurted out that he wanted to marry you.

SARA (*forgetting her anger—eagerly*). He told you that?

MELODY. Yes, and he said he had told his mother, and she had said all she wanted was his happiness but she felt in fairness to you and to himself—and I presume she also meant to both families concerned—he should test his love and yours by letting a decent interval of time elapse before your marriage. She mentioned a year, I believe.

SARA (*angrily*). Ah! Didn't I guess that would be her trick!

MELODY (*lifting his eyebrows—coldly*). Trick? In my opinion, the lady displayed more common sense and knowledge of the world than I thought she possessed. The reasons she gave him are sound and show a consideration for your good name which ought to inspire gratitude in you and not suspicion.

SARA. Arrah, don't tell me she's made a fool of you again! A lot of consideration she has for me!

MELODY. She pointed out to him that if you were the daughter of some family in their own little Yankee clique, there would be no question of a hasty marriage, and so he owed it to you—

SARA. I see. She's the clever one!

MELODY. Another reason was—and here your Simon stammered so embarrassedly I had trouble making him out—she warned him a sudden wedding would look damnably suspicious and start a lot of evil-minded gossip.

SARA (*tensely*). Oh, she's clever, all right! But I'll beat her.

MELODY. I told him I agreed with his mother. It is obvious that were there a sudden wedding without a suitable period of betrothal, everyone would believe—

SARA. I don't care what they believe! Tell me this! Did she get him to promise her he'd wait? (*Before he can answer—bitterly*) But of course she did! She'd never have left till she got that out of him!

MELODY (*ignores this*). I told him I appreciated the honor he did me in asking for your hand, but he must understand that I could not commit myself until I had talked to his father and was assured the necessary financial arrangements could be concluded to our mutual satisfaction. There was the amount of settlement to be agreed upon, for instance.

SARA. That dream, again! God pity you! (*She laughs helplessly and a bit hysterically.*) And God help Simon. He must have thought you'd gone out of your mind! What did he say?

MELODY. He said nothing, naturally. He is well bred and he knows this is a matter he must leave to his father to discuss. There is also the equally important matter of how generous an allowance Henry Harford is willing to settle on his son. I did not mention this to Simon, of course, not wishing to embarrass him further with talk of money.

SARA. Thank God for that, at least! (*She giggles hysterically.*)

MELODY (*quietly*). May I ask what you find so ridiculous in an old established custom? Simon is an elder son, the heir to his father's estate. No matter what their differences in the past may have been, now that Simon has decided to marry and settle down his father will wish to do the fair thing by him. He will realize, too, that although there is no more honorable calling than that of poet and philosopher, which his son has chosen to pursue, there is no decent living to be gained by its practice. So naturally he will settle an allowance on Simon, and I shall insist it be a generous one, befitting your position as my daughter. I will tolerate no niggardly trader's haggling on his part.

SARA (*stares at him fascinatedly, on the edge of helpless, hysterical laughter*). I suppose it would never occur to you that old Harford might not think it an honor to have his son marry your daughter.

MELODY (*calmly*). No, it would never occur to me—and if it should occur to him, I would damned soon disabuse his mind. Who is he but a money-grubbing trader? I would remind him that I was born in a castle and there was a time when I possessed wealth and position, and an estate compared to which any Yankee upstart's home in this country is but a hovel stuck in a cabbage patch. I would remind him that you, my daughter, were born in a castle!

SARA (*impulsively, with a proud toss of her head*). Well, that's no more than the truth. (*Then furious with herself and him.*) Och, what crazy blather! (*She springs to her feet.*) I've had enough of your mad dreams!

MELODY. Wait! I haven't finished yet. (*He speaks quietly, but as he goes on there is an increasing vindictiveness in his tone.*) There was another reason why I told young Harford I could not make a final decision. I wished time to reflect on a further aspect of this proposed marriage. Well, I have been reflecting, watching you and examining your conduct, without prejudice, trying to be fair to you and make every possible allowance— (*He pauses.*) Well, to be brutally frank, my dear, all I can see in you is a common, greedy, scheming, cunning peasant girl, whose only thought is money and who has shamelessly thrown herself at a young man's head because his family happens to possess a little wealth and position.

SARA (*trying to control herself*). I see your game, Father. I told you when you were drunk like this— But this time, I won't give you the satisfaction— (*Then she bursts out angrily.*) It's a lie! I love Simon, or I'd never—

MELODY (*as if she hadn't spoken*). So, I have about made up my mind to decline for you Simon Harford's request for your hand in marriage.

SARA (*jeers angrily now*). Oh, you have, have you? As if I cared a damn what you— !

MELODY. As a gentleman, I feel I have a duty, in honor, to Simon. Such a marriage would be a tragic misalliance for him—and God knows I know the sordid tragedy of such a union.

SARA. It's Mother has had the tragedy!

MELODY. I hold young Harford in too high esteem. I cannot stand by and let him commit himself irrevocably to what could only bring him disgust and bitterness, and ruin to all his dreams.

SARA. So I'm not good enough for him, you've decided now?

MELODY. That is apparent from your every act. No one, no matter how charitably inclined, could mistake you for a lady. I have tried to make you one. It was an impossible task. God Himself cannot transform a sow's ear into a silk purse!

SARA (furiously). Father!

MELODY. Young Harford needs to be saved from himself. I can understand his physical infatuation. You are pretty. So was your mother pretty once. But marriage is another matter. The man who would be the ideal husband for you, from a standpoint of conduct and character, is Mickey Maloy, my bartender, and I will be happy to give him my parental blessing—

SARA. Let you stop now, Father!

MELODY. You and he would be congenial. You can match tongues together. He's a healthy animal. He can give you a raft of peasant brats to squeal and fight with the pigs on the mud floor of your hovel.

SARA. It's the dirty hut in which your father was born and raised you're remembering, isn't it?

MELODY (stung to fury, glares at her with hatred. His voice quivers but is deadly quiet). Of course, if you trick Harford into getting you with child, I could not refuse my consent. (Letting go, he bangs his fist on the table.) No, by God, even then, when I remember my own experience, I'll be damned if I could with a good conscience advise him to marry you!

SARA (glaring back at him with hatred). You drunken devil! (She makes a threatening move toward him, raising her hand as if she were going to slap his face— then she controls herself and speaks with quiet, biting sarcasm.) Consent or not, I want to thank you for your kind fatherly advice on how to trick Simon. I don't think I'll need it but if the worst comes to the worst I promise you I'll remember—

MELODY (coldly, his face expressionless). I believe I have said all I wished to say to you. (He gets up and bows stiffly.) If you will excuse me, I shall join Corporal Cregan. (He goes to the bar door. SARA turns and goes quietly out right, forgetting to clear the few remaining dishes on the center table. His back turned, he does not see her go. With his hand on the knob of the bar door, he hesitates. For a second he breaks—torturedly.) Sara! (Then quietly.) There are things I said which I regret—even now. I— I trust you will overlook— As your mother knows, it's the liquor talking, not— I must admit that, due to my celebrating the anniversary, my brain is a bit addled by whiskey—as you said. (He waits, hoping for a word of forgiveness. Finally, he glances over his shoulder. As he discovers she is not there and has not heard him, for a second he crumbles, his soldierly erectness sags and his face falls. He looks sad and hopeless and bitter and old, his eyes wandering dully. But, as in the two preceding acts, the mirror attracts him, and as he moves from the bar door to stand before it he assumes his arrogant, Byronic pose again. He repeats in each detail his pantomime before the mirror. He speaks proudly.) Myself to the bitter end! No weakening, so help me God! (There is a knock on the street door but he does not hear it. He starts his familiar incantation quotes from Byron.)
"I have not loved the World, nor the World me;
I have not flattered its rank breath, nor bowed
To its idolatries a patient knee . . ."
(The knock on the door is repeated more loudly. MELODY starts guiltily and steps quickly away from the mirror. His embarrassment is transformed into resentful anger. He calls.) Come in, damn you! Do you expect a lackey to open the door for you? (The door opens and NICHOLAS GADSBY comes in. GADSBY is in his late forties, short, stout, with a big, bald head, round, florid face, and small, blue eyes. A rigidly conservative, best-family attorney, he is stiffly correct in dress and man-

ner, dryly portentous in speech, and extremely conscious of his professional authority and dignity. Now, however, he is venturing on an unfamiliar ground and is by no means as sure of himself as his manner indicates. The unexpected vision of MELODY *in his uniform startles him and for a second he stands, as close to gaping as he can be,* impressed by MELODY's *handsome distinction.* MELODY, *in his turn, is surprised. He had not thought the intruder would be a gentleman. He unbends, although his tone is still a bit curt. He bows a bit stiffly, and* GADSBY *finds himself returning the bow.*) Your pardon, sir. When I called, I thought it was one of the damned riffraff mistaking the barroom door. Pray be seated, sir. (GADSBY *comes forward and takes the chair at the head of the center table, glancing at the few dirty dishes on it with distaste.* MELODY *says*) Your pardon again, sir. We have been feasting late, which accounts for the disarray. I will summon a servant to inquire your pleasure.

GADSBY (*beginning to recover his aplomb —shortly*). Thank you, but I want nothing, sir. I came here to seek a private interview with the proprietor of this tavern, by name, Melody. (*He adds a bit hesitantly*) Are you, by any chance, he?

MELODY (*stiffens arrogantly*). I am not, sir. But if you wish to see Major Cornelius Melody, one time of His Majesty's Seventh Dragoons, who served with honor under the Duke of Wellington in Spain, I am he.

GADSBY (*dryly*). Very well, sir. Major Melody, then.

MELODY (*does not like his tone—insolently sarcastic*). And whom have I the honor of addressing?

(*As* GADSBY *is about to reply,* SARA *enters from right, having remembered the dishes,* MELODY *ignores her as he would a servant.* GADSBY *examines her carefully as she gathers up the dishes. She notices him staring at her and gives him a resentful, suspicious glance. She carries the dishes out, right, to the kitchen, but a moment later she can be seen just inside the hall at right, listening. Meanwhile, as soon as he thinks she has gone,* GADSBY *speaks.*)

GADSBY (*with affected casualness*). A pretty young woman. Is she your daughter,

sir? I seemed to detect a resemblance—

MELODY (*angrily*). No! Do I look to you, sir, like a man who would permit his daughter to work as a waitress? Resemblance to me? You must be blind, sir. (*Coldly.*) I am still waiting for you to inform me who you are and why you should wish to see me.

GADSBY (*hands him a card—extremely nettled by* MELODY's *manner—curtly*). My card, sir.

MELODY (*glances at the card*). Nicholas Gadsby. (*He flips it aside disdainfully.*) Attorney, eh? The devil take all your tribe, say I. I have small liking for your profession, sir, and I cannot imagine what business you can have with me. The damned thieves of the law did their worst to me many years ago in Ireland. I have little left to tempt you. So I do not see— (*Suddenly an idea comes to him. He stares at* GADSBY, *then goes on in a more friendly tone.*) That is, unless— Do you happen by any chance to represent the father of young Simon Harford?

GADSBY (*indignant at* MELODY's *insults to his profession—with a thinly veiled sneer*). Ah, then you were expecting— That makes things easier. We need not beat about the bush. I do represent Mr. Henry Harford, sir.

MELODY (*thawing out, in his total misunderstanding of the situation*). Then accept my apologies, sir, for my animadversions against your profession. I am afraid I may be prejudiced. In the army, we used to say we suffered more casualties from your attacks at home than the French ever inflicted. (*He sits down on the chair on* GADSBY's *left, at rear of table —remarking with careless pride*) A word of explanation as to why you find me in uniform. It is the anniversary of the battle of Talavera, sir, and—

GADSBY (*interrupts dryly*). Indeed, sir? But I must tell you my time is short. With your permission, we will proceed at once to the matter in hand.

MELODY (*controlling his angry discomfiture—coldly*). I think I can hazard a guess as to what that matter is. You have come about the settlement?

GADSBY (*misunderstanding him, replies in a tone almost openly contemptuous*). Exactly, sir. Mr. Harford was of the opinion, and I agreed with him, that a settlement would be foremost in **your** mind.

MELODY (*scowls at his tone but, as he completely misunderstands* GADSBY's *meaning, he forces himself to bow politely*). It does me honor, sir, that Mr. Harford appreciates he is dealing with a gentleman and has the breeding to know how these matters are properly arranged. (GADSBY *stares at him, absolutely flabbergasted by what he considers a piece of the most shameless effrontery.* MELODY *leans toward him confidentially.*) I will be frank with you, sir. The devil of it is, this comes at a difficult time for me. Temporary, of course, but I cannot deny I am pinched at the moment—devilishly pinched. But no matter. Where my only child's happiness is at stake, I am prepared to make every possible effort. I will sign a note of hand, no matter how ruinous the interest demanded by the scoundrelly moneylenders. By the way, what amount does Mr. Harford think proper? Anything in reason—

GADSBY (*listening in utter confusion, finally gets the idea* MELODY *is making him the butt of a joke—fuming*). I do not know what you are talking about, sir, unless you think to make a fool of me! If this is what is known as Irish wit—

MELODY (*bewildered for a second—then in a threatening tone*). Take care, sir, and watch your words or I warn you you will repent them, no matter whom you represent! No damned pettifogging dog can insult me with impunity! (*As* GADSBY *draws back apprehensively, he adds with insulting disdain*) As for making a fool of you, sir, I would be the fool if I attempted to improve on God's handiwork!

GADSBY (*ignoring the insults, forces a placating tone*). I wish no quarrel with you, sir. I cannot for the life of me see— I fear we are dealing at cross-purposes. Will you tell me plainly what you mean by your talk of settlement?

MELODY. Obviously, I mean the settlement I am prepared to make on my daughter. (*As* GADSBY *only looks more dumfounded, he continues sharply.*) Is not your purpose in coming here to arrange, on Mr. Harford's behalf, for the marriage of his son with my daughter?

GADSBY. Marriage? Good God, no! Nothing of the kind!

MELODY (*dumfounded*). Then what have you come for?

GADSBY (*feeling he has now the upper hand—sharply*). To inform you that Mr. Henry Harford is unalterably opposed to any further relationship between his son and your daughter, whatever the nature of that relationship in the past.

MELODY (*leans forward threateningly*). By the Immortal, sir, if you dare insinuate—!

GADSBY (*draws back again, but he is no coward and is determined to carry out his instructions*). I insinuate nothing, sir. I am here on Mr. Harford's behalf, to make you an offer. That is what I thought you were expecting when you mentioned a settlement. Mr. Harford is prepared to pay you the sum of three thousand dollars—provided, mark you, that you and your daughter sign an agreement I have drawn up which specifies that you relinquish all claims, of whatever nature. And also provided you agree to leave this part of the country at once with your family. Mr. Harford suggests it would be advisable that you go West—to Ohio, say.

MELODY (*so overcome by a rising tide of savage, humiliated fury, he can only stammer hoarsely*). So Henry Harford does me the honor—to suggest that, does he?

GADSBY (*watching him uneasily, attempts a reasonable, persuasive tone*). Surely you could not have spoken seriously when you talked of marriage. There is such a difference in station. The idea is preposterous. If you knew Mr. Harford, you would realize he would never countenance—

MELODY (*his pent-up rage bursts out—smashing his fist on the table*). Know him? By the Immortal God, I'll know him soon! And he'll know me! (*He springs to his feet.*) But first, you Yankee scum, I'll deal with you! (*He draws back his fist to smash* GADSBY *in the face, but* SARA *has run from the door at right and she grabs his arm. She is almost as furious as he is and there are tears of humiliated pride in her eyes.*)

SARA. Father! Don't! He's only a paid lackey. Where is your pride that you'd dirty your hands on the like of him?

(*While she is talking the door from the bar opens and* ROCHE, O'DOWD, *and* CREGAN *crowd into the room.* MICKEY *stands in the doorway.* NORA *follows* SARA *in from right.*)

ROCHE (*with drunken enthusiasm*). It's

a fight! For the love of God, clout the damned Yankee, Major!

MELODY (*controls himself—his voice shaking*). You are right, Sara. It would be beneath me to touch such a vile lickspittle. But he won't get off scot-free. (*Sharply, a commander ordering his soldiers*) Here you, Roche and O'Dowd! Get hold of him! (*They do so with enthusiasm and yank* GADSBY *from his chair.*)

GADSBY. You drunken ruffians! Take your hands off me!

MELODY (*addressing him—in his quiet, threatening tone now*). You may tell the swindling trader, Harford, who employs you that he'll hear from me! (*To* ROCHE *and* O'DOWD.) Throw this thing out! Kick it down to the crossroads!

ROCHE. Hurroo! (*He and* O'DOWD *run* GADSBY *to the door at rear.* CREGAN *jumps ahead, grinning, and opens the door for them.*)

GADSBY (*struggling futilely as they rush him through the door*). You scoundrels! Take your hands off me! Take—

(MELODY *looks after them. The two women watch him,* NORA *frightened,* SARA *with a strange look of satisfied pride.*)

CREGAN (*in the doorway, looking out— laughing*). Oh, it'd do your heart good, Con, to see the way they're kicking his butt down the street! (*He comes in and shuts the door.*)

MELODY (*his rage welling again, as his mind dwells on his humiliation—starting to pace up and down*). It's with his master I have to deal, and, by the Powers, I'll deal with him! You'll come with me, Jamie. I'll want you for a witness. He'll apologize to me—more than that, he'll come back here this very night and apologize publicly to my daughter, or else he meets me in the morning! By God, I'll face him at ten paces or across a handkerchief! I'll put a bullet through him, so help me, Christ!

NORA (*breaks into dirgelike wail*). God forgive you, Con, is it a duel again— murtherin' or gettin' murthered?

MELODY. Be quiet, woman! Go back to your kitchen! Go, do you hear me!

(NORA *turns obediently toward the door at right, beginning to cry.*)

SARA (*puts an arm around her mother. She is staring at* MELODY *apprehensively now*). There, Mother, don't worry. Father knows that's all foolishness. He's only

talking. Go on now in the kitchen and sit down and rest, Mother. (NORA *goes out right.* SARA *closes the door after her and comes back.*)

MELODY (*turns on her with bitter anger*). Only talking, am I? It's the first time in my life I ever heard anyone say Con Melody was a coward! It remains for my own daughter— !

SARA (*placatingly*). I didn't say that, Father. But can't you see—you're not in Ireland in the old days now. The days of duels are long past and dead, in this part of America anyway. Harford will never fight you. He—

MELODY. He won't, won't he? By God, I'll make him! I'll take a whip. I'll drag him out of his house and lash him down the street for all his neighbors to see! He'll apologize, or he'll fight, or I'll brand him a craven before the world!

SARA (*frightened now*). But you'll never be let see him! His servants will keep you out! He'll have the police arrest you, and it'll be in the papers about another drunken Mick raising a crazy row! (*She appeals to* CREGAN.) Tell him I'm telling the truth, Jamie. You've still got some sober sense in you. Maybe he'll listen to you.

CREGAN (*glances at* MELODY *uneasily*). Maybe Sara's right, Major.

MELODY. When I want your opinion, I'll ask for it! (*Sneeringly*) Of course, if you've become such a coward you're afraid to go with me—

CREGAN (*stung*). Coward, is ut? I'll go, and be damned to you!

SARA. Jamie, you fool! Oh, it's like talking to crazy men! (*She grabs her father's arm—pleadingly*) Don't do it, Father, for the love of God! Have I ever asked you anything? Well, I ask you to heed me now! I'll beg you on my knees, if you like! Isn't it me you'd fight about, and haven't I a right to decide? You punished that lawyer for the insult. You had him thrown out of here like a tramp. Isn't that your answer to old Harford that insults him? It's for him to challenge you, if he dares, isn't it? Why can't you leave it at that and wait—

MELODY (*shaking off her hand—angrily*). You talk like a scheming peasant! It's a question of my honor!

SARA. No! It's a question of my happiness, and I won't have your mad interfering—! (*Desperately forcing herself to reason with him again*) Listen, Father! If you'll keep out of it, I'll show you how I'll make a fool of old Harford! Simon won't let anything his father does keep him from marrying me. His mother is the only one who might have the influence over him to come between us. She's only watching for a good excuse to turn Simon against marrying me, and if you go raising a drunken row at their house, and make a public scandal, shouting you want to murder his father, can't you see what a chance that will give her?

MELODY (*raging*). That damned, insolent Yankee bitch! She's all the more reason. Marry, did you say? You dare to think there can be any question now of your marrying the son of a man who has insulted my honor—and yours?

SARA (*defiantly*). Yes, I dare to think it! I love Simon and I'm going to marry him!

MELODY. And I say you're not! If he wasn't sick, I'd— But I'll get him out of here tomorrow! I forbid you ever to see him again! If you dare disobey me I'll— ! (*Beginning to lose all control of himself*) If you dare defy me—for the sake of the dirty money you think you can beg from his family, if you're his wife— !

SARA (*fiercely*). You lie! (*Then with quiet intensity*) Yes. I defy you or anyone who tries to come between us!

MELODY. You'd sell your pride as my daughter— ! (*His face convulsed by fury*) You filthy peasant slut! You whore! I'll see you dead first— ! By the living God, I'd kill you myself! (*He makes a threatening move toward her.*)

SARA (*shrinks back frightenedly*). Father! (*Then she stands and faces him defiantly.*)

CREGAN (*steps between them*). Con! In the name of God! (MELODY's *fit of insane fury leaves him. He stands panting for breath, shuddering with the effort to regain some sort of poise.* CREGAN *speaks, his only thought to get him away from* SARA.) If we're going after old Harford, Major, we'd better go. That thief of a lawyer will warn him—

MELODY (*seizing on this—hoarsely*). Yes, let's go. Let's go, Jamie. Come along, Corporal. A stirrup cup, and we'll be off. If the mare wasn't lame, I'd ride alone—

but we can get a rig at the livery stable. Don't let me forget to stop at the barn for my whip. (*By the time he finishes speaking, he has himself in hand again and his ungovernable fury has gone. There is a look of cool, menacing vengefulness in his face. He turns toward the bar door.*)

SARA (*helplessly*). Father! (*Desperately, as a last, frantic threat*) You'll force me to go to Simon—and do what you said!

(*If he hears this, he gives no sign of it. He strides into the bar.* CREGAN *follows him, closing the door.* SARA *stares before her, the look of defiant desperation hardening on her face. The street door is flung open and* O'DOWD *and* ROCHE *pile in, laughing uproariously.*)

ROCHE. Hurroo!

O'DOWD. The army is back, Major, with the foe flying in retreat. (*He sees* MELODY *is not there—to* SARA.) Where's himself? (SARA *appears not to see or hear him.*)

ROCHE (*after a quick glance at her*). Lave her be. He'll be in the bar. Come on. (*He goes to the bar.*)

O'DOWD (*following him, speaks over his shoulder to* SARA). You should have seen the Yank! His coachman had to help him in his rig at the corner—and Roche gave the coachman a clout too, for good measure! (*He disappears, laughing, slamming the door behind him.* NORA *opens the door at right and looks in cautiously. Seeing* SARA *alone, she comes in.*)

NORA. Sara. (*She comes over to her.*) Sara. (*She takes hold of her arm—whispers uneasily.*) Where's himself?

SARA (*dully*). I couldn't stop him.

NORA. I could have told you you was wastin' breath. (*With a queer pride*) The divil himself couldn't kape Con Melody from a duel! (*Then mournfully*) It's like the auld times come again, and the same worry and sorrow. Even in the days before ivir I'd spoke a word to him, or done more than make him a bow when he'd ride past on his hunter, I used to lie awake and pray for him when I'd hear he was fightin' a duel in the mornin'. (*She smiles a shy, gentle smile.*) I was in love with him even then. (SARA *starts to say something bitter but what she sees in her mother's face stops her.* NORA *goes on, with a feeble attempt at boastful confidence.*) But I'll not worry this time, and let you not, either. There wasn't a man in Galway was his equal with a pistol, and what chance will this auld stick av a Yankee have against him? (*There is a noise of boisterous farewells from the bar and the noise of an outer door shutting.* NORA *starts.*) That's him leavin'! (*Her mouth pulls down pitiably. She starts for the bar with a sob.*) Ah, Con darlin', don't—! (*She stops, shaking her head helplessly.*) But what's the good? (*She sinks on a chair with a weary sigh.*)

SARA (*bitterly, aloud to herself more than to her mother*). No good. Let him go his way—and I'll go mine. (*Tensely*) I won't let him destroy my life with his madness, after all the plans I've made and the dreams I've dreamed. I'll show him I can play at the game of gentleman's honor too! (NORA *has not listened. She is sunk in memories of old fears and her present worry about the duel.* SARA *hesitates—then, keeping her face turned away from her mother, touches her shoulder.*) I'm going upstairs to bed, Mother.

NORA (*starts—then indignantly*). To bed, is it? You can think of sleepin' when he's—

SARA. I didn't say sleep, but I can lie down and try to rest. (*Still avoiding looking at her mother*) I'm dead tired, Mother.

NORA (*tenderly solicitous now, puts an arm around her*). You must be, darlin'. It's been the divil's own day for you, with all— (*With sudden remorse*) God forgive me, darlin'. I was forgettin' about you and the Harford lad. (*Miserably*) Oh, God help us! (*Suddenly with a flash of her strange, fierce pride in the power of love*) Never mind! If there's true love between you, you'll not let a duel or anything in the world kape you from each other, whatever the cost! Don't I know!

SARA (*kisses her impulsively, then looks away again*). You're going to sit up and wait down here?

NORA. I am. I'd be destroyed with fear lying down in the dark. Here, the noise of them in the bar kapes up my spirits, in a way.

SARA. Yes, you'd better stay here. Good night, Mother.

NORA. Good night, darlin'.

(SARA *goes out at right, closing the door behind her.*)

CURTAIN

ACT FOUR

SCENE. *The same. It is around midnight. The room is in darkness except for one candle on the table, center. From the bar comes the sound of* PATCH RILEY'S *pipes playing a reel and the stamp of dancing feet.*

NORA *sits at the foot of the table at center. She is hunched up in an old shawl, her arms crossed over her breast, hugging herself as if she were cold. She looks on the verge of collapse from physical fatigue and hours of worry. She starts as the door from the bar is opened. It is* MICKEY. *He closes the door behind him, shutting out an uproar of music and drunken voices. He has a decanter of whiskey and a glass in his hand. He has been drinking, but is not drunk.*

———

NORA (*eagerly*). There's news of himself?

MALOY (*putting the decanter and glass on the table*). Sorra a bit. Don't be worryin' now. Sure, it's not so late yet.

NORA (*dully*). It's aisy for you to say—

MALOY. I came in to see how you was, and bring you a taste to put heart in you. (*As she shakes her head*) Oh, I know you don't indulge, but I've known you once in a while, and you need it this night. (*As she again shakes her head—with kindly bullying*) Come now, don't be stubborn. I'm the doctor and I highly recommend a drop to drive out black thoughts and rheumatism.

NORA. Well—maybe—a taste, only.

MALOY. That's the talkin'. (*He pours a small drink and hands it to her.*) Drink hearty, now.

NORA (*takes a sip, then puts the glass on the table and pushes it away listlessly*). I've no taste for anything. But I thank you for the thought. You're a kind lad, Mickey.

MALOY. Here's news to cheer you. The word has got round among the boys, and they've come in to wait for Cregan and himself. (*With enthusiasm*) There'll be more money taken over the bar than any night since this shebeen started!

NORA. That's good.

MALOY. If they do hate Con Melody, he's Irish, and they hate the Yanks worse. They're all hopin' he's bate the livin' lights out of Harford.

NORA (*with belligerent spirit*). And so he has, I know that!

MALOY (*grins*). That's the talk. I'm glad to see you roused from your worryin'. (*Turning away*) I'd better get back. I left O'Dowd to tend bar and I'll wager he has three drinks stolen already. (*He hesitates.*) Sara's not been down?

NORA. No.

MALOY (*resentfully*). It's a wonder she wouldn't have more thought for you than to lave you sit up alone.

NORA (*stiffens defensively*). I made her go to bed. She was droppin' with tiredness and destroyed with worry. She must have fallen asleep, like the young can. None of your talk against Sara, now!

MALOY (*starts an exasperated retort*). The divil take— (*He stops and grins at her with affection.*) There's no batin' you, Nora. Sure, it'd be the joy av me life to have a mother like you to fight for me—or, better still, a wife like you.

NORA (*a sweet smile of pleased coquetry lights up her drawn face*). Arrah, save your blarney for the young girls!

MALOY. The divil take young girls. You're worth a hundred av thim.

NORA (*with a toss of her head*). Get along with you! (MICKEY *grins with satisfaction at having cheered her up and goes in the bar, closing the door. As soon as he is gone, she sinks back into apprehensive brooding.*)

(SARA *appears silently in the doorway at right. She wears a faded old wrapper over her nightgown, slippers on her bare feet. Her hair is down over her shoulders, reaching to her waist. There is a change in her. All the bitterness and defiance have disappeared from her face. It looks gentle and calm and at the same time dreamily happy and exultant. She is much prettier than she has ever been before. She stands looking at her mother, and suddenly she becomes shy and uncertain —as if, now that she'd come this far, she had half a mind to retreat before her mother discovered her. But NORA senses her presence and looks up.*)

NORA (*dully*). Ah, it's you, darlin'! (*Then gratefully*) Praise be, you've come at last! I'm sick with worry and I've got to the place where I can't bear waitin' alone, listenin' to drunks dancin' and cele-bratin'. (SARA *comes to her.* NORA *breaks. Tears well from her eyes.*) It's cruel, it

is! There's no heart or thought for himself in divil a one av thim. (*She starts to sob.* SARA *hugs her and kisses her cheek gently. But she doesn't speak. It is as if she were afraid her voice would give her away.* NORA *stops sobbing. Her mood changes to resentment and she speaks as if* SARA *had spoken.*) Don't tell me not to worry. You're as bad as Mickey. The Yankee didn't apologize or your father'd been back here long since. It's a duel, that's certain, and he must have taken a room in the city so he'll be near the ground. I hope he'll sleep, but I'm feared he'll stay up drinkin', and at the dawn he'll have had too much to shoot his best and maybe— (*Then defiantly self-reas-suringly*) Arrah, I'm the fool! It's himself can keep his head clear and his eyes sharp, no matter what he's taken! (*Pushing* SARA *away—with nervous peevishness.*) Let go of me. You've hardened not to care. I'd rather stay alone. (*She grabs* SARA's *hand.*) No. Don't heed me. Sit down, darlin'. (SARA *sits down on her left at rear of table. She pats her mother's hand, but remains silent, her expression dreamily happy, as if she heard* NORA's *words but they had no meaning for her.* NORA *goes on worriedly again.*) But if he's staying in the city, why hasn't he sent Jamie Cregan back for his duelin' pistols? I know he'd nivir fight with any others. (*Resentful now at* MELODY) Or you'd think he'd send Jamie or someone back with a word for me. He knows well how tormented I'd be waiting. (*Bitterly*) Arrah, don't talk like a loon! Has he ever cared for anyone except himself and his pride? Sure, he'd never stoop to think of me, the grand gentleman in his red livery av bloody England! His pride, in-dade! What is it but a lie? What's in his veins, God pity him, but the blood of thievin' auld Ned Melody who kept a dirty shebeen? (*Then is horrified at her-self as if she had blasphemed.*) No! I won't say it! I've nivir! It would break his heart if he heard me! I'm the only one in the world he knows nivir sneers at his dreams! (*Working herself to rebellion again*) All the same, I won't stay here the rist of the night worryin' my heart out for a man who—it isn't only fear over the duel. It's because I'm afraid it's God's punishment, all the sorrow and trouble that's come on us, and I have the black tormint in my mind that it's the fault of the mortal sin I did with him unmarried, and the promise he made me make to leave the Church that's kept me from ever confessin' to a priest. (*She pauses— dully*) Go to a doctor, you say, to cure the rheumantism. Sure, what's rheumatism but a pain in your body? I could bear ten of it. It's the pain of guilt in my soul. Can a doctor's medicine cure that? No, only a priest of Almighty God— (*With aroused rebellion again*) It would serve Con right if I took the chance now and broke my promise and woke up the priest to hear my confession and give me God's forgiveness that'd bring my soul peace and comfort so I wouldn't feel the three of us were damned. (*Yearningly*) Oh, if I only had the courage! (*She rises suddenly from her chair—with brave defiance*) I'll do it, so I will! I'm going to the priest's, Sara. (*She starts for the street door—gets halfway to it and stops.*)

SARA (*a strange, tenderly amused smile on her lips—teasingly*). Well, why don't you go, Mother?

NORA (*defiantly*). Ain't I goin'? (*She takes a few more steps toward the door —stops again—she mutters beatenly.*) God forgive me, I can't. What's the use pretendin'?

SARA (*as before*). No use at all, Mother. I've found that out.

NORA (*as if she hadn't heard, comes back slowly*). He'd feel I'd betrayed him and my word and my love for him—and for all his scorn, he knows my love is all he has in the world to comfort him. (*Then spiritedly, with a proud toss of her head*) And it's my honor, too! It's not for his sake at all! Divil mend him, he always prates as if he had all the honor there is, but I've mine, too, as proud as his. (*She sits down in the same chair.*)

SARA (*softly*). Yes, the honor of her love to a woman. I've learned about that too, Mother.

NORA (*as if this were the first time she was really conscious of* SARA *speaking, and even now had not heard what she said— irritably*). So you've found your tongue, have you? Thank God. You're cold comfort, sitting silent like a statue, and me making talk to myself. (*Regarding her as if she hadn't really seen her before—resentfully*) Musha but it's pleased and pretty you look, as if there wasn't a care

in the world, while your poor father—

SARA (*dreamily amused, as if this no longer had any importance or connection with her*). I know it's not use telling you there won't be any duel, Mother, and it's crazy to give it a thought. You're living in Ireland long ago, like Father. But maybe you'll take Simon's word for it, if you won't mine. He said his father would be paralyzed with indignation just at the thought he'd ever fight a duel. It's against the law.

NORA (*scornfully*). Och, who cares for the law? He must be a coward. (*She looks relieved.*) Well, if the young lad said that, maybe it's true.

SARA. Of course it's true, Mother.

NORA. Your father'd be satisfied with Harford's apology and that'd end it.

SARA (*helplessly*). Oh, Mother! (*Then quickly*) Yes, I'm sure it ended hours ago.

NORA (*intent on her hope*). And you think what's keeping him out is he and Jamie would take a power av drinks to celebrate.

SARA. They'd drink, that's sure, whatever happened. (*She adds dreamily*) But that doesn't matter now at all.

NORA (*stares at her—wonderingly*). You've a queer way of talking, as if you'd been asleep and was still half in a dream.

SARA. In a dream right enough, Mother, and it isn't half of me that's in it but all of me, body and soul. And it's a dream that's true, and always will be to the end of life, and I'll never wake from it.

NORA. Sure, what's come over you at all?

SARA (*gets up impulsively and comes around in back of her mother's chair and slips to her knees and puts her arms about her—giving her a hug*). Joy. That's what's come over me. I'm happy, Mother. I'm happy because I know now Simon is mine, and no one can ever take him from me.

NORA (*at first her only reaction is pleased satisfaction*). God be thanked! It was a great sorrow tormentin' me that the duel would come between you. (*Defiantly*) Honor or not, why should the children have their lives and their love destroyed!

SARA. I was a great fool to fear his mother could turn him against me, no matter what happened.

NORA. You've had a talk with the lad?

SARA. I have. That's where I've been.

NORA. You've been in his room ever since you went up?

SARA. Almost. After I'd got upstairs it took me a while to get up my courage.

NORA (*rebukingly*). All this time—in the dead of the night!

SARA (*teasingly*). I'm his nurse, aren't I? I've a right.

NORA. That's no excuse!

SARA (*her face hardening*). Excuse? I had the best in the world. Would you have me do nothing to save my happiness and my chance in life, when I thought there was danger they'd be ruined forever? Don't you want me to have love and be happy, Mother?

NORA (*melting*). I do, darlin'. I'd give my life— (*Then rebuking again*) Were you the way you are, in only a nightgown and wrapper?

SARA (*gaily*). I was—and Simon liked my costume, if you don't, although he turned red as a beet when I came in.

NORA. Small wonder he did! Shame on you!

SARA. He was trying to read a book of poetry, but he couldn't he was that worried hoping I'd come to say goodnight, and being frightened I wouldn't. (*She laughs tenderly.*) Oh, it was the cutest thing I've ever done, Mother, not to see him at all since his mother left. He kept waiting for me and when I didn't come, he got scared to death that his kissing me this morning had made me angry. So he was wild with joy to see me—

NORA. In your bare legs with only your nightgown and wrapper to cover your nakedness! Where's your modesty?

SARA (*gaily teasing*). I had it with me, Mother, though I'd tried hard to leave it behind. I got as red as he was. (*She laughs.*) Oh, Mother, it's a great joke on me. Here I'd gone to his room with my mind made up to be as bold as any street woman and tempt him because I knew his honor would make him marry me right away if— (*She laughs.*) And then all I could do was stand and gape at him and blush!

NORA. Oh. (*Rebukingly*) I'm glad you had the dacency to blush.

SARA. It was Simon spoke first, and once he started, all he'd been holding back came out. The waiting for me, and the fear he'd had made him forget all his shyness, and he said he loved me and asked me to marry him the first day we could. Without knowing how it happened, there I was with his arms around me and mine around him and his lips on my lips and it was heaven, Mother.

NORA (*moved by the shining happiness in* SARA's *face*). God bless the two av you.

SARA. Then I was crying and telling him how afraid I'd been his mother hated me, Father's madness about the duel would give her a good chance to come between us; Simon said no one could ever come between us and his mother would never try to, now she knew he loved me, which was what she came over to find out. He said all she wanted was for him to be free to do as he pleased, and she only suggested he wait a year, she didn't make him promise. And Simon said I was foolish to think she would take the duel craziness serious. She'd only be amused at the joke it would be on his father, after he'd been so sure he could buy us off, if he had to call the police to save him.

NORA (*aroused at the mention of police*). Call the police, is it? The coward!

SARA (*goes on, unheedingly*). Simon was terribly angry at his father for that. And at Father too when I told how he threatened he'd kill me. But we didn't talk of it much. We had better things to discuss. (*She smiles tenderly.*)

NORA (*belligerently*). A lot Con Melody cares for police, and him in a rage! Not the whole dirty force av thim will dare interfere with him!

SARA (*goes on as if she hadn't heard*). And then Simon told me how scared he'd been I didn't love him and wouldn't marry him. I was so beautiful, he said, and he wasn't handsome at all. So I kissed him and told him he was the handsomest in the world, and he is. And he said he wasn't worthy because he had so little to offer, and was a failure at what he'd hoped he could be, a poet. So I kissed him and told him he was too a poet, and always would be, and it was what I loved most about him.

NORA. The police! Let one av thim lay his dirty hand on Con Melody, and he'll knock him senseless with one blow.

SARA. Then Simon said how poor he was, and he'd never accept a penny from his father, even if he offered it. And I told him never mind, that if we had to live in a hut, or sleep in the grass of a field without a roof to our heads, and work our hands to the bone, or starve itself, I'd be in heaven and sing with the joy of our love! (*She looks up at her mother.*) And I meant it, Mother! I meant every word of it from the bottom of my heart!

NORA (*answers vaguely from her pre-occupation with the police—patting* SARA's *hair mechanically*). Av course you did, darlin'.

SARA. But he kissed me and said it wouldn't be as bad as that, he'd been thinking and he'd had an offer from an old college friend who'd inherited a cotton mill and who wants Simon to be equal partners if he'll take complete charge of it. It's only a small mill and that's what tempts Simon. He said maybe I couldn't believe it but he knows from his experience working for his father he has the ability for trade, though he hates it, and he could easily make a living for us from this mill—just enough to be comfortable, and he'd have time over to write his book, and keep his wisdom, and never let himself become a slave to the greed for more than enough that is the curse of mankind. Then he said he was afraid maybe I'd think it was weakness in him, not wisdom, and could I be happy with enough and no more. So I kissed him and said all I wanted in life was his love, and whatever meant happiness to him would be my only ambition. (*She looks up at her mother again—exultantly*) And I meant it, Mother! With all my heart and soul!

NORA (*as before, patting her hair*). I know, darlin'.

SARA. Isn't that a joke on me, with all my crazy dreams of riches and a grand estate and me a haughty lady riding around in a carriage with coachman and footman! (*She laughs at herself.*) Wasn't I the fool to think that had any meaning at all when you're in love? You were right, Mother. I knew nothing of love, or the pride a woman can take in giving everything—the pride in her own love! I was only an ignorant, silly girl boasting, but I'm a woman now, Mother, and I know.

NORA (*as before, mechanically*). I'm sure you do, darlin'. (*She mutters fumingly to herself.*) Let the police try it!

He'll whip them back to their kennels, the dirty curs!

SARA (*lost in her happiness*). And then we put out the light and talked about how soon we'd get married, and how happy we'd be the rest of our lives together, and we'd have children—and he forgot whatever shyness was left in the dark and said he meant all the bold things he'd written in the poems I'd seen. And I confessed that I was up to every scheme to get him, because I loved him so much there wasn't anything I wouldn't do to make sure he was mine. And all the time we were kissing each other, wild with happiness. And— (*She stops abruptly and looks down guiltily.*)

NORA (*as before*). Yes, darlin', I know.

SARA (*guiltily, keeping her eyes down*). You—know, Mother?

NORA (*abruptly comes out of her pre-occupation, startled and uneasy*). I know what? What are you sayin'? Look up at me! (*She pulls* SARA's *head back so she can look down in her face—falteringly*) I can see— You let him! You wicked, sinful girl!

SARA (*defiantly and proudly*). There was no letting about it, only love making the two of us!

NORA (*helplessly resigned already but feeling it her duty to rebuke*). Ain't you ashamed to boast— ?

SARA. No! There was no shame in it! (*Proudly*) Ashamed? You know I'm not! Haven't you told me of the pride in your love? Were you ashamed?

NORA (*weakly*). I was. I was dead with shame.

SARA. You were not! You were proud like me!

NORA. But it's a mortal sin. God will punish you—

SARA. Let Him! If He'd say to me, for every time you kiss Simon you'll have a thousand years in hell, I wouldn't care, I'd wear out my lips kissing him!

NORA (*frightenedly*). Whist, now! He might hear you.

SARA. Wouldn't you have said the same—?

NORA (*distractedly*). Will you stop! Don't torment me with your sinful questions! I won't answer you!

SARA (*hugging her*). All right. Forgive me, Mother. (*A pause—smilingly*) It was Simon who felt guilty and repentant. If he'd had his way, he'd be out of bed now, and the two of us would be walking around in the night, trying to wake up someone who could marry us. But I was so drunk with love, I'd lost all thought or care about marriage. I'd got to the place where all you know or care is that you belong to love, and you can't call your soul your own any more, let alone your body, and you're proud you've given them to love. (*She pauses—then teasing lovingly*) Sure, I've always known you're the sweetest woman in the world, Mother, but I never suspected you were a wise woman too, until I knew tonight the truth of what you said this morning, that a woman can forgive whatever the man she loves could do and still love him, because it was through him she found the love in herself; that, in one way, he doesn't count at all, because it's love, your own love, you love in him, and to keep that your pride will do anything. (*She smiles with a self-mocking happiness.*) It's love's slaves we are, Mother, not men's—and wouldn't it shame their boasting and vanity if we ever let them know our secret? (*She laughs—then suddenly looks guilty.*) But I'm talking great nonsense. I'm glad Simon can't hear me. (*She pauses.* NORA *is worrying and hasn't listened.* SARA *goes on.*) Yes, I can even understand now—a little anyway—how you can still love Father and be proud of it, in spite of what he is.

NORA (*at the mention of* MELODY, *comes out of her brooding*). Hush, now! (*Miserably*) God help us, Sara, why doesn't he come, what's happened to him?

SARA (*gets to her feet exasperatedly*). Don't be a fool, Mother. (*Bitterly*) Nothing's happened except he's made a public disgrace of himself, for Simon's mother to sneer at. If she wanted revenge on him, I'm sure she's had her fill of it. Well, I don't care. He deserves it. I warned him and I begged him, and got called a peasant slut and a whore for my pains. All I hope now is that whatever happened wakes him from his lies and mad dreams so he'll have to face the truth of himself in that mirror. (*Sneeringly*) But there's devil a chance he'll ever let that happen. Instead, he'll come home as drunk as two lords, boasting of his glorious victory over old Harford, whatever the truth is!

(*But* NORA *isn't listening. She has heard the click of the latch on the street door at rear.*)

NORA (*excitedly*). Look, Sara! (*The door is opened slowly and* JAMIE CREGAN *sticks his head in cautiously to peer around the room. His face is battered, nose red and swollen, lips cut and puffed, and one eye so blackened it is almost closed.* NORA's *first reaction is a cry of relief.*) Praise be to the Saints, you're back, Jamie!

CREGAN (*puts a finger to his lips—cautioningly*). Whist!

NORA (*frightenedly*). Jamie! Where's himself?

CREGAN (*sharply*). Whist, I'm telling you! (*In a whisper*) I've got him in a rig outside, but I had to make sure no one was here. Lock the bar door, Sara, and I'll bring him in.

(*She goes and turns the key in the door, her expression contemptuous.* CREGAN *then disappears, leaving the street door half open.*)

NORA. Did you see Jamie's face? They've been fightin' terrible. Oh, I'm afraid, Sara.

SARA. Afraid of what? It's only what I told you to expect. A crazy row—and now he's paralyzed drunk.

(CREGAN *appears in the doorway at rear. He is half leading, half supporting* MELODY. *The latter moves haltingly and woodenly. But his movements do not seem those of drunkenness. It is more as if a sudden shock or stroke had shattered his coordination and left him in a stupor. His scarlet uniform is filthy and torn and pulled awry. The pallor of his face is ghasty. He has a cut over his left eye, a blue swelling on his left cheekbone, and his lips are cut and bloody. From a big raw bruise on his forehead, near the temple, trickles of dried blood run down to his jaw. Both his hands are swollen, with skinned knuckles, as are* CREGAN's. *His eyes are empty and lifeless. He stares at his wife and daughter as if he did not recognize them.*)

NORA (*rushes and puts her arm around him*). Con, darlin'! Are you hurted bad? (*He pushes her away without looking at her. He walks dazedly to his chair at the head of the center table.* NORA *follows him, breaking into lamentation.*) Con, don't you know me? Oh, God help us, look at his head!

SARA. Be quiet, Mother. Do you want them in the bar to know he's come home —the way he is. (*She gives her father a look of disgust.*)

CREGAN. Ay, that's it, Sara. We've got to rouse him first. His pride'd nivir forgive us if we let thim see him dead bate like this.

(*There is a pause. They stare at him and he stares sightlessly at the table top.* NORA *stands close by his side, behind the table, on his right,* SARA *behind her on her right,* CREGAN *at right of* SARA.)

SARA. He's drunk, isn't that all it is, Jamie?

CREGAN (*sharply*). He's not. He's not taken a drop since we left here. It's the clouts on the head he got, that's what ails him. A taste of whiskey would bring him back, if he'd only take it, but he won't.

SARA (*gives her father a puzzled, uneasy glance*). He won't?

NORA (*gets the decanter and a glass and hands them to* CREGAN). Here. Try and make him.

CREGAN (*pours out a big drink and puts it before* MELODY—*coaxingly*). Drink this now, Major, and you'll be right as rain! (MELODY *does not seem to notice. His expression remains blank and dead.* CREGAN *scratches his head puzzledly.*) He won't. That's the way he's been all the way back when I tried to persuade him. (*Then irritably*) Well, if he won't, I will, be your leave. I'm needin' it bad. (*He downs the whiskey, and pours out another—to* NORA *and* SARA) It's the divil's own rampage we've had.

SARA (*quietly contemptuous, but still with the look of puzzled uneasiness at her father*). From your looks it must have been.

CREGAN (*indignantly*). You're takin' it cool enough, and you seein' the marks av the batin' we got! (*He downs his second drink—boastfully.*) But if we're marked, there's others is marked worse and some av thim is police!

NORA. God be praised! The dirty cowards!

SARA. Be quiet, Mother. Tell us what happened, Jamie.

CREGAN. Faix, what didn't happen? Be the rock av Cashel, I've nivir engaged in a livelier shindy! We had no trouble findin' where Harford lived. It's a grand mansion, with a big walled garden behind it, and we wint to the front door. A flunky in livery answered wid two others behind. A big black naygur one was. That pig av a lawyer must have warned Harford to expect us. Con spoke wid the airs av a lord. "Kindly inform your master," he says, "that Major Cornelius Melody, late of His Majesty's Seventh Dragoons, respectfully requests a word with him." Well, the flunky put an insolent sneer on him. "Mr. Harford won't see you," he says. I could see Con's rage risin' but he kept polite. "Tell him," he says, "if he knows what's good for him he'll see me. For if he don't, I'll come in and see him." "Ye will, will ye?" says the flunky, "I'll have you know Mr. Harford don't allow drunken Micks to come here disturbing him. The police have been informed," he says, "and you'll be arrested if you make trouble." Then he started to shut the door. "Anyway, you've come to the wrong door," he says, "the place for the loiks av you is the servants' entrance."

NORA (*angrily*). Och, the impident divil!

SARA (*in spite of herself her temper has been rising. She looks at* MELODY *with angry scorn*). You let Harford's servants insult you! (*Then quickly*) But it serves you right! I knew what would happen! I warned you!

CREGAN. Let thim be damned! Kape your mouth shut, and lave me tell it, and you'll see if we let them! When he'd said that, the flunky tried to slam the door in our faces, but Con was too quick. He pushed it back on him and lept in the hall, roarin' mad, and hit the flunky a cut with his whip across his ugly mug that set him screaming like a stuck pig!

NORA (*enthusiastically*). Good for you, Con darlin'!

SARA (*humiliatedly*). Mother! Don't! (*To* MELODY *with biting scorn*) The famous duelist—in a drunken brawl with butlers and coachmen!

(*But he is staring sightlessly at the table top as if he didn't see her or know her.*)

CREGAN (*angrily, pouring himself another drink*). Shut your mouth, Sara, and don't be trying to plague him. You're wastin' breath anyway, the way he is. He doesn't know you or hear you. And don't put on lady's airs about fighting when you're the whole cause of it.

SARA (*angrily*). It's a lie! You know I tried to stop—

CREGAN (*gulps down his drink, ignoring this, and turns to* NORA—*enthusiastically*). Wait till you hear, Nora! (*He plunges into the midst of battle again.*) The naygur hit me a clout that had my head dizzy. He'd have had me down only Con broke the butt av the whip over his black skull and knocked him to his knees. Then the third man punched Con and I gave him a kick where it'd do him least good, and he rolled on the floor, grabbin' his guts. The naygur was in again and grabbed me, but Con came at him and knocked him down. Be the mortal, we had the three av thim licked, and we'd have dragged auld Harford from his burrow and tanned his Yankee hide if the police hadn't come!

NORA (*furiously*). Arrah, the dirthy cowards! Always takin' sides with the rich Yanks against the poor Irish!

SARA (*more and more humiliated and angry and torn by conflicting emotions— pleadingly*). Mother! Can't you keep still?

CREGAN. Four av thim wid clubs came behind us. They grabbed us before we knew it and dragged us into the street. Con broke away and hit the one that held him, and I gave one a knee in his belly. And then, glory be, there was a fight! Oh, it'd done your heart good to see himself! He was worth two men, lettin' out right and left, roarin' wid rage and cursin' like a trooper—

MELODY (*without looking up or any change in his dazed expression, suddenly speaks in a jeering mumble to himself*). Bravely done, Major Melody! The Commander of the Forces honors your exceptional gallantry! Like the glorious field of Talavera! Like the charge on the French square! Cursing like a drunken, foul-mouthed son of a thieving shebeen keeper who sprang from the filth of a peasant hovel, with pigs on the floor— with that pale Yankee bitch watching from a window, sneering with disgust!

NORA (*frightenedly*). God preserve us, it's crazed he is!

SARA (*stares at him startled and wondering. For a second there is angry pity in her eyes. She makes an impulsive move toward him*). Father! (*Then her face hardening*) He isn't crazed, Mother. He's

come to his senses for once in his life! (*To* MELODY) So she was sneering, was she? I don't blame her! I'm glad you've been taught a lesson! (*Then vindictively*) But I've taught her one, too. She'll soon sneer from the wrong side of her mouth!

CREGAN (*angrily*). Will you shut your gab, Sara! Lave him be and don't heed him. It's the same crazy blather he's talked every once in a while since they brought him to—about the Harford woman—and speakin' av the pigs and his father one minute, and his pride and honor and his mate the next. (*He takes up the story again.*) Well, anyways, they was too much for us, the four av thim wid clubs. The last thing I saw before I was knocked senseless was three av thim clubbing Con. But, be the Powers, we wint down fightin' to the last for the glory av auld Ireland!

MELODY (*in a jeering mutter to himself*). Like a rum-soaked trooper, brawling before a brothel on a Saturday night, puking in the gutter!

SARA (*strickenly*). Don't, Father!

CREGAN (*indignantly to* MELODY). We wasn't in condition. If we had been—but they knocked us senseless and rode us to the station and locked us up. And we'd be there yet if Harford hadn't made thim turn us loose, for he's rich and has influence. Small thanks to him! He was afraid the row would get in the paper and put shame on him. (MELODY *laughs crazily and springs to his feet. He sways dizzily, clutching his head—then goes toward the door at left front.*)

NORA. Con! Where are you goin'? (*She starts after him and grabs his arm. He shakes her hand off roughly as if he did not recognize her.*)

CREGAN. He don't know you. Don't cross him now, Nora. Sure, he's only goin' upstairs to bed. (*Wheedlingly*) You know what's best for you, don't you, Major?

(MELODY *feels his way gropingly through the door and disappears, leaving it open.*)

SARA (*uneasy, but consoling her mother*). Jamie's right, Mother. If he'll fall asleep, that's the best thing— (*Abruptly she is terrified.*) Oh God, maybe he'll take revenge on Simon— (*She rushes to the door and stands listening—with relief*) No, he's gone to his room. (*She comes back—a bit ashamed.*) I'm a fool. He'd never harm a sick man, no matter— (*She takes her mother's arm—gently*) Don't stand there, Mother. Sit down. You're tired enough—

NORA (*frightenedly*). I've never heard him talk like that in all the years—with that crazy dead look in his eyes. Oh, I'm afeered, Sara. Lave go of me. I've got to make sure he's gone to bed. (*She goes quickly to the door and disappears.* SARA *makes a move to follow her.*)

CREGAN (*roughly*). Stay here, unless you're a fool, Sara. He might come to all av a sudden and give you a hell av a thrashin'. Troth, you deserve one. You're to blame for what's happened. Wasn't he fightin' to revenge the insults to you? (*He sprawls on a chair at rear of the table at center.*)

SARA (*sitting down at rear of the small table at left front—angrily*). I'll thank you to mind your own business, Jamie Cregan. Just because you're a relation—

CREGAN (*harshly*). Och, to hell with your airs! (*He pours out a drink and downs it. He is becoming drunk again.*)

SARA. I can revenge my own insults, and I have! I've beaten the Harfords— and he's only made a fool of himself for her to sneer at. But I've beaten her and I'll sneer last! (*She pauses, a hard, triumphant smile on her lips. It fades. She gives a little bewildered laugh.*) God forgive me, what a way to think of— I must be crazy, too.

CREGAN (*drunkenly*). Ah, don't be talkin'! Didn't the two of us lick them all! And Con's all right. He's all right, I'm sayin'! It's only the club on the head makes him quare a while. I've seen it often before. Ay, and felt it meself. I remember at a fair in the auld country I was clouted with the butt av a whip and I didn't remember a thing for hours, but they told me after I never stopped gabbin' but went around tellin' every stranger all my secrets. (*He pauses.* SARA *hasn't listened. He goes on uneasily.*) All the same, it's no fun listening to his mad blather about the pale bitch, as he calls her, like she was a ghost, haunting and scorning him. And his gab about his beautiful thoroughbred mare is madder still, raving what a grand, beautiful lady she is, with her slender ankles and dainty feet, sobbin' and beggin' her forgiveness

and talkin' of dishonor and death— (*He shrinks superstitiously—then angrily, reaching for the decanter*) Och, be damned to this night!

(*Before he can pour a drink,* NORA *comes hurrying in from the door at left front.*)

NORA (*breathless and frightened*). He's come down! He pushed me away like he didn't see me. He's gone out to the barn. Go after him, Jamie.

CREGAN (*drunkenly*). I won't. He's all right. Lave him alone.

SARA (*jeeringly*). Sure, he's only gone to pay a call on his sweetheart, the mare, Mother, and hasn't he slept in her stall many a time when he was dead drunk, and she never even kicked him?

NORA (*distractedly*). Will you shut up, the two av you! I heard him openin' the closet in his room where he keeps his auld set of duelin' pistols, and he was carryin' the box when he came down—

CREGAN (*scrambles hastily to his feet*). Oh, the lunatic!

NORA. He'll ride the mare back to Harford's! He'll murther someone! For the love av God, stop him, Jamie!

CREGAN (*drunkenly belligerent*). Be Christ, I'll stop him for you, Nora, pistols or no pistols! (*He walks a bit unsteadily out the door at left front.*)

SARA (*stands tensely—bursts out with a strange triumphant pride*). Then he's not beaten! (*Suddenly she is overcome by a bitter, tortured revulsion of feeling.*) Merciful God, what am I thinking? As if he hadn't done enough to destroy— (*Distractedly*) Oh, the mad fool! I wish he was— (*From the yard, off left front, there is the muffled crack of a pistol shot hardly perceptible above the noise in the barroom. But* SARA *and* NORA *both hear it and stand frozen with horror.* SARA *babbles hysterically.*) I didn't mean it, Mother! I didn't!

NORA (*numb with fright—mumbles stupidly*). A shot!

SARA. You know I didn't mean it, Mother!

NORA. A shot! God help us, he's kilt Jamie!

SARA (*stammers*). No—not Jamie— (*Wildly*) Oh, I can't bear waiting! I've got to know— (*She rushes to the door at left front—then stops frightenedly.*) I'm afraid to know! I'm afraid—

NORA (*mutters stupidly*). Not Jamie? Then who else? (*She begins to tremble —in a horrified whisper*) Sara! You think— Oh, God have mercy!

SARA. Will you hush, Mother! I'm trying to hear— (*She retreats quickly into the room and backs around the table at left front until she is beside her mother.*) Someone's at the yard door. It'll be Jamie coming to tell us—

NORA. It's a lie! He'd nivir. He'd nivir!

(*They stand paralyzed by terror, clinging to each other, staring at the open door. There is a moment's pause in which the sound of drunken roistering in the bar seems louder. Then* MELODY *appears in the doorway with* CREGAN *behind him.* CREGAN *has him by the shoulder and pushes him roughly into the room, like a bouncer handling a drunk.* CREGAN *is shaken by the experience he has just been through and his reaction is to make him drunkenly angry at* MELODY. *In his free hand is a dueling pistol.* MELODY's *face is like gray wax. His body is limp, his feet drag, his eyes seem to have no sight. He appears completely possessed by a paralyzing stupor.*)

SARA (*impulsively*). Father! Oh, thank God! (*She takes one step toward him— then her expression begins to harden.*)

NORA (*sobs with relief*). Oh, praise God you're alive! Sara and me was dead with fear— (*She goes toward them.*) Con! Con, darlin'!

CREGAN (*dumps* MELODY *down on the nearest chair at left of the small table— roughly, his voice trembling*). Let you sit still now, Con Melody, and behave like a gintleman! (*To* NORA) Here he is for ye, Nora, and you're welcome, bad luck to him! (*He moves back as* NORA *comes and puts her arms around* MELODY *and hugs him tenderly.*)

NORA. Oh, Con, Con, I was so afeered for you! (*He does not seem to hear or see her, but she goes on crooning to him comfortingly as if he were a sick child.*)

CREGAN. He was in the stable. He'd this pistol in his hand, with the mate to it on the floor beside the mare. (*He shudders and puts the pistol on the table shakenly.*) It's mad he's grown entirely! Let you take care av him now, his wife and daughter! I've had enough. I'm no damned keeper av lunatics! (*He turns toward the barroom.*)

SARA. Wait, Jamie. We heard a shot. What was it?

CREGAN (*angrily*). Ask him, not me! (*Then with bewildered horror*) He kilt the poor mare, the mad fool! (SARA *stares at him in stunned amazement.*) I found him on the floor with her head in his lap, and her dead. He was sobbing like a soul in hell— (*He shudders.*) Let me get away from the sight of him where there's men in their right senses laughing and singing! (*He unlocks the barroom door.*) And don't be afraid, Sara, that I'll tell the boys a word av this. I'll talk of our fight in the city only, because it's all I want to remember.

(*He jerks open the door and goes in the bar, slamming the door quickly behind him. A roar of welcome is heard as the crowd greets his arrival.* SARA *locks the door again. She comes back to the center table, staring at* MELODY, *an hysterical, sneering grin making her lips quiver and twitch.*)

SARA. What a fool I was to be afraid! I might know you'd never do it as long as a drink of whiskey was left in the world! So it was the mare you shot? (*She bursts into uncontrollable, hysterical laughter. It penetrates* MELODY's *stupor and he stiffens rigidly on his chair, but his eyes remain fixed on the table top.*)

NORA. Sara! Stop! For the love av God, how can you laugh—!

SARA. I can't—help it, Mother. Didn't you hear—Jamie? It was the mare he shot! (*She gives way to laughter again.*)

NORA (*distractedly*). Stop it, I'm sayin'! (SARA *puts her hand over her mouth to shut off the sound of her laughing, but her shoulders still shake.* NORA *sinks on the chair at rear of the table. She mutters dazedly.*) Kilt his beautiful mare? He must be mad entirely.

MELODY (*suddenly speaks, without looking up, in the broadest brogue, his voice coarse and harsh*). Lave Sara laugh. Sure, who could blame her? I'm roarin' meself inside me. It's the damnedest joke a man ivir played on himself since time began.

(*They stare at him.* SARA's *laughter stops. She is startled and repelled by his brogue. Then she stares at him suspiciously, her face hardening.*)

SARA. What joke? Do you think murdering the poor mare a good joke?

(MELODY *stiffens for a second, but that*

is all. He doesn't look up or reply.)

NORA (*frightened*). Look at the dead face on him, Sara. He's like a corpse. (*She reaches out and touches one of his hands on the table top with a furtive tenderness—pleadingly*) Con, darlin'. Don't!

MELODY (*looks up at her. His expression changes so that his face loses all its remaining distinction and appears vulgar and common, with a loose, leering grin on his swollen lips*). Let you not worry, Allanah. Sure, I'm no corpse, and with a few drinks in me, I'll soon be lively enough to suit you.

NORA (*miserably confused*). Will you listen to him, Sara—puttin' on the brogue to torment us.

SARA (*growing more uneasy but sneering*). Pay no heed to him, Mother. He's play-acting to amuse himself. If he's that cruel and shameless after what he's done—

NORA (*defensively*). No, it's the blow on the head he got fightin' the police.

MELODY (*vulgarly*). The blow, me foot! That's Jamie Cregan's blather. Sure, it'd take more than a few clubs on the head to darken my wits long. Me brains, if I have any, is clear as a bell. And I'm not puttin' on brogue to tormint you, me darlint. Nor play-actin', Sara. That was the Major's game. It's quare, surely, for the two av ye to object when I talk in me natural tongue, and yours, and don't put on airs loike the late lamented auld liar and lunatic, Major Cornelius Melody, av His Majesty's Seventh Dragoons, used to do.

NORA. God save us, Sara, will you listen!

MELODY. But he's dead now, and his last bit av lyin' pride is murthered and stinkin'. (*He pats* NORA's *hand with what seems to be genuine comforting affection.*) So let you be aisy, darlint. He'll nivir again hurt you with his sneers, and his pretindin' he's a gintleman, blatherin' about pride and honor, and his boastin' av duels in the days that's gone, and his showin' off before the Yankees, and thim laughin' at him, prancing around drunk on his beautiful thoroughbred mare— (*He gulps as if he were choking back a sob.*) For she's dead, too, poor baste.

SARA (*this is becoming unbearable for her—tensely*). Why—why did you kill her?

MELODY. Why did the Major, you mean! Be Christ, you're stupider than I thought you, if you can't see that. Wasn't she the livin' reminder, so to spake, av all his lyin' boasts and dreams? He meant to kill her first wid one pistol, and then himself wid the other. But faix, he saw the shot that killed her had finished him, too. There wasn't much pride left in the auld lunatic, anyway, and seeing her die made an end av him. So he didn't bother shooting himself, because it'd be a mad thing to waste a good bullet on a corpse! (*He laughs coarsely.*)

SARA (*tensely*). Father! Stop it!

MELODY. Didn't I tell you there was a great joke in it? Well, that's the joke. (*He begins to laugh again but he chokes on a stifled sob. Suddenly his face loses the coarse, leering, brutal expression and is full of anguished grief. He speaks without brogue, not to them but aloud to himself.*) Blessed Christ, the look in her eyes by the lantern light with life ebbing out of them—wondering and sad, but still trustful, not reproaching me—with no fear in them—proud, understanding pride —loving me—she saw I was dying with her. She understood! She forgave me! (*He starts to sob but wrenches himself out of it and speaks in broad, jeering brogue.*) Begorra, if that wasn't the mad Major's ghost speakin'! But be damned to him, he won't haunt me long, if I know it! I intind to live at my ease from now on and not let the dead bother me, but enjoy life in my proper station as auld Nick Melody's son. I'll bury his Major's damned red livery av bloody England deep in the ground and he can haunt its grave if he likes, and boast to the lonely night av Talavera and the ladies of Spain and fightin' the French! (*With a leer*) Troth, I think the boys is right when they say he stole the uniform and he nivir fought under Wellington at all. He was a terrible liar, as I remember him.

NORA. Con, darlin', don't be grievin' about the mare. Sure, you can get another. I'll manage—

SARA. Mother! Hush! (*To* MELODY, *furiously*) Father, will you stop this mad game you're playing—?

MELODY (*roughly*). Game, is it? You'll find it's no game. It was the Major played a game all his life, the crazy auld loon, and cheated only himself. But I'll be content to stay meself in the proper station I was born to, from this day on. (*With a cunning leer at* SARA.) And it's meself feels it me duty to give you a bit av fatherly advice, Sara darlint, while my mind is on it. I know you've great ambition, so remember it's to hell wid honor if ye want to rise in this world. Remember the blood in your veins and be your grandfather's true descendent. There was an able man for you! Be Jaysus, he nivir felt anything beneath him that could gain him something, and for lyin' tricks to swindle the bloody fools of gintry, there wasn't his match in Ireland, and he ended up wid a grand estate, and a castle, and a pile av gold in the bank.

SARA (*distractedly*). Oh, I hate you!

NORA. Sara!

MELODY (*goes on as if he hadn't heard*). I know he'd advise that to give you a first step up, darlint, you must make the young Yankee gintleman have you in his bed, and afther he's had you, weep great tears and appeal to his honor to marry you and save yours. Be God, he'll nivir resist that, if I know him, for he's a young fool, full av dacency and dreams, and looney, too, wid a touch av the poet in him. Oh, it'll be aisy for you—

SARA (*goaded beyond bearing*). I'll make you stop your dirty brogue and your play-acting! (*She leans toward him and speaks with taunting vindictiveness, in broad brogue herself.*) Thank you kindly but I've already taken your wise advice, Father. I made him have me in his bed, while you was out drunk fightin' the police!

NORA (*frightenedly*). Sara! Hault your brazen tongue!

MELODY (*his body stiffens on his chair and the coarse leer vanishes from his face. It becomes his old face. His eyes fix on her in a threatening stare. He speaks slowly, with difficulty keeping his words in brogue*). Did you now, God bless you! I might have known you'd not take any chance that the auld loon av a Major, going out to revenge an insult to you, would spoil your schemes. (*He forces a horrible grin.*) Be the living God, it's me should be proud this night that one av the Yankee gintry has stooped to be seduced by my slut av a daughter! (*Still keeping*

his eyes fixed on hers, he begins to rise from his chair, his right hand groping along the table top until it clutches the dueling pistol. He aims it at SARA's heart, like an automaton, his eyes as cold, deadly, and merciless as they must have been in his duels of long ago. SARA is terrified but she stands unflinchingly.*)

NORA (*horror-stricken, lunges from her chair and grabs his arm*). Con! For the love av God! Would you be murthering Sara?

(*A dazed look comes over his face. He grows limp and sinks back on his chair and lets the pistol slide from his fingers on the table. He draws a shuddering breath—then laughs hoarsely.*)

MELODY (*with a coarse leer*). Murtherin' Sara, is it? Are ye daft, Nora? Sure, all I want is to congratulate her!

SARA (*hopelessly*). Oh! (*She sinks down on her chair at rear of the center table and covers her face with her hands.*)

NORA (*with pitifully well-meant reassurance*). It's all right, Con. The young lad wants to marry her as soon as can be, she told me, and he did before.

MELODY. Musha, but that's kind of him! Be God, we ought to be proud av our daughter, Nora. Lave it to her to get what she wants by hook or crook. And won't we be proud watchin' her rise in the world till she's a grand lady!

NORA (*simply*). We will, surely.

SARA. Mother!

MELODY. She'll have some trouble, rootin' out his dreams. He's set in his proud, noble ways, but she'll find the right trick! I'd lay a pound, if I had one, to a shilling she'll see the day when she'll wear fine silks and drive in a carriage wid a naygur coachman behind spankin' thoroughbreds, her nose in the air; and she'll live in a Yankee mansion, as big as a castle, on a grand estate av stately woodland and soft green meadows and a lake. (*With a leering chuckle*) Be the Saints, I'll start her on her way by making her a wedding present av the Major's place where he let her young gintleman build his cabin—the land the Yankees swindled him into buyin' for his American estate, the mad fool! (*He glances at the dueling pistol—jeeringly.*) Speakin' av the departed, may his soul roast in hell, what am I doin' wid his pistol? Be God, I don't need pistols. Me fists, or a club if it's handy, is enough. Didn't me and Jamie lick a whole regiment av police this night?

NORA (*stoutly*). You did, and if there wasn't so many av thim—

MELODY (*turns to her—grinningly*). That's the talk, darlint! Sure, there's divil a more loyal wife in the whole world— (*He pauses, staring at her—then suddenly kisses her on the lips, roughly but with a strange real tenderness.*) and I love you.

NORA (*with amazed, unthinking joy*). Oh, Con!

MELODY (*grinning again*). I've meant to tell you often, only the Major, damn him, had me under his proud thumb. (*He pulls her over and kisses her hair.*)

NORA. Is it kissin' my hair— !

MELODY. I am. Why wouldn't I? You have beautiful hair, God bless you! And don't remember what the Major used to tell you. The gintleman's sneers he put on is buried with him. I'll be a real husband to you, and help ye run this she-been, instead of being a sponge. I'll fire Mickey and tend the bar myself, like my father's son ought to.

NORA. You'll not! I'll nivir let you!

MELODY (*leering cunningly*). Well, I offered, remember. It's you refused. Sure, I'm not in love with work, I'll confess, and maybe you're right not to trust me too near the whiskey. (*He licks his lips.*) Be Jaysus, that reminds me. I've not had a taste for hours. I'm dyin' av thirst.

NORA (*starts to rise*). I'll get you—

MELODY (*pushes her back on her chair*). Ye'll not. I want company and singin' and dancin' and great laughter. I'll join the boys in the bar and help Cousin Jamie celebrate our wonderful shindy and the police. (*He gets up. His old soldierly bearing is gone. He slouches and his movements are shambling and clumsy, his big hairy hands dangling at his sides. In his torn, disheveled, dirt-stained uniform, he looks like a loutish, grinning clown.*)

NORA. You ought to go to bed, Con darlin', with your head hurted.

MELODY. Me head? Faix, it was nivir so clear while the Major lived to torment me, makin' me tell mad lies to excuse his divilments. (*He grins.*) And I ain't tired a bit. I'm fresh as a man new born. So I'll say goodnight to you, darlint. (*He bends and kisses her.* SARA *has lifted her tear-stained face from her hands and is staring at him with a strange, anguished look of desperation. He leers at her.*) And you go to bed, too, Sara. Troth, you deserve a long, dreamless slape after all you've accomplished this day.

SARA. Please! Oh, Father, I can't bear— Won't you be yourself again?

MELODY (*threatening her good-humoredly*). Let you kape your mouth closed, ye slut, and not talk like you was ashamed of me, your father. I'm not the Major who was too much of a gintleman to lay hand on you. Faix, I'll give you a box on the ear that'll teach you respect, if ye kape on trying to raise the dead! (*She stares at him, sick and desperate. He starts toward the bar door.*)

SARA (*springs to her feet*). Father! Don't go in with those drunken scum! Don't let them hear and see you! You can drink all you like here. Jamie will come and keep you company. He'll laugh and sing and help you celebrate Talavera—

MELODY (*roughly*). To hell wid Talavera! (*His eyes are fastened on the mirror. He leers into it.*) Be Jaysus, if it ain't the mirror the auld loon was always admirin' his mug in while he spouted Byron to pretend himself was a lord wid a touch av the poet— (*He strikes a pose which is a vulgar burlesque of his old before-the-mirror one and recites in mocking brogue.*)

"I have not loved the World, nor the World me; ,
I have not flatthered uts rank breath, nor bowed
To uts idolatries a pashunt knee,
Nor coined me cheek to smiles,— nor cried aloud
In worship av an echo: in the crowd
They couldn't deem me one av such —I stood
Among thim, but not av thim . . ."
(*He guffaws contemptuously.*) Be Christ, if he wasn't the joke av the world, the Major. He should have been a clown in a circus. God rest his soul in the flames av tormint! (*Roughly.*) But to hell wid the dead. (*The noise in the bar rises to an uproar of laughter as if* JAMIE *had just made some climactic point in his story.* MELODY *looks away from the mirror to the bar door.*) Be God, I'm alive

and in the crowd they *can* deem me one av such! I'll be among thim and av thim, too—and make up for the lonely dog's life the Major led me. (*He goes to the bar door.*)

SARA (*starts toward him—beseechingly*). Father! Don't put this final shame on yourself. You're not drunk now. There's no excuse you can give yourself. You'll be as dead to yourself after, as if you'd shot yourself along with the mare!

MELODY (*leering—with a wink at* NORA). Listen to her, Nora, reproachin' me because I'm not drunk. Troth, that's a condition soon mended. (*He puts his hand on the knob of the door.*)

SARA. Father!

NORA (*has given way to such complete physical exhaustion, she hardly hears, much less comprehends what is said— dully*). Lave him alone, Sara. It's best.

MELODY (*as another roar is heard from the bar*). I'm missin' a lot av fun. Be God, I've a bit of news to tell the boys that'll make them roar the house down. The Major's passin' to his eternal rest has set me free to jine the Democrats, and I'll vote for Andy Jackson, the friend av the common men like me, God bless him! (*He grins with anticipation.*) Wait till the boys hear that! (*He starts to turn the knob.*)

SARA (*rushes to him and grabs his arm*). No! I won't let you! It's my pride, too! (*She stammers.*) Listen! Forgive me, Father! I know it's my fault—always sneering and insulting you—but I only meant the lies in it. The truth—Talavera —the Duke praising your bravery—an officer in his army—even the ladies in Spain—deep down that's been my pride, too—that I was your daughter. So don't— I'll do anything you ask— I'll even tell Simon—that after his father's insult to you—I'm too proud to marry a Yankee coward's son!

MELODY (*has been visibly crumbling as he listens until he appears to have no character left in which to hide and defend himself. He cries wildly and despairingly, as if he saw his last hope of escape suddenly cut off*). Sara! For the love of God, stop—let me go— !

NORA (*dully*). Lave your poor father be. It's best.

(*In a flash* MELODY *recovers and is the leering peasant again.*)

SARA (*with bitter hopelessness*). Oh, Mother! Why couldn't you be still!

MELODY (*roughly*). Why can't you, ye mean. I warned ye what ye'd get if ye kept on interferin' and tryin' to raise the dead. (*He cuffs her on the side of the head. It is more of a playful push than a blow, but it knocks her off balance back to the end of the table at center.*)

NORA (*aroused—bewilderedly*). God forgive you, Con! (*Angrily*) Don't you be hittin' Sara now. I've put up with a lot but I won't—

MELODY (*with rough good nature*). Shut up, darlint. I won't have to again. (*He grins leeringly at* SARA.) That'll teach you, me proud Sara! I know you won't try raisin' the dead any more. And let me hear no more gab out of you about not marryin' the young lad upstairs. Be Jaysus, haven't ye any honor? Ye seduced him and ye'll make an honest gentleman av him if I have to march ye both by the scruff av the neck to the nearest church. (*He chuckles—then leeringly.*) And now with your permission, ladies both, I'll join me good friends in the bar. (*He opens the door and passes into the bar, closing the door behind him. There is a roar of welcoming drunken shouts, pounding of glasses on bar and tables, then quiet as if he had raised a hand for silence, followed by his voice greeting them and ordering drinks, and other roars of acclaim mingled with the music of* RILEY's *pipes.* SARA *remains standing by the side of the center table, her shoulders bowed, her head hanging, staring at the floor.*)

NORA (*overcome by physical exhaustion again, sighs*). Don't mind his giving you a slap. He's still quare in his head. But he'll sing and laugh and drink a power av whiskey and slape sound after, and tomorrow he'll be himself again—maybe.

SARA (*dully—aloud to herself rather than to her mother*). No. He'll never be. He's beaten at last and he wants to stay beaten. Well, I did my best. Though why I did, I don't know. I must have his crazy pride in me. (*She lifts her head, her face hardening—bitterly*) I mean, the late Major Melody's pride. I mean, I did have it. Now it's dead—thank God— and I'll make a better wife for Simon.

(*There is a sudden lull in the noise from the bar, as if someone had called for silence—then* MELODY's *voice is plainly heard in the silence as he shouts a toast:* "Here's to our next President, Andy Jackson! Hurroo for Auld Hickory, God bless him!" *There is a drunken chorus of answering "hurroos" that shakes the walls.*)

NORA. Glory be to God, cheerin' for Andy Jackson! Did you hear him, Sara?

SARA (*her face hard*). I heard someone. But it wasn't anyone I ever knew or want to know.

NORA (*as if she hadn't heard*). Ah well, that's good. They won't all be hatin' him now. (*She pauses—her tired, worn face becomes suddenly shy and tender.*) Did you hear him tellin' me he loved me, Sara? Did you see him kiss me on the mouth—and then kiss my hair? (*She gives a little, soft laugh.*) Sure, he must have gone mad altogether!

SARA (*stares at her mother. Her face softens*). No, Mother, I know he meant it. He'll keep on meaning it, too, Mother. He'll be free too, now. (*She smiles strangely.*) Maybe I deserved the slap for interfering.

NORA (*preoccupied with her own thoughts*). And if he wants to kape on makin' game of everyone, puttin' on the brogue and actin' like one av thim in there— (*She nods toward the bar.*) Well, why shouldn't he if it brings him peace and company in his loneliness? God pity him, he's had to live all his life alone in the hell av pride. (*Proudly*) And I'll play any game he likes and give him love in it. Haven't I always? (*She smiles.*) Sure, I have no pride at all—except that.

SARA (*stares at her—moved*). You're a strange, noble woman, Mother. I'll try and be like you. (*She comes over and hugs her—then she smiles tenderly.*) I'll wager Simon never heard the shot or anything. He was sleeping like a baby when I left him. A cannon wouldn't wake him. (*In the bar,* RILEY *starts playing a reel on his pipes and there is the stamp of dancing feet. For a moment* SARA's *face becomes hard and bitter again. She tries to be mocking.*) Faith, Patch Riley don't know it but he's playing a requiem for the dead. (*Her voice trembles.*) May the hero of Talavera rest in peace! (*She breaks down and sobs, hiding her face on her mother's shoulder—bewilderedly*) But why should I cry, Mother? Why do I mourn for him?

NORA (*at once forgetting her own exhaustion, is all tender, loving help and comfort*). Don't, darlin', don't. You're destroyed with tiredness, that's all. Come on to bed, now, and I'll help you undress and tuck you in. (*Trying to rouse her—in a teasing tone*) Shame on you to cry when you have love. What would the young lad think of you?

CURTAIN

THE NIGHT OF THE IGUANA

Tennessee Williams

Presented by Charles Bowden, in association with Violla Rubber, at the Royale Theatre in New York on December 28, 1961, with the following cast:

MAXINE FAULK   Bette Davis
PEDRO   James Farentino
PANCHO   Christopher Jones
REVEREND SHANNON   Patrick O'Neal
HANK   Theseus George
HERR FAHRENKOPF   Heinz Hohenwald
FRAU FAHRENKOPF   Lucy Landau

WOLFGANG   Bruce Glover
HILDA   Laryssa Lauret
JUDITH FELLOWS   Patricia Roe
HANNAH JELKES   Margaret Leighton
CHARLOTTE GOODALL   Lane Bradbury
JONATHAN COFFIN (NONNO)   Alan Webb
JAKE LATTA   Louis Guss

Directed by Frank Corsaro
Setting by Oliver Smith
Costumes by Noel Taylor
Lighting by Jean Rosenthal

Production owned and presented by "The Night of the Iguana" Joint Venture (the joint venture consisting of Charles Bowden and Two Rivers Enterprises, Inc.).

THE CAREER of Tennessee Williams is too well known in the theatre to require the extensive notice it is possible to give it. A brief recapitulation for the record would say that he was born in Columbus, Mississippi, in 1914, the son of mismatched parents, the mother a cultivated woman and daughter of an Episcopalian clergyman, the father a more or less typical American go-getter who would have preferred to get his son into business and into general conformity with Main Street. The family tension, also reflected in the disturbed character of a loved sister long ago institutionalized, has been variously translated and transmuted in the body of Mr. Williams' work.

After a rather desultory education in St. Louis, where he spent much of his youth, and graduation from the State University of Iowa, he clerked in a shoe factory, operated an elevator in an office, and worked in hotels, movie houses, and restaurants. His first professionally produced play, *Battle of Angels,* was completed in an advanced seminar for playwrights given in 1940 by Theresa Helburn and John Gassner, both of the Theatre Guild. It was quickly optioned for production by the Guild and assigned to Margaret Webster to direct—no doubt as a tribute to her success in staging poetic drama ever since her superb *Richard II* production with Maurice Evans excelling in the title role. Although the play, owing to a series of difficulties during the tryout in Boston, was not brought to New York, Tennessee Williams, who had been writing fiction, verse, and drama assiduously since boyhood, proceeded to dramatize a D. H. Lawrence story with a friend, Donald Windham. The play, called *You Touched Me,* was staged by the late Guthrie McClintic with his customary skill and sensitivity, and had a moderate run on Broadway. But the author's fortunes first underwent a change for the better and his enormous talent first won general recognition in 1945 with the Eddie Dowling production of *The Glass Menagerie,* starring Laurette Taylor.

Thereafter, he moved from success to success, attaining worldwide repute with *A Streetcar Named Desire* (1947), *Summer and Smoke* (1948), *The Rose Tattoo* (1951), *Cat on a Hot Tin Roof* (1955), and *The Night of the Iguana* (1962), and receiving qualified appreciation for several other long plays (*Camino Real, Orpheus Descending, Sweet Bird of Youth, Period of Adjustment*) and a few remarkable one-acters. His most recently produced play, *The Milk Train Doesn't Stop Here Anymore* in the season of 1962-63, too hastily thrust on Broadway after a tryout production at the Spoleto Festival in Italy in 1962, disappointed his friends and pleased the growing number of his detractors.

The Night of the Iguana is the expanded version of the shorter play tried out at the Spoleto Festival the summer before, but the author's essential concept remained unchanged. The defeated characters with whom the playwright sympathizes are entrapped by life like the iguana of the title—the lizard captured and tormented by the natives of Acapulco and kept overnight for eating the next day. "Eating" has preyed on the author's mind, as may be seen also in the cannibalism theme of *Suddenly Last Summer,* produced during the same period. Symbol-hunting critics and amateur psychoanalysts are welcome to make of this what they will, so far as I am concerned. The effectiveness of the play comes in any case not from the author's perfunctory treatment of the "eaters" but from the nature of those who are "eaten," and effectiveness stems as much from the life of these characters as from their author's dramatic skill and poetic imagination. The corrective for overpraise of the author's dramatic impact may well be Alan Downer's trenchant complaint that "Williams has become a kind of latter-day Belasco with his genius for making effective theatrical statements of the intellectual clichés of the day." (*Quarterly Journal of Speech,* October, 1962, p. 265.) I take it that Mr. Downer had in mind chiefly the reliance on sexual motivations and relationships. The corrective to undervaluing the author's atmospheric power and suggestiveness might be the reflection that in the American theatre very few playwrights have even approached Tennessee Williams' ability to make one feel that the theatre is a form of poetry no matter how much melodramatic motion it entails.

SCENE. *The play takes place in the summer of 1940 in a rather rustic and very Bohemian hotel, the Costa Verde, which, as its name implies, sits on a jungle-covered hilltop overlooking the "caleta," or "morning beach" of Puerto Barrio in Mexico. But this is decidedly not the Puerto Barrio of today. At that time—twenty years ago—the west coast of Mexico had not yet become the Las Vegas and Miami Beach of Mexico. The villages were still predominantly primitive Indian villages, and the still-water morning beach of Puerto Barrio and the rain forests above it were among the world's wildest and loveliest populated places.*

The setting for the play is the wide verandah of the hotel. This roofed verandah, enclosed by a railing, runs around all four sides of the somewhat dilapidated, tropical-style frame structure, but on the stage we see only the front and one side. Below the verandah, which is slightly raised above the stage level, are shrubs with vivid trumpet-shaped flowers and a few cactus plants, while at the sides we see the foliage of the encroaching jungle. A tall coconut palm slants upward at one side, its trunk notched for a climber to chop down coconuts for rum-cocos. In the back wall of the verandah are the doors of a line of small cubicle bedrooms which are screened with mosquito-net curtains. For the night scenes they are lighted from within, so that each cubicle appears as a little interior stage, the curtains giving a misty effect to their dim inside lighting. A path which goes down through the rain forest to the highway and the beach, its opening masked by foliage, leads off from one side of the verandah. A canvas hammock is strung from posts on the verandah and there are a few old wicker rockers and rattan lounging chairs at one side.

ACT ONE

As the curtain rises, there are sounds of a party of excited female tourists arriving by bus on the road down the hill below the Costa Verde Hotel. MRS. MAXINE FAULK, *the proprietor of the hotel, comes around the turn of the verandah. She is a stout, swarthy woman in her middle forties—affable and rapaciously lusty. She is wearing a pair of levis and a blouse that is half unbuttoned. She is followed by* PEDRO, *a Mexican of about twenty—slim and attractive. He is an employee in the hotel and also her casual lover.* PEDRO *is stuffing his shirt under the belt of his pants and sweating as if he had been working hard in the sun.* MRS. FAULK *looks down the hill and is pleased by the sight of someone coming up from the tourist bus below.*

MAXINE (*calling out*). Shannon! (*A man's voice from below answers: "Hi!"*) Hah! (MAXINE *always laughs with a single harsh, loud bark, opening her mouth like a seal expecting a fish to be thrown to it.*) My spies told me that you were back under the border! (*To* PEDRO) Anda, hombre, anda! (MAXINE's *delight expands and vibrates in her as* SHANNON *labors up the hill to the hotel. He does not appear on the jungle path for a minute or two after the shouting between them starts.*) Hah! My spies told me you went through Saltillo last week with a busload of women—a whole busload of females, all females, hah! How many you laid so far? Hah!

SHANNON (*from below, panting*). Great Caesar's ghost . . . stop . . . shouting!

MAXINE. No wonder your ass is dragging, hah!

SHANNON. Tell the kid to help me up with this bag.

MAXINE (*shouting directions*). Pedro! Anda—la maléta. Pancho, no seas flojo! Va y trae el equipaje del señor.

(PANCHO, *another young Mexican, comes around the verandah and trots down the jungle path.* PEDRO *has climbed up a coconut tree with a machete and is chopping down nuts for rum-cocos.*)

SHANNON (*shouting, below*). Fred? Hey, Fred!

MAXINE (*with a momentary gravity*). Fred can't hear you, Shannon. (*She goes over and picks up a coconut, shaking it against her ear to see if it has milk in it.*)

SHANNON (*still below*). Where is Fred—gone fishing?

(MAXINE *lops the end off a coconut with the machete, as* PANCHO *trots up to the verandah with* SHANNON's *bag—a beat-up Gladstone covered with travel stickers from all over the world. Then* SHANNON *appears, in a crumpled white linen suit.*)

He is panting, sweating and wild-eyed. About thirty-five, SHANNON *is "black Irish." His nervous state is terribly apparent; he is a young man who has cracked up before and is going to crack up again—perhaps repeatedly.*)

MAXINE. Well! Lemme look at you!

SHANNON. Don't look at me, get dressed!

MAXINE. Gee, you look like you had it!

SHANNON. You look like you been having it, too. Get dressed!

MAXINE. Hell, I'm dressed. I never dress in September. Don't you know I never dress in September?

SHANNON. Well, just, just—button your shirt up.

MAXINE. How long you been off it, Shannon?

SHANNON. Off what?

MAXINE. The wagon . . .

SHANNON. Hell, I'm dizzy with fever. Hundred and three this morning in Cuernavaca.

MAXINE. Watcha got wrong with you?

SHANNON. Fever . . . fever . . . Where's Fred?

MAXINE. Dead.

SHANNON. Did you say *dead?*

MAXINE. That's what I said. Fred is dead.

SHANNON. How?

MAXINE. Less'n two weeks ago, Fred cut his hand on a fishhook, it got infected, infection got in his blood stream, and he was dead inside of forty-eight hours. (*To* PANCHO) Vete!

SHANNON. Holy smoke. . . .

MAXINE. I can't quite realize it yet. . . .

SHANNON. You don't seem—inconsolable about it.

MAXINE. Fred was an old man, baby. Ten years older'n me. We hadn't had sex together in. . . .

SHANNON. What's that got to do with it?

MAXINE. Lie down and have a rum-coco.

SHANNON. No, no. I want a cold beer. If I start drinking rum-cocos now I won't stop drinking rum-cocos. So Fred is dead? I looked forward to lying in this hammock and talking to Fred.

MAXINE. Well Fred's not talking now, Shannon. A diabetic gets a blood infection, he goes like that without a decent hospital in less'n a week. (*A bus horn is heard blowing from below.*) Why don't your busload of women come on up here? They're blowing the bus horn down there.

SHANNON. Let 'em blow it, blow it. . . . (*He sways a little.*) I got a fever. (*He goes to the top of the path, divides the flowering bushes and shouts down the hill to the bus.*) Hank! Hank! Get them out of the bus and bring 'em up here! Tell 'em the rates are OK. Tell 'em the. . . . (*His voice gives out, and he stumbles back to the verandah, where he sinks down onto the low steps, panting.*) Absolutely the worst party I've ever been out with in ten years of conducting tours. For God's sake, help me with 'em because I can't go on. I got to rest here a while. (*She gives him a cold beer.*) Thanks. Look and see if they're getting out of the bus. (*She crosses to the masking foliage and separates it to look down the hill.*) Are they getting out of the bus or are they staying in it, the stingy-daughters of—bitches. . . . Schoolteachers at a Baptist Female College in Blowing Rock, Texas. Eleven, eleven of them.

MAXINE. A football squad of old maids.

SHANNON. Yeah, and I'm the football. Are they out of the bus?

MAXINE. One's gotten out—she's going into the bushes.

SHANNON. Well, I've got the ignition key to the bus in my pocket—this pocket —so they can't continue without me unless they walk.

MAXINE. They're still blowin' that horn.

SHANNON. Fantastic. I can't lose this party. Blake Tours has put me on probation because I had a bad party last month that tried to get me sacked and I am now on probation with Blake Tours. If I lose this party I'll be sacked for sure . . . Ah, my God, are they still all in the bus? (*He heaves himself off the steps and staggers back to the path, dividing the foliage to look down it, then shouts.*) Hank! Get them out of the busssss! Bring them up heeee-re!

HANK's VOICE (*from below*). They wanta go back in toooooowwww-n.

SHANNON. They *can't* go back in toooowwwwn!—Whew—Five years ago this summer I was conducting round-the-world tours for Cook's. Exclusive groups of retired Wall Street financiers. We traveled in fleets of Pierce Arrows and Hispano Suizas.—Are they getting out of the bus?

MAXINE. You're going to pieces, are you?

SHANNON. No! Gone! Gone! (*He rises and shouts down the hill again.*) Hank! come up here! Come on up here a minute! I wanta talk to you about this situation!— Incredible, fantastic . . . (*He drops back on the steps, his head falling into his hands.*)

MAXINE. They're not getting out of the bus.—Shannon . . . you're not in a nervous condition to cope with this party, Shannon, so let them go and you stay.

SHANNON. You know my situation: I lose this job, what's next? There's nothing lower than Blake Tours, Maxine honey.—Are they getting out of the bus? Are they getting out of it now?

MAXINE. Man's comin' up the hill.

SHANNON. Aw. Hank. You gotta help me with him.

MAXINE. I'll give him a rum-coco.

(HANK *comes grinning onto the verandah.*)

HANK. Shannon, them ladies are not gonna come up here, so you better come on back to the bus.

SHANNON. Fantastic.—I'm not going down to the bus and I've got the ignition key to the bus in my pocket. It's going to stay in my pocket for the next three days.

HANK. You can't get away with that, Shannon. Hell, they'll walk back to town if you don't give up the bus key.

SHANNON. They'd drop like flies from sunstrokes on that road. . . . Fantastic, absolutely fantastic . . . (*Panting and sweating, he drops a hand on* HANK's *shoulder.*) Hank, I want your co-operation. Can I have it? Because when you're out with a difficult party like this, the tour conductor—me—and the guide— you—have got to stick together to control the situations as they come up against us. It's a test of strength between two men, in this case, and a busload of old wet *hens!* You know that, don't you?

HANK. Well. . . . (*He chuckles.*) There's this kid that's crying on the back seat all the time, and that's what's rucked up the deal. Hell, I don't know if you did or you didn't but they all think that you did 'cause the kid keeps crying.

SHANNON. *Hank? Look!* I don't care what they think. A tour conducted by T.

Lawrence Shannon is in his charge, completely—where to go, when to go, every detail of it. Otherwise I resign. So go on back down there and get them out of that bus before they suffocate in it. Haul them out by force if necessary and herd them up here. Hear me? Don't give me any argument about it. Mrs. Faulk, honey? Give him a menu, give him one of your sample menus to show the ladies. She's got a Chinaman cook here, you won't believe the menu. The cook's from Shanghai, handled the kitchen at an exclusive club there. I got him here for her, and he's a bug, a fanatic about—whew!— continental cuisine . . . can even make beef Strogonoff and thermidor dishes. Mrs. Faulk, honey? Hand him one of those—whew!—one of those fantastic sample menus. (MAXINE *chuckles, as if perpetrating a practical joke, as she hands him a sheet of paper.*) Thanks. Now, here. Go on back down there and show them this fantastic menu. Describe the view from the hill, and . . . (HANK *accepts the menu with a chuckling shake of the head.*) And have a cold Carta Blanca and. . . .

HANK. You better go down with me.

SHANNON. I can't leave this verandah for at least forty-eight hours. *What in blazes is this?* A little animated cartoon by Hieronymus Bosch?

(*The German family which is staying at the hotel, the* FAHRENKOPFS, *their daughter and son-in-law, suddenly make a startling, dreamlike entrance upon the scene. They troop around the verandah, then turn down into the jungle path. They are all dressed in the minimal concession to decency and all are pink and gold like baroque cupids in various sizes —Rubensesque, splendidly physical. The bride,* HILDA, *walks astride a big inflated rubber horse which has an ecstatic smile and great winking eyes. She shouts "Horsey, horsey, giddap!" as she waddles astride it, followed by her Wagnerian-tenor bridegroom,* WOLFGANG, *and her father,* HERR FAHRENKOPF, *a tank manufacturer from Frankfurt. He is carrying a portable shortwave radio, which is tuned in to the crackle and guttural voices of a German broadcast reporting the Battle of Britain.* FRAU FAHRENKOPF, *bursting with rich, healthy fat and carrying a basket of food for a picnic at the beach, brings up the rear. They begin to sing a Nazi marching song.*)

SHANNON. Aw—Nazis. How come there's so many of them down here lately?

MAXINE. Mexico's the front door to South America—and the back door to the States, that's why.

SHANNON. Aw, and you're setting yourself up here as a receptionist at both doors, now that Fred's dead? (MAXINE *comes over and sits down on him in the hammock.*) Get off my pelvis before you crack it. If you want to crack something, crack some ice for my forehead. (*She removes a chunk of ice from her glass and massages his forehead with it.*)—Ah, God. . . .

MAXINE (*chuckling*). Ha, so you took the young chick and the old hens are squawking about it, Shannon?

SHANNON. The kid asked for it, no kidding, but she's seventeen—less, a month less'n seventeen. So it's serious, it's very serious, because the kid is not just emotionally precocious, she's a musical prodigy, too.

MAXINE. What's that got to do with it?

SHANNON. Here's what it's got to do with it, she's traveling under the wing, the military escort, of this, this—butch vocal teacher who organizes little community sings in the bus. Ah, God! I'm surprised they're not singing now, they must've already suffocated. Or they'd be singing some morale-boosting number like "She's a Jolly Good Fellow" or "Pop Goes the Weasel."—Oh, God. . . . (MAXINE *chuckles up and down the scale.*) And each night after supper, after the complaints about the supper and the check-up on the checks by the math instructor, and the vomiting of the supper by several ladies, who have inspected the kitchen—then the kid, the canary, will give a vocal recital. She opens her mouth and out flies Carrie Jacobs Bond or Ethelbert Nevin. I mean after a day of one indescribable torment after another, such as three blowouts, and a leaking radiator in Tierra Caliente. . . . (*He sits up slowly in the hammock as these recollections gather force.*) And an evening climb up sierras, through torrents of rain, around hairpin turns over gorges and chasms measureless to man, and with a thermos-jug under the driver's seat which the Baptist College ladies think is filled with icewater but which I know is filled with iced tequila—I mean after such a day has finally come to a close, the musical prodigy, Miss Charlotte Goodall, right after supper, before there's a chance to escape, will give a heartbreaking and earsplitting rendition of Carrie Jacobs Bond's "End of a Perfect Day"—with absolutely no humor. . . .

MAXINE. Hah!

SHANNON. Yeah, "Hah!" Last night—no, night before last, the bus burned out its brake linings in Chilpancingo. This town has a hotel . . . this hotel has a piano, which hasn't been tuned since they shot Maximilian. This Texas songbird opens her mouth and out flies "I Love You Truly," and it flies straight at *me,* with *gestures,* all right at *me,* till her chaperone, this Diesel-driven vocal instructor of hers, slams the piano lid down and hauls her out of the mess hall. But as she's hauled out Miss Bird-Girl opens her mouth and out flies, "Larry, Larry, I love you, I love you truly!" That night, when I went to my room, I found that I had a roommate.

MAXINE. The musical prodigy had moved in with you?

SHANNON. The *spook* had moved in with me. In that hot room with one bed, the width of an ironing board and about as hard, the spook was up there on it, sweating, stinking, grinning up at me.

MAXINE. Aw, the spook. (*She chuckles.*) So you've got the spook with you again.

SHANNON. That's right, he's the only passenger that got off the bus with me, honey.

MAXINE. Is he here now?

SHANNON. Not far.

MAXINE. On the verandah?

SHANNON. He might be on the other side of the verandah. Oh, he's around somewhere, but he's like the Sioux Indians in the Wild West fiction, he doesn't attack before sundown, he's an after-sundown shadow. . . . (SHANNON *wriggles out of the hammock as the bus horn gives one last, long protesting blast.*)

MAXINE. I have a little shadow
That goes in and out with me,
And what can be the use of him
Is more than I can see.

He's very, very like me,
From his heels up to his head,
And he always hops before me

When I hop into my bed.

SHANNON. That's the truth. He sure hops in the bed with me.

MAXINE. When you're sleeping alone, or . . . ?

SHANNON. I haven't slept in three nights.

MAXINE. Aw, you will tonight, baby.

(*The bus horn sounds again.* SHANNON *rises and squints down the hill at the bus.*)

SHANNON. How long's it take to sweat the faculty of a Baptist Female College out of a bus that's parked in the sun when it's a hundred degrees in the shade?

MAXINE. They're staggering out of it now.

SHANNON. Yeah, I've won *this* round, I reckon. What're they doing down there, can you see?

MAXINE. They're crowding around your pal Hank.

SHANNON. Tearing him to pieces?

MAXINE. One of them's slapped him, he's ducked back into the bus, and she is starting up here.

SHANNON. Oh, Great Caesar's ghost, it's the butch vocal teacher.

MISS FELLOWES (*in a strident voice, from below*). Shannon! Shannon!

SHANNON. For God's sake, help me with her.

MAXINE. You know I'll help you, baby, but why don't you lay off the young ones and cultivate an interest in normal grown-up women?

MISS FELLOWES (*her voice coming nearer*). Shannon!

SHANNON (*shouting down the hill*). Come on up, Miss Fellowes, everything's fixed. (*To* MAXINE) Oh, God, here she comes chargin' up the hill like a bull elephant on a rampage!

(MISS FELLOWES *thrashes through the foliage at the top of the jungle path.*)

SHANNON. Miss Fellowes, never do that! Not at high noon in a tropical country in summer. Never charge up a hill like you were leading a troop of cavalry attacking an almost impregnable. . . .

MISS FELLOWES (*panting and furious*). I don't want advice or instructions, I want the *bus key*!

SHANNON. Mrs. Faulk, this is Miss Judith Fellowes.

MISS FELLOWES. Is this man making a deal with you?

MAXINE. I don't know what you—

MISS FELLOWES. Is this man getting a

kickback out of you?

MAXINE. Nobody gets any kickback out of me. I turn away more people than—

MISS FELLOWES (*cutting in*). This isn't the Ambos Mundos. It says in the brochure that in Puerto Barrio we stay at the Ambos Mundos in the heart of the city.

SHANNON. Yes, on the plaza—tell her about the plaza.

MAXINE. What about the plaza?

SHANNON. It's hot, noisy, stinking, swarming with flies. Pariah dogs dying in the—

MISS FELLOWES. How is this place better?

SHANNON. The view from this verandah is equal and I think better than the view from Victoria Peak in Hong Kong, the view from the roof-terrace of the Sultan's palace in—

MISS FELLOWES (*cutting in*). I want the view of a clean bed, a bathroom with plumbing that works, and food that is eatable and digestible and not contaminated by filthy—

SHANNON. *Miss Fellowes!*

MISS FELLOWES. Take your hand off my arm.

SHANNON. Look at this sample menu. The cook is a Chinese imported from Shanghai by *me!* Sent here by *me,* year before last, in nineteen thirty-eight. He was the chef at the Royal Colonial Club in—

MISS FELLOWES (*cutting in*). You got a telephone here?

MAXINE. Sure, in the office.

MISS FELLOWES. I want to use it— I'll call collect. Where's the office?

MAXINE (*to* PANCHO). Llevala al telefono!

(*With* PANCHO *showing her the way,* MISS FELLOWES *stalks off around the verandah to the office.* SHANNON *falls back, sighing desperately, against the verandah wall.*)

MAXINE. Hah!

SHANNON. Why did you have to . . . ?

MAXINE. Huh?

SHANNON. Come out looking like this! For you it's funny but for me it's. . . .

MAXINE. This is how I *look*. What's wrong with how I *look*?

SHANNON. I told you to button your shirt. Are you so proud of your boobs that you won't button your shirt up?—Go in the office and see if she's calling Blake

Tours to get me fired.

MAXINE. She better not unless she pays for the call. (*She goes around the turn of the verandah.*)

(MISS HANNAH JELKES *appears below the verandah steps and stops short as* SHANNON *turns to the wall, pounding his fist against it with a sobbing sound in his throat.*)

HANNAH. Excuse me.

(SHANNON *looks down at her, dazed.* HANNAH *is remarkable-looking—ethereal, almost ghostly. She suggests a Gothic cathedral image of a medieval saint, but animated. She could be thirty, she could be forty: she is totally feminine and yet androgynous-looking—almost timeless. She is wearing a cotton print dress and has a bag slung on a strap over her shoulder.*)

HANNAH. Is this the Costa Verde Hotel?

SHANNON (*suddenly pacified by her appearance*). Yes. Yes, it is.

HANNAH. Are you . . . you're not, the hotel manager, are you?

SHANNON. No. She'll be right back.

HANNAH. Thank you. Do you have any idea if they have two vacancies here? One for myself and one for my grandfather who's waiting in a taxi down there on the road. I didn't want to bring him up the hill—till I'd made sure they have rooms for us first.

SHANNON. Well, there's plenty of room here out-of-season—like now.

HANNAH. Good! Wonderful! I'll get him out of the taxi.

SHANNON. Need any help?

HANNAH. No, thank you. We'll make it all right. (*She gives him a pleasant nod and goes back off down the path through the rain forest. A coconut plops to the ground; a parrot screams at a distance.* SHANNON *drops into the hammock and stretches out. Then* MAXINE *reappears.*)

SHANNON. How about the call? Did she make a phone call?

MAXINE. She called a judge in Texas —Blowing Rock, Texas. Collect.

SHANNON. She's trying to get me fired and she is also trying to pin on me a rape charge, a charge of statutory rape.

MAXINE. What's "statutory rape"? I've never known what that was.

SHANNON. That's when a man is seduced by a girl under twenty. (*She chuckles.*) It's not funny, Maxine honey.

MAXINE. Why do you want the young ones—or think that you do?

SHANNON. I don't want any, any—regardless of age.

MAXINE. Then why do you take them, Shannon? (*He swallows but does not answer.*)—Huh, Shannon.

SHANNON. People need human contact, Maxine honey.

MAXINE. What size shoe do you wear?

SHANNON. I don't get the point of that question.

MAXINE. These shoes are shot and if I remember correctly, you travel with only one pair. Fred's estate included one good pair of shoes and your feet look about his size.

SHANNON. I loved ole Fred but I don't want to fill his shoes, honey.

(*She has removed* SHANNON'S *beat-up, English-made oxfords.*)

MAXINE. Your socks are shot. Fred's socks would fit you, too, Shannon. (*She opens his collar.*) Aw-aw, I see you got on your gold cross. That's a bad sign, it means you're thinkin' again about goin' back to the Church.

SHANNON. This is my last tour, Maxine. I wrote my old Bishop this morning a complete confession and a complete capitulation.

(*She takes a letter from his damp shirt pocket.*)

MAXINE. If this is the letter, baby, you've sweated through it, so the old bugger couldn't read it even if you mailed it to him this time. (*She has started around the verandah, and goes off as* HANK *reappears up the hill-path, mopping his face.* SHANNON'S *relaxed position in the hammock aggravates* HANK *sorely.*)

HANK. Will you get your ass out of that hammock?

SHANNON. No, I will not.

HANK. Shannon, git out of that hammock! (*He kicks at* SHANNON'S *hips in the hammock.*)

SHANNON. Hank, if you can't function under rough circumstances, you are in the wrong racket, man. I gave you instructions, the instructions were simple. I said get them out of the bus and. . . .

(MAXINE *comes back with a kettle of water, a towel and other shaving equipment.*)

HANK. Out of the hammock, Shannon! (*He kicks* SHANNON *again, harder.*)

SHANNON (*warningly*). That's enough,

Hank. A little familiarity goes a long way, but not as far as you're going. (MAXINE *starts lathering his face.*) What's this, what are you . . . ?

MAXINE. Haven't you ever had a shave-and-haircut by a lady barber?

HANK. The kid has gone into hysterics.

MAXINE. Hold still, Shannon.

SHANNON. Hank, hysteria is a natural phenomenon, the common denominator of the female nature. It's the big female weapon, and the test of a man is his ability to cope with it, and I can't believe you can't. If I believed that you couldn't, I would not be able—

MAXINE. Hold still!

SHANNON. I'm holding still. (*To* HANK) No, I wouldn't be able to take you out with me again. So go on back down there and—

HANK. You want me to go back down there and tell them you're getting a shave up here in a hammock?

MAXINE. Tell them that Reverend Larry is going back to the Church so they can go back to the Female College in Texas.

HANK. I want another beer.

MAXINE. Help yourself, piggly-wiggly, the cooler's in my office right around there. (*She points around the corner of the verandah.*)

SHANNON (*as* HANK *goes off*). It's horrible how you got to bluff and keep bluffing even when hollering "Help!" is all you're up to, Maxine. *You cut me!*

MAXINE. You didn't hold still.

SHANNON. Just trim the beard a little.

MAXINE. I know. Baby, tonight we'll go night-swimming, whether it storms or not.

SHANNON. Ah, God. . . .

MAXINE. The Mexican kids are wonderful night-swimmers. . . . Hah, when I found 'em they were taking the two-hundred-foot dives off the Quebrada, but the Quebrada Hotel kicked 'em out for being over-attentive to the lady guests there. That's how I got hold of them.

SHANNON. Maxine, you're bigger than life and twice as unnatural, honey.

MAXINE. No one's bigger than life-size, Shannon, or even ever that big, except maybe Fred. (*She shouts* "Fred?" *and gets a faint answering echo from an adjoining hill.*) Little Sir Echo is all that answers for him now, Shannon, but. . . . (*She pats some bay rum on his face.*)

Dear old Fred was always a mystery to me. He was so patient and tolerent with me that it was insulting to me. A man and a woman have got to challenge each other, y'know what I mean. I mean I hired those diving-boys from the Quebrada six months before Fred died, and did he care? Did he give a damn when I started night-swimming with them? No. He'd go night-*fishing,* all night, and when I got up the next day, he'd be preparing to go out fishing again, but he just caught the fish and threw them back in the sea.

(HANK *returns and sits drinking his beer on the steps.*)

SHANNON. The mystery of old Fred was simple. He was just cool and decent, that's all the mystery of him. . . . Get your pair of night-swimmers to grab my ladies' luggage out of the bus before the vocal-teacher gets off the phone and stops them.

MAXINE (*shouting*). Pedro! Pancho! Muchachos! Trae las maletas al anejo! Pronto! (*The Mexican boys start down the path.* MAXINE *sits in the hammock beside* SHANNON.) You I'll put in Fred's old room, next to me.

SHANNON. You want me in his socks and his shoes and in his room next to you? (*He stares at her with a shocked surmise of her intentions toward him, then flops back down in the hammock with an incredulous laugh.*) Oh no, honey. I've just been hanging on till I could get in this hammock on this verandah over the rain forest and the still-water beach, that's all that can pull me through this last tour in a condition to go back to my . . . original . . . vocation.

MAXINE. Hah, you still have some rational moments when you face the fact that churchgoers don't go to church to hear atheistical sermons.

SHANNON. Goddamit, I never preached an atheistical sermon in a church in my life, and. . . .

(MISS FELLOWS *has charged out of the office and rounds the verandah to bear down on* SHANNON *and* MAXINE, *who jumps up out of the hammock.*)

MISS FELLOWES. I've completed my call, which I made collect to Texas.

(MAXINE *shrugs, going by her around the verandah.* MISS FELLOWES *runs across the verandah.*)

SHANNON (*sitting up in the hammock*).

Excuse me, Miss Fellowes, for not getting out of this hammock, but I . . . Miss Fellowes? Please sit down a minute, I want to confess something to you.

MISS FELLOWES. *That* ought to be in-t'restin'! *What?*

SHANNON. Just that—well, like every-one else, at some point or other in life, my life has cracked up on me.

MISS FELLOWES. How does that compensate *us?*

SHANNON. I don't think I know what you mean by *compensate,* Miss Fellowes. (*He props himself up and gazes at her with the gentlest bewilderment, calculated to melt a heart of stone.*) I mean I've just confessed to you that I'm at the end of my rope, and you say, "How does that compensate *us?*" Please, Miss Fellowes. Don't make me feel that any adult hu-man being puts personal compensation before the dreadful, bare fact of a man at the end of his rope who still has to try to go on, to continue, as if he'd never been better or stronger in his whole ex-istence. No, don't do that, it would. . . .

MISS FELLOWES. It would *what?*

SHANNON. Shake if not shatter every-thing left of my faith in essential . . . human . . . *goodness!*

MAXINE (*returning, with a pair of socks*). Hah!

MISS FELLOWES. Can you sit there, I mean lie there—yeah, I mean *lie* there . . . ! and talk to me about—

MAXINE. Hah!

MISS FELLOWES. "Essential human good-ness"? Why, just plain human decency is beyond your imagination, Shannon, so lie there, lie there and *lie* there, we're *going!*

SHANNON (*rising from the hammock*). Miss Fellowes, I thought that I was con-ducting this party, not you.

MISS FELLOWES. You? You just now *ad-mitted* you're incompetent, as well as. . . .

MAXINE. Hah.

SHANNON. Maxine, will you—

MISS FELLOWES (*cutting in with cold, righteous fury*). Shannon, we girls have worked and slaved all year at Baptist Fe-male College for this Mexican tour, and the tour is a cheat!

SHANNON (*to himself*). Fantastic!

MISS FELLOWES. Yes, *cheat!* You haven't stuck to the schedule and you haven't stuck to the itinerary advertised in the brochure which Blake Tours put out. Now either Blake Tours is cheating us or you are cheating Blake Tours, and I'm putting wheels in motion—I don't care *what* it costs me—I'm. . . .

SHANNON. Oh, Miss Fellowes, isn't it just as plain to you as it is to me that your hysterical insults, which are not at all easy for any born and bred gentleman to accept, are not . . . *motivated, provoked* by . . . anything as *trivial* as the, the . . . the motivations that you're . . . *ascribing* them to? Now can't we talk about the *real, true* cause of. . . .

MISS FELLOWES. Cause of *what?*

(CHARLOTTE GOODALL *appears at the top of the hill.*)

SHANNON. —Cause of your *rage* Miss Fellowes, your—

MISS FELLOWES. *Charlotte!* Stay down the hill in the *bus!*

CHARLOTTE. Judy, they're—

MISS FELLOWES. *Obey me! Down!*

(CHARLOTTE *retreats from view like a well-trained dog.* MISS FELLOWES *charges back to* SHANNON *who has gotten out of the hammock. He places a conciliatory hand on her arm.*)

MISS FELLOWES. *Take your hand off my arm!*

MAXINE. Hah!

SHANNON. *Fantastic.* Miss Fellowes, please! No more shouting? Please? Now I really must ask you to let this party of ladies come up here and judge the ac-commodations for themselves and com-pare them with what they saw passing through town. Miss Fellowes, there is such a thing as charm and beauty in some places, as much as there's nothing but dull, ugly imitation of highway motels in Texas and—

(MISS FELLOWES *charges over to the path to see if* CHARLOTTE *has obeyed her.* SHANNON *follows, still propitiatory.* MAXINE *says "Hah," but she gives him an affec-tionate little pat as he goes by her. He pushes her hand away as he continues his appeal to* MISS FELLOWES.)

MISS FELLOWES. I've taken a look at those rooms and they'd make a room at the "Y" look like a suite at the Ritz.

SHANNON. Miss Fellowes, I am employed by Blake Tours and so I'm not in a posi-tion to tell you quite frankly what mis-takes they've made in their advertising brochure. They just don't know Mexico.

I do. I know it as well as I know five out of all six continents on the—

MISS FELLOWES. *Continent! Mexico?* You never even studied geography if you—

SHANNON. My degree from Sewanee is *Doctor of Divinity,* but for the past ten years geography's been my *specialty,* Miss Fellowes, honey! Name any tourist agency I haven't worked for! You couldn't! I'm only, now, with Blake Tours because I—

MISS FELLOWES. Because you *what?* Couldn't keep your hands off innocent, under-age girls in your —

SHANNON. Now, Miss Fellowes. . . . (*He touches her arm again.*)

MISS FELLOWES. Take your hand off my arm!

SHANNON. For days I've known you were furious and unhappy, but—

MISS FELLOWES. *Oh!* You think it's just *me* that's unhappy! Hauled in that stifling bus over the byways, off the highways, shook up and bumped up so you could get your rake-off, is that what you—

SHANNON. What I know is, all I know is, that you are the *leader* of the *insurrection!*

MISS FELLOWES. All of the girls in this party have dysentery!

SHANNON. That you can't hold me to blame for.

MISS FELLOWES. I *do* hold you to blame for it.

SHANNON. Before we entered Mexico, at New Laredo, Texas, I called you ladies together in the depot on the Texas side of the border and I passed out mimeographed sheets of instructions on what to eat and what *not* to eat, what to drink, what *not* to drink in the—

MISS FELLOWES. It's not *what* we ate but *where* we ate that gave us dysentery!

SHANNON (*shaking his head like a metronome*). It is not dysentery.

MISS FELLOWES. The result of eating in places that would be condemned by the Board of Health in—

SHANNON. Now wait a minute—

MISS FELLOWES. For disregarding all rules of sanitation.

SHANNON. It is not dysentery, it is not amoebic, it's nothing at all but—

MAXINE. Montezuma's Revenge! That's what we call it.

SHANNON. I even passed out pills. I passed out bottles of Enteroviaform because I knew that some of you ladies

would rather be victims of Montezuma's Revenge than spend cinco centavos on bottled water in stations.

MISS FELLOWES. You sold those pills at a profit of fifty cents per bottle.

MAXINE. Hah-hah! (*She knocks off the end of a coconut with the machete, preparing a rum-coco.*)

SHANNON. Now fun is fun, Miss Fellowes, but an accusation like that—

MISS FELLOWES. I *priced* them in *pharmacies,* because I suspected that—

SHANNON. Miss Fellowes, I am a gentleman, and as a gentleman I can't be insulted like this. I mean I can't accept insults of that kind even from a member of a tour that I am conducting. And, Miss Fellowes, I think you might also remember, you might try to remember, that you're speaking to an ordained minister of the Church.

MISS FELLOWES. *De-*frocked! But still trying to pass himself off as a minister!

MAXINE. How about a rum-coco? We give a complimentary rum-coco to all our guests here. (*Her offer is apparently unheard. She shrugs and drinks the rum-coco herself.*)

SHANNON. —Miss Fellowes? In every party there is always one individual that's discontented, that is not satisfied with all I do to make the tour more . . . unique— to make it different from the ordinary, to give it a personal thing, the Shannon touch.

MISS FELLOWES. The gyp touch, the touch of a defrocked minister.

SHANNON. Miss Fellowes, don't, don't, don't . . . do what . . . you're doing! (*He is on the verge of hysteria, he makes some incoherent sounds, gesticulates with clenched fists, then stumbles wildly across the verandah and leans panting for breath against a post.*) Don't! Break! *Human! Pride!*

VOICE FROM DOWN THE HILL (*a very Texan accent*). Judy? They're taking our luggage!

MISS FELLOWES (*shouting down the hill*). Girls! Girls! Don't let those boys touch your luggage. Don't let them bring your luggage in this dump!

GIRL'S VOICE (*from below*). Judy! We can't stop them!

MAXINE. Those kids don't understand English.

MISS FELLOWES (*wild with rage*). Will

you please tell those boys to take that luggage back down to the bus? (*She calls to the party below again.*) Girls! Hold onto your luggage, don't let them take it away! We're going to drive back to A-cap-ul-co! *You hear?*

GIRL'S VOICE. Judy, they want a swim, first!

MISS FELLOWES. I'll be right back. (*She rushes off, shouting at the Mexican boys.*) You! Boys! Muchachos! *You carry that luggage back down!*

(*The voices continue, fading.* SHANNON *moves brokenly across the verandah.* MAXINE *shakes her head.*)

MAXINE. Shannon, give 'em the bus key and let 'em go.

SHANNON. And me do what?

MAXINE. Stay here.

SHANNON. In Fred's old bedroom— yeah, in Fred's old bedroom.

MAXINE. You could do worse.

SHANNON. Could I? Well, then, I'll do worse, I'll . . . do worse.

MAXINE. Aw now, baby.

SHANNON. If I could do worse, I'll do worse. . . . (*He grips the section of railing by the verandah steps and stares with wide, lost eyes. His chest heaves like a spent runner's and he is bathed in sweat.*)

MAXINE. Give me that ignition key. I'll take it down to the driver while you bathe and rest and have a rum-coco, baby.

(SHANNON *simply shakes his head slightly. Harsh bird cries sound in the rain forest. Voices are heard on the path.*)

HANNAH. Nonno, you've lost your sun glasses.

NONNO. No. Took them off. No sun.

(HANNAH *appears at the top of the path, pushing her grandfather,* NONNO, *in a wheelchair. He is a very old man but has a powerful voice for his age and always seems to be shouting something of importance.* NONNO *is a poet and a showman. There is a good kind of pride and he has it, carrying it like a banner wherever he goes. He is immaculately dressed—a linen suit, white as his thick poet's hair; a black string tie; and he is holding a black cane with a gold crook.*)

NONNO. Which way is the sea?

HANNAH. Right down below the hill, Nonno. (*He turns in the wheelchair and raises a hand to shield his eyes.*) We can't see it from here. (*The old man is deaf, and she shouts to make him hear.*)

NONNO. I can feel it and smell it. (*A murmur of wind sweeps through the rain forest.*) It's the cradle of life. (*He is shouting, too.*) Life began in the sea.

MAXINE. These two with your party?

SHANNON. No.

MAXINE. They look like a pair of loonies.

SHANNON. Shut up.

(SHANNON *looks at* HANNAH *and* NONNO *steadily, with a relief of tension almost like that of someone going under hypnosis. The old man still squints down the path, blindly, but* HANNAH *is facing the verandah with a proud person's hope of acceptance when it is desperately needed.*)

HANNAH. How do you do.

MAXINE. Hello.

HANNAH. Have you ever tried pushing a gentleman in a wheelchair uphill through a rain forest?

MAXINE. Nope, and I wouldn't even try it *downhill.*

HANNAH. Well, now that we've made it, I don't regret the effort. What a view for a painter! (*She looks about her, panting, digging into her shoulder-bag for a handkerchief, aware that her face is flushed and sweating.*) They told me in town that this was the ideal place for a painter, and they weren't—*whew*—exaggerating!

SHANNON. You've got a scratch on your forehead.

HANNAH. Oh, is that what I felt.

SHANNON. Better put iodine on it.

HANNAH. Yes, I'll attend to that—*whew* —later, thank you.

MAXINE. Anything I can do for you?

HANNAH. I'm looking for the manager of the hotel.

MAXINE. Me—speaking.

HANNAH. Oh, *you're* the manager, *good!* How do you do, I'm Hannah Jelkes, Mrs. . . .

MAXINE. Faulk, Maxine Faulk. What can I do for you folks? (*Her tone indicates no desire to do anything for them.*)

HANNAH (*turning quickly to her grandfather*). Nonno, the manager is a *lady* from the *States.*

(NONNO *lifts a branch of wild orchids from his lap, ceremonially, with the instinctive gallantry of his kind.*)

NONNO (*shouting*). Give the lady these —botanical curiosities!—you picked on the way up.

HANNAH. I believe they're wild orchids,

isn't that what they are?

SHANNON. Laelia tibicina.

HANNAH. Oh!

NONNO. But tell her, Hannah, tell her to keep them in the icebox till after dark, they draw bees in the sun! (*He rubs a sting on his chin with a rueful chuckle.*)

MAXINE. Are you all looking for rooms here?

HANNAH. Yes, we are, but we've come without reservations.

MAXINE. Well, honey, the Costa Verde is closed in September—except for a few special guests, so. . . .

SHANNON. They're special guests, for God's sake.

MAXINE. I thought you said they didn't come with your party.

HANNAH. Please let us be special guests.

MAXINE. *Watch out!*

(NONNO *has started struggling out of the wheelchair.* SHANNON *rushes over to keep him from falling.* HANNAH *has started toward him, too, then seeing that* SHANNON *has caught him, she turns back to* MAXINE.)

HANNAH. In twenty-five years of travel this is the first time we've ever arrived at a place without advance reservations.

MAXINE. Honey, that old man ought to be in a hospital.

HANNAH. Oh, no, no, he just sprained his ankle a little in Taxco this morning. He just needs a good night's rest, he'll be on his feet tomorrow. His recuperative powers are absolutely amazing for someone who is ninety-seven years *young*.

SHANNON. Easy, Grampa. Hang on. (*He is supporting the old man up to the veranda.*) Two steps. One! Two! Now you've made it, Grampa.

(NONNO *keeps chuckling breathlessly as* SHANNON *gets him onto the verandah and into a wicker rocker.*)

HANNAH (*breaking in quickly*). I can't tell you how much I appreciate your taking us in here now. It's—providential.

MAXINE. Well, I can't send that old man back down the hill—right now—but like I told you the Costa Verde's practically closed in September. I just take in a few folks as a special accommodation and we operate on a special basis this month.

NONNO (*cutting in abruptly and loudly*). Hannah, tell the lady that my perambulator is temporary. I will soon be ready to crawl and then to toddle and before long I will be leaping around here like an—

old—mountain—goat, ha-ha-ha-ha. . . .

HANNAH. Yes, I explained that, Grandfather.

NONNO. I don't like being on wheels.

HANNAH. Yes, my grandfather feels that the decline of the western world began with the invention of the wheel. (*She laughs heartily, but* MAXINE's *look is unresponsive.*)

NONNO. And tell the manager . . . the, uh, lady . . . that I know some hotels don't want to take dogs, cats or monkeys and some don't even solicit the patronage of infants in their late nineties who arrive in perambulators with flowers instead of rattles . . . (*He chuckles with a sort of fearful, slightly mad quality.* HANNAH *perhaps has the impulse to clap a hand over his mouth at this moment but must stand there smiling and smiling and smiling.*) . . . and a brandy flask instead of a teething ring, but tell her that these, uh, concessions to man's seventh age are only temporary, and. . . .

HANNAH. Nonno, I told her the wheelchair's because of a sprained ankle, Nonno!

SHANNON (*to himself*). Fantastic.

NONNO. And after my siesta, I'll wheel it back down the hill, I'll kick it back down the hill, right into the sea, and tell her. . . .

HANNAH. Yes? What, Nonno? (*She has stopped smiling now. Her tone and her look are frankly desperate.*) What shall I tell her now, Nonno?

NONNO. Tell her that if she'll forgive my disgraceful longevity and this . . . temporary decrepitude . . . I will present her with the last signed . . . compitty (*he means "copy"*) of my first volume of verse, published in . . . when, Hannah?

HANNAH (*hopelessly*). The day that President Ulysses S. Grant was inaugurated, Nonno.

NONNO. *Morning Trumpet!* Where is it—you have it, give it to her right now.

HANNAH. Later, a little later! (*Then she turns to* MAXINE *and* SHANNON.) My grandfather is the poet Jonathan Coffin. He is ninety-seven years *young* and will be ninety-eight years *young* the fifth of next month, October.

MAXINE. Old folks are remarkable, yep. The office phone's ringing—excuse me, I'll be right back. (*She goes around the verandah.*)

NONNO. Did I talk too much?

HANNAH [quietly, to SHANNON]. I'm afraid that he did. I don't think she's going to take us.

SHANNON. She'll take you. Don't worry about it.

HANNAH. Nobody would take us in town, and if we don't get in here, I would have to wheel him back down through the rain forest, and then *what,* then *where?* There would just be the road, and no direction to move in, except out to sea—and I doubt that we could make it divide before us.

SHANNON. That won't be necessary. I have a little influence with the patrona.

HANNAH. Oh, then, do use it, please. Her eyes said *no* in big blue capital letters.

(SHANNON *pours some water from a pitcher on the verandah and hands it to the old man.*)

NONNO. What is this—libation?

SHANNON. Some icewater, Grampa.

HANNAH. Oh, that's kind of you. Thank you. I'd better give him a couple of salt tablets to wash down with it. (*Briskly she removes a bottle from her shoulder-bag.*) Won't you have some? I see you're perspiring, too. You have to be careful not to become dehydrated in the hot seasons under the Tropic of Cancer.

SHANNON (*pouring another glass of water.*) Are you a little *financially* dehydrated, too?

HANNAH. That's right. Bone-dry, and I think the patrona suspects it. It's a logical assumption, since I pushed him up here myself, and the patrona has the look of a very logical woman. I am sure she knows that we couldn't afford to hire the taxi driver to help us up here.

MAXINE (*calling from the back*). Pancho?

HANNAH. A woman's practicality when she's managing something is harder than a man's for another woman to cope with, so if you have influence with her, please do use it. Please try to convince her that my grandfather will be on his feet tomorrow, if not tonight, and with any luck whatsoever, the money situation will be solved just as quickly. Oh, here she comes back, do help us!

(*Involuntarily,* HANNAH *seizes hold of* SHANNON's *wrist as* MAXINE *stalks back onto the verandah, still shouting for* PAN-CHO. *The Mexican boy reappears, sucking a juicy peeled mango—its juice running down his chin onto his throat.*)

MAXINE. Pancho, run down to the beach and tell Herr Fahrenkopf that the German Embassy's waiting on the phone for him. (PANCHO *stares at her blankly until she repeats the order in Spanish.*) Dile a Herr Fahrenkopf que la embajada alemana lo llama al telefono. Corre, corre! (PANCHO *starts indolently down the path, still sucking noisily on the mango.*) I said run! Corre, corre! (*He goes into a leisurely loping pace and disappears through the foliage.*)

HANNAH. What graceful people they are!

MAXINE. Yeah, they're graceful like cats, and just as dependable, too.

HANNAH. Shall we, uh, . . . *register* now?

MAXINE. You all can register later but I'll have to collect six dollars from you first if you want to put your names in the pot for supper. That's how I've got to operate here out of season.

HANNAH. Six? Dollars?

MAXINE. Yeah, three each. In season we operate on the continental plan but out of season like this we change to the modified American plan.

HANNAH. Oh, what is the, uh . . . modification of it? (*She gives* SHANNON *a quick glance of appeal as she stalls for time, but his attention has turned inward as the bus horn blows down the hill.*)

MAXINE. Just two meals are included instead of all three.

HANNAH (*moving closer to* SHANNON *and raising her voice*). Breakfast and dinner?

MAXINE. A continental breakfast and a cold lunch.

SHANNON (*aside*). Yeah, very cold—cracked ice—if you crack it yourself.

HANNAH (*reflectively*). Not dinner.

MAXINE. No! Not dinner.

HANNAH. Oh, I see, uh, but . . . we, uh, operate on a special basis ourselves. I'd better explain it to you.

MAXINE. How do you mean "operate," —on what "basis"?

HANNAH. Here's our card. I think you may have heard of us. (*She presents the card to* MAXINE.) We've had a good many write-ups. My grandfather is the oldest living and practicing poet. *And* he gives recitations. I . . . paint . . . water colors and I'm a "quick sketch artist." We travel together. We pay our way as we go by my grandfather's recitations and the sale of my water colors and quick character sketches in charcoal or pastel.

SHANNON (*to himself*). I have fever.

HANNAH. I usually pass among the tables at lunch and dinner in a hotel. I wear an artist's smock—picturesquely dabbed with paint—wide Byronic collar and flowing silk tie. I don't push myself on people. I just display my work and smile at them sweetly and if they invite me to do so sit down to make a quick character sketch in pastel or charcoal. If not? Smile sweetly and go on.

SHANNON. What does Grandpa do?

HANNAH. We pass among the tables together slowly. I introduce him as the world's oldest living and practicing poet. If invited, he gives a recitation of a poem. Unfortunately all of his poems were written a long time ago. But do you know, he has started a new poem? For the first time in twenty years he's started another poem!

SHANNON. Hasn't finished it yet?

HANNAH. He still has inspiration, but his power of concentration has weakened a little, of course.

MAXINE. Right now he's not concentrating.

SHANNON. Grandpa's catchin' forty winks. Grampa? Let's hit the sack.

MAXINE. Now wait a minute. I'm going to call a taxi for these folks to take them back to town.

HANNAH. Please don't do that. We tried every hotel in town and they wouldn't take us. I'm afraid I have to place myself at your . . . mercy.

(*With infinite gentleness* SHANNON *has roused the old man and is leading him into one of the cubicles back of the verandah. Distant cries of bathers are heard from the beach. The afternoon light is fading very fast now as the sun has dropped behind an island hilltop out to sea.*)

MAXINE. Looks like you're in for one night. Just one.

HANNAH. Thank you.

MAXINE. The old man's in number 4. You take 3. Where's your luggage—no luggage?

HANNAH. I hid it behind some palmettos at the foot of the path.

SHANNON (*shouting to* PANCHO): Bring up her luggage. Tu, flojo . . . las maletas . . . baja las palmas. Vamos! (*The Mexican boys rush down the path.*) Maxine honey, would you cash a postdated check for me?

MAXINE (*shrewdly*). Yeah—mañana, maybe.

SHANNON. Thanks—generosity is the cornerstone of your nature.

(MAXINE *utters her one-note bark of a laugh as she marches around the corner of the verandah.*)

HANNAH. I'm dreadfully afraid my grandfather had a slight stroke in those high passes through the sierras. (*She says this with the coolness of someone saying that it may rain before nightfall. An instant later, a long, long sigh of wind sweeps the hillside. The bathers are heard shouting below.*)

SHANNON. Very old people get these little "cerebral accidents," as they call them. They're not regular strokes, they're just little cerebral . . . incidents. The symptoms clear up so quickly that sometimes the old people don't even know they've had them.

(*They exchange this quiet talk without looking at each other. The Mexican boys crash back through the bushes at the top of the path, bearing some pieces of ancient luggage fantastically plastered with hotel and travel stickers indicating a vast range of wandering. The boys deposit the luggage near the steps.*)

SHANNON. How many times have you been around the world?

HANNAH. Almost as many times as the world's been around the sun, and I feel as if I had gone the whole way on foot.

SHANNON (*picking up her luggage*). What's your cell number?

HANNAH (*smiling faintly*). I believe she said it was cell number 3.

SHANNON. She probably gave you the one with the leaky roof. (*He carries the bags into the cubicle.* MAXINE *is visible to the audience only as she appears outside the door to her office on the wing of the verandah.*) But you won't find out till it rains and then it'll be too late to do much about it but swim out of it. (HANNAH *laughs wanly. Her fatigue is now very plain.* SHANNON *comes back out with her luggage.*) Yep, she gave you the one with the leaky roof so you take mine and. . . .

HANNAH. Oh, no, no, Mr. Shannon, I'll find a dry spot if it rains.

MAXINE (*from around the corner of the verandah.*) Shannon!

(*A bit of pantomime occurs between* HANNAH *and* SHANNON. *He wants to put her luggage in cubicle number 5. She catches hold of his arm, indicating by gesture toward the back that it is necessary to avoid displeasing the proprietor.* MAXINE *shouts his name louder.* SHANNON *surrenders to* HANNAH's *pleading and puts her luggage back in the leaky cubicle number 3.*)

HANNAH. Thank you so much, Mr. Shannon. (*She disappears behind the mosquito netting.* MAXINE *advances to the verandah angle as* SHANNON *starts toward his own cubicle.*)

MAXINE (*mimicking* HANNAH's *voice*). "Thank you so much, Mr. Shannon."

SHANNON. Don't be bitchy. Some people say thank you sincerely. (*He goes past her and down the steps from the end of the verandah.*) I'm going down for a swim now.

MAXINE. The water's blood temperature this time of day.

SHANNON. Yeah, well, I have a fever so it'll seem cooler to me. (*He crosses rapidly to the jungle path leading to the beach.*)

MAXINE (*following him*). Wait for me, I'll. . . .

(*She means she will go down with him, but he ignores her call and disappears into the foliage.* MAXINE *shrugs angrily and goes back onto the verandah. She faces out, gripping the railing tightly and glaring into the blaze of the sunset as if it were a personal enemy. Then the ocean breathes a long cooling breath up the hill, as* NONNO's *voice is heard from his cubicle.*)

NONNO. How calmly does the orange branch
Observe the sky begin to blanch,
Without a cry, without a prayer,
With no expression of despair. . . .

(*And from a beach cantina in the distance a marimba band is heard playing a popular song of that summer of 1940, "Palabras de Mujer"—which means "Words of Women."*)

SLOW DIM OUT AND SLOW CURTAIN

ACT TWO

Several hours later: near sunset.

The scene is bathed in a deep golden, almost coppery light; the heavy tropical foliage gleams with wetness from a recent rain.

MAXINE *comes around the turn of the verandah. To the formalities of evening she has made the concession of changing from levis to clean white cotton pants, and from a blue work shirt to a pink one. She is about to set up the folding card-tables for the evening meal which is served on the verandah. All the while she is talking, she is setting up tables, etc.*

———

MAXINE. Miss Jelkes?

(HANNAH *lifts the mosquito net over the door of cubicle number 3.*)

HANNAH. Yes, Mrs. Faulk?

MAXINE. Can I speak to you while I set up these tables for supper?

HANNAH. Of course, you may. I wanted to speak to you, too. (*She comes out. She is now wearing her artist's smock.*)

MAXINE. Good.

HANNAH. I just wanted to ask you if there's a tub-bath Grandfather could use. A shower is fine for me—I prefer a shower to a tub—but for my grandfather there is some danger of falling down in a shower and at his age, although he says he is made out of India rubber, a broken hipbone would be a very serious matter, so I. . . .

MAXINE. What I wanted to say is I called up the Casa de Huéspedes about you and your Grampa, and I can get you in there.

HANNAH. Oh, but we don't want to move!

MAXINE. The Costa Verde isn't the right place for you. Y'see, we cater to folks that like to rough it a little, and—well, frankly, we cater to younger people.

(HANNAH *has started unfolding a card-table.*)

HANNAH. Oh yes . . . uh . . . well . . . the, uh, Casa de Huéspedes, that means a, uh, sort of a rooming house, Mrs. Faulk?

MAXINE. Boarding house. They feed you, they'll even feed you on credit.

HANNAH. Where is it located?

MAXINE. It has a central location. You could get a doctor there quick if the old man took sick on you. You got to think about that.

HANNAH. Yes, I—(*She nods gravely, more to herself than* MAXINE.)—I *have* thought about that, but. . . .

MAXINE. What are you doing?

HANNAH. Making myself useful.

MAXINE. Don't do that. I don't accept help from guests here.

(HANNAH *hesitates, but goes on setting the tables.*)

HANNAH. Oh, please, let me. Knife and fork on one side, spoon on the . . . ? (*Her voice dies out.*)

MAXINE. Just put the plates on the napkins so they don't blow away.

HANNAH. Yes, it is getting breezy on the verandah. (*She continues setting the table.*)

MAXINE. Hurricane winds are already hitting up coast.

HANNAH. We've been through several typhoons in the Orient. Sometimes *outside* disturbances like that are an almost welcome distraction from *inside* disturbances, aren't they? (*This is said almost to herself. She finishes putting the plates on the paper napkins.*) When do you want us to leave here, Mrs. Faulk?

MAXINE. The boys'll move you in my station wagon tomorrow—no charge for the service.

HANNAH. That is very kind of you. (MAXINE *starts away.*) Mrs. Faulk?

MAXINE (*turning back to her with obvious reluctance*). Huh?

HANNAH. Do you know jade?

MAXINE. Jade?

HANNAH. Yes.

MAXINE. Why?

HANNAH. I have a small but interesting collection of jade pieces. I asked if you know jade because in jade it's the craftsmanship, the carving of the jade, that's most important about it. (*She has removed a jade ornament from her blouse.*) This one, for instance—a mircle of carving. Tiny as it is, it has two figures carved on it—the legendary Prince Ahk and Princess Angh, and a heron flying above them. The artist that carved it probably received for this miraculously delicate workmanship, well, I would say perhaps the price of a month's supply of rice for his family, but the merchant who employed him sold it, I would guess, for at least three hundred pounds sterling to an English lady who got tired of it and gave it to me, perhaps because I painted her not as she was at that time but as I could see she must have looked in her youth. Can you see the carving?

MAXINE. Yeah, honey, but I'm not operating a hock shop here, I'm trying to run a hotel.

HANNAH. I know, but couldn't you just accept it as security for a few day's stay here?

MAXINE. You're completely broke, are you?

HANNAH. Yes, we are—completely.

MAXINE. You say that like you're proud of it.

HANNAH. I'm not proud of it or ashamed of it either. It just happens to be what's happened to us, which has never happened before in all our travels.

MAXINE (*grudgingly*). You're telling the truth, I reckon, but I told you the truth, too, when I told you, when you came here, that I had just lost my husband and he'd left me in such a financial hole that if living didn't mean more to me than money, I'd might as well have been dropped in the ocean with him.

HANNAH. Ocean?

MAXINE (*peacefully philosophical about it.*) I carried out his burial instructions exactly. Yep, my husband, Fred Faulk, was the greatest game fisherman on the West Coast of Mexico—he'd racked up unbeatable records in sailfish, tarpon, kingfish, barracuda—and on his deathbed, last week, he requested to be dropped in the sea, yeah, right out there in that bay, not even sewed up in canvas, just in his fisherman outfit. So now old Freddie the Fisherman is feeding the fish —fishes' revenge on old Freddie. How about that, I ask you?

HANNAH (*regarding* MAXINE *sharply*). I doubt that he regrets it.

MAXINE. I do. It gives me the shivers.

(*She is distracted by the German party singing a marching song on the path up from the beach.* SHANNON *appears at the top of the path, a wet beachrobe clinging to him.* MAXINE's *whole concentration shifts abruptly to him. She freezes and blazes with it like an exposed power line. For a moment the "hot light" is concentrated on her tense, furious figure.* HANNAH *provides a visual counterpoint. She clenches her eyes shut for a moment, and when they open, it is on a look of stoical despair of the refuge she has unsuccessfully fought for. Then* SHANNON *approaches the verandah and the scene is his.)*

SHANNON. Here they come up, your conquerors of the world, Maxine honey, singing "Horst Wessel." (*He chuckles fiercely, and starts toward the verandah steps.*)

MAXINE. Shannon, wash that sand off you before you come on the verandah.

(*The Germans are heard singing the "Horst Wessel" marching song. Soon they appear, trooping up from the beach like an animated canvas by Rubens. They are all nearly nude, pinked and bronzed by the sun. The women have decked themselves with garlands of pale green seaweed, glistening wet, and the Munich-opera bridegroom is blowing on a great conch shell. His father-in-law, the tank manufacturer, has his portable radio, which is still transmitting a shortwave broadcast about the Battle of Britain, now at its climax.*)

HILDA (*capering, astride her rubber horse*). Horsey, horsey, horsey!

HERR FAHRENKOPF (*ecstatically*). London is burning, the heart of London's on fire! (*WOLFGANG turns a handspring onto the verandah and walks on his hands a few paces, then tumbles over with a great whoop.* MAXINE *laughs delightedly with the Germans.*) Beer, beer, beer!

FRAU FAHRENKOPF. Tonight champagne!

(*The euphoric horseplay and shouting continue as they gambol around the turn of the verandah.* SHANNON *has come onto the porch.* MAXINE's *laughter dies out a little sadly, with envy.*)

SHANNON. You're turning this place into the Mexican Berchtesgaden, Maxine honey?

MAXINE. I told you to wash that sand off. (*Shouts for beer from the Germans draw her around the verandah corner.*)

HANNAH. Mr. Shannon, do you happen to know the Casa de Huéspedes, or anything about it, I mean? (*SHANNON stares at her somewhat blankly.*) We are, uh, thinking of . . . *moving* there tomorrow. Do you, uh, recommend it?

SHANNON. I recommend it along with the Black Hole of Calcutta and the Siberian salt mines.

HANNAH (*nodding reflectively*). I suspected as much. Mr. Shannon, in your touring party, do you think there might be anyone interested in my water colors? Or in my character sketches?

SHANNON. I doubt it. I doubt that they're corny enough to please my ladies. *Oh-oh! Great Caesar's ghost. . . .*

(*This exclamation is prompted by the shrill, approaching call of his name.* CHARLOTTE *appears from the rear, coming from the hotel annex, and rushes like a teen-age Medea toward the verandah.* SHANNON *ducks into his cubicle, slamming the door so quickly that a corner of the mosquito netting is caught and sticks out, flirtatiously.* CHARLOTTE *rushes onto the verandah.*)

CHARLOTTE. *Larry!*

HANNAH. Are you looking for someone, dear?

CHARLOTTE. Yeah, the man conducting our tour, Larry Shannon.

HANNAH. Oh, Mr. Shannon. I think he went down to the beach.

CHARLOTTE. I just now saw him coming up from the beach. (*She is tense and trembling, and her eyes keep darting up and down the verandah.*)

HANNAH. Oh. Well. . . . But. . . .

CHARLOTTE. Larry? Larry! (*Her shouts startle the rain-forest birds into a clamorous moment.*)

HANNAH. Would you like to leave a message for him, dear?

CHARLOTTE. No. I'm staying right here till he comes out of wherever he's hiding.

HANNAH. Why don't you just sit down, dear. I'm an artist, a painter. I was just sorting out my water colors and sketches in this portfolio, and look what I've come across. (*She selects a sketch and holds it up.*)

SHANNON (*from inside the cubicle*). Oh, God!

CHARLOTTE (*darting to the cubicle*). Larry, let me in there!

(*She beats on the door of the cubicle as* HERR FAHRENKOPF *comes around the verandah with his portable radio. He is bug-eyed with excitement over the news broadcast in German.*)

HANNAH. Guten abend.

HERR FAHRENKOPF *jerks his head with a toothy grin, raising a hand for silence.* HANNAH *nods agreeably and approaches him with her portfolio of drawings. He maintains the grin as she displays one picture after another.* HANNAH *is uncertain whether the grin is for the pictures or the news broadcast. He stares at the pictures, jerking his head from time to time. It is rather like the pantomime of showing lantern slides.*)

CHARLOTTE (*suddenly crying out again*). Larry, open this door and let me in! I know you're in there, Larry!

HERR FAHRENKOPF. Silence, please, for one moment! This is a recording of Der Führer addressing the Reichstag just . . . (*He glances at his wristwatch.*) . . . eight hours ago, today, transmitted by Deutsches Nachrichtenbüro to Mexico City. Please! Quiet, bitte!

(*A human voice like a mad dog's bark emerges from the static momentarily.* CHARLOTTE *goes on pounding on* SHANNON's *door.* HANNAH *suggests in pantomime that they go to the back verandah, but* HERR FAHRENKOPF *despairs of hearing the broadcast. As he rises to leave, the light catches his polished glasses so that he appears for a moment to have electric light bulbs in his forehead. Then he ducks his head in a genial little bow and goes out beyond the verandah, where he performs some muscle-flexing movement of a formalized nature, like the preliminary stances of Japanese Suma wrestlers.*)

HANNAH. May I show you my work on the other verandah? (HANNAH *had started to follow* HERR FAHRENKOPF *with her portfolio, but the sketches fall out, and she stops to gather them from the floor with the sad, preoccupied air of a lonely child picking flowers.*)

(SHANNON's *head slowly, furtively, appears through the window of his cubicle. He draws quickly back as* CHARLOTTE *darts that way, stepping on* HANNAH's *spilt sketches.* HANNAH *utters a soft cry of protest, which is drowned by* CHARLOTTE's *renewed clamor.*)

CHARLOTTE. Larry, Larry, Judy's looking for me. Let me come in, Larry, before she finds me here!

SHANNON. You can't come in. Stop shouting and I'll come out.

CHARLOTTE. All right, come out.

SHANNON. Stand back from the door so I *can.*

(*She moves a little aside and he emerges from his cubicle like a man entering a place of execution. He leans*

against the wall, mopping the sweat off his face with a handkerchief.)

SHANNON. How does Miss Fellowes know what happened that night? Did you tell her?

CHARLOTTE. I didn't tell her, she guessed.

SHANNON. Guessing isn't knowing. If she is just guessing, that means she doesn't know—I mean if you're not lying, if you didn't tell her.

(HANNAH *has finished picking up her drawings and moves quietly over to the far side of the verandah.*)

CHARLOTTE. Don't talk to me like that.

SHANNON. Don't complicate my life now, please, for God's sake, don't complicate my life now.

CHARLOTTE. Why have you changed like this?

SHANNON. I have a fever. Don't complicate my . . . fever.

CHARLOTTE. You act like you hated me now.

SHANNON. You're going to get me kicked out of Blake Tours, Charlotte.

CHARLOTTE. Judy is, not me.

SHANNON. Why did you sing "I Love You Truly" at me?

CHARLOTTE. Because I do love you truly!

SHANNON. Honey girl, don't you know that nothing worse could happen to a girl in your, your . . . unstable condition . . . than to get emotionally mixed up with a man in my unstable condition, huh?

CHARLOTTE. No, no, no, I—

SHANNON (*cutting through*). Two unstable conditions can set a whole world on fire, can blow it up, past repair, and that is just as true between two people as it's true between. . . .

CHARLOTTE. All I know is you've got to marry me, Larry, after what happened between us in Mexico City!

SHANNON. A man in my condition can't marry, it isn't decent or legal. He's lucky if he can even hold onto his job. (*He keeps catching hold of her hands and plucking them off his shoulders.*) I'm almost out of my mind, can't you see that, honey?

CHARLOTTE. I don't believe you don't love me.

SHANNON. Honey, it's almost impossible for anybody to believe they're not loved by someone they believe they love, but, honey, I love *nobody*. I'm like that, it isn't my fault. When I brought you home that night I told you goodnight in the hall, just kissed you on the cheek like the little girl that you are, but the instant I opened my door, you rushed into my room and I couldn't get you out of it, not even when I, oh God, tried to scare you out of it by, oh God, don't you remember?

(MISS FELLOWES' *voice is heard from back of the hotel calling,* "Charlotte!")

CHARLOTTE. Yes, I remember that after making love to me, you hit me, Larry, you struck me in the face, and you twisted my arm to make me kneel on the floor and pray with you for forgiveness.

SHANNON. I do that, I do that always when I, when . . . I don't have a dime left in my nervous emotional bank account— I can't write a check on it, now.

CHARLOTTE. Larry, let me help you!

MISS FELLOWES (*approaching*). Charlotte, Charlotte, Charlie!

CHARLOTTE. Help me and let me help you!

SHANNON. The helpless can't help the helpless!

CHARLOTTE. Let me in, Judy's coming!

SHANNON. Let me go. Go away! (*He thrusts her violently back and rushes into his cubicle, slamming and bolting the door—though the gauze netting is left sticking out. As* MISS FELLOWES *charges onto the verandah,* CHARLOTTE *runs into the next cubicle, and* HANNAH *moves over from where she has been watching and meets her in the center.*)

MISS FELLOWES. Shannon, Shannon! Where are you?

HANNAH. I think Mr. Shannon has gone down to the beach.

MISS FELLOWES. Was Charlotte Goodall with him? A young blonde girl in our party—was she with him?

HANNAH. No, nobody was with him, he was completely alone.

MISS FELLOWES. I heard a door slam.

HANNAH. That was mine.

MISS FELLOWES (*pointing to the door with the gauze sticking out*). Is this yours?

HANNAH. Yes, mine. I rushed out to catch the sunset.

(*At this moment* MISS FELLOWES *hears* CHARLOTTE *sobbing in* HANNAH's *cubicle. She throws the door open.*)

MISS FELLOWES. Charlotte! Come out of there, Charlie! (*She has seized* CHARLOTTE *by the wrist.*) What's your word worth— nothing? You promised you'd stay away from him! (CHARLOTTE *frees her arm, sobbing bitterly.* MISS FELLOWES *seizes her again, tighter, and starts dragging her away.*) I have talked to your father about this man by long distance and he's getting out a warrant for his arrest, if he dare try coming back to the States after this!

CHARLOTTE. I don't care.

MISS FELLOWES. I do! I'm responsible for you.

CHARLOTTE. I don't want to go back to Texas!

MISS FELLOWES. Yes, you do! And you will! (*She takes* CHARLOTTE *firmly by the arm and drags her away behind the hotel.* HANNAH *comes out of her cubicle, where she had gone when* MISS FELLOWES *pulled* CHARLOTTE *out of it.*)

SHANNON (*from his cubicle*). Ah, God. . . .

(HANNAH *crosses to his cubicle and knocks by the door.*)

HANNAH. The coast is clear now, Mr. Shannon.

(SHANNON *does not answer or appear. She sets down her portfolio to pick up* NONNO's *white linen suit, which she had pressed and hung on the verandah. She crosses to his cubicle with it, and calls in.*)

HANNAH. Nonno? It's almost time for supper! There's going to be a lovely, stormy sunset in a few minutes.

NONNO (*from within*). Coming!

HANNAH. So is Christmas, Nonno.

NONNO. So is the Fourth of July!

HANNAH. We're past the Fourth of July. Hallowe'en comes next and then Thanksgiving. I hope you'll come forth sooner. (*She lifts the gauze net over his cubicle door.*) Here's your suit, I've pressed it. (*She enters the cubicle.*)

NONNO. It's mighty dark in here, Hannah.

HANNAH. I'll turn the light on for you.

(SHANNON *comes out of his cubicle, like the survivor of a plane crash, bringing out with him several pieces of his clerical garb. The black heavy silk bib is loosely fastened about his panting, sweating chest. He hangs over it a heavy gold cross with an amethyst center and attempts to fasten on a starched round collar. Now* HANNAH *comes back out of* NONNO's *cubicle, adjusting the flowing silk tie which goes with her "artist" costume. For a moment they both face front, adjusting their two outfits. They are like two actors in a play which is about to fold on the road, preparing gravely for a performance which may be the last one.)*

HANNAH (*glancing at* SHANNON). Are you planning to conduct church services of some kind here tonight, Mr. Shannon?

SHANNON. Goddamit, please help me with this! (*He means the round collar.*)

HANNAH (*crossing behind him*). If you're not going to conduct a church service, why get into that uncomfortable outfit?

SHANNON. Because I've been accused of being defrocked and of lying about it, that's why. I want to show the ladies that I'm still a clocked—*frocked!*—minister of the. . . .

HANNAH. Isn't that lovely gold cross enough to convince the ladies?

SHANNON. No, they know I redeemed it from a Mexico City pawnshop, and they suspect that that's where I got it in the first place.

HANNAH. Hold still just a minute. (*She is behind him, trying to fasten the collar.*) There now, let's hope it stays on. The button hole is so frayed I'm afraid that it won't hold the button. (*Her fear is instantly confirmed: the button pops out.*)

SHANNON. Where'd it go?

HANNAH. Here, right under. . . . (*She picks it up.* SHANNON *rips the collar off, crumples it and hurls it off the verandah. Then he falls into the hammock, panting and twisting.* HANNAH *quietly opens her sketch pad and begins to sketch him. He doesn't at first notice what she is doing.*)

HANNAH (*as she sketches*). How long have you been inactive in the, uh, Church, Mr. Shannon?

SHANNON. What's that got to do with the price of rice in China?

HANNAH (*gently*). Nothing.

SHANNON. What's it got to do with the price of coffee beans in Brazil?

HANNAH. I retract the question. With apologies.

SHANNON. To answer your question politely, I have been inactive in the Church for all but one year since I was ordained a minister of the Church.

HANNAH (*sketching rapidly and moving forward a bit to see his face better*). Well, that's quite a sabbatical, Mr. Shannon.

SHANNON. Yeah, that's . . . quite a . . . sabbatical.

(NONNO's *voice is heard from his cubicle repeating a line of poetry several times.*)

SHANNON. Is your grandfather talking to himself in there?

HANNAH. No, he composes out loud. He has to commit his lines to memory because he can't see to write them or read them.

SHANNON. Sounds like he's stuck on one line.

HANNAH. Yes. I'm afraid his memory is failing. Memory failure is his greatest dread. [*She says this almost coolly, as if it didn't matter.*]

SHANNON. Are you drawing me?

HANNAH. Trying to. You're a very difficult subject. When the Mexican painter Siqueiros did his portrait of the American poet Hart Crane he had to paint him with closed eyes because he couldn't paint his eyes open—there was too much suffering in them and he couldn't paint it.

SHANNON. Sorry, but I'm not going to close my eyes for you. I'm hypnotizing myself—at least trying to—by looking at the light on the orange tree . . . leaves.

HANNAH. That's all right. I can paint your eyes open.

SHANNON. I had one parish one year and then I wasn't defrocked but I was . . . locked out of my church.

HANNAH. Oh . . . Why did they lock you out of it?

SHANNON. Fornication and heresy . . . in the same week.

HANNAH (*sketching rapidly*). What were the circumstances of the . . . uh . . . first offense?

SHANNON. Yeah, the fornication came first, preceded the heresy by several days. A very young Sunday-school teacher asked to see me privately in my study. A pretty little thing—no chance in the world—only child, and both of her parents were spinsters, almost identical spinsters wearing clothes of the opposite sexes. Fooling some of the people some of the time but not me—none of the time. . . . (*He is pacing the verandah with gathering agitation, and the all-inclusive mockery that his guilt produces.*) Well, she declared herself to me—wildly.

HANNAH. A declaration of love?

SHANNON. Don't make *fun* of me, honey!

HANNAH. I wasn't.

SHANNON. The natural, or unnatural, attraction of one . . . lunatic for . . . another . . . that's all it was. I was the goddamnedest prig in those days that even you could imagine. I said, let's kneel down together and pray and we did, we knelt down, but all of a sudden the kneeling position turned to a reclining position on the rug of my study and . . . When we got up? I struck her. Yes, I did, I struck her in the face and called her a damned little tramp. So she ran home. I heard the next day she'd cut herself with her father's straightblade razor. Yeah, the paternal spinster shaved.

HANNAH. Fatally?

SHANNON. Just broke the skin surface enough to bleed a little, but it made a scandal.

HANNAH. Yes, I can imagine that it . . . provoked some comment.

SHANNON. That it did, it did that. (*He pauses a moment in his fierce pacing as if the recollection still appalled him.*) So the next Sunday when I climbed into the pulpit and looked down over all of those smug, disapproving, accusing faces uplifted, I had an impulse to shake them—so I shook them. I had a prepared sermon—meek, apologetic—I threw it away, tossed it into the chancel. Look here, I said, I shouted, I'm tired of conducting services in praise and worship of a senile delinquent—yeah, that's what I said, I shouted! All your Western theologies, the whole mythology of them, are based on the concept of God as a *senile delinquent* and, by God, I will not and cannot continue to conduct services in praise and worship of this, this . . . this. . . .

HANNAH (*quietly*). Senile delinquent?

SHANNON. Yeah, this angry, petulant old man. I mean he's represented like a bad-tempered childish old, old, sick, peevish man—I mean like the sort of old man in a nursing home that's putting together a jigsaw puzzle and can't put it together and gets furious at it and kicks over the table. Yes, I tell you they *do* that, all our theologies do it—accuse God of being a cruel, senile delinquent, blaming the world and brutally punishing all he created for his own faults in construction, and then, ha-ha, yeah—a thunderstorm broke that Sunday. . . .

HANNAH. You mean *outside* the church?

SHANNON. Yep, it was wilder than I was! And out they slithered, they slithered out of their pews to their shiny black cockroach sedans, ha-ha, and I shouted after them, hell, I even followed them halfway out of the church, shouting after them as they. . . . (*He stops with a gasp for breath.*)

HANNAH. Slithered out?

SHANNON. I shouted after them, go on, go home and close your house windows, all your windows and doors, against the truth about God!

HANNAH. Oh, my heavens. Which is just what they did—poor things.

SHANNON. Miss Jelkes honey, Pleasant Valley, Virginia, was an exclusive suburb of a large city and these poor things were not poor—materially speaking.

HANNAH (*smiling a bit*). What was the, uh, upshot of it?

SHANNON. Upshot of it? Well, I wasn't defrocked. I was just locked out of the church in Pleasant Valley, Virginia, and put in a nice little private asylum to recuperate from a complete nervous breakdown as they preferred to regard it, and then, and then I . . . I entered my present line—tours of God's world conducted by a minister of God with a cross and a round collar to prove it. Collecting evidence!

HANNAH. Evidence of what, Mr. Shannon?

SHANNON (*a touch shyly now*). My personal idea of God, not as a senile delinquent, but as a. . . .

HANNAH. Incomplete sentence.

SHANNON. It's going to storm tonight—a terrific electric storm. Then you will see the Reverend T. Lawrence Shannon's conception of God Almighty paying a visit to the world he created. I want to go back to the Church and preach the gospel of God as Lightning and Thunder . . . and also stray dogs vivisected and . . . and . . . and. . . . (*He points out suddenly toward the sea.*) That's him! There he is now! (*He is pointing out at a blaze, a majestic apocalypse of gold light, shafting the sky as the sun drops into the*

Pacific.) His oblivious majesty—and *here I am* on this . . . dilapidated verandah of a cheap hotel, out of season, in a country caught and destroyed in its flesh and corrupted in its spirit by its gold-hungry Conquistadors that bore the flag of the Inquisition along with the Cross of Christ. Yes . . . and. . . . (*There is a pause.*)

HANNAH. Mr. Shannon . . . ?

SHANNON. Yes . . . ?

HANNAH (*smiling a little*). I have a strong feeling you will go back to the Church with this evidence you've been collecting, but when you do and it's a black Sunday morning, look out over the congregation, over the smug, complacent faces for a few old, very old faces, looking up at you, as you begin your sermon, with eyes like a piercing cry for something to still look up to, something to still believe in. And then I think you'll not shout what you say you shouted that black Sunday in Pleasant Valley, Virginia. I think you will throw away the violent, furious sermon, you'll toss *it* into the chancel, and talk about . . . no, maybe talk about . . . nothing . . . just. . . .

SHANNON. What?

HANNAH. Lead them beside still waters because you know how badly they need the still waters, Mr. Shannon.

(*There is a moment of silence between them.*)

SHANNON. Lemme see that thing. (*He seizes the sketch pad from her and is visibly impressed by what he sees. There is another moment which is prolonged to* HANNAH's *embarrassment.*)

HANNAH. Where did you say the patrona put your party of ladies?

SHANNON. She had her . . . Mexican concubines put their luggage in the annex.

HANNAH. Where is the annex?

SHANNON. Right down the hill back of here, but all of my ladies except the teen-age Medea and the older Medea have gone out in a glass-bottomed boat to observe the . . . submarine marvels.

HANNAH. Well, when they come back to the annex they're going to observe my water colors with some marvelous submarine prices marked on the mattings.

SHANNON. By God, you're a hustler, aren't you, you're a fantastic cool hustler.

HANNAH. Yes, like *you*, Mr. Shannon.

(*She gently removes her sketch pad from his grasp.*) Oh, Mr. Shannon, if Nonno, Grandfather, comes out of his cell number 4 before I get back, will you please look out for him for me? I won't be longer than three shakes of a lively sheep's tail. (*She snatches up her portfolio and goes briskly off the verandah.*)

SHANNON. Fantastic, absolutely fantastic.

(*There is a windy sound in the rain forest and a flicker of gold light like a silent scattering of gold coins on the verandah; then the sound of shouting voices. The Mexican boys appear with a wildly agitated creature—a captive iguana tied up in a shirt. They crouch down by the cactus clumps that are growing below the verandah and hitch the iguana to a post with a piece of rope.* MAXINE *is attracted by the commotion and appears on the verandah above them.*)

PEDRO. Tenemos fiesta! *

PANCHO. Comeremos bien.

PEDRO. Damela, damela! Yo la ataré.

PANCHO. *Yo la cojí—yo la ataré!*

PEDRO. Lo que vas a *hacer* es dejarla escapar.

MAXINE. Ammarla fuerte! Ole, ole! No la dejes escapar. Dejala moverse! (*To* SHANNON) They caught an iguana.

SHANNON. I've noticed they did that, Maxine.

(*She is holding her drink deliberately close to him. The Germans have heard the commotion and crowd onto the verandah.* FRAU FAHRENKOPF *rushes over to* MAXINE.)

FRAU FAHRENKOPF. What is this? What's going on? A snake? Did they catch a snake?

MAXINE. No. *Lizard.*

FRAU FAHRENKOPF (*with exaggerated revulsion*). Ouuu . . . lizard! (*She strikes a grotesque attitude of terror as if she were threatened by Jack the Ripper.*)

SHANNON [*to* MAXINE]. You like iguana meat, don't you?

FRAU FAHRENKOPF. Eat? *Eat?* A big *lizard?*

MAXINE. Yes, they're mighty good eating—taste like white meat of chicken.

---

* We're going to have a feast! / We'll eat good. / Give it to me! I'll tie it up. / I caught it—*I'll* tie it up! / You'll only let it get away. / Tie it up right! Ole, ole! Don't let it get away. Give it enough room!

(FRAU FAHRENKOPF *rushes back to her family. They talk excitedly in German about the iguana.*)

SHANNON. If you mean Mexican chicken, that's no recommendation. Mexican chickens are scavengers and they taste like what they scavenge.

MAXINE. Naw, I mean Texas chicken.

SHANNON (*dreamily*). Texas . . . chicken. . . . (*He paces restlessly down the verandah.* MAXINE *divides her attention between his tall, lean figure, that seems incapable of stillness, and the wriggling bodies of the Mexican boys lying on their stomachs half under the verandah—as if she were mentally comparing two opposite attractions to her simple, sensual nature.* SHANNON *turns at the end of the verandah and sees her eyes fixed on him.*)

SHANNON. What is the sex of this iguana, Maxine?

MAXINE. Hah, who cares about the sex of an iguana . . . (*He passes close by her.*) . . . except another . . . iguana?

SHANNON. Haven't you heard the limerick about iguanas? (*He removes her drink from her hand and it seems as if he might drink it, but he only sniffs it, with an expression of repugnance. She chuckles.*)

There was a young gaucho named Bruno
Who said about love, This I do know:
Women are fine, and sheep are divine,
But iguanas are—*Numero Uno!*

(*On* "Numero Uno" SHANNON *empties* MAXINE's *drink over the railing, deliberately onto the humped, wriggling posterior of* PEDRO, *who springs up with angry protests.*)

PEDRO. Me cágo . . . hijo de la . . .

SHANNON. Qué? Qué?

MAXINE. Véte!

(SHANNON *laughs viciously. The iguana escapes and both boys rush shouting after it. One of them dives on it and recaptures it at the edge of the jungle.*)

PANCHO. La iguana se escapé.*

MAXINE. Cojela, cojela! La cojíste? Si no la cojes, te morderá el culo. La cojíste?

PEDRO. La cojí.

(*The boys wriggle back under the verandah with the iguana.*)

MAXINE (*returning to* SHANNON). I

---

* The iguana's escaped. / Get it, get it! Have you got it? If you don't, it'll bite your behind. Have you got it? / He's got it.

---

thought you were gonna break down and take a drink, Reverend.

SHANNON. Just the odor of liquor makes me feel nauseated.

MAXINE. You couldn't smell it if you got it *in* you. (*She touches his sweating forehead. He brushes her hand off like an insect.*) Hah! (*She crosses over to the liquor cart, and he looks after her with a sadistic grin.*)

SHANNON. Maxine honey, whoever told you that you look good in tight pants was not a sincere friend of yours. (*He turns away. At the same instant, a crash and a hoarse, startled outcry are heard from* NONNO's *cubicle.*)

MAXINE. I knew it, I *knew* it! The old man's took a fall!

(SHANNON *rushes into the cubicle, followed by* MAXINE.)

(*The light has been gradually, steadily dimming during the incident of the iguana's escape. There is, in effect, a division of scenes here, though it is accomplished without a blackout or curtain. As* SHANNON *and* MAXINE *enter* NONNO's *cubicle,* HERR FAHRENKOPF *appears on the now twilit verandah. He turns on an outsize light fixture that is suspended from overhead, a full pearly-moon of a light globe that gives an unearthly luster to the scene. The great pearly globe is decorated by night insects, large but gossamer moths that have immolated themselves on its surface: the light through their wings gives them an opalescent color, a touch of fantasy.*)

(*Now* SHANNON *leads the old poet out of his cubicle, onto the facing verandah. The old man is impeccably dressed in snow-white linen with a black string tie. His leonine mane of hair gleams like silver as he passes under the globe.*)

NONNO. No bones broke, I'm made out of India rubber!

SHANNON. A traveler-born falls down many times in his travels.

NONNO. Hannah? (*His vision and other senses have so far deteriorated that he thinks he is being led out by* HANNAH.) I'm pretty sure I'm going to finish it here.

SHANNON (*shouting, gently*). I've got the same feeling, Grampa.

(MAXINE *follows them out of the cubicle.*)

NONNO. I've never been surer of anything in my life.

SHANNON (*gently and wryly*). I've never been surer of anything in mine either.

(HERR FAHRENKOPF *has been listening with an expression of entrancement to his portable radio, held close to his ear, the sound unrealistically low. Now he turns it off and makes an excited speech.*)

HERR FAHRENKOPF. The London fires have spread all the way from the heart of London to the Channel coast! Goering, Field Marshall Goering, calls it "the new phase of conquest!" *Super-firebombs! Each night!*

(NONNO *catches only the excited tone of this announcement and interprets it as a request for a recitation. He strikes the floor with his cane, throws back his silver-maned head and begins the delivery in a grand, declamatory style.*)

NONNO:

Youth must be wanton, youth must be quick,

Dance to the candle while lasteth the wick,

Youth must be foolish and. . . .

(NONNO *falters on the line, a look of confusion and fear on his face. The Germans are amused.* WOLFGANG *goes up to* NONNO *and shouts into his face.*)

WOLFGANG. Sir? What is your age? How old?

(HANNAH, *who has just returned to the verandah, rushes up to her grandfather and answers for him.*)

HANNAH. He is ninety-seven years *young!*

HERR FAHRENKOPF. How old?

HANNAH. Ninety-seven—almost a *century young!*

(HERR FAHRENKOPF *repeats this information to his beaming wife and* HILDA *in German.*)

NONNO (*cutting in on the Germans*). Youth must be foolish and mirthful and blind,

Gaze not before and glance not behind,

Mark not. . . .

(*He falters again.*)

HANNAH (*prompting him, holding tightly onto his arm*).

Mark not the shadow that darkens the way—

(*They recite the next lines together.*)

Regret not the glitter of any lost day,

But laugh with no reason except the red wine,

For youth must be youthful and foolish and blind!

(*The Germans are loudly amused.* WOLFGANG *applauds directly in the old poet's face.* NONNO *makes a little unsteady bow, leaning forward precariously on his cane.* SHANNON *takes a firm hold of his arm as* HANNAH *turns to the Germans, opening her portfolio of sketches and addressing* WOLFGANG.)

HANNAH. Am I right in thinking you are on your honeymoon? [*There is no response, and she repeats the question in German while* FRAU FAHRENKOPF *laughs and nods vehemently.*] Habe ich recht dass Sie auf Ihrer Hochzeitsreise sind? Was für eine hübsche junge Braut! Ich mache Pastell-Skizzen . . . darf ich, würden Sie mir erlauben . . . ? Wurden Sie, bitte . . . bitte. . . .

(HERR FAHRENKOPF *bursts into a Nazi marching song and leads his party to the champagne bucket on the table at the left.* SHANNON *has steered* NONNO *to the other table.*)

NONNO (*exhilarated*). Hannah! What was the *take?*

HANNAH (*embarrassed*). Grandfather, sit down, please stop shouting!

NONNO. Hah? Did they cross your palm with silver or paper, Hannah?

HANNAH (*almost desperately*). Nonno! No more shouting! Sit down at the table. It's time to *eat!*

SHANNON. Chow time, Grampa.

NONNO (*confused but still shouting*). How much did they come across with?

HANNAH. Nonno! *Please!*

NONNO. Did they, did you . . . sell 'em a . . . water color?

HANNAH. No sale, Grandfather!

MAXINE. Hah!

(HANNAH *turns to* SHANNON, *her usual composure shattered, or nearly so.*)

HANNAH. He won't sit down or stop shouting.

NONNO (*blinking and beaming with the grotesque suggestion of an old coquette*). Hah? How rich did we strike it, Hannah?

SHANNON. *You* sit down, Miss Jelkes. (*He says it with gentle authority, to which she yields. He takes hold of the old man's forearm and places in his hand a crumpled Mexican bill.*) Sir? Sir? (*He is shouting.*) Five! Dollars! I'm putting it in your pocket.

HANNAH. We can't accept . . . gratuities, Mr. Shannon.

SHANNON. Hell, I gave him five pesos.

NONNO. Mighty good for one poem!

SHANNON. Sir? Sir? The *pecuniary rewards* of a *poem* are *grossly inferior* to its *merits, always!* (*He is being fiercely, almost mockingly tender with the old man—a thing we are when the pathos of the old, the ancient, the dying is such a wound to our own* (*savagely beleaguered*) *nerves and sensibilities that this outside demand on us is beyond our collateral, our emotional reserve. This is as true of* HANNAH *as it is of* SHANNON, *of course. They have both overdrawn their reserves at this point of the encounter between them.*)

NONNO. Hah? Yes. . . . (*He is worn out now, but still shouting.*) We're going to clean up in this place!

SHANNON. You bet you're going to clean up here!

(MAXINE *utters her one-note bark of a laugh.* SHANNON *throws a hard roll at her. She wanders amiably back toward the German table.*)

NONNO (*tottering, panting, hanging onto* SHANNON's *arm, thinking it is* HANNAH's). Is the, the . . . diningroom . . . crowded? (*He looks blindly about with wild surmise.*)

SHANNON. Yes, it's filled to capacity! There's a big crowd at the door! (*His voice doesn't penetrate the old man's deafness.*)

NONNO. If there's a cocktail lounge, Hannah, we ought to . . . work that . . . first. Strike while the iron is hot, ho, ho, while it's hot. . . . (*This is like a delirium—only as strong a woman as* HANNAH *could remain outwardly impassive.*)

HANNAH. He thinks you're me, Mr. Shannon. Help him into a chair. Please stay with him a minute, I. . . . (*She moves away from the table and breathes as if she has just been dragged up half-drowned from the sea.* SHANNON *eases the old man into a chair. Almost at once* NONNO's *feverish vitality collapses and he starts drifting back toward half sleep.*)

SHANNON (*crossing to* HANNAH). What're you breathing like that for?

HANNAH. Some people take a drink, some take a pill. I just take a few deep breaths.

SHANNON. You're making too much out of this. It's a natural thing in a man as old as Grampa.

HANNAH. I know, I know. He's had more than one of these little "cerebral accidents" as you call them, and all in the last few months. He was amazing till lately. I had to show his passport to prove that he was the oldest living and practicing poet on earth. We did well, we made expenses and *more!* But . . . when I saw he was failing, I tried to persuade him to go back to Nantucket, but he conducts our tours. He said, "No, *Mexico!*" So here we are on this windy hilltop like a pair of scarecrows. . . . The bus from Mexico City broke down at an altitude of 15,000 feet above sea level. That's when I think the latest cerebral incident happened. It isn't so much the loss of hearing and sight but the . . . dimming out of the mind that I can't bear, because until lately, just lately, his mind was amazingly clear. But yesterday? In Taxco? I spent nearly all we had left on the wheelchair for him and still he insisted that we go on with the trip till we got to the sea, the . . . cradle of life as he calls it. . . . (*She suddenly notices* NONNO, *sunk in hs chair as if lifeless. She draws a sharp breath, and goes quietly to him.*)

SHANNON (*to the Mexican boys.*) Servicio! Aqui! (*The force of his order proves effective: they serve the fish course.*)

HANNAH. What a kind man you are. I don't know how to thank you, Mr. Shannon. I'm going to wake him up now. Nonno! (*She claps her hands quietly at his ear. The old man rouses with a confused, breathless chuckle.*) Nonno, linen napkins. (*She removes a napkin from the pocket of her smock.*) I always carry one with me, you see, in case we run into paper napkins as sometimes happens, you see. . . .

NONNO. Wonderful place here. . . . I hope it is à la carte, Hannah, I want a very light supper so I won't get sleepy. I'm going to work after supper. I'm going to finish it here.

HANNAH. Nonno? We've made a friend here. Nonno, this is the Reverend Mr. Shannon.

NONNO (*struggling out of his confu-*

sion). Reverend?

HANNAH (*shouting to him*). Mr. Shannon's an Episcopal clergyman, Nonno.

NONNO. A man of God?

HANNAH. A man of God, on vacation.

NONNO. Hannah, tell him I'm too old to baptize and too young to bury but on the market for marriage to a rich widow, fat, fair and forty. (NONNO *is delighted by all of his own little jokes. One can see him exchanging these pleasantries with the rocking-chair brigades of summer hotels at the turn of the century—and with professors' wives at little colleges in New England. But now it has become somewhat grotesque in a touching way, this desire to please, this playful manner, these venerable jokes.* SHANNON *goes along with it. The old man touches something in him which is outside of his concern with himself. This part of the scene, which is played in a "scherzo" mood, has an accompanying windy obligato on the hilltop—all through it we hear the wind from the sea gradually rising, sweeping up the hill through the rain forest, and there are fitful glimmers of lightning in the sky.*) But very few ladies ever go past forty if you believe 'em, ho, ho! Ask him to . . . give the blessing. Mexican food needs blessing.

SHANNON. Sir, you give the blessing. I'll be right with you. (*He has broken one of his shoe laces.*)

NONNO. Tell him I will oblige him on one condition.

SHANNON. What condition, sir?

NONNO. That you'll keep my daughter company when I retire after dinner. I go to bed with the chickens and get up with the roosters, ho, ho! So you're a man of God. A benedict or a bachelor?

SHANNON. Bachelor, sir. No sane and civilized woman would have me, Mr. Coffin.

NONNO. What did he say, Hannah?

HANNAH (*embarrassed*). Nonno, give the blessing.

NONNO (*not hearing this*). I call her my daughter, but she's my daughter's daughter. We've been in charge of each other since she lost both her parents in the very first automobile crash on the island of Nantucket.

HANNAH. Nonno, give the blessing.

NONNO. She isn't a modern flapper, she isn't modern and she—doesn't flap, but

she was brought up to be a wonderful wife and mother. But . . . I'm a selfish old man so I've kept her all to myself.

HANNAH (*shouting into his ear*). Nonno, Nonno, the blessing!

NONNO (*rising with an effort*). Yes, the blessing. Bless this food to our use, and ourselves to Thy service. Amen. (*He totters back into his chair.*)

SHANNON. Amen.

(NONNO's *mind starts drifting, his head drooping forward. He murmurs to himself.*)

SHANNON. How good is the old man's poetry?

HANNAH. My grandfather was a fairly well-known minor poet before the First World War and for a little while after.

SHANNON. In the minor league, huh?

HANNAH. Yes, a minor league poet with a major league spirit. I'm proud to be his granddaughter. . . . (*She draws a pack of cigarettes from her pocket, then replaces it immediately without taking a cigarette.*)

NONNO (*very confused*). Hannah, it's too hot for . . . hot cereals this . . . morning. . . . (*He shakes his head several times with a rueful chuckle.*)

HANNAH. He's not quite back, you see, he thinks it's morning. (*She says this as if making an embarrassing admission, with a quick, frightened smile at* SHANNON.)

SHANNON. Fantastic—*fantastic*.

HANNAH. That word "fantastic" seems to be your favorite word, Mr. Shannon.

SHANNON (*looking out gloomily from the verandah*). Yeah, well, you know we —live on two levels, Miss Jelkes, the realistic level and the fantastic level, and which is the real one, really. . . .

HANNAH. I would say both, Mr. Shannon.

SHANNON. But when you live on the fantastic level as I have lately but have got to operate on the realistic level, that's when you're spooked, that's the spook. . . . (*This is said as if it were a private reflection.*) I thought I'd shake the spook here but conditions have changed here. I didn't know the patrona had turned to a widow, a sort of bright widow spider. (*He chuckles almost like* NONNO.)

(MAXINE *has pushed one of those gay little brass-and-glass liquor carts around the corner of the verandah. It is laden with an ice bucket, coconuts and a variety of liquors. She hums gaily to herself as she pushes the cart close to the table.)*

MAXINE. Cocktails, anybody?

HANNAH. No, thank you, Mrs. Faulk, I don't think we care for any.

SHANNON. People don't drink cocktails between the fish and the entrée, Maxine honey.

MAXINE. Grampa needs a toddy to wake him up. Old folks need a toddy to pick 'em up. *(She shouts into the old man's ear.)* Grampa! How about a toddy? *(Her hips are thrust out at* SHANNON.*)*

SHANNON. Maxine, your ass—excuse me, Miss Jelkes—your hips, Maxine, are too fat for this verandah.

MAXINE. Hah! Mexicans like 'em, if I can judge by the pokes and pinches I get in the buses to town. And so do the Germans. Ev'ry time I go near Herr Fahrenkopf he gives me a pinch or a goose.

SHANNON. Then go near him again for another goose.

MAXINE. Hah! I'm mixing Grampa a Manhattan with two cherries in it so he'll live through dinner.

SHANNON. Go on back to your Nazis, I'll mix the Manhattan for him. *(He goes to the liquor cart.)*

MAXINE *(to* HANNAH*).* How about you, honey, a little soda with lime juice?

HANNAH. Nothing for me, thank you.

SHANNON. Don't make nervous people more nervous, Maxine.

MAXINE. You better let me mix that toddy for Grampa, you're making a mess of it, Shannon. *(With a snort of fury, he thrusts the liquor cart like a battering ram at her belly. Some of the bottles fall off it; she thrusts it right back at him.)*

HANNAH. Mrs. Faulk, Mr. Shannon, this is childish, please stop it!

(The Germans are attracted by the disturbance. They cluster around, laughing delightedly. SHANNON *and* MAXINE *seize opposite ends of the rolling liquor cart and thrust it toward each other, both grinning fiercely as gladiators in mortal combat. The Germans shriek with laughter and chatter in German.)*

HANNAH. Mr. Shannon, stop it! *(She appeals to the Germans.)* Bitte! Nehmen Sie die Spirituosen weg. Bitte, nehmen Sie sie weg.

*(*SHANNON *has wrested the cart from* MAXINE *and pushed it at the Germans.*

They scream delightedly. The cart crashes into the wall of the verandah. SHANNON *leaps down the steps and runs into the foliage. Birds scream in the rain forest. Then sudden quiet returns to the verandah as the Germans go back to their own table.)*

MAXINE. Crazy, black Irish protestant son of a . . . protestant!

HANNAH. Mrs. Faulk, he's putting up a struggle not to drink.

MAXINE. Don't interfere. You're an interfering woman.

HANNAH. Mr. Shannon is dangerously . . . disturbed.

MAXINE. I know how to handle him, honey—you just met him today. Here's Grampa's Manhattan cocktail with two cherries in it.

HANNAH. Please don't call him Grampa.

MAXINE. Shannon calls him Grampa.

HANNAH *(taking the drink).* He doesn't make it sound condescending, but you *do.* My grandfather is a gentleman in the true sense of the word, he is a *gentle man.*

MAXINE. What are you?

HANNAH. I am his granddaughter.

MAXINE. Is that all you are?

HANNAH. I think it's enough to be.

MAXINE. Yeah, but you're also a deadbeat, using that dying old man for a front to get in places without the cash to pay even one day in advance. Why, you're dragging him around with you like Mexican beggars carry around a sick baby to put the touch on the tourists.

HANNAH. I told you I had no money.

MAXINE. Yes, and I told you that I was a widow—recent. In such a financial hole they might as well have buried me with my husband.

*(*SHANNON *reappears from the jungle foliage but remains unnoticed by* HANNAH *and* MAXINE.*)*

HANNAH *(with forced calm).* Tomorrow morning, at daybreak, I will go into town. I will set up my easel in the plaza and peddle my water colors and sketch tourists. I am not a weak person, my failure here isn't typical of me.

MAXINE. I'm not a weak person either.

HANNAH. No. By no means, no. Your strength is awe-inspiring.

MAXINE. You're goddam right about that, but how do you think you'll get to Acapulco without the cabfare or even the busfare there?

HANNAH. I will go on shanks' mare, Mrs. Faulk—islanders are good walkers. And if you doubt my word for it, if you really think I came here as a deadbeat, then I will put my grandfather back in his wheelchair and push him back down this hill to the road and all the way back into town.

MAXINE. Ten miles, with a storm coming up?

HANNAH. Yes, I would—I will. (*She is dominating* MAXINE *in this exchange. Both stand beside the table.* NONNO's *head is drooping back into sleep.*)

MAXINE. I wouldn't let you.

HANNAH. But you've made it clear that you don't want us to stay here for one night even.

MAXINE. The storm would blow that old man out of his wheelchair like a dead leaf.

HANNAH. He would prefer that to staying where he's not welcome, and I would prefer it for him, and for myself, Mrs. Faulk. (*She turns to the Mexican boys.*) Where is his wheelchair? Where is my grandfather's wheelchair?

(*This exchange has roused the old man. He struggles up from his chair, confused, strikes the floor with his cane and starts declaiming a poem.*)

NONNO. Love's an old remembered song
A drunken fiddler plays,
Stumbling crazily along
Crooked alleyways.

When his heart is mad with music
He will play the—

HANNAH. Nonno, not now, Nonno! He thought someone asked for a poem. (*She gets him back into the chair.* HANNAH *and* MAXINE *are still unaware of* SHANNON.)

MAXINE. Calm down, honey.

HANNAH. I'm perfectly calm, Mrs. Faulk.

MAXINE. I'm *not*. That's the trouble.

HANNAH. I understand that, Mrs. Faulk. You lost your husband just lately. I think you probably miss him more than you know.

MAXINE. No, the trouble is Shannon.

HANNAH. You mean his nervous state and his . . . ?

MAXINE. No, I just mean Shannon. I want you to lay off him, honey. You're not for Shannon and Shannon isn't for you.

HANNAH. Mrs. Faulk, I'm a New England spinster who is pushing forty.

MAXINE. I got the vibrations between you—I'm very good at catching vibrations between people—and there sure was a vibration between you and Shannon the moment you got here. That, just that, believe me, nothing but that has made this . . . misunderstanding between us. So if you just don't mess with Shannon, you and your Grampa can stay on here as long as you want to, honey.

HANNAH. Oh, Mrs. Faulk, do I look like a *vamp*?

MAXINE. They come in all types. I've had all types of them here.

(SHANNON *comes over to the table.*)

SHANNON. Maxine, I told you don't make nervous people more nervous, but you wouldn't listen.

MAXINE. What you need is a drink.

SHANNON. Let me decide about that.

HANNAH. Won't you sit down with us, Mr. Shannon, and eat something? Please. You'll feel better.

SHANNON. I'm not hungry right now.

HANNAH. Well, just sit down with us, won't you?

(SHANNON *sits down with* HANNAH.)

MAXINE (*warningly to* HANNAH). O.K. O.K. . . .

NONNO (*rousing a bit and mumbling*). Wonderful . . . wonderful place here.

(MAXINE *retires from the table and wheels the liquor cart over to the German party.*)

SHANNON. Would you have gone through with it?

HANNAH. Haven't you ever played poker, Mr. Shannon?

SHANNON. You mean you were bluffing?

HANNAH. Let's say I was drawing to an inside straight. (*The wind rises and sweeps up the hill like a great waking sigh from the ocean.*) It *is* going to storm. I hope your ladies aren't still out in that, that . . . glass-bottomed boat, observing the, uh, submarine . . . marvels.

SHANNON. That's because you don't know these ladies. However, they're back from the boat trip. They're down at the cantina, dancing together to the jukebox and hatching new plots to get me kicked out of Blake Tours.

HANNAH. What would you do if you. . . .

SHANNON. Got the sack? Go back to

the Church or take the long swim to China. (HANNAH *removes a crumpled pack of cigarettes from her pocket. She discovers only two left in the pack and decides to save them for later. She returns the pack to her pocket.*) May I have one of your cigarettes, Miss Jelkes? (*She offers him the pack. He takes it from her and crumples it and throws it off the verandah.*) Never smoke those, they're made out of tobacco from cigarette stubs that beggars pick up off sidewalks and out of gutters in Mexico City. (*He produces a tin of English cigarettes.*) Have these—Benson and Hedges, imported, in an airtight tin, my luxury in my life.

HANNAH. Why—thank you, I will, since you have thrown mine away.

SHANNON. I'm going to tell you something about yourself. You are a lady, a *real* one and a *great* one.

HANNAH. What have I done to merit that compliment from you?

SHANNON. It isn't a compliment, it's just a report on what I've noticed about you at a time when it's hard for me to notice anything outside myself. You took out those Mexican cigarettes, you found you just had two left, you can't afford to buy a new pack of even that cheap brand, so you put them away for later. Right?

HANNAH. Mercilessly accurate, Mr. Shannon.

SHANNON. But when I asked you for one, you offered it to me without a sign of reluctance.

HANNAH. Aren't you making a big point out of a small matter?

SHANNON. Just the opposite, honey, I'm making a small point out of a very large matter. (SHANNON *has put a cigarette in his lips but has no matches.* HANNAH *has some and she lights his cigarette for him.*) How'd you learn how to light a match in the wind?

HANNAH. Oh, I've learned lots of useful little things like that. I wish I'd learned some *big* ones.

SHANNON. Such as what?

HANNAH. How to help you, Mr. Shannon. . . .

SHANNON. Now I know why I came here!

HANNAH. To meet someone who can light a match in the wind?

SHANNON (*looking down at the table, his voice choking*). To meet someone who wants to *help me*, Miss Jelkes. . . . (*He makes a quick, embarrassed turn in the chair, as if to avoid her seeing that he has tears in his eyes. She regards him steadily and tenderly, as she would her grandfather.*)

HANNAH. Has it been so long since anyone has wanted to help you, or have you just. . . .

SHANNON. Have I—what?

HANNAH. Just been so much involved with a struggle in yourself that you haven't noticed when people have wanted to help you, the little they can? I know people torture each other many times like devils, but sometimes they do see and know each other, you know, and then, if they're decent, they do want to help each other all that they can. Now will you please help *me*? Take care of Nonno while I remove my water colors from the annex verandah because the storm is coming up by leaps and bounds now.

(*He gives a quick, jerky nod, dropping his face briefly into the cup of his hands. She murmurs "Thank you" and springs up, starting along the verandah. Halfway across, as the storm closes in upon the hilltop with a thunderclap and a sound of rain coming,* HANNAH *turns to look back at the table.* SHANNON *has risen and gone around the table to* NONNO.)

SHANNON. Grampa? Nonno? Let's get up before the rain hits us, Grampa.

NONNO. What? What?

(SHANNON *gets the old man out of his chair and shepherds him to the back of the verandah as* HANNAH *rushes toward the annex. The Mexican boys hastily clear the table, fold it up and lean it against the wall.* SHANNON *and* NONNO *turn and face toward the storm, like brave men facing a firing squad.* MAXINE *is excitedly giving orders to the boys.*)

MAXINE. Pronto, pronto, muchachos! Pronto, pronto!* Llevaros todas las cosas! Pronto, pronto! Recoje los platos! Apurate con el mantel!

PEDRO. Nos estamos dando prisa!

PANCHO. Que el chubasco lave los platos!

(*The German party look on the storm*

---

* Hurry, hurry, boys! Pick everything up! Get the plates! Hurry with the table cloth! / We are hurrying! / Let the storm wash the plates!

as a Wagnerian climax. They rise from
their table as the boys come to clear it,
and start singing exultantly. The storm,
with its white convulsions of light, is like
a giant white bird attacking the hilltop
of the Costa Verde. HANNAH reappears
with her water colors clutched against her
chest.)

SHANNON. Got them?

HANNAH. Yes, just in time. Here is your
God, Mr. Shannon.

SHANNON (quietly). Yes, I see him, I
hear him, I know him. And if he doesn't
know that I know him, let him strike
me dead with a bolt of his lightning.
(He moves away from the wall to the
edge of the verandah as a fine silver sheet
of rain descends off the sloping roof,
catching the light and dimming the figures
behind it. Now everything is silver, delicately lustrous. SHANNON extends his hands
under the rainfall, turning them in it as
if to cool them. Then he cups them to
catch the water in his palms and bathes
his forehead with it. The rainfall increases.
The sound of the marimba band at the
beach cantina is brought up the hill by
the wind. SHANNON lowers his hands from
his burning forehead and stretches them
out through the rain's silver sheet as if
he were reaching for something outside
and beyond himself. Then nothing is
visible but these reaching-out hands. A
pure white flash of lightning reveals
HANNAH and NONNO against the wall, behind SHANNON, and the electric globe suspended from the roof goes out, the power
extinguished by the storm. A clear shaft
of light stays on SHANNON's reaching-out
hands till the stage curtain has fallen,
slowly.)

INTERMISSION

NOTE: In staging, the plastic elements
should be restrained so that they don't
take precedence over the more important
human values. It should not seem like
an "effect curtain." The faint, windy
music of the marimba band from the
cantina should continue as the house-lights
are brought up for the intermission.

ACT THREE

The verandah, several hours later. Cubicles number 3, 4, and 5 are dimly lighted

within. We see HANNAH in number 3,
and NONNO in number 4. SHANNON, who
has taken off his shirt, is seated at a
table on the verandah, writing a letter
to his Bishop. All but this table have
been folded and stacked against the wall
and MAXINE is putting the hammock back
up which had been taken down for dinner. The electric power is still off and
the cubicles are lighted by oil lamps. The
sky has cleared completely, the moon is
making for full and it bathes the scene
in an almost garish silver which is inten-
sified by the wetness from the recent
rainstorm. Everything is drenched—there
are pools of silver here and there on the
floor of the verandah. At one side a
smudge pot is burning to repel the mos-
quitoes, which are particularly vicious
after a tropical downpour when the wind
is exhausted.

SHANNON is working feverishly on the
letter to the Bishop, now and then slapping at a mosquito on his bare torso. He
is shiny with perspiration, still breathing
like a spent runner, muttering to himself
as he writes and sometimes suddenly
drawing a loud deep breath and simultaneously throwing back his head to stare
up wildly at the night sky. HANNAH is
seated on a straight-back chair behind the
mosquito netting in her cubicle—very
straight herself, holding a small book in
her hands but looking steadily over it at
SHANNON, like a guardian angel. Her hair
has been let down. NONNO can be seen
in his cubicle rocking back and forth on
the edge of the narrow bed as he goes
over and over the lines of his first new
poem in "twenty-some years"—which he
knows is his last one.

Now and then the sound of distant
music drifts up from the beach cantina.

MAXINE. Workin' on your sermon for
next Sunday, Rev'rend?

SHANNON. I'm writing a very important
letter, Maxine. (He means don't disturb
me.)

MAXINE. Who to, Shannon?

SHANNON. The Dean of the Divinity
School at Sewanee. (MAXINE repeats
"Sewanee" to herself, tolerantly.) Yes,
and I'd appreciate it very much, Maxine
honey, if you'd get Pedro or Pancho to
drive into town with it tonight so it will
go out first thing in the morning.

MAXINE. The kids took off in the station wagon already—for some cold beers and hot whores at the cantina.

SHANNON. "Fred's dead"—he's lucky. . . .

MAXINE. Don't misunderstand me about Fred, baby. I miss him, but we'd not only stopped sleeping together, we'd stopped talking together except in grunts —no quarrels, no misunderstandings, but if we exchanged two grunts in the course of a day, it was a long conversation we'd had that day between us.

SHANNON. Fred knew when I was spooked—wouldn't have to tell him. He'd just look at me and say, "Well, Shannon, you're spooked."

MAXINE. Yeah, well, Fred and me'd reached the point of just grunting.

SHANNON. Maybe he thought you'd turned into a pig, Maxine.

MAXINE. Hah! You know damn well that Fred respected me, Shannon, like I did Fred. We just, well, you know . . . age difference. . . .

SHANNON. Well, you've got Pedro and Pancho.

MAXINE. Employees. They don't respect me enough. When you let employees get too free with you, personally, they stop respecting you, Shannon. And it's, well, it's . . . humiliating—not to be . . . respected.

SHANNON. Then take more bus trips to town for the Mexican pokes and the pinches, or get Herr Fahrenkopf to "respect" you, honey.

MAXINE. Hah! You kill me. I been thinking lately of selling out here and going back to the States, to Texas, and operating a tourist camp outside some live town like Houston or Dallas, on a highway, and renting out cabins to business executives wanting a comfortable little intimate little place to give a little after-hours dictation to their cute little secretaries that can't type or write shorthand. Complimentary rum-cocos—bathrooms with bidets. I'll introduce the bidet to the States.

SHANNON. Does everything have to wind up on that level with you, Maxine?

MAXINE. Yes and no, baby. I know the difference between loving someone and just sleeping with someone—even I know about that. (*He starts to rise.*) We've both reached a point where we've got to settle for something that works for us in our lives—even if it isn't on the highest kind of level.

SHANNON. I don't want to rot.

MAXINE. You wouldn't. I wouldn't let you! I know your psychological history. I remember one of your conversations on this verandah with Fred. You was explaining to him how your problems first started. You told him that Mama, your Mama, used to send you to bed before you was ready to sleep—so you practiced the little boy's vice, you amused yourself with yourself. And once she caught you at it and whaled your backside with the back side of a hairbrush because she said she had to punish you for it because it made God mad as much as it did Mama, and she had to punish you for it so God wouldn't punish you for it harder than she would.

SHANNON. I was talking to Fred.

MAXINE. Yeah, but I heard it, all of it. You said you loved God and Mama and so you quit it to please them, but it was your secret pleasure and you harbored a secret resentment against Mama and God for making you give it up. And so you got back at God by preaching atheistical sermons and you got back at Mama by starting to lay young girls.

SHANNON. I have never delivered an atheistical sermon, and never would or could when I go back to the Church.

MAXINE. You're not going back to no Church. Did you mention the charge of statutory rape to the Divinity Dean?

SHANNON (*thrusting his chair back so vehemently that it topples over*). Why don't you *let up* on me? You haven't let up on me since I got here this morning! *Let up on me!* Will you please *let up* on me?

MAXINE (*smiling serenely into his rage*). Aw baby. . . .

SHANNON. What do you mean by "aw baby"? What do you want out of me, Maxine honey?

MAXINE. Just to do this. (*She runs her fingers through his hair. He thrusts her hand away.*)

SHANNON. Ah, God. (*Words fail him. He shakes his head with a slight, helpless laugh and goes down the steps from the verandah.*)

MAXINE. The Chinaman in the kitchen says, "No sweat.". . . "No sweat." He says that's all his philosophy. All the Chinese philosophy in three words, "Mei yoo guanchi"—which is Chinese for "No sweat.". . . With your record and a charge of statutory rape hanging over you in Texas, how could you go to a church except to the Holy Rollers with some lively young female rollers and a bushel of hay on the church floor?

SHANNON. I'll drive into town in the bus to post this letter tonight. (*He has started toward the path. There are sounds below. He divides the masking foliage with his hands and looks down the hill.*)

MAXINE (*descending the steps from the verandah*). Watch out for the spook, he's out there.

SHANNON. My ladies are up to something. They're all down there on the road, around the bus.

MAXINE. They're running out on you, Shannon.

(*She comes up beside him. He draws back and she looks down the hill. The light in number 3 cubicle comes on and HANNAH rises from the little table that she had cleared for letter-writing. She removes her Kabuki robe from a hook and puts it on as an actor puts on a costume in his dressing room. NONNO's cubicle is also lighted dimly. He sits on the edge of his cot, rocking slightly back and forth, uttering an indistinguishable mumble of lines from his poem.*)

MAXINE. Yeah. There's a little fat man down there that looks like Jake Latta to me. Yep, that's Jake, that's Latta. I reckon Blake Tours has sent him here to take over your party, Shannon. (SHANNON *looks out over the jungle and lights a cigarette with jerky fingers.*) Well, let him do it. No sweat! He's coming up here now. Want me to handle it for you?

SHANNON. I'll handle it for myself. You keep out of it, please.

(*He speaks with a desperate composure.* HANNAH *stands just behind the curtain of her cubicle, motionless as a painted figure, during the scene that follows.* JAKE LATTA *comes puffing up the verandah steps, beaming genially.*)

LATTA. Hi there, Larry.

SHANNON. Hello, Jake. (*He folds his letter into an envelope.*) Mrs. Faulk honey, this goes air special.

MAXINE. First you'd better address it.

SHANNON. Oh! (SHANNON *laughs and snatches the letter back, fumbling in his pocket for an address book, his fingers shaking uncontrollably.* LATTA *winks at* MAXINE. *She smiles tolerantly.*)

LATTA. How's our boy doin', Maxine?

MAXINE. He'd feel better if I could get him to take a drink.

LATTA. Can't you get a drink down him?

MAXINE. Nope, not even a rum-coco.

LATTA. Let's have a rum-coco, Larry.

SHANNON. You have a rum-coco, Jake. I have a party of ladies to take care of. And I've discovered that situations come up in this business that call for cold, sober judgment. How about you? Haven't you ever made that discovery, Jake? What're you doing here? Are you here with a party?

LATTA. I'm here to pick up your party, Larry boy.

SHANNON. That's interesting! On whose authority, Jake?

LATTA. Blake Tours wired me in Cuernavaca to pick up your party here and put them together with mine cause you'd had this little nervous upset of yours and. . . .

SHANNON. Show me the wire! Huh?

LATTA. The bus driver says you took the ignition key to the bus.

SHANNON. That's right. I have the ignition key to the bus and I have this party and neither the bus or the party will pull out of here till I say so.

LATTA. Larry, you're a sick boy. Don't give me trouble.

SHANNON. What jail did they bail you out of, you fat zero?

LATTA. Let's have the bus key, Larry.

SHANNON. Where did they dig you up? You've got no party in Cuernavaca, you haven't been out with a party since 'thirty-seven.

LATTA. Just give me the bus key. Larry.

SHANNON. In a pig's—snout!—like yours!

LATTA. Where is the reverend's bedroom, Mrs. Faulk?

SHANNON. The bus key is in my pocket. (*He slaps his pants pocket fiercely.*) Here, right here, in my pocket! Want it? Try and get it, Fatso!

LATTA. What language for a reverend to use, Mrs. Faulk. . . .

SHANNON (*holding up the key*). See it? (*He thrusts it back into his pocket.*) Now go back wherever you crawled from.

My party of ladies is staying here three more days because several of them are in no condition to travel and neither—neither am I.

LATTA. They're getting in the bus now.

SHANNON. How are you going to start it?

LATTA. Larry, don't make me call the bus driver up here to hold you down while I get the key away from you. You want to see the wire from Blake Tours? Here. (*He produces the wire.*) Read it.

SHANNON. You sent that wire to yourself.

LATTA. From Houston?

SHANNON. You had it sent you from Houston. What's that prove? Why, Blake Tours was nothing, *nothing!*—till they got me. You think they'd let me go?—Ho, ho! Latta, it's caught up with you, Latta, all the whores and tequila have hit your brain now, Latta. (LATTA *shouts down the hill for the bus driver.*) Don't you realize what I mean to Blake Tours? Haven't you seen the brochure in which they mention, they brag, that special parties are conducted by the Reverend T. Lawrence Shannon, D.D., noted world traveler, lecturer, son of a minister and grandson of a bishop, and the direct descendant of two colonial governors? (MISS FELLOWES *appears at the verandah steps.*) Miss Fellowes has read the brochure, she's memorized the brochure. She knows what it says about me.

MISS FELLOWES (*to* LATTA). Have you got the bus key?

LATTA. Bus driver's going to get it away from him, lady. (*He lights a cigar with dirty, shaky fingers.*)

SHANNON. Ha-ha-ha-ha-ha! (*His laughter shakes him back against the verandah wall.*)

LATTA. He's gone. (*He touches his forehead.*)

SHANNON. Why, those ladies . . . have had . . . some of them, most of them if not all of them . . . for the first time in their lives the advantage of contact, social contact, with a gentleman born and bred, whom under no other circumstances they could have possibly met . . . let alone be given the chance to insult and accuse and. . . .

MISS FELLOWES. Shannon! The girls are in the bus and we want to go now, so give up that key. Now!

(HANK, *the bus driver, appears at the top of the path, whistling casually: he is not noticed at first.*)

SHANNON. If I didn't have a decent sense of responsibility to these parties I take out, I would gladly turn over your party—because I don't like your party—to this degenerate here, this Jake Latta of the gutter-rat Lattas. Yes, I would—I would surrender the bus key in my pocket, even to Latta, but I am not that irresponsible, no, I'm not, to the parties that I take out, regardless of the party's treatment of me. I still feel responsible for them till I get them back wherever I picked them up. (HANK *comes onto the verandah.*) Hi, Hank. Are you friend or foe?

HANK. Larry, I got to get that ignition key now so we can get moving down there.

SHANNON. Oh! Then *foe!* I'm disappointed, Hank. I thought you were friend, not foe. (HANK *puts a wrestler's armlock on* SHANNON *and* LATTA *removes the bus key from his pocket.* HANNAH *raises a hand to her eyes.*) O.K., O.K., you've got the bus key. By force. I feel exonerated now of all responsibility. Take the bus and the ladies in it and go. Hey, Jake, did you know they had lesbians in Texas—without the dikes the plains of Texas would be engulfed by the Gulf. (*He nods his head violently toward* MISS FELLOWES, *who springs forward and slaps him.*) Thank you, Miss Fellowes, Latta, hold on a minute. I will not be stranded here. I've had unusual expenses on this trip. Right now I don't have my fare back to Houston or even to Mexico City. Now if there's any truth in your statement that Blake Tours have really authorized you to take over my party, then I am sure they have . . . (*He draws a breath, almost gasping.*) . . . I'm sure they must have given you something in the . . . the nature of . . . *severance* pay? Or at least enough to get me back to the States?

LATTA. I got no money for you.

SHANNON. I hate to question your word, but. . . .

LATTA. We'll drive you back to Mexico City. You can sit up front with the driver.

SHANNON. *You* would do that, Latta. *I'd* find it *humiliating*. Now! Give me my severance pay!

LATTA. Blake Tours is having to refund those ladies half the price of the tour. That's your severance pay. And Miss Fellowes tells me you got plenty of money out of this young girl you seduced in. . . .

SHANNON. Miss Fellowes, did you really make such a . . . ?

MISS FELLOWES. When Charlotte returned that night, she'd cashed two traveler's checks.

SHANNON. After I had spent all my own cash.

MISS FELLOWES. On what? Whores in the filthy places you took her through?

SHANNON. Miss Charlotte cashed two ten-dollar traveler's checks because I had spent all the cash I had on me. And I've never had to, I've certainly never desired to, have relations with whores.

MISS FELLOWES. You took her through ghastly places, such as. . . .

SHANNON. I showed her what she wanted me to show her. Ask her! I showed her San Juan de Letran, I showed her Tenampa and some other places not listed in the Blake Tours brochure. I showed her more than the floating gardens at Xochimilco, Maximilian's Palace, and the mad Empress Carlotta's little homesick chapel, Our Lady of Guadalupe, the monument to Juarez, the relics of the Aztec civilization, the sword of Cortez, the headdress of Montezuma. I showed her what she told me she wanted to see. Where is she? Where is Miss . . . oh, down there with the ladies. (*He leans over the rail and shouts down.*) Charlotte! Charlotte! (MISS FELLOWES *seizes his arm and thrusts him away from the verandah rail.*)

MISS FELLOWES. Don't you dare!

SHANNON. Dare what?

MISS FELLOWES. Call her, speak to her, go near her, you, you . . . *filthy!*

(MAXINE *reappears at the corner of the verandah, with the ceremonial rapidity of a cuckoo bursting from a clock to announce the hour. She just stands there with an incongruous grin, her big eyes unblinking, as if they were painted on her round beaming face.* HANNAH *holds a gold-lacquered Japanese fan motionless but open in one hand; the other hand touches the netting at the cubicle door as if she were checking an impulse to rush to* SHANNON's *defense. Her attitude has the style of a Kabuki dancer's pose.* SHANNON's *manner becomes courtly again.*)

SHANNON. Oh, all right, I won't. I only wanted her to confirm my story that I took her out that night at her request, not at my . . . suggestion. All that I did was offer my services to her when *she* told *me* she'd like to see things not listed in the brochure, not usually witnessed by ordinary tourists such as. . . .

MISS FELLOWES. Your hotel bedroom? Later? That too? She came back *flea-bitten!*

SHANNON. Oh, now, don't exaggerate, please. Nobody ever got any fleas off Shannon.

MISS FELLOWES. Her clothes had to be fumigated!

SHANNON. I understand your annoyance, but you are going too far when you try to make out that I gave Charlotte fleas. I don't deny that. . . .

MISS FELLOWES. Wait till they get my *report!*

SHANNON. I don't deny that it's possible to get fleabites on a tour of inspection of what lies under the public surface of cities, off the grand boulevards, away from the nightclubs, even away from Diego Rivera's murals, but. . . .

MISS FELLOWES. Oh, preach that in a pulpit, Reverend Shannon *de*-frocked!

SHANNON (*ominously*). You've said that once too often. (*He seizes her arm.*) This time before witnesses. Miss Jelkes? Miss Jelkes!

(HANNAH *opens the curtain of her cubicle.*)

HANNAH. Yes, Mr. Shannon, what is it?

SHANNON. You heard what this. . . .

MISS FELLOWES. Shannon! Take your hand off my arm!

SHANNON. Miss Jelkes, just tell me, did you hear what she . . . (*His voice stops oddly with a choked sobbing sound. He runs at the wall and pounds it with his fists.*)

MISS FELLOWES. I spent this entire afternoon and over twenty dollars checking up on this impostor, with long-distance phone calls.

HANNAH. Not impostor—you mustn't say things like that.

MISS FELLOWES. You were locked out of your church!—for atheism and seducing of girls!

SHANNON (*turning about*). In front of God and witnesses, you are lying, lying!

LATTA. Miss Fellowes, I want you to know that Blake Tours was deceived about this character's background and

Blake Tours will see that he is black-listed from now on at every travel agency in the States.

SHANNON. How about Africa, Asia, Australia? The whole world, Latta, God's world, has been the range of my travels. I haven't stuck to the schedules of the brochures and I've always allowed the ones that were willing to see, to *see!*— the underworlds of all places, and if they had hearts to be touched, feelings to feel with, I gave them a priceless chance to feel and be touched. And none will ever forget it, none of them, ever, never! (*The passion of his speech imposes a little stillness.*)

LATTA. Go on, lie back in your hammock, that's all you're good for, Shannon. (*He goes to the top of the path and shouts down the hill.*) O.K., let's get cracking. Get that luggage strapped on top of the bus, we're moving! (*He starts down the hill with* MISS FELLOWES.)

NONNO (*incongruously, from his cubicle*).

How calmly does the orange branch
Observe the sky begin to blanch. . . .

(SHANNON *sucks in his breath with an abrupt, fierce sound. He rushes off the verandah and down the path toward the road.* HANNAH *calls after him, with a restraining gesture.* MAXINE *appears on the verandah. Then a great commotion commences below the hill, with shrieks of outrage and squeals of shocked laughter.*)

MAXINE (*rushing to the path*). Shannon! Shannon! Get back up here, get back up here. Pedro, Pancho, traerme a Shannon. Que está haciendo allí? Oh, my God! Stop him, for God's sake, somebody stop him!

(SHANNON *returns panting and spent. He is followed by* MAXINE.)

MAXINE. Shannon, go in your room and stay there until that party's gone.

SHANNON. Don't give me orders.

MAXINE. You do what I tell you to do or I'll have you removed—you know where.

SHANNON. Don't push me, don't pull at me, Maxine.

MAXINE. All right, do as I say.

SHANNON. Shannon obeys only Shannon.

MAXINE. You'll sing a different tune if they put you where they put you in 'thirty-six. Remember 'thirty-six, Shannon?

SHANNON. O.K., Maxine, just . . . let me breathe alone, please. I won't go but I will lie in the . . . hammock.

MAXINE. Go into Fred's room where I can watch you.

SHANNON. Later, Maxine, not yet.

MAXINE. Why do you always come here to crack up, Shannon?

SHANNON. It's the hammock, Maxine, the hammock by the rain forest.

MAXINE. Shannon, go in your room and stay there until I get back. Oh, my God, the money. They haven't paid the mother-grabbin' bill. I got to go back down there and collect their goddam bill before they. . . . Pancho, vijilalo, entiendes? (*She rushes back down the hill, shouting "Hey! Just a minute down there!"*)

SHANNON. What did I do? (*He shakes his head, stunned.*) I don't know what I did.

(HANNAH *opens the screen of her cubicle but doesn't come out. She is softly lighted so that she looks, again, like a medieval sculpture of a saint. Her pale gold hair catches the soft light. She has let it down and still holds the silver-backed brush with which she was brushing it.*)

SHANNON. God almighty, I . . . what did I do? I don't know what I did. (*He turns to the Mexican boys who have come back up the path.*) Que hice? Que hice?

(*There is breathless, spasmodic laughter from the boys as* PANCHO *informs him that he pissed on the ladies' luggage.*)

PANCHO. Tú measte en las maletas de las señoras!

(SHANNON *tries to laugh with the boys, while they bend double with amusement.* SHANNON's *laughter dies out in little choked spasms. Down the hill,* MAXINE's *voice is raised in angry altercation with* JAKE LATTA. MISS FELLOWES' *voice is lifted and then there is a general rhubarb to which is added the roar of the bus motor.*)

SHANNON. There go my ladies, ha, ha! There go my . . . (*He turns about to meet* HANNAH's *grave, compassionate gaze. He tries to laugh again. She shakes her head with a slight restraining gesture and drops the curtain so that her softly luminous figure is seen as through a mist.*) . . . ladies, the last of my—ha, ha! (*He bends far over the verandah rail, then straightens violently and with an animal outcry begins to pull at the chain suspending the gold cross about his neck.* PANCHO *watches indifferently as the chain cuts the back of* SHANNON's *neck.* HANNAH *rushes out to him.*)

HANNAH. Mr. Shannon, stop that! You're cutting yourself doing that. That isn't necessary, so stop it! (*To* PANCHO.) Agarrale las manos! (PANCHO *makes a half-hearted effort to comply, but* SHANNON *kicks at him and goes on with the furious self-laceration.*) Shannon, let me do it, let me take it off you. Can I take it off you? (*He drops his arms. She struggles with the clasp of the chain but her fingers are too shaky to work it.*)

SHANNON. No, no, it won't come off, I'll have to break it off me.

HANNAH. No, no, wait—I've got it. (*She has now removed it.*)

SHANNON. Thanks. Keep it. Goodbye! (*He starts toward the path down to the beach.*)

HANNAH. Where are you going? What are you going to do?

SHANNON. I'm going swimming. I'm going to swim out to China!

HANNAH. No, no, not tonight, Shannon! Tomorrow . . . tomorrow, Shannon!

(*But he divides the trumpet-flowered bushes and passes through them.* HANNAH *rushes after him, screaming for* "Mrs. Faulk." MAXINE *can be heard shouting for the Mexican boys.*)

MAXINE. Muchachos, cojerlo! Atarlo! Está loco. Traerlo aqui. Catch him, he's crazy. Bring him back and tie him up!

(*In a few moments* SHANNON *is hauled back through the bushes and onto the verandah by* MAXINE *and the boys. They rope him into the hammock. His struggle is probably not much of a real struggle—histrionics mostly. But* HANNAH *stands wringing her hands by the steps as* SHANNON, *gasping for breath, is tied up.*)

HANNAH. The ropes are too tight on his chest!

MAXINE. No, they're not. He's acting, acting. He likes it! I know this black Irish bastard like nobody ever knowed him, so you keep out of it, honey. He cracks up like this so regular that you can set a calendar by it. Every eighteen months he does it, and twice he's done it here and I've had to pay for his medical care. Now I'm going to call in town to get a doctor to come out here and give him a knockout injection, and if he's not better tomorrow he's going into the Casa de Locos

again like he did the last time he cracked up on me!

(*There is a moment of silence.*)

SHANNON. Miss Jelkes?

HANNAH. Yes.

SHANNON. Where are you?

HANNAH. I'm right here behind you. Can I do anything for you?

SHANNON. Sit here where I can see you. Don't stop talking. I have to fight this panic.

(*There is a pause. She moves a chair beside his hammock. The Germans troop up from the beach. They are delighted by the drama that* SHANNON *has provided. In their scanty swimsuits they parade onto the verandah and gather about* SHANNON's *captive figure as if they were looking at a funny animal in a zoo. Their talk is in German except when they speak directly to* SHANNON *or* HANNAH. *Their heavily handsome figures gleam with oily wetness and they keep chuckling lubriciously.*)

HANNAH. Please! Will you be so kind as to leave him alone?

(*They pretend not to understand her.* FRAU FAHRENKOPF *bends over* SHANNON *in his hammock and speaks to him loudly and slowly in English.*)

FRAU FAHRENKOPF. Is this true you make pee-pee all over the suitcases of the ladies from Texas? Hah? Hah? You run down there to the bus and right in front of the ladies you pees all over the luggage of the ladies from Texas?

(HANNAH's *indignant protest is drowned in the Rabelaisian laughter of the Germans.*)

HERR FAHRENKOPF. Thees is vunderbar, vunderbar! Hah? Thees is a epic gesture! Hah? Thees is the way to demonstrate to ladies that you are a American gentleman! Hah? (*He turns to the others and makes a ribald comment. The two women shriek with amusement,* HILDA *falling back into the arms of* WOLFGANG, *who catches her with his hands over her almost nude breasts.*)

HANNAH (*calling out*). Mrs. Faulk! Mrs. Faulk! (*She rushes to the verandah angle as* MAXINE *appears there.*) Will you please ask these people to leave him alone. They're tormenting him like an animal in a trap.

(*The Germans are already trooping around the verandah, laughing and caper-*

ing gaily.)

SHANNON (*suddenly, in a great shout*). Regression to infantilism, ha, ha, regression to infantilism . . . The infantile protest, ha, ha, ha, the infantile expression of rage at Mama and rage at God and rage at the goddam crib, and rage at the everything, rage at the . . . everything. . . . Regression to infantilism. . . .

(*Now all have left but* HANNAH *and* SHANNON.)

SHANNON. Untie me.

HANNAH. Not yet.

SHANNON. I can't stand being tied up.

HANNAH. You'll have to stand it a while.

SHANNON. It makes me panicky.

HANNAH. I know.

SHANNON. A man can die of panic.

HANNAH. Not if he enjoys it as much as you, Mr. Shannon. (*She goes into her cubicle directly behind his hammock. The cubicle is lighted and we see her removing a small teapot and a tin of tea from her suitcase on the cot, then a little alcohol burner. She comes back out with these articles.*)

SHANNON. What did you mean by that insulting remark?

HANNAH. What remark, Mr. Shannon?

SHANNON. That I enjoy it.

HANNAH. Oh . . . that.

SHANNON. Yes. That.

HANNAH. That wasn't meant as an insult, just an observation. I don't judge people, I draw them. That's all I do, just draw them, but in order to draw them I have to observe them, don't I?

SHANNON. And you've observed, you think you've observed, that I like being tied in this hammock, trussed up in it like a hog being hauled off to the slaughter house, Miss Jelkes.

HANNAH. Who wouldn't like to suffer and atone for the sins of himself and the world if it could be done in a hammock with ropes instead of nails, on a hill that's so much lovelier than Golgotha, the Place of the Skull, Mr. Shannon? There's something almost voluptuous in the way that you twist and groan in that hammock—no nails, no blood, no death. Isn't that a comparatively comfortable, almost voluptuous kind of crucifixion to suffer for the guilt of the world, Mr. Shannon? (*She strikes a match to light the alcohol burner. A pure blue jet of flame springs up to cast a flickering, rather unearthly glow on their section of the verandah. The glow is delicately refracted by the subtle, faded colors of her robe—a robe given to her by a Kabuki actor who posed for her in Japan.*)

SHANNON. Why have you turned against me all of a sudden, when I need you the most?

HANNAH. I haven't turned against you at all, Mr. Shannon. I'm just attempting to give you a character sketch of yourself, in words instead of pastel crayons or charcoal.

SHANNON. You're certainly suddenly very sure of some New England spinsterish attitudes that I didn't know you had in you. I thought that you were an *emancipated* Puritan, Miss Jelkes.

HANNAH. Who is . . . ever . . . completely?

SHANNON. I thought you were sexless but you've suddenly turned into a woman. Know how I know that? Because you, not me—not me—are taking pleasure in my tied-up condition. All women, whether they face it or not, want to see a man in a tied-up situation. They work at it all their lives, to get a man in a tied-up situation. Their lives are fulfilled, they're satisfied at last, when they get a man, or as many men as they can, in the tied-up situation. (HANNAH *leaves the alcohol burner and teapot and moves to the railing where she grips a verandah post and draws a few deep breaths.*) You don't like this observation of you? The shoe's too tight for comfort when it's on your own foot, Miss Jelkes? Some deep breaths again—feeling panic?

HANNAH (*recovering and returning to the burner*). I'd like to untie you right now, but let me wait till you've passed through your present disturbance. You're still indulging yourself in your . . . your Passion Play performance. I can't help observing this self-indulgence in you.

SHANNON. What rotten indulgence?

HANNAH. Well, your busload of ladies from the female college in Texas. I don't like those ladies any more than you do, but after all, they did save up all year to make this Mexican tour, to stay in stuffy hotels and eat the food they're used to. They want to be at home away from home, but you . . . you indulged yourself, Mr. Shannon. You did conduct the tour as if it was just for you, for your own pleasure.

SHANNON. Hell, what pleasure—going through hell all the way?

HANNAH. Yes, but comforted, now and then, weren't you, by the little musical prodigy under the wing of the college vocal instructor?

SHANNON. Funny, ha-ha funny! Nantucket spinsters have their wry humor, don't they?

HANNAH. Yes, they do. They have to.

SHANNON (*becoming progressively quieter under the cool influence of her voice behind him*). I can't see what you're up to, Miss Jelkes honey, but I'd almost swear you're making a pot of tea over there.

HANNAH. That is just what I'm doing.

SHANNON. Does this strike you as the right time for a tea party?

HANNAH. This isn't plain tea, this is poppyseed tea.

SHANNON. Are you a slave to the poppy?

HANNAH. It's a mild, sedative drink that helps you get through nights that are hard for you to get through and I'm making it for my grandfather and myself as well as for you, Mr. Shannon. Because, for all three of us, this won't be an easy night to get through. Can't you hear him in his cell number 4, mumbling over and over and over the lines of his new poem? It's like a blind man climbing a staircase that goes to nowhere, that just falls off into space, and I hate to say what it is. . . . (*She draws a few deep breaths behind him.*)

SHANNON. Put some hemlock in his poppyseed tea tonight so he won't wake up tomorrow for the removal to the Casa de Huéspedes. Do that act of mercy. Put in the hemlock and I will consecrate it, turn it to God's blood. Hell, if you'll get me out of this hammock I'll serve it to him myself, I'll be your accomplice in this act of mercy. I'll say, "Take and drink this, the blood of our—

HANNAH. Stop it! Stop being childishly cruel! I can't stand for a person that I respect to talk and behave like a small, cruel boy, Mr. Shannon.

SHANNON. What've you found to respect in me, Miss . . . Thin-Standing-Up-Female-Buddha?

HANNAH. I respect a person that has had to fight and howl for his decency and his—

SHANNON. *What* decency?

HANNAH. Yes, for his decency and his bit of goodness, much more than I respect the lucky ones that just had theirs handed out to them at birth and never afterwards snatched away from them by . . . unbearable . . . torments, I. . . .

SHANNON. You *respect* me?

HANNAH. I do.

SHANNON. But you just said that I'm taking pleasure in a . . . voluptuous crucifixion without nails. A . . . what? . . . painless atonement for the—

HANNAH (*cutting in*). Yes, but I think—

SHANNON. Untie me!

HANNAH. Soon, soon. Be patient.

SHANNON. Now!

HANNAH. Not quite yet, Mr. Shannon. Not till I'm reasonably sure that you won't swim out to China, because, you see, I think you think of the . . . "the long swim to China" as another painless atonement. I mean I don't think you think you'd be intercepted by sharks and barracudas before you got far past the barrier reef. And I'm afraid you *would* be. It's as simple as that, if that is simple.

SHANNON. What's simple?

HANNAH. Nothing, except for simpletons, Mr. Shannon.

SHANNON. Do you believe in people being tied up?

HANNAH. Only when they might take the long swim to China.

SHANNON. All right, Miss Thin-Standing-Up-Female-Buddha, just light a Benson & Hedges cigarette for me and put it in my mouth and take it out when you hear me choking on it—if that doesn't seem to you like another bit of voluptuous self-crucifixion.

HANNAH (*looking about the verandah*). I will, but . . . where did I put them?

SHANNON. I have a pack of my own in my pocket.

HANNAH. Which pocket?

SHANNON. I don't know which pocket, you'll have to frisk me for it. (*She pats his jacket pocket.*)

HANNAH. They're not in your coat-pocket.

SHANNON. Then look for them in my pants' pockets.

(*She hesitates to put her hand in his pants' pockets, for a moment. HANNAH has always had a sort of fastidiousness, a re-*

luctance, toward intimate physical contact. But after the momentary fastidious hesitation, she puts her hands in his pants' pocket and draws out the cigarette pack.)

SHANNON. Now light it for me and put it in my mouth. (*She complies with these directions. Almost at once he chokes and the cigarette is expelled.*)

HANNAH. You've dropped it on you—where is it?

SHANNON (*twisting and lunging about in the hammock*). It's under me, under me, burning. Untie me, for God's sake, will you—it's burning me through my pants!

HANNAH. Raise your hips so I can—

SHANNON. I can't, the ropes are too tight. Untie me, untieeeee meeeeee!

HANNAH. I've found it, I've got it!

(*But* SHANNON'S *shout has brought* MAXINE *out of her office. She rushes onto the verandah and sits on* SHANNON'S *legs.*)

MAXINE. Now hear this, you crazy black Irish mick, you! You Protestant black Irish looney, I've called up Lopez, Doc Lopez. Remember him—the man in the dirty white jacket that come here the last time you cracked up here? And hauled you off to the Casa de Locos? Where they threw you into that cell with nothing in it but a bucket and straw and a water pipe? That you crawled up the water pipe? And dropped head-down on the floor and got a concussion? Yeah, and I told him you were back here to crack up again and if you didn't quiet down here tonight you should be hauled out in the morning.

SHANNON (*cutting in, with the honking sound of a panicky goose*). Off, off, off, off, off!

HANNAH. Oh, Mrs. Faulk, Mr. Shannon won't quiet down till he's left alone in the hammock.

MAXINE. Then why don't *you* leave him alone?

HANNAH. I'm not sitting on him and he . . . has to be cared for by someone.

MAXINE. And the someone is *you?*

HANNAH. A long time ago, Mrs. Faulk, I had experience with someone in Mr. Shannon's condition, so I know how necessary it is to let them be quiet for a while.

MAXINE. He wasn't quiet, he was shouting.

HANNAH. He will quiet down again.

I'm preparing a sedative tea for him, Mrs. Faulk.

MAXINE. Yeah, I see. Put it out. Nobody cooks here but the Chinaman in the kitchen.

HANNAH. This is just a little alcohol burner, a spirit lamp, Mrs. Faulk.

MAXINE. I know what it is. It goes out! (*She blows out the flame under the burner.*)

SHANNON. Maxine honey? [*He speaks quietly now.*] Stop persecuting this lady. You can't intimidate her. A bitch is no match for a lady except in a brass bed, honey, and sometimes not even there.

(*The Germans are heard shouting for beer—a case of it to take down to the beach.*)

WOLFGANG. Eine Kiste Carta Blanca.

FRAU FAHRENKOPF. Wir haben genug gehabt . . . vielleicht nicht.

HERR FAHRENKOPF. Nein! Niemals genug.

HILDA. Mutter du bist dick . . . aber wir sind es nicht.

SHANNON. Maxine, you're neglecting your duties as a beerhall waitress. (*His tone is deceptively gentle.*) They want a case of Carta Blanca to carry down to the beach, so give it to 'em . . . and tonight, when the moon's gone down, if you'll let me out of this hammock, I'll try to imagine you as a . . . as a nymph in her teens.

MAXINE. A fat lot of good you'd be in your present condition.

SHANNON. Don't be a sexual snob at your age, honey.

MAXINE. Hah! (*But the unflattering offer has pleased her realistically modest soul, so she goes back to the Germans.*)

SHANNON. Now let me try a bit of your poppyseed tea, Miss Jelkes.

HANNAH. I ran out of sugar, but I had some ginger, some sugared ginger. (*She pours a cup of tea and sips it.*) Oh, it's not well brewed yet, but try to drink some now and the—(*She lights the burner again.*)—the second cup will be better. (*She crouches by the hammock and presses the cup to his lips. He raises his head to sip it, but he gags and chokes.*)

SHANNON. *Caesar's ghost!*—it could be chased by the witches' brew from Macbeth.

HANNAH. Yes, I know, it's still bitter.

(*The Germans appear on the wing of the verandah and go trooping down to the beach, for a beer festival and a moonlight swim. Even in the relative dark they have a luminous color, an almost phosphorescent pink and gold color of skin. They carry with them a case of Carta Blanca beer and the fantastically painted rubber horse. On their faces are smiles of euphoria as they move like a dream-image, starting to sing a marching song as they go.*)

SHANNON. Fiends out of hell with the . . . voices of . . . angels.

HANNAH. Yes, they call it "the logic of contradictions," Mr. Shannon.

SHANNON (*lunging suddenly forward and undoing the loosened ropes*). Out! Free! Unassisted!

HANNAH. Yes, I never doubted that you could get loose, Mr. Shannon.

SHANNON. Thanks for your help, anyhow.

HANNAH. Where are you going?

(*He has crossed to the liquor cart.*)

SHANNON. Not far. To the liquor cart to make myself a rum-coco.

HANNAH. Oh. . . .

SHANNON (*at the liquor cart*). Coconut? Check. Machete? Check. Rum? Double check! Ice? The ice-bucket's empty. O.K., it's a night for warm drinks. Miss Jelkes? Would you care to have your complimentary rum-coco?

HANNAH. No thank you, Mr. Shannon.

SHANNON. You don't mind me having mine?

HANNAH. Not at all, Mr. Shannon.

SHANNON. You don't disapprove of this weakness, this self-indulgence?

HANNAH. Liquor isn't your problem, Mr. Shannon.

SHANNON. What is my problem, Miss Jelkes?

HANNAH. The oldest one in the world —the need to believe in something or in someone—almost anyone—almost anything . . . something.

SHANNON. Your voice sounds hopeless about it.

HANNAH. No, I'm not hopeless about it. In fact, I've discovered something to believe in.

SHANNON. Something like . . . God?

HANNAH. No.

SHANNON. What?

HANNAH. Broken gates between people so they can reach each other, even if it's just for one night only.

SHANNON. One night stands, huh?

HANNAH. One night . . . communication between them on a verandah outside their . . . separate cubicles, Mr. Shannon.

SHANNON. You don't mean physically, do you?

HANNAH. No.

SHANNON. I didn't think so. Then what?

HANNAH. A little understanding exchanged between them, a wanting to help each other through nights like this.

SHANNON. Who was the someone you told the widow you'd helped long ago to get through a crack-up like this one I'm going through?

HANNAH. Oh . . . that. Myself.

SHANNON. You?

HANNAH. Yes. I can help you because I've been through what you are going through now. I had something like your spook—I just had a different name for him. I called him the blue devil, and . . . oh . . . we had quite a battle, quite a contest between us.

SHANNON. Which you obviously won.

HANNAH. I couldn't afford to lose.

SHANNON. How'd you beat your blue devil?

HANNAH. I showed him that I could endure him and I made him respect my endurance.

SHANNON. How?

HANNAH. Just by, just by . . . enduring. Endurance is something that spooks and blue devils respect. And they respect all the tricks that panicky people use to outlast and outwit their panic.

SHANNON. Like poppyseed tea?

HANNAH. Poppyseed tea or rum-cocos or just a few deep breaths. Anything, everything, that we take to give them the slip, and so to keep on going.

SHANNON. To where?

HANNAH. To somewhere like this, perhaps. This verandah over the rain forest and the still-water beach, after long, difficult travels. And I don't mean just travels about the world, the earth's surface. I mean . . . subterranean travels, the . . . the journeys that the spooked and bedevilled people are forced to take through the . . . the *unlighted* sides of their natures.

SHANNON. Don't tell me you have a dark side to your nature. (*He says this sardonically.*)

HANNAH. I'm sure I don't have to tell a man as experienced and knowledgeable as you, Mr. Shannon, that everything has its shadowy side? (*She glances up at him and observes that she doesn't have his attention. He is gazing tensely at something off the verandah. It is the kind of abstraction, not vague but fiercely concentrated, that occurs in madness. She turns to look where he's looking. She closes her eyes for a moment and draws a deep breath, then goes on speaking in a voice like a hypnotist's, as if the words didn't matter, since he is not listening to her so much as to the tone and the cadence of her voice.*)

HANNAH. Everything in the whole solar system has a shadowy side to it except the sun itself—the sun is the single exception. You're not listening, are you?

SHANNON (*as if replying to her*). The spook is in the rain forest. (*He suddenly hurls his coconut shell with great violence off the verandah, creating a commotion among the jungle birds.*) Good shot—it caught him right on the kisser and his teeth flew out like popcorn from a popper.

HANNAH. Has he gone off—to the dentist?

SHANNON. He's retreated a little way away for a little while, but when I buzz for my breakfast tomorrow, he'll bring it in to me with a grin that'll curdle the milk in the coffee and he'll stink like a . . . a gringo drunk in a Mexican jail who's slept all night in his vomit.

HANNAH. If you wake up before I'm out, I'll bring your coffee in to you . . . if you call me.

SHANNON (*his attention returns to her*). No, you'll be gone, God help me.

HANNAH. Maybe and maybe not. I might think of something tomorrow to placate the widow.

SHANNON. The widow's implacable, honey.

HANNAH. I think I'll think of something because I have to. I can't let Nonno be moved to the Casa de Huéspedes, Mr. Shannon. Not any more than I could let you take the long swim out to China. You know that. Not if I can prevent it, and when I have to be resourceful, I can

be very resourceful.

SHANNON. How'd you get over your crack-up?

HANNAH. I never cracked up, I couldn't afford to. Of course, I nearly did once. I was young once, Mr. Shannon, but I was one of those people who can be young without really having their youth, and not to have your youth when you are young is naturally very disturbing. But I was lucky. My work, this occupational therapy that I gave myself—painting and doing quick character sketches—made me look out of myself, not in, and gradually, at the far end of the tunnel that I was struggling out of I began to see this faint, very faint gray light—the light of the world outside me—and I kept climbing toward it. I had to.

SHANNON. Did it stay a gray light?

HANNAH. No, no, it turned white.

SHANNON. Only white, never gold?

HANNAH. No, it stayed only white, but white is a very good light to see at the end of a long black tunnel you thought would be neverending, that only God or Death could put a stop to, especially when you . . . since I was . . . far from sure about God.

SHANNON. You're still unsure about him?

HANNAH. Not as unsure as I was. You see, in my profession I have to look hard and close at human faces in order to catch something in them before they get restless and call out, "Waiter, the check, we're leaving." Of course sometimes, a few times, I just see blobs of wet dough that pass for human faces, with bits of jelly for eyes. Then I cue in Nonno to give a recitation, because I can't draw such faces. But those aren't the usual faces, I don't think they're even real. Most times I *do* see something, and I can catch it—I *can*, like I caught something in your face when I sketched you this afternoon with your eyes open. Are you still listening to me? (*He crouches beside her chair, looking up at her intently.*) In Shanghai, Shannon, there is a place that's called the House for the Dying—the old and penniless dying, whose younger, penniless living children and grandchildren take them there for them to get through with their dying on pallets, on straw mats. The first time I went there it shocked me, I ran away from it. But

I came back later and I saw that their children and grandchildren and the custodians of the place had put little comforts beside their death-pallets, little flowers and opium candies and religious emblems. That made me able to stay to draw their dying faces. Sometimes only their eyes were still alive, but, Mr. Shannon, those eyes of the penniless dying with those last little comforts beside them, I tell you, Mr. Shannon, those eyes looked up with their last dim life left in them as clear as the stars in the Southern Cross, Mr. Shannon. And now . . . now I am going to say something to you that will sound like something that only the spinster granddaughter of a minor romantic poet is likely to say. . . . Nothing I've ever seen has seemed as beautiful to me, not even the view from this verandah between the sky and the still-water beach, and lately . . . lately my grandfather's eyes have looked up at me like that. . . . (*She rises abruptly and crosses to the front of the verandah.*) Tell me, what is that sound I keep hearing down there?

SHANNON. There's a marimba band at the cantina on the beach.

HANNAH. I don't mean that, I mean that scraping, scuffling sound that I keep hearing under the verandah.

SHANNON. Oh, that. The Mexican boys that work here have caught an iguana and tied it up under the verandah, hitched it to a post, and naturally of course it's trying to scramble away. But it's got to the end of its rope, and get any further it cannot. Ha-ha—that's it. (*He quotes from* NONNO's *poem:* "And still the orange," etc.) Do you have any life of your own—besides your water colors and sketches and your travels with Grampa?

HANNAH. We make a home for each other, my grandfather and I. Do you know what I mean by a home? I don't mean a regular home. I mean I don't mean what other people mean when they speak of a home, because I don't regard a home as a . . . well, as a place, a building . . . a house . . . of wood, bricks, stone. I think of a home as being a thing that two people have between them in which each can . . . well, nest–rest–live in, emotionally speaking. Does that make any sense to you, Mr. Shannon?

SHANNON. Yeah, complete. But. . . .

HANNAH. Another incomplete sentence.

SHANNON. We better leave it that way. I might've said something to hurt you.

HANNAH. I'm not thin skinned, Mr. Shannon.

SHANNON. No, well, then, I'll say it. . . . (*He moves to the liquor cart.*) When a bird builds a nest to rest in and live in, it doesn't built it in a . . . a falling-down tree.

HANNAH. I'm not a bird, Mr. Shannon.

SHANNON. I was making an analogy, Miss Jelkes.

HANNAH. I thought you were making yourself another rum-coco, Mr. Shannon.

SHANNON. Both. When a bird builds a nest, it builds it with an eye for the . . . the relative permanence of the location, and also for the purpose of mating and propagating its species.

HANNAH. I still say that I'm not a bird, Mr. Shannon, I'm a human being and when a member of that fantastic species builds a nest in the heart of another, the question of permanence isn't the first or even the last thing that's considered . . . necessarily? . . . always? Nonno and I have been continually reminded of the impermanence of things lately. We go back to a hotel where we've been many times before and it isn't there any more. It's been demolished and there's one of those glassy, brassy new ones. Or if the old one's still there, the manager or the Maitre D who always welcomed us back so cordially before has been replaced by someone new who looks at us with suspicion.

SHANNON. Yeah, but you still had each other.

HANNAH. Yes. We did.

SHANNON. But when the old gentleman goes?

HANNAH. Yes?

SHANNON. What will you do? Stop?

HANNAH. Stop or go on . . . probably go on.

SHANNON. Alone? Checking into hotels alone, eating alone at tables for one in a corner, the tables waiters call aces.

HANNAH. Thank you for your sympathy, Mr. Shannon, but in my profession I'm obliged to make quick contacts with strangers who turn to friends very quickly.

SHANNON. Customers aren't friends.

HANNAH. They turn to friends, if

they're friendly.

SHANNON. Yeah, but how will it seem to be traveling alone after so many years of traveling with. . . .

HANNAH. I will know how it feels when I feel it—and don't say alone as if nobody had ever gone on alone. For instance, you.

SHANNON. I've always traveled with trainloads, planeloads and busloads of tourists.

HANNAH. That doesn't mean you're still not really alone.

SHANNON. I never fail to make an intimate connection with someone in my parties.

HANNAH. Yes, the youngest young lady, and I was on the verandah this afternoon when the latest of these young ladies gave a demonstration of how lonely the intimate connection has always been for you. The episode in the cold, inhuman hotel room, Mr. Shannon, for which you despise the lady almost as much as you despise yourself. Afterwards you are so polite to the lady that I'm sure it must chill her to the bone, the scrupulous little attentions that you pay her in return for your little enjoyment of her. The gentleman-of-Virginia act that you put on for her, your noblesse oblige treatment of her . . . Oh no, Mr. Shannon, don't kid yourself that you ever travel with someone. You have always traveled alone except for your spook, as you call it. He's your traveling companion. Nothing, nobody else has traveled with you.

SHANNON. Thank you for your sympathy, Miss Jelkes.

HANNAH. You're welcome, Mr. Shannon. And now I think I had better warm up the poppyseed tea for Nonno. Only a good night's sleep could make it possible for him to go on from here tomorrow.

SHANNON. Yes, well, if the conversation is over—I think I'll go down for a swim now.

HANNAH. To China?

SHANNON. No, not to China, just to the little island out here with the sleepy bar on it . . . called the Cantina Serena.

HANNAH. Why?

SHANNON. Because I'm not a nice drunk and I was about to ask you a not nice question.

HANNAH. Ask it. There's no set limit on questions here tonight.

SHANNON. And no set limit on answers?

HANNAH. None I can think of between you and me, Mr. Shannon.

SHANNON. That I will take you up on.

HANNAH. Do.

SHANNON. It's a bargain.

HANNAH. Only do lie back down in the hammock and drink a full cup of the poppyseed tea this time. It's warmer now and the sugared ginger will make it easier to get down.

SHANNON. All right. The question is this: have you never had in your life any kind of a lovelife? (HANNAH *stiffens for a moment.*) I thought you said there was no limit set on questions.

HANNAH. We'll make a bargain—I will answer your question *after* you've had a full cup of the poppyseed tea so you'll be able to get the good night's sleep you need, too. It's fairly warm now and the sugared ginger's made it much more— (*She sips the cup.*)—palatable.

SHANNON. You think I'm going to drift into dreamland so you can welch on the bargain? (*He accepts the cup from her.*)

HANNAH. I'm not a welcher on bargains. Drink it all. All. *All!*

SHANNON (*with a disgusted grimace as he drains the cup*). Great Caesar's ghost. (*He tosses the cup off the verandah and falls into the hammock, chuckling.*) The oriental idea of a Mickey Finn, huh? Sit down where I can see you, Miss Jelkes honey. (*She sits down in a straight-back chair, some distance from the hammock.*) Where I can *see* you! I don't have an x-ray eye in the back of my head, Miss Jelkes. (*She moves the chair alongside the hammock.*) Further, further, up further. (*She complies.*) There now. Answer the question now, Miss Jelkes honey.

HANNAH. Would you mind repeating the question.

SHANNON (*slowly, with emphasis*). Have you never had in all of your life and your travels any experience, any encounter, with what Larry-the-crackpot Shannon thinks of as a lovelife?

HANNAH. There are . . . worse things than chastity, Mr. Shannon.

SHANNON. Yeah, lunacy and death are both a little worse, *maybe!* But chastity isn't a thing that a beautiful woman or an attractive man falls into like a booby trap or an overgrown gopher hole, is it? (*There is a pause.*) I still think you are welching on the bargain and I. . . . (*He starts out of the hammock.*)

HANNAH. Mr. Shannon, this night is just as hard for me to get through as it is for you to get through. But it's you that are welching on the bargain, you're not staying in the hammock. Lie back down in the hammock. Now. Yes. Yes, I have had two experiences, well, encounters, with. . . .

SHANNON. *Two,* did you say?

HANNAH. Yes, I said two. And I wasn't exaggerating and don't you say "fantastic" before I've told you both stories. When I was sixteen, your favorite age, Mr. Shannon, each Saturday afternoon my grandfather Nonno would give me thirty cents, my allowance, my pay for my secretarial and housekeeping duties. Twenty-five cents for admission to the Saturday matinee at the Nantucket movie theatre and five cents extra for a bag of popcorn, Mr. Shannon. I'd sit at the almost empty back of the movie theatre so that the popcorn munching wouldn't disturb the other movie patrons. Well . . . one afternoon a young man sat down beside me and pushed his . . . knee against mine and . . . I moved over two seats but he moved over beside me and continued this . . . pressure! I jumped up and screamed, Mr. Shannon. He was arrested for molesting a minor.

SHANNON. Is he still in the Nantucket jail?

HANNAH. No. I got him out. I told the police that it was a Clara Bow picture— it *was* a Clara Bow picture—and I was just overexcited.

SHANNON. Fantastic.

HANNAH. Yes, very! The second experience is much more recent, only two years ago, when Nonno and I were operating at the Raffles Hotel in Singapore, and doing very well there, making expenses and more. One evening in the Palm Court of the Raffles we met this middle-aged, sort of nondescript Australian salesman. You know—plump, bald-spotted, with a bad attempt at speaking with an upper-class accent and terribly overfriendly. He was alone and looked lonely. Grandfather said him a poem and I did a quick character sketch that was shamelessly flattering of him. He paid me more than my usual asking price and gave my grandfather five Malayan dol-

lars, yes, and he even purchased one of my water colors. Then it was Nonno's bedtime. The Aussie salesman asked me out in a sampan with him. Well, he'd been so generous . . . I accepted. I did, I accepted. Grandfather went up to bed and I went out in the sampan with this ladies' underwear salesman. I noticed that he became more and more. . . .

SHANNON. What?

HANNAH. Well . . . *agitated* . . . as the afterglow of the sunset faded out on the water. (*She laughs with a delicate sadness.*) Well, finally, eventually, he leaned toward me . . . we were vis-à-vis in the sampan . . . and he looked intensely, passionately into my eyes. (*She laughs again.*) And he said to me: "Miss Jelkes? Will you do me a favor? Will you do something for me?" "What?" said I. "Well," said he, "if I turn my back, if I look the other way, will you take off some piece of your clothes and let me hold it, just hold it?"

SHANNON. Fantastic!

HANNAH. Then he said, "It will just take a few seconds." "Just a few seconds for what?" I asked him. (*She gives the same laugh again.*) He didn't say for what, but. . . .

SHANNON. His satisfaction?

HANNAH. Yes.

SHANNON. What did you do—in a situation like that?

HANNAH. I . . . gratified his request, I did! And he kept his promise. He did keep his back turned till I said ready and threw him . . . the part of my clothes.

SHANNON. What did he do with it?

HANNAH. He didn't move, except to seize the article he'd requested. I looked the other way while his satisfaction took place.

SHANNON. Watch out for commercial travelers in the Far East. Is that the moral, Miss Jelkes honey?

HANNAH. Oh, no, the moral is oriental. Accept whatever situation you cannot improve.

SHANNON. "When it's inevitable, lean back and enjoy it—is that it?

HANNAH. He'd bought a water color. The incident was embarrassing, not violent. I left and returned unmolested. Oh, and the funniest part of all is that when we got back to the Raffles Hotel, he took the piece of apparel out of his pocket like a bashful boy producing an apple for his schoolteacher and tried to slip it into my hand in the elevator. I wouldn't accept it. I whispered, "Oh, please keep it, Mr. Willoughby!" He'd paid the asking price for my water color and somehow the little experience had been rather touching, I mean it was so *lonely,* out there in the sampan with violet streaks in the sky and this little middle-aged Australian making sounds like he was dying of asthma! And the planet Venus coming serenely out of a fair-weather cloud, over the Straits of Malacca. . . .

SHANNON. And that experience . . . you call that a. . . .

HANNAH. A love experience? Yes. I do call it one.

(*He regards her with incredulity, peering into her face so closely that she is embarrassed and becomes defensive.*)

SHANNON. That, that . . . sad, dirty little episode, you call it a . . . ?

HANNAH (*cutting in sharply*). Sad it certainly was—for the odd little man—but why do you call it "dirty"?

SHANNON. How did you feel when you went into your bedroom?

HANNAH. Confused, I . . . a little confused, I suppose. . . . I'd known about loneliness—but not that degree or . . . depth of it.

SHANNON. You mean it didn't *disgust* you?

HANNAH. Nothing human disgusts me unless it's unkind, violent. And I told you how gentle he was—apologetic, shy, and really very, well, *delicate* about it. However, I do grant you it was on the rather fantastic level.

SHANNON. You're. . . .

HANNAH. I am *what?* "Fantastic"?

(*While they have been talking,* NONNO's *voice has been heard now and then, mumbling, from his cubicle. Suddenly it becomes loud and clear.*)

NONNO. And finally the broken stem,
The plummeting to earth and then. . . .

(*His voice subsides to its mumble.* SHANNON, *standing behind* HANNAH, *places his hand on her throat.*)

HANNAH. What is that for? Are you about to strangle me, Mr. Shannon?

SHANNON. You can't stand to be touched?

HANNAH. Save it for the widow. It isn't for me.

SHANNON. Yes, you're right. (*He removes his hand.*) I could do it with Mrs. Faulk, the inconsolable widow, but I couldn't with you.

HANNAH (*dryly and lightly*). Spinster's loss, widow's gain, Mr. Shannon.

SHANNON. Or widow's loss, spinster's gain. Anyhow it sounds like some old parlor game in a Virginia or Nantucket Island parlor. But . . . I wonder something. . . .

HANNAH. What do you wonder?

SHANNON. If we couldn't . . . *travel* together, I mean just *travel* together?

HANNAH. Could we? In your opinion?

SHANNON. Why not, I don't see why not.

HANNAH. I think the impracticality of the idea will appear much clearer to you in the morning, Mr. Shannon. (*She folds her dimly gold-lacquered fan and rises from her chair.*) Morning can always be counted on to bring us back to a more realistic level. . . . Good night, Mr. Shannon. I have to pack before I'm too tired to.

SHANNON. Don't leave me out here alone yet.

HANNAH. I have to pack now so I can get up at daybreak and try my luck in the plaza.

SHANNON. You won't sell a water color or sketch in that blazing hot plaza tomorrow. Miss Jelkes honey, I don't think you're operating on the realistic level.

HANNAH. Would I be if I thought we could travel together?

SHANNON. I still don't see why we couldn't.

HANNAH. Mr. Shannon, you're not well enough to travel anywhere with anybody right now. Does that sound cruel of me?

SHANNON. You mean that I'm stuck here for good? Winding up with the . . . inconsolable widow?

HANNAH. We all wind up with something or with someone, and if it's someone instead of just something, we're lucky, perhaps . . . unusually lucky. (*She starts to enter her cubicle, then turns to him again in the doorway.*) Oh, and tomorrow. . . . (*She touches her forehead as if a little confused as well as exhausted.*)

SHANNON. What about tomorrow?

HANNAH (*with difficulty*). I think it might be better, tomorrow, if we avoid showing any particular interest in each other, because Mrs. Faulk is a morbidly jealous woman.

SHANNON. *Is* she?

HANNAH. Yes, she seems to have misunderstood our . . . sympathetic interest in each other. So I think we'd better avoid any more long talks on the verandah. I mean till she's thoroughly reassured it might be better if we just say good morning or good night to each other.

SHANNON. We don't even have to say that.

HANNAH. I will, but you don't have to answer.

SHANNON (*savagely*). How about walltappings between us by way of communication? You know, like convicts in separate cells communicate with each other by tapping on the walls of the cells? One tap: I'm here. Two taps: are you there? Three taps: yes, I am. Four taps: that's good, we're together. *Christ!* . . . Here, take this. (*He snatches the gold cross from his pocket.*) Take my gold cross and hock it, it's 22-carat gold.

HANNAH. What do you, what are you . . . ?

SHANNON. There's a fine amethyst in it, it'll pay your travel expenses back to the States.

HANNAH. Mr. Shannon, you're making no sense at all now.

SHANNON. Neither are you, Miss Jelkes, talking about tomorrow, and. . . .

HANNAH. All I was saying was. . . .

SHANNON. You won't *be* here tomorrow! Had you forgotten you won't be here tomorrow?

HANNAH (*with a slight, shocked laugh*). Yes, I *had*, I'd *forgotten!*

SHANNON. The widow wants you out and out you'll go, even if you sell your water colors like hotcakes to the pariah dogs in the plaza. (*He stares at her, shaking his head hopelessly.*)

HANNAH. I suppose you're right, Mr. Shannon. I must be too tired to think or I've contracted your fever. . . . It had actually slipped my mind for a moment that—

NONNO (*abruptly, from his cubicle*). Hannah!

HANNAH (*rushing to his door*). Yes, what is it, Nonno? (*He doesn't hear her and repeats her name louder.*) Here I am, I'm here.

NONNO. Don't come in yet, but stay where I can call you.

HANNAH. Yes, I'll *hear* you, Nonno. (*She turns toward* SHANNON, *drawing a deep breath.*)

SHANNON. Listen, if you don't take this gold cross that I never want on me again, I'm going to pitch it off the verandah at the spook in the rain forest. (*He raises an arm to throw it, but she catches his arm to restrain him.*)

HANNAH. All right, Mr. Shannon, I'll take it, I'll hold it for you.

SHANNON. Hock it, honey, you've got to.

HANNAH. Well, if I do, I'll mail the pawn ticket to you so you can redeem it, because you'll want it again, when you've gotten over your fever. (*She moves blindly down the verandah and starts to enter the wrong cubicle.*)

SHANNON. That isn't your cell, you went past it. (*His voice is gentle again.*)

HANNAH. I did, I'm sorry. I've never been this tired in all my life. (*She turns to face him again. He stares into her face. She looks blindly out, past him.*) *Never!* (*There is a slight pause.*) What did you say is making that constant, dry, scuffling sound beneath the verandah?

SHANNON. I told you.

HANNAH. I didn't hear you.

SHANNON. I'll get my flashlight, I'll show you. (*He lurches rapidly into his cubicle and back out with a flashlight.*) It's an iguana. I'll show you. . . . See? The iguana? At the end of its rope? Trying to go on past the end of its goddam rope? Like *you!* Like *me!* Like Grampa with his last poem!

(*In the pause which follows singing is heard from the beach.*)

HANNAH. What is a—what—iguana?

SHANNON. It's a kind of lizard—a big one, a giant one. The Mexican kids caught it and tied it up.

HANNAH. Why did they tie it up?

SHANNON. Because that's what they do. They tie them up and fatten them up and then eat them up, when they're ready for eating. They're a delicacy. Taste like white meat of chicken. At least the Mexicans think so. And also the kids, the Mexican kids, have a lot of fun with them, poking out their eyes with sticks and burning their tails with matches.

You know? Fun? Like that?

HANNAH. Mr. Shannon, please go down and cut it loose!

SHANNON. I can't do that.

HANNAH. Why can't you?

SHANNON. Mrs. Faulk wants to eat it. I've got to please Mrs. Faulk, I am at her mercy. I am at her disposal.

HANNAH. I don't understand. I mean I don't understand how anyone could eat a big lizard.

SHANNON. Don't be so critical. If you got hungry enough you'd eat it too. You'd be surprised what people will eat if hungry. There's a lot of hungry people still in the world. Many have died of starvation, but a lot are still living and hungry, believe you me, if you will take my word for it. Why, when I was conducting a party of—*ladies?*—yes, ladies . . . through a country that shall be nameless but in this world, we were passing by rubberneck bus along a tropical coast when we saw a great mound of . . . well, the smell was unpleasant. One of my ladies said, "Oh, Larry, what is that?" My name being Lawrence, the most familiar ladies sometimes call me Larry. I didn't use the four letter word for what the great mound was. I didn't think it was necessary to say it. Then she noticed, and I noticed too, a pair of very old natives of this nameless country, practically naked except for a few filthy rags, creeping and crawling about this mound of . . . and . . . occasionally stopping to pick something out of it, and pop it into their mouths. What? Bits of undigested . . . food particles, Miss Jelkes. (*There is silence for a moment. She makes a gagging sound in her throat and rushes the length of the verandah to the wooden steps and disappears for a while.* SHANNON *continues, to himself and the moon.*) Now why did I tell her that? Because it's true? That's no reason to tell her, because it's true. Yeah. Because it's true was a good reason not to tell her. Except . . . I think I first *faced* it in that nameless country. The gradual, rapid, natural, unnatural—predestined, accidental—cracking up and going to pieces of young Mr. T. Lawrence Shannon, yes, still *young* Mr. T. Lawrence Shannon, by which rapid-slow process . . . his final tour of ladies through tropical countries. . . . Why did I say "tropical"? Hell! Yes! It's

always been tropical countries I took ladies through. Does that, does that—huh?—signify something, I wonder? Maybe. Fast decay is a thing of hot climates, steamy, hot, wet climates, and I run back to them like a. . . . Incomplete sentence. . . . Always seducing a lady or two, or three or four or five ladies in the party, but really ravaging her first by pointing out to her the—what?—horrors? Yes, horrors!—of the tropical country being conducted a tour through. My . . . brain's going out now, like a failing —power. . . . So I stay here, I reckon, and live off la patrona for the rest of my life. Well, she's old enough to predecease me. She could check out of here first, and I imagine that after a couple of years of having to satisfy her I might be prepared for the shock of her passing on. . . . Cruelty . . . pity. What is it? . . . Don't know, all I know is. . . .

HANNAH (*from below the verandah*). You're talking to yourself.

SHANNON. No. To you. I knew you could hear me out there, but not being able to see you I could say it easier, you know . . . ?

NONNO. A chronicle no longer gold,
A bargaining with mist and mould. . . .

HANNAH (*coming back onto the verandah*). I took a closer look at the iguana down there.

SHANNON. You did? How did you like it? Charming? Attractive?

HANNAH. No, it's not an attractive creature. Nevertheless I think it should be cut loose.

SHANNON. Iguanas have been known to bite their tails off when they're tied up by their tails.

HANNAH. This one is tied by its throat. It can't bite its own head off to escape from the end of the rope, Mr. Shannon. Can you look at me and tell me truthfully that you don't know it's able to feel pain and panic?

SHANNON. You mean it's one of God's creatures?

HANNAH. If you want to put it that way, yes, it is. Mr. Shannon, will you please cut it loose, set it free? Because if you don't, I will.

SHANNON. Can you look at *me* and tell *me* truthfully that this reptilian creature, tied up down there, doesn't mostly disturb you because of its parallel situation to your Grampa's dying-out effort to finish one last poem, Miss Jelkes?

HANNAH. Yes, I. . . .

SHANNON. Never mind completing that sentence. We'll play God tonight like kids play house with old broken crates and boxes. All right? Now Shannon is going to go down there with his machete and cut the damn lizard loose so it can run back to its bushes because God won't do it and we are going to play God here.

HANNAH. I knew you'd do that. And I thank you.

(SHANNON *goes down the two steps from the verandah with the machete. He crouches beside the cactus that hides the iguana and cuts the rope with a quick, hard stroke of the machete. He turns to look after its flight, as the low, excited mumble in cubicle 3 grows louder. Then* NONNO's *voice turns to a sudden shout.*)

NONNO. Hannah! Hannah! (*She rushes to him, as he wheels himself out of his cubicle onto the verandah.*)

HANNAH. Grandfather! What is it?

NONNO. I! believe! it is! *finished!* Quick, before I forget it—pencil, paper! Quick! please! Ready?

HANNAH. Yes. All ready, grandfather.

NONNO (*in a loud, exalted voice*).
How calmly does the orange branch
Observe the sky begin to blanch
Without a cry, without a prayer,
With no betrayal of despair.

Sometime while night obscures the tree
The zenith of its life will be
Gone past forever, and from thence
A second history will commence.

A chronicle no longer gold,
A bargaining with mist and mould,
And finally the broken stem
The plummeting to earth; and then

An intercourse not well designed
For beings of a golden kind
Whose native green must arch above
The earth's obscene, corrupting love.

And still the ripe fruit and the branch
Observe the sky begin to blanch
Without a cry, without a prayer,
With no betrayal of despair.

O Courage, could you not as well
Select a second place to dwell,

Not only in that golden tree
But in the frightened heart of me?

Have you got it?

HANNAH. Yes!

NONNO. All of it?

HANNAH. Every word of it.

NONNO. It is *finished?*

HANNAH. Yes.

NONNO. Oh! God! Finally finished?

HANNAH. Yes, finally finished. (*She is crying. The singing voices flow up from the beach.*)

NONNO. After waiting so long!

HANNAH. Yes, we waited so long.

NONNO. And it's good! It is *good?*

HANNAH. It's—it's. . . .

NONNO. What?

HANNAH. Beautiful, grandfather! (*She springs up, a fist to her mouth.*) Oh, grandfather, I am so happy for you. Thank you for writing such a lovely poem! It was worth the long wait. Can you sleep now, grandfather?

NONNO. You'll have it typewritten to-morrow?

HANNAH. Yes. I'll have it typed up and send it off to *Harper's.*

NONNO. Hah? I didn't hear that, Han-nah.

HANNAH (*shouting*). I'll have it typed up tomorrow, and mail it to *Harper's* tomorrow! They've been waiting for it a long time, too! You know!

NONNO. Yes, I'd like to pray now.

HANNAH. Good night. Sleep now, Grandfather. You've finished your love-liest poem.

NONNO (*faintly, drifting off*). Yes, thanks and praise . . .

(MAXINE *comes around the front of the verandah, followed by* PEDRO *playing a harmonica softly. She is prepared for a night swim, a vividly striped towel thrown over her shoulders. It is apparent that the night's progress has mellowed her spirit: her face wears a faint smile which is suggestive of those cool, impersonal, all-comprehending smiles on the carved heads of Egyptian or Oriental deities. Bearing a rum-coco, she approaches the hammock, discovers it empty, the ropes on the floor, and calls softly to* PEDRO.)

MAXINE. Shannon ha escapado! (PEDRO *goes on playing dreamily. She throws back her head and shouts.*) SHANNON! (*The call is echoed by the hill beyond.*

PEDRO *advances a few steps and points under the verandah.*)

PEDRO. Miré. Allé 'hasta Shannon.

(SHANNON *comes into view from below the verandah, the severed rope and machete dangling from his hands.*)

MAXINE. What are you doing down there, Shannon?

SHANNON. I cut loose one of God's creatures at the end of the rope.

(HANNAH, *who has stood motionless with closed eyes behind the wicker chair, goes quietly toward the cubicles and out of the moon's glare.*)

MAXINE (*tolerantly*). What'd you do that for, Shannon.

SHANNON. So that one of God's creatures could scramble home safe and free. . . . A little act of grace, Maxine.

MAXINE (*smiling a bit more definitely*). C'mon up here, Shannon. I want to talk to you.

SHANNON (*starting to climb onto the verandah, as* MAXINE *rattles the ice in the coconut shell*). What d'ya want to talk about, Widow Faulk?

MAXINE. Let's go down and swim in that liquid moonlight.

SHANNON. Where did you pick up that poetic expression?

(MAXINE *glances back at* PEDRO *and dismisses him with,* "Vamos." *He leaves with a shrug, the harmonica fading out.*)

MAXINE. Shannon, I want you to stay with me.

SHANNON (*taking the rum-coco from her*). You want a drinking companion?

MAXINE. No, I just want you to stay here, because I'm alone here now and I need somebody to help me manage the place.

(HANNAH *strikes a match for a cigarette.*)

SHANNON (*looking toward her*). I want to remember that face. I won't see it again.

MAXINE. Let's go down to the beach.

SHANNON. I can make it down the hill, but not back up.

MAXINE. I'll get you back up the hill. (*They have started off now, toward the path down through the rain forest.*) I've got five more years, maybe ten, to make this place attractive to the male clientele, the middle-aged ones at least. And you can take care of the women that are

with them. That's what you can do, you know that, Shannon.

(*He chuckles happily. They are now on the path,* MAXINE *half leading half supporting him. Their voices fade as* HANNAH *goes into* NONNO's *cubicle and comes back with a shawl, her cigarette left inside. She pauses between the door and the wicker chair and speaks to herself and the sky.*)

HANNAH. Oh, God, can't we stop now? Finally? Please let us. It's so quiet here, now.

(*She starts to put the shawl about* NONNO, *but at the same moment his head drops to the side. With a soft intake of breath, she extends a hand before his mouth to see if he is still breathing. He isn't. In a panicky moment, she looks right and left for someone to call to. There's no one. Then she bends to press her head to the crown of* NONNO's *and the curtain starts to descend.*)

THE END

NAZI MARCHING SONG

Heute wollen wir ein Liedlein singen,
Trinken wollen wir den kuehlen Wein;
Und die Glaeser sollen dazu klingen,
Denn es muss, es muss geschieden sein.

Gib' mir deine Hand,
Deine weisse Hand,
Leb'wohl, mein Schatz, leb'wohl, mein
     Schatz
Lebe wohl, lebe wohl,
Denn wir fahren. Boom! Boom!
Denn wir fahren. Boom! Boom!
Denn wir fahren gegen Engelland. Boom!
     Boom!

Let's sing a little song today,
And drink some cool wine;
The glasses should be ringing
Since we must, we must part.

Give me your hand,
Your white hand,
Farewell, my love, farewell,
Farewell, farewell,
Since we're going—
Since we're going—
Since we're going against England.

THE DARK AT THE TOP
OF THE STAIRS

William Inge

Presented by Saint Subber and Elia Kazan at The Music Box in New York on December 5, 1957, with the following cast:

CORA FLOOD, *a young housewife*
    Theresa Wright
RUBIN FLOOD, *her husband* Pat Hingle
SONNY FLOOD, *the ten-year-old son*
    Charles Saari
BOY OUTSIDE   Jonathan Shawn
REENIE FLOOD, *the sixteen-year-old daughter*   Judith Robinson
FLIRT CONROY, *a flapper friend of Reenie's*
    Evans Evans

MORRIS LACEY, *Cora's brother-in-law*
    Frank Overton
LOTTIE LACEY, *Cora's older sister*
    Eileen Heckart
PUNKY GIVENS, *Flirt's boy friend*
    Carl Reindel
SAMMY GOLDENBAUM, *Punky's friend*
    Timmy Everett
CHAUFFEUR   Anthony Ray

Directed by Elia Kazan
Setting by Ben Edwards
Costumes by Lucinda Ballard
Lighting by Jean Rosenthal

The home of Rubin Flood, his wife and two children, in a small Oklahoma town close to Oklahoma City. The time is the early 1920's.

ACT ONE. A Monday afternoon in early spring.
ACT TWO. After dinner, the following Friday.
ACT THREE. The next day, late afternoon.

---

the British Empire, including the Dominion of Canada, and all other countries of the Copyright Union and the Universal Copyright Convention, is subject to royalty. All rights, including professional, amateur, motion picture, recitation, lecturing, public reading, radio and television broadcasting, and the rights of translation into foreign languages are strictly reserved. Particular emphasis is paid on the question of readings, permission for which must be secured from the author's agent in writing. All inquiries should be addressed to the author's representative, Audrey Wood, c/o Ashley-Steiner, Inc., 555 Madison Avenue, New York 22, N. Y.

The amateur acting rights of *The Dark at the Top of the Stairs* are controlled exclusively by the Dramatists Play Service, 14 East 38th Street, New York 16, N. Y., without whose permission in writing no amateur performance of it may be made.

WILLIAM INGE is another playwright who needs no introduction to readers of the Best American Plays series. *The Dark at the Top of the Stairs* was the culmination of a series of successes that began modestly in 1950 with a notable Theatre Guild production of his "little" (by Broadway standards) but affecting drama of domestic infelicity, *Come Back, Little Sheba*. It was not his first play; he had attracted the present editor's interest twice before with plays that qualified more for regional than Broadway production. Despite his previous experience with the entertainment business as the drama and film reviewer for the St. Louis *Star-Times*, it took Mr. Inge, a very modest and quietly troubled man, a little time before he felt confident enough to enlarge his gambit. By then, however, he also allowed himself to be nudged by Main Stem production exigencies into accommodating his playwriting to popular appeal. This was evident in his first two substantial successes—*Picnic*, produced in 1953, which won him both the New York Drama Critics Circle Award and the Pulitzer Prize, and *Bus Stop*, produced in 1955.

Although not entranced with his public triumphs (he had mixed feelings about *Picnic* because, yielding to persuasion, he had substituted an "upbeat" romantic ending for the original "downbeat" one), Mr. Inge could not resist the almost irresistibly dynamic director Elia Kazan's positive response to a third play, *The Dark at the Top of the Stairs*, based on a modestly affecting early piece dealing with domestic troubles. Perhaps less seduction by Broadway expertise, which ensured great success, would have averted Louis Kronenberger's astute complaint that "No mood enveloped the play because it kept reverting to parlor comedy and domestic vaudeville . . . things that instead of deepening the serious scenes emphasized them too much by contrast." This may not, however, be as noticeable in a reading of the play and in a less Broadway-slanted production than the one Mr. Kronenberger, then reviewing for *Time*, had seen.

The expansion of the piece gave William Inge another hit and some of his friends, including the present editor, some qualms, especially concerning the facile resolution of the action and intensification of earlier scenes by an intrusive episode between the daughter of the family and a doubly-alienated young cadet. But enthusiasm greeted the play with hardly a reservation in most quarters, and the author, whose bent had been reflective, became that ideal of Broadway show business, a playwright with a reputation for having no failures. Naturally such a reputation could not be maintained without some interruption, and his plays *A Loss of Roses* and *Natural Affection* of the past three years had unsuccessful productions; at the same time, the mass media had marked him for their own purposes and laid claim to his services. It did not seem that he would be allowed to retreat into the shell from which he had hatched his most cherishable scenes and characterizations, of which there are not a few in *The Dark at the Top of the Stairs*.*

* For a recent appreciative yet critical estimate of Inge's recent work, especially the present play, the reader can consult the essay "William Inge and the Subtragic Muse" in John Gassner's *Theatre at the Crossroads* (1960), pages 167-173. Penetrative criticism will be found in Louis Kronenberger's paragraphs on the play in his yearbook, *The Best Plays of 1957-58*, published by Dodd, Mead & Co. in 1958, pp. 15-16.

ACT ONE

SCENE: *The setting for the entire play is the home of* RUBIN FLOOD *and his wife and two children, in a small Oklahoma town close to Oklahoma City. The time is the early 1920's, during an oil boom in the area. The house is comfortable and commodious, with probably eight or nine rooms. It is one of those square, frame houses built earlier in the century, that stand secure as blocks, symbols of respectability and material comfort.*

All we see of the FLOODS' *house is the living room, where the action of the play takes place. There is a flight of stairs at the far left. At the top of them is the upstairs hallway, which is not accessible to windows and sunlight. During the daytime scenes, this small area is in semi-darkness, and at night it is black. When the hallway is lighted, we can see the feet of the characters who happen to be there. We are conscious of this area throughout the play, as though it holds some possible threat to the characters.*

On the far right, downstairs, is the outside entrance, with a small hallway one must go through before coming into the living room.

In the middle of the living room is a wicker table and two comfortable wicker chairs, placed one on each side. Upstage center are sliding doors leading into the parlor, where we see a player piano. To the left of these doors and under the stairway, is a swinging door leading into the dining room. Extreme downstage left is a fireplace and a large comfortable leather chair. This area is considered RUBIN'S. *In the rest of the room are book shelves, a desk, a few small tables and portraits of* CORA FLOOD's *mother and father. Through a large window at the back, we see part of the front porch to the house, and can see characters coming and going.*

As for the atmosphere of the room, despite the moodiness of shadowy corners and Victorian (more or less) furnishings, there is an implied comfort and hospitality.

When the curtain goes up, it is a late Monday afternoon in the early spring, about five o'clock. Outside, the sun is setting, but the room is still filled with soft, warm light.

The stage is empty when the curtain rises. CORA *and* RUBIN *are both upstairs, he preparing to leave on a business trip.*

———

CORA (*off*). Rubin!

RUBIN (*off*). Yah!

CORA (*off*). How many times do I have to tell you to rinse your hands before you dry them on a towel! You leave the bathroom looking like a wild horse had been using it. (RUBIN *laughs.*) I can smell the bay rum clear over here. My! You're certainly getting spruced up!

RUBIN (*starting downstairs, carrying a suitcase. He is quite a good-looking man of thirty-six, still robust, dressed in Western clothes—a big Stetson, boots, narrow trousers, colorful shirt and string tie*). I gotta look good for my customers.

CORA (*calling down to him*). How long will you be gone this time?

RUBIN. I oughta be home end of the week. Saturday.

CORA (*calling down*). That's better than you usually do. Where will you be?

RUBIN (*goes to his corner, where he keeps his business paraphernalia*). I've made out my route for ya. I've left it on the mantel.

NEWSBOY (*calling into house from outside*). Hey, Mr. Flood. Jonsey says your tire's ready at the garage.

RUBIN. O.K., Ed, I'll be down to get it.

CORA (*coming downstairs*). Rubin, you've waited this long to go, why don't you wait now until morning? Here it is almost suppertime. You won't be able to see any customers tonight, no matter where you go. Wait until morning. I'll get up early and fix you breakfast. I'll fix you biscuits, Rubin.

RUBIN. I shoulda been out first thing this mornin'. Monday, and I'm just gettin' away. I can make it to Muskogee tonight and be there first thing in the mornin'. I can finish up by noon and then get on to Chicasha.

CORA. I wish you were home more, Rubin.

RUBIN. I gotta make a livin'.

CORA. Other men make a living without traveling all over the country selling harness.

RUBIN. The way other men make a livin' is *their* business. I gotta make mine the best way I know how. I can't be no schoolmaster like your old man was when he brung you all out here from Pennsylvania. I can't be no dentist like your brother-in-law Morris. I was raised on a ranch and thought I'd spend my life on it. Sellin' harness is about all I'm prepared for . . . as long as there's any harness to sell.

CORA (*with a trace of self-pity*). I envy women who have their husbands with them all the time. I never have anyone to take me any place. I live like a widow.

RUBIN. What do you want me to do? Give up my job and stay home here to pleasure you every day?

CORA (*she is often disturbed by his language*). Rubin! Don't say that.

RUBIN. Jesus Christ, ya talk like a man had nothin' else to do but stay home and entertain you.

CORA. Rubin! It's not just myself I'm thinking of. It's the children. We have a daughter sixteen years old now. Do you realize that? Yes. Reenie's sixteen. And Sonny's ten. Sometimes they act like they didn't have a father.

RUBIN (*sits at table to sharpen his knife*). You're always tellin' me how good they do at school. The girl plays the piano, don't she? And the boy does somethin', too. Gets up and speaks pieces, or somethin' like that? (*In* CORA's *sewing basket he finds a sock on which to wipe his knife.*)

CORA (*again she is shocked*). Rubin! Not on a clean sock!

RUBIN. Seems to me you all get along all right without me.

CORA. Rubin, I worry about them. Reenie's so shy of people her own age, I don't know what to make of her. She's got no confidence at all. And I don't know how to give her any, but you could. Her eyes light up like candles every time you go near her.

RUBIN (*a little embarrassed*). Come on now, Cora.

CORA. It's true . . . and the boy. Other boys tease him and call him names, Rubin. He doesn't know how to get along with them.

RUBIN. He ought beat the tar outa the other boys.

CORA. He's not like you, Rubin. He's not like anyone I ever knew. He needs a father, Rubin. So does Reenie. Kids need a father when they're growing up, same as they need a mother.

RUBIN. You din allus talk like that. God almighty, when those kids was born, you hugged 'em so close to ya, ya made me think they was your own personal property, and I din have nothin' to do with 'em at all.

CORA. Rubin, that's not so.

RUBIN. The hell it ain't. Ya pampered 'em so much and coddled 'em, they thought I was just bein' mean if I tried to drill some sense into their heads.

CORA. Rubin. Don't say that.

RUBIN. You're always kissin' and makin' over the boy until I sometimes wonder who's top man around here.

CORA. Rubin!

RUBIN. I just said I wonder.

CORA. If I kept the kids too close to me, it's only because you weren't there, and I had to have *someone* close to me. I had to have *some*one.

RUBIN. You're like an old mare Pa used to have on the ranch. Never wanted to give up her colts. By God, she'd keep 'em locked inside her and make all us men dig inside her with our hands to get 'em out. She never wanted to let 'em go.

CORA (*a little repelled by the comparison*). Rubin, I don't like what you just said.

RUBIN. Well, she was a good mare in every other way.

CORA. You talk shamefully at times.

RUBIN. Well . . . I got my own way of sayin' things and it's pretty hard to change.

CORA (*watching him primp before the mirror*). You like being out on the road, don't you? You like to pretend you're still a young cowboy.

RUBIN. It wasn't a bad life.

CORA. Rubin, there are ever so many things you could do in town. Mr. Binny down here on the corner makes a very good living just selling groceries to the neighborhood people. We could find a store like that, Rubin, and the kids and I could help you, too. You'd be happier doing something like that, Rubin. I know you would.

RUBIN. Don't tell me how t' be happy. I told you over and over, I ain't gonna spend my life cooped up in no store.

CORA. Or a filling station, Rubin. You could run a filling station or a garage . . .

RUBIN. God damn it, Cora. I don't mean

to have that kinda life. I just wasn't cut out for it. Now, quit pickin' at me. We been married seventeen years now. It seems t'me, you'd be ready t'accept me the way I am, or start lookin' for a new man.

CORA. I don't want a new man. You know that.

RUBIN. Then start tryin' to put up with the one you got.

CORA. I do try.

RUBIN. 'Cause he ain't gonna change. Kiss me g'bye. (*Playfully rough with her*) You come here and kiss me. (*He grabs her in a fast embrace, and they kiss.*)

CORA (*cautiously*). Rubin, you've got to leave me some money.

RUBIN. How much you gonna need?

CORA. Uh . . . could you let me have maybe twenty-five dollars?

RUBIN (*hitting the ceiling*). Twenty-five dollars? I'm only gonna be gone till Saturday.

CORA. I have a lot of expenses this week, and . . .

RUBIN. *I* pay the bills.

CORA. I take care of the utilities, Rubin. And we have a big gas bill this month, last month was so cold. And Reenie's invited to a big birthday party out at the country club. The Ralston girl, and Reenie has to take her a present.

RUBIN. Me? Buy presents for Harry Ralston's girl when he owns half this town?

CORA. I don't often ask for this much.

RUBIN (*taking a bill from his wallet*). Twenty's the best I can do.

CORA. Thank you, Rubin. The Ralstons are giving Mary Jane a big dance. (*Finding a button loose on his coat*) Here, let me fix that.

RUBIN. Cora, that'll be all right.

CORA. It'll only take a minute, sit down. (*They sit, and* CORA *takes needle and thread from her sewing basket.*) They're having a dance orchestra from Oklahoma City.

RUBIN. Harry and Peg Ralston puttin' on the dog now, are they?

CORA. Oh, yes. I hardly ever see Peg any more.

RUBIN. I guess they don't have time for any of their old friends, now that they've got so much money.

CORA. Anyway, they've asked Reenie to

the party, I'm thankful for that.

RUBIN. The country club, huh? By God, I'd die in the poorhouse 'fore I'd ever do what Harry Ralston done.

CORA. Now, Rubin . . .

RUBIN. I mean it. He shot hisself in the foot to collect enough insurance money to make his first investment in oil.

CORA. Do you believe all those stories?

RUBIN. Hell, yes, I believe it. I know it for a fact. He shot hisself in the foot. He oughta be in jail now. Instead, he's a social leader, givin' parties out at the country club. And I'm supposed to feel proud he invited my daughter. Hurry up.

CORA. I ran into Peg downtown during the winter. My, she was wearing a beautiful fur coat. Gray squirrel. And she was wearing a lot of lovely jewelry, too.

RUBIN. She's spendin' his money as fast as old Harry makes it.

CORA. Why shouldn't she have a few nice things?

RUBIN. They tell me they both started drinkin' now. They go out to those country club parties and get drunk as lords.

CORA. Peg didn't used to be like that.

RUBIN. They're all like that now. The town's gone oil-boom crazy. Chamber of Commerce says we're the wealthiest town per capita in all the Southwest. I guess they're not exaggeratin' much, either, with all this oil money, those damned Indians ridin' around in their limousines, gettin' all that money from the government, millions of dollars. Millions of dollars, and nobody knows what to do with it. Come on, hurry up now . . .

CORA (*finishing with the button*). Rubin, if you want to make an investment, if you should hear of something absolutely sure, you can take that money Mama left me when she died. Two thousand dollars, Rubin. You can make an investment with that.

RUBIN. There ain't no such thing as a *sure thing* in the oil business.

CORA. Isn't there?

RUBIN. No. Ya can make a million dollars or lose your ass overnight.

CORA. Rubin, you don't have to use words like that.

RUBIN. I do a good job supportin' ya, don't I?

CORA. Of course.

RUBIN. Then let's let well enough alone.

CORA. I was only thinking, it makes

you feel kind of left out to be poor these days.

(*Suddenly, from outside, we hear the sounds of young boys' jeering voices.*)

BOYS' VOICES.
Sonny Flood! His name is mud!
Sonny runs home to Mama!
Sonny plays with paper dolls!
Sonny Flood, his name is mud!

CORA. See, there! (*She jumps up nervously and runs outside to face her son's accosters.*) You boys run along. My Sonny hasn't done anything to hurt you. You go home now or I'll call your mothers, every last one of you. You should be ashamed of yourselves, picking on a boy who's smaller than you are.

(SONNY *comes running into the house now. It is hard to discern his feelings.*)

RUBIN (*follows* CORA *out to the porch*). Cora, cut it out.

CORA. I can't stand quietly by while they're picking on my boy!

RUBIN. It's *his* battle. He's gotta fight it out for hisself.

CORA. If they touch one hair of that boy's head I'll destroy them.

VOICE (*one last heckler*). Sonny Flood, his name is mud!

CORA. I'll destroy them. (CORA *re-enters the house.*)

VOICE. Sonny Flood, his name is mud.

RUBIN (*still on the porch*). Hey, come here, you fat butterball.

BOY. Hi, Mr. Flood.

RUBIN. How you doin', Jonathan? Let me see how you're growin'. (*He lifts the boy up.*) Gettin' fat as a pig. Say hello to your pa for me. (*The boy runs off and* RUBIN *comes back inside.*)

CORA. Sonny, did they hurt you?

SONNY. No.

CORA. What started it this time?

SONNY. I don't know.

CORA. Did you say anything to make them mad?

SONNY. No.

CORA. They're just jealous because you make better grades than they do. They're just jealous, the little beasts.

RUBIN. Son!

SONNY. Huh?

RUBIN. Want me to teach you how to put up a good fight?

SONNY (*turning away from his father*). I don't think so.

RUBIN (*to* CORA). What else can I do?

Buy him a shotgun?

CORA. There should be *something* we can do. *Something.*

RUBIN. Everybody's gotta figure out his own way of handlin' things, Cora. Whether he fights or whether he runs.

CORA. I hate for anything to make me feel so helpless.

RUBIN. I gotta be goin'.

CORA. Say good-bye to your father, Sonny.

RUBIN (*making a point of being friendly*). Good-bye, son.

SONNY (*diffidently*). G'bye.

RUBIN (*giving up*). Oh, hell.

CORA. Isn't there anything you can say to him?

RUBIN. Cora, if that boy wants me to help him, he's gotta come to me and tell me how. I never know what's on his mind.

CORA. You're just not interested.

RUBIN. Oh, hell, I give up. I plain give up. (*Exasperated,* RUBIN *bolts outside,* CORA *anxiously following him to the door.*)

CORA. Rubin . . . Rubin . . . (*We hear* RUBIN's *car drive off.* CORA *comes back inside.*) Why don't you listen to your father, Sonny? Why don't you let him help you?

SONNY. Where's Reenie?

CORA. She's downtown. Your father isn't here very often. Why don't you try and get along with him when he is?

SONNY (*wanting to evade the issue*). I don't know.

CORA. Most boys your age *worship* their fathers.

SONNY. I like him, all right. Where are my movie stars?

CORA. Forget your movie stars for a minute. You have a father to be proud of, Sonny. He and his family were pioneers. They fought Indians and buffalo, and they settled this country when it was just a wilderness. Why, if there was a movie about them, you couldn't wait to see it.

SONNY. Mom, it just makes it worse when you come out and tell those boys you're going to call their mothers.

CORA. You just won't listen to me, will you? You just won't listen to anyone. You're so set in your ways.

SONNY. I want my movie stars.

CORA. I put them in the book shelves

when I was straightening up this morning. The only pastime you have is coming home here and playing with those pictures of movie stars.

(SONNY *gets out his scrapbook and spreads it on the floor.*)

SONNY. I like them.

CORA. That's all the friends you have. Not real friends at all. Just *pictures* of all the lovely friends you'd *like* to have. There's a mighty big difference between pictures of people and the way people are.

SONNY. I like pictures.

CORA. Maybe you should get out and play with the other boys more often, Sonny.

SONNY. They play stupid games.

CORA. People distrust you if you don't play the same games they do, Sonny. It's the same after you grow up.

SONNY. I'm not going to play games just to make them like me.

CORA (*suddenly warm and affectionate*). Come to me, Sonny. I wish I understood you better, boy.

SONNY. I don't see why.

CORA (*caressing him*). No, I don't suppose you do. You're a speckled egg, and the old hen that laid you can't help wondering how you got in the nest. But I love you, Sonny. More than anything else in the world.

SONNY. Mom, can I go to a movie tonight?

CORA. You know the rules. One movie a week, on Friday night.

SONNY. Please, Mom. It's a real special movie tonight. Honest, I just *got* to see it.

CORA. Oh, I bet. It's always something special and you've just got to see it like your very life depended on it. No. You're supposed to study on week nights. Now, stay home and study.

SONNY. I've already got all my lessons.

CORA. You have to speak at Mrs. Stanford's tea party next Saturday. Why don't you memorize a new recitation?

SONNY. I can't find anything I like.

CORA. Oh! I found a cute little poem in the Oklahoma City paper this morning. It's about a little boy who hates to take castor oil. It starts off:
"Of all the nasty things, gee whiz!
I think the very worst there is . . ."

SONNY (*obviously bored*). I want to do something serious.

CORA. Serious! Like what?

SONNY. I dunno.

CORA. Goodness, it seems to me we've got enough serious things in the world without you getting up to recite sad pieces.

(*Outside the window, we see* FLIRT *and* REENIE *come onto the porch, giggling.*)

SONNY. I'm tired of all those stupid pieces you cut out of the papers.

CORA. My goodness! Aren't we getting superior! Oh, here's your sister, Sonny. Be a little gentleman and open the door for her.

REENIE (*sticking her head in through the door, asking cautiously*). Is Daddy gone, Mom?

CORA. Yes, he's gone. The coast is clear.

REENIE (*runs to* CORA *excitedly. She is a plain girl with no conscious desire to be anything else*). Oh, Mom, it's the prettiest dress I ever had.

CORA. Bring it in.

REENIE. Come on in, Flirt.

FLIRT (*enters carrying a large dress box. She is a vivacious young flapper of the era*). Hello, Mrs. Flood.

CORA. Hello, Flirt. (FLIRT *opens the box.*)

REENIE. And they took up the hem and took in the waist so that it fits me just perfectly now.

FLIRT. I think it's simply scrumptious, Mrs. Flood.

CORA. Thank you, Flirt. Hold it up, Reenie.

FLIRT. Yes, hold it up.

REENIE (*holding the dress before her*). Is Dad going to be awfully mad, Mom?

CORA. I told you, he's not going to know anything about it for a while, Reenie. He gave me some money before he left, enough for me to make a small down payment. My, I bet Flirt thinks we're terrible, plotting this way.

FLIRT. Shucks, no. Mama and I do the same thing.

REENIE. Oh, Mom. You should see the dress Flirt got.

FLIRT. It's all red, with spangles on it, and a real short skirt. It's just darling. Daddy says he feels like disowning me in it.

CORA. Did you buy your dress at Delman's, too, Flirt?

FLIRT (*she can't help boasting an advantage*). No. Mama takes me into Oklahoma City to buy all my clothes.

CORA. Oh!

SONNY (*feeling the dress*). Look, it's got stars.

REENIE (*snapping angrily*). Sonny, take your dirty hands off my new dress.

SONNY (*ready to start a fight any time REENIE is*). My hands are *not* dirty! So there.

REENIE. You make me mad. Why don't you go outdoors and play ball instead of staying in the house all the time, spying on everything I do. Mother, why don't you make him go out and play?

SONNY. It's my house as much as it's yours, and I've got as much right to be here as you do. So there!

CORA (*always distressed by their fighting*). Reenie. He only wanted to touch the dress. He likes pretty things, too.

FLIRT. Gee whiz, he hasn't done anything, Reenie.

CORA. Of course he hasn't. You kids are just antagonistic to each other. You scrap all the time.

SONNY. I hate you.

REENIE. I hate you, too.

CORA. Now stop that. Is that any way for a brother and sister to talk? I'm not going to have any more of it. Flirt, are you taking the Ralston girl a birthday present?

FLIRT. Mama got me a compact to give her. It's the only thing we could think of. She already has everything under the sun.

CORA. Yes, I suppose so. Her parents are so wealthy now. Well, I'll have to shop for something for Reenie to take her.

FLIRT. You know, my folks knew the Ralstons before he made all his money. Mama says Mrs. Ralston used to clerk in a millinery store downtown.

CORA. Yes, I knew her then.

FLIRT. And my daddy says that Mr. Ralston was so crazy to make money in oil that he shot himself in the foot. Isn't that awful?

SONNY. Why did he do that? (*REENIE goes into the parlor to try on her dress. SONNY sits at the table. FLIRT fascinates him.*)

FLIRT. So he could collect enough insurance money to make his first investment in oil. Did you hear that story, too, Mrs. Flood?

CORA. Oh, yes . . . you hear all kinds of stories about the Ralstons now.

FLIRT. And you know, some of the women out at the country club didn't want to give Mr. Ralston a membership because they disapproved of *her*.

CORA. Is that so?

FLIRT. But when you've got as much money as the Ralstons do, I guess you can be a member of *anything*. I just hate Mary Jane Ralston. Some of the boys at school think she's pretty but I think she's a *cow*. I'm not being jealous, either. I guess if I had as much money to spend on clothes as she does, I'd have been voted the prettiest girl in school, too. Anyway, I'm absolutely positive she peroxides her hair.

CORA. Really?

REENIE (*poking her head out between the sliding doors*). Are you sure?

FLIRT. Yes. Because she and I play on the same volley ball team in gym class, and her locker is right next to mine, and . . .

CORA (*reminding her of SONNY's presence*). Flirt!

FLIRT. Isn't it terrible for me to say all these things, when I'm going to her birthday party? But I don't care. She just invited me because she had to. Because my daddy's her daddy's lawyer.

SONNY (*as REENIE comes out of parlor wearing her new dress, he makes a grotesque face and props his feet on the table*). Ugh . . .

CORA. Oh, Reenie! it's lovely. Sonny, take your feet down. Let me see! Oh, Reenie. He did a fine job. Flirt! tell me more about the young man who's taking Reenie to the party.

FLIRT. He's a Jew, Mrs. Flood.

CORA. Oh, he is?

REENIE. Do you think it's all right for me to go out with a Jew, Mom?

CORA. Why, of course, dear, if he's a nice boy.

FLIRT. His name is Sammy Goldenbaum, and he comes from Hollywood, California, and his mother's a moving-picture actress.

CORA. Really?

REENIE. Flirt just found that out, Mom. I didn't know it before.

SONNY (*all ears*). A moving-picture actress!

FLIRT. Yes, but she just plays itsy-bitsy

parts in pictures. I saw her once. She played a real stuck-up society woman, and she was Gloria Swanson's rival. You see, they were in love with the same man, Thomas Meighan, and she told all these lies about Gloria Swanson to make people think Gloria Swanson wasn't nice, so she could marry Thomas Meighan herself. But Thomas Meighan found out all about it, finally, and . . .

REENIE. Mom, what's a Jewish person like?

CORA. Well, I never knew many Jewish people, Reenie, but . . .

FLIRT. I've heard that some of them can be awful fast with girls.

CORA. I'm sure they're just like any other people.

FLIRT (*dancing coquettishly about room*). They don't believe in Christianity.

CORA. Most of them don't.

REENIE. But do they act different?

CORA (*not really knowing*). Well . . .

FLIRT. My daddy says they always try to get the best of you in business.

CORA. There are lots of very nice Jewish people, Reenie.

FLIRT. Oh, sure! Gee whiz, of course.

REENIE. I don't know what to expect.

FLIRT. Kid, he's a *boy*. That's all you have to know.

CORA. There are Jewish families over in Oklahoma City, but I guess there aren't any here in town.

FLIRT. Oh, yes there are, Mrs. Flood. The Lewises are Jewish, only they changed their name from Levin so no one would know.

CORA. I guess I did hear that some place.

REENIE. Mom, I feel sort of scared to go out with someone so different.

FLIRT (*she never seems aware of her casual offensiveness*). Oh, you're crazy, Reenie. Gee whiz, I'd never go steady with a Jewish boy, but I'd sure take a date with one—if I didn't have any other way of going.

CORA. Now, Reenie, I'm sure that any friend of the Givens boy is nice, whether he's Jewish or not. And besides, his mother's a movie actress. Think of that.

FLIRT. Yes, but not a famous one.

CORA (*to* REENIE). Now, you have a nice date to the party, and a lovely new dress to wear. You can be sure you'll have a good time.

FLIRT. Gosh, yes! After all, a party's a party. And it's out at the country club, and they're having a swell dance orchestra from Oklahoma City, and they're giving favors. I can't wait. Fix your hair real cute and you'll look all right. (*Looks at her wrist watch.*) Oh, heck! I've got to go home.

CORA. Do you want to stay here for supper, Flirt?

FLIRT. No. It's my night to fix supper for the folks. My mother makes me fix supper once a week, cook's night out. She says it's good for me to learn something about home-making. Isn't that crazy? The only think I know how to cook is salmon loaf. I learned how to make it in domestic science class. I've made salmon loaf every Monday night now for the whole year. Kid, can you help me study for that stupid old civics test we're having next week?

REENIE. I guess so.

FLIRT. Civics! Why can't they teach us something in that old school that'd do us some good?

CORA. Good-bye, Flirt.

FLIRT. Good-bye, Mrs. Flood, good-bye, Reenie. Oh, Sonny, you come over to *my* house and play sometime. I know how to be nice to little boys.

CORA. Good-bye! (FLIRT *exits.*) Sonny, you've got to go to the store now if we're going to have anything for supper tonight.

SONNY. Mom! Can I get a candy bar?

CORA. Wouldn't you rather have the nickel to put in your piggy bank?

SONNY. No—I want a candy bar.

CORA. All right. If you promise not to eat it before supper.

REENIE. I want one, too. I want a nut Hershey.

CORA. Bring one for Reenie, too.

SONNY. She can get her own candy bar.

REENIE. He's mean, Mom.

SONNY. I don't care. She makes me mad, and I don't like her.

CORA. Sonny, she's your sister.

SONNY. I don't care. I don't like her. (*He exits.*)

CORA. Oh, God, some day you kids are going to be sorry. When you can't even get along with people in your own family, how can you expect to get along with people out in the world? (*Goes to the window and looks out, protectively.*)

Poor Sonny, every time he leaves the house, those neighborhood bullies pick on him. I guess they've all gone home now.

(REENIE *takes off her new dress and throws it on a chair.*)

REENIE. I don't know if I like Flirt or not.

CORA (*comes away from the window*). Why, what's the matter?

REENIE. The only reason she likes me is because I help her with her studies. (REENIE *goes into the parlor, gets her daytime clothes, and comes back into the living room to put them on.*)

CORA. Why do you say that?

REENIE. I just do.

CORA. You don't think *anyone* likes you, do you?

REENIE. Mom, maybe we shouldn't have bought the dress.

CORA. What?

REENIE. I mean it, Mom. Dad'd be awful mad if he knew.

CORA. I told you, he's not going to know.

REENIE. Won't he be here the night of the party?

CORA. No. And even if he were, he wouldn't notice the dress was new unless you told him about it.

REENIE. Just the same, Mom, I don't feel right about it.

CORA. Why don't you feel right?

REENIE. Because . . . the dress cost so much, and what good is it going to do me? I never have a good time at those dances, anyway. No one ever dances with me.

CORA. This time it's going to be different. You've got a new dress, and you've got a nice young man coming here all the way from California to be your escort. Think of it. Why, most young girls would be too excited to breathe.

REENIE. It's just a *blind* date.

CORA. What are you talking about?

REENIE. They give blind dates to all the girls in town that nobody else wants to take.

CORA. Daughter, I'm sure that's not so.

REENIE. Oh, Mom, you just don't know.

CORA. I do too.

RENNIE. Besides, he's Jewish. I never knew a Jewish boy before. I'm scared.

CORA. Daughter, you're just looking for excuses. You just don't want to go, do you? Reenie, don't you want to have friends?

REENIE. Yes, but . . .

CORA. You're not going to make friends just staying home playing the piano, or going to the library studying your lessons. I'm glad you're studious and talented, but those things aren't enough just in themselves.

REENIE. I don't want to talk about it any more.

CORA. You're going to have to talk about these things someday. Where are you going?

REENIE. To practice the piano. (*She goes into the parlor and starts playing scales.*)

CORA (*angrily impatient*). That's where you spend half your life, *practicing* at the piano. (REENIE *bangs on piano exasperatedly and exits to dining room.*) But will you get up and play for people so they'll know how talented you are? No. You hide your light under a bushel. You stay home and play behind closed doors, where no one can hear you except your own family. All you do is *pity* yourself at the piano. That's all. You go in there and pity yourself, playing all those sad pieces.

(REENIE *comes out of dining room, and calms herself by watering her plants.*)

REENIE. Mom, I just couldn't get up before an audience and play. I just couldn't.

CORA. Why couldn't you? What good is it for your father to have bought the piano? What use is it? (REENIE *begins to sob.*) Now, don't cry, Reenie. I'm sorry. (REENIE *goes into parlor and resumes her monotonous scales.* CORA *goes to telephone.*) Long distance? Give me three-six-oh-seven-J in Oklahoma City, please. (*There is a wait of several moments.*) Hello, Lottie. . . . Lottie, can you and Morris come over to dinner Friday night? I haven't seen you for so long, I want to talk with you, Lottie. I've just got to see some of my own flesh and blood. (*We hear* RUBIN's *car slam to a stop outside; the car door slams and then he comes stomping up to the front porch.*) Reenie's going to a big party out at the country club, and I thought I'd have a nice dinner first. . . . Rubin won't be here and I'll want company. Please come. Oh, I'm so glad. I'll be looking forward to seeing you.

RUBIN (*bursting into the house*). What the hell's been goin' on behind my back? (*Sees the innocent dress lying on a chair.*) There it is!

CORA (*her phone call over*). Rubin!

RUBIN (*displaying the dress as evidence*). So this is what ya wanted the extra money for. Fine feathers! Fine feathers! And ya buy 'em when my back is turned.

CORA. Rubin, we were going to tell you. . . .

RUBIN. A man has t'go downtown and talk with some of his pals before he knows what's goin' on in his own family.

CORA. Who told you?

RUBIN. That's all right who told me. I got my own ways a findin' out what goes on when my back is turned.

CORA. You didn't leave town at all. You've been down to that dirty old pool hall.

RUBIN. I got a right to go to the pool hall whenever I damn please.

CORA. I thought you were in such a hurry to get out of town. Oh, yes, you had to get to Muskogee tonight.

RUBIN. I can still make it to Muskogee. (*Finds the price tag on the dress.*) Nineteen seventy-five! Lord have mercy! Nineteen seventy-five.

CORA. Did Loren Delman come into the pool hall while you were there? Did he? Did he tell you? If he did I'll never buy anything in that store again.

RUBIN. That'd suit me just fine.

CORA. Oh, why couldn't he have kept his mouth shut? I was going to pay for the dress a little at a time, and . . .

RUBIN. "The finest dress I had in the store," he says, walkin' into the Arcade with a big cigar stuck in his mouth, wearin' a suit of fine tailored clothes. "I just sold your wife the finest dress I had in the store."

CORA. Oh, that makes me furious.

RUBIN. Jesus Christ, woman, whatta you take me for, one a those millionaire oil men? Is that what you think you're married to?

REENIE (*pokes her head in through parlor door, speaking with tears and anxiety*). I told you he'd be mad, Mom. Let's take the dress back, Mom. I don't want to go to the party anyhow.

CORA (*angrily impatient*). Get back in that parlor, Reenie, and don't come in

here until I tell you to. (CORA *slams the parlor doors shut.*)

RUBIN. See there! That girl don't even want the dress. It's *you*, puttin' all these high-fallutin' ideas in her head about parties, and dresses and nonsense.

CORA. Rubin, of course Reenie doesn't want to go to the party. She never wants to go any place. All she wants to do is lock herself in the parlor and practice at the piano, or go to the library and hide her nose in a book. After all, she's going to want to get married one of these days, isn't she? And where's she going to look for a husband? In the public library?

(RUBIN *goes to his corner, sits in his big leather chair, and draws a pint of whiskey out of his desk drawer.*)

RUBIN. I bought her a fine dress . . . just a little while back.

CORA. Oh, you did?

RUBIN. Yes, I did.

CORA. That's news to me. When?

RUBIN. Just a few months ago. Sure I did.

CORA. I certainly never saw it. What'd it look like?

RUBIN. It was white.

CORA. Rubin Flood, that was the dress you bought her three years ago when she graduated from the eighth grade. And she hasn't had a new dress since then, except for a few school clothes.

RUBIN. Why couldn't she wear the white dress to the party?

CORA. Because she's grown three inches since you got her that dress, and besides I cut it up two years ago and dyed it black and made her a skirt out of it to wear with a middy.

RUBIN. Just the same, I ain't got money to throw away on no party togs. I just ain't got it.

CORA. Oh, no. You don't have money when we need something here at home, do you?

RUBIN. I'm tellin' ya, right now I don't.

CORA. But you always have money for a bottle of bootleg whiskey when you want it, don't you? And I daresay you've got money for a few other things, too, that I needn't mention just at present.

RUBIN. What're ya talkin' about?

CORA. *You* know what I'm talking about.

RUBIN. The hell I do.

CORA. I know what goes on when you

go out on the road. You may tell me you spruce up for your customers, but I happen to know better. Do you think I'm a fool?

RUBIN. I don't know what you're talkin' about.

CORA. I happen to have friends, decent, self-respecting people, who tell me a few things that happen when you visit Ponca City.

RUBIN. You mean the Werpel sisters!

CORA. It's all right, who I mean. I have friends over there. That's all I need to say.

RUBIN. Those nosy old maids, the Werpel sisters! God damn! Have they been runnin' to you with stories?

CORA. Maybe you don't have money to buy your daughter a new dress, but it seems you have money to take Mavis Pruitt to dinner whenever you're over there, and to a movie afterwards, and give her presents.

RUBIN. I've known Mavis . . . Pruitt ever since I was a boy! What harm is there if I take her to a movie?

CORA. You're always too tired to take *me* to a movie when you come home.

RUBIN. Life's different out on the road.

CORA. I bet it is.

RUBIN. Besides, I din ask her. She come into the Gibson House one night when I was havin' my dinner. What could I do but let her join me?

CORA. She went to the Gibson House because she knew *you* were there. I know what kind of woman she is.

RUBIN. She's not as bad as she's painted. That poor woman's had a hard time of it, too.

CORA. Oh, she has!

RUBIN. Yes, she has. I feel sorry for her.

CORA. Oh, you do!

RUBIN. Yes, I do. Is there any law that says I can't feel sorry for Mavis Pruitt?

CORA. She's had her eye on you ever since I can remember.

RUBIN. Oh, shoot!

CORA. What happened to the man she left town with after we were married?

RUBIN. He ran off and left her.

CORA. For good reason, too, I bet. I also heard that she was seen sporting a pair of black-bottom hose shortly after you left town, and that you were seen buying such a pair of hose at the Globe Dry Goods Store.

RUBIN. By God, you got yourself a real detective service goin', haven't you?

CORA. I don't ask people to tell me these things. I wish to God they didn't.

RUBIN. All right. I bought her a pair of hose. I admit it. It was her birthday. The hose cost me sixty-eight cents. They made that poor woman happy. After all, I've known her ever since I was a boy. Besides, I was a li'l more flush then.

CORA. How do you think it makes me feel when people tell me things like that?

RUBIN. Ya oughtn'ta listen.

CORA. How can I help it?

RUBIN (*he has to stop to remember to call Mavis Pruitt by her full name, to keep* CORA *from suspecting too much familiarity between them*). There's nothin' 'tween me and Mavis . . . Pruitt . . . Mavis Pruitt, nothin' for you to worry about.

CORA. There's probably a woman like her in every town you visit. That's why you want to get out of town, to go frisking over the country like a young stallion.

RUBIN. You just hush your mouth. The daughter'll hear you.

CORA (*indulging in a little self-pity*). A lot you care about your daughter. A lot you care about any of us.

RUBIN. You don't think I care for ya unless I set ya on my knee and nuzzle ya.

CORA. What you need for a wife is a squaw. Why didn't you marry one of those Indian women out on the reservation? Yes. She'd make you rich now, too, wouldn't she? And you wouldn't have to pay any attention to her at all.

(SONNY *is seen coming onto porch.*)

RUBIN. All right. Maybe that's what I *shoulda* done.

CORA. Oh. So you want to throw it up to me!

RUBIN. Throw what?

(SONNY *quietly enters the room, carrying a sack of groceries.* CORA *and* RUBIN *are too far into battle to notice him.*)

CORA. You know what, Rubin Flood.

RUBIN. I don't know nothin'.

CORA. You never *wanted* to marry me.

RUBIN. I never said that.

CORA. It's true, isn't it?

RUBIN. I'm tellin' ya, it ain't.

CORA. It is. I've felt it all these years.

(SONNY *crosses and goes through the parlor into the dining room, still unobserved by* RUBIN *and* CORA.)

RUBIN. All right. If you're so determined to think it, then go ahead. I admit, in some ways I din wanna marry nobody. Can't ya understand how a man feels, givin' up his freedom?

CORA. And how does a woman feel, knowing her husband married her only because . . . because he . . . (CORA *now spots* REENIE *spying between the parlor doors. She screams at her.*) Reenie, get away from there!

RUBIN. None of this is what we was arguin' about in the first place. We was arguin' about the dress. Ya gotta take it back.

CORA. *I won't.*

RUBIN. *Ya will.*

CORA. Reenie's going to wear her new dress to the party, or you'll have to bury me.

RUBIN. You'll take that dress back to Loren Delman, or I'm leavin' this house for good and never comin' back.

CORA. Go on. You're only home half the time as it is. We can get along without you the rest of the time.

RUBIN. Then that's what you're gonna do. There'll be ice-cream parlors in hell before I come back to this place and listen to your jaw. (*He bolts into the hallway.*)

CORA. Get out! Get out and go to Ponca City. Mavis Pruitt is waiting. She's probably getting lonesome without you.

(SONNY *quietly enters from the dining room, and watches.*)

RUBIN. By God, Cora, it's all I can do to keep from hittin' you when you talk like that.

CORA (*following him into hallway, taunting him. Here they are both unseen by audience*). Go on and hit me! You wouldn't dare! (*But he does dare. We hear the sound of his blow, which sends* CORA *reeling back into parlor.*) Rubin!

(REENIE *watches from the parlor.* SONNY *is still in the living room.*)

RUBIN. I'll go to Ponca City, and drink booze and take Mavis to the movies, and raise every kind of hell I can think of. T'hell with you! (*He bolts outside.*)

CORA (*running to the door*). Don't you ever set foot in this house again, Rubin Flood. I'll never forget what you've said. Never! Don't you ever come back inside this house again!

(*We hear* RUBIN'S *car drive off now.*

CORA *returns to the living room, still too dazed to be sure what has happened.*)

SONNY. Gee, Mom. That was the worst fight you ever had, wasn't it?

CORA. How long have you been standing there, Sonny?

SONNY. Since he hit you.

REENIE (*coming forth*). Did he mean it about not coming back? Oh, Mom, why did you have to say all those things? I love Daddy. Why do you say those things to him?

CORA. Oh, God, I hate for you kids to see us fight this way.

SONNY. What did he mean, he didn't want to marry you?

CORA. You're not old enough to understand these things, Sonny.

SONNY. Did he hurt you, Mom. Did he?

CORA. I'm still too mad to know whether he did or not.

REENIE. I don't think he'll ever come back. What'll we do, Mom?

CORA. Now, don't worry, Reenie.

REENIE. Will we have to go to the poorhouse?

CORA. No, of course not. Now, quit worrying.

REENIE. But if Daddy doesn't come back?

CORA. I still have the money my mother left me, haven't I? And if worst comes to worst we can always go to Oklahoma City and move in with your Aunt Lottie and Uncle Morris.

SONNY (*jumping up and down in glee*). Goody, goody, goody. I wanta move to Oklahoma City.

REENIE. Listen to him, Mom. He's *glad* Daddy's gone. He's *glad.*

SONNY. I don't care. I wanta move to Oklahoma City.

REENIE. I don't. *This* is home. *This* is. And I don't want to move.

CORA. Now, children!

REENIE. I hate you.

SONNY. I hate you, too. So there! Oklahoma City! Oklahoma City! I wanta move to Oklahoma City!

CORA. Stop it! There's been enough fighting in this house for one night. Reenie, take your dress upstairs and hang it in the closet.

REENIE. I hate the old dress now. It's the cause of all the trouble. I hate it.

CORA. You do what I tell you. You take that dress upstairs and hang it in the closet. You're going to go to that party if I have to take you there myself. (REENIE *starts upstairs.*) The next time you're invited to a party. I'll let you go in a hand-me-down.

SONNY (*with the joy of discovering a new continent*). Oklahoma City.

CORA (*wearily*). I'll go out and fix supper, although I don't imagine any of us will feel like eating.

SONNY. I do. I'm hungry.

CORA (*a little amused*). Are you? Good. Come to me, Sonny! (*With a sudden need for affection*) Do you love me, boy? Do you love your old mom?

SONNY. More than all the world with a fence around it.

CORA (*clasping him to her*). Oh, God, what would I do without you kids? I hope you'll always love me, Sonny. I hope you always will. (REENIE *comes downstairs.*) Where are you going, daughter?

(REENIE *looks disdainfully at them, and marches into the parlor, where, in a moment, we hear her playing a lovely Chopin nocturne.*)

SONNY. Mom, I'm going to sell my autographed photograph of Fatty Arbuckle. Millicent Dalrymple said she'd give me fifteen cents for it. And Fatty Arbuckle isn't one of my favorites any more. If I sold the photograph, I'd have enough to go to the movie tonight and buy a sack of popcorn, besides.

CORA (*lying on the floor beside him*). If the world was falling to pieces all about you, you'd still want to go to the movies, wouldn't you?

SONNY. I don't see why not.

CORA. Your mother's unhappy, Sonny. Doesn't that mean anything to you?

SONNY. Well . . . I'm sorry.

CORA. I want you kids near me tonight. Can't you understand? Oh, God, wouldn't it be nice if life were as sweet as music! (*For a moment, mother and son lie together in each other's arms. Then* CORA *stands, as though fearing her own indulgence, and takes* SONNY *by the hand.*) Come! Help me set the table, Sonny.

CURTAIN

ACT TWO

SCENE: *At rise of curtain, we hear a banging rendition of "Smiles" coming from the parlor, where* LOTTIE *is at the piano,* SONNY *by her side, both singing in hearty voices.* REENIE *stands listlessly watching, drying a dish.* MORRIS *sits in* RUBIN'S *chair, working one of those baffling little hand puzzles, which has got the best of him.* LOTTIE *proves to be a big, fleshy woman, a few years older than* CORA. *She wears a gaudy dress and lots of costume jewelry.* MORRIS *is a big defeated-looking man of wrecked virility.*

LOTTIE *and* SONNY (*singing*). "There are smiles that make us happy . . ."

CORA (*coming into living room from kitchen*). I won't need you to help me with the dishes, Reenie. I want you to go upstairs now and get ready for your party. (*Calls into parlor.*) Sonny! Sonny!

MORRIS. Sure was a good dinner, Cora.

CORA. What, Morris?

MORRIS (*trying to make himself heard above the piano*). I said, it sure was a good dinner.

CORA. Thank you, Morris. Now go and get dressed, Reenie. (REENIE *reluctantly goes upstairs.*) Sonny! Sonny! Lottie, will you please stop that racket. A body can't hear himself think.

(LOTTIE *and* SONNY *finish the chorus.*)

CORA. Sonny, I said you've got to help me in the kitchen.

SONNY. Why can't Reenie?

CORA. She cleared the table for me, and now she has to bathe and get ready for her party.

SONNY. I have to do everything around here.

LOTTIE (*in the voice one uses to indulge a child*). I think it's a shame. (SONNY *and* CORA *exit into the dining room.* LOTTIE *comes into the living room. To* MORRIS) Cora always was jealous because I could play the piano and she couldn't. (*Looks to see if* CORA *is out of hearing distance.*) Do I have something to tell you! Do you know why she asked us over here? (*She hurries over to* MORRIS.)

MORRIS. For dinner.

LOTTIE. No! She and Rubin have had another fight. She told me all about it while I was in the kitchen helping her get dinner on the table.

MORRIS. What about, this time?

LOTTIE. About a new dress she bought for Reenie. But what difference does that make? They could fight about anything.

Only this time he hit her.

MORRIS. He did?

LOTTIE. Don't tell her I told you. Poor Cora. I guess maybe she has a hard time with Rubin.

MORRIS. Has Rubin walked out again?

LOTTIE. You guessed it. Do you know what she wants to do now, honey? She wants to bring the kids over to Oklahoma City to live *with us!* She says I suggested they do that some time ago. I guess maybe I did, but my God, I never thought they'd do it. We'd be perfectly miserable with her and the two kids living with us, wouldn't we, Morris? With only one extra bedroom, one of 'em would have to sleep on the davenport in the living room, and then what would happen when your patients started coming in the morning?

MORRIS. Yah. It wouldn't work out very well.

LOTTIE. No. Oh, my! The way she pampers those kids, Morris. If she had her way, she'd spoil 'em rotten.

MORRIS. What did you tell her, honey?

LOTTIE. Well, I haven't told her anything yet. I was so flabbergasted when she asked me, I just hemmed . . . (SONNY *enters the parlor to put away a big vase that* CORA *has just washed.* LOTTIE *sees him.*) Hi! Honey.

SONNY. They got me working again.

LOTTIE. I think it's terrible.

(SONNY *exits into the dining room.*)

LOTTIE. . . . and hawed until I could think of something to say. Oh, Morris, put away that puzzle and listen to me. She's going to come to you sometime this evening and ask you about it, and all you need to say is, "I'm leaving all that in Lottie's hands, Cora." Can you remember that? Just say it real nice, like it was none of your business.

MORRIS. I'll remember.

LOTTIE. You say you will, but will you?

MORRIS. Yes, honey.

LOTTIE. I don't know. You're so afraid of hurting people's feelings.

MORRIS. That's not so.

LOTTIE. Oh, it is too. Don't I know! You had to go to see some psychologist over in Oklahoma City because you were so afraid of hurting your patients when you drilled their teeth. Now, confess it. It was actually making you sick, that you had to drill your patients' teeth and hurt them.

MORRIS. Honey, I wasn't really *sick* about it.

LOTTIE. You were too. Now remember what I say. Don't get *soft-hearted* at the last minute and tell Cora to bring the kids and come on over. My God, Morris, we'd be in the loony bin in less than two days with them in the house. Cora may be my own flesh and blood but I couldn't live with her to save my life. And I love those kids of hers. I do, Morris. But I couldn't live with them. They'd drive me crazy. You, too. You know they would.

CORA (*enters the parlor to put napkins in the sideboard*). Almost finished.

LOTTIE. You shoulda let me help you. (*But* CORA *has returned to the kitchen.*) Cora said something to me about her getting a job at one of the big department stores over in Oklahoma City. Can you see her doin' a thing like that? I can't. "Cora," I said, "you wouldn't last two days at that kind of work, on your feet all day, taking people's sass." Well, I don't know if I convinced her or not, but I gave her something to think about. (*Sneaks back to parlor door to see if* CORA *is within earshot, then comes back to* MORRIS, *speaking in a very confidential voice.*) Morris? Do you think Rubin still plays around with Mavis Pruitt over in Ponca City?

MORRIS (*clamming up*). I don't know, honey.

LOTTIE. You do too.

MORRIS. I'm telling you, I don't.

LOTTIE. You men, you tell each other everything, but you all want to protect each other. And wild horses and screaming ravens couldn't get you to talk.

MORRIS. Well, whatever Rubin does . . . like that . . . is *his* business.

LOTTIE. My! Don't we sound righteous all of a sudden! Well, I bet anything he still sees her.

MORRIS. Well, don't you let on to Cora.

LOTTIE. I won't. Did I ever tell you about the first time she met Rubin?

MORRIS. Yes, honey.

LOTTIE. I did not! Cora and I were coming out of the five-and-ten. She'd wanted to buy a little lace to put on a dress. And here comes Rubin, like a picture of Sin, riding down the street on a shiny black horse. My God, he was handsome. Neither of us knew who he was.

But he looked at Cora and smiled, and Cora began to get all nervous and fluttery. And do you know what? He came by the house that very night and wanted to see her. Mama and Papa didn't know what to do. They stood around like they were afraid of Rubin. But Cora went out riding with him. He'd brought a buggy with him. And six weeks later they were married. Mama and Papa were worried sick. Rubin's people were all right, but they were ranchers. Kind of wild. And Cora only seventeen, not out of high school. I think that's the reason Papa had his stroke, don't you, Morris?

MORRIS. Maybe . . .

LOTTIE. I do. They just felt like Cora might as well be dead as married to a man like Rubin. But Cora was always a determined creature. Mama and Papa were no match for her when she wanted her own way.

MORRIS. Well, I like Rubin.

LOTTIE. I do, too, honey. I'm not saying anything against him. And he's made a lot better husband than I ever thought he would. But I'm glad *I'm* not married to him. I'd be worried to death all the time. I'm glad I'm married to a nice man I can trust.

(MORRIS *does not know how to respond to this endearment. He crosses the room troubledly.*)

MORRIS. What'll Cora do if Rubin doesn't come back?

LOTTIE. Well, that's not our problem, honey.

MORRIS. Yes, but just the same, I . . .

LOTTIE. Listen, she's got a nice big house here, hasn't she? She can take in roomers if she has to. And Mama left her two thousand dollars when she died, didn't she? Yes, Cora was the baby, so Mama left the money to her. I'm not going to worry.

REENIE (*upstairs*). Aunt Lottie!

MORRIS. All right. I was just wondering.

LOTTIE. Now, remember. All you've got to say is, "I'm leaving all that to Lottie, Cora."

MORRIS. Yes, honey.

(REENIE *comes downstairs looking somewhat wan and frightened.*)

LOTTIE. Shhhh! (*Now she turns to* REENIE *with a prepared smile.*) Well, honey, aren't you getting ready for your party? Morris and I are dying to see your new dress.

REENIE. I don't feel well. I wish I didn't have to go.

LOTTIE (*alarmed*). You don't feel well? Did you tell your mother?

REENIE. Yes. But she won't believe me. I wish you'd tell her, Aunt Lottie.

LOTTIE (*rushes excitedly into dining room, where we hear her speaking to* CORA). Cora! Reenie says she isn't feeling well. Cora, I think maybe she shouldn't go to the party. She says she doesn't want to go. Cora, what do you think is wrong?

CORA (*enters living room from dining room—followed by* LOTTIE). There's nothing wrong with the child, Lottie.

LOTTIE. But she says she isn't feeling well, Cora. (*Turns to* REENIE.) Come here, honey, let me see if you've got a temperature. No. Not a sign of temperature. Stick out your tongue. Are you sick at your stomach?

REENIE. Kind of.

LOTTIE. My God, Cora. Her little hands are like ice.

CORA (*quite calm and wise*). There's nothing wrong with the child, Lottie. She gets to feeling like this every time she goes to a party.

LOTTIE. She's not going to have a very good time if she doesn't feel well.

CORA. It's something she's got to get over, Lottie. Plans are already made now. I got her the dress and she's got a date with a boy who's come here all the way from California. Now, I'm not going to let her play sick and not go. The Ralston girl would never invite Reenie to another party as long as she lived if she backed out now.

(*Her strategy defeated,* REENIE *goes back up the stairs.*)

LOTTIE. It's awful funny when a young girl doesn't want to go to a party, don't you think so, Morris? (*She watches* REENIE's *departure, puzzledly.*) I just thought of something. I've got a bottle of perfume I'm going to give her. It's Coty's L'Origan. Finest perfume made. One of the big drugstores in Oklahoma City was having an anniversary sale. With each box of Coty's face powder, they gave you a little bottle of perfume, stuck right on top of the box. Morris, run out to the car and get me that package. It's on the back seat. I'll take it upstairs to Reenie. It'll make her feel good, don't you think?

CORA. That's very thoughtful of you, Lottie.

MORRIS (*on his way to door*). You'll have her smelling like a fancy woman.

LOTTIE (*with a sudden bite*). How do *you* know what a fancy woman smells like?

MORRIS. I can make a joke, can't I? (MORRIS *exits.* CORA *and* LOTTIE *sit on either side of the table.*)

LOTTIE. It was a wonderful dinner, Cora.

CORA. I'm glad you thought so. It all tasted like ashes to me.

LOTTIE. Oh, now, Cora, quit taking on.

CORA. Seventeen years we've been married, Lottie, and we still can't get along.

LOTTIE. What are you talking about? Why, I've known times when you got along just fine . . . for months at a time.

CORA. When Rubin was gone.

LOTTIE. Cora, that's not so.

CORA. Lottie, it's not good for kids to see their parents fighting.

LOTTIE. Cora, you've got the two nicest kids in the whole world. Why, they're wonderful children, Cora.

CORA. I worry about them, Lottie . . . You saw Reenie just now. Here she is, sick because she's going to a party, when most girls her age would be tickled to death. And the other boys tease Sonny so.

LOTTIE. Oh, Reenie'll get over that. So will Sonny.

CORA. Kids don't just "get over" these things, in some magic way. These troubles stay with kids sometimes, and affect their lives when they grow up.

MORRIS (*returns with a small package*). This what you want?

LOTTIE. Yes. Reenie—I've got something for you, Reenie. I've got something here to make you smell good. Real French perfume. Morris says it'll make you smell like a fancy woman. (*She goes running upstairs, exuding her own brand of warmth and affection.*)

CORA. Lottie's awful good-hearted, Morris.

MORRIS. She thinks an awful lot of your kids, Cora.

CORA. I know she does. Morris, I've been thinking, wouldn't it be nice if Sonny and Reenie could go to those big schools you have in Oklahoma City? I mean . . .

LOTTIE (*hurrying back downstairs*). Cora, I wish you'd let me curl Reenie's hair for her. I could have her looking like a real baby doll. I'm an artist at it. Last week, Morris took me to a party at the Shrine, and everybody told me I had the prettiest head of hair at the whole party.

CORA. Go on and do it.

LOTTIE. I can't right now. She's in the bathtub. When are you going to get your hair bobbed, Cora?

CORA. Rubin doesn't like bobbed hair.

LOTTIE. Oh, he doesn't! You like my bobbed hair, don't you, Morris?

MORRIS. It's all right, honey.

LOTTIE. I'll be darned if I'd let any man tell me whether I could bob my hair or not. Why, I wouldn't go back to long hair now for anything. Morris says maybe I should take up smoking cigarettes now. Would you believe it, Cora? Women all over Oklahoma City are smoking cigarettes now. Isn't that disgraceful? What in God's name are we all coming to?

CORA (*there is too much on her mind for her to partake now of* LOTTIE's *small talk*). I . . . I'd better finish up in the kitchen. (*She exits through the dining-room door.*)

LOTTIE. Morris, I don't know what to do. I just can't bear to see little Cora so unhappy.

MORRIS. After all, it's not your worry, honey.

LOTTIE. Oh, I know, but in a way it *is* my worry. I mean, I've always looked after Cora, ever since we were girls. I took her to her teacher the first day of school. I gave up the wishbone for her every time we had fried chicken. She was the baby of the family, and I guess we all felt we had to pamper her.

MORRIS. Honey, if you want to take in her and the kids, it's up to you. We'd manage somehow.

LOTTIE. Oh, God, Morris! Life'd be miserable.

SONNY (*enters through parlor*). Wanta see my movie stars, Aunt Lottie?

LOTTIE. I guess so, honey. (SONNY *goes into parlor to get scrapbook as* LOTTIE *turns to* MORRIS *with a private voice.*) Every time we come over here we've got to look at his movie stars.

MORRIS. Got any of Norma Talmadge?

SONNY (*spreading the scrapbook on the floor before them*). Sure.

LOTTIE. Norma Talmadge, Norma Talmadge! That's all you ever think about is Norma Talmadge. I don't know what you see in her. Besides, she's a Catholic.

MORRIS. Honey, you've just got a bug about the Catholics.

LOTTIE. Oh I do, do I! Maybe you'd like to marry Norma Talmadge someday and then let the Pope tell you what to do the rest of your life, making you swear to leave all your money to the church, and bring up all your children Catholic, and then join the Knights of Columbus and take an oath to go out and kill all the nice Protestant women when the day comes for the Catholics to take over the world.

(CORA *enters the parlor on her way to the sideboard, then wanders into the living room.*)

MORRIS. Honey, where do you pick up these stories?

LOTTIE. Well, it's the truth. Marietta Flagmeyer told me. Cora, Marietta has this very close friend who used to be a Catholic but isn't any more. She even joined a convent, but she ran away because she found out all those things and wouldn't stand for them. This friend told Marietta that the Catholics keep the basements of their churches filled with guns and all kinds of ammunition . . .

CORA (*she has heard* LOTTIE's *rantings before*). Lottie! (*She shakes her head hopelessly and returns to the parlor, on her way to the kitchen.*)

LOTTIE. . . . because some day they plan to rise and take over the world, and kill off all the rest of us who don't want to be Catholics. I believe every word of it, too.

MORRIS. Well . . . I still like Norma Talmadge. Got any of Bebe Daniels?

SONNY. Yes. (*He hands* MORRIS *a picture, which* LOTTIE *snaps up first for an approving look.*)

LOTTIE. I don't know what you see in her. (*She now passes the picture on to* MORRIS.)

MORRIS. You don't like any of the women stars, honey.

LOTTIE. I guess I don't. I hear they're all a bunch of trollops. (*To* SONNY) Honey, when is your daddy coming home?

SONNY. Oh, he's not coming back at all. He and Mom had a fight. Here's one of your favorites, Aunt Lottie. (*He hands her a picture.*)

LOTTIE. Who? Rudolph Valentino. He's not one of my favorites at all.

MORRIS. You saw *The Sheik* four times.

LOTTIE. That's just because Marietta Flagmeyer wanted me to keep her company.

MORRIS. Rudolph Valentino must be a Catholic, too. He's an Eyetalian.

LOTTIE. But he's not a Catholic. Marietta's friend has a book that lists all the people in Hollywood who are Catholics. (*She studies the picture very intently.*) You know, it scares me a little to look at him. Those eyes, that seem to be laughing at you, and all those white teeth. I think it's a sin for a man to be as pretty as he is. Why, I'd be scared to death to let a man like him touch me. (CORA *returns now, without her apron; she is carrying a paper bag.*) But you know, they say he's really a very nice man. Cora, do you know there's this woman over in Oklahoma City who worships Rudolph Valentino? That's the truth. Marietta knows her. She's made a little shrine to him down in her basement, and she keeps the room filled with candles and she goes down there every day and says a little prayer for him.

CORA. I thought you were going to fix Reenie's hair.

LOTTIE. Oh, yes. I guess she's out of the bathtub now.

CORA (*puts the bag on the table*). There's a lot of fried chicken left, Lottie. I brought you some to take home with you.

LOTTIE. Won't you and the kids want it?

CORA. They won't eat anything but the breast.

LOTTIE. Thanks, Cora.

CORA. Sonny, I don't want your pictures all over the floor when the young people come by for Reenie.

SONNY. All right.

MORRIS (*as* LOTTIE *takes a drumstick out of the bag*). Honey, you just ate.

LOTTIE. Don't scold me, Daddy. (*She whispers boldly to him before starting upstairs.*) Remember what I told you, Morris. (*Now she goes hurrying up the stairs.*) Reenie! I'm coming up to fix your hair. I'm going to turn you into a real baby doll.

REENIE (*upstairs*). I'm in here, Aunt

Lottie.

(MORRIS *draws over to the door, as though hoping to evade* CORA.)

CORA. Morris . . . Morris! I suppose Lottie told you what's happened.

MORRIS. Well, uh . . . yes, Cora . . . she said something about it.

CORA. I guess now that maybe my folks were right, Morris. I shouldn't have married Rubin.

MORRIS. You're going to forget all this squabble after a while, Cora. So's Rubin.

CORA. I don't think we *should* forget it. I don't think we should *try* to come back together. I think I've failed.

MORRIS. Now, Cora, I think you're exaggerating things in your own mind.

CORA. Morris, I'm only thirty-four. That's still young. I thought I'd like to take the kids to Oklahoma City and put them in school there, and get myself a job in one of the department stores. I know I've never done work like that, but I think I'd like it, and . . . it seems to me that I've got to, Morris. I've got to.

MORRIS. Well, Cora . . . maybe . . .

LOTTIE (*upstairs we see her feet treading the hallway*). Let's go into the bathroom, Reenie, where the light's better.

MORRIS. It's awful hard, Cora, being on your feet all day.

CORA. But I'd get used to it.

MORRIS. Well . . . it's hard for me to advise you, Cora.

CORA. Morris, I was wondering if maybe the kids and I could come and live with you and Lottie for a while. Just for a while. Until we got used to the city. Until I got myself a job and we felt more or less at home.

MORRIS. Well, I . . . uh . . .

CORA. I promise we wouldn't be any bother. I mean, I'd keep things straightened up after the kids, and do as much of the cooking as Lottie wanted me to do.

MORRIS. Well, I . . . uh . . .

CORA. I just don't know what else the kids and I can do, Morris.

MORRIS. Yes. Well . . . Cora, I don't know just what to say.

CORA. Would we be too much in the way, Morris?

MORRIS. Oh, no. Of course not, Cora. But . . .

CORA (*hopefully*). I think we could manage. And I'd pay our share of the bills. I'd insist on that.

(FLIRT, PUNKY and SAMMY *are seen through the window, coming onto the porch.*)

MORRIS. Well, Cora, I . . .

LOTTIE (*comes hurtling halfway down the stairs, full of anxiety*). Cora, Reenie's sick. She's vomiting all over the bathroom. (*She bustles back upstairs as* CORA *starts to follow.*)

CORA. Oh, my God! (*The doorbell rings, catching* CORA *for a moment.*) Oh, dear! It's the young people after Reenie. Sonny, put on your manners and answer the door. (SONNY *runs to the door, stopping to turn on the porch light before opening it. We see the three young people on the porch outside—*FLIRT *in dazzling party dress, and the two boys in uniforms from a nearby military academy. One boy,* PUNKY GIVENS, *is seen drinking from a flask, preparing himself to meet people. Inside,* CORA *starts upstairs in worried concern.*) Oh, dear! What could be wrong with the child? Morris, try to entertain the young people until I get back. (CORA *goes off.* SONNY *swings open the door.*)

SONNY. Won't you come in?

FLIRT (*comes dancing into the hallway, bringing the atmosphere of a chilly spring night with her*). Hi, Sonny! Is your sister ready?

SONNY. Not yet.

FLIRT. Oh, shucks! (*Sticks her head out the door.*) Come on in, fellows. We're going to have to wait. (PUNKY GIVENS *and* SAMMY GOLDENBAUM *make a colorful entrance. Both are dressed in uniforms of lustrous blue, which fit them like smooth upholstery.* FLIRT *begins the introductions.*) Sammy, this is Sonny Flood, Reenie's little brother.

(SAMMY GOLDENBAUM *steps forth correctly, his plumed headgear in his hand. He is a darkly beautiful young man of seventeen, with lustrous black hair, black eyes and a captivating smile. Yet, something about him seems a little foreign, at least in comparison with the Midwestern company in which he now finds himself. He could be a Persian prince, strayed from his native kingdom. But he has become adept over the years in adapting himself, and he shows an eagerness to make friends and to be liked.*)

SAMMY. Hi, Sonny!

SONNY (*shaking hands*). Hi!

FLIRT (*bringing* PUNKY *up from the rear*). And this is Punky Givens. (*She all but drags him from the dark corner of the hallway to face the lighted room full of people. For* PUNKY *is a disappointment as a human being. The military academy has done nothing as yet for his posture, and he wears his uniform as though embarrassed by its splendor. He offers a limp hand when being introduced, mumbles some incoherent greeting, and then retires in hopes that no one will notice him. These introductions made,* FLIRT *now notices* MORRIS.) Oh, hello! I'm Flirt Conroy. How're you?

MORRIS. How d'ya do? I'm Morris Lacey. Reenie's uncle. From Oklahoma City.

FLIRT. Oh, yes, I've heard her speak about you. Fellows, this is Dr. Lacey. He's Reenie's uncle. From Oklahoma City.

SAMMY (*crossing the room to present himself to* MORRIS, *he is brisk and alert, even though his speech betrays a slight stammer*). How do you do, sir? My name is G-Goldenbaum. Sammy, they call me.

MORRIS. Glad to know you, Sammy.

FLIRT. And this is Punky Givens. (*Nudging him*) Stand up straight, Punky.

MORRIS. Glad to know you, Punky. (PUNKY *mumbles.* MORRIS *now feels the burden of his responsibility as temporary host.*) Uh . . . anyone care for a Life Saver? (*He offers a pack from his pocket, but no one is interested.* LOTTIE *comes bustling down the stairs, eager to take over the situation, exuberantly babbling inconsequentials all the way down.*)

LOTTIE. Hello, everyone! I'm Lottie Lacey, Reenie's aunt. I'm Cora Flood's sister. From Oklahoma City. Oklahoma City's a great big town now. People say in another ten years it's going to be the biggest city in the whole United States, bigger even than New York or Chicago. You're the little Conroy girl, aren't you? I've heard my sister speak of you. My! What a pretty red dress. Have you all met my husband? Dr. Lacey. He's a dentist. Come over to Oklahoma City and he'll pull all your teeth. (*She laughs heartily, and then her eyes slowly widen at the magnificent uniforms.*) My goodness! Aren't those handsome getups?

SAMMY (*stepping forth*). How do you do, ma'am? I'm Sammy Goldenbaum. From California.

LOTTIE. Oh, yes. Cora told me about the yonng man from California. He's from Hollywood, Morris. His mother's in the movies. Has she played in anything I might have seen?

SAMMY. She was in T-Thomas Meighan's last picture. Her name is Gertrude Vanderhof. It was a very small part. She isn't a star or anything.

LOTTIE. Gertrude Vanderhof! Did we see Thomas Meighan's last picture, Morris? I don't believe so. I like Thomas Meighan, but we don't have time to see *all* the movies. Do you think you ever saw Gertrude Vanderhof in anything, Morris? (LOTTIE *seems to refer to her husband on every topic without waiting for his judgment. Nevertheless,* MORRIS *mulls over this last query as* FLIRT *interrupts.*)

FLIRT. Mrs. Lacey, have you met Punky Givens?

LOTTIE. How do you do? I've heard my sister speak of you. Your people are very prominent in town, aren't they? Yes, I've heard Cora speak of them. (PUNKY *offers a hand and mumbles.*) What did you say? (*He repeats his mumble.* LOTTIE *is still at sea but makes the best of things.*) Thank you very much.

(*At the top of the stairs, we see* REENIE's *feet trying to get up the courage to bring her down, and we hear* CORA *coaxing her.*)

CORA (*off*). Go on, Reenie.

(*But* REENIE *can't make it yet. The feet go scurrying back to safety.*)

LOTTIE (*trying to avoid embarrassment*). Well, I'm afraid you're all going to have to wait a few minutes. Reenie isn't quite ready.

CORA (*upstairs*). Reenie, not another word.

LOTTIE. Cora's upstairs now, helping her. I guess you'll have to entertain yourselves a while. Do any of you play mahjong? (*She notices the bag of fried chicken, and hides it under the table.*)

FLIRT. I want to play some music. Got any new piano rolls, Sonny?

SONNY. A few. (*They run into the parlor, to the piano.*)

FLIRT. Gee, I wish you had a Victrola like we do.

LOTTIE (*sitting, turning her attention to* SAMMY). My, you're a long way from home, aren't you?

SAMMY. Yes, ma'am.

LOTTIE. Morris and I went to California once. A Shriners' convention. Oh, we thought it was perfectly wonderful, all those oranges and things. Didn't we, Morris? I should think you'd want to go home on your spring vacation.

SAMMY. Well, I . . . I guess I don't really have a home . . . Mrs. Lacey.

(SONNY *wanders back from the parlor.* SAMMY *fills him with curiosity and fascination.*)

LOTTIE. Did you tell me your mother lived out there?

SAMMY. Yes, but, you see, she's pretty busy in moving pictures, and . . . Oh, she feels awfully bad that she doesn't have more time for me. Really she does. But she doesn't have a place where I could stay right now . . . and . . . But, it's not *her* fault.

LOTTIE. Where's your father?

SAMMY. Oh, I never knew him.

LOTTIE. You never knew your father?

SAMMY. No. You see, he died before I was born. My mother has been married . . . a few times since then. But I never met any of her husbands . . . although they were all very fine gentlemen.

LOTTIE. Well—I just never knew anyone who didn't have a home. Do you spend your whole life in military academies?

SAMMY. Just about. I bet I've been in almost every military academy in the whole country. Well, I take that back. There's some I didn't go to. I mean . . . there's some that wouldn't take me.

SONNY (*out of the innocent blue*). My mother says you're a Jew.

LOTTIE (*aghast*). Sonny!

SAMMY. Well . . . yes, Sonny. I guess I am.

LOTTIE (*consolingly*). That's perfectly all right. Why, we don't think a thing about a person's being Jewish, do we, Morris?

MORRIS. No. Of course not.

SAMMY. My father was Jewish. Mother told me. Mother isn't Jewish at all. Oh, my mother has the most beautiful blond hair. I guess I take after my father . . . in looks, anyhow. He was an actor, too, but he got killed in an automobile acci-

dent.

LOTTIE. That's too bad. Sonny, I think you should apologize.

SONNY. Did I say something bad?

SAMMY. Oh, that's all right. It doesn't bother me that I'm Jewish. Not any more. I guess it used to a little . . . Yes, it did used to a little.

LOTTIE (*who must find a remedy for everything*). You know what you ought to do? You ought to join the Christian Science church. Now, I'm not a member myself, but I know this Jewish woman over in Oklahoma City, and she was very, very unhappy, wasn't she, Morris? But she joined the Christian Science church and has been perfectly happy ever since.

SONNY. I didn't mean to say anything wrong.

SAMMY. You didn't say anything wrong, Sonny.

(*The piano begins playing "The Sheik of Araby" with precise, automatic rhythm.* FLIRT *dances in from the parlor.*)

FLIRT. Come on, Punky, let's dance. (*She sings.*) The Sheik of Araby—boom—boom—boom—his heart belongs to me. Come *on,* Punky.

SAMMY (*always courteous, to* LOTTIE). Would you care to dance, ma'am?

LOTTIE. Me? Good heavens, no. I haven't danced since I was a girl. But I certainly appreciate your asking. Isn't he respectful, Morris? (LOTTIE *exits to dining room.*)

SAMMY. Wanta wild West ride, Sonny? (*He kneels on the floor, permitting* SONNY *to straddle his back. Then* SAMMY *kicks his feet in the air like a wild colt, as* SONNY *holds to him tight.*)

FLIRT (*at the back of the room, instructs* PUNKY *in the intricacies of a new step*). No, Punky. That's not it. You take one step to the left and then *dip.* See? Oh, it's a wonderful step, and all the kids are doing it.

LOTTIE (*enters from kitchen with a plate of cookies, which she offers to* SAMMY *and* SONNY). Would you like a cookie?

SAMMY (*getting to his feet, the ride over*). Gee, that gets to be pretty strenuous.

(FLIRT *and* PUNKY *now retire to the parlor where they indulge in a little private lovemaking.*)

SONNY. Where did you get those clothes?

SAMMY. They gave them to me at the academy, Sonny.

FLIRT (*protesting* PUNKY'S *advances*). Punky, *don't.*

(LOTTIE *observes this little intimacy, having just started into the parlor with the plate of cookies. It rouses some of her righteousness.*)

SAMMY. No. I take that back. They didn't *give* them to me. They never give you anything at that place. I paid for them. Plenty!

SONNY. Why do you wear a sword?

SAMMY (*pulls the sword from its sheath, like a buccaneer, and goes charging about the room in search of imagined villains*). I wear a sword to protect myself! See! To kill off all the villains in the world. (*He frightens* LOTTIE.) Oh, don't worry, ma'am. It's not sharp. I couldn't hurt anyone with it, even if I wanted to. We just wear them for show.

SONNY (*jumping up and down*). Can I have a sword? I want a sword.

SAMMY. Do you, Sonny? Do you want a sword? Here, Sonny, I'll give you *my* sword, for all the good it'll do you.

LOTTIE (*to* MORRIS). Cora will probably buy Sonny a sword now. (*Now* SONNY *takes the sword and imitates the actions of* SAMMY. LOTTIE *is apprehensive.*) Now, you be careful, Sonny.

SAMMY. What do you want a sword for, Sonny?

SONNY (*with a lunge*). To *show* people.

LOTTIE. Sonny! Be careful with that thing.

SAMMY. And what do you want to show people, Sonny?

SONNY. I just want to *show* 'em. (*He places the sword between his arm and his chest, then drops to the floor, the sword rising far above his body, giving the appearance that he is impaled.* LOTTIE *is horrified.*)

LOTTIE. Oh, darling—put it down. Sonny, please don't play with that nasty thing any more.

(SONNY *rises now and laughs with* SAMMY. LOTTIE *puts the sword away in the parlor, where she again comes upon* FLIRT *and* PUNKY, *now engaged in more serious necking. Morally outraged, she runs up the stairs to inform* CORA.)

SAMMY (*kneeling beside* SONNY, *as*

though to make himself a physical equal*). What'll we do now, Sonny? Are there any games you want to play? Do you want to fight Indians? or set bear traps? or go flying over volcanoes? or climb the Alps?

SONNY (*eagerly*). Yes . . . yes.

SAMMY. Gee, so do I, Sonny. But we can't. Not tonight anyway. What else can we do?

SONNY. I can show you my movie stars.

SAMMY. I've had enough of movie stars. What else?

SONNY. I can speak a piece.

SAMMY. You can? (*Jumps to his feet.*) Hey, everyone! Stop the music. Sonny's going to speak a piece. (SAMMY *stops the piano, which* FLIRT *finds quite annoying.*)

LOTTIE (*hurrying downstairs*). Did you hear that, Morris? Sonny's going to speak a piece.

FLIRT (*to* SAMMY). Hey, what are you doing?

SAMMY (*to* SONNY). Where do you want to stand, sir?

LOTTIE. He's got a little platform in the parlor where he practices.

SAMMY (*having taken over as impresario*). Into the parlor, everyone. Into the parlor to hear Sonny speak his piece.

FLIRT (*pulling* PUNKY'S *arm*). Come on, Punky. Come on. We *have* to listen, don't we?

SAMMY. Quiet, everyone. Quiet!

(*All enter the parlor, except* MORRIS, *who crosses toward the door, as though he hoped to escape, as* SONNY *begins the famous soliloquy with boyish fervor.* MORRIS *looks as though he might share some of Hamlet's woes. After* SONNY *begins,* CORA *starts down the stairs with* REENIE.)

SONNY.

"To be, or not to be: that is the question:
Whether 'tis nobler in the mind to suffer
The slings and arrows of outrageous fortune,
Or to take arms against a sea of troubles,
And by opposing end them? To die: to sleep;
No more; and, by a sleep to say we end
The heart-ache and the thousand natural shocks
That flesh is heir to, 'tis a consummation
Devoutly to be wish'd. To die, to sleep;
To sleep: perchance to dream: ay, there's the rub,

For in that sleep of death what dreams
  may come
When we have shuffled off this mortal
  coil,
Must give us pause. . . ."

CORA (*while* SONNY *is reciting*). Oh,
Sonny's reciting. Why, he's reciting
Shakespeare. He must have gotten out
that dusty volume of Shakespeare over
in the bookcase, and memorized that
speech all on his own. (*Points to* SAMMY
in the parlor.) Reenie, there's your young
man. Isn't he handsome? Now you're going to have a good time. I can feel it in
my bones.

(SONNY *and* CORA *finish speaking at the
same time. There is immediate loud acclaim for* SONNY.)

SAMMY. That was *won*derful, Sonny.

(*All come into the living room now,*
SAMMY *carrying* SONNY *on his shoulders
like a triumphant hero.*)

LOTTIE. He's a second Jackie Coogan.

FLIRT. That was just wonderful, Sonny.

LOTTIE. Cora, you should have been
here. Sonny recited Shakespeare. It was
just wonderful.

CORA. Yes. I heard him.

SAMMY. Sonny's a genius. I'm going to
take you to Hollywood, Sonny, and put
you in the movies. You'll be the greatest
actor out there, Sonny.

FLIRT. Oh, I think Shakespeare's just
wonderful. I'm going to read him sometime, really I am.

CORA (*going to* SAMMY). Good evening,
young man. I'm Mrs. Flood.

SAMMY (*putting* SONNY *down*). Beg
your pardon, ma'am. I'm Sammy Goldenbaum.

CORA. Welcome. I see my son's been
entertaining you.

SAMMY. He sure has, ma'am.

CORA. He started speaking pieces about
a year ago. Just picked it up. Some people think he's talented.

SAMMY. I think so, too, ma'am. Very.

CORA (*brings* REENIE *forth*). Reenie!
Sammy, this is my daughter Reenie.

SAMMY. Good evening, Reenie.

REENIE (*reluctantly*). Good evening.

SAMMY. You certainly look nice. That's
a very beautiful dress.

FLIRT. Isn't it cute! I helped her pick
it out. (CORA *quietly grabs* FLIRT's *arm
and prevents her from taking over.*)
Ouch!

SAMMY. Gee! I didn't expect you to be
. . . like you are. I mean . . . well, Punky
told me you were a friend of Flirt's, so I
just naturally thought you'd be . . . well,
kind of like Flirt is. Although Flirt is a
very nice girl. I didn't mean to imply
anything against her. But . . . *you're* very
nice, too, in a different way.

REENIE (*still a little distrustful*). Thank
you . . .

SAMMY. Would you call me *Sammy?*

REENIE. Sammy.

SAMMY. And may I call you Reenie?

REENIE. I guess so.

SAMMY. It's awfully nice of you to let
me take you to the party. I know just how
a girl feels, going out with some crazy
guy she doesn't even know.

REENIE. Oh . . . that's all right. After
all, you don't know anything about me,
either.

SAMMY. You know, I've never been to
many parties, have you?

REENIE. Not many.

SAMMY. I always worry that maybe people aren't going to like me, when I go
to a party. Isn't that crazy? Do you ever
get kind of a sick feeling in the pit of
your stomach when you dread things?
Gee, I wouldn't want to miss a party for
anything. But every time I go to one, I
have to reason with myself to keep from
feeling that the whole world's against me.
See, I've spent almost my whole life in
military academies. My mother doesn't
have a place for me, where she lives. She
. . . she just doesn't know what else to
do with me. But you mustn't misunderstand about my mother. She's really a
very lovely person. I guess every boy
thinks his mother is very beautiful, but
my mother really is. She tells me in every
letter she writes how sorry she is that we
can't be together more, but she has to
think of her work. One time we were
together, though. She met me in San
Francisco once, and we were together
for two whole days. She let me take her
to dinner and to a show and to dance.
Just like we were sweethearts. It was the
most wonderful time I ever had. And
then I had to go back to the old military
academy. Every time I walk into the
barracks, I get kind of a depressed feeling. It's got hard stone walls. Pictures of
generals hanging all over . . . oh, they're
very fine gentlemen, but they all look so

kind of hard-boiled and stern . . . you know what I mean. (CORA *and* LOTTIE *stand together, listening to* SAMMY's *speech with motherly expressions.* FLIRT *is bored.* PUNKY *is half asleep, and now he gives a sudden, audible yawn that startles everyone.*) Well, gee! I guess I've bored you enough, telling you about myself.

CORA *and* LOTTIE. Oh, no. You haven't either.

FLIRT (*impatient to get to the party*). Come on, kids. Let's hurry.

SAMMY (*tenderly, to* REENIE). Are you ready?

CORA (*as though fearing* REENIE *might bolt and run*). Reenie?

REENIE. Yes.

SAMMY. May I help you into your wrap?

(*The word "wrap" is a false glorification of her Sunday coat, which he offers her, helping her into it.*)

REENIE. Thank you.

CORA (*whispering to* LOTTIE). I wish I could have bought her one of those little fur jackets like Flirt is wearing.

FLIRT. Stand up straight, Punky, and say good night to everyone.

(PUNKY *tries again, but remains inarticulate.*)

CORA (*assuming that* PUNKY *said good night*). Good night, Punky. Tell your mother hello for me.

FLIRT. Very pleased to have met you, Mr. and Mrs. Lacey. Good night, Mrs. Flood.

CORA. Good night, Flirt.

LOTTIE *and* MORRIS. Good night.

SONNY (*pulling at* SAMMY's *coat tails*). Do you have to go?

SAMMY. I'm afraid I do, Sonny.

SONNY. Can I go, too? Please? Can I go, too?

SAMMY. Gee, I don't know. (*He thinks a moment and then consults* FLIRT *and* PUNKY.) Hey, is there any reason Sonny can't come along? I promise to look after him. Think what a great time he'd have.

(FLIRT *and* PUNKY *look dubious.*)

SONNY (*takes his welcome immediately for granted and dances about the room joyously*). Goody, goody! I'm going to the party. I'm going to the party.

REENIE (*running to* CORA's *side*). Mother, I'm not going if Sonny goes too. Other girls don't have to be bothered by their little brothers.

CORA. I agree with you, daughter.

FLIRT (*she loves to lash out when she has a victim*). No. It's not a kids' party, Sammy. That was a stupid idea. I think you should mind your own business.

CORA (*trying to cool* FLIRT's *temper*). Now, Flirt.

FLIRT (*to* REENIE). He's always trying to boss everyone.

CORA (*to* SAMMY). I guess Sonny'd better not go.

SONNY (*crying, jumping in protest*). I want to go to the party. I want to go to the party.

SAMMY (*trying to be consoling*). I guess it was a pretty dumb idea, Sonny.

SONNY. I WANT TO GO TO THE PARTY! I WANT TO GO TO THE PARTY! (SONNY *flies into a real tantrum now, throws himself on the floor, pounding the floor with his fists and kicking it with his toes, his face red with rage.* CORA *and* LOTTIE *flutter about him like nervous hens.*)

CORA. Sonny! Sonny! Stop it this instant. Sonny, I'll not let you go to another movie for a whole month if you don't stop.

LOTTIE. Oh, what'll I do? Oh, here, Sonny, do you want a little cookie, sweetheart?

FLIRT. Now we'll never get there.

CORA. I never can do a thing with him when he throws one of these tantrums.

SAMMY (*quietly goes to* SONNY's *side and speaks in a voice that is firm with authority, yet still thoughtful and considerate*). Sonny, that's no way to behave.

SONNY (*suddenly quiet*). Isn't it?

SAMMY. No, Sonny. You mustn't ever act like that.

SONNY (*more reasonable now*). But I want to go to the party.

SAMMY. But if you act that way, no one's *ever* going to ask you to a party.

SONNY. Aren't they?

SAMMY. No, Sonny. You have to be a good boy before people ask you to parties. Even then, they don't always ask you.

SONNY. I love parties more than anything else in the world.

SAMMY. So do I, Sonny. I love parties, too. But there's lots of parties I can't go to.

SONNY. Honest?

SAMMY. Honest. It was wrong of me to

suggest that you go to the party tonight. You're not old enough yet. You'll be old enough someday though, and then you can go to all the parties you like.

SONNY. Can I?

SAMMY. Sure. Now, I tell you what I'll do. I'll gather up all the favors I can find at the party. Want me to? And I'll give them to your sister to bring home to you. And then you can have a party here all by yourself. Would you like that? You can throw a big party in Sammy's honor, without any old grown-ups around to interfere. Will that make you happy?

SONNY. Yes, yes.

SAMMY. O.K. Are we still buddies?

SONNY. Yes.

SAMMY. Forever and ever?

SONNY. Forever and ever. (SONNY *impulsively hugs him.*)

SAMMY. Gee! I love kids.

CORA (*awed as though by a miracle*). You're the first person in the entire world who's ever been able to do a thing with the boy when he goes into one of his tantrums.

SAMMY. You know, it's funny, but . . . I always seem to know just how kids feel.

FLIRT (*still impatient*). Come on, Sammy. (FLIRT *and* PUNKY *exit.*)

CORA. Good night, Sammy. I hope you'll be able to come back sometime.

SAMMY. Thank you, ma'am. It's very nice to feel welcome.

LOTTIE *and* MORRIS. Good night. Come over to see us sometime in Oklahoma City. It's a big town. You can stay in the extra bedroom. I hope you like cats.

CORA (*while* LOTTIE *and* MORRIS *are speaking*). Oh, Reenie, don't forget your present. You're feeling better now, aren't you?

REENIE. Yes, Mom.

SAMMY (*breaking away from* LOTTIE *and* MORRIS). Excuse me. (SAMMY *offers* REENIE *his arm now, and together they walk proudly out.*)

CORA (*after they exit*). Why, that's the nicest young man I ever met.

LOTTIE. I thought so, too, Cora. And my goodness, he was handsome. Morris says he felt sorry for him, though.

CORA. Sorry? Oh, Morris.

LOTTIE. He seemed like a perfectly happy boy to me. But Morris says he looked like a very unhappy boy to him. What makes you think that, Morris?

MORRIS. Oh . . . I don't know.

CORA. Unhappy? Why, he made himself right at home, didn't he?

LOTTIE. I should say he did. He was laughing and enjoying himself. But Morris says sometimes the people who act the happiest are really the saddest.

CORA. Oh, Morris.

LOTTIE. Morris, I think you make these things up. Ever since you went to that psychologist, you've gone around imagining everyone's unhappy. (MORRIS *quietly gets up and walks to the door, leaving* LOTTIE *to wonder if she has said anything wrong.*) Where are you going, Morris?

MORRIS. Thought I'd go out for a little walk, honey. (MORRIS *exits.*)

LOTTIE (*following him to the door*). Oh. Well, don't be gone long. We've got to get started back soon.

CORA. Oh, please don't talk about going.

LOTTIE. My God, Cora, we can't stay here all night. (*She peers out the window now, wondering about* MORRIS.) Morris is funny, Cora. Sometimes he just gets up like that and walks away. I never know why. Sometimes he's gone for hours at a time. He says the walk helps his digestion, but I think it's because he just wants to get away from me at times. Did you ever notice how he is with people? Like tonight. He sat there when all the young people were here, and he didn't say hardly a word. His mind was a thousand miles away. Like he was thinking about something. He seems to be always thinking about something.

CORA. Morris is nice to you. You've got no right to complain.

LOTTIE. He's nice to me . . . in *some* ways.

CORA. Good heavens, Lottie! He gave you those red patent-leather slippers, and that fox neckpiece . . . you should be grateful.

LOTTIE. I know, but . . . there's *some* things he hasn't given me.

CORA. Lottie! That's not his fault. You've got no right to hold that against him!

LOTTIE. Oh, it's just fine for you to talk. You've got two nice kids to keep you company. What have I got but a house full of cats?

CORA. Lottie, you always claimed you never wanted children.

LOTTIE. Well . . . what else can I say to people?

CORA (*this is something of a revelation to her*). I just never knew.

LOTTIE (*having suddenly decided to say it*). Cora . . . I can't let you and the kids come over and live with us.

CORA (*this is a blow to her*). Oh . . . Lottie.

LOTTIE. I'm sorry, Cora. I just can't do it.

CORA. Lottie, I was depending on you . . .

LOTTIE. Maybe you've depended on me too much. Ever since you were a baby, you've run to me with your problems, and now I've got problems of my own.

CORA. What am I going to do, Lottie?

LOTTIE. Call up Rubin and ask him to come back. Beg him to come back, if you have to get down on your knees.

CORA. I mustn't do that, Lottie.

LOTTIE. Why not?

CORA. Because we just can't keep from fighting, Lottie. You know that. I just don't think it's right, our still going on that way.

LOTTIE. Do you still love him?

CORA. Oh . . . don't ask me, Lottie.

LOTTIE. Do you?

CORA. Oh . . . yes.

LOTTIE. Cora, I don't think you should listen to the stories those old Werpel sisters tell you.

CORA. He's as good as admitted it, Lottie.

LOTTIE. Well, Cora, I don't think it means he likes you any the less, because he's seen Mavis Pruitt a few times.

CORA. No . . . I know he loves me.

LOTTIE (*asking very cautiously*). Does he still want to be intimate?

CORA. That's only animal, Lottie. I couldn't indulge myself that way if I didn't feel he was being honorable.

LOTTIE (*breaks into a sudden raucous laugh*). My God, a big handsome buck like Rubin! Who cares if he's honorable?

CORA (*a little shocked*). Lottie!

LOTTIE (*we see now a sudden lewdness in* LOTTIE *that has not been discernible before*). Cora, did you hear what the old maid said to the burglar? You see, the burglar came walking into her bedroom with this big, long billy club and . . .

CORA. Lottie!

LOTTIE (*laughing so hard she can hardly finish the story*). And the old maid . . . she was so green she didn't know what was happening to her, she said . . .

CORA. Lottie! That's enough. That's enough.

LOTTIE (*shamed now*). Shucks, Cora. I don't see what's wrong in having a little fun just telling stories.

CORA. Sometimes you talk shamefully, Lottie, and when I think of the way Mama and Papa brought us up . . .

LOTTIE. Oh, Mama and Papa, Mama and Papa! Maybe they didn't know as much as we gave them credit for.

CORA. You're changed since you were a girl, Lottie.

LOTTIE. What if I am!

CORA. I never heard such talk.

LOTTIE. Well, that's all it is. It's only talk. Talk, talk, talk.

CORA. Lottie, are you sure you can't take us in?

LOTTIE. It'd mean the end of my marriage too, Cora. You don't understand Morris. He's always nice and quiet around people, so afraid of hurting people's feelings. But he's the most nervous man around the house you ever saw. He'd try to make the best of it if you and the kids came over, but he'd go to pieces. I know he would.

CORA. Honest?

LOTTIE. I'm not joking, Cora. My God, you're not the only one who has problems. Don't think that for a minute.

CORA. A few moments ago, you said *you* had problems, Lottie . . .

LOTTIE. Problems enough.

CORA. Tell me, Lottie.

LOTTIE. Oh, why should I?

CORA. Doesn't Morris ever make love to you any more?

LOTTIE (*it takes her several moments to admit it*). . . . No. It's been over three years since he even touched me . . . that way.

CORA (*another revelation*). Lottie!

LOTTIE. It's the God's truth, Cora.

CORA. Lottie! What's wrong?

LOTTIE. How do I know what's wrong? How does anyone ever know what's wrong with anyone else?

CORA. I mean . . . is there another woman?

LOTTIE. Not unless she visits him from the spirit world. (*This releases her humor again and she is diverted by another story.*) Oh, say, Cora, did I tell you about this woman over in Oklahoma City who's been holding séances? Well, Marietta went to her and . . . (*But suddenly, again, she loses her humor and makes another sad admission.*) Oh, no there isn't another woman. Sometimes I wish there was.

CORA. Lottie, you don't mean that.

LOTTIE. How the hell do *you* know what I mean? He's around the house all day long, now that he's got his dental office in the dining room. Day and night, day and night. Sometimes I get tired of looking at him.

CORA. Oh, Lottie . . . I'd always felt you and Morris were so devoted to each other. I've always felt you had an almost perfect marriage.

LOTTIE. Oh, we're still devoted, still call each other "honey," just like we did on our honeymoon.

CORA. But what happened? Something must have happened to . . .

LOTTIE. Did you notice the way Morris got up out of his chair suddenly and just walked away, with no explanation at all? Well, something inside Morris did the same thing several years ago. Something inside him just got up and went for a walk, and never came back.

CORA. I . . . just don't understand.

LOTTIE. Sometimes I wonder if maybe I've been too bossy. Could be. But then, I always supposed that Morris *liked* me because I was bossy.

CORA. I always envied you, having a husband you could boss.

LOTTIE. Yes, I can boss Morris because he just isn't there any more to fight back. He doesn't care any more if I boss him or not.

CORA. Just the same, he never hit you.

LOTTIE. I wish he would.

CORA. Lottie!

LOTTIE. I do. I wish to God someone *loved* me enough to hit me. You and Rubin fight. Oh, God I'd like a good fight. Anything'd be better than this *nothing*. Morris and I go around always being so sweet to each other, but sometimes I wonder maybe he'd like to kill me.

CORA. Lottie, you don't mean it.

LOTTIE. Do you remember how Mama and Papa used to caution us about men, Cora?

CORA. Yes, I remember.

LOTTIE. My God, they had me so afraid of ever giving in to a man, I was petrified.

CORA. So was I.

LOTTIE. Yes, you were until Rubin came along and practically raped you.

CORA. Lottie! I don't want Sonny to hear talk like that.

LOTTIE. Why not? Let him hear!

CORA (*newly aghast at her sister's boldness*). Lottie!

LOTTIE. Why do we feel we always have to protect kids?

CORA. Keep your voice down. Rubin never did anything like that.

LOTTIE. Didn't he?

CORA. Of course not!

LOTTIE. My God, Cora, he had you pregnant inside of two weeks after he started seeing you.

CORA. Sssh.

LOTTIE. I never told. I never even told Morris. My God, do you remember how Mama and Papa carried on when they found out?

CORA. I remember.

LOTTIE. And Papa had his stroke just a month after you were married. Oh, I just thought Rubin was the wickedest man alive.

CORA. I never blamed Rubin for that. I was crazy in love with him. He just swept me off my feet and made all my objections seem kinda silly. He even made Mama and Papa seem silly.

LOTTIE. Maybe I shoulda married a man like that. I don't know. Maybe it was as much my fault as Morris'. Maybe I didn't . . . respond right . . . from the very first.

CORA. What do you mean, Lottie?

LOTTIE. Cora, I'll tell you something. Something I've never told another living soul. I never did enjoy it the way some women . . . say they do.

CORA. Lottie! You?

LOTTIE. Why do you say *me* like that? Because I talk kinda dirty at times? But that's all it is, is talk. I talk all the time just to convince myself that I'm alive. And I stuff myself with victuals just to feel I've got something inside me. And I'm full of all kinds of crazy curiosity about . . . all the things in life I seem to have missed out on. Now I'm telling you the truth, Cora. Nothing ever really happened to me while it was going on.

CORA. Lottie . . .

LOTTIE. That first night Morris and I

were together, right after we were married, when we were in bed together for the first time, after it was all over, and he had fallen asleep, I lay there in bed wondering what in the world all the cautioning had been about. Nothing had happened to me at all, and I thought Mama and Papa musta been makin' things up.

CORA. Oh, Lottie!

LOTTIE. So, don't come to me for sympathy, Cora. I'm not the person to give it to you.

(*Outside there is a low rumble of thunder.* SONNY *enters from the dining room with a cup of flour paste and his scrapbook.* MORRIS *returns from his walk, his face mysterious and grave.*)

MORRIS. We'd better be starting back now, honey. It looks like rain.

CORA. Oh, don't talk about leaving. Can't you and Lottie stay all night? I'd get up early and fix you breakfast. I'll fix you biscuits.

MORRIS. I can't, Cora. I got patients coming first thing in the morning.

LOTTIE. And I have to go home to let out the cats.

MORRIS. It was a wonderful dinner, Cora.

CORA. Thank you, Morris.

LOTTIE (*on a sudden impulse, she springs to her feet, hoists her skirt to her waist, and begins wrestling with her corset*). My God, I'm gonna take off this corset and ride back home in comfort.

CORA (*runs protectively to* SONNY, *and stands between him and* LOTTIE, *to prevent his seeing this display*). Sonny! Turn your head.

LOTTIE. My God! That feels good. (*She rolls the corset under her arm and rubs the flesh on her stomach in appreciation of its new freedom. Then she reaches for the bag of fried chicken.*) Thanks for the fried chicken, Cora. Oh, good! A gizzard. (*She brings out a gizzard to gnaw on.*) It was a wonderful dinner. You're a better cook than I am.

CORA. That's not so.

LOTTIE. Kiss me good-bye, Sonny.

SONNY. Good-bye, Aunt Lottie.

LOTTIE (*hugging him close*). Good night, darling.

MORRIS. That was a fine recitation, Edwin Booth.

SONNY. Thank you, Uncle Morris.

LOTTIE (*facing her husband with a bright smile, as though nothing but happiness had ever passed between them*). I'm ready, Daddy.

MORRIS. All right, Mama. Good of you to have us, Cora.

CORA. Glad you could come, Morris.

LOTTIE (*at the door, thinks of one last piece of news she must impart to her sister before leaving*). Oh, Cora! I forgot to tell you. Mamie Keeler's in the hospital.

MORRIS (*goes out on the porch now*). Looks like it's gonna rain any minute now.

CORA. What's wrong?

LOTTIE. Some kind of female trouble.

CORA. Oh . . . that's too bad.

(*But* LOTTIE *can tell by the sound of* CORA's *voice that she is too preoccupied now with her own worries to care about Mamie Keeler.*)

LOTTIE. Oh, God, Cora . . . I just can't go off and leave you this way.

CORA. I'll be all right, Lottie.

LOTTIE. Look, Cora . . . if you and the kids wanta come over and stay with us . . . we'll manage somehow . . .

CORA. Oh, thank you, Lottie. (*They embrace as though recognizing the bond of their blood.*) But I'm going to work this out for myself, Lottie.

LOTTIE. Good-bye, Cora.

MORRIS (*from outside*). It's beginning to rain, honey.

LOTTIE (*hurrying out the door*). Hold your horses, Morris. I'm coming. Don't be impatient now. (*They exit. Now* CORA *returns to the center of the room, feeling somehow deserted.*)

SONNY. It's always so quiet after company leaves, isn't it?

CORA. Hush, Sonny. I'm trying to think.

(*From outside, we hear the sound of* MORRIS' *car driving off, and then the sound of the rain and the wind.*)

SONNY. Let's move to California, Mom. Please, let's move to California.

(*But* CORA *has made a sudden decision. She rushes to the telephone.*)

CORA. Long distance. (*A moment's wait.*) This is Mrs. Flood, three-two-one. I want to talk to Mr. Rubin Flood at the Hotel Boomerang in Blackwell . . . Yes, I'll wait.

SONNY (*in an innocent voice*). I bet he

isn't there. I bet anything.

CORA. Hello? He isn't? Would you ask them if he's been there this week? (*A moment's wait.*) He hasn't! Oh . . . Well, please tell him, if he does come, to cal his family immediately. It's very important. (*A fallen expression on her face, she sits for a moment, wondering what next move to make. Then she hears a car approaching from the distance. She jumps up and runs to the window.*)

SONNY. It isn't Dad. I can always tell the sound of his car.

(CORA *comes back to the middle of the room.*)

CORA. Run along to bed now, Sonny. It's late. I have to go out and empty the pan under the ice box.

(CORA *goes out through the dining-room door.* SONNY *walks slowly, hesitantly, to the foot of the stairs and stands there, looking up at the blackness at the top. He stands there several moments, unable to force himself to go further. From the kitchen we hear* CORA's *muffled sobs.* SONNY *cries out in fear.*)

SONNY. Mom!

(CORA *returns now, not wanting* SONNY *to know she has been crying.*)

CORA. Sonny, I thought I told you to go upstairs (*She looks at him now and sees his embarrassed fear.*) Sonny, why are you so afraid of the dark?

SONNY. 'Cause . . . you can't see what's in front of you. And it might be something awful.

CORA. You're the man of the house now, Sonny. You mustn't be afraid.

SONNY. I'm not afraid . . . if someone's with me.

(CORA *walks over to him and takes his hand.*)

CORA. Come, boy. We'll go up together.

(*They start up the stairs to face the darkness hovering there like an omen.*)

CURTAIN

ACT THREE

SCENE: *It is the next day, late afternoon. Outside, there is a drizzling rain that has continued through the day.* REENIE *has not dressed all day. She sits by the fire in her robe, rubbing her* freshly *shampooed hair with a towel.* CORA *enters from the dining room, wearing a comfortable old kimono. She looks at the tray by* REENIE's *side.*

———

CORA. Reenie! Is that all you feel like eating?

REENIE. Yes.

CORA. But that's all you've had all day, Reenie. You don't eat enough to keep a bird alive.

REENIE. I . . . I'm not hungry, Mom.

CORA. Now quit feeling sorry for yourself, just because you didn't have a good time last night.

REENIE. Mom, is Dad coming back?

CORA. I don't know. I tried to call him last night but couldn't get him.

REENIE. Aren't you mad at him any more?

CORA. No . . . I'm not mad.

REENIE. Even though he hit you?

CORA. Even though he hit me. I was defying him to do it . . . and he did. I can't blame him now.

REENIE. Do you think he *will* be back, Mom?

CORA. This is the day he was supposed to come back. It's almost suppertime and he still isn't here.

REENIE. But it's been raining, Mom. I'll bet the roads are bad.

CORA. You love your father, don't you?

REENIE. Yes.

CORA. Well, I'm glad. The people we love aren't always perfect, are they? But if we love them, we have to take them as they are. After all, I guess I'm not perfect, either.

REENIE. You are too, Mom. You're absolutely perfect, in every way.

CORA. No, I'm not, Reenie. I . . . I have my own score to settle for. I've always accused your father of neglecting you kids, but maybe I've hurt you more with pampering. You . . . and Sonny, too.

REENIE. What do you mean, Mom?

CORA. Oh, nothing. I can't say anything more about it right now. Forget it. (*For some reason we don't yet know, she tries to change the subject.*) Are you feeling a little better now?

REENIE. I guess so.

CORA. Well, the world isn't going to end just because your young man went off and left you.

REENIE. Oh, Mom. It was the most

humiliating thing that ever happened to me.

CORA. Where do you think Sammy went?

REENIE. He went out to the cars at intermission time with some other girl.

CORA. To spoon?

REENIE. They call it *necking*.

CORA. Are you sure of this?

REENIE. Mom, that's what all the boys do at intermission time. They take girls and go out to the cars. Some of them don't even come back for the rest of the dance.

CORA. But are you sure Sammy did that? Did you see him?

REENIE. No, Mom. I just know that's what he did.

CORA. Wouldn't *you* have gone out to one of the cars with him?

REENIE (*with self-disparagement*). Oh. Mom.

CORA. What makes you say "Oh, Mom" that way?

REENIE. He wouldn't have liked *me* that way.

CORA. But why? Why not?

RENNIE. I'm just not *hot stuff* like the other girls.

CORA. Reenie, what an expression! You're pretty. You're every bit as pretty as Flirt or Mary Jane. Half a woman's beauty is in her confidence.

REENIE. Oh, Mom.

CORA. Reenie, I've tried to raise you proper, but . . . you're sixteen now. It's perfectly natural if a boy wants to kiss you, and you let him. It's all right if you *like* the boy.

REENIE (*a hesitant admission*). Oh . . . Sammy kissed me.

CORA (*quite surprised*). He did?

REENIE. On the way out to the party, in Punky's car. Flirt and Punky were in the front seat, Sammy and I in the back. Punky had a flask . . .

CORA. The little devil!

REENIE. Mom, most of those wealthy boys who go away to school are kind of wild.

CORA. Go on.

REENIE. Well, Punky and Flirt started necking, very first thing. Flirt, I don't mean to be tattling, but she *is* kind of fast.

CORA. I guessed as much. You aren't tattling.

REENIE. Well, Sammy and I felt kind of embarrassed, with no one else to talk to, and so he took my hand. Oh, he was very nice about it, Mom. And then he put an arm around me, and said . . . "May I kiss you, Reenie?" And I was so surprised, I said yes before I knew *what* I was saying. And he kissed me. Was it all right, Mom?

CORA. Did you like the young man? That's the important thing.

REENIE. Yes, I . . . I liked him . . . very much. (*She sobs helplessly.*) Oh, Mom.

CORA. There, there, Reenie dear. If he's the kind of young man who goes around kissing all the girls, you don't want to worry about him any more. You did right to leave the party!

REENIE. Did I, Mom?

CORA. Of course you did. I'm very disappointed in Sammy. I thought he was such a nice boy. But I guess appearances can be deceiving.

REENIE. Oh Mom!

CORA. There, there, dear. There are plenty of other young men in the world. You're young. You're not going to have to worry.

REENIE (*struggling to her feet*). Mom, I don't think I ever want to get married.

CORA. Reenie!

REENIE. I mean it, Mom.

CORA. You're too young to make a decision like that.

REENIE. I'm serious.

CORA. What makes you say such a thing? Tell me.

REENIE. I don't want to fight with anyone, like you and Daddy.

CORA. Oh, God.

REENIE. Every time you and Daddy fight, I just feel that the whole house is going to cave in all around me.

CORA. Then I *am* to blame.

REENIE. And I think I'd be lots happier, just by myself, teaching school, or working in an office building.

CORA. No, daughter. You need someone after you grow up. You need someone.

REENIE. But I don't want to. I don't *want* to need anyone, ever in my life. It's a horrible feeling to need someone.

CORA (*disturbed*). Daughter!

REENIE. Anyway, the only times I'm really happy are when I'm alone, practicing at the piano or studying in the library.

CORA. Weren't you happy last night when Sammy kissed you?

REENIE. I guess you can't count on happiness like that.

CORA. Daughter, when you start getting older, you'll find yourself getting lonely and you'll want someone; someone who'll hear you if you get sick and cry out in the night; and someone to give you love and let you give your love back to him in return. Oh, I'd hate to see any child of mine miss that in life. (*There is a moment of quiet realization between them. Then we hear the sound of a car drawing up to the house.* CORA, *running to the window, is as excited as a girl.*) That must be your father! No, it's Sonny. In a big limousine. He's getting out of the car as if he owned it. Mrs. Stanford must have sent him home with her chauffeur. (*She gives "chauffeur" its American pronunciation.* SONNY, *in his Sunday suit, bursts in to the house waving a five-dollar bill in his mother's face.*)

SONNY. Mom. Look, Mom! Mrs. Stanford gave me five dollars for speaking my piece. See? Five whole dollars. She said I was the most talented little boy she ever saw. See, Mom? Then she got out her pocketbook and gave me five whole dollars. See?

CORA. I declare. Why, Sonny, I'm proud of you, boy. That's the very first money you ever earned, and I'm very proud.

SONNY. And Mrs. Stanford sent me home with her chauffeur, too, Mom. (*He gives the word its French pronunciation.*) That's the way you're supposed to pronounce it, chauffeur. It's French.

CORA. If you spend any more time at Mrs. Stanford's, you'll be getting too high-hat to come home. (*She notices* REENIE *starting upstairs.*) We'll talk later, Reenie. (REENIE *exits.* CORA *again turns her attention to* SONNY.) Did you have anything to eat?

SONNY. Oh, Mom, it was just delicious. She had all kinds of little sandwiches. Gee, they were good. And cocoa, too, Mom, with lots of whipped cream on top, in little white cups with gold edges. Gee, they were pretty. And lots of little cakes, too, with pink frosting and green. And ice cream, too. I just ate and ate and ate.

CORA. Good. That means I won't have to get you any supper.

SONNY. No. I don't want any supper. I'm going to the movies tonight. And to the Royal Candy Kitchen afterwards, to buy myself a great big sundae with chocolate and marshmallow and cherries and . . .

CORA. Now, wait a minute, Sonny. This is the first money you've ever earned in your life, and I think you should save it.

SONNY. Oh, Mom!

CORA. I mean it. Five dollars is a lot of money, and I'm not going to let you squander it on movies and sundaes. You'll thank me for this some day. (*She takes his piggy bank from the bookcase.*)

SONNY. I will not. I will not thank you!

CORA. Sonny. (*She takes the bill from him and drops it into the bank.* SONNY *is wild at the injustice.*)

SONNY. Look what you've done. I hate you! I wanta see the movie. I've just gotta see the movie. If I can't see the movie, I'll kill myself.

CORA. Such foolish talk!

SONNY. I mean it. I'll kill myself.

CORA. Now, be quiet, Sonny. I want to have a little talk.

SONNY. Can I sell the milk bottles for money?

CORA. No! Now quit pestering me about the movies. You've already talked me into letting you see one movie this week. I have scarcely any money now, and I can't spare a cent. (SONNY *is badly frustrated. He finds the favors that* SAMMY *promised him, displayed on the settee. He throws a handful of confetti recklessly into the air, then dons a paper hat, and blows violently on a paper horn.*) Sonny! Stop that racket! You're going to have to clean up that mess.

SONNY. You won't let me have any fun at all.

CORA. The young man was very thoughtful to have sent you the favors. I wish he had been as thoughtful in other ways.

SONNY. Didn't Reenie have a good time at the party last night?

CORA. No.

SONNY. Serves her right. Serves her right.

CORA. Sonny! I'm not going to have any more talk like that. If you and your sister can't get along, you can at least have a little respect for one another. Now, come here, Sonny, I want to talk serious for a little while. (SONNY *taunts her with the horn.*) Will you go sit down?

SONNY. What's the matter? (*He sits opposite her at the table.*)

CORA. Nothing. I just want to talk a while.

SONNY (*suddenly solemn and apprehensive*). Have I done something bad?

CORA. Well, I don't know if you have or if I have. Anyway, we've got to talk about it. Sonny, you mustn't come crawling into my bed any more. I let you do it last night, but I shouldn't have. It was wrong.

SONNY. I was scared.

CORA. Just the same, that's not to happen again, Sonny. It's not the same when a boy your age comes crawling into bed with his mother. You can't expect me to mean as much to you as when you were a baby. Can you understand, Sonny? (*He looks away from her with unconscious guilt. She studies him.*) I think you're older in your feelings than I ever realized. You're a funny mixture, Sonny. In some ways, shy as your sister. In other ways, bold as a pirate.

SONNY. I don't like you any more at all.

CORA. Sonny!

SONNY. I don't care. You make me mad.

CORA (*going to him*). Oh, God, I've kept you too close to me, Sonny. Too close. I'll take the blame, boy. But don't be mad. Your mother still loves you, Sonny. (*But she sees that they are at an impasse.*) Well, we won't talk about it any more. Run along to the store now, before it closes. (*We see* FLIRT's *face in the door window. She is knocking on the door and calling for* REENIE. CORA *hurries to let her in.*) Flirt!

FLIRT (*rushing inside*). Where's Reenie? Reenie . . . Reenie. Oh, Mrs. Flood, I have the most awful news.

CORA. What is it, Flirt?

FLIRT (FLIRT's *face, her whole body are contorted by shock and confused grief*). Oh, it's so awful.

CORA. Tell me.

FLIRT. Is Reenie here? I've got to tell her, too.

CORA (*calls upstairs*). Reenie, can you come down? Flirt is here.

REENIE (*off*). I'm coming.

FLIRT. Oh, Mrs. Flood, it's the most

awful thing that ever happened in this town. It's the most awful thing I ever heard of happening anywhere.

CORA. Did something happen to you, or your family? . . .

FLIRT. No, it's Sammy.

CORA. Sammy? . . .

REENIE (*coming downstairs*). What is it, Flirt?

FLIRT. Kid! Sammy Goldenbaum . . . killed himself.

(*There is a long silence.*)

CORA. Where did you hear this, Flirt?

FLIRT. Mrs. Givens told me. The hotel people over in Oklahoma City called her about it just a little while ago. They found a letter in Sammy's suitcase Mrs. Givens had written him, inviting him to come home with Punky.

CORA. Oklahoma City?

FLIRT. He went over there last night after he left the party. He took the midnight train. That's what they figured out, because he registered at the hotel this morning at two o'clock.

CORA. How . . . did he do it, Flirt?

FLIRT (*hides her face in her hands as though hiding from the hideous reality of it*). He . . . Oh, I just can't.

CORA. There, there, honey.

FLIRT. Oh, I'm such a silly about things. He . . . he jumped out of the window . . . on the fourteenth floor . . . and landed on the pavement below.

CORA. Oh, my God.

FLIRT. Oh . . . it's really the most terrible thing that ever happened to me. I never did know anyone who killed himself before.

CORA. Does anyone have any idea what made him do it?

FLIRT. No! Punky says that he used to get kind of moody at times, but Punky never expected him to do anything like *this.*

CORA. Why did he go to Oklahoma City in the middle of the night?

FLIRT. No one knows that either . . . for sure. But one thing did happen at the party. He was dancing with Mary Jane Ralston . . . that cow . . . just before intermission . . . and Mrs. Ralston . . . she'd had too much to drink . . . comes out in the middle of the floor and stops them.

CORA. What for?

FLIRT. Well, you know how Mrs. Ralston is. No one takes her very serious even if she does have money. Anyway, she came right out in the middle of the floor and gave Sammy a bawling out . . .

CORA. A bawling out? Why?

FLIRT. She said she wasn't giving this party for Jews, and she didn't intend for her daughter to dance with a Jew, and besides, Jews weren't allowed in the country club anyway. And that's not so. They are too allowed in the country club. Maybe they're not permitted to be members, but they're certainly allowed as guests. Everyone knows that. (*She turns now to* REENIE, *who has sat numb in a chair since* FLIRT's *shocking announcement.*) Where were you when it all happened?

REENIE. I . . . I . . . (*But she is inarticulate.*)

CORA. Reenie wasn't feeling well. She left the party and came home.

FLIRT. The other kids told me Sammy was looking for you everywhere. He was going around asking everyone, Where's Reenie?

CORA. That . . . that's too bad.

FLIRT (*turning to* CORA). . . . But a thing like that isn't serious enough to make a boy kill himself, is it?

CORA. Well . . . he did.

FLIRT. An old blabbermouth like Mrs. Ralston?

CORA. She was a stranger to Sammy. She probably sounded like the voice of the world.

FLIRT. Gee . . . I just don't understand things like that. Do you know something else, Mrs. Flood? They called Sammy's mother way out in California, and told her, and I guess she was terribly sorry and everything, but she told them to go on and have the funeral in Oklahoma City, that she'd pay all the expenses, but she wouldn't be able to come for it because she was working. And she cried over the telephone and asked them please to try and keep her name out of the papers, because she said it wasn't generally known that she had a son.

CORA. There won't be anyone Sammy knows at the funeral, will there?

FLIRT. Mrs. Givens said Punky and his daddy could drive us over for it. Will you come, Reenie? (REENIE *nods.*) Do you wanta come, too, Sonny? (SONNY *nods.*) Well . . . it'll be day after tomor-

row, in the afternoon. We'll all have to get excused from school, Oh, gee, it all makes me feel so kind of *strange.* Doesn't it *you,* kid? I think I'll go to Sunday School tomorrow. Do you wanta go with me, Reenie? (REENIE *nods yes.*) Oh, I feel just terrible. (FLIRT *bolts out the front door, as though wanting to run away from all that is tragic or sorrowful in life.* CORA *keeps silent for several moments, her eyes on* REENIE.)

CORA. Where were you when Sammy went off?

REENIE (*twisting with grief*). Stop it, Mom!

CORA. Tell me. Where were you?

REENIE. Don't, Mom!

CORA (*commanding*). *Tell* me.

REENIE. I . . . was up in . . . the girls' room.

CORA. Where did you leave Sammy?

REENIE. As soon as we got to the party, Sammy and I started dancing. He danced three straight dances with me, Mom. Nobody cut in. I didn't think anybody was ever going to cut in, Mom. I got to feeling so humiliated I didn't know what to do. I just couldn't bear for Sammy to think that no one liked me.

CORA. Dear God!

REENIE. So I told Sammy there was someone at the party I had to talk to. Then I took him over to Mary Jane Ralston and . . . introduced him to her . . . and told him to dance with her.

CORA. Reenie!

REENIE. I . . . I thought he'd like her.

CORA. But you said that *you* liked Sammy. You told me you did.

REENIE. But, Mom, I just couldn't *bear* for him to think I was such a wallflower.

CORA. You ran off and *hid,* when an ounce of thoughtfulness, one or two kind words, might have saved him.

REENIE. I didn't *know.* I didn't *know.*

CORA. A nice young man like that, bright and pleasant, handsome as a prince, caught out here in this sandy soil without a friend to his name and no one to turn to when some thoughtless fool attacks him and he takes it to heart. (REENIE *sobs uncontrollably.*) Tears aren't going to do any good now, Reenie. Now, you listen to me. I've heard all I intend to listen to about being so shy and sensitive and afraid of people. I can't respect those feelings any more. They're nothing but selfishness. (REENIE *starts to bolt from the room, just as* FLIRT *did, but* CORA's *voice holds her.*) Reenie! It's a fine thing when we have so little confidence in ourselves, we can't stop to think of the other person.

SONNY (*who has been a silent listener until now*). I *hate* people.

CORA. Sonny!

SONNY. I *do.*

CORA. Then you're just as bad as Peg Ralston.

SONNY. How can you keep from hating?

CORA. There are all kinds of people in the world. And you have to live with them all. God never promised us any different. The bad people, you don't hate. You're only sorry they have to be. Now, run along to the store before it closes.

(SONNY *goes out, and finds himself again confronted by the jeers of the neighborhood boys, which sound like the voices that have plagued humanity from the beginning of time.*)

BOY'S VOICES.
Sissy Sonny!
Sonny Flood! His name is mud!
Sonny plays with dolls!
Sonny loves his mama!

(*Hearing the voices,* CORA *runs to the door, but stops herself from going further.*)

CORA. I guess I can't go through life protecting him from bullies. (*She goes to* REENIE.) I'm sorry I spoke so harshly to you, Reenie.

REENIE. He asked for *me* . . . for *me.* The only time anyone ever *wanted* me, or *needed* me, in my entire life. And I wasn't there. I didn't stop once to think of . . . Sammy. I've always thought I was the only person in the world who had any feelings at all.

CORA. Well . . . you're not, if that's any comfort. Where are you going, dear?

REENIE (*resignedly*). I haven't done anything to my room all day. I . . . I still have to make my bed. (REENIE *exits upstairs.*)

CORA (*calling after her*). It's Saturday. Change the linens. I put them in the attic to dry. (CORA *goes into the parlor to pull down the shades.* RUBIN *enters from the dining room. He is in his stocking feet, and is carrying several bags, which he drops onto the floor with a clatter.* CORA *comes running from the*

parlor.) My God!

RUBIN. I scare ya?

CORA. Rubin! I hate to be frightened so.

RUBIN. I din *mean* to frighten ya.

CORA. I didn't hear you drive in.

RUBIN. I didn't.

CORA. Where's the car?

RUBIN. It ain't runnin' right. Left it downtown at the garage. I walked home.

CORA. Why did you come in the back way?

RUBIN. Cora, what difference does it make if I come in the back way or the front way, or down the chimney? My boots was covered with mud. So I left 'em out on the back porch. I din wanta track up your nice, clean house. Now, wasn't that thoughtful of me?

CORA. Did you get my message?

RUBIN. What message?

CORA (*a little haughty*). Oh . . . nothing.

RUBIN. What message you talkin' about?

CORA. The route you left me said you'd be in Blackwell last night. I called you there, but . . . Well, I suppose you had better places to be.

RUBIN. That's right. I did. What'd ya call me for?

CORA (*hurt*). I don't know now. You'll be wanting a hot bath. I'll go turn on the water tank. (CORA *exits through dining-room door.* RUBIN *sits in his big chair and drops his face into his hands with a look of sad discouragement. Then he begins to unpack one of the bags, taking out small pieces of harness and tossing them on the floor. In a few moments,* CORA *returns.*) What made you decide to come back?

RUBIN. I lost my job.

CORA. What?

RUBIN. I said I lost my job.

CORA. Rubin! You've always sold more harness for the company than any of the other salesmen.

RUBIN. Yah. The on'y trouble is, *no* one's selling much harness today because no one's buyin' it. People are buyin' automobiles. Harness salesmen are . . . things of the past.

CORA. Do you mean . . . your company's going out of business?

RUBIN. That's it! You won the kewpie doll.

CORA. Oh, Rubin!

RUBIN. So that's why ya couldn't get me in Blackwell last night. I went somewhere else, regardless of what you were thinkin', lookin' for a job.

CORA (*a little embarrassed with regret*). Oh . . . I apologize, Rubin.

RUBIN. Oh, that's all right. You have to get in your li'l digs ev'ry once in a while. I'm used to 'em.

CORA. I'm really awfully sorry. Believe me.

RUBIN. I was in Tulsa, talkin' to some men at the Southwest Supply Company. They're hirin' lotsa new men to go out in the fields and sell their equipment.

CORA (*seizing her opportunity*). Rubin Flood, now that you've lost one traveling job, I'm not going to let you take another. You go downtown the first thing Monday morning and talk to John Fraser. He's bought out all the Curley Cue markets in town, and he needs men to manage them. He'd give you a job in a minute. Now, you do what I say, Rubin.

RUBIN (*he looks at her for several moments before getting to his feet*). God damn! I come home here t'apologize to you for hittin' ya. I been feelin' all week like the meanest critter alive, because I took a sock at a woman. My wife, at that. I walked in here ready to *beg* ya to forgive me. Now I feel like doin' it all over again. Don't you realize you can't talk to a man like that? Don't you realize that every time you talk that way, I just gotta go out and raise more hell, just to prove to myself I'm a free man? Don't you know that when you talk to a man like that, you're not givin' him credit for havin' any brains, or any guts, or a spine, or . . . or a few other body parts that are pretty important, too? All these years we been married, you never once really admitted to yourself what kinda man I am. No, ya keep talkin' to me like I was the kinda man you think I *oughta* be. (*He grabs her by the shoulders.*) Look at me. Don't you know who I am? Don't you know who I am?

CORA. Rubin, you're hurting me.

RUBIN. I'm takin' the job if I can get it. It's a damn good job, pays good money.

CORA. I don't care about money.

RUBIN. No, you don't! Not until you see Peg Ralston come waltzin' down the street in a new fur coat, and then you start wonderin' why old Rubin don't shoot hisself in the foot to make a lot of money.

CORA. Rubin, I promise you I'll never envy Peg Ralston another thing, as long as I live.

RUBIN. Did it ever occur to you that maybe I feel like a cheapskate because I can't buy you no fur coat? Did you ever stop to think maybe I'd like to be able to send my kids away to a fine college?

CORA. All I'm asking is for you to give them something of *yourself*.

RUBIN. God damn it! What have *I* got to give 'em? In this day and age, what's a man like me got to give? With the whole world so all-fired crazy about makin' money, how can *any* man, unless he's got a million dollars stuck in his pocket, feel he's got anything else to give that's very important?

CORA. Rubin!

RUBIN. I mean it, Cora.

CORA. I never realized you had such doubts.

RUBIN. The new job is work I've never done. Work I never even thought of doin'. Learnin' about all that goddamn machinery, and how to get out there and demonstrate it. Working with different kinds of men, that's smarter than I am, that think fast and talk sharp and mean all business. Men I can't sit around and chew tobacco with and joke with like I did m' old customers. I . . . I don't like 'em. I don't know if I'm *gonna* like them.

CORA. But you just said you wanted the job.

RUBIN. I don't like them, but I'm gonna join them. A fellow's gotta get into the swim. There's nothing else to do. But I'm scared. I don't know how I'll make out. I . . . I'm scared.

CORA. I never supposed you had it *in* you to fear.

RUBIN. I s'pose all this time you been thinkin' you was married to one a them movin'-pitcher fellas that jump off bridges and hold up trains and shoot Indians, and are never scared a nothin'. Times are changin', Cora, and I dunno where they're goin'. When I was a boy, there wasn't much more to this town than a post office. I on'y had six years a schoolin' cause that's all the Old Man thought I'd ever need. Now look at things. School buildin's, churches, fine stores, movie theatres, a country club. Men becomin' millionaires overnight, drivin' down the street in big limousines, goin' out to the country club and gettin' drunk, acting like they was the lords of creation. I dunno what to think of things now, Cora. I'm a stranger in the very land I was born in.

CORA (*trying to restore his pride*). Your folks pioneered this country.

RUBIN. Sometimes I wonder if it's not a lot easier to pioneer a country than it is to settle down in it. I look at the town now and don't recognize anything in it. I come home here, and I still have to get used to the piano, and the telephone, and the gas stove, and the lace curtains at the windows, the carpets on the floor. All these things are still *new* to me. I dunno what to make of 'em. How can *I* feel I've got anything to give to my children when the world's as strange to me as it is to them?

CORA (*with a new awareness of him*). Rubin!

RUBIN. I'm doin' the best I can, Cora. Can't ya understand that? I'm doin' the best I can.

CORA. Yes, Rubin. I know you are.

RUBIN. Now, there's a few more things I gotta say . . . I wanna apologize. I'm sorry I hit ya, Cora. I'm awful sorry.

CORA. I know I provoked you, Rubin.

RUBIN. You provoked me, but . . . I still shouldn'ta hit ya. It wasn't manly.

CORA. I'm not holding it against you, Rubin.

RUBIN. And I'm sorry I made such a fuss about you gettin' the girl a new dress. But I was awful worried about losin' my job then, and I din have much money left in the bank.

CORA. Rubin, if I'd known that, I wouldn't have *thought* of buying the dress. You should have told me, Rubin.

RUBIN. I din wanta make you worry, too.

CORA. But that's what I'm for.

RUBIN. That's all I gotta say, Cora, except that . . . I love ya. You're a good woman and I couldn't git along without you.

CORA. I love you, too, Rubin. And I couldn't get along without you another day.

RUBIN. You're clean, and dainty. Give a man a feeling of decency . . . and order . . . and respect.

CORA. Thank you, Rubin.

RUBIN. Just don't get the idea you can rearrange *me* like ya do the house, whenever ya wanta put it in order.

CORA. I'll remember. (*There is a short silence between them now, filled with new understanding.*) When you have fears about things, please tell me, Rubin.

RUBIN. It's hard for a man t'admit his fears, even to hisself.

CORA. Why? Why?

RUBIN. He's always afraid of endin' up like . . . like your brother-in-law Morris.

CORA. Oh! (CORA *has a new appreciation of him. She runs to him, throwing her arms about him in a fast embrace. A glow of satisfaction radiates from* RUBIN, *to have his woman back in his arms.*)

RUBIN. Oh, my goodness. (RUBIN *carries* CORA *center, where they sit like honeymooners, she on his lap; and he kisses her.* SONNY *returns now with a sack of groceries, and stands staring at his parents until they become aware of him.*) H'lo, son.

SONNY. Hi!

CORA. Take the groceries to the kitchen, Sonny. (*Obediently,* SONNY *starts for the dining-room door.*) Rubin, Mrs. Stanford paid Sonny five dollars this afternoon for speaking a piece at her tea party.

RUBIN. I'll be damned. He'll be makin' more money than his Old Man.

(SONNY *exits now through dining-room door.*)

CORA. Be nice to him, Rubin. Show him you want to be his friend.

RUBIN. I'm nice to that boy, ain't I?

CORA. Sometimes you do talk awfully rough and bad-natured.

RUBIN. Well . . . *life's* rough. *Life's* bad-natured.

CORA. I know. And I keep trying to pretend it isn't.

RUBIN. I'll remind ya.

CORA. Every time I see the kids go out of the house, I worry . . . like I was watching them go out into life, and they seem so young and helpless.

RUBIN. But ya gotta let 'em go, Cora. Ya can't hold 'em.

CORA. I've always felt I could give them life like a present, all wrapped in white, with every promise of happiness inside.

RUBIN. That ain't the way it works.

CORA. No. All I can promise them is life itself. (*With this realization, she gets off* RUBIN'S *lap.*) I'd better go to the kitchen and put the groceries away.

RUBIN (*grabs her to him, not willing to let her go*). T'hell with the groceries!

CORA (*a maidenly protest*). Rubin!

RUBIN (*caressing her*). Is there any chance of us bein' alone t'night?

CORA (*secretively*). I think Reenie plans to go to the library. If you give Sonny a dime, I'm sure he'll go to the movies.

RUBIN. It's a deal. (*He tries again to re-engage her in lovemaking.*)

CORA. Now, Rubin, be patient. (*She exits through the dining-room door as REENIE comes running downstairs.*)

REENIE. Did I hear Daddy?

RUBIN. Hello, daughter.

REENIE (*she runs into his arms and he lifts her high in the air*). Oh, Daddy!

RUBIN. Well, how's my girl?

REENIE. I feel better now that you're home, Daddy.

RUBIN. Thank ya, daughter.

REENIE. I've been practicing a new piece, Daddy. It's Chopin. Do you want me to play it for you?

RUBIN. Sure. I like sweet music same as anyone.

REENIE. I can't play it quite perfect yet, but almost. (*REENIE goes into parlor and in a moment we hear another wistful piece by Chopin.*)

RUBIN. That's all right. (SONNY *now returns and stands far right. RUBIN, center, faces him. They look at each other with wonder and just a little resentment. But RUBIN goes to SONNY, making the effort to offer himself.*) Son, your mom tells me you do real well, goin' around speaking pieces, gettin' to be a reg'lar Jackie Coogan. I got a customer has a daughter does real well at that kinda thing. Gets up before people and whistles.

SONNY. Whistles?

RUBIN. Yah! Like birds. Every kinda bird ya ever heard of. Maybe you'd like to meet her sometime.

SONNY. Oh, maybe.

(RUBIN *feels himself on uncertain ground with his son.*)

RUBIN. Your mom said maybe you'd like to go to the movie tonight. I guess I could spare you the money. (*He digs into his pocket.*)

SONNY. I've changed my mind. I don't want to now. (SONNY *turns from his father.*)

RUBIN (*looks at his son as though realizing sadly the breach between them. With a feeling of failure, he puts a warm hand on* SONNY's *shoulder*). Oh! Well, I ain't gonna argue. (*He walks out, and as he passes the parlor, he speaks to* REENIE.) That's real purty, daughter.

REENIE. Thank you, Daddy.

RUBIN (*opens dining-room door and speaks to* CORA). Cora, those kids ain't goin' to the movies. Come on now.

CORA (*off*). I'll be up in a minute, Rubin.

RUBIN (*closing the door behind him, speaking to* REENIE *and* SONNY). I'm goin' upstairs now, and have my bath.

(REENIE *and* SONNY *watch him all the way as he goes upstairs.*)

SONNY. They always want to be alone.

REENIE. All married people do, crazy.

(SONNY *impulsively sticks out his tongue at her. But she ignores him, picking up one of the favors, a reminder of* SAMMY, *and fondling it tenderly.* SONNY *begins to feel regret.*)

SONNY. I'm sorry I made a face at you, Reenie.

REENIE (*sobbing softly*). Go on and make as many faces as you like. I'm not going to fight with you any more.

SONNY. Don't cry, Reenie.

REENIE. I didn't know Sammy had even remembered the favors until I started to go. Then I went to find my coat, and there they were, sticking out of my pocket. At the very moment he was putting them there . . . he must have had in mind doing what he did.

SONNY (*with a burst of new generosity*). You! You keep the favors, Reenie.

REENIE. He promised them to *you.*

SONNY. Just the same . . . *you* keep them, Reenie.

REENIE. Do you mean it?

SONNY. Yes.

REENIE. You never were thoughtful like this . . . before.

(CORA *comes through the dining-room door now, hears the children's plans, and stands unobserved, listening.*)

SONNY. Reenie, do you want to go to the movie tonight? It's Mae Murray in *Fascination,* and there's an *Our Gang Comedy* first.

REENIE. I don't feel I should.

SONNY. When I feel bad, I just *have* to go to the movies. I just *have* to.

REENIE. I was supposed to go to the

library tonight.

SONNY. Please go with me, Reenie. Please.

REENIE. Do you really want me?

SONNY. Yes, Reenie. Yes.

REENIE. Where would you get the money to take *me*, Sonny? I have to pay adult admission. It's thirty-five cents.

SONNY. I've got all the money we'll need. (*He runs for his piggy bank as* CORA *makes a quick return to the dining room.*)

REENIE. Sonny! Mother told you you had to save that money.

SONNY. I don't care. She's not going to boss me for the rest of my life. It's *my* money, and I've got a right to spend it. (*With a heroic gesture of defiance, he throws the piggy bank smashing against the fireplace, its pieces scattering on the floor.*)

REENIE. Sonny!

SONNY (*finding his five-dollar bill in the rubble*). And we'll have enough for popcorn, too, and for ice cream afterwards at the Royal Candy Kitchen.

(*Now we see* CORA *in the parlor again, a silent witness.*)

REENIE. I feel very proud to be treated by my little brother.

SONNY. Let's hurry. The comedy starts at seven o'clock and I don't want to miss it.

REENIE. We can stay for the second show if we miss the comedy.

SONNY. Oh, I want to stay for the second show, anyway. I always see the comedy twice.

CORA (*coming forth now*). Are you children going some place?

REENIE. We're going to the movie, Mom.

CORA. Together?

REENIE. Yes.

CORA. Well . . . that's nice.

REENIE. Darn it. I left my rubbers out on the porch. (*She exits.*)

RUBIN (*from upstairs*). Cora!

CORA. I'll be up in a minute, Rubin. (*She turns thoughtfully to her son.*) Have you forgiven your mother, Sonny?

SONNY (*inscrutable*). Oh . . . maybe.

CORA. Your mother still loves you, Sonny. (*She puts an arm around him but he avoids her embrace.*)

SONNY. Don't Mom.

CORA. All right. I understand.

RUBIN (*upstairs, growing more impatient*). Cora! Come on, honey!

CORA (*calling back to him*). I'll be up in a minute, Rubin. (SONNY *looks at her with accusing eyes.*) Good-bye, Sonny!

(REENIE *sticks her head in the door from outside.*)

REENIE. Hurry up, Sonny!

RUBIN. Come on, Cora!

(CORA *starts up the stairs to her husband, stopping for one final look at her departing son. And* SONNY, *just before going out the door, stops for one final look at his mother, his face full of confused understanding. Then he hurries out to* REENIE, *and* CORA, *like a shy maiden, starts up the stairs, where we see* RUBIN's *naked feet standing in the warm light at the top.*)

CORA. I'm coming, Rubin. I'm coming.

CURTAIN

WHO'S AFRAID OF VIRGINIA WOOLF?

Edward Albee

First presented by Richard Barr and Clinton Wilder for Theatre 1963 at the Billy Rose Theatre, New York, on October 13, 1962, with the following cast:

MARTHA Uta Hagen

GEORGE Arthur Hill

NICK George Grizzard

HONEY Melinda Dillon

Original matinee cast:

MARTHA Kate Reid

GEORGE Sheppard Strudwick

NICK Bill Berger

HONEY Avra Tetrides

NOTE: Nancy Kelly substituted for Uta Hagen during the summer of 1963; and later played the role of Martha in the national touring company.

Directed by Alan Schneider
Designed by William Ritmar

THE DETAILS of Edward Franklin Albee's life, his being the adopted child of a well-to-do family well known in show business, his having been sent to the Hotchkiss private school, his having had a difficult childhood and kept himself going with odd jobs as a short-order cook, copy boy, and clerk, his having perhaps more than his share of problems attendant upon youth—all this I pass by, resolved to provide no grist to the amateur analysts who infest the world of theatre. (Though I like Jerry Tallmer's saying in the New York *Post* that "Albee writes from his own interior in metaphor.") So far as the present editor is concerned, our present business is only to know that Edward Albee was born on March 12, 1928, that he spent much of his early youth writing poetry and fiction, and then turned to writing plays.

His first produced play, written in his thirtieth year, was the remarkable long one-act piece, *The Zoo Story,* the theme of which is loneliness carried to the point of desperation. The subject was brilliantly evoked if perhaps melodramatically resolved in a nevertheless distinctly original climactic scene. Due to the circuitous circulation of the manuscript among friends in Europe, *The Zoo Story* was first produced in Berlin on September 28, 1959. The American premiere came several months later, on January 14, 1960, when the play was produced at the Provincetown Playhouse in Greenwich Village on a twin bill with Samuel Beckett's *Krapp's Last Tape,* by Richard Barr, a former member of John Houseman and Orson Welles' famous Mercury Theatre of the late 1930's. Barr and his Broadway-seasoned partner, Clinton Wilder, subsequently presented Mr. Albee's *surréaliste* one-act satire on conformity, *The American Dream,* in 1960. To this Ionesco-like play (clever and, I believe, also moving), they ultimately added another Albee one-acter, *The Death of Bessie Smith,* which had also had its world premiere in Berlin (in 1959), a too loosely organized yet uncommonly piercing piece. The two playlets made up a well-attended off-Broadway attraction and won for their author a citation and cash prize in June, 1961, the Lola D'Annunzio Award, from a jury of critics. Another one-acter, the fourteen-minute miniature drama, *The Sandbox,* written for the Spoleto "Festival of Two Worlds" (but not produced at Spoleto), proved to be completely entrancing yet meaningful when presented on the stage and on a television program in 1960.

Harold Clurman, in covering *The Zoo Story* for *The Nation,* wrote that "Albee's play is the introduction to what could prove to be an important talent of the American stage." When *Who's Afraid of Virginia Woolf?* opened October 13, 1962, under the Richard Barr and Clinton Wilder ("Theatre 1963") management, Mr. Clurman proved to be a good prophet, as did the Lola D'Annunzio jury that had singled out Albee as the most promising newcomer to the American stage. The success of the lengthy and taxing new play (so taxing, in fact, that a different cast was assembled for the matinee performances) was an unmistakable triumph for the author, especially since this trenchant three-and-a-half hour drama had to overcome public uneasiness caused by its uncongenial subject matter and the vigor and occasionally disconcerting language with which it was treated. In view of the excellence of the Broadway production staged by Alan Schneider with Uta Hagen and Arthur Hill in the evening performances, Mr. Albee could share his honors with them. But there were enough of these to spare. They came with impressive frequency toward the end of the 1962-63 season. Virtually the only available award the play did not receive was the Pulitzer Prize recommended by the Pulitzer Prize jury of John Mason Brown and John Gassner, who promptly resigned when their recommendation was rejected by the Pulitzer Prize Advisory Board.

Because the play also encountered some determined resistance, and since both its structure and texture appear to have been insufficiently appreciated even by admirers, I reproduce passages from my long review of an excellent Columbia recording in 1963 which appeared in the June 29 issue of *The Saturday Review.*

"Entire episodes exist as verbal structures in Albee's play and the phrases mesh with each other not so much as logically connected statements but as spontaneous utterances carrying pertinent moods, attitudes, or intentions. Albee's short phrases and sentences make up a series of musico-dramatic movements perhaps even more distinctly related than they could be in a visual production because the text comes at us naked, so to speak—that is, as pure sound.

"In Act III, for example, there are several of these movements. The first is Martha's desperation, expressed in a drunken soliloquy (it has its own unique broken rhythm); the second is her disillusionment with men, starting with a teasing colloquy with her would-be but ultimately inadequate lover Nick and culminating in a monologue the keynote of which is 'I am the Earth Mother, and you're all flops. . . . I pass my life in crummy, totally pointless infidelities . . . *would*-be infidelities.' A new rhythm is established in a second, rather analytical, conversation with Nick concerning her attitude toward her husband George, 'who has made the hideous, the hurting, the insulting mistake of loving me and must be punished for it.' It is followed by the teasing rhythms of reducing Nick to the lowly status of a 'houseboy' in compelling him to answer the doorbell, and of herself being teased and insulted by the mounting aggressiveness of her nearly cuckolded husband George. Then the beat quickens, the pulse grows uneven, and the voices strain toward a climax of violence as Martha strives to preserve her illusion of motherhood while George endeavors to strip her of it, the struggle culminating in the strong counterpoint of Martha's dramatizing the illusioned son while her husband recites the Latin prayers for the dead—that is, for the son who had never existed except in their imagination and whom he now proposes to 'kill.' Finally, there is the denouement or 'falling action' starting with the ominous quietness of George's 'I am afraid our boy isn't coming home for his birthday' and concluding with the fragmented sentences with which Martha reluctantly relinquishes her hitherto fiercely defended illusion. After that episode, when the two guests, Nick and his wife, depart, the lines assigned to the emotionally drained Martha and George rarely exceed two-word speeches of 'I'm cold' and 'It's late,' and the play closes with Martha's dully spoken monosyllabic response to the 'Who's Afraid of Virginia Woolf?' ditty sung by her husband 'I . . . am . . . George . . . I . . . am. . . .'

"It is not particularly space-consuming to point out that, in spite of its great length and almost musical fluidity, *Who's Afraid of Virginia Woolf?* is a notably concentrated and carefully constructed drama.

"An irritable middle-aged couple, notably articulate but also inebriated, comes home from a party, and before long the husband and wife, George and Martha, are slashing away at each other, mercilessly exposing themselves and two guests, a younger and seemingly happier but actually just as miserable couple. The battle attains sensational intensity because the principals are not only sufficiently aroused but, as Albee declares in the Columbia Records brochure, 'intelligent and sensitive enough to build proper weapons for their war with each other.' The struggle fluctuates, with dubious victory falling first to one side, then to the other, until the antagonists are sufficiently self-revealed and purged to arrive at a tentative reconciliation. Hosts and their guests in conventional American society (which Albee satirized previously in *The American Dream*) go in for 'fun and games,' and it is under the pretense of 'fun and games' that the action proceeds. One movement is a 'Get the Host' game in which Martha is the aggressor against George in the presence of the visitors. A second movement, a 'get the guests' game, is directed against the visitors by the humiliated George, who resents the smugness of his guest and university colleague, the biologist Nick, on personal and general grounds. Nick, infuriated by revelations of his own unsatisfactory domestic life, and Martha, who is also out for vengeance, collaborate on the third game, in which Nick supposedly makes a cuckold of George—that is, 'gets' the hostess, Martha. In the final movement, George counterattacks with a climactic 'bringing up baby' game that 'brings up' the crucial fact that Martha and he have never had a son and could not have a child. After all the devastating 'fun' they have been having and the 'games' the history professor George and his wife have been playing from midnight to dawn they are brought to the point of renouncing the game they have been playing privately for some twenty-three years. The time for illusions is over, at last, and the husband and wife will have to make the best of whatever reality there is for them, facing life together, even if the thought of 'Just . . . us?' fills Martha with misgivings.

"An exegesis on this conclusion, and indeed on the entire play, is a distinct possibility. It is perhaps even a necessity for those who sense that a larger gambit than Martha's and George's 'games' is being played and would like to have it spelled out for them once the 'fun' (and there is plenty of comedy in the text) becomes grim. Symbol or image hunters can have a field day with the play." *

Also, since I believe readers and playgoers able to leave their barbed-wire defenses of right- or left-wing moralism for a while will profit from an analysis written by a professed "layman" for his own and his friends' pleasure, I am pleased to be able to reprint an article written by Dr. Harold Lamport of Westport, who—I hasten to add— is not a practicing psychoanalyst or psychologist but research associate in *physiology* at the Yale University Medical Center in New Haven. I am grateful to Dr. Lamport for permission to reprint his fine essay virtually intact, and I expect that the reader will be too—as he will also be by a statement by Albee especially relevant to the resolution of the play. He is reported to have said to Jerry Tallmer, interviewing him in the *Post* (Nov. 4, 1962), *"We must try to claw our way into compassion."* This is a true insight into a play which was originally called *Exorcism* and culminates in an act bearing the same title.

WHO'S AFRAID OF VIRGINIA WOOLF?

by Harold Lamport

(December 22, 1962)

"It is easy to accept Albee's play as a drama of marital conflict, concerned primarily with deep character development, the portrayal by a misogynist of Strindberg stripe of the mutual destructiveness of a couple ill-suited to marriage. Some critics have regarded the homosexual components of the history professor husband as the primary element in the raging battle between the sexes shown by Albee on the stage and regard Albee's goal in this play that of the naturalist, the description of this battle and its protagonists. Such purpose seems to me better exemplified in *The Shrike,* a play seen on Broadway several years earlier, in which a mordantly destructive woman works the ruin of her husband and his permanent incarceration within a mental institution.

"That Albee meant more by his play is revealed in its title. From the advance publicity we learned that other titles were considered before production because of possible legal objections to the use of the name of an author who died recently. Albee is said to have insisted on retaining the title if at all possible because of its importance to the play and Leonard Woolf, his wife's executor, gave permission.

" 'Who's afraid of Virginia Woolf?' are the words of a humorous song danced and sung by faculty wives at a faculty party. Several times the two faculty wives of the two couples joke about this song-and-dance and sing snatches of it, regarding it as extremely hilarious, more so than the men. Later, it becomes the battle song of the historian whenever he is moved to defy his destructive wife. One is constrained to regard these words with deep curiosity; they must contain in condensed form much of what Albee's play is about, perhaps telling even more than Albee himself is aware. Of course, in seeking the profounder meaning of such a nonsense phrase (a little reminiscent of the single-sentence irrational problems of Zen Buddhism), one examines one's own associations in the hope that they will duplicate, after subtraction of the purely personal, what Albee meant and—if he succeeded as a playwright—what he communicated to his audience even if inchoate in their minds.

"Superficially, 'Who's afraid of Virginia Woolf?' suggests to me: Who's afraid of the intellectual woman, since Virginia Woolf in the English-speaking literary world represents such a woman, able to lead as a critic and a writer among the most cerebral of men. As sung by the faculty wives, the refrain seems dual and ambivalent: we faculty wives—witness our light-hearted song-and-dance—are really not so intellectual as Virginia Woolf and we are a little jealous and afraid of the intellectual type whom our husbands may prefer; and, less clearly, speaking for our men, though intellectuals (mostly), they are often insecure as males in the presence of the intellectually out-

* Reprinted from *The Saturday Review* (June 29, 1963) by permission of the editors.

standing woman and *they* are afraid of the Virginia Woolf in us, since we are not as unintellectual as our song-and-dance may make us seem—we could compete effectively with them if we permitted ourselves to. My guess is that the first statement is what the audience hears, particularly the women, and the second is what the men hear, particularly the two professors in the play, who didn't think the skit funny.

"Virginia Woolf might be replaced by other famous women of intellectual stamp (but offhand a good substitute is hard to find), yet Albee was insistent. The reason, I think, is that the phrase is a parody of the nursery song from the fable of the piglets: 'Who's afraid of the big bad wolf?' As we know, the piglets were very *much* afraid of the wolf—and with good reason: Their song certainly was a whistling-in-the-dark to keep up their courage. Certainly the success of the wolf in the fable is known to us all. The allusive pun on Virginia Woolf's name adds zest to the words of the song-and-dance routine and to the title of Albee's play.

"Various means of expressing hostility, aside from the most overt—the historian's abortive attempt to choke his wife—are employed in the play. But the method that draws blood, that shatters each character, one by one, is the statement of an unpleasant, hidden truth either to the concerned individual alone or before others where its impact is to castigate that individual without mercy.

The crowning betrayal, the last salvo that so utterly unhinges his sadistic wife, is the historian's disclosure to his guests that their son is imaginary, a delusion he had permitted his wife and shared with her only so long as their agreed *folie-à-deux* rule of keeping it secret was honored. Strangely, after all the in-fighting in which she was the aggressor, disregarding his repeated warnings of retribution, she pleads to be allowed to keep this delusion, but he has been too sorely tried and for him resolution of their violent encounter requires this final victory after so many prior defeats.

"The young biologist's wife has been finally exposed, not as the sweet young thing she first seemed, but as an alcoholic, the wealthy heiress of a peculating preacher, an hysteric who vomits with little provocation and whose false pregnancy before marriage at first was offered by her husband to the historian as the pretext for his spuriously magnanimous marriage. However, the young biologist is shown to be a go-getter who wanted the help of a rich wife in getting to the top, one who accepts the role of a gigolo (gratuitously revealed to his wife) and toady to gain advancement.

"The historian's academic failure has been related before all to a character defect obviously derived from his great guilt over his fantasies of killing his parents (to what extent there is a basis in fact is not clear). And the historian's wife, the daughter of the president of the college, she more than any lays herself bare and is bared as she attacks all. Her inordinate love of her father is said to be unreciprocated, her desire to marry a man who vicariously would fulfill her desire to inherit her father's power and position are found to have been frustrated by the wrong choice of mate. It is she who burns with unhappiness, who has leaned on the invention of a son to provide her a way to satisfy some of her drive towards the role of masculinity.

"The penchant of the intellectual for introspection and for learning the truths about others' inner thoughts is a dangerous sport, terribly destructive when the truths so discovered are wantonly revealed. In *Who's Afraid of Virginia Woolf?* the devastating impact of publicly exposing the truth, whether already known or not to those most intimately concerned, is made frightfully clear. Is not the cruel exposure of the secret truth (or falsehood) on which our self-respect rests the villain of the play? Is he not the wolf we foolishly or sadistically release without adequate realization of the consequences? . . .

"The relationship between the history professor and his wife is fascinating. Slowly, it becomes apparent that along with their headlong hate there is also love. Why else are they still together? They understand and appreciate one another even though each is a tortured person. They play the same games, they say—and it is true. The professor rejects the wet smacky kiss tendered by his wife because it would excite him too much sexually when the biologist and wife are momentarily expected. Later, sourly regarding the fiasco of her seduction of the not-so-potent biologist, she compliments her husband on his greater virility. There is a healthy carnal element in their marriage. And when almost mortally wounded by her husband's killing off the fantasy of the son, she still turns to him for compassion and support. He provides them. Their relationship is an incredible inferno of sado-masochism: their most violent attacks are not without a loving component and each provides the other with the opportunity for expressing these ambivalent feelings. With brief insight, she says it well:

" 'George who is good to me, and whom I revile; who understands me, and whom I push off; who can make me laugh, and I choke it back in my throat; who can hold me, at night, so that it's warm, and whom I will bite so there's blood; who keeps learning the games we play as quickly as I can change the rules; who can make me happy and I do not wish to be happy . . . who has made the hideous, the hurting, the insulting mistake of loving me and must be punished for it . . . who tolerates, which is intolerable; who is kind, which is cruel; who understands, which is beyond comprehension. . . .' "

THE SCENE. The living room of a house on the campus of a small New England college.

ACT ONE:

FUN AND GAMES

Set in darkness. Crash against front door. MARTHA'S *laughter heard. Front door opens, lights are switched on.* MARTHA *enters, followed by* GEORGE.

———

MARTHA. *Jesus.* . . .

GEORGE. . . . Shhhhhhh. . . .

MARTHA. . . . H. Christ. . . .

GEORGE. For God's sake, Martha, it's two o'clock in the. . . .

MARTHA. Oh, George!

GEORGE. Well, I'm *sorry,* but. . . .

MARTHA. What a cluck! What a cluck you are.

GEORGE. It's late, you know? Late.

MARTHA (*looks about the room. Imitates Bette Davis*). What a dump. Hey, what's that from? "What a dump!"

GEORGE. How would I know what. . . .

MARTHA. Aw, come on! What's it from? *You* know. . . .

GEORGE . . . Martha. . . .

MARTHA. WHAT'S IT FROM, FOR CHRIST'S SAKE?

GEORGE (*wearily*). What's what from?

MARTHA. I just told you; I just did it. "What a dump!" Hunh? What's that from?

GEORGE. I haven't the faintest idea what. . . .

MARTHA. Dumbbell! It's from some goddamn Bette Davis picture . . . some goddamn Warner Brothers epic. . . .

GEORGE. *I* can't remember all the pictures that. . . .

MARTHA. Nobody's asking you to remember every single goddamn Warner Brothers epic . . . just one! One single little epic! Bette Davis gets peritonitis in the end . . . she's got this big black fright wig she wears all through the picture and she gets peritonitis, and she's married to Joseph Cotten or something. . . .

GEORGE . . . Some*body.* . . .

MARTHA . . . some*body* . . . and she wants to go to Chicago all the time, 'cause she's in love with that actor with the scar. . . . But she gets sick, and she sits down in front of her dressing table. . . .

GEORGE. What actor? What scar?

MARTHA. *I* can't remember his name, for God's sake. What's the name of the *picture?* I want to know what the name of the *picture* is. She sits down in front of her dressing table . . . and she's got this peritonitis . . . and she tries to put her lipstick on, but she can't . . . and she gets it all over her face . . . but she decides to go to Chicago anyway, and. . . .

GEORGE. *Chicago!* It's called *Chicago.*

MARTHA. Hunh? What . . . what is?

GEORGE. The picture . . . it's called *Chicago.* . . .

MARTHA. Good grief! Don't you know *anything?* Chicago was a 'thirties musical, starring little Miss Alice *Faye.* Don't you know *anything?*

GEORGE. Well, that was probably before my *time,* but. . . .

MARTHA. Can it! Just cut that out! This picture . . . Bette Davis comes home from a hard day at the grocery store. . . .

GEORGE. She works in a grocery store?

MARTHA. She's a housewife; she buys things . . . and she comes home with the groceries, and she walks into the modest living room of the modest cottage modest Joseph Cotten has set her up in. . . .

GEORGE. Are they married?

MARTHA (*impatiently*). Yes. They're married. To each other. Cluck! And she comes in, and she looks around, and she puts her groceries down, and she says, "What a dump!"

GEORGE (*pause*). Oh.

MARTHA (*pause*). She's discontent.

GEORGE (*pause*). Oh.

MARTHA (*pause*). Well, what's the name of the picture?

GEORGE. I really don't know, Martha. . . .

MARTHA. Well, think!

GEORGE. I'm tired, dear . . . it's late . . . and besides. . . .

MARTHA. I don't know what you're so tired about . . . you haven't *done* anything all day; you didn't have any classes, or anything. . . .

GEORGE. Well, I'm tired. . . . If your father didn't set up these goddamn Saturday night orgies all the time. . . .

MARTHA. Well, that's too bad about you, George. . . .

GEORGE (*grumbling*). Well, that's how it is, anyway.

MARTHA. You didn't *do* anything; you never *do* anything; you never *mix*. You just sit around and *talk*.

GEORGE. What do you want me to do? Do you want me to act like you? Do you want me to go around all night *braying* at everybody, the way you do?

MARTHA (*braying*). I DON'T BRAY!

GEORGE (*softly*). All right . . . you don't bray.

MARTHA (*hurt*). I do not *bray*.

GEORGE. All right. I said you didn't bray.

MARTHA (*pouting*). Make me a drink.

GEORGE. What?

MARTHA (*still softly*). I said, make me a drink.

GEORGE (*moving to the portable bar*). Well, I don't suppose a nightcap'd kill either one of us. . . .

MARTHA. A nightcap! Are you kidding? We've got guests.

GEORGE (*disbelieving*). We've got what?

MARTHA. Guests. GUESTS.

GEORGE. GUESTS!

MARTHA. Yes . . . guests . . . people. . . . We've got guests coming over.

GEORGE. When?

MARTHA. NOW!

GEORGE. Good Lord, Martha . . . do you know what time it. . . . *Who's* coming over?

MARTHA. What's-their-name.

GEORGE. Who?

MARTHA. WHAT'S-THEIR-NAME!

GEORGE. Who what's-their-name?

MARTHA. I don't know what their name is, George. . . . You met them tonight . . . they're new . . . he's in the math department, or something. . . .

GEORGE. Who . . . who are these people?

MARTHA. You met them tonight, George.

GEORGE. I don't remember meeting anyone tonight. . . .

MARTHA. Well you did . . . Will you give me my drink, please. . . . He's in the math department . . . about thirty, blond, and. . . .

GEORGE . . . and good-looking. . . .

MARTHA. Yes . . . and good-looking. . . .

GEORGE. It figures.

MARTHA . . . and his wife's a mousey little type, without any hips, or anything.

GEORGE (*vaguely*). Oh.

MARTHA. You remember them now?

GEORGE. Yes, I guess so, Martha. . . . But why in God's name are they coming over here now?

MARTHA (*in a so-there voice*). Because Daddy said we should be nice to them, that's why.

GEORGE (*defeated*). Oh, Lord.

MARTHA. May I have my drink, please? Daddy said we should be nice to them. Thank you.

GEORGE. But why now? It's after two o'clock in the morning, and. . . .

MARTHA. Because Daddy said we should be nice to them!

GEORGE. Yes. But I'm sure your father didn't mean we were supposed to stay up all *night* with these people. I mean, we could have them over some Sunday or something. . . .

MARTHA. Well, never mind. . . . Besides, it *is* Sunday. Very early Sunday.

GEORGE. I mean . . . it's ridiculous. . . .

MARTHA. Well, it's *done*!

GEORGE (*resigned and exasperated*). All right. Well . . . where are they? If we've got guests, where are they?

MARTHA. They'll be here soon.

GEORGE. What did they do . . . go home and get some sleep first, or something?

MARTHA. They'll *be* here!

GEORGE. I wish you'd *tell* me about something sometime. . . . I wish you'd stop *springing* things on me all the time.

MARTHA. I don't *spring* things on you all the time.

GEORGE. Yes, you do . . . you really do . . . you're always *springing* things on me.

MARTHA (*friendly-patronizing*). Oh, George!

GEORGE. Always.

MARTHA. Poor Georgie-Porgie, put-upon pie! (*As he sulks*) Awwwwww . . . what are you doing? Are you sulking? Hunh? Let me see . . . are you sulking? Is that what you're doing?

GEORGE (*very quietly*). Never mind, Martha. . . .

MARTHA. AWWWWWWWWWW!

GEORGE. Just don't bother yourself. . . .

MARTHA. AWWWWWWWWWWW! (*No re-action.*) Hey! (*No reaction.*) HEY! (GEORGE *looks at her, put-upon.*) Hey. (*She sings.*)

Who's afraid of Virginia Woolf,
        Virginia Woolf,
        Virginia Woolf. . . .

Ha, ha, ha, HA! (*No reaction.*) What's the matter . . . didn't you think that was funny? Hunh? (*Defiantly*) I thought it was a scream . . . a real scream. You didn't like it, hunh?

GEORGE. It was all right, Martha. . . .

MARTHA. You laughed your head off when you heard it at the party.

GEORGE. I smiled. I didn't laugh my head off . . . I smiled, you know? . . . it was all right.

MARTHA (*gazing into her drink*). You laughed your goddamn head off.

GEORGE. It was all right. . . .

MARTHA (*ugly*). It was a scream!

GEORGE (*patiently*). It was very funny; yes.

MARTHA (*after a moment's consideration*). You make me puke!

GEORGE. What?

MARTHA. Uh . . . you make me puke!

GEORGE (*thinks about it . . . then . . .*) That wasn't a very nice thing to say, Martha.

MARTHA. That wasn't *what*?

GEORGE . . . a very nice thing to say.

MARTHA. I like your anger. I think that's what I like about you most . . . your anger. You're such a . . . such a simp! You don't even have the . . . the what? . . .

GEORGE. . . . . guts? . . .

MARTHA. PHRASEMAKER! (*Pause . . . then they both laugh.*) Hey, put some more ice in my drink, will you? You never put any ice in my drink. Why is that, hunh?

GEORGE (*takes her drink*). I always put ice in your drink. You eat it, that's all. It's that habit you have . . . chewing your ice cubes . . . like a cocker spaniel. You'll crack your big teeth.

MARTHA. THEY'RE MY BIG TEETH!

GEORGE. Some of them . . . some of them.

MARTHA. I've got more teeth than you've got.

GEORGE. Two more.

MARTHA. Well, two more's a lot more.

GEORGE. I suppose it is. I suppose it's pretty remarkable . . . considering how old you are.

MARTHA. YOU CUT THAT OUT! (*Pause.*) You're not so young yourself.

GEORGE (*with boyish pleasure . . . a chant*). I'm six years younger than you are. . . . I always have been and I always will be.

MARTHA (*glumly*). Well . . . you're going bald.

GEORGE. So are you. (*Pause . . . they both laugh.*) Hello, honey.

MARTHA. Hello. C'mon over here and give your Mommy a big sloppy kiss.

GEORGE. . . . . oh, now. . . .

MARTHA. I WANT A BIG SLOPPY KISS!

GEORGE (*preoccupied*). I don't *want* to kiss you, Martha. Where *are* these people? Where are these *people* you invited over?

MARTHA. They stayed on to talk to Daddy. . . . They'll be here. . . . *Why* don't you want to kiss me?

GEORGE (*too matter-of-fact*). Well, dear, if I kissed you I'd get all excited . . . I'd get beside myself, and I'd take you, by force, right here on the living room rug, and then our little guests would walk in, and . . . well, just think what your father would say about *that*.

MARTHA. You pig!

GEORGE (*haughtily*). Oink! Oink!

MARTHA. Ha, ha, ha, HA! Make me another drink . . . lover.

GEORGE (*taking her glass*). My God, you can swill it down, can't you?

MARTHA (*imitating a tiny child*). I'm firsty.

GEORGE. Jesus!

MARTHA (*swinging around*). Look, sweetheart, I can drink you under any goddamn table you want . . . so don't worry about me!

GEORGE. Martha, I gave you the prize years ago. . . . There isn't an abomination award going that you. . . .

MARTHA. I swear . . . if you existed I'd divorce you. . . .

GEORGE. Well, just stay on your feet, that's all. . . . These people are your guests, you know, and. . . .

MARTHA. I can't even see you . . . I haven't been able to see you for years. . . .

GEORGE. . . . . if you pass out, or throw up, or something. . . .

MARTHA. . . . . I mean, you're a blank, a cipher. . . .

GEORGE. . . . . and try to keep your clothes on, too. There aren't many more sickening sights than you with a couple of drinks in you and your skirt up over your head, you know. . . .

MARTHA. . . . . a zero. . . .

GEORGE. . . . . your *head*s, I should

say. . . .

(*The front doorbell chimes.*)

MARTHA. Party! Party!

GEORGE (*murderously*). I'm really looking forward to this, Martha. . . .

MARTHA (*same*). Go answer the door.

GEORGE (*not moving*). You answer it.

MARTHA. Get to that door, you. (*He does not move.*) I'll fix you, you. . . .

GEORGE (*fake-spits*). . . . to you. . . .

(*Door chime again.*)

MARTHA (*shouting . . . to the door*). C'MON IN! (*To* GEORGE, *between her teeth*) I said, get over there!

GEORGE (*moves a little toward the door, smiling slightly*). All right, love . . . whatever love wants. (*Stops.*) Just don't start on the bit, that's all.

MARTHA. The bit? The bit? What kind of language is that? What are you talking about?

GEORGE. The bit. Just don't start in on the bit.

MARTHA. You imitating one of your students, for God's sake? What are you trying to do? WHAT BIT?

GEORGE. Just don't start in on the bit about the kid, that's all.

MARTHA. What do you take me for?

GEORGE. Much too much.

MARTHA (*really angered*). Yeah? Well, I'll start in on the kid if I want to.

GEORGE. Just leave the kid out of this.

MARTHA (*threatening*). He's mine as much as he is yours. I'll talk about him if I want to.

GEORGE. I'd advise against it, Martha.

MARTHA. Well, good for you. (*Knock.*) C'mon in. Get over there and open the door!

GEORGE. You've been advised.

MARTHA. Yeah . . . sure. Get over there!

GEORGE (*moving toward the door*). All right, love . . . whatever love wants. Isn't it nice the way some people have manners, though, even in this day and age? Isn't it nice that some people won't just come breaking into other people's houses even if they *do* hear some sub-human monster yowling at 'em from inside . . . ?

MARTHA. SCREW YOU!

(*Simultaneously with* MARTHA's *last remark,* GEORGE *flings open the front door.* HONEY *and* NICK *are framed in the entrance. There is a brief silence, then. . . .*)

GEORGE (*ostensibly a pleased recognition of* HONEY *and* NICK, *but really satisfaction at having* MARTHA's *explosion overheard*). Ahhhhhhhhh!

MARTHA (*a little too loud . . . to cover*). HI! Hi, there . . . c'mon in!

HONEY *and* NICK (*ad lib*). Hello, here we are . . . hi . . . etc.

GEORGE (*very matter-of-factly*). You must be our little guests.

MARTHA. Ha, ha, ha, HA! Just ignore old sour-puss over there. C'mon in, kids . . . give your coats and stuff to sour-puss.

NICK (*without expression*). Well, now, perhaps we shouldn't have come. . . .

HONEY. Yes . . . it *is* late, and. . . .

MARTHA. Late! Are you kidding? Throw your stuff down anywhere and c'mon in.

GEORGE (*vaguely . . . walking away*). Anywhere . . . furniture, floor . . . doesn't make any difference around this place.

NICK (*to* HONEY). I told you we shouldn't have come.

MARTHA (*stentorian*). I said c'mon in! Now c'mon!

HONEY (*giggling a little as she and* NICK *advance*). Oh, dear.

GEORGE (*imitating* HONEY's *giggle*). Hee, hee, hee, hee.

MARTHA (*swinging on* GEORGE). Look, muckmouth . . . you cut that out!

GEORGE (*innocence and hurt*). Martha! (*To* HONEY *and* NICK) Martha's a devil with language; she really is.

MARTHA. Hey, *kids* . . . sit down.

HONEY (*as she sits*). Oh, isn't this lovely!

NICK (*perfunctorily*). Yes indeed . . . very handsome.

MARTHA. Well, thanks.

NICK (*indicating the abstract painting*). Who . . . who did the . . . ?

MARTHA. That? Oh, that's by. . . .

GEORGE. . . . some Greek with a mustache Martha attacked one night in. . . .

HONEY (*to save the situation*). Oh, ho, ho, ho, HO.

NICK. It's got a . . . a. . . .

GEORGE. A quiet intensity?

NICK. Well, no . . . a. . . .

GEORGE. Oh. (*Pause*) Well, then a certain noisy relaxed quality, maybe?

NICK (*knows what* GEORGE *is doing, but stays grimly, coolly polite*). No. What I meant was. . . .

GEORGE. How about . . . uh . . . a quietly noisy relaxed intensity.

HONEY. Dear! You're being joshed.

NICK (*cold*). I'm aware of that.

(*A brief, awkward silence.*)

GEORGE (*truly*). I *am* sorry.

(NICK *nods condescending forgiveness.*)

GEORGE. What it is, actually, is it's a pictorial representation of the order of Martha's mind.

MARTHA. Ha, ha, ha, HA! Make the kids a drink, George. What do you want, kids? What do you want to drink, hunh?

NICK. Honey? What would you like?

HONEY. I don't know, dear . . . A little brandy, maybe. "Never mix—never worry." (*She giggles.*)

GEORGE. Brandy? Just brandy? Simple; simple. (*Moves to the portable bar.*) What about you . . . uh. . . .

NICK. Bourbon on the rocks, if you don't mind.

GEORGE (*as he makes drinks*). Mind? No, I don't mind. I don't think I mind. Martha? Rubbing alcohol for you?

MARTHA. Sure. "Never mix—never worry."

GEORGE. Martha's tastes in liquor have come down . . . simplified over the years . . . crystallized. Back when I was courting Martha—well, don't know if that's exactly the right word for it—but back when I was courting Martha. . . .

MARTHA (*cheerfully*). Screw, sweetie!

GEORGE (*returning with* HONEY *and* NICK's *drinks*). At any rate, back when I was courting Martha, she'd order the damnedest things! You wouldn't believe it! We'd go into a bar . . . you know, a *bar* . . . a whiskey, beer, and bourbon *bar* . . . and what she'd do would be, she'd screw up her face, think real hard, and come up with . . . brandy Alexanders, creme de cacao frappes, gimlets, flaming punch bowls . . . seven-layer liqueur things.

MARTHA. They were good . . . I liked them.

GEORGE. Real lady-like little drinkies.

MARTHA. Hey, where's my rubbing alcohol?

GEORGE (*returning to the portable bar*). But the years have brought to Martha a sense of essentials . . . the knowledge that cream is for coffee, lime juice for pies . . . and alcohol (*Brings* MARTHA *her drink.*) pure and simple . . . here you are, angel . . . for the pure and simple. (*Raises his glass.*) For the mind's blind eye, the heart's ease, and the liver's craw. Down the hatch, all.

MARTHA (*to them all*). Cheers, dears. (*They all drink.*) You have a poetic nature, George . . . a Dylan Thomas-y quality that gets me right where I live.

GEORGE. Vulgar girl! With guests here!

MARTHA. Ha, ha, ha, HA! (*To* HONEY *and* NICK) Hey; hey! (*Sings, conducts with her drink in her hand.* HONEY *joins in toward the end.*)

Who's afraid of Virginia Woolf,
>   Virginia Woolf,
>   Virginia Woolf,
Who's afraid of Virginia Woolf. . . .

(MARTHA *and* HONEY *laugh;* NICK *smiles.*)

HONEY. Oh, wasn't that funny? That was so funny. . . .

NICK (*snapping to*). Yes . . . yes, it was.

MARTHA. I thought I'd bust a gut; I really did. . . . I really thought I'd bust a gut laughing. George didn't like it. . . . George didn't think it was funny at all.

GEORGE. Lord, Martha, do we have to go through this again?

MARTHA. I'm trying to shame you into a sense of humor, angel, that's all.

GEORGE (*over-patiently, to* HONEY *and* NICK). Martha didn't think I laughed loud enough. Martha thinks that unless . . . as she demurely puts it . . . that unless you "bust a gut" you aren't amused. You know? Unless you carry on like a hyena you aren't having any fun.

HONEY. Well, I certainly had fun . . . it was a *wonderful* party.

NICK (*attempting enthusiasm*). Yes . . . it certainly was.

HONEY (*to* MARTHA). And your father! Oh! He is so marvelous!

NICK (*as above*). Yes . . . yes, he is.

HONEY. Oh, I tell you.

MARTHA (*genuinely proud*). He's quite a guy, isn't he? Quite a guy.

GEORGE (*at* NICK). And you'd better believe it!

HONEY (*admonishing* GEORGE). Ohhhh-hhhhh! He's a wonderful man.

GEORGE. I'm not trying to tear him down. He's a God, we all know that.

MARTHA. You lay off my father!

GEORGE. Yes, love. (*To* NICK.) All I mean is . . . when you've had as many of these faculty parties as I have. . . .

NICK (*killing the attempted rapport*). I rather appreciated it. I mean, aside from enjoying it, I appreciated it. You know, when you're new at a place . . . (GEORGE *eyes him suspiciously.*) Meeting everyone, getting introduced around . . . getting to know some of the men. . . . When I was teaching in Kansas. . . .

HONEY. You won't believe it, but we had to make our way all by *ourselves* . . . isn't that right, dear?

NICK. Yes, it is. . . . We. . . .

HONEY. . . . We had to make our own way. . . . I had to go up to wives . . . in the library, or at the supermarket . . . and say, "Hello, I'm new here . . . you must be Mrs. So-and-so, Doctor So-and-so's wife." It really wasn't very nice at all.

MARTHA. Well, *Daddy* knows how to run things.

NICK (*not enough enthusiasm*). He's a remarkable man.

MARTHA. You bet your sweet life.

GEORGE (*to* NICK . . . *a confidence, but not whispered*). Let me tell you a secret, baby. There are easier things in the world, if you happen to be teaching at a university, there are easier things than being married to the daughter of the president of that university. There are easier things in this world.

MARTHA (*loud . . . to no one in particular*). It *should* be an extraordinary opportunity . . . for *some* men it would be the chance of a lifetime!

GEORGE (*to* NICK . . . *a solemn wink*). There are, believe me, easier things in this world.

NICK. Well, I can understand how it might make for some . . . awkwardness, perhaps . . . conceivably, but. . . .

MARTHA. *Some* men would give their right arm for the chance!

GEORGE (*quietly*). Alas, Martha, in reality it works out that the sacrifice is usually of a somewhat more private portion of the anatomy.

MARTHA (*a snarl of dismissal and contempt*). NYYYYAAAAHHHHH!

HONEY (*rising quickly*). I wonder if you could show me where the . . . (*Her voice trails off.*)

GEORGE (*to* MARTHA, *indicating* HONEY). Martha. . . .

NICK (*to* HONEY). Are you all right?

HONEY. Of course, dear. I want to . . . put some powder on my nose.

GEORGE (*as* MARTHA *is not getting up*).

Martha, won't you show her where we keep the . . . euphemism?

MARTHA. Hm? What? Oh! Sure! (*Rises.*) I'm sorry, c'mon. I want to show you the house.

HONEY. I think I'd like to. . . .

MARTHA. . . . wash up? Sure . . . c'mon with me. (*Takes* HONEY *by the arm. To the men*) You two do some men talk for a while.

HONEY (*to* NICK). We'll be back, dear.

MARTHA (*to* GEORGE). Honestly, George, you burn me up!

GEORGE (*happily*). All right.

MARTHA. You really do, George.

GEORGE. O.K. Martha . . . O.K. Just . . . trot along.

MARTHA. You really do.

GEORGE. Just don't shoot your mouth off . . . about . . . you-know-what.

MARTHA (*surprisingly vehement*). I'll talk about any goddamn thing I want to, George!

GEORGE. O.K. O.K. Vanish.

MARTHA. Any goddamn thing I want to! (*Practically dragging* HONEY *out with her*) C'mon. . . .

GEORGE. Vanish. (*The women have gone.*) So? What'll it be?

NICK. Oh, I don't know . . . I'll stick to bourbon, I guess.

GEORGE (*takes* NICK'S *glass, goes to portable bar*). That what you were drinking over at Parnassus?

NICK. Over at. . . ?

GEORGE. Parnassus.

NICK. I don't understand. . . .

GEORGE. Skip it. (*Hands him his drink.*) One bourbon.

NICK. Thanks.

GEORGE. It's just a private joke between li'l ol' Martha and me. (*They sit.*) So? (*Pause*) So . . . you're in the math department, eh?

NICK. No . . . uh, no.

GEORGE. Martha said you were. I think that's what she said. (*Not too friendly*) What made you decide to be a teacher?

NICK. Oh . . . well, the same things that . . . uh . . . motivated you, I imagine.

GEORGE. What were they?

NICK (*formal*). Pardon?

GEORGE. I said, what were they? What were the things that motivated me?

NICK (*laughing uneasily*). Well . . . I'm sure I don't know.

GEORGE. You just finished saying that the things that motivated you were the same things that motivated me.

NICK (*with a little pique*). I said I *imagined* they were.

GEORGE. Oh. (*Off-hand*) Did you? (*Pause*) Well. . . . (*Pause*) You like it here?

NICK (*looking about the room*). Yes . . . it's . . . it's fine.

GEORGE. I mean the University.

NICK. Oh. . . . I thought you meant. . . .

GEORGE. Yes . . . I can see you did. (*Pause*) I meant the University.

NICK. Well, I . . . I like it . . . fine. (*As* GEORGE *just stares at him*) Just fine. (*Same*) You . . . you've been here quite a long time, haven't you?

GEORGE (*absently, as if he had not heard*). What? Oh . . . yes. Ever since I married . . . uh, What's-her-name . . . uh, Martha. Even before that. (*Pause*) Forever. (*To himself*) Dashed hopes, and good intentions. Good, better, best, bested. (*Back to* NICK) How do you like that for a declension, young man? Eh?

NICK. Sir, I'm sorry if we. . . .

GEORGE (*with an edge in his voice*). You didn't answer my question.

NICK. Sir?

GEORGE. Don't you condescend to me! (*Toying with him*) I asked you how you liked that for a declension: Good; better; best; bested. Hm? Well?

NICK (*with some distaste*). I really don't know what to say.

GEORGE (*feigned incredulousness*). You really don't know what to *say*?

NICK (*snapping it out*). All right . . . what do you want me to say? Do you want me to say it's funny, so you can contradict me and say it's sad? or do you want me to say it's sad so you can turn around and say no, it's funny. You can play that damn little game any way you want to, you know!

GEORGE (*feigned awe*). Very good! Very good!

NICK (*even angrier than before*). And when my wife comes back, I think we'll just. . . .

GEORGE (*sincere*). Now, now . . . calm down, my boy. Just . . . calm . . . down. (*Pause*) All right? (*Pause*) You want another drink? Here, give me your glass.

NICK. I still have one. I *do* think that

when my wife comes downstairs. . . .

GEORGE. Here . . . I'll freshen it. Give me your glass. (*Takes it.*)

NICK. What I mean is . . . you two . . . you and your wife . . . seem to be having *some* sort of a. . . .

GEORGE. Martha and I are having . . . nothing. Martha and I are merely . . . exercising . . . that's all . . . we're merely walking what's left of our wits. Don't pay any attention to it.

NICK (*undecided*). Still. . . .

GEORGE (*an abrupt change of pace*). Well, now . . . let's sit down and talk, hunh?

NICK (*cool again*). It's just that I don't like to . . . become involved . . . (*An afterthought*) uh . . . in other people's affairs.

GEORGE (*comforting a child*). Well, you'll get over that . . . small college and all. Musical beds is the faculty sport around here.

NICK. Sir?

GEORGE. I said, musical beds is the faculty. . . . Never mind. I wish you wouldn't go "Sir" like that . . . not with the question mark at the end of it. You know? Sir? I know it's meant to be a sign of respect for your (*Winces*) elders . . . but . . . uh . . . the way you do it. . . . Sir? . . . Madam?

NICK (*with a small, noncommittal smile*). No disrespect intended.

GEORGE. How old *are* you?

NICK. Twenty-eight.

GEORGE. I'm forty something. (*Waits for reaction . . . gets none.*) Aren't you surprised? I mean . . . don't I look older? Doesn't this . . . *gray* quality suggest the fifties? Don't I sort of fade into backgrounds . . . get lost in the cigarette smoke? Hunh?

NICK (*looking around for an ashtray*). I think you look . . . fine.

GEORGE. I've always been lean . . . I haven't put on five pounds since I was your age. I don't have a paunch, either. . . . What I've got . . . I've got this little distension just below the belt . . . but it's hard . . . It's not soft flesh. I use the handball courts. How much do *you* weigh?

NICK. I. . . .

GEORGE. Hundred and fifty-five, sixty . . . something like that? Do you play handball?

NICK. Well, yes . . . no . . . I mean, not

very well.

GEORGE. Well, then . . . we shall play some time. Martha is a hundred and eight . . . years *old*. She weighs somewhat more than that. How old is *your* wife?

NICK (*a little bewildered*). She's twenty-six.

GEORGE. Martha is a remarkable woman. I would imagine she weighs around a hundred and ten.

NICK. Your . . . wife . . . weighs . . . ?

GEORGE No, no, my boy. Yours! *Your* wife. My wife is Martha.

NICK. Yes . . . I know.

GEORGE. If you were married to Martha you would know what it means. (*Pause*) But then, if I were married to your wife I would know what that means, too . . . wouldn't I?

NICK (*after a pause*). Yes.

GEORGE Martha says you're in the Math Department, or something.

NICK (*as if for the hundredth time*). No . . . I'm not.

GEORGE. Martha is seldom mistaken . . . maybe you *should* be in the Math Department, or something.

NICK. I'm a biologist. I'm in the Biology Department.

GEORGE (*after a pause*). Oh. (*Then, as if remembering something*) OH!

NICK. Sir?

GEORGE. You're the one! You're the one's going to make all that trouble . . . making everyone the same, rearranging the chromozones, or whatever it is. Isn't that right?

NICK (*with that small smile*). Not exactly: chromo*somes*.

GEORGE. I'm very mistrustful. Do you believe . . . (*Shifting in his chair*) . . . do you believe that people learn nothing from history? Not that there is nothing to learn, mind you, but that people learn nothing? I am in the History Department.

NICK. Well. . . .

GEORGE. I am a Doctor. A.B. . . . M.A. . . . PH.D. . . . ABMAPHID! Abmaphid has been variously described as a wasting disease of the frontal lobes, and as a wonder drug. It is actually both. I'm really very mistrustful. Biology, hunh? (NICK *does not answer . . . nods . . . looks.*) I read somewhere that science fiction is really not fiction at all . . . that you peo-ple are arranging my genes, so that everyone will be like everyone else. Now, I won't have that! It would be a . . . shame. I mean . . . look at me! Is it really such a good idea . . . if everyone was forty something and looked fifty-five? You didn't answer my question about history.

NICK. This genetic business you're talking about. . . .

GEORGE. Oh, that. (*Dismisses it with a wave of his hand.*) That's very upsetting . . . very . . . disappointing. But history is a great deal more . . . disappointing. I am in the History Department.

NICK. Yes . . . you told me.

GEORGE. I know I told you. . . . I shall probably tell you several more times. Martha tells me often, that I am *in* the History Department . . . as opposed to *being* the History Department . . . in the sense of *running* the History Department. I do not run the History Department.

NICK. Well, I don't run the Biology Department.

GEORGE. You're twenty-one!

NICK. Twenty-eight.

GEORGE. Twenty-eight! Perhaps when you're forty something and look fifty-five, you will run the History Department. . . .

NICK. . . . Biology. . . .

GEORGE. . . . the Biology Department. I *did* run the History Department, for four years, during the war, but that was because everybody was away. Then . . . everybody came back . . . because nobody got killed. That's New England for you. Isn't that amazing? Not one single man in this whole place got his head shot off. That's pretty irrational. (*Broods.*) Your wife *doesn't* have any hips . . . has she . . . does she?

NICK. What?

GEORGE. I don't mean to suggest that I'm hip-happy. . . . I'm not one of those thirty-six, twenty-two, seventy-eight men. No-siree . . . not me. Everything in proportion. I was implying that your wife is . . . slim-hipped.

NICK. Yes . . . she is.

GEORGE (*looking at the ceiling*). What are they *doing* up there? I assume that's where they are.

NICK (*false heartiness*). You know women.

GEORGE (*gives* NICK *a long stare, of feigned incredulity . . . then his attention moves*). Not one son-of-a-bitch got killed. Of course, nobody bombed Washington. No . . . that's not fair. You have any kids?

NICK. Uh . . . no . . . not yet. (*Pause*) You?

GEORGE (*a kind of challenge*). That's for me to know and you to find out.

NICK. Indeed?

GEORGE. No kids, hunh?

NICK. Not yet.

GEORGE. People do . . . uh . . . have kids. That's what I meant about history. You people are going to make them in test tubes, aren't you? You biologists. Babies. Then the rest of us . . . them as wants to . . . can screw to their heart's content. What will happen to the tax deduction? Has anyone figured that out yet? (NICK, *who can think of nothing better to do, laughs mildly.*) But you *are* going to have kids . . . anyway. In spite of history.

NICK (*hedging*). Yes . . . certainly. We . . . want to wait . . . a little . . . until we're settled.

GEORGE. And this . . . (*With a handsweep taking in not only the room, the house, but the whole countryside*) . . . this is your heart's content—Illyria . . . Penguin Island . . . Gomorrah. . . . You think you're going to be happy here in New Carthage, eh?

NICK (*a little defensively*). I hope we'll stay here.

GEORGE. And every definition has its boundaries, eh? Well, it isn't a bad college, I guess. I mean . . . it'll do. It isn't M.I.T. . . . it isn't U.C.L.A. . . . it isn't the Sorbonne . . . or Moscow U. either, for that matter.

NICK. I don't mean . . . forever.

GEORGE. Well, don't you let that get bandied about. The old man wouldn't like it. Martha's father expects loyalty and devotion out of his . . . staff. I was going to use another word. Martha's father expects his . . . staff . . . to cling to the walls of this place, like the ivy . . . to come here and grow old . . . to fall in the line of service. One man, a professor of Latin and Elocution, actually fell in the cafeteria line, one lunch. He was buried, as many of us have been, and as many more of us will be, under the shrubbery around the chapel. It is said . . . and I have no reason to doubt it . . . that we make excellent fertilizer. But the old man is not going to be buried under the shrubbery . . . the old man is not going to die. Martha's father has the staying power of one of those Micronesian tortoises. There are rumors . . . which you must not breathe in front of Martha, for she foams at the mouth . . . that the old man, her father, is over two hundred years old. There is probably an irony involved in this, but I am not drunk enough to figure out what it is. How many kids you going to have?

NICK. I . . . I don't know. . . . My wife is. . . .

GEORGE. Slim-hipped. (*Rises*) Have a drink.

NICK. Yes.

GEORGE. MARTHA! (*No answer*) DAMN IT! (*To* NICK) You asked me if I knew women. . . . Well, one of the things *I* do *not* know about them is what they talk about while the men are talking. (*Vaguely*) I must find out some time.

MARTHA'S VOICE. WHADD'YA WANT?

GEORGE (*to* NICK). Isn't that a wonderful sound? What I mean is . . . what do you think they really *talk* about . . . or don't you care?

NICK. Themselves, I would imagine.

MARTHA'S VOICE. GEORGE?

GEORGE (*to* NICK). Do you find women . . . puzzling?

NICK. Well . . . yes and no.

GEORGE (*with a knowing nod*). Unhhunh. (*Moves toward the hall, almost bumps into* HONEY, *re-entering.*) Oh! Well, here's one of you, at least. (HONEY *moves toward* NICK. GEORGE *goes to the hall.*)

HONEY (to GEORGE). She'll be right down. (*To* NICK) You must see this house, dear . . . this is such a wonderful old house.

NICK. Yes, I. . . .

GEORGE. MARTHA!

MARTHA'S VOICE. FOR CHRIST'S SAKE, HANG ON A MINUTE, WILL YOU?

HONEY (*to* GEORGE). She'll be right down . . . she's changing.

GEORGE (*incredulous*). She's *what*? She's changing?

HONEY. Yes.

GEORGE. Her clothes?

HONEY. Her dress.

GEORGE (*suspicious*). Why?

HONEY (*with a nervous little laugh*). Why, I imagine she wants to be . . . comfortable.

GEORGE (*with a threatening look toward the hall*). Oh, she does, does she?

HONEY. Well, heavens, I should think. . . .

GEORGE. YOU DON'T KNOW!

NICK (*as* HONEY *starts*). You feel all right?

HONEY (*reassuring, but with the echo of a whine. A long-practiced tone*). Oh, yes, dear . . . perfectly fine.

GEORGE (*fuming . . . to himself*). So she wants to be comfortable, does she? Well, we'll see about that.

HONEY (*to* GEORGE, *brightly*). I didn't know until just a minute ago that you had a *son*.

GEORGE (*wheeling, as if struck from behind*). WHAT?

HONEY. A son! I hadn't known.

NICK. You to know and me to find out. Well, he must be quite a big. . . .

HONEY. Twenty-one . . . twenty-one tomorrow . . . tomorrow's his birthday.

NICK (*a victorious smile*). Well!

GEORGE (*to* HONEY). She told you about him?

HONEY (*flustered*). Well, yes. Well, I mean. . . .

GEORGE (*nailing it down*). She told you about him.

HONEY (*a nervous giggle*). Yes.

GEORGE (*strangely*). You say she's changing?

HONEY. Yes.

GEORGE. And she mentioned . . . ?

HONEY (*cheerful, but a little puzzled*). . . . your son's birthday . . . yes.

GEORGE (*more or less to himself*). O.K., Martha . . . O.K.

NICK. You look pale, Honey. Do you want a . . . ?

HONEY. Yes, dear . . . a little more brandy, maybe. Just a drop.

GEORGE. O.K., Martha.

NICK. May I use the . . . uh . . . bar?

GEORGE. Hm? Oh, yes . . . yes . . . by all means. Drink away . . . you'll need it as the years go on. (*For* MARTHA, *as if she were in the room*) You goddam destructive. . . .

HONEY (*to cover*). What time is it, dear?

NICK. Two-thirty.

HONEY. Oh, it's so late . . . we *should* be getting home.

GEORGE (*nastily, but he is so preoccupied he hardly notices his own tone*). For what? You keeping the babysitter up, or something?

NICK (*almost a warning*). I told you we didn't have children.

GEORGE. Hm? (*Realizing*) Oh, I'm sorry. I wasn't even listening . . . or thinking . . . (*With a flick of his hand*) . . . whichever one applies.

NICK (*softly, to* HONEY). We'll go in a little while.

GEORGE (*driving*). Oh no, now . . . you mustn't. Martha is changing . . . and Martha is not changing for *me*. Martha hasn't changed for *me* in years. If Martha is changing, it means we'll be here for . . . days. You are being accorded an honor, and you must not forget that Martha is the daughter of our beloved boss. She is his . . . right ball, you might say.

NICK. You might not understand this . . . but I wish you wouldn't talk that way in front of my wife.

HONEY. Oh, now. . . .

GEORGE (*incredulous*). Really? Well, you're quite right . . . We'll leave that sort of talk to Martha.

MARTHA (*entering*). What sort of talk? (MARTHA *has changed her clothes, and she looks, now, more comfortable and . . . and this is most important . . . most voluptuous*)

GEORGE. There you are, my pet.

NICK (*impressed; rising*). Well, now. . . .

GEORGE. Why, Martha . . . your Sunday chapel dress!

HONEY (*slightly disapproving*). Oh, that's most attractive.

MARTHA (*showing off*). You like it? Good! (*To* GEORGE) What the hell do you mean screaming up the stairs at me like that?

GEORGE. We got lonely, darling . . . we got lonely for the soft purr of your little voice.

MARTHA (*deciding not to rise to it*). Oh. Well, then, you just trot over to the barie-poo. . . .

GEORGE (*taking the tone from her*). . . . and make your little mommy a gweat big dwink.

MARTHA (*giggles*). That's right (*To*

NICK) Well, did you two have a nice little talk? You men solve the problems of the world, as usual?

NICK. Well, no, we. . .

GEORGE (*quickly*). What we did, actually, if you really want to know, what we did actually is try to figure out what you two were talking about.

(HONEY *giggles*, MARTHA *laughs*.)

MARTHA (*to* HONEY). Aren't they something? Aren't these . . . (*Cheerfully disdainful*) . . . men the absolute end? (*To* GEORGE) Why didn't you sneak upstairs and listen in?

GEORGE. Oh, I wouldn't have *listened*, Martha. . . . I would have *peeked*.

(HONEY *giggles*, MARTHA *laughs*.)

NICK (*to* GEORGE, *with false heartiness*). It's a conspiracy.

GEORGE. And now we'll never know. Shucks!

MARTHA (*to* NICK, *as* HONEY *beams*). Hey, you must be quite a boy, getting your Masters when you were . . . what? . . . twelve? You hear that, George?

NICK. Twelve-and-a-half, actually. No, nineteen really. (*To* HONEY) Honey, you needn't have mentioned that. It. . . .

HONEY. Ohhh . . . I'm *proud* of you. . . .

GEORGE (*seriously, if sadly*). That's very . . . impressive.

MARTHA (*aggressively*). You're damned right!

GEORGE (*between his teeth*). I said I was impressed, Martha. I'm beside myself with jealousy. What do you want me to do, throw up? (*To* NICK) That really is very impressive. (*To* HONEY) You should be right proud.

HONEY (*coy*). Oh, he's a pretty nice fella.

GEORGE (*to* NICK). I wouldn't be surprised if you *did* take over the History Department one of these days.

NICK. The Biology Department.

GEORGE. The *Biology* Department . . . of course. I seem preoccupied with history. Oh! What a remark. (*He strikes a pose, his hand over his heart, his head raised, his voice stentorian.*) "I am preoccupied with history."

MARTHA (*as* HONEY *and* NICK *chuckle*). Ha, ha, ha, HA!

GEORGE (*with some disgust*). I think I'll make *myself* a drink.

MARTHA. George is not preoccupied with history. . . . George is preoccupied with the *History Department*. George is preoccupied with the History Department because. . . .

GEORGE. . . . because he is *not* the History Department, but is only *in* the History Department. We know, Martha . . . we went all through it while you were upstairs . . . getting up. There's no need to go through it again.

MARTHA. That's right, baby . . . keep it clean. (*To the others*) George is bogged down in the History Department. He's an old bog in the History Department, that's what George is. A bog. . . . A fen. . . . A G.D. swamp Ha, ha, ha, HA! A SWAMP! Hey, swamp! Hey SWAMPY!

GEORGE (*with a great effort controls himself . . then as if she had said nothing more than "George, dear". . . .*) Yes, Martha? Can I get you something?

MARTHA (*amused at his game*). Well . . . uh . . . sure, you can light my cigarette, if you're of a mind to.

GEORGE (*considers, then moves off*). No . . . there are limits. I mean, man can put up with only so much without he descends a rung or two on the old evolutionary ladder . . . (*Now a quick aside to* NICK) . . . which is up your line . . . (*Then back to* MARTHA) . . . sinks, Martha, and it's a funny ladder . . . you can't reverse yourself . . . start back up once you're descending. (MARTHA *blows him an arrogant kiss.*) Now . . . I'll hold your hand when it's dark and you're afraid of the bogey man, and I'll tote your gin bottles out after midnight, so no one'll see . . . but I will not light your cigarette. And that, as they say, is that.

(*Brief silence*)

MARTHA (*under her breath*). Jesus! (*Then, immediately, to* NICK) Hey, you played football, hunh?

HONEY (*as* NICK *seems sunk in thought*). Dear. . . .

NICK. Oh! Oh, yes . . . I was a . . . quarterback . . . but I was much more . . . adept . . . at boxing, really.

MARTHA (*with great enthusiasm*). BOXING! You hear that, George?

GEORGE (*resignedly*). Yes, Martha.

MARTHA (*to* NICK, *with peculiar intensity and enthusiasm*). You musta been pretty good at it . . . I mean, you don't look like you got hit in the face at all.

HONEY (*proudly*). He was intercollegiate state middleweight champion.

NICK (*embarrassed*). Honey. . . .

HONEY. Well, you were.

MARTHA You look like you still got a pretty good body *now*, too . . . is that right? Have you?

GEORGE (*intensely*). Martha . . . decency forbids. . . .

MARTHA (*to* GEORGE . . . *still staring at* NICK, *though*). SHUT UP! (*Now, back to* NICK) Well, have you? Have you kept your body?

NICK (*unselfconscious . . . almost encouraging her*). It's still pretty good. I work out.

MARTHA (*with a half-smile*). Do you!

NICK. Yeah.

HONEY. Oh, yes . . . he has a very . . . firm body.

MARTHA (*still with that smile . . . a private communication with* NICK). Have you! Oh, I think that's very nice.

NICK (*narcissistic, but not directly for* MARTHA). Well, you never know . . . (*Shrugs.*) . . . you know . . . once you have it. . . .

MARTHA. . . . you never know when it's going to come in handy.

NICK. I was going to say . . . why give it up until you have to.

MARTHA I couldn't agree with you more. (*They both smile, and there is a rapport of some unformed sort, established.*) I couldn't agree with you more.

GEORGE. Martha, your obscenity is more than. . . .

MARTHA. George, here, doesn't cotton much to body talk . . . do you sweetheart? (*No reply*) George isn't too happy when we get to muscle. You know . . . flat bellies, pectorals. . . .

GEORGE (*to* HONEY). Would you like to take a walk around the garden?

HONEY (*chiding*). Oh, now. . . .

GEORGE (*incredulous*). You're amused? (*Shrugs.*) All right.

MARTHA. Paunchy over there isn't too happy when the conversation moves to muscle. How much do you weigh?

NICK. A hundred and fifty-five, a hundred and. . . .

MARTHA. Still at the old middleweight limit, eh? That's pretty good. (*Swings around.*) Hey George, tell 'em about the boxing match *we* had.

GEORGE (*slamming his drink down, moving toward the hall*). Christ!

MARTHA. George! Tell 'em about it!

GEORGE (*with a sick look on his face*). You tell them, Martha. You're good at it. (*Exits.*)

HONEY. Is he . . . all right?

MARTHA (*laughs*). Him? Oh, sure. George and I had this boxing match . . . Oh, Lord, twenty years ago . . . a couple of years after we were married.

NICK. A boxing match? The two of you?

HONEY. Really?

MARTHA. Yup . . . the two of us . . . really.

HONEY (*with a little shivery giggle of anticipation*). I can't magine it.

MARTHA. Well, like I say, it was twenty years ago, and it wasn't in a ring, or anything like that, you know what I mean. It was wartime, and Daddy was on this physical fitness kick . . . Daddy's always admired physical fitness . . . says a man is only part brain . . . he has a body, too, and it's his responsibility to keep both of them up . . . you know?

NICK. Unh-hunh.

MARTHA. Says the brain can't work unless the body's working, too.

NICK. Well, that's not exactly so. . . .

MARTHA. Well, maybe that *isn't* what he says . . . something like it. *But* . . . it was wartime, and Daddy got the idea all the men should learn how to box . . . self-defense. I suppose the idea was if the Germans landed on the coast, or something, the whole faculty'd go out and punch 'em to death. . . . I don't know.

NICK. It was probably more the principle of the thing.

MARTHA. No kidding. Anyway, so Daddy had a couple of us over one Sunday and we went out in the back, and Daddy put on the gloves himself. Daddy's a strong man. . . . Well, *you* know.

NICK. Yes . . . yes.

MARTHA And he asked George to box with him Aaaaannnnd . . . George didn't *want* to . . . probably something about not wanting to bloody-up his meal ticket. . . .

NICK. Unh-hunh.

MARTHA. . . . Anyway, George said he didn't want to, and Daddy was saying, "Come on, young man . . . what sort of son-in-law *are* you?" . . . and stuff like that.

NICK. Yeah.

MARTHA. So, while this was going on . . . I don't know why I *did* it . . . I got into a pair of gloves myself . . . you know, I didn't lace 'em up, or anything . . . and I snuck up behind George, just kidding, and I yelled "Hey George!" and at the same time I let go sort of a round-house right . . . just kidding, you know?

NICK. Unh-hunh.

MARTHA. . . . and George wheeled around real quick, and he caught it right in the jaw . . . POW! (NICK *laughs*.) I hadn't meant it . . . honestly. Anyway . . . POW! Right in the jaw . . . and he was off balance . . . he must have been . . . and he stumbled back a few steps, and then, CRASH, he landed . . . flat . . . in a huckleberry bush! (NICK *laughs*. HONEY *goes* tsk, tsk, tsk, tsk, *and shakes her head*.) It was awful, really. It was funny, but it was awful. (*She thinks, gives a muffled laugh in rueful contemplation of the incident.*) I think it's colored our whole life. Really I do! It's an excuse, anyway. (GEORGE *enters now, his hands behind his back. No one sees him.*) It's what he uses for being bogged down, anyway . . . why he hasn't *gone* anywhere.

(GEORGE *advances.* HONEY *sees him.*)

MARTHA. And it was an *accident* . . . a real, goddamn accident!

(GEORGE *takes from behind his back a short-barreled shotgun, and calmly aims it at the back of* MARTHA's *head.* HONEY *screams . . . rises.* NICK *rises, and, simultaneously,* MARTHA *turns her head to face* GEORGE. GEORGE *pulls the trigger.*)

GEORGE. POW!!! (*Pop! From the barrel of the gun blossoms a large red and yellow Chinese parasol.* HONEY *screams again, this time less, and mostly from relief and confusion.*) You're dead! Pow! You're dead!

NICK (*laughing*). Good Lord. (HONEY *is beside herself.* MARTHA *laughs too . . . almost breaks down, her great laugh booming.* GEORGE *joins in the general laughter and confusion. It dies, eventually.*)

HONEY. Oh! My goodness!

MARTHA (*joyously*). Where'd you get that, you bastard?

NICK (*his hand out for the gun*). Let me see that, will you?

(GEORGE *hands him the gun.*)

HONEY. I've never been so frightened in my life! Never!

GEORGE (*a trifle abstracted*). Oh, I've had it awhile. Did you like that?

MARTHA (*giggling*). You bastard.

HONEY (*wanting attention*). I've *never* been so frightened . . . never.

NICK. This is quite a gadget.

GEORGE (*leaning over* MARTHA). You liked that, did you?

MARTHA. Yeah . . . that was pretty good. (*Softer*) C'mon . . . give me a kiss.

GEORGE (*indicating* NICK *and* HONEY). Later, sweetie. (*But* MARTHA *will not be dissuaded. They kiss,* GEORGE *standing, leaning over* MARTHA's *chair. She takes his hand, places it on her stage-side breast. He breaks away.*) Oh-ho! That's what you're after, is it? What are we going to have . . . blue games for the guests? Hunh? Hunh?

MARTHA (*angry-hurt*). You . . . prick!

GEORGE (*a Pyrrhic victory*). Everything in its place, Martha . . . everything in its own good time.

MARTHA (*an unspoken epithet*). You. . . .

GEORGE (*over to* NICK, *who still has the gun*). Here, let me show you . . . it goes back in, like this. (*Closes the parasol, reinserts it in the gun.*)

NICK. That's damn clever.

GEORGE (*puts the gun down*). Drinks now! Drinks for all! (*Takes* NICK's *glass without question . . . goes to* MARTHA.)

MARTHA (*still angry-hurt*). I'm not finished.

HONEY (*as* GEORGE *puts out his hand for her glass*). Oh, I think I need *something.*

(*He takes her glass, moves back to the portable bar.*)

NICK. Is that Japanese?

GEORGE. Probably.

HONEY (*to* MARTHA). I was never so frightened in my life. Weren't you frightened? Just for a second?

MARTHA (*smothering her rage at* GEORGE). I don't remember.

HONEY. Ohhhh, now . . . I bet you were.

GEORGE. Did you really think I was going to kill you, Martha?

MARTHA (*dripping contempt*). You? . . . Kill me? . . . That's a laugh.

GEORGE. Well, now, I might . . . some day.

MARTHA. Fat chance.

NICK (*as* GEORGE *hands him his drink*). Where's the john?

GEORGE. Through the hall there . . . and down to your left.

HONEY. Don't you come back with any guns, or anything, now.

NICK (*laughs*). Oh, no.

MARTHA. You don't need any props, do you, baby?

NICK. Unh-unh.

MARTHA (*suggestive*). I'll bet not. No fake Jap gun for you, eh?

NICK (*smiles at* MARTHA. *Then, to* GEORGE, *indicating a side table near the hall*). May I leave my drink here?

GEORGE (*as* NICK EXITS *without waiting for a reply*). Yeah . . . sure . . . why not? We've got half-filled glasses everywhere in the house, wherever Martha forgets she's left them . . . in the linen closet, on the edge of the bathtub. . . . . I even found one in the freezer, once.

MARTHA (*amused in spite of herself*). You did not!

GEORGE. *Yes* I did.

MARTHA (*ibid*). You did *not!*

GEORGE (*giving* HONEY *her brandy*). Yes I *did*. (*To* HONEY.) Brandy doesn't give you a hangover?

HONEY. I never mix. And then, I don't drink very much, either.

GEORGE (*grimaces behind her back*). Oh . . . that's good. Your . . . your husband was telling me all about the . . . chromosomes.

MARTHA (*ugly*). The what?

GEORGE. The chromosomes, Martha . . . the genes, or whatever they are. (*To* HONEY) You've got quite a . . . terrifying husband.

HONEY (*as if she's being joshed*). Ohhhhhhhhh. . . .

GEORGE. No, really. He's quite terrifying, with his chromosomes, and all.

MARTHA. He's in the Math Department.

GEORGE. No, Martha . . . he's a biologist.

MARTHA (*her voice rising*). He's in the *Math* Department!

HONEY (*timidly*). Uh . . . biology.

MARTHA (*unconvinced*). Are *you* sure?

HONEY (*with a little giggle*). Well, I ought to. (*Then as an afterthought*) Be.

MARTHA (*grumpy*). I suppose *so*. I don't know who said he was in the Math Department.

GEORGE. You did, Martha.

MARTHA (*by way of irritable explana-* *tion*). Well, I can't be expected to remember *everything*. I meet fifteen new teachers and their goddamn wives . . . present company outlawed, of course . . . (HONEY *nods, smiles sillily*.) . . . and I'm supposed to remember *everything*. (*Pause*) So? He's a biologist. Good for him. Biology's even better. It's less . . . abstruse.

GEORGE. Abstract.

MARTHA. ABSTRUSE! In the sense of recondite. (*Sticks her tongue out at* GEORGE.) Don't you tell me words. Biology's even better. It's . . . right at the *meat* of things. (NICK *reenters*.) You're right at the meat of things, baby.

NICK (*taking his drink from the side table*). Oh?

HONEY (*with that giggle*).They thought you were in the Math Department.

NICK. Well, maybe I ought to be.

MARTHA. You stay right where you are . . . you stay right at the . . . *meat* of things.

GEORGE. You're obsessed with that phrase, Martha. . . . It's ugly.

MARTHA (*ignoring* GEORGE . . . *to* NICK). You stay right there. (*Laughs*.) Hell, you can take over the History Department just as easy from there as anywhere else. God knows, *some*body's going to take over the History Department, *some* day, and it ain't going to be Georgie-boy, there . . . that's for sure. Are ya, swampy . . . are ya, hunh?

GEORGE. In my mind, Martha, you are buried in cement, right up to your neck. (MARTHA *giggles*.) No . . . right up to your nose . . . that's much quieter.

MARTHA (*to* NICK). Georgie-boy, here, says you're terrifying. Why are you terrifying?

NICK (*with a small smile*). I didn't know I was.

HONEY (*a little thickly*). It's because of your chromosomes, dear.

NICK. Oh, the chromosome business. . . .

MARTHA (*to* NICK). What's all this about chromosomes?

NICK. Well, chromosomes are. . . .

MARTHA. I know what chromosomes are, sweetie, I love 'em.

NICK. Oh. . . . Well, then.

GEORGE. Martha eats them . . . for breakfast . . . she sprinkles them on her cereal. (*To* MARTHA, *now*) It's very simple, Martha, this young man is working on a system whereby chromosomes can be altered . . . well not all by himself—he probably has one or two co-conspirators—the genetic makeup of a sperm cell changed, reordered . . . *to* order, actually . . . for hair and eye color, stature, potency . . . I imagine . . . hairiness, features, health . . . and *mind.* Most important . . . Mind. All imbalances will be corrected, sifted out . . . propensity for various diseases will be gone, longevity assured. We will have a race of men . . . test-tube-bred . . . incubator-born . . . superb and sublime.

MARTHA (*impressed*). Hunh!

HONEY. How exciting!

GEORGE. *But!* Everyone will tend to be rather the same. . . . Alike. Everyone . . . and I'm sure I'm not wrong here . . . will tend to look like this young man *here.*

MARTHA. *That's* not a bad idea.

NICK (*impatient*). All right, now. . . .

GEORGE. It will, on the surface of it, be all rather pretty . . . quite jolly. But of course there will be a dank side to it, too. A certain amount of regulation will be necessary . . . uh . . . for the experiment to succeed. A certain number of sperm tubes will have to be cut.

MARTHA. Hunh! . . .

GEORGE. Millions upon millions of them . . . millions of tiny little slicing operations that will leave just the smallest scar, on the underside of the scrotum (MARTHA *laughs.*) but which will assure the sterility of the imperfect . . . the ugly, the stupid . . . the . . . unfit.

NICK (*grimly*). Now look . . . !

GEORGE. . . . with this, we will have, in time, a race of glorious men.

MARTHA. Hunh!

GEORGE. I suspect we will not have much music, much painting, but we will have a civilization of men, smooth, blond, and right at the middleweight limit.

MARTHA. Awww. . . .

GEORGE. . . . a race of scientists and mathematicians, each dedicated to and working for the greater glory of the super-civilization.

MARTHA. Goody.

GEORGE. There will be a certain . . . loss of liberty, I imagine, as a result of this experiment . . . but diversity will no longer be the goal. Cultures and races will eventually vanish . . . the ants will take over the world.

NICK. Are you finished?

GEORGE (*ignoring him*). And I, naturally, am rather opposed to all this. History, which is my field . . . history, of which I am one of the most famous bogs. . . .

MARTHA. Ha, ha, HA!

GEORGE. . . . will lose its glorious variety and unpredictability. I, and with me the . . . the surprise, the multiplexity, the sea-changing rhythm of . . . history, will be eliminated. There will be order and constancy . . . and I am unalterably opposed to it. I will not give up Berlin!

MARTHA. You'll give up Berlin, sweetheart. You going to defend it with your paunch?

HONEY. I don't see what Berlin has to *do* with anything.

GEORGE. There is a saloon in West Berlin where the barstools are five feet high. And the earth . . . the floor . . . is . . . so . . . far . . . below you. I will not give up things like that. No . . . I won't. I will fight you, young man . . . one hand on my scrotum, to be sure . . . but with my free hand I will battle you to the death.

MARTHA (*mocking, laughing*). Bravo!

NICK (*to* GEORGE). That's right. And I am going to be the wave of the future.

MARTHA. You bet you are, baby.

HONEY (*quite drunk—to* NICK). I don't see why you want to do all those things, dear. You never told me.

NICK (*angry*). Oh for God's sake!

HONEY (*shocked*). OH!

GEORGE. The most profound indication of a social malignancy . . . no sense of humor. None of the monoliths could take a joke. Read history. I know something about history.

NICK (*to* GEORGE, *trying to make light of it all*). You . . . you don't know much about science, do you?

GEORGE. I know something about history. I know when I'm being threatened.

MARTHA (*salaciously—to* NICK). So, everyone's going to look like you, eh?

NICK. Oh, sure. I'm going to be a personal screwing machine!

MARTHA. Isn't that nice.

HONEY (*her hands over her ears*). Dear, you mustn't . . . you mustn't . . . you mustn't.

NICK (*impatiently*). I'm sorry, Honey.

HONEY. Such language. It's. . . .

NICK. I'm *sorry*. All right?

HONEY (*pouting*). Well . . . all right. (*Suddenly she giggles insanely, subsides. To* GEORGE) . . . When is your son? (*Giggles again.*)

GEORGE. What?

NICK (*distastefully*). Something about your son.

GEORGE. SON!

HONEY. When is . . . where is your son . . . coming home? (*Giggles.*)

GREORGE. Ohhhh. (*Too formal*) Martha? When is our son coming home?

MARTHA. Never mind.

GEORGE. No, no . . . I want to know . . . you brought it out into the open. When is he coming home, Martha?

MARTHA. I said never mind. I'm sorry I brought it up.

GEORGE. Him up . . . not it. You brought *him* up. Well, more or less. When's the little bugger going to appear, hunh? I mean isn't tomorrow meant to be his birthday, or something?

MARTHA. I don't want to talk about it!

GEORGE (*falsely innocent*). But Martha. . . .

MARTHA. I DON'T WANT TO TALK ABOUT IT!

GEORGE. I'll bet you don't. (*To* HONEY *and* NICK) Martha does not want to talk about it . . . him. Martha is sorry she brought it up . . . him.

HONEY (*idiotically*). When's the little bugger coming home? (*Giggles.*)

GEORGE. Yes, Martha . . . since you had the bad taste to bring the matter up in the first place . . . when *is* the little bugger coming home?

NICK. Honey, do you think you . . . ?

MARTHA. George talks disparagingly about the little bugger because . . . well, because he has problems.

GEORGE. The little bugger has problems? What problems has the little bugger got?

MARTHA. Not the little bugger . . . stop calling him that! You! You've got problems.

GEORGE (*feigned disdain*). I've never heard of anything more ridiculous in my life.

HONEY. Neither have I!

NICK. Honey. . . .

MARTHA. George's biggest problem about the little . . . ha, ha, ha, HA! . . .

about our son, about our great big son, is that deep down in the private-most pit of his gut, he's not completely sure it's his own kid.

GEORGE (*deeply serious*). My God, you're a wicked woman.

MARTHA. And I've told you a million times, baby . . . I wouldn't conceive with anyone but you . . . you know that, baby.

GEORGE. A deeply wicked person.

HONEY (*deep in drunken grief*). My, my, my, my. Oh, my.

NICK. I'm not sure that this is a subject for. . . .

GEORGE. Martha's lying. I want you to know that, right now. Martha's lying. (MARTHA *laughs.*) There are very few things in this world that I *am* sure of . . . national boundaries, the level of the ocean, political allegiances, practical morality . . . none of these would I stake my stick on any more . . . but the one thing in this whole sinking world that I am sure of is my partnership, my chromosomological partnership in the . . . creation of our . . . blond-eyed, blue-haired . . . son.

HONEY. Oh, I'm so glad!

MARTHA. That was a very pretty speech, George.

GEORGE. Thank you, Martha.

MARTHA. You rose to the occasion . . . good. Real good.

HONEY. Well . . . real well.

NICK. Honey. . . .

GEORGE. Martha knows . . . she knows better.

MARTHA (*proudly*). I know better. I been to college like everybody else.

GEORGE. Martha been to college. Martha been to a convent when she were a little twig of a thing, too.

MARTHA. And I was an atheist. (*Uncertainly*) I still am.

GEORGE. Not an atheist, Martha . . . a pagan. (*To* HONEY *and* NICK) Martha is the only true pagan on the eastern seaboard. (MARTHA *laughs.*)

HONEY. Oh, that's nice. Isn't that nice, dear?

NICK (*humoring her*). Yes . . . wonderful.

GEORGE. And Martha paints blue circles around her things.

NICK. You do?

MARTHA (*defensively, for the joke's sake*). Sometimes. (*Beckoning*) You wanna see?

GEORGE (*admonishing*). Tut, tut, tut.

MARTHA. Tut, tut yourself . . . you old floozie!

HONEY. He's not a floozie . . . he can't be a floozie . . . you're a floozie. (*Giggles.*)

MARTHA (*shaking a finger at* HONEY). Now you watch yourself!

HONEY (*cheerfully*). All right. I'd like a nipper of brandy, please.

NICK. Honey, I think you've had enough, now. . . .

GEORGE. Nonsense! Everybody's ready, I think. (*Takes glasses, etc.*)

HONEY (*echoing* GEORGE). Nonsense.

NICK (*shrugging*). O.K.

MARTHA (*to* GEORGE). Our son does *not* have blue hair . . . or blue eyes, for that matter. He has green eyes . . . like me.

GEORGE. He has blue eyes, Martha.

MARTHA (*determined*). Green.

GEORGE (*patronizing*). Blue, Martha.

MARTHA (*ugly*). GREEN! (*To* HONEY *and* NICK.) He has the loveliest green eyes . . . they aren't all flaked with brown and gray, you know . . . hazel . . . they're real green . . . deep, pure green eyes . . . like mine.

NICK (*peers*). Your eyes are . . . brown, aren't they?

MARTHA. Green! (*A little too fast*) Well, in some lights they look brown, but they're green. Not green like his . . . more hazel. George has watery blue eyes . . . milky blue.

GEORGE. Make up your mind, Martha.

MARTHA. I was giving you the benefit of the doubt. (*Now back to the others*) Daddy has green eyes, too.

GEORGE. He does not! Your father has tiny red eyes . . . like a white mouse. In fact, he *is* a white mouse.

MARTHA. You wouldn't dare say a thing like that if he was here! You're a coward!

GEORGE (*to* HONEY *and* NICK). You know . . . that great shock of white hair, and those little beady red eyes . . . a great big white mouse.

MARTHA. George hates Daddy . . . not for anything Daddy's done to him, but for his own. . . .

GEORGE (*nodding . . . finishing it for her*). . . . . inadequacies.

MARTHA (*cheerfully*). That's right. You hit it . . . right on the snout. (*Seeing*

GEORGE *exiting.*) Where do you think *you're* going?

GEORGE. We need some more booze, angel.

MARTHA. Oh. (*Pause*) So, go.

GEORGE (*exiting*). Thank you.

MARTHA (*seeing that* GEORGE *has gone*). He's a good bartender . . . a good bar nurse. The S.O.B., he hates my father. You know that?

NICK (*trying to make light of it*). Oh, come on.

MARTHA (*offended*). You think I'm kidding? You think I'm joking? I never joke . . . I don't have a sense of humor. (*Almost pouting*) I have a fine sense of the ridiculous, but no sense of humor. (*Affirmatively*) I have no sense of humor!

HONEY (*happily*). I haven't, either.

NICK (*half-heartedly*). Yes, you have, Honey . . . a quiet one.

HONEY (*proudly*). Thank you.

MARTHA. You want to know *why* the S.O.B. hates my father? You want me to tell you? All right. . . . I will now tell you why the S.O.B. hates my father.

HONEY (*swinging to some sort of attention*). Oh, good!

MARTHA (*sternly, to* HONEY). *Some* people feed on the calamities of others.

HONEY (*offended*). They do not!

NICK. Honey. . . .

MARTHA. All right! Shut up! Both of you! (*Pause*) All right, now. Mommy died early, see, and I sort of grew up with Daddy. (*Pause—thinks.*) . . . I went away to school, and stuff, but I more or less grew up with him. Jesus, I admired that guy! I worshipped him . . . I absolutely worshipped him. I still do. And he was pretty fond of me, too . . . you know? We had a real . . . rapport going . . . a real rapport.

NICK. Yeah, yeah.

MARTHA. And Daddy built this college . . . I mean, he built it up from what it was . . . it's his whole life. He *is* the college.

NICK. Unh-hunh.

MARTHA. The college is him. You know what the endowment was when he took over, and what it is *now*? You look it up some time.

NICK. I know . . . I read about it. . . .

MARTHA. Shut up and listen . . . (*As an afterthought*) . . . cutie. So after I got done with college and stuff, I came back here and sort of . . . sat around, for a while. I wasn't married, or anything. Wellllll, I'd *been* married . . . sort of . . . for a week, my sophomore year at Miss Muff's Academy for Young Ladies . . . college. A kind of junior Lady Chatterly arrangement, as it turned out . . . the marriage. (NICK *laughs.*) He mowed the lawn at Miss Muff's, sitting up there, all naked, on a big power mower, mowing away. But Daddy and Miss Muff got together and put an end to that . . . real quick . . . annulled . . . which is a laugh . . . because theoretically you can't get an annullment if there's entrance. Ha! Anyway, so I was revirginized, finished at Miss Muff's . . . where they had one less gardener's boy, and a real shame, that was . . . and I came back here and sort of sat around for a while. I was hostess for Daddy and I took care of him . . . and it was . . . nice. It was very nice.

NICK. Yes . . . yes.

MARTHA. What do you mean, yes, yes? How would you know? (NICK *shrugs helplessly.*) Lover. (NICK *smiles a little.*) And I got the idea, about then, that I'd marry into the college . . . which didn't seem to be quite as stupid as it turned out. I mean, Daddy had a sense of history . . . of . . . continuation. . . . Why don't you come over here and sit by me?

NICK (*indicating* HONEY, *who is barely with it*). I . . . don't think I . . . should. . . . I. . . .

MARTHA. Suit yourself. A sense of continuation . . . history . . . and he'd always had it in the back of his mind to . . . *groom* someone to take over . . . some time, when he quit. A succession . . . you know what I mean?

NICK. Yes, I do.

MARTHA. Which is natural enough. When you've made something, you want to pass it on, to somebody. So, I was sort of on the lookout, for . . . prospects with the new men. An heir-apparent. (*Laughs.*) It wasn't *Daddy's* idea that I had to necessarily marry the guy. I mean, I wasn't the albatross . . . you didn't have to take me to get the prize, or anything like that. It was something *I* had in the back of *my* mind. And a lot of the new men were married . . . naturally.

NICK. Sure.

MARTHA (*with a strange smile*). Like you, baby.

HONEY (*a mindless echo*). Like you, baby.

MARTHA (*ironically*). But then George came along . . . along come George.

GEORGE (*reentering, with liquor*). And along came George, bearing hooch. What are you doing now, Martha?

MARTHA (*unfazed*). I'm telling a story. Sit down . . . you'll learn something.

GEORGE (*stays standing. Puts the liquor on the portable bar*). All rightie.

HONEY. You've come back!

GEORGE. That's right.

HONEY. Dear! He's come back!

NICK. Yes, I see . . . I see.

MARTHA. Where was I?

HONEY. I'm *so* glad.

NICK. Shhhhh.

HONEY (*imitating him*). Shhhhh.

MARTHA. Oh yeah. And along came George. That's right. WHO was young . . . intelligent . . . and . . . bushy-tailed, and . . . sort of cute . . . if you can imagine it. . . .

GEORGE. . . . and younger than you. . . .

MARTHA. . . . and younger than me. . . .

GEORGE. . . . by six years. . . .

MARTHA. . . . by six years. . . . It doesn't bother me, George. . . . And along he came, bright-eyed, into the History Department. And you know what I did, dumb cluck that I am? You know what I did? I fell for him.

HONEY (*dreamy*). Oh, that's nice.

GEORGE. Yes, she did. You should have seen it. She'd sit outside of my room, on the lawn, at night, and she'd howl and claw at the turf . . . I couldn't work.

MARTHA (*laughs, really amused*). I actually fell for him . . . it . . . that, there.

GEORGE. Martha's a Romantic at heart.

MARTHA. That I am. So, I actually fell for him. And the match seemed . . . practical, too. You know, Daddy was looking for someone to. . . .

GEORGE. Just a minute, Martha. . . .

MARTHA. . . . take over, some time, when he was ready to. . . .

GEORGE (*stony*). Just a minute, Martha.

MARTHA. . . . retire, and so I thought. . . .

GEORGE. STOP IT, MARTHA!

MARTHA (*irritated*). Whadda you want?

GEORGE (*too patiently*). I'd thought you were telling the story of our courtship, Martha . . . I didn't know you were going to start in on the other business.

MARTHA (*so-thereish*). Well, I am!

GEORGE. I wouldn't, if I were you.

MARTHA. Oh . . . you wouldn't? Well, you're not!

GEORGE. Now, you've already sprung a leak about you-know-what. . . .

MARTHA (*a duck*). What? What?

GEORGE. . . . about the apple of our eye . . . the sprout . . . the little bugger . . . (*Spits it out.*) . . . our *son* . . . and if you start in on this other business, I warn you, Martha, it's going to make me angry.

MARTHA (*laughing at him*). Oh, it is, is it?

GEORGE. I warn you.

MARTHA (*incredulous*). You *what?*

GEORGE (*very quietly*). I warn you.

NICK. Do you really think we have to go through . . . ?

MARTHA. I stand warned! (*Pause . . . then, to* HONEY *and* NICK) So, anyway, I married the S.O.B., and I had it all planned out. . . . He was the groom . . . he was going to be groomed. He'd take over some day . . . first, he'd take over the History Department, and then, when Daddy retired, he'd take over the college . . . you know? That's the way it was supposed to be. (*To* GEORGE, *who is at the portable bar with his back to her*) You getting angry, baby? Hunh? (*Now back*) That's the way it was *supposed* to be. Very simple. And Daddy seemed to think it was a pretty good idea, too. For a while. Until he watched for a couple of years! (*To* GEORGE *again*) You getting angrier? (*Now back*) Until he watched for a couple of years and started thinking maybe it wasn't such a good idea after all . . . that maybe Georgie-boy didn't have the stuff . . . that he didn't have it in him!

GEORGE (*still with his back to them all*). Stop it, Martha.

MARTHA (*viciously triumphant*). The hell I will! You see, George didn't have much . . . push . . . he wasn't particularly . . . aggressive. In fact he was sort of a .. (*Spits the word at* GEORGE's *back.*) . . . a FLOP! A great . . . big . . . fat . . . FLOP!

(CRASH! *Immediately after* Flop! GEORGE *breaks a bottle against the portable bar and stands there, still with his back to them all, holding the remains of the bottle by the neck. There is a silence, with* everyone frozen. Then. . . .)

GEORGE (*almost crying*). I said stop, Martha.

MARTHA (*after considering what course to take*). I hope that was an empty bottle, George. You don't want to waste good liquor . . . not on your salary. (GEORGE *drops the broken bottle on the floor, not moving.*) Not on an Associate Professor's salary. (*To* NICK *and* HONEY) I mean, he'd be . . . no good . . . at trustees' dinners, fund raising. He didn't have any . . . personality, you know what I mean? Which was disappointing to Daddy, as you can imagine. So, here I am, stuck with this flop. . . .

GEORGE (*turning around*). . . . don't go on, Martha. . . .

MARTHA. . . . this BOG in the History Department. . . .

GEORGE. . . . don't, Martha, don't. . . .

MARTHA (*her voice rising to match his*). . . . who's married to the President's daughter, who's expected to *be* somebody, not just some nobody, some bookworm, somebody who's so damn . . . contemplative, he can't make anything out of himself, somebody without the *guts* to make anybody proud of him . . . ALL RIGHT, GEORGE!

GEORGE (*under her, then covering, to drown her*). I said, don't. All right . . . all right: (*Sings.*)
Who's afraid of Virginia Woolf,
   Virginia Woolf,
   Virginia Woolf,
Who's afraid of Virginia Woolf,
 early in the morning.

GEORGE *and* HONEY (*who joins him drunkenly*).
Who's afraid of Virginia Woolf,
   Virginia Woolf,
   Virginia Woolf . . . (*etc.*)

MARTHA. STOP IT!

(*A brief silence.*)

HONEY (*rising, moving toward the hall*). I'm going to be sick . . . I'm going to be sick . . . I'm going to vomit. (*Exits.*)

NICK (*going after her*). Oh, for God's sake! (*Exits.*)

MARTHA (*going after them, looks back at* GEORGE, *contemptuously*). Jesus! (*Exits.* GEORGE *is alone on stage.*)

CURTAIN

ACT TWO:

WALPURGISNACHT

GEORGE, *by himself:* NICK *reenters.*

———

NICK (*after a silence*). I . . . guess . . . she's all right. (*No answer*) She . . . really shouldn't drink. (*No answer*) She's . . . frail. (*No answer*) Uh . . . slim-hipped, as you'd have it. (GEORGE *smiles vaguely.*) I'm really very sorry.

GEORGE (*quietly*). Where's my little yum yum? Where's Martha?

NICK. She's making coffee . . . in the kitchen. She . . . gets sick quite easily.

GEORGE (*preoccupied*). Martha? Oh no, Martha hasn't been sick a day in her life, unless you count the time she spends in the rest home. . . .

NICK (*he, too, quietly*). No, no; *my* wife . . . *my* wife gets sick quite easily. Your wife is Martha.

GEORGE (*with some rue*). Oh, yes . . . I know.

NICK (*a statement of fact*). She doesn't really spend any time in a rest home.

GEORGE. Your wife?

NICK. No. Yours.

GEORGE. Oh! Mine. (*Pause*) No, no, she doesn't . . . *I* would; I mean if I were . . . her . . . she . . . *I* would. But I'm not . . . and so I don't. (*Pause*) I'd like to, though. It gets pretty bouncy around here sometimes.

NICK (*coolly*). Yes . . . I'm sure.

GEORGE. Well, you saw an example of it.

NICK. I try not to. . . .

GEORGE. Get involved. Um? Isn't that right?

NICK. Yes . . . that's right.

GEORGE. I'd imagine not.

NICK. I find it . . . embarrassing.

GEORGE (*sarcastic*). Oh, you do, hunh?

NICK. Yes. Really. Quite.

GEORGE (*mimicking him*). Yes. Really. Quite. (*Then aloud, but to himself*) IT'S DISGUSTING!

NICK. Now look! I didn't have anything. . . .

GEORGE. DISGUSTING! (*Quietly, but with great intensity*) Do you think I like having that . . . whatever-it-is . . . ridiculing me, tearing me down, in front of . . . (*Waves his hand in a gesture of contemptuous dismissal.*) YOU? Do you think I *care* for it?

NICK (*cold—unfriendly*). Well, no . . . I don't imagine you care for it at all.

GEORGE. Oh, you don't imagine it, hunh?

NICK (*antagonistic*). No . . . I don't. I don't imagine you do!

GEORGE (*withering*). Your sympathy disarms me . . . your . . . your compassion makes me weep! Large, salty, unscientific tears!

NICK (*with great disdain*). I just don't see why you feel you have to subject *other* people to it.

GEORGE. *I?*

NICK. If you and your . . . wife . . . want to go at each other, like a couple of. . . .

GEORGE. *I?* Why *I* want to!

NICK. . . . animals, I don't see why you don't do it when there aren't any. . . .

GEORGE (*laughing through his anger*). Why, you smug, self-righteous little. . . .

NICK (*a genuine threat*). CAN . . . IT . . . MISTER! (*Silence*) Just . . . watch it!

GEORGE. . . . scientist.

NICK. I've never hit an older man.

GEORGE (*considers it*). Oh. (*Pause*) You just hit younger men . . . and children . . . women . . . birds. (*Sees that* NICK *is not amused.*) Well, you're quite right, of course. It isn't the prettiest spectacle . . . seeing a couple of middle-age types hacking away at each other, all red in the face and winded, missing half the time.

NICK. Oh, you two don't miss . . . you two are pretty good. Impressive.

GEORGE. And impressive things impress you, don't they? You're . . . easily impressed . . . sort of a . . . pragmatic idealism.

NICK (*a tight smile*). No, it's that sometimes I can admire things that I don't admire. Now, flagellation isn't my idea of good times, but. . . .

GEORGE. . . . but you can admire a good flagellator . . . a real pro.

NICK. Unh-hunh . . . yeah.

GEORGE. Your wife throws up a lot, eh?

NICK. I didn't say that. . . . I said she gets sick quite easily.

GEORGE. Oh. I thought by sick you meant. . . .

NICK. Well, it's true. . . . She . . . she does throw up a lot. Once she starts . . . there's practically no stopping her. . . . I mean, she'll go right on . . . for hours.

Not all the time, but . . . regularly.

GEORGE. You can tell time by her, hunh?

NICK. Just about.

GEORGE. Drink?

NICK. Sure. (*With no emotion, except the faintest distaste, as* GEORGE *takes his glass to the bar*) I married her because she was pregnant.

GEORGE. (*Pause*) Oh? (*Pause*) But you said you didn't have any children . . . When I asked you, you said. . . .

NICK. She wasn't . . . really. It was a hysterical pregnancy. She blew up, and then she went down.

GEORGE. And while she was up, you married her.

NICK. And then she went down. (*They both laugh, and are a little surprised that they do.*)

GEORGE. Uh . . . Bourbon *is* right.

NICK. Uh . . . yes, Bourbon.

GEORGE (*at the bar, still*). When I was sixteen and going to prep school, during the Punic Wars, a bunch of us used to go into New York on the first day of vacations, before we fanned out to our homes, and in the evening this bunch of us used to go to this gin mill owned by the gangster-father of one of us—for this was during the Great Experiment, or Prohibition, as it is more frequently called, and it was a bad time for the liquor lobby, but a fine time for the crooks and the cops—and we would go to this gin mill, and we would drink with the grown-ups and listen to the jazz. And one time, in the bunch of us, there was this boy who was fifteen, and he had killed his mother with a shotgun some years before—accidentally, completely accidentally, without even an unconscious motivation, I have no doubt, no doubt at all—and this one evening this boy went with us, and we ordered our drinks, and when it came his turn he said, I'll have bergin . . . give me some bergin, please . . . bergin and water. Well, we all laughed . . . he was blond and he had the face of a cherub, and we all laughed, and his cheeks went red and the color rose in his neck, and the assistant crook who had taken our order told people at the next table what the boy had said, and then they laughed, and then more people were told and the laughter grew, and more laughter, and no one

was laughing more than us, and none of us more than the boy who had shot his mother. And soon, everyone in the gin mill knew what the laughter was about, and everyone started ordering bergin, and laughing when they ordered it. And soon, of course, the laughter became less general, but it did not subside, entirely, for a very long time, for always at this table or that someone would order bergin and a new area of laughter would rise. We drank free that night, and we were bought champagne by the management, by the gangster-father of one of us. And, of course, we suffered the next day, each of us, alone, on his train, away from New York, each of us with a grown-up's hangover . . . but it was the grandest day of my . . . youth. (*Hands* NICK *a drink on the word.*)

NICK (*very quietly*). Thank you. What . . . what happened to the boy . . . the boy who had shot his mother?

GEORGE. I won't tell you.

NICK. All right.

GEORGE. The following summer, on a country road, with his learner's permit in his pocket and his father on the front seat to his right, he swerved the car, to avoid a porcupine, and drove straight into a large tree.

NICK (*faintly pleading*). No.

GEORGE. He was not killed, of course. And in the hospital, when he was conscious and out of danger, and when they told him that his father *was* dead, he began to laugh, I have been told, and his laughter grew and he would not stop, and it was not until after they jammed a needle in his arm, not until after that, until his consciousness slipped away from him, that his laughter subsided . . . stopped. And when he was recovered from his injuries enough so that he could be moved without damage should he struggle, he was put in an asylum. That was thirty years ago.

NICK. Is he . . . still there?

GEORGE. Oh, yes. And I'm told that for these thirty years he has . . . not . . . uttered . . . one . . . sound. (*A rather long silence: five seconds, please.*) MARTHA! (*Pause*) MARTHA!

NICK. I told you . . . she's making coffee.

GEORGE. For your hysterical wife, who goes up and down.

NICK. Went. Up and down.

GEORGE. Went. No more?

NICK. No more. Nothing.

GEORGE (*after a sympathetic pause*). The saddest thing about men. . . . Well, no, one of the saddest things about men is the way they age . . . some of them. Do you know what it is with insane people? Do you? . . . the quiet ones?

NICK. No.

GEORGE. They don't change . . . they don't grow old.

NICK. They must.

GEORGE. Well, eventually, probably, yes. But they don't . . . in the usual sense. They maintain a . . . a firm-skinned serenity . . . the . . . the under-use of everything leaves them . . . quite whole.

NICK Are you recommending it?

GEORGE No. Some things are sad, though. (*Imitates a pep-talker.*) But ya jest gotta buck up an' face 'em, 'at's all. Buck up! (*Pause*) Martha doesn't have hysterical pregnancies.

NICK. My wife had *one*.

GEORGE. Yes. Martha doesn't have pregnancies at all.

NICK. Well, no . . . I don't imagine so . . . now. Do you have any other kids? Do you have any daughters, or anything?

GEORGE (*as if it's a great joke*). Do we have any *what*?

NICK. Do you have any . . . I mean, do you have only one . . . kid . . . uh . . . your son?

GEORGE (*with a private knowledge*). Oh no . . . just one . . . one boy . . . our son.

NICK. Well . . . (*Shrugs.*) . . . that's nice.

GEORGE. Oh ho, ho. Yes, well, he's a . . . comfort, a bean bag.

NICK. A what?

GEORGE. A bean bag. Bean bag. You wouldn't understand. (*Over-distinct*) Bean . . . bag.

NICK. I *heard* you . . . I didn't say I was deaf . . . I said I didn't understand.

GEORGE. You didn't say that at all.

NICK. I meant I was *implying* I didn't understand. (*Under his breath*) For Christ's sake!

GEORGE. You're getting testy.

NICK (*testy*). I'm sorry.

GEORGE. All I said was, our son . . . the apple of our three eyes, Martha being a Cyclops . . . our son is a bean bag, and you get testy.

NICK. I'm sorry! It's late, I'm tired, I've been drinking since nine o'clock, my wife is vomiting, there's been a lot of screaming going on around here. . . .

GEORGE. And so you're testy. Naturally. Don't . . . worry about it. Anybody who comes here ends up getting . . . testy. It's expected . . . don't be upset.

NICK (*testy*) I'm not upset!

GEORGE. You're testy.

NICK. Yes.

GEORGE. I'd like to set you straight about something . . . while the little ladies are out of the room . . . I'd like to set you straight about what Martha said.

NICK. I don't . . . make judgments, so there's no need, really, unless you. . . .

GEORGE. Well, I want to. I know you don't like to become involved . . . I know you like to . . . preserve your scientific detachment in the face of—for lack of a better word—Life . . . and all . . . but still, I want to tell you.

NICK (*a tight, formal smile*). I'm a . . . guest. You go right ahead.

GEORGE (*mocking appreciation*). Oh . . . well, thanks. Now! That makes me feel all warm and runny inside.

NICK. Well, if you're going to . . .

MARTHA'S VOICE. HEY!

NICK. . . . if you're going to start that kind of stuff again. . . .

GEORGE. Hark! Forest sounds.

NICK. Hm?

GEORGE. Animal noises.

MARTHA (*sticking her head in*). Hey!

NICK. Oh!

GEORGE. Well, here's nursie.

MARTHA (*to* NICK). We're sitting up . . . we're having coffee, and we'll be back in.

NICK (*not rising*). Oh . . . is there anything I should do?

MARTHA. Nayh. You just stay here and listen to George's side of things. Bore yourself to death.

GEORGE. Monstre!

MARTHA. Cochon!

GEORGE. Bête!

MARTHA. Canaille!

GEORGE. Putain!

MARTHA (*with a gesture of contemptuous dismissal*). Yaaaahhhh! You two types amuse yourselves . . . we'll be in. (*As she goes*) You clean up the mess you made, George?

GEORGE (MARTHA *goes.* GEORGE *speaks to the empty hallway*). No, Martha, I did not clean up the mess I made. I've been trying for years to clean up the mess I made.

NICK. Have you?

GEORGE. Hm?

NICK. *Have* you been trying for years?

GEORGE (*after a long pause . . . looking at him*). Accommodation, malleability, adjustment . . . those do seem to be in the order of things, don't they?

NICK. Don't try to put me in the same class with you!

GEORGE (*pause*). Oh. (*Pause*) No, of course not. Things are simpler with you . . . you marry a woman because she's all blown up . . . while I, in my clumsy, old-fashioned way. . . .

NICK. There was more to it than that!

GEORGE. Sure! I'll bet she has money, too!

NICK (*looks hurt. Then, determined, after a pause*). Yes.

GEORGE. Yes? (*Joyfully*) YES! You mean I was right? I hit it?

NICK. Well, you see. . . .

GEORGE. My God, what archery! First try, too. How about that!

NICK. You see. . . .

GEORGE. There were other things.

NICK. Yes.

GEORGE. To compensate.

NICK. Yes.

GEORGE. There always are. (*Sees that* NICK *is reacting badly.*) No, I'm sure there are. I didn't mean to be . . . flip. There are *always* compensating factors . . . as in the case of Martha and myself. . . . Now, on the surface of it. . . .

NICK. We sort of grew up together, you know. . . .

GEORGE. . . . it looks to be a kind of knock-about, drag-out affair, on the *surface* of it. . . .

NICK. We knew each other from, oh God, I don't know, when we were *six,* or something. . . .

GEORGE. . . . but somewhere back there, at the beginning of it, right when I first came to New Carthage, back then. . . .

NICK (*with some irritation*). I'm *sorry.*

GEORGE. Hm? Oh. No, no . . . *I'm* sorry.

NICK. No . . . it's . . . it's all right.

GEORGE. No . . . you go ahead.

NICK. No . . . please.

GEORGE. I insist. . . . You're a guest. You go first.

NICK. Well, it seems a little silly . . . now.

GEORGE. Nonsense! (*Pause*) But if you were six, she must have been four, or something.

NICK. Maybe I was eight . . . she was six. We . . . we used to play . . . doctor.

GEORGE. That's a good healthy heterosexual beginning.

NICK (*laughing*). Yup.

GEORGE. The scientist even then, eh?

NICK (*laughs*). Yeah. And it was . . . always taken for granted . . . you know . . . by our families, and by us, too, I guess. And . . . so, we did.

GEORGE. (*Pause*) Did what?

NICK. We got married.

GEORGE. When you were eight?

NICK. No. No, of course not. Much later.

GEORGE. I wondered.

NICK. I wouldn't say there was any . . . particular *passion* between us, even at the beginning . . . of our marriage, I mean.

GEORGE. Well, certainly no surprise, no earth-shaking discoveries, after doctor, and all.

NICK (*uncertainly*). No. . . .

GEORGE. Everything's all pretty much the same, anyway . . . in *spite* of what they say about Chinese women.

NICK. What is that?

GEORGE. Let me freshen you up. (*Takes* NICK's *glass.*)

NICK. Oh, thanks. After a while you don't get any drunker, do you?

GEORGE. Well, you *do* . . . but it's different . . . everything slows down. . . . you get sodden. . . . unless you can upchuck . . . like your wife . . . then you can sort of start all over again.

NICK. Everybody drinks a lot here in the East. (*Thinks about it.*) Everybody drinks a lot in the Middle West, too.

GEORGE. We drink a great deal in this country, and I suspect we'll be drinking a great deal more, too . . . if we survive. We should be Arabs or Italians . . . the Arabs don't drink, and the Italians don't get drunk much, except on religious holidays. We should live on Crete, or something.

NICK (*sarcastically . . . as if killing a joke*). And that, of course, would make us cretins.

GEORGE (*mild surprise*). So it would. (*Hands* NICK *his drink.*) Tell me about your wife's money.

NICK (*suddenly suspicious*). Why?

GEORGE. Well . . . don't, then.

NICK. What do you want to know about my wife's money for? (*Ugly*) Hunh?

GEORGE. Well, I thought it would be nice.

NICK. No you didn't.

GEORGE (*still deceptively bland*). All right. . . . I want to know about your wife's money because . . . well, because I'm fascinated by the methodology . . . by the pragmatic accommodation by which you wave-of-the-future boys are going to take over.

NICK. You're starting in again.

GEORGE. Am I? No I'm not. Look . . . Martha has money too. I mean, her father's been robbing this place blind for years, and. . . .

NICK. No, he hasn't. He has not.

GEORGE. He hasn't?

NICK. No.

GEORGE (*shrugs*). Very well. . . . Martha's father has *not* been robbing this place blind for years, and Martha does not have any money. O.K.?

NICK. We were talking about *my* wife's money . . . not yours.

GEORGE. O.K. . . . talk.

NICK. No. (*Pause*) My father-in-law . . . was a man of the Lord, and he was very rich.

GEORGE. What faith?

NICK. He . . . my father-in-law . . . was called by God when he was six, or something, and he started preaching, and he baptized people, and he saved them, and he traveled around a lot, and he became pretty famous . . . not like some of them, but he became pretty famous . . . and when he died he had a lot of money.

GEORGE. God's money.

NICK. No . . . his own.

GEORGE. What happened to God's money?

NICK. He spent God's money . . . and he saved his own. He built hospitals, and he sent off Mercy ships, and he brought the outhouses indoors, and he brought the people outdoors, into the sun, and he built three churches, or whatever they were, and two of them burned down . . .

and he ended up pretty rich.

GEORGE (*after considering it*). Well, I think that's very nice.

NICK. Yes. (*Pause. Giggles a little.*) And so, my wife's got some money.

GEORGE. But not God's money.

NICK. No. Her own.

GEORGE. Well, I think that's very nice. (NICK *giggles a little.*) *Martha's* got money because Martha's father's second wife . . . not Martha's mother, but after Martha's mother died . . . was a very old lady with warts who was very rich.

NICK. She was a witch.

GEORGE. She was a *good* witch, and she married the white mouse . . . (NICK *begins to giggle.*) . . . with the tiny red eyes . . . and he must have nibbled her warts, or something like that, because she went up in a puff of smoke almost immediately. POUF!

NICK. POUF!

GEORGE. POUF! And all that was left, aside from some wart medicine, was a big fat will. . . . A peach pie, with some for the township of New Carthage, some for the college, some for Martha's daddy, and just this much for Martha.

NICK (*quite beside himself*). Maybe . . . maybe my father-in-law and the witch with the warts should have gotten together, because he was a mouse, too.

GEORGE (*urging* NICK *on*). He was?

NICK (*breaking down*). Sure . . . he was a church mouse! (*They both laugh a great deal, but it is sad laughter . . . eventually they subside, fall silent.*) Your wife never mentioned a stepmother.

GEORGE (*considers it*). Well . . . maybe it isn't true.

NICK (*narrowing his eyes*). And maybe it is.

GEORGE. Might be . . . might not. Well, I think your story's a lot nicer . . . about your pumped-up little wife, and your father-in-law who was a priest. . . .

NICK. He was not a priest . . . he was a man of God.

GEORGE. Yes.

NICK. And my wife wasn't pumped up . . . she blew up.

GEORGE. Yes, yes.

NICK (*giggling*). Get things straight.

GEORGE. I'm sorry . . . I will. I'm sorry.

NICK. O.K.

GEORGE. You realize, of course, that I've been drawing you out on this stuff, not because I'm interested in your terrible lifehood, but only because you represent a direct and pertinent threat to my livelihood, and I want to get the goods on you.

NICK (*still amused*). Sure . . . sure.

GEORGE. I mean . . . I've warned you . . . you stand warned.

NICK. I stand warned. (*Laughs.*) It's you sneaky types worry me the most, you know. You ineffectual sons of bitches . . . you're the worst.

GEORGE. Yes . . . we are. Sneaky. An elbow in your steely-blue eye . . . a knee in your solid gold groin . . . we're the worst.

NICK. Yup.

GEORGE. Well, I'm glad you don't believe me. . . . I know you've got history on your side, and all. . . .

NICK. Unh-unh. *You've* got history on *your* side. . . . I've got biology on mine. History, biology.

GEORGE. I know the difference.

NICK. You don't act it.

GEORGE. No? I thought we'd decided that you'd take over the History Department first, before you took over the whole works. You know . . . a step at a time.

NICK (*stretching . . . luxuriating . . . playing the game*). Nyaah . . . what I thought I'd do is . . . I'd sort of insinuate myself generally, play around for a while, find all the weak spots, shore 'em up, but with my own name plate on 'em . . . become sort of a fact, and then turn into a . . . a what . . . ?

GEORGE. An inevitability.

NICK. Exactly. . . . An inevitability. You know. . . . Take over a few courses from the older men, start some special groups for myself . . . plow a few pertinent wives. . . .

GEORGE. Now that's it! You can take over all the courses you want to, and get as much of the young elite together in the gymnasium as you like, but until you start plowing pertinent wives, you really aren't working. The way to a man's heart is through his wife's belly, and don't you forget it.

NICK (*playing along*). Yeah. . . . I know.

GEORGE. And the women around here are no better than puntas—you know, South American ladies of the night. You know what they do in South America

. . . in Rio? The puntas? Do you know? They hiss . . . like geese. . . . They stand around in the street and they hiss at you . . . like a bunch of geese.

NICK. Gangle.

GEORGE. Hm?

NICK. Gangle . . . gangle of geese . . . not bunch . . . gangle.

GEORGE. Well, if you're going to get all cute about it, all ornithological, it's gaggle . . . not gangle, *gaggle*.

NICK. Gaggle? Not gangle?

ᵛGEORGE. Yes, gaggle.

NICK (*crestfallen*). Oh.

GEORGE. Oh. Yes. . . . Well they stand around on the street and they hiss at you, like a bunch of geese. All the faculty wives, downtown in New Carthage, in front of the A&P, hissing away like a bunch of geese. That's the way to power —plow 'em all!

NICK (*still playing along*). I'll bet you're right.

GEORGE. Well, I am.

NICK. And I'll bet your wife's the biggest goose in the gangle, isn't she . . . ? Her father president, and all.

GEORGE. You bet your historical inevitability she is!

NICK. Yessirree. (*Rubs his hands together.*) Well now, I'd just better get her off in a corner and mount her like a goddam dog, eh?

GEORGE. Why, you'd certainly better.

NICK (*looks at GEORGE a minute, his expression a little sick*). You know, I almost think you're serious.

GEORGE (*toasting him*). No, baby . . . *you* almost think you're serious, and it scares the hell out of you.

NICK (*exploding in disbelief*). ME!

GEORGE (*quietly*). Yes . . . you.

NICK. You're kidding!

GEORGE (*like a father*). I wish I were. . . . I'll give you some good advice if you want me to. . . .

NICK. Good advice! From you? Oh boy! (*Starts to laugh.*)

GEORGE. You haven't learned yet. . . . Take it whenever you can get it. . . . Listen to me, now.

NICK. Come off it!

GEORGE. I'm giving you good advice, now.

NICK. Good God . . . !

GEORGE. There's quicksand here, and you'll be dragged down, just as. . . .

NICK. Oh boy . . . !

GEORGE. . . . before you know it . . . sucked down. . . . (NICK *laughs derisively*.) You disgust me on principle, and you're a smug son of a bitch personally, but I'm trying to give you a survival kit. DO YOU HEAR ME?

NICK (*still laughing*). I hear you. You come in loud.

GEORGE. ALL RIGHT!

NICK. Hey, Honey.

GEORGE (*silence. Then quietly*). All right . . . O.K. You want to play it by ear, right? Everything's going to work out anyway, because the time-table's history, right?

NICK. Right . . . right. You just tend to your knitting, grandma. . . . I'll be O.K.

GEORGE (*after a silence*). I've tried to . . . tried to reach you . . . to. . . .

NICK (*contemptuously*). . . . make contact?

GEORGE. Yes.

NICK (*still*). . . . communicate?

GEORGE. Yes. Exactly.

NICK. Aw . . . that *is* touching . . . is . . . downright moving . . . that's what it is. (*With sudden vehemence*) UP YOURS!

GEORGE (*brief pause*). Hm?

NICK (*threatening*). You heard me!

GEORGE (*at NICK, not to him*). You take the trouble to construct a civilization . . . to . . . to build a society, based on the principles of . . . of principle . . . you endeavor to make communicable sense out of natural order, morality out of the unnatural disorder of man's mind . . . you make government and art, and realize that they are, must be, both the same . . . you bring things to the saddest of all points . . . to the point where there *is* something to lose . . . then all at once, through all the music, through all the sensible sounds of men building, attempting, comes the *Dies Irae*. And what is it? What does the trumpet sound? Up yours. I suppose there's justice to it, after all the years. . . . Up yours.

NICK (*brief pause . . . then applauding*). Ha, ha! Bravo! Ha, ha! (*Laughs on.*)

(*And* MARTHA *reenters, leading* HONEY, *who is wan but smiling bravely.*)

HONEY (*grandly*). Thank you . . . thank you.

MARTHA. Here we are, a little shaky, but on our feet.

GEORGE. Goodie.

NICK. What? Oh . . . OH! Hi, Honey . . . you better?

HONEY. A little bit, dear. . . . I'd better sit down, though.

NICK. Sure . . . c'mon . . . you sit by me.

HONEY. Thank you, dear.

GEORGE (*beneath his breath*). Touching . . . touching.

MARTHA (*to* GEORGE). Well? Aren't you going to apologize?

GEORGE (*squinting*). For what, Martha?

MARTHA. For making the little lady throw up.

GEORGE. I did not make her throw up.

MARTHA. You most certainly did!

GEORGE. I did not!

HONEY (*papal gesture*). No, now . . . no.

MARTHA (*to* GEORGE). Well, who do you think did . . . Sexy over there? You think he made his *own* little wife sick?

GEORGE (*helpfully*). Well, you make *me* sick.

MARTHA. THAT'S DIFFERENT!

HONEY. No, now. I . . . I throw up . . . I mean, I get sick . . . occasionally, all by myself . . . without any reason.

GEORGE. Is that a fact?

NICK. You're . . . you're delicate, Honey.

HONEY (*proudly*). I've always done it.

GEORGE. Like Big Ben.

NICK (*a warning*). Watch it!

HONEY. And the doctors say there's nothing wrong with me . . . organically. You know?

NICK. Of course there isn't.

HONEY. Why, just before we got married, I developed . . . appendicitis . . . or everybody *thought* it was appendicitis . . . but it turned out to be . . . it was a . . . (*Laughs briefly.*) . . . false alarm.

(GEORGE *and* NICK *exchange glances.*)

MARTHA (*to* GEORGE). Get me a drink. (GEORGE *moves to the bar.*) George makes everybody sick. . . . When our son was just a little boy, he used to. . . .

GEORGE. Don't, Martha. . . .

MARTHA. . . . he used to throw up all the time, because of George. . . .

GEORGE. I said, don't!

MARTHA. It got so bad that whenever

George came into the room he'd start right in retching, and. . . .

GEORGE. . . . the real reason (*Spits out the words.*) our son . . . used to throw up all the time, wife and lover, was nothing more complicated than that he couldn't stand you fiddling at him all the time, breaking into his bedroom with your kimono flying, fiddling at him all the time, with your liquor breath on him, and your hands all over his. . . .

MARTHA. YEAH? And I suppose that's why he ran away from home twice in one month, too. (*Now to the guests*) Twice in one month! Six times in one year!

GEORGE (*also to the guests*). Our son ran away from home all the time because Martha here used to corner him.

MARTHA (*braying*). I NEVER CORNERED THE SON OF A BITCH IN MY LIFE!

GEORGE (*handing* MARTHA *her drink*). He used to run up to me when I'd get home, and he'd say, "Mama's always coming at me." That's what he'd say.

MARTHA. Liar!

GEORGE (*shrugging*). Well, that's the way it was . . . you were always coming at him. I thought it was very embarrassing.

NICK. If you thought it was so embarrassing, what are you talking about it for?

HONEY (*admonishing*). Dear . . . !

MARTHA. Yeah! (*To* NICK) Thanks, sweetheart.

GEORGE (*to them all*). I didn't want to talk about him at all . . . I would have been perfectly happy not to discuss the whole subject. . . . I never want to talk about it.

MARTHA. Yes you do.

GEORGE. When we're alone, maybe.

MARTHA. We're alone!

GEORGE. Uh . . . no, love . . . we've got guests.

MARTHA (*with a covetous look at* NICK). We sure have.

HONEY. Could I have a little brandy? I think I'd like a little brandy.

NICK. Do you think you should?

HONEY. Oh yes . . . yes, dear.

GEORGE (*moving to the bar again*). Sure! Fill 'er up!

NICK. Honey, I don't think you. . . .

HONEY (*petulance creeping in*). It will steady me, *dear*. I feel a little unsteady.

GEORGE. Hell, you can't walk steady on half a bottle . . . got to do it right.

HONEY. Yes. (*To* MARTHA) I love brandy . . . I really do.

MARTHA (*somewhat abstracted*). Good for you.

NICK (*giving up*). Well, if you think it's a good idea. . . .

HONEY (*really testy*). I know what's best for me, dear.

NICK (*not even pleasant*). Yes . . . I'm sure you do.

HONEY (GEORGE *hands her a brandy*). Oh, goodie! Thank you. (*To* NICK) Of course I do, dear.

GEORGE (*pensively*). I used to drink brandy.

MARTHA (*privately*). You used to drink bergin, too.

GEORGE (*sharp*). Shut up, Martha!

MARTHA (*her hand over her mouth in a little-girl gesture*). Oooooops.

NICK (*something having clicked, vaguely*). Hm?

GEORGE (*burying it*). Nothing . . . nothing.

MARTHA (*she, too*). You two men have it out while we were gone? George tell you his side of things? He bring you to tears, hunh?

NICK. Well . . . no. . . .

GEORGE. No, what we did, actually, was . . . we sort of danced around.

MARTHA. Oh, yeah? Cute!

HONEY. Oh, I love dancing.

NICK. He didn't mean that, Honey.

HONEY. Well, I didn't think he did! Two grown men dancing . . . heavens!

MARTHA. You mean he didn't start in on how he would have amounted to something if it hadn't been for Daddy? How his high moral sense wouldn't even let him *try* to better himself? No?

NICK (*qualified*). No. . . .

MARTHA. And he didn't run on about how he tried to publish a goddam book, and Daddy wouldn't let him.

NICK. A book? No.

GEORGE. Please, Martha. . . .

NICK (*egging her on*). A book? What book?

GEORGE (*pleading*). Please. Just a book.

MARTHA (*mock incredulity*). Just a book!

GEORGE. *Please,* Martha!

MARTHA (*almost disappointed*). Well, I guess you didn't get the whole sad story.

What's the matter with you, George? You given up?

GEORGE (*calm . . . serious*). No . . . no. It's just I've got to figure out some new way to fight you, Martha. Guerilla tactics, maybe . . . internal subversion . . . I don't know. Something.

MARTHA. Well, you figure it out, and let me know when you do.

GEORGE (*cheery*). All right, love.

HONEY. Why don't we dance? I'd love some dancing.

NICK. Honey. . . .

HONEY. I would! I'd love some dancing.

NICK. Honey. . . .

HONEY. I *want* some! I want some dancing!

GEORGE. All right . . . ! For heaven's sake . . . we'll have some dancing.

HONEY (*all sweetness again; to MAR-THA*). Oh, I'm so glad . . . I just love dancing. Don't you?

MARTHA (*with a glance at NICK*). Yeah . . . yeah, that's not a bad idea.

NICK (*genuinely nervous*). Gee.

GEORGE. Gee.

HONEY. I dance like the wind.

MARTHA (*without comment*). Yeah?

GEORGE (*picking a record*). Martha had her daguerrotype in the paper once . . . oh, 'bout twenty-five years ago. . . . Seems she took second prize in one o' them seven-day dancin' contest things . . . biceps all bulging, holding up her partner.

MARTHA. Will you put a record on and shut up?

GEORGE. Certainly, love. (*To all*) How are we going to work this? Mixed doubles?

MARTHA. Well, you certainly don't think I'm going to dance with *you,* do you?

GEORGE (*considers it*). Noooooo . . . not with him around . . . that's for sure. And not with twinkle-toes here, either.

HONEY. I'll dance with anyone. . . . I'll dance by myself.

NICK. Honey. . . .

HONEY. I dance like the wind.

GEORGE. All right, kiddies . . . choose up and hit the sack.

(*Music starts. . . . Second movement, Beethoven's 7th Symphony*)

HONEY (*up, dancing by herself*). De, de de de *da* da, da-da de, da *da*-da de da . . . wonderful . . . !

NICK. Honey. . . .

MARTHA. All right, George . . . cut that out!

HONEY. Dum, de de da da, da-da de, dum de *da* da da. . . . Wheeeee . . . !

MARTHA. Cut it out, George!

GEORGE (*pretending not to hear*). What, Martha? What?

NICK. Honey. . . .

MARTHA (*as GEORGE turns up the volume*). CUT IT OUT, GEORGE!

GEORGE. WHAT?

MARTHA (*gets up, moves quickly, threateningly, to GEORGE*). All right, you son of a bitch. . . .

GEORGE (*record off, at once. Quietly*). What did you say, love?

MARTHA. You son of a. . . .

HONEY (*in an arrested posture*). You stopped! Why did you stop?

NICK. Honey. . . .

HONEY (*to NICK, snapping*). Stop that!

GEORGE. I thought it was fitting, Martha.

MARTHA. Oh you did, hunh?

HONEY. You're always *at* me when I'm having a good time.

NICK (*trying to remain civil*). I'm sorry, Honey.

HONEY. Just . . . leave me alone!

GEORGE. Well, why don't *you* choose, Martha? (*Moves away from the phonograph . . . leaves it to MARTHA.*) Martha's going to run things . . . the little lady's going to lead the band.

HONEY. I like to dance and you don't want me to.

NICK. *I* like you to dance.

HONEY. Just . . . leave me alone. (*She sits . . . takes a drink.*)

GEORGE. Martha's going to put on some rhythm she understands . . . Sacre du Printemps, maybe. (*Moves . . . sits by HONEY.*) Hi, sexy.

HONEY (*a little giggle-scream*). Ooooooohhhhh!

GEORGE (*laughs mockingly*). Ha, ha, ha, ha, ha. Choose it, Martha . . . do your stuff!

MARTHA (*concentrating on the machine*). You're damn right!

GEORGE (*to HONEY*). You want to dance with me, angel-tits?

NICK. What did you call my wife?

GEORGE (*derisively*). Oh boy!

HONEY (*petulantly*). No! If I can't do my interpretive dance, I don't want to dance with anyone. I'll just sit here and.

. . . (*Shrugs . . . drinks.*)

MARTHA (*record on . . . a jazzy slow pop tune*). O.K. stuff, let's go. (*Grabs* NICK.)

NICK. Hm? Oh . . . hi.

MARTHA. Hi. (*They dance, close together, slowly.*)

HONEY (*pouting*). We'll just sit here and watch.

GEORGE. That's *right!*

MARTHA (*to* NICK). Hey, you *are* strong, aren't you?

NICK. Unh-hunh.

MARTHA. I like that.

NICK. Unh-hunh.

HONEY. They're dancing like they've danced before.

GEORGE. It's a familiar dance . . . they both know it. . . .

MARTHA. Don't be shy.

NICK. I'm . . . not. . . .

GEORGE (*to* HONEY). It's a very old ritual, monkey-nipples . . . old as they come.

HONEY. I . . . I don't know what you mean.

NICK *and* MARTHA *move apart now, and dance on either side of where* GEORGE *and* HONEY *are sitting; they face each other, and while their feet move but little, their bodies undulate congruently. . . . It is as if they were pressed together.*)

MARTHA. I like the way you move.

NICK. I like the way you move, too.

GEORGE (*to* HONEY). They like the way they move.

HONEY (*not entirely with it*). That's nice.

MARTHA (*to* NICK). I'm surprised George didn't give you his side of things.

GEORGE (*to* HONEY). Aren't they cute?

NICK. Well, he didn't.

MARTHA. That surprises me. (*Perhaps* MARTHA's *statements are more or less in time to the music.*)

NICK. Does it?

MARTHA. Yeah . . . he usually does . . . when he gets the chance.

NICK. Well, what do you know.

MARTHA. It's really a very sad story.

GEORGE. You have ugly talents, Martha.

NICK. Is it?

MARTHA. It would make you weep.

GEORGE. Hideous gifts.

NICK. Is that so?

GEORGE. Don't encourage her.

MARTHA. Encourage me.

NICK. Go on.

(*They may undulate toward each other and then move back.*)

GEORGE. I warn you . . . don't encourage her.

MARTHA. He warns you . . . don't encourage me.

NICK. I heard him . . . tell me more.

MARTHA (*consciously making rhymed speech*).

Well, Georgie-boy had lots of big ambitions

In spite of something funny in his past. . . .

GEORGE (*quietly warning*). Martha. . . .

MARTHA.

Which Georgie-boy here turned into a novel. . . .

His first attempt and also his last. . . .

Hey! I rhymed! I rhymed!

GEORGE. I warn you, Martha.

NICK. Yeah . . . you rhymed. Go on, go on.

MARTHA. But Daddy took a look at Georgie's novel. . . .

GEORGE. You're looking for a punch in the mouth. . . . You know that, Martha.

MARTHA. Do tell . . . and he was very shocked by what he read.

NICK. He was?

MARTHA. Yes . . . he was. . . . A novel all about a naughty boychild. . . .

GEORGE (*rising*). I will not tolerate this!

NICK (*offhand, to* GEORGE). Oh, can it.

MARTHA. . . . ha, ha!

naughty boychild

who . . . uh . . . who killed his mother and his father dead.

GEORGE. STOP IT, MARTHA!

MARTHA. And Daddy said . . . Look here, I will not let you publish such a thing. . . .

GEORGE (*rushes to phonograph . . . rips the record off*). That's it! The dancing's over. That's it. Go on now!

NICK. What do you think you're doing, hunh?

HONEY (*happily*). Violence! Violence!

MARTHA (*loud: a pronouncement*). And Daddy said . . . Look here, kid, you don't think for a second I'm going to let you publish this crap, do you? Not on your life, baby . . . not while you're teaching here. . . . You publish that goddam book and you're out . . . on your ass!

GEORGE. DESIST! DESIST!

MARTHA. Ha, ha, ha, HA!

NICK (*laughing*). De . . . sist!

HONEY. Oh, violence . . . violence!

MARTHA. Why, the idea! A teacher at a respected, conservative institution like this, in a town like New Carthage, publishing a book like that? If you respect your position here, young man, young . . . whippersnapper, you'll just withdraw that manuscript. . . .

GEORGE. I will not be made mock of!

NICK. He will not be made mock of, for Christ's sake. (*Laughs.*)

(HONEY *joins in the laughter, not knowing exactly why.*)

GEORGE. I will not! (*All three are laughing at him. Infuriated*) THE GAME IS OVER!

MARTHA (*pushing on*). Imagine such a thing! A book about a boy who murders his mother and kills his father, and pretends it's all an accident!

HONEY (*beside herself with glee*). An accident!

NICK (*remembering something related*). Hey . . . wait a minute. . . .

MARTHA (*her own voice now*). And you want to know the clincher? You want to know what big brave Georgie said to Daddy?

GEORGE. NO! NO! NO! NO!

NICK. Wait a minute now. . . .

MARTHA. Georgie said . . . but Daddy . . . I mean . . . ha, ha, ha, ha . . . but *Sir* it isn't a *novel* at all. . . . (*Other voice*) Not a novel? (*Mimicking* GEORGE'S *voice*) No, sir . . . it isn't a novel at all. . . .

GEORGE (*advancing on her*). You will not say this!

NICK (*sensing the danger*). Hey.

MARTHA. The hell I won't. Keep away from me, you bastard! (*Backs off a little . . . uses* GEORGE'S *voice again.*) No, sir, this isn't a novel at all . . . this is the truth . . . this really happened. . . . TO ME!

GEORGE (*on her*). I'LL KILL YOU! (*Grabs her by the throat. They struggle.*)

NICK. HEY! (*Comes between them.*)

HONEY (*wildly*). VIOLENCE! VIOLENCE! (GEORGE, MARTHA, *and* NICK *struggle . . . yells, etc.*)

MARTHA. IT HAPPENED! TO ME! TO ME!

GEORGE. YOU SATANIC BITCH!

NICK. STOP THAT! STOP THAT!

HONEY. VIOLENCE! VIOLENCE!

(*The other three struggle.* GEORGE'S *hands are on* MARTHA'S *throat.* NICK *grabs him, tears him from* MARTHA, *throws him on the floor.* GEORGE, *on the floor;* NICK *over him;* MARTHA *to one side, her hand on her throat.*)

NICK. That's enough now!

HONEY (*disappointment in her voice*). Oh . . . oh . . . oh. . . .

GEORGE *drags himself into a chair. He is hurt, but it is more a profound humiliation than a physical injury.*)

GEORGE (*they watch him . . . a pause. . . .*) All right . . . all right . . . very quiet now . . . we will all be . . . very quiet.

MARTHA (*softly, with a slow shaking of her head*). Murderer. Mur . . . der . . . er.

NICK (*softly to* MARTHA). O.K. now . . . that's enough.

(*A brief silence. They all move around a little, self-consciously, like wrestlers flexing after a fall.*)

GEORGE (*composure seemingly recovered, but there is a great nervous intensity*). Well! That's one game. What shall we do now, hunh? (MARTHA *and* NICK *laugh nervously.*) Oh come on . . . let's think of something else. We've played Humiliate the Host . . . we've gone through that one . . . what shall we do now?

NICK. Aw . . . look. . . .

GEORGE. AW LOOK! (*Whines it.*) Awww . . . looooook. (*Alert*) I mean, come on! We must know other games, college-type types like us . . . that can't be the . . . limit of our vocabulary, can it?

NICK. I think maybe. . . .

GEORGE. Let's see now . . . what else can we do? There are other games. How about . . . how about . . . Hump the Hostess? HUNH?? How about that? How about Hump the Hostess? (*To* NICK) You wanna play that one? You wanna play Hump the Hostess? HUNH? HUNH?

NICK (*a little frightened*). Calm down, now.

(MARTHA *giggles quietly.*)

GEORGE. Or is that for later . . . mount her like a goddamn dog?

HONEY (*wildly toasting everybody*). Hump the Hostess!

NICK (*to* HONEY . . . *sharply*). Just shut up . . . will you?

(HONEY *does, her glass in mid-air.*)

GEORGE. You don't wanna play that

now, hunh? You wanna save that game till later? Well, what'll we play now? We gotta play a game.

MARTHA (*quietly*). Portrait of a man drowning.

GEORGE (*affirmatively, but to none of them*). I am not drowning.

HONEY (*to NICK, tearfully indignant*). You told me to shut up!

NICK (*impatiently*). I'm sorry.

HONEY (*between her teeth*). No you're not.

NICK (*to HONEY, even more impatiently*). I'm sorry.

GEORGE (*claps his hands together, once, loud*). I've got it! I'll tell you what game we'll play. We're done with Humiliate the Host . . . this round, anyway . . . we're done with that . . . and we don't want to play Hump the Hostess, yet . . . not yet . . . so I know what we'll play. . . . We'll play a round of Get the Guests. How about that? How about a little game of Get the Guests?

MARTHA (*turning away, a little disgusted*). Jesus, George.

GEORGE. Book dropper! Child mentioner!

HONEY. I don't like these games.

NICK. Yeah. . . . I think maybe we've had enough of games, now. . . .

GEORGE. Oh, no . . . oh, no . . . we haven't. We've had only one game. . . . Now we're going to have another. You can't fly on one game.

NICK. I think maybe. . . .

GEORGE (*with great authority*). SILENCE! (*It is respected.*) Now, how are we going to play Get the Guests?

MARTHA. For God's sake, George. . . .

GEORGE. You be quiet! (MARTHA *shrugs.*) I wonder. . . . I wonder. (*Puzzles . . . then. . . .*) O.K.! Well . . . Martha . . . in her indiscreet way . . . well, not really indiscreet, because Martha is a naïve, at heart . . . anyway, Martha told you all about my first novel. True or false? Hunh? I mean, true or false that there ever was such a thing. HA! But, Martha told you about it . . . my first novel, my . . . memory book . . . which I'd sort of preferred she hadn't, but hell, that's blood under the bridge. BUT! what she didn't do . . . what Martha didn't tell you about is she didn't tell us all about my *second* novel. (MARTHA *looks at him with puzzled curiosity.*) No,

you didn't know about that, did you, Martha? About my second novel, true or false. True or false?

MARTHA (*sincerely*). No.

GEORGE. *No.* (*He starts quietly but as he goes on, his tone becomes harsher, his voice louder.*) Well, it's an allegory, really —probably—but it can be read as straight, cozy prose . . . and it's all about a nice young couple who come out of the Middle West. It's a bucolic you see. AND, this nice young couple comes out of the Middle West, and he's blond and about thirty, and he's a scientist, a teacher, a scientist . . . and his mouse is a wifey little type who gargles brandy all the time . . . and. . . .

NICK. Just a minute here. . . .

GEORGE. . . .and they got to know each other when they was only teensie little types, and they used to get under the vanity table and poke around, and. . . .

NICK. I said JUST A MINUTE!

GEORGE. This is my game! You played yours . . . you people. This is my game!

HONEY (*dreamy*). I want to hear the story. I love stories.

MARTHA. George, for heaven's sake. . . .

GEORGE. AND! And Mousie's father was a holy man, see, and he ran sort of a traveling clip joint, based on Christ and all those girls, and he took the faithful . . . that's all . . . just took 'em. . . .

HONEY (*puzzling*). This is familiar.

NICK (*voice shaking a little*). No kidding!

GEORGE. . . . and he died eventually, Mousie's pa, and they pried him open, and all sorts of money fell out. . . . Jesus money, Mary money. . . . LOOT!

HONEY (*dreamy, puzzling*). I've heard this story before.

NICK (*with quiet intensity . . . to waken her*). Honey. . . .

GEORGE. But that's in the backwash, in the early part of the book. Anyway, Blondie and his frau out of the plain states came. (*Chuckles.*)

MARTHA. Very funny, George. . . .

GEORGE. . . . thank you . . . and settled in a town just like nouveau Carthage here. . . .

NICK (*threatening*). I don't think you'd better go on, mister. . . .

GEORGE. Do you not!

NICK (*less certainly*). No. I . . . I don't think you'd better.

HONEY. I love familiar stories . . . they're the best.

GEORGE. How right you are. But Blondie was in disguise, really, all got up as a teacher, 'cause his baggage ticket had bigger things writ on it . . . H.I. HI! Historical inevitability.

NICK. There's no need for you to go any further, now. . . .

HONEY (*puzzling to make sense out of what she is hearing*). Let them go on.

GEORGE. We shall. And he had this baggage with him, and part of this baggage was in the form of his mouse. . . .

NICK. We don't have to listen to this!

HONEY. Why not?

GEORGE. Your bride has a point. And one of the things nobody could understand about Blondie was his baggage . . . his mouse, I mean, here he was, pan-Kansas swimming champeen, or something, and he had this mouse, of whom he was solicitous to a point that faileth human understanding . . . given that she was sort of a simp, in the long run. . . .

NICK. This isn't fair of you. . . .

GEORGE. Perhaps not. Like, as I said, his mouse, she tooted brandy immodestly and spent half of her time in the up-chuck. . . .

HONEY (*focussing*). I know these people. . . .

GEORGE. Do you! . . . But she was a money baggage amongst other things . . . Godly money ripped from the golden teeth of the unfaithful, a pragmatic extension of the big dream . . . and she was put up with. . . .

HONEY (*some terror*). I don't like this story. . . .

NICK (*surprisingly pleading*). Please . . . please don't.

MARTHA. Maybe you better stop, George. . . .

GEORGE. . . . and she was put up with. . . . STOP? Ha-ha.

NICK. Please . . . please don't.

GEORGE. Beg, baby.

MARTHA. George. . . .

GEORGE. . . . and . . . oh, we get a flashback here, to How They Got Married.

NICK. NO!

GEORGE (*triumphant*). YES!

NICK (*almost whining*). Why?

GEORGE. How They Got Married. Well, how they got married is this. . . . The Mouse got all puffed up one day, and she

went over to Blondie's house, and she stuck out her puff, and she said . . . look at me.

HONEY (*white . . . on her feet*). I . . . don't . . . like this.

NICK (*to* GEORGE). Stop it!

GEORGE. Look at me . . . I'm all puffed up. Oh my goodness, said Blondie. . . .

HONEY (*as from a distance*). . . . and so they were married. . . .

GEORGE. . . . and so they were married. . . .

HONEY. . . . and then. . . .

GEORGE. . . . and then. . . .

HONEY (*hysteria*). WHAT? . . . and then, WHAT?

NICK. NO! No!

GEORGE (*as if to a baby*). . . . and then the puff went *away* . . . like magic . . . pouf!

NICK (*almost sick*). Jesus God. . . .

HONEY. . . . the puff went away. . . .

GEORGE (*softly*). . . . pouf.

NICK. Honey . . . I didn't mean to . . . honestly, I didn't mean to. . . .

HONEY. You . . . you told them. . . .

NICK. Honey . . . I didn't mean to. . . .

HONEY (*with outlandish horror*). You . . . told them! You told them! OOOOHHHH! Oh, no, no, no, no! You couldn't have told them . . . oh, noooo!

NICK. Honey, I didn't mean to. . . .

HONEY (*grabbing at her belly*). Ohhhhh . . . nooooo.

NICK. Honey . . . baby . . . I'm sorry . . . I didn't mean to. . . .

GEORGE (*abruptly and with some disgust*). And that's how you play Get the Guests.

HONEY. I'm going to . . . I'm going to be . . . sick. . . .

GEORGE. Naturally!

NICK. Honey. . . .

HONEY (*hysterical*). Leave me alone . . . I'm going . . . to . . . be . . . sick. (*She runs out of the room.*)

MARTHA (*shaking her head, watching* HONEY's *retreating form*). God Almighty.

GEORGE (*shrugging*). The patterns of history.

NICK (*quietly shaking*). You shouldn't have done that . . . you shouldn't have done that at all.

GEORGE (*calmly*). I hate hypocrisy.

NICK. That was cruel . . . and vicious. . . .

GEORGE. . . . she'll get over it. . . .

NICK. . . . and damaging . . . !

GEORGE. . . . she'll recover. . . .

NICK. DAMAGING!! TO ME!!

GEORGE (*with wonder*). To you!

NICK. TO ME!!

GEORGE. To you!!

NICK. YES!!

GEORGE. Oh beautiful . . . beautiful. By God, you gotta have a swine to show you where the truffles are. (*So calmly*) Well, you just rearrange your alliances, boy. You just pick up the pieces where you can . . . you just look around and make the best of things . . . you scramble back up on your feet.

MARTHA (*quietly, to* NICK). Go look after your wife.

GEORGE. Yeah . . . go pick up the pieces and plan some new strategy.

NICK (*to* GEORGE, *as he moves toward the hall*). You're going to regret this.

GEORGE. Probably. I regret everything.

NICK. I mean, I'm going to make you regret this.

GEORGE (*softly*). No doubt. Acute embarrassment, eh?

NICK. I'll play the charades like you've got 'em set up. . . . I'll play in your language. . . . I'll be what you say I am.

GEORGE. You are already . . . you just don't know it.

NICK (*shaking within*). No . . . no. Not really. But I'll *be* it, mister. . . . I'll show you something come to life you'll wish you hadn't set up.

GEORGE. Go clean up the mess.

NICK (*quietly . . . intensely*). You just wait, mister. (*He exits. Pause.* GEORGE *smiles at* MARTHA.)

MARTHA. Very good, George.

GEORGE. Thank you, Martha.

MARTHA. Really good.

GEORGE. I'm glad you liked it.

MARTHA. I mean. . . . You did a good job . . . you really fixed it.

GEORGE. Unh-hunh.

MARTHA. It's the most . . . life you've shown in a long time.

GEORGE. You bring out the best in me, baby.

MARTHA. Yeah . . . pigmy hunting!

GEORGE. PIGMY!

MARTHA. You're really a bastard.

GEORGE. I? I?

MARTHA. Yeah . . . you.

GEORGE. Baby, if quarterback there is a pigmy, you've certainly changed your style. What are you after now . . . giants?

MARTHA. You make me sick.

GEORGE. It's perfectly all right for you. . . . I mean, you can make your own rules . . . you can go around like a hopped-up Arab, slashing away at everything in sight, scarring up half the world if you want to. But somebody else try it . . . no sir!

MARTHA. You miserable. . . .

GEORGE (*mocking*). Why baby, I did it all for you. I thought you'd like it, sweetheart . . . it's sort of to your taste . . . blood, carnage and all. Why, I thought you'd get all excited . . . sort of heave and pant and come running at me, your melons bobbling.

MARTHA. You've really screwed up, George.

GEORGE (*spitting it out*). Oh, for God's sake, Martha!

MARTHA. I mean it . . . you really have.

GEORGE (*barely contained anger now*). You can sit there in that chair of yours, you can sit there with the gin running out of your mouth, and you can humiliate me, you can tear me apart . . . ALL NIGHT . . . and that's perfectly all right . . . that's O.K. . . .

MARTHA. YOU CAN STAND IT!

GEORGE. I CANNOT STAND IT!

MARTHA. YOU CAN STAND IT!! YOU MARRIED ME FOR IT!!

(*A silence*)

GEORGE (*quietly*). That is a desperately sick lie.

MARTHA. DON'T YOU KNOW IT, EVEN YET?

GEORGE (*shaking his head*). Oh . . . Martha.

MARTHA. My arm has gotten tired whipping you.

GEORGE (*stares at her in disbelief*). You're mad.

MARTHA. For twenty-three years!

GEORGE. You're deluded . . . Martha, you're deluded.

MARTHA. IT'S NOT WHAT I'VE WANTED!

GEORGE. I thought at least you were . . . on to yourself. I didn't know. I . . . didn't know.

MARTHA (*anger taking over*). I'm on to myself.

GEORGE (*as if she were some sort of bug*). No . . . no . . . you're . . . sick.

MARTHA (*rises—screams*). I'LL SHOW YOU WHO'S SICK!

GEORGE. All right, Martha . . . you're going too far.

MARTHA (*screams again*). I'LL SHOW YOU WHO'S SICK. I'LL SHOW YOU.

GEORGE (*he shakes her*). Stop it! (*Pushes her back in her chair.*) Now, stop it!

MARTHA (*calmer*). I'll show you who's sick. (*Calmer*) Boy, you're really having a field day, hunh? Well, I'm going to finish you . . . before I'm through with you. . . .

GEORGE. . . . you and the quarterback . . . you both gonna finish me . . . ?

MARTHA. . . . before I'm through with you you'll wish you'd died in that automobile, you bastard.

GEORGE (*emphasizing with his forefinger*). And you'll wish you'd never mentioned our son!

MARTHA (*dripping contempt*). You. . . .

GEORGE. Now, I said I warned you.

MARTHA. I'm impressed.

GEORGE. I warned you not to go too far.

MARTHA. I'm just beginning.

GEORGE (*calmly, matter-of-factly*). I'm numbed enough . . . and I don't mean by liquor, though maybe that's been part of the process—a gradual, over-the-years going to sleep of the brain cells—I'm numbed enough, now, to be able to take you when we're alone. I don't listen to you . . . or when I *do* listen to you, I sift everything, I bring everything down to reflex response, so I don't really *hear* you, which is the only way to manage it. But you've taken a new tack, Martha, over the past couple of centuries—or however long it's been I've lived in this house with you—that makes it just too much . . . too much. I don't mind your dirty underthings in public . . . well, I *do* mind, but I've reconciled myself to that . . . but you've moved bag and baggage into your own fantasy world now, and you've started playing variations on your own distortions, and, as a result. . . .

MARTHA. Nuts!

GEORGE. Yes . . . you have.

MARTHA. Nuts!

GEORGE. Well, you can go on like that as long as you want to. And, when you're done. . . .

MARTHA. Have you ever listened to your sentences, George? Have you ever listened to the way you talk? You're so frigging . . . convoluted . . . that's what you are.

You talk like you were writing one of your stupid papers.

GEORGE. Actually, I'm rather worried about you. About your mind.

MARTHA. Don't you worry about my mind, sweetheart!

GEORGE. I think I'll have you committed.

MARTHA. You WHAT?

GEORGE (*quietly . . . distinctly*). I think I'll have you committed.

MARTHA (*breaks into long laughter*). Oh baby, aren't you something!

GEORGE. I've got to find some way to really get at you.

MARTHA. You've got at me, George . . . you don't have to do anything. Twenty-three years of you has been quite enough.

GEORGE. Will you go quietly, then?

MARTHA. You know what's happened, George? You want to know what's *really happened*? (*Snaps her fingers.*) It's snapped, finally. Not me . . . *it*. The whole arrangement. You can go along . . . forever, and everything's . . . manageable. You make all sorts of excuses to yourself . . . *you* know . . . this is life . . . the hell with it . . . maybe tomorrow he'll be dead . . . maybe tomorrow *you'll* be dead . . . all sorts of excuses. But then, one day, one night, something happens . . . and SNAP! It breaks. And you just don't give a damn anymore. I've tried with you, baby . . . really, I've tried.

GEORGE. Come off it, Martha.

MARTHA. I've tried . . . I've really tried.

GEORGE (*with some awe*). You're a monster . . . you *are*.

MARTHA. I'm loud, and I'm vulgar, and I wear the pants in this house because somebody's got to, but I am *not* a monster. I am *not*.

GEORGE. You're a spoiled, self-indulgent, willful, dirty-minded, liquor-ridden. . . .

MARTHA. SNAP! It went snap. Look, I'm not going to try to get through to you any more. . . . I'm not going to try. There was a second back there, maybe, there was a second, just a second, when I could have gotten through to you, when maybe we could have cut through all this crap. But that's past, and now I'm not going to try.

GEORGE. Once a month, Martha! I've gotten used to it . . . once a month and we get misunderstood Martha, the good-hearted girl underneath the barnacles, the little Miss that the touch of kindness'd bring to bloom again. And I've believed it more times than I want to remember, because I don't want to think I'm that much of a sucker. I don't believe you . . . I just don't believe you. There is no moment . . . there is no moment any more when we could . . . come together.

MARTHA (*armed again*). Well, maybe you're right, baby. You can't come together with nothing, and you're nothing! SNAP! It went snap tonight at Daddy's party. (*Dripping contempt, but there is fury and loss under it.*) I sat there at Daddy's party, and I watched you . . . I watched you sitting there, and I watched the younger men around you, the men who were going to go somewhere. And I sat there and I watched you, and *you* weren't *there!* And it snapped! It finally snapped! And I'm going to howl it out, and I'm not going to give a damn what I do, and I'm going to make the damned biggest explosion you ever heard.

GEORGE (*very pointedly*). You try it and I'll beat you at your own game.

MARTHA (*hopefully*). Is that a threat, George? Hunh?

GEORGE. That's a threat, Martha.

MARTHA (*fake-spits at him*). You're going to get it, baby.

GEORGE. Be careful, Martha . . . I'll rip you to pieces.

MARTHA. You aren't man enough . . . you haven't got the guts.

GEORGE. Total war?

MARTHA. Total.

(*Silence. They both seem relieved . . . elated.* NICK *reenters.*)

NICK (*brushing his hands off*). Well . . . she's . . . resting.

GEORGE (*quietly amused at* NICK's *calm, off-hand manner*). Oh?

MARTHA. Yeah? She all right?

NICK. I think so . . . now. I'm . . . terribly sorry. . . .

MARTHA. Forget about it.

GEORGE. Happens all the time around here.

NICK. She'll be all right.

MARTHA. She lying down? You put her upstairs? On a bed?

NICK (*making himself a drink*). Well, no, actually. Uh . . . may I? She's . . . in the bathroom . . . on the bathroom floor . . . she's lying there.

GEORGE (*considers it*). Well . . . that's

not very nice.

NICK. She likes it. She says it's . . . cool.

GEORGE. Still, I don't think. . . .

MARTHA (*overruling him*). If she wants to lie on the bathroom floor, let her. (*To* NICK, *seriously*) Maybe she'd be more comfortable in the tub?

NICK (*he, too, seriously*). No, she says she likes the floor . . . she took up the mat, and she's lying on the tiles. She . . . she lies on the floor a lot . . . she really does.

MARTHA (*pause*). Oh.

NICK. She . . . she gets lots of headaches and things, and she always lies on the floor. (*To* GEORGE) Is there . . . ice?

GEORGE. What?

NICK. Ice. Is there ice?

GEORGE (*as if the word were unfamiliar to him*). Ice?

NICK. Ice. Yes.

MARTHA. Ice.

GEORGE (*as if he suddenly understood*). Ice!

MARTHA. Attaboy.

GEORGE (*without moving*). Oh, yes . . . I'll get some.

MARTHA. Well, go. (*Mugging . . . to* NICK) Besides, we want to be alone.

GEORGE (*moving to take the bucket*). I wouldn't be surprised, Martha . . . I wouldn't be surprised.

MARTHA (*as if insulted*). Oh, you wouldn't, hunh?

GEORGE. Not a bit, Martha.

MARTHA (*violent*). NO?

GEORGE (*he too*). NO! (*Quietly again*) You'll try anything, Martha. (*Picks up the ice bucket.*)

NICK (*to cover*). Actually, she's very . . . frail, and. . . .

GEORGE. . . . slim-hipped.

NICK (*remembering*). Yes . . . exactly.

GEORGE (*at the hallway . . . not kindly*). That why you don't have any kids? (*He exits.*)

NICK (*to* GEORGE's *retreating form*). Well, I don't know that that's . . . (*Trails off.*) . . . if that has anything to do with any . . . thing.

MARTHA. Well, if it does, who cares? Hunh?

NICK. Pardon?

(MARTHA *blows him a kiss.*)

NICK (*still concerned with* GEORGE's *remark*). I . . . what? . . . I'm sorry.

MARTHA. I said . . . (*Blows him another kiss.*)

NICK (*uncomfortable*). Oh . . . yes.

MARTHA. Hey . . . hand me a cigarette . . . lover. (NICK *fishes in his pocket.*) That's a good boy. (*He gives her one.*) Unh . . . thanks. (*He lights it for her. As he does, she slips her hand between his legs, somewhere between the knee and the crotch, bringing her hand around to the outside of his leg.*) Ummmmmmmm. (*He seems uncertain, but does not move. She smiles, moves her hand a little.*) Now, for being such a good boy, you can give me a kiss. C'mon.

NICK (*nervously*). Look . . . I don't think we should. . . .

MARTHA. C'mon, baby . . . a friendly kiss.

NICK (*still uncertain*). Well. . . .

MARTHA. . . . you won't get hurt, little boy. . . .

NICK. . . . not so little. . . .

MARTHA. I'll bet you're not. C'mon. . . .

NICK (*weakening*). But what if he should come back in, and . . . or . . . ?

MARTHA (*all the while her hand is moving up and down his leg*). George? Don't worry about him. Besides, who could object to a friendly little kiss? It's all in the faculty. (*They both laugh, quietly . . .* NICK *a little nervously.*) We're a close-knit family here . . . Daddy always says so. . . . Daddy wants us to get to know each other . . . that's what he had the party for tonight. So c'mon . . . let's get to know each other a little bit.

NICK. It isn't that I don't want to . . . believe me. . . .

MARTHA. You're a scientist, aren't you? C'mon . . . make an experiment . . . make a little experiment. Experiment on old Martha.

NICK (*giving in*). . . . not very old. . . .

MARTHA. That's right, not very old, but lots of good experience . . . lots of it.

NICK. I'll . . . I'll bet.

MARTHA (*as they draw slowly closer*). It'll be a nice change for you, too.

NICK. Yes, it would.

MARTHA. And you could go back to your little wife all refreshed.

NICK (*closer . . . almost whispering*). She wouldn't know the difference.

MARTHA. Well, nobody else's going to know, either. (*They come together. What might have been a joke rapidly becomes serious, with* MARTHA *urging it in that direction. There is no frenetic quality, but rather a slow, continually involving intertwining. Perhaps* MARTHA *is still more or less in her chair, and* NICK *is sort of beside and on the chair.*)

(GEORGE *enters . . . stops . . . watches a moment . . . smiles . . . laughs silently, nods his head, turns, exits, without being noticed.*)

(NICK, *who has already had his hand on* MARTHA'S *breast, now puts his hand inside her dress.*)

MARTHA (*slowing him down*). Hey . . . hey. Take it easy, boy. Down, baby. Don't rush it, hunh?

NICK (*his eyes still closed*). Oh, c'mon, now. . . .

MARTHA (*pushing him away*). Unh-unh. Later, baby . . . later.

NICK. I told you . . . I'm a biologist.

MARTHA (*soothing him*). I know. I can tell. Later, hunh?

(GEORGE *is heard off-stage, singing* "Who's afraid of Virginia Woolf?" MARTHA *and* NICK *go apart,* NICK *wiping his mouth,* MARTHA *checking her clothes. Safely later,* GEORGE *reenters with the ice bucket.*)

GEORGE. . . . of Virginia Woolf,
Virginia Woolf,
Virginia. . . .
. . . ah! Here we are . . . ice for the lamps of China, Manchuria thrown in. (*To* NICK) You better watch those yellow bastards, my love . . . they aren't amused. Why don't you come on over to our side, and we'll blow the hell out of 'em. Then we can split up the money between us and be on Easy Street. What d'ya say?

NICK (*not at all sure what is being talked about*). Well . . . sure. Hey! Ice!

GEORGE (*with hideously false enthusiasm*). Right! (*Now to* MARTHA, *purring*) Hello, Martha . . . my dove. . . . You look . . . radiant.

MARTHA (*off-hand*). Thank you.

GEORGE (*very cheerful*). Well now, let me see. I've got the ice. . . .

MARTHA. . . . gotten. . . .

GEORGE. *Got*, Martha. Got is perfectly correct . . . it's just a little . . . archaic, like you.

MARTHA (*suspicious*). What are you so cheerful about?

GEORGE (*ignoring the remark*). Let's

see now . . . I've got the ice. Can I make someone a drink? Martha, can I make you a drink?

MARTHA (*bravura*). Yeah, why not?

GEORGE (*taking her glass*). Indeed . . . why not? (*Examines the glass.*) Martha! You've been nibbling away at the glass.

MARTHA. I have not!

GEORGE (*to* NICK, *who is at the bar*). I see you're making your own, which is fine . . . fine. I'll just hootch up Martha, here, and then we'll be all set.

MARTHA (*suspicious*). All set for what?

GEORGE (*pause . . . considers*). Why, I don't know. We're having a party, aren't we? (*To* NICK, *who has moved from the bar*) I passed your wife in the hall. I mean, I passed the john and I looked in on her. Peaceful . . . so peaceful. Sound asleep . . . and she's actually . . . sucking her thumb.

MARTHA. Awwwwww!

GEORGE. Rolled up like a fetus, sucking away.

NICK (*a little uncomfortably*). I suppose she's all right.

GEORGE (*expansively*). Of course she is! (*Hands* MARTHA *her drink.*) There you are.

MARTHA (*still on her guard*). Thanks.

GEORGE. And now one for me. It's my turn.

MARTHA. Never, baby . . . it's never your turn.

GEORGE (*too cheerful*). Oh, now, I wouldn't say that, Martha.

MARTHA. You moving on the principle the worm turns? Well, the worm part's O.K. . . . cause that fits you fine, but the turning part . . . unh-unh! You're in a straight line, buddy-boy, and it doesn't lead anywhere . . . (*A vague after-thought*) . . . except maybe the grave.

GEORGE (*chuckles, takes his drink*). Well, you just hold that thought, Martha . . . hug it close . . . run your hands over it. Me, I'm going to sit down . . . if you'll excuse me. . . . I'm going to sit down over there and read a book. (*He moves to a chair facing away from the center of the room, but not too far from the front door.*)

MARTHA. You're gonna do *what*?

GEORGE (*quietly, distinctly*). I am going to read a book. Read. Read. Read? You've heard of it? (*Picks up a book.*)

MARTHA (*standing*). Whaddya mean you're gonna read? What's the matter with you?

GEORGE (*too calmly*). There's nothing the matter with me, Martha. . . . I'm going to read a book. That's all.

MARTHA (*oddly furious*). We've got company!

GEORGE (*over-patiently*). I know, my dear . . . (*Looks at his watch.*) . . . but . . . it's after four o'clock, and I always read around this time. Now, you . . . (*Dismisses her with a little wave.*) . . . go about your business. . . . I'll sit here very quietly. . . .

MARTHA. You read in the afternoon! You read at four o'clock in the afternoon . . . you don't read at four o'clock in the morning! Nobody reads at four o'clock in the morning!

GEORGE (*absorbing himself in his book*). Now, now, now.

MARTHA (*incredulously, to* NICK). He's going to read a book. . . . The son of a bitch is going to read a book!

NICK (*smiling a little*). So it would seem. (*Moves to* MARTHA, *puts his arm around her waist.* GEORGE *cannot see this, of course.*)

MARTHA (*getting an idea*). Well, we can amuse ourselves, can't we?

NICK. I imagine so.

MARTHA. We're going to amuse ourselves, George.

GEORGE (*not looking up*). Unh-hunh. That's nice.

MARTHA. You might not like it.

GEORGE (*never looking up*). No, no, now . . . you go right ahead . . . you entertain your guests.

MARTHA. I'm going to entertain myself, too.

GEORGE. Good . . . good.

MARTHA. Ha, ha. You're a riot, George.

GEORGE. Unh-hunh.

MARTHA. Well, I'm a riot, too, George.

GEORGE. Yes you are, Martha.

(NICK *takes* MARTHA's *hand, pulls her to him. They stop for a moment, then kiss, not briefly.*)

MARTHA (*after*). You know what I'm doing, George?

GEORGE. No, Martha . . . what are you doing?

MARTHA. I'm entertaining. I'm entertaining one of the guests. I'm necking with one of the guests.

GEORGE (*seemingly relaxed and pre-*

occupied, never looking). Oh, that's nice. Which one?

MARTHA (*livid*). Oh, by God you're funny. (*Breaks away from* NICK . . . *moves into* GEORGE's *side-line of vision by herself. Her balance is none too good, and she bumps into or brushes against the door chimes by the door. They chime.*)

GEORGE. Someone at the door, Martha.

MARTHA. Never mind that. I said I was necking with one of the guests.

GEORGE. Good . . . good. You go right on.

MARTHA (*pauses . . . not knowing quite what to do*). Good?

GEORGE. Yes, good . . . good for you.

MARTHA (*her eyes narrowing, her voice becoming hard*). Oh, I see what you're up to, you lousy little. . . .

GEORGE. I'm up to page a hundred and. . . .

MARTHA. Cut it! Just cut it out! (*She hits against the door chimes again; they chime.*) Goddam bongs.

GEORGE. They're chimes, Martha. Why don't you go back to your necking and stop bothering me? I want to read.

MARTHA. Why, you miserable. . . . I'll show you.

GEORGE (*swings around to face her . . . says, with great loathing*). No . . . show him, Martha . . . he hasn't seen it. *Maybe* he hasn't seen it. (*Turns to* NICK.) You haven't seen it yet, have you?

NICK (*turning away, a look of disgust on his face*). I . . . I have no respect for you.

GEORGE. And none for yourself, either. . . . (*Indicating* MARTHA) I don't know what the younger generation's coming to.

NICK. You don't . . . you don't even. . . .

GEORGE. Care? You're quite right. . . . I couldn't care less. So, you just take this bag of laundry here, throw her over your shoulder, and. . . .

NICK. You're disgusting.

GEORGE (*incredulous*). Because *you're* going to hump Martha, *I'm* disgusting? (*He breaks down in ridiculing laughter.*)

MARTHA (*to* GEORGE). You Mother! (*To* NICK.) Go wait for me, hunh? Go wait for me in the kitchen. (*But* NICK *does not move.* MARTHA *goes to him, puts her arms around him.*) C'mon, baby . . . please. Wait for me . . . in the kitchen . . . be a good baby. (NICK *takes her kiss,*

glares at GEORGE . . . *who has turned his back again . . . and exits.* MARTHA *swings around to* GEORGE.) Now you listen to me. . . .

GEORGE. I'd rather read, Martha, if you don't mind. . . .

MARTHA (*her anger has her close to tears, her frustration to fury*). Well, I do mind. Now, you pay attention to me! You come off this kick you're on, or I swear to God I'll do it. I swear to God I'll follow that guy into the kitchen, and then I'll take him upstairs, and. . . .

GEORGE (*swinging around to her again . . . loud . . . loathing*). SO WHAT, MARTHA?

MARTHA (*considers him for a moment . . . then, nodding her head, backing off slowly*). O.K. . . . O.K. . . . You asked for it . . . and you're going to get it.

GEORGE (*softly, sadly*). Lord, Martha, if you want the boy that much . . . have him . . . but do it honestly, will you? Don't cover it over with all this . . . all this . . . footwork.

MARTHA (*hopeless*). I'll make you sorry you made me want to marry you. (*At the hallway*) I'll make you regret the day you ever decided to come to this college. I'll make you sorry you ever let yourself down. (*She exits.*)

(*Silence.* GEORGE *sits still, staring straight ahead. Listening . . . but there is no sound. Outwardly calm, he returns to his book, reads a moment, then looks up . . . considers. . . .*)

GEORGE. "And the west, encumbered by crippling alliances, and burdened with a morality too rigid to accommodate itself to the swing of events, must . . . eventually . . . fall." (*He laughs, briefly, ruefully . . . rises, with the book in his hand. He stands still . . . then, quickly, he gathers all the fury he has been containing within himself . . . he shakes . . . he looks at the book in his hand and, with a cry that is part growl, part howl, he hurls it at the chimes. They crash against one another, ringing wildly. A brief pause, then* HONEY *enters.*)

HONEY (*the worse for wear, half asleep, still sick, weak, still staggering a little . . . vaguely, in something of a dream world*). Bells. Ringing. I've been hearing bells.

GEORGE. Jesus!

HONEY. I couldn't sleep . . . for the bells. Ding-ding, bong . . . it woke me up. What time is it?

GEORGE (*quietly beside himself*). Don't bother me.

HONEY (*confused and frightened*). I was asleep, and the bells started . . . they BOOMED! Poe-bells . . . they were Poe-bells . . . Bing-bing-bong-BOOM!

GEORGE. BOOM!

HONEY. I was asleep, and I was dreaming of . . . something . . . and I heard the sounds coming, and I didn't know what it was.

GEORGE (*never quite to her*). It was the sound of bodies. . . .

HONEY. And I didn't want to wake up, but the sound kept coming. . . .

GEORGE. . . . go back to sleep. . . .

HONEY. . . . and it FRIGHTENED ME!

GEORGE (*quietly . . . to* MARTHA, *as if she were in the room*). I'm going to get you . . . Martha.

HONEY. And it was so . . . cold. The wind was . . . the wind was so cold! And I was lying somewhere, and the covers kept slipping away from me, and I didn't want them to. . . .

GEORGE. Somehow, Martha.

HONEY. . . . and there was someone there . . . !

GEORGE. There was no one there.

HONEY (*frightened*). And I didn't want someone there. . . . I was . . . naked . . . !

GEORGE. You don't know what's going on, do you?

HONEY (*still with her dream*). I DON'T WANT ANY . . . NO . . . !

GEORGE. You don't know what's been going on around here while you been having your snoozette, do you.

HONEY. NO! . . . I DON'T WANT ANY . . . I DON'T WANT THEM. . . . GO 'WAY. . . . (*Begins to cry.*) I DON'T WANT . . . ANY . . . CHILDREN. . . . I . . . don't . . . want . . . any . . . children. I'm afraid! I don't want to be hurt. . . . PLEASE!

GEORGE (*nodding his head . . . speaks with compassion*). I should have known.

HONEY (*snapping awake from her reverie*). What! What?

GEORGE. I should have known . . . the whole business . . . the headaches . . . the whining . . . the. . . .

HONEY (*terrified*). What are you talking about?

GEORGE (*ugly again*). Does *he* know that? Does that . . . stud you're married to know about that, hunh?

HONEY. About what? Stay away from me!

GEORGE. Don't worry, baby . . . I wouldn't. . . . Oh, my God, that *would* be a joke, wouldn't it! But don't worry, baby. HEY! How you do it? Hunh? How do you make your secret little murders stud-boy doesn't know about, hunh? Pills? PILLS? You got a secret supply of pills? Or what? Apple jelly? WILL POWER?

HONEY. I feel sick.

GEORGE. You going to throw up again? You going to lie down on the cold tiles, your knees pulled up under your chin, your thumb stuck in your mouth . . . ?

HONEY (*panicked*). Where is he?

GEORGE. Where's who? There's nobody here, baby.

HONEY. I want my husband! I want a drink!

GEORGE. Well, you just crawl over to the bar and make yourself one. (*From offstage comes the sound of* MARTHA's *laughter and the crashing of dishes. Yelling.*) That's right! Go at it!

HONEY. I want . . . something. . . .

GEORGE. You know what's going on in there, little Miss? Hunh? You hear all that? You know what's going on in there?

HONEY. I don't want to know anything!

GEORGE. There are a couple of people in there. . . . (MARTHA's *laughter again.*) . . . they are in there, in the kitchen. . . . Right there, with the onion skins and the coffee grounds . . . sort of . . . sort of a . . . sort of a dry run for the wave of the future.

HONEY (*beside herself*). I . . . don't . . . understand . . . you. . . .

GEORGE (*a hideous elation*). It's very simple. . . . When people can't abide things as they are, when they can't abide the present, they do one of two things . . . either they . . . either they turn to a contemplation of the past, as I have done, or they set about to . . . alter the future. And when you want to change something . . . you BANG! BANG! BANG! BANG!

HONEY. Stop it!

GEORGE. And you, you simpering bitch . . . you don't want *children*?

HONEY. You leave me . . . alone. Who . . . WHO RANG?

GEORGE. What?

HONEY. What were the bells? Who

rang?

GEORGE. You don't want to know, do you? You don't want to listen to it, hunh?

HONEY (*shivering*). I don't want to listen to you. . . . I want to know who rang.

GEORGE. Your husband is . . . and you want to know who *rang?*

HONEY. Who rang? Someone rang!

GEORGE (*his jaw drops open . . . he is whirling with an idea*). . . . Someone. . . .

HONEY. RANG!

GEORGE. . . . someone . . . rang . . . yes . . . yessss. . . .

HONEY. The . . . bells . . . rang. . . .

GEORGE (*his mind racing ahead*). The bells rang . . . and it was someone. . . .

HONEY. Somebody. . . .

GEORGE (*he is home, now*). . . . somebody rang . . . it was somebody . . . with . . . I'VE GOT IT! I'VE GOT IT, MARTHA . . . ! Somebody with a message . . . and the message was . . . our son . . . OUR SON! (*Almost whispered*) It was a message . . . the bells rang and it was a message, and it was about . . . our son . . . and the message . . . was . . . and the message was . . . our . . . son . . . is . . . DEAD!

HONEY (*almost sick*). Oh . . . no.

GEORGE (*cementing it in his mind*). Our son is . . . dead. . . . And . . . Martha doesn't know. . . . I haven't told . . . Martha.

HONEY. No . . . no . . . no.

GEORGE (*slowly, deliberately*). Our son is dead, and Martha doesn't know.

HONEY. Oh. God in heaven . . . no.

GEORGE (*to* HONEY . . . *slowly, deliberately, dispassionately*). And you're not going to tell her.

HONEY (*in tears*). Your son is dead.

GEORGE. I'll tell her myself . . . in good time. I'll tell her myself.

HONEY (*so faintly*). I'm going to be sick.

GEORGE (*turning away from her . . . he, too, softly*). Are you? That's nice. (MARTHA's *laugh is heard again.*) Oh, listen to that.

HONEY. I'm going to die.

GEORGE (*quite by himself now*). Good . . . good . . . you go right ahead. (*Very softly, so* MARTHA *could not possibly hear*) Martha? Martha? I have some . . . terrible news for you. (*There is a strange half-smile on his lips.*) It's about our . . .

son. He's dead. Can you hear me, Martha? Our boy is dead. (*He begins to laugh, very softly . . . it is mixed with crying.*)

CURTAIN

ACT THREE:

THE EXORCISM

MARTHA *enters, talking to herself.*

———

MARTHA. Hey, hey. . . . Where is everybody . . . ? (*It is evident she is not bothered.*) So? Drop me; pluck me like a goddamn . . . whatever-it-is . . . creeping vine, and throw me over your shoulder like an old shoe . . . George? (*Looks about her.*) George? (*Silence*) George! What are you doing: Hiding, or something? (*Silence*) GEORGE!! (*Silence*) Oh, fa Chri . . . . . . (*Goes to the bar, makes herself a drink and amuses herself with the following performance.*) Deserted! Abandon-ed! Left out in the cold like an old pussycat. HA! Can I get you a drink, Martha? Why, thank you, George; that's very kind of you. No, Martha, no; why I'd do anything for you. Would you, George? Why, I'd do anything for you, too. Would you, Martha? Why, certainly, George. Martha, I've misjudged you. And I've misjudged you, too, George. WHERE IS EVERYBODY!!! Hump the Hostess! (*Laughs greatly at this, falls into a chair; calms down, looks defeated, says, softly.*) Fat chance. (*Even softer*) Fat chance. (*Baby-talk now.*) Daddy? Daddy? Martha is abandon-ed. Left to her own vices at . . . (*Peers at a clock.*) . . . something o'clock in the old A.M. Daddy White-Mouse; do you really have red eyes? Do you? Let me see. Ohhhhh! You do! You do! Daddy, you have red eyes . . . because you cry all the time, don't you, Daddy? Yes; you do. You cry alllll the time. I'LL GIVE ALL YOU BASTARDS FIVE TO COME OUT FROM WHERE YOU'RE HIDING!! (*Pause*) I cry all the time too, Daddy. I cry alllll the time; but deep inside, so no one can see me. I cry all the time. And Georgie cries all the time, too. We both cry all the time, and then, what we do, we cry, and we take our tears, and we put 'em in the ice box, in the goddamn ice trays (*Begins to laugh.*) until they're all frozen

(*Laughs even more.*) and then . . . we put them . . . in our . . . drinks. (*More laughter, which is something else, too. After sobering silence*) Up the drain, down the spout, dead, gone and forgotten. . . . Up the spout, not down the spout; *up* the spout: THE POKER NIGHT. Up the spout. . . . (*Sadly*) I've got windshield wipers on my eyes, because I married you . . . baby! . . . Martha, you'll be a song-writer yet. (*Jiggles the ice in her glass.*) CLINK! (*Does it again.*) CLINK! (*Giggles, repeats it several times.*) CLINK! . . . CLINK! . . . CLINK! . . . CLINK!

(NICK *enters while* MARTHA *is clinking; he stands in the hall entrance and watches her; finally he comes in.*)

NICK. My God, you've gone crazy too.

MARTHA. Clink?

NICK. I said, you've gone crazy too.

MARTHA (*considers it*). Probably . . . probably.

NICK. You've all gone crazy: I come downstairs, and what happens. . . .

MARTHA. What happens?

NICK. . . . my wife's gone into the can with a liquor bottle, and she winks at me . . . winks at me! . . .

MARTHA (*sadly*). She's never wunk at you; what a shame. . . .

NICK. She is lying down on the floor again, the tiles, all curled up, and she starts peeling the label off the liquor bottle, the brandy bottle. . . .

MARTHA. . . . we'll never get the deposit back that way. . . .

NICK. . . . and I ask her what she's doing, and she goes: shhhhhh!, nobody knows I'm here; and I come back in here, and you're sitting there going Clink!, for God's sake. Clink!

MARTHA. CLINK!

NICK. You've all gone crazy.

MARTHA. Yes. Sad but true.

NICK. Where is your husband?

MARTHA. He is vanish-ed. Pouf!

NICK. You're all crazy: nuts.

MARTHA (*affects a brogue*). Awww, 'tis the refuge we take when the unreality of the world weighs too heavy on our tiny heads. (*Normal voice again*) Relax; sink into it; you're no better than anybody else.

NICK (*wearily*). I think I am.

MARTHA (*her glass to her mouth*). You're certainly a flop in some departments.

NICK (*wincing*). I beg your par-

don . . . ?

MARTHA (*Unnecessarily loud*). I said, you're certainly a flop in some. . . .

NICK (*he, too, too loud*). I'm sorry you're disappointed.

MARTHA (*braying*). I didn't say I was disappointed! Stupid!

NICK. You should try me some time when we haven't been drinking for ten hours, and maybe. . . .

MARTHA (*still braying*). I wasn't talking about your potential; I was talking about your goddamn performance.

NICK (*softly*). Oh.

MARTHA (*she softer, too*). Your potential's fine. It's dandy. (*Wiggles her eyebrows.*) Absolutely dandy. I haven't seen such a dandy potential in a long time. Oh, but baby, you sure are a flop.

NICK (*snapping it out*). Everybody's a flop to you! Your husband's a flop, *I'm a* flop. . . .

MARTHA (*dismissing him*). You're all flops. I am the Earth Mother, and you're all flops. (*More or less to herself*) I disgust me. I pass my life in crummy, totally pointless infidelities . . . (*Laughs ruefully.*) *would*-be infidelities. Hump the Hostess? That's a laugh. A bunch of boozed-up . . . impotent lunk-heads. Martha makes goo-goo eyes, and the lunk-heads grin, and roll their beautiful, beautiful eyes back, and grin some more, and Martha licks her chops, and the lunk-heads slap over to the bar to pick up a little courage *and* they pick up a little courage, and they bounce back over to old Martha, who does a little dance for them, which heats them all up . . . mentally . . . and so they slap over to the bar again, and pick up a little more courage, and their wives and sweethearts stick their noses up in the air . . . right through the ceiling, sometimes . . . which sends the lunk-heads back to the soda fountain again where they fuel up some more, while Martha-poo sits there with her dress up over her head . . . suffocating—you don't know how *stuffy* it is with your dress up over your head—suffocating! waiting for the lunk-heads; so, *finally* they get their courage up . . . but that's all, baby! Oh my, there is sometimes some very nice potential, but, oh my! My, my, my. (*Brightly*) But that's how it is in a civilized society. (*To herself again*) All the gorgeous lunk-heads.

Poor babies. (*To* NICK, *now; earnestly*)
There is only one man in my life who
has ever . . . made me happy. Do you
know that? One!

NICK. The . . . the what-do-you-call-it?
. . . uh . . . the lawn mower, or something?

MARTHA. No; I'd forgotten him. But
when I think about him and me it's
almost like being a voyeur. Hunh. No;
I didn't mean him; I meant George, of
course. (*No response from* NICK) Uh
. . . George; my husband.

NICK (*disbelieving*). You're kidding.

MARTHA. Am I?

NICK. You must be. Him?

MARTHA. Him.

NICK (*as if in on a joke*). Sure; sure.

MARTHA. You don't believe it.

NICK (*mocking*). Why, of course I do.

MARTHA. You always deal in appearances?

NICK (*derisively*). Oh, for God's
sake. . . .

MARTHA. . . . George who is out somewhere there in the dark. . . . George who
is good to me, and whom I revile; who
understands me, and whom I push off;
who can make me laugh, and I choke it
back in my throat; who can hold me, at
night, so that it's warm, and whom I
will bite so there's blood; who keeps
learning the games we play as quickly as
I can change the rules; who can make
me happy and I do not wish to be happy,
and yes I do wish to be happy. George
and Martha: sad, sad, sad.

NICK (*echoing, still not believing*). Sad.

MARTHA. . . . whom I will not forgive
for having come to rest; for having seen
me and having said: yes, this will do;
who has made the hideous, the hurting,
the insulting mistake of loving me and
must be punished for it. George and
Martha: sad, sad, sad.

NICK (*puzzled*). Sad.

MARTHA. . . . who tolerates, which is intolerable; who is kind, which is cruel;
who understands, which is beyond comprehension. . . .

NICK. George and Martha: sad, sad, sad.

MARTHA. Some day . . . hah! some *night*
. . . some stupid, liquor-ridden night . . .
I will go too far . . . and I'll either break
the man's back . . . or push him off for
good . . . which is what I deserve.

NICK. I don't think he's got a vertebra

intact.

MARTHA (*laughing at him*). You don't,
huh? You don't think so. Oh, little boy,
you got yourself hunched over that
microphone of yours. . . .

NICK. Microscope. . . .

MARTHA. . . . yes . . . and you don't see
anything, do you? You see everything but
the goddamn mind; you see all the little
specs and crap, but you don't see what
goes on, do you?

NICK. I know when a man's had his
back broken; I can see that.

MARTHA. Can you!

NICK. You're damn right.

MARTHA. Oh . . . you know so little.
And you're going to take over the world,
hunh?

NICK. All right, now. . . .

MARTHA. You think a man's got his
back broken 'cause he makes like a clown
and walks bent, hunh? Is that *really* all
you know?

NICK. I said, all *right!*

MARTHA. Ohhhh! The stallion's mad,
hunh. The gelding's all upset. Ha, ha, ha,
HA!

NICK (*softly; wounded*). You . . . you
swing wild, don't you.

MARTHA (*triumphant*). HAH!

NICK. Just . . . anywhere.

MARTHA. HAH! I'm a Gatling gun.
Hahahahahahahahaha!

NICK (*in wonder*). Aimless . . . butch-
ery. Pointless.

MARTHA. Aw! You poor little bastard.

NICK. Hit out at everything.

(*The door chimes chime.*)

MARTHA. Go answer the door.

NICK (*amazed*). What did you say?

MARTHA. I said, go answer the door.
What are you, deaf?

NICK (*trying to get it straight*). You
. . . want me . . . to go answer the door?

MARTHA. That's right, lunk-head; answer the door. There must be something
you can do well; or, are you too drunk to
do that, too? Can't you get the latch up,
either?

NICK. Look, there's no need. . . .

(*Door chimes again*)

MARTHA (*shouting*). Answer it!
(*Softer*) You can be houseboy around
here for a while. You can start off being
houseboy right now.

NICK. Look, lady, I'm no flunky to you.

MARTHA (*cheerfully*). Sure you are!

You're ambitious, aren't you, boy? You didn't chase me around the kitchen and up the goddamn stairs out of mad, driven passion, did you now? You were thinking a little bit about your career, weren't you? Well, you can just houseboy your way up the ladder for a while.

NICK. There's no limit to you, is there? (*Door chimes again*)

MARTHA (*calmly, surely*). No, baby; none. Go answer the door. (NICK *hesitates.*) Look, boy; once you stick your nose in it, you're not going to pull out just whenever you feel like it. You're in for a while. Now, git!

NICK. Aimless . . . wanton . . . pointless. . . .

MARTHA. Now, now, now; just do what you're told; show old Martha there's something you *can* do. Hunh? Atta boy.

NICK (*considers, gives in, moves toward the door. Chimes again*). I'm coming, for Christ's sake!

MARTHA (*claps her hands*). Ha HA! Wonderful; marvelous. (*Sings.*) "Just a gigolo, everywhere I go, people always say. . . ."

NICK. STOP THAT!

MARTHA (*giggles*). Sorry, baby; go on now; open the little door.

NICK (*with great rue*). Christ. (*He flings open the door, and a hand thrusts into the opening a great bunch of snapdragons; they stay there for a moment.* NICK *strains his eyes to see who is behind them.*)

MARTHA. Oh, how lovely!

GEORGE (*appearing in the doorway, the snapdragons covering his face; speaks in a hideously cracked falsetto*). Flores; flores para los muertos. Flores.

MARTHA. Ha, ha, ha HA!

GEORGE (*A step into the room; lowers the flowers; sees* NICK; *his face becomes gleeful; he opens his arms*). Sonny! You've come home for your birthday! At last!

NICK (*backing off*). Stay away from me.

MARTHA. Ha, ha, ha, HA! That's the houseboy, for God's sake.

GEORGE. Really? That's not our own little sonny-Jim? Our own little all-American something-or-other?

MARTHA (*giggling*). Well, I certainly hope not; he's been acting awful funny, if he is.

GEORGE (*almost manic*). Ohhhh! I'll bet! Chippie-chippie-chippie, hunh? (*Affecting embarrassment*) I . . . I brungya dese flowers, Mart'a, 'cause I . . . wull, 'cause you'se . . . awwwwww hell. Gee.

MARTHA. Pansies! Rosemary! Violence! My wedding bouquet!

NICK (*starting to move away*). Well, if you two kids don't mind, I think I'll just. . . .

MARTHA. Ach! You just stay where you are. Make my hubby a drink.

NICK. I don't think I will.

GEORGE. No, Martha, no; that would be too much; he's your houseboy, baby, not mine.

NICK. I'm nobody's houseboy. . . .

GEORGE *and* MARTHA. . . . Now! (*Sing.*) I'm nobody's houseboy now. . . . (*Both laugh.*)

NICK. Vicious. . . .

GEORGE (*finishing it for him*). . . . children. Hunh? That right? Vicious children, with their oh-so-sad games, hop-scotching their way through life, etcetera, etcetera. Is that it?

NICK. Something like it.

GEORGE. Screw, baby.

MARTHA. Him can't. Him too fulla booze.

GEORGE. Weally? (*Handing the snapdragons to* NICK) Here; dump these in some gin. (NICK *takes them, looks at them, drops them on the floor at his feet.*)

MARTHA (*sham dismay*). Awwwwww.

GEORGE. What a terrible thing to do . . . to Martha's snapdragons.

MARTHA. Is that what they are?

GEORGE. Yup. And here I went out into the moonlight to pick 'em for Martha tonight, and for our sonny-boy tomorrow, for his birfday.

MARTHA (*passing on information*). There is no moon now. I saw it go down from the bedroom.

GEORGE (*feigned glee*). From the bedroom! (*Normal tone*) Well, there was a moon.

MARTHA (*too patient; laughing a little*). There couldn't have been a moon.

GEORGE. Well, there was. There is.

MARTHA. There is no moon; the moon went / down.

GEORGE. There is a moon; the moon is up.

MARTHA (*straining to keep civil*). I'm afraid you're mistaken.

GEORGE (*too cheerful*). No; no.

MARTHA (*between her teeth*). There is no goddamn moon.

GEORGE. My dear Martha . . . I did not pick snapdragons in the stony dark. I did not go stumbling around Daddy's greenhouse in the pitch.

MARTHA. Yes . . . you did. You would.

GEORGE. Martha, I do not pick flowers in the blink. I have never robbed a hothouse without there is a light from heaven.

MARTHA (*with finality*). There is no moon; the moon went down.

GEORGE (*with great logic*). That may very well be, Chastity; the moon may very well have gone down . . . but it came back up.

MARTHA. The moon does *not* come back up; when the moon has gone down it stays down.

GEORGE (*getting a little ugly*). You don't know anything. IF the moon went down, then it came back up.

MARTHA. BULL!

GEORGE. Ignorance! Such . . . ignorance.

MARTHA. Watch who you're calling ignorant!

GEORGE. Once . . . once, when I was sailing past Majorca, drinking on deck with a correspondent who was talking about Roosevelt, the moon went down, thought about it for a little . . . considered it, you know what I mean? . . . and then, POP, came up again. Just like that.

MARTHA. That is not true! That is such a lie!

GEORGE. You must not call everything a lie, Martha. (*To* NICK) Must she?

NICK. Hell, I don't know when you people are lying, or what.

MARTHA. You're damned right!

GEORGE. You're not supposed to.

MARTHA. Right!

GEORGE. At any rate, I was sailing past Majorca. . . .

MARTHA. You never sailed past Majorca. . . .

GEORGE. Martha. . . .

MARTHA. You were never in the goddamn Mediterranean at all . . . ever. . . .

GEORGE. I certainly was! My Mommy and Daddy took me there as a college graduation present.

MARTHA. Nuts!

NICK. Was this after you killed them?

(GEORGE *and* MARTHA *swing around and look at him; there is a brief, ugly pause.*)

GEORGE (*defiantly*). Maybe.

MARTHA. Yeah; maybe not, too.

NICK. Jesus!

(GEORGE *swoops down, picks up the bunch of snapdragons, shakes them like a feather duster in* NICK's *face, and moves away a little.*)

GEORGE. HAH!

NICK. Damn you.

GEORGE (*to* NICK). Truth and illusion. Who knows the difference, eh toots? Eh?

MARTHA. You were never in the Mediterranean . . . truth or illusion . . . either way.

GEORGE. If I wasn't in the Mediterranean, how did I get to the Aegean? Hunh?

MARTHA. OVERLAND!

NICK. Yeah!

GEORGE. Don't you side with her, houseboy.

NICK. I am not a houseboy.

GEORGE. Look! I know the game! You don't make it in the sack, you're a houseboy.

NICK. I AM NOT A HOUSEBOY!

GEORGE. No? Well, then you must have made it in the sack. Yes? (*He is breathing a little heavy; behaving a little manic.*) Yes? Someone's lying around here; somebody isn't playing the game straight. Yes? Come on; come on; who's lying? Martha? Come on!

NICK (*after a pause; to* MARTHA, *quietly with intense pleading*). Tell him I'm not a houseboy.

MARTHA (*after a pause, quietly, lowering her head*). No; you're not a houseboy.

GEORGE (*with great, sad relief*). So be it.

MARTHA (*pleading*). Truth and illusion, George; you don't know the difference.

GEORGE. No; but we must carry on as though we did.

MARTHA. Amen.

GEORGE (*flourishing the flowers*). SNAP WENT THE DRAGONS!! (NICK *and* MARTHA *laugh weakly.*) Hunh? Here we go round the mulberry bush, hunh?

NICK (*tenderly, to* MARTHA). Thank you.

MARTHA. Skip it.

GEORGE (*loud*). I said, here we go

round the mulberry bush!

MARTHA (*impatiently*). Yeah, yeah; we know; snap go the dragons.

GEORGE (*taking a snapdragon, throwing it, spearlike, stem-first at* MARTHA). SNAP!

MARTHA. Don't, George.

GEORGE (*throws another*). SNAP!

NICK. Don't do that.

GEORGE. Shut up, stud.

NICK. I'm not a stud!

GEORGE (*throws one at* NICK). SNAP! Then you're a houseboy. Which is it? Which are you? Hunh? Make up your mind. Either way. . . . (*Throws another at him.*) SNAP! . . . *you disgust me.*

MARTHA. Does it matter to you, George!?

GEORGE (*throws one at her*). SNAP! No, actually, it doesn't. Either way . . . I've had it.

MARTHA. Stop throwing those goddamn things at me!

GEORGE. Either way. (*Throws another at her.*) SNAP!

NICK (*to* MARTHA). Do you want me to . . . do something to him?

MARTHA. You leave him alone!

GEORGE. If you're a houseboy, baby, you can pick up after me; if you're a stud, you can go protect your plow. Either way. Either way. . . . Everything.

NICK. Oh for God's. . . .

MARTHA (*a little afraid*). Truth or illusion, George. Doesn't it matter to you . . . at all?

GEORGE (*without throwing anything*). SNAP! (*Silence*) You got your answer, baby?

MARTHA (*sadly*). Got it.

GEORGE. You just gird your blue-veined loins, girl. (*Sees* NICK *moving toward the hall.*) Now; we got one more game to play. And it's called bringing up baby.

NICK (*more-or-less under his breath*). Oh, for Lord's sake. . . .

MARTHA. George. . . .

GEORGE. I don't want any fuss. (*To* NICK) You don't want any scandal around here, do you, big boy? You don't want to wreck things, do you? Hunh? You want to keep to your time table, don't you? Then sit! (NICK *sits. To* MARTHA) And you, pretty Miss, you like fun and games, don't you? You're a sport from way back, aren't you?

MARTHA (*quietly, giving in*). All right, George; all right.

GEORGE (*seeing them both cowed; purrs*). Goooooooood; gooooood. (*Looks about him.*) But, we're not all here. (*Snaps his fingers a couple of times at* NICK.) You; you . . . uh . . . you; your little wifelet isn't here.

NICK. Look; she's had a rough night, now; she's in the can, and she's. . . .

GEORGE. Well, we can't play without everyone here. Now that's a fact. We gotta have your little wife. (*Hog-calls toward the hall.*) sooowwwiiieee!! soooowwwiiieee!!

NICK (*as* MARTHA *giggles nervously*). Cut that!

GEORGE (*swinging around, facing him*). Then get your butt out of that chair and bring the little dip back in here. (*As* NICK *does not move*) Now be a good puppy. Fetch, good puppy, go fetch. (NICK *rises, opens his mouth to say something, thinks better of it, exits.*) One more game.

MARTHA (*after* NICK *goes*). I don't like what's going to happen.

GEORGE (*surprisingly tender*). Do you know what it is?

MARTHA (*pathetic*). No. But I don't like it.

GEORGE. Maybe you will, Martha.

MARTHA. No.

GEORGE. Oh, it's a real fun game, Martha.

MARTHA (*pleading*). No more games.

GEORGE (*quietly triumphant*). One more, Martha. One more game, and then beddie-bye. Everybody pack up his tools and baggage and stuff and go home. And you and me, well, we gonna climb them well-worn stairs.

MARTHA (*almost in tears*). No, George; no.

GEORGE (*soothing*). Yes, baby.

MARTHA. No, George; please?

GEORGE. It'll all be done with before you know it.

MARTHA. No, George.

GEORGE. No climb stairs with Georgie?

MARTHA (*a sleepy child*). No more games . . . please. It's games I don't want. No more games.

GEORGE. Aw, sure you do, Martha . . . original game-girl and all, 'course you do.

MARTHA. Ugly games . . . ugly. And now this new one?

GEORGE (*stroking her hair*). You'll love it, baby.

MARTHA. No, George.

GEORGE. You'll have a ball.

MARTHA (*tenderly; moves to touch him*). Please, George, no more games; I. . . .

GEORGE (*slapping her moving hand with vehemence*). Don't you touch me! You keep your paws clean for the undergraduates!

MARTHA (*a cry of alarm, but faint*).

GEORGE (*grabbing her hair, pulling her head back*). Now, you listen to me, Martha; you have had quite an evening . . . quite a night for yourself, and you can't just cut it off whenever you've got enough blood in your mouth. We are going on, and I'm going to have at you, and it's going to make your performance tonight look like an Easter pageant. Now I want you to get yourself a little alert. (*Slaps her lightly with his free hand.*) I want a little life in you, baby. (*Again*)

MARTHA (*struggling*). Stop it!

GEORGE (*again*). Pull yourself together! (*Again*) I want you on your feet and slugging, sweetheart, because I'm going to knock you around, and I want you up for it. (*Again; he pulls away, releases her; she rises.*)

MARTHA. All right, George. What do you want, George?

GEORGE. An equal battle, baby; that's all.

MARTHA. You'll get it!

GEORGE. I want you mad.

MARTHA. I'M MAD!!

GEORGE. Get madder!

MARTHA. DON'T WORRY ABOUT IT!

GEORGE. Good for you, girl; now we're going to play this one to the death.

MARTHA. Yours!

GEORGE. You'd be surprised. Now, here come the tots; you be ready for this.

MARTHA (*she paces, actually looks a bit like a fighter*). I'm ready for you.

(NICK *and* HONEY *re-enter;* NICK *supporting* HONEY, *who still retains her brandy bottle and glass.*)

NICK (*unhappily*). Here we are.

HONEY (*cheerfully*). Hip, hop. Hip, hop.

NICK. You a bunny, Honey? (*She laughs greatly, sits.*)

HONEY. I'm a bunny, Honey.

GEORGE (*to* HONEY). Well, now, how's the bunny?

HONEY. Bunny funny! (*She laughs again.*)

NICK (*under his breath*). Jesus.

GEORGE. Bunny funny? Good for bunny!

MARTHA. Come on, George!

GEORGE (*to* MARTHA). Honey funny bunny! (HONEY *screams with laughter.*)

NICK. Jesus God. . . .

GEORGE (*slaps his hands together, once*). All right! Here we go! Last game! All sit. (NICK *sits.*) Sit down, Martha. This is a civilized game.

MARTHA (*cocks her fist, doesn't swing. Sits*). Just get on with it.

HONEY (*to* GEORGE). I've decided I don't remember anything. (*To* NICK) Hello, dear.

GEORGE. Hunh? What?

MARTHA. It's almost dawn, for God's sake. . . .

HONEY (*ibid*). I don't remember anything, and you don't remember anything, either. Hello, dear.

GEORGE. You what?

HONEY (*ibid, an edge creeping into her voice*). You heard me, nothing. Hello, dear.

GEORGE (*to* HONEY, *referring to* NICK). You do know that's your husband, there, don't you?

HONEY (*with great dignity*). Well, I certainly know *that*.

GEORGE (*close to* HONEY's *ear*). It's just some things you can't remember . . . hunh?

HONEY (*a great laugh to cover; then quietly, intensely to* GEORGE). Don't remember; not *can't*. (*At* NICK, *cheerfully*) Hello, dear.

GEORGE (*to* NICK). Well, speak to your little wifelet, your little bunny, for God's sake.

NICK (*softly, embarrassed*). Hello, Honey.

GEORGE. Awww, that was nice. I think we've been having a . . . a real good evening . . . all things considered. . . . We've sat around, and got to know each other, and had fun and games . . . curl-up-on-the-floor, for example. . . .

HONEY. . . . the tiles. . . .

GEORGE. . . . the tiles. . . . Snap the Dragon.

HONEY. . . . peel the label. . . .

GEORGE. . . . peel the . . . what?

MARTHA. Label. Peel the label.

HONEY (*apologetically, holding up her brandy bottle*). I peel labels.

GEORGE. We all peel labels, sweetie; and when you get through the skin, all three layers, through the muscle, slosh aside the organs (*An aside to* NICK) them which is still sloshable—(*Back to* HONEY) and get down to bone . . . you know what you do then?

HONEY (*terribly interested*). No.

GEORGE. When you get down to bone, you haven't got all the way, yet. There's something inside the bone . . . the marrow . . . and that's what you gotta get at. (*A strange smile at* MARTHA)

HONEY. Oh! I see.

GEORGE. The marrow. But bones are pretty resilient, especially in the young. Now, take our son. . . .

HONEY (*strangely*). Who?

GEORGE. Our son. . . . Martha's and my little joy!

NICK (*moving toward the bar*). Do you mind if I . . . ?

GEORGE. No, no; you go right ahead.

MARTHA. George. . . .

GEORGE (*too kindly*). Yes, Martha?

MARTHA. Just what are you doing?

GEORGE. Why love, I was talking about our son.

MARTHA. Don't.

GEORGE. Isn't Martha something? Here we are, on the eve of our boy's homecoming, the eve of his twenty-first birfday, the eve of his majority . . . and Martha says don't talk about him.

MARTHA. Just . . . don't.

GEORGE. But I want to, Martha! It's very important we talk about him. Now bunny and the . . . well, whichever he is . . . here don't know much about junior, and I think they should.

MARTHA. Just . . . don't.

GEORGE. (*snapping his fingers at* NICK). You. Hey, you! You want to play bringing up baby, don't you!

NICK (*hardly civil*). Were you snapping at me?

GEORGE. That's right. (*Instructing him*) *You* want to hear about our bouncey boy.

NICK (*pause; then shortly*). Yeah; sure.

GEORGE (*to* HONEY). And you, my dear? You want to hear about him, too, don't you.

HONEY (*pretending not to understand*). Whom?

GEORGE. Martha's and my son.

HONEY (*nervously*). Oh, you have a child?

(MARTHA *and* NICK *laugh uncomfortably.*)

GEORGE. Oh, indeed; do we ever! Do you want to talk about him, Martha, or shall I? Hunh?

MARTHA (*a smile that is a sneer*). Don't, George.

GEORGE. All rightie. Well, now; let's see. He's a nice kid, really, in spite of his home life; I mean, most kids'd grow up neurotic, what with Martha here carrying on the way she does: sleeping 'till four in the P.M., climbing all over the poor bastard, trying to break the bathroom door down to wash him in the tub when he's sixteen, dragging strangers into the house at all hours.

MARTHA (*rising*). O.K. YOU!

GEORGE (*mock concern*). Martha!

MARTHA. That's enough!

GEORGE. Well, do you want to take over?

HONEY (*to* NICK). Why would anybody want to wash somebody who's sixteen years old?

NICK (*slamming his drink down*). Oh, for Christ's sake, Honey!

HONEY (*stage whisper*). Well, why?!

GEORGE. Because it's her baby-poo.

MARTHA. ALL RIGHT!! (*By rote; a kind of almost-tearful recitation*) Our son. You want our son? You'll have it.

GEORGE. You want a drink, Martha?

MARTHA (*pathetically*). Yes.

NICK (*to* MARTHA *kindly*). We don't have to hear about it . . . if you don't want to.

GEORGE. Who says so? You in a position to set the rules around here?

NICK (*pause; tight-lipped*). No.

GEORGE. Good boy; you'll go far. All right, Martha; your recitation, please.

MARTHA (*from far away*). What, George?

GEORGE (*prompting*). "Our son. . . ."

MARTHA. All right. Our son. Our son was born in a September night, a night not unlike tonight, though tomorrow, and twenty . . . one . . . years ago.

GEORGE (*beginning of quiet asides*). You see? I told you.

MARTHA. It was an easy birth. . . .

GEORGE. Oh, Martha; no. You labored

. . . how you labored.

MARTHA. It was an easy birth . . . once it had been . . . accepted, relaxed into.

GEORGE. Ah . . . yes. Better.

MARTHA. It was an easy birth, once it had been accepted, and I was young.

GEORGE. And I was younger. . . . (*Laughs quietly to himself.*)

MARTHA. And I was young, and he was a healthy child, a red, bawling child, with slippery firm limbs. . . .

GEORGE. . . . Martha thinks she saw him at delivery. . . .

MARTHA. . . . with slippery, firm limbs, and a full head of black, fine, fine hair which, oh, later, later, became blond as the sun, our son.

GEORGE. He was a healthy child.

MARTHA. And I had wanted a child . . . oh, I had wanted a child.

GEORGE (*prodding her*). A son? A daughter?

MARTHA. A child! (*Quieter*) A child. And I had my child.

GEORGE. Our child.

MARTHA (*with great sadness*). Our child. And we raised him . . . (*Laughs, briefly, bitterly.*) yes, we did; we raised him. . . .

GEORGE. With teddy bears and an antique bassinet from Austria . . . and *no nurse.*

MARTHA. . . . with teddy bears and transparent floating goldfish, and a pale blue bed with cane at the headboard when he was older, cane which he wore through . . . finally . . . with his little hands . . . in his . . . sleep. . . .

GEORGE. . . . nightmares. . . .

MARTHA. . . . *sleep.* . . . He was a restless child. . . .

GEORGE (*soft chuckle, head-shaking of disbelief*). . . . Oh Lord . . .

MARTHA. . . . sleep . . . and a croup tent . . . a pale green croup tent, and the shining kettle hissing in the one light of the room that time he was sick . . . those four days . . . and animal crackers, and the bow and arrow he kept under his bed. . . .

GEORGE. . . . the arrows with rubber cups at their tip. . . .

MARTHA. . . . at their tip, which he kept beneath his bed. . . .

GEORGE. Why? Why, Martha?

MARTHA. . . . for fear . . . for fear of. . . .

GEORGE. For fear. Just that: for fear.

MARTHA (*vaguely waving him off; going on*). . . . and . . . and sandwiches on Sunday night, and Saturdays . . . (*Pleased recollection*) . . . and Saturdays the banana boat, the whole peeled banana, scooped out on top, with green grapes for the crew, a double line of green grapes, and along the sides, stuck to the boat with toothpicks, orange slices. . . . SHIELDS.

GEORGE. And for the oar?

MARTHA (*uncertainly*). A . . . carrot?

GEORGE. Or a swizzle stick, whatever was easier.

MARTHA. No. A carrot. And his eyes were green . . . green with . . . if you peered so deep into them . . . so deep . . . bronze . . . bronze parentheses around the irises . . . such green eyes!

GEORGE. . . . blue, green, brown. . . .

MARTHA. . . . and he loved the sun! . . . He was tan before and after everyone . . . and in the sun his hair . . . became . . . fleece.

GEORGE (*echoing her*). . . . fleece. . . .

MARTHA. . . . beautiful, beautiful boy.

GEORGE. Absolve, Domine, animas, omnium fidelium defunctorum ab omni vinculo delictorum.

MARTHA. . . . and school . . . and summer camp . . . and sledding . . . and swimming. . . .

GEORGE. Et gratia tua illis succurrente, mereantur evadere judicium ultionis.

MARTHA (*laughing, to herself*). . . . and how he broke his arm . . . how funny it was . . . oh, no, it hurt him! . . . but, oh, it was funny . . . in a field, his very first cow, the first he'd ever seen . . . and he went into the field, to the cow, where the cow was grazing, head down, busy . . . and he moo'd at it! (*Laughs ibid.*) He moo'd at it . . . and the beast, oh, surprised, swung its head up and moo'd at him, all three years of him, and he ran, startled, and he stumbled . . . fell . . . and broke his poor arm. (*Laughs, ibid.*) Poor lamb.

GEORGE. Et lucis aeternae beatitudine perfrui.

MARTHA. George cried! Helpless . . . George . . . cried. I carried the poor lamb. George snuffling beside me. I carried the child, having fashioned a sling . . . and across the great fields.

GEORGE. In Paradisum deducant te Angeli.

MARTHA. And as he grew . . . and as he grew . . . oh! so wise! . . . he walked evenly between us . . . (*She spreads her hands.*) . . . a hand out to each of us for what we could offer by way of support, affection, teaching, even love . . . and these hands, still, to hold us off a bit, for mutual protection, to protect us all from George's . . . weakness . . . and my . . . necessary greater strength . . . to protect himself . . . and *us.*

GEORGE. In memoria aeterna erit justus: ab auditione mala non timebit.

MARTHA. So wise; so wise.

NICK (*to* GEORGE). What is this? What are you doing?

GEORGE. Shhhhh.

HONEY. Shhhhh.

NICK (*shrugging*). O.K.

MARTHA. So beautiful; so wise.

GEORGE (*laughs quietly*). All truth being relative.

MARTHA. It was true! Beautiful; wise; perfect.

GEORGE. There's a real mother talking.

HONEY (*suddenly; almost tearfully*). I want a child.

NICK. Honey. . . .

HONEY (*more forcefully*). I want a child!

GEORGE. On principle?

HONEY (*in tears*). I want a child. I want a baby.

MARTHA (*waiting out the interruption, not really paying it any mind*). Of course, this state, this perfection . . . couldn't last. Not with George . . . not with George around.

GEORGE (*to the others*). There; you see? I knew she'd shift.

HONEY. Be still!

GEORGE (*mock awe*). Sorry . . . mother.

NICK. Can't you be still?

GEORGE (*making a sign at* NICK). Dominus vobiscum.

MARTHA. Not with George around. A drowning man takes down those nearest. George tried, but, oh, God, how I fought him. God, how I fought him.

GEORGE (*a satisfied laugh*). Ahhhhhhh.

MARTHA. Lesser states can't stand those above them. Weakness, imperfection cries out against strength, goodness and innocence. And George tried.

GEORGE. How did I try, Martha? How did I try?

MARTHA. How did you . . . what? . . . No! No . . . he grew . . our son grew . . . up; he is grown up; he is away at school, college. He is fine, everything is fine.

GEORGE (*mocking*). Oh, come on, Martha!

MARTHA. No. That's all.

GEORGE. Just a minute! You can't cut a story off like that, sweetheart. You started to say something . . . now you say it!

MARTHA. No!

GEORGE. Well, I will.

MARTHA. No!

GEORGE. You see, Martha, here, stops just when the going gets good . . . just when things start getting a little rough. Now, Martha here, is a misunderstood little girl; she really is. Not only does she have a husband who is a bog . . . a younger-than-she-is bog albeit . . . not only does she have a husband who is a bog, she has as well a tiny problem with spiritous liquors—like she can't get enough. . . .

MARTHA (*without energy*). No more, George.

GEORGE. . . . and on top of all that, poor weighed-down girl, PLUS a father who really doesn't give a damn whether she lives or dies, who couldn't care less *what* happens to his only daughter . . . on top of all that she has a *son*. She has a son who fought her every inch of the way, who didn't want to be turned into a weapon against his father, who didn't want to be used as a goddamn club whenever Martha didn't get things like she wanted them!

MARTHA (*rising to it*). Lies! Lies!

GEORGE. Lies? All right. A son who would *not* disown his father, who came to him for advice, for information, for love that wasn't mixed with sickness— and you know what I mean, Martha!— who could not tolerate the slashing, braying residue that called itself his MOTHER. MOTHER? HAH!!

MARTHA (*cold*). All right, you. A son who was so ashamed of his father he asked me once if it—possibly—wasn't true, as he had heard, from some cruel boys, maybe, that he was not our child; who could not tolerate the shabby failure his father had become. . . .

GEORGE. Lies!

MARTHA. Lies? Who would not bring his girl friends to the house. . . .

GEORGE. . . . in shame of his mother. . . .

MARTHA. . . . of his father! Who writes letters only to me!

GEORGE. Oh, so you think! To me! At my office!

MARTHA. Liar!

GEORGE. I have a stack of them!

MARTHA. YOU HAVE NO LETTERS!

GEORGE. And you have?

MARTHA. He has no letters. A son . . . a son who spends his summers away . . . away from his family . . . ON ANY PRETEXT . . . because he can't stand the shadow of a man flickering around the edges of a house. . . .

GEORGE. . . . who spends his summers away . . . and he does! . . . who spends his summers away because there isn't room for him in a house full of empty bottles, lies, strange men, and a harridan who. . . .

MARTHA. Liar!!

GEORGE. Liar?

MARTHA. . . . A son who I have raised as best I can against . . . vicious odds, against the corruption of weakness and petty revenges. . . .

GEORGE. . . . A son who is, deep in his gut, sorry to have been born. . . .

(*Both together*)

MARTHA. I have tried, oh God I have tried; the one thing . . . the one thing I've tried to carry pure and unscathed through the sewer of this marriage; through the sick nights, and the pathetic, stupid days, through the derision and the laughter . . . *God,* the laughter, through one failure after another, one failure compounding another failure, each attempt more sickening, more numbing than the one before; the one thing, the one *person* I have tried to protect, to raise above the mire of this vile, crushing marriage; the one light in all this hopeless . . . *dark*ness . . . our SON.

GEORGE. Libera me, Domine, de morte aeterna, in die illa tremenda; Quando caei movendi sunt et terra: Dum veneris judicare saeculum per ignem. Tremens factus sum ego, et timeo, dum discussio venerit, atque ventura ira. Quando caeli movendi sunt et terra. Dies illa, dies irae, calamitatis et miseriae; dies magna et amara valde. Dum veneris judicare saeculum per ignem. Requiem aeternam dona eis, Domine: et lux perpetua luceat eis. Libera me Domine de morte aeterna in die illa tremenda: quando caeli movendi sunt et terra; Dum veneris judicare saeculum per ignem.

(*End together*)

HONEY (*her hands to her ears*). STOP IT!! STOP IT!!

GEORGE (*with a hand sign*). Kyrie, eleison. Christe, eleison. Kyrie, eleison.

HONEY. JUST STOP IT!!

GEORGE. Why, baby? Don't you like it?

HONEY (*quite hysterical*). You . . . can't . . . do . . . this!

GEORGE (*triumphant*). Who says!

HONEY. I! Say!

GEORGE. Tell us why, baby.

HONEY. No!

NICK. Is this game over?

HONEY. Yes! Yes, it is.

GEORGE. Ho-ho! Not by a long shot. (*To* MARTHA) We got a little surprise for you, baby. It's about sunny-Jim.

MARTHA. No more, George.

GEORGE. YES!

NICK. Leave her be!

GEORGE. I'M RUNNING THIS SHOW! (*To* MARTHA) Sweetheart, I'm afraid I've got some bad news for you . . . for us, of course. Some rather sad news.

(HONEY *begins weeping, head in hands.*)

MARTHA (*afraid, suspicious*). What is this?

GEORGE (*oh, so patiently*). Well, Martha, while you were out of the room, while the . . . two of you were out of the room . . . I mean, I don't know where, hell, you both must have been somewhere (*Little laugh*). . . . While you were out of the room, for a while . . . well, Missey and I were sittin' here havin' a little talk, you know: a chaw and a talk . . . and the doorbell rang. . . .

HONEY (*head still in hands*). Chimed.

GEORGE. Chimed . . . and . . . well, it's hard to tell you, Martha. . . .

MARTHA (*a strange throaty voice*). Tell me.

HONEY. Please . . . don't.

MARTHA. Tell me.

GEORGE. . . . and . . . what it was . . . it was good old Western Union, some little boy about seventy.

MARTHA (*involved*). Crazy Billy?

GEORGE. Yes, Martha, that's right . . .

crazy Billy . . . and he had a telegram, and it was for us, and I have to tell you about it.

MARTHA (*as if from a distance*). Why didn't they phone it? Why did they bring it; why didn't they telephone it?

GEORGE. Some telegrams you have to deliver, Martha; some telegrams you can't phone.

MARTHA (*rising*). What do mean?

GEORGE. Martha. . . . I can hardly bring myself to say it. . . .

HONEY. Don't.

GEORGE (*to* HONEY). Do you want to do it?

HONEY (*defending herself against an attack of bees*). No no no no no.

GEORGE (*sighing heavily*). All right. Well, Martha . . . I'm afraid our boy isn't coming home for his birthday.

MARTHA. Of course he is.

GEORGE. No, Martha.

MARTHA. Of course he is. I say he is!

GEORGE. He . . . can't.

MARTHA. He is! I say so!

GEORGE. Martha . . . (*Long pause*) . . . our son is . . . dead. (*Silence*) He was . . . killed . . . late in the afternoon. . . . (*Silence. A tiny chuckle*) on a country road, with his learner's permit in his pocket, he swerved, to avoid a porcupine, and drove straight into a. . . .

MARTHA (*rigid fury*). YOU . . . CAN'T . . . DO . . . THAT!

GEORGE. . . . large tree.

MARTHA. YOU CANNOT DO THAT!

NICK (*softly*). Oh, my God. (HONEY *is weeping louder.*)

GEORGE (*quietly, dispassionately*). I thought you should know.

NICK. Oh my God; no.

MARTHA (*quivering with rage and loss*). NO! NO! YOU CANNOT DO THAT! YOU CAN'T DECIDE THAT FOR YOURSELF! I WILL NOT LET YOU DO THAT!

GEORGE. We'll have to leave around noon, I suppose. . . .

MARTHA. I WILL NOT LET YOU DECIDE THESE THINGS!

GEORGE. . . . because there are matters of identification, naturally, and arrangements to be made. . . .

MARTHA (*leaping at* GEORGE, *but ineffectual*). YOU CAN'T DO THIS! (NICK *rises, grabs hold of* MARTHA, *pins her arms behind her back.*) I WON'T LET YOU DO THIS, GET YOUR HANDS OFF ME!

GEORGE (*as* NICK *holds on; right in* MARTHA's *face*). You don't seem to understand, Martha; I haven't done anything. Now, pull yourself together. Our son is DEAD! Can you get that into your head?

MARTHA. YOU CAN'T DECIDE THESE THINGS.

NICK. Lady, please.

MARTHA. LET ME GO!

GEORGE. Now listen, Martha; listen carefully. We got a telegram; there was a car accident, and he's dead. POUF! Just like that! Now, how do you like it?

MARTHA (*a howl which weakens into a moan*). NOOOOOOooooooo.

GEORGE (*to* NICK). Let her go. (MARTHA *slumps to the floor in a sitting position.*) She'll be all right now.

MARTHA (*pathetic*). No; no, he is *not* dead; he is not *dead*.

GEORGE. He is dead. Kyrie, eleison. Christe, eleison. Kyrie, eleison.

MARTHA. You *cannot*. You may not decide these things.

NICK (*leaning over her; tenderly*). He hasn't decided anything, lady. It's not his doing. He doesn't have the power. . . .

GEORGE. That's right, Martha; I'm not a God. I don't have the power over life and death, do I?

MARTHA. YOU CAN'T KILL HIM! YOU CAN'T HAVE HIM DIE!

HONEY. Lady . . . please. . . .

MARTHA. YOU CAN'T! ·

GEORGE. There was a telegram, Martha.

MARTHA (*up; facing him*). Show it to me! Show me the telegram!

GEORGE (*long pause; then, with a straight face*). I ate it.

MARTHA (*a pause; then with the greatest disbelief possible, tinged with hysteria*). What did you just say to me?

GEORGE (*barely able to stop exploding with laughter*). I . . . ate . . . it.

(MARTHA *stares at him for a long moment, then spits in his face.*)

GEORGE (*with a smile*). Good for you, Martha.

NICK (*to* GEORGE). Do you think that's the way to treat her at a time like this? Making an ugly goddamn joke like that? Hunh?

GEORGE (*snapping his fingers at* HONEY). Did I eat the telegram or did I not?

HONEY (*terrified*). Yes; yes, you ate it. I watched . . . I watched you . . . you

. . . you ate it all down.

GEORGE (*prompting*). . . . like a good boy.

HONEY. . . . like a . . . g-g-g-good . . . boy. Yes.

MARTHA (*to* GEORGE, *coldly*). You're not going to get away with this.

GEORGE (*with disgust*). YOU KNOW THE RULES, MARTHA! FOR CHRIST'S SAKE, YOU KNOW THE RULES!

MARTHA. NO!

NICK. (*with the beginnings of a knowledge he cannot face*). What are you two talking about?

GEORGE. I can kill him, Martha, if I want to.

MARTHA. HE IS OUR CHILD!

GEORGE. Oh yes, and you bore him, and it was a good delivery. . . .

MARTHA. HE IS OUR CHILD!

GEORGE. AND I HAVE KILLED HIM!

MARTHA. NO!

GEORGE. YES!

(*Long silence*)

NICK (*very quietly*). I think I understand this.

GEORGE (*ibid*). Do you?

NICK (*ibid*). Jesus Christ, I think I understand this.

GEORGE (*ibid*). Good for you, buster.

NICK (*violently*). JESUS CHRIST I THINK I UNDERSTAND THIS!

MARTHA (*great sadness and loss*). You have no right . . . you have no right at all. . . .

GEORGE (*tenderly*). I have the right, Martha. We never spoke of it; that's all. I could kill him any time I wanted to.

MARTHA. But why? Why?

GEORGE. You broke our rule, baby. You mentioned him . . . you mentioned him to someone else.

MARTHA (*tearfully*). I did *not*. I never did.

GEORGE. Yes, you did.

MARTHA. Who? WHO?!

HONEY (*crying*). To me. You mentioned him to me.

MARTHA (*crying*). I FORGET! Sometimes . . . sometimes when it's night, when it's late, and . . . and everybody else is . . . talking . . . I forget and I . . . want to mention him . . . but I . . . HOLD ON . . . I hold on . . . but I've wanted to . . . so often . . . oh, George, you've *pushed* it . . . there was no need . . . there was no need for *this*. I *ment*ioned him . . . all

right . . . but you didn't have to push it over the EDGE. You didn't have to . . . kill him.

GEORGE. Requiescat in pace.

HONEY. Amen.

MARTHA. You didn't have to have him die, George.

GEORGE. Requiem aeternam dona eis, Domine.

HONEY. Et lux perpetua luceat eis.

MARTHA. That wasn't . . . needed.

(*A long silence*)

GEORGE (*softly*). It will be dawn soon. I think the party's over.

NICK (*to* GEORGE; *quietly*). You couldn't have . . . any?

GEORGE. *We* couldn't.

MARTHA (*a hint of communion in this*). *We* couldn't.

GEORGE (*to* NICK *and* HONEY). Home to bed, children; it's way past your bedtime.

NICK (*his hand out to* HONEY). Honey?

HONEY (*rising, moving to him*). Yes.

GEORGE (MARTHA *is sitting on the floor by a chair now*). You two go now.

NICK. Yes.

HONEY. Yes.

NICK. I'd like to. . . .

GEORGE. Good night.

NICK (*pause*). Good night.

(NICK *and* HONEY *exit;* GEORGE *closes the door after them; looks around the room; sighs, picks up a glass or two, takes it to the bar.*)

(*This whole last section very softly, very slowly.*)

GEORGE. Do you want anything, Martha?

MARTHA (*still looking away*). No . . . nothing.

GEORGE. All right. (*Pause*) Time for bed.

MARTHA. Yes.

GEORGE. Are you tired?

MARTHA. Yes.

GEORGE. I am.

MARTHA. Yes.

GEORGE. Sunday tomorrow; all day.

MARTHA. Yes. (*a long silence between them*) Did you . . . did you . . . have to?

GEORGE (*pause*). Yes.

MARTHA. It was . . . ? You had to?

GEORGE (*pause*). Yes.

MARTHA. I don't know.

GEORGE. It was . . . time.

MARTHA. Was it?

GEORGE. Yes.

MARTHA (*pause*). I'm cold.

GEORGE. It's late.

MARTHA. Yes.

GEORGE (*long silence*). It will be better.

MARTHA (*long silence*). I don't . . . know.

GEORGE. It will be . . . maybe.

MARTHA. I'm . . . not . . . sure.

GEORGE. No.

MARTHA. Just. . . . us?

GEORGE. Yes.

MARTHA. I don't suppose, maybe, we could. . . .

GEORGE. No, Martha.

MARTHA. Yes. No.

GEORGE. Are you all right?

MARTHA. Yes. No.

GEORGE (*puts his hand gently on her shoulder; she puts her head back and he sings to her, very softly*).

Who's afraid of Virginia Woolf
Virginia Woolf
Virginia Woolf,

MARTHA. I . . . am . . . George. . . .

GEORGE. Who's afraid of Virginia Woolf. . . .

MARTHA. I . . . am . . . George. . . . I . . . am. . . .

(GEORGE *nods, slowly.*)

(*Silence; tableau*)

CURTAIN

THE ROPE DANCERS

Morton Wishengrad

Presented by The Playwrights' Company
and Gilbert Miller at the Cort Theatre in New York
on November 20, 1957, with the following cast:

LIZZIE HYLAND	Beverly Lunsford	JAMES HYLAND	Art Carney
MARGARET HYLAND	Siobhan McKenna	LAMESHNIK	Joseph Julian
THE MOVING MAN	William Edmondson	THE COP	Joseph Boland
MRS. FARROW	Joan Blondell	DR. JACOBSON	Theodore Bikel
CLEMENTINE	Barbara Ellen Myers		

Directed by Peter Hall
Designed by Boris Aronson
Costumes by Patricia Zipprodt

SCENE. New York. The turn of the century.

ACT ONE. An afternoon in early October.

ACT TWO. SCENE I. Immediately thereafter. SCENE II. Half an hour later.
SCENE III. Half an hour later.

ACT THREE. Two hours later.

A GNARLED, strong play by an author (Morton Wishengrad, born in 1914) whose faults are the defects of his virtues of reflectiveness and passion for truth-telling, *The Rope Dancers* fared unexpectedly well on Broadway. One cannot but suspect that the decent run achieved by the play was due to the factors scholars call identification and recognition and can be more simply denoted as insight and sympathy. These qualities were his by natural right of experience as a hard-pressed and unwell man who earned his living precariously but with absolute devotion to the highest standards of Biblical ethics and humanism in writing one of the most distinguished and long-running public-service radio series, "The Eternal Light." Some of these radio programs were collected under the same title and published by Crown Publishers in 1947.

His other radio scripts were also pitched on the altitudes of moral renewal; some of the better known were "Land of the Free," "The Jeffersonian Heritage," and "Cavalcade of America," the N.B.C. "Our American Heritage" series in which he voiced his anger at a flaccid society along the lines of his complaint (in an interview, in the fall of 1959) that "No one cares anymore. We live in a public relations society with a public relations President." A favorite quotation of his was his hero Jefferson's declaration, inscribed on the Jefferson Memorial, "I have sworn upon the altar of God eternal hostility against every form of tyranny over the minds of men." Wishengrad grew up during the Depression and developed his social idealism in that serious testing period. One of the occupations of his youth was working for the New York shipping clerks' union and included painting picket signs; there was also a time when he became a member of the Young People's Socialist League, then familiarly called, if I am not mistaken, the "Yipsels."

Renouncing his hope of becoming a physician because he lacked the means for financing an expensive education, he began to write as well as to teach. He became educational director of Local 91 of the progressive International Ladies' Garment Workers Union, and he wrote the script of the pro-labor movie *With These Hands* at the special request of David Dubinksy, president of the union. In 1944 he left his job with the union to write documentary radio scripts on the Red Cross and many other subjects. The "Eternal Light" scripts on Jewish history and Judaic ideals grew in distinction as they mounted in number; he wrote over 150 of these radio plays.

In the course of his work, Wishengrad came across a report on a little girl at New York's Bellevue Hospital who had been born with six fingers and had St. Vitus' dance. He based a radio play on this report under the title of *Lizzie and the Whiskers*. But it was turned down for "Cavalcade of America" by the sponsoring company—probably, the author reflected in his *Post* interview with no little scorn, because some vice-president at Du Pont thought it was un-American for a girl to have six fingers just as death and sickness have become un-American "because they break the success pattern." Ultimately, after getting the play done on the "Eternal Light" program, Wishengrad adapted the story and transformed it under the title of *The Rope Dancers,* which is about a great deal more than a girl with six fingers.* He was forty-three years old when *The Rope Dancers* opened in the fall of 1957. It was the only play of his that Morton Wishengrad lived to see on Broadway.

To those who may be troubled by the death of the child as an adventitious and possibly anticlimactic detail, one may recommend an interview with the author conducted by Miss Frances Herridge of the New York *Post* (December 26, 1957). "Margaret the wife and mother," Miss Herridge writes, "is the strong-minded puritan who attributes the deformity of her six-fingered child to her husband's philandering and her own secret enjoyment of sex. The mother devotes her life to hiding this stigma of shame from the world, and when a kindly doctor removes the finger, the child dies from the shock. But Wishengrad does not think of it as tragic. The child's death, he says, is the birth of Margaret's marriage, and the play ends on the hope of a happy home at last."

Still, there can be no denying that Wishengrad set himself an extremely difficult

* The reader may wish to read a review of *The Rope Dancers* by the present editor in the essay "Clinic and Symbol in Wishengrad's *Rope Dancers"* on pages 161-164 in John Gassner's *Theatre at the Crossroads* (Holt, Rinehart and Winston, 1960).

task (*it is simply not true that those who write and produce for Broadway invariably look for an easy way of making a dollar*), and Richard Watts, Jr., was quite correct in saying, in the same newspaper, that "Possibly only Eugene O'Neill could have taken this particular material and, by the strength of his monumental theatrical drive, given it the desperate tragic sense it demanded." The problems in writing this play are not the result of Broadway opportunism or of a lack of insight on the part of the author, whose point is so well made when he lets the puritanical Margaret say to her philandering husband, "You are such an innocent in your sin, and I am such a whore in my virtue." It is in the development of the action that Wishengrad could be faulted, and Thomas Barbour paid him a proper compliment (in the *Hudson Review,* Spring, 1958, p. 117) in calling *The Rope Dancers* "one of the most uncompromising plays I have seen." Mr. Barbour predicted that if Mr. Wishengrad could maintain his integrity in the hurly-burly of Broadway, he might yet, in that respect at least, confirm his leading lady's (Siobhan McKenna's) premature contention that he was the finest American playwright since O'Neill. Unfortunately the prediction could not be tested; Morton Wishengrad died on February 12, 1963.

ACT ONE

The time is an afternoon in early October, the turn of the century.

As the curtain rises we see the two-room flat of Margaret Hyland on the fifth floor of a New York tenement.

It is a kitchen and a bedroom in a single setting. The kitchen is large and the main room, and—most important—it is provided with a window on the street.

The bedroom window looks out upon a shaft and there is a rickety fire escape with a ladder going up to the roof.

Both rooms are a disorder of boxes, bundles, odds and ends of furniture . . . The Hylands are moving in.

Against the wall of the bedroom lean a mattress and a spring. And as we look a girl is placing books in a bookcase which will stand near where the bed will be.

———

LIZZIE. (*singing to herself—by rote*). President, President Rutherford Hayes, Grew a beard in twenty-eight days.

(*From the hall outside* MARGARET HYLAND *comes into the kitchen carrying a tailor's dummy. She places it in a corner of the room, rapidly removes her hat and coat and goes to a packing barrel, which shows signs of having been half-emptied.*)

MARGARET (*calling*). I almost forgot the dummy.

LIZZIE. What?

MARGARET. I almost forgot the dummy.

LIZZIE (*from the bedroom*). I was wondering why you went out again.

MARGARET. I don't trust that moving man.

LIZZIE. He's a nice man. You can tell by the way he talks to his horse. He told me he never takes jobs that are too big —because of the horse.

MARGARET. He's careless with furniture. (*At thirty-three,* MARGARET HYLAND *is careworn. Once she must have been a handsome woman, but life has made her acid and too quick to defend herself against its attack.*) What are you doing in there?

LIZZIE. Arranging my books.

MARGARET. That's for the last. Come here and help me with the dishes. (LIZZIE *puts the remainder of the books on top of the bookcase. It is an effort for her to do so—she is frail. We see her better*

when she comes into the kitchen, a pale, delicate child of eleven dressed in white, with white shoes and a white bow in her hair . . . as if she were going to a wedding, and not moving into a tenement apartment on the fifth floor.*) I told you the books would get you dirty.

LIZZIE (*she brushes the skirt of her dress with a sweep of her hand—her right hand. The distinguishing feature of her dress is that it has an unusual but rather attractive pocket on the left side, and in this pocket* LIZZIE *keeps her hand*). Why do I have to wear a white dress on moving day?

MARGARET. Because my child always wears a white dress.

(*We hear a noise from the hall—the heavy tread of footsteps coming up and a banging of furniture against a wall.*)

MOVING MAN (*coming up*). These goddam narrow steps.

(MARGARET *puts her head outside the door and calls in a voice of exasperation.*)

MARGARET. You're an experienced moving man. Why can't you be careful?

(*The* MOVING MAN *comes in, his shirt wet with perspiration. He is carrying a brass bedstead—the double-bed size—an ironing board, and a collection of pots tied together with a rope.*)

MOVING MAN. It's heavy work.

(MARGARET *takes the ironing board.*)

MARGARET. Why do you have to carry so many things at once! (*She leans it against a wall.*)

MOVING MAN. I don't like to climb stairs. Where do you want the bed?

MARGARET. There is this kitchen and there is that bedroom—where do you think I want it? (MOVING MAN *looks her full in the face, and then with great deliberation he lets the pots and pans fall with a great clatter to the floor.*) Don't you do that to my things. You be careful with the rest of it.

MOVING MAN (*going into the bedroom*). That's all there is, that's the last of the load. (*He starts to assemble the bedstead.*)

MARGARET (*grudgingly*). You're careless but you're quick. I will say that.

MOVING MAN (*dryly*). Put it in my tip.

(LIZZIE *has shriveled at the acid in her mother's voice. Now, furtively, she finds a paper bag on a chair and from it she takes out some bread and starts to the bedroom.*)

MARGARET (*unpacking*). Where are you going?

LIZZIE (*hiding the bread*). I forgot something in there. (*She skips into the bedroom and whispers to the* MOVING MAN:) Mister. (*She touches him.*)

MOVING MAN (*not looking up*). What is it?

LIZZIE. I brought you bread and jelly. (*The resentment ebbs from his face as he sees the girl and the bread in her hand. He is about to refuse it but her look changes his mind.*)

MOVING MAN. It's just what I want. (*He looks at the dainty slice with some misgivings and then puts it all into his mouth. With her right hand,* LIZZIE *pulls a chair up.*)

LIZZIE. Sit down when you eat.

MOVING MAN (*he gulps and the entire mouthful goes down*). When you sit, the food only goes to here. (*He points to his abdomen.*) When you stand, it goes down all the way. In my line of work a man has got to think of his feet.

MARGARET (*with her anger*). What's taking so long in there!

MOVING MAN (*with his anger*). Lady, I'm trying to put this bed together.

MARGARET (*she takes quick steps to the bedroom doorway*). I didn't ask you to. I asked you to move us from Lispenard Street and that is all. Don't think I'm going to pay you for doing something I didn't ask and that I can do myself.

MOVING MAN (*curtly*). All right, Mrs. Hyland, then I'm done—pay me. (*MARGARET HYLAND goes to a cupboard in the kitchen. Shielding with her body the ensuing operation she finds a breadbox, and in the breadbox a paper, and in the paper her pocketbook—from which she takes out an old cotton change purse. She brings the change purse toward the* MOVING MAN, *who meets her belligerently in the center of the kitchen. Carefully she undoes a large safety pin which secures the change purse. She puts the pin in her mouth and counts out three and a half dollars in bills and coins. Not bothering to count it:*) Next time you move, call another moving man.

MARGARET. Count it.

MOVING MAN (*putting the money in his pocket. To* LIZZIE). So long, kid. (*He starts for the door.*)

MARGARET. Here's your tip. (*She goes to him and gives him a dime.*)

MOVING MAN (*examining it*). Five flights of stairs!

MARGARET. That's a good tip. (*He looks at her with contempt and goes to* LIZZIE, *who shies away from him. He pursues her. Her left hand is still in the pocket of her dress. He drops the coin into the pocket, turns and exits.*)

MOVING MAN (*going off*). Cheap! Goddam cheap. Five flights of stairs and a lousy ten-cent tip.

(MARGARET *instantly goes to the door, locks it first with a key and then with a chain.*)

MARGARET (*turning to* LIZZIE). You can keep the ten cents.

LIZZIE (*she returns it to her mother, her voice tight with reproach*). He was a nice man.

MARGARET. You mean he was a fool. Keep it.

LIZZIE. It doesn't belong to me.

MARGARET. You're another fool.

LIZZIE (*turning her back*). You aren't; you have the ten cents.

(MARGARET *imploringly holds the dime out to* LIZZIE, *who never turns.* MARGARET *puts the coin in her change purse, thinks better of it and puts it instead on the table. She closes the purse and fastens it with the safety pin.*)

MARGARET. You always wanted a window on the street. Well—there it is. (LIZZIE *goes to the window . . . while her mother goes through the secret operation of hiding the change purse in the pocketbook and restoring the pocketbook to the paper bag in the breadbox, etc.*) Don't lean out too far.

LIZZIE (*from the window*). What?

MARGARET. I said, don't lean out too far.

LIZZIE. I won't. (*With more animation.*) They're wading in the horse trough.

MARGARET. Who?

LIZZIE (*craning to see*). Some boys and girls. They're playing.

MARGARET (*as she goes toward a packing barrel*). If they were my children I'd find something for them to do with their time.

LIZZIE (*dully*). I know . . . they're just silly kids. (*Turning to her.*) Ma, where's my jump-rope?

MARGARET. There's more important things than jump-ropes to be unpacked.

(*Five flights below from the street we hear a chanting voice.*)

THE RAG MAN'S VOICE. I cash clothes. I buy, I cash . . . I cash clothes. (*He continues like this.*)

LIZZIE (*looking out the window*). It's the same crazy rag man we had on Lispenard Street. What's he doing here?

MARGARET (*working all the while*). Earning his living by the sweat of his brow. He's a hardworking man. But he needn't stop for me. When I get through with clothes, there's nothing left . . . not even rags. (*From this point and to the final curtain,* MARGARET *is constantly at work and under her skillful hands the bare flat is put in order. She works for a moment now. We hear the thin yap of a poodle.*)

LIZZIE (*leaning out*). The people on the third have got a little white poodle dog.

MARGARET. They're never clean . . . shedding all over.

LIZZIE. I'll bet it has a cute face.

MARGARET. When it rains, they have a smell. Don't lean out. Shut the window and help me unpack. (LIZZIE *tries to close the window with one hand.* MARGARET, *a look of sudden tenderness on her face, goes to the window and helps her.* LIZZIE *runs to the table, and still using only one hand, tries to remove a small stack of dishes.* MARGARET *nods, a nod of reassurance.* LIZZIE *removes the hand from the pocket—it is a mittened hand. She takes up the dishes and starts toward the cupboard.*) What are you doing?

LIZZIE. Putting them in the cupboard.

MARGARET. You know better than that. Put them on the sink.

LIZZIE. You washed them before we moved . . . in scalding water.

MARGARET. I'm going to wash them again. And then I'm going to wash the cupboard again. I'm going to scrub this flat from top to bottom. I don't live in other people's dirt.

(LIZZIE *responds with the mechanical flattery expected of her.*)

LIZZIE. You're clean, Ma. You're the cleanest thing I ever saw.

MARGARET (*pleased*). I'm going to make you a nice new dress, just as soon as I finish the shirtwaist for Mrs. Bernard and the velvet coat.

LIZZIE. You work too hard.

MARGARET. To work is to pray.

LIZZIE. I wish I could help you sew. Then you wouldn't have to stay up nights.

MARGARET. Tell that to James Hyland. He always said I complain. . . . This is my lot in life, this is what I am, and I must be grateful for good health and for what I have. If your father had been a man like other men, I wouldn't have to take in sewing. If! It's a big word. (*The recollection of* JAMES HYLAND *angers her and she turns sharply on* LIZZIE.) I don't care if I never see him again. (*The look of misery on* LIZZIE's *face infuriates her.*) Don't stand there like a wooden stick. If you're going to help me, help me, if not go and sit on a chair and read your books.

LIZZIE. I don't want to read. I want to help you.

MARGARET. I don't need anyone to help me. I'm capable of helping myself. I earn my own piece of bread. I take no favors from anyone. I moved by myself. I'll unpack myself. I don't need his help. I don't need his daughter's help, I don't need anybody's help. (*Yelling.*) And I don't need that look from you, Lizzie Hyland. I don't keep you in white dresses for that kind of look.

LIZZIE. I'm sorry I looked.

MARGARET. But you're not sorry I'm yelling.

LIZZIE (*belligerently*). I love my father.

MARGARET. Of course! Because I'm the bad one, I'm the mean one, I'm the witch.

LIZZIE. I never said that.

MARGARET. That's what you think. Go on, deny it. Your mother—the witch.

LIZZIE. Please. I can't talk to you when you're like this.

MARGARET (*working herself up into a fury*). You can't deny it. That's what you think of me. The mean one, the bad one. You do, say it—you do. Hate me, Lizzie, hate me, but don't lie to me or I'll take a strap and lay your back open . . . because God hates a liar. And I won't have any lies in this new house. No more lies. No more lies. I want this to be a clean house. I want this to be a good house . . . I want . . . (*Suddenly she stops.*) Oh, my God! Someday I'll take a knife and cut it out.

LIZZIE (*afraid*). Ma!

MARGARET. The evil tongue in my face . . . I swear I'll bite it off with my own teeth.

LIZZIE. Don't talk like that.

MARGARET. The only thing it's good for is to tear living pieces out of people. (LIZZIE *runs to her mother and holds her fiercely . . .* MARGARET *doesn't cry, but the posture of her body, the clenching of her hands is louder than a cry.*)

LIZZIE (*whispering*). You're a good mother. (*She reaches up with her mittened hand and she strokes her mother's face . . . They both startle at a knock on the door.*)

MRS. FARROW's VOICE. Hello in there . . . We're the people on the fourth—come to say hello.

(MARGARET *shakes her head violently . . .* LIZZIE *whispers urgently:*)

LIZZIE. Yes, Ma. We're in a new house. You promised.

MARGARET (*with a great effort, calling out*). Just a minute, I'll open the door. (*She looks searchingly in* LIZZIE's *face. Then she moistens a corner of her apron in her mouth and wipes a smudge off* LIZZIE's *face. It is no kiss, and yet the look that goes between them is a kiss.* LIZZIE *puts her left hand back in the pocket and* MARGARET *unlocks and unchains the door, admitting to our view* MRS. FARROW *and her daughter,* CLEMENTINE. *Where* MARGARET *is spare,* MRS. FARROW *is ample. Where* MARGARET *is angular of face and figure,* MRS. FARROW *is all curve and comfort. Buttons are cheerfully missing from her blouse and if she is aware of the coffee stains on it or of the egg on her daughter's chin, she makes no sign.* CLEMENTINE *is* LIZZIE's *height, although two years younger, unkempt, unclean, but cheerful and nosy.*)

MRS. FARROW. Hello, there! I'm no sparrow but my name is Farrow and this is my daughter Clementine.

MARGARET. How do you do?

CLEMENTINE (*showing it*). We brought you a cake. (*She raises it higher.*)

MARGARET (*stiffly*). Thank you very much. That's very kind of you. I'm sure we'll enjoy it.

MRS. FARROW (*scratching her head dubiously*). Clementine baked it. It's the feeling that's put into the dough. (*When* MARGARET *shows no disposition to ask them in,* MRS. FARROW *employs her one stratagem. With one swift hand she propels* CLEMENTINE *into the room.*) Say hello to the new kid. When you want

them to shut up, they jabber.

CLEMENTINE (*sizing* LIZZIE *up*). Hello.

LIZZIE (*afraid*). Hello.

MRS. FARROW. Don't just hold the cake in your hands, put it on the table. (CLEMENTINE *puts it on the table and swipes the dime.*) Now say something friendly.

CLEMENTINE (*she picks her nose*). You haven't got any brothers or sisters. Only one bed came up the stairs.

MRS. FARROW. Don't pick your nose in other people's houses, it ain't ladylike.

CLEMENTINE (*to her mother*). The moving man was cursing all the way down on account of her mother only offered him a ten-cent tip.

MRS. FARROW. Don't say "her mother"! (*Craftily*) Her mother's name is . . .

MARGARET (*grudging it*). Mrs. Hyland.

MRS. FARROW (*triumphant*). We're pleased to make your acquaintance and you'll find this a friendly tenement. People take an interest. You're not English?

MARGARET. No we are not English.

MRS. FARROW (*to* CLEMENTINE). I told you they were Irish. (*To* MARGARET.) My own grandmother was born in Mayo. You wouldn't be from Mayo?

MARGARET. No.

MRS. FARROW. County Kerry? (MARGARET *makes no answer.*) Clare? Cork? Sligo? (*To* LIZZIE.) Kilkenny?

MARGARET (*putting a stop to the nonsense*). I am from the North, Mrs. Farrow.

MRS. FARROW (*with infinite tact*). That's a fine rocking chair you've got. (*She goes to it and tries it and pushes* CLEMENTINE *into it. The* FARROWS *are in possession.*)

MARGARET. I would ask you to come in but we're not fixed up yet.

MRS. FARROW (*a merry laugh*). I've had four children born here and I'm still not fixed up. It's true the back is sunnier, but the front has a window on the street. You couldn't give me the back for no rent and a dollar besides. (*Goes to the window.*) I could sit in the window from my first cup of coffee until bedtime. It's my pleasure. If you ever want to talk to me just open the window and yell Farrow or Sparrow and I'll answer. (*Suddenly*) She's shy, ain't she?

MARGARET. What did you say?

MRS. FARROW. Your girl. She's shy and she's pale. Instead of that pretty Sunday dress and a bow in her hair, she ought to be out in the horse trough with my kids. Oats all over the cobblestones and the cool running water. It's just like the country. (LIZZIE *lights up.*) Clementine, you take her down.

MARGARET. No.

CLEMENTINE. Come on, I'll take you. (*She grabs* LIZZIE *and pulls her toward the door.*)

MARGARET (*with anger*). No.

MRS. FARROW. It ain't no trouble for Clementine. She wants to.

MARGARET. I said no.

MRS. FARROW. Yes, that's what you did say, didn't you? And no is no. We better go before my supper burns on the fire. (*Beckoning to her daughter.*) Come on, Clementine. (*She goes to the door and stops as she passes* LIZZIE . . . *Her face softens.*) What's your name?

LIZZIE. Lizzie.

MRS. FARROW. For Elizabeth?

LIZZIE. Yes, ma'am.

MRS. FARROW. Mine's nine. How old are you?

LIZZIE. Eleven. (*She runs to her mother.*)

MRS. FARROW. You're real nice with your hair done up in that bow. Clementine'll call for you in the morning.

MARGARET (*sharply*). What for?

MRS. FARROW. School. I remember what it's like—being a new kid in a school. Clementine'll be glad to . . .

MARGARET (*breaking in*). Lizzie isn't going to school.

MRS. FARROW (*not understanding*). People are sure different. I can't wait to get mine out of the house. It's like takin' off a corset. Well, she can take her the day after.

MARGARET. I know you mean to help, Mrs. Farrow, but I don't think you understand. Lizzie didn't go to public school where we lived, and there's no reason for her to go to public school here.

MRS. FARROW. There sure is: there's the truant officer.

CLEMENTINE. Hey, Ma, if she don't go, there's no reason I have to go.

MRS. FARROW. There's two reasons. First, it's the law, and second, I ain't havin' you around the house; and third, (*She claps* CLEMENTINE *on the behind.*) you put the dime back on the table. (CLEMENTINE *marches.*) You have to watch them all the time or they'll swipe

your birthmarks. I've got a big pot of potato soup on the stove. I'll bring you some.

MARGARET. That's kind of you, Mrs. Farrow. Thank you. But we don't need anything.

(MRS. FARROW *looks at her carefully.*)

MRS. FARROW. You must be lucky. (*Turning to* LIZZIE.) Welcome to the block, Lizzie, I hope you like it here. (*She goes out and* CLEMENTINE, *who dawdles, is yanked out by her mother.* MARGARET *closes the door and turns the key in the lock once more and chains the door. All the tension suddenly ebbs out of her . . . She turns toward* LIZZIE.)

MARGARET. I wanted to, I tried. (LIZZIE *answers by going to a rocker and sitting stiffly on the edge of the chair . . . to make herself as uncomfortable as possible.*) I know. You don't have to say it to me. She wanted to be a neighbor and I behaved as I always behave. But she didn't notice. I watched her. She didn't notice a thing. Only your white dress and your white shoes and your pretty bow, and she was eaten with jealousy. (LIZZIE *begins to rock herself—and seated as she is, it is a rocking without pleasure or purpose, other than to infuriate.*) Don't sit rocking like that; you'll fall. (LIZZIE *persists.*) Stop rocking like that. (LIZZIE *stops abruptly.*) It makes me nervous.

LIZZIE. I stopped.

MARGARET. You just going to sit like that?

LIZZIE. I can stand. (*She does.*)

MARGARET (*shrieks*). Stop punishing me.

LIZZIE (*with injured innocence*). Standing?

MARGARET. Lizzie, please. Don't let's hate each other in the new house. We can begin all over again. Like nothing ever happened. Not like mother and daughter. Like two loving sisters. (LIZZIE *goes into the bedroom and just stands there.* MARGARET *looks at her, all her yearning and need in her face . . . Only at such moments when she is unobserved does she dare to exhibit her humanity. She bends now and unties the pots and pans and she holds the rope up.*) Lizzie! . . . Lizzie! . . . (LIZZIE *goes to the door to look.*) You were sure I'd leave it behind, but I didn't. (LIZZIE *runs in with a rap-*

turous expression. She begins to skip rope, rapidly, with great skill. Anxiously:) Not too fast— (LIZZIE *abates her speed.)* And not too long. You mustn't get overtired, Lizzie, it's the only thing I ask. Stop before you get tired. It's important.

(But LIZZIE *doesn't hear . . . All she is aware of when she skips rope are the words and the rhymes that spring up in her own ear. She skips now with the merest flip of her wrist, the barest rising of her toes . . . It is the economy of energy with which her intelligence answers her physical frailty. Now she begins to chant what she has improvised.)*

LIZZIE. President, President, Rutherford Hayes,
Grew a beard in twenty-eight days.
Shaved it off to grow another
Made a pillow for his mother.

MARGARET *(donning coat and hat).* Lizzie, I have to go down to the store.

LIZZIE *(she stops skipping).* What for?

MARGARET. Because there isn't anything in the house for supper. You like potato soup? (LIZZIE's *look has too many questions in it . . . She casts her eyes down.)* I know. I'll go down to her in the morning. I promise. I'll knock on her door . . . I'll say it's a nice day, isn't it? We'll talk, we'll be friends. You'll see . . . I'll bring her a napkin for a present . . . or the blue dish your father won that time at the seashore. It's quite simple.

LIZZIE. Go to her now.

MARGARET. I can't. *(Concerned)* Look how tired you are.

LIZZIE. She may not be home tomorrow.

MARGARET. She's always home . . . sitting in the window. She said so. Your lips are blue again.

LIZZIE. Why can't you do it now?

MARGARET *(yelling it).* Because she's a slob! *(She goes to the door and opens it . . . Her voice is agonized again.)* Lock the door on the chain. *(She takes a step out and returns . . . a note of entreaty in her voice.)* Listen to me, Lizzie . . . There are no buttons missing on my blouse . . . and no coffee stains. Put the jump-rope away. I want you to rest. It's important for you to rest, do you hear? And . . . *(She goes out.)* . . . lock the door on the chain. (MARGARET *disappears from view.)*

*(*LIZZIE *closes the door, but she neither turns the key nor fastens the chain. Then,*

even in her rebellion, she remembers something. She runs to the cupboard and opens it. She finds the breadbox, the paper in it, and inside the paper: her mother's pocketbook. She starts back to the door with it, opens the door, runs out.)

LIZZIE *(automatically).* Ma, you forgot your money. *(She returns, allows herself a small shrug . . . and this time she does turn the key and fasten the door chain. She returns the pocketbook to its place in the breadbox, takes up her jump-rope and begins to skip as before.)*
There once was a girl,
Her name was Lizzie,
She skipped, she jumped,
Till she was dizzy,
Her dress was white,
Her blood was red,
She skipped, she jumped,
(A considerable pause.)
Till she was dead.

(And now LIZZIE *accelerates the pace of her jumping. She goes faster and faster . . . the rope becomes a blur . . . it is a virtuoso performance of a rope dancer. And as she dances, descending the fire ladder from the roof comes* JAMES HYLAND. *He peers through the window, and raps a cane conspiratorially on the window frame.* LIZZIE *drops her jump-rope.)*

LIZZIE *(frightened).* Who's there?

JAMES. Open sesame!

LIZZIE *(her face transformed).* Pa! *(She races into the bedroom, holding wide her arms. And on the other side of the window,* JAMES *outspreads his own arms.* LIZZIE *breathlessly undoes the window catch, and on either side of the window, father and daughter push up the window together. He vaults into the room, and she flings herself into his arms.)* You were hiding on the roof.

JAMES. Not hiding, my dear, biding. Biding my time. *(They execute a little dance . . . laughing.)* And when your esteemed mother folded her tent like the Arab and silently stole away, I concluded that the time was propitious for a visit to a certain Elizabeth Pamela Ursula Hyland. (LIZZIE *curtsies to him. He bows. He spies the paper bag on the chair.)* This much I do say for Margaret Hyland: she still dresses you in flawless white. *(He puts his foot on the bedstead. Now he studies the room and then he focuses his inquiry upon his daughter. In the voice of a schoolmaster*) Are you reading?

LIZZIE. Oh, yes.

JAMES. Good! . . . wherever one goes . . . one reads. (*To the paper bag.*) En garde! (*Stabs it with his cane.*) Right through the heart! (*Presents his cane to* LIZZIE.) So, she moved again!

LIZZIE. I was going to write you a letter.

JAMES (*deliberately*). I believe you. (*He picks up the neatly tied bundle upon which his foot has been resting.*) A remarkable specimen of womanhood, your mother! Let her inhabit a place but for an hour and it is invested with that exquisite perfume which is next to godliness . . . soap. There are some, though, who prefer the smell of humanity. (*He tosses an imaginary object into the air and catches it in the paper bag. Despite her knowledge of his tricks,* LIZZIE *is taken in. She looks inside, finds only an empty paper bag, and giggles.*)

LIZZIE. Oh, Pa! Where have you been?

JAMES (*gradually, as he crumples the paper bag*). Elsewhere! (*He stalks into the kitchen,* LIZZIE *at his heels. The grandeur goes as swiftly as it has come. We see* JAMES HYLAND *for what he is . . . flamboyant but frayed at the edges, like his coat and with a button missing.*) A window on the street! (*He goes to it and throws the window open.*)

THE RAG MAN'S VOICE (*from below*). I cash clothes. I buy clothes. I cash.

JAMES (*shuts the window*). Ah, the turning wheels of commerce . . . the din of the bazaar, the grinding of the market place! Vanity of vanities, you've grown an inch!

LIZZIE. Did you get that job?

JAMES. What job?

LIZZIE. With the magician.

JAMES. Oh! The magician! (*Hides the crumpled bag under his arm.*) He disappeared. (*He goes to the stove and without too much hope he uncovers a pot.*)

LIZZIE. There isn't anything.

JAMES. I have already dined. (*He replaces the lid.*) Have you missed me?

LIZZIE. I have missed you.

JAMES. Who is Elizabeth and what is she?

LIZZIE. Why, don't you know, you foolish man? The Queen of Merrie England,

and in her hand is the sceptre of her affection!

JAMES (*bows*). And to which chantry or chapel did you say the Queen Mother went?

LIZZIE. To the greengrocer's, m'lord, or mayhap t'was to the vintner's.

JAMES (*the game has lost its zest*). Not to the vintner's . . . not your Ma. (*He sits . . . All the weariness flows back into his face.*)

LIZZIE (*going to him . . . troubled*). Don't be so tired.

JAMES. I only look tired. It happens when I'm thinking.

LIZZIE. Of me?

JAMES (*nods*). Of you, of her, of me . . . we happy three. How is she?

LIZZIE. She misses you.

JAMES. Like the cured lung misses consumption. It is pleasant up on that roof. (*Noticing the pallor of her face—the blue lace of her veins.*) You must go up sometimes and sit there. The sun is warm. Sit in the sun as much as you can. It is good for the paleness in your cheek. (*Sighs.*) I could have been a fine physician.

LIZZIE. Will you be there, if I go up?

JAMES. There will be times. Do you eat eggs?

LIZZIE (*searching his pockets*). What book did you bring me?

JAMES. How do you know I brought you a book?

LIZZIE. You always do. (*He gazes at her—famished.*) Why do you look at me like that?

JAMES. When you were little, and choking with croup and we thought you were dying . . . and a whole day once and a whole night we took turns steaming a kettle over your crib . . . and when I thought you were going to die, I bent down and kissed you . . . wanting to leave the whole of my breath in you, and to die in your stead . . . but you got well . . . and I didn't die.

LIZZIE. You sound sorry.

JAMES. It would have been so noble an ending.

LIZZIE. What's the book you brought?

(*He is about to take it out of his pocket when there is a knock on the door.*)

JAMES (*on his feet ready to fly*). Who is that?

MRS. FARROW'S VOICE. It's me again. I had to come.

LIZZIE. Her name is Mrs. Farrow. She's the fourth floor.

JAMES (*fixing his tie*). Oh!

LIZZIE. Her blouse has coffee stains.

JAMES. For shame!

(LIZZIE *unchains and unlocks the door.*)

MRS. FARROW (*appearing in the doorway*). I had to come straight back and bring you some of my potato soup . . . (*She stops when she sees* JAMES HYLAND.) In-the-way-again-Farrow!

JAMES (*with a gallant bow he relieves her of the bowl*). Not at all, dear lady, and do come in. I am James Hyland, the child's father.

MRS. FARROW (*genuinely surprised*). I could have sworn she was a widow.

JAMES. I am an agreeable man in most things—but in that I could not oblige her. (*He stirs the contents of the bowl with the spoon and sniffs it gratifyingly.*) Do be seated, Madam.

MRS. FARROW. I can't stay. But you sit down.

JAMES. Thank you. (*He must . . . he is so weary and hungry.*) The rule of my character is never to stand when I can sit, never to sit, when I can lie down, never to be awake, when I can be asleep, never to sleep when I can be dead.

MRS. FARROW. You are a funny man.

JAMES. It requires effort. (*He takes a spoonful of soup—he closes his eyes in gratification.*)

MRS. FARROW (*anxiously*). Is it good?

JAMES (*he assumes his mountebank's role with a self-contempt at once cynical yet amiable*). My dear Mrs. Farrow, we must arrange, you and I, for a large issue of both common and preferred stock, the proceeds of which will be dedicated to the erection of a huge manufactory crowded from floor to ceiling with immense vats where this potato soup of yours will be on the boil by day and night according to your own secret recipe —which incidentally must be filed without delay in the United States Patent Office. Inevitably we shall become licensed purveyors to his recently crowned Britannic Majesty, Edward the Seventh . . . and a newer, finer, nobler race of British kings will be bred upon this royal soup.

MRS. FARROW. I'm glad you like it.

JAMES. It wants salt. (*She tests the salt-cellar on her wrist and he seizes her hand, turns it, and his soup is salted.*) A pinch.

MRS. FARROW. You are the one, Mr. Hyland, aren't you?

JAMES. Only, Mrs. Farrow, if you are two. "You must sit down," says Love, "and taste my meat. So I do sit and eat." (*He takes another spoonful.*)

MRS. FARROW (*she sighs at him*). And there I was fretting I wasn't going to like my new neighbors on the fifth. (*At his expression, she changes her own.*) There . . . did I say something wrong!

JAMES (*simply and sadly*). No, Mrs. Farrow . . . but I must tell you we are not together. (*The mountebank again*) To put the matter briefly, I occupy another domicile. (*He shovels the soup into his mouth.*)

MRS. FARROW. You're hungry.

JAMES (*shaking his head*). Not at all. But this is ambrosia!

MRS. FARROW. I wish Mr. Farrow thought so.

JAMES. There *is* a Mr. Farrow?

MRS. FARROW. And five little sparrows.

JAMES. You destroy me.

MRS. FARROW (*giggles*). Tell me, Mr. Hyland . . . what line of business do you follow?

JAMES (*a sweeping gesture*). The curvature of the earth. At the present time I am at liberty.

(*In all this* LIZZIE *has been as fascinated as* MRS. FARROW . . . *more so perhaps, because there is something about her mother which inhibits the flow of* JAMES HYLAND'S *verbal juices. Now, fearful of her mother's return,* LIZZIE *goes to the window and posts watch.*)

MRS. FARROW. A woman has no greater pleasure . . . than to feed a man.

JAMES. The converse is of equal importance to the race; a man has no greater pleasure than to satisfy his hunger. Madam, may I bring you a pillow. Is that chair quite comfortable?

MRS. FARROW. Oh, yes.

JAMES. Splendid! Just now we spoke of hunger, you and I. Let me relate a professional experience. Years ago, in my travels I came upon a place of famine. And in this land of famine, we found a child. One small living child who, even as we watched, reached out his hand to play with the flickering light of day . . . and we saw the face of the child as his hand grasped a sunbeam . . . and the child opened his hand . . . and it was empty . . . and the brightness was gone. This was hunger! They turned to me, "Hyland," they said, "Go back . . . tell them." I did. I went up and down the Ladies' Auxiliaries of the Atlantic Seaboard. "There is an invisible guest at my table," I told them, "and at your table as well." And they wept. All except one woman . . . in the second row near the aisle. She sat this way . . . like this . . . (*He shows her, folding his arms across his chest.*) We were in the basement of a church in New Bedford, Massachusetts, and she sat as a stone sits, and never shed a tear. I looked her full in the face and I said, "Ladies, I have seen husbands without wives, and wives without husbands, and children crying, 'Mother'!" They broke their hearts and opened their pocketbooks. But not this woman. She sat stoic, ungiving. The strings of my tongue were cut loose. And as I spoke, tears began to flow between the aisles of chairs and there was a great sobbing. They pulled off their wedding rings, those other women, and flung them at me. But not this one. She sat like this. And when I could no longer bear it, I looked at her, and said, "Give me your wedding ring." "I'm not married." "Then at least why don't you cry?" I shouted . . . And, Mrs. Farrow, do you know what she answered? "I'm not a member!"

MRS. FARROW. What happened to the hungry child?

JAMES. Who?

MRS. FARROW. The hungry child?

JAMES. Oh! He developed a running nose and became a sharpshooter. Which reminds me of another incident.

MRS. FARROW (*admiringly*). You have a story for everything, haven't you?

JAMES (*lowering his voice*). It seems so, doesn't it? But I believe I can trust you. I am like that young sharpshooter who was acclaimed the greatest marksman in the civilized world. Three professors with beards came to investigate this remarkable phenomenon. There it was . . . one thousand bullets and every single bullet exactly in the center of every single bull's eye. And shall I tell you the secret of it?

MRS. FARROW. Oh, yes.

JAMES. I am like that young lad. First

I shoot . . . and then—around the bullet . . . (*He makes a revolving, circling motion with his right index finger.*) . . . I paint the bull's eye. (MRS. FARROW *laughs —a laugh of admiration and contentment.*) My dear . . . (*He rises and goes to her.*) You have that rarest, that most blessed, most precious quality which our Maker can bestow upon womankind . . . (*He takes her hand in his own.*) You listen. (*He speaks now with utter seriousness.*) This afternoon you have reminded me of something I had forgotten . . .

MRS. FARROW. What, Mr. Hyland?

JAMES. That I'm a man. (*Between them there oscillates a look of recognition— male and female—and at this moment* MARGARET HYLAND *appears in the doorway . . . They turn when they grow aware of her, but not before she has had sufficient opportunity to digest the tableau.*)

MARGARET. So you found us.

LIZZIE (*when the silence becomes unendurable*). You came back for your pocketbook.

MARGARET. The man in the store wanted to trust me but I wouldn't have it. For what you eat you must pay.

MRS. FARROW. I brought you some of my potato soup.

MARGARET. Thank you. Well, James, you have words for everyone else . . . have you no word for me?

JAMES (*slowly*). You look the same, Margaret.

MARGARET. I am the same.

MRS. FARROW. If you will excuse me, I must go down.

MARGARET. You are excused, Mrs. Farrow.

(MRS. FARROW *clenches one hand—but it is helplessness rather than anger. She exits, with a look of curosity at* JAMES HYLAND.)

MARGARET (*to* LIZZIE *who is on the way to the window*). Where are you going? Go to the bedroom. I want to speak to your father alone.

LIZZIE. There's no bed to lie down on.

MARGARET. There is a chair.

(LIZZIE *looks imploringly at her mother . . . and trembles the slightest bit.*)

LIZZIE. Yes, Ma. (*She goes toward the bedroom . . . and as she goes she drags her right leg.*)

MARGARET. Walk right.

LIZZIE. What?

MARGARET (*points*). You're dragging your leg.

LIZZIE. Oh. (*To her father*) You'll come back again, won't you?

JAMES. I will.

MARGARET. He will not.

LIZZIE. Please, Ma.

MARGARET. Go to your room.

JAMES (*when* LIZZIE *doesn't budge*). Do what she tells you.

(LIZZIE *goes . . . finally.* MARGARET *follows and closes the door.* LIZZIE *kneels before her books, unseeing; her eyes are blind with tears.*)

MARGARET. She never dragged her leg until just now. Why did you have to come back?

JAMES. I had to see my little girl.

MARGARET. For four months you haven't had to see her.

JAMES. I wasn't able to come before today.

MARGARET (*searching his face*). Yes. Four months in the workhouse could make a man look pale.

JAMES. It could.

MARGARET. So they finally found you drunk in the gutter and sent you to Blackwell's Island.

JAMES. I would like to sit down for a while. May I?

MARGARET. For a while.

JAMES (*as he slumps into a chair*). That's not like you, Margaret, to be vague! Let us limit our compassion. Shall we say five minutes? Four and a half?

MARGARET. Take off your jacket.

JAMES. What?

MARGARET. Your jacket.

JAMES (*nonplussed. But she has already found thread, needle, thimble and a button. He takes off his jacket, gives it to her, watching. She begins to sew with extraordinary rapidity*). Thank you, Margaret. For a man who is lonely, romance often begins in a public restaurant . . . with a waitress. Why? She brings his food; she serves it to him . . . a very feminine thing. Like sewing on a button. You cannot resist the mending, can you?

MARGARET. I can resist anything.

JAMES. Don't be too sure. The ancients had a saying: "More than the calf needs to suckle does the cow need to give suck." Margaret, do you know what I did this morning? On a whim, I took the cable car to Fort George. We used to do that, didn't we? The first year! And do you remember when we looked down, how we used to see our own shape in the grass? I went to the place and I looked down and I couldn't find my shape.

MARGARET. Why did you come back?

JAMES. To find my shape.

MARGARET. Go back to that woman.

JAMES. She is not my family.

MARGARET. Go back to the others.

JAMES. Margaret, visits with Lizzie no longer satisfy me.

MARGARET. We have no marriage.

JAMES. I can sleep in the kitchen again. (*She bites off the thread of her sewing.*) Someone has to teach her.

MARGARET. I still take in sewing. I can hire a teacher.

JAMES. Hire me.

MARGARET (*she puts his jacket down and takes up a carefully wrapped package. She strips off the paper and in her hand we see a coat she has been making, a coat whose red velvet opulence is in striking contrast to the bareness of the kitchen and its self-disciplined poverty. As* JAMES *watches she drapes the coat on the dummy with elegant hands, the hands of a woman whose creative talent equals his own. And now, having demonstrated her proofs, she makes her answer*). You would be the last.

JAMES. I taught in a school once.

MARGARET. Three weeks.

JAMES. I am better than any teacher you could hire. Why won't you let me teach her?

MARGARET. Because I won't have you in my house.

JAMES (*as* LIZZIE *startles in the bedroom*). What have I done that is so beyond forgiving?

MARGARET. The mark that is on her flesh.

JAMES (*helplessly*). I can speak to anyone in the world but not to you.

MARGARET. Because you're a coward, James Hyland, and afraid of what I know. I wash and I scrub, but no matter how many times I wash and I scrub, it doesn't wash away. So let me have my hate, and leave us, and never come back.

(*The bedroom door is flung open and* LIZZIE *appears.*)

LIZZIE. Don't talk like that to my

father! You have no right to talk like that to him.

MARGARET. I'm his wife. (*She turns on* JAMES *with contempt.*) Have you a place to sleep tonight?

JAMES. Yes.

MARGARET. You are a liar, James Hyland. You have always been a liar. Show me the money in your pocket to buy a night's lodging. Show me.

JAMES. Don't Margaret, not in front of the child.

MARGARET. I will give you fifty cents and then you'll go.

JAMES. Good-by, Lizzie . . . (*He starts for the door, then wavers.*)

MARGARET (*he flings the door open . . . but instead of going out he stands there.* MARGARET *rises as he shuts it again*). I'll get the money.

LIZZIE (*crying*). Go, Pa. Please go.

MARGARET. He can't, Lizzie. Shall I tell you why? Because your father knows that fifty cents is forty-nine cents more than pride. James Hyland, you stand there dumb! Where are all the books you read, the stories, the jokes, the bragging! Did you brag to Mrs. Farrow and make her laugh? I will pay fifty cents to laugh. A dollar. Make me laugh, James. Tell me one of your stories. (*Shouting it*) Well . . . did you spend it all on Mrs. Farrow? Is there nothing left for me! (*She goes to him, close . . . her body taut like a drawn bow.*) Where are all the words?

JAMES (*he shakes his head*). You choke me, Margaret.

MARGARET. Good. Tell me a story full of your choking words.

JAMES. What you do to me.

MARGARET. I'll tell you what you do to me . . . my fastidious James Hyland who always had to carry two clean handkerchiefs . . . you choke me. (*He reaches to her—touching her lips, and her body arches at his touch, her eyes close; then, with rage, she swings her arm down like the blade of guillotine—down and hard, flinging back his reaching hand.*) I am no rag doll for your fingers to touch . . . I am five flights above the street. These are my four walls. My rent is paid in advance! So you go! And let me shut the door! And turn the key! And draw the chain across!

JAMES (*looks beseechingly for a re-prieve . . . but no soft look comes to mitigate the decree. He looks now to* LIZZIE . . . *She turns her back to him*). Good-by, Lizzie. (*When she doesn't answer, he walks around* MARGARET, *careful not to brush against her, and he takes a book from his coat and places it on the table.*) Lizzie, I did bring you a book. "The Lady of the Lake" by Sir Walter Scott. It's hardly a major work . . . (*Despising himself for talking.*) but the children do read it in the schools . . . for some unaccountable reason. I'll leave it on the table.

LIZZIE. You don't have to bother.

JAMES. But I must. It is our defense against the schoolmasters and their truant officers.

LIZZIE (*in a voice like* MARGARET HYLAND'S). I don't want anything from you. Nothing. Not a thing.

JAMES. I'll leave it anyhow.

MARGARET. Leave it and go.

JAMES. Lizzie . . .

(LIZZIE *takes a step toward him.*)

MARGARET (*stepping between them*). He will be all right. He heals. He will walk downstairs broken-hearted, but on the corner a man will say, "Sir, can you tell me the hour?" and he will deliver a talk on time—so full of quotations, he'll be invited to the nearest tavern for a glass of sherry from Spain.

JAMES. Why do you have to do this?

MARGARET. Because if I am a devil, I want her to know the devil is a devil because the devil has a memory. I want to tell her all the times I sent you downstairs to buy bread and you met a man on the street. Or you argued a case for a lawyer, or wrote a prescription for a medical doctor, and all the time I sat with a baby in my arms and waited . . . while you talked . . . and I knew what all those people were thinking . . . how lucky I was to be married to James Hyland. (*She grabs his arm as he starts for the door again.*)

JAMES. I never hurt anyone.

MARGARET. Didn't you?

JAMES. Let her love me a little.

MARGARET. Only as much as you're entitled.

(LIZZIE *is like a wall against him. He has nothing now . . . He goes emptily to the door, turns the knob, and opens it to show us* CLEMENTINE, *who has been lis-*

tening.)

CLEMENTINE (*unperturbed by her discovery*). Hello.

MARGARET (*yanking her into the kitchen*). What were you doing out there?

CLEMENTINE. There's two men on the next block. One is a cop. They're askin' for somebody called Elizabeth Ursula Hyland. (*She points a dirty finger at* LIZZIE.) Isn't that her?

MARGARET. Go away from her. Go down to your own house.

CLEMENTINE. They're asking . . . and they'll be coming.

MARGARET. Don't you ever wash your face? Don't you ever comb your hair? You sneak. You thief . . . you slob's daughter . . .

JAMES. Margaret!

CLEMENTINE. (*she touches her face where the words have burned her. And she looks at* LIZZIE . . . *who holds two hands to cover her ears against the sounds of this new humiliation. . . . and the malice comes into* CLEMENTINE's *mouth, and she makes a stone of it*). Why does she wear that glove on her hand?

(JAMES HYLAND *reaches out his own hand as if to pull the words down from the air which suspends them on a vibration . . . but* MARGARET *knows that the words, having been spoken, are irrevocable.*

(LIZZIE *holds her ears and shuts her eyes . . . and a trembling comes over her like a shudder of thought.*

(*And seeing* LIZZIE's *trembling, all that is pent up, and bitter, and without hope, and loveless in the life of* MARGARET HYLAND *issues from her throat . . .*)

MARGARET (*to* CLEMENTINE). I hope you die.

CURTAIN

ACT TWO

SCENE ONE

Immediately thereafter.
CLEMENTINE *is running out.*

———

CLEMENTINE. Ma, Ma, Ma!

(MARGARET *at the door in an instant, shutting it against the world.*)

LIZZIE (*wildly*). The truant officer!

JAMES (*cradling* LIZZIE *in his arms*). Don't worry about the truant officer. Not one teenie-weenie bit.

LIZZIE. You don't have to talk to me like that.

JAMES. I'm sorry.

LIZZIE. I'm not a baby.

JAMES. Forgive me, darling. I keep forgetting.

(MARGARET, *as* LIZZIE *coughs, fills a glass at the sink and hurries with it to* JAMES. *Without waiting, she rushes into bedroom.* MARGARET *lifts the bedspring and manoeuvres it into place. He turns his head to the sound she makes.*)

JAMES (*calling into the bedroom*). You hold Lizzie . . . I'll do that, Margaret.

MARGARET. What?

JAMES. I said I will do that for you.

MARGARET (*contemptuously*). When did you learn? (*She continues with her work—the spring in place, she hoists the mattress onto it, brushing away some imaginary dust . . . even in her agonized haste she cannot omit this step . . . and she finds sheets, pillow, pillowcase, and quilt.*)

JAMES. Have another sip of water.

LIZZIE. No.

JAMES. It's good water. It comes down to us when God cries for people.

LIZZIE (*her anger melts . . . a tired little child now wanting only to be held*). It hurts when I swallow.

JAMES (*and his love for her instructs him . . . he rests her cheek against his own and for a few moments he gives her the benison of his silence.* MARGARET *works furiously in the next room. He rocks her a little*). When God created us and called us Man, I think He assumed a little too much.

LIZZIE (*she doesn't know why, but this touches her terribly. She shows him her mittened hand*). Why?

JAMES. Ask no questions. Ask no questions.

LIZZIE (*exploding at him*). Why do you let her talk to you like that!

JAMES. Margaret Hyland is a truthful woman.

LIZZIE. Stop it.

JAMES. When you were little, I used to hold you like this and tell you a story.

LIZZIE. I don't want a story. I'm too old.

JAMES. What do you want?

LIZZIE. (*and she doesn't know it, but she sounds like her mother*). Why do you never say a word back? Not even one word!

JAMES. What is there to say?

LIZZIE. You're my father!

JAMES. I'm a bag of wind.

LIZZIE. (*she beats her mittened fist against his chest*). You are my father. You are my father. My father.

JAMES. Lizzie, you're hurting me.

LIZZIE. I want to. (*Suddenly she throws her arms around him.*) Take me away.

JAMES. Where?

LIZZIE. Anywhere.

JAMES. I would disappoint you. (*He starts to unbutton her dress.*)

LIZZIE. I want you to take me away.

JAMES (*he shakes his head*). I never learned to make a dollar. Who would give me spending money? (*She pushes herself out of his arms.*)

LIZZIE. I don't want you to hold me any more. (*She goes to the table, finds the dime, and brings it to him.*) It's a dime.

JAMES (*crushed*). Not you, Lizzie, please.

MARGARET (*running out of the bedroom*). At the very least you might have taken off her clothes. (*She strips the dress off* LIZZIE, *who shivers.*)

JAMES. She's cold.

MARGARET (*working furiously*). Warm her with the hot wind that blows from your mouth.

LIZZIE (*slamming the dime on the table*). How long will you let her talk like that to you?

MARGARET. As long as he lives. Hurry, Lizzie! Please! For God's sake, hurry!

(LIZZIE *tears herself out of her mother's grasp and runs to her father.*)

LIZZIE. Oh, Pa. Pa. (*She kisses him.*)

JAMES. Margaret, let her go to school with other children.

LIZZIE. No.

(*He is holding her mittened hand and she pulls away. The mitten is in his hand.* LIZZIE *screams;* MARGARET *seizes the exposed hand and, like some wild creature with its maimed young, she kisses the hand over and over again.*)

JAMES (*turning his back*). Don't do that!

(MARGARET *for once is bewildered. She pulls the mitten out of his hand and*

gives it to LIZZIE.)

MARGARET. It's all right. (*Bemused*) Lizzie, your bed is made.

LIZZIE. I know, Mama. (*She drags her leg across the kitchen to the bedroom, and gets into bed and covers herself.*)

MARGARET. You shouldn't have uncovered her. It was wrong.

JAMES. It is nothing, Margaret. It's a trivial thing she has.

MARGARET. God's punishment, James Hyland, is never a trivial thing.

JAMES. What is it? A little girl was born with six fingers on her left . . . (*But he never finishes the rest, because* MARGARET's *hand is over his mouth . . . And as they stand there this way, we hear the unmistakable sound of footsteps on the stairway, and voices.*)

LAMESHNIK (*off*). Two more and then we're through for the day.

COP (*off*). Yeah!

LAMESHNIK. Where did you say it was?

COP. The door at the top of the stairs.

(*We hear a knock. The knock is repeated. She looks across at* JAMES *when the knock is repeated a third time.*)

MARGARET (*almost gently*). Sit down. (*She puts a book in his hand and indicates the chair.*)

JAMES. When was the last time your hand touched my mouth! (*He sits down.*)

MARGARET (*the knocking now becomes a banging and a rattling of the door. She calls out as much to* JAMES *as to the other intruders*). You're breaking my door in . . . it isn't your property!

LAMESHNIK's VOICE. Then open it, Mrs. Hyland.

MARGARET. Who are you? What do you want in my house?

LAMESHNIK's VOICE. My name is Lameshnik. I am a truant officer.

(MARGARET *turns the key in the lock, but she does not unfasten the door chain. When he opens the door it goes only as far as the chain permits.*)

LAMESHNIK (*his face is half-visible*). You're wasting your own time. I've got papers from the Board of Education. (*He thrusts a paper at her through the aperture. She doesn't bother to take it, although she does read it.*)

MARGARET. You can't come into my house without an order from the Court.

LAMESHNIK (*he withdraws the first paper and substitutes for it an official-look-*

ing document). We thought of that, Mrs. Hyland.

MARGARET. You still can't come in. (*The document is withdrawn.*)

THE COP'S VOICE. Step away from the door, Lady.

MARGARET. What for?

THE COP'S VOICE. Move away or you'll get hurt.

MARGARET. Wait. (*She unchains the door and admits them. They come in . . . a man in a derby and a policeman.*)

LAMESHNIK. Why do you make so much trouble for people?

MARGARET. What fine thing are you going to do for my child that I shouldn't make trouble for you?

LAMESHNIK. Your kid goes to school five days a week, gets the whole summer for a vacation. That isn't the Raymond Street Jail. (*Pointing to bedroom*) In there?

MARGARET (*blocking the way*). My daughter is sick.

LAMESHNIK (*producing it*). Yeah. I have the record. In Canal Street, sick. In Hudson Street, sick. In Lispenard Street, sick. For a sick kid you certainly travel her around, don't you?

(*The COP has made good use of LAMESHNIK's recitation to work his way into the bedroom: he verifies LIZZIE's condition.*)

COP. The kid *is* sick.

LAMESHNIK (*he walks to the chair, where LIZZIE's dress has been forgotten, and he calls to the COP in a voice that is curiously contented*). Yeah?

COP. She's covered with a quilt.

LAMESHNIK (*contentedly*). That only means she's in bed.

COP. She's not wearing a dress.

LAMESHNIK (*he picks up the dress*). Isn't she?

COP. No.

LAMESHNIK. How about her shoes?

COP (*looks under the bed, then he feels her feet through the quilt, and an oath bursts from him*). Well, I'll be damned.

LAMESHNIK. Find something, Kelleher?

COP. Two shoes . . . one on each foot.

LAMESHNIK (*to MARGARET*). All right now?

MARGARET (*she takes the dress from him*). You must like your job.

LAMESHNIK. I have nothing to be ashamed of. Get your kid dressed.

MARGARET. No.

LAMESHNIK (*pulls the dress back*). All right. I've got two girls of my own. I can dress her. (*He starts for the bedroom and then he pauses to inspect JAMES HYLAND.*) Are you the girl's father? (*JAMES nods.*) It is the duty of the father to support the child, it is the duty of the State to educate the child. (*He has expounded the philosophy he has learned by rote. Now he adds his own view.*) Why do you let this woman interfere with the duty of the State? (*He waits for JAMES HYLAND to answer.*) You sure don't have much to say, do you! (*MARGARET laughs.*) Did I say something funny?

MARGARET. Silent James Hyland! I have lived to see the day.

(*Stung, JAMES rises, put his unread book on the table and walks away.*)

LAMESHNIK. All right, let's not fool around any more. One of us gets the kid dressed. Which one?

MARGARET. Don't go into that room.

LAMESHNIK. That's agreeable with me. You go in. (*Offers the dress.*)

MARGARET. Don't force me.

LAMESHNIK. Come on, Lady.

MARGARET. I'm telling you not to force me.

LAMESHNIK. I don't know what's in your mind, Lady. We'll have to take a chance. (*He starts for the door—but JAMES, having made his own decision, reaches out and stops him.*)

JAMES (*peremptorily*). One moment!

LAMESHNIK. What the hell for?

JAMES. Mister Lameshnik: You have come to this house the minister plenipotentiary, so to speak, of the educational conscience of this metropolis, so I would ask you . . . what is the purpose of the public school system? And further, what is the meaning of the compulsory education law? The raison d'être?

LAMESHNIK (*he takes off his derby*). I guess I made a mistake about you.

JAMES. Sir, why did you break in here?

LAMESHNIK. Who broke in? She opened the door.

JAMES. I stand corrected. Even so, would you be good enough to answer the question put to you?

LAMESHNIK. Mister, what are you talking about? What question?

JAMES. Why is there a civil statute, and criminal penalties if the statute is disobeyed, to compel the education of the young? Why? To guarantee that whatever is latent within the child will be kindled and encouraged. Educate. E, meaning *out,* and duco, I *lead.* Educate— to lead out—therefore, to draw out what is already there. Let us see what is there, and what has been drawn out. (*A glad shout*) Lizzie, come.

MARGARET. Maniac, what do you think you are doing! Stay where you are, Lizzie.

LIZZIE (*she runs in to her father*). What do you want? (MARGARET *touches her, and* LIZZIE *shakes it off.*) I'm all right, Ma. What is it?

JAMES. Lizzie, what is the Latin for father?

LIZZIE (*but she faces the policeman, and answers her father only after she has put down her fear of the uniform*). Pater.

JAMES. The French word for house?

LIZZIE. La maison. (*Her mood now becomes gay.*)

JAMES. How do you pronounce s-c-h-i-s-m?

LIZZIE. Sizm.

JAMES (*to* LAMESHNIK). As guardian of our culture, Mr. Lameshnik, would you tell us who wrote *King Lear?* (*Correcting himself hastily*) No, I beg your pardon, that is too simple a question. (LIZZIE *nods.*) It is an unworthy test. (*He thinks.*) What is the most celebrated work of William Blake?

LAMESHNIK. Who?

JAMES. Surely you have heard of William Blake? (*He allows them a moment.*) Lizzie, what is the most famous work of William Blake?

LIZZIE. "Songs of . . ."

JAMES (*stops her*). Tell the Board of Education.

LIZZIE. "Songs of Innocence."

JAMES (*imperiously*). How do you know?

LIZZIE. I read it in a book.

JAMES. And the Board of Education gave you the book?

LIZZIE. Oh, no! You did.

JAMES (*to the* COP). Officer, you are the defender of morality, the club in your belt a testimony to the fate of the evildoer. Tell us, therefore . . . Mr. Kelleher, who wrote *The Spirit of the Laws?* (*The* COP's *jaw is agape.* JAMES *turns to* LIZZIE

—*and she preens herself.*)

LIZZIE. Montesquieu.

JAMES (*the humbly arrogant tone of the proud schoolmaster towards his beloved pupil*). Now then, attend me: The Epistle to Dr. Arbuthnot!

LIZZIE (*gaily*).
" 'Shut, shut, the door, good John,'
    fatigued, I said,
'Tie up the knocker, say I'm sick, I'm
    dead.' "

(*They laugh. He takes her hand and kisses her cheek.*)

JAMES. Lizzie, what never faileth?

LIZZIE. Charity.

JAMES. Next time when I tell you you're beautiful, never deny it.

LIZZIE. I'm not beautiful.

LAMESHNIK. Are you finished?

JAMES. One final question! Lizzie . . . what said her kinsman Boaz to gentle Ruth?

(MARGARET *stiffens.*)

LIZZIE. "Tarry this night."

JAMES (*goes from* LIZZIE *to the truant officer and the* COP). Could you do half as well?

COP. I'm a political appointment.

JAMES. Ah, yes! Gentlemen, I submit that to this date the education of Elizabeth Hyland has been accomplished in her own home, and not at all to the detriment of the State nor to her own disadvantage. You came unbidden, hurling imprecations. Now have the civility to depart, only this time quietly, if you please, and not in the distempered manner of your coming; for there are good neighbors below, with small children, and a poodle dog on the third floor fearful of strangers.

LAMESHNIK (*to* LIZZIE). Put your clothes on, Elizabeth.

(MARGARET *smiles grimly: giving no charity, asking none, she has never doubted the outcome.*)

JAMES. You cannot be serious.

LAMESHNIK. The kid has got to go to school.

JAMES. Why?

LAMESHNIK. It's the law. (LAMESHNIK *replaces the derby on his head—a gesture of unmistakable finality. To* LIZZIE, *who has begun to tremble*) Now, Elizabeth, you and your Ma'll go uptown with me, and you'll talk to some people. They won't hurt you. (*He holds the dress out to her.*) Now you go in there and put this on.

(LIZZIE *trembles violently.*)

JAMES (*placing his arm around her*). Lizzie, what is it? What's the matter, darling?

(LIZZIE *attempts to speak—her jaw works but no intelligible sound comes out. She wheels and drags herself into the bedroom.* MARGARET *hurries in after her. She helps* LIZZIE *onto the bed.*)

MARGARET. Don't worry, Lizzie, no one's going to take you away from here. (*She hurries back to the kitchen.*) You said you had children of your own.

LAMESHNIK. Two boys and two girls. And the four of them put together—and they're my own kids—don't know half as much as she's got in her little finger. Why are you afraid to send her to school? Why does . . . why does she always keep one hand in her pocket?

MARGARET. Shut up.

LAMESHNIK. I was only asking why she . . .

MARGARET (*drowning him out*). Shut, shut, shut, shut up. Shut up!

LAMESHNIK. Kelleher, go inside and bring the kid out. If you have to carry her, carry her.

(*As the* COP *starts for the bedroom,* MARGARET *runs to the window, throws it open.*)

MARGARET. Leave my house, or I jump.

LAMESHNIK. Lady, don't be crazy.

COP (*simultaneously*). For God's sakes, woman!

MARGARET (*stepping into the window*). If you don't leave—both of you—I jump.

LIZZIE (*from the bedroom door*). Mama! Mama! Mama!

MARGARET. I warn you.

JAMES. Margaret . . . don't.

MARGARET. Who are you to tell me anything?

JAMES. I'm still her father. A child has two parents.

MARGARET (*she grasps the window sash as though she would break it in her hands*). I am both her parents. I am my own husband.

LIZZIE (*runs into the kitchen*). Ma. Ma. Ma. (*She becomes convulsive—holding onto the table, then falling to the kitchen floor . . . a little child with two shaking, uncontrollable arms.*)

MARGARET. Lizzie! (*She runs from the window.*) For God's sake, Lizzie, stop it. For God's sake. (*She drops to the kitchen floor trying to smother with her own body the convulsion of the child.*) Lizzie, for God's sake, Lizzie, Lizzie, for God's sake!

THE CURTAIN IS LOWERED

SCENE TWO

Half an hour later.

In the bedroom LIZZIE *is cradled in* JAMES HYLAND's *arms.* MARGARET *is in the rocker, her back to the audience, listening wearily as* JAMES *sings to* LIZZIE.

———

JAMES (*his singing is not a particularly good voice but his voice, his words, his emotion*).
I will tell you a dream you'll understand,
Rounder than gladness, whiter than sand,
A dream for my Lizzie to hold in her hand,
When she sleeps, when she sleeps.
Petal of roses to slipper your feet,
Wool of a lamb to pillow your cheek,
Eyes of a fawn to watch while you sleep,
While you sleep, while you sleep.

(MRS. FARROW *enters with a bottle of whiskey. She listens to* JAMES *for a moment before going to* MARGARET.)
So dream your father will come again,
And dream he is near;
His arms to keep you from hurt and pain,
To keep you from fear.

I will give you a dream to hold in your eyes,
To kiss your sorrows, to mend your sighs.
To shine like a moon till your star will arise,
Go to sleep, go to sleep, go to sleep.

(*He continues, humming and singing softly.*)

MRS. FARROW (*speaking over the final quatrain*). I keep coming back, don't I? When Clementine came down and told me your curse, I swore the ground would open before I ever spoke to you again. But you're a woman like me, so there's whiskey on the table. I leave the bottle.

MARGARET. I do not take strong spirits.

MRS. FARROW. Let your man have the whiskey. (*Grudgingly*) You need something yourself till Clementine comes with the doctor. Coffee ain't no trouble for me. I've got some hot on the fire.

MARGARET. Hot coffee would be good.
Thank you. (*She turns slightly toward
the door, listening to* JAMES HYLAND's *lullaby.*) I don't want a doctor in this house.
I want no strangers.

MRS. FARROW. What kind of a mother
are you to want no doctor for a kid
that's took so bad?

MARGARET. The kind of mother I am.

MRS. FARROW. Well, the doctor will come
because they're bringing him. And you
better be glad, goddamit, because he's
Dr. Jacobson.

MARGARET. He is nothing to me.

MRS. FARROW. Now you be decent to
him, Mrs. Hyland—he saved my little
Timmy from the milk fever.

MARGARET. You said you were going to
bring me a cup of coffee. If you intend
to bring it . . . bring it.

MRS. FARROW. I'll spit in the cup to
sweeten it. Can't you take a kindness
from no one?

MARGARET. No one.

MRS. FARROW. Well, I'm a slob. I'll
bring the coffee. (*She exits.*)

(JAMES HYLAND, *still enfolding* LIZZIE
*in his arms, now sings the last four lines
of the song.*)

JAMES. So many times I held you like
this in my arms. You were smaller than
a small Amen in a little prayerbook, and
people marveled at the lovely thing a
man carried. You wore a mitten over
your hand, it is true, but you walked
when you were seven months, and you
spoke when you were nine months.
To shine like a moon till your star will
arise
Go to sleep, go to sleep, go to sleep.

(MRS. FARROW *has returned with the
coffee. But while* JAMES HYLAND *reprises
the song, she can make no sound and
take no step.*)

MRS. FARROW. A man like that!

MARGARET. What is the good of him!
Your man works!

MRS. FARROW. After work he drinks
beer.

MARGARET. But only beer.

MRS. FARROW. Until he is belched to
sleep.

MARGARET. Even so, he works.

MRS. FARROW. Peter Farrow's a hard-working man but if James Hyland asked
me I'd go away with him in an hour.

(MARGARET *rises, takes the cup, carries
it to the sink and pours out its contents.
She rinses it and puts it into* MRS. FARROW's *hand.*)

MARGARET. You kept your word . . .
(MRS. FARROW *looks at her with curiosity.*)
You spit in my cup.

(MRS. FARROW *regards her for a stupefied moment . . . then exits.*)

JACOBSON (*off*). Hello, Mrs. Farrow.
Is it up here?

(MARGARET *stands motionless, and turns
only when there is a sound in the doorway. It is* DR. ISAAC JACOBSON.)

MARGARET (*it is a statement*). Dr. Jacobson.

JACOBSON. One day I will have a patient who lives on the first floor. Mrs.
Hyland?

MARGARET (*a bare nod*). My daughter
is in there.

JACOBSON. I was told she was in convulsion.

MARGARET (*answering his unspoken
question*). She is with her father.

(*He looks at her curiously as he removes his coat.*)

JACOBSON. How old is the child?

MARGARET. Eleven.

JACOBSON. Have there been any previous seizures . . . similar to this one?

MARGARET. No. Never. Dr. Jacobson, I
didn't send for you.

JACOBSON. I understand. Now if you
will excuse me . . . (*Standing where she
is, she bars his way. He will not go
around her and she will not step aside.
He looks at her without speaking . . .
and he yields. He goes around her to the
bedroom and for a moment he is so filled
with wonderment over this woman that
he cannot see* LIZZIE *in the arms of* JAMES
HYLAND.)

JAMES (*rousing him*). We are glad you
came.

(JACOBSON *sees them now.*)

JACOBSON (*he looks into* LIZZIE's *eyes
. . . he places his fingers on the pulse in
her throat*). My dear, I am a friend. Are
you able to speak? What's your name?

JAMES (*answering for her*). Elizabeth.

JACOBSON. Let her answer. (*To* LIZZIE)
Is it painful for you to swallow?

JAMES. It is, Doctor. (*Aware of* JACOBSON's *exasperation*) I beg your pardon.

(*In the next room,* MARGARET *draws
closer, straining to hear above the noise*

of her own heart.)

JACOBSON. Does it hurt when you swallow? (*She nods.*) And you don't feel like talking? (*She shakes her head.*) Because you're sleepy? (*She nods.*) We want you to sleep. We're not going to disturb you. (*From his bag he takes a stethoscope and listens, frowning a little, to* LIZZIE*'s heart.*) Very good. (JAMES, *however, is hardly convinced. He looks inquiringly at* DR. JACOBSON, *whose only reply is:*) I should like a tablespoon, please.

JAMES. Yes. (*He goes out.*)

MARGARET. You left her alone with him! You fool.

JAMES. Yes, I left her alone with him. I want a tablespoon. (*She finds a spoon in great haste and gives it to him . . . He returns with it to* JACOBSON, *who pours some medicine out of a bottle that he has taken from his bag.*)

JACOBSON. I want you to drink some of this.

JAMES. It's medicine, Lizzie, it will make you better.

JACOBSON (*when she makes no move*). I would hate to have to use force. Now let me see . . . relax your fingers . . .

(*She opens her mouth . . . and he inserts the tablespoon between her trembling lips. She makes a face and* JAMES *starts for the sink again . . . but* MARGARET *is already near the bedroom door, a glass of water in her hand.*)

MARGARET. Doctor, can't you see! My daughter is upset!

(LIZZIE *drinks noisily, with difficulty.*)

JACOBSON. Very well. I'm going to visit you again after you wake up. (*And all three of them,* JAMES, MARGARET, *and* LIZZIE *register their own varied reactions to this warning. Aware of the sudden new tension,* JACOBSON *is at a loss.*) We're going to let you sleep. Please, may I wash my hands?

(MARGARET *nods and* JACOBSON *goes out to the sink.* JAMES *follows and goes to the table and sits down before the whiskey. He pours some into the glass.*)

JACOBSON. How did all this begin, Mr. Hyland?

JAMES (*for once in his life he understates the thing*). It has been a bad day for her. (*He raises the whiskey in the glass.*) Dr. Jacobson, would you care for a drink?

JACOBSON (*waving it aside*). I want to hear about the child.

JAMES (*holding the glass in his hands*). She's been overwrought all day. The moving from Lispenard Street, the strain of meeting new people . . . the truant officer . . . other things. And then her mother noticed it . . .

JACOBSON. Noticed what?

JAMES. That she was dragging her leg. (*As one colleague to another*) The first prodromal symptom? (JACOBSON *looks at him curiously and nods. Dying for the whiskey:*) Then difficulty in swallowing, followed by the twitching . . . convulsive, every muscle in her body. If it hadn't stopped, I would have tried a mustard bath.

JACOBSON. Would you?

JAMES (*his eyes riveted on the whiskey*). Yes. (*Looking up*) Is there something more I can tell you?

JACOBSON. My compliments, Mr. Hyland. You have presented a classical description of the onset of a disease. (JAMES *drinks the whiskey, and refills the glass.*) Tell me, Mr. Hyland, did you ever study medicine?

JAMES (*his head flies up like a setter at the point*). You are an observant man.

JACOBSON (*warily*). You studied medicine.

JAMES. No!

JACOBSON (*going to him*). Where did you learn about mustard bath therapy in convulsions?

JAMES. I read. (*He stares at* MARGARET *and then picks up the brimming whiskey glass and pours its contents back into the bottle.* MARGARET, *seeing him cork the bottle, is shaken out of her ironclad silence.*)

MARGARET. Doctor . . . (JACOBSON *turns to her.*) What is the name for Lizzie's sickness? . . . If there is a name?

JACOBSON. It is too soon to say. But it could be St. Vitus' Dance. It used to be much worse. (*He takes his coat and starts to put it on.*) In the Middle Ages, in Swabia—not many miles from where I myself was born—there was an epidemic . . . arms and legs dancing, out of control . . . It must have been something to witness! The Jews were blamed for it. Tens—hundreds—thousands—dancing in the streets—a dancing dementia. And the poor suffering men and women danced into the chapels of St. Vitus which were all over the countryside . . . and they prayed for healing. (*He goes to the bedroom and looks carefully at* LIZZIE. *Then he comes back.*) Well, I have patients waiting in my office. I will come back later. (*Going to the door*) As for the truant officer, you will not be disturbed again. I will see to that. (*Exits.*)

MARGARET (*when his footsteps have ceased to echo*). All she has eaten all day is a little bread and jelly.

JAMES. I'll go to the store.

MARGARET. After you come back . . . you leave.

JAMES. Do I?

MARGARET. This time I want no misunderstanding.

JAMES. I will not leave until she wakes up and I can kiss her again. I make that a condition.

MARGARET (*she smiles faintly*). You use such words. Very well, the kiss is the condition!

JAMES. Margaret, what is it that has made you so strong and me such a weakling?

MARGARET. Thirteen years of the same marriage. (*She goes to the breadbox, where through force of long habit she shields what she does.*)

JAMES (*releasing his anger in the taunt*). Be careful, Margaret.

MARGARET. You can see where I hide my money. It is not a money-cheat you are.

JAMES. You must still be careful. You could grow absentminded and find between two dollar bills some of the love you keep hidden.

MARGARET (*she separates two dollar bills and holds them apart*). There is no love hidden away.

JAMES. Not even for Lizzie?

MARGARET. I can't help loving her . . . but to be a mother is an animal thing. You're a man! What would you know of the thing that tears the belly? (*She thinks of the time.*) I was jealous of the midwife when she washed her. But mine was the first joy of her—mine was the first kiss. I held her in my arms and we slept. (*Unconsciously she rocks her body back and forth and her eyes close. Then the rocking stops and her eyes open wide.*) I wonder if it happens to the others! After the first sleep. You wake up and you hold the child to nurse and you see what you've given birth. Two eyes. A nose. A mouth. Little ears. Fingernails. I kissed the fingernails. (*And her body becomes rigid.*) The finger of God's wrath! (*She remains silent—and* JAMES *has no tongue for speech.*) To be a mother is an animal thing. I can't help loving her. But I don't lie to myself that she loves me back.

JAMES. Margaret . . . what do you have left?

MARGARET (*with quiet acceptance*). My own spite. (*She opens her fist and regards the crumpled dollar bills.*) Here. Buy for her . . . milk, bread, meat—whatever you want.

JAMES (*making no move for the money*). Margaret, I loved you once.

MARGARET. Did you?

JAMES. You loved me once.

MARGARET. Did I?

JAMES. The two years before Lizzie was born.

MARGARET. Nothing.

JAMES. I still know those two years. I know a woman who wore a lavender dress and waved to ships. I know evenings . . . when you read the pages I had written. You never told me if they were good, but you didn't have to speak. . . . Margaret, I wrote good things in those pages. You knew that, didn't you? You knew that whatever lies I lied . . . not the written word.

MARGARET. Yes.

JAMES. You believed in me a little.

MARGARET. Why did you spoil it?

JAMES. I did?

MARGARET. I never asked you for a dollar. It was enough to see that you worked. Why did you never finish anything?

JAMES. What does a writer do when it doesn't come?

MARGARET. He struggles. (*She aches with the memory of it.*) The neighbor's children going out to the factories and a grown man sleeping in the afternoon. And then going out—to taverns.

JAMES. I couldn't bear your silence.

MARGARET. You could have earned a living as a writer.

JAMES. And you regret the living—as I regret the writer.

MARGARET. That's what they call wit. I'm a plain woman, James.

JAMES. It is difficult for you to smile;

and your chin is too definite, your cheek-bones are too wide—but you're not a plain woman.

MARGARET (*crossing to the sink*). The store is downstairs.

JAMES. Have you no curiosity about where I've been for four months?

MARGARET. No.

JAMES. That isn't true. I was in Gouverneur Hospital. I had pneumonia. The second year we were married I had pneumonia. Do you remember? I had a terrible fever.

MARGARET. Don't.

JAMES. Don't what?

MARGARET. Don't *use* that.

JAMES. But it was the best time. The best! (*She turns away.*) Whatever happened when Lizzie was conceived, don't deny the memory of the good years.

MARGARET. They were few and I have pawned them with my wedding ring. (*She shows him her naked finger.*) You are a man, you can pretend as much as you wish. (*Her lip curls.*) Not even a man. If you had a man's intestines, you would make your fist a hammer and smash my mouth.

JAMES. Is that what you want from me?

MARGARET. Yes. If you are a man, smash my face, and let us have a little peace.

(*He takes the money*—MARGARET's *hand is open, her palm supplicating; but he goes, and she stands alone as:*)

THE CURTAIN IS LOWERED

SCENE THREE

A half hour later; the light is dim. LIZZIE *sleeps in her bed, her room darkened. In the half-light of the kitchen* MARGARET *is working on the velvet coat draped on the tailor's dummy. Now she removes the coat and brings it with her to her worktable. She tiptoes into* LIZ-ZIE's *room and kisses the sleeping child; then she tiptoes back and, unmindful of the gathering darkness, she begins to sew buttons onto the coat. Enter* JAMES HY-LAND, *carrying a bag of groceries. He puts the bag down on the sink. She allows him, with her own wordless irony, to undertake the housewifely duty of re-moving the groceries from the bag, plac-ing them on a shelf. She is content to sew.*

When he is finished he stands aimlessly for a moment and watches her flying needle.

———

JAMES. You don't have to work now.

MARGARET. It quiets me. (*After a moment*) And we need the money. (*She sews—swiftly in spite of fatigue and darkness. He goes to the stove and finds a match. He lights the overhead gas fixture. She looks up and nods. It is a garish light, and by it the room looks naked.*)

JAMES (*he waits for her to say something . . . then he goes to the rocking chair and sits down, and from his pocket he takes a book and begins to read. But he cannot abide the censure of her silence . . . He goes to* LIZZIE's *room*). I thought I heard her stir . . . I said, I thought I heard her stir.

MARGARET. I heard what you said.

(*He walks back to his chair.*)

JAMES. That wasn't true. I didn't hear anything.

MARGARET (*nods . . . and sews. He goes back to his book*). James, which is harder for you?

JAMES. Harder?

MARGARET. To endure silence or to tell the truth?

JAMES. I don't know. They are both difficult.

MARGARET. I didn't say difficult, I said hard.

JAMES. The words are the same.

MARGARET (*shaking her head*). I am hard, you are difficult.

JAMES (*laughs ruefully*). You sew, with a sharp needle.

MARGARET (*she laughs . . . her laugh is even a little humorous*). It's a pity I'm your wife, I would have been an amusing companion. (*She resumes her sewing.*) What are you pretending to read?

JAMES. A new book.

MARGARET. Where did you get it?

JAMES. Yes. It might amuse you. I was in a public place frequented by certain well-known literary figures. I overheard two gentlemen discussing this book. I ventured to express an opinion, and then I—uh—

MARGARET. Talked.

JAMES (*he laughs*). After about an hour one of the gentlemen took it into his head to ask me if I had read the book, and I rather surprised myself by confessing that I had only read the critical notices. So he said, "Sir, anyone who can discourse with such authority on the basis of the notices, should at least read the book." So he gave it to me as a present. (*After a reflective moment*) Why did you say I was pretending to read it?

MARGARET. If you were dead in your coffin, you would pretend you were dead and in your coffin.

JAMES. That's what first attracted me to you: your pathological urge to tell the truth. (*Going to her*) Margaret, what attracted you to me?

MARGARET. Why should I tell you that?

JAMES. Because you have never told me.

MARGARET. It's done now.

JAMES. That makes it more important. The only things no one can take away are the things we've lost forever. Tell me what I've lost so I can have it.

MARGARET (*she resumes her sewing*). I have work.

JAMES (*watches her sew for a moment*). I used to read to you when you sewed. Shall I read to you now?

MARGARET. Since you must either talk or die, you might as well read.

JAMES (*he is angry and considers what to do . . . and concludes that she is right and that he might as well read . . . So he does*). "When Zarathustra came into the next city, he found many people gathered together, for they had been called that they should see a rope dancer."

MARGARET. A rope dancer!

JAMES. A tight rope. (*She nods and goes back to her sewing.*) "And Zarathustra spoke: 'Man is a cord above an abyss. A perilous arriving, a perilous traveling, a perilous looking backward, a perilous trembling and standing still. What is great in man is that he is a bridge and no goal. . . . What can be loved in man is that he is a going over and a going under. I love them that are great in scorn . . . *Saying the words by heart as he looks up from the page*) '. . . for these are they that are great in ·reverence.'"

(*She looks up at him. Her body tenses at his nearness.*)

MARGARET. I have sewing to do.

JAMES. So have I, so have I.

MARGARET. Don't read any more.

JAMES (*he puts the book down and rises*). I believe I'll go out in the hall for a minute and smoke. (*He waits for her answer.*) Would you mind very much if I smoked in here? (*She shrugs. From inside his coat pocket* JAMES HYLAND *brings forth a battered cigar-case, and goes to the stove for a stick match. He lights his cigar and puffs with deep satisfaction.*)

MARGARET. That smell . . . in my house!

JAMES (*going to the sink*). I will put it out.

MARGARET (*shaking her head*). No. I like it. (*Softly*) It smells of a man. (*He throws the cigar away and goes to her now and touches her hair with his fingertips, and she allows it.*) You always did it.

JAMES. Did I?

MARGARET. Always quoted other people to me. All the time.

JAMES. Your literary bedfellow. Is your virtue loathsome to you?

MARGARET. You're still quoting.

JAMES. I waited four months.

MARGARET. What do you want from me?

JAMES. Mrs. Hyland's Margaret. (*He lifts her from her chair, and turns her until she faces him. He strokes her cheek and she allows it.*)

MARGARET (*yielding*). Why don't you ever speak so I can understand?

JAMES. Not everything can be explained: there is mystery. (*He touches his fingertips to her neck. She shivers . . . and she flees—to the dummy and her work.*) What was it, the first time we met in your cousin's house in Belfast? Was it the way I talked?

MARGARET. No.

JAMES. What was it?

MARGARET. I looked at you and you were there.

JAMES. You never should have let me walk you home.

MARGARET. Never.

JAMES. Grapes from a pushcart. A pennysworth! Do you remember what I said?

MARGARET. "Margaret, I bring you grapes of Eshcol, and my mouth is filled with water!"

JAMES. I look at you, I look. Such a penalty to pay for eyes! (*He bends and kisses . . . her breast!*)

LIZZIE. Ma! (MARGARET *startles.*) Ma!

MARGARET. I've forgotten Lizzie. (*And as she hurries to the bedroom, there is a knock on the door.*)

JACOBSON (*off*). It's Dr. Jacobson.

(JAMES *goes to the door.*)

MARGARET (*in the bedroom*). What is it, Lizzie, did you have a dream?

LIZZIE. I wasn't sleeping.

JACOBSON (*in the kitchen*). How is the child?

JAMES. She seems better, Doctor.

JACOBSON (*taking off his coat*). Good. I want to take another look. (JACOBSON *crosses to the bedroom, and as* JAMES *follows:*) How are you, Mr. Hyland?

JAMES. Very well, thank you.

JACOBSON (*entering the bedroom*). Well, Elizabeth—you look better than the first time I saw you. How do you feel?

LIZZIE. Better.

JACOBSON. You will never be a bore. Do you know what a bore is? When you ask him how he feels, he tells you.

JAMES. Voltaire!

JACOBSON. I beg your pardon.

JAMES. Voltaire said it a long time ago. Not your words, of course. His own paraphrase.

JACOBSON (*to* LIZZIE). You have a learned father.

(LIZZIE *doesn't answer and unable to tolerate a conversational void,* JAMES HYLAND *blurts his own answer.*)

JAMES. I have a learned daughter.

JACOBSON. Yes, I am sure her teachers think so.

(LIZZIE *stiffens, and looks imploringly at her mother.*)

MARGARET. It's all right, Lizzie. Dr. Jacobson isn't going to ask you any more questions.

JACOBSON. Of course not. We'll just take your pulse. (*He reaches for the wrist near him, but* LIZZIE *thrusts her arm under her body.*) I can't take your pulse if you hide your wrist from me. (LIZZIE *extends her right wrist to him, like a duellist extending a rapier across the body.* JACOBSON *looks curiously from one to the other, waiting for them to explain this extraordinary behavior. When they show their unity of silence, he takes her pulse . . . Its wild rhythm shocks him.*) Child, tell your pulse not to be afraid of me. (*He places his ear against his heart . . . listens a moment.*) If my examination is going to frighten you, I'll go away again, if that's what you want. It's more important for you to be calm,

than for me to examine you.

MARGARET. You're a good man.

JACOBSON (*without any emphasis*). I'm a doctor. Please, Mrs. Hyland, may I speak with you for a moment?

MARGARET. Yes. (*She goes into the kitchen,* JACOBSON *covers* LIZZIE *hastily and follows* MARGARET. JAMES *pulls the covers up and kneels at* LIZZIE'S *side.*)

JACOBSON. Mrs. Hy—(*Closes the door.*) Mrs. Hyland, you must explain it to me.

MARGARET. What?

JACOBSON. Her terrible fright.

MARGARET. I can't explain it.

JACOBSON. You mean you will not.

MARGARET (*she regards him for a moment*). Let me pay you for your two visits. (*She starts for the place where her purse is.*)

JACOBSON. I have not even begun my examination.

MARGARET. You saw how she is.

JACOBSON. I will be patient. I'm used to small chidren who are frightened of my stethoscope, but not a girl of her age. Has she been like this with every doctor?

MARGARET. It was a mistake to let you come here. I will get the money.

JACOBSON. I am dismissed . . . and sent down to my carriage.

MARGARET. Lizzie will be all right . . . after you are gone.

JACOBSON. Quite apart from the St. Vitus' Dance, your daughter requires medical care. Mrs. Hyland, I'll go now, because I do not wish to excite her. But I will come again and you must allow it.

MARGARET. I cannot allow it. I must not.

JACOBSON. You have no choice. Your daughter needs me.

MARGARET. I cannot allow it.

JACOBSON. (*he studies her and his face empties*). My fee is one dollar for each house visit. That will be two dollars, Mrs. Hyland.

(*She goes to her purse—the operation as before.*)

LIZZIE. Pa, don't hold me any more.

JAMES (*he puts her down*). All right. Can I bring you something?

LIZZIE. My jump-rope.

JAMES (*happily*). I don't know where it is.

LIZZIE. Ask Ma.

JAMES (*he goes out*). Margaret, Lizzie wants her jump-rope.

MARGARET. I must pay Dr. Jacobson

first.

JAMES (*surprised*). Are you leaving, sir?

JACOBSON. So it seems. Mr. Hyland, is there anything *you* would like to tell me about your daughter's history?

(JAMES *is afraid to answer.* LIZZIE *gets out of bed and goes trembling to the doorway. They are focused upon themselves and cannot see her.*)

JAMES (*he looks at* MARGARET). No . . . there's nothing to tell. Nothing you don't already know.

MARGARET. You see, Doctor?

JACOBSON. I see that you and your husband are united in silence.

MARGARET. We are hardly united.

LIZZIE (*in the doorway*). I asked for my jump-rope.

MARGARET (*sharply*). What are you doing out of bed?

LIZZIE. I want Dr. Jacobson to see how I jump rope. (*As* MARGARET *runs to her.*) I'm all right, Mama. I feel fine. (*She wards her off.*) Dr. Jacobson, do you know that it's a special kind of jump-rope? I make up jumping rhymes with it. (*As* MARGARET *tries to lead her back to her bed, desperately*)

Boss Billy Tweed skipped out of jail. They put him back in without any bail . . .

MARGARET. All right, Lizzie. You've told the doctor a jump-rhyme.

LIZZIE. But that was such a short one. (*And before her mother can stop her, she blurts out the rhyme—clapping her hands so that he can see the mitten:*)

Wild Bill Hickok,
Needle and thread,
Shot a man,
Full of lead.
Man had a brother named McCall,
Shot Wild Bill
And that was all.

(*Wildly*) Dr. Jacobson, don't you think if I went to school, I'd be promoted and never left back?

MARGARET. You're being selfish, Lizzie. Dr. Jacobson has many patients who need him.

LIZZIE. But I have to tell him why I don't go to school. I wear a mitten to cover my left hand. (*She raises her hand and pulls her mitten off and extends the fist that she has made of her left hand.*) Count.

(*He takes her fist in his own gentle hands.*)

JACOBSON. Your hand is warm from the glove.

LIZZIE. Not a glove. A mitten.

JACOBSON. Is that all? Now shall we go back to bed?

LIZZIE. You didn't listen.

JACOBSON. All right. That's not so terrible.

LIZZIE (*weeping with hopelessness, she runs to* JAMES). Pa, make him understand that my name is Elizabeth Pamela Ursula Hyland and I have six fingers.

JACOBSON. My name is Isaac Jacobson. I am a Jew.

MARGARET (*whispering it*). No, Dr. Jacobson, not the same thing.

JAMES. We have kept her covered for eleven years.

JACOBSON. What a waste of life! We all wear a glove over something. Every day! You should see them in my office! The people who are ashamed. The ones who have no teeth, or too much hair. The short ones, the fat ones, the disappointed ones. They don't talk about it. It's hard for us to come into the presence of another and stand naked. Elizabeth, you have nothing to be ashamed of.

MARGARET. Evil is on her hand.

JACOBSON. Evil is in the mind.

(LIZZIE *steps away from him and puts her hand in* MARGARET'S *who automatically begins to cover* LIZZIE'S *hand.* JACOBSON *regards them, this mother and daughter joined by sickness, and he reaches out and snatches the mitten from* MARGARET'S *hand.*)

JACOBSON. No, not anymore! (*Flings the mitten on the table.* LIZZIE *thrusts her mother away and takes a trembling step toward the doctor.*) Don't be frightened. (LIZZIE'S *trembling becomes a convulsive seizure; she stumbles toward* JACOBSON, *her arms flailing, independent of her will, insane;* JACOBSON *watches her as she is about to fall. He smothers her in his arms and calls urgently:*) Please. My bag! (*And he runs with the convulsive child into the bedroom.* MARGARET *follows, opening his bag as she runs.* JACOBSON *holds* LIZZIE *on the bed with one bear-like arm; and as she thrashes from side to side, swinging like some wild human pendulum, he finds chloroform and gauze in his bag, and manages somehow to get*

the bottle open and the gauze dampened.)
Now I want you to inhale. Breathe in!
(*And despite the paroxysm the child
obeys, and he encourages her.*) Again,
again. Breathe . . . breathe . . . breathe
. . . that's the way. Good. All the way.
Good. (*His face is averted, and his own
deep breathing joins with the child's.*)
Again. Good. Again. Good.

(MARGARET *watches, her whole body in
rhythm with the pain of her child. But*
JAMES *cannot watch. He is turned away,
shrunken, sick. They stand this way—
immobile, exhausted; and* LIZZIE *begins
to sleep.*)

MARGARET (*to* JAMES). St. Vitus'
Dance?

JAMES. Yes.

MARGARET. And they named it after a
saint! (*She goes out and sits heavily on
a kitchen chair.* JACOBSON *raises one of*
LIZZIE'S *eyes and sees that she is sleeping.
He caps the chloroform bottle and goes
out.* JAMES *remains with* LIZZIE, *covering
her, listening.*) She never had anything
like that before.

JACOBSON. Yes. But now it will happen again.

MARGARET. Often?

JACOBSON. The greatest frequency is at
her age. And girls have it more than
boys. Fair girls or with red hair! Interesting. When the symptoms are severe,
chloroform or chloral inhalations. We
have nothing else.

MARGARET. Does the chloroform cure?

JACOBSON. It makes it easier for her,
but it doesn't cure.

MARGARET. What is the cure for the St.
Vitus' Dance?

JACOBSON. You mean, what is it that
makes her mind so afraid her body tries
to run away? You can answer that, Mrs.
Hyland.

MARGARET. There must be a cure. Her
body can't stand that anymore.

(JAMES *is now with them, in the
kitchen.*)

JACOBSON (*he reopens his medical bag,
goes with it to* LIZZIE'S *door and looks
in for a moment*). She would feel no
pain.

MARGARET. What are you thinking?

JACOBSON. She is deeply anesthetized.

MARGARET. Tell me what you're thinking.

JACOBSON. Well, what do we know of

St. Vitus' Dance? An infection? We're
not sure. Something produced by a microbe? Possibly. But if it is a microbe, of
what type? No one has ever described
it. And yet the possibility exists that the
germ could be . . . fright.

JAMES. Lizzie has always been frightened.

JACOBSON. How lucky she is . . . that
her fright is merely a finger!

JAMES. Do you think it would cure
her?

JACOBSON. I have no right to think
anything. But we should try.

JAMES (*putting the decision to her*).
Margaret?

MARGARET. Every birthday I bake her a
cake, I light a candle, and when she blows
the candle out, I die a little. Half her
nights I stand in the dark to hear if she
breathes. You mustn't touch her with
your knife.

JACOBSON. It would be minor surgery.

MARGARET. She has no blood to spare.

JACOBSON. Modern surgery is fast. There
will be little bleeding. It will be healed
in two weeks.

MARGARET. No.

JACOBSON. Why are you so afraid? This
is hardly an operation! I don't have to do
it in a hospital. Not even in my own
office. I can do it right now. Here. Everything I need is in this bag. Why do you
insist on your daughter's sickness?

MARGARET. Is that what I do?

JACOBSON. Yes. You insist.

MARGARET. Then don't ask me any
more.

JAMES. Do it, Dr. Jacobson!

JACOBSON. Good. Good. (*He goes to
the table, examines it.*) I will need a
larger table. (*Remembering*) Mrs. Farrow has such a table. (*To* JAMES) Help
me carry it up. (*The two men exit, and
we hear the sound of their footsteps as
they go down.*)

MARGARET (*alone now, she discovers the
jump-rope on the table. She holds it by
the ends . . . and as it forms a wide loop
for jumping, she smiles strangely. She
swings the rope back and forth. Chanting to herself*).

There once was a girl,
Her name was Lizzie,
She skipped, she jumped,
Till she was dizzy;
Her dress was white,

Her blood was red,
She skipped, she jumped
Till she was dead!
(*Then, violently, the arc of the rope
comes high. She snaps it viciously against
her neck, and with a cruel twist she
swings a loop around her neck and holding the rope she forces her arms out wide
. . . and she lifts her face and beseeches
the Jehovah of her judgment.*) Pull it
tight for me. I have no more strength.

CURTAIN

ACT THREE

*It is two hours later. The time is eight
o'clock.*

*The full light of the kitchen is upon
the tailor's dummy which has been
brought downstage, and which now
shows that even in this brief space of
elapsed time* MARGARET's *fingers have not
been idle. The coat has buttons now, and
button-holes, and on each lapel there is a
bit of trimming. The coat, nearly done,
is a creation of considerable imagination
and dramatically reveals* MARGARET's *in-
nate, essential elegance.*

*The room has been tidied. Whatever
the disorder of* MARGARET's *emotion, there
can be no disorder in her house. Her absence from the flat only emphasizes this
fact.*

JAMES HYLAND *is also absent. In possession, and sitting in a rocker before the
window on the street, is* MRS. FARROW,
reading a child's picture book.

*The bedroom is darkened, but in its
dim light we can see* LIZZIE *sleeping. She
stirs once and the whiteness of the band-
age on her left hand shines like something
luminous.*

After a moment CLEMENTINE *appears in
the kitchen doorway and stands there,
looking at the mother who has betrayed
her. She makes a small noise, and her
mother turns and sees her.*

CLEMENTINE (*picking her nose*). Pa's
home.

MRS. FARROW (*without enthusiasm*).
Hallelujah. When did he come in?

CLEMENTINE. About ten minutes ago.
He wants to know when you're coming
down to your own house.

MRS. FARROW. Didn't you tell him? As
soon as one of them gets back. There's a
sick child here.

CLEMENTINE. I told him. He wants to
know when the hell you're coming down.
He's sore.

MRS. FARROW. He'll get over it. The
dockwalloper! What is he sore about?

CLEMENTINE. He worked overtime and
he wants his supper.

MRS. FARROW. Don't talk so loud. Come
in before you wake her up.

CLEMENTINE. If I so much as set foot
in this house he'll break every goddam
bone in my goddam body.

MRS. FARROW (*rising and going toward*
CLEMENTINE *with murder in her heart*).
Clementine Farrow, you told him.

CLEMENTINE. The whole goddam thing.
(*Spotting the table and running to it*)
Hey, that's our furniture!

MRS. FARROW. Oh shut up, you silly.
Did you have to tell him?

CLEMENTINE. She said to me, I hope
you die. (MRS. FARROW *embraces her.*) He
wants to know when you're coming
down.

MRS. FARROW. Mr. Hyland never came
back and the woman had to bring some
sewing work to a lady. With the girl so
sick, no matter what the woman is, I
will be a Christian.

CLEMENTINE. He wants to know if they
have to do it on your head before you
know it ain't raining? You better come
down, he wants his supper. He's got that
look on his face.

MRS. FARROW. You tell your father I'll
come down when I get there. The woman
out of the window half the day and the
child operated, . . . and all Peter Farrow
can think of is his own fat belly. Tell
him to read your brothers a story.

CLEMENTINE (*her jaw falls open*).
What?

MRS. FARROW. What do you mean what!
You tell your father to stop snapping his
suspenders and to read the kids a story.

CLEMENTINE. How?

MRS. FARROW. Out of a book.

CLEMENTINE. He'd kill me.

MRS. FARROW (*she knows her man*).
Peter Farrow won't kill nobody.

PETER FARROW (*off*). I'm waiting for
my goddam supper.

MRS. FARROW (*runs to window and yells
down*). You got two hands. You and your

big mouth.

LIZZIE. Mrs. Farrow!

MRS. FARROW. Look what we've done! We woke her up! (*Not harshly*) Go down to your father, Clementine. (*Making her joke*) Go on, before I cut off your head and put on a button. (*She pushes* CLEMENTINE *out.* CLEMENTINE *exits.*)

LIZZIE. Mrs. Farrow!

MRS. FARROW. I'm coming, Lizzie. (MRS. FARROW *turns up the bedroom light and hurries to* LIZZIE . . . *She touches her forehead.*) Poor child, you're soaked with your own sweat. (*She finds a towel and begins to mop* LIZZIE's *face and neck.*)

LIZZIE (*after a moment*). Pa is gone.

MRS. FARROW. That's because you're better. He'll be back.

LIZZIE. I'm not a little baby. She sent him away.

MRS. FARROW. He'll be back.

LIZZIE. She told him to go. He kissed me and he went. He's never coming back again.

MRS. FARROW. Where did you get such a idea!

LIZZIE. He went away forever. I heard him say it.

MRS. FARROW. You had a foolish dream.

LIZZIE. It's a dream only when he comes back. She won't let him.

MRS. FARROW. You mustn't feel such things and say such things about your own mother. She had to bring a shirtwaist to a Mrs. Bernard. She said she couldn't afford to lose a steady customer. I saw the shirtwaist. Your mother does fine work. You have to give her credit.

LIZZIE. I know about my mother. You don't have to tell me. (*Irrelevantly*) Mrs. Farrow, do you know that James Hyland is one of the finest unpublished poets in America?

MRS. FARROW. You don't say!

LIZZIE. He talks his poems. He's a deep man. He once talked a poem about marriage: "Kiss a girl and say a prayer, get a child your tears to wear." That was the whole poem.

(MRS. FARROW *finishes with the towel . . . now she takes a comb, puts* LIZZIE's *head against her bosom, and combs* LIZZIE's *hair.*)

MRS. FARROW. I'll bring you a looking glass. When you see how pretty you look, you'll feel better. You do feel better, don't you?

LIZZIE. I have pain in my . . . ! I want to sleep. It's a funny feeling.

MRS. FARROW. That's from the stuff the doctor gave you.

LIZZIE. I have a funny taste in my mouth.

MRS. FARROW. You're thirsty, that's what it is. (*Puts comb down.*) You just close your eyes for a second. (*She hurries to the washstand and returns with a glass of water. She puts her arm under* LIZZIE, *holding* LIZZIE's *head against her breast.*) Drink it slow.

LIZZIE (*drinks a little*). It still hurts when I swallow.

MRS. FARROW. A little more? It's good for you.

(LIZZIE *drinks again.*)

LIZZIE. Thank you, Mrs. Farrow.

MRS. FARROW. You're welcome. Your body is so thin.

LIZZIE. You have a soft bosom.

(MRS. FARROW's *eyes fill with tears.*)

MRS. FARROW. Poor little girl, you're starved! (*She turns the light down again, and continues to stand near the bed listening to the sound of the breathing child.*)

(*Minus his shabby jacket, his watch and chain,* JAMES HYLAND *enters from the hall, humming. He is in high and alcoholic humor, which does not diminish when he is confronted by the tailor's dummy wearing the velvet coat.*)

JAMES (*drunkenly, to the dummy*). "Each morning sees some task begun. Each evening sees it close: Something attempted, something done, Has earned a night's repose . . ." Madam, shall we dance? (*And he dances with the dummy as his partner until* MRS. FARROW *steps out of the darkened bedroom—and bangs the washbasin on the sink.*) I thought you were Margaret.

MRS. FARROW. She's gone out to deliver a shirtwaist.

JAMES. She left her alone!

MRS. FARROW. So did you!

JAMES. You know why she went? To prove how strong she is.

MRS. FARROW. She went because the shirtwaist was promised. She knocked on my door and she asked me to sit with the child.

JAMES. She did that?

MRS. FARROW. She did!

JAMES. That's a great deal for Margaret Hyland. (*He lurches toward the door of* LIZZIE's *room.*)

MRS. FARROW (*stopping him*). Lizzie wants to sleep!

JAMES (*stopping*). That's a blessing.

MRS. FARROW. You and Dr. Jacobson come for my table! Mr. Hyland, what has happened here?

JAMES. An occasion for rejoicing and singing of hosannas.

MRS. FARROW. What has happened?

JAMES. I will tell you when I return.

MRS. FARROW. You're going out again!

JAMES. Just for two seconds. (*He exits and after a moment he returns carrying a live parrot in a cage. As parrots go, it is not a particularly attractive bird, nor is its plumage especially gay. But it is a parrot, and it is alive. Triumphantly:*) Well, what do you think of it, Mrs. Farrow?

MRS. FARROW. You went from the child for that?

JAMES. Margaret would never permit a dog or a cat or even a goldfish to enter her house. Lizzie always wanted a pet.

MRS. FARROW (*coldly*). Where did you buy it?

JAMES. Oh, he couldn't be bought. His price is far above rubies.

MRS. FARROW. Lizzie was asking for you.

JAMES. Don't you like the parrot? I got him from a Tierra del Fuego missionary. He dropped anchor in the East River to take on Bibles and distilled water. We began by exchanging views on eschatology and one dogma led to another. He was so overwhelmed nothing would satisfy him but that I instantly accept the bird.

MRS. FARROW. Does it talk?

JAMES (*he whistles and caws, and at the look of delight on* MRS. FARROW's *face, he sighs*). Alas, that was only me. The bird speaks only Italian. (*He takes a stiff drink of whiskey.*) His name is Bill. But I believe we're going to change it to George Psalmanazar, who in the days of Samuel Johnson spent some months in Christ's Church in Oxford teaching the rudiments of Formosan to the English heathen. He's a very old bird, Mrs. Farrow.

MRS. FARROW (*sniffing*). He smells like an old bird, Mr. Hyland.

JAMES. You are disappointed because the bird doesn't talk. Be of good cheer, Mrs. Farrow, for tomorrow I shall purchase an Italian grammar and in a fortnight, the bird will be singing Bellini.

MRS. FARROW (*with cunning*). Where's your coat?

JAMES. I see I must tell you the truth. (*Making a desperate effort*) This noble bird belonged to a company of travelling opera singers who were buried in an avalanche north of Central City. The only survivors were George and the tenor, who lost his voice from the shock, and is now employed as a masseur in a Turkish bath on Houston Street.

MRS. FARROW. Your wife waited. You told her you were going out for a few minutes. That ain't right.

JAMES. But there was something I had to get for my daughter.

MRS. FARROW (*with scorn*). A goddam pigeon that don't speak English.

JAMES. A ring. (*From his vest pocket he takes out the ring and shows it to her.*) A golden ring for my Lizzie to wear on her hand.

MRS. FARROW (*takes it*). It's brass. A gimcrack for five cents!

(MARGARET *enters. She shows no surprise, only weariness. She goes silently to* LIZZIE's *door, opens it and looks in.* MRS. FARROW *goes to her.*)

MARGARET (*whispering*). How's Lizzie?

MRS. FARROW. She took a little water.

MARGARET. That's good. (*Studies the sleeping child.*) Thank you, Mrs. Farrow. (*Closes door softly and wearily removes her hat, her gloves, her worn coat.* JAMES *shows her the ring on his hand and she looks at him in helpless wonder —this incurable romantic. He picks up the parrot, and starts with it toward the door.*)

JAMES. I bought it for Lizzie.

MARGARET. I understand.

(*He puts the parrot out in the hall and goes into the darkened bedroom and puts the ring on top of a book.*)

MRS. FARROW. No one has ever told me.

MARGARET (*dully*). What?

MRS. FARROW. About Lizzie!

MARGARET. She was born with six fingers and I hid it in a mitten. (*She sits, holding her things.*) No one to play with, so she jumped rope. Dancing with a rope, on a rope, without any rope at all. Her whole body dancing. Today she had fits and they call it St. Vitus' Dance. (*She runs her fingers over her shabby coat.*) James and I, we gave her what we didn't give each other, and maybe she didn't need that. She has always been torn between us, and we are always running from each other; and who is always left behind and caught? The child. (MRS. FARROW *impulsively holds out her hand, and* MARGARET *takes it; two women holding each other by the hand this moment of their lives.*) Oh, Mrs. Farrow! We strong ones, we have no chance against the James Hylands! We are always right and they are always loved.

MRS. FARROW. You call down if you need me. Any time. (*She goes.*)

(*From a paper bag* MARGARET *removes some binding and places it on her work-table. Then, wearily, she removes the coat from the dummy and places it on her lap and begins to pin the binding to the coat.*)

LIZZIE (*opening her eyes*). Pa!

JAMES. Darling, darling.

LIZZIE. You came back!

JAMES. Darling, darling, do you know what day of your life this is? (*Turns up the light.*)

LIZZIE. No.

JAMES. It is the day of your birth. (*He goes to her bed and kisses her.*) No mitten for your hand. Never again. (MARGARET *has risen from her chair . . . her fists holding back her own terrible yearning to be with her daughter. But she will allow* JAMES *this moment, for it is due him, and she knows it.*) While you were asleep—without your knowing it, without any pain—Dr. Jacobson took it off.

LIZZIE. You're sure?

JAMES. Sure, sure, sure!

LIZZIE. Does *she* know?

JAMES. She helped the doctor. Now you are like everyone else. And I bought you a ring to wear. A golden ring. From now on, darling, everything will be different. You'll have dresses without pockets. I'm going to rip off all the pockets.

LIZZIE. No. (*Desperately.*) You mustn't take away my pockets!

JAMES (*he lifts her bandaged hand and shows it to her*). But there's nothing to hide anymore.

LIZZIE. I need my pockets. I've got to have my pockets. (*He yields, and kisses*

her numbly—*defeated.*) Let me sleep.

JAMES (*entering the kitchen*). I wiped the sweat from her head and she held up her hand . . .

MARGARET. I heard.

JAMES. I showed her the ring and I kissed her.

MARGARET (*she goes to her sewing table and picks up the coat*). I saw it.

JAMES. Today—this one time—it will not kill you.

MARGARET (*sewing*). What?

JAMES. To kiss your own daughter.

MARGARET (*the mechanics of her own syndrome*). For what reason?

JAMES. My God, must love have a reason! Kiss her to show your love.

MARGARET. I've never been a demonstrative woman.

JAMES. Try.

MARGARET. I did. Many times. But you were always there before me. Holding her. You held her so tight you squeezed me dry.

(*He goes and pulls the coat from her.*)

JAMES. Go in. Take her in your arms. Make amends.

MARGARET. Don't I sew for her bread. (*Taking the coat back.*)

JAMES. I marvel. I marvel that someone as sweet and so pure came out of you . . . I marvel!

(*She resumes her sewing . . . She bites off a thread and then:*)

MARGARET (*evenly*). I have sewing to do and you are standing in my light.

JAMES. Is there no softness in you?

MARGARET. None whatsoever.

JAMES (*clenching his fist and looking down on her hair*). Not even in your hair. (*Touching it.*) God knows, it has been a bitter life for you . . . There should be at least one finger of gray in your hair. You will not even yield to age.

MARGARET. I cannot yield to anything.

JAMES. You will have to yield: the finger is off her hand. You will have to find some new madness. Lizzie and I will walk in the street now. She won't be timid with the world. She will wear my ring. I'm a worthless husband but I can be father enough to teach her to laugh. I feel good. (*He picks up the bottle.*)

MARGARET. Celebrate. Fill your glass, my friend.

JAMES. No. You want me drunk. My breath a stink. And I know why. So that we can stand together before the Magistrate . . . and the child between us . . . to choose between her thrifty mother, and the drunken braggart who is her father.

MARGARET. We make progress. You will be irresponsible, it is true, and a bragger, but no longer drunken. It is something.

JAMES. "I love them that are great in scorn . . . for these are they that are great in reverence."

MARGARET. You are a fool to repeat that.

JAMES. I was a fool before that. Yet, there was a time, Margaret, when I could have been better than a fool. Had there been a kiss instead of silence.

MARGARET. You kissing man! How old does a man have to be before he stops looking for the nipple!

JAMES. Margaret, let me be the only thing I am. A father is more than a husband. A mother is more than a wife! For the sake of the child, Margaret, we can still do it, even now.

MARGARET. Don't beg.

JAMES (*shouting*). How many years do you want me to pay? I'm a family man.

MARGARET. You are shouting at me.

JAMES. It's time.

MARGARET. You will wake up Lizzie . . . the same way, eleven and a half years ago, that your sin awoke her in my womb and marked her with shame. (*He slaps her.*)

JAMES. Why did you stop being a woman the moment you became a mother? (*She turns away.*) Not even when you die will you be more beautiful than when you carried Lizzie. Your hair was soft, there was a shining on your cheek. The smell of you made me want you day and night. Why did you pull away from my touch! Did you think I would have harmed you?

MARGARET. The night Lizzie was conceived you were drunk.

JAMES. Eleven years of hell for that!

MARGARET. It was an afternoon when I found you pretending to work. For five weeks you had not written one line. I whipped you with my tongue. Oh, I know how to do that, don't I? So you ran to a tavern. When a man has no comfort in his house he has the right to look for comfort in a glass. I grant you that. You see how I've changed! I wanted to tell you I was sorry. I waited up. But how could I tell you? You were drunk. So I let you come to me instead and that was better than talking.

JAMES. I don't remember. (*Turns away from her.*)

MARGARET. I am cursed with memory. You were drunk in the afternoon, and in the evening you went to a whore. And then you came to me—still wet with the whore—and fathered your child—and you bragged! You gentle, gentle man, you family man, you bragged. (*He begins to cry.*) Cry, James Hyland, wash yourself clean with tears. But I cannot. "When lust hath conceived, it bringeth forth sin; and sin when it is finished, bringeth forth death."

JAMES. That isn't true.

MARGARET. It is Scripture. It is true. We are judged and we are punished.

JAMES. We?

MARGARET. Yes, we.

JAMES. I went to the whore; what did you do? Why are you punished?

MARGARET. I lusted for you. And I reveled in my own lust.

JAMES (*he stares at her incredulously*). All these years! It wasn't me you were punishing, it was Margaret Hyland. For finding pleasure in her own husband! Margaret, you've been wearing a mitten. God is your sixth finger.

MARGARET. And He is a jealous God and great in scorn.

JAMES. To deny the woman in yourself for demons, monsters!

MARGARET. Even as Lizzie was born monstrous.

JAMES (*furious, he grabs her shoulder and throws her violently to the floor*). Margaret, you're mad; but you're not going to make my daughter mad. The sickness of this house was cut off on that table. From now on I stay.

MARGARET. You will not stay because I will drive you from this house. (*She begins to disrobe.*) You remember a Margaret that loved you, but let me show you the kind of woman I am. I can play the whore. (*Throws her blouse to the floor, and unfastens her skirt.*) Let us be animal and animal with each other; let me disgust you. (*Throwing her skirt down*) The last illusion of James Hyland. (*She kisses him with passion.*) James, when a man is with a whore, is the blood money paid before or after? (*With a sob*) I have been curious about that. (*She kisses him again, her kisses descending from his lips; she falls to her knees, embracing him.*)

JAMES. Margaret, don't do that!

MARGARET (*kissing him again*). Does it burn? I am burned. Did you suppose I was cold? It is the cold ones that get rid of their husbands by having many babies.

JAMES. You wanted me to go! (*He takes one step and she forbids another by holding him around the knees.*)

MARGARET. My floor is clean enough to eat from. (*She rips her skirt in two, and spreads it on the floor, their nuptial bed. She sits on it, inviting him, shameless. JAMES stares at her, pitying her. Then he turns his back.*) You are such an innocent in your sin and I am such a whore in my virtue. (*She commences to sob. He turns, slowly. He touches his hand to her shoulder, gently; and he lifts her to her feet. She backs away from him, and stares at her torn clothes, and covers her face in shame.*) I'm all right now. (*She goes to the sink.*) I'll be very good. (*She fills the basin with water and goes to LIZZIE's room.*)

(*JAMES would follow her, but there is a knock. JAMES opens the door . . . It is not DR. JACOBSON who stands there but MRS. FARROW.*)

MRS. FARROW. Dr. Jacobson is on the third with Mrs. August. He'll be right up. (*MRS. FARROW starts to leave.*)

MARGARET (*she dips the cloth into the bowl, wrings it out. Something in LIZZIE's attitude stops her short. She touches LIZZIE with her fingertips. And her voice is a trumpet of death*). James. James! (*He runs into the bedroom. MRS. FARROW comes back.*) She is so cold.

JAMES (*kneeling*). Lizzie . . . darling . . . (*He takes her hand.*) Sweetheart . . . we mustn't play games. (*He looks at the hand—this cold lifeless thing.*) Lizzie, this is wrong.

MARGARET. Lizzie . . . it's your mother.

(*DR. JACOBSON enters the kitchen. He puts his bag wearily on the table . . . and then something in MRS. FARROW's attitude catches him.*)

JACOBSON (*sharply*). What!

MRS. FARROW. I don't know.

(*He grabs his bag and runs into the bedroom . . . There are no words in the room. JACOBSON does what a doctor will do: the controlled response of the trained physician. Yet, even as he strains to hear the beating of a dead heart there is a tremor in his own practiced hand, and his knees turn to water.*)

JACOBSON. It was only a minor operation. It . . . (*Unbidden from his lips, unsummoned, the immemorial words of his ancestors:*) Boruch dayan emes . . . (*He looks with stricken eyes at the child.*)

MARGARET (*on her knees*). Forgiveness, God, forgiveness! Forgiveness for the living who destroy their own! (*She kisses the dead lips.*)

JAMES. Doctor, why? You have got to tell me why!

JACOBSON. Mr. Hyland, I am just a man. We die. Only God knows why. Perhaps you cannot take eleven years of deformity and cut it off with just a knife. (*He sits slowly, numbly on the bedroom chair. MRS. FARROW moves into the bedroom doorway.*)

MARGARET. We must wash her clean. (*MARGARET dips the cloth but it has become too heavy for her hand.*) I am not able. (*Her voice is like a child's.*) Mrs. Farrow . . . please . . . the kindness of a neighbor.

(*MRS. FARROW takes the cloth and goes to the bed, where she kneels, and crosses herself and quietly weeps. JAMES leads MARGARET away, into the kitchen. He is forced to half-carry her—her feet are lead.*)

MARGARET. She never knew how much I loved her.

JAMES. She knew, she knew. Have mercy on yourself.

MARGARET. Hold me, James.

JAMES. We will still be a family.

CLEMENTINE (*appearing suddenly in the doorway*). Ma, I found a parrot in the hall. (*She sees MARGARET, stricken, in her petticoat.*) Ma!

MARGARET (*called from her grief by the sight of the child she had cursed—the living child. She lifts her torn dress and touches CLEMENTINE gently on the cheek.*) I tore my dress . . . I'll need to mend it. I sew, you know.

CURTAIN

LOOK HOMEWARD, ANGEL

Ketti Frings

Based on the novel by THOMAS WOLFE

Presented by Kermit Bloomgarden and Theatre 200, Inc.,
at the Ethel Barrymore Theatre, New York, on November 28th, 1957,
with the following cast:

BEN GANT Arthur Hill

MRS. MARIE "FATTY" PERT
    Florence Sundstrom

HELEN GANT BARTON Rosemary Murphy

HUGH BARTON Leonard Stone

ELIZA GANT Jo Van Fleet

WILL PENTLAND Tom Flatley Reynolds

EUGENE GANT Anthony Perkins

JAKE CLATT Joseph Bernard

MRS. CLATT Mary Farrell

FLORRY MANGLE Elizabeth Lawrence

MRS. SNOWDEN Julia Johnston

MR. FARREL Dwight Marfield

MISS BROWN Susan Torrey

LAURA JAMES Frances Hyland

W. O. GANT Hugh Griffith

DR. MAGUIRE Victor Kilian

TARKINTON Jack Sheehan

MADAME ELIZABETH Bibi Osterwald

LUKE GANT Arthur Storch

Directed by George Roy Hill
Settings and lighting by Jo Mielziner
Costumes by Motley

The town of Altamont, in the State of North Carolina, in the fall of the
year nineteen hundred and sixteen.

ACT ONE. SCENE 1: The Dixieland Boarding House; a fall afternoon.
SCENE 2: The same; that evening.

ACT TWO. SCENE 1: Gant's marble yard and shop; one week later.
SCENE 2: The Dixieland Boarding House; the next night.

ACT THREE. The Dixieland Boarding House; two weeks later.

Where the play is available for amateur production royalty will be quoted on application to Samuel French, Inc., at 25 West 45th Street, New York 36, N. Y., or at 7623 Sunset Boulevard, Hollywood 46, Calif., or to Samuel French (Canada), Ltd., 27 Grenville Street, Toronto 5, Ontario, Canada, one week before the date when the play is given.

Stock royalty quoted on application to Samuel French, Inc.

For all other rights than those stipulated above, apply to Pincus Berner, Administrator, C.T.A., of the Estate of Thomas Wolfe, 25 West 43rd Street, New York 36, N. Y., and Friend & Reiskind, 375 Park Avenue, New York, N. Y.

Particular emphasis is laid on the question of amateur or professional readings, permission for which must be secured in writing from Samuel French, Inc.

IT WOULD have been difficult to believe that so effective a dramatization of Thomas Wolfe's *Look Homeward, Angel* could have been made without distortion of that comprehensively detailed novel of a sensitive young giant and his turbulent family. Even if there would be no distortion for the sake of dramatic cohesion, the dramatization was bound to produce an effect of amputation; surely one would be aware of missing events in any playwright's effort to pack a huge novel into a two-hour play. That, except for some loss of language (compensated for by good acting and by excision of the novelist-narrator's occasional fustian), the dramatization proved to be so satisfactory may be attributed to the skill of the adapter, Ketti Frings, an author of fiction herself who, like Thomas Wolfe, had been attracted to the theatre as a playwright. She first attracted attention during World War II with *Mr. Sycamore*, a dramatization which the Theatre Guild produced at some risk, since the subject of this delicate little play, which dealt with a mailman's transformation into a tree, was more suitable for inclusion in Ovid's *Metamorphoses* than for presentation in a Shubert playhouse. Mrs. Frings returned to Hollywood after the short, unhappy run of *Mr. Sycamore*, which was one of the Theatre Guild's and the present editor's mistakes; and it was there she remained, turning out reputable screen adaptations of William Inge's *Come Back, Little Sheba* and Joseph Kramm's Broadway success *The Shrike*, before her intrepid dramatization of *Look Homeward, Angel* settled down for a long run at the Ethel Barrymore Theatre under the expert guardianship of Kermit Bloomgarden. Mrs. Frings met with the approval of the New York Drama Critics Circle and the Pulitzer Prize board, both of which gave awards to her dramatization as the best American play of the year.

It is to be hoped the ghost of Thomas Wolfe was somewhat appeased. Like Henry James this natural novelist had hoped to succeed as a playwright, and he had studied the craft under Frederick H. Koch at the University of North Carolina and for three years under George Pierce Baker in his Workshop 47 at Harvard. Wolfe wrote a number of short and long plays, one of which, *Welcome to Our City,* was held under option by the Theatre Guild of New York in 1923. But his only dramatic success was a posthumous one, when his family drama *Mannerhouse* was translated and produced in Germany.

A factor in the success of the dramatization that should not be overlooked is Jo Mielziner's setting, which made it possible to play different scenes simultaneously. But the feat of unifying the action of the novel started with Mrs. Frings' ability to condense it into a period of a few weeks and to relate the gangling seventeen-year-old protagonist's development to the events of that period. It is a testimony to the adapter's craftsmanship that she was able to crowd together with barely an indication of contrivance, as the late Wolcott Gibbs put it, "such diverse material as a boy's first love, a shocking death in the family, the final disintegration of a marriage, and the culmination not only of a woman's fierce conflict between greed and her need to be loved but of her son's equally agonized struggle to escape from the surroundings that are destroying him both as a man and as an artist." The least the novel became in Mrs. Frings' capable hands is a workable family drama, although it is more than that—a young artist's discovery of reality. In one respect it is even an improvement on the autobiographical flamboyance, the self-centeredness, of the novelist.

ACT ONE

SCENE ONE

SCENE: *The Dixieland Boarding House; a fall afternoon. The house is a flimsily constructed frame house of fifteen draughty, various-sized rooms. It has a rambling, unplanned gabular appearance, and is painted a dirty yellow. Most of its furniture is badly worn and out of style. The beds are chipped enamel-covered iron. There are accordion hat trees, cracked mirrors, an occasional plant. On the typically Southern veranda which embraces the front and one side of the house, there are chairs, rockers, and a woodbox. There is a sign above the door, electrically lighted at night:* DIXIELAND— ROOMS AND BOARD. *In the center of the house, slightly raised, is a turntable on which all the bedroom scenes are played. At the back of the house a walk approaches the rear of the veranda. There is a side door and near it a circular yard seat. Also down front of the bedroom is a table and a chair. The street itself has a feeling of great trees hanging over it. Occasionally during the play, the stillness is broken by the rustle of autumn leaves, and the poignant wail of a train whistle. The Curtain rises in darkness. After a moment we hear* EUGENE's *voice coming from his room. Seated, he is glimpsed, writing, surrounded by books.*

EUGENE. "Ben" by Eugene Gant. . . . My brother Ben's face is like a piece of slightly yellow ivory. (*Lights come up on the veranda where* BEN GANT, *30, delicate and sensitive, the most refined of the Gants, and forever a stranger among them, is seated on the front steps reading a newspaper. He is sometimes scowling and surly, but he is the hero protector of those he loves, with quiet authority and a passion for home which is fundamental. At times he speaks to the side over his shoulder, in a peculiar mannerism of speech, as though he were addressing a familiar unseen presence.*)
His high, white forehead is knotted fiercely by an old man's scowl.
His mouth is like a knife.
His smile the flicker of light across the blade.
His face is like a blade, and a knife, and a flicker of light.

And when he fastens his hard white fingers
And his scowling eyes upon a thing he wants to fix,
He sniffs with sharp and private concentration.
(*Lights now reveal* MARIE "FATTY" PERT, *43, seated near* BEN *in her rocker. She is a generous, somewhat boozy woman, knitting a pair of men's socks and tenderly regarding* BEN.)
Thus women looking, feel a well of tenderness
For his pointed, bumpy, always scowling face. . . .
(EUGENE *continues writing.*)
BEN. Somebody's got to drive the Huns from the skies. Poor old England can't be expected to do it alone.
MRS. PERT. It's their mess, isn't it?
BEN. It says here there's an American flying corps forming in Canada.
MRS. PERT. Ben Gant, what are you thinking of?
BEN. All my life in this one little burg, Fatty! Besides getting away, I'd be doing my bit.
MRS. PERT. Would they take you so old?
BEN. This article says eighteen to thirty-two.
MRS. PERT. Aren't the physical standards pretty high?
BEN. Listen to her! I'm in good condition!
MRS. PERT. You're twenty pounds underweight! I never saw anyone like you for not eating.
BEN. Maguire gave me a thorough checkup this spring!
MRS. PERT. How would your family feel if you went?
BEN. What family? The batty boarders? (*Takes her hand.*) Apologies, Fatty. I never associate you with them. Except for Gene, nobody'd know I was gone. (*Looks up, dreamily.*) To fly up there in the wonderful world of the sky. Up with the angels.
(HELEN GANT BARTON *and her husband* HUGH *enter from the house.* HELEN *is gaunt, raw-boned, in her middle twenties, often nervous, intense, irritable and abusive, though basically generous, the hysteria of excitement constantly lurking in her. It is a spiritual and physical necessity for her to exhaust herself in service to others, though her grievances, especially*

in her service to her mother, are many. HUGH *is a cash-register salesman, simple, sweet, extremely warmhearted. He carries a newspaper, a tray with a coffee pot and cups and saucers, which* HELEN *helps him set on a table. They have been arguing.*)

HUGH. We should never have agreed to live here for one day—that's the answer. You work yourself to the bone—for what?

HELEN (*busy putting cups in saucers*). Mrs. Pert, the other boarders have almost finished dinner!

MRS. PERT. What's the dessert, Helen?

HELEN. Charlotte Russe.

HUGH. They're like children with a tapeworm. (*Crosses and sits woodbox down right.*)

BEN. Fatty, I told you you'd better get in there!

MRS. PERT. I was trying to do without, but I'm afraid that calls me. (*Rises.*) See you later, Ben. (*She leaves her knitting on the chair, exits inside.*)

HELEN. Ben, where is Mama?

BEN. How should I know?

HELEN. I've had to serve the entire dinner alone!

HUGH. Look at me, holes in my socks, a trouser button missing—and before I married you I had the reputation of being "dapper."

HELEN. I bet she's off somewhere with Uncle Will, and *I'm* left in the kitchen to slave for a crowd of old cheap boarders! That's her tactic!

HUGH. "Dapper Hugh Barton"—it said so in the newspaper when we were married.

HELEN (*crosses to* BEN, *who pays no attention*). You know that, don't you, *don't you?* And do I ever hear her say a word of thanks? Do I get—do I get as much as a go-to-hell for it? No. "Why, pshaw, child," she'll say, "I work more than anybody!" And most times, damn her, she does.

BOARDERS (*offstage, calling, ringing the service bell*). Helen. Helen!

HELEN. You come in, Hugh, and help me! (*Exits into the house.*)

BEN. How are the cash registers selling, Hugh?

HUGH. Putting the cigar box out of business. I got a good order in Raleigh last week. I've already put away nine

hundred dollars toward our own little house.

BEN (*rises*). You ought to have one, Hugh. You and Helen. (*Crossing toward wicker unit down left where he has left his coat.*)

HUGH (*looking at part of newspaper*). I guess they don't have to advertise the good jobs, do they? The really big jobs—they wouldn't be here in the newspaper, would they?

BEN. Why?

HUGH. If there was something good here in town—not on the road so much—maybe then I could talk Helen into moving away. Ben— (*Rises.*) you hear things around the paper—

HELEN (*off*). Hugh! Hugh!

BEN. I'll keep my ears open, Hugh.

HUGH. Well, I guess I don't want to make Helen any madder at me. Thanks, Ben. (*Exits inside.*)

(*An automobile is heard off, driving up, stopping.* BEN *moves down to the yard seat, reads his newspaper. The car door slams.*)

ELIZA (*off*). I'll vow I never saw such a man. What little we have got, I've had to fight for tooth and nail, tooth and nail! (ELIZA GANT *enters with* WILL PENTLAND, *her brother.* ELIZA, *57, is of Scotch descent, with all the acquisitiveness and fancied premonitions of the Scotch. She is mercurial, with dauntless energy, greed and love. She has an odd way of talking, pursing her lips, and she characteristically uses her right hand in a point-making gesture, fist enclosed, forefinger extended. These mannerisms are often imitated by those who hate and love her.* ELIZA *is carrying some fall leaves, a real estate circular and two small potted plants.* WILL *is paunchy, successful, secure, a real estate broker. He carries a small tray with several flower pots, geranium cuttings, and a can of peat moss therein, which he places on woodbox. They do not notice* BEN.) Like the fellow says, there's no fool like an old fool! Of course Mr. Gant's been a fool all his life. Pshaw! If I hadn't kept after him all these years we wouldn't have a stick to call our own.

WILL. You had to have an "artistic" husband. (*Places flower pots on table above* PERT'S *rocker.*)

ELIZA (*crosses to left of* WILL). Artistic. I have my opinion about that. Why, Will, the money that man squanders every year on liquor alone would buy all kinds of good downtown property, to say nothing of paying off this place. We could be well-to-do people now if we'd started at the very beginning.

WILL (*he fixes a cutting into one of the pots and places it on the porch rail right*). You've given him every opportunity.

ELIZA. He's always hated the idea of owning anything—couldn't bear it, he told me once—'cause of some bad trade he made when he was a young man up in Pennsylvania. If I'd been in the picture then, you can bet your bottom dollar there'd been no loss.

WILL (*chuckling*). Or the loss'd been on the other side.

ELIZA (*moving him front of her to the steps*). That's a *good* one! You know us Pentlands! Well, I'm going to get after Mr. Gant right today about that bank offer.

WILL (*in yard right of right porch pillar*). Let me know when you've warmed him up enough for me to talk to him.

ELIZA (*on porch step*). It'll take a good deal of warming up, I can tell you. He's so blamed stubborn about that precious old marble yard, but I'll do it!

WILL. Give me a jingle when you want to look at that farm property. (*Exiting*) I'll drive you out there.

ELIZA. Thanks, Will! I appreciate it. (*Places leaves, brochure and purse on left porch pillar. Sees* BEN.) Ben! What are you doing home at this hour?

BEN. I'm working afternoons this week.

ELIZA. Oh. (*Somewhat worriedly. Crossing onto porch for two small flower pots.*) Will you get dinner downtown?

BEN. I usually do.

ELIZA (*crossing into yard to right of center table*). You always sound so short with me, Ben. Why is that? You don't even look at me. You know I can't stand not being looked at by the person I'm talking to. Don't you feel well?

BEN. I feel good.

(*A train whistle is heard in the distance.*)

ELIZA. Oh, pshaw, there's the midday train now! Has Eugene gone to the station?

BEN. How should I know?

ELIZA (*crossing left. Calling up to* EUGENE's *room*). Eugene, are you up in your room? Eugene? (EUGENE, *hearing his mother's voice, rises from his chair, turns toward the window, but he doesn't answer, and* ELIZA *does not see him.* EUGENE *is 17, the youngest of the Gants, tall, awkward, with a craving for knowledge and love. During the following he leaves his room. Crossing toward porch right*) Eugene! I'll vow, that boy! Just when I need him— (*Notices* MRS. PERT's *knitting.*) Ben, I hope you haven't been lying around here wasting time with that Mrs. Pert again?

BEN. Listen to her! It's the nicest time I spend.

ELIZA (*crossing to right of him*). I tell you what: it doesn't look right, Ben. What must the other boarders think? A woman her age—a drinking woman—married. Can't you find someone young and pretty and free to be with? I don't understand it. You're the best looking boy I've got.

BEN (*more pleasantly*). If it'll make you feel better, Mama, I'll look around.

ELIZA (*relieved by the change in his mood, smiles. She also notices the sprawled newspaper. Crossing to right of center table*). That's Mr. Clatt's newspaper. You know he's finicky about reading it first. Fold it up before you go. (*During the above,* EUGENE *is seen coming down the stairs from his room. Now limping slightly, he starts to sneak out the side door, but* ELIZA *spots him.*) Eugene, where are you sneaking to? Come out here.

EUGENE (*comes out to left of center table*). Yes, Mama?

ELIZA. The train's just coming in. Now you hurry over to that depot.

EUGENE. Today? I did it yesterday.

ELIZA. Every day until every room is filled. The advertising cards are on the hall table. Go get them. (EUGENE, *disgruntled, goes into the entry hall to get the cards from a small stand.* ELIZA *strips some dead leaves off a plant.*) I declare, seventeen is an impossible age. I don't know why he complains. He hasn't anything else to do. Spending his time up there scribbling, dreaming.

BEN. The other boarding houses send their porters to the trains.

ELIZA. Never you mind, Ben Gant, you used to do it. It's little enough I've ever asked of you boys. (*To* EUGENE *as he comes from the hall.*) Have you got the cards? (*Crosses onto porch to flower tray.*)

EUGENE (*crossing left*). In my pocket.

ELIZA (*holding out her hand*). Let me see them. Let me see them!

EUGENE (*in yard front of left pillar. Takes cards from pocket, reads*). "Stay at Dixieland, Altamont's Homiest Boarding House."—It should be homeliest.

ELIZA. Eugene!

EUGENE. I hate drumming up trade! It's deceptive and it's begging.

ELIZA. Oh, my—my! Dreamer Eugene Gant, what do you think the world is all about? We are all—all of us—selling something. Now you get over to the depot right this minute. And for heaven's sake, boy, spruce up, shoulders back! Look like you *are* somebody! (EUGENE *starts off.*) And smile! Look pleasant! (EUGENE *grins, maniacally.*)

BEN (*suddenly, as he watches* EUGENE *limping*). Gene! What are you walking like that for?

EUGENE. Like what?

BEN (*rises*). What are you limping for? My God, those are my shoes you've got on! I threw them out yesterday!

ELIZA (*busy at flower tray*). They're practically brand new.

BEN. They're too small for *me,* they must be killing him.

EUGENE. Ben, please!

ELIZA (*takes flower tray to up right table*). Maybe you can afford to throw out brand-new shoes.

BEN. Mama, for God's sake, you ask him to walk straight, how can he? His toes must be like pretzels!

EUGENE. They're all right. I'll get used to them.

BEN (*throwing down his paper*). My God, it's a damned disgrace, sending him out on the streets like a hired man. Gene should be *on* that train, going to college!

ELIZA (*crossing to right of center table with can of peat moss*). That's enough—that's just enough of that! You haven't a family to provide for like I have, Ben Gant. Now I don't want to hear another word about it! Gene will go to college when we can afford it. This year he can help Papa at the shop.

BEN. I thought you were going to "warm up" Papa, so he'll sell the shop.

ELIZA. Ben Gant, that wasn't intended for your ears. I'd appreciate it if you wouldn't mention it to Mr. Gant until I have. Hurry off now, son, get us a customer!

EUGENE (*crossing to left of center table*). Why should Papa sell his shop?

ELIZA (*packing moss in flower pots*). Now, you're too young to worry about my business. You tend to yours.

EUGENE. What business do I have to attend to, Mama?

ELIZA. Well, get busy, get busy! Help your Papa at the shop.

EUGENE. I don't want to be a stonecutter.

ELIZA. Well, go back to delivering newspapers. Work for Uncle Will in his real estate office. But keep the ball rolling, child. Now hurry on or you'll be late! (EUGENE *exits.*)

HELEN (*entering from hall right*). Mama, dinner's practically over! I'm no slave!

ELIZA. I'll be right in, Helen. (HELEN *exits, slamming door.* ELIZA *sighs. For a moment, left alone with* BEN, *she becomes herself, a deeply troubled woman.*) What's the matter with him, Ben? What's wrong with that boy? (*Crosses to pillar for purse, leaves and brochure.*) What's the matter with all of you? I certainly don't know. I tell you what, sometimes I get frightened. Seems as if every one of you's at the end of something, dissatisfied, and wants something else. But it just can't be. A house divided against itself cannot stand. I'll vow, I don't know what we're all coming to. (*Approaches side door left, pauses.*) If you like, this once, as long as you're home, why don't you eat here? I'm sure there's plenty left over.

BEN. No, thank you, Mama. (*He starts off.*)

ELIZA. A good hot meal!

BEN (*tosses paper on center table*). I've got to get over there.

ELIZA. Ben, are you sure you feel all right?

BEN. I feel fine.

ELIZA. Well, have a nice day at the paper, son.

(BEN *exits,* ELIZA *looks after him, then hearing the voices of the boarders, exits into the house by the side door. The boarders, ushered by* HELEN, *enter through the front door. They are:* JAKE CLATT, *30, an insensitive boor.* MRS. CLATT,

60, JAKE's mother, with a coarse smile and dyed hair. She is deaf and carries a cane. FLORRY MANGLE, *29, wistful, humorless, interested in* JAKE. MRS. SNOWDEN, *50, quiet, unobtrusive, lonely. Takes her coffee, sits up right.* MISS BROWN, *36, prim on the surface, but with the marks of the amateur prostitute.* MR. FARREL, *60, a retired dancing master, new to Dixieland.*)

MRS. CLATT. I ate too much again.

HELEN (*loudly to* MRS. CLATT, *as she crosses to table with fresh pot of coffee*). Help yourself to coffee, please, Mrs. Clatt. I'm short-handed today.

MRS. CLATT (*brandishing her cane at* MR. FARREL, *who is about to sit chair down right*). Not there, that's my chair! That one's free, since the school teacher left.

MISS BROWN (*at front of porch door*). You're a teacher too, aren't you, Mr. Farrel?

MR. FARREL. Of the dance. Retired.

MISS BROWN. I hope you'll stay with us for a while. Where are you from?

MR. FARREL. Tampa.

MISS BROWN. Do you know the Castle Walk, Mr. Farrel? I'd love to learn it! (*They stroll down to the yard seat left.*)

MRS. CLATT. I don't know what Mrs. Gant makes this coffee of. (*Crosses, sits down right.*) There isn't a bean invented tastes like this.

JAKE (*on porch up right center*). Couldn't you make it for us sometime, Helen?

HELEN. My mother always make the coffee here.

(HUGH *and* MRS. PERT *enter. The others seat themselves.*)

MRS. PERT. That was scrumptious dessert, but oh dear! (*Sits in her rocker.*)

JAKE (*down right center on porch*). Yes, it was good, if only the servings were bigger.

MRS. CLATT. I'm told the best boarding house food in town is down the street at Mrs. Haskell's.

JAKE. That's right, Mother. That's what I heard.

HUGH (*crossing to yard to left of* MRS. PERT). Then move in to Mrs. Haskell's!

HELEN (*with a shove*). Hugh! (*She exits.*)

MISS MANGLE (*seated right of door*). I spent one season there, but I prefer it here. It's more informal and entertaining.

JAKE (*seated woodbox*). Not lately. It's been over a month since Mrs. Gant had to have Mr. Molasses Edward, and his two Dixie Ramblers evicted for not paying their rent. She certainly loves to see the police swarm around!

LAURA JAMES, *23, carrying a suitcase, and a Dixieland advertising card, enters. She is attractive, but not beautiful. She advances to the steps.*)

MISS MANGLE. Don't you?

JAKE. I like excitement—why shouldn't I?

MISS MANGLE. Other people's excitement. Don't you ever want excitement of your own? I do.

(MRS. CLATT *sees* LAURA; *nudges her son into attention.* HUGH *turns to her.*)

LAURA. Good afternoon!

HUGH. Good afternoon!

LAURA. Is the proprietor here?

HUGH. I'll call her. (*Calls inside.*) Mrs. Gant! Customer! (*To* LAURA) Please come right up.

JAKE (*leaping to* LAURA). Here, let me take that suitcase. It must be heavy for you.

LAURA. Thank you.

(JAKE *takes* LAURA's *suitcase. Puts it on porch right of right pillar. The other boarders look her over, whisper.* ELIZA, *wearing an apron, places the leaves in a vase, on the hall table, enters. At first raking glance she doubts that* LAURA, *so young and different, is a true prospect.*)

ELIZA. Yes?

LAURA. Are you the proprietor?

ELIZA. Mrs. Eliza Gant—that's right.

LAURA (*crossing to left of* ELIZA *on porch*). I found this card on the sidewalk.

ELIZA (*takes card*). On the sidewalk! And you're looking for a room?

LAURA. If you have one for me.

ELIZA (*taking her to chair left of center table which* HUGH *has pulled out for her*). Of course I have, dear—a nice quiet room. You just sit down here and have yourself a cup of my *good* coffee, while I go and open it up, so I can show it to you. Hugh, you take care of the young lady. This is Mr. Barton, my son-in-law.

LAURA. How do you do, Mr. Barton? I'm Laura James.

ELIZA (*turns at steps*). Laura—why that's a *good* Scotch name. Are you Scotch?

LAURA. On one side.

ELIZA (*crosses back to her*). Pshaw! I could have told you were the Scotch the minute I laid eyes on you. I'm Scotch too. Well, isn't that nice? (*Makes introductions.* HUGH *crosses porch for coffee.*) Miss James, Mr. Clatt—(*Each acknowledges the introduction according to his personality.*) His mother, Mrs. Clatt, Mrs. Snowden, Miss Mangle, Mr. Farrel—(*Disapprovingly notices* MISS BROWN *flirting with* MR. FARREL.) Miss Brown—Miss Brown! and Mrs. Pert. Where do you come from, dear?

LAURA. I live in Richmond.

(MISS BROWN *and* MR. FARREL *exit down right practicing the Castle Walk, eventually reappear at the rear of the veranda up right.*)

ELIZA. Richmond! Now that's a pleasant city—but hot! Not like it is here, cool and refreshing in these hills. You haven't come to Altamont for a cure, have you, dear?

LAURA. I'm healthy, if that's what you mean. But I've been working hard and I need a rest.

ELIZA (*as* HUGH *approaches with coffee*). Here's your coffee.

LAURA (*takes coffee*). Thank you, Mr. Barton. What are your rates, Mrs. Gant?

EUGENE (*off*). Mama! (*Runs up the back walk, around the veranda.*)

ELIZA. Suppose I show you the room first.

EUGENE. Mama!

ELIZA (*crossing above* LAURA *to right of her*). I declare that child either crawls like a snail or speeds like a fire engine—

EUGENE (*pulls* ELIZA *off left away from the others*). Can I speak to you, Mama?

ELIZA. I don't see you limping *now*, when you're not trying to get sympathy. Don't think I don't know your little tricks to—

EUGENE (*urgently*). Mama, Papa's been at Laughran's again. Doctor Maguire is trying to steer him home now.

ELIZA (*momentarily stabbed*). The doctor? Is he sick or is he drunk?

EUGENE. He's rip roaring! He's awful. He kicked Uncle Will again!

(HUGH *and* JAKE *have seated* LAURA *left of center table*—LAURA *removes her hat. Offstage are the sounds of a small riot approaching. The occasional bull yell of* GANT, *children chanting "Old Man Gant came home drunk," a dog barking,* etc.)

ELIZA (*weakly*). I don't think I can stand it again. A *new* young lady, too. (EUGENE *turns to see* LAURA, *who, with the other boarders, have heard the approaching* GANT.) Oh, Eugene, why do they keep bringing him home? Take him to a state institution, throw him in the gutter, I don't care. I don't know what to do any more. What'll I do, child?

EUGENE. At least it's been a month this time.

GANT (*off*). Mountain Grills! Stay away from me!

JAKE CLATT. My God, Mr. Gant's on the loose again! (*Crosses onto porch.*)

MISS MANGLE. Oh dear, oh dear—

MRS. CLATT. What? What is it?

JAKE CLATT (*shouting*). The old boy's on the loose again!

EUGENE (*crossing up to the boarders*). Would you go inside, all of you, please?

MRS. CLATT. I haven't finished my coffee.

EUGENE. You can wait in the parlor. Please, just until we get him upstairs!

JAKE CLATT (*crosses porch up right*). And miss the show?

MISS BROWN. Come along, Mr. Farrel. Let's clear the deck for the old geezer.

MR. FARREL. Perhaps there is some way I can help?

MISS BROWN. I wouldn't recommend it, Mr. Farrel.

JAKE CLATT. Look at him, he's really got a snootful this time!

(EUGENE *urges several of the boarders inside, where they cram in the hallway.* JAKE *and* MRS. CLATT *remain on the porch.* LAURA, *not knowing where to go, remains with* HUGH *outside.*)

GANT (*from up the walk in the back, bellowing like a wounded bull. Off*). Mountain Grills! Mountain Grills! Fiends, not friends! Don't push me! *Get away from me!*

DR. MAGUIRE (*off*). All right then, Gant, if you can walk, walk! (ELIZA *stands downstage, stiff and straight.* W. O. GANT, *60, clatters up the back veranda steps, his arms flailing. At heart he is a far wanderer and a minstrel but he has degraded his life with libertinism and drink. In him still, though, there is a monstrous fumbling for life. He is accompanied by* DR. MAGUIRE, *unkempt but kind, and by* TARKINTON, *disreputably dressed, a crony, also drunk but navigating, and by* WILL

PENTLAND.) Here we are, Gant; let's go in the back way.

(WILL *precedes* GANT *and crosses to yard down right.* GANT *pushes the* DOCTOR *aside, plunges headlong along the veranda, scattering rockers, flower pots, etc.*)

GANT. Where are you? Where are you? The lowest of the low—boarding house swine! Merciful God, what a travesty! That it should come to this! (*Stumbles, almost falls, bursts into maniacal laughter.*)

EUGENE. Papa, come on—Papa, please! (EUGENE *tries to take* GANT *by the arm;* GANT *flings him aside.*)

GANT (*with a sweeping gesture*). "Waken lords and ladies gay
On the mountain dawns the day—"
(*Stumbles,* GENE *catches him.* MRS. CLATT *screams and dashes into the hall.*) Don't let me disturb your little tete-a-tete. Go right ahead, help yourself. (*Tosses* GENE *toward* PERT's *rocker.*) Another helping of mashed potatoes, Mrs. Clatt? Put another tire around your middle— (EUGENE *tries to catch* GANT's *flailing arms.*)

ELIZA (*crossing to left of left pillar*). Mr. Gant, I'd be ashamed, I'd be ashamed.

GANT. Who speaks?

ELIZA. I thought you were sick.

GANT. I am not sick, Madame; I am in a wild, blind fury. (*Raises a chair aloft, threatening* ELIZA. EUGENE *and the* DOCTOR *grab it away from him.* LAURA, *urged by* HUGH, *retreats to down left unit.*)

ELIZA. Dr. Maguire, get him in the house.

DR. MAGUIRE (*right of* GANT). Come on, Gant, let me help you.

GANT. Just one moment! You don't think I know my own home when I see it? This is not where I live. I reside at 92 *Woodson Street.*

DR. MAGUIRE. That was some years ago. This is your home now, Gant.

GANT. This barn? This damnable, this awful, this murderous and bloody barn—home? Holy hell, what a travesty on nature! A-h-h-h! (*He maniacally lunges to the yard after* ELIZA. GENE *halts him.*)

WILL. Why don't we carry him in?

DR. MAGUIRE. You keep out of this, Pentland. You're the one who enrages him.

GANT (*tossing* GENE *onto steps*). Pentland—now that's a name for you! (*Pivots, searching for him.*) Where are you, Will Pentland? (*Sees him, staggers toward him.*) You're a Mountain Grill! Your father was a Mountain Grill and a horse thief, and he was hanged in the public square.

(*While* HUGH *holds* GANT, EUGENE *brings a cup of coffee.*)

EUGENE (*left of* GANT). Papa, wouldn't you like some coffee? There's some right here.

GANT. Hah! Some of Mrs. Gant's *good* coffee? (*He kicks at the coffee cup.* EUGENE *backs away.*) Ahh! I'll take some of that *good* bourbon, if you have it, son.

DR. MAGUIRE (*crosses, puts bag on* PERT *rocker*). Get him a drink! Maybe he'll pass out.

GANT. Drink!

ELIZA (*stopping* GENE *at door*). Gene! Dr. Maguire, you know there isn't a drop of alcohol in this house!

LAURA. I have some. (LAURA *quickly opens her handbag, takes from it a small vial, crosses to the* DOCTOR.) I always carry it in case of a train accident.

GANT (*lunges toward her*). Well, what are we waiting for, let's have it!

DR. MAGUIRE (*taking the vial*). Good God, this won't fill one of his teeth.

GANT (*roars*). Well, let's have it! (LAURA *backs away in fear.*)

DR. MAGUIRE. You can have it, Gant—but you'll have to come up onto the veranda to drink it—

GANT. Mountain Grills! Vipers! Lowest of the low! I'll stand here until you take me home. (HELEN *enters from up right.*) Isn't anybody going to take me home?

HELEN (*crossing to right of* GANT). Papa! Why have you been drinking again when you know what it does to you?

GANT (*weakens, leans against her*). Helen—I have a pain right here.

HELEN. Of course you do. Come with me now. I'll put you to bed, and bring you some soup. (HELEN *takes the huge man's arm, leads him toward the veranda.* HELEN's *success with* GANT *etches itself deeply into* ELIZA's *face.*)

GANT (*weakly*). Got to sit down— (*Sits on edge of porch, left of left pillar, pats space beside him.*) Sit down, Helen, you and me. (*She sits step right of* GANT. GENE *sits table left of* GANT.) Sit and talk. Would you like to hear some Keats—beautiful Keats?

ELIZA (*crossing up to veranda, angrily*).

He's got his audience now. That's all he wants.

EUGENE. Mama, he's sick!

ELIZA (*on porch step*). Mr. Gant, if you feel so bad, why don't you act nice and go inside? The whole neighborhood's watching you.

GANT (*wildly sings*). "Old man Gant came home drunk—" (TARKINTON *joins him*.) "Old man Gant came home drunk —"

TARKINTON (*singing, waving his arms. Seated chair which* GENE *had taken from* GANT *and placed left of woodbox*). "Old man Gant came home—" (*His joy fades as he sees* ELIZA *glaring at him*.)

ELIZ. Were you drinking with him too, Mr. Tarkinton?

TARKINTON. Sev-eral of us were, Mrs. Gant, I regret to say.

ELIZA (*pulling* TARKINTON *to his feet*). I'll have Tim Laughran thrown. in jail for this.

TARKINTON. He started out so peaceable like—

ELIZA (*pushing him toward rear exit of veranda*). I've warned him for the last time.

TARKINTON. Just on beer!

ELIZA. *Get off my premises!*

(TARKINTON *exits.* GANT *groans.* DOCTOR *to yard right of* HELEN.)

HELEN. Dr. Maguire's here to give you something for your pain, Papa.

GANT. Doctors! Thieves and bloodsuckers! (DOCTOR *crosses to bag*.) "The paths of glory lead but to the grave."—Gray's Elegy. Only four cents a letter on any tombstone you choose, by the master carver— Any orders? (*He groans with pain*.) It's the devil's own pitchfork. Don't let them put me under the knife— promise me, daughter. Promise me! (HELEN *nods. With a giant effort,* GANT *pulls himself up*.) "Over the stones, rattle his bones! He's only a beggar that nobody owns."

DR. MAGUIRE. Good God, he's on his feet again.

EUGENE. Hugh, let's get him in the house.

GANT (*throwing off* HUGH *and* EUGENE). I see it! I see it! Do you see the Dark Man's shadow? There! There he stands— the Grim Reaper—as I always knew he would. So you've come at last to take the old man home? Jesus, have mercy on my soul! (GANT *falls to the ground. There is an agonized silence.* EUGENE, THE DOCTOR, *and* HUGH *rush to him*.)

ELIZA (*anxiously, above right pillar*). Dr. Maguire.

DR. MAGUIRE (*feels* GANT's *heart*). He's just passed out, Mrs. Gant. Men, let's carry him up!

(HUGH, WILL, MAGUIRE *and* EUGENE *lift the heavy body, quickly carry* GANT *inside.* HELEN *follows.* ELIZA, *saddened and miserable, starts to gather the coffee cups.* LAURA *picks up her suitcase and starts off.* ELIZA *turns, sees her*.)

ELIZA. Oh, Miss James. I was going to show you that room, wasn't I? (*Crosses, seizes* LAURA's *suitcase*.)

LAURA. Hmmmmmm?

ELIZA (*right center*). I think you'll enjoy it here. It's quiet and peaceful—oh, nobody pays any mind to Mr. Gant. I'll tell you: we don't have occurrences like this every day.

LAURA. Well, how much is it?

ELIZA. Twenty—fifteen dollars a week. Three meals a day, and the use of electricity and the bath. Do you want me to show it to you?

LAURA. No, I'm sure it will be all right.

ELIZA (*starting in, turns back*). That's in advance, that is.

LAURA (*opens her purse, takes out a roll of one-dollar bills, puts them one by one into* ELIZA's *outstretched hand*.) One, two, three—I always keep my money in one-dollar bills—it feels like it's more.

ELIZA (*almost cheerful again*). Oh, I know what you mean. (MR. FARREL *enters by the side door with his suitcase. He is hoping to sneak out.* ELIZA *sees him as the paying business continues. Crossing to left of* LAURA.) Mr. Farrel! Where are you going? Mr. Farrel, you've paid for a week in advance! (MR. FARREL *wordlessly gestures that it's all too much for him, exits*.) Well, they come and they go. And you're here now, isn't that nice?

LAURA. . . . Nine . . . ten. . . .

BEN (*enters from the other direction, hurriedly*). I heard about Father—how is he? (*Crosses to porch*.)

ELIZA. Drunk. Dr. Maguire's taking care of him now. Ben, this is Miss James —this is my son, Ben Gant.

BEN (*impressed by her looks, nods*). Miss James.

LAURA (*barely looking at* BEN, *nods*).

—fourteen, fifteen. There.

ELIZA (*puts the money in bosom of her dress*). Thank you, dear. Miss James is going to stay with us a while, we hope! I'll take you up, dear. You'll be cozy and comfortable here. (*They start inside.*) I'll show you the rest of the house later.

LAURA (*turning in doorway*). Nice to have met you, Mr. Gant. (ELIZA *and* LAURA *exit.*)

BEN (*imitating* LAURA's *disinterest, as he picks up cup of coffee*). Nice to have met you, Mr. Gant. (*Shrugs, sits woodbox and lights cigarette.*)

WILL (*enters from the house, still sweating. Left of* BEN). That father of yours. Do you know he kicked me? I don't want to tell you where. Why don't you watch out for him more, Ben? It's up to you boys, for your mother's sake—for Dixieland. I warned her about him—a born wanderer like he is, and a widower. But you can't advise women—not when it comes to love and sex. (*He starts off, stops up right.*) You might thank me for my help. No one else has.

BEN. Thank you, Uncle Will.

WILL. Bunch of ungrateful Gants. You're the only one of them who has any class. (*Exits up right.*)

EUGENE (*enters*). Did you hear about it, Ben?

BEN. There isn't a soul in town who hasn't.

EUGENE (*crossing into yard*). What's it all about? It doesn't make sense. Can you figure it out, Ben? Why does he do it?

BEN. How should I know? (*Drinks his coffee.*) Is Maguire almost through?

EUGENE (*hurt, not understanding* BEN's *preoccupation*). Ben, remember in the morning when we used to walk together and you were teaching me the paper route? We talked a lot then.

BEN. Listen to him! We're talking.

EUGENE (*crosses, sits step*). If he hates it so much here, why does he stay?

BEN. You stupid little fool, it's like being caught in a photograph. Your face is there, and no matter how hard you try, how are you going to step out of a photograph? (DOCTOR MAGUIRE *enters.*) Shut up now, will you. Hello, Doc. (*Rises, leaves coffee on woodbox.*)

DR. MAGUIRE (*entering, putting on cap*). Your sister sure can handle that old goat like a lamb! The funny thing though is that people like him. He's a good man, when sober.

BEN. Is he all right?

DR. MAGUIRE (*taking bag, crossing to yard down right*). He's going to be.

BEN (*crossing yard to left of down right*). Can I speak to you a minute about me? If you have a minute.

DR. MAGUIRE. Shoot, Ben.

BEN (*to* EUGENE, *who has seated himself right of door*). Haven't you got something else to do?

EUGENE. No.

(BEN *crosses to right of center table.*)

DR. MAGUIRE (*crossing to right of* BEN). What's the matter—you got pyorrhea of the toenails or is it something more private?

BEN. I'm tired of pushing daisies here. I want to push them somewhere else.

DR. MAGUIRE. What's that supposed to mean?

BEN. I suppose you've heard there's a war going on in Europe? I've decided to enlist in Canada.

EUGENE (*rises*). What do you want to do that for?

BEN (*to* EUGENE). You keep out of this.

DR. MAGUIRE. It is a good question, Ben. Do you want to save the world? This world?

BEN. In Christ's name, Maguire, you'll recommend me, won't you? You examined me just a couple of months ago.

DR. MAGUIRE (*crosses, puts down his bag on right pillar*). Well, let's see, for a war the requirements are somewhat different. Stick out your chest. (BEN *does so; the* DOCTOR *looks him over.*) Feet? Good arch, but pigeon-toed.

BEN. Since when do you need toes to shoot a gun?

DR. MAGUIRE (*crossing to him*). How're your teeth, son?

BEN. Aren't you overdoing it, Doc? (BEN *draws back his lips and shows two rows of hard white grinders. Unexpectedly* MAGUIRE *prods* BEN's *solar plexus with a strong yellow finger and* BEN's *distended chest collapses. He sinks to the veranda edge, coughing.*)

EUGENE. What did you do that for?

DR. MAGUIRE (*crosses for bag*). They'll have to save this world without you, Ben.

BEN (*rises, grabs the* DOCTOR). What do you mean?

DR. MAGUIRE. That's all. That's all.

BEN. You're saying I'm not all right?

DR. MAGUIRE (*turns to him*). Who said you weren't all right?

BEN (*left of down right*). Quit your kidding.

DR. MAGUIRE. What's the rush? We may get into this war ourselves before too long. Wait a bit. (*To* EUGENE.) Isn't that right, son? (*Turns for bag.*)

BEN (*grabs his right arm*). I want to know. Am I all right or not?

DR. MAGUIRE. Yes, Ben, you're all right. Why, you're one of the most all right people I know. (*Carefully, as he feels* BEN's *arm.*) You're a little run down, that's all. You need some meat on those bones. (BEN *breaks from him, moves away left.*) You can't exist with a cup of coffee in one hand and a cigarette in the other. Besides, the Altamont air is good for you. Stick around. Big breaths, Ben, big breaths. (*Picks up his bag.*)

BEN. Thanks. As a doctor, you're a fine first baseman.

DR. MAGUIRE. Take it easy. Try not to care too much. (*Exits down right.* BEN *puts out cigarette in coffee cup on center table.*)

EUGENE (*crosses to right of* BEN). He's right. You should try to look after yourself more, Ben. (*Tries to comfort* BEN. BEN *avoids his touch, lurches away.*)

BEN. He doesn't have any spirit about this war, that's all that's the matter with him. (*Recovers his coffee, drinks.* EUGENE *studies him.*)

EUGENE. I didn't know you wanted to get away from here so badly.

BEN (*looks over at* EUGENE, *puts down coffee on right pillar. Crosses to yard*). Come here, you little bum. (EUGENE *approaches close.*) My God, haven't you got a clean shirt? (*He gets out some money.*) Here, take this and go get that damn long hair cut off, and get some shoes that fit, for God's sake, you look like a lousy tramp—

EUGENE (*backing away left*). Ben, I can't keep taking money from you.

BEN. What else have you got me for? (*The brothers roughhouse playfully with the money,* EUGENE *giggling. Then with sudden intense ferocity* BEN *seizes* EUGENE's *arms, shakes him.*) You listen to me. You go to college, understand? Don't settle for anyone or anything—

learn your lesson from me! I'm a hack on a hick paper—I'll never be anything else. You can be. Get money out of them, any way you can! Beg it, take it, steal it, but get it from them somehow. Get it and get away from them. To hell with them all! (BEN *coughs.* EUGENE *tries to help him.* BEN *escapes, sits tiredly on the veranda's edge.* EUGENE *disconsolately sinks into nearby chair left of center table.*) Neither Luke, nor Stevie, nor I made it. But you can, Gene. I let her hold on and hold on until it was too late. Don't let that happen to you. And Gene, don't try to please everyone—please yourself. (BEN *studies* EUGENE, *realizes his confusion and depression. Then, noticing* LAURA's *hat which she has left on the yard table, points to it.*) Where's she from?

EUGENE (*follows* BEN's *gaze to* LAURA's *hat, picks it up, sniffs it*). I don't know. I don't even know her name.

BEN. Miss James. I'll have to announce her arrival in my "society" column. (*Takes hat from* EUGENE, *admires it.*) The firm young line of spring—budding, tender, virginal. "Like something swift, with wings, which hovers in a wood—among the feathery trees, suspected, but uncaught, unseen." Exquisite. (*Returns hat to table, rises.*) Want to walk downtown with me? I'll buy you a cup of mocha.

EUGENE. Maybe I ought to stay here.

BEN (*ruffling* EUGENE's *hair. Crossing for coffee*). With her around I don't blame you. I dream of elegant women myself, all the time.

EUGENE (*rising*). You do? But, Ben, if you dream of elegant women, how is it, well—

BEN (*on porch*). Mrs. Pert? Fatty's a happy woman—there's no pain in her she feels she has to unload onto someone else. Besides she's as adorable as a duck; don't you think so?

EUGENE. I guess you're right. I like her —myself—sure.

BEN (*replaces coffee cup on tray, crosses to yard down right*). Some day you'll find out what it means. I've got to get back to work.

EUGENE (*front of left pillar*). Ben, I'm glad they won't take you in Canada.

BEN (*with that upward glance*). Listen to him! I was crazy to think of going. I have to bring you up first, don't I? (BEN *exits.*)

MISS BROWN (*dressed for a stroll, carrying a parasol, she enters from the house*). Gene! You haven't even said hello to me today.

EUGENE. Hello, Miss Brown.

MISS BROWN (*crosses to yard down right*). My, everything's quiet again. Lovely warm day, isn't it? (MISS BROWN *sings and dances sensuously for* EUGENE.)*
"Pony boy, pony boy,
Won't you be my pony boy?
Don't say no, can't we go
Right across the plains?"
(MISS BROWN *approaches* EUGENE, *he backs away from her, stumbling against the table. She starts out through rear veranda.*)
"Marry me, carry me—
Far away with you!
Giddy-ap, giddy-ap, giddy-ap. Oh!
My pony boy!"
(MISS BROWN *exits.* EUGENE *sits in the yard, takes off one shoe and rubs his aching toes.* LAURA *enters, picks up her hat, sees* EUGENE. EUGENE *hides his shoeless foot.* MISS BROWN'S VOICE *from offstage, receding in distance.*)
"Pony boy, pony boy
Mmmm, mmm, mmm—Mmmm, mmm, mmm,
Marry me, carry me
Giddy-ap, giddy-ap, giddy-ap. Oh!
My pony boy."
(*At the door,* LAURA *looks again at* EUGENE, *smiles, exits.*)

CURTAIN

SCENE Two

SCENE: *The same; that evening. The night is sensuous, warm. A light storm is threatening. Long, swaying tree shadows project themselves on the house. Seated on the side veranda are* JAKE, MRS. CLATT, FLORRY, MISS BROWN, *and* MRS. SNOWDEN. MRS. PERT *is seated in her rocker,* BEN *left of her. They are drinking beer.* MRS. PERT *measures the socks she is knitting against* BEN's *shoe.* JAKE CLATT *softly plays the ukulele and sings.* EUGENE *is*

---

* "My Pony Boy" used by special permission of copyright owner, Jerry Vogel Music Co., Inc., New York 36, N. Y.
Far away with you

sitting on the side door steps, lonely, yearning. Glasses of lemonade have replaced the noontime coffee cups. And a phonograph replaces the flower tray on the up right center table on the porch.

JAKE (*singing "K-K-K-Katy"*).* "K-K-K-aty, K-K-Katy," etc. (*As* JAKE *finishes,* FLORRY *gently applauds.* JAKE *starts softly strumming something else.*)

MRS. PERT (*to* BEN, *quietly*). I know you talked to the doctor today. What did he say? Tell Fatty.

BEN. I'm out before I'm in. Oh, I know you're pleased, but you don't know how it feels to be the weakling. All the other members of this family—they're steers, mountain goats, eagles. Except Father, lately—unless he's drunk. Do you know, though, I still think of him as I thought of him as a little boy—a Titan! The house on Woodson Street that he built for Mama with his own hands, the great armloads of food he carried home—the giant fires he used to build. The women he loved at Madame Elizabeth's. Two and three a night, I heard.

MRS. PERT. It's nice for parents to have their children think of them as they were young. (*As* BEN *chuckles*) I mean, that's the way I'd like my children to think of me. Oh, you know what I mean.

BEN (*laughs with his typical glance upward*). Listen to her!

MRS. PERT. Ben, who are you always talking to, like that? (*Imitates* BEN *looking up over his shoulder.*)

BEN. Who, him? (*She nods.*) That's Grover, my twin. It was a habit I got into, while he was still alive.

MRS. PERT. I wish you'd known me when I was young. I was some different.

BEN. I bet you weren't half as nice and warm and round as you are now.

MRS. PERT. Ben, don't ever let your mother hear you say those things. What could she think?

BEN. Who cares what she thinks?

MRS. PERT. Dear, I only hope when the right girl comes along you won't be sorry for the affection you've lavished on me.

---

* "K-K-K-Katy," words and music by Geoffrey O'Hara © 1918, copyright renewal 1945 Leo Feist, Inc. Used by permission of the copyright owner solely for the purpose of printing in this edition. CAUTION: Permission to include this song in any performance of this play must be obtained from Leo Feist, Inc., 1540 Broadway, New York 36, N. Y.

BEN. I don't want the "right girl." Like some more beer? I've got another bottle.

MRS. PERT. Love some more, honey.

(BEN *rises, searches under the yard table for the bottle he has hidden, realizes it's not there, suspiciously looks at* EUGENE. EUGENE *innocently gestures, then reaches behind him and tosses the beer bottle to* BEN. BEN *and* FATTY *laugh.* BEN *returns with the beer to* FATTY *as* LAURA *enters from the house.*)

JAKE (*rising expectantly*). Good evening, Miss James.

LAURA. Good evening.

JAKE. Won't you sit down? (*Indicates woodbox where he has been sitting.*)

MRS. CLATT (*as* LAURA *seems about to choose a chair*). That's Mr. Farrel's. Yours is back there!

JAKE (*loudly. Moves up left of her*). Mr. Farrel has left, Mother.

MRS. CLATT. What?

JAKE. Never mind. (*To* LAURA.) No sense in being formal. Won't you sing with me, Miss James?

LAURA. I love music, but I have no talent for it. (*Moves toward rear of veranda, away from the others.* JAKE *places uke on woodbox.*)

FLORRY (*to* JAKE). I love to sing.

(JAKE *ignores* FLORRY, *follows after* LAURA, FLORRY *tugging at* JAKE's *coat.*)

MRS. SNOWDEN (*to* JAKE *as he passes*). Do you know Indiana Lullaby? It's a lovely song.

(JAKE *and* LAURA *exit.*)

BEN. I'm comfortable when I'm with you, Fatty.

MRS. PERT. That's good, so'm I.

BEN. People don't understand. Jelly roll isn't everything, is it?

MRS. PERT. Ben Gant, what kind of a vulgar phrase is that?

BEN. It's a Stumptown word. I used to deliver papers there. Sometimes those negra women don't have money to pay their bill, so they pay you in jelly roll.

MRS. PERT. Ben—your little brother's right over there listening!

BEN (*glances toward* EUGENE). Gene knows all about jelly roll, don't you? Where do you think he's been all his life —in Mama's front parlor?

EUGENE. Oh, come on, Ben. (*Embarrassed laugh.*)

BEN (*laughs*). There's another word I remember in the eighth grade. We had a thin, anxious-looking teacher. The boys had a poem about her. (*Quotes.*)
"Old Miss Groody
Has good toody."

MRS. PERT. Ben, stop it! (*They both laugh.* EUGENE *joins in.* LAURA *has managed to lose* JAKE, *has strolled around the back of the house. She enters to* EUGENE *from the side door.*)

LAURA. Good evening.

EUGENE. What!

LAURA. I said good evening.

EUGENE (*flustered*). Goodyado. (*Rises, moves down left of her.*)

LAURA. I beg your pardon?

EUGENE. I mean—I meant to say good evening, how do you do?

LAURA. Goodyado! I like that much better. Goodyado! (*They shake hands,* LAURA *reacting to* EUGENE's *giant grip.* EUGENE *sits left on unit.*) Don't you think that's funny?

EUGENE. It's about as funny as most things I do.

LAURA. May I sit down?

EUGENE (*leaping up*). Please.

LAURA (*as she sits*). I'm Laura James.

EUGENE. I know. My name's Eugene Gant.

LAURA. You know, I've seen you before.

EUGENE. Yes, earlier this afternoon.

LAURA. I mean before that. I saw you throw those advertising cards in the gutter.

EUGENE. You did?

LAURA. I was coming from the station. You know where the train crosses the street? You were just standing there staring at it. I walked right by you and smiled at you. I never got such a snub before in my whole life. My, you must be crazy about trains.

EUGENE (*sits left of her*). You stood right beside me? (BEN *plays a record on the phonograph.*) Where are you from?

LAURA. Richmond, Virginia.

EUGENE. Richmond! That's a big city, isn't it?

LAURA. It's pretty big.

EUGENE. How many people?

LAURA. Oh, about a hundred and twenty thousand, I'd say.

EUGENE. Are there a lot of pretty parks and boulevards?

LAURA. Oh, yes—

EUGENE. And fine tall buildings, with elevators?

LAURA. Yes, it's quite a metropolis.

EUGENE. Theatres and things like that?

LAURA. A lot of good shows come to Richmond. Are you interested in shows?

EUGENE. You have a big library. Did you know it has over a hundred thousand books in it?

LAURA. No, I didn't know that.

EUGENE. Well, it does. I read that somewhere. It would take a long time to read a hundred thousand books, wouldn't it?

LAURA. Yes, it would.

EUGENE. I figure about twenty years. How many books do they let you take out at one time?

LAURA. I really don't know.

EUGENE. They only let you take out two here!

LAURA. That's too bad.

EUGENE. You have some great colleges in Virginia. Did you know that William and Mary is the second oldest college in the country?

LAURA. Is it? What's the oldest?

EUGENE. Harvard! I'd like to study there! First Chapel Hill. That's our state university. Then Harvard. I'd like to study all over the world, learn all its languages. I love words, don't you?

LAURA. Yes; yes, I do.

EUGENE. Are you laughing at me?

LAURA. Of course not.

EUGENE. You are smiling a lot!

LAURA. I'm smiling because I'm enjoying myself. I like talking to you.

EUGENE. I like talking to you, too. I always talk better with older people.

LAURA. Oh!

EUGENE. They know so much more.

LAURA. Like me?

EUGENE. Yes. You're very interesting.

LAURA. Am I?

EUGENE. Oh yes! You're very interesting!

(JACK CLATT *approaches,* FLORRY MANGLE *hovering anxiously on the veranda.*)

JAKE. Miss James?

LAURA. Yes, Mr. Platt?

JAKE. Clatt.

LAURA. Clatt.

JAKE. Jake Clatt! It's a lovely evening. Would you like to take a stroll?

LAURA. It feels to me like it's going to rain.

JAKE (*looking at the sky*). Oh, I don't know.

EUGENE (*rising, moving in between* LAURA *and* JAKE). It's going to rain, all right.

JAKE. Oh, I wouldn't be so sure!

LAURA. Perhaps some other time, Mr. Clatt.

JAKE. Certainly. Good night, Miss James. Good night, sonny.

(EUGENE *glares after* JAKE, *who returns to the veranda under* FLORRY's *jealous stare. The other boarders have disappeared.* JAKE *and* FLORRY *exit,* FLORRY *hugging* JAKE's *ukulele in her arms. Only* FATTY *and* BEN *still sit on the steps. A train whistle moans mournfully in the distance.* EUGENE *cocks an ear, listens.*)

LAURA. You do like trains, don't you?

EUGENE. Mama took us on one to St. Louis to the Fair, when I was only five. Have you ever touched one?

LAURA. What?

EUGENE. A locomotive. Have you put your hand on one? You have to feel things to fully understand them.

LAURA. Aren't they rather hot?

EUGENE. Even a cold one, standing in a station yard. You know what you feel? You feel the shining steel rails under it— and the rails send a message right into your hand—a message of all the mountains that engine ever passed—all the flowing rivers, the forests, the towns, all the houses, the people, the washlines flapping in the fresh cool breeze—the beauty of the people in the way they live and the way they work—a farmer waving from his field, a kid from the school yard —the faraway places it roars through at night, places you don't even know, can hardly imagine. Do you believe it? You feel the rhythm of a whole life, a whole country clicking through your hand.

LAURA (*impressed*). I'm not sure we all would. I believe *you* do.

(*There is a moment while* LAURA *looks at* EUGENE. BEN *moves up to the veranda and the phonograph plays another record.* EUGENE *and* LAURA *speak simultaneously.*)

EUGENE. How long do you plan to stay here—?

LAURA. How old are you, Gene?

EUGENE. I'm sorry—please. (*Draws a chair close to* LAURA, *straddles it, facing her.*)

LAURA. No, you.

EUGENE. How long do you plan to stay here, Miss James?

LAURA. My name is Laura. I wish you'd call me that.

EUGENE. Laura. It's a lovely name. Do you know what it means?

LAURA. No.

EUGENE. I read a book once on the meaning of names. Laura is the laurel. The Greek symbol of victory.

LAURA. Victory. Maybe some day I'll live up to that! (*After a second*) What does Eugene mean?

EUGENE. Oh, I forget.

LAURA. *You, forget?*

EUGENE. It means "well born."

LAURA. How old are you?

EUGENE. Why?

LAURA. I'm always curious about people's ages.

EUGENE. So am I. How old are you?

LAURA. I'm twenty-one. You?

EUGENE. Nineteen. Will you be staying here long?

LAURA. I don't know exactly.

EUGENE. You're only twenty-one?

LAURA. How old did you think I was?

EUGENE. Oh, about that. About twenty-one, I'd say. That's not old at all!

LAURA (*laughs*). I don't feel it is!

EUGENE. I was afraid you might think I was too young for you to waste time with like this!

LAURA. I don't think nineteen is young at all!

EUGENE. It isn't, really, is it?

LAURA (*rises*). Gene, if we keep rushing together like this, we're going to have a collision.

(LAURA *moves away from* EUGENE. *He follows her. They sit together on the side steps, reaching with whispers toward each other. The turntable revolves, removing* EUGENE's *room and revealing* GANT's *room. As it does so:*)

FATTY. Ben, what's your full name?

BEN. Benjamin Harrison Gant. Why?

FATTY. I though Ben was short for benign.

BEN. Benign! Listen to her!

(*They laugh. The lights come up in* GANT's *bedroom.* ELIZA, *carrying a pitcher and a glass, enters.* GANT *is in bed, turned away from her.*)

GANT. Helen?

ELIZA (*bitterly*). No, it's not Helen, Mr. Gant. (*She pours a glass of water.*)

GANT (*without turning*). If that's water, take it away. (*She leaves glass and pitcher on dresser.*)

ELIZA. Why aren't you asleep? Do you have any pain?

GANT. None but the everyday pain of thinking. You wouldn't know what that is.

ELIZA. I wouldn't know? (*She starts picking up* GANT's *strewn socks and shoes.*)

GANT. How could you? You're always so busy puttering.

ELIZA. All the work I do around here, and you call it puttering?

GANT. Some people are doers, some are thinkers.

ELIZA (*neatly rearranging his vest on the back of the chair*). Somebody has to *do*, Mr. Gant. Somebody has to. Oh! I know you look on yourself as some kind of artist fella—but personally, a man who has to be brought maudlin through the streets—screaming curses—if you call that artistic!

GANT. The hell hound is at it again. Shut up, woman!

ELIZA. Mr. Gant, I came in here to see if there was something I could do for you. Only pity in my heart. Now will you please turn over and look at me when I talk to you? You know I can't stand being turned away from!

GANT. You're a bloody monster, you would drink my heart's blood!

ELIZA. You don't mean that—we've come this far together; I guess we can continue to the end. (*Picks up socks she has placed on bed.*) You know I was thinking only this morning about that first day we met. Do you realize it was thirty-one years ago, come July?

GANT (*groaning*). Merciful God, thirty-one long miserable years!

ELIZA. I can remember like it was yesterday. I'd just come down from Cousin Sally's and I passed by your shop and there you were. I'll vow you looked as big as one of your tombstones—and as dusty—with a wild and dangerous look in your eye. You were romantic in those days—like the fellow says, a regular courtin' fool—"Miss Pentland," you said, "you have come into this hot and grubby shop like a cooling summer shower—like a cooling summer shower." That's just what you said!

GANT. And you've been a wet blanket ever since.

ELIZA. I forgive you your little jokes, Mr. Gant. I forgive your little jokes. (*She sits chair. Starts to fold his nightgown.*)

GANT. Do you? (*Slowly turns towards her and looks at her finally.*) Do you ever forgive me, Eliza? If I could make you understand something. I was such a strong man. I was dozing just now, dreaming of the past. The far past. The people and the place I came from. Those great barns of Pennsylvania. The order, the thrift, the plenty. It all started out so right, there. There I was a man who set out to get order and position in life. And what have I come to? Only rioting and confusion, searching and wandering. There was so much before, so much. Now it's all closing in. My God, Eliza, where has it all gone? Why am I here, now, at the rag end of my life? The years are all blotted and blurred—my youth a red waste —I've gotten old, an old man. But why here? Why here?

ELIZA. You belong here, Mr. Gant, that's why! You belong here. (*She touches his hand.*)

GANT (*throws away her hand*). And as I get weaker and weaker, you get stronger and stronger!

ELIZA (*rise, puts folded nightgown in dresser*). Pshaw! If you feel that way, it's because you have no position in life. If you'd ever listened to me once, things would have been different. You didn't believe me, did you, when I told you that little, old marble shop of yours would be worth a fortune some day? Will and I happened to be downtown this morning— (GANT *groans. Picks up his robe from bed.*)—and old Mr. Beecham from the bank stopped us on the street and he said, "Mrs. Gant, the bank is looking for a site to build a big new office building, and do you know the one we have our eye on?" And I said, "No." "We have our eye on Mr. Gant's shop, and we're willing to pay twenty thousand dollars for it!" Now what do you think of that? (*She sits chair, starts to mend robe.*)

GANT. And you came in here with only pity in your heart!

ELIZA. Well, I'll tell you what, twenty thousand dollars is a lot of money! Like the fellow says, "It ain't hay!"

GANT. And my angel, my Carrara angel? You were going to sell her too?

ELIZA. The angel, the angel, the angel! I'm so tired of hearing about that angel!

GANT. You always have been. Money dribbled from your honeyed lips. But never a word about my angel. I've started twenty pieces of marble trying to capture her. But my life's work doesn't interest you.

ELIZA. If you haven't been able to do it in all these years, don't you think your gift as a stone cutter may be limited?

GANT. Yes, Mrs. Gant, it may be limited. It may be limited.

ELIZA. Then why don't you sell the shop? We can pay off the mortgage at Dixieland and then just set back big as you please and live off the income from the boarders the rest of our lives!

GANT (*furiously, he all but leaps from the bed*). Oh, holy hell; Wow-ee! The boarders! That parade of incognito pimps and prostitutes, calling themselves penniless dancing masters, pining widows, part-time teachers and God knows what all! Woman, have mercy! That shop is my last refuge on earth. I beg you—let me die in peace! You won't have long to wait. You can do what you please with it after I'm gone. But give me a little comfort now. *And leave me my work!* At least my first wife understood what it meant to me. (*He sentimentally seeks the plump pillow.*) Cynthia, Cynthia . . .

ELIZA (*coldly*). You promised me you would never mention her name to me again. (*There is a long silence.* ELIZA *bites the sewing thread, rises and tosses robe on bed.*) Mr. Gant, I guess I never will understand you. I guess that's just the way it is. Good night. Try to get some sleep. (*She tucks the bed clothes about him.*) I reckon it's like the fellow says, some people never get to understand each other—not in this life. (*Exits and stands outside* GANT's *door, trying to pull herself together.*)

GANT (*moans*). Oh-h-h, I curse the day I was given life by that blood-thirsty monster up above. Oh-h-h, Jesus! I beg of you. I know I've been bad. Forgive me. Have mercy and pity upon me. Give me another chance in Jesus' name. . . . Oh-h-h!

(*The turntable removes* GANT's *room, replacing it with* EUGENE's *room. Lights come up on the veranda.* LAURA *and* EUGENE *still sit on the side steps.* FATTY *and* BEN, *seated as earlier, are softly laughing.* ELIZA, *bitterly warped by her scene with* GANT, *enters. She starts gathering up the boarders' lemonade glasses.*)

MRS. PERT (*a little giddy*). Why, if it

isn't Mrs. Gant! Why don't you sit down and join us for a while?

ELIZA (*her sweeping glance takes in the beer glasses*). I've told you before, Mrs. Pert, I don't tolerate drinking at Dixieland!

BEN. Oh, Mama, for God's sake—

ELIZA. You two can be heard all over the house with your carrying on.

BEN. Carrying on—listen to her!

ELIZA (*angrily turns off phonograph*). You're keeping the boarders awake.

BEN. They just went in!

ELIZA. As I came past your door just now, Mrs. Pert, there was a light under it. If you're going to spend all night out here, there's no sense in wasting electricity.

BEN. The Lord said, "Let there be light," even if it's only 40 watts.

ELIZA. Don't you get on your high horse with me, Ben Gant. You're not the one who has to pay the bills! If you did, you'd laugh out of the other side of your mouth. I don't like any such talk. You've squandered every penny you've ever earned because you've never known the value of a dollar!

BEN. The value of a dollar! (*Rises, goes into hall to get his jacket.*) Oh what the hell's the use of it, anyway? Come on, Fatty, let's go for a stroll.

FATTY (*rises. Crosses to yard right of right pillar*). Whatever you say, Ben, old Fatty's willing.

ELIZA (*attacking FATTY; on step left of her*). I don't want any butt-ins from you, do you understand? You're just a paying boarder here. That's all. You're not a member of my family, and never will be, no matter what low methods you try!

EUGENE (*leaving LAURA, miserably*). Mama, please.

ELIZA (*crosses to EUGENE*). I'm only trying to keep decency and order here, and this is the thanks I get! You should all get down on your knees and be grateful to me!

BEN (*coming out of hall, slamming the screen door*). What am I supposed to be grateful for? For what?

FATTY (*trying to stop it*). Ben, Ben, come on.

BEN (*on step right of ELIZA*). For selling the house that Papa built with his own hands and moving us into this drafty barn where we share our roof, our food, our pleasures, our privacy so that you

can be Queen Bee? Is that what I'm supposed to be grateful for?

ELIZA (*picks up bottle and glasses from left of left pillar*). It's that vile liquor that's talking!

EUGENE. Let's stop it! For God's sake, let's stop it! Mama, go to bed, please. Ben— (*Sees that LAURA has exited into the house. He frantically looks after her.*)

BEN. Look at your kid there! You've had him out on the streets since he was eight years old—collecting bottles, selling papers —anything that would bring in a penny.

ELIZA. Gene is old enough to earn his keep!

BEN. Then he's old enough for you to let go of him! But no, you'd rather hang on to him like a piece of property! Maybe he'll grow in value, you can turn a quick trade on him, make a profit on him. He isn't a son, he's an investment! You're so penny-mad that— (*Shifting the bottles and glasses into one hand, ELIZA slaps BEN. There is a long silence. They stare at each other.*) Come on, Fatty. (*BEN exits, past FATTY, down the street.*)

FATTY. He didn't mean it, Mrs. Gant. (*She follows BEN.*) Ben? Ben, wait for Fatty! (*Exits.*)

EUGENE (*quietly, miserably*). Mama. Mama. Mama!

ELIZA. Well, she put him up to it! He never used to talk to me like that. You stood right there and saw it. Now I'll just ask you: was it my fault? Well, was it?

EUGENE (*looks after LAURA*). Mama, Mama, in God's name go to bed, won't you? Just go to bed and forget about it, won't you?

ELIZA (*crossing porch, placing bottles, glasses on tray*). All of you. Every single one of you. Your father, then Ben, now you—you all blame me. And not one of you has any idea, any idea—you don't know what I've had to put up with all these years.

EUGENE. Oh Mama, stop! Please stop!

ELIZA (*sinking onto the steps left of right pillar*). I've done the best I could. I've done the best I could. Your father's never given me a moment's peace. Nobody knows what I've been through with him. Nobody knows, child, nobody knows.

EUGENE (*sits beside her*). I know, Mama. I do know. Forget about it! It's all right.

ELIZA. You just can't realize. You don't

know what a day like this does to me. Ben and I used to be so close—especially after little Grover died. I don't think a mother and son were ever closer. You don't remember when he was a youngster, the little notes he was always writing me. I'd find them slipped under my door, when he got up early to go on his paper route. . . . "Good morning, Mama!" . . . "Have a nice day, Mama." We were so close . . .

EUGENE (*gently*). It's late. You're tired.

ELIZA (*managing to pull herself together*). Well, like the fellow says, it's no use crying over *that* spilt milk. I have all those napkins and towels to iron for tomorrow.

EUGENE (*rises, looking toward* LAURA's *room*). The boarders can get along without new napkins tomorrow. Mama, why don't you get some sleep?

ELIZA (*rises*). Well, I tell you what: I'm not going to spend my life slaving away here for a bunch of boarders. They needn't think it. I'm going to sit back and take things as easy as any of them. One of these days you may just find us Gants living in a big house in Doak Park. I've got the lot—the best lot out there. I made the trade with old Mr. Doak himself the other day. What about that? (*She laughs.*) He said, "Mrs. Gant, I can't trust any of my agents with you. If I'm to make anything on this deal, I've got to look out. You're the sharpest trader in this town!" "Why, pshaw, Mr. Doak," I said (I never let on I believed him or anything), "all I want is a fair return on my investment. I believe in everyone making his profit and giving the other fellow a chance. Keep the ball a-rolling," I said, laughing as big as you please! (*She laughs again in recollection.*) "You're the sharpest trader in this town." That's exactly his words. Oh, dear— (EUGENE *joins her laughter.*) Well—I'd better get at those napkins. Are you coming in, child?

EUGENE (*rises, looks toward* LAURA's *room*). In a little while.

ELIZA. Don't forget to turn off the sign. Good night, son. (EUGENE *returns to* ELIZA. *She kisses him.*) Get a *good* night's sleep, boy. You mustn't neglect your health. (*She starts in.*)

EUGENE. Don't work too late. (*Starts toward the side door.*)

ELIZA. Gene, you know where Sunset Terrace runs up the hill? At the top of the rise? Right above Dick Webster's place. That's my lot. You know where I mean, don't you?

EUGENE. Yes, Mama.

ELIZA. And that's where we'll build— right on the very top. I tell you what, though, in another five years that lot'll bring twice the value. You mark my words!

EUGENE. Yes, Mama. Now, for God's sake, go and finish your work so you can get to sleep!

ELIZA. No sir, they needn't think I'm going to slave away all my life. I've got plans, same as the next fellow! You'll see. (*Offstage, the church chimes start to sound the midnight hour.*) Well, good night, son.

EUGENE. Good night, Mama. . . . (ELIZA *exits.* EUGENE *calls with desperate softness.*) Laura—Laura! (*Gives up, turns away.* LAURA *enters through the side door.* EUGENE *turns, sees her.*) Did you hear all that? I'm sorry, Laura.

LAURA. What's there to be sorry about?

EUGENE. Would you like to take a walk?

LAURA. It's a lovely evening.

EUGENE. It might rain.

LAURA. I love the rain.

(EUGENE *and* LAURA *hold out their hands to each other.* EUGENE *approaches her, takes her hand. They go off together D. L. For a moment the stage is silent.* ELIZA *enters with an envelope in her hand.*)

ELIZA. See, looky here—I made a map of it. Sunset Terrace goes— (*She looks around.*) Gene? Eugene? (*She looks up towards* EUGENE's *room.*) Gene, I asked you to turn out the sign! That boy. I don't know what I'm going to do with him. (*Goes into the hall, turns out the sign and stands for a moment. Offstage, a passerby is whistling "Genevieve."* ELIZA *comes down to the edge of the veranda and looks out into the night in the direction taken by* BEN *and* FATTY.) Ben? Ben?

SLOW CURTAIN

ACT TWO

SCENE ONE

SCENE: GANT's *marble yard and shop, a week later. Under a high wide shed is the sign:* W. O. GANT—STONE CARVER. *The shed is on a back street, behind the town square. In the distance can be seen the outline of Dixieland. Inside the shed, are slabs of marble and granite and some finished monuments—an urn, a couchant lamb and several angels. The largest and most prominent monument is a delicately carved angel of a lustrous white Carrara marble, with an especially beautiful smiling countenance. There is a cutting area down right, protected from the sun by a shade, where* EUGENE, *wearing one of his father's aprons, is discovered operating a pedalled emery wheel. At the other side of the shed is an office with a grimy desk, a telephone, and a curtain into another room beyond. A sidewalk runs between the shed and a picket fence upstage. Near the office is a stone seat, bearing the inscription, "Rest here in peace."* ELIZA *enters from the street right. The prim shabbiness of her dress is in contrast to her energetic mood and walk.*

ELIZA (*crosses to office, calls inside*). Mr. Gant! Mr. Gant!

EUGENE (*stops wheel, calls*). Papa's not here now, Mama.

ELIZA (*approaches* EUGENE *just as he accidentally blows some marble dust in her face*). Where is he? Gene, you know I can't stand that marble dust—will you step out here where I can talk to you? Besides, I can't stand not to see the face I'm talking to. My goodness, spruce up, boy—how many times do I have to tell you? Shoulders back—like you *are* somebody. And smile, look pleasant. (EUGENE *gives that idiotic grin.* ELIZA *indicates Laughran is off up left.*) O pshaw! I hope your father's not over at you-know-where again.

EUGENE. He went to buy a newspaper for the obituaries.

ELIZA. How enterprising of him! But he won't follow up on it. Oh no, he says it's ghoulish to contact the bereaved ones right off. I declare, tombstones are no business anyway, any more—in this day and age people die too slowly. (EUGENE *crosses with stencil letter and chalk to left of center table.* ELIZA *sinks onto stone seat, leans back; for a brief instant seems actually to rest.*) I tell you what, this feels good. I wish I had as much time as some folks and could sit outside and enjoy the air. (*Notices* EUGENE *looking at her dress,*

as he works lettering a marble slab.) What are you looking at? I don't have a rent, do I?

EUGENE. I was just noticing you have on your dealing and bargaining costume again.

ELIZA. Eugene Gant, whatever do you mean by that? Don't I look all right? Heaven knows, I always try to look neatly respectable.

EUGENE (*crosses to right unit for chalk*). Come on, Mama.

ELIZA. What! I declare! I might have a better dress than this, but law's sake, there's some places it don't pay to advertise it! Oh, Gene, you're smart, smart, I tell you! You've got a future ahead of you, child.

EUGENE (*crossing to left of center table*). Mama, what kind of a future have I got if I can't get an education?

ELIZA. Pshaw, boy, you'll get your education if my plans work out! I'll tell you what, though—in the meantime, it wouldn't hurt you to work in Uncle Will's office, would it?

EUGENE (*working*). I don't know anything about real estate, Mama.

ELIZA. What do you have to know? Buying and selling is an instinct, and you've got it. You've got my eye for looking and seeing and remembering, and that's what's important. Why there isn't a vital statistic about a soul in Altamont I don't carry right in my head. What they make, what they owe—what they're hiding, what they show! (GENE *crosses to right unit for stencil letter and then back to Center table. She laughs, enjoying her cleverness.*) You see, Eugene, I'm a poet, too—"a poet and I don't know it, but my feet show it—they're longfellows!" (*She leans back, chuckles.*) Oh dear, I can't get a smile out of you this morning. You've been so strange all this last week. (*Rises, slaps him on his back.*) Gene, stand with your shoulders back. If you go humped over, you'll get lung trouble sure as you're born. (*Moves upstage, looks toward the town center where she presumes* GANT *is.*) That's one thing about your papa: he always carried himself straight as a rod. Of course, he's not as straight now as he used to be— Gene, *what* in the world are you standing on one foot and then the other for? Do you have to go to the bathroom?

EUGENE. Mama! Asking me that at my age!

ELIZA. Then why are you fidgeting? It's not often we have a nice chance to chat like this.

EUGENE. Papa's paying me thirty cents an hour!

ELIZA. Paying you? How did you manage that?

EUGENE. I told him I needed the money.

ELIZA. For heaven's sake, what for? You've got your room and board.

EUGENE. Don't you think I need new clothes for one thing?

ELIZA. Pshaw! The way you're still growing? It doesn't pay. (EUGENE *returns to work. She purses her lips, looks at him significantly.*) Has my baby gone and got himself a girl?

EUGENE (*exasperated, sits on table*). What of it? What if it were true? Haven't I as much right as anyone?

ELIZA. Pshaw! You're too young to think of girls, especially that Miss James. She's practically a mature woman compared to you. I don't think you realize how young you are, just because you're tall and read a lot of books. (*Sounds of car off right.* ELIZA *looks off.*) Pshaw! That's your Uncle Will come for me. Say, how long does it take your father to buy a newspaper, anyway?

EUGENE. He said he'd be right back. Is it something important?

ELIZA (*crosses for purse and stole she has left on bench*). Oh, I've got plans, Gene, for him, plans for all of us. Well, tell him I'll be back. Second thought, don't tell him, I'll just catch him. I want you to be here, too. Work hard, child!

(ELIZA *exits, the car leaves.* EUGENE *approaches the Carrara angel, touches the draped folds over her breast.* GANT *enters upper left, watches smiling. He has had a few beers, but he is not drunk.* EUGENE *becomes aware of* GANT's *presence, starts guiltily. Crosses down right.*)

GANT (*crossing to angel*). I've done that myself many a time, son. Many a time. Well, what did your mother have to say?

EUGENE. Did you see her?

GANT (*crossing to unit left for apron*). I've been sitting over at Laughran's waiting for her to leave. What a long-winded bag!

EUGENE. You promised the doctor you wouldn't go to Laughran's.

GANT (*putting on his apron*). What difference does it make? A couple of beers won't hurt what I've got. Was that Will Pentland she went off with?

EUGENE. Yes.

GANT (*upper left center*). Aha! And she said she'd be back?

EUGENE. Yes.

GANT. I have a mind what she's up to. She'll be back with freshly drawn-up papers tucked in her bosom. Yes, when you touch the breast of Miss Eliza, you feel the sharp crackle of bills of sale— (*Crosses to angel.*) not like the bosom of this angel. She begins to look better after a bath, doesn't she? I've been neglecting her lately. My, how she gleams!

EUGENE (*sits below angel*). Papa, you were young when you got married, weren't you?

GANT. What?

EUGENE. When did you get married?

GANT (*crossing to left of center table to work*). It was thirty-one bitter years ago when your mother first came wriggling around that corner at me like a snake on her belly—

EUGENE. I don't mean Mama. How old were you when you were first married? To Cynthia?

GANT. By God, you better not let your mother hear you say that name!

EUGENE. I want to know—how old were you?

GANT (*crossing down right center*). Well, I must have been twenty-eight. Ah, Cynthia, Cynthia!

EUGENE. You loved her, didn't you, Papa?

GANT. She had a real glowing beauty. Sweet, noble, proud, and yet soft, soft— she died in her bloom.

EUGENE. She was older than you, wasn't she?

GANT. Yes. Ten years.

EUGENE. Ten years! But it didn't make any difference, did it?

GANT (*confidingly*). She was a skinny, mean, tubercular old hag who nearly drove me out of my mind! (*Crosses to center table to work.*)

EUGENE (*shocked*). Then why do you talk about her the way you do? To Mama?

GANT. Because I'm a bastard, Gene. I'm a bastard! (LAURA *enters upper right carrying a picnic basket, her mood some-*

what restless.) Say, isn't this a pretty little somebody looking for you?

EUGENE (*crosses to her*). Laura!

LAURA (*left of* GANT). Hello, Mr. Gant.

GANT. Hello!

LAURA (*crossing to right of angel*). Hello, Gene. So this is your shop?

GANT (*a step toward her*). This is a real pleasure. It's not often I see *smiling* people around here. Haven't you got fed up with our little resort, young lady?

LAURA. I'm really just beginning to enjoy it here.

GANT. What do you find to enjoy about it?

LAURA. Oh, the countryside is beautiful. Gene and I have had lots of pleasant walks in the hills.

GANT. Oh, so it's Gene who makes it pleasant for you, hey?

EUGENE. Come on, Papa! Hah, hah— (*Embarrassed laugh and turns away.*)

GANT. You're fond of Gene, aren't you?

LAURA. He's very nice and intelligent.

GANT. Gene's a good boy—our best.

LAURA (*looking around*). My, isn't this shop interesting? How did you happen to become a stone cutter, Mr. Gant?

(EUGENE *puts apron on bench, studies* LAURA *during this, sensing her evasiveness to him.*)

GANT. Well, I guess you'd call it a passion with some people. When I was a boy Gene's age, I happened to pass a shop something like this. (*Of the angel*) And this very angel was there. She's Carrara marble— (*Sits right on center table.*) from Italy. And as I looked at her smiling face, I felt, more than anything in the world, I wanted to carve delicately with a chisel. It was as though, if I could do that, I could bring something of me out onto a piece of marble. Oh, the reminiscences of the old always bore the young.

LAURA. No, they don't.

GANT. So I walked into that shop, and asked the stone cutter if I could become an apprentice. Well, I worked there for five years. When I left, I bought the angel. (*He looks at the angel with longing.*) I've hardly had her out of my sight, since. I bet I've started twenty pieces of marble, but I've never been able to capture her. . . . I guess there's no use trying any more— (*He becomes silent, morose. Sensitively* EUGENE *touches* GANT's *shoulder, looks at* LAURA.)

EUGENE. Would you like to look around, Laura?

LAURA. I'm afraid I'm bothering you at your work.

GANT (*looks at* EUGENE, *coming out of his distant thought and mood*). No, no. Show her about, Gene. (*Suddenly decisive.*) I have some other things I must do—(*Starts toward office, pauses.*)— though some people find looking at tombstones depressing. Still we all come to them in the end. (GANT *exits.*)

EUGENE. Why do you think you might be bothering me?

LAURA. You are supposed to be working.

EUGENE (*a step to her*). You came here to see me. What's happened, Laura? Something's different today.

LAURA (*crossing left, puts picnic basket on marble slab down right*). Oh, don't pay any attention to me. I just—I don't know.

EUGENE. What's in the basket?

LAURA. I asked Helen to pack us a picnic lunch.

EUGENE (*crosses for basket and takes her hand*). Good! Let's go!

LAURA (*pulling away*). Not now.

EUGENE (*puts his arm around her*). What is it, Laura? What's the matter? Have I done something wrong?

LAURA (*shakes her head*). Gene, Helen knows about us! And your father too. He—

EUGENE. I don't care—I want the whole world to know. (*Picks up basket.*) Here, let's go.

LAURA (*pulling away*). No. Let's not talk about it. (*Sits on stool, near slab.*) This is pretty marble. Where's it from?

EUGENE. Laura, you don't give a damn where that marble came from!

LAURA (*starts to cry*). Oh, Gene, I'm so ashamed, so ashamed.

EUGENE (*sits beside her on slab*). Laura, my darling, what is it?

LAURA. Gene, I lied to you—I'm twenty-three years old.

EUGENE. Is that all?

LAURA. You're not nineteen either. You're seventeen.

EUGENE. I'm a thousand years old, all the love I've stored up for you. (*Again puts his arms around her.*)

LAURA (*struggling away*). I'm an older woman—

EUGENE. In God's name, what does that have to do with us?

LAURA. There have to be rules!

EUGENE. Rules are made by jealous people. They make rules to love by so even those with no talent for it can at least pretend. We don't need rules. We don't have to pretend. Oh, Laura, my sweet, what we have is so beautiful, so rare . . . how often in life can you find it?

LAURA (*escaping his arms, rises, crosses down right center and turns to him*). Eugene, you're a young boy, a whole world just waiting for you.

EUGENE. You are my world, Laura. You always will be. Don't let anything destroy us. Don't leave me alone. I've always been alone.

LAURA. It's what you want, dear. It's what you'll always want. You couldn't stand anything else. You'd get so tired of me. You'll forget—you'll forget.

EUGENE. I'll never forget. I won't live long enough. (*Takes her in his arms, kisses her.*) Will you forget?

LAURA (*as he holds her*). Oh my darling, every word, every touch, how could I?

EUGENE. Then nothing has changed. Has it? Has it?

MADAME ELIZABETH'S VOICE (*off*). Good morning! (MADAME ELIZABETH, *38, the town madame, enters along the street upper left. She is well-clad, carries herself stylishly. She sees* EUGENE *and* LAURA, *stops as they break from each other.*)

EUGENE. Good morning, Madame Elizabeth.

MADAME ELIZABETH (*closing her parasol*). Is Mr. Gant here?

EUGENE. He's inside.

MADAME ELIZABETH. Well, don't let me keep you from what you're doing. (*Approaches office, calls.*) Mr. Gant! (*Places parasol down left of bench. Crosses to angel.*)

(LAURA *and* EUGENE *exit into yard down right.* GENE *carrying off down right stool.* GANT, *changed into another, better pair of trousers, tying his tie, enters.*)

GANT. Elizabeth, my dear Elizabeth! Well, this is a surprise! (*Seizes her hands.*)

MADAME ELIZABETH (*sentimentally looking him over*). Six years, W.O. Six years —except to nod to. Time, what a thief you are.

GANT. He hasn't stolen from you— you're still as handsome and stylish as ever. Won't you sit down?

MADAME ELIZABETH (*crossing to bench down left center*). Oh, W.O.—you and your gallant manners. But I'm no chicken any more, and no one knows it better than I do. If you only knew how often we talk about you up on Eagle Crescent. What a man you were! Wild! Bacchus himself. You remember the song you used to sing?

GANT. Life was many songs in those days, Elizabeth.

MADAME ELIZABETH. But when you got liquored up enough—don't you remember? Of course I can't boom it out like you do. (*Sings, imitating* GANT. GANT *joins her.*)

"Up in that back room, boys,
Up in *that* back room
All those kisses and those hugs
Among the fleas and bugs
In the evening's gloom, boys,
I pity your sad doom.
Up in that back room, boys,
Up in *that* back room."

(*Both laugh.* GANT *gives her an affectionate fanny slap.*)

GANT. The loss of all that, that's the worst, Elizabeth.

MADAME ELIZABETH (*sitting on the bench downstage*). Oh, W.O., W.O.! We do miss you.

GANT (*joining her on the bench*). How are all the girls, Elizabeth?

MADAME ELIZABETH (*suddenly distressed*). That's what I came to see you about. I lost one of them last night. (*Takes handkerchief from her pocket, quietly cries into it.*)

GANT. Oh. I'm sorry to hear that.

MADAME ELIZABETH. Sick only three days. I'd have done anything in the world for her. A doctor and two trained nurses by her all the time.

GANT. Too bad. Too bad. Which one was it?

MADAME ELIZABETH. Since your time, W.O. We called her Lily.

GANT. Tch—tch—tch! Lily.

MADAME ELIZABETH. I couldn't have loved her more if she had been my own daughter. Twenty-two. A child, a mere child. And not a relative who would do anything for her. Her mother died when she was thirteen, and her father is a mean old bastard who wouldn't even come to her death-bed.

GANT. He will be punished.

MADAME ELIZABETH. As sure as there's a God in heaven—the old bastard! I hope he rots! Such a fine girl, such a bright future for her. She had more opportunities than I ever had—and you know what I've done here. I'm a rich woman today, W.O. Why, not even your wife owns more property than I do. I beg your pardon—I hope you don't mind my speaking of her— (GANT *gestures to go right ahead.*) Mrs. Gant and I both understand that property is what makes a person hold one's head up! And Lily could have had all that too. Poor Lily! No one knows how much I'll miss her. (*A moment's quiet.* GANT *is respecting her grief.*)

GANT. There! There! (*As he comfortingly pats her hand*) I suppose you'll be wanting something for her grave? (*As* MADAME ELIZABETH *nods, he rises, crossing to left of lamb.*) Here's a sweet lamb —couchant lamb, it's called. "Couchant" means lying-down in French. That should be appropriate.

MADAME ELIZABETH. No, I've already made up my mind— (*Rises, moves toward the Carrara angel.*) I want that angel.

GANT (*crosses to left of her*). You don't want *her*, Elizabeth. Why, she's a white elephant. Nobody can afford to buy her!

MADAME ELIZABETH. I can and I want her.

GANT (*crossing right*). My dear Elizabeth, I have other fine angels. What about this one? My own carving.

MADAME ELIZABETH. No. Ever since I first saw that angel, I thought, when somebody who means something to me goes, she's going to be on the grave.

GANT. That angel's not for sale, Elizabeth.

MADAME ELIZABETH. Then why should you have her out here?

GANT. The truth is, I've promised her to someone.

MADAME ELIZABETH (*crossing to bench for her purse then back to angel*). I'll buy her from whoever you promised and give them a profit. Cash on the line. Who did you sell it to?

GANT (*crossing to right of her with urn*). My dear Madame Elizabeth, here is a nice expensive Egyptian urn. Your beloved Lily would like that.

MADAME ELIZABETH. Egyptian urns— pah! Pee pots! I want the angel!

GANT (*with growing intensity, angrily replaces urn on unit*). It's not for sale! Anything you like—*everything* you like —I'll give it to you—I'll make you a present, for old times' sake. But not my angel!

MADAME ELIZABETH. Now, let's not waste any more time over this. How much, W.O.?

GANT. She's Carrara marble from Italy, and too good for any whore! (*He calls.*) Eugene—Eugene!

MADAME ELIZABETH (*furious*). Why you old libertine, how dare you speak to me like that?

EUGENE (*entering, with* LAURA). What is it, Father? What's the matter?

MADAME ELIZABETH. Your father's a stubborn old nut, that's what!

GANT (*crosses toward office, turns*). I'm sorry if I've offended you.

MADAME ELIZABETH. You have, W.O., deeply!

GANT. Gene, will you be so kind and see if you can wait upon the Madame? (*Exits into the inner room of the office.*)

MADAME ELIZABETH (*crossing left*). I've heard the trouble your mother has with the old terror—now I believe it! All I'm asking is that he sells me that angel— for one of my dear girls who's gone—a dear, young girl in the flower of her life —(*Of* LAURA) like this young girl here—

EUGENE (*upper center*). Madame Elizabeth, I believe Papa is saving that angel for his own grave.

MADAME ELIZABETH (*sits on bench*). Oh-h-h, why didn't he say so? Why didn't he tell me? Poor, poor W.O. Well, of course in that case— (*She partially recovers; to* LAURA.) If you were to think of *your* death, dear—if you can, I mean, and we never know, we never know—is there something here that would appeal to you?

LAURA (*crosses to right of center table. Looks around*). I like the little lamb.

MADAME ELIZABETH. Lambs are for children, aren't they?

EUGENE (*stoops left of lamb*). Lambs are for anybody. Put your hand on it. Feel it. (MADAME ELIZABETH's *hand strokes across the lamb.*) Isn't it cool and content and restful? And you could have a poem engraved on the base.

MADAME ELIZABETH. A poem—

EUGENE. Let's see if we can find something you'd like. (*Picks up book from desk.*) Here's a book of Fifty Fine Memorial Poems. (MADAME ELIZABETH *still strokes the lamb;* EUGENE *finds a poem.*) See if you like this— (*Reads.*)
"She went away in beauty's flower,
Before her youth was spent;
Ere life and love had lived their hour,
God called her—and she went."
(MADAME ELIZABETH *sobs.*)
"Yet whispers faith upon the wind;
No grief to her was given.
She left your love and went to find
A greater one in heaven."

MADAME ELIZABETH (*quoting, through her heartfelt tears*). "She left *your* love and went to find a greater one in heaven. . . ." (*Rises, addresses* EUGENE.) I hope you never lose someone you love, boy. (*Gets parasol.*) Well, let me know when the little lying-down lamb is ready. (*She nods with majestic dignity to* LAURA, *exits.* WILL *and* ELIZA *enter, look off in the direction taken by* MADAME ELIZABETH.)

ELIZA. Don't stare after her, Will! You know who that is. (*To* EUGENE) Was that shameless woman here to see your father?

EUGENE. One of the girls at Eagle Crescent died. She bought a monument.

ELIZA. Oh she did! She bought one! Well, your father certainly has to deal with all kinds of people. Will, go in and tell Mr. Gant that we're here. (WILL *exits.* ELIZA *looks at* LAURA.) Oh, Miss James, it's five minutes to dinner time at Dixieland, and you know the rules about being late.

EUGENE (*crosses to pick up basket*). Laura and I are going on a picnic.

ELIZA. Not now, you're not. (*To* LAURA) My dear, I want to talk privately to Mr. Gant—to Eugene, too, and I've asked Ben to join us.

EUGENE. We've made plans, Mama.

ELIZA (*beside bench*). Son, this is a family conference.

LAURA. Gene, please—I'll wait for you over at Woodruff's. Please. (LAURA *and* EUGENE *stroll off up right whispering.* WILL *enters from office paring his nails.*)

ELIZA. Is he in there?

WILL. He's there. We've got him cornered. (*They chuckle.* BEN, *looking feverish and ill, enters up left.*)

BEN. Hello, Uncle Will. Hello, Mama—you look like you just swallowed fifty or a hundred acres. What did you buy today?

ELIZA. Now, Ben, it just happens that today we're selling—I hope we are, anyway.

BEN. What's it all about?

ELIZA (*crossing to center*). You just sit down there. I may not need you, but I want you to be here.

BEN (*sits beneath the angel*). I hope it won't take long.

GANT (*enters. He wears a coat of carefully brushed black wool, a tie, and carries his hat which he leaves just inside the office*). Good morning, Miss Eliza.

ELIZA. My, how elegant! Aren't we burning a river this morning?

GANT (*places hat on office stool, crosses to left of center table*). I heard you were out here, Miss Eliza. I so seldom have a visit from you! (*He gestures the tribute.*)

ELIZA. That's most gracious. You may all sit down now. Gene! Will! (EUGENE *enters, sits on center table.* WILL *sits on office step.* GANT *moves a chair to center.*) Now, Mr. Gant—

GANT (*as he places chair left of center table and sits*). This isn't one of your temperance meetings?

ELIZA (*a bit surprised. Putting stole and purse on bench*). Our private temperance problem—that's a part of it, yes. Mr. Gant, how old are you?

GANT. I've lost track.

ELIZA. You're sixty years old in December. And if Dr. Maguire were here, he could tell you—

GANT. I've heard what Doc Maguire has to tell me. I shouldn't be lifting these marbles. I shouldn't be drinking liquor. I should take a nice long rest.

ELIZA. Then you save me a great deal of argument about that. Now, Gene— (*Crosses over to* EUGENE *above center table.*)

EUGENE. Yes, Mama? (*Rises.*)

ELIZA. You want to go to college, don't you?

EUGENE. Very much.

ELIZA. Well, I figure that four years at Chapel Hill will cost thirty-four hundred dollars—but of course you'll have to wait on table. Otherwise it would be forty-four hundred dollars, which is ridiculous

—at the moment we don't even have thirty-four hundred dollars—

GANT. Oh, for God's sake, get to the point, Miss Eliza. Have you got the papers from the bank?

ELIZA (*crosses to left of him*). Why, what do you mean, what papers?

GANT. You know what I mean. Fish for them, woman! (*Pointing to her bosom.*) *Go ahead, fish for them.* (ELIZA *turns her back, from her bosom fishes out a large envelope.* GANT *laughs, a roaring bitter laugh, leaps up to* EUGENE *who joins the laughter.*)

ELIZA (*angrily*). What in the world are you two hyenas laughing at?

GANT. Oh, as you would say, Miss Eliza, that's a good one, that's a *good* one.

ELIZA. Well, I am glad to see you in a *good* mood.

GANT (*crossing down right center*). So the bank wants this little old lot, here? That's what you told me, didn't you? Though I can't for the life of me see why.

WILL. There's a new business street going through here in a few months.

GANT (*crosses to right of her*). Let me see the check.

ELIZA (*takes check from envelope, hands it to him*). Well, it's for twenty thousand dollars. Will had to guarantee it personally for me to bring it here. Did you ever see anything like it? Two, zero, coma, zero—zero—zero—decimal—zero—zero!

GANT. "W. O. Gant." It seems to be in good order, all right.

ELIZA. Well—it is—and Will's looked over this deed, and it's all in order too, isn't it, Will? (*Hands the deed to* GANT.) Give me your pen, Will.

WILL (*hands* ELIZA *the pen*). And I just had it filled.

GANT (*examining the deed. Crosses, sits center*). This fine print—I really do need glasses.

ELIZA. You can trust Will. (*Puts pen on work table.*) He's been all over it, Mr. Gant!

WILL (*looks at angel*). What about the marble stock and the monuments?

ELIZA. They're not included.

EUGENE. Papa—the years you've spent here—all your fine work. Please don't give it up.

ELIZA. Now, Gene, your father knows what he's doing.

EUGENE. But he's such a fine stone cutter!

GANT. You think my work is fine, son?

EUGENE. Isn't it, Ben? (GANT *crosses down right into the marble yard, looking about.*)

ELIZA. Your father knows his duty to all of us—and to himself—

EUGENE. There isn't a cemetery in the state that isn't filled with his work—you can always recognize it. Clean, and pure and beautiful. Why should he give it up?

ELIZA. Why, law, I don't say he should give it up entirely. He can have another little shop further out of town!

EUGENE. But he's too old to transplant now, Mama. This is his street. Everyone knows him here. People pass by. Mr. Jannadeau's shop next door, and Woodruff's across the way—All the people and places Papa knows!

GANT. And Tim Laughran's down the block!

ELIZA (*crosses down to* GANT). Oh, yes. That's another reason for getting rid of this place. Put yourself out of temptation's way, Mr. Gant.

GANT (*sits on slab*). I certainly do love it here.

EUGENE. Don't give it up, Papa.

BEN. What do you want to do to him, Mama?

ELIZA. Now, looky here—you are a fine stone cutter—why, haven't I always said so? But it's time you rested. You want to live a long time, don't you? (*Sits beside him on slab.*)

GANT. Well, sometimes, I'm not sure.

ELIZA. Well, you do—and I want you to live a long time—we all want to! People can talk about a short but sweet life, but we all want to live! Look at me, I'm fifty-seven years old. I've borne nine children, raised six of them, and worked hard all my life. I'd like to back up and rest a little myself. And we can, Mr. Gant. If you'll just sign that little slip of paper. I guarantee, in a year from now, you'll have completely forgotten this dingy, crooked, dusty yard. Won't he, Ben? Won't he? Ben!

BEN. Some people have trouble forgetting some things, Mama.

ELIZA. Why, pshaw, I'm going to *see* to it that he forgets it. I'll have time to look after you. Won't I, Mr. Gant?

GANT. You're right about one thing, Miss Eliza—that I can't dispute. You have worked hard. (*Rises, moves to center work table.*)

EUGENE. Papa, please, don't do it. (GANT *sits at work table, signs the deed.* ELIZA *crosses to him, picks it up.*)

ELIZA. Thank you, Mr. Gant. Now the check. You know what I'm going to do? I'm going to plan a great, glorious celebration. (*Gives the deed to* WILL, *speaks to* EUGENE.) We'll ask your brother Luke to come home, if the Navy will let him out. And we'll invite Stevie, and Daisy and her husband, too, except if she brings those whiny children of hers. (*Notices* GANT *just looking at the check.*) Turn it over, Mr. Gant. Sign it on the back.

GANT. Why do I have to sign it?

ELIZA. Endorse it, that's all. "W. O. Gant," like it's written on the front of the check.

GANT. That can wait until I offer it, can't it?

ELIZA. To clear the check, Mr. Gant!

GANT. I'm not used to these things. How do you clear it?

ELIZA. You sign it—I'll deposit it in the Dixieland account, then we draw checks on it.

GANT. We?

ELIZA. Yes. You draw what you want. I'll draw what we need for Gene's college —for Dixieland, and for anything else we need.

GANT (*rises, crosses to office*). I think I'll wait to cash it until I get to Chapel Hill. The bank has a branch there, doesn't it, Will? (*Gives* WILL *his pen.*)

ELIZA. Why would you want to cash it in Chapel Hill?

GANT. This is my check, isn't it? I'm the one who had the foresight to buy this little pie-cornered lot thirty-one years ago for four hundred dollars—money from the estate of Cynthia L. Gant, deceased. I guess I'm entitled to the profit.

ELIZA. Now, Mr. Gant, if you're thinking to get my dander up!

GANT (*picks up hat, puts it on*). Miss Eliza, I've been wanting to get away from here for a long time. I'm taking Gene with me. (*Crosses to* EUGENE.) I'm going to put him in that college there at Chapel Hill.

EUGENE. Now?

GANT. Now! And then I'm going to travel—and when Gene's free in the summer, we'll travel together. (*Crosses back to* ELIZA.) And there's nothing in this whole wide world that you're going to do to to stop me. And I can just see the word Dixieland forming on your cursed lips. What about Dixieland? Nothing for Dixieland? *No, not one god-damn red cent!* You've plenty of property of your own you can sell. If it's rest and comfort you really want, sell it, woman, sell it! But I think you like working hard, because then that makes us all feel sorry for you. And I do feel sorry for you too, from the bottom of my heart. (*Puts check in pocket.*) Well, Eugene!

EUGENE. Papa, I can't go now.

GANT. Why not? You haven't got any better clothes . . . so you might as well go as you are. I guess we'll say our good-byes. (*Addresses the angel.*) So long, dear Carrara angel. I'll arrange for us to be together again some day. Good-bye, Ben— Tell Helen—tell Helen I'll write to her. (*Shakes hands with* BEN.)

ELIZA (*leaping at* GANT). I won't let you do this. I won't let you.

EUGENE. MAMA!

ELIZA (*seizes check from* GANT's *pocket, tears it up, flings it on the ground*). All right, all right, all right! There's your check. I guess there's nothing to prevent you from going to the bank and trying to get another check, but it won't work because I'm going to put an injunction against you. I'll prove you're not responsible to sell this property, or even to own it. I'll get guardianship over you! Everyone knows the times you've been to the cure—the threats you've made to me —the times you've tried to kill me—I'll tell them. You're a madman, Mr. Gant, a madman. You're not going to get away with this. I'll fight you tooth and nail, tooth and nail. And I'll win. (*Trembling, she picks up her handbag from the stone seat.*)

GANT. All the things you've said about me are true, Eliza. I've only brought you pain. Why don't you let me go?

ELIZA. Because you're my husband, Mr. Gant! You're my husband. Thirty-one years together and we'll go on—we must go on. A house divided against itself cannot stand. We must try to understand and love each other. We must try. . . . (*Exits up right.*)

GANT (*quietly*). Take her home, will you, Will? (WILL *hurries after* ELIZA. *A long moment.* BEN, *weak and feverish, dries his forehead with his handkerchief.* GANT *sinks into a chair.*) Eugene, go over to Laughran's and get me a bottle. You heard me.

EUGENE. No, Papa.

GANT. Are you still paddling along after your mother?

BEN. Leave Gene alone. If you want to get sick, do it yourself.

GANT. Ungrateful sons! Oh, the sad waste of years, the red wound of all our mistakes. (*Rises, exits up left.* EUGENE *looks after him.*)

BEN. The fallen Titan. He might have succeeded if he hadn't tried to take you. He could still make it, but he won't try again.

EUGENE. They loved each other once. They must have had one moment in time that was perfect. What happened? It frightens me, Ben; how can something so perfect turn into this torture?

BEN. They're strangers. They don't know each other. No one ever really comes to know anyone.

EUGENE (*sits center table*). That's not true. I know you—I know Laura.

BEN. Listen to him! No matter what arms may clasp us, what heart may warm us, what mouth may kiss us, we remain strangers. We never escape it. Never, never, never. (*Closes eyes, leans back.*)

EUGENE. Ben! Hey, Ben? (*Worriedly crosses down to* BEN, *feels his face.*) Ben, you're burning up! Come on— (*Tries to lift him.*) Put your arms around me. I'm going to take you home.

BEN (*sinks back*). Can't. It's all right, I'm just tired.

EUGENE (*takes* BEN's *coat from his lap and puts it around his shoulders*). Why didn't you tell somebody you're sick, you crazy idiot! (*Again tries to lift* BEN.)

BEN. To hell with them, Gene. To hell with them all. Don't give a damn for anything. Nothing gives a damn for you. There are a lot of bad days, there are a lot of good ones— (EUGENE *rushes into the office, picks up the telephone.*) That's all there is . . . a lot of days . . . My God, is there no freedom on this earth?

EUGENE (*into telephone*). Get me Dr. Maguire quickly. *It's my brother Ben!*

BEN (*stirs, in anguish, looks up at the Carrara angel*). And still you smile. . . .

CURTAIN

ACT TWO
SCENE TWO

SCENE: *The Dixieland Boarding House; the next night. A painful tenseness grips the house.* LAURA *and* EUGENE *sit together on the yard seat down left.* MRS. PERT *sits motionless in a rocker near the front door.* HUGH *slowly walks about. The inside hall is lighted; as is* BEN's *room, which we see for the first time. There* DR. MAGUIRE *and* HELEN *are hovering over* BEN's *still body.* GANT *is at the hall telephone.*

GANT (*shouting into telephone*). Second class seaman, Luke Gant. G-A-N-T— Gant! (*Angrily*) I don't know why you can't hear me.

HUGH (*crosses to door*). W.O., you don't have to shout because it's long distance.

GANT. Shut up, Hugh, I know what I'm doing. (*Into telephone*) Do what? I am standing back from the telephone. All right, all right. . . . (*Moves telephone away from him, lower.*) Can you hear me now? Of all the perversities. Very well, I will repeat. Yesterday I sent a telegram to my son, Luke Gant, to come home, that his brother Ben has pneumonia. Can you tell me if—oh, he did leave? Why didn't he let us know? All right! Thank you. Thank you very much. (*Hangs up, joins the others on the veranda.*)

HUGH. They gave him leave?

GANT. If he made good connections he ought to be here by now.

HUGH. Ben'll be all right, W.O.

GANT (*crosses to sit wicker stool down right.* HUGH *sits woodbox*). I remember when little Grover was ill in St. Louis, and Eliza sent for me. I didn't get there on time.

ELIZA (*enters from the house*). Did you reach him?

GANT. He's on his way.

ELIZA (*at center on porch*). It's all nonsense, of course. Ben is far from dying. But you do like to dramatize, Mr. Gant. Still, it will be good to see Luke—

EUGENE (*crosses to* ELIZA). Mama, when can I see Ben?

ELIZA. When the doctor says. I'll tell

you what: when you go in there, don't make out like Ben is sick. Just make a big joke of it—laugh as big as you please—

EUGENE (*groans, sits left of left pillar*). Mama!

ELIZA. Well, it's the sick one's frame of mind that counts. I remember when I was teaching school in Hominy township, I had pneumonia. Nobody expected me to live, but I—did—I got through it somehow. I remember one day I was sitting down—I reckon I was convalescing as the fella says. Old Doc Fletcher had been there—and as he left I saw him shake his head at my cousin Sally. "Why, Eliza, what on earth," she says, just as soon as he had gone, "he tells me you're spitting up blood every time you cough; you've got consumption as sure as you live!" "Pshaw!" I said. I remember I was just determined to make a big joke of it. "I don't believe a word of it," I said. "Not one single word." And it was because I didn't believe it that *I got well.*

GANT (*quietly*). Eliza, don't run on so.

HELEN (*appears on veranda*). The doctor says Mama can come in for a few minutes, but no one else yet.

EUGENE (*rises, take* HELEN'S *hand*). How is he?

HELEN. You know Dr. Maguire. If you can get anything out of him. . . . (ELIZA *takes a big breath; she and* HELEN *go in.*)

GANT (*moans worriedly*). Oh God, I don't like the feel of it. I don't like the feel of it.

BEN (*weakly*). Maguire, if you don't stop hanging over me I'll smother to death.

MAGUIRE (*to the women as they enter*). With both of you in here soaking up oxygen, leave that door open. (ELIZA *advances slowly to* BEN, *swallows a gasp at the sight of the tortured, wasted body.* BEN'S *eyes are closed.*)

HELEN (*foot of bed*). Mama's here, Ben.

ELIZA (*speaking as though to a baby*). Why hello, son—did you think I wasn't ever coming in to see you?

HELEN (*after a pause*). Ben, Mama's here.

ELIZA (*to* MAGUIRE). Can't he talk? Why doesn't he look at me?

MAGUIRE (*head of bed*). Ben, you can hear what's going on, can't you?

BEN (*quietly, his eyes still closed*). I wish you'd all get out and leave me alone.

ELIZA. What kind of talk is that? You have to be looked after, son!

BEN. Then let Mrs. Pert look after me.

HELEN. Ben!

BEN. Maguire, where's Fatty? I want to see Fatty.

HELEN (*crosses center of bed.* ELIZA *turns away up left*). Ben, how can you talk that way? Your mother and your sister? If it weren't for that woman you wouldn't be sick now. Drinking, carousing with her night after night—

BEN (*yells with dwindling strength*). Fatty! Fatty! (*On the veranda* MRS. PERT *stands quickly, then enters house toward* BEN'S *room.*)

HELEN (*to* BEN). You ought to be ashamed of yourself!

DR. MAGUIRE. Mrs. Gant, we need some more cold cloths. Why don't you—

HELEN (*crosses angrily to* MAGUIRE). Fiend! Do you have to add to her misery? When you need something, ask me. (ELIZA *starting out of* BEN'S *room, meets* FATTY *in doorway.* FATTY *hesitates.*)

DR. MAGUIRE. That's all right, Mrs. Pert.

BEN (*immediately turns toward her*). Fatty?

DR. MAGUIRE. Ben seems to want you here, that's all I care about. (*To* HELEN) You'll be called if you're needed.

HELEN. This is the last time you come into this house, Dr. Maguire!

(HELEN *leaves the room. Outside* BEN'S *door* ELIZA *hands some cold cloths to* HELEN.)

BEN. Fatty, stay by me. Sing to me. "A Baby's Prayer at Twilight."

FATTY (*sitting beside him*). Sh-h-h, Ben. Be quiet, dear. Save yourself.

BEN. Hold my hand, Fatty.

FATTY (*takes his hand, sings*).*
"Just a baby's prayer at twilight
When lights are low
A baby's years
Are filled with tears
Hmmmmm hmmmmm hmmmmmm."

---

* "Just a Baby's Prayer at Twilight," words by Sam M. Lewis and Joe Young, music by M. K. Jerome. © 1918. Copyright renewal 1946. Mills Music, Inc., and Warlock Music, Inc. Used by permission of the copyright owners solely for the purpose of printing in this edition. CAUTION: Permission to include this song in any performance of this play must be obtained from Mills Music, Inc., 1619 Broadway, New York 19, N. Y.

(HELEN *re-enters* BEN's *room. Places cloths on bureau. Hearing the voice,* EUGENE *stands, looks up toward* BEN's *room.* HELEN *and* ELIZA *appear on the veranda,* HELEN *comforting her mother.*)

EUGENE. How does he seem, Mama?

ELIZA (*right of* HELEN). He couldn't stand to see me worrying. That's what it was, you know. He couldn't stand to see me worrying about him.

GANT (*groaning*). Oh Jesus, it's fearful—that this should be put on me, old and sick as I am—

HELEN (*in blazing fury. Crosses to left of him*). You shut your mouth this minute, you damned old man! I've spent my life taking care of you! Everything's been done for you—everything—and you'll be here when we're all gone—so don't let us hear anything about your sickness, you selfish old man—it makes me furious!

DR. MAGUIRE (*appearing on veranda*). If any of you are interested, Ben is a little better.

EUGENE. Thank God!

HELEN. Ben is better? Why didn't you say so before?

ELIZA. I could have told you! I could have told you! I had a feeling all along!

DR. MAGUIRE (*crosses down steps*). I'll be back in a little while.

GANT. Well! We can all relax now.

DR. MAGUIRE (*motions* EUGENE *away from the others to down left*). Eugene, it's both lungs now. I can't tell them. But see to it that they stay around. I'm going next door and phone for some oxygen. It may ease it a little for him. It won't be long. (*He gives* EUGENE *a fond, strengthening touch, exits.*)

GANT (*in doorway*). What about Luke? Luke'll be furious when he finds out he came all this way for nothing!

ELIZA (*R. of him*). For nothing? You call Ben's getting well "for nothing"?

GANT. Oh, you know what I mean, Miss Eliza. I'm going to take a little nap.

ELIZA. You're going to take a little nip, that's what you mean.

GANT. You can come up and search my room if you don't believe me. (*Exits into house.*)

(EUGENE *stands, dazed and miserable, forces himself during the following scene.* JAKE *and* FLORRY *enter from rear veranda where* HELEN *and* HUGH *have moved to.*)

ELIZA (*excitedly*). Mr. Clatt, Miss Mangle—did you hear? Ben is getting better! The crisis is past!

JAKE. We're so happy for you, Mrs. Gant.

ELIZA. I knew all along—something told me. Oh, not that he didn't have a very high fever—I admit that—but my second sense—

LUKE (*off right*). Hello—o—o there!

ELIZA (*peering off*). Luke. (*Rushes down steps.*) Luke! Luke Gant!

(*The boarders melt into the background as* LUKE GANT *enters, wearing a Navy uniform and carrying a lightly packed duffle bag, which he places on wicker stool down right. He is attractive, slight, lighted by an enormous love of humor and life, and adored by everyone. He is the son who got away early, but he still carries the marks of a distressing childhood; he sometimes stutters.*)

LUKE. Mama, Mama! (*Swings her around.*)

HUGH (*right of him in yard*). Well, if it isn't the sailor himself! How are you?

LUKE (*shaking hands with* HUGH). I'm fine, Hugh! How goes it?

ELIZA. Aren't you going to kiss your old mother?

LUKE. Old? You're getting younger and stronger by the minute. (*Kisses her.*)

ELIZA. I am, I am, son. I feel it—now that Ben's going to get well.

LUKE. The old boy is better?

HELEN (*R. of R. pillar*). Luke!

LUKE. Helen!

HELEN (*leaps into his arms from porch*). How's my boy?

LUKE. S-s-slick as a puppy's belly. I thought you all might need cheering up. I brought you some ice cream from Woodruff's! (*Gives carton of ice cream to* HELEN.)

HELEN. Naturally; you wouldn't be Luke Gant if you didn't!

EUGENE (*crosses to center*). Welcome home, Luke!

LUKE (*crosses to him. They shake hands*). My God, doesn't anybody buy you any clothes—and look at that hair. Mama, he looks like an orphan! Cut off those damn big feet of his, he'd go up in the air!

EUGENE. How long have you got, Luke?

LUKE. Can you s-s-stand me for twenty-four hours? (*Sees* LAURA, *crosses to her.*) Who's this?

ELIZA (*following*). That's Miss James from Virginia. Laura, this is another of my sons, Luke Gant.

LAURA (*shaking hands*). How do you do, Mr. Gant?

LUKE. How do you do?

ELIZA (*drawing* LUKE *away*). All right, just come along here, and behave yourself.

HELEN. I'd better dish up the ice cream before it melts. (*Exits into house.*)

LUKE (*calling after* HELEN *from porch*). Maybe Ben would like some. I got pistachio especially for him.

ELIZA (*to* HELEN, *left of left pillar*). Tell your father the admiral is here!

LUKE. Can I see Ben, now?

ELIZA. Well, the truth is, that Mrs. Pert is in there with him now.

LUKE. Mrs. Pert is? (*Looks at the others.*)

HUGH (*crosses onto porch with duffle bag. Sits woodbox*). I wouldn't go into it, Luke. It's a somewhat "fraught" subject.

LUKE. Oh boy, oh boy, I know what that is! Still the same old happy household? (LUKE *and* ELIZA *sit on the veranda edge.*)

ELIZA. Nonsense. I have nothing against the woman except she's getting too many ideas that she's a fixture here. First thing in the morning I'm going to ask her to move.

LUKE. Doesn't she pay her rent?

ELIZA. Oh, she pays it.

LUKE (*laughs*). Then you're never going to ask her to move—don't kid me! The paying customers are what counts around here! Aren't they, Mama?

ELIZA. Luke Gant, there are certain standards I have to keep up, for the reputation of Dixieland!

LUKE (*never unkindly*). What kind of standards? The old dope fiend who hung himself in the same bedroom where Ben had to sleep for eight years after he cut him down? And all those amateur femme fatales who bask under your protection here, waylaying us in the hall, the bathroom—Mama, we never had a s-s-safe moment! And people think you find out about life in the Navy!

ELIZA (*playfully*). I'm warning you, Luke! It's a good thing I know you're teasing.

(HELEN *enters with plates, dishes up ice cream.*)

LUKE. Remember the early mornings when Ben and Gene and I used to take the paper route together, remember, Gene? Old Ben used to make up stories for us about all the sleeping people in all the sleeping houses! He always used to throw the papers as lightly as he could because he hated to wake them. Remember, Gene?

HELEN (*offering* HUGH *ice cream*). And that book of baseball stories Ben used to read to us by the hour—what was it, Gene?

EUGENE (*in tears*). *You Know Me, Al,* by Ring Lardner.

ELIZA (*leaping to* EUGENE). Eugene. Child, what is it? What is it!

MRS. PERT (*enters hurriedly*). Mrs. Gant! Mrs. Gant!

HELEN. What is it, Mrs. Pert?

MRS. PERT. He can't get his breath!

HUGH. Gene, get the doctor! (HELEN *and* ELIZA *follow* MRS. PERT *into the house.*)

ELIZA. You ridiculous woman! The doctor said he was better. (EUGENE *exits to get* DR. MAGUIRE. GANT *enters side door.*)

GANT. What the hell's all the commotion about? (*Sees* LUKE.) Luke! Welcome home!

LUKE (*as they shake hands right center*). Papa—Ben's not doing so well.

GANT (*crosses to right pillar*). Jesus, have mercy! That I should have to bear this in my old age. Not another one—first Grover, now Ben . . .

LUKE (*on porch above him*). For God's sake, Papa, try to behave decently, for Ben's sake! (EUGENE *and* DR. MAGUIRE *enter hurriedly.*)

GANT (*seizing* DR. MAGUIRE). Maguire, you got to save him—you got to save him. (DR. MAGUIRE *pushes past* GANT *into the house, enters* BEN'S *room where the three women are gathered,* MRS. PERT *standing nearest* BEN *at the head of the bed.*)

DR. MAGUIRE. You women step back, give him air. (*Bends over* BEN.)

GANT (*collapsing on to the porch right of right pillar*). When the old die, no one cares. But the young . . . the young . . .

EUGENE (*sits left of him on steps.* LUKE *sits rocker*). I would care, Papa.

BEN. It's one way—to step out of—

the photograph—isn't it, Fatty?

FATTY. Hush, Ben, don't say that!

HELEN (*to* DR. MAGUIRE; *right of him*). There must be something you can do!

DR. MAGUIRE (*straightens up*). Not all the king's horses, not all the doctors in the world can help him now.

HELEN. Have you tried everything? Everything?

DR. MAGUIRE (*turns upstage*). My dear girl! He's drowning! Drowning!

ELIZA (*in deep pain, moving from foot of bed*). Mrs. Pert, you're standing in my place— (FATTY *moves away.* ELIZA *steps close to* BEN, *sits.*) Ben—son.

(*She reaches to touch him. His head turns toward her, drops. There is a last rattling, drowning sound.* BEN *dies.* DR. MAGUIRE *checks his heart.*)

DR. MAGUIRE. It's over. It's all over.

HELEN (*racked, exits to veranda; tries to stifle her sobs*). He's gone. Ben's gone.

(ELIZA *sits stool and takes* BEN's *hand.* FATTY *puts the socks she has been knitting at* BEN's *feet and exits upstairs.* HELEN *falls into* EUGENE's *arms.* DR. MAGUIRE, *carrying his doctor's bag, appears in the hall, puts a match to his chewed cigar.*)

EUGENE (*crossing to right of* DR. MAGUIRE). Did he say anything? Did he say anything at the end?

DR. MAGUIRE. What were you expecting him to say?

EUGENE. I don't know. I just wondered.

DR. MAGUIRE. If he found what he was looking for? I doubt that, Gene. At least he didn't say anything.

(EUGENE *leaves and goes into* BEN's *room.* DR. MAGUIRE *comes out into the veranda.*)

LUKE. How long have you known, Doc?

DR. MAGUIRE. For two days—from the beginning. Since I first saw him at three in the morning in the Uneeda Lunch with a cup of coffee in one hand and a cigarette in the other.

GANT. Was there nothing to be done?

DR. MAGUIRE. My dear, dear Gant, we can't turn back the days that have gone. We can't turn back to the hours when our lungs were sound, our blood hot, our bodies young. We are a flash of fire—a brain, a heart, a spirit. And we are three cents' worth of lime and iron—which we cannot get back. (*He shakes his head.*) We can believe in the nothingness of life. We can believe in the nothingness of death, and of a life after death. But who can believe in the nothingness of Ben?

HELEN. Come on, Papa, there's nothing more to sit up for. Let me put you to bed. Come along.

(*She takes the old man and leads him gently into the house, as* DR. MAGUIRE *exits.* HUGH *and* LUKE *exit after* HELEN *and* GANT. *Only* LAURA *is left, still sitting on the yard seat.* EUGENE, *who has been standing in the corner in* BEN's *room, goes to his mother, who is holding* BEN's *hand tightly.*)

EUGENE. Mama?

ELIZA. He doesn't turn away from me any more.

EUGENE (*takes her hand, tries gently to disengage* BEN's). Mama, you've got to let go. You've got to let go, Mama! (ELIZA *shakes her head, her rough clasp tightening.* EUGENE *leaves the room, comes out to the veranda. There, slowly, he sinks to his knees, prays.* LAURA *watches him, her heart going out to him.*) Whoever You are, be good to Ben tonight. Whoever You are, be good to Ben tonight . . . Whoever You are . . . be good to Ben tonight . . . be good to Ben tonight. . . .

SLOW CURTAIN

ACT THREE

SCENE: *The Dixieland Boarding House; two weeks later. The house is seen in a soft early light. From offstage, a newsboy, whistling, throws four tightly wadded newspapers onto the veranda—plop—plop—plop—plop. The whistling and his steps fade away. The lights come up dimly in* LAURA's *room.* LAURA *is in bed in her nightgown.* EUGENE *is at the foot of the bed by the window, looking out. He takes his shirt from the bedpost, puts it on.*

LAURA (*stirring*). Gene? What was that?

EUGENE (*head of* LAURA's *bed*). Soaks Baker with the morning papers. Plop-plop-plop-plop—how I used to love that sound. Every time the heavy bag getting lighter. I'll always feel sorry for people who have to carry things. (*Sighs.*) It's getting light, it's nearly dawn.

LAURA. Don't go yet. (*Reaches for his hand.*)

EUGENE. Do you think I want to on your last morning here? Mama gets up so early. Do you know that every morning before she cooks breakfast she visits Ben's grave? (*Sits on bed, takes her in his arms.*)

LAURA. Gene, Gene.

EUGENE. Oh Laura, I love you so. When I'm close to you like this, it's so natural. Are all men like me? Tell me.

LAURA. I've told you I've never known anyone like you.

EUGENE (*as* LAURA *turns away*). But you have known men? It would be strange if you hadn't. A woman so beautiful, so loving. You make me feel like I only used to dream of feeling. I've hardly thought to daydream in weeks—except about us.

LAURA. What did you used to dream?

EUGENE. I always wanted to be the winner, the general, the spearhead of victory! Then following that I wanted to be loved. Victory and love! Unbeaten and beloved. And I am that now, truly! Laura, will you marry me?

LAURA (*moving away*). Oh, darling!

EUGENE. You knew I was going to ask you, didn't you? You knew I couldn't let you go even for a day.

LAURA. Yes, I knew.

EUGENE. You're happy with me. You know I make you happy. And I'm so complete with you. Do you know that three hundred dollars Ben left me? He would want me to use it for us. I'll go with you to Richmond today. I'll meet your parents, so they won't think I'm an irresponsible fool who's stolen you. That may be a little hard to prove—but there is a job I can get. Would you mind living in Altamont?

LAURA (*moving into his arms*). I don't care where I live. Just keep holding me.

EUGENE. I am going to have to tell Mama first.

LAURA. Let's not worry about that now. Tell me about us.

EUGENE. All the treasures the world has in store for us? We'll see and know them all. . . . All the things and the places I've read about. There isn't a state in this country we won't know. The great names of Arizona, Texas, Colorado, California—we'll ride the freights to get there if we have to. And we'll go to Europe, and beyond—the cool, green land of Shakespeare, the gloomy forests of Gaul, the great Assyrian plains where Alexander feasted—the crumbling walls of Babylon, the palaces of the kings of Egypt, the towering white crags of Switzerland. My God, Laura, there might not be time enough for all!

LAURA. There will be time enough, darling.

(*From a far distance, they hear the whistle of a train as it passes.*)

EUGENE. The Richmond train leaves at noon. I'll have to get packed.

LAURA. You do love trains, don't you?

EUGENE. I love only you. Will you have confidence in me, the unbeaten and beloved?

LAURA. Yes, darling, I will have confidence in you.

EUGENE. I'll never have to sneak out of this room again. (*Rises, moves to the door.* LAURA, *on her knees, reaches toward him.*)

LAURA. Eugene! (*He comes back to her.*) I will love you always. (*They kiss.* EUGENE *exits.* LAURA *leaps from the bed, hurries after him.*) Gene!

(ELIZA *has come out the side door, putting on sweater, takes flowers out of a bucket preparing to take them to* BEN's *grave.* EUGENE *enters the hallway, lifts the phone receiver. He doesn't see* ELIZA. *Lights dim down on* LAURA's *room as she gets slippers and exits.*)

EUGENE (*into telephone*). Good morning. Three-two, please— Hello, Uncle Will? This is Eugene— Yes, I know how early it is— You know that position you offered me? I've decided to take it.

ELIZA (*pleased, to herself*). Well, can you imagine!

EUGENE (*into telephone*). I've thought it over, and that's what I'd like to do, for a while anyway— That's right— That's fine— Well, you see, I'm getting married— (ELIZA *freezes in pain at center.*) Yes, married—to Miss James. We're going to Richmond for a few days. We're leaving on the noon train— Thanks, Uncle Will. Thanks a lot. (*Hangs up and starts to go back upstairs.*)

ELIZA. Eugene!

EUGENE (*coming out to her slowly*). Well, now—with your second sense, I thought you would have guessed it, Mama.

ELIZA (*sits left of left pillar*). Why didn't I know, why didn't I see?

EUGENE (*kneels at pillar*). I'm sorry, Mama, but we couldn't wait any longer.

ELIZA. Gene, child, don't make this mistake. She's so much older than you. Don't throw yourself away, boy!

EUGENE. Mama, there's no use arguing. Nothing you can say will change my mind.

ELIZA (*desperately*). And my plans for you? What of my plans for you?

EUGENE. Mama, I don't want your plans, I've got my own life to live! (*Moves to right on porch.* ELIZA *follows.*)

ELIZA. But you don't know! Gene, listen, you know that Stumptown property of mine? I sold it just yesterday so you could go to Chapel Hill— You know I've always wanted you to have an education. You can have it now, child, you can have it.

EUGENE. It's too late, Mama, it's too late!

ELIZA. Why law, child, it's never too late for anything! It's what Ben wanted, you know.

EUGENE. Laura and I are leaving, Mama. I'm going up to get packed. (*She turns away from his kiss and he exits into house.*)

ELIZA. Gene! (ELIZA *stands looking after him a moment, then quickly enters the hall, lifts the telephone receiver.*) Three-two, please. (*Waits.*)

HELEN (*enters from the kitchen, with a broom with which she sweeps the veranda*). What are you calling Uncle Will so early for?

ELIZA (*into phone*). Will? No, no, I know—I heard— Yes, I know it's early— Listen, Will, I want you to do something for me. You know my Stumptown property? I want you to sell it— Now, this morning— Will, don't argue with me— I don't care what it's worth. Call Cash Rankin, he's been after me for weeks to sell— Well, I know what I want to do— I'll explain it to you later— Just do what I say and let me know. (*She hangs up.*)

(LAURA *re-enters her bedroom.*)

HELEN. Well, it's never too early in the morning to turn a trade, is it? What are you selling?

ELIZA. Some property I own.

HELEN. Maybe you can put a little of that money into getting somebody else to help you at that altar of yours, the kitchen stove.

ELIZA (*puts sweater on hall chair*). Helen, get breakfast started, will you? I'll be in later. And if Gene comes down,

keep him in there, will you?

HELEN. Oh, all right. You let me know when I can let him out! (*Exits into house.*)

(ELIZA *appears at door of* LAURA's *room.* LAURA *is dressed and is packing her suitcase on the bed.*)

LAURA. Oh, Mrs. Gant. I've been expecting you. Come in. (*As* ELIZA *enters.*)

ELIZA. I should think you would.

LAURA. Mrs. Gant, before you say anything—

ELIZA. I'll vow I can't believe a mature woman—at a time of trouble like this— would take advantage of a child, a mere child—

LAURA. Mrs. Gant, will you please listen?

ELIZA (*tossing her nightgown from head of bed into suitcase*). I will listen to nothing. You just pack your things and get out of this house. I should have known what you were from the first minute I set eyes on you . . . "I'm looking for a room, Mrs. Gant . . ." Why, butter wouldn't melt in your mouth—

LAURA (*slowly, distinctly*). Mrs. Gant, I am not marrying Eugene. I'm not. I wish with all my heart I could!

ELIZA (*turning to dresser*). You can't lie out of it. Gene just told me.

LAURA. I am engaged to be married to a young man in Richmond.

ELIZA. What kind of a wicked game are you playing with my child?

LAURA (*sits bed*. ELIZA *sits chair left*). Mrs. Gant, this isn't easy. I should have told Gene long ago—but I didn't. A girl about to get married suddenly finds herself facing responsibilities. I never liked responsibilities. Gene knows how I am. I like music, I like to walk in the woods, I like—to dream. I know I'm older than Gene, but in many ways I'm younger. The thought of marriage frightened me. I told my fiancé I needed time to think it over. I fell in love with Eugene. I found the kind of romance I'd never known before, but I've also found that it isn't the answer. Gene is a wonderful boy, Mrs. Gant. He must go to college. He must have room to expand and grow, to find himself. He mustn't be tied down at this point in his life. He needs the whole world to wander in—and I know now that I need a home, I need children —I need a husband. (*Rises, closes bag.*) For people like me there are rules, very good rules for marriage and for happiness—and I've broken enough of them. I telephoned Philip last night. He's arriving at the depot on that early train. We're going on to Charleston together, and we'll be married there. He loves me, and I will love him too after a while. (*Takes note from desk.*) I left this note for Eugene. I couldn't just tell him. (*Gives it to* ELIZA. *Crosses for bag, puts it down left of head of bed. Gets hat and purse from bureau.*) Will you say good-bye to Mr. Gant for me, and tell him I hope he feels better? And my good-byes to Mr. Clatt and the others? And to Helen. Especially to Helen. She works so hard. (*Looks around.*) Good-bye, little room. I've been happy here. (*Picks up suitcase, faces* ELIZA.) Some day you're going to let him go, too. Good-bye, Mrs. Gant. (*She exits.*)

(*During the above* HUGH *has entered the veranda, is seated, reading the newspaper.* LAURA *enters from the house, looks back lingeringly, then, hearing the approaching train, hurries off toward the station down left.* HELEN *enters, drinking coffee.*)

HELEN. Mama? Now, where on earth! Hugh, have you seen Mama?

HUGH. Umph.

HELEN (*crosses upstage on porch*). Do you know she was on the phone just now selling some property? Imagine—at this hour! And she leaves me to slave in the kitchen. . . . Do you know where she is?

HUGH. You know, they don't advertise the good jobs in here, not the really big ones.

GANT (*entering in his suspenders, sleepily rubbing his jaw*). Isn't breakfast ready yet?

HELEN. Papa, how many times has Mama told you, you wait until the boarders have had theirs! And don't you dare appear in front of them in your suspenders, do you hear?

GANT. Merciful God! What a way to greet the day! (*He exits.*)

HELEN (*calling after* GANT). Papa, do you know where Mama is?

(HELEN *exits after* GANT. EUGENE *enters downstairs, carrying his suitcase, stops at* LAURA's *door, knocks.* ELIZA *has just laid* LAURA's *letter on the bed.*)

EUGENE. Laura? Laura? (*Enters to* ELIZA.) Mama! Where's Laura? Where is she?

ELIZA. She's gone.

EUGENE. Gone? Where?

ELIZA. She just walked out on you, child. Just walked out on you. (*Shakes her finger at him.*) I could have told you, the minute I laid eyes on her—

EUGENE (*seizing* ELIZA's *hand*). You sent her away.

ELIZA. I never did. She just walked out on you, child. (EUGENE *breaks for the door.* ELIZA *picks up the letter, runs after him.*) Gene! Eugene! Wait!

EUGENE (*runs down to the veranda*). Laura— (*Looks up street.*) Laura— (*As* HUGH *points toward station, starts off that way.*) Laura—

ELIZA (*entering, waving the letter*). Wait! Wait! She left you this. Gene! (EUGENE *turns, sees the letter.*) She left you this. Read it, child. (EUGENE *crosses to* ELIZA, *takes the letter, reads it as the train is heard leaving station.*) You see, it's no use. It's no use. (EUGENE *crosses slowly to the yard seat, sits.* ELIZA *watches him.* HELEN *enters through the front door.*)

HELEN. Mama, there you are! Where have you been? We've got to start getting breakfast. (*As* ELIZA *waves her to silence*) What's the matter?

ELIZA. That Miss James. She and Eugene—

HELEN (*laughs*). Oh my God, Mama, have you just found out about that? What about it?

ELIZA. She's gone.

HELEN. What?

ELIZA. She just walked out on him.

HELEN (*crosses to* EUGENE). Oh ho, so that's it, is it? Has your girl gone and left you, huh? Huh? (*Tickles his ribs; he turns, clasps her knees.*) Why, Gene, forget about it! You're only a kid yet. She's a grown woman.

ELIZA (*crossing above to left of* EUGENE). Helen's right. Why, child, I wouldn't let a girl get the best of me. She was just fooling you all the time, just leading you on, wasn't she, Helen?

HELEN. You'll forget her in a week, Gene.

ELIZA. Why, of course you will. Pshaw, this was just puppy love. Like the fellow says, there's plenty good fish in the sea, as ever came out of it.

HELEN. Cheer up, you're not the only man got fooled in his life!

HUGH (*from behind his paper*). By

God, that's the truth! (HELEN *and* ELIZA *glare at him.*)

ELIZA. Helen, go inside, I'll be in in a minute.

HELEN. Oh, all right. Hugh, you come in and help me. (HELEN *exits, followed by* HUGH.)

ELIZA (*sits beside* EUGENE, *his back still turned to her*). Gene. You know what I'd do if I were you? I'd just show her I was a good sport, that's what! I wouldn't let on to her that it affected me one bit. I'd write her just as big as you please and laugh about the whole thing.

EUGENE. Oh, God, Mama, please, leave me alone, leave me alone!

ELIZA. Why, I'd be ashamed to let any girl get my goat like that. When you get older, you'll just look back on this and laugh. You'll see. You'll be going to college next year, and you won't remember a thing about it. (EUGENE *turns, looks at her.*) I told you I'd sold that Stumptown property, and I have. This year's term has started already but next year—

EUGENE. Mama, *now! Now!* I've wasted enough time!

ELIZA. What are you talking about? Why you're a child yet, there's plenty of time yet—

EUGENE (*rises, walks about her, beggingly*). Mama, Mama, what is it? What more do you want from me? Do you want to strangle and drown me completely? Do you want more string? Do you want me to collect more bottles? Tell me what you want! Do you want more property? Do you want the town? Is that it?

ELIZA. Why, I don't know what you're talking about, boy. If I hadn't tried to accumulate a little something, none of you would have had a roof to call your own.

EUGENE (*right center*). A roof to call our own? Good God, I never had a bed to call my own! I never had a room to call my own! I never had a quilt to call my own that wasn't taken from me to warm the mob that rocks on that porch and grumbles.

ELIZA (*rises, looking for an escape*). Now you may sneer at the boarders if you like—

EUGENE. No, I can't. There's not breath or strength enough in me to sneer at them all I like. Ever since I was this

high, and you sent me to the store for the groceries, I used to think, "This food is not for us—it's for them!" Mama, making us wait until they've eaten, all these years—feeding us on *their* leftovers —do you know what it does to us?— when it's you we wanted for us, *you* we needed for us. Why? Why?

ELIZA (*trembling*). They don't hurt me like the rest of you do—they wouldn't talk to me like you are, for one thing. (*Starts toward side door.*)

EUGENE. Because they don't care— they're strangers. They don't give a damn about you! They'll talk like this about you behind your back—I've heard them do that plenty!

ELIZA (*turns*). What? What? What kind of things do they say about me?

EUGENE. What does it matter what they say—*they* say! Doesn't it matter to you what I say? (*Takes her in his arms, holds her.*)

ELIZA (*beginning to weep*). I don't understand.

EUGENE (*releases her, moves away*). Oh, it's easy to cry now, Mama, but it won't do you any good! I've done as much work for my wages as you deserve. I've given you fair value for your money, I thank you for nothing. (*Crosses up to the veranda.*)

ELIZA (*crosses to left of left pillar*). What's that? What are you saying!

EUGENE. I said I thank you for nothing, but I take that back. Yes, I have a great deal to be thankful for. I give thanks for every hour of loneliness I've had here, for every dirty cell you ever gave me to sleep in, for the ten million hours of indifference, and for these two minutes of cheap advice.

ELIZA. You will be punished if there's a just God in Heaven.

EUGENE. Oh, there is! I'm sure there is! Because I have been punished. By God, I shall spend the rest of my life getting my heart back, healing and forgetting every scar you put upon me when I was a child. The first move I ever made after the cradle was to crawl for the door. And every move I ever made since has been an effort to escape. And now, at last I am free from all of you. And I shall get me some order out of this chaos. I shall find my way out of it yet, though it takes me twenty years more—alone. (*Starts for door.*)

ELIZA. Gene! Gene, you're not leaving?

EUGENE. Ah, you were not looking, were you? I've already gone.

(EUGENE *exits into the house.* ELIZA *sits on the veranda edge, stunned.* GANT, *wearing a vest over his suspenders, enters.*)

GANT. Now do you suppose I can get some breakfast? (ELIZA *doesn't answer.*) Well, do you mind if I make a fire in the fireplace? (*Goes to woodbox, muttering.*) If I can't get any food to keep me alive, I can get a little warmth out of this drafty barn! (*Starts collecting wood from box.*) Some day I'm going to burn up this house—just pile in all the logs that old grate'll hold—and all the furniture—and all the wooden-headed people around here —and some kerosene—till this old barn takes off like a giant cinder blazing through the sky. That would show them —all fifteen miserable rooms—burning, blistering—

ELIZA. I wish you would, Mr. Gant. I just wish you would.

GANT. You think I'm joking.

ELIZA. No, I don't.

GANT. If I just get drunk enough, I will!

ELIZA (*rises, faces house*). Serve it right —miserable, unholy house!

GANT. Why, Miss Eliza!

ELIZA. I'll do it myself— (*With demoniacal strength she shakes the left pillar by the steps.*) I'll tear you down! I'll kill you, house, kill you! I'll shake you to pieces!

GANT. Let me help you, Mrs. Gant! (*Picks up* MRS. PERT's *rocker, crashes it.*)

HELEN (*entering hurriedly*). Eliza Gant, have you gone mad!

GANT (*drops wood, starts tearing at the other post.*) God-damned barn! Thief! Travesty on nature

ELIZA. God-damned barn!—(*Hits latticed panels under the veranda left with stick of wood.*)

HELEN (*calls inside*). Hugh, come out here!

WILL (*entering from rear of veranda*). My God, what are they doing?

GANT (*screaming up at house. Brandishing torn pillar*). Clatt—Mangle—Brown— Come out of there, you rats, all of you —come out, come out, wherever you are!

(*The boarders begin to yell and squeal from inside.*)

ELIZA (*hysterically imitating* GANT; *crossing left*). Come out, come out, wherever you are!

HUGH (*entering*). What's going on?

GANT (*breaking off the newel post; crosses to right center*). We're tearing down this murderous trap, that's what. Hand me the hatchet, Hugh. It's in the woodbox.

HUGH. Fine! Fine! (*Dashes to woodbox, takes out hatchet.*)

(*Boarders enter downstairs in various stages of undress.*)

MISS BROWN. Call the police.

MRS. CLATT. Let's get to Mrs. Haskell's!

JAKE. Gant's off his nut!

GANT (*chasing them off left, threatening the boarders*). Squeal, you croaking bastards. Croak and run! Run for your lives!

BOARDERS (*ad lib as they scurry off.*) The house is falling down!—It's a tornado! —Ladies' Temperance Society, humph!— Has anyone called the police?—(*etc.*)

HUGH (*yard right center*). Here's the hatchet, W.O.

GANT (*leaping for it. Tossing pillar up right center*). Give it to me.

WILL (*right of* HUGH, *grabbing for hatchet*). Stop it, Gant—stop this! Have you all lost your minds?

ELIZA (*throwing flower pot after the boarders.*) Go to Mrs. Haskell's!

HELEN. Mama!

GANT (*brandishing hatchet at* JAKE *and* MRS. CLATT *as they exit porch up right*). Look at 'em run! And they haven't even had breakfast. Run, scatterbrains, empty-bellies!

JAKE. I'll sue you for this, Gant, I'll sue you for this! (*Exits.*)

(MRS. SNOWDEN *enters through front door,* GANT *whirls on her.*)

GANT. So you don't like the food here? So you don't like my wife's coffee! (MRS. SNOWDEN, *screaming, hastily retreats.*)

ELIZA (*lifting a chair to hurl after the boarders*). Why, law, that's good coffee! (HELEN *seizes* ELIZA's *arms, stops her.* ELIZA's *sensibilities slowly return.*)

GANT. Look at 'em run! Oh, Miss Eliza, what a woman you are! (*Roaring with laughter, he crosses down to* ELIZA, *is about to embrace her, sees her sober, shocked face.*)

ELIZA (*picking up broken pillar*). Mr. Gant, Mr. Gant, what have you done? What have you done?

GANT. What have I done? What have

I— Merciful God, woman!

ELIZA (*tosses pillar onto porch left*). Just look at this mess! And the boarders have all gone!

HELEN (*left of* ELIZA). I don't know what got into you, Papa.

GANT (*speechless, turns to* HUGH *on porch right*). Merciful God! What got into me? Didn't she just stand there herself and—

ELIZA. Helen, go get the boarders, tell them he's been drinking, tell them anything, but get them back!

WILL (*down right*). I never saw such an exhibition.

ELIZA. Will, go with Helen. Tell them we all apologize. They'll listen to you. Hugh, help me clean up this mess. (HELEN *and* WILL *exit after the boarders up right*.)

GANT. Let them go, Miss Eliza. *Let the boarders go!* (ELIZA *stands rigid.* GANT *waits anxiously.*)

ELIZA (*on porch center*). I just don't know what came over me.

GANT (*crosses—flings the hatchet in the woodbox.* ELIZA *crosses to see damage to veranda lattice.*) Merciful God! (EUGENE *enters with his suitcase.*) Where are you going?

EUGENE. I'm going to school at Chapel Hill, Papa.

GANT. You are? (*He looks at* ELIZA.)

EUGENE. Mama promised me the money. She sold her Stumptown property.

GANT (*crosses to right of her*). Oh? By God, maybe it isn't going to be such a god-damned miserable day, after all! Got any money, son?

EUGENE (*in yard, right of* GANT). I've got Ben's money. Thanks, Papa.

GANT (*takes money from his pocket, tucks it into* EUGENE's *pocket*). Well, go, Gene. Go for both of us. Keep right on going.

EUGENE. I will, Papa. Good-bye.

GANT (*as they shake hands*). Good-bye, Gene. (*Starts into house, turns.*) You're going to bust loose, boy—you're going to bust loose, all over this dreary planet!

(GANT *exits.* EUGENE *crosses to right of* ELIZA, *who starts picking up the debris.*)

ELIZA. I reckon you've made up your mind all right.

EUGENE. Yes, Mama, I have. (*Crosses down left.*)

ELIZA (*crosses to porch, slamming wood in woodbox*). Well, I'll deposit the money in the Chapel Hill Bank for you. I tell you what! It looks mighty funny, though, that you can't just stay a day or two more with Ben gone and all. It seems you'll do anything to get away from me. That's all right, I know your mind's made up and I'm not complaining! It seems all I've ever been fit for around here is to cook and sew. That's all the use any of you have ever had for me—

EUGENE. Mama, don't think you can work on my feelings here at the last minute.

ELIZA. It seems I've hardly laid eyes on you all summer long— (*Replacing wood in woodbox and picking up rocker.* EUGENE *turns to her.*) Well, when you get up there, you want to look up your Uncle Emerson and Aunt Lucy. Your Aunt Lucy took a great liking to you when they were down here, and when you're in a strange town it's mighty good sometimes to have someone you know. And say, when you see your Uncle Emerson, you might just tell him not to be surprised to see me any time now. (*She nods pertly at him.*) I reckon I can pick right up and light out the same as the next fellow when I get ready. I'm not going to spend all my days slaving away for a lot of boarders—it don't pay. If I can turn a couple of trades here this fall, I just may start out to see the world like I always intended to. I was talking to Cash Rankin the other day—he said, "Why, Mrs. Gant," he said, "if I had your head for figures, I'd be a rich man in—" (*Her talk drifts off.* EUGENE *stands looking at her. There is another terrible silence between them. She points at him with her finger, finally her old loose masculine gesture. Crossing to left on porch.*) Here's the thing I'm going to do. You know that lot of mine on Sunset Terrace, right above Dick Webster's place? Well, I been thinking. If we started to build there right away, we could be in our own house by spring. I've been thinking about it a lot lately. . . . (*There is another silence.*) I hate to see you go, son.

EUGENE. Good-bye, Mama.

ELIZA. Try to be happy, child, try to be a little more happy. . . . (*She turns and, with unsteady step, starts into the house.*)

EUGENE. MAMA! (*He drops the valise, takes the steps in a single bound, catching*

ELIZA's *rough hands, which she had held clasped across her body, and drawing them to his breast.*) GOOD-BYE . . . GOOD-BYE . . . GOOD-BYE . . . MAMA . . .

ELIZA (*holding him*). Poor child . . . poor child . . . poor child. (*Huskily, faintly*) We must try to love one another. (*Finally* EUGENE *moves from her, picks up the valise, as the lights start dimming, holding a spot on her.* ELIZA *seems to recede in the distance as into his memory.*) Now for Heaven's sake, spruce up, boy, spruce up! Throw your shoulders back! And smile, look pleasant! Let them know up there that you *are* somebody!

(ELIZA's *voice fades, the set is black. A spot holds on* EUGENE.)

EPILOGUE

BEN's VOICE. So you're finally going, Gene?

EUGENE. Ben? Is that you, Ben?

BEN's VOICE. Who did you think it was, you little idiot? Do you know why you're going, or are you just taking a ride on a train?

EUGENE (*looking up and front right*). I know. Of course I know why I'm going. There's nothing here for me. Ben, what really happens? Everything is going. Everything changes and passes away. Can you remember some of the things I do?

I've already forgotten the old faces. I forget the names of people I knew for years. I get their faces mixed. I get their heads stuck on other people's bodies. I think one man has said what another said. And I forget. There is something I have lost and can't remember.

BEN's VOICE. The things you have forgotten and are trying to remember is the child that you were. He's gone, Gene, as I am gone. And will never return. No matter where you search for him, in a million streets, in a thousand cities.

EUGENE. Then I'll search for an end to hunger, and the happy land!

BEN's VOICE. Ah, there is no happy land. There is no end to hunger!

EUGENE. Ben, help me! You must have an answer. Help me, and I won't go searching for it.

BEN's VOICE. You little fool, what do you want to find out there?

EUGENE. *I want to find the world. Where is the world?*

BEN's VOICE (*fading*). The world is nowhere, Gene. . . .

EUGENE. Ben, wait! Answer me!

BEN's VOICE. The world is nowhere, no one, Gene. *You* are your world.

(*The train whistle sounds. Lights reveal Dixieland in dim silhouette.* EUGENE, *without looking back, exits.*)

CURTAIN

ALL THE WAY HOME

Tad Mosel

Based on *A Death in the Family* by JAMES AGEE

Presented by Fred Coe in association with Arthur Cantor
at the Belasco Theatre, New York, on November 30, 1960,
with the following cast:

RUFUS John Megna	JESSIE FOLLET Georgia Simmons
BOYS Larry Provost	JIM-WILSON Christopher Month
Jeff Conaway	AUNT SADIE FOLLET Dorrit Kelton
Gary Morgan	GREAT-GREAT-GRANMAW Lylah Tiffany
Robert Ader	CATHERINE LYNCH Lillian Gish
JAY FOLLET Arthur Hill	AUNT HANNAH LYNCH Aline MacMahon
MARY FOLLET Colleen Dewhurst	JOEL LYNCH Thomas Chalmers
RALPH FOLLET Clifton James	ANDREW LYNCH Tom Wheatley
SALLY FOLLET Lenka Peterson	FATHER JACKSON Art Smith
JOHN HENRY FOLLET Edwin Wolfe	

Directed by Arthur Penn
Settings and lighting by David Hays
Costumes by Raymond Sovey

The action takes place in and around Knoxville, Tennessee,
and covers a period of four days in May of 1915.
ACT ONE. The first day.
ACT TWO. The second day.
ACT THREE. Two days later.

ALL THE WAY HOME is based upon the autobiographical novel *A Death in the Family* by James Agee, the Southern-born film critic, journalist, and screen writer (scenarist of *The African Queen, The Night of the Hunter,* and *The Quiet One*) who died in 1955 at the age of forty-six. The adapter, Tad Mosel, who must be credited with the organization and technique of the play as well as with many fine adjustments to the stage, was already widely experienced in dramatic media, especially in television, to which he turned after graduation from Amherst and post-graduate studies at the Yale University's School of Drama and Columbia University's now defunct School of Dramatic Arts.

The play received an unusual amount of support from New York reviewers, who wanted it to stay on the boards when the attendance thinned out early in the course of the production. A Pulitzer Prize also helped to extend the run of a play that, aside from the sadness of the principal action, had pockets of stasis in outward action. But outweighing the defects, rather unavoidable once Mr. Mosel had made the courageous decision to dramatize Agee's book, were the humanity and honesty of the adapter's presentation of character, which he refrained from adulterating with plot manipulations for the purpose of providing "action" at any cost. It is hard to determine whether the favorable reviews were influenced by what Mr. Mosel put into the play or what he refrained from putting into it.

A particularly astute criticism was made by the genial critic and author George Oppenheimer (*Newsday,* Dec. 14, 1960) when he wrote, "I feel one of its [the adaptation's] shortcomings is that, despite a first act of careful preparation, the relationship between the wife and the husband, who is soon to be killed in an automobile accident, is not too clearly defined. It is evident that there are areas of conflict between them, but they are stated rather than explored." There are other relationships, however, that were splendidly realized in the play: the visit to the ancestral old crone which brings us close to elemental reality in a play about life and death, the wife's explosion of wrath at her husband's accident, and, generally, the little son's tender and humorous encounter with life which ends up as an encounter with death for which the only possible shield is love. It is for these and other dramatic elements, as well as for the rare quality of simple honesty in the play, that the New York Drama Critics Circle Award and the Pulitzer Prize went to *All the Way Home* in the spring of 1961.

The Setting of the Play

The Follets live in a mixed sort of neighborhood, fairly solidly lower middle class, with one or two juts apiece on either side of that. The houses correspond: middle-sized, gracefully fretted wood houses built in the late nineties and early nineteen hundreds, with small front and side and more spacious back yards, and porches, and trees in the yards. These are soft-wooded trees, poplars, tulip trees, cottonwoods. There are fences around one or two of the houses, but mainly the yards run into each other with only now and then a low hedge that isn't doing very well.

The stage itself is encircled by a high cyclorama of vertical grey clapboards, suggesting perhaps the walls of a house, the paling of a gigantic fence, or even the sky. It is a background for the action of the play, dim, indistinguishable at times, bright and sunny at others, but always unobtrusive.

The structure of the Follets' two story house fills most of the stage. The living room is stage left, with an upright piano against the cyclorama, a Morris chair and a davenport facing the audience. The kitchen is stage center, with a table and two chairs, a sink, an ice box, a small cupboard, and a telephone. The stairs rise to the second floor upstage, between the living room and the kitchen. There are two bedrooms upstairs, the larger one belongs to Mary and Jay, center stage, over the kitchen, and containing a double bed and a bureau. Rufus's room is stage left, over the living room, with a small child's bed, a rocking chair, and a decorated trunk. Only the furniture mentioned is visible. Only the most necessary properties are used.

There are no interior or exterior walls to the house, and window shades suspended in mid-air suggest windows. The characters move from room to room, into the house or out of the house, without regard to placement of doors. If a character upstairs wishes to speak to a character in the yard, he merely steps to the edge of the second story and calls down to him. Sometimes the characters cannot hear what is going on in another room, and at other times the rooms join together to become a single acting area.

The only solid wall on the stage is the upstage wall of the kitchen, behind which is an escape area for the actors. From the kitchen, a practical door in this wall leads to the bathroom. At the foot of the stairs, another door opens into a closet. By going around the other side of the stairs, the characters presumably go into the other downstairs rooms of the house.

Stage right, between the structure of the house and the cyclorama, there is an open area with an old-fashioned swing suspended from the flies. Sometimes this area is the Follets' yard, sometimes it is a streetcar stop (when the swing becomes the waiting bench), and once it is Great-Great-Granmaw's yard. Below the house, running across the front of the stage, there is another shallow areas which is sometimes part of the Follets' yard, sometimes a sidewalk, and once it is a road.

ACT ONE

AT RISE: RUFUS, *aged six, in the yard. Four older boys wearing rakish gaudy caps dance around him, jumping up and down with ferocious joy, shoving their fingers at his chest, his stomach and face, screaming and chanting.* JAY *enters and watches, unseen by them.*

———

RUFUS (*as the curtain rises, one clear frantic call*). My name is Rufus!

BOYS (*together*). Nigger's name, nigger's name, nigger's name!

RUFUS. Rufus! Rufus!

FIRST BOY (*as the others chant "nigger's name!"*).

Nigger, nigger, black as tar,

Tried to ride a 'lectric car,

Car broke down and broke his back,

Poor nigger wanted his nickel back!

RUFUS. I'm Rufus!

BOYS (*together*).

Uh-Rufus, uh-Rastus, uh-Johnson, uh-Brown,

Uh-what ya gonna do when the rent comes 'roun'?

Uh-Rufus, uh-Rastus, uh-Johnson, uh-Brown,

Uh-what ya gonna do when the rent comes 'roun'?

(RUFUS *makes one desperate effort to*

escape, running straight into JAY's *arms*.)

FIRST BOY. Nigger name! Hey, we're gonna catch hell! (*They scramble off, and* JAY *looks after them, glowering. Then he puts his hand on* RUFUS's *head and smiles down at him.*)

JAY. What in the world you doin', Google Eyes?

RUFUS. I wish my name was Google Eyes.

JAY. No you don't, because that's a funny name. You wouldn't want to be called by a funny name.

RUFUS. Rufus is a funny name.

JAY. No honey, it ain't.

RUFUS. It's a nigger's name.

JAY (*looking out over the valley*). Look, we got a nice clear day for the outing, don't we. You can see all the way to North Knoxville. And if you squint your eyes you can see the North Pole. Squint your eyes. (*They both squint for a moment.*) See the Pole? (RUFUS *nods, enchanted.*) And see that puff o' smoke comin' up over the hill? That means there'll be a train along the viaduct any minute. The one-oh-seven.

MARY (*off*). Rufus—?

RUFUS. Mama's calling me.

JAY (*taking his hand, in high good spirits*). Let's just watch that train go by! (*They both look out.*) You know, Rufus is a very fine old name, Rufus. Some colored people take it too, but that is perfectly all right and nothing for them to be ashamed of, or for white people to be ashamed of who take it. You were given that name because it was your Great-Grandfather Lynch's name, your mama's grandfather, and it's a name to be proud of. You're proud of it, ain't you?

RUFUS. Yes, sir.

JAY. Then you got to stand up for it. Can you spell brave?

RUFUS. B-r-a-v-e.

JAY. Now proud.

RUFUS. P-r-o-u-d.

JAY. That's the one. Just keep spellin' that.

RUFUS. P-r-o-u-d.

JAY. You know what I'm proud of?

RUFUS (*guessing*). Mama?

JAY. You, too. Why you're only six years old, and you can read and spell like I couldn't when I was twicet your age.

RUFUS (*looking off, after the boys*). I wish you could be proud of me because I'm brave.

JAY. One of these days you'll get those boys to shake you by the hand. When a man shakes you by the hand, that means you've won him over. (*He puts out his hand.* RUFUS *grabs it.*) Hold on there, y'only got me by the ends of the fingers. Push your thumb clear up against mine, that's it—then wrap your fingers as far's you can around the palm of my hand, right to the other side, if you can. Now squeeze. Not too much, that's just braggin'. Just enough to show you mean what you're doin'. Now shake. (*They solemnly shake, and* JAY *looks off excitedly.*) There she goes, right on time!

(*With a burst of good spirits, he begins to sing.*)

"Oh, I hear them train cars a-rumblin',
And, they're mighty near at hand,
I hear that train come a-rumblin',
Come a-rumblin' through the land!"

(*He lifts* RUFUS *to his shoulders.*)

"Git on board, little children,
Git on board, little children,
Git on board, little children,
There's room for many and more!"

(*As he sings, the lights come up on the house.* MARY FOLLET *is placing bowls of flowers in the living room.*)

"Oh, I look a way down yonder,
And, uh-what do you reckon I see,
A band of shinin' angels
A-comin' after me!"

(MARY *gets a tray of glasses from the kitchen table and joins them in the yard, singing along with* JAY, *achieving some pleasing harmonies.*)

JAY & MARY (*singing*).

"Git on board, little children,
Git on board, little children,
Git on board, little children,
There's room for many and more!"

(*As they finish the song.* JAY *swings* RUFUS *lightly to the ground.*)

RUFUS. Here comes the one-oh-seven! (*He chugs into the house like a train and settles into the Morris chair with his coloring book.*)

MARY. Don't you go away, Rufus! Your daddy's *people* will be here any minute! (*Turning to* JAY, *as if with a very amusing confidence she has been saving for him.*) Ralph just called up on the telephone!

JAY. Where from?

MARY. You know Ralph! He wasn't ten blocks away, just down town. But instead of coming right on, he went to all the trouble of parking the machine, going in some place and calling up to say they were *almost* here! (*She laughs and places the tray on the ground beside the swing.*)

JAY (*laughing with her*). Did you ever know anyone to get such a kick outa telephones?

MARY. If you ask me, he was in a saloon. Probably didn't want to telephone at all, if you know what I mean, but used it as an excuse to Sally for stopping, and then once he was in there he felt he'd better *really* call us, because Sally'd find out from us if he didn't and then she'd know that wasn't why he stopped!

JAY (*whistling*). You sure can complicate a thought, Mama!

MARY. You know what I mean!

JAY (*grinning*). Did he say anything about knockin' Kaiser Wilhelm's block off?

MARY. No, thank goodness, he was *very pleasant!* (*She laughs.*)

JAY. Then I reckon we'll still have a nice day.

MARY (*seriously*). When they get here, Jay, you won't—I mean you won't let Ralph influence you?

JAY. Oh, I might hoist a few with him!

MARY (*uncertainly*). Jay—?

JAY. Sure, you and the others go on to Great-Granmaw's! I figure Ralph and I'll stay here and have ourselves a bender! I'm just ripe for it!

MARY. Don't say that, even in fun!

JAY (*laughing, putting his arms around her*). Aw now Mary, you don't ever worry about me any more, do you?

MARY. I just don't like jokes about that particular subject.

JAY. And you know what I don't like? Super-intendents! No sir, I don't like people lookin' down on me, thinkin' they got to keep an eye on me.

MARY (*shocked*). Was I looking down on you?

JAY. Why, you was about ten feet off the ground!

MARY (*crushed*). Honestly, Jay?

JAY. Two feet.

MARY. Well, *shame* on me. And I *certainly* thank you for pointing it out.

JAY (*impulsively holding her close, singing in her ear*). "I got a gal and a sugar babe, too—My honey, my baby . . ."

MARY. That awful song! (*She laughs.*)

JAY. I guess I know how to get on the good side of you, don't I?

MARY. I guess you do! (*He kisses her. She steps back primly, really tremendously pleased.*) Well, I certainly hope the neighbors enjoyed that! (*And she turns briskly into the living room.*) Rufus, I had this room all straightened up for your daddy's *people!*

JAY (*following*). They won't be coming in here, Mary.

MARY. I want them to be able to if they want to, don't I?

JAY (*scraping his pipe into the ashtray*). Rufus'll clean up the mess he made, won't you, honey?

MARY. And will *you* clean up the mess *you're* making with that pipe? Honestly, Jay!

JAY (*picking up the dirtied ashtray, looking around, not knowing what to do with it*). Rufus, did you ever think of starting a collection of pipe scrapelings?

RUFUS (*at once interested*). Scrapelings?

JAY. Sure, that's what they're called.

MARY. Really, Jay!

JAY. You wrap 'em up in a little piece of paper and you mark 'em with the date and whose pipe they come out of, then you put 'em away in some secret hiding place where no one'll ever find 'em.

MARY (*laughing*). All *right*, Jay!

RUFUS. Please, Mama, may I?

MARY. Of course you may, just don't spill them all over everything! And get your feet off your daddy's chair—! (*She stoops to pick up the coloring book.*)

JAY. Rufus, don't make your mama pick up after you—

MARY (*straightening up quickly*). Oh—!

JAY. What is it, honey?

MARY. It just made me dizzy for a moment—

JAY. Here, you sit right down.

RUFUS. What's the matter, Mama?

JAY. Are you all right now?

MARY. Of course I am. It was just a thing of the minute. It's to be expected from now on.

RUFUS (*demanding*). What's the *matter?*

MARY. Mama just stooped over very

quickly, that's all, and it made the room go around. (RUFUS *stoops over very quickly and straightens up hopefully.*)

RUFUS. It's not going around.

MARY. Not for *you*, dear—

JAY. Why don't you tell him, Mary?

MARY. Oh Jay, please—!

RUFUS. Tell me what?

MARY. There, you *see*?

JAY. He has to find out some time.

MARY. But not *now*—!

RUFUS. Find out what, Mama?

JAY. Won't be long before he sees for himself that *something's* happening.

MARY (*flaring*). Not if you don't bring it to his attention!

JAY. I'd have told him weeks ago if you'd let me!

MARY. I wanted to talk to Father Jackson first.

JAY. You don't need any priest to tell you how to talk to your own boy.

MARY. Jay, I don't want him asking q-u-e-s-t-i-o-n-s!

JAY. That won't do y'any good, Mama, he can out-spell the both of us put together.

(RUFUS *has been looking from one to the other during this. There is now a silence.*)

RUFUS. I can get dizzy on a swing! Or if I turn around in circles fast like this—! (*He whirls.*) Look Mama, *I'm* gettin' dizzy! Look!

MARY. Rufus. (*He stops whirling.*) Come here to Mama. (*She takes him on her lap.*) Rufus—after a while you're going to have a wonderful surprise.

RUFUS. Like a present?

MARY. Something. Only very much nicer.

RUFUS. What's it going to *be*?

MARY. If I told you, it wouldn't be a surprise any more, would it?

(JAY *begins to frown.*)

RUFUS. Will I get it today?

MARY. No dear, not for a long time yet.

RUFUS. When summer vacation starts?

MARY. Not till after summer vacation *ends,* and you've gone back to school. Not even till after you've cut out your pumpkin for Halloween.

RUFUS. Where is it now?

MARY. It's in heaven. Still up in heaven.

JAY. Tell him it's right here with us.

RUFUS. Right *here*— (*He looks quickly under the davenport and under the piano.*)

JAY (*stopping him*). For the next few months, Rufus, you and I've got to take special care of Mama. (*He cups his hands as if holding a very fragile object.*) We've got to treat her like something that might just break. (RUFUS *looks wonderingly into the cup of* JAY's *hands.*)

MARY. I think we've told him enough for the time being. He knows there's a surprise coming for us from heaven, and he has something to look forward to.

JAY. If we don't tell him all of it, honey, the older boys will in the streets. Would you like that?

RUFUS (*astounded*). What do *they* know?

MARY. Nothing dear, nothing at all!

RUFUS (*excitedly*). Is it a cap, Mama? Is the surprise a cap?

MARY (*finding an outlet for her irritation*). Rufus, I've told you again and again you can't *have* one of those cheap flashy caps! And I've told you to stay away from those rowdy boys!

JAY. What if *they* won't stay away from *him*?

MARY (*hugging* RUFUS). Now darling, will you do Mama a favor? There's a lunch hamper on the kitchen table, and I want you to take it out by the alley so it'll be all ready to put in Uncle Ralph's car. Will you do that?

RUFUS. Do I have to?

JAY. Do what your mama says, Rufus. (*During the following,* RUFUS *struggles off with the hamper. There is an uncomfortable silence between* MARY *and* JAY.)

JAY. I think it'd make him feel more grown up if he had a cap like the older boys.

MARY. He's not grown up, Jay.

JAY. It's kind of hard for a fellow to know where he stands around here. You tell him to stay away from the older boys, and I tell him to win 'em over. You say the surprise is up in the sky some place, I say it's right here on earth. Yes sir, it sure is hard for a fellow to know what's going on.

MARY. He's just a *child*.

JAY. All that about priests and *heaven* —! Sets my teeth on edge.

MARY. Oh Jay, sometimes I pray—

JAY. That's your privilege.

MARY. Now I can't say what I was going to say.

JAY. I'm listening.

MARY. But you're keeping your distance. As you always do when these things come up. There's a space of about a hundred miles between us.

JAY. And you've got that pursed-*up* look. That preachy pursed-up look.

(*Another awkward silence. Neither one gives in. Finally she goes to him.*)

MARY. When the baby comes, it'll be time enough for him to hear about it, Jay. (*She puts her arms around his waist and leans against him. He does not respond.*)

JAY. Sure, Mary.

MARY (*stepping back, hurt, going to the kitchen*). I thought we'd all have a glass of something cold before we start. (*He bangs his pipe loudly into the ashtray while she gets the lemonade pitcher from the icebox. She stops in the middle of the kitchen and closes her eyes.*) Oh Lord, in Thy mercy, Who can do all things, close this gulf between us. Make us one in *Thee* as we are in earthly wedlock. For Jesus' sake, Amen. (*She crosses herself.* JAY *has followed and heard. She turns and sees him looking at her. There is a sudden loud whooping, off, and* RUFUS *runs in.*)

RUFUS. They're here, they're here! (*He tugs at his father to get him outside, then runs off again.*)

MARY. That's not Ralph's car!

JAY (*laughing*). But that sure is Ralph gettin' out! (*He hurries excitedly to the yard to meet* RALPH FOLLET, *his brother.*) Hey there, Ralph!

RALPH. We made it, Jay, safe and sound!

JAY (*eagerly*). Where'd you get the car?

RALPH. D'you like 'er?

JAY (*impressed*). Chalmers, ain't it?

RALPH. Goes like sixty, Jay!

JAY (*laughing*). What're you tryin' t'do, make me look like a piker?

RALPH (*punching at him*). Well, y'are a piker, ya piker, with your ole Tin Lizzy! (*Dashing to* MARY *who has come out with the pitcher of lemonade.*) How ya been, sweetheart!

MARY. I'm fine, Ralph!

RALPH (*admiringly*). I gotta hug ya, just gotta hug ya! (*He grabs her.*) You can hug Sally if you want to, Jay! *Ever'*body hugs *my* wife!

MARY (*pulls away from his whiskey breath*). I thought we'd have a glass of something cold before we start, Ralph!

RALPH. Did I do somethin' wrong, Mary?

MARY. Goodness sakes, *no!* Just tell the rest of them to get out of the car before they suffocate!

RALPH (*yelling*). Come on, ever'body, Mary's got us a glass of somethin' cold! And isn't it just like you, Mary! I was sayin' to them as we were drivin' along, I'll bet Jay's wife thinks of havin' somethin' cold waitin'—

(RUFUS *runs in crying.*)

RUFUS. Daddy, Daddy !

JAY. Why, what's the trouble honey? (*Squatting to* RUFUS's *level.*) What you cryin' about? Wuzza matter, honey? (*He takes out his handkerchief.*)

RALPH. Oh, Jay, y'oughtn't ever to call a boy "honey"!

JAY (*to* RUFUS). Come on, blow. You know your mama don't like you to swallah that stuff.

MARY. What is it, Rufus, what's happened?

(RUFUS *hides from her.*)

JAY. I reckon it ain't fit for ladies' ears, Mary. Maybe you better turn your back.

MARY (*turning away*). Oh, for goodness *sakes!*

JAY. Now *tell* Daddy. (RUFUS *whispers in his ear.*) Is that all? Why, is that all it is?

MARY. What is it, Jay?

JAY (*standing, as* RUFUS *hides his face in shame*). It seems that Rufus, here, has had a little accident.

MARY. Accident—?

RALPH. Did my Jim-Wilson hit him? Because if he did—

JAY. No Ralph, nothin' like that. You know, Mary. An accident.

MARY. Oh Rufus, you're too *old* for that! And I had you all dressed up for your daddy's people. Jay, you'll have to help him change.

JAY. He's old enough to manage by himself.

RALPH (*with a whoop of delight*). *That* kind of an accident?

JAY. Musta been the excitement of the day.

RALPH. Oh that's rich, that is! (*In a sing-song*) Rufus is a baby, Rufus is a baby!

(RUFUS *runs into the house.*)

JAY. That'll do, Ralph!

RALPH (*laughing happily as* SALLY, JIM-WILSON, JESSIE *and* JOHN HENRY *come in from the car.* JESSIE *carries a small rubber inner tube*). Did y'hear that ever'body? Rufus had an accident! That's how my Chalmers affects people, they take one look at it and wet their britches!

SALLY. Ralph!

RALPH. Pee their pants!

(*There is sudden loud activity as everybody greets one another.*)

SALLY (*to* MARY). I think I'll take him right inside, Mary, and get it over with— (*She and* JIM-WILSON *start for the house.*)

MARY. You'll find everything ready for you, Sally, make yourself at home— Mama Follet, how good to see you!

RALPH (*simultaneously with above*). Find a chair for Paw to sit down, Jay, he shouldn't stand around too much— this is what I like, all the Follets in one yard—where you goin', Sally?

JESSIE (*to* MARY, *simultaneously with above*). I reckon I'll just never get used to ridin' in automobiles, Mary, m'ear's all plugged up—not that Ralph ain't a good driver—

JAY (*simultaneously with above*). You sit down right over here, Paw, and rest yourself—

RALPH (*shouting*). Sally! (*All talking, greeting and movement stop.*) I asked you where you were goin'!

SALLY. I'm taking Jim-Wilson to the bathroom before we have any more accidents.

RALPH. Oh. Well, I just like you to answer me when I ask you a question! (SALLY *and* JIM-WILSON *continue on with* RALPH *following as far as the kitchen.*) Did you hear me, Sally? I just like you to answer when I ask you a question! (*She is gone, and as the others talk in the yard,* RALPH *takes out a pint from his pocket and has a swallow.*)

JESSIE. Here Paw, you better sit on your tube. (*She helps him to rise halfway and puts the inner tube underneath him.*)

MARY. Will you have something cold to drink, Mama Follet?

JESSIE. Wait on Paw first, if you will, Mary dear. I know how parched he gets. How's your breath, Paw?

JOHN HENRY. Pretty fair.

JAY. You haven't had any more of your attacks, have you, Paw?

JOHN HENRY. Not since that time last fall, Jay. (*He and* JESSIE *knock on the wood of their chairs.*)

JAY (*grinning*). Maw sure does spoil you then.

JESSIE. When you come close to losing someone, that's the way you do.

JAY. Some easy life, I'll say!

JESSIE. I'm sure Mary spoils you enough.

MARY (*serving*). Oh no, I think Jay spoils me!

JESSIE. So he should with another baby on the way. (*Eyeing her appraisingly.*) It don't show yet, do it, Mary. (MARY *laughs, embarrassed, and smooths her dress.*) Well, some show early, some show late. Ralph showed almost afore I knew he was there. Jay, you was a kicker. You all right, Paw?

JOHN HENRY. Pretty good.

MARY (*calling, as she returns to the tray of glasses*). Ralph, are you in there?

RALPH (*in the kitchen, quickly putting the bottle into his pocket*). Be right with yuh, Mary!

MARY. Do you want some lemonade?

RALPH (*bustling out*). Thank yuh, Mary, I'm dry's a bone.

(MARY *serves them lemonade.*)

JAY. Things must be pretty good for you, Ralph, if you can afford to go out and buy a new Chalmers.

RALPH. Oh yes, Jay, considerin' the state of the world 'n' all, Ralph Follet's doin' fine, just fine!

JESSIE (*shaking her head*). Tst tst.

RALPH. Aw right, Maw, so I borrowed the money, but in this day and age you got to be in a sound financial situation to borrow money! (*Turning to* JAY *enthusiastically.*) Why Jay, I walked into Ed Briggs' office at the bank in LaFollette, and he says "You want to buy a car, Ralph? Take whatever you need!" That's how highly thought of I am in *that* bank!

JAY. I'm surprised he didn't give you the keys to the safe, Ralph.

RALPH (*to his parents, gratified*). You hear what Jay said?

JOHN HENRY. I reckon Ed Briggs knew what he was doin'. An undertaker's always a good risk.

RALPH. It wasn't that, Paw!

JOHN HENRY (*bewildered*). I'm tryin'

to give you a compliment, son.

JESSIE. Paw's right. Only thing you can be sure of in life is, people go on dyin'.

MARY. Oh Mama Follet, I'd rather say they go on being born.

JESSIE (*nodding*). That too, Mary, they got to be born afore they can die.

RALPH. Ed Briggs give me that money because it was *me* askin' for it! Why there's other undertakers in LaFollette he wouldn't give the time o' day to!

JESSIE. Just the same, your paw never owed a cent in his life, Ralph, did you, Paw? (SALLY *comes out of the house.*)

JOHN HENRY. I'm even thinkin' maybe the farm'll be free and clear afore I die, Jay.

JAY. You worked hard for it, Paw.

JOHN HENRY (*vaguely*). *You* owe any money, Jay?

RALPH (*before* JAY *can answer*). What if he don't, *I* happen to want to give *Sally* some of life's refinements! I don't like the idea *my* wife ridin' around town in some old Tin Lizzy!

MARY (*laughing*). Why, Ralph, I just love our Ford!

SALLY. I never get to ride around town in *anything*! *He's* always off some place! He only bought that new car because of you, Jay, so he'd have a better one than yours, and don't let him tell you different!

MARY. I'm certainly anxious to *ride* in it! Aren't you, Jay?

JAY (*grinning at her*). Just can't wait!

RALPH (*angrily to* SALLY). And what're *you* doin' at home while I'm out in the car on *business,* just tell me that!

MARY. Why don't we get started! (*Calling.*) Rufus—?

RALPH. The trouble with my wife is she don't appreciate how I try to please her! (*To* SALLY) You ask Maw the things she's had to do without all her life and see how lucky y'are!

JESSIE. Now I know one thing I *can* do without, and that's any more of this talk.

JAY. Sure Ralph, come on! We've all been lookin' forward to a good time to-day!

RALPH (*sulking*). I'm *havin'* a good time. (*As* JIM-WILSON *comes out; snapping at him*) Get out here, Jim-Wilson, and start enjoyin' yourself.

SALLY (*to* JIM-WILSON). Would you like some lemonade, dear?

RALPH. My God, she just gets him all drained out and she fills him up again!

MARY. Did you see Rufus in there, Jim-Wilson?

RALPH (*sing-song*). Rufus is a baby, Rufus is a baby!

MARY. Please Ralph, that's enough of that.

RALPH. Rufus is a ba-by!

MARY. Ralph, you're to stop!

RALPH. Just teasin', Mary!

MARY. Well, you're to stop it, what*ever* it is! The child had a perfectly normal accident!

RALPH. Why, Jim-Wilson hasn't had an accident like that in years, and he's younger'n Rufus by 'leven months!

MARY (*angrily*). I don't care what Jim-Wilson does! (*Catching herself.*) I didn't mean that, of course, Sally. (*Stooping quickly to hug* JIM-WILSON.) Aunt Mary cares the *world* about Jim-Wilson!

RALPH (*laughing*). God-damn it, why is it ever'thin' I say today gets me into trouble!

MARY (*flaring again*). And I'll thank you not to take the Lord's name in vain!

RALPH (*exploding*). This family ain't Catholics and I'll take the Lord's name any way that comes to mind!

(*There is a shocked silence.*)

JESSIE. Tst tst.

JAY. You sure like to hit all bases, don't you, Ralph.

RALPH. I'm sorry for what I said, Jay. (*Crossing shyly, apologetically to* MARY) Mary, Jim-Wilson does pee his pants ever' day without fail.

JAY. Then I think you oughta get Rufus out here and apologize to him for making fun of him.

RALPH. Sure, Jay, of course. (*Calling*) Rufus? Come on out here, Rufus! (RUFUS *steals down the stairs from his room.*) This is your Uncle Ralph callin' to you. I promise not t'tease y'any more. D'you hear me, Rufus? (RUFUS *comes out of the house.*) There he is! Looky here. (*He digs into his pocket and pulls out a business card.*) I got somethin' for you. Take it. (RUFUS *takes the card and looks at it.* RALPH *reads it for him.*) "Ralph Follet, Mortician." We friends again? (RUFUS *looks to* JAY *who pantomimes shaking hands.* RUFUS *puts out his hand and* RALPH *takes it. They shake.* RALPH *sinks to his knees, pretending to writhe in the strength of* RUFUS's *grip.*) Oh-o-o-ooh—! (RUFUS *laughs and squeezes harder.* RALPH *howls in mock pain.* JAY *laughs and* MARY *laughs.* RALPH *leaps to his feet with an exuberant whoop.*) That's what I like, ever'body friends again! All the Follets is friends, ain't we, Mary?

MARY. Of course we are, Ralph!

JESSIE (*rising, helping* JOHN HENRY *up*). If we're goin' t'get there this afternoon, we'd best get started.

RALPH. Maw's right! Come on ever'-body, pile in the Chalmers! Jay, you and Mary sit up front with me and Rufus! (*He lifts* RUFUS *high in the air.*) You can sit on my lap, Rufus, and maybe I'll even let you steer!

SALLY. I think Jay ought to drive.

(*It rings through the happy activity, and all movement stops as everybody looks to* RALPH.)

RALPH (*incredulous, dropping* RUFUS *to the ground*). Drive *my* car?

SALLY. You're in no fit condition to drive it.

RALPH. Well, nobody else is goin' to drive it, I'll tell you that! Not *my* car!

SALLY. Can we go in your car, Jay?

RALPH. His old Tin Lizzy? We couldn't even all get in it!

SALLY. I'd rather be a little crowded and have Jay drive.

RALPH. Jay this an' Jay that, ever'body always lookin' up to Jay, askin' *Jay's* advice, lettin' *Jay* do the drivin'! Well, let me tell you, there's been times when you wouldn't ride with him neither! *He's* been hauled outa the gutter more times'n you can count *and* put in jail *and* worse!

SALLY. You go ahead in the Chalmers, Ralph, and the rest of us'll follow with Jay in his car.

RALPH (*beside himself*). And you'll be sittin' up there next to him, I suppose, rubbin' legs with him! So it's *Jay* you're after now!

JAY. That thought never once came into Sally's head and you know it. So dry up!

RALPH. Don't think you're the only one she's after, either! Don't get no swelled head it's just you! It's any man with a flat belly, that's who it is! Any man at all, so long as his belly don't get in the way! (JAY *attempts to take his arm, but* RALPH *swings wildly at him.*) God-damn your flat belly! (*He stumbles towards the*

house, turning back for only a moment.) I've a good mind t'go over there an' punch that Kaiser Wilhelm in the nose! Then maybe the lotta y'll treat me with a little respect! (*He goes into the kitchen and a deep sigh seems to pass among the people in the yard. He takes out his pint and has a swallow.*)

JESSIE. Better let me make you comfortable again, Paw. (*She puts the inner tube under him.*)

SALLY. Every time he sets out to enjoy himself he—gets so unhappy.

MARY. I'll look after him, Jay. (*She starts for the house.*)

JAY (*stopping her*). I reckon you've had to do enough of that kinda lookin' after people—for your time. (*He goes into the kitchen to find* RALPH *staring fixedly at his hands.* MARY *crosses to the swing with* RUFUS. *Then she joins* SALLY *on the swing.* RUFUS *and* JIM-WILSON *go to play in the yard behind them.*)

RALPH. Smell my hands, Jay, go ahead, smell 'em.

JAY. Now there's nothin' on your hands, Ralph.

RALPH. Yes there is, Jay, it's that f'maldehyde. *I* can't smell it but ever'body else can. I scrub 'em and scrub 'em, and I can't ever get rid of that smell. Why last night I went to the picture show, and I was sittin' there next t'this girl and she got up and moved. It was that smell, Jay, don't you think?

JAY. Go on, Ralph, you're the worst tail chaser in LaFollette!

RALPH (*angrily*). It was 'at smell made her move, I tell yuh! It's terrible t'work with it ever' day of your life, and then even when you go out for a good time t'have it go along with yuh. The picture show was good though. Charlie. You like Charlie?

JAY. Sure do.

RALPH. Last night he put a bag of eggs in the seat of his pants and then forgot and sat on 'em. (*He pantomimes this and sits in chair at the table.*)

JAY (*laughing*). Rufus and I seen that one.

RALPH (*laughing with him*). You 'n' I like lotsa the same things, Jay, maybe we're more brothers than we seem.

JAY. I reckon people'd know we was brothers.

RALPH. Thank yuh for that. (*Taking*

up the bottle.) Well, outside they're thinkin' he's been in there long enough for two drinks, and I've only had one. If that's what they're goin' to think, I might's well *have* two! (*He drinks.*)

JAY. You sure can hold it, Ralph.

RALPH (*pushing the bottle across the table to him*). He'p yourself.

JAY. Ever'body's waitin' on us, Ralph!

RALPH. Go on, Jay, Mary can't see. I tell you what, I'll keep watch for yuh!

JAY. It ain't that. (*He shoves the bottle at Ralph who grabs it from him.*)

RALPH. So God-damned reformed, ain't you!

JAY. I'm just thinkin' of you. If you keep pullin' away at that bottle, it ain't goin' to last you through the day. And I know that feelin' when the bottle's empty and you ain't full.

RALPH (*close to tears*). I want it to be empty, Jay. I'm no good when I'm like this. No good at all. I'm mean and I'm reckless. I'm not even real. *I wish this bottle was empty!*

(*After a short silence,* JAY *grabs the bottle from him, drinks the last of the whiskey and drops the bottle loudly into the trash can.*)

JAY. Empty. Now are you ready to go?

RALPH. How's it make you feel, Jay?

JAY. That little bit don't make me feel anything.

RALPH. If you had a lot?

JAY. Come on, Ralph, it's gettin' late. If we're going to get to Great-Granmaw's and back before dark, we got to start.

RALPH. I ain't movin' from this spot till you tell me how it makes you feel!

JAY. Well, if I had as much as you, Ralph, I'd go quiet. So quiet, I could hear the tickin' of the earth. And I'd be young as ever I could remember, and nothin' bad had ever happened to me or ever would. I wouldn't dare talk to no one, of course, for fear they'd show me the lie. And after a while it'd get lonesome in there all by myself, and I'd go off like a fire-cracker. If you happened to be standin' by, you'd get a few powder burns, let me tell you.

RALPH. What made you change, Jay? Was it Mary's religion?

JAY. Mary's religion is her own.

RALPH. How'd you do it, then?

JAY. I made a vow to myself. I said if I ever get drunk again, I'll kill myself.

RALPH. Oh Jay. That's a strong vow.

JAY. Couldn't afford to leave myself any loopholes.

RALPH. Don't y'ever get thirsty?

JAY. There's too many reasons why I don't want to kill myself.

RALPH. What reasons?

JAY. There's two of 'em right out in the yard. (*Grinning*) As a matter of fact, two'n a half.

RUFUS (*outside*). Daddy!

JAY (*his patience beginning to go*). Now come on, Ralph, I promised them an outing today! They been lookin' forward to it for weeks, and I'm not goin' to disappoint them!

RALPH. I got reasons out in the yard too, don't I, Jay?

JAY (*giving him a towel, briskly*). Now wipe off your face. You worked yourself into a sweat.

(RALPH *wipes his face.*)

RALPH. I could take that vow of yours, couldn't I, Jay?

JAY. Nobody's goin' to try and stop you!

RALPH. I'm takin' that vow this minute! Stand back! (*He stands up and straightens himself.*) Or Jay, maybe I could just take a vow that if ever I get drunk again I'll take your vow.

JAY. You better think on it, Ralph, that's a pretty serious step!

RALPH (*enthusiastically*). All right, Jay, I tell you what! I hereby take a vow—to think on it!

JAY. Good for you! (*They come outside.*) All set everybody?

SALLY. Which car are we going in?

JAY. Why, the Chalmers, of course. I wouldn't pass up a chance to ride in a Chalmers!

RALPH. But I've asked Jay to do the drivin'! I'm going to ride on the running board!

SALLY. Oh, Ralph!

RALPH. I got to point out the route to Jay, because I'm the only one remembers how to get there!

(*They begin to arrange themselves on two benches which vaguely represent the Chalmers.* SALLY *is on the upstage end of the rear bench,* JESSIE *next to her,* JOHN HENRY *downstage holding* RUFUS *on his lap.* JAY *is on the downstage end of the front bench with* MARY *beside him, hold-*

ing JIM-WILSON *in her lap.* RALPH *stands above them on the "running board."*)

JESSIE. Be sure you do remember, Ralph. We don't want to get lost in those mountains.

JOHN HENRY. There used to be cats back in those mountains. We called 'em painters then, Rufus. That's the same as a panther.

JAY. They was around here when I was a boy, Paw. And there still is bear, they claim. (JIM-WILSON *whimpers.*) Don't you fret, Jim-Wilson, we ain't likely to see any.

MARY. When was the last time all of you saw Great-Granmaw?

RALPH. I was the last to see her! I come out one day about twenty years ago!

MARY. Twenty years! Why for goodness sake, Ralph, you certainly have a wonderful memory to find the way!

RALPH (*pleased*). I've always had a pretty good memory.

MARY. Why, that's *remarkable!* How long since you came out here, Jay?

JAY. I'm a-studyin' it. Nearly thirteen years. The last time was just before I went to Panama.

MARY. Then *you* were the last one to see her!

RALPH. Wait a minute, seems to me I seen her since then!

JOHN HENRY. Are you sure that's the place, Ralph? That don't look like I remember it.

RALPH. Oh that's it all right! Why sure! Only we come up on it from behind!

MARY. She doesn't live there alone, does she?

JOHN HENRY. My sister Sadie give her life to her. She wouldn't come and live with any of us. I raised my family in this cabin, she said, I lived all my life from fourteen years on and I aim to die here. That must have been a good thirty-five, most, a good forty years ago, Grampaw died.

(SADIE *has begun slowly to push* GREAT-GRANMAW *in a home-made wheelchair from upstage right to down right apron.*)

MARY. Goodness' sakes, and she was an old woman then!

JAY. She's a hundred and three years old. Hundred and three or hundred and four, she never could remember for sure which. But she knows she wasn't born later than eighteen twelve. And she always reckoned it might of been eighteen eleven.

MARY. Do you know what she is, Rufus? She's Grampa Follet's grandmother!

JOHN HENRY. That's a fact, Rufus. Woulda never believed you'd hear *me* call nobody Granmaw, now would you?

RUFUS. No sir.

JOHN HENRY. Well, you're gonna!

RALPH (*picking* JIM-WILSON *up from* MARY's *lap*). Are you listenin' to all this, Jim-Wilson.

JAY. She's an old, old lady.

RALPH (*an echo, awed*). Old.

(AUNT SADIE *comes to meet them, they all stand.*)

SADIE. Lord God. (*She looks from one to the other.*) Lord God.

JOHN HENRY. Howdy, Sadie.

SADIE. Howdy, John Henry.

JOHN HENRY. Thought maybe you wouldn'ta knowed us.

SADIE. I know'd you all the minute I laid eyes on you. Just couldn't believe it. Howdy, Jessie.

JESSIE. It's good to see you, Sadie.

JAY. Howdy, Aunt Sadie.

SADIE. Howdy, Jay. You Jay's brother?

RALPH. I'm Ralph, Aunt Sadie.

SADIE. Howdy, Ralph.

RALPH. That's my machine we come in. And this is my bride Sally. (*Glancing shyly at* SALLY) That's how I thinka her.

SADIE (*looking at* SALLY). Pretty.

JAY. And this is Mary, Aunt Sadie. Mary, this is Aunt Sadie.

SADIE. I'm proud to know you. I figured it must be you. And Rufus.

MARY (*to* RUFUS). Say hello to Aunt Sadie.

RUFUS. Hello, Aunt Sadie.

RALPH. Jim-Wilson? Step up and kiss your Aunt Sadie and give her a hug. *This* is *my* boy, Aunt Sadie.

(SADIE *snorts and grabs* JIM-WILSON's *hand, scaring him back to* SALLY's *skirts. Then she stands back.*)

SADIE. Lord God.

JAY. How's Granmaw?

SADIE. Good's we got any right to expect. But don't feel put out if she don't know none-a-yews. She mought and she mought not. Half the time she don't even know me.

RALPH. Poor old soul.

SADIE. So if I was you-all, I'd come up

on her kind of easy. Bin a coon's age since she seen so many folks at oncet. Me either. Mought skeer her if you all come a-whoopin' up on her in a flock.

JAY. Whyn't you go see her the first? Paw? You're the eldest.

JOHN HENRY. 'Tain't me she wants to see. Hit's the younguns'd tickle her most.

SADIE. Reckon that's true, if she can take notice. (*To* JAY) She shore like to cracked her heels when she heard *yore* boy was borned. Proud as Lucifer. 'Cause that was the first.

MARY. I know. Fifth generation that made.

RALPH. Sally and I lost a baby the year *before* Rufus was born. That *woulda* been the first.

SADIE (*to* JAY). She always seemed to take a shine to you.

JAY. I always did take a shine to her.

SADIE. Did you get her postcard?

JAY. What postcard?

SADIE. When yore boy was borned.

MARY. Why, no!

SADIE. She told me what to write on one a them postcards and put hit in the mail to both a yews and I done it. Didn't you never git it?

JAY. First I've heard tell of it.

MARY. What street did you send it to, Aunt Sadie? Because we moved just before Rufus was born—

SADIE. Never sent it to no street. Never knowed I needed to, Jay working for the Post Office.

JAY. Why, I quit working for the post office a long time back, Aunt Sadie. I'm in law now, for Mary's paw.

SADIE. Well, I reckon that's how come then. 'Cause I just sent it to "Post Office, Cristobal, Canal Zone, Panama." And I spelt it right, too C-r-i—

MARY. Oh.

JAY. Aw—why Aunt Sadie, I thought you'd a known. I been living in Knoxvul since before I was married even.

SADIE (*looking at him keenly, almost angrily, then nodding several times*). Well, they might just as well put me out to grass. Let me lay down and give me both barls threw the head.

MARY. Why, Aunt Sadie.

SADIE. I knowed that like I knowed my own name and it plumb slipped my mind.

MARY. Oh, what a shame.

SADIE. If I git like that, too, then who's a-goana look out for *her?*

RALPH. What did she say on the postcard, Aunt Sadie?

SADIE. Lemme figger. Bin so long ago. (*She thinks for a moment.*) "I bin borned again," she says. "Love, Great-Granmaw."

MARY. Born again. Why that's beautiful.

SADIE. Mebbe. I always figgered bein' borned oncet was enough. (*She goes to* GREAT-GRANMAW.) Granmaw, ya got company. (*The old woman does not move.* SADIE *speaks loudly but does not shout.*) It's Jay and his wife and the others come up from Knoxvul to see you. (*The hands crawl in the lap and the face turns toward the younger woman. A thin, dry cackling, but no words.*) She knows ye. Come on over, Jay. (JAY, MARY *and* RUFUS *advance slowly, shyly.*) I'll tell her about the resta yuns in a minute.

RALPH (*herding the others back further*). Aunt Sadie'll tell her about us in a minute.

SADIE. Don't holler. It only skeers her. Just talk loud and plain right up next her ear.

MARY. I know. My mother is deaf.

JAY (*bending close to* GRANMAW's *ear*). Granmaw? (*He draws away a little where she can see him.* GREAT-GRANMAW *looks straight into his eyes and her eyes and face never change.* JAY *leans forward again and gently kisses her on the mouth. Then he draws back again, smiling a little anxiously. He speaks into her ear.*) I'm Jay. John Henry's boy.

(*The old lady's hands crawl on her skirt. Her mouth opens and shuts, emitting the low dry croaking. But her eyes do not change.*)

SADIE (*quietly*). I figure she knows you.

JAY. She can't talk any more, can she?

SADIE. Times she can. Times she can't. Ain't only so seldom call for talk, reckon she loses the hang of it. But I figger she knows ye and I'm tickled she does.

JAY. Come here, Rufus.

MARY. Go to him. (*She gives* RUFUS *a gentle push toward* JAY.)

JAY. Just call her Granmaw. Get right up to her ear like you do to Granmaw Lynch and say, "Granmaw, I'm Rufus."

(RUFUS *walks over to* GRANMAW *as quietly as if she is asleep. He stands on tiptoe and puts his mouth to her ear.*)

RUFUS. Granmaw, I'm Rufus.

JAY. Come out where she can see you.
(RUFUS *draws back and stands still further on tiptoe, leaning across where she can see him.*)

RUFUS. I'm Rufus.

(*Suddenly the old eyes dart a little and look straight into his, not changing expression.*)

JAY. Tell her "I'm Jay's boy Rufus."

RUFUS. I'm Jay's boy Rufus.

JAY. Now kiss her.

(RUFUS *kisses her. Suddenly the old woman's hands grip his arms and shoulders, drawing him closer, looking at him, almost glaring and suddenly she is smiling so hard that her chin and nose almost touch, and her eyes fill with light and almost giggle with joy. And again the croaking gurgle, making shapes that are surely words but incomprehensible words, and she holds him even more tightly and cocks her head to one side. With sudden love,* RUFUS *kisses her again.*)

MARY (*whispering, frightened*). Jay—!

JAY. Let them be.

(*After a moment,* SADIE *gently disengages* GRANMAW's *hands from* RUFUS's *arms.* RUFUS *steps back with his parents, and the three of them edge away toward the others. They are now a good distance from* GRANMAW, *watching intently as* SADIE *bends over her.* GRANMAW's *face settles back into its former expression, as if nothing had taken place.*)

MARY (*hushed*). Is she all right?

SADIE. All she knows is somethin's been took from her.

(*A silence, and in the silence, the lights dim on* GRANMAW, *leaving the family gazing at empty space.*)

JOHN HENRY. We won't none of us ever see Granmaw again.

JAY. I wouldn't be surprised, Paw. (*He goes into the house and up to* RUFUS's *room.*)

JOHN HENRY. The hand of death is comin' close to this family. (JIM-WILSON *whimpers.*)

RALPH (*reverently*). Well—when her time comes, I'll be—honored to 'ficiate. Free of charge. (RALPH, SALLY *and* JIM-WILSON *go off.*)

RUFUS. Mama? Do you know what happened?

MARY. What, dear?

RUFUS. Great-great-granmaw had an accident. (MARY *looks down at him.*) When I kissed her. (MARY *looks away, close to tears.*) Isn't she too old for that? (MARY *takes his hand and leads him off.*) Isn't she, Mama?

JESSIE. How's your breath, Paw?

JOHN HENRY. Pretty fair.

(*They exit and the lights dim.* JAY *has been singing softly; now the lights come up on him as he stands by* RUFUS's *bed singing him to sleep. He holds a tattered cloth dog in his hands.*)

JAY (*singing*).

Every time the sun goes down,
'Nother dollar made for Betsy Brown.
Sugar Babe.
There's a good old saying, Lord, ever'-
   body know
You can't track a rabbit when there ain't
   no snow.
Sugar Babe.

(MARY *comes out of the bathroom in her nightgown. As she goes upstairs, her voice joins his in clear, graceful harmonies. The lights come up on their bedroom. She pulls the shade, brushes her hair, turns down the bed and sits on it to braid her hair.*)

Now it ain't going to rain and it ain't
   going to snow.
The sun's going to shine and the wind's
   going to blow.
Sugar Babe.

(*He looks down at* RUFUS's *bed and speaks softly.*) 'Sleep now, Google-Eyes? (*There is no answer. He quietly leaves the room. The light fades there. He joins* MARY.) Look what I found.

MARY. What, dear?

JAY. His ole dog Jackie.

MARY (*taking it*). Goodness sakes, where was it?

JAY. Back in a corner under the crib. I was scarin' the Boogee Man outa there.

MARY. The *crib!* Shame on *me!*

JAY. Poor ole Jackie.

MARY. Is Rufus asleep?

JAY. Yeah, he's asleep.

MARY. What was the matter with him?

JAY. Bad dream, I reckon. (*He starts to undo his necktie.*) Pore little ole Jackie, so lonesome and thrown away. Remember when I got him?

MARY. Of course I do. You took such pleasure in picking him out.

JAY. Little ole Jackie was bigger'n Rufus. And I had to explain. "It's a dog,"

I had to say. Only "dog" was too big a word in those days. I gave you too soon, Jackie. And here it is too late. Left behind with the baby crib. (*He picks up the toy from the bed.*)

MARY. I'm certainly glad we kept that crib. It'll save buying a new one.

JAY (*tossing the toy to the floor*). Back to the corner with you, Jackie.

MARY. Don't leave it there, darling. (He *retrieves the dog.*) What is it, Jay?

JAY. Nothin'. (*He stands in the middle of the room, the dog in his hands. She waits.*) I reckon it's just seein' Great-Granmaw again and rememberin' the summers I had out there. And it's seein' Paw begin to shrink up, and watchin' Ralph. And it's feelin' Rufus growin' bigger, and singin' those sad ole songs. And findin' Jackie. It's just the day, Mary.

MARY. It's been a long one.

(JAY *pulls at the dog and a piece comes off in his hand.*)

JAY. Jackie's ear come off. It's enough to make a man thirsty. (*Abruptly, grimly, he dashes* JACKIE *to the floor and runs downstairs where he takes a whiskey bottle from the hall closet.* MARY *picks up her robe and hurries down to find him standing in the living room, staring at the bottle. He goes into the kitchen.*) How far we all come, Mary. How far we all come away from ourselves. So far, so much between, you can't even remember where you started or what you had in mind or where you thought you were goin'. All you know is you were headin' *some* place. (*He hefts the bottle, as if testing its weight.*) One way you do remember. (*He puts the bottle on the kitchen table.*) You have a boy or a girl of your own, and now and then you sing to them or hold them, and you know how they feel, and it's almost the same as if you were your own self again. Just think, Mary, my paw used to sing to me. And before my time, even before I was dreamed of in this world, his daddy or his mother used to sing to him, and away on back through the mountains, back past Great-Granmaw, away on back through the years, right on back to Adam, only nobody ever sang to Adam.

MARY. God did.

JAY. Maybe God did.

MARY. We're supposed to come away

from ourselves, Jay. That's the whole point. We're supposed to come away to— (*She stops herself.*)

JAY. I know. To God.

(*She nods.*)

MARY. I don't see how you can *feel* the way you do and not believe in Him.

JAY. We come from people, Mary, and in time they fall away from us, like Great-Granmaw. We give birth to others, and in time they *grow* away from us, like Rufus will. (*He picks up the bottle.*) When we're about eighty years old, you'n me, all we'll have left is us. And that's what I believe in. (*He puts the bottle back in the closet.*) Maybe that's it. Maybe that's where we're heading—to each other. And the sad thing all our lives is the distance between us. But maybe if we keep goin' in the direction we think is right, maybe we can't ever get all the way there, but at least we can make that distance less'n it was. (*She goes to him and they embrace.*) You'll catch cole down here like that. Now wait'll I warm up the bed for you. (*He runs upstairs and rubs his hands swiftly between the sheets. She follows him and sits on the bed. He kneels before her, removes her slippers and warms her feet in his hands.*) When I was a youngster on the farm, on cold nights we all used to pile into one bed together. Finally I was too big for that, but I wasn't too big to cry at bein' left alone in a big cold bed all by myself. An' my maw, she brought me her own pillah and she put it under the covers next to me. And she said to pretend it was one o' *them* keepin' me warm through the night and watchin' over me. Pore Maw. She slep' without a pillar for a coupla months there. (*He takes her in his arms and kisses her.*) Now *your* job is to get the *other* side o' the bed warm for *me!* (*Under the covers,* MARY *runs her hands on* JAY's *side of the bed and warms it. There is the sudden sharp ring of the telephone downstairs. All sound, all movement stops for a moment. The ring is repeated.* MARY *sits up in bed and* JAY *goes out grumbling.*) Now who could that be this time o' night? (*He goes down to the kitchen and answers the telephone.*) Hello—? Yeah, Central, this is Jay Follet—put 'im through. Hello, Ralph? What's the trouble? Ralph? Sure I can hear you, what's the matter? Are you cryin', Ralph? (*Impatiently*) Paw? Listen, Ralph, I 'preciate your calling and you're *not* putting me out—now tell me about Paw. (*He listens.*) I should come up, huh? (*Suddenly angry*) Hold on, Ralph, you hold on there! I'm glad I'm not where I could hit you—! If Paw's that bad you know damn well I'm comin' so don't give me none o' that! Will you stop *cryin'!* Now listen to me, Ralph, I want you to get it straight I'm not tryin' to jump on you, but sometimes you're likely to exaggerate and—no, I don't think you're alyin' to me—and no, I don't think you're drunk! I just want you to think for a minute! *Just how sick is he really*, Ralph? (*In a fury*) *Think*, God-damn it! (MARY *has followed him downstairs, turned on the kitchen light, lighted the stove, put a few fresh grounds into the coffee pot and placed it on the flame. She is now sitting in the chair left of the table, listening.*) Listen, Ralph, I know you wouldn'ta phoned if you didn't think it was serious.

MARY (*whispering*). Is Sally there?

JAY. Is Sally out to the farm? And 'course Maw's there.

MARY. Doctor?

JAY. And the doctor? What's he say?—From the way you tell me that, I suspect the doctor said a *good* chance. (*Now anxious to hang up*) Look here, Ralph, I'm talkin' too much. I'm startin' right on up. I ought to be there by—what time is it now?

MARY (*looking at living-room clock*). It's eleven-thirty.

JAY. It's eleven-thirty, Ralph. I ought to be there by two, two-thirty. Well, I'm afraid that's the best my ole Tin Lizzy can make it, Ralph. You tell Maw I'm comin' right on up quick's I can.

MARY. Is he conscious?

JAY. Is he conscious? Well, if he gets conscious, just let him know I'm comin'! That's all right, Ralph. Don't mention it—Mary understands . . . Good-bye, Ralph. That's all right . . . Thanks for calling. *Good-bye, Ralph!* (*He hangs up.*) My God, talkin' to him's like tryin' to put socks on an octopus.

MARY. Is it very grave?

JAY. Lord knows. I can't be sure of anything with Ralph, but I can't afford to take the risk.

MARY (*to table with cup and saucer*). Of course not.

JAY. What're *you* up to?

MARY. I'm fixing you something to eat.

JAY. Aw, honey, I'll get a bite on the way if I want to.

MARY. In one of those all-night lunchrooms? Sakes alive!

JAY. It'll be quicker, honest it will. (*He goes upstairs.*)

MARY. I don't want your mother to think I don't feed you. (*She checks the coffee, runs into the living room, selects a pipe from the rack on the piano, picks up* JAY's *tobacco pouch and returns to the kitchen, putting them on the table by the cup and saucer. She returns to the stove to tend the coffee. During this,* JAY *has been putting on his vest and coat in their bedroom. He is about to go out of the room when he sees the rumpled bed. He smooths out the covers, pulling them high to keep in the warmth. Then, on a sudden thought, he puts his pillow well down under the covers where he would normally sleep. He leaves the room, looks in briefly on* RUFUS, *then goes down into the living room. He selects a pipe, searches vainly for his tobacco pouch and enters the kitchen.*)

JAY. Have you seen my tobacco—aw, you had it all ready for me.

MARY. I had to guess which pipe you wanted to take.

JAY (*picking up her choice, slipping his own into his pocket*). Just the one I was looking for.

MARY (*pleased*). It's the one I gave you. (*Pulling back a chair at the table*) At least you have time for a cup of coffee. (*As he hesitates*) It's the way you like it. (*He grins and sits. She pours the coffee.*) The pot's choked *full* of old grounds, and I added some new.

JAY (*sipping*). Now that's *coffee*.

MARY. I'd as soon watch you drink sulfuric acid.

JAY. The outing musta been too much for him. Paw just sits there so quiet any more we don't always know what's going on underneath. He got home and just collapsed.

MARY. Isn't it funny, Jay. This afternoon he was saying we'd be losing your great-grandmother soon. And now it turns out your father's the one in danger.

JAY. I guess we never know who's in

danger. (*She fills his cup again.*) You got a birthday coming up. What would you like to do?

MARY. Why Jay. Why—you nice thing. Why—

JAY. You think it over. Whatever you'd like best. Within reason, of course. I'll see we manage it. (*Then as they both remember*) That is, of course, if everything goes the way we hope it will, up home. (*He goes into living room where he scrapes out his pipe. She follows him.*)

MARY. It's time, isn't it? You're almost looking forward to it, aren't you, Jay? The all-night lunchroom. Driving through the night when everybody else is asleep, going fast.

JAY. I just know I have to go, Mary. So I'm anxious to get started.

MARY (*giving him a hug*). Don't drive too fast.

JAY (*pointing to the ashtray*). Scrapelings for him to find in the morning. For his collection.

MARY. I wonder if we should wake him up. I'm afraid he's going to be disappointed you didn't tell him good-bye.

JAY. I've looked in on him. Tell you what. Tell him, don't promise him or anything, of course, but tell him I'm practically sure to be back before he's asleep tomorrow night. Tell him I'll do my best.

MARY. All right, Jay. Give my love to your mother. Tell her they're both in my thoughts and wishes constantly. And your father, of course, if he's—well enough to talk.

(*By now they are at the back door.*)

JAY. Don't you come any further.

MARY (*feeling a chill*). It was so warm this afternoon. (*He kisses her.*) I wish I could go with you, Jay. In whatever happens.

JAY. Why'd you add that?

MARY. It's the way I feel.

(*He kisses her again.*)

JAY. I'll let you know quick's I can, if it's serious. (*He goes across the yard rapidly. She stands in the door. He stops, halfway.*) Hey, how's your money?

MARY (*thinking quickly*). All right, thank you.

JAY. Tell *him* I'll even try to make it for supper!

MARY. All right, dear.

JAY. Goodnight.

MARY. Goodnight.

(*He goes to the edge of the stage and turns back once more.*)

JAY (*in a loud whisper*). I keep forgettin' to tell you! I want this next one to be a girl! (*He goes. She stands waiting in the door, but is chilled again and goes inside, turns off stove and kitchen light, goes upstairs. She sees the lump on the bed, pulls back the covers wonderingly, then she smiles.*)

MARY. The dear. Why, the dear. (*She gets into bed and hugs the pillow as . . .*)

THE CURTAIN FALLS

ACT TWO

AT RISE: *Catherine is sitting in chair left of kitchen table. Mary is measuring a slipcover which she is making for the living room davenport.*

———

CATHERINE. Father Jackson and I have had the loveliest afternoon planning aid to war-stricken Europe. And since we were all to come here for supper, I saw no reason for going home, only to come out again. So I thought I'd stop by early, Mary dear, and we could have a nice quiet chat.

MARY. Lovely, Mama.

CATHERINE (*lifting her ear trumpet*). Beg pardon?

MARY (*loudly into trumpet*). We can have a nice quiet chat!

CATHERINE. Lovely. Of course when your papa finds out I've been with Father Jackson, there's no telling what he'll say. (*Dropping her ear trumpet firmly to her lap*) Well, I simply shan't listen. (*The telephone rings and MARY starts for the kitchen.*) Bathroom?

MARY. Telephone!! (*She answers.*) Hello? Yes, Central, go ahead—Jay? Jay darling, I've been so anxious all day. How's your father? Oh dear, then you went all that way for nothing. Now there's no sense in getting angry about it, darling, you know Ralph—just be thankful your father's all right. (*RUFUS runs down the stairs and starts to tiptoe out.*) Rufus, come say hello to Grandma Lynch. (*He puts out his hand to CATHERINE who hugs him.*) Where's your hat?

RUFUS. I forgot.

MARY. Well, *get* it, darling.

(RUFUS *goes into the living room where he pulls his hat out from under his jacket where he has hidden it.*)

MARY. What's that, dear? Oh then you'll definitely be here for supper—the family's coming up

CATHERINE (*overlapping*). If that's Jay, give him my love.

MARY. Yes, Mama's here already and she sends her love. The others are coming up later and Andrew has a present for me that they're all being very mysterious about, so do try to make it, Jay. Well, don't hurry, not if it means driving fast, because I can hold supper—I'd rather hold it than have you race—all right, darling, we'll see you very soon then—thank you for calling—goodbye. (*She hangs up and speaks into* CATHERINE'*s ear trumpet.*) Excuse me! (*She goes into the living room.*) Rufus, what are you doing under there—? You're supposed to be at the streetcar stop.

RUFUS (*climbing out from under the piano bench where he has been searching for something*). I was looking for the surprise.

MARY. The surprise?

RUFUS. Daddy said it was in here some place.

MARY. Oh Rufus, oh darling—!

RUFUS. He said so, didn't he?

MARY (*adjusting his hat*). Now don't ask questions, darling, you *can't* keep Aunt Hannah waiting. That was Daddy on the telephone and Grampa Follet's going to be all right! Isn't that wonderful? And Daddy said he'd be home in time for supper—think of that, Rufus! You'll see him before you go to bed! (*Stepping back to survey his appearance*) Now—what are you going to say to Aunt Hannah?

RUFUS (*as if reciting a piece in school*). I am glad to go shopping with you—

MARY. *So* glad.

RUFUS. I am so glad to go shopping with you, Aunt Hannah, and thank you for—

MARY. Thank you *very much*.

RUFUS. And thank you very much for thinking of me.

MARY. Now say it all together.

RUFUS. I - am - so - glad - to - go - shopping - with - you - Aunt - Hannah - and - thank - you - very - much - for -

thinking - of - me!

MARY (*laughs and kisses him*). And be sure to help with her parcels.

(RUFUS *goes out to the yard.*)

CATHERINE. You always dress him so well, Mary dear.

(*She and* MARY *go into the back part of the house. Alone,* RUFUS *takes off his hat and stuffs it contemptuously under his jacket. The lights dim in the house.*)

RUFUS (*placing one foot ahead of the other, balances, and sings softly*). "I'm a little busy bee, busy bee, busy bee,

I'm a little busy bee, singing in the clover!"

(*The older boys enter, pushing a home-made cart with an elaborate, mast-like steering rod.*)

FIRST BOY. Hey Busy bee—

SECOND BOY. Bzz-bzz-bzz!

FIRST BOY. What's your name?

RUFUS. You know.

FIRST BOY. No I don't. Tell me.

SECOND BOY. Bzzzzzzzzzzzz—!

RUFUS. I told you yesterday.

FIRST BOY. No honest! I don't know your name!

THIRD BOY. He wouldn't ast you if he knowed it already, would he?

RUFUS. You're just trying to tease me.

SECOND BOY. I don't think he's got a name at all! He's a no-name nothin'!

THIRD BOY. No-name nothin'!

FIRST BOY. Leave 'im alone! Stop pickin' on 'im! What d'you mean, pickin' ona little kid like that! Pick on someone your own size!

THIRD BOY (*the picture of innocence*). I didn't mean nothin'!

FIRST BOY. Don't pay no 'tention to *them!* (RUFUS *looks longingly at the cart.*) Yeah, get on up. (RUFUS *climbs on eagerly, tests the steering rod, then puts out his hand gratefully.*) What you puttin' your hand out for?

RUFUS. So you can shake it.

(*The boys giggle, but the first boy shushes them up.*)

FIRST BOY. I'll tell you what—I'll shake your hand if you'll tell me your name.

RUFUS (*suddenly bold*). I'll tell you my name if you'll answer a question!

FIRST BOY. What question?

RUFUS. You've got to promise to answer it first.

FIRST BOY. Cross my heart and body!

Now what's your name?

(RUFUS *looks from one to the other. They wait, respectful and interested.*)

RUFUS. It's Rufus.

(*The minute it is out of his mouth, the boys scream and jeer.*)

THE BOYS. Nigger name! Nigger name! Nigger name!

RUFUS. It is not either! I got it from my Great-Grampa Lynch!

THIRD BOY. Then your grampa's a nigger too! (*They run through all their chants, adding "Rufus's Grampa's a nigger!"*)

RUFUS. It's my *great*-grampa and he is *not!*

THE BOY. He's a ning-ger! He's a ning-ger!

(HANNAH LYNCH *is suddenly in their midst.*)

HANNAH (*peering nearsightedly*). Now what's all *this!*

(*The boys, at once subdued, murmur "Afternoon, ma'am!" and "We gotta go!" and "Yeah, it's time!" backing away and suddenly running off.*)

RUFUS (*yelling after them*). You didn't answer my question—!

HANNAH (*observing his distraught state*). Never mind, Rufus, see what I've brought you. (*She gives him a small bag. He looks inside. She waits for him to be pleased. But he turns to look after the departed boys.*) Well—?

RUFUS. They didn't play fair.

HANNAH. There are chocolate drops in there, Rufus, and speckled pennies and I don't know what all. I was almost *late* picking them out.

RUFUS (*clutching the bag*). Thank you, Aunt Hannah.

HANNAH. Don't you think it would be polite to offer me one?

RUFUS. Will you have a piece of my candy, Aunt Hannah?

HANNAH. Why, thank you, Rufus, for thinking of me. I'd like a chocolate drop, if you'll pick it out for me. My eyes, you know. (*He digs for the candy. She looks up the street.*) How many street cars have we missed?

RUFUS. I don't know.

HANNAH. What was the question you wanted to ask those boys? Perhaps I can help you.

RUFUS. Mama says we've got a surprise coming to our house.

HANNAH. Why were you going to ask those boys about it?

RUFUS. Because Daddy said if Mama didn't tell me about it, I'd find out from the older boys in the street.

HANNAH. And she didn't tell you?

RUFUS. She and Daddy had a fight about it, and now Mama won't let me ask questions at all.

HANNAH. I see. (*She considers this for a moment.*) Rufus, aren't you going to eat your candy?

RUFUS. The teacher says we should send things to the Belgian orphans.

HANNAH. Well, that's very generous of you, but I bought the candy for *you,* in case you grow tired of traipsing from store to store, for we have a great deal of shopping to do this afternoon. A scarf for your mother's birthday—you mustn't tell her!—and something called A Grammar of Ornament for your Uncle Andrew, and bunion pads for me, and hooks and eyes—

RUFUS (*eagerly*). Can I watch you pare your bunions?

HANNAH. We'll see. But for the time being, I'm sure the Belgian orphans wouldn't mind if you had one piece of their candy.

RUFUS. Would *you* like another piece of my candy, Aunt Hannah?

HANNAH. Thank you, Rufus, a speckled penny this time I think.

(*He gives her one.*)

RUFUS. What do those boys know about a surprise that's coming to our house, Aunt Hannah? Did Daddy tell them?

HANNAH. Of course not. They don't know a thing.

RUFUS. Daddy said they did.

HANNAH. He didn't mean they *knew* exactly, he just meant they— (*She stops, at a loss, and takes her glasses off, holding them up to the light.*) Rufus, I'm sure your mother saw to it that you had a clean handkerchief before you came out of the house.

RUFUS (*excitedly*). Can I clean your glasses, Aunt Hannah?

HANNAH. If you'll promise to be *very* careful.

RUFUS. I promise!

HANNAH (*handing him the glasses*). I'll hold the candy for you. (*He gives her the bag of candy and she munches absent-mindedly during the following.*) Rufus,

I know about the surprise.

RUFUS (*astonished*). You *do*?

HANNAH. Oh yes. And I could tell you about it. But there are certain things that should only be told by certain people. For instance, your teacher should be the one to tell you about arithmetic, because she knows about it. And a Priest, or a Minister, should be the one to tell you about God because he's a *man* of God. And your mama and daddy are the only ones to tell you about this particular surprise. Oh, there are others who'd be *willing* to tell you about it, if you ask them. But you mustn't ask them.

RUFUS. Why not, Aunt Hannah?

HANNAH. Because they wouldn't tell it right.

RUFUS. Wouldn't *you* tell it right?

HANNAH (*after a moment*). Breathe on the lenses, child. That's right. (*She holds out her hand and he gives her the glasses.*) You wait for your mama to explain. You'll be glad later on. (*Her glasses are on now and she leans close to peer at him.*) *There* you are! (*He laughs, delighted.*) What's that bunchy place under your jacket?

RUFUS (*guilty*). My hat.

HANNAH. Well, let's put it on. (*She pulls out and smooths the rumpled hat, examining it distastefully.*) Where *does* your mother buy your clothes? (*She looks at the label inside his jacket collar.*) Millers? (*He nods. She plunks the hat on his head.*) Hmp. *Women's clothes* cut to fit little boys. After we've done our shopping on Gay Street, I think we'll go around to Market Street.

RUFUS (*intrigued*). Mama won't go on Market Street.

HANNAH. We're going into Harbison's there. (*With satisfaction*) I hear they're *very* sporty. And I'm going to buy you a cap. (*He is speechless.*) Or is there something else you'd rather have?

RUFUS (*passionately*). Oh no—no!

HANNAH (*pleased*). We'll see what we can do about it. (*Taking her change purse from her bag*) Now, Rufus, when a gentleman takes a lady out for an afternoon of shopping *he's* the one to pay for everything. So I'm going to let you carry my money. First of all, you'll need streetcar fares— (*She puts two coins into the palm of his hand.*) Five cents for you and five cents for me. Or would you rather walk? Then you can keep the streetcar fares for yourself.

RUFUS (*in seventh heaven*). Oh - Aunt - Hannah - I'm - so - glad - to - go - shopping - with - you - and - thank - you - very - much - for - thinking - of - me!

HANNAH. Your mother told you to say that, didn't she?

RUFUS (*tugging her hand*). I forgot.

HANNAH (*as they start off*). I know direct quotation when I hear it.

(*The lights dim. A small light comes up on* MARY, *sitting by* RUFUS's *bed, singing him to sleep.*)

MARY (*singing*).

Go tell Aunt Rhoda, go tell Aunt Rhoda,
Go tell Aunt Rhoda that the old grey goose is dead.

One she's been savin', the one she's been savin',
Yes, the one she's been savin' to make a feather bed.

Old gander's weepin', the old gander's weepin',
Oh, the old gander's weepin' because his wife is dead.

The goslins are mournin', the goslins are mournin',
The goslins are mournin' because their mother's dead.

She died in the mill-pond, she died in the mill-pond,
She died in the mill-pond from standin' on her head.

Go tell Aunt Rhoda, oh go tell Aunt Rhoda,
Oh, go tell Aunt Rhoda the old grey goose is dead.

(*The lights have come up on the living room where* CATHERINE *sits at the piano, running her fingers over the keys but playing no music.* JOEL LYNCH *comes into the room and watches her.* ANDREW LYNCH *comes into the yard by the swing and spreads a quilt on the ground. During the following,* HANNAH *enters the kitchen from the unseen dining room, the last of the supper dishes in her hands.*)

CATHERINE. I wish you wouldn't stand there, Joel. I can't do my best when I'm being watched.

JOEL (*loudly*). What the devil do you think you're playing?

CATHERINE. "The Burning Of Rome."

JOEL. Well, let's hear it, then!

CATHERINE (*impatiently*). Rufus is asleep! (*She turns a page and goes on "playing."*)

JOEL. Good God! (*He crosses out to the yard.*)

ANDREW. You know, Papa, we've got to face the possibility, you and I, that Jay is drunk somewhere and be ready for it!

JOEL. Rot!

ANDREW. Mary's thinking it though—ever since supper—and she's worried, I can tell, Papa—she's got what Jay calls that pursed-up look. Shall I go look for him?

JOEL. Where would you look?

ANDREW. He used to like those places down off Market Square. It's lively down there at night, Papa, with the farmers rolling into town and the smell of salt and leather and fresh vegetables and whiskey!

JOEL. If that's where he is, let the man come home on his own. It will be hard enough for him when he gets here. You might as well learn, Andrew, it's the way of our women to try to break their men with piety.

ANDREW. Or is it the way of our men, Papa, to try to break their women with impiety. (JOEL *snorts.*) I'm just asking. I've never been able to decide who I am, your son or Mama's.

JOEL. Not everyone has such a wide choice.

(MARY *has stopped singing, come down the stairs and now passes through the kitchen.*)

MARY. Rufus is finally asleep. He was terribly disappointed that Jay hadn't come home.

HANNAH. He'll be along soon.

(MARY *crosses out to yard.*)

MARY (*she sits beside* JOEL *on the swing*). Do you think I've been deserted, Papa? Do you think my husband's gone away, never to return? Will you take care of me again, Papa, if I'm deserted? Will you let me come home again and sit on your lap and cry for my lost love?

JOEL. No, daughter.

MARY. Why not, Papa?

JOEL. Because you'll never be deserted.

MARY. You always defend Jay, don't you, Papa?

JOEL. I always thought highly of him. From the first.

MARY. You'd praise Jay to the skies on the one hand, and on the other, why practically in the same breath, you'd be telling me one reason after another why it would be plain foolhardy to marry him.

JOEL. Isn't it possible that I meant both things?

MARY. I don't see how.

JOEL. You learned how yourself, Mary.

MARY. Is that what I've learned?

JOEL. I've taken Jay into the office. That shows confidence.

MARY. And he's teaching himself law! Your confidence is justified!

JOEL (*laughing*). That's what I wanted. To hear you defend him!

MARY. Me defend him—? Why, Papa, why—I couldn't ever defend Jay enough! Oh Papa, in these past few months we've come to a—a kind of harmoniousness that is so beautiful I've no business talking about it. It's only the gulfs between us. If I could fill them in, it would all be perfect. I want life to be perfect, Papa. (*Looking off*) Why doesn't he come home? (*Turning back to them*) Andrew, I'm ready to see that present now!

ANDREW (*going into the living room as the others follow,* HANNAH *joins them from the kitchen*). I should make you wait for your birthday, Mary, it was meant to be a birthday present.

MARY. What is it, a new picture you've done?

JOEL. I think you'll like it, Mary.

HANNAH. Yes, Mary!

MARY. Oh, you've all seen it!

(*They agree with "Oh yes!" and "Andrew showed it to us at breakfast!" and* MARY *says "That's no fair!" There is a festive, family air.* CATHERINE *turns to face the group, putting her trumpet to her ear.*)

ANDREW. Mama, will you give us a nice fanfare for the unveiling?

JOEL. She didn't hear you, Andrew.

MARY (*into* CATHERINE'S *trumpet*). Mama, Andrew wonders if you'd play us a fanfare! (CATHERINE *does so.* ANDREW *removes the wrapping from the picture, which turns out to be a painting of* JAY. *There is silence. They all look at* MARY'S *reaction.*) Oh Andrew. It's Jay.

ANDREW. Do you like it?

MARY. It *is* Jay!

HANNAH. I think Andrew caught a very good likeness.

JOEL. Especially around the mouth and chin.

MARY. Yes, right in through there, especially!

ANDREW. The eyes were the hardest. They always are unless the subject sits for you, and I didn't want Jay to do that because then you'd both have known. I've been making sketches for months.

MARY. He wouldn't have done it anyhow. Imagine Jay sitting still for an artist!

HANNAH. The picture has great dignity.

JOEL. So has Jay.

MARY (*hugging* ANDREW). Oh Andrew, I just love it! Thank you!

(RUFUS *runs down the stairs calling.*)

RUFUS. Daddy! Daddy!

MARY. Oh dear!

HANNAH. I guess we *were* making a racket.

(RUFUS *runs into the room, wearing his night shirt and a thunderous fleecy check cap in jade green, canary yellow, black and white, which sticks out inches to either side above his ears and has a great scoop of a visor beneath which his face is all but lost.*)

CATHERINE. There's little Rufus!

RUFUS. Did Daddy come home yet?

MARY. No dear, what made you think so?

RUFUS. I woke up. I wanted to show him my cap!

MARY. Rufus, I told you not to wear that cap to bed! (*Exasperated*) Aunt Hannah! I'll never *forgive* you.

(HANNAH *smiles rather secretly and shrugs.*)

CATHERINE. Rufus, come give Grandma a good hug! (RUFUS *goes to her and hugs her. She vigorously slaps his back.*) Mmmmm-mm. Nice little boy! (*Over his shoulder to* MARY, *gently reproving.*) Mary dear, do you think he ought to wear his cap to *bed*?

(*They all laugh. The telephone rings.*)

MARY. Maybe that's Jay. (*She goes quickly to the kitchen.*)

CATHERINE (*discreetly to* HANNAH). Bathroom?

RUFUS (*loudly*). Telephone!

(CATHERINE *nods and smiles.*)

MARY (*at telephone*). Hello—?

CATHERINE (*taking* RUFUS's *hand*). Come along, Rufus, let *Grandma* put you to bed *this* time! (*She takes him upstairs.*)

MARY (*loudly*). Hello! Will you please talk a little louder! I can't hear— I said I can't hear you!

JOEL. It's long distance all right.

HANNAH. Oh dear, his father's worse.

ANDREW. At least we know where he is!

(*They try not to listen, focusing on the portrait, but gradually they are caught by what they can hear.*)

MARY. Yes, that's better, thank you. Yes, this is she, what is it? (*A long silence*) Yes—I heard you. (*She stares dumbly at the telephone, then rallies.*) Yes, there's my brother. Where should he come to? (*Closing her eyes, concentrating, memorizing*) Brannicks—left of the Pike—Bell's Bridge. Do you have a doctor? A *doctor*, do you have one? All right then—my brother will come out just as fast as he can. Thank you—very much for calling. Goodnight. (*She hangs up and stands for a moment, her hand still on the telephone. Then she slowly turns to the others.*) Andrew, there's been an— that was a man from Powell's Station, about twelve miles out towards LaFollette, and he says—he says Jay has met with a very serious accident. He wants—he said they want some man of his family to come out just as soon as possible and —help bring him in, I guess.

ANDREW. Shall I get Dr. Dekalb?

MARY. He says no. Just you.

ANDREW. I guess there's a doctor already there.

MARY. I guess so.

ANDREW. Where do I go?

MARY. Powell's Station, out on the Pike toward—

ANDREW. I know, but exactly where? Didn't he say?

MARY. Brannick's Blacksmith Shop. B-r-a-n-n-i-c-k. He said they'll keep the lights on and you can't miss it. It's just to the left of the Pike, just this side of Bell's Bridge.

ANDREW. I won't be any longer than I have to.

MARY. Bless you. I'll—we'll get everything ready here in case—you know—he's well enough to be brought home.

ANDREW. Good. I'll phone the minute I know anything. Anything.

MARY. Bless you, dear.

(ANDREW *goes.*)

JOEL. Where is he hurt?

MARY. He didn't say.

JOEL. Well didn't you ask—?

HANNAH. Joel.

JOEL. No matter.

MARY. Where's Mama?

JOEL. Upstairs with Rufus.

MARY. Keep her up there, will you, Papa—? Just a few minutes till I— Make sure Rufus is asleep, be sure he's asleep, then tell her what's happened. And talk as softly as you can and still have her know what you're saying.

JOEL. Would you like us to go home, Mary?

MARY. No!

JOEL. We'll keep out of the way—

MARY. It's not that—it's just that with Mama it's so very hard to talk.

HANNAH. For heaven's sake, Joel, go along.

(*He goes upstairs and sits with* CATHERINE *in* RUFUS'S *room.*)

MARY. What time is it, Aunt Hannah?

HANNAH. About ten twenty-five.

MARY. Let's see, Andrew drives pretty fast, though not so fast as Jay, but he'll be driving better than usual tonight, and it's just over twelve miles. That would be—supposing he goes thirty miles an hour, that's twelve miles—let's see, six times four is twenty-four, six times five's thirty, twice twelve is twenty-four—sakes alive, I was always dreadful at figures.

HANNAH. It's only twelve miles. We should hear very soon.

MARY (*abruptly*). Let's have some tea.

HANNAH. Why not let me— (*She stops.*)

MARY (*blankly*). What?

HANNAH. Just let me know if there's anything I can help with.

MARY. Not a thing, thank you. (*She goes into the kitchen, and during the following lights the stove, puts the kettle on to boil, takes down the box of tea, finds the strainer, the cups and saucers.* HANNAH *watches, her hands folded.*) We'll make up the downstairs bedroom. Remember he stayed there when his poor back was sprained. It's better than upstairs, near the kitchen and the bathroom and no stairs to climb. He's always saying we must get the bathroom upstairs but we never do. And of course, if need be, that is if

he needs a nurse, we can put her in the dining room and eat in here, or even set up a cot right in the room with him and put up a screen. Or if she minds that, why she can just sleep on the living room davenport and keep the door open in between. Don't you think so?

HANNAH. Certainly.

MARY. Of course it's very possible he'll have to be taken straight to a hospital. The man did say it was serious, after all. Sugar and milk—(*She gets them.*)—or lemon. I don't know if I have any lemons, Aunt Hannah—

HANNAH. Milk is fine for me.

MARY. Me too. Would you like some Zuzus? (*She gets them from the cupboard.*) Or bread and butter, or toast? I could toast some.

HANNAH. Just tea will do.

MARY. Well, here are the Zuzus. (*She puts them on the table.*)

HANNAH. Thank you.

MARY. Goodness sakes, the watched *pot!* (*She stands by the stove, motionless.*)

HANNAH. I hope you didn't really mind my giving Rufus that cap, Mary.

MARY (*vaguely*). Heavens no, you were good to do it.

HANNAH. I'm sure if you had realized how much he wanted one, you'd have given it to him yourself long ago.

MARY (*forcing concentration*). Of course. Oh yes. But *Harbisons,* isn't that where you got it? I hear it' so tough, how did you ever dare go *in?*

HANNAH. Fortunately, I'm so blind I couldn't see what might hurt me. I just sailed up to the nearest man and said, "Where do I go, please, to find a cap for my nephew." And he said, "I'm no clerk, Ma'am, I'm a customer myself." And I said, "Then why aren't you wearing a hat?" He had no answer to *that,* of course, so—

MARY. Why didn't he tell me?

HANNAH. Who?

MARY. That man on the telephone! Why didn't I ask? I didn't even ask! *How* serious? *Where* is he hurt? Papa noticed it!

HANNAH. You couldn't think.

MARY. Is he living or dead? (*She has said it.*)

HANNAH. That we simply have to wait and find out.

MARY. Of course we have to wait!

That's what's so unbearable!

HANNAH. Try if you can to find a mercy in it.

MARY. A *mercy*—?

HANNAH. A little time to prepare ourselves.

MARY. I'm sorry, Aunt Hannah, you're quite right. (*She sits at the table.*)

CATHERINE (*crossing to head of stairs, followed by* JOEL). I'm going down to see if there isn't something I can do for poor dear Mary. (JOEL *stops her.*) But it's my place to, isn't it, Joel? (*She looks at him rather anxiously. He nods. She goes on down the stairs.*)

MARY. I don't know's I really want any tea but I think it's a good idea to drink something warm while we're waiting, don't you?

HANNAH. I'd like some.

CATHERINE (*going to* MARY). I've decided there is no cause for alarm, Mary dear. Jay is perfectly all right, I'm sure. And Andrew was simply too overjoyed with relief to bother to phone and is bringing Jay straight home instead for a wonderful surprise. That would be like Andrew. And like Jay to go along with the surprise and enjoy it, just laugh at how scared we've been. Of course, we shall have to scold them both. (*She nods brightly, having solved everything, and goes into the living room to sit with* JOEL *on the davenport.*) Joel, what Andrew's doing is coming in with Jay's poor body to the undertaker's. Roberts, probably. Although they do say that new man over on Euclid Avenue is very good. But our family has always used Roberts.

MARY. Did Rufus pick out the cap all by himself?

HANNAH. You don't think I chose that monstrosity, do you? (*She laughs.*) At first he picked a very genteel little serge, but I smelled the hypocrisy behind it, and forgive an old woman, Mary, but I said, "Do you really like that one or do you just think it will please your mother?" Then he revealed his true taste. But I was switched if I was going to boss him.

MARY (*who has not listened*). Either he's badly hurt but he'll live. Or he is so terribly hurt that he will die from it, maybe after a long, terrible struggle, maybe breathing his last at this very minute and wondering where I am, why I'm not there. Or he was already gone when the man called. Of course it's just what we have no earthly business guessing about. And I'm not going to say he's dead until I know for sure that he is.

HANNAH. Certainly not.

MARY. But I'm all but certain that he is, all the same. (*After a moment*) Oh I do beseech my God that it be not so! (*Turning to* HANNAH, *lost, scared*) Aunt Hannah, can we kneel down for a moment? (HANNAH *does not respond.*) Aunt Hannah—?

HANNAH (*sighing*). No Mary.

MARY (*bewildered*). Why not—?

HANNAH. It's too easy. As you say, it's one thing or the other. But no matter what it is, there's not one thing in this world or the next that we can do or hope or guess at or wish or pray that can change it one iota. Because whatever it is, *is*. That's all. And all there is now is to be ready for it, strong enough for it, whatever it may be. That's all that matters because it's all that's possible.

MARY. I'm *trying* to be ready—!

HANNAH. Your beliefs have never been truly tested. God has come easily to you. He's going to come harder now. But if you wait until you can't go on without Him, you'll find Him. When you *have* to pray, we'll pray.

MARY. Goodness sakes, why don't I get his room ready. (*She goes off to back part of the house.*)

HANNAH (*alone*). It's your turn now.

CATHERINE (*in the living room*). What time is it, Joel?

JOEL. Twelve forty-five. A quarter of one!

CATHERINE. Andrew's had time to get there and back, hasn't he, Joel?

JOEL. Twice!

CATHERINE. Don't shout at me, Joel. Just speak distinctly and I can hear you. (*She crosses to the piano for her ear trumpet.*) Just think, Joel, it will be a posthumous baby.

JOEL. Good—God, woman.

CATHERINE. We haven't had a posthumous birth in the family since—your cousin Hetty was posthumous, wasn't she? Of course, your uncle Henry was killed in the War Between the States.

(MARY, *who has joined* HANNAH *in the kitchen, begins to pray.*)

HANNAH. Our Father, Who art in Heaven— (*As they say the prayer,* AN-

DREW *enters and rushes to* HANNAH'S *arms. He holds her so close that she gasps.*) Mary!

MARY. He's dead, Andrew, isn't he? He was dead when you got there.

ANDREW (*he has withdrawn to the swing*). He was instantly killed!

(*She starts to go limp. He rushes to her.*)

MARY. Papa—! Mama—! (*He supports her as best he can into the living room where the others take her from him and seat her on the davenport.*)

CATHERINE. There there there, Mary, dear, there there!

HANNAH (*she goes to get water and then smelling salts*). Sit down, Mary—!

JOEL. It's hell, Mary, just plain hell!

ANDREW (*hysterically*). Instantly, Papa! Instantly! (*Snapping his fingers again and again.*) Instantly! Quick as that! Quick as that! He was at this blacksmith's shop and they made me look at him! Instantly! This reeking horseblanket and they made me look! I'd never seen a dead man before and it was Jay! Instantly! The flat of the hand! The flat of the hand of death, the flat of the hand—! (*He is now slapping the seat of a kitchen chair.*)

JOEL. For God's sake, Andrew, think of your sister!

MARY. What happened, Andrew?

HANNAH. Give yourself a minute, Mary, just a minute—

CATHERINE (*waving the smelling salts past* MARY's *nose*). This will clear your head—

MARY (*brushing the salts aside*). I don't want it, Mama, I want to hear what happened! Andrew?

ANDREW (*as if suddenly realizing*). I have to tell you—?

JOEL. Tell her!

ANDREW. I can't, I can't be the one—!

JOEL. What *happened*?

ANDREW. I don't even know how to begin—!

JOEL. Just begin!

ANDREW. Where?

JOEL. Anywhere.

ANDREW. Well—he was alone, for one thing—

MARY. Of course he was alone, I *know* that.

ANDREW. I just meant—there was no one else in the accident, or other automobiles—

MARY. I want to hear about *Jay!*

ANDREW. I'm *trying* to tell you—!

JOEL. *What caused the accident?*

ANDREW (*shouting*). A cotter pin!

MARY. What's a cotter pin?

ANDREW. You wouldn't understand, Mary, you don't know about automobiles—

MARY. Papa, make him tell me!

ANDREW. All *right*, it's just something that holds the steering mechanism together like this— (*Holds up his knuckles.*) There'd be a hole through the knuckles and that's where the cotter pin goes like a hairpin and you open the ends flat and spread them—

MARY. I *understand!*

ANDREW. *The cotter pin fell out.*

MARY. What happened then?

ANDREW. Nobody was there, we can't say. He just lost control of the auto!

MARY. Who found him?

ANDREW. The man who telephoned you.

MARY. Who was he?

ANDREW. I don't know his name.

MARY. I wish you did.

ANDREW. He was driving in toward town about nine o'clock and he heard Jay coming up from behind terrifically fast— All of a sudden he said he heard a terrifying noise and then dead silence. He turned around and drove back—

MARY. Where was this?

ANDREW. Just the other side of Bell's Bridge—

MARY. Where you come down that sort of angle?

ANDREW. That's the place. He'd been thrown absolutely clear of the auto as it ran off the road. And the car had gone up an eight-foot embankment, then tumbled back, bottom-side up, right next to him, without even grazing him. They think when the cotter pin fell out, he must have been thrown forward very hard, so he struck his chin one sharp blow against the steering wheel, and that must have killed him . . .

MARY (*putting her hand to his mouth*). Killed— (*Then, after a long moment*) I'll never see him again. Never. Never, never, never, never. (*She moves into the living room. The others watch helplessly, unable to comfort or even touch her, for when they try, she tears herself away from them, then she falls to her knees in front of* JAY's *portrait in the armchair. She is completely dissolved, moaning and cry-ing.* CATHERINE *kneels beside her and puts her arms around her.*)

CATHERINE. There, there, Mary. We're all here.

MARY (*now completely drained*). Thank heaven for that, Mama. (*Weakly*) Andrew, I want whiskey.

HANNAH. It'll do her good.

JOEL. Do us all good.

ANDREW. I'll go down home and get some.

MARY. No— (*She points vaguely to the hall closet.* HANNAH *gets the bottle as* AN-DREW *is getting glasses. In his haste, he drops one into the sink and it breaks. They pour some for* MARY *but she holds up her glass for more. Then she gulps it several times. Eventually*) Did you— what did he look like—?

ANDREW. His clothes were hardly even rumpled.

MARY (*nodding*). His brown suit.

ANDREW (*at a loss*). He was lying on his back.

MARY. His face?

ANDREW. Just a little blue bruise on the lower lip.

MARY (*hurt*). Is that all?

ANDREW. And a cut so small they can sew it up with one stitch.

MARY. Where?

ANDREW. The exact point of his chin.

MARY (*touching her father's chin*). Point of the chin, Papa.

ANDREW. The doctor said death was in-stantaneous. Concussion of the brain. (*She turns away and he stops for a mo-ment. Then she gulps her whiskey and turns back.*) He can't have suffered, Mary, not a fraction of a second. I asked about that very particularly because I knew you'd want to be sure. I saw his face. There wasn't a glimmer of pain in it. Only a kind of surprise. Startled.

MARY (*nodding*). I imagine so.

ANDREW. It was just a chance in a mil-lion. Just that one tiny area, at just a cer-tain angle, and just a certain sharpness of impact on the chin. If it had been even half an inch to one side, he'd be alive this minute.

JOEL (*watching* MARY). Shut up, An-drew.

ANDREW. What'd I say, Papa?

MARY. Have a little mercy! A little mercy!

ANDREW. I'm so sorry, Mary—

HANNAH. Let her cry.

ANDREW. I'm so sorry.

MARY. O God, forgive me! Forgive me! Forgive me! It's just more than I can bear! Just more than I can bear. Forgive me!

ANDREW. Forgive *you*! I say, O God if you exist, God-damn you!

HANNAH. Andrew! (*A silence*) Mary, listen to me. There's nothing to ask for-giveness for. There's nothing to ask for-giveness for, Mary. Do you hear me, do you hear me, Mary?

MARY. I spoke to Him as if He had no mercy.

HANNAH. Andrew was just—

MARY. To *God*. As if He were trying to rub it in. Torment me! That's what I asked forgiveness for.

CATHERINE. There there, Mary.

HANNAH. Listen Mary, Our Lord on the Cross, do you remember?

MARY. My God, my God, why hast Thou forsaken me?

HANNAH. Yes. And then did He ask forgiveness?

MARY. He was God. He didn't have to.

HANNAH. He was human too. And He didn't ask it. Nor was it asked of Him to ask it. No more are you. And no more should you. You're wrong. You're terribly mistaken. What was it He said instead? The very next thing?

MARY. Father, into Thy hands— (*She stops.*)

HANNAH. Father, into Thy hands I commend my spirit.

MARY. I commend— (*She stops again, then after a moment, looks up at* HANNAH *deeply hurt and bewildered.*) You've never had anything *but* God, Aunt Han-nah. I had a husband. I was married to a *man*. I won't *have* God in his place. (*She turns away to find herself facing the pic-ture.*) Nor that picture, Andrew. I never saw that face in my life before tonight. Jay's face had eyes and mouth. Put it in the hall closet, Papa. (JOEL *takes the por-trait from the room.*)

CATHERINE. Try not to suffer too much, Mary.

MARY (*with a sudden, irrational an-ger*). That's right, Mama, keep your ear trumpet in your lap! Shut out whatever might be unpleasant! Think of having voices to hear and not listening! (*Stop-*

ping, again with that un-understanding hurt) I want more whiskey.

HANNAH. Let me fix you one good hot toddy so you'll sleep.

MARY. I want a *lot* more whiskey!

ANDREW. You'll make yourself drunk, Mary.

MARY (*grabbing the bottle angrily*). Let me!

HANNAH. You've tomorrow to reckon with!

MARY (*pouring herself a good drink*). What's tomorrow! I'm going to get just as drunk as I can. (*She gulps silently, broodingly for a long moment.*)

CATHERINE (*suddenly very cheerful, rather chatty*). Mother always said that in times of stress, the best thing to drink was buttermilk.

(*They look at her and each other in astonishment, and then* MARY *begins to laugh.*)

MARY. Buttermilk! (ANDREW *laughs, and then* HANNAH. JOEL *returns and is caught into the contagion of this somewhat hysterical laughter, and they all roar, laughing their heads off, while* CATHERINE *sits disapproving of the levity and somehow uneasily suspecting that for some reason they are laughing at her, but in courtesy and reproof, and in an expectation of hearing the joke, smiling and lifting her trumpet. The laughter quiets down.*)

JOEL. What are we laughing at?

(*And they are off again, giving themselves to their laughter, willing it to continue.*)

ANDREW. Buttermilk!

JOEL. What's so funny about buttermilk?

(*And they laugh all the harder.*)

HANNAH. Now this is terrible! We're not going to laugh any more! We're going to stop it!

MARY. Aunt Hannah's right! Andrew, stop making me laugh!

ANDREW (*tickling her*). You stop making *me* laugh!

MARY. You started it!

HANNAH (*clapping her hands*). Children! Children!

(*They make a great effort to stop, and suddenly thoroughly enjoy giving in to it again. Finally they quiet down, holding their sides, moaning and drying their eyes, unable to laugh any more.*)

CATHERINE (*very primly rising to get the whiskey bottle, corking it and putting it away*). I have never in my life been so thoroughly shocked and astonished.

(*And they are off again, laughing harder than ever, hugging* CATHERINE, *kissing her, petting her, leaning on each other, trying to catch their breaths.*)

MARY (*suddenly, loudly*). Listen!

(*All the laughing stops and they look to her.*)

ANDREW. What is it?

MARY. Just listen.

JOEL. What's up?

MARY. Quiet, Papa, please. There's something.

ANDREW. I can't hear anything.

HANNAH (*who has been watching her closely*). Mary does.

ANDREW. There is something.

MARY. It's in the kitchen.

ANDREW. I'll go see—

MARY. Wait, Andrew, don't, not yet.

CATHERINE. Has somebody come into the house?

ANDREW. What made you think so, Mama?

CATHERINE. Why, how stupid of me. I thought I heard. Footsteps. I must be getting old and dippy.

ANDREW. Sssh!

MARY. It's Jay.

HANNAH (*watching her*). Of course it is.

JOEL (*thundering*). What—!

MARY. Now he's come into the room with us.

ANDREW. Mary—!

MARY. It's Jay, Andrew, who else would be coming here tonight so terribly worried, so terribly concerned for us, and restless. Feel the restlessness.

ANDREW. You mean you can—

MARY. I mean it simply feels like his presence.

ANDREW. Do you feel anything, Papa?

JOEL. I feel goose bumps, of course. But that's from looking at your faces.

MARY. He's going upstairs.

JOEL. You've got to stop this, Mary.

MARY. Quiet, Papa! He's in Rufus's room.

JOEL. For God's sake, Mary, you're having hallucinations.

HANNAH. Joel, I know that God in a wheelbarrow wouldn't convince you, but Mary *knows* what she is experiencing.

ANDREW. I believe it! I really do!

JOEL. I see you've decided whose son you are.

MARY. Please stop talking about it, please. It just means so much more than we can say. I'd just like to be quiet in the house, by myself. (*She goes upstairs singing "Sugar Babe" softly. The others start to leave.*)

HANNAH. Andrew, when you get home, telephone Jay's people and tell them how it happened.

(MARY *is in* RUFUS's *room. She suddenly calls down to them as they cross the yard.*)

MARY. Andrew! (*They stop and look up at her.*) Where is he? Dear God, where is he?

ANDREW (*vaguely*). What d'you mean?

MARY. Where did you take him?

ANDREW. Oh. To Roberts.

MARY. Roberts. Yes. Bless you. (JOEL, CATHERINE *and* ANDREW *go.* HANNAH *sinks wearily to a chair in the kitchen.* MARY *turns into her own room, wandering, hopefully, half frightened.*) Jay, darling? Dear heart? Are you here? (*She has moved around and now stands on the threshold of* RUFUS's *room again.*) Jay? (*She stops, seeing the little boy sitting up in bed, staring at her. She sinks to the trunk.*) Dear God.

CURTAIN

ACT THREE

AT RISE: RUFUS *is alone in his bedroom, dressed in a black suit and cap.*

He goes into his mother's room, down the stairs, into the kitchen, then into the living room. No one is around. He takes off his cap, puts it on the sofa, then from under his jacket takes out his gaudy cap, puts it on and goes out into the street. The boys enter from down right on their way to school. The first boy runs past.

———

RUFUS. My daddy's dead! (*The boy ignores him.*) My daddy's dead!

SECOND BOY. Huh! Betcha he ain't!

RUFUS. Why he is so.

SECOND BOY. Where's your satchel at? You're just making up a lie so you can lay outa school.

RUFUS. I am not laying out, I'm just staying out, because my daddy's dead!

(*The third boy has joined them.*)

THIRD BOY. He can lay out because his daddy got killed.

(RUFUS *looks at him gratefully. And the third boy seems to regard him with something like respect.*)

FIRST BOY. How do *you* know?

THIRD BOY. 'Cause my daddy seen it in the paper. Can't your daddy read?

RUFUS (*astounded*). The *news*paper—?

THIRD BOY. Sure, your daddy got his *name* in the paper. Yours too.

FIRST BOY (*with growing respect*). His name's in the paper? Rufus's?

THIRD BOY. Him and his daddy both, right in the paper.

RUFUS. He was killed instantly. (*He snaps his fingers.*)

THIRD BOY. What you get for drivin' a auto when you're drunk, that's what my daddy says.

RUFUS. What's drunk?

SECOND BOY. What's *drunk?* Drunk is fulla good ole whiskey. (*He staggers around in circles, weak-kneed, head lolling.*) 'At's what drunk is.

RUFUS. Then he wasn't.

SECOND BOY. How do *you* know?

RUFUS. Because my daddy never walked like that.

THIRD BOY. How'd he get killed if he wasn't drunk?

RUFUS. He had a fatal accident.

SECOND BOY. How'd he *have* a fatal accident if he wasn't drunk?

RUFUS. It was kuhkushon.

SECOND BOY. Hell, you don't even know what you're talkin' about!

FIRST BOY (*simultaneously*). Don't even know how his own daddy got killed!

(*They scoff and jeer.* RUFUS *begins to think he has lost his audience.*)

THIRD BOY. My daddy says we gotta feel sorry for Rufus here 'cause he's an orphan.

RUFUS. I am?

THIRD BOY. Sure, like the Belgian kids, on'y worse, 'cause that's *war,* and my daddy says any kid that's made an orphan just 'cause his daddy gets drunk is a *pore kid.*

FIRST BOY. He says his daddy *wasn't* drunk.

SECOND BOY. Yeah.

RUFUS. Maybe he was a little.

FIRST BOY. Izzat so?

RUFUS. I remember now.

THIRD BOY. Sure he was.

SECOND BOY. Good ole whiskey.

THIRD BOY. Pore kid. My daddy says his ole Tin Lizzy run up a eight foot embankment—

RUFUS (*bravely*). That's all you know about it.

FIRST BOY (*to* THIRD). Let *him* tell it.

SECOND BOY. Yeah, *you* tell it, Rufus.

THIRD BOY. Well, come on and tell us then.

RUFUS. Well—it wasn't any old Tin Lizzy he was driving, in the first place, it was a—a Chalmers. And my daddy was going like sixty!

SECOND BOY. 'Cause he was drunk.

RUFUS (*nodding*). Good ole whiskey.

THIRD BOY. Pore kid.

RUFUS (*now completely confident*). And then the auto didn't run up any eight foot embank—emb—what you said —either, it ran up a—a pole.

THIRD BOY. A *pole?*

RUFUS (*jumping up on the swing*). A hundred feet high!

(*Doubts have now set in among the three boys.*)

SECOND BOY. Aw, what kinduva pole is that?

RUFUS. The *north* pole. (*They stare at him blankly to see if it is an old joke, but he is too excited to notice. He points off.*) Out there! If you squint your eyes you can see it! (*He squints searchingly, and the three boys look at one another. One makes circles with his forefinger at the side of his head, another silently blubbers his lower lip, another rolls his eyeballs back so that only the whites are showing.*) Can you see it?

THE THREE BOYS. Oh yeah! Sure, Rufus! We see it! So that's the North Pole! Hmmm! Always wondered where it was!

RUFUS. And my daddy's auto ran up it and fell right back on top of my daddy like—(*Suddenly he jumps from the swing.*)—whomp! And that joggled his brain loose in his head and it—fell out and the hand of death came down out of the sky and scooped it up. (*Now somewhat out of breath*) And that's kuhku-shon.

FOURTH BOY (*running on*). Hey, I'm waitin' on you.

FIRST BOY (*edging off*). Yeah. Sure, Rufus. Well, we gotta go. (RUFUS *quickly puts out his hand with supreme confidence. The* FIRST BOY *shakes it hurriedly.*) S'long, Rufus.

SECOND BOY (*shaking* RUFUS's *hand*). That's a nice new cap you got, Rufus.

THIRD BOY (*shaking hands*). We'll be seeing yuh, Rufus.

(*They hurry off, looking back over their shoulders at him, talking among themselves, one saying "Whomp!" and clapping his hands together, another blubbering his lower lip, another staggering, whether in imitation of a drunk or an imbecile, it is hard to say.* RUFUS *looks after them, beaming with pride.*)

RUFUS. P-r-o-u-d. (*He scuffs into the living room, making up a bright little song, almost jigging.*) B-r-a-v-e-p-r-o-u-d! (*He puts one of his father's pipes in his mouth, finds a newspaper and sits in the Morris chair to read.*) "He is sur-sur-vived by his wi-wife, Mary." Mama has her name in the paper. "And a son Rufus." Me. (*He thinks for a moment, then carefully folds the newspaper. He stops, suddenly struck.*) My daddy's dead. Whomp. (*He swings his legs, thinking it through.*) He can't ever come home. Not tomorrow or the next day. Or the next day or the next day or the next day. Or the next day or the next day or the next day or the next day or the next day or the next day. (*As he continues the odd chant, he begins to cry. He throws the pipe, the newspaper and the ashtray.*) Whomp! Whomp! Good ole whiskey! Whomp! (*He kicks the Morris chair, bangs at the furniture.*) Good ole whiskey! Good ole whiskey! Good ole whiskey!

(MARY, *in her dressing gown, comes from the back part of the house, followed by* HANNAH *in deepest mourning.*)

MARY. Rufus!

RUFUS (*escaping her, running into the kitchen, hiding under the table*). Good ole whiskey! Good ole whiskey! Good ole whiskey!

MARY (*pulling him out from under the table, sitting in a chair, cradling him*). Darling, who have you been talking to?

RUFUS. My daddy's dead. It says so in the newspaper.

MARY. Oh darling, darling! Now Rufus, Aunt Hannah is going to take you down to Grandma Lynch's for the rest of the morning. Mama will come by later, and then we'll go and see Daddy just once more, so you can say good-bye to him. (*She kisses him.*) You be very good and very quiet.

RUFUS. How could he have a fatal accident if he wasn't drunk.

MARY (*suddenly turning away from him*). Hannah. (HANNAH *takes* RUFUS *by the hand, and they go off.* MARY *looks after them, then goes into the back part of the house. After a moment,* RALPH'S *voice is heard, off.*)

RALPH. Don't you fret, ever'body, I'm goana see us through this grievous day! (*He enters, followed by* JOHN HENRY *and* JESSIE, SALLY *and* JIM-WILSON. *At the same time,* JOEL, CATHERINE *and* ANDREW *enter from the other side of the stage. All but* SALLY *are in deepest black, and she is self-conscious in navy blue.*) Get in here, Jim-Wilson, you're goana spend th'afternoon with your cousin Rufus and you play nice with him! Andrew, m'Chalmers is right out front and I'm goana drive Mary and Paw and Maw and you follow me with the others. You all right, Paw? Try to be brave, Maw, try to be brave.

JESSIE (*making* JOHN HENRY *comfortable in the living room*). Leave me be, Ralph.

RALPH. Cry your heart out, Maw. It's natural at a time like this. I'm goana be two sons to you now. I'm goana be as many sons as you want.

JESSIE (*wearily*). Jes' leave me be.

(*The two families are now seated in the living room.*)

RALPH (*awkwardly*). Well, if anybody needs me, I'll be right outside. (*He goes to the yard and sits on the swing. He takes out his bottle and has a good swallow.*)

SALLY. I feel so bad about my dress, Mother Follet.

JESSIE. You look fine, Sally.

SALLY (*ashamed*). I wish it was black.

JESSIE. Imagine bein' young enough not to have a black dress. Imagine that Miz Lynch.

CATHERINE. What is it, Joel?

JOEL. *Black dresses.*

CATHERINE. Oh. (*She looks around the room.*) Is anybody speaking?

JOEL. No, Catherine.

CATHERINE. When I was a girl in Michigan, the dressmaker and the milliner used to come to the house. They were almost the first to arrive. After the Priest, of course, but before the undertaker. They filled in that gap. Nobody ever knew how they *knew* when to come, for they were never summoned—they just appeared, as if they had an extra sense about such things. And they always wore purple to show they weren't of the tragedy but in sympathy to it. (*She looks from one to the other. They seem to be waiting. She nods and smiles.*) I've finished.

JESSIE. If a woman has a usual life, one black dress will see her through it.

CATHERINE. Beg pardon?

JESSIE (*sympathetically*). She really *don't* hear good, do she?

JOEL (*after a pause*). In Japan they say white is the color of mourning.

JESSIE. Now that wouldn't seem right.

JOEL. Black wouldn't seem right to them.

JESSIE. You all right, Paw?

JOHN HENRY. There's Granmaw sittin' up on that mountain for a hundred and three years. And here's me with two attacks to m'credit. And still, Jay's the one that gets took. (*He shakes his head sadly.*) Not Jay. Never Jay.

JESSIE. Now, Paw.

JOHN HENRY. I was all *ready* to go.

(RALPH *sits up in the swing and hides his bottle as* HANNAH *and* RUFUS *enter the yard, followed by* MARY *and* FATHER JACKSON. RALPH *struggles to his feet.*)

RALPH. There he is, the poor little fatherless child.

RUFUS. I saw my daddy, Uncle Ralph.

RALPH. Don't you cry, honey, your Uncle Ralph is here.

MARY. Ralph, I'd like you to meet Father Jackson. This is my brother-in-law, Mr. Follet.

JACKSON. How do you do?

RALPH. How do you do, sir. Can I—take your hat?

JACKSON (*taking off his hat*). Thank you.

HANNAH. That won't be necessary, Father. We're leaving again directly.

RALPH. Was everything all right down to Roberts', Mary? (*To* FATHER JACKSON) What d'you think of that, sir? With the deceased's only brother an undertaker and willin' to do the generous thing, free of charge, still she puts him in the hands of a stranger. Did y'ever hear of such a thing's that?

JACKSON. It's right for your brother to be buried here, Mr. Follet, where his home was.

RALPH. Now that just plain don't make sense! Jay spent over two-thirds of his life in LaFollette and less'n one-third in Knoxvul! I figgered it out! (*Turning on* MARY) You just didn't think of me! You never even thought of me, did yuh?

MARY. No.

RALPH. My own brother! My own brother!

MARY. My own—only husband.

RALPH. All right for you. Mary. (*He stumbles upstage, taking out his bottle.*) All right for you. (*He mumbles under his breath.* MARY *looks at him for a moment, then the procession continues into the living room.*)

CATHERINE. There's little Rufus!

RUFUS. I saw my daddy!

JESSIE. Come to Granmaw, Rufus.

CATHERINE. Come sit on Grandma's lap.

JESSIE. Well, I never!

JOEL. She didn't hear you, Mrs. Follet. No offense.

JESSIE. I keep forgettin'!

JOEL (*rising*). Is it time, Mary?

MARY. Yes, Papa.

SALLY. I'll put Jim-Wilson in Rufus's room for his nap, if that's all right, Mary.

MARY. It's all right, Sally. (SALLY *takes* JIM-WILSON *upstairs.*) Rufus, Mama has to leave you now. You're to be a good boy and stay with Grandma Lynch. (JOEL *offers his arm to* MARY.)

RALPH (*in the yard, his mumbling reaching a shout, he smashes his bottle against the back fence*). I'm glad he's dead!

(MARY *has started to take* JOEL'S *arm. Now she suddenly turns out of the room and into the yard to confront* RALPH.)

MARY. Was he drunk?

HANNAH (*following her*). Mary!

RALPH. On top of ever'thin' else, a priest.

MARY. Was my husband drunk?

RALPH. A Follet in the hands of a priest!

MARY. *Was he drunk!* I have to know. You were with him all afternoon. Tell me!

RALPH. I ain't goanna tell yuh, Mary.

(*She strikes out at him, but he catches her wrist.*)

RALPH. You thought of me all right, the night he died, even. And you just didn't want me. I ain't goanna tell you nothin'!

HANNAH. We must go, Mary!

RALPH. I ain't goanna tell you nothin'!

(MARY *returns to the living room, stands a moment, then goes quickly up to her room.*)

JOEL (*as* HANNAH *starts up after* MARY). What's she going to do—?

(HANNAH *gestures silence without stopping. She goes up to find* MARY *in her room.*)

SALLY (*running out to* RALPH, *handing him his bowler*). Are you all right to drive, Ralph—?

RALPH. Well—nobody else is goanna drive my Chalmers, let me tell you! (*He goes off followed by* SALLY.)

HANNAH. Mary, the service is due to start in a very few minutes.

MARY. I'm going to stay here in this room.

HANNAH. Shall I send Father Jackson up to you?

MARY. No.

(ANDREW *has come up the stairs.*)

ANDREW. Is she coming?

HANNAH. The rest of you get in the cars. We'll come when we can.

(ANDREW *goes back downstairs, and during the following, all but* CATHERINE *and* RUFUS *file out.*)

MARY. Why don't they all leave. You too, Hannah. For I'm not going.

HANNAH (*touching her shoulder*). I'm staying here.

MARY. If you are, please don't touch me. (*In a sudden rage*) That miserable Ralph! Damn him! You were right, Hannah, God is coming harder to me now. And Jay, too! I can't seem to find either one of them. (HANNAH *stands back quietly.* MARY *gets a necktie from the bureau and scrutinizes the label.*) This necktie was bought in Chattanooga some place. When, do you suppose? Sometimes when he went off like that, he was said to be seen as far as Clairborne County. But Chattanooga— Whatever made Jay do it, *ever!* The night we moved into this house, where did he *go!* And when he first went to work in Papa's office—! (*Stopping, remembering, more softly*) Not when Rufus was born, though. He was very dearly close to me then, very. But other times, he'd feel himself being closed in, watched by superintendents, he'd say, and— There was always a special quietness about him afterwards, when he came home, as if he were very far away from where he'd been, but very far away from me, too, working his way back, but keeping his distance.

HANNAH. Let the man rest, Mary.

MARY. I want him to rest.

HANNAH (*angrily*). Aren't you even going to attend the funeral!

MARY. Do you think he'll rest simply by lowering him into the ground? I won't watch it. How *can* he when he was *lost* on the very day he died!

HANNAH. You don't know that he was *lost,* or drunk, or *what* he was.

MARY (*after a moment*). No. That's just what I don't know.

HANNAH. And *that's* what you can't bear.

MARY (*after an even longer moment*). I never knew. Not for sure. There were times we *all* knew about, of course, but there were other times when it wasn't always the whiskey. He'd be gone for a night, or a day, or even two, and I'd know he hadn't touched a drop. And it wasn't any of the other things that come to a woman's mind, either, in case you're thinking that.

HANNAH. I wasn't thinking that.

MARY. Those are easy enemies. It was Market Square. And talking to country people about country secrets that go way on back through the mountains. And anyone who'd sing his sad old songs with him. Or all-night lunch rooms. What's an all-night lunch room for, he'd say, except to sit in all night. And drink coffee so strong it would burn your ribs. And it was locomotives, I suppose, and railroad people, and going fast, and even Charlie Chaplin. What's wrong with Charlie, he'd ask me, not because he didn't know what I'd say, but to make me say it. He's so nasty, I'd say, so vulgar, with his nasty little cane, hooking up skirts. And Jay would laugh and go off to see Charlie Chaplin and not come home. Where he went, I can't even imagine, for he'd never tell me. It was always easier to put everything down to whiskey.

HANNAH. To put it down to an enemy.

MARY. Why couldn't I let him have those things, whatever they were, if they meant something to him. Why can't I let him have them now. The dear. He always worked his way back.

(ANDREW *runs in, to the foot of the stairs.*)

ANDREW (*in a loud whisper*). Aunt Hannah, we can't wait any longer.

HANNAH (*at the top*). All *right*, Andrew.

(ANDREW *goes off again.*)

MARY. They must be suffocating in those cars. (*She smooths the bed for a moment, then straightens up.*) I'm glad Ralph didn't tell me. I must just accept not knowing, mustn't I? I must let Jay *have* what I don't know. (*She picks up her hat and veil and looks at them.*) What if he was drunk. What in the world if he was. Did I honestly think *that* was a gulf? *This* is a gulf! (*She tears a rent in the veil.*) If he was drunk, Hannah, just *if* he was, I hope he loved being. Speeding along in the night—singing at the top of his lungs—racing because he loved to go fast—racing to us because he loved us. And for the time, enjoying—reveling in a freedom that was his, that no place or person, that nothing in this world could ever give him or take away from him. Let's hope that's how it was, Hannah, how he looked death itself in the face. In his strength. (*She puts on the hat and pulls the veil over her face, goes down the stairs.* HANNAH *follows her into the yard.*) That's what we'll put on the gravestone, Hannah. In his strength. (*They go off.*)

(CATHERINE *comes downstage into the living room, looks to make sure that no one is around, sits on the bench at the piano, and carefully opens the keyboard cover. She is silently running her fingers over the keys when* RUFUS *comes into the room and taps her back.*)

RUFUS. Look Grandma! (*He shows her a drawing he has just made.*)

CATHERINE. Oh, that's very nice. Is it you?

RUFUS. It's a Belgian.

CATHERINE. Isn't he wearing your new cap?

RUFUS. He's a norphan.

CATHERINE. What are all these riches coming down from the sky?

RUFUS. Those are letters and presents

from children all over the world because they feel sorry for him.

CATHERINE. Why, some day, Rufus, you may be an artist like your Uncle Andrew. For the time being, of course, I think it would be *polite* for you to *say* you want to go into law, as your grandfather did and as your dear father was doing. Just for a time. That would only be showing *respect*.

(JOEL *and* ANDREW *come into the living room.* JOEL *bangs his hat on the end-table.*)

JOEL. Priggish, mealy-mouthed son-of-a-bitch! I tell you, Andrew, it's enough to make a man retch up his soul!

CATHERINE (*to* ANDREW). Was it a lovely funeral, dear?

JOEL. That Jackson! *Father* Jackson, as he insists on being called! Not a *word* would he say over Jay's body, let alone read a service! Because he'd never been baptized. A rule of the Church! Some church!

CATHERINE. Andrew, is there something I should be hearing?

ANDREW. Absolutely not, Mama! Come on, Rufus! (*He takes* RUFUS *into the yard where the swing is.*)

JOEL. You come to one simple single act of Christian charity, and what happens! The rules of the Church forbid it! He's not a member of our little club! I only care, mind you, for Mary's sake! (*He sits beside* CATHERINE *on the davenport.*)

CATHERINE. Joel, I don't know what you're saying, but I wish you wouldn't say it. Wait until we get home, dear, where what you say won't matter.

JOEL. Good God!

(*In the yard,* ANDREW *lifts* RUFUS *over the back of the swing and seats him.*)

ANDREW. I tell you, Rufus, if anything ever makes me believe in God, or Life after Death, it'll be what happened this afternoon in Greenwood Cemetery. There were a lot of clouds, but they were blowing fast, so there was lots of sunshine too. Right when they began to lower your father into the ground, into his grave, a cloud came over and there was a shadow just like iron, and a perfectly magnificent butterfly settled on the coffin, just rested there, right over the breast, and stayed there, just barely making his wings breathe like a heart. He stayed there all the way down, Rufus, until it

grated against the bottom like a—rowboat. And just when it did, the sun came out just dazzling bright and he flew up and out of that—hole in the ground, straight up into the sky, so high I couldn't even see him any more. Don't you think that's wonderful, Rufus?

RUFUS. Yes, sir.

ANDREW. If there are any such things as miracles, then *that's* surely miraculous. (*Slowly shaking his head, under his breath*) A damned *miracle*.

(*The Follets enter the kitchen.* SALLY *goes up to* RUFUS's *room to sit by the sleeping* JIM-WILSON. JESSIE *and* JOHN HENRY *sit at the kitchen table.* RALPH *enters just as* MARY *and* HANNAH *come in from the other direction. When he sees* MARY, *he takes refuge in the bathroom.* HANNAH *goes upstairs while* MARY *stops in the living room to speak to her father.*)

MARY (*lifting her veil back*). So many people there, Papa, did you notice? I didn't know half of them. We don't always realize, do we, how many others love the people we love. (*She goes upstairs, to join* HANNAH, *removes her hat and looks at herself in the mirror.*) Rufus says my face looks like my best china tea-cup. You know, Hannah, the one Jay mended for me so many times. He's beginning to say things like that now, and I don't know where he gets them. (*She starts to put the hat away, but stops.*) People fall away from us, and in time, others grow away from us. That is simply what living is, isn't it? (*She puts the hat on the bureau.*)

HANNAH (*now sitting on the bed*). Why don't you rest?

MARY. You're the one, you haven't stopped for three days.

HANNAH. I'm not tired.

MARY. You must be dead—the words that come to mind.

HANNAH. Not dead. Older perhaps. I'm content to be.

MARY. Well, you're going to lie down for just a minute.

HANNAH. There's supper to be fixed for that mob.

MARY. Not yet.

HANNAH. Perhaps just for a moment. (*She lies down.*)

MARY. Hannah, I love and revere everyone in this world who has ever suffered. I truly do, even those who have failed to endure.

HANNAH. I like the way you call me Hannah now, instead of Aunt Hannah.

MARY. We're that much closer.

HANNAH. Will you let me know when it's time to get started again?

MARY. I'll let you know. (*She takes* HANNAH's *glasses off, puts them on the bureau, looks in on* SALLY *and* JIM-WILSON *in* RUFUS's *room. During this,* RALPH *comes out of the bathroom, goes into the yard and off stage.*)

SALLY. He sleeps too much, Mary. He just sleeps and sleeps.

(MARY *leaves them, stops in front of the stairs as if looking out of upstairs hall window.*)

MARY. Be with us all you can, my darling, my dearest. This is good-bye. (*During the following,* MARY *comes down the stairs, takes the portrait of* JAY *from the hall closet.*)

CATHERINE (*in the living room*). I quite agree with you, Joel.

JOEL. I didn't say anything.

CATHERINE. Somebody did.

JOEL. What did they say?

CATHERINE (*primly*). They said how fortunate we have been, you and I, to have lived so many years without losing each other.

JOEL. I did say it.

CATHERINE. I must have been mistaken.

JOEL. You weren't mistaken, Catherine. That's-what-I-said!

CATHERINE (*patting his hand several times*). Never mind, dear.

(JOEL *and* CATHERINE *watch* MARY *as she enters with* JAY's *portrait, but she seems unaware of their presence. She places it on the music rack of the piano, steps back and gazes at the picture.*)

JESSIE (*in the kitchen*). How's your breath, Paw?

JOHN HENRY. Pretty fair.

(MARY *squeezes* JOEL's *hand, touches* CATHERINE's *cheek, goes into the kitchen where* JESSIE *and* JOHN HENRY *are sitting. She kisses his forehead and the top of* JESSIE's *head, then goes out into the yard where she hugs* ANDREW.)

MARY. You can actually *feel* summer coming on.

ANDREW. At last.

MARY. There's just one more thing, Andrew. Would you keep an eye on Ralph for the rest of the day? (ANDREW *groans.*)

He has to drive his family back to La-Follette tonight, and goodness sakes, we don't want any accidents.

(ANDREW *goes off to hunt for* RALPH. MARY *sits on the swing beside* RUFUS.)

MARY. My, you can see all the way to North Knoxville.

RUFUS. Mama?

MARY. Yes?

RUFUS. We sur—sur—

MARY. What are you trying to say?

RUFUS. We sur—*vived,* didn't we, Mama?

MARY. Why yes, darling, we survived.

RUFUS. Am I a norphan now?

MARY. An *orphan*—?

RUFUS. Like the Belgians?

MARY. Of *course* you're not an orphan, Rufus. Orphans haven't got *either* a father or a mother.

RUFUS. Am I half a norphan then?

MARY. Rufus, orphans don't have anybody to love them or take care of them, and you *do!* Oh darling, Mama's wanted to see more of you these last days, a lot more. But you do know how much she loves you, with all her heart and soul, all her life—you know that, don't you?

RUFUS. Will we still get the surprise, Mama?

MARY. I promised you, didn't I? Did you ever know me to break a promise? (*He shakes his head. They get up from the swing.*) Well then, the surprise will come, just as I said. And do you want to know what it's going to be, Rufus?

RUFUS (*eagerly*). What?

MARY. A baby. (*He considers this, not too enthusiastically, and looks down at the ground.*) You're going to have a baby sister. Or it may turn out to be a brother, but I dearly hope it will be a sister. Isn't that wonderful?

RUFUS (*figuring it through*). If I'm half a norphan, Mama, then the baby will be half a norphan, and the two of us together will be a *whole* norphan.

MARY (*impatiently*). Rufus, you're to stop *wanting* to be an *orphan!* Goodness sakes! You be thankful you're not! They sound lucky to you because they're far away and everybody talks about them right now. But they're very, very unhappy little children. Do you hear?

RUFUS. Yes, Mama. (*Retaining, however, a few private hopes.*)

MARY. Good.

RUFUS. Why can't we get the baby right away?

MARY. The time will pass more quickly than you think, much more quickly. And when it does—when she does come to us, you must help her all you can.

RUFUS. Why?

MARY. Because she'll be just beginning. She'll have so much to learn, and I'm counting on you to teach her, because you're so much older and have had so much more experience. She'll be very small and lost, you see, and very delicate.

RUFUS. Like a butterfly?

MARY (*somewhat mystified*). Why, that's a very beautiful thought, Rufus, a very grown-up way to put it.

RUFUS (*excitedly*). Look Mama, there's a train crossing the viaduck!

MARY. It's time to go home, darling.

RUFUS. Let's just watch that train go by. (*He watches excitedly. She looks off, not in the same direction. Pointing at the train, he slowly walks across the stage and sings "Get On Board Little Chil-dren," under his breath.*) Where's the baby now, Mama?

MARY. Up in Heaven . . . (*She changes her mind, walks towards him and puts her hand to her waist.*) Right here. (*She takes his hand and places it on her waist.*) Yes, darling. Right here. (*She kneels down to him and holds him by the shoulders.*) You see, Rufus, when a grown man and woman love each other, truly love each other, as Daddy and Mother did, then they get married, and that's the beginning of a family. (*The lights are now up full on the house with all the Folletts and Lynches in the various rooms.* MARY *turns and leads* RUFUS *home as the curtain begins to fall.*) It will happen to you one day, before you know it, so I want you to listen very carefully to everything I'm going to tell you because I think it's time you knew about it, and I want you to ask questions if you don't understand. Will you do that, darling?

THE CURTAIN IS DOWN

SILENT NIGHT, LONELY NIGHT

Robert Anderson

Presented by The Playwrights' Company
at the Morosco Theatre, New York, on December 3, 1959,
with the following cast:

KATHERINE Barbara Bel Geddes   JANET Lois Nettleton
MAE Eda Heinemann   PHILIP Bill Berger
JOHN Henry Fonda   JERRY Peter De Visé

Directed by Peter Glenville
Production designed and lighted by Jo Mielziner
Costumes by Theoni V. Aldridge

SCENE. A room in a Colonial Inn in a New England town.
ACT ONE. SCENE 1. Christmas Eve. SCENE 2. Later that evening.
ACT TWO. SCENE 1. Later that night. SCENE 2. Christmas morning.

ONE of the most intelligent and cultivated of Broadway playwrights, who has also given Hollywood the benefit of his sensibility and skill without disgrace, Robert Anderson does not conform to the patterns and folklore of show business. This is as evident in a film assignment such as *A Nun's Story* as in plays such as *All Summer Long* and *Tea and Sympathy*. *Silent Night, Lonely Night,* presented during the season of 1959-1960, confirmed his atypicality. It was a "small" play carried essentially by two lonely characters drawn to each other on an especially lonely night but tied to absent characters by bonds of memory, conscience, and a sense of obligation they cannot ignore. Whatever else they may feel, and regardless of their loneliness, they remain what they must be, a lady and a gentleman. This type of play, with its unavoidable attenuation of outward action, does not ordinarily draw large audiences. But for better or worse, which to this possibly partial editor is "for the better," this is the Robert Anderson whom we confront every now and then in the Broadway emporium.

Born in 1917 of what used to be called "good family," Robert Anderson was educated at Phillips Exeter and then at Harvard, where he took two degrees and subsequently taught. World War II, in which he served as a naval officer, broke the progress of his seemingly foreordained career. He became a recognized young playwright with a play written while he was in service, *Marching Home,* which won first prize in a National Theatre Conference contest in 1944 and was produced next year at the University of Iowa theatre. Fellowships and subsidies followed, a play (*Love Revisited*) was given a production at the Westport Country Playhouse in 1950, and *All Summer Long,* a dramatization of Donald Wetzel's family novel *A Wreath and Curse,* was staged by Alan Schneider at Zelda Fichandler's Washington Arena Theatre in 1953 and won acclaim for its sensitivity. Then came Anderson's official Broadway introduction with the Elia Kazan production of *Tea and Sympathy,* which became the first hit of the 1953-54 season. *All Summer Long* also reached Broadway in 1954 but fared less well in New York than had been expected; and *Silent Night, Lonely Night,* while received with respect, had but a modest run. But it was representative of qualities many a playgoer would be pleased to find more frequently in the raw and raucous world that the commercial theatre has become with the rise of theatre costs, the multiplication of musicals, and the growth of hit-crazy and theatre-party crazed audiences upon which Broadway has come to depend too often and too much.

It is distinctly to the credit rather than discredit of the author that explanations of *Silent Night, Lonely Night* would be absurdly superfluous. This is the work of a mature and responsible writer who let his heart and sympathetic intelligence talk out for him under the quiet control of taste and normal tact, without effort to overheat the emotions or to artificially activate the plot for the purpose of providing excitement for the Broadway public. It is this quality of authenticity and artistic balance, which adverse criticism tended to describe variously as detachment, verbosity, and lack of "action" or "movement," that is the treasurable quality of the play. From it derive dramatic experience and insight within the author's self-imposed limits. Our theatre and our society are not favorable to the emergence of writers like Robert Anderson who don't emerge into the limelight with acid in the soul, poison on their tongue, and dynamite in their pockets. He is by natural inclination definitely a gentleman in the age of literary assassins.

ACT ONE

SCENE ONE

A bedroom in an old colonial inn in a New England town.

It is a warm and comfortable room, full of atmosphere and mood. A fireplace is downstage right. Upstage there is the entrance from the hall, and in the center of the back wall a door to an adjoining room, which is locked. A window and the door to bathroom in stage left wall.

The time is Christmas Eve, the present.

KATHERINE JOHNSON *is an attractive well-dressed woman in her mid-thirties. There is much of the girl in her; a certain trusting innocence that is easily bewildered. She is sitting on the floor in front of the fireplace, playing solitaire. She is also smoking, and a whisky and water is on the floor beside her. She is not concentrating on the cards, or the smoking, or the drinking. They are mechanical actions. She comes to the end of the deck, and takes a puff on the cigarette and a drink of whisky, and doesn't go back to the cards. She just sits looking into the fire and beyond it into her own troubled thoughts.*

A town clock chimes the hour: seven o'clock. She puts out the cigarette in an ash tray and picks the ash tray up along with her drink and sets both on bureau. For a moment she fingers and looks at a letter which is lying open there—it is obviously what is bothering her. Then she tosses it down again as though she were not going to let it bother her. She picks up a pack of cigarettes lying among some things which have been fished out of her purse earlier, but then puts down the cigarettes, picks up the drink and fluffs up a couple of ribbons on two Christmas presents which are lying on the bureau. Then goes to the window and looks out. There is nothing there to interest her. She makes up her mind to do something, and goes to the telephone.

KATHERINE. Uh . . . Yes. Could you tell me, if there's a movie house in the village? . . . Could you . . . I see, around eight. Thank you . . . No, I don't care what's playing . . . but, I see, thank you. Can I walk from here? . . . Fine, thank you.

(She hangs up. The door from the hall opens and MAE *wheels in a room-service table with dinner for one set up and a small vase with a sprig of holly in it.* MAE *is a perfectly matter-of-fact woman in her fifties, who does her job well, rarely looks at anyone when she talks to him, and keeps busy straightening the room, poking the fire, emptying ash trays and generally tidying up.)*

MAE. Sorry to be so long . . . We're a little short-handed in the kitchen tonight.

KATHERINE. That's all right.

MAE. The regular guests have gone home for Christmas . . . so they let some of the help have Christmas Eve off.

KATHERINE. Of course.

MAE. I suppose the manager figures everyone's got a home is in it.

KATHERINE. Yes.

MAE *(uncovering dishes)*. I think that's everything . . . Soup, roast beef, no gravy, salad . . . Shall I bring coffee later?

KATHERINE. No, thanks. This will be fine. I'm sorry to be keeping you.

MAE. I haven't anyplace to go.

KATHERINE. Oh.

MAE *(indicating the studio couch)*. When you want the bed made up, let me know.

KATHERINE. I can manage that, thank you.

MAE *(touching the holly)*. This was the cook's idea . . . Holly for you and the gentleman next door and mistletoe for the newlyweds on the top floor.

KATHERINE. Oh, do we have newlyweds?

MAE. Yes. Strange place for a honeymoon. But then I don't know. Maybe it isn't.

KATHERINE. If they like it . . .

MAE. They've been complaining of the cold ever since they arrived. Got two electric heaters in their room right now.

KATHERINE. It's too bad they can't have this room with the fire. It's rather wasted on me.

MAE. They probably aren't conscious what room they're in. *(She pokes the fire.)* There's a double feature at the movie, if that interests you. Starts at eight fifteen.

KATHERINE. Yes, I've checked. Thank you.

MAE. The gentleman next door says it's very entertaining. He's been twice.

KATHERINE. Really?

MAE. The bill changes tomorrow. He says that's a good one too. He's seen it where he lives, but he says he's planning to go again. Poor man. His wife's in the hospital up on the hill. It's so sad. Afternoon show usually starts at two. I imagine Christmas won't make any difference. It's just another Tuesday as far as they're concerned.

KATHERINE. Thank you for all the information.

MAE (*adjusting the window shade and straightening the curtain*). That's the only important information in the town . . . What time the movies begin and what time the trains leave for Boston. Excuse me for going on like this, living alone I chatter a lot when I'm let loose.

KATHERINE. I've enjoyed it. . . . Won't you stay?

MAE. You mean . . .

KATHERINE. Yes . . . While I eat my dinner. I'd be grateful if you would.

MAE. No, I couldn't do that. Thank you all the same. I'm covering for most of the married help, and though I'd like to, I . . . well . . . (*She switches on the bedside radio.*) There should be Christmas carols on this somewhere. It seems to me there's been nothing but Christmas carols since Thanksgiving. (*She gets "O Little Town of Bethlehem."*) There . . . (*She surveys her handiwork.*) I guess this is what they call a home away from home.

KATHERINE. Thank you.

MAE (*going*). Anything you want, please call . . . I'll count it a favor if you keep me busy tonight.

KATHERINE. Thank you. (MAE *exits.* KATHERINE *moves over to look at the dinner for one. She looks at it with a dread. The Christmas carols get on her nerves, and she moves quickly to the radio and turns it off. She picks up her cigarettes and moves back to the table and sits down, opening her napkin and spreading it on her lap. She tries to eat a spoonful of soup, but it is tasteless in her mouth. She picks up a cracker and nibbles the edge of it, but she can't continue. She tries to fight the terrible loneliness welling up in her. She is a girl used to controlling her emotions and she'll do it this time too. But suddenly she can't. She buries her head in her hands, elbows on the table, and suddenly she gives a half-*involuntary strangled cry.*) Help! (*She is shocked at herself, and claps her hand over her mouth. Her eyes open wide to see if anyone heard. For a moment, there is nothing. Then there is a tentative knock at the door. She sits, frightened.*)

JOHN (*outside*). Hello? (*She doesn't know what to do. She is alert, waiting. Again a knock, a little louder.*) Hello? (KATHERINE *rises and goes into the bathroom, half-closing the door behind her.* JOHN *knocks again and half-opens the door.*) I'm sorry, but I thought I heard . . . (*He hears the water start to run in the bathroom. He enters, leaving the door open. He is a man in his early forties. He goes nearer the bathroom door.*) Did you call for help?

KATHERINE (*offstage. The water is turned off for a moment*). Everything is all right, thank you. (*The water is turned on again.* JOHN *is not quite satisfied with her answer. He looks around for a moment at the unfinished game of solitaire, the uneaten dinner. He sees the purse and its contents spilled out on the bureau, pokes his finger around the contents, and finds the bottle of pills. He looks at the key chain with its odd pendant. He goes to the hall door and closes it, staying on the inside. When* KATHERINE *hears the door close, she comes from the bathroom, dabbing her eyes. She is surprised to find him still there.*) Oh . . .

JOHN. I'm sorry. I just wanted to make sure everything was all right.

(*There is obviously an immediate contact between these two people, arising from the occasion, their own moods, and the strangeness of the situation in which they meet—a certain unguarded nakedness of feeling on her part, a natural instinct of protecting on his.*)

KATHERINE. Thank you. (*She goes to the bureau for a clean handkerchief.*)

JOHN. I'm in the next room and . . .

KATHERINE. Yes. Thank you. I'm sorry I disturbed you.

JOHN. Is there something I can do?

KATHERINE. No. But thank you.

JOHN (*realizing that there must be something he can do if her embarrassment can be forgotten, he smiles*). I could never stand to see a woman cry.

KATHERINE. It's very silly and a bore. I don't very often. (*She has taken out a cigarette. He lights it.*) Oh, thank you.

It's very embarrassing.

JOHN (*trying to lighten the situation*). It's a woman's prerogative.

KATHERINE. Still very sloppy. Self-indulgent.

JOHN. My name's John Sparrow. (KATHERINE *smiles as she hears the name*.) Yes . . . It's always good for a smile.

KATHERINE. I didn't mean to—

JOHN. —No, I like it. It's a name that gives my friends endless opportunities to exercise their wit . . . You know, the fallen sparrow, et cetera. (KATHERINE *smiles, liking him. But then her smile dies, and she turns away to the ash tray.* JOHN *tries to keep her interested and amused.*) I see you aren't doing any better with your dinner than I am. I was eating my dinner, or trying to . . .

KATHERINE. I just didn't seem to . . . (*She finishes with a shrug and a gesture.*)

JOHN. My mother, who lived alone a great deal of her life, used to say, the most important part of any meal is someone to eat it with. (KATHERINE *smiles reluctantly again, appreciative of this man's efforts.*) My mother didn't mind ending sentences with prepositions. As a matter of fact, she rarely ended sentences at all. She was a chatterer. (KATHERINE *just smiles at him.*) Is this your first meal here?

KATHERINE. Yes.

JOHN. The food's really very good. (*Touching the holly*) I see they tried to cheer up your tray too.

KATHERINE. Yes.

JOHN. Somehow I resent their forcing Christmas cheer down my throat. Don't you?

KATHERINE. I guess they're only trying to be kind.

JOHN (*looking at the food*). That looks awfully good. I've always been a great one for eating off other people's plates.

KATHERINE. Your dinner must be getting cold.

JOHN. Yes. (*Suddenly and directly*) May I bring it in here?

KATHERINE (*flustered*). I'm going out.

JOHN. Oh, I see.

KATHERINE. To the movies.

JOHN. Oh. So am I. Eight fifteen.

KATHERINE. But I understand you've seen the show twice already.

JOHN. How did you know?

KATHERINE. The maid. She said you recommended it.

JOHN. It put me to sleep twice . . . which is what I wanted it to do. I go to the movies a great deal.

KATHERINE. Yes, so do I lately.

JOHN. Back in college I used to go to three double features on Saturdays. It was sort of a drug just to get through Saturdays. That was before I met my wife, the girl who was to become my wife. (KATHERINE *hesitates a moment, wondering whether or not to mention the hospital.* JOHN *continues matter-of-factly.*) She's dead.

KATHERINE (*looks at him, surprised*). Oh . . . I'm sorry.

JOHN (*making nothing of it*). Five years ago. Thank you. May I bring my dinner in?

KATHERINE (*thinks for a moment. She has never done anything like this before —instinctive and impulsive—and she is afraid, but there is such directness in him that to refuse his suggestion would be rude*). Yes. I'm sorry to be so . . . But . . .

JOHN. May I ask you your name?

KATHERINE. Katherine Johnson.

JOHN. Thank you. I'll be right back, Mrs. Johnson.

KATHERINE (*she realizes that he has noticed her wedding ring. She calls after him*). Perhaps it would be better if we went to the dining room . . . (*But he has gone. She stands there not knowing quite what she's doing. Then she moves her tray, and puts up the other drop leaf of the table to make room for his tray.*)

JOHN (*in a moment, he re-enters, carrying the tray expertly on his shoulder, and carrying a bottle of Scotch in his other hand*). I worked my way through school doing this. (*Sets the tray down on the space she's cleared.*) Thanks . . . One day I spilled a chocolate sundae down the back of the wife of the headmaster . . . She was very decent and wore the dress in again the following week to show me I hadn't hurt it.

KATHERINE (*helping him arrange things*). That was nice of her.

JOHN. I hope you drink Scotch. I've been sitting in there staring at this bottle longingly, but not daring to open it alone . . . sooner or later I would have.

KATHERINE. You're stronger than I was . . . I've had one.

JOHN. Another?

KATHERINE. Not just now, thanks.

JOHN (*making himself one*). Some people think drinking alone is very decadent. I just think it's very dangerous . . . I heard you turn on the Christmas carols for a moment.

KATHERINE. The maid turned them on. I turned them off.

JOHN. I agree with you. They're murderous when you're lonely. (*He pauses a moment—then, simply*) I'm lonely. I'm assuming you are too. (*He smiles.*)

KATHERINE (*is about to say something, but then she just smiles. She is touched by this man. She drinks off a little water from her glass, and holds it out*). I will take a little, thank you.

JOHN (*pours a little Scotch into the glass*). Well, what shall it be? . . . Absent friends? . . . Snow for Christmas? . . . Or just that we manage to struggle through the evening without becoming public or private nuisances?

(KATHERINE *is suddenly sad, and turns away.*)

JOHN (*goes on quickly*). I'm sorry. Let's make it snow for Christmas . . . and an early dawn. (*He drinks, turns his attention away from her so she can recover without embarrassment.*) The roast beef has been very good here for twenty-five years. I came to school here and my folks used to visit me once a year and bring me here to the Inn for a feed. (*He looks to see if she has recovered, but she has just barely, so he goes on.*) Disgusting how children can eat. I had a nephew visiting me once . . . twenty years old. Ate a huge breakfast and then for a finish settled down with a Milky Way.

KATHERINE. You came to school here?

JOHN. Yes. About twenty-five years ago. A quarter of a century. Ugly phrase isn't it? I'm forty and I have intimations of mortality. (KATHERINE *smiles at this as she sits down and starts to eat, listening to him.*) It's a wonderful age, really. You're old enough to sense it's not going to last forever, yet young enough to do most of the things you could do at twenty . . . I think I have an appetite. For which, many thanks. (KATHERINE *starts to eat the soup.*) Shall I have Mae warm that up for you?

KATHERINE. No, it's fine. Thank you.

JOHN. Here, let me move some of this stuff away. Nothing less appetizing than a jammed tray. (*He jumps up, and moves things to another table.*)

KATHERINE. Please sit down.

JOHN. It's my waiter's instinct.

KATHERINE. Please.

JOHN (*sits and eats a mouthful—then*). Shall we do without the holly . . . or . . . No, I think it's rather nice now. Only we can consolidate it. (*Puts the sprigs together, with difficulty.*) Damned hard stuff to arrange, holly. I don't know if you're aware of that or not. There. (*He eats a mouthful and smiles at her. She manages something of a smile back.*) Do you play a lot of solitaire?

KATHERINE (*remembering the game set up by the fire*). Yes.

JOHN. My wife loved solitaire . . . We used to play double solitaire. I noticed you had a move you hadn't made.

KATHERINE. I just got tired of it . . . I didn't try to finish.

(*They eat in silence for a moment.*)

JOHN. Sometimes we used to . . . (*Suddenly stops, looks up, listening, very serious.*) Was that the phone? (*He listens for a moment, then rises quickly.*) I mean the phone in my room. (*He moves toward the door to the adjoining room.*) Did you hear the phone? (*He listens tensely for a moment, standing at the door.*) No, I guess not. (*His mood has changed. He doesn't return to the table.*) May I bum one of your cigarettes now?

KATHERINE. Of course.

JOHN (*he picks up the pack from the dresser*). I noticed this strange gadget on your key chain. May I ask what it is?

KATHERINE. It's the eye of God.

JOHN. What?

KATHERINE. In Europe in saloons and bars they used to have little porcelain plaques with an eye painted on it . . . it was called the eye of God. It was to remind people that the eye of God was on them.

JOHN. Hm.

KATHERINE. My father found this little one shaped like a charm and gave it to me when he gave me my first housekey.

JOHN. That's slightly terrifying.

KATHERINE. Yes.

JOHN. I don't know as I approve of that. (*Holds it up.*) Kind of like a neon light blinking, "No!" . . . "No!" . . . "No!"

KATHERINE. I guess that's what he

meant it to be.

JOHN (*returns to the table*). I believe they should paste a big label on youth! "Perishable. Use at once!" . . . When I was a student here, my life seemed fenced around with "No's". . . . I have a friend who has a little child, and when the child reaches for something he might break or shouldn't have, the mother says, "No, Becky. That's a No-no." My youth seemed to be filled with "No-no's." I wonder if it's the same for the boys here now.

KATHERINE. I have a son here now.

JOHN. Oh?

KATHERINE. Thirteen. Just beginning.

JOHN. It sounds silly to say, it's hard to believe . . . But I've said it.

KATHERINE. That's why I'm here. He's been sick in the Infirmary.

JOHN. That's too bad.

KATHERINE. Oh, he's all right now, but they won't let him out until tomorrow. Something about his temperature being down forty-eight hours before they'll discharge him.

JOHN. I seem to remember that sort of thing.

KATHERINE. I stayed with him until they sent me away . . . gave him one of his Christmas presents . . . A recorder . . . you know . . . (*She demonstrates.*) He's quite a whiz at it.

JOHN. And when he gets out tomorrow?

KATHERINE. He goes to Boston and flies to London to join his father for the holidays. My husband's on a business trip there. He's an engineer.

JOHN. You said, "He's going."

KATHERINE (*flustered*). Yes . . . I'm going to put him on a plane in Boston . . . I . . . I can't go just now.

JOHN (*notes that she is flustered and goes on*). They make quite a thing of Christmas abroad . . . Paris doesn't do so much, but Rome and London . . .

KATHERINE. You've spent Christmas in many places.

JOHN. Yes. I guess I have.

KATHERINE (*gently prying*). Did your wife like traveling?

JOHN. Uh . . . I was alone. It was since.

KATHERINE. Oh.

JOHN (*rising to change the subject, he indicates the Scotch*). Could I interest you in . . . ?

KATHERINE. No, thank you. (*JOHN hesitates over his own glass now.*) I don't suppose you have a son in the Infirmary too?

JOHN. No.

KATHERINE. Do you have children?

JOHN (*behind her back, he hesitates a moment, then quickly*). We had a daughter. Yes. Born a few years after the war. She was killed in an accident.

KATHERINE. I'm terribly sorry.

JOHN (*too quickly and urgently*). No, please. Please don't be sorry. I don't . . . Don't be sorry. It was all quite awhile ago. (*Now he does pour himself a light drink. Nervously, he goes on, with some banter.*) You know my family motto is *Dum spiro, spero.* Do you know Latin?

KATHERINE. I did in college, but . . .

JOHN. While I breathe I hope. While there's life, there's hope. Somehow my friends found out about this, and it became "Don't spearo Sparrow." (*He knows this isn't very funny and smiles.*) They thought it terribly funny.

KATHERINE. It *is* funny. It's also a nice motto. *Dum spiro, spero.* Is that it?

JOHN. Yes. *Spiro,* I breathe . . . *Spero,* I hope,

KATHERINE (*mulling it over*). *Spero.* (*Looks at him.*) Sparrow. (*Smiles.*) It's nice to have a name so close to Hope.

JOHN (*still bantering*). It's greater than Charity, isn't it? Or is it? I can't quite remember. Hope in myself, Charity in others.

KATHERINE. And Faith in what?

JOHN. In the morning.

KATHERINE. Yes. That's good. Faith in the morning.

JOHN. You're from the West, aren't you? California?

KATHERINE. How did you know?

JOHN. Oh, it's a different race out there. Sun-touched gods and goddesses.

KATHERINE. You're from . . . ?

JOHN. Born in New York. Educated up here in New England. Lived here for quite a while with four years out for the war. I've wandered quite a bit.

KATHERINE. What are you?

JOHN (*smiling*). I wish I knew.

KATHERINE. I mean, what do you do?

JOHN. Ah. At cocktail parties I tell people I'm a writer. That shuts them up, because they've never heard of me, and it embarrasses people to talk to a writer they've never read.

KATHERINE. You're a writer then?

JOHN. I wanted to be a writer. But I had a family that didn't think it was quite right to say you wanted to be a writer, so I said I wanted to be a teacher, and you know the classic phrase, write on the side. The war interrupted it very nicely. I was a flier . . . Navy, in the Pacific. Came back and became a newspaper man whose specialty was aviation.

KATHERINE. That's what you are now?

JOHN. Yes, more or less free-lance.

KATHERINE. And the writing?

JOHN. I did my duty and wrote my book after the war. Everyone said it should have sold better. It didn't.

KATHERINE. What was it called?

JOHN. *The Comfort of Your Company*.

KATHERINE. It sounds like something I'd like to read.

JOHN. Why?

KATHERINE (*flustered at what might have been a too revealing statement*). I don't know. I guess it's the kind of title I like.

JOHN. So did I.

KATHERINE. Kind of title you hardly have to read the book.

JOHN. A lot of people agreed with you. They read the title and had had it.

KATHERINE. Was it based on personal experience?

JOHN. Thinly disguised to protect people living and dead. Are you from San Francisco?

KATHERINE. Yes.

JOHN. I thought so.

KATHERINE. Why?

JOHN. San Francisco women have . . . Oh, a style, yet also a womanliness that is fast disappearing . . .

KATHERINE. Was the story set in San Francisco?

JOHN. Yes. It might have been you.

KATHERINE. I was married.

JOHN. So was I. So was she.

KATHERINE. Oh.

JOHN. It was just before Christmas. We were shoving off the next day . . . and I'd sat in a phone booth in the St. Francis trying to reach my wife back East . . . to say good-bye. I waited about five hours to get through, and then she wasn't in. No reason why she should have been . . . she was out for the evening and no one knew where . . . So I started drinking with the fellows in the bar, and suddenly it came over me that I had to say good-bye to someone, some girl. It was a big thing. I was going off to war, and I wanted to say good-bye. Only girl I knew was a girl I'd been out with with another officer on my ship. She was married, had a baby, and her husband was in the Pacific . . . So I called her up, but she had to stay home and take care of the baby. So I bought everything I could find, flowers, champagne, something for the baby, and even a couple of books, because we'd talked about poetry . . . and I took one of those wild streetcars out to her place. We sat on the couch and she played records, Jerome Kern, and we drank and I looked at the pictures of her husband's ship. She hadn't seen him in over a year, and we were both lonesome and sick inside. I knew from the way she looked at me, we both wanted to help each other over a tough spot. And she asked me if I'd like to dance, but I knew I couldn't, because if I ever held her in my arms even in dancing . . . And after all, we were decent, and her husband was in the Pacific, and her baby in the next room. Anyway, I finally got up to go home, and I shook hands with her . . . wanting to hold her and feel her warmth and give and take whatever comfort we had for each other. But we didn't. We shook hands and I left, and went back to my ship. I sailed the next day and was away for two years.

KATHERINE. And that was the story too?

JOHN. No. In the story he stayed the night. I wrote it that way because I knew that's what I should have done. You see a writer gets a second chance. Not very satisfying, but still . . . In those days I felt if I ever slept with anyone else, I'd never be able to be with my wife again. (KATHERINE *looks at him at this, expecting him to go on. It is obviously an important point to her*.) I'm sorry. The conversation got a little out of hand.

KATHERINE. It's all right.

JOHN (*he gets up to get himself another of her cigarettes—changes his tone back to the bantering again*). I'll get you a carton in the morning. For your stocking. Do you open presents on Christmas Eve or Christmas Day in your family?

KATHERINE. Christmas Day.

JOHN. My wife's family opened them

Christmas Eve, mine Christmas Day. So we compromised and did it Christmas Eve. (*Notices the artistically wrapped presents.*) My wife wrapped packages beautifully.

MAE (*in the next room*). Mr. Sparrow? Are you there?

JOHN. Did you order coffee?

KATHERINE. No.

JOHN (*starts towards the hall door*). Mae . . . (*Stops. To* KATHERINE) Perhaps it embarrasses you?

KATHERINE (*it is a new experience for her, but she has committed herself*). No.

JOHN (*at the door*). Mae, will you bring it in here, please? (MAE *comes in, taking no notice that they are together. She acts as though it were the most usual thing in the world.* JOHN *turns to* KATHERINE.) Sure you won't change your mind?

KATHERINE. No, but I would like this thermos filled with coffee for the morning.

MAE. I'll take care of it. (*Looks at the fire on her way out.*) If you need any more wood for the fire just ask for it.

JOHN *and* KATHERINE. Yes, thank— (*They look at each other.* JOHN *smiles, embarrassed, realizing it's not his fire.*)

KATHERINE. I think there'll be enough, thanks.

JOHN. Oh, Mae, I've invited the newlyweds for a drink later on, so would you see I have glasses and ice and soda.

MAE. Ice, soda . . . yes . . . Four glasses. (KATHERINE *registers on the "four"; so does* JOHN.) They're out walking just now in the snow. (*She leaves.*)

JOHN. The help keeps track of every move those poor people make.

KATHERINE (*laughs*). I know.

JOHN. Barbaric custom, honeymoons.

KATHERINE. Yes.

JOHN. Newlyweds do something to a place. They fill it with a sort of infectious sensuality.

KATHERINE (*smiling*). I understand they've been freezing to death.

JOHN (*laughs*). I met the groom in the bar on my way in.

KATHERINE. Alone?

JOHN. Yes. He was having a stiff whisky and was buried in his gun catalogue as though it were his only contact with a fast disappearing reality. (KATHERINE *laughs.*) He grabbed hold of me as though he were the Ancient Mariner. It turns out we're fraternity brothers at the school here . . . fifteen years apart, but still . . . (*He gives himself the fraternal handshake.*) I think he saw in me the terrible future, and I saw in him the lovely past. Anyway, when he said, "There's still nothing to do around this town at night," I stifled my sympathetic laughter and asked them up for a drink later on . . . if they still had nothing better to do. (KATHERINE *is laughing freely now. She looks at him.* JOHN *continues, seriously.*) I'm glad you're laughing.

KATHERINE (*she stops laughing slowly, and smiles*). Yes. Thank you.

JOHN (*looks at his watch*). It takes ten minutes to walk to the movies.

KATHERINE. Oh, yes.

JOHN. You still want to go to the movies?

KATHERINE (*she realizes how pleasant it is just to sit and talk, but she thinks the movies are best*). Yes.

JOHN (*going*). I'll just get my coat and tell the operator where I can be reached in case there's a call. (*He goes.*)

KATHERINE (*this concern for a call puzzles her. She puts on her coat and has almost reached the door when her phone rings. She stops, looks at it, and then returns and picks up the phone*). Yes? . . . London? . . . Wait a minute. (*She is upset.*) Just a minute . . . Tell him . . . tell London I can't accept the call . . . No . . . Tell them you can't reach me . . . Thank you . . . (*She hangs up the phone slowly.*)

JOHN (*having put on his coat, he sticks his head in through the hall door*). Coming?

(*There is a slight pause. Then—*)

KATHERINE. Yes. (*She throws her scarf around her neck as she exits after him.*)

CURTAIN

Scene Two

As the curtain rises, we see the room lit only with one light and the glow from the fire.

The dinner things have been replaced by the set-ups for the four drinks—an ice bucket, soda, and glasses.

There is talk offstage, as the four people approach the doors.

JOHN (*offstage*). I hope everybody likes Scotch.

JANET *and* PHILIP. Yes, that's fine . . . That'll be great.

KATHERINE (*opening her door*). I'll just leave my coat in my room. Janet, do you want to—(*She snaps on another light.*)

JOHN (*has entered his own room. We hear him calling out*). Didn't I ask for ice and things for drinks?

KATHERINE (*sees the ice and glasses*). Mae left the tray and things in here. I'll bring them in.

(JANET, *still in her overcoat, goes out of* JOHN'S *room, goes through the hall and comes into* KATHERINE'S *room through the main door. She is bright-eyed, twenty-one and assured.*)

JANET. Can I help?

KATHERINE. No. But come in.

JANET. This is a lovely room.

KATHERINE. Yes. It's a shame you can't have it. When I leave tomorrow, why don't you take over?

JANET. I'm afraid we couldn't swing it. Up under the eaves for us.

KATHERINE (*running a comb through her hair*). Oh, make him splurge for your honeymoon. It's terribly important.

JANET. Oh, he'd splurge. It's me. I want to save the money for something, oh, I don't know, anyway something permanent.

KATHERINE. You'll find a honeymoon turns out to be quite permanent.

JANET. Yes, I guess it is.

KATHERINE. Would you let me make you a present of it for a few days? I assure you I can afford it.

JANET. That's sweet of you. No. Philip's parents offered to stake us to a grand honeymoon, but we're making them buy us a hi-fi and oodles of records instead.

KATHERINE. It's just that young people never seem to realize how important honeymoons are till they're over. I know I was full of bright ideas about not wasting the time or money, and . . . well . . .

JANET. I agree with you, but it's not as though Philip and I hadn't . . . I mean . . . (*Embarrassed*) Well, you know.

KATHERINE (*not sure she does*). Oh, yes. (*Takes the tray and starts toward the hall door. She indicates the bathroom.*) Do you want to go in there or anything, before we . . .

JANET. No, but can't we stay in here? This room is so much more pleasant.

(*We can hear* JOHN *unbolting one of the double doors that separate the rooms. He knocks.*)

JANET. Oh. Shall I? (*She moves to open the adjoining door.*)

KATHERINE. Oh. Uh, of course.

(JOHN *enters with the bottle.*)

JOHN. May I leave the door open so I can hear the phone?

KATHERINE (*a little taken aback by this moving in. She sets the tray down*). Uh . . . yes. Of course.

JANET (*as* PHILIP *comes in*). You know, Phil, this would be a wonderful color scheme for the living room at the farm.

(KATHERINE *closes the hall door.*)

JOHN (*busying himself with the drinks*). Oh, have you a farm?

JANET. Not yet. Just a four flight walk-up on West Tenth Street with a flowerpot on the ledge. But one day we're going to have a remodeled barn or something like that . . . not in any fancy district like Westport or Bucks County, but someplace simple.

KATHERINE. Sounds wonderful. Fixing your first house is one of the great experiences.

PHILIP (*taking a drink to* JANET). There's a little matter of money first.

KATHERINE. Well, get good pieces slowly. You think you're just getting something temporary and you end up having it for life.

(*Each time* KATHERINE *says something,* JOHN *gets a little more information about her. And each time he says something, no matter how casual, it registers on her.*)

JANET. We're not so keen on good pieces as we are on keeping it simple. I'll take orange crates and a big house full of books and records and children. (*She smiles.*)

JOHN (*giving a drink to* KATHERINE). That's charming.

JANET (*she studies the colors and furnishings as she goes on*). My mother and dad, and Philip's, live in a clutter of Things with a capital T. Accumulated junk. Possessions which they spend a fortune to house and keep clean. And they're always bickering about the high cost of living. Sorry, Philip. At least mine are.

PHILIP. Yes, mine too. (*Puts his arm around her to soften the criticism.*) But I'm afraid our fifty-year program is hardly of general interest.

KATHERINE. I think it's wonderful. I'm very touched by it.

JANET. I know. You think it won't work. Well, we'll make it work.

KATHERINE. Of course you will. And I didn't mean that at all. I'd like to send you a wedding present. Some records maybe.

JOHN. What's your line of work, Philip?

PHILIP. Oh, I'm just finishing off business school, and then I have a job in New York.

JANET. Philip's always embarrassed to mention it, and I tell him it's ridiculous. There can be sincere advertising men.

JOHN. Of course.

JANET. Just as long as we don't try to pretend that it's of earth-shaking importance. It's a means to an end. If Philip and I can live the kind of life we want on some slogan that he dreams up, what's wrong with that?

KATHERINE. Nothing at all.

JANET. My father has a friend who lived his entire life on the strength of one slogan he thought up. I've forgotten which one it is, but you all know it.

JOHN. When better cars are built . . . ?

JANET. No.

KATHERINE. It's smart to be thrifty?

JANET. No. Well, it doesn't matter. Philip is embarrassed because he wanted to be a concert pianist, but his father talked him out of it. But we're going to have a piano. His mother is giving us one, and it can always be a hobby for him.

PHILIP. Jan, honey . . . these things are important to us, but—

JOHN. —I hope these things are always important to everyone. (*He raises his glass to toast this idea.*)

KATHERINE. And I hope you never quite achieve them all. (*She raises her glass.*)

PHILIP. Really?

KATHERINE. Yes. (*She notices* JOHN *is looking at her.*)

JANET. Why?

KATHERINE (*shrugs*). It's better that way.

JANET. I guess I have talked an awful lot. I'm sorry.

JOHN. Please. We're loving it.

JANET. You're not laughing at us?

KATHERINE (*moved by their bright innocence*). No, of course we're not.

JANET. The trouble with me is I've always been terribly enthusiastic about anything I . . . (*She has started to look for a handkerchief in her pocket and now brings it out with a shower of confetti.*) Oh, I'm sorry. (*She tries to pick up the confetti.*)

KATHERINE. Please leave it. (*She looks at it almost fondly.*)

JANET. My brother got into my suitcase and filled it with confetti.

KATHERINE (*helping* JANET *pour some into an ashtray*). You'll never get rid of it. It will show up years from now on some dismal winter afternoon when you're packing to go home to Mother.

JANET. My brother's a poet, or he's trying to be a poet. Anyway, he's living in Greenwich Village. We expect to have a lot of wonderful evenings together.

JOHN. I'm sure you will have.

KATHERINE. Where were you married?

PHILIP. Well, we wanted to have a quiet wedding up here. Past two years we've been up here on weekends a lot . . . (*Checks himself, embarrassed.*) I mean . . .

JANET (*to* KATHERINE). That's what I meant.

KATHERINE. Oh, yes.

PHILIP. What?

JANET. Just something I'd said to Mrs. Johnson about why we weren't splurging on a honeymoon. I'm sorry I interrupted.

(PHILIP *looks to* JOHN *for a clue.* JOHN *shrugs his ignorance.*)

PHILIP (*disconcerted, goes on*). Anyway, we wanted a quiet wedding up here, because this place means something to us, but Jan's family thought . . .

JANET. It's true. It was my family's fault.

PHILIP. Anyway, it turned out to be quite a hassle.

JANET. Terrifying.

PHILIP. Janet tried to pretend it wasn't happening by carrying on a rapid-fire conversation with one of her bridesmaids about the United Nations . . .

JANET. How do you know? You were at the other end of the church.

PHILIP. I was told. Besides it went on all during the wedding breakfast, only by then the subject had switched to foreign aid.

JANET (*to* KATHERINE). Well, did you manage to get a quiet wedding?

KATHERINE. No.

JOHN. I managed it. (*Smiles smugly.*) Or I should say, we did.

JANET. Oh . . . Yes, of course.

JOHN. We had the perfect marriage. Early June . . . small New England town . . . little white church with the sun coming through . . . and just the two of us. That's something to have had.

KATHERINE. It must have been lovely.

JOHN. And a minister who said very simply that marriages are not made in Heaven.

PHILIP. Did our minister say anything? I don't remember.

JANET. Yes, lots. But I don't remember either.

PHILIP. You told him how wonderful it was.

JANET. Well what are you going to say? A man stands up there and talks for ten minutes . . .

PHILIP. I think he said he'd send us a copy of it.

JANET. Oh, well good. I guess. (*Gently needling him—obviously, they share a joke.*) We didn't bring along *enough* to read. (PHILIP *laughs, and then frowns because the others won't understand.*) I mean . . .

JOHN (*smiling*). We all do it . . . We all bring along books on our honeymoons so that they won't be a complete waste of time. (*They all laugh, the young ones in embarrassment. To* KATHERINE) What did you take on your honeymoon?

KATHERINE. *War and Peace.*

JOHN. You must have had a long honeymoon.

KATHERINE. I did. But I haven't read *War and Peace* yet.

JANET. Well, for your information, we haven't cracked our books either.

JOHN. Good . . . Will you have another drink?

(JANET *and* PHILIP *look at each other.*)

JANET. Uh . . . I don't think so, thanks.

PHILIP. We'd better be running along.

JANET. I haven't finished all my thank-you notes yet.

PHILIP. Uh . . . yes . . . Besides it's way after eleven.

JANET (*holding out a hand to say good night*). I apologize if I've been a bore.

KATHERINE. I'm sorry you feel you need to apologize. We're jealous. At least I am. Merry Christmas.

JANET. Merry Christmas, and thank you. I didn't find out anything about you except you're going tomorrow. (*To* JOHN.) Are you going too?

JOHN. No. I'm staying.

JANET (*confused*). Oh. (*She looks from* KATHERINE *to* JOHN.)

JOHN. Mrs. Johnson and I just met, at dinnertime.

JANET. Oh, then we're all strangers.

JOHN. Yes.

PHILIP. Good night. Merry Christmas. Thank you. Sorry we didn't get a chance to talk about the fraternity.

JOHN. Maybe we'll meet again in the bar . . .

PHILIP (*puts a finger to his lips and coughs slightly*). Uh . . .

JOHN. Oh, sorry. (*He gives the fraternity handshake.*) Good night.

JANET. Please don't laugh at us when we go.

KATHERINE. We're much more likely to cry.

JANET. Why do people cry at weddings?

KATHERINE. Oh . . . someday you may know. I hope not.

JANET. I don't understand that.

KATHERINE. Good.

PHILIP. I had a coat.

JOHN. Oh, yes, you left it in my room. (*He goes into his own room.*)

PHILIP (*as he follows* JOHN). Sorry. I'm always the one who says good night and then exits into the coat closet. (*He goes into* JOHN's *room.*)

JANET (*at the hall door, leaving*). Did I make a fool of myself? Going on and on?

KATHERINE. Of course not.

JANET. It's just that you're the first people we've talked to in five days. (KATHERINE *kisses her on the cheek, and sees her out.* JANET *joins* PHILIP *in the hall.*) Good night.

KATHERINE. Good night.

(JANET *closes the hall door.* KATHERINE *picks up the solitaire cards. In a few moments,* JOHN *appears in the connecting door to his room, fully conscious of the situation. He pauses there a moment.*)

JOHN. Do you think they'll make it?

KATHERINE. Who knows? Let's hope so.

JOHN. I always speculate at weddings . . . Is she still in love with someone who wouldn't marry her? Who does he dream about? What happens now that it's no longer stolen weekends, but guaranteed weeks, months and years? . . . What happens? (*He comes in.*) I never saw a more militant bride.

KATHERINE. Weren't you and your wife that way?

JOHN. Oh, determined for the good life, yes. Not simplicity. She was not a simple girl. I was the one who always was trying to find one great simple guiding truth on the head of a pin.

KATHERINE. Did you ever find it?

JOHN. No. At the moment I'm a man who's done almost everything and knows nothing.

KATHERINE. That's very sad.

JOHN. I always thought, if I had just a little more experience I'd finally know it.

KATHERINE. What?

JOHN. I don't know. Whatever it is. Some certainty. But all I found was a rage of contradictions . . . a saddening but somehow beautiful complexity . . . You whistle beautifully.

KATHERINE. What do you mean?

JOHN. You've been whistling ever since we met those two coming out of the movies.

KATHERINE. I have a feeling you've been whistling too.

JOHN. Hell, we're a world of whistlers. (*Toasts.*) To the whistling walking wounded.

KATHERINE. There's comfort in that. *"The Comfort of Your Company."*

JOHN. Thanks for remembering. (*Looks outside.*) Well, we got what we wished for. It's snowing.

KATHERINE. That's right. We wished for snow, didn't we?

JOHN. Among other things.

KATHERINE (*looking out the window with him*). Is that one of the school buildings up there, with all the lights on?

JOHN. I think it's . . . a hospital.

KATHERINE (*looks at him*). Oh.

JOHN (*pulling the curtains*). Somehow now we've got the snow I don't want it. Do you mind?

KATHERINE. No.

(*There is an awkward moment between them.*)

JOHN. I'll just finish my drink.

KATHERINE. What? Oh, yes.

JOHN (*he walks past the dresser and sees the bottle of pills still there*). Were you about to try suicide when you called for help?

KATHERINE. I don't know what I was going to do. I just suddenly found myself crying for help.

JOHN. I've had it right there so many times. (*He touches his mouth.*)

KATHERINE. I've always bottled up. I couldn't believe it when I heard myself crying out like that.

JOHN. I imagine if we could hear all the stifled cries for help in the world, it would be deafening . . . Help . . . Help . . . Help.

KATHERINE. Somehow I always thought it cowardly to cry out. I'm ashamed of myself now.

JOHN (*after a moment of looking at each other*). Nietzsche said the thought of suicide got a lot of people through a lot of terrible nights . . . Have you ever actually tried it?

KATHERINE. No, not really. I suppose, like most people, I've thought about it.

JOHN. I never quite had the courage to gobble all those sleeping pills or pull a trigger or jump. I beachcombed for a year, after my wife . . . died, and I used to put it in the lap of Fate. I'd get fairly drunk and then I'd go in swimming in the surf at night. If Fate wanted me, she could have me. She didn't want me. She always threw me up on the beach with the seaweed.

KATHERINE. Why did *you* want to commit suicide?

JOHN. Oh, general feeling of worthlessness, I guess . . . I can't imagine you ever had that feeling.

KATHERINE. You can't?

JOHN. No. (*Waits for her to go on, but she doesn't.*) In the movies tonight, the sad picture, you cried out of all proportion to—

KATHERINE. —I know. I'm sorry.

JOHN. I told you I couldn't stand to see a woman cry.

KATHERINE. Yes.

JOHN. And when I took your hand . . .

KATHERINE (*not wanting to go on with it*). Please. (*She has turned away. It will take more opening up on his own part before she will open up. He switches on the radio.*)

JOHN. I wonder if they're through with their carols yet. (*Gets soft dance music.*) Mmmm. I don't know. Is that worse than the carols or better? (KATHERINE *smiles and shrugs.*) Does that happen to be a song that brings up pleasant or unpleasant memories?

KATHERINE. No.

JOHN. Then it can stand. Somehow I feel nights like this should be in a vacuum, having no relation to past or future . . . (*Getting back to the subject*) I never cried for help . . . but for years I had the desperate impulse to reach out a lonely hand to touch someone. The night in San Francisco in the war, when I went back to my ship, I wanted to reach out and touch the head of the girl who sat in front of me on the bus. (*In remembering, he has reached out his hand. He takes its back.*) I didn't.

KATHERINE (*after a long moment*). Maybe I'd better say something. It may sound ridiculous, but . . . Oh, no, it *is* ridiculous.

JOHN. Say it.

KATHERINE. No. (*He waits for her, not helping her out of her spot.*) Oh, all right. I . . . I'm very lonely . . . and I'm quite miserable and all that . . . but it's only fair to tell you I'm not going to spend the night with you. (JOHN *smiles.* KATHERINE *is now swept up in confusion.*) You see it *is* ridiculous. But I only thought it fair to tell you, so that you'd . . . well, know. Now I suppose I've spoiled everything, and you're going to think what kind of woman is this who goes around assuming that every man wants to . . . It's just that . . . I don't know.

JOHN. It's very touching that you should feel that you had to say that.

KATHERINE (*running on, having trapped herself into making revelations*). I've never been with anyone but my husband, and I . . . My God, why should that sound prudish? Why should I feel I have to apologize for that. It's just that . . .

JOHN. Don't apologize.

KATHERINE. I'm not apologizing. It's just that, in this day and age, I seem like an anachronism. What the kids call a . . . a square. Isn't that the word?

JOHN. Yes, that's the word.

KATHERINE (*suddenly defending herself violently*). Well, I'd rather be that than a whore. (*She realizes that her defense is out of all proportion and has no relation to anything that's been said. She turns away.*) I'm sorry. (*She snaps off the radio.*)

JOHN. Who's made you feel embarrassed about it? Someone.

KATHERINE. Yes, I suppose they have. My husband's away a great deal . . . sometimes months. In the beginning, I stayed home, I mean I didn't go out to parties when he was away . . . Then I started to go to my friends' homes, and of course they'd be very considerate and have a man to pick me up, take me home . . . very often husbands of my friends who were away visiting parents, or just out of town. I got quite a view of a lot of marriages.

JOHN. And you learned to make your little speech.

KATHERINE. Yes. I was shocked at how glibly people talked about going to bed together. As though you could fall in love in an hour.

JOHN. You think people go to bed together only because they're in love?

KATHERINE (*she looks at him for a moment*). You obviously don't think so.

JOHN. There are a lot of other reasons besides love . . . Reassurance, courage, loneliness, comfort . . . for protection against the horrors of the night.

KATHERINE. You've been with a lot of women.

JOHN. Yes. Too many, if that doesn't sound ridiculous coming from a man.

KATHERINE. You see, you do the same thing I do. You apologize for your feeling that there could be too many . . .

JOHN. What I said sounded smug as I said it.

KATHERINE (*these are things she has never had a chance to talk about before, and they spill out . . .*). There was one man . . . no, there were two . . . but there was this one man. I knew him and his wife. They were both my friends . . . and then his wife got sick, and it was hopeless, and she was five or six months in the hospital . . . dying. And this man, he was younger than I was . . . I used to go to the hospital to see his wife, and when she'd fall asleep for the night, I'd go out for a drink with him, sometimes bring him home for a sandwich, listen to him talk about how much he loved his wife, and he did. Why are you smiling?

JOHN. What did you do? . . . I know

the answer, don't I? Because you said you'd only—

KATHERINE. —I didn't. He didn't love me. (*Defensive again*) Any woman would have done. A prostitute. (JOHN *shakes his head "No."*) Why not?

JOHN (*too strongly*). Because with a prostitute it's a kind of mockery, and it leaves you more lonely than ever.

KATHERINE (*thinks over his protest*). You think I should have done it.

JOHN. I have no right to think what anyone else should or should not do.

KATHERINE. Well, I didn't. And I've hated myself ever since.

JOHN. That's too bad. I mean, hating yourself.

KATHERINE. But I believe there is a book, a book we live by, and if we don't live by it, then we should stop saying we do, and throw it away and start all over again.

JOHN. You've tried to live by the book.

KATHERINE. Yes. I'm not strong enough to make up my own rules as I go along. I wish I were. I sometimes wish to God I were.

JOHN. Yeah. The Eleventh Commandment is a tough one to live by. (KATHERINE *looks at him inquiringly*.) Don't Get Caught . . . Funny thing is, you go around being afraid someone else is going to catch you, and you end up catching yourself.

KATHERINE. My mother . . . (*Stops herself.*) Anyway, my father took me away from her when I was seven. I don't know if she's dead or alive. I think she's dead. They say I look like her. (*Her fear is clear from this statement.*)

JOHN. And your father gave you the eye of God, which has always said "No."

KATHERINE. Yes. It has always said "No." (*She smiles.*) That was the other time . . . I started to write poetry some years after I was married. I had been class poet at college . . . it was the only talent I had . . . and the home wasn't enough any more . . . We'd promised to love, honor and succeed . . . and he'd succeeded . . . So I wrote poetry . . . which I could never have published, because it turned out to be too personal. But I did send it to a young poet whose work I admired, and we corresponded . . . and one day he came to San Francisco to give a reading of his poetry. And he

wanted to meet me. We had drinks after the reading. I don't know what he expected to find. I don't know what I expected to find . . . He was staying overnight in a hotel, and my husband was away on one of his trips. My God, no one stays home any more, do they? . . . And it was quite obvious what was happening over the drinks. We were talking about verse forms, but we knew each other very intimately through our poetry . . . and we were falling in love . . . At which point I opened my purse to get a cigarette, and nestled in the bottom with the lipstick and aspirin and Kleenex . . . the eye of God looked up at me.

JOHN. And said "No."

KATHERINE. No. It was more specific that time. "Thou shalt not commit adultery."

JOHN. And have you hated yourself ever since?

KATHERINE (*smiles*). No, not hate. Regret, maybe. But my husband came home the next day and I made him cancel all his appointments and take me to lunch . . . And I wanted him to spend the afternoon with me after lunch, but he couldn't do that, so I went and had my hair done . . . I wonder if husbands realize when their wives suddenly show up at the office and ask to be taken to lunch . . . I wonder if they realize it's a cry for help, for protection.

JOHN. I think you've been steering through the narrows and shoals with wonderful dexterity . . .

KATHERINE. And I got halfway home.

JOHN. What do you mean?

KATHERINE. I didn't quite make it, but I did get halfway home. Now? (*She shakes her head.*) Next time you ask me if I want a drink, I don't.

JOHN. You're not high. You're just . . .

KATHERINE. Like the militant bride, I haven't talked with anyone in five days, or five years . . . or ever, like this. Why did you stop me whistling?

JOHN. Because of the way you held my hand in the movies.

KATHERINE (*goes to her purse on the bureau*). I think I'd better take one of my unwinders. (*She takes out a pill box and fishes for a pill.*)

JOHN. What's that?

KATHERINE. I don't know exactly what

they are, but they unwind me, get me ready for sleep . . . sometimes. If they don't, then I have others . . .

JOHN. Yes, I saw those.

KATHERINE. It's funny. Usually people unload on me. I'm sorry. I'm really sorry. You won't think so much of San Francisco ladies after this. Out there I'm famous for not even giving my name except at the point of a gun.

JOHN. I'm flattered and touched that you'd talk to me like this.

KATHERINE. I gather you've heard many astounding stories about marriage. I suppose most of them are the same.

JOHN (*he holds up his thumb*). Like thumbs, all alike. Like thumb prints, all different.

KATHERINE. Who said that?

JOHN. I'm afraid I did.

KATHERINE. What are you doing here alone in a God-forsaken spot on Christmas Eve?

JOHN (*thinks for a moment*). I'm evading the kindness of friends, and enjoying the kindness of a stranger.

KATHERINE. I know what you mean.

JOHN. I could have toddled along to friends' houses to help them trim the tree. But I decided not to this year.

KATHERINE. I can understand.

JOHN. Christmastime and Thanksgiving . . . it's an offense against something or other to be single. My wife and I used to gather in our friends who were alone. I never realized how lonely we were making them feel. It's much better to be with strangers . . . to make your own "family" as it were, for a few hours.

KATHERINE. Yes.

JOHN. I was in Paris one year at Christmas. And New Year's Eve in the subways, all the single men and women were headed for parties with their nicely wrapped bottles under their arms. Their tickets of admission.

KATHERINE. Where were you going?

JOHN. I don't remember where I was going. But I know where I ended up. Did you know the French don't sing "Auld Lang Syne"? I got very maudlin about old acquaintances, and the girl had never heard of it. (*He starts to whistle it, then stops.*)

KATHERINE. You manage to find compatible strangers wherever you are.

(*They look at each other a long moment. He is suddenly serious, a little hurt by this. He moves away.*)

JOHN. That kind of woman is easy to find.

KATHERINE. A man as attractive as you, I should think—

JOHN (*bluntly, directly*). I've made it a practice for two years not to sleep with anyone I could possibly care for.

KATHERINE. How terrible!

JOHN. There are more terrible things. (*He moves away.*) I don't know why I told you that. I suppose it's because you told me you had no intention of sleeping with me. I just wanted to put your mind at rest. (*Goes to the bottle.*) You sure you won't have some more?

KATHERINE. I seem to be suddenly sobered. All right.

(*He pours for her and gives her ice.*)

JOHN (*as he pours, he starts to smile*). I'm sorry. That was uncalled for. Very ungentlemanly.

KATHERINE. I think I asked for it.

JOHN. Seems impossible to think this is the same little gentleman who used to push his mother's chair to the table downstairs in the dining room.

KATHERINE. I would like to have seen you then.

JOHN. No you wouldn't have. I was a very proper little prig. Mortally afraid of anything even slightly off the straight and narrow, and hiding my fear behind a pompous self-righteousness. How could the seniors make love to the town girls down by the river on spring evenings . . . When all the time I was aching to do it myself. So much morality is just lack of opportunity, or lack of courage, or lack of appetite . . . Lest you draw the wrong conclusions, mine was lack of courage.

KATHERINE (*smiles*). So I gathered from what you said earlier. (*The clock outside starts to strike twelve.*) It's Christmas.

JOHN. Yes. Officially. (*Draws the curtains aside a bit.*) When I was a student here I used to lie awake at night listening to those bells. The simplicity of the half-awake dreams I used to make up for myself!

KATHERINE. That someday you would find the answer on the head of a pin?

JOHN. Oh, no. I knew the answer in those days. Do right, work hard. Be honest, and there'd be a big reward for you on Prize Day . . . Now I know there is no Prize Day. My wife was as near to being a saint as anyone could be on this earth, and there was no Prize Day for her. (*He has suddenly blurted this forth. He looks up, surprised, then smiles and holds up his glass.*) But there are small comforts along the way. You said you'd gotten halfway home. What did you mean?

KATHERINE. I changed the subject.

JOHN. I'm changing it back again . . . if I may.

KATHERINE. My father once told me that one should be very careful what one writes or says late at night. You are.

JOHN. Yes, I am.

KATHERINE (*she sits at the desk, and draws the letter from the pigeonhole and just places it in front of her*). Two days ago, just before I left California, I got a letter from my husband. It's very touching, really . . . touching, and yet to me, terrifying. I mean, I know a husband can't be away as much as he is without something happening, but a woman always expects or hopes it's something meaningless . . . or she tries not to think about it at all . . . Some friends of mine came back from London and tattled.

JOHN. I'm sorry.

KATHERINE. He knew they would. So he wrote me this letter. (*She picks up the letter and reads a bit from it.*) "It's a defenseless position, but I won't come crawling with this over my head for the rest of my life. And I can't blame you if you want a divorce. But I hope you won't. It happened, and, to be honest, it's happened before. I'm bewildered and feel terribly isolated. I have tried. I have seen hundreds of movies alone in all the languages of the world. I know I have put you in an impossible situation . . ." (*She almost breaks.*)

JOHN. He's very honest.

KATHERINE. Yes. He's honest and honorable. I think sometimes that's why he married me. I was the first girl he'd . . . been with . . . and I think he never questioned that that meant marriage. Oh, that sounds dreadful. We were in love. In college I had a little apartment, and he made it his home. I think when senior year was over, we just didn't know what else to do. We were neither one of us very adventurous, and I guess we were

both glad to find a safe harbor. We'd had a wonderful relationship, and we didn't want it to end. But it did end with marriage, in a sense, with the first bills and responsibilities. My friends who have seen her say she looks like me. Strange.

JOHN. What are you going to do?

KATHERINE. I don't know. (*She goes to the window.*) It's a terrible decision to have to make.

JOHN. That's why you're not going to London, then?

KATHERINE. Yes . . . My husband called earlier this evening, but I wouldn't take the call. I need time.

JOHN. You're thinking of leaving him then?

KATHERINE. Yes. (*Turns to him, defensively.*) I committed myself to the marriage. Do you know what that means?

JOHN. Yes.

KATHERINE. It wasn't a one-foot-in, one-foot-out, ready-to-jump sort of thing . . . as long as it's convenient, as long as it doesn't get in the way of my self-expression. I think I terrified him with my sense of dedication. I wanted to dedicate my life blindly. It frightened him. He wanted the more loosely knit relationship we'd had in college . . . I wanted to fulfill his life as he would fulfill mine . . . not just have a . . . a marriage of convenience . . . not just friends who slept together! . . . I sound so bitchy. But I'm hurt . . . You don't say anything.

JOHN. I don't know anything to say.

KATHERINE. Somehow it's all right until someone gives you the feeling you're being cheated . . . I had an aunt who thought she'd been happily married till she read an article about sex enjoyment. After that she thought she'd had a terrible marriage and got a divorce. Now she's alone someplace in an apartment hotel and spends her evenings walking her dog. (*They smile sadly at this.*) Why do you sleep only with women you can't care for?

JOHN. I've told my story too many times to too many people.

KATHERINE. Were you happily married?

JOHN. Yes.

KATHERINE. Then why didn't you marry again?

JOHN (*not wishing to go into this*). I could explain your husband to you.

KATHERINE. No.

JOHN. I'd like to.

KATHERINE. Nobody needs to explain longing and desire to me. Were you faithful to your wife?

JOHN. Yes.

KATHERINE. You said there'd been no Prize Day for her. (JOHN *doesn't answer.*) How long were you married?

JOHN. Oh, 1940 . . . nineteen years.

KATHERINE. But you said she'd been dead five years.

JOHN. Did I? (*He looks at her a moment, then moves toward his door. She watches him, puzzled. He sees her sleeping pills on the desk.*) May I have a couple of your sleeping pills? I forgot mine.

KATHERINE (*going to the desk and giving him one*). Yes . . . One should do.

JOHN (*looks at the pill in his hand*). Mine are pink . . . though I've had some luck with the yellow and white ones. Can't take the blue ones. Thank you. Good night. (*He goes to his door.*)

KATHERINE. Good night.

(*She goes to her bed, thinking he has gone . . . and sits. JOHN stands in his doorway, watching her. He sees her bury her head in her hands. He is touched by this misery, and moves back into the room and sits and then lies on the couch. She turns around and watches him.*)

JOHN. I don't particularly want to be alone tonight. Do you mind? (KATHERINE *smiles and shakes her head "No."*) Christmas Eve is Hell, isn't it? (*She smiles at him.*) The Fourth of July is much easier.

(KATHERINE *takes a blanket from the top of her bed, and comes over to the couch. She turns out the lights near the couch, and puts the blanket over him. As she pulls it up around his shoulders, he turns away. She looks at him, surprised, wondering. She crosses to her bed, and sits down and starts taking off her shoes, as*

THE CURTAIN FALLS

ACT TWO

SCENE ONE

As the curtain rises, the only light in the room is from the fireplace. JOHN *is asleep on the couch, restless and mumbling in his sleep.*

KATHERINE *is still in her sweater and skirt, and is lying on the bed with a blanket over her. She is propped up on one elbow, watching* JOHN *and listening to him. Then she lies back on the pillow.*

In the distance a town clock strikes five.

———

JOHN (*suddenly he sits bolt upright and listens. He looks over at* KATHERINE, *but thinks she is asleep. His main attention is elsewhere. He throws off the blanket and jumps up and goes to his door and listens. He hears nothing, but he goes into his room, and we hear him at the phone.*) Hello . . . I'm sorry to disturb you, but I'm expecting a call and I thought I heard the phone . . . You're sure . . . All right. Thank you. (*We hear him hanging up.* KATHERINE, *puzzled by this, sits up and looks toward his door. In a moment, he comes back in.*) Sorry. I thought my phone was ringing. (*He walks over to light her cigarette.*)

KATHERINE. That's all right . . . Thanks. (JOHN *moves an ash tray to the edge of her bed.*) Thanks.

JOHN. Did you sleep at all?

KATHERINE. A little.

JOHN. Sorry to wake you up.

KATHERINE. I was awake.

JOHN. Oh.

KATHERINE. I was listening to you moan in your sleep.

JOHN (*shaking his head*). Oh . . . Just crack me one when I do that. Doctor told my wife it was no good waking me up by talking to me . . . Just slap me hard. Apparently that gets down to the subconscious where the moaning is going on. So next time crack me one.

KATHERINE (*smiling*). Yes. I'll remember next time.

JOHN (*smiles when he realizes how foolish it was to say "next time."*) That's right. Well . . . (KATHERINE *swings around and sits on the bed. He notices that she's still dressed.*) I'm afraid I messed up your night for you. Kept you from getting properly to bed.

KATHERINE. This is the way I wanted it.

JOHN. Really?

KATHERINE. It was nice to wake up and see you . . . to see somebody, sleeping there.

JOHN. It's terrible.

KATHERINE. What?

JOHN. To be part of a woman's life again.

KATHERINE. Terrible?

JOHN (*smiles*). Yes. Quiet like this. Just sharing the room. Someone to talk to at night when you wake up . . . when you're frightened of the dark . . . Someone to get an ash tray for.

KATHERINE. But there have been many women.

JOHN. Yes. But they always got up and went home. Or I got up and went home . . . There's a certain mystical thing about spending the night . . . I've never spent a night like this before.

KATHERINE. Neither have I.

JOHN (*turns and looks through the curtains*). It's stopped snowing . . .

". . . the world, which seems
To lie before us like a land of dreams,
So various, so beautiful, so new,
Hath really neither joy, nor love, nor light,
Nor"—

What? I don't remember. I think I used to recite that to my first girl . . . and I wrote it in a letter to my wife during the war . . . My wife and I, we bought two copies of the same book of poems, *The Golden Treasury,* and we marked each one with a date . . . and while I was away, we were going to read the same poem at the same hour of the day.

KATHERINE. How nice.

JOHN. Of course it took quite a bit of planning, figuring out changes in time, and international date lines, et cetera . . . I was reading, "Shall I compare thee to a summer's day," when we were hit by a torpedo.

KATHERINE. Your wife sounds as though she had been very much a kindred spirit, as though you were very close.

JOHN (*smiles*). She stopped me from going to three double features on Saturdays. (*He picks up her cigarette from the ash tray and takes a puff.*)

KATHERINE (*smiles*). How old were you when you met her?

JOHN. A very innocent eighteen.

KATHERINE. My God!

JOHN. Yes, my God! To really fall in love for the first time at eighteen, and suddenly to have your whole life fall into focus. It's a miracle, isn't it? That only happens once. You don't ask, Am I in love? Is this real? Will it last? It suddenly just pours over you like sunshine . . . and you breathe deeply as though for the first time. And you're wide open. You confess your sins, and she confesses hers. My God, what little sins . . . and you forgive each other and fall into each other's arms.

KATHERINE. Did you really have it like that?

JOHN. Yes, so help me God. It seemed to be four years of spring. She lived with her family in Boston, but they were always away, around the world, or abroad, and so we were like children playing house on Beacon Hill. I'd been a very mediocre student, and suddenly, nothing but A's. At first the college thought I was cheating . . . but I was only in love. And there seemed to be time for everything in those days. We sailed at Marblehead, we skied in New Hampshire, and we lay in each other's arms for hours and hours just filled with the wonder of it. All we could say was, "It's wonderful, isn't it?" . . . "It's marvelous, isn't it?" . . . "Aren't we lucky?" . . . Went to the theatre, up in the second balcony . . . once a month Sunday lunches at the Ritz and a walk up the Charles River, and then the long afternoon in front of the fire in her living room . . . Every summer I went to summer school to be near her. My parents marveled at my thirst for knowledge . . . But surely you had this too. All young lovers do.

KATHERINE. No.

JOHN. I can't believe it.

KATHERINE. I believe you.

JOHN. Sorry. I'm truly sorry.

KATHERINE. Don't misunderstand. We had a wonderful time. But it wasn't like that. It wasn't his temperament, or perhaps mine.

JOHN. I have letters we wrote each other. It didn't seem enough to see each other every day. We wrote letters too, and handed them to each other. It seemed silly at the time. I've grown grateful for that silliness. One should commit one's love to paper. Like photographs, love letters grow in importance . . . "Oh, did I look like that?" . . . "Did you look like that?" . . . Friends of mine had movies taken of their garden wedding. When they showed the film to their children fifteen years later, the oldest said, "My, Daddy loved Mommy then, didn't he?" One should commit one's love to paper. Though sometimes it's . . . (*A new thought darkens his mind, and he stops.*)

KATHERINE. Dangerous.

JOHN. Yes.

KATHERINE. —One day my husband came across my poems. It was like coming across the truth locked in a drawer. I had expressed my loneliness so directly, almost nakedly.

JOHN. What did your husband say?

KATHERINE. It's not what you think. I looked into a window from the garden, and saw he was reading them. He didn't see me. I went upstairs to our room, and waited. I lay down and stared out the window and waited. He came up in a while and looked at me. I could see he'd been crying. He lay down beside me and held me in his arms. It almost killed me. He didn't say anything. He just held me for a very long while. He never said anything about them.

JOHN. The footsteps of doves.

KATHERINE. What?

JOHN. Someone said, "The great crises in our lives come not with the sound of thunder and lightning, but quietly like the footsteps of doves."

KATHERINE. Yes.

JOHN. Like sun suddenly breaking over you . . . or night.

KATHERINE. For quite a while after that, we were very gentle towards each other. I, because I knew I had hurt him. He, because he realized now my loneliness in our relationship.

JOHN. I always treated my wife so that people wouldn't know we were married. I think early in my life I was frightened by a middle-aged couple at a summer resort. They sat just opposite me in the dining room, and they never talked. I've seen couples in Paris and Rome, on that long-saved-for holiday together, staring at their plates, and wondering why they'd come. I often thought they should have swapped wives for the trip.

KATHERINE. But you chattered.

JOHN. Yes. Like a magpie. Or I'd just smile at her. Or I'd tease her. Anything to keep contact. I wanted to prove against all the evidence around me that it could work. On a rainy afternoon for no reason I'd send her some spring flowers . . .

There were hundreds of anniversaries to remember. The day we met, the day we first kissed, the day we first slept together . . . the day we decided to get married. You know. Every couple has them.

KATHERINE. You really worked at it, didn't you?

JOHN. I hate looking into a flower shop and seeing a lovely bunch of white lilacs or the first tulips, and not having anyone to send them to. I hate having nothing to give you.

KATHERINE. You've given me a great deal already. You've given me this night.

JOHN. No. I've taken that . . . from you.

KATHERINE. It's nice that we should both feel that way.

JOHN. Yes. (*They look at each other for a moment, then* JOHN *goes to the window and looks out.*) We're almost through it without disturbance, public or private.

KATHERINE. Yes.

JOHN (*looking out the window*). You know, when my wife first . . . first after my wife died, people were very kind and did everything for me . . . always asked what else they could do. I couldn't ask a woman what I really wanted . . . "Come home and be with me all night. Just let me hold you all night." . . . What I wanted was to hold someone.

KATHERINE. When I go visit my father, who's in his seventies, he always says, "Just hold me a little for a moment . . . Let me hold you."

JOHN. Yes. Hold me . . . Hold me . . . Help . . . Help.

KATHERINE (*after looking at him a long moment*). Your wife is not dead, is she?

JOHN. What?

KATHERINE. Your wife is not dead. She's in that hospital up there, isn't she?

JOHN. Yes. How did you know?

KATHERINE. The maid told me.

JOHN. You've been very patient then.

KATHERINE. Do you want to tell me about her? (*When she gets no answer, she goes on.*) I feel you've been waiting . . . inviting questions and then shying away from them. Why do you say she's dead? Is it very serious? I mean your wife's illness.

JOHN. Yes, serious but not fatal.

KATHERINE. The phone call you keep

expecting then is . . . ?

JOHN. Yes.

KATHERINE. But if it's not fatal?

JOHN (*with difficulty, but unemotionally*). My wife is . . . The hospital is a sanitarium . . . My wife is insane.

KATHERINE. Oh, I see.

JOHN. If I'd told you that earlier on, I would have found the evening intolerable.

KATHERINE. Why?

JOHN. Just the way you looked at me now.

KATHERINE. How long has she been there?

JOHN. Five years.

KATHERINE. And what hope is there?

JOHN (*ignoring this piecemeal questioning*). I told you we'd had a wonderful marriage. We did. A lovely daughter of five.

KATHERINE. Oh, yes . . . the accident.

JOHN. Yes, in a sense. The accident of my becoming infatuated with another woman after fourteen years of marriage. Don't ask me why or how. I've spent five years trying to rationalize what I did. But I did. I became helplessly, shamefully infatuated. Nothing happened. She was married and didn't really care for me. I wrote her many letters, many, many letters. And one day, for the first time, she wrote me a letter . . . My wife for some reason opened it. The address looked like Mrs. instead of Mr. . . . I don't know. And quite naturally, quite humanly she read it . . . It was a letter telling me that I must not love her . . . this woman telling me . . . While she had been reading the letter, our child had wandered into the neighbor's property and had fallen into the pool and drowned . . . Four months later, we brought my wife up here . . . (KATHERINE *makes a move toward him of sympathy. Sensing the move, he turns deftly away.*) I didn't think that was a story for a Christmas Eve. As a matter of fact, I don't any longer think it's a story for any time. It's much easier to say she died.

KATHERINE. It sounds silly to say, "I'm so sorry."

JOHN. Please don't say it. I'm sick of pity! . . . When it started happening to my wife, everyone was full of sympathy and pity. I wanted to tell them about the letter . . . to show them that I had driven her insane. But I couldn't . . . I wanted to kill the woman who had written the letter. I wanted to kill myself. And all the time there was pity. And I accepted their pity, and hated myself for needing it. How wonderfully ready women are to heal by the laying on of hands and lips. My God, how healing.

KATHERINE. So you have run away from comfort, from pity.

JOHN. At first I tried to visit my wife every day. But she didn't know who I was, and seemed to be worse when I saw her. The doctors suggested I stay away for a long while. I did. I left the country and started wandering . . . I looked for and found solace in sensation . . . I wanted to hit bottom. Have you ever had that feeling?

KATHERINE. No.

JOHN (*drily, but with self-contempt*). I became a scavenger. I scavenged off unhappy marriages. Having destroyed my own marriage, I wanted to prove that other marriages could be destroyed . . . Did you know it's ridiculously easy to be a lover? . . . Especially if you've been married. You know all the little sufferings that a wife endures, that you've made your own wife endure . . . I almost succeeded in making a mockery of everything, in reaching absolute zero . . . Then one morning in Lisbon I knew. I knew that this rock bottom I'd been trying to reach was not rock, was not something you'd spring back from alive and purged . . . It was muck and swallowed you up . . . And I came home.

KATHERINE. Is there a chance your wife will get well?

JOHN. No. But when the doctors all say "No," you begin to believe in mysteries, superstitions. You remember, "If I can walk home without stepping on a crack in the sidewalk . . ."

KATHERINE. I remember.

JOHN. I don't know why . . . perhaps because of the thing that started it, the letter, but I began to think that as long as I didn't love anyone else, or sleep with anyone I cared about, she would somehow know I loved her and get well. (KATHERINE *half-frowns, half-smiles at this idea.*) I know it's ridiculous. But what else is there? And when there is nothing else, there's got to be something.

KATHERINE. Yes, of course.

JOHN (*after a moment—the final*

horror). When a person has been more or less continuously insane for five years . . .

KATHERINE. Yes?

JOHN. There can be an annulment.

KATHERINE. I didn't know that.

JOHN. Neither did I. My wife found this out . . . in one of her sane periods.

KATHERINE. I see.

JOHN. Every time I've come up here the last months when she's been halfway . . . right, she's said she would manage, in some way she would manage to kill herself if I didn't get an annulment . . . that she is ruining my life . . . How can I make her see that now she is my life? She is the condition of my life. How can I make her see that the more I tried to destroy the meaning of marriage, the closer I came to its true meaning? . . . Maybe it's guilt that binds me. I think it's love.

KATHERINE. She might improve, get well, if . . .

JOHN. Could you do it?

KATHERINE. An annulment?

JOHN. Yes.

KATHERINE. No. I guess not.

JOHN. Well I did. I did it . . . I took it to her yesterday.

KATHERINE. Did she understand it?

JOHN. When I gave it to her, she was calm and smiling. I kneeled down beside her and said, "Here it is. It's what you wanted. But as far as I'm concerned, I'm still married to you. I couldn't live without you." . . . She said, "No, Jack. No. Don't say that. No." . . . I start to argue, to explain. You start, you know, and you think they're talking perfect sense, and then you know they're not. I never know when I go to see her if she's going to spit at me, or hold out her arms and say, "Here's my boy." And I don't know which is real . . . Anyway, now it's done . . . How can you annul your life?

KATHERINE. It's just a word.

JOHN. I've tried to get through to her to talk to her about the letter, but each time she clouds over. She slips away into another time. "Darling, you talked in your sleep last night, but I didn't have the heart to slap you." . . . Then some days she sleeps for hours and hours and they get afraid and slap her awake, gently, but they slap her and ask, "Who are you? What's your name?" And she looks around like a startled child and says, "Jennifer Sparrow" . . . and when they smile approval, she smiles back and goes to sleep again . . . Who are you? . . . Who are you? . . . I wake up some nights, bolt upright, and I think they're slapping me, and I find myself calling out . . . "John Sparrow. I'm John Sparrow."

KATHERINE. You must have loved her very much.

JOHN. Yes, and also hated her very much too, I imagine. Or why did I . . . Husbands and wives shouldn't be allowed to testify in or out of court as to the nature of their marriage. What they give is not truth, but guilt or shame or remorse, or memories tempered to what they can live with . . . "Who are you sleeping with, Jack?" she asks. I try not to answer, but she knows. She knows me. She loved it in me, the reaching out, the need to be part of a woman's life.

KATHERINE. And what do you tell her?

JOHN. No one I can care for . . . And she cries. (*There is a long moment of silence. He has told the story again, and he hates himself for having told it, but he knows he had to tell it. Finally—*) Well, the sun's somewhere over there . . . We got through the night without incident . . . Congratulations.

KATHERINE (*weakly*). Congratulations.

JOHN. Who cried "Help" anyway? . . . I'm sorry for my long and boring story.

KATHERINE (*flatly*). I'm sorry for mine.

JOHN. Now you can see why I haven't told that story for two years . . . Merry Christmas.

KATHERINE. Yes. Merry Christmas.

(JOHN *moves toward his door. As he passes her, she turns and looks at him. He stops. They look at each other for a moment, and then she touches his cheek with her hand.*)

JOHN. Please . . . I'm sick of pity.

KATHERINE. Why do you have to give it a name? I want to hold you. I want you to hold me. (*They are suddenly in each other's arms, kissing desperately, and holding each other with gratitude. He kisses her hair, her eyes, and suddenly she starts to cry, and she goes out of control. She turns from him to hide her tears, and she goes to her bed and sits, turned away from him. He looks down at her for a moment. He leans over and strokes her* hair, comforting her. He holds her head against his thigh. The passion is suddenly gone. Through her subsiding tears) I'm sorry. I'll be all right in a minute. (He crouches beside her, and puts his arms around her, comforting her gently.) It's not easy . . . I've never been with . . .

JOHN (very quietly). I'll go now.

KATHERINE (with a little move, she stops him from going). I'll be all right. Just hold me a minute. I'll be all right. (JOHN holds her quietly, wondering, waiting. A shudder as her crying finally stops, and she looks at him again.) Thank you. (A look of infinite pity comes into her face, and she reaches toward his face with her hand, as though to bestow a mercy.)

JOHN. I don't want your pity.

KATHERINE. I want yours.

(Overwhelmed by the simple honesty of this, he takes her in his arms.)

CURTAIN

SCENE TWO

As the curtain rises, MAE is carrying in a tray with breakfast. The curtains are drawn back. It is about half-past nine in the morning.

Throughout, MAE is not surprised at anything. She takes everything in her stride, and is perhaps a little pleased at the turn in events.

She puts the tray down, picks up the glasses from night before, and puts them on the tray with the ice bucket.

She folds up the extra blanket and puts it over couch.

KATHERINE's suitcase is packed and open on the couch.

In a moment, KATHERINE comes in from the bathroom. She is wearing a skirt, and is buttoning her blouse.

———

KATHERINE. Good morning, Mae.

MAE. Good morning. Merry Christmas.

KATHERINE. Merry Christmas. You are working around the clock, aren't you?

MAE. I'll get my rest tomorrow when everyone else is working. I love it that way.

KATHERINE. Makes you feel quite wicked, doesn't it?

MAE. Absolutely sinful.

KATHERINE. It's a lovely morning, isn't it?

MAE. Nippy.

KATHERINE. A real old-fashioned Christmas.

MAE (poking around the tray). I spared you the morning papers. It's filled with the usual, murders, robberies and disasters.

KATHERINE. Thank you.

MAE. They said downstairs you'd be leaving this morning.

KATHERINE (looks for a moment at JOHN's door, which is closed). Yes.

MAE. That's too bad. (Still busying herself around the room.) Did you enjoy the movies?

KATHERINE. Yes. Very much.

MAE (noticing the wrappings on the Christmas presents, as she empties an ash tray). The stores do beautiful wrappings these days, don't they?

KATHERINE (modestly proud). I did those myself.

MAE. Did you? Must have taken you hours. Mr. Sparrow's having God's own time in there trying to tie bows on his presents. Cutting the ribbons with old razor blades, too. (MAE shudders. KATHERINE looks in the direction of the door.) I'm afraid his poor wife won't know the difference. It's a shame, isn't it?

KATHERINE. Yes.

MAE. Every time he comes here, I always wish there was something I could do. But . . . (She shrugs.)

KATHERINE. I'm sure he appreciates it.

MAE (on her way out). Well, if there's anything you want . . .

KATHERINE (slips a bill into MAE's apron pocket). If I don't see you again, thank you. You've made me feel very much at home.

MAE. Thank you. It's been nice talking with you. I hope you have a very happy New Year . . . and keep well.

KATHERINE. Thank you. (MAE goes out, closing the door behind her. KATHERINE waits for a moment, takes a sip of coffee, then goes to JOHN's door and listens for a moment. She tries to open the door, but it is bolted. She knocks, tentatively, but gets no answer. She moves away, puzzled. In a moment, the door is opened, JOHN stands in the doorway, with Christmas paper in his hands. They look at each other for a moment, uncertain.) Good morning.

JOHN. Good morning.

KATHERINE. Mae said you were wrapping Christmas presents.

JOHN (*glad that intimate talk is avoided for the moment*). Yes. I'm terrible at it.

KATHERINE. Maybe I could help you.

JOHN. Would you? (*He brings in the paper, ribbons and a box with small presents in it and sets them on the stool.* KATHERINE *watches him carefully during all this. Is it to be just casual talk this morning?*) I'm all thumbs when it comes to this kind of thing. I've already cut myself once. (*He looks at his finger as he holds it out, then looks up at her. She has not looked at the finger, but has continued to look at him. They look at each other a moment, and then gently hold each other. There is sadness in this holding, yet a desire to be close, to say the things that will be said.*)

KATHERINE. When I went to sleep . . . you left.

JOHN. Yes.

KATHERINE. When I woke up, I went to your door. You'd bolted it. (JOHN *shakes his head "Yes." He would rather not have to delve into all this, but it is inevitable, and he is awkward, yet loving, and not wanting to hurt.*) I thought I would wake up so full of remorse and guilt. I woke up as easily as I went to sleep . . . And you'd gone. (*She looks at him and sees his inability to say anything.*) I'm sorry. Should I not say—

JOHN (*holding her, sorry to have stopped her lyrical outburst*). Yes . . . Yes. Go on.

KATHERINE. Do I look very much like your wife?

JOHN (*knows what's coming*). Not very much. No. A little. Yes.

KATHERINE. You didn't really want to be with me last night, did you?

JOHN. How can you say that?

KATHERINE. You were being compassionate, and then suddenly I was your wife. (*He holds her, wishing to soften the pain that he may have given her.*) I suppose I should have been hurt when you called me by her name . . .

JOHN. I don't know why I did that.

KATHERINE. I do. For the first time in two years you were sleeping with someone you could care for. You were sleeping with your wife. And I was honored . . . and suddenly it became quite simple and beautiful.

JOHN (*he looks at her, moved by what she's said*). God, you're sweet.

KATHERINE. I wish you'd stayed. Did you think that by getting up and going . . . did you think by doing that you could somehow turn me into a whore?

JOHN. Don't say that.

KATHERINE. Such a terrible instinct to destroy it.

JOHN. Yes, I know.

KATHERINE. How I envy your wife to have been loved so much.

JOHN (*moved by her sweetness*). There are so many things I'd like to say to you.

KATHERINE. Say them.

JOHN (*looks at her, wanting to say them, but the words won't come*). I can't.

KATHERINE. It's all right.

JOHN. No, it isn't. A woman likes to hear the words, and I like to say them. Not to say them somehow leaves everything incomplete . . . But I've spoiled them for myself. It's the only honesty I have left. Not to call things by the wrong names . . . I would like to say how wonderful it would be to be married to you. But then I know I don't mean that. I have a wife I love as a wife.

KATHERINE. But you must let someone love you. And don't be ashamed of letting her love you for the hurt you've suffered . . .

JOHN. And the hurt I've given?

KATHERINE. Yes. None of us goes far without hurting. Teach us to forgive ourselves . . .

JOHN. I'm not free to love that way. I don't want to be free to love that way. It's better to say "Never" than to play around the fringes of caring. (KATHERINE *looks at him. It seems such a waste. He reaches out and touches her hand.*) It's so hard for us to understand the terms on which other people settle their lives. (*They look at each other a moment, and then he breaks it by reaching into the box and pulling out a particularly ghastly attempt at a bow.*) I've been trying to follow instructions on how to make a fancy bow. The directions say a ten-year-old can do it. I can't.

KATHERINE (*kneels on the floor and starts to tie a bow on a small present*). When do you go to the hospital?

JOHN. In a little while, I guess.

KATHERINE. There was no call, was there?

JOHN. No.

KATHERINE. You were afraid, weren't you, that—

JOHN. Yes. I'm always afraid she might kill herself. Now with the annulment, I'm more afraid than ever. (*He goes to the window, and holds back the curtains for a moment.*) I remember how many times she begged me to do something she really didn't want—for my own good— But sometimes they call to say that it's a good day, and I should hurry over.

KATHERINE. I can imagine those are wonderful days.

JOHN. Yes. We don't realize how important it is to have someone to remember with. Without her I have no past.

KATHERINE (*holding up the present*). How does that look?

JOHN. Great . . . Very fancy. Maybe too fancy.

KATHERINE (*not looking at him*). Yes, I see. I suppose it's impossible to keep secrecy out of adultery. (*Looks up at him.*) I'll never think of this as adultery.

JOHN (*touched by everything this woman says, he smiles at her*). Thank you.

KATHERINE (*stops making the bow*). No, this is too good. You'd better do the ribbons.

JOHN. I'd better do it all. I'm famous for my wrappings. My presents are always good for a laugh. (*He takes a charm bracelet, and some paper and ribbons and sits with them in his hand for a moment.*) How easily we talk about death and suicide when we're young. My wife and I made a pact, "If ever I get an incurable disease, kill me and make it look like suicide." . . . It's a way of making love, isn't it? In the health and vigor of youth, I put my life in your hands. That's how much I love you. My wife always used to say, "I want to die first. I couldn't live without you." She said it a lot. We'd get into quite an argument as to who was going to die first. She was very sentimental. (*Toward the end of this, he has put the charm bracelet in the middle of the paper, pulled up the sides of the paper, and twisted a length of ribbon around it and knotted it.*)

KATHERINE. She found the right man.

JOHN. I guess most people do . . . There. (*He holds up his crude wrapping. KATHERINE is moved, but smiles.*) Is it really so ghastly?

KATHERINE. No. It's just that . . . No. It's beautiful. (*She has to turn away from him.*)

JOHN. After all, it's the spirit of the thing, not the wrapping.

KATHERINE. Yes.

JOHN. If you ever get a present without a card and wrapped like this you'll know who sent it.

KATHERINE (*looks at him seriously*). Yes. I'll know.

JOHN. Have you heard from your boy?

KATHERINE. The Infirmary called to say they had released him, and he had gone to his room to pack.

JOHN. Did your husband try to call again?

KATHERINE. Yes, this morning. But there was a mix-up. The call wasn't completed. (*As though in answer to his unasked question.*) I'm going to him. To London.

JOHN. That's good.

KATHERINE. Yes.

JOHN. The beautiful complexity.

KATHERINE (*not looking at him*). I'd always thought of adultery as shared ecstasy . . . shared excitement . . . I'd never realized it could be shared sadness . . .

JOHN. Yes.

KATHERINE. What will you do tonight?

JOHN. I don't know. Probably go to the movies. (*They look at each other as time runs out.*)

KATHERINE. When my son comes . . .

JOHN. Yes, I know. I'd like to write.

KATHERINE. No.

JOHN. I was going to send you a copy of my book.

KATHERINE. I wonder if I have to read it now. I'll find a copy. *The Comfort of Your Company.*

JOHN. Yes.

KATHERINE. Maybe someday . . . maybe we could be friends.

JOHN. I'm no good as a friend.

KATHERINE. That's sad.

JOHN. Yes.

KATHERINE. What's going to happen to you?

JOHN. I'm fine.

KATHERINE. Yes, of course. We're all fine . . . I don't want to say "Good-bye."

JOHN. It's impossible, isn't it?

KATHERINE. You knew it would be.

JOHN. Yes.

KATHERINE. I'll know next time . . . Just let me say "I love you." (*Shakes his head.*) Don't be angry. I do. This moment I do . . . I don't care about what's going to come . . . but I couldn't leave with that all choked up in me . . . (*The phone rings.*) This will be London. (*She hesitates for a moment, then goes to the phone and picks it up.* JOHN *makes a gesture—Does she want him to get out? She shakes her head "No."*) Hello . . . Oh, yes. Thank you. (*She hangs up.*) My son is on his way up. (*Smiles.*) I knew it would be like this.

JOHN (*approaching her*). I would like to give you something . . . something silly to . . .

KATHERINE. I'll remember.

JOHN. I have nothing. (*All he has found in his pocket is a penny.*) A penny. (*He holds it out to show her.*)

KATHERINE (*reaching for it*). I'll take that.

JOHN. Give me something.

KATHERINE. I have nothing either . . . (*Reaches in her pocket.*) A handkerchief . . . (*She holds it out. He takes it.*)

JERRY (*offstage*). Hey, Mom. (*The sound of running feet outside.*)

KATHERINE. I'll send him on an errand or something for a moment . . . (JOHN *moving casually toward his door, shakes his head "No."* KATHERINE *continues urgently.*) Yes.

JERRY (*outside. He knocks heavily on the door*). Mom . . . it's Jerry.

KATHERINE (*whispers*). I'll knock.

(JOHN *stops at his door a moment, and looks at her, then exits, closing the door behind him.*)

JERRY (*outside*). Mom. (*He knocks again.*)

KATHERINE (*opens the door*). Yes, Jerry, come in.

JERRY (*a nice, open-faced boy of thirteen comes in. He is carrying a couple of wrapped gifts*). Merry Christmas, Mom. (*He gives her a bear hug and a kiss on the cheek.*)

KATHERINE. Merry Christmas, Jerry. How are you feeling?

JERRY. Terrific. Here. (*He holds out a flower box for her.*)

KATHERINE (*taking it*). What's this?

JERRY. I know you don't like that kind very much, but it's all I could get.

KATHERINE (*opening the box*). What is it?

JERRY. You'll see.

KATHERINE (*she takes out a single gardenia corsage*). Oh, it's lovely, Jerry. Thank you. (*She kisses him on the cheek.*)

JERRY. Is it okay?

KATHERINE. You know it is.

JERRY. Here's something else. (*He shoves a small box at her.*)

KATHERINE. Goodness. What is it?

JERRY. Whatever it is, it's mighty small.

KATHERINE (*unwrapping present*). Good things come in small packages. (*She has unwrapped a small bottle of perfume.*) Oh, how nice.

JERRY. That's your kind of perfume, isn't it?

KATHERINE. It sure is. You're very observant. How did you get it in the Infirmary?

JERRY. A fellow got it for me. I got something for Dad too. It's in my suitcase downstairs. Hey, we gotta go.

KATHERINE. This is wonderful, Jerry. Thank you.

JERRY. I'm sorry it's so small, but holy cat, that stuff's expensive.

KATHERINE. A little goes a long way. I won't open it now. I'll keep it for London.

JERRY. Okay.

KATHERINE. I'd better finish dressing. I'm all packed except a few things.

JERRY (*noticing* JOHN's *things on the dresser*). What's this stuff?

KATHERINE. Oh . . . don't go peeking. I mean . . .

JERRY (*teasing*). What is it?

KATHERINE (*herding him away*). Now come on, play fair . . . Over there's a present for you. Open that. (JERRY *makes a beeline for the presents. The phone rings.* KATHERINE *picks it up.*) Hello. Yes, this is Mrs. Johnson. I'll hold on. (*To* JERRY) It's London. (*Then, into the phone*) Yes, Dick . . . Hello . . . Yes, I know you have. (*A long pause, after which she interrupts him to let him know she can't talk. He has obviously said that he has been trying to reach her.*) Yes, but . . . Jerry's here. Yes . . . He looks fine.

JERRY (*he has opened his present, and loves it. It is a camera*). Hey, Mom. (*He rushes over and throws his arms around his mother and kisses her.*) Thanks, Mom. Gee, that's great.

KATHERINE (*into the phone*). That's Jerry being grateful.

JERRY (*into the phone* KATHERINE *is still holding*). Hi, Dad . . . Be right there. Hey, Merry Christmas. (*Takes the phone.*) I got a crazy present for you . . . What? . . . Oh, I'm fine. (*He hands the phone back to his mother, and studies his camera.*)

KATHERINE (*at the phone*). He looks a little pale, but they says it's all right for him to come . . . We're both coming. (*She listens a moment to his reaction of pleasure, and smiles.*) We're practically out the door . . . Yes, it will be good to see you too.

JERRY (*impulsively taking the phone from* KATHERINE). Hey, Dad, I've grown a whole inch. And I've put a half-inch on my muscle . . . the right arm . . . Okay. (*He hands the phone back.*)

KATHERINE (*into the phone*). What are those beeps? . . . Oh, well we'd better save the money. The plumber finally came . . . No, I won't tell you how much it cost. I don't want to spoil your Christmas . . . Yes, I forgot too. Merry Christmas . . . It's a nice day here too, so everything should be all right . . . Here he is. (*To* JERRY) He wants to say something to you. (*Into the phone*) Tomorrow then. (*She gives the phone to* JERRY *and goes on packing.*)

JERRY (*into the phone*). Yes, Dad . . . Yeah. I'll take care of her . . . Right . . . Right . . . She looks fine . . . Right. Okay, Dad . . . See you tomorrow . . . Oh, Dad, I got a new girl . . . I'll tell you about her. I got her picture. Give you something to live for . . . 'Bye. (*He hangs up.*) Gosh, you can hear just as clear . . .

KATHERINE. Darling, tuck this robe in the top and close it up while I finish. (*She goes into the bathroom to get her compact.*)

JERRY (*packing*). You got more tissue paper than clothes in here . . . Where's the rest of your stuff?

KATHERINE. At the station in Boston.

JERRY. Did you say close it up?

KATHERINE. Yes, and you can take it downstairs. I'll meet you. Get a cab.

JERRY. I told them to have one waiting. (*Looks out the window.*) It's there.

KATHERINE. I'll just be another minute . . . so you go ahead.

JERRY. Dad told me not to let you out of my sight. I'm responsible, he says.

KATHERINE. Well, you be responsible downstairs.

JERRY. That's your old trick . . . "I'm ready," you say, and a half-hour later you appear. (*He gets her coats.*) How many coats you got?

KATHERINE. You never know what kind of weather we're going to run into. Daddy says it's spring in London.

JERRY. I got one coat, period.

KATHERINE (*coming back in*). With a woman it's different. You take two coats and I'll take two . . . and run along.

JERRY. We got about three minutes, Mom.

KATHERINE. Jerry, come on. Do what I tell you to do. Run along with the bag. I'll be right there. See, I'm all ready.

JERRY. Then why don't you come along now?

KATHERINE (*not too sternly. A little smile*). Jerry, vamoose.

JERRY. Dad said . . .

KATHERINE. Mother says.

JERRY (*takes the suitcase and starts to go*). Okay, but if you're not down in thirty seconds, there's going to be hell to pay, mother or no mother. (*As he goes, he starts counting.*) One, and two and three and . . .

(KATHERINE *is alone for a moment. She picks up pocketbook, and moves toward* JOHN's *room. She opens the door to go in when the phone in his room rings. She turns back into her room, afraid, wondering, listening.*)

JOHN (*in his room*). Yes? . . . Hello, Doctor . . . Oh, that's great. I'll be right over . . . I understand, but a day's a day, isn't it? . . . Tell her, I'll— What? . . . Hello, Jennifer . . . How are you? . . . Yes, it's Christmas. Merry Christmas to you . . . (KATHERINE *turns toward the door to the hall, and waits there a moment. She is smiling and she is crying.*) I got a whole raft of presents for you . . . Yes, my crazy wrapping. Wait till you see . . . Ghastly . . . This is wonderful, Jennifer . . . My God, it's so wonderful.

KATHERINE *goes into the hall, and*

THE CURTAIN IS DOWN

TWO FOR THE SEESAW

William Gibson

Presented by Fred Coe at the Booth Theatre, New York,
on January 16, 1958, with the following cast:

JERRY RYAN Henry Fonda   GITTEL MOSCA Anne Bancroft

The action takes place this past year, between fall and spring, in two
rooms—Jerry's and Gittel's—in New York City.

ACT ONE. SCENE 1: Both rooms. September, late afternoon. SCENE 2:
  Gittel's room. Midnight, the same day. SCENE 3: Both rooms. Day-
  break following.
ACT TWO. SCENE 1: Jerry's room. October, dusk. SCENE 2: Both rooms.
  December, noon. SCENE 3: Gittel's room. February, a Saturday night.
ACT THREE. SCENE 1: Gittel's room. March, midday. SCENE 2: Jerry's
  room. May, dusk. SCENE 3: Both rooms. A few days later, afternoon.

Directed by Arthur Penn
Settings by George Jenkins
Costumes by Virginia Volland

WILLIAM GIBSON had apparently been getting along in the world very nicely as an independent writer. He had published verse, and he had made reputation as well as money on a novel, *The Cobweb,* which was bought after publication by a motion-picture company. He was also living peacefully in Stockbridge, Massachusetts, where his wife, a psychoanalyst, was attached to the celebrated Austen Riggs Center —happily remote from New York City, where he had spent his first twenty years, and where he had attended the City College and dreamed of becoming a college teacher. But he incautiously wrote a two-character comedy, *Two for the Seesaw,* entrusted it to the producing hands of that able drama graduate from Yale Fred Coe, now a successful producer, who in turn entrusted it to Arthur Penn, one of the country's ablest stage directors. Even worse luck! The producers enlisted the aid of Henry Fonda, an actor who has a way of appearing in "hit" films and plays, and Anne Bancroft, a hitherto unknown young lady who acquired the habit of performing her role so well that she became one of the country's leading actresses almost effortlessly and has since won all sorts of prizes in leading roles.

There was no help for it!—*Two for the Seesaw* simply had to become a hit, and Mr. Gibson was snared for Broadway even before the run of that play was over. With Miss Anne Bancroft in mind he proceeded to develop a second play, *The Miracle Worker,* out of a television script he had written about Annie Sullivan, the woman who opened the world that had been closed to little Helen Keller when she became blind, deaf, and consequently virtually mute, too, in infancy. *The Miracle Worker,* the pulsing drama of a young teacher's heroic struggle with a refractory child close to savagery who later became a distinguished woman despite her handicap, proved to be an even greater success on the stage and the screen than *Two for the Seesaw.*

Publication of the last-mentioned play by the firm of Alfred A. Knopf was, however, a double victory for the author. The reader was treated not only to a Broadway success in print, but to a fierce and funny anti-Broadway crusade under the title of *The Seesaw Log,* which makes excellent reading. In it Mr. Gibson describes a playwright's dismay at the mills of Broadway production which grind out successes and failures with equal indifference to an author's sensibilities, nerves, and integrity for the sake of ensuring a commercial success. (It was an honest and touching cry one heard in the author's comment that "The play grew more and more effective and I felt less and less fulfilled as a writer.") And Mr. Gibson's puzzlement grew amusingly, though without actually resolving any problems, when he reflected that his yielding to pressure had brought good results—"that the hammering my script and head had undergone . . . had issued in a much better play." This autobiographical chronicle did not, however, inhibit the author's next collaboration with the same producer and director in the fabrication of a hit. Mr. Gibson was trapped into becoming a successful Broadway author even though, just to square things, he became an unsuccessful off-Broadway one with a satiric fantasy called *Dinny and the Witches.* And Mr. Gibson, who was unusual among playwrights in resenting Broadway success, proved to be unusual as well in attaining it in mid-Manhattan and not attaining it in Greenwich Village.

Comment on *Two for the Seesaw,* one of the most enjoyable Broadway comedies of any season and especially noteworthy for the original characterization of Gittel, the heroine, would be superfluous here. Let the reader enjoy himself—and let the buyer beware only if he goes out shopping not for fun and felicity but for profundity and sociology.*

---

* For the reader who wants to involve himself in somber exercises, the editor unblushingly recommends his own essay, *"Two for the Seesaw* and *The Seesaw Log"* in his book *Theatre at the Crossroads,* pages 211-217 (Holt, Rinehart and Winston, 1960) and the broadside delivered with pyrotechnical skill by John Simon in the August 1960 issue (Number 15) of The Mid-Century, published by the Mid-Century Book Society, pages 15-22; see also Sol Stein's note in the same issue, pages 1-3.

THE SET *consists of two rooms, angled toward each other, but in no way related; they are in different buildings, a few miles apart, in New York.*

The room on stage right is JERRY RYAN'S *and is the tiny living room of a bleak two-room flat in a lower East Side tenement. It contains principally a narrow couch with a kitchen chair at its side, and at the beginning has the depressing air of having been moved into recently and minimally; the telephone for instance sits on the bare floor. In the right wall is a window through which we see nearby rooftops. In the rear wall is a doorway which opens into a kitchen so dark it is practically indecipherable; in this kitchen is a gas range, a covered bathtub, and the entrance door of the flat. The left wall of the room towards stage center is omitted or fragmented, so as not to obstruct our view of the other room on the stage.*

The room on stage left is GITTEL MOSCA'S *and is the living room of a flat in a run-down brownstone in midtown. It is on a lower level than Jerry's, is larger and lighter, and has a pleasantly untidy and cluttered air of having been lived in for some time; though furnished in very ordinary taste, it speaks of human comfort and warmth. Downstage in the left wall is the entrance door, and upstage a doorway into the kitchen, which is partly visible. The room contains among other things a studio double bed, a night table with lamp and phone, a bureau, chairs, and a dress dummy and sewing machine in the corner; there is also a window which looks out upon the street.*

ACT ONE

SCENE ONE

Both rooms. It is a late afternoon in September; the windows of both rooms are open, and the sounds of traffic float in.
GITTEL'S *room is empty.*

In the other room JERRY *is sitting on his couch, cigarette in hand, searching with his finger down the phone book open between his feet.* JERRY *is a long fellow in his thirties, attractive, with an underlayer of melancholy and, deeper, a lurking anger; his manner of dress, which is casually conservative, is too prosperous*

for this drab and disorderly room. The couch is unmade, the kitchen chair next to it has a typewriter on it and is hung with clothes, a handsome suitcase is open on the unswept floor, and the dust is gathering in bunches along the baseboard. Now JERRY *finds the number he wants, and dials.*

The phone in GITTEL'S *room rings.*

On the fourth ring JERRY *hangs up. Simultaneously there has been a rattle of key and knob at* GITTEL'S *door; she runs in, not stopping to set down her bag of groceries, and grabs the phone.*

GITTEL (*out of breath*). Yeah, hello? (*She waits a second.*) Oh, hell. (*She hangs up. She is a dark, thin girl of indeterminate age, too eccentric to be called pretty, nervous, uncouth, and engaging by virtue of some indestructible cheerfulness in her; all her clothes—denim skirt, peasant blouse, sandals—are somehow misfits, and everything she does has the jerky and lightweight intensity of a bird on the ground.*)

Now she and JERRY *go about their separate business.*

JERRY *lifts the suitcase onto the couch, and taking out his clothes—a fine jacket, a fine suit, a fine topcoat—begins hanging them on a clothes rod set catty-corner between two walls; while he is putting some shoes down, the rod slips out of one support and everything falls on his head.*)

JERRY. Oh, you son of a bitch. (*He lets it all lie, and returns into the kitchen. He comes back with a block of wood, hammer, and nails; he nails the block any which way under the socket on one wall, puts the rod back in place, and hangs the clothes up again; this time the rod holds. Meanwhile* GITTEL, *on her way to the kitchen with her bag of groceries, has stopped in front of the dress dummy and looks critically at a gaudy bodice pinned together on it; she stands unmoving for a minute, then with her free hand unpins the collar and commences to work. After a while she steps back, and is disgusted.*)

GITTEL. Oh, for Christ sakes. (*She gives up, slaps the pins down, and continues on to the kitchen, where we see her pour out a panful of milk and set it to warm on a gas burner; she puts the other groceries away in cupboard and icebox.* JERRY *finishes with his clothes, turns to regard the phone, sits on the couch, checks the* same number, and dials it once more. *The phone in* GITTEL's *room rings.* GITTEL *runs back and answers it just as* JERRY *is about to hang up after two rings.*) Yeah, hello?

(JERRY's *voice when we hear it now is well-educated, with a deadpan mockery in it that is essentially detached.*)

JERRY. Gittel Mosca, please.

GITTEL. It's me, who's this?

JERRY. This is Jerry Ryan. We met across eight or nine unidentified bodies last night at Oscar's. I'm a slight acquaintance of his from back home.

GITTEL. Oh?

JERRY. I say slight, about 170 pounds. Six one. (*Waits; then elaborately*) Red beard—

GITTEL. Oh, you were the fella in the dark hat that didn't say anything!

JERRY. You must know some very bright hats. I overheard you talk about a frigidaire you want to sell. Be all right if I stop by for a look?

GITTEL. At that frigidaire?

JERRY. It's all I had in mind, to begin with.

GITTEL. It's not a frigidaire, it's an icebox.

JERRY. Good enough. No electric bill, a product of American know-how. I could be there in about—

GITTEL. I gave it away!

JERRY (*a pause, stymied*). Oh. Not very kind of you.

GITTEL. I just helped him lug it home. Some jerk I never saw in my life, Sophie sent him over, so I let him have it just to get rid of the goddam thing. Why didn't you ask me last night?

JERRY. I didn't want to be among the quick. Last night.

GITTEL. Huh?

JERRY. I changed my mind and life today, great day, I thought I'd start by putting my nose in on you for a look.

GITTEL. It just isn't here.

JERRY. So you said. (*A pause, both waiting.*) Yes. Thanks anyway.

GITTEL. Sure. (JERRY *hangs up.*) Oh, hell. (*She hangs up too.* JERRY *after a morose moment gets up, fingers in his pack of cigarettes, finds it empty. En route to the window with it he bumps his knee against the couch; he lifts his foot and shoves it back, it jars the wall, the clothes rod is jogged out of the other*

support, *and the clothes fall on the floor.*)

JERRY. Agh, you son of a bitch! (*He grabs the rod and brings it down over his knee; it only bends, flies up in his face. He attacks it again, can't break it, trips over it, and doesn't know where to get rid of it, in a rage which is comic, until suddenly he throws a short punch into the window, not comic; the glass flies. He stands, grimly considers his fist, his surroundings, his state of mind, gets away from the window, walks into the phone on the floor, regards it, gathers it up, and dials. Meanwhile* GITTEL's *milk boils over as she is removing her sandals. She jumps up, and is hurrying toward the kitchen when her phone rings.*)

GITTEL. Oh, for Christ sakes. (*She is undecided, then hurries back and grabs up the phone.*) Just a minute, will you, I'm boiling over. (*She lays it down, hurries into the kitchen, turns the milk off, and comes back to the phone.*) Milk all over the goddam stove, yeah? (JERRY *sits with his eyes closed, the mouthpiece against his eyebrows.*) Hello? (JERRY *separates his face and the mouthpiece.*) Hello, is anybody on this line?

JERRY. No.

GITTEL. Huh? (JERRY *hangs up.*) Hey! (*She stares at the phone in her hand, then replaces it. She decides to shrug it off and go back to her milk, which she cools off by adding more from the container; but she stands in the doorway sipping it for only a second, then makes for the phone. She dials, and waits.* JERRY *walking in his room finds his hand is bleeding a bit, wraps it in his handkerchief, and has a private argument, not liking himself.*)

JERRY. You brokenhearted fly, *begin*. (*He gazes around the bare room, answers himself mordantly.*) Begin what? The conquest of the Sunday *Times*? (*He shoves the suitcase off the couch, lies down and extracts section after section of newspaper from under him, flinging them away.* GITTEL *gets an answer.*)

GITTEL. Sophie. Is Oscar there? . . . Well, listen, that hat-type friend of his last night, the long one, what's his number? . . . Look, girl, will you drag your mind up out of your girdle and go see if Oscar's got it written down?

(JERRY's *legs are overhanging, he moves back, but now his head bumps the wall. He gets to his feet and considers the couch grimly, muttering.)*

JERRY. Six feet of man, five feet of couch, calls for a new man. (*He stands the suitcase on end at the couch foot, lies down again with his feet out upon it, and extracts and flings away a final section of newspaper.* GITTEL *scribbles.*)

GITTEL. 69 what? Yeah, yeah, yeah, very funny. (*She clicks down, and immediately dials it.* JERRY's *phone rings. His head lifts to regard it, and he lets it ring another time before he leans over to pick it up.*)

JERRY (*guardedly*). Yes?

GITTEL (*quickly, a little nervous*). Look, I been thinking here about that icebox, what we could do is I could take you around the corner where this character lives, if you offer him a buck or two he might turn loose of it, and it's worth five easy, what do you say? (JERRY *on his elbow mulls her over.*) Hey, you still with me?

JERRY. I don't know yet, I might be against you. I'm not in the book, how did you get my number?

GITTEL. Sophie gave me it. Now about this icebox, I mean for nothing I let this kid have a real bargain, you could afford to make it worth his while, what do you think?

JERRY. I think you can't be calling about an icebox you had to help someone carry through the streets to get rid of.

GITTEL. What do you mean?

JERRY. You're calling either because like me you have nothing better to do, or because you're under the misap—

GITTEL (*indignantly*). I got eleven different things I could be doing!

JERRY. Different isn't better, why aren't we doing them? Or because you're under the misapprehension it was me who just hung up on you.

GITTEL (*confused*). Uh—it wasn't?

JERRY. Whoever it was had a reason. Question now is what's yours? If a man calls up to say he's not calling up, a girl who calls him back can be either lonely, solicitous, prying, a help or a nuisance—

GITTEL. Look, how'd I get in the wrong here?

JERRY. —and I'm curious to know which.

GITTEL. Did you call me up about this icebox or not?

JERRY. Not.

(GITTEL *bangs the phone down, gets up, and tears her scrap of paper with his number into bits; she throws them into the wastebasket.* JERRY *after a surprised moment finds this somewhat amusing, smiles in spite of himself, clicks down, and dials back.* GITTEL's *phone rings, and she comes to answer it;* JERRY's *manner now is rather teasing.*)

GITTEL. Yeah, hello?

JERRY. I said I didn't call you about an icebox.

GITTEL (*darkly*). Whaat?

JERRY. It seems I did, but I didn't.

GITTEL. Look, I can't follow this whole conversation. You called—

JERRY. I called because the only female voice I've heard on this phone is the robot lady with the correct time, and I'm going off my nut in solitary here. I called to make contact.

GITTEL. Oh!

JERRY. With someone of the weaker sex who's weaker.

GITTEL (*pause*). Okay, here I am. (JERRY *ponders it.*) Contact!

JERRY. I called to invite you to dinner tonight. And a show.

GITTEL. So why didn't you?

JERRY. I was afraid you'd say yes or no.

GITTEL. Huh? I would of said sure.

JERRY. See what I mean? All right, which show? It's Sunday, we'll have to see what—

GITTEL. Well, now I'm *not* so sure.

JERRY. Why?

GITTEL. I don't know if I want to get involved now, you sound awful complicated to me!

JERRY. How? Man calls to invite you to dinner via the icebox, you say there isn't any icebox, he waits to be invited in without the icebox, you show no interest in anything but the icebox, you call him back to invite him to invite you via the icebox again, he expresses interest in your personality, not your icebox, you're so devoted to the icebox you hang up. What's complicated?

GITTEL (*a pause*). Look, what's your point?

JERRY (*dryly*). I'm kind of pointless, how are you?

GITTEL. I mean I'm the girl, right? You're the man, make up your mind. *Then* ask me to dinner, and I'll make up my mind.

JERRY. My point is I've been trying to make up my mind for a month here.

GITTEL. What, to ask me to dinner?

JERRY. To climb off a certain piece of flypaper. It's a beginning. (*Pause*) I mean once you break a leg in five places you hesitate to step out.

GITTEL. Oh!

JERRY. It's one night in the year I don't want to eat alone. (*Another pause*) The reason I hung up was I didn't want to say please. Help me.

GITTEL. Well. How'd you expect to pick me up?

JERRY. How far east are you?

GITTEL. Off Second.

JERRY. I'll be there in half an hour.

GITTEL. Maybe you shouldn't, is it okay enough to?

JERRY. Is what okay enough to?

GITTEL. Your leg.

JERRY. What leg? Oh. (*He is deadpan.*) I don't know, it seems to have affected my head. I'll see you. (*He hangs up, replaces the phone on his couch. GITTEL stares, shakes her head, glances at an alarm clock on the night table, hangs up hurriedly, and darts out her door into the hall, where from another room we hear the bathtub water being turned on. Meanwhile JERRY's mood has lightened; he picks up his fallen clothes and lays them across the couch, brushes his jacket off, and slips into it. He is on his way out with his hat when the phone rings, and he comes back to answer it, thinking it is GITTEL and speaking dryly into the mouthpiece.*) I'm as sane as you are, stop worrying. (*Then his faces changes, becomes guarded.*) Yes, this is Mr. Ry— (*His mouth sets. After a second*) Who's calling from Omaha? (*Suddenly he hangs up. He stands over the phone, his hand upon it, until it begins to ring again; then he puts his hat on slowly, and walks out of the room. He pulls the kitchen light out, and leaves, closing the outer door. The phone continues to ring.*)

Scene Two

GITTEL's *room. It is close to midnight the same day, and both rooms are dark, except for the lights of the city in the sky beyond their open windows. The faint sounds of metropolitan night are audible.*

Under GITTEL's *door there is a line of yellow light from the hall, where presently we hear voices and footsteps; the door is unlocked, and* GITTEL *comes in with* JERRY *behind her, both silhouetted. Their mood is light, though* JERRY's *manner remains essentially ironic and preoccupied.*

GITTEL. Look out for the furniture. Got to be a bat to find your way around *this* goddam room in the dark.

JERRY. Some of my best friends are bats. And the rest are cuckoos. The— Oogh!

GITTEL. There. (*She clicks on a lamp which gives a cozy light, and tosses her purse and a theater program on the bed.* JERRY *is holding a carton of cokes and a bag, and rubbing his shin with his bandaged hand;* GITTEL *comes back, grinning.*) So whyn't you listen?

JERRY (*surrenders the things*). No place like home, be it ever so deadly. Sixty per cent of the accidents in this country occur in the home. (GITTEL *takes the things into her kitchen.*) Doesn't include ruptured marriages. Be safe, be homeless.

GITTEL (*calling in, amused*). What'll you have, coke or beer, Jerry?

JERRY. Anything you're having that's wet.

GITTEL. I'm having warm milk.

JERRY (*with doubt*). Warm milk. (*He considers it, putting his hat on the dress dummy while* GITTEL *in the kitchen lights the gas under a potful.*) I think I'm too old for you. I'll have a hell-bent coke.

GITTEL. Coke's got caffeine in it, maybe I'll give you a beer better, huh?

JERRY. Better for what?

GITTEL. It's more relaxing. You had three cups of coffee at dinner, a coke now makes—

JERRY. Gittel, call off the St. Bernards. I mean let's not nurse me, I've been taken care of to shreds. (GITTEL *is brought back to the doorway by his tone, which has an edge.*) Coke, and damn the torpedoes.

GITTEL. You said you don't sleep. So you *won't* sleep. (*She goes back into the kitchen.* JERRY *thinks it over, dryly.*)

JERRY. It's a non-income-producing habit. If you guarantee I'll sleep with beer, you can give me beer.

(GITTEL *comes back into the doorway.*)

GITTEL. Look, let's start all over, on

your own. Coke or beer?

JERRY. Warm milk.

GITTEL. Now listen—

JERRY. If I'm relaxing I don't want to be *casual* about it.

(GITTEL, *shaking her head, goes back into the kitchen; she continues from there, while* JERRY *explores the room.*)

GITTEL. What kind of bed you got you don't sleep?

JERRY. A couch I got at the Salvation Army, eight dollars.

GITTEL. Well, my God, no wonder! Take a feel of that bed. (*She comes into the doorway, points with a mug;* JERRY *stops to eye the bed.*) You know how much I paid for that mattress alone? Fifty-nine bucks! Sears' best.

JERRY. Six lovely feet long and wide enough for two, isn't it?

GITTEL. Yeah, well, that's one thing I'd never be without is a good bed, you just got to get yourself a good bed. (*She goes back into the kitchen.*) I mean figure it out, you're in it a third of your life.

JERRY (*dryly*). You lead a very puritanical life, by that estimate.

GITTEL. How come? Oh. Okay, half!

JERRY (*interested*). Hm. Well, I've been spending most of my nights here on the jewel-like bridges. I can't afford fifty-nine dollars just to make my bedbugs comfy.

GITTEL. You got bedbugs? (*She comes in frowning, with a box of cookies and two mugs of milk, and hands him one.*)

JERRY. Among other things eating me at night.

GITTEL. You out of work, Jerry?

JERRY (*inspecting his milk*). I know why I'm drinking this, why are you?

GITTEL. Oh, I got an ulcer. (*She indicates her chest, explains.*) In the duodenum.

JERRY. Serious? (GITTEL *shrugging wags her head, makes herself comfortable on the bed, her legs under her.*) I thought ulcers in women went out with the bicycle built for two, isn't it a man's disease nowadays?

GITTEL (*philosophically*). Well, I got it!

JERRY. Well, which are you, the old-fashioned type or the manly type?

GITTEL. Why, what's the difference?

JERRY. Present difference might be whether I drink this and go, or stay all night. (*He cocks an eye at her, and* GITTEL *eyes him back unperturbed, a moment of frank speculation, both ways.*)

GITTEL. You don't exactly lead up to things, do you?

JERRY. Oh, I've been *up* for hours, pawing the ground. The only question is which way to run. (*He moves away from this subject, which leaves her perplexed; he stops to regard the gaudy bodice on the dress dummy, his manner dry and light.*) Speaking of blind as a bat, who is this for?

GITTEL. Dance costume, some kid she's at the Education Alliance next Sunday.

JERRY. Has no bottom part, this kid she has no bottom parts?

GITTEL. Goes with tights, natch!

JERRY (*at the sewing machine*). Good idea. And here you earn an immodest living, hm?

GITTEL (*dubiously*). Mmm. Half and half.

JERRY. Why, what's the other half?

GITTEL. The other half I'm unemployed!

JERRY (*at photos on a wall*). Well, the answer is simple, longer costumes. Aha, acrobats. Who's the black beauty with cramps?

GITTEL. That's me.

JERRY. You?

GITTEL. Yeah, don't act so surprised! I'm dancing.

JERRY. Oh. Yes, I see. I had the impression you'd given up that line of work, or vice versa.

GITTEL (*indignant*). No! That's what I *am*. Ye gods, I studied with Jose for years.

JERRY. Jose who?

GITTEL (*staring*). Are you serious?

JERRY. Good question. You mean this is the real you.

GITTEL. Well, if it isn't I sure wasted a lot of seven-fifties a week!

JERRY. And Mr. America here would be your ex-mistake?

GITTEL. Who?

JERRY. Your husband.

GITTEL. Nah, Wally wasn't around long enough to *snap* a picture. That's Larry.

JERRY (*sagely*). Oh. The present mistake. (*He contemplates the photos.*) Somehow there's more *of* the real you. Do you have such nice legs?

GITTEL. Sure! Well, I mean I did, but that's some time back, before I got sick,

I lost a lot of weight since then.

JERRY (*on tiptoe at one photo's neckline*). With your old-fashioned duodenum? Can almost make it out in this one—

GITTEL. No, ulcers you put *on* weight. That diet, ye gods, six meals a day, the last hemorrhage I had I put on eighteen pounds. I looked very good. (JERRY *turns to her with a frown*.) Everybody said!

JERRY. The last.

GITTEL. Yeah, I hope it's the last. I got just so much blood!

JERRY. It is serious. How many hemorrhages have you had?

GITTEL. Two. Then when I never looked healthier in my life, they had to operate on me.

JERRY. For the ulcer?

GITTEL. Appendicitis! (*She becomes self-conscious under his continued gaze; she laughs.*) No kidding, I'm a physical wreck, practically.

(*After a moment* JERRY *raises his milk to her.*)

JERRY. To your physique. As is, without appendix. I couldn't resist another ounce. (*He drinks to her, and* GITTEL *cheerfully acknowledges it with a sip of her own.*)

GITTEL. So okay, that's what's wrong with me, what's wrong with you?

JERRY. Me? Not a thing.

GITTEL. How'd you break your leg in five places?

JERRY. Oh, my leg. It broke with grief. (*He empties the mug, sets it down, stops at her radio and clicks it on, sees that it lights up, clicks it off, and moves on, taking out a cigar.*)

GITTEL. Look, whyn't you settle down and rest up? (JERRY *turns to her, she anticipates him.*) I'm not nursing, it just makes me nervous to watch!

JERRY (*dryly*). I have two rates of motion, the other is collapse. The last lady who invited me to settle down I couldn't get up for nine years. (*He drops in a chair apart from her, unwrapping the cigar;* GITTEL *stares.*)

GITTEL. Who was that?

JERRY. Her name escapes me. The question at hand is how we're to make up our mind.

GITTEL. About what?

JERRY. About my staying over. I appreciate the invitation, but I'm not sure you should insist. On the other hand, it's very pleasant here and I can't plead any prior engagements.

GITTEL (*a pause*). I don't get you, Jerry.

JERRY. I only sound hard to get. No one's had much trouble.

GITTEL. I mean first you can't say if you even want to eat with me, the next minute, bing, into bed. Only it's all talk, how come?

JERRY. It's exploratory talk. Like the old lady who said how do I know what I think till I hear what I say.

GITTEL. Ahuh. Is that the way you decide everything?

JERRY. How?

GITTEL. In your head?

JERRY. Well, I have a little gray thingamajig in there supposed to save me false moves. Where do you decide things?

GITTEL. Well, that one not in my head! I mean a couple of false moves might get you further.

JERRY (*studies her for a moment*). Don't rush me. I think I should examine what I'm getting into.

GITTEL (*eyebrows up*). Who said yes, yet?

JERRY. And so should you. What if all I can afford is a—(*He waves a hand at the photos.*)—lady on a picture, not a whole human being with hemorrhages and so on?

GITTEL (*indignantly*). So who's giving them to you?

JERRY. Well. I'm burning my bridges before me. Maybe we could have a little music to obscure the future, I've missed that too.

GITTEL. My God, you haven't got a radio even?

JERRY. No, why?

GITTEL. Everybody's got a radio! (*He lights the cigar.* GITTEL *stares at him, till the radio comes in under her hand; she dials around to some music.*) Listen, are you really broke?

JERRY (*inspecting the cigar*). What kind of a name is Gittel? Has an exotic ring, Eskimo or—

GITTEL. Polish. Are you?

JERRY. Polish?

GITTEL. Broke!

JERRY. Why do you ask?

GITTEL. I just want to know if that's what's keeping you up nights, and if so what'd we eat out and go to a show for?

I mean we could of gone Dutch at least.

JERRY (*deadpan*). I thought you were Italian.

GITTEL. Who, me? Jewish!

JERRY. Mosca?

GITTEL. Oh, *that's* exotic. It's my stage name.

JERRY. What stage are you in?

GITTEL. Huh?

JERRY. What's your real name?

GITTEL. Too long. For the marquees, Moscowitz.

JERRY. So you became a witzless Italian. Is that where you were born?

GITTEL. Italy?

JERRY. Poland.

GITTEL (*indignantly*). I was born in the Bronx. Listen, whyn't you get unemployed insurance? It's what I do.

JERRY. Well. For one thing, I'm not a legal resident of this state.

GITTEL. Oh. (*She considers it.*) So what state are you from, legally?

JERRY. Nebraska.

GITTEL. Nebraska. That's somewhere out in California, isn't it?

JERRY. I think it's Nevada that's in California.

GITTEL. I mean, you're a long ways from home. You don't know anybody here you can borrow from?

(JERRY *in his chair appraises her steadily.*)

JERRY. Only you. (*A quiet moment, their eyes not leaving each other.* GITTEL *then picks up his mug, to refill it, debating.*)

GITTEL. How much do you need?

JERRY (*eyes down*). You're a very generous girl. (*Then he gets to his feet, his voice flattening; he walks away from her.*) Much too generous. Don't play the fairy godmother, the wolf will eat you up.

GITTEL. You said you were broke!

JERRY. No, you said I was broke. The unromantic fact is that last year I made fifteen thousand dollars.

GITTEL (*staring*). Doing what?

JERRY. I'm an attorney.

GITTEL. You mean a lawyer?

JERRY. Attorney. To be exotic.

GITTEL (*indignant*). I got eighteen bucks to get me through the month, what am I helping you out for?

JERRY (*indifferent, at the window*). Offhand I think you enjoy feeding stray wolves.

GITTEL. What?

JERRY. I think you're a born victim.

GITTEL. Of who?

JERRY. Yourself.

GITTEL (*staring*). Am I wrong or have you got a nerve? I felt sorry for you, what's so terrible?

JERRY (*turning*). For me.

GITTEL. Sure.

JERRY. How old are you?

GITTEL. Twenty-nine, so?

JERRY. So. Don't talk like twenty-eight. At thirty you're over the hill, half a life gone, there's very little in this room to show for it. I think it's time you worried about your worries.

GITTEL (*scowling*). I do! I got plans!

JERRY. What plans?

GITTEL. Several! I'm starting right away with this Larry, we're going to work up a whole goddam dance recital, why shouldn't we be the new Humphrey and Weidman? I'm hunting everywhere for a cheap loft to fix up a studio, I can rent it out for classes too. Not to mention I'll probably do the costumes for a show downtown, Oscar's in a new theater bunch there, he says he can—

JERRY (*flatly*). None of this will happen. (*This is true enough to take the wind out of* GITTEL *for a moment.*)

GITTEL (*incensed*). So I'll think up something else! Why are you riding me for?

JERRY. Seriously?

GITTEL. Yeah!

JERRY (*evenly*). Because I enjoy you, life is short, and if you're spending it like a sailor on a spree you might as well spend some on me, but all I probably mean is trouble, I can be here today and gone tomorrow, and I'd rather not be responsible for an ingenuous little nitwit like you. In one word.

GITTEL (*scowling*). What's ingenuous mean, smart?

JERRY. Dumb. Naïve.

GITTEL. Oh, for Christ sakes. I had a room of my own in the Village at sixteen, what do you think, to play potsy? All those reasons, I think you're just scared!

JERRY (*a pause, levelly*). Do you sleep with him?

GITTEL. Who?

JERRY. Mr. America. Larry.

GITTEL. He's a *dancer*.

JERRY. So you said.

GITTEL. I mean we're very good friends and all that, but my God. You think I'm peculiar or something? (*Her eyes widen.*) Are you?

JERRY. Am I what?

GITTEL. Queer?

JERRY (*a pause, shakes his head*). Oh, you've gone too far. (*He puts down the cigar.*) No one's in your life now?

GITTEL. No, I'm free as a bird, goddam it.

JERRY. I'm free as a worm. We can keep it as simple as that, an item of diet. (*His hands gesture for her, and* GITTEL *readily comes;* JERRY *kisses her. It begins temperately enough, but as* GITTEL *co-operates it becomes a wholehearted and protracted undertaking. It is* GITTEL *who slides out of it, leaving* JERRY *with his hands trembling; she is a bit jittery herself.*)

GITTEL. Brother. How long you been on the wagon?

JERRY. A year.

GITTEL (*staring*). Where you been, in jail? (JERRY *reaches, grasping her arms this time inexorably. He kisses her again; she resists weakly, responds, resists very weakly, and gives up, hanging loosely in his hands until they part mouths for air.*) Look, let's not get all worked up if we're not going to finish it, huh?

JERRY. Who's not going to, huh.

GITTEL. I mean you just have another cookie to calm down, and then maybe you better go.

JERRY. Go!

GITTEL. Please.

(JERRY *releases her. A silence.*)

JERRY. Is that what you meant by a false move would get me further?

GITTEL. No, I—

JERRY. Go where? (*He turns away, very annoyed, finds himself at the radio, and mocks her.*) Back to a room without a radio?

GITTEL (*weakly*). Radio costs nineteen ninety-five—

JERRY. That's cheap enough. I had the impression you'd been inviting me all night. To buy a radio? (*He snaps the radio off, and walks.*)

GITTEL (*defensive*). I got an ironclad rule I wouldn't sleep with God Almighty on the first date, you want me to be *promiscuous*? In the second place you—walk

around too much—(*She works up some indignation.*)—and in the third place I can't stand cigars in the first place, and in the fourth place I tell you my whole life practically and what do I hear out of you, no news at all, why should I hit the hay right away with someone I don't know if he's— (JERRY *wheels on her so bitingly it stops her like a blow.*)

JERRY. *Because I'm drowning in cement here!*

GITTEL. Where?

JERRY. This town! (*He paces, talking through his teeth, more to himself than to her.*) I haven't passed a word with a living soul for a month, until I called Oscar—and we never liked one another! Everyone else I knew here has moved to Connecticut, Vermont, the Arctic Circle. I've worn out a pair of shoes in the museums. And a pair of pants in bad movies. And if I hike over another beautiful bridge here by my lonesome, so help me, I'll jump off! So I go back to my cell, twenty-one dollars a month, with garbage pails in the hall they'll find me gassed to death by some morning. (*He turns on her.*) And I can't *spend* nineteen ninety-five on a radio!

GITTEL (*the neighbors*). Sssh! Why?

JERRY (*hissing*). Because I came east with five hundred dollars. I'm living on three-fifty a day here now.

GITTEL (*hissing*). You spent about sixteen-eighty on me tonight!

JERRY (*hissing*). I splurged.

GITTEL. What, on me?

JERRY. On me. I was thirty-three years old today. (GITTEL *is speechless. He lifts up his cigar, dourly.*) So, I bought myself a dollar cigar.

GITTEL. It's your *birthday*?

JERRY. Sorry it—exploded. (*He crushes it out in the ash tray.*)

GITTEL (*alarmed*). So don't ruin it! You got to buy yourself a present on your birthday, my God? Whyn't you tell me?

JERRY. Why, you'd like to give me one?

GITTEL. Sure!

JERRY. Thank you. (*He retrieves his hat from the dummy.*) I'm not hinting for handouts, from crackpot lovable waifs. Just don't tell a man go when you've been indicating come all night, it's not ladylike. (*He walks toward the door.*)

GITTEL (*stung*). So what do you think

you been doing right along?

JERRY (*stops*). What?

GITTEL. Hinting for handouts! It's what *you* been doing all night!

JERRY. Are you talking to me?

GITTEL. Sure. All these hints, unhappy, bedbugs, broke—

JERRY. Unhappy bedbugs!

GITTEL. Unhappy! Bedbugs!

JERRY. What in God's name are you dreaming—

GITTEL. Like this minute, if I don't sleep with you they'll find you dead?

JERRY (*astonished*). Who said that?

GITTEL. You did. With the garbage?

JERRY. Oh, cut it out. I—

GITTEL. Or off a bridge, you're so lonely? That's the *last* thing you said?

JERRY. I was—I— (*But he breaks off, staring at her in less disbelief.*) That was —campaign oratory. You call that all night?

GITTEL. The *first* thing you said was help me. On the phone. Right?

(JERRY *stares, almost speechless, though he makes one more convictionless try.*)

JERRY. I—said I *wouldn't* say that, I—

GITTEL. Oh, come on! You said help me, I said sure. (JERRY *cannot remove his eyes from her, at a loss for words.*) I'm not complaining, I'm used to all kinds, but what do you call me names, you want it both ways? (JERRY *still stares at her, but something has opened in him that now takes him away from her, downstage, his fingers at his brow, almost in a daze.* GITTEL *becomes concerned.*) Hey. I say something hurt your feelings?

JERRY (*with an effort*). Yes, slightly. I— (*He shakes his head, abandons the attempt at irony. Low*) I'm remembering. Something from—(*It comes from far away, his tone now simple and vulnerable.*)—thirteen years ago yesterday. I was walking across the campus of Nebraska U, with a beautiful auburn-haired girl whose father was a sizable wheel in the state. The girl and I were—intimate that summer, and I was telling her I'd have to leave school, no family to help me. The next day—my birthday—was the luckiest in my life, I got the George Norris scholarship. It kept me in school, and I became a lawyer. The girl and I— continued. (*He stops.* GITTEL *waits.*)

GITTEL. That's the whole story?

JERRY. I married her.

GITTEL (*darkly*). You got a *wife*?

JERRY. Had a wife. She's divorcing me out there.

GITTEL (*contrite*). Oh. You too, huh?

JERRY. Me too. It was just before we married I learned that Lucian—her father —had wangled that scholarship for me. You know what I said?

GITTEL. What?

JERRY. Nothing. (*He opens his hands, helplessly.*) It's absolutely true, the— point you made, you made your point.

GITTEL. Which?

JERRY. I ask for handouts. I never *saw* it happening before, right under my nose. (*He shakes his head, finds his hat again, and walks once more to the door.*)

GITTEL. So where you going now?

JERRY. Back to solitary. (*Beset*) There I go again!

GITTEL. So don't. Ye gods, if you hate it so much you don't want to go back there on your birthday, stay over. I got a couch in the back room, you take the bed. Maybe a good night's sleep you'll feel better in the morning, huh? (JERRY *stares unseeing.*) You want to stay?

JERRY. Stay?

GITTEL. So you'll get a good night's sleep. You'll feel better in the morning.

JERRY. You mean, put you out?

GITTEL. It's not out, I fit that couch. I mean you got—long legs, you know?

JERRY. Yes. (GITTEL *is eyeing his legs, with interest. When their eyes meet it is as though for the first time, really: something warmer passes between them, they are both shy about it.*) Both of them.

GITTEL. Yeah, well, I— You mind my sheets? (*She yanks the bedspread down, takes a pillow, gathers things up.*) I put them on clean yesterday and I had a bath.

JERRY. No. It's kind of you to offer, kind of absurd, but kind—

GITTEL. What do you mean absurd? You got a lousy bed, tomorrow you'll get some kerosene and see where they come out of the wall.

JERRY. Gittel. You're a very sweet girl—

GITTEL (*embarrassed*). Well—you're a very sweet girl, too. The john's right out there behind you—

JERRY. —but all I proposed was a change of bedmates.

GITTEL. Listen, all *I* got in mind is a good night's sleep you'll feel better in the morning—

JERRY (*simultaneously with her*). —feel better in the morning. No doubt.

GITTEL (*all settled*). So okay! (*She turns with her armful into the kitchen, puts out the light there.*)

JERRY. Gittel!

GITTEL (*within*). What?

JERRY. I can't.

GITTEL (*within*). I'm all packed!

JERRY (*a pause*). Crazy. (*Nevertheless, the bed attracts his eye; he turns back from it.*) Gittel! (GITTEL *reappears, still with her armful.*) Look, agree with me. It would be an act of—frailty to stay after—

GITTEL. What, on your birthday? (*She goes back in.* JERRY *considers this argument for a long moment, contemplates the bed and the room around it, and sighs.*)

JERRY. Gittel. (GITTEL *reappears; his tone is humble.*) Should I really stay?

GITTEL. Look, don't nudya me! You want to stay?

JERRY (*a pause*). I haven't been in a place that smelled of—human living in a month. Of course I want to stay.

GITTEL. So stay! (GITTEL *takes the hat out of his hand, drops it on the bed, gives him a towel, and disappears beyond the kitchen again. When* JERRY *opens the towel, it has a large hole in it. He shakes his head, amused, and rather forlorn.*)

JERRY. I feel ridiculous. (*He walks out into the hall, leaving the door open. After a moment* GITTEL *comes back through the kitchen, still with her armful.*)

GITTEL. Listen, I— (*She sees the room is empty, stops, stares at his hat on the bed. She scowls at it, debating. Then she shakes her head, no, no, and walks back toward the kitchen with her armful. But on the threshold she halts. After a second she turns back, and stands to give the hat another stare. Finally she sighs, and with an air of disgusted resignation mutters to herself.*) Oh, what the hell, happy birthday. (*And she puts everything back, her clothes back in the drawer, the clock back on the table, the pillow back in place alongside the other on the bed. She unbuttons and takes off her blouse, hangs it dangling on a chair, sits on the bed to remove her sandals, stands to slip her skirt off, walks in her half-slip and bra to a drawer again, takes out pajama-tops,* and at this moment hears JERRY *in the hall; she skedaddles with the pajama-tops into the darkness beyond the kitchen.*)

JERRY *returns, and walks around, restive. It is a moment before he accidentally kicks one of* GITTEL's *sandals, stares at them, then at her skirt on the floor, then at her pillow next to his, and looking toward the kitchen, comprehends her intention. He takes up her blouse in his fingers. Bringing it to his face, he inhales the odor of woman again; he rubs it against his cheek, thinking, scowling. At last he comes out of the other end of some maze, and tells himself grittily:*)

JERRY. It's, not, a, beginning. (*He hangs the blouse back on the chair, turns, picks up his hat from the bed, and walks straight out into the hall, closing the door behind him.*)

After a moment GITTEL *peers in from the kitchen, clad in the pajama-tops and carrying her underthings; she sees the room is still empty and comes in. Quickly she clicks off the lamp, turns down the sheet, has her knee up to get in, remembers, and kneels around to the foot of the bed with her hand outstretched for* JERRY's *hat. It is not there. She searches, baffled, then sees the door is now closed; she scrambles over the bed to it, looks along the hall to the john and then down over the bannister. Two stories down, there is the closing of the street door.*

GITTEL *comes back into her doorway, where she stands silhouetted; after a perplexed moment she slaps her thigh, in resignation.*)

SCENE THREE

Both rooms. It is several hours later, and the first light of dawn is just beginning to pick out the furniture in both rooms.

GITTEL *is in her bed, asleep, with the blanket and sheet pulled up over her ears.*

JERRY's *room is empty, but after a moment we hear* JERRY *letting himself in at his door. When he opens it, he spies and bends to pick up a telegram waiting inside the threshold. He comes into his living room staring at it, unkempt, needing a shave, weary from walking all night, but relatively lighthearted. He takes the telegram to the broken window, tears the envelope open, then pauses in the act of lifting the message out, and presently shoves it back in, tosses it onto his couch, and lights a cigarette. He walks around a few steps, then stands deliberating between the telegram and the phone, and suddenly sits to the phone. He dials, waits.*

The phone in GITTEL's *room rings.* GITTEL *rolls around before she is altogether awake, her hand fumbling till it finds the phone.*

GITTEL (*eyes closed*). Yeah, h'lo. (JERRY *considers how to begin.*) H'lo!

JERRY (*dryly*). About that icebox. I think you let that other jerk have it too cheap.

GITTEL. Whah?

JERRY. If you keep handing things out to the first comer, judgment day will find you without an icebox to your name, morally speaking.

GITTEL (*jerking up*). Jerry! Hey, you all right? I called you two three times, no answer.

JERRY. I tried another bridge. Queensboro, it opens a vast new territory to— (*He catches himself, breaks off.*) I was about to say get lost in, but that's my last hint. I walked out on you, Gittel.

GITTEL. Yeah. I noticed!

JERRY. What changed your ironclad rule?

GITTEL. Oh—I couldn't resist your goddam hat!

JERRY. I should have left it for you. I thought it was something else.

GITTEL. Like what?

JERRY. Charity. I think your trouble is running the community chest.

GITTEL. Huh?

JERRY. My trouble is my wife does understand me. You lit a fair-sized birthday candle under me tonight, it cast a light backwards all the way to Omaha, Nevada.

GITTEL. How?

JERRY. Tess—her name is Tess, it comes back to me from time to time—also smothered me in loving kindnesses. But my God, if I hinted for them it's not all her fault. I needn't have gone into her father's law office. I needn't have let him set us up in a handsome house in Fairacres. It poisoned the well.

GITTEL (*scowling*). Well?

JERRY. Well—we had running water, but not much monogamy. I had to be

heroic with some wife, no matter whose, and Tess now is marrying someone else, a colleague of mine who— (*He breaks this off.*) That's another chapter. I wanted to say only that tonight half my like looks like a handout, and I finally walked out on one. From you.

GITTEL. Oh. *I* thought it was something else.

JERRY. Such as?

GITTEL. I figured you figured I wasn't— (*She takes a breath.*) I mean maybe you didn't think I was— You know.

JERRY. No.

GITTEL. Attractive!

JERRY (*a pause*). Oh, God. And you still called me two or three times?

GITTEL (*she has her pride*). *Two* times.

JERRY. Why?

GITTEL. Well, you disappear like that, I got worried about you.

JERRY. Gittel. (*His tone is gentle, very affectionate, for the first time genuinely heedful of her; the relationship is taking on a quite different color.*) Gittel, I'll tell you two truths. One, you're attractive, two, you don't look out for yourself.

GITTEL. Sure I do.

JERRY. No. If you did you'd object more.

GITTEL. What to?

JERRY. So many things. This minute, this very minute, why aren't you taking my head off about the time?

GITTEL. Why, what time is it?

JERRY. Little before five. It takes practice, go ahead.

GITTEL. Go ahead what?

JERRY. Practice. Protest. Enter an objection.

GITTEL. Huh?

JERRY. *Holler* at me!

GITTEL. What for?

JERRY. It's a hell of an hour to phone anyone. Who do I think I am, waking you up this time of night, my father-in-law? It shows no respect for you, you resent it, say so!

GITTEL. Look, what are you hollering at me for?

JERRY (*mildly*). Your own good.

GITTEL. I don't like to holler at people, it makes me nervous. Anyway, I'm glad you phoned.

JERRY. Why?

GITTEL (*exasperated*). What makes you so dumb? *I was worried about you!*

JERRY. That's better.

GITTEL. Better!

JERRY. All you need is practice. Go ahead.

GITTEL (*irately*). Who's practicing? What do you think, I'm nuts, you know what time it is, is that what you call me up five o'clock in the morning to practice hollering?

JERRY (*amused*). No, I called to say don't give anything else away. Until I see you.

GITTEL. What?

JERRY. I'm asking whether you'd—care to try being half of a pair?

GITTEL (*a pause*). Look, let's not go through all *that* again!

JERRY. On my terms, this time. And I don't mean as a handout.

GITTEL. So what do you mean?

JERRY. That *I'd*—like to look out for you. Hemorrhages notwithstanding. (GITTEL *stares at the phone.*) Will you let me? (GITTEL *shakes her head, too uncertain about her feelings to know what to say; she is touched, and also wants to snicker.*)

GITTEL. I'm—I— Why?

JERRY. I think you can use me. Not that I'll be such a bargain, a lot of me is still tied up in the—civil wars. I thought I'd tell you the whole mess, if you'd have breakfast with me.

GITTEL. Where?

JERRY. Here. Will you come?

GITTEL. Well, I'm having a tooth pulled out eight-fifteen. I mean I'll be spitting a lot of goddam blood, we won't be able to *do* anything.

JERRY. Will you come?

GITTEL. Sure I'll come.

JERRY (*a pause, gently*). I'll look for you. (*He is about to hang up, when he has an afterthought.*) Gittel.

GITTEL. Yeah?

JERRY. What do you do when a tooth bleeds?

GITTEL (*concerned*). Why, you got one?

JERRY. Oh, you're a character. I'm talking about *yours*.

GITTEL. Oh. Let it bleed, why? It dries up.

JERRY. I knew I'd have a use for that icebox. I'll have a cake of ice in the sink.

GITTEL. What for?

JERRY. For the ice bag I'll buy for your tooth.

GITTEL (*a pause, amused*). You're start-ing right in, huh?

JERRY. Not a minute to lose. It's a new day, in my thirty-fourth year, and I feel like a rising lark. Get some sleep, now. (*He hangs up.* GITTEL *sits for a moment, then also hangs up and shakes her head in a kind of wonderment.*)

GITTEL. Sonofabitch. (*Presently she gets up and goes into her kitchen, pours herself some milk from the pot, and comes back; she settles in bed with it.*)

(JERRY *sets his phone on the floor and remains smiling, until his eyes again encounter the telegram. He picks it up, fingers it. Finally he draws it out, takes it to the window, and reads it. He goes over it twice in silence; the third time he reads it aloud to himself, without expression.*)

JERRY. "I called to say happy birthday you stinker don't shut me out God help both of us but will you remember I love you I do Tess." (*After a second he perceives the telegram is trembling. He crumples it in his hand, and drops it slowly out the broken window. He returns to his couch, transfers his clothes to the chair, and lies down to finish his cigarette.*

Each lies alone with his thoughts in the bleak light of daybreak, JERRY *smoking and* GITTEL *sipping her milk; the only sound is some distant church clock ringing five.*)

ACT TWO

SCENE ONE

JERRY's *room. It is October now, early evening, dusk.*

GITTEL's *room is much the same, with her bed unmade and two pillows rumpled; but a transformation has overtaken* JERRY's. *It has been fixed up inexpensively, and now is tidy, pleasant, livable, with bedspread, wall lamp, throw rugs, burlap drapes, stained fruit crates for shelving—all improvements in the peasant style of* GITTEL's *garb. Near the window there is a bridge table with two chairs, set for dinner.* GITTEL's *little radio is playing on a shelf, WNYC, symphonic music.*

The light in the kitchen is on, now agreeably shaded; out here GITTEL, *wearing a dishtowel for an apron, is preparing dinner. She comes in carrying a bowlful of salad, sets it on the table, and stands listening thoughtfully to the music; she then has a kind of slow convulsion, which after a moment we see is a modern-dance movement, because she stops, is dissatisfied, scratches her head, tries another, gives it up, and returns to the kitchen. Here she opens the gas-range oven to peer in, does some basting, closes it. In the middle of her next turn she halts, listens towards the door, then skedaddles back in and hastily begins lighting two candles on the table. We then see* JERRY *opening the outer door.*

GITTEL (*calling happily*). Hiya, baby.

JERRY. Hi. (*He stops to sniff the oven, looks in.*) Hmm. Smells good, who's in here? Chicken!

GITTEL. And salad, and potatoes, and wine's on the ice.

JERRY. Wine, well. (*Coming into the doorway he leans there, just taking her in at the candles; he is in street clothes and hat, with a legal tome or two under his arm, and some parcels.*) What are we launching, me?

GITTEL. I got a bargain, sixty-nine cents a bottle. Must of been getting kind of old. (*She comes to kiss his amused face above her, and his arm draws her in.*) What's so funny?

JERRY. You are, infant. (*He spies the window over her shoulder.*) You put up curtains for me!

GITTEL. Sure, what do you think I come over for, just to see you?

JERRY. Very cozy. Last couple of weeks you've turned this into the show place of the nation. You're better than wine, you improve with age.

GITTEL. What's in the bag?

JERRY. Everything's in the bag.

GITTEL. I mean this bag.

JERRY. Don't move!

GITTEL (*alarmed*). Huh?

JERRY. Careful. Back in one inch.

GITTEL. Why?

JERRY (*soberly*). Because all afternoon I've been totally surrounded by lawbooks, and I like it much better being totally surrounded by you. I got your thread. (*He jiggles a bag at her ear.*)

GITTEL. Oh, good. You see Frank Taubman, Jerry?

JERRY. I did. And dessert. (*He jiggles another bag.*) Soya cake. Salt-free, butter-free, flavor-free.

GITTEL. Well, what'd he say?

JERRY. You'll hear. And a piece of the moon. From me, to you. (*He deposits the third bag in her hand.*)

GITTEL. A present?

JERRY. Just a piece of the moon. (GITTEL *unwraps it at the candles, while* JERRY *gets rid of his books and hat, takes off his jacket.*)

GITTEL. I can't wait to see what's in it, what's in it?

JERRY (*deadpan*). Well, it turns out this way, she opens this box from her lover thinking it's candy but it's really the preserved brains of her unfaithful father, who has run away to join this gang of juvenile delinquents, she recognizes him instantly and lets out an unearthly shriek—

GITTEL (*blankly, lifts it*). A cake of soap?

JERRY (*approaching*). Supposed to be the preserved brains of—

GITTEL. What's the matter, I smell?

JERRY. Good idea, let's investigate. (*He puts his nose in her hair from behind, his arms around her waist.*)

GITTEL. I mean what kind of present is a cake of soap, I need a bath?

JERRY. What kind of present is a— Did you look at the box?

GITTEL. No.

JERRY. Read the soap.

GITTEL (*by candlelight*). Channel number—

JERRY. Channel number five, it's a TV sample. Chanel number five, girl, you're holding a two-fifty soap bubble there.

GITTEL (*aghast*). Two-fif— For *one* cake of soap?

JERRY. Don't you dare take a bath with that. We're going to eat it, spoonful by spoonful. Instead of that soya cake.

GITTEL. You know sometimes I think the nutty one of this twosome some of us think I am is you? Two-fifty, we won't eat!

JERRY. We'll eat, it will be a feast. How's your belly?

GITTEL. Oh, fine. I took some banthine, it went away.

JERRY. Didn't all go away. Here's some.

GITTEL. Some what?

JERRY. Belly.

GITTEL. Oh. You think I'm too fat.

JERRY. Good God, no.

GITTEL. You think I'm too skinny?

JERRY (*dryly*). I think you're a sacred vessel of womanhood.

GITTEL. Ahuh. Sexy as all get-out, that's why you buy me a hunk of soap.

JERRY. Buoyant in the bow, swively in the stern, and spicy in the hatch, how's that?

GITTEL. S'pretty good. (*They have been kissing; now* GITTEL *cocks her head back.*) You think I'm *too* sexy?

JERRY. Hm?

GITTEL. I mean oversexed?

JERRY. I think you're a mixed-up girl. Calmly considered, your bottom is tops.

GITTEL. Some vessel. Sounds like a shipwreck. (*She kisses him again. When they come up for air, she slides out of his hands.*) Anyway! You're getting a phone call soon. Long-distance.

JERRY. Who from?

GITTEL (*brightly*). Your wife. (*She inhales at the soap again.*) This her kind, Jerry?

JERRY (*a pause*). No. And I seldom gave her gifts, she was—amply supplied.

GITTEL. Okay. (*She takes the soap out into the kitchen, busies herself at the oven.* JERRY *stands alone, not moving, for a long moment; then he calls out, sounding casual.*)

JERRY. When did she call?

GITTEL (*calling in*). Soon's I got here. Said she'd call back eight o'clock. (*JERRY looks at his wristwatch, stares at the phone, clears the litter off the table, glances again at the phone, and goes to his window, to gaze out.* GITTEL *comes back in, bearing a casserole of chicken and a bowlful of French fries to the table, with cheerful chatter.*) She must have money to burn, huh? I mean *two* long-distant phone calls, ye gods. You know I only made one long-distant phone call in my whole life? (*She stands serving out their portions.*) Tallahassee, that's in Florida, right after we were married. Wally had a job there. I mean he said he had a job, when I found out it was really a redhead he went back to I didn't drop dead either, but I called him up—

JERRY. I don't think I care to talk to her. (GITTEL *continues serving, but frowning over it.*) Gittel.

GITTEL. So don't. Anyway I got the bill,

that's when I did drop dead.

JERRY. I won't answer.

GITTEL (*presently*). All right. You want to get the wine?

JERRY. With pleasure. (*He turns the radio on, and goes into the kitchen.*) Let's drink life to the dregs, the whole sixty-nine cents worth. I have something for us to toast. I had a long session this afternon with Frank—(GITTEL *meanwhile stares at the phone, then switches the radio off; the mood in the room changes, and the phone now begins to haunt what they do and say.* JERRY *returns with the wine and a corkscrew.*) What's the matter, honey?

GITTEL (*sits*). I don't see any crowd.

JERRY. That I said I wouldn't answer?

GITTEL. Nothing's the matter!

JERRY. It's dead and buried. (*He uncorks the bottle.*) Six feet under, the coffin is sealed, the headstone is paid for, I'd rather not open it all up again. (*Lightly*) Let's change the subject to something pleasant. How are you making out on your recital?

GITTEL. That's pleasant? I looked at that loft again—the goddam bastard still wants a two-year lease and won't come down a cent. I mean I haven't got that kind of gelt. It's a very fine dance studio, for Rockefeller.

JERRY. You don't need Rockefeller, you have Fort Knox here.

GITTEL. Where?

JERRY (*taps his brow*). I had a long session with Frank Taubman this afternoon.

GITTEL. So what'd he tell you? (*But her look is on the phone.*)

JERRY. That if I'm not a member of the New York Bar he could offer me only some briefs to prepare.

GITTEL. Oh.

JERRY. I'll go down with you in the morning and we'll give this goddam bastard two months rent.

GITTEL. Out of what?

JERRY. I accepted them. It pays per brief, we'll be papering the walls with gelt.

GITTEL. I'll get the loft when *I* get a job. (*Her look again is on the phone; this time* JERRY *notices.*)

JERRY (*a pause*). It didn't say anything.

GITTEL. Huh?

JERRY. The phone.

GITTEL. Yeah. I heard Schrafft's was putting on girls, I'm going to see about it tomorrow.

JERRY. Schrafft's. Waiting on table?

GITTEL. Whatever they got. I worked the candy counter for them last year, I put on seven pounds. It's very good candy.

JERRY. Do me a small favor, let me do you a small favor?

GITTEL. Sure. Like what?

JERRY. Like stake you to Loft's instead of Schrafft's. You know how much I can earn doing briefs? A hundred a week, I'll *buy* you candy. It's absurd for you to work at Schrafft's.

GITTEL. What have you got against Schrafft's?

JERRY. I'm afraid someone there will eat *you* up. No Schrafft's, the prosecution rests. (*They eat again.*) You know this chicken is fabulous? What makes it taste like gin?

GITTEL. Gin.

JERRY. Fabulous. You can sew, you can cook, you—(*He suddenly takes note, ominously.*) What are we doing eating French fries?

GITTEL. You like them.

JERRY. Not after you were up half the night with a bellyache.

GITTEL (*indignant*). You said they were your favorite.

JERRY (*mildly*). My favorite will put holes in *your* stomach lining. And your stomach lining is my favorite, how many did you eat?

GITTEL. Three.

JERRY (*rises*). Three too many.

GITTEL. I love them.

JERRY (*hesitates*). Four is all you get. (*He lifts the potatoes from her plate in his fingers, drops one back and takes the bowlful out into the kitchen.*)

GITTEL. Hey! (*But the protest is weak, she contents herself with snaring others from* JERRY'S *plate in his absence, and pops them into her mouth. He comes back with a slice or two of bread.*)

JERRY. Here. Instead. You need starch to soak up the acids, honey, I've been reading up on the whole pathology of ulcers and you simply don't know what to do with your acids. In medical parlance we call this a half-acid diagnosis. Let's stick to what *you* can eat, hm?

GITTEL (*her mouth full*). Certainly!

(JERRY *about to sit consults his wristwatch, frowns, glances at the phone; then, sitting, finds* GITTEL's *eyes on him.*) It didn't say anything!

JERRY. What?

GITTEL. The phone.

JERRY. Not going to, either. I was just thinking I'd forgotten the sound of her voice. How did she sound?

GITTEL (*scowling*). What do you mean how did she sound?

JERRY (*bored*). Only how did she sound, don't—

GITTEL. Lovely, she sounded lovely! You want to hear how she sounds, talk to her. What are you scared of? (JERRY *puts down his fork, and contemplates her.*)

JERRY (*evenly*). You really want me to answer it, don't you?

GITTEL. Who, me?

JERRY. Why?

GITTEL. Why not?

JERRY. Because I'm in a state of grace here in a garden of Eden with you and a stuffed chicken. Adam and Eve, and you know what that twelve hundred miles of phone cable is? the snake. Why let it in, it was enough work getting rid of the bedbugs.

GITTEL. Why do you hate her so?

JERRY. I don't, let's change the subject. (*They eat again.*) I'll go with you about this loft tomorrow. Tell the man I'm your lawyer, I handle nothing but your leases, I'll negotiate the whole transaction. I'll even bring my brief case.

GITTEL. What kind of bread is this?

JERRY. Health bread. For our health.

GITTEL. Gee, they must cut this right off a *stump*, huh? (JERRY *sits back and enjoys her.*)

JERRY. You're a bug. A water bug, this way, that, what did I do to have you in my blood stream? Look. I'm saying if you're a dancer it's time to do something about it, the days are going—

GITTEL (*vehemently*). Of course I'm a dancer, it's driving me crazy! Everybody else is getting famous, all I'm getting is repair bills from Singer's!

JERRY. All right then, I can lead a hand with the loft. You go to work on the recital, I go to work on the briefs.

GITTEL. What's doing briefs?

JERRY. Researching a case for precedents. (GITTEL *is uncomprehending, so he clarifies it.*) When one cuke brings suit against another cuke, the court can't decide which cuke is cukier until it hears how two other cukes made out in *another* court in 1888.

GITTEL. So is that fun?

JERRY. Not unless you have a nose-in-the-book talent. But I needn't be writing briefs for the rest of my life, I can practice in court here any time I take the state Bar exam.

GITTEL. So whyn't you take it?

JERRY (*smiles*). It makes me nervous.

GITTEL. Aah. You'd knock them dead.

JERRY. What makes you think so?

GITTEL (*serenely*). I got my impressions.

JERRY. I barely know the traffic laws here. Statutory law *varies*, from state to state, I—

GITTEL. So what, you could study up.

JERRY (*dryly*). I'm a little old to go back to school.

GITTEL. Every day you read in the paper, some grandma going to NYU, eleven grandchildren, seventy years—

JERRY. Do I look like somebody's grandma? I'm not *that* old, but I've been a practicing—(*But he breaks off and leans back to regard her for a moment. Then*) How do you do it?

GITTEL. What?

JERRY. We begin with my saying I'll lend a hand, and end one minute later with you putting me through college.

GITTEL. I don't need a hand, I'll make out! (JERRY *is displeased with this, and after a moment lowers his face to his plate.*) You got to take the exam sometime, no?

JERRY. No.

GITTEL. So what'll you be here in your old age?

JERRY. Don't rush me into the grave. I'm not living that far ahead.

(GITTEL *is displeased with this, and after a moment lowers her face to her plate. They eat.* GITTEL *then bounces up, marches into the kitchen, returns with the bowl of potatoes, and drops a fistful into her plate.*)

GITTEL. What are you, on vacation here? (*She sits.* JERRY *reaches over, puts the fistful back into the bowl, rises, and carries it out again to the kitchen. He returns without it.*)

JERRY. Not necessarily, but I *might* die somewhere else. Be a shame to go to all the trouble of taking the Bar exam in New York and die in New Jersey. I'd have to commute. (*He sits.* GITTEL *rises, and marches toward the kitchen again; but* JERRY *catches her wrist, pulls her onto his lap.*) Look, look. (*He reaches a long arm out to the couch, catches up one of the legal tomes, and deposits it open on* GITTEL's *thighs. She scowls at the text.*)

GITTEL. What?

JERRY. This is Clevenger. Civil Practice Act of New York, what I don't know fills this little volume and a library full besides. To take the Bar exam here. For two days in this state they lift open the top of your skull and stare in. Now—

GITTEL. Jerry, you know what I think you got too much of? Lack of confidence!

JERRY. Oh, great.

GITTEL. I mean ye gods, you were such a popular lawyer in Nevada, what's the difference?

JERRY. Nebraska, dear. (*He kisses her neck.*)

GITTEL. Nebraska, so what's the difference?

JERRY. About a thousand miles. You know you have a two-fifty smell without that damned soap?

GITTEL (*squirms*). Giving me goose-pimples. Jerry, now I'm talking seri—(JERRY *turns her face, kisses her; after a moment she comes up for breath.*) —ous, how come you were so popular there if—

JERRY (*kissing her throat*). I shot in the mid-seventies.

GITTEL (*stares*). Shot what?

JERRY (*kissing her chin*). Birdies.

GITTEL. That made you *popular*?

JERRY. In the butterfly set. (*He kisses her mouth; this time she comes up with her eyes closed, takes a breath, and gives up.*)

GITTEL. Oh, damn you. (*She seizes his ears and kisses him fiercely; Clevenger slides to the floor, unnoticed, and the kiss goes on. Now the phone rings.* GITTEL's *head comes up. After a second* JERRY *draws it down with his hand, but the next ring brings her up scowling at it.*) Phone's ringing.

JERRY (*lightly*). I don't want the world in. (*He draws her to him again; it rings again.*)

GITTEL. I can't!

(JERRY *puts her aside on her feet, gets*

up, crosses, takes the phone off the hook, drops it to hang and comes back.)

JERRY. Better?

GITTEL. Oh, for Christ sakes. (*She ducks past him, and picks up the phone, combative.*) Yeah, hello. . . .

JERRY (*outraged*). Put down that phone!

GITTEL. . . . So whyn't you call sooner— . . . (JERRY *coming swiftly snatches the phone from her, ready to slam it down.*) It's *Larry*! (JERRY *stares at her, lifts the phone to his ear, listens, then hands it to her, and walks away.*) Hello? . . . No, we thought it was the—landlord. So what'd the Y say? . . . *How much?* . . . (JERRY *stands staring out the window, which is now dark with night;* GITTEL's *eyes are on him.*) Well, listen, I can't— . . . No, maybe we'll try Henry Street, but I can't think about it now. . . . I'm in the middle of eating, Larry, I'll call you back later. . . . No, I can't swing the loft yet, but I can't go into all that now. (*She hangs up and stands over the phone.* JERRY *leaves the window; at the table he drains his tumbler of wine in one swallow, sets it down. They stand silent for a moment,* GITTEL *not taking her eyes from him.*)

JERRY (*curtly*). I'm sorry I shouted.

GITTEL. What did that bitch do to you?

JERRY (*rounding*). Bitch? (*Grimly, then*) Married me, helped put me through law school, stood by me in pinches. Loved me, if anyone did or could. She was never a bitch, don't call her that again.

GITTEL (*nettled*). That's why you left Nebraska, she was so nice?

JERRY. I left because I couldn't take being in the same town with her and her fiancé.

GITTEL. So you ran away.

JERRY. If that's what you call starting over from bedrock, yes, I ran away.

GITTEL. So stop running, it's the Atlantic Ocean already.

JERRY. No one's running now.

GITTEL. You're running, why can't you talk to her on the phone?

(JERRY *turns to look at her.*)

JERRY. Ask it of me. Don't do it for me, ask it of me, perhaps I'll do it for you. Do you want me to?

GITTEL. She's your wife.

JERRY. Do you want me to?

GITTEL. It's your phone.

JERRY. Do *you* want me to? Yes or no!

GITTEL. No!

JERRY (*a pause*). You want me to work here for Frank Taubman?

GITTEL. No.

JERRY. What *do* you want from me?

GITTEL. Not a goddam thing. (*She lights a cigarette, takes a drag.* JERRY *passing removes it from her lips, and* GITTEL, *very annoyed, shakes another from his pack while he is stubbing the first out.*)

JERRY. Why do you smoke, you know it's not good for your stomach.

GITTEL. I'll keep track of my own stomach, we been together almost thirty years now, we get by! (*She strikes the match to the new cigarette and* JERRY *turns. He observes her, not moving a muscle, until it comes in an outburst.*)

JERRY. Don't be such a damfool tower of strength!

GITTEL. What!

JERRY. I'm sick of it too, idiotic act of taking care of you and your weak stomach. Weak, you're as tough as wire.

GITTEL. So one of us better be!

(JERRY *stares at her grimly; when he speaks now it is level, but unsparing.*)

JERRY. And one of us better not be. You don't get by, you only tell yourself lies. From day to day, sure, job to job, man to man, you get by. And nothing sticks, they take off to Tallahassee. Did you pay his train fare? (*This is a mock question, but* GITTEL's *open mouth is a real answer.*) My God, you did! You pay the freight, and every bum climbs on for a free ride. And you never know why the ride is over, do you? I'll tell you why, when a man offers you a hand up you put a donation into it. Why don't you spit in it? So they use you and walk out. How many of them have you slept with on their way through, twenty-five? (*He waits.*) Fifty? (GITTEL *only stares, now he is inexorable.*) Five hundred? It's not a lark any more, you're not a kid, you're on the edge of a nightmare, and you're all alone. Who cares, but me? Don't spit in my hand, Gittel, whether you know it or not you need it. And make one claim, one real claim on a man, he just might surprise you. (*He waits:* GITTEL *continues to stare, palely, not answering.* JERRY's *voice is hard:*) Do you get my point?

GITTEL (*shaken*). Sure. (*Then she re-*

acts, leap-frogging over her own feelings)
You're a *terrific* lawyer, what are you
bashful about?

JERRY. You didn't understand one
word I—

GITTEL. Sure I did, and if I was the jury
I'd send me up for five years, no kidding.
(*She rises, escaping toward the kitchen;*
JERRY *catches her wrists.*)

JERRY. *I'm* not kidding!

GITTEL. So what do you want? Let go
my—

JERRY. Need someone!

GITTEL. Let me go, Jerry, you're hurting—

JERRY. Need someone!

GITTEL. For what? Let go my arms or
I'll yell!

JERRY. You won't yell. Now you—

GITTEL. *Help!* (JERRY *drops her wrists.*
She stumbles away from him, tears of
pain in her eyes, and inspects her wrists.)

JERRY. You little lunatic, someone will
come.

GITTEL. Nobody'll come, it's New York.
(*But her voice is trembling as she shows*
her arm.) Look, I'm going to be all black
and blue, you big ape! I ought to get out
of here before you slug me.

JERRY. Slug you. Is that something
you've learned to expect from your ro-
mances?

GITTEL. I expect the worst! When it
comes to men I expect the worst! (*Now*
she is struggling against the tears.)
Whyn't you pick up the phone if you're
so goddam strong?

JERRY. Do you want me to?

GITTEL. I don't know where I stand
here, it's a big question mark, why should
I stick my neck out?

JERRY (*inexorably*). Do you want me
to?

GITTEL. I *will* get a job too, what's
such a crime, just—cause I—won't—(*And*
finally the tears come; helpless with sobs
she turns away, trying to keep her weep-
ing as private as she can, and failing.)

JERRY (*moved*). Gittel, I—shouldn't
have said all that—

GITTEL (*wheeling on him*). All right,
all right, I can scream my head off here
and nobody comes, who can I count on
besides me?

JERRY. Me, Gittel. (*The phone rings.*
JERRY *alone turns his eyes to it; he stands*
unmoving. GITTEL *gets her sobbing in*
hand, and waits on his decision. It rings
again, and at last she speaks.*)

GITTEL. You. Lean on you I'll fall in a
big hole in Nevada somewhere. (*She*
comes to the table to crush the cigarette,
but JERRY *stops her hand; he takes the*
cigarette from her, goes with it to the
phone, and lifts the receiver.)

JERRY. Yes? . . . Yes, speaking. . . . (*A*
pause, while the connection is made; GIT-
TEL *stands, and* JERRY *takes a much-*
needed drag. His head comes up with
the voice at the other end.) Hello, Tess.
. . . (*His own voice starts out deliberately*
casual.) No, I didn't care to talk to you
the other times, I'm doing it now by
special request. . . . What's that, woman's
intuition? . . . Yes, she is. . . . (GITTEL
now moves to clear the dishes from the
table, very quietly; she takes a stack out
to the kitchen.) Her name's Gittel . . . I
do, very much. . . . I didn't plan to be
celibate the rest of my days, wouldn't do
you any good. . . . And a year of it in
your house didn't do me any good. . . .
(*Sardonically*) Oh, I'll be glad to represent you in the divorce. If your father
will represent me, I need a good lawyer
to help take him to the cleaners. . . .
(*Now more irritable*) Oh, tell him to
stuff it up his—safe-deposit box, if I need
money I can earn it . . . I have a job, I
accepted one today. A girl, an apartment,
a job adds up to a life, I'm beginning.
. . . I have no intention of contesting
the divorce, tell Lucian he can file any
time, I'll enter a voluntary appearance.
The sooner the better . . . I'm not interested in being *friends* with you and your
fiancé, you'll have to put up with each
other. . . . (*Now through his teeth:*) Tess,
you can't sink a knife in me and hope to
leave a tender afterglow. . . . (*Watching*
him with the cigarette we see what this
conversation is coming to cost him; he
controls himself. Now weary:) Tess, are
you calling me halfway across the continent to talk about the furniture? . . . If
the house is haunted burn it, we'll split
the insurance. . . . (GITTEL *comes back in*
to clear what remains on the table. Now
shakily) I'm not unfeeling, *I* don't want
to be haunted either, my God, you made
a choice, get your hand out of my bowels!
. . . (GITTEL *stiffens at this.* JERRY *closes*
his eyes in pain.) Tess. . . . Don't. . . .
Please—plea— . . . (TESS *hangs up.* JERRY

looks at the phone, and slowly replaces it; he is drenched in sweat, and sudden tears confuse his eyes; when he lifts his hand for a prolonged drag, the cigarette is shaking. He does not look at GITTEL. *She reaches with her fingers and pinches out each of the candles; the room goes dark except for the light from the kitchen.* GITTEL *without a word lies face down on the couch, and does not stir.*) Gittel. (GITTEL *is silent.* JERRY *comes to stand above her, puts a hand on her hair; she huddles away.*) Gittel, I—

GITTEL (*suddenly*). It's not what you think!

JERRY. What isn't?

GITTEL. Larry says the Y wants six hundred and twenty-five bucks for one night, that's where we been saying we'd give it. I can't even get up sixty-five a month for a lousy loft! (*Another silence.*)

JERRY (*shakily*). No. Let's look at the snake. (*He tugs the string to the overhead bulb, and its naked light floods the room. He stands, unsteady.*) Gittel. Turn around. Please. (*She lies unmoving.*) *Look at me!* (*She rolls half around now, to face him with her eyes smouldering.*) Don't pretend. It hurts, let me see it hurts—

GITTEL. What, what?

JERRY. How I can—drown in that well. I need you.

GITTEL. For what?

JERRY. Give me something to hold onto! How do I climb out, where do I get a—foothold here, who do I work *for,* what do I build on? I'm in limbo here and I'm—shaking inside. Gittel. Need *me* for something, if it's only a lousy loft.

(GITTEL *keeps her eyes on him for a long moment; then she comes through in kind, almost inaudibly.*)

GITTEL. Sure it hurts. I'll never hear you tell me that.

JERRY. What?

GITTEL. That I got a—hand inside you.

JERRY (*a pause*). Meet me halfway.

(*Presently* GITTEL *smiles, wryly.*)

GITTEL. You mean in that loft, huh? Okay. Now put out that goddam light, will you? (JERRY *tugs it out.*) C'mere, you—French fry potato. (*He comes, she clasps him around the neck, and pulls him down upon her; and they lie in the haven, rack, forcing-bed of each other's arms.*)

SCENE TWO

Both rooms. It is several weeks later, noon, a cold December day. In both rooms the heat is now on—in GITTEL'S *from a gas heater affixed to the wall, in* JERRY'S *from a new kerosene stove in the center of the floor.*

GITTEL'S *room is empty, the door ajar.* JERRY *is in his room, lying in a spread of legs and legal papers on the couch, with the telephone receiver tucked at his shoulder, in the middle of a conversation.*

JERRY. . . . Yes. . . . Well, that was the issue in McCuller *v.* Iowa Transfer, if a claimant not the consignee enters— . . . That's right, they appealed and it was reversed. This outfit doesn't stand a Chinaman's chance of collecting out there, Mr. Taubman, I don't— . . . Hm? . . . All right: Frank. I don't think we should even consider a settlement . . . It's not going out on a limb. Though many a lawyer would have a fresh view of things from the end of a limb, I— . . . Why, thank you. . . . No, the surprise is finding myself such an expert here on Midwest jurisprudence. . . . I see what it proves, it proves an expert is a damn fool a long way from home. . . . (*The phone in* GITTEL'S *room rings.*) No, taking the Bar exam is something I need about as badly as a brain operation, what for? . . . Why should they admit me to the Bar on motion? . . . I'm familiar with the procedure, you sponsor me and I deliver a truckload of Nebraska affidavits. Maybe I can get the affidavits, I'm doubtful about the truck. . . . If it saves me taking the Bar exam why not, but why should you sponsor— . . . Full time. I see. . . . How much would you pay me?—just to keep it symbolic. . . . 6500 what, two-dollar bills? . . . Not enough, Mr.—Frank. If I'm useful to have around full time I'm worth at least 7500, and to nail me down will take eight, so we'd have to begin talking at nine. . . . (GITTEL'S *phone rings again.*) I might be very serious, I'm interested in being nailed down. . . . But not to the cross, by a Bar exam. If you'll sponsor me on motion, I'll certainly see what affidavits I can dig out of Omaha— . . .

(GITTEL *meanwhile runs in from the hall, to answer her phone; she is clad in a nondescript wrap, and we see her coun-*

tenance is adorned with a white mustache-smear and goatee-dab of bleaching cream. Her mood is listless.)

GITTEL. Yeah, hello? . . . Oh, Sophie, hiya. . . .

JERRY (glancing at wristwatch). . . . Yes, I can take a cab up. . . .

GITTEL. . . . Good thing you called, how long am I supposed to leave this stuff on? I look like a goddam Kentucky colonel here. . . .

JERRY. . . . No, I was going to bring this Wharton brief in after lunch anyway. . . .

GITTEL. . . . It itches. . . .

JERRY. . . . All right, men's grill at the St. Regis, quarter past. . . .

GITTEL. . . . What old friend? . . . Sam? . . .

JERRY. . . . Yes. See you. (He clicks down, again consults his watch, and dials.)

GITTEL. . . . What'd you tell him I'm going steady for? I mean how do you know I'm going steady if I don't know? . . . So let me shoo them off. . . . I don't know what I sound worried about, I sound worried? . . .

JERRY (busy signal). Come on, Sophie, get off that damned line. (He hangs up, and without collecting his things walks out of his flat.)

GITTEL. . . . Well, my stomach's been giving me a pain in the behind. . . . No, everything's peachy. . . . Oh, she's going to marry someone else. . . . I don't know how I get involved in such a mix-up, anyway it's not such a mix-up. . . . No, Wally was different. . . . Milton was different. . . . Which Max? . . . (She locates her mug of milk, and takes a swallow.) Look, did anybody ever buy me a loft before? . . . Yeah, he used to bring me a Mr. Goodbar, that one still owes me seventy-two bucks I'll never see again. The fact is I'm a born victim! Here I am, practically thirty years old, I'm just finding it out. . . . (JERRY returns with a fistful of mail, among which is a feminine blue envelope; it stops him. He discards the others, rips it open and reads it, troubledly.) So who's against going steady? . . . What do you think, I'm crazy? Take him home to meet Momma he'll leave New York in a balloon. . . . You don't understand—he plays golf, for instance. I never knew anybody per-

sonally played golf. . . . Oh, what do you know? . . . He's got a lot on the ball! He busts his brains all day over these briefs he's doing, then he comes down the loft and sweeps up for me, what do you think of that? . . . Sure! I made twenty-two bucks on that loft this month, and Molly's got this kids' class she's going to move in this week. . . .

(JERRY consults his watch again; he returns to the phone and dials, one digit.)

JERRY. Operator, I want to call Omaha, Nebraska, Atlantic 5756. . . .

GITTEL (dispirited). . . . Yeah, I been working on my recital. Well, trying to. . . .

JERRY. . . . Algonquin 4-6099. . . .

GITTEL. . . . It's hard to get started again after so long, you know? . . .

JERRY. . . . Call me back, please. (He hangs up, then slowly lifts the letter to his nostrils, in a faraway nostalgia.)

GITTEL. . . . Maybe I'll take up golf instead. . . . Sure he talks to her. . . . About the divorce, she won't get off the pot! . . . Sophie, I told him talk to her, he has to talk with her, what are you bending my ear about? . . . Sophie, you're getting me mad. . . . Cause you're pestering me! . . . So don't be such a friend, be an enemy and don't pester me! (She hangs up irately, and commences to dial again. Before she completes the round, JERRY's phone rings; he answers it.)

JERRY. Yes? . . . All right. . . .

GITTEL (busy signal). Oh, nuts. (She hangs up, gathers some clothes, and goes into her back room.)

JERRY. . . . Hi, Ruth, is your boss in? . . . Tell him it's his son-in-law. The retiring one. . . . Thank you, Ruth, I miss you folks too. . . . Hello, Lucian, how are you, don't answer that question. . . . (He moves the phone out from his ear.) No, I have a job, thanks, in fact I'm applying for admission to the New York Bar on motion. . . . Sure, tell Tess. She thinks the only feet I can stand on are hers. . . . I'm calling about her. I have a letter from her here, it has a St. Joe postmark. What's she doing in St. Joe? . . . (He moves the phone out from his ear.) Well, it didn't walk down there and mail itself. I've had a call in to her since Wednesday, there's nobody in the house. When did you see her, Lucian? . . . Drives where for three days? . . .

Just drives? . . . I wish you'd spend more time around her, you're better than nothing . . . I mean your idea of solicitude is a loud voice, Lucian, just talking to you on the phone is like a workout with dumbbells. . . . (*He moves the phone out from his ear.*) Money isn't enough. I have too much to say on that, though, sometime I'll call you collect. . . . She's not all right, I can smell it between the lines here. . . . What girl? . . . Of course I have a girl here, I told Tess so. . . . You mean it's since *then* she's so— . . . Devastated by what? . . . My God, Lucian, I waited for a year, a solid year, till I didn't have an ounce of self-respect left in me! One ounce, I packed with it. . . . Is that her word, abandoned? Tell me how I can abandon another man's bride, I'll come to the wedding. . . . Lucian, listen. Keep an eye on her, will you? That's all I called to say. . . . And give her my best. (GITTEL *comes out of her back room, dressed for the street.* JERRY *hangs up, collects his topcoat, hat, and brief case, consults his watch, then hurries to dial.* GITTEL *picks up her phone, commences to dial, and* JERRY *gets a busy signal.*) Oh, hell. (*He hangs up, as* GITTEL *completes dialing, and hastens out of his flat. His phone now rings once, twice, while* GITTEL *in her room stares at her phone with mounting indignation. On the third ring* JERRY *comes running back in, and grabs up his phone just in time to hear* GITTEL *addressing hers.*)

GITTEL. Ye gods, you were just there!

JERRY. I'm here.

GITTEL. Oh, Jerry!

JERRY. I called twice. Hasn't Sophie got anything better to do than to talk to you?

GITTEL. No. I called *three* times, who you been yakking with?

JERRY. I was talking to Omaha.

GITTEL. What, *again?*

(*A pause.*)

JERRY. What does that mean? I had a peculiar letter from Tess, she—

GITTEL. You ask her about the divorce?

JERRY. No. It was Lucian, I didn't get to the divorce. Tess seems sunk, her father says she—

GITTEL (*hastily*). Jerry, I'm on my way to the loft, I got to hurry, what are you calling me about?

JERRY. I thought you were calling me.

GITTEL. Who?

JERRY. Never mind. I called Lucian because I had to know what's going on out there, he says Tess has shut herself off from—

GITTEL (*interrupting*). Jerry, I got to run, you give me a ring tomorrow.

JERRY (*staring*). What about tonight?

GITTEL. It's Friday, after the loft I'm going to Momma's.

JERRY. What's special about Friday?

GITTEL. Gefüllte fish, good-bye.

JERRY (*protesting*). Hey, we had a dinner—(*But* GITTEL *hangs up.* JERRY *looks at the empty phone, his voice dying.*)—date. (*After a moment he also hangs up.* GITTEL *backs away from her phone, while* JERRY *glances at his watch; each is reluctant to leave.* GITTEL *halts,* JERRY *hesitates over his phone, both are tempted to try again; but neither does. After a melancholy moment they turn and leave, in opposite directions.*)

SCENE THREE

GITTEL's *room. It is February now, a Saturday night, late. Both rooms are dark, and the glow of the city plays in the snowy night outside the windows.*

For a moment there is no movement in either room.

Then there is the sound of a key at GITTEL's *and the door swings open.* GITTEL *is silhouetted in the doorway, alone and motionless, resting against the jamb from brow to pelvis; then she pushes away, and comes unsteadily in. There is a sprinkling of snow on her hair and overcoat. She lets her purse drop on the floor, weaves her way around the bed without light except from the hall, and in the kitchen gets herself a glass of water at the sink; she drinks it, fills another, brings it in, and sits on the bed, with head bowed in her hand. After a moment she reaches to click on the lamp, takes up her address book, and searches for a number. She dials it, and waits; when she speaks her voice is tired and tipsy.*

GITTEL. Dr. Segen there? . . . *I'm* calling, who are you? I mean are you really there or are you one of these answering nuisances? . . . So can you reach Dr. Segen for me? . . . Yeah, it's an emergency. . . . Gittel Mosca, I used to be a patient of his, will you tell him I'm very sick? . . . Canal 6-2098. . . . Thanks. (*She gets rid of the phone, and still in her overcoat, drops back onto the bed. The lamplight is in her eyes, and she puts up a fumbling hand to click it off. She lies in the dark, an arm over her face. After a second* JERRY *in topcoat and hat comes silently up, around the bannister in the hall, and into the doorway, where he stands. The snow has accumulated thickly on him. He sees* GITTEL's *purse on the floor, picks it up, sees the key still in the lock, and draws it out; it is this sound that brings* GITTEL *up on her elbow, startled, apprehensive.*) Oh! Hiya, Jerry. Where'd you blow in from? (JERRY *regards her, his manner is heavy and grim, and hers turns light.*) How was *your* party, have a good time?

JERRY. Not as good as you. Are you drunk, at least?

GITTEL (*with a giggle*). I had a couple, yeah. I had this terrible thirst all night, you know, I didn't stop to think. I mean think to stop.

(JERRY *drops the key in her purse, tosses it on the bed, and closes the door; he walks to the window, silent, where he leans against the casing, not removing his hat.*)

JERRY (*then*). Let's get it over with, who was the wrestler?

GITTEL. What wrestler?

JERRY. The fat-necked one who brought you home just now.

GITTEL. Jake? (*She sits up.*) He's not a wrestler, he's a very modern painter.

JERRY. That's why you kiss him goodnight, you're a patroness of the arts?

GITTEL (*staring*). Where were you?

JERRY. One jump behind you. In more ways than one.

GITTEL. I didn't kiss him, he kissed me. Didn't you go to Frank Taubman's party —(*She pushes herself to her feet, changes her mind, and sits again, shivering.*) Light the gas, will you, honey, I'm awful cold.

(JERRY *after a moment takes out matches, and kneels to the gas heater. When it comes on, it illuminates* GITTEL *drinking the glass of water in one gulp;* JERRY *rising sees her, and comes over to grip her wrist.*)

JERRY. You've drunk enough.

GITTEL. It's water! (JERRY *pries her fingers loose, and tastes it. He gives it back.* GITTEL *grins.*) What's the matter, you

don't trust me?

JERRY. Trust you. You were in his cellar in Bleecker Street for an hour.

GITTEL (*staring*). How do you know?

JERRY. What was he showing you, great paintings, great wrestling holds, what? (GITTEL *does not answer, and* JERRY *yanks on the lamp, sits opposite her on the bed, and turns her face into the light.*) What? (*She only reads his eyes and* JERRY *reads hers, a long moment in which she might almost cry on his shoulder, but she ends it with a rueful little snigger.*)

GITTEL. So what do you see, your fortune?

JERRY. Yours. And not one I want to see. You look trampled, is that what you're in training to be?

GITTEL (*irked*). Ye gods, I had about six drinks, you think I'm ruined for life?

JERRY. I don't mean anything so wholesome as drink. You slept with him, didn't you?

GITTEL. Whyn't you take off your hat and stay awhile? (*She pushes his hat back from his eyes, then touches his temple and cheek.*) Poor Jerry, you—

JERRY (*puts her hand down*). You slept with him.

GITTEL. You want to cry? I want to cry.

JERRY (*grimly*). Differences aren't soluble in tears, this city would be one flat mud pie. *Did* you sleep with him? (*But* GITTEL *rolls away into a pillow, her back to him.*)

GITTEL. We both know I'm dumb, whyn't you talk plain words a normal dumb person could understand?

JERRY. How plain, one syllable?

GITTEL. Yeah.

JERRY. Fine. Did he lay you? (GITTEL *lies averted in silence, her eyes open.*) I asked did he—

GITTEL. So what if he did, that's the end of the world? (*Now she does rise, to get away from him, though she is wobbly, and soon drops into a chair.* JERRY *puts his fingers to his eyes, and remains on the bed; it takes him time to come to terms with this.*)

JERRY. Maybe. Of this world. (*But he can't hold the anger in, he smacks the glass off the night table and is on his feet, bewildered and savage, to confront her.*) Why? *Why?*

GITTEL (*wearily*). What's it matter?

JERRY. It matters because I'm at a crossroads and which way I send my life pack-ing turns on you! And so are you, you want to watch *your* life float down the sewer out to sea? You care so little?

GITTEL. I don't know, I—

JERRY. For me?

GITTEL. Oh, Jerry, I—

JERRY. For yourself?

GITTEL. Myself, I got other things to worry—

JERRY. Why did you *want* to?

GITTEL. I don't *know* why! Anyway who said I did?

JERRY (*glaring at her*). You'll drive *me* to drink. *Did you or didn't you?*

GITTEL. Well, he may of slept with me, but I didn't sleep with him.

(JERRY *stares at her, tight-lipped for patience.*)

JERRY. All right, let's go back. Why did you go home with him?

GITTEL. It's a long story, I used to go with Jake two three years ago—

JERRY. Not that far back. Get to to-night.

GITTEL. So tonight I had a couple of drinks too many, I guess it was—just a case of old lang syne.

JERRY. Old lang syne—

GITTEL. *You* know.

JERRY. Yes, I'm an expert in it, espe-cially tonight. Why did you drink?

GITTEL (*bored*). You're supposed to be at the Taubman's having a good time.

JERRY. Is that why?

GITTEL. Nah, who wants to go there, for God's sake.

JERRY. I went about this trouble with the affidavits. I left as soon as I could to pick you up at Sophie's, you were just com-ing out with him, giggling like a pony.

GITTEL (*indignantly*). I was plastered, I said so, you want a *written* confession?

JERRY. You don't get plastered and flush us down the drain for no reason, and Taubman's party isn't it. I'm after the—(*She gets up wearily, again to move away from him.*) Don't walk away from me! I'm talking to you.

GITTEL. So go ahead, talk. Lawyers, boy.

JERRY. Because when something hap-pens to me *twice* I like to know why. I'm after the reason, what did I do this time, what's your complaint?

GITTEL. Who's complaining? *You* are!

JERRY. My God, I have no right?

GITTEL. Don't get off the subject.

JERRY. It's the subject, I'm talking about you and me.

GITTEL. Well, I'm talking about your wife!

(*A silence.* GITTEL *walks, rubbing her stomach with the heel of her hand.* JERRY *quiets down, then:*)

JERRY. All right, let's talk about her. She's interested in you too, I feel like an intercom. What about her?

GITTEL. I saw your last month's phone bill. Omaha Neb 9.81, Omaha Neb 12.63 —Whyn't you tell me you were the world's champion talkers?

JERRY. I like to keep in touch, Gittel, she's having a very rough time.

GITTEL. So who isn't? I got a headache, lemme alone.

JERRY. What's your case, I'm unfaith-ful to you with my wife over the phone, it's the phone bill pushes you into bed with this what's his name jerk?

GITTEL. Jake.

JERRY. Jerk! It could be you're pushing me into Grand Central for a ticket back, has that thought struck you? Is that what you want, to cut me loose? So you can try anything in pants in New York you've overlook—(*But* GITTEL *has flopped across the bed, face down, and lies still and miserable.* JERRY *contemplates her, his anger going, compassion coming, un-til he resigns himself with a sigh.*) All right. All right, it can wait till tomor-row. We'll battle it out when you're on your feet. (*He drops his hat on a chair, comes over to the bed, kneels and begins untying her shoes. This kindness sends* GITTEL *off into a misery, her shoulders quiver, and she whimpers.*)

GITTEL. Oh, Jerry—

JERRY. What's the matter?

GITTEL. You don't like me any more.

JERRY. I hate you, isn't that passion-ate enough? Turn over. (GITTEL *turns over, and he starts to unbutton her over-coat; her hands come up, his ignore them.*)

GITTEL. I can do it.

JERRY. It's a huge favor, have the grace not to, hm?

GITTEL (*desisting*). You don't hate me.

JERRY. I wouldn't say so.

GITTEL. You just feel sorry for me.

JERRY. What makes you think you're so pathetic? Pull.

GITTEL (*freeing one arm*). Ever saw

me dancing around that loft, boy, you'd think I was pathetic. I been sitting on that goddam floor so many hours I'm getting a callus, I wait for ideas to show up like I'm—*marooned* or something. So the dawn came, after all these years, you know what's wrong?

JERRY (*pausing, gently*). You're not a dancer?

GITTEL (*staring*). How'd you know?

JERRY. I didn't. I meant that loft as a help, not just to puncture a bubble.

GITTEL. So if I'm not a dancer, what am I?

JERRY. Is that why you got crocked? Turn over. (GITTEL *turns back over, and he slips the coat from her other arm and off; he begins to unbutton her blouse in back*.) Will you drink coffee if I make some?

GITTEL (*shuddering*). No.

JERRY. Or an emetic? Get the stuff off your stomach?

GITTEL. You mean vomit?

JERRY. Yes.

(GITTEL *now, breaking away from his fingers in sudden vexation, rolls up to glare at his face*.)

GITTEL. Why we always talking about my stomach? I got no other charms? (JERRY *reaches again*.) Get away! (*She pulls the still-buttoned blouse over her head, gets stuck, and struggles blindly*.)

JERRY (*compassionately*). Gittel. (*His hands come again, but when she feels them she kicks out fiercely at him*.)

GITTEL (*muffled*). I don't want your goddam favors! (*One of her kicks lands in his thigh, and stops him.* GITTEL *then yanks the blouse off with a rip, slings it anywhere, which happens to be at him, drags the coat over her head on her way down, and lies still. A silence*.)

JERRY (*then*). I'm sorry you don't. I could use it. (*He retrieves the blouse, draws the sleeves right side out, and hangs it over a chair, then stands regarding her*.) That's how you intend to sleep it off? (GITTEL *under the coat neither moves nor answers*.) Gittel? (*Again no answer*) You want me to stay or go? (*After a wait* JERRY *walks to his hat, picks it up*.) Go. (*He looks at the gas heater, pauses*.) Shall I leave the gas on? (*No response from under* GITTEL's *coat*.) Yes. You need me for anything? (*He waits*.) No. Of course not. (*Presently he* puts the lamp out, walks around the bed to the door, and opens it. But he stands. Then he bangs it shut again, throws his hat back at the chair and walks in again after it. GITTEL *then sits up to see the closed door, and gives a wail of abandonment*.)

GITTEL. Jerry—Jerry—

JERRY (*behind her*). What? (GITTEL *rolls around, to see him staring out the window*.)

GITTEL (*indignant*). What are you still here?

JERRY. I *can't* put it off till tomorrow. (*He catches up a newspaper and rolls it in his hands as he paces, grimly.* GITTEL *kneels up on the bed and regards him*.)

GITTEL. What's ailing *you*?

JERRY. I have to talk. I called home today.

GITTEL. So what'd she say for herself this time?

JERRY. I didn't talk to her. (*He paces*.) I can't get the court affidavits I need there unless I ask her father to pull strings for me. I called to ask, and couldn't get my tongue in the old groove.

GITTEL. So hooray.

JERRY. Yes, hooray. It means the Appellate Division here won't admit me, on motion. I want my day in court. I've got to get out from behind that pile of books into a courtroom, and I'm at a dead end here. With one way out, the March Bar exam.

GITTEL. So take it.

JERRY. I'm *scared*. I've been under Lucian's wing all my professional life, I'm not sure myself what's in my skull besides his coattails, if I take that exam I'm putting everything I am in the scales. If I flunk it, what?

GITTEL. What else can you do?

JERRY (*slowly*). I can live where I *am* a member of the Bar.

(GITTEL *stares at him, and neither moves; then she sits back on her heels*.)

GITTEL (*unbelieving*). You want to go back. (*The phone rings.* GITTEL *glances at it with sharp nervousness, knowing who it is, then back at* JERRY.) Go on.

JERRY. Answer it.

GITTEL. No. Go on. (*It rings again, and* JERRY *walks to it, the roll of newspaper in his hand*.) Let it ring! I won't talk to anybody. (*Her alarmed vehemence stops* JERRY, *he stares at her. The phone rings a few times throughout the following, then ceases.*)

JERRY (*sharply*). Who is it, this late, him?

GITTEL. I don't know. So you going or not?

JERRY (*angered*). Why not? I can make three times the money I earn here, to do the work I'm starved for, it tempts me and what's so tempting here, Jake? Beat my head against a Bar exam when I'm building here on what, Jake, kicks in the belly, quicksand? (GITTEL *offers no answer. He turns back to the window.* GITTEL *now digs in her purse for a bottle of banthine tablets.*)

GITTEL. What do you think *I'm* up to my neck in here, not quicksand? (*She goes out into the kitchen, where she puts on the light and sets a pot of milk up to warm;* JERRY *turns after her.*)

JERRY. All right, then tell me that! If something sticks in your throat you can't spit it out? It's so much quicker to hop in with the first gorilla you meet instead? How *dare* you treat yourself like a hand-me-down snotrag any bum can blow his nose in? (GITTEL *is shaken by this; but she avoids him and comes back in, cool as metal, unscrewing her bottle of tablets.*)

GITTEL. Okay. When?

JERRY. When what?

GITTEL. When you going?

JERRY (*heavily*). Look. Don't rush *me* off to Tallahassee. I don't turn loose so easy.

GITTEL. Well, I got to make my plans.

JERRY. What plans, now?

GITTEL (*unconcernedly*). I'll probably hook up with Jake again. He's got a lot to give a girl, if you know what I mean, you'd be surprised. (JERRY *stands like a statue,* GITTEL *with a not unmalicious twinkle gazing back at him. Then his arm leaps up with the roll of newspaper to crack her across the side of the head, it knocks her off balance and the bottle of tablets flies out of her hand in a shower; she falls on the bed.*)

JERRY (*furious*). That's not all I mean to you! *Now tell the truth, once!* (GITTEL *holds her cheek, never taking her eyes from him.* JERRY *then looks around, stoops and picks up the tablets and bottle, reads the label, sees what it is. He goes into the kitchen. He pours her milk into the*

mug, *and brings it back in. He hands her the mug, which* GITTEL *takes, still staring at his face while he weighs the tablets in his palm.*) How many?

GITTEL. Two. (JERRY *gives her two, and she swallows them with a mouthful of milk. He replaces the others in the bottle.*)

JERRY. If your stomach's bothering you, why don't you go to a doctor?

GITTEL. What do I want to go to the doctor? He tells me don't have emotions. (JERRY *screws the cap back on the bottle, tosses it on the bed, and regards her.*)

JERRY. How bad is it?

GITTEL. It's not bad!

JERRY. Did I hurt you?

GITTEL. Sure you hurt me. What do you think my head's made, out of tin? (*She waits.*) You didn't say you're sorry.

JERRY. You had it coming. Didn't you?

GITTEL. Sure.

JERRY. I'm sorry.

(GITTEL *now takes a sip of milk, holding it in both hands like a child; then she looks up at him with a grin.*)

GITTEL. You see? I said you'd slug me and you did.

JERRY. Makes you so happy I'll oblige every hour.

GITTEL (*ruefully*). Who's happy? Boy, what a smack. (*She explores her cheek, tentatively, with one palm.*) Okay, so you're *not* going! (*She eyes him cheerfully, but* JERRY *turns away from her.*)

JERRY. I didn't finish. (*He stands at the window, to gaze down at the street.*) Now the divorce plea is in, Tess is in a— tailspin. Lucian thinks she won't remarry.

(*This is worse than being hit, and* GITTEL *can only sit and stare.*)

GITTEL (*at last*). Oh, brother. You stand a chance?

JERRY. Maybe. (*But he shakes his head, suddenly wretched at the window.*) I don't know what or where I stand, what to put behind me, what's ahead, am I coming or going, so help me, I— (*He breaks it off.* GITTEL *hugs her shoulders together, she is cold; it takes her a moment to find desperation enough to try to go over the edge.*)

GITTEL. All right, Jerry, I'll tell you the truth. I— (*She looks for where to begin.*) About tonight and Jake, I—did want to go to Frank Taubman's. Only I don't fit in with your classy friends. Like she would.

(JERRY *turns and looks at her.*)

JERRY. What?

GITTEL. What do you think, I don't know? (*She is hugging herself, shivering a little as she makes herself more naked, but trying to smile.*) I mean all I am is what I am. Like Wally, he wanted me to get braces on my teeth, I said so face it, I got a couple of buck teeth, what did I keep it, such a secret? I said you got to take me the way I am, I got these teeth.

JERRY. You're a beautiful girl. Don't you know that?

GITTEL. But I'm not her. And she's all you been thinking about since the minute we met.

JERRY. No.

GITTEL. Yes. So what's Jake, a—piece of penny candy. It's like when I was a kid, we used to neck in the vestibule, she's inside you and I'm always in the vestibule! You never gave me a chance. Okay, but then you say need you. I need you, I *need* you, who has to say everything in black and white? (*She rises to confront him, pressing the heel of her hand into her stomach.*) But if you want I should of just laid down and said jump on me, no, Jerry. No. Cause I knew all the time you had it in the back of your head to—prove something to her—

JERRY. To myself.

GITTEL. To her. Everything you gave me was to show her, you couldn't wait for a goddam *letter* to get to her. So when *you*—ask *me* to—hand myself over on a platter— (*She has endeavored to be dispassionate, but now it is welling up to a huge accusatory outcry:*) For what? For *what*? What'll I *get*? Jake, I pay a penny, get a penny candy, but you, you're a—big ten-buck box and all I'll get is the cellophane! *You shortchange people, Jerry!* (JERRY *takes this indictment moveless, but rocked, staring at her.* GITTEL *hugs herself, tense, waiting till she has hold of herself.*) And that's the truth. That's what you did *this* time. (*A silence. She waits upon him, intent, still tense, so much hangs on this; while he absorbs it painfully in his entire anatomy.*)

JERRY (*then*). You mean I want a—complete surrender. And don't give one.

GITTEL. Yeah. Is that all I said?

(JERRY *closes his eyes on her.*)

JERRY. This time. And last time too. Because I shortchanged her also, didn't I?

GITTEL (*desperate*). I'm not talking about *her* now, that's exactly what I'm talking about! (*But it takes* JERRY *unhearing away from her to the bureau, averted.* GITTEL *gives up, sits, slaps her chair, and puts her head in her hands.*)

JERRY. It's true. God help me, it's true, half of me isn't in this town.

GITTEL. So I tried Jake.

JERRY. Of course.

GITTEL. Okay, a snotrag. So we're both flops.

JERRY. Both? (*And presently he nods. But when he turns his gaze to her, and takes in her forlorn figure, his eyes moisten.*) No. Not altogether. (*He comes to stand behind her; she does not lift her head.*) All these months I've been telling you one thing, infant, you live wrong. I wanted to make you over. Now I'll tell you the other thing, how you live right. (*He gazes down at her hair, moves his hand to touch it, refrains.*) You're a gift. Not a flop, a gift. Out of the blue. God knows there aren't many like you, so when he makes one it's for many poor buggers. Me among many. (*He shakes his head, slowly.*) The men don't matter. I promise you, *the men don't matter.* If they use you and walk out, they walk out with something of you, in them, that helps. Forget them, not one of them has dirtied you. Not one has possessed you, nobody's even got close. I said a beautiful girl, I didn't mean skin deep, there you're a delight. Anyone can see. And underneath is a street brawler. That some can see. But under the street brawler is something as fresh and crazy and timid as a colt, and virginal. No one's been there, not even me. And why you lock them out is—not my business. (*He finds his hat, stands with it, not looking at her now.*) What you've given me is—something I can make out with, from here on. And more. More. But what I've given you has been—What? A gift of *me*, but half of it's a fraud, and it puts you in bed with bums. That colt needs an unstinting hand, infant. Not Jake, not me. (*He walks to the door, opens it, pauses, looking for a final word, and gives it across his shoulder.*) I love your buck teeth. (*After a moment he starts out, and* GITTEL's *head comes up.* JERRY *is on the stairs when she stumbles around her chair, and cries out the doorway after him.*)

GITTEL. Jerry! Don't go! (JERRY *halts, not turning.*) The main thing *I* did in Jake's was—faint in the john. That's when I found I— (*Her voice breaks, the tremor in it is out as a sob.*) I'm bleeding, Jerry!

JERRY (*wheels on the stairs*). What!

GITTEL. It's why I was so thirsty, I'm—scared, Jerry, this time I'm scared to be bleeding—

JERRY. Gittel! (*He runs back in, to grip her up by the arms; she leans on him.*)

GITTEL. Help me, Jerry!

JERRY (*stricken*). Who's your doctor?

GITTEL. It's all right, you just got to get me to the hospital—

JERRY. *Who's your doctor?*

GITTEL. Segen. In my book, it was him calling, I didn't want you to know—

JERRY. You *lunatic.* Lie down, you—crazy, crazy—nitwit— (*He turns her to the bed, where she lies down;* JERRY *sits with her, and looks for the number in her book.*)

GITTEL (*weeping*). Jerry, don't hate my guts.

JERRY. Why didn't you *tell* me?

GITTEL. I didn't want to trap you—trap you in anything you—

JERRY. Trap me? *Trap* me?

GITTEL. I hate my goddam guts, I'm so ashamed, but don't leave—

JERRY. Oh God, shut up, you—lunatic girl—

GITTEL. Don't leave me, don't leave me—

JERRY. I'm not leaving! (*He finds the number, bends to her face on his knee.*) I'm *here,* infant. Take it easy, can't you see I'm here? (*He kisses her; then he commences to dial with his free hand,* GITTEL *pressing the other to her cheek.*)

ACT THREE

SCENE ONE

GITTEL's *room. It is March now, midday, sunny and warm.*

JERRY's *room has an unused look—the window is closed and the shade pulled*

down, *a pillow in its bare ticking lies on the couch, the curtain drawn back on the clothes-closet corner reveals chiefly empty hangers.*

In GITTEL's *room the window is open and the sunlight streams in. The furniture has been rearranged.* JERRY's *suitcase is in a corner. The sewing machine and dress dummy are gone, and in their place is a table littered with lawbooks, mimeographed sheets and syllabuses, notebooks, pencils in a jar, a desk lamp,* JERRY's *portable typewriter, a coffee cup, a dirty plate or two, a saucer full of butts. The night table by* GITTEL's *bed has become a medicine table, studded with bottles and glasses, including one of milk; a new and more expensive radio is also on it, playing softly.*

GITTEL *herself in a cotton nightgown is in bed, pale, thin, and glum. She lies with her head turned to gaze out the window. The hefty book she has been trying to read rests on her lap, her finger in it, and she is not hearing the radio, until the music stops and the announcer begins, cheerfully. What he has to say is that this is* WQXR, *the radio station of* The New York Times, *to be fully informed read* The New York Times, *and wouldn't she like to have* The New York Times *delivered every morning before breakfast so she could enjoy its worldwide coverage while sipping her coffee, join the really smart people who—*

GITTEL (*disgusted*). Aah, shut up, what do you know. (*She dials him out, and gets some music elsewhere; but she is in no mood to listen, and clicks it off altogether. She then opens the book again, and scowls with an effort of concentration over the page. But she heaves first a gloomy sigh, and next the book: it hits the floor and almost hits a flinching* JERRY, *who is opening the door with his foot, his arms laden with lawbooks and groceries, his topcoat over his shoulder, his hat back on his head.* GITTEL *brightens at once.*)

JERRY. Hold your fire, I'm unarmed!

GITTEL. Jerry, honey, I thought you'd never be home.

(JERRY *bends to kiss her, then drops his lawbooks and coat and a gift box on the table. Throughout the scene he attends to a variety of chores in an unpausing flow, without leisure really to* stop once; he is in something of a fever of good spirits. He indicates the gift box.)

JERRY. I came home a roundabout way, to bring you something from China. Though they met me more than half-way.

GITTEL. You don't have to bring presents.

JERRY. After lunch. I got in a tangle with old Kruger on this Lever contract, I have to be back by one. (He bears the groceries out to the kitchen.)

GITTEL (darkly). That's two minutes ago.

JERRY. Yes, if I hurry I'll be late. I had a great morning though, I bore down on the old barracuda and he only opened his mouth like a goldfish. All those barracudas seem to be shrinking, lately, must be the humidity. What kind of morning did you have?

GITTEL. So so.

JERRY (not approving). Just lay here?

GITTEL. I almost got up to go to the john.

JERRY. Ah, that will be the day, won't it?

GITTEL. Yeah. Be in all the newsreels. (JERRY in silence in the kitchen lights the oven, unwraps a small steak, slides it under the broiler.) I'll try for the john tomorrow, Jerry, I'm pretty wobbly.

JERRY. What do you expect the first time, to climb Mount Everest?

GITTEL (a pause). That's what they go up there for? (She gazes out the open window, while JERRY opens a can of potatoes, and dumps them in a pot to warm.) You know where I'd like to be this minute?

JERRY. In bed, or you'd be out of it.

GITTEL. Central Park. On the grass. I don't get any use out of Central Park, you know? Specially a day like this, I mean here spring isn't even here and spring is here.

(JERRY comes back in, unknotting his tie, en route to the bureau to rummage in its drawers.)

JERRY. I'll make you a proposition, will you shoot for the stairs by Friday afternoon?

GITTEL (uneasily). Why?

JERRY. I called Dr. Segen again this morning, he emphatically recommended a change of venue. I'll take you to Central Park in a cab Friday afternoon, is it a date?

GITTEL. What's Friday afternoon?

JERRY. The exam's over, I'd like to collapse in Central Park myself. Be down to get you in a taxi, honey, straight from the Bar exam. Date?

GITTEL (evading it). One thing I'll be glad when that exam's over, maybe you'll stop running long enough to say hello.

JERRY (obliges, with a smile). Hello. Date?

GITTEL (scowling). I just sit on the edge here, I feel like my stomach's a—cracked egg or something. I don't want any more leaks.

(JERRY gives her a severe eye while he hangs his jacket over a chair and takes a batch of mail out of its pocket.)

JERRY. Doctor says if you don't get out of bed this week all your blood will rust. I really couldn't afford that hello, I didn't have a minute yet to look into who's writing me what here. (He hurries through the envelopes, discarding them one by one onto the bed.) Harper's wants me to buy their complete works, haven't time to read why. Hospital bill, ouch. Smoke it after dinner, on the gas stove. Clerk of the District Court, Omaha— (But this one stops him short. He carries it away from her, rips it open, unfolds a legal document, in blue backing distinctive enough to be remembered later, and stares at it.)

GITTEL. Anything?

JERRY (a silence). Legal stuff. Coming out of my ears these days, I— (He finds it difficult to lift his eyes from it, it takes him an effort, but he drops document and envelope on the table and gets back into stride.) Here, before I forget. (From his jacket he brings a check out and over to GITTEL.) I let Molly's class in the loft, she gave me a check for you. She'll leave the key over the door, I'll pick it up before cram-school.

GITTEL. Gee, Jerry, you shouldn't take time. (She takes his hand as well as the check, and puts her cheek to it.) You're okay.

JERRY. It's your money I'm after, infant.

GITTEL (brightly). Yeah, it pays to be a big fat capitalist, huh? Lay here, it just rolls in.

JERRY (stooping). And this rolls out.

Get up today or forever hold your peas. (*He comes up with a bedpan from under the bed, and bears it into the back room, while* GITTEL *stares.*)

GITTEL. Hey, what's the—My God, I lost a quart of blood!

JERRY. I bought you three pints, that's a handsome enough profit. Capitalists who aren't satisfied with fifty per cent end up in the federal hoosegow. (*On his way back he picks up the book and a mimeographed exam sheet that has fallen out of it.*) What are you doing with this exam, boning up for me?

GITTEL. Just looking.

JERRY (*scanning*). '53, I'll have to go through this one tonight. (*He drops the novel and exam sheet back on the bed, strips to the waist, now at last removes his hat and sets it on the desk lamp, and collects the dirty plates and saucer of butts, while* GITTEL *watches him.*)

GITTEL. When you going to get some sleep? You're getting skinny!

JERRY. Muscle, I'm all muscle these days. And that reminds me, if you don't get off your rear end soon I'll be advertising in the Sunbathers Gazette for one that works. (*He bears the plates into the kitchen, where he next opens the oven and turns the steak over.*)

GITTEL (*scowling*). Mine works.

JERRY. Unemployed. You think unemployed insurance can go on in perpetuity? (*This is only kidding, while he proceeds to splash water into his face at the sink; but* GITTEL *staring into the future is so despondent she has to shake it off.*)

GITTEL. So when have you got any time, *now?*

JERRY. Three-thirty Friday after the battle, mother. Date?

GITTEL. In Central Park?

JERRY (*not hearing*). And at your service, from then on in.

GITTEL (*glumly*). For how long?

JERRY. Hey?

GITTEL. I said for how long.

JERRY. Can't hear you. (*He turns off the water and comes in, drying his face with a towel.*) Hm?

GITTEL. I said I love you. (JERRY *stands absolutely still for a long moment. Then* GITTEL *lowers her eyes.*) Hell, I don't have to say it, do I? You know it.

JERRY (*gently*). Yes.

GITTEL. I'll try not to say it too often.

Twice a week.

JERRY. You can't say it too often, it's part of my new muscle.

GITTEL. Maybe getting sick was the biggest favor I ever did you, huh?

JERRY. I think we can manage without. The big favor is to get back on your feet, Gittel. (GITTEL'S *eyes are down.* JERRY *glances at his watch, bends to kiss her cheek, and crosses to the bureau.*)

GITTEL (*low*). What's the percentage?

(JERRY *opening a drawer frowns. He then takes out a laundered shirt, removes the cardboard, and slips into the shirt.*)

JERRY. The percentage is one hundred.

GITTEL. I don't mean to get better, I mean—

JERRY. I know what you mean. When I said I'd like to look out for you what do you think *I* meant, a thirty-day option? (*Buttoning his shirt he goes back into the kitchen, where he turns the potatoes off and puts a plate in the oven to warm.*) You ready for lunch?

GITTEL. You eat already?

JERRY. I'll take a sandwich into the office. You wouldn't care to spring to your feet and run around the plate three times, work up an appetite? (*He waits on her in the doorway; she does not meet his eyes.*)

GITTEL. I got an appetite.

JERRY. A hm. (*Presently he turns back into the kitchen, where he prepares a tray—tumbler of milk, paper napkin, silverware, and the meal on a plate.*)

GITTEL. You ought to have more than a sandwich, Jerry, you get sick too we'll really be up the goddam creek. Get a malted, too, huh? And tell him make it a guggle-muggle while he's at it.

JERRY. A what?

GITTEL. It's with a beat-up egg. I mean two whole days of exam, you got to keep your strength up for those cruds.

(JERRY *brings in the tray, and places it on her lap in bed.*)

JERRY. The condemned man ate a hearty guggle-muggle and lived another thirty-four years. I don't intend to get sick, infant, even to get you up. (*He collects papers and books on the table, slipping them into his brief case, and pauses over the legal document he has dropped there; he takes it up, and with his back to* GITTEL *reads it again, grimly.*)

GITTEL. Jerry.

JERRY. Yes.

GITTEL (*painfully*). I'm not just taking advantage, you know, I'm—I mean since you been living here I'm—Nobody ever took care of me so good, it sort of weakens your will power, you know? (JERRY *looks over his shoulder at her, then back at the document; he is deliberating between them.*)

JERRY. Strengthens mine.

GITTEL. I mean I'm kind of in the habit of—seeing your neckties around, now. I'll miss them.

(*A silence,* JERRY *weighing the document and something else, much heavier, in himself.*)

JERRY (*then*). Why do you think I'm taking this Bar exam, you boob, to lift legal dumbbells? I intend to live here, work here, be used. Lot of my life I've been cold from being unused.

GITTEL. I'm scared of afterwards, Jerry.

JERRY. What's afterwards?

GITTEL. I get up out of here, all the goddam neckties go back to your place. I'm scared to—live alone, again. Now.

(JERRY *stands for a long moment with the document. Then abruptly and decisively he wads it into his briefcase, sits, thrusts books and papers away to clear space, and writes.*)

JERRY. Eat your lunch.

(GITTEL *obeys, for a mouthful or two, but watches him perplexedly.*)

GITTEL. What are you writing?

JERRY. A promissory note. I promise you, conversation at meals. (*When he is finished he folds the paper; standing, he takes up the gift box.*) And other items, less elevating. (*He lifts out a Chinese bed jacket of brocaded silk.* GITTEL *drops her fork.*)

GITTEL. Hey! That's *beautiful*, what is it?

JERRY. Something to remember me by, till six o'clock.

GITTEL. A bed jacket! Ye gods, I'll never get up. (*She wiggles her fingers for it, but* JERRY *holds up the folded paper.*)

JERRY. This is a letter to my landlord. (*He slips it into the pocket of the bed jacket.*) For *you* to mail. By hand.

GITTEL. Huh?

JERRY. At the corner. As soon as you're on your feet to make it down there.

GITTEL. Why, what's it say? (*Her eyes widen.*) Get a new tenant! Huh?

JERRY. See for yourself.

GITTEL. You'll move the neckties in for keeps?

JERRY. See for yourself. (*From across the room he holds the bed jacket ready for her, the letter poking out prominently.*)

GITTEL (*reproachfully*). Jerry.

JERRY. Come and get it.

GITTEL (*reproachfully*). Jerry, I got to be on my feet to get you?

JERRY. Maybe. Better find out, hm? (GITTEL *shakes her head.*) Is it so out of the question that I want to keep the goddam neckties here? Come on. (GITTEL *just gazes at him, her eyes moist.*) Come. Come and get it.

(GITTEL *puts the tray aside, moves her legs to the edge, and sits still.*) Come on, honey. (GITTEL *stands, unsteady for a moment, then moves toward him, afraid of her belly, afraid of her legs, the progress of someone who hasn't walked in a month; but she gets to him and the letter, unfolds it, and reads.*)

GITTEL. You're giving up your flat.

JERRY. Save rent.

GITTEL (*a pause*). You're really ruining me, Jerry! (*She keeps her face averted, on the verge of tears.*) I didn't use to be a —bitch of a—lousy blackmailer. (*Another pause.*) And I'm not going to be either! Enough is enough! (*And with sudden resolution she tears the letter into pieces.*)

JERRY (*equably*). That's how you waste forest resources? Now I'll have to write another.

GITTEL. Not unless you want to!

JERRY. I want to. (*His arms wrap her in the bed jacket, and hold her. He kisses her, studies her eyes; she searches his. Then he glances at his watch, pats her cheek, and reaches for his brief case.*) Don't overdo a good thing. Lie down soon. Chew your lunch before swallowing. Take your medicine. Don't tackle the stairs alone. Button up your overcoat, you belong to me. (*He is on his way to the door, when her small voice stops him.*)

GITTEL. Jerry. I do. You know I do, now?

JERRY. Yes. I know that, infant.

GITTEL. I love you. (JERRY *stands inarticulate, until she releases him:*) That's twice, there, I used up the whole week!

JERRY (*lightly*). I may need to hear it

again before that Bar exam. For muscle.

GITTEL. You'll pass.

JERRY. Hell, I'll blow all the answers out of my brilliant nose. (*He blows her a kiss and is out the door, gone, leaving her on her feet in the room, shaking her head after him, in her Chinese silk, like a rainbow, half radiance, half tears. She fingers his coat, sits, and brings it to her face; she is much troubled.*)

SCENE TWO

JERRY's *room. It is May, almost summer now, a hot muggy dusk, and eight months since this affair began. Once again the windows of both rooms are open—*JERRY's *from the top—and the sounds of traffic float in.*

In GITTEL's *room the only change is that the table is cleared of all* JERRY's *exam preparations, the night table is cleared of medicines, the bed is made.*

JERRY's *flat however is a shambles. Packing is in progress, nothing is in its place, cartons stand here and there. In the kitchen* JERRY *in his shirt sleeves is slowly wrapping dishware in newspaper; in the living room* GITTEL—*barefoot and back to normal, but with a stratum of gloom underneath—is folding linens into a carton. This separate activity goes on for an interval of silence, until* JERRY *calls in; his voice is rather dispirited, and so is hers.*

JERRY. What about these pots, honey? You want them packed separate?

GITTEL. Separate from what?

JERRY. Dishes.

GITTEL. Guess so. I mean, sure. (*They go back to packing in silence. Both are sweaty with the prosaic drudgery of packing, and depressed, but neither is admitting this; there is an atmosphere of something being avoided. Then* GITTEL *stands on a chair to take down the clothes-closet curtain, and in the process jogs one support of the rod with its remaining clothes; it falls.* GITTEL *grabs it.*) Help! (JERRY *drops what he is doing, and comes at once, on the run.*)

JERRY. What's wrong?

GITTEL. This cruddy pole. S'all.

JERRY (*relieved*). Oh, I thought you— (*He stops himself, takes the rod and clothes off her hands, and lays them on the couch.*) Never did get around to fixing that thing permanently. Guess I never believed it was permanent, all it takes is two screws and a—(*He becomes aware of her eyes moody on him.*) Hm?

GITTEL. Nothing. (*They gaze at each other a moment, something unsaid between them. Then* JERRY *grips her at the waist, and lifts her down.*)

JERRY. You stay on the ground, squirrel.

GITTEL (*irked*). Why?

JERRY. Because I've climbed Long's Peak four times. I'm used to these rare altitudes. (*He climbs the chair, and begins to unhook the curtain.*)

GITTEL. What'd you think, I was doing a nose dive? No such luck.

JERRY (*another gaze*). What kind of cheery remark is that?

GITTEL. I mean *bad* luck.

JERRY. Oh. I thought you meant good bad luck.

GITTEL. What's Long's Peak?

JERRY. Mountain. Front Range, Colorado. Fourteen thousand feet, up on all fours, down on all fives.

GITTEL (*a pause*). I been up the Empire State nineteen times, so what?

(JERRY *smiles, shakes his head, and turns to hand her the curtain.*)

JERRY. Here. (*But* GITTEL *is on her way out to the kitchen, in a mood.* JERRY *stares, tosses the curtain onto the couch mattress, bare in its ticking, and considers the window drapes.*) You want this other one down?

GITTEL (*out of sight*). What other one?

JERRY. Window curtain.

GITTEL. D'you want it down?

JERRY (*puzzled*). Yes, I want it down.

GITTEL. So take it down!

JERRY (*frowning*). What's eating you?

GITTEL. A banana!

JERRY. What?

GITTEL. A banana. (*She comes in again, eating a banana.*) Want a bite?

JERRY. I said, what's eating *you.* (*He moves the chair to the window, gets up again, and works on the burlap drapes.*)

GITTEL. Oh, *me.* What's eating *you.*

JERRY. I asked you first.

GITTEL. I mean what's eating me is figuring out what's eating you.

JERRY. I see. Well, what's eating me is figuring out what's eating you. Which just about exhausts that investigation. Be altogether fruitless except for the banana.

Want these brackets too? (GITTEL *not re-plying bites at the banana, and* JERRY *looks from the brackets down to her.*) Hm?

GITTEL. *I* don't want a goddam thing. D'*you* want them?

JERRY (*a pause*). Correction. Do *we* want them?

GITTEL. We sure do. Cost good money, can always use them.

JERRY. That's right, ten cents a pair. I'll get a screwdriver. (*He comes down, to head for the kitchen.*)

GITTEL. So then don't!

JERRY. I mean what do we need *all* this junk for? We have your curtains there, we're not going to—

GITTEL. What junk? (*She is handling the drapes, pinches up a piece.*) That's good stuff, forty-seven cents a yard reduced, I could make eleven different things out of it.

JERRY. Name ten.

GITTEL. Anything. Bedspread, cushions, pocketbook, I was even thinking I'd make you some neckties.

JERRY (*very dubious*). Well.

GITTEL. You don't want?

JERRY. I just don't see myself appearing in court in a red burlap necktie. (*He goes into the kitchen.* GITTEL *takes up the banana again for a last bite, slings the peel straight across the room out the open window, and sits gloomily on the couch.* JERRY *returning with the screwdriver studies her as he passes.*) Maybe we ought to knock off for tonight, infant. You look tired.

GITTEL (*testily*). I'm not tired!

JERRY. Then why so down?

GITTEL. *Who's* down? I'm in sixth heaven! (JERRY *stops to eye her before mounting the chair.*) Just don't rush to the rescue. You're killing me with kindness. (JERRY *after a moment plunges the screwdriver by the handle straight into the chair, and lets it stand;* GITTEL's *eyes widen. But* JERRY *shows no further vehemence, and when he speaks it is calmly enough.*)

JERRY. That's in exchange for all the little needles.

GITTEL (*sullen*). I'm sorry.

JERRY. We're supposed to be joyfully packing to be together. Why act as though—

GITTEL. Nobody around here's *enjoying* this. Every frigging towel I put in that box I feel worse.

JERRY (*dryly*). It's a chore, who likes to break up a happy home? (*He fishes in his shirt pocket for cigarettes.*) Though in a peculiar way it has been. I won't forget *this* first-aid station in a hurry.

GITTEL. There's always the next one.

JERRY. What next one?

GITTEL. The one we're fixing up for me. (JERRY *looks at her, lights the cigarette, and to avoid the topic mounts the chair again with the screwdriver.* GITTEL *takes a fresh breath and dives in, very brightly.*) Look, Jerry, whyn't we just, sort of, get married and get the goddam thing over with, huh?

(JERRY *half-turns, to gaze at her over his shoulder.*)

JERRY. Bigamy? Big of you, I mean, I have one wife now.

GITTEL. I mean *after* the divorce. I'm not going to be just a ball and chain, now you passed that Bar exam you know the first thing I'm going to do? Take up shorthand!

JERRY. Shorthand is the one thing this romance has lacked from the beginning.

GITTEL. So when you open your law office, there I am! A goddam secretary, you're really going to save dough on me. And soon as I make enough out of that loft I'm going to fix up the flat for us, real nice.

JERRY. It's real nice.

GITTEL. Stinks.

JERRY. What stinks about it?

GITTEL. It's a dump, you think I don't know that? My God, how can you entertain somebody a cockroach committee comes out of the sink to see who's here? Hasn't been an exterminator in there since Babe Ruth.

JERRY. Who are we exterminating?

GITTEL. Huh?

JERRY. I meant to say entertaining.

GITTEL. Well, anybody you need to. Customers! Partners, the Taubmans, maybe *criminals,* you don't know who yet, but you can't have a dump for them. Can you?

JERRY (*a pause*). No. I couldn't think of representing some dope addict who'd just murdered his mother and have him see a cockroach. Here's the brackets. (*But* GITTEL *is folding the drapes to put in the carton, and he steps down with them.*)

GITTEL. Who knows, maybe later on we'll move to a real apartment house even. You know one thing I always wanted to live in a house with?

JERRY. Me?

GITTEL. An elevator! With an elevator you can invite anybody.

(JERRY *drops the brackets in her purse, next to her little radio. The radio stops him, he contemplates it, rubs it with his thumb, and then finds* GITTEL'S *eye on him.*)

JERRY (*smiles*). Remembering the day you left this at the door. We kept each other company many a wee hour, I hate to see it end up all alone in some closet.

GITTEL. Nah, we'll use it.

JERRY (*mildly*). If you have in mind plastic neckties, they're also out. I have room for it in with the pots. (*He takes the radio out into the kitchen.* GITTEL *on her knees begins on another carton, loading in books, papers, a miscellany.*)

GITTEL (*calling out*). What about this stuff, Jerry, bills? Gas, phone—

JERRY (*out of sight*). Leave them out where I'll see them, I don't think I paid those yet.

GITTEL (*discarding them*). What do you want to pay them, all they can do is shut it off if you do or you don't. Letters—(*She unfolds one, on feminine blue stationery.*) "Jerry dearest, I—" Whoops. (*She shuts in a hurry, not reading it, but as she puts it away she comes to a legal document in blue backing that tickles her memory: the last time she saw it was in her room, in* JERRY'S *hands. She reads, frowning, her lips moving at first soundlessly, then becoming audible.*) "—although the plaintiff has conducted herself as a true and faithful wife to the defendant, the said defendant has been guilty. Of acts of cruelty toward the plaintiff, destroying the—" (*Now* JERRY *is standing in the doorway, a cup in his hand.*) "—peace of mind of the plaintiff and the objects of—matrimony. It is hereby ordered, adjudged—"

(JERRY *completes it from memory.*)

JERRY (*slowly*). —and decreed by the Court that the bonds of matrimony heretofore existing are severed and held for naught. And that the said plaintiff is granted an absolute divorce from the defendant. Unquote.

(*A silence*)

GITTEL. So why didn't you tell me, Jerry.

JERRY (*a pause*). I had to live with it. A while longer. Digest it. Let it grow out with my fingernails, till I was—rid of it.

(*Another pause*)

GITTEL. You didn't want me to know.

JERRY. Not till I was—on top of it. Do you know what the sense of never is? Never again, not even once? Never is a deep hole, it takes time to—close over.

GITTEL. Then what'll you do?

JERRY. Then?

GITTEL. Yeah. Then.

JERRY (*a pause, gently*). I think I'll do one thing at a time.

GITTEL. What?

JERRY. Pack this cup. (*He comes to the carton with it, kneeling near her.*)

GITTEL. You sonofabitch. (JERRY *wheels on his knee to confront her.*) You tell her about *me*? That you moved in?

JERRY (*whitely*). Yes.

GITTEL. Because I had a hemorrhage?

JERRY. I'm *not* a sonofabitch—

GITTEL. *Did you tell her I had a hemorrhage?*

JERRY. Yes.

GITTEL. And you didn't tell me about this (*She slings the decree straight into his face.* JERRY *squats, rigid.* GITTEL *then scrambles up and makes for her shoes.* JERRY *rising slams the cup into the carton of crockery.*) Smash them all, who needs them?

JERRY. What are you off on this time?

GITTEL. I'm getting out of here, you— you goddam—(*But the grief breaks through, and she wails to him out of loss:*) Jerry, *why* didn't you *tell* me?

JERRY. I couldn't.

(GITTEL *gazing at him takes this in; then she finishes putting her shoes on, and makes a beeline for her bag.*)

GITTEL. Yeah. You only tell her about me. My God, even when you *divorce* her it's a secret you have with her! One of these days you'll marry me, she'll know it and I won't! (*But when she turns to the doorway,* JERRY *is planted in it, blocking her.*)

JERRY. You're not leaving.

GITTEL. Jerry, look out!

JERRY. Sit down.

GITTEL. You look out or I'll let you

have it, Jerry!

JERRY. Go ahead, street brawler. (GITTEL *slaps him across the face, he is unmoving; she slaps him again backhand, he is like a statue; she then wheels looking for a weapon, comes up from the carton with the broken cup, and charges his face, but hesitates.* JERRY *stands moveless, waiting.*) Do. I'll beat your behind off. (GITTEL *flinging the cup past him throws herself averted on the couch, tearful with rage.*)

GITTEL. Sonofabitch, all my life I never yet could beat up one goddam man, it's just *no* fair!

JERRY. Why do you think I told her about the hemorrhage?

GITTEL. To prove something to her on *me,* now.

JERRY. Like what?

GITTEL. How you're so wonderful, looking after me, you don't need her help.

JERRY. I told her because she asked *my* help. She wants me home.

(GITTEL *rolls over, to stare at him.*)

GITTEL. She does.

JERRY. When at last she really needs me, and I'm enough my own man to help, I had to say no. And why.

GITTEL (*a deep breath*). Okay, Jerry. You said make a claim, right?

JERRY. Yes.

GITTEL. So I'm going to make it.

JERRY. All right.

GITTEL. I want you here. I want *all* of you here. I don't want half a hunk of you, I want—I mean it's—(*With difficulty.*) It's leap year, Jerry, tell the truth. *Would* you—ever say—I love you? Once.

JERRY (*pained*). It's a lifetime promise, infant, I've only said it once. (*But the moment he turns again to the kitchen, her voice rises after him:*)

GITTEL. Jerry, Jerry, give me a break, will you? Don't kid me along. Is that a friend? (*This word nails him, he turns back with his eyes moist.*) I'll tell you straight, you move in I just—won't give up on you marrying me. You—you let me have it straight, too. (*He stands, gazing at her.*) Jerry, you my friend?

JERRY (*finally*). I'm your friend. Here it is, straight. You say love, I think you mean *in* love. I mean so much more by that word now—

GITTEL. I mean wanting. Somebody. So bad—

JERRY. Not wanting. Love is having, having had, having had so—deeply, daily, year in and out, that a man and woman exchange—guts, minds, memories, exchange—eyes. Love is seeing through the other's eyes. So because she likes bridges I never see a bridge here without grief, that her eyes are not looking. A hundred things like that. Not simply friend, some ways my mortal enemy, but *wife,* and ingrown. (*He looks down at the decree.*) What *could* I tell you about this—piece of paper, that the bonds of matrimony are *not* severed? Why would I—love my right hand, if I lost it? That's what love is. To me, now.

(GITTEL *keeps her eyes on him for a long moment, then she closes them.*)

GITTEL. You ever tell her that?

JERRY. No. I should have told her years ago. I didn't know it then.

(GITTEL *rolls up; she climbs the chair at the window and hangs gazing out, to find her way through this.*)

GITTEL. You'll never marry me, Jerry.

JERRY. I can't, infant.

GITTEL. So what kind of competition can I give her, have a hemorrhage twice a year? Trap you that way, be *more* of a cripple, one month to another? Get half of you by being a wreck on your hands, will that keep you around?

JERRY. As long as you need me, I'll be around.

(GITTEL *turns on the chair, staring at him, as it dawns on her.*)

GITTEL. And you'll move in. Even now.

JERRY. What's in me to give, without shortchanging, I'll give—

GITTEL. My God, *I'm* in a goddam trap! (*A pause; then* JERRY *nods.*) You're one, all right, I could—lose a leg or something in you.

JERRY. Yes, you could lose—a lot of time. You're a growing girl, and of the two things I really want, one is to see you grow. And bear your fruit.

GITTEL. And the other is—

JERRY. Tess.

GITTEL. Jerry, Jerry, Jerry. (*She regards him, her eyes blinking; this is hard to say.*) I don't *want* the short end. I want somebody'll—say to me what you just said about her. (*She gets down, retrieving her bag, and stands not looking at him.*) What do you say we—give each other the gate, huh, Jerry? (*She moves to pass him in the doorway; but he stops her, to take her face between his palms, and search her eyes.*)

JERRY. For whose sake?

GITTEL. Jerry, I haven't taken one happy breath since that hemorrhage. I want to get out of here and *breathe. (After a moment* JERRY *lets her go. She brushes quickly past him, through the kitchen and out of the flat. He turns in the doorway, looking after her, with his hands up on the jambs, unmoving as the lights dim.*)

SCENE THREE

Both rooms. It is a few days later, a gray afternoon.

JERRY's *room is cleaned out, altogether bare except for his suitcase and portable typewriter standing there, and the phone on the floor near them.* JERRY *is not in sight, though we may hear him in the kitchen.*

GITTEL *is in her room, taking the dance photos of herself down from the wall. She is engaged in this without feeling, almost without awareness; it is something to do while she waits. What she is waiting for is the phone, as we see from her eyes. She takes the photos to her night table and drops them in a drawer, then walks nervously round and round her room, eyeing her alarm clock, eyeing her phone.*

Meanwhile a match has been lighted in JERRY's *dark kitchen,* JERRY *making a last survey of it. When he comes in, he is in street clothes and hat; he is shaking the match out, his other arm cradles a few last toilet articles, shaving cream, brush, razor. He kneels at the typewriter case, and fits these articles carefully in. Then he consults his wrist watch. He stands over the phone a heavy moment, picks it up, and dials.*

The phone in GITTEL's *room rings, and she flies to sit on her bed.*

GITTEL. Yeah, hello?

JERRY (*a pause*). Honey, I'm—all packed here, I—

GITTEL (*softly*). Hiya, Jerry.

JERRY (*a pause*). Some cartons of—odds and ends in the kitchen here, the key will be with the janitor. If you want anything.

GITTEL. I won't want anything.

JERRY. If you do. (*A pause*) Look, if you do, I mean anything—important, Gittel, I'm at the Commodore Hotel in Lincoln, I don't have the number, long-distance will give it to you. Lincoln, Nebraska. *Not* Nevada.

GITTEL. Not Nevada.

JERRY. And not Omaha, I'm not walking back into that mistake, ever again. As soon as I get an office and a phone I'll send you the number. Now if you—if you need anything in a hurry, I mean instantly, will you call Frank Taubman? You won't have to explain anything, it's taken care of, just call him.

GITTEL (*a pause*). Yeah.

JERRY. No. Promise.

GITTEL. I promise. (*A pause*) Jerry, I'm all right now. You just—you just get what you want out there, huh?

JERRY. I'll try. It's back to the wars. My terms are steep, I won't work for Lucian, I won't live in Omaha, and all we'll have is what I earn. I'm beginning very—modestly, a desk and a phone and a pencil. And what's in my head.

GITTEL. It's a lot.

JERRY. But I won't shortchange her. It has to be a new deal, on both sides.

GITTEL. I'm rooting for you, Jerry.

JERRY. No backsliding. By you either, Gittel, don't you give up either, hm?

GITTEL. Oh, I don't! I bounce up, like a —jack in the box, you know?

JERRY. I'm rooting for you, too. It's a big city and you're the salt of the earth, just don't waste it, he's around some corner. You'll find him.

GITTEL. I'm looking. I got a better opinion of myself now, I'm going to propose more often. I'll send you a birthday card now and then, huh?

JERRY. Now and then.

GITTEL. Twice a week!

(JERRY *pinches his eyes, he is shaky.*)

JERRY. Gittel. What am I doing, I— moments here I think I—

GITTEL. You're doing right, Jerry. I mean *I* don't want any handouts either, you know? That's no favor.

JERRY. If I know anything I know that.

GITTEL. And I'm not going to be just giving them out, from now on. I want somebody'll take care of me who's all mine. You taught me that. And nobody like Sam or Jake, between them they couldn't take care of a chiclet. I mean, things look a lot different to me, Jerry, you did me a world of good.

JERRY. Did I really? Golly, if I could think each of us—helped somehow, helped a bit—

GITTEL. You been a great help, Jerry, it's the first affair I—come out with more than I went in. I mean, wherever this guy is, he'll owe you!

JERRY (*a pause, humbly*). Thank you for that. And she'll owe you more than she'll know. After—(*He tries to recall it.*) After the verb to love, to help is—

GITTEL (*a pause*). What, Jerry?

JERRY. —the sweetest in the tongue. Somebody said it. Well. (*He looks at his watch.*) Well. So long, infant.

(GITTEL *tries to say it, but her eyes are full, her heart is in her mouth, and she struggles to keep it from overflowing there; she cannot.*)

GITTEL. *I love you, Jerry!* (JERRY *is rigid; it takes her a moment to go on.*) Long as you *live* I want you to remember the last thing you heard out of me was I love you!

JERRY (*long pause*). I love you too, Gittel. (*He hangs up, and for a moment there is no movement.*

Then JERRY *puts the phone down, and lights himself a cigarette; his first drag tells us how much he needs it. After another, he kneels again, shuts the typewriter case, stands with it and the suitcase in either hand, and gives the room a final check.*

GITTEL *meanwhile has not hung up; she clicks down, then rapidly dials again. But the minute it rings once, she claps the phone down.*

JERRY *is on his way out with typewriter and suitcase when the single ring comes. He stops, not putting either down, just staring at the phone for a long minute.* GITTEL *sits, head high, eyes closed. Neither moves.*

Then GITTEL *takes her hand off the phone. And* JERRY *turns, and walks out of his flat.*)

MARY, MARY

Jean Kerr

Presented by Roger L. Stevens in
association with Lyn Austin, at the
Helen Hayes Theatre in New York on
March 8, 1961, with the following cast:

BOB MC KELLAWAY Barry Nelson   OSCAR NELSON John Cromwell
MARY MC KELLAWAY Barbara Bel Geddes   DIRK WINSTON Michael Rennie
TIFFANY RICHARDS Betsy von Furstenberg

ACT ONE: A Saturday morning in winter.
ACT TWO: Saturday night, late.
ACT THREE: Sunday morning.

Directed by Joseph Anthony
Designed by Oliver Smith
Costumes by Theoni V. Aldridge
Lighting by Peggy Clark

THE dangers of *Mary, Mary* when exposed to critics who look upon Broadway as a den of middlebrow and middle-aged iniquity (and they have at least the warrant of zeal for their acerbity) are twofold. Mrs. Kerr's play proved to be vastly successful with the public, therefore had to be iniquitous! At the same time, it invited suspicion of soap-opera problematics, which is what it could become when viewed with the interest of marriage-counselors; after all, wasn't there a marriage to be repaired? A large, earnestly-put question rated a headline over a picture-story in *Life* magazine, which read "Can Witty Women Win in Love?" Whatever problem this may pose in the American home (and it doesn't seem much of a problem so long as wit seems in short supply in most American households), it poses another one in the American theatre. How can a notion ideal for a skit in a sophisticated revue be expanded into a full-length play? Fortunately Mrs. Kerr has enough zest for herself and her characters, too—even for the understandably irritated husband who complains that his wife has been wifely only "on and off—between jokes." Fortunately, too, Mrs. Jean Kerr, who is the tempered mother of five sons, has too much tartness to be trapped into a soap-opera even if she is concerned with domestic relations and can create winning characters who need only to be tenderized a little to be devoured by the hucksters.

At one time four companies grossing $162,247 in a single week were presenting her comedy to the American public, for which we can only hope she will be forgiven. No one in show business has repaired a broken marriage with less ostentation and with less expenditure of concern. In Mrs. Kerr's case this is doubly commendable since she did not altogether invent her heroine but based her upon observation. "I am not very inventive," she told Henry Hewes of the *Saturday Review*, ". . . almost everything I write is only a slightly exaggerated version of something I have observed." So far as subject and plot are concerned, she wasn't particularly original either in *Mary, Mary*, but she was able to give almost everything in it the high polish without which there can be no high comedy. *Mary, Mary* is an exceptionally well written and well organized example of this vanishing commodity.

Jean Kerr, who is Mrs. Walter Kerr in private life, can be claimed for the publishing trade as well as the stage. She was until the success of *Mary, Mary* best known as the author of the popular and extremely amusing books *Please Don't Eat the Daisies* and *The Snake Has All the Lines*. Mrs. Kerr is a natural-born writer and a master (should one say mistress?) of feminine wit, in which a tolerant understanding of human foibles is a large part. Inevitably attracted to the stage and involved in the donnybrook known as the professional or commercial theatre, she did not confine her writing to the library. She wrote sketches for a revue (*Touch and Go*) and the book for the musical *Goldilocks* with Walter Kerr, and collaborated with Eleanor Brooke on *King of Hearts*. This comedy, which opened at the Lyceum Theatre on April 1, 1954, profitably deflated an inflated public character, and scored a Broadway run of 279 performances. *Mary, Mary* was not of course received without qualification, even by its friends. Louis Kronenberger, who took pleasure in the play, referred not unkindly to the "thin ice of the narrative" on which the play skated, and more reservedly only to "the too thick icing of its bon-mots." But its appeal to the playgoing public in New York and in other cities continued to be unmistakable.

SETTING. *The action takes place in* BOB MC KELLAWAY's *living room, which is also an office away from the office, in a New York apartment building. The place is well kept, and obviously belongs to a man of taste and intelligence, but it is neither chic nor overly expensive. When the lights are lowered, it has a cozy, domestic feel to it, as though it had already been shared with a woman, though* BOB *is a bachelor at the moment and has let his homework rather overrun the place. He is a publisher by profession, heading his own small company, and he has a cluttered desk at one side of the room. Otherwise the customary sofa, chairs, liquor cabinet, bookshelves, a fish tank, and so on. There are entrances to five other areas: a main door to the outside corridor, a door to the bedroom, one to the kitchen, one to a linen closet, and one to what is obviously a cubbyhole filled with business files.*

ACT ONE

AT RISE: BOB *is on the telephone. Several morning newspapers, open to the book page, are spread out in front of him. He dials a number.*

———

BOB. I want to speak to Mr. Howard Nieman. (*The doorbell rings once, perfunctorily.*) Okay, I'll hold on.

TIFFANY (*letting herself in at the front door; she carries a jar of wheat germ*). Bob!

BOB. Hi, honey.

TIFFANY (*leaving the door ajar and coming into the room apprehensively*). I've read the reviews. How are you feeling?

BOB. I'm not exactly dancing with glee.

TIFFANY. Well, it's not fair!

BOB (*rising, phone in hand*). Shhhh! This is Nieman. I'm waiting for him to get off the other line.

TIFFANY (*coming to* BOB *at the desk*). But it isn't fair. You publish books of quality and distinction and you should get the credit.

BOB. You're one hundred percent correct and beautiful besides. (*They kiss. Into the phone.*) Hello, Howard! How are you? (*He sits, pulling newspapers toward him.*) Yes, sure I read the notices. Well, Howard, we were both hoping for a better break, but on the other hand there are a lot of good quotes here. (*Running his finger down a page and having some difficulty finding a decent quote*) "A magician with words" and so forth. (TIFFANY *hangs her coat on the railing, and quietly feeds wheat germ to the fish.*) And with a book like yours we can hope for something more in the weeklies. I'm confident we'll go into another printing. What did you think about the notices? Sure, we all wish Orville Prescott would write a novel. Look, Howard, please calm down. I hope you're not going around talking this way. Well, for one thing, people don't read reviews that carefully. All you do is spread the bad word. (*Rises, fidgeting.*) Let me give you some advice from Jake Cooper, in publicity. In his coarse but memorable phrase, nobody knows you've got a boil on your behind if you don't tell them. (BOB *listens a second longer, then shrugs and hangs up.*)

TIFFANY. What did he say?

BOB. He said the boil was not on his behind. (*Picks up a newspaper.*) It was on page 34 of the New York *Times*.

TIFFANY. Why shouldn't he be mad? It's a wonderful book!

BOB. That's what I like. Loyalty. (*Suddenly remembering, picking up a box of candy.*) I have a present for you and I forgot about it.

TIFFANY. A present?

BOB. It's Valentine's Day. (*Bringing her the box*) Did you forget? To the sweet. Will you be my valentine? (*Kiss.*)

TIFFANY. Sure I'll be your valentine. (*Pulls* BOB *down onto the sofa. He is kissing her as* OSCAR *appears from the corridor with a brief case.*)

OSCAR (*pushing the door wider*). The door is open. Shall I come in?

BOB. Oh, Oscar—by all means. Tiffany, I want you to meet Oscar Nelson. My old friend and my new tax lawyer.

TIFFANY. Hello.

BOB. And this is Tiffany Richards. We're getting married next month.

OSCAR. And she'll be deductible. (*Comes down to shake hands with* TIFFANY.) Congratulations. (BOB *closes the door.*)

TIFFANY. Well, I'm very happy he's got you as a tax lawyer. Don't you think it's just outrageous—the government investigating his back taxes just like he was Frank Sinatra?

OSCAR. Under the law we're all equals.

BOB. Oscar—think of that clunk from the FBI who came charging in here and accused me of fleecing the government of six thousand dollars!

OSCAR. Wait, wait, wait. In the first place, this clunk is not from the FBI. He's from the Internal Revenue Service, a small but real distinction. In the second place, he is not accusing you of anything. He is merely asking you to produce proof that this six thousand dollars was legitimate professional expenses.

BOB. All I can tell you is that I'm not coughing up any six thousand dollars. I'll move to Alaska.

OSCAR. You're too late. It's come into the Union.

TIFFANY. Darling, there's nothing to be upset about. Mr. Nelson will handle this man. (*Rises.*) Now *I'm* going to get you your midafternoon cocktail. (*To* OSCAR.) Would you like one?

OSCAR. Not this early, thank you.

TIFFANY. It's not alcohol. It's raw milk, brewer's yeast, and wheat germ.

OSCAR. Not this early, thank you.

BOB (*aware of* OSCAR's *expression*). It does sound awful, but it's incredible the energy it gives you.

OSCAR. I'll have to try it sometime.

TIFFANY. You have no intention of trying it. And you know what? You should, because you're definitely undernourished. Look at your ears.

OSCAR. What about them? I know they stick out.

TIFFANY. They're whitish. Here, let me look at your fingernails. (*She picks up his hand.*) See how pale they are? A really healthy person will have pink ears and pink fingernails. Another thing—a healthy person will have a tongue the color of beefsteak.

OSCAR (*backing away, hand to mouth*). No, no—I will spare you that.

TIFFANY. I'm going to bring you a cocktail, and you try it. (*She goes off to the kitchen and closes the door.*)

BOB. You think that's a lot of damn nonsense.

OSCAR. How did you know?

BOB. Because that's what I thought, in the beginning. But I have seen the results and I am completely sold. And if you want to know— I *love* being clucked over.

OSCAR. I'm delighted to hear it. And your ears were never lovelier. Now, shall we get down to business? (*Goes to the desk with his brief case.*)

BOB. Please, let's. I'm in a real mess, Oscar. Actually, it's been a muddle ever since I started to pay alimony. And now this tax thing. What am I going to do? You probably read those notices today. I won't make anything on the Nieman book. Somewhere, something's got to give. And it's got to be straightened out before Tiffany and I get married.

OSCAR (*spreading out various papers on the desk*). We'll see what we can do.

BOB. What I want is a bird's-eye view of my whole financial picture. What I'm spending. What I should be spending. Where I should be cutting corners.

OSCAR. All right. I've already come to a few conclusions, but I'll want to look at your files— (*Makes a gesture toward the inner office.*)

BOB. Thanks, Oscar. And I appreciate your coming over here on a Saturday. In fact, I appreciate your taking on this whole dumb job. I didn't think you would.

OSCAR. Why not?

BOB. Well. (*Glancing toward the kitchen door.*) You wouldn't handle the divorce.

OSCAR. Bob, how could I have handled the divorce? Mary was just as much my friend as you were. Besides, I never thought you'd go through with it. I thought of you as the golden couple— smiling over steaming bowls of Campbell's chicken soup—

BOB. Oh, brother.

OSCAR. What happened?

BOB (*with a shrug*). What happens to any marriage. You're in love, and then you're not in love. I married Mary because she was so direct and straightforward and said just exactly what she meant.

OSCAR. And why did you divorce her?

BOB. Because she was so direct and straightforward and said just exactly what she meant.

OSCAR. When did you see her last?

BOB. Eight, nine months ago.

OSCAR. Well, you're going to see her this afternoon.

BOB. Like hell!

OSCAR. Bob, I called Mary in Philadelphia and asked her—as a special favor

—to come up here this afternoon.

BOB. But why would you do that? Why in God's name would you—?

OSCAR. Why? Because you have five thousand dollars' worth of canceled checks that you can neither identify nor explain. Some of them Mary signed. I'm hoping that her memory will be a little better than yours.

BOB (*searching for an out*). But I've got an appointment here in ten minutes. Do you remember Dirk Winston?

OSCAR. The movie actor? Sure.

BOB. We were in the Navy together. Now he's moved into this building.

OSCAR. Well, it's nice you two old sailors can get together. There ought to be many a salty story, many a hearty laugh.

BOB. You don't get the picture. He's written a book.

OSCAR. A book?

BOB. That's right. The story of his life in three hundred and eighteen ungrammatical pages. (*Hands him a manuscript from the low bookcase.*)

OSCAR (*glancing at it*). *Life Among the Oranges.* Not a bad title.

BOB. It's all right, I suppose. (*Picks up a small bowl of dried apricots and begins to eat one, nervously.*) I can't imagine it on our lists.

OSCAR. I gather you're not going to do it.

BOB. Of course I'm not going to do it. But I dread talking to him. There is no right way to tell an author you don't want to publish his book.

OSCAR. If it's not going to be sweet, make it short. I can take Mary into the office—

BOB. Oh—Mary. (*Suddenly turning on* OSCAR) Don't you leave me alone with her for one minute, do you hear?

OSCAR. She's only five feet three.

BOB. Never mind that. (*Going to the file cabinet, upset, and picking up a set of galleys.*) And when will I get to these galleys? They have to be back to the printer on Monday.

OSCAR. What are you eating?

BOB. Dried apricots. (OSCAR *remains silent.*) They're full of vitamin C.

OSCAR. The things I'm learning today! (*Indicating the galleys* BOB *is fretting over.*) What's that one like?

BOB. It's absolutely fascinating. I want you to read it. (*Enthusing, partly to distract himself*) It's told in the first person, and when the story opens we're coming back from a funeral. But only gradually do we come to realize that the narrator of the story is the dead man.

OSCAR. It sounds sensitive, very sensitive.

BOB (*an extravagant little flare-up*). Oscar, I can think of only one sure way to clean up this business! A new series. I could take the great sex novels—*Lady Chatterley, Peyton Place*—and have them rewritten for the ten-to-twelve age group.

(TIFFANY *enters with drinks, bringing one to* BOB.)

TIFFANY. It took me longer because the Waring Blendor was broken. . . .

BOB. Thank you, darling.

TIFFANY. And I had to use an egg beater. (*Handing a glass to* OSCAR, *who rises.*) You've *got* to *taste* it, anyway. (*He doesn't.*)

BOB (*taking over*). Honey, I want you to put on your new gray bonnet and get out of here.

TIFFANY (*surprised*). Bob! Aren't we driving up to Goshen? Dad's expecting us!

BOB. Certainly. I'll pick you up at five-thirty. No, make it six.

TIFFANY (*really puzzled*). But why do I have to *go*?

BOB. Because in my winning, boyish way, I'm asking you to.

TIFFANY. I know why! Because that sexy movie actor is coming. You think in ten minutes I'll be sitting on his lap giving little growls of rapture.

BOB. Nonsense. Why should you care about vulgar good looks when you have me? No—(*With a sigh and moving away from her*)—the truth is my ex-wife is descending upon me this afternoon.

OSCAR. It was my suggestion. I thought she might be able to shed some light on this tax matter.

TIFFANY (*abruptly*). I'm delighted. I want to meet her. I've always wanted to meet her.

BOB. Well, you're not *going* to meet her—

TIFFANY (*sitting down, firmly, in a chair*). Yes, I am.

(OSCAR, *sensing that he'd better, slips away into the inner office with his papers and closes the door.*)

BOB. Darling, you are a sweet, reasonable girl, and I insist that you stay in character. Besides, I have those galleys to finish. (*As though to conclude the matter*) Kiss me, and stop all this nonsense.

TIFFANY. (*deliberately refusing to move*). I won't. I am not going to turn into Joan Fontaine.

BOB. What the hell are you talking about?

TIFFANY. Don't you remember Joan Fontaine in *Rebecca*? She was always thinking about the first Mrs. de Winter. She used to imagine that she could see her ghost on the staircase with that straight black Indian hair floating behind her. Don't you remember? And she'd shudder when she saw the monogram on the silver brushes.

BOB (*with a snort*). Silver brushes! Mary used to use plastic combs with little tails, and she'd crack off the tails so they'd fit in her purse. And her hair was tied back in a bun. Tiffany—this is so silly!

TIFFANY. I'll tell you another reason why I ought to meet Mary. We'd probably have a lot in common. Daddy says that a man goes on making the same mistake indefinitely.

BOB. Is that supposed to be an epigram? Because I don't get it.

TIFFANY. Practically everybody Daddy knows is divorced. It's not that they're worse than other people, they're just richer. And you do begin to see the pattern. You know Howard Pepper. When he divorced his first wife, everybody said "Oh, what he endured with Maggie! It was hell on earth!" Then when he married the new girl, everybody said "She's so *good* for him." Except when you met her she looked like Maggie, she talked like Maggie, it was Maggie all over again. And now his *third* wife—

BOB. Okay, okay. I get the whole ghastly picture. But I promise you on my sacred oath as a Yale man that you don't resemble my ex-wife in any way, shape, or form.

TIFFANY. Is that good?

BOB (*relaxing for a moment with* TIFFANY *on the sofa*). Good? It's a benediction from heaven. You—sweet, idiot child—soothe my feathers. Mary always, always ruffled them. Life with Mary was like being in a phone booth with an open umbrella—no matter which way you turned, you got it in the eye.

TIFFANY. Well, at last—a plain statement! Now that you've opened up a little, tell me, where did you meet her? Who introduced you?

BOB. I don't think we *were* introduced.

TIFFANY. You picked her up.

BOB. In a way. Do you remember that novel we published—*Our Kingdom Come*? It was sort of an allegory—the pilot of the plane turned out to be God?

TIFFANY. I don't think so.

BOB. Well, they made a play out of it. So of course I had to go to the opening night. And it was awful. Really grisly. After the second act, we were all standing out on the sidewalk. We were too stunned to talk. In fact, there didn't seem to be anything to say. Finally this girl spoke. She was standing there by herself in a polo coat, smoking—and she said, "Well, it's *not* uneven." So I laughed, and we started to talk—

TIFFANY. And you said, "We don't have to go back in there, let's have a drink—"

BOB. See? I don't have to tell you. You know. (*Rises and gets her coat.*)

TIFFANY (*rising, too, pursuing the subject*). Did you kiss her that night?

BOB. Come on. Put on your coat. You're just stalling for time.

TIFFANY. I'll bet you did.

BOB. What?

TIFFANY. Kiss her that night.

BOB. I didn't kiss her for weeks.

TIFFANY. I don't believe it. You kissed me on the second night—in the elevator—do you remember?

BOB (*thinking of* MARY). Oh, I made certain fumbling attempts—but she'd make some little joke, like, "Let's not start something we can't finish in a cab on Forty-fourth Street"—

TIFFANY. Well, for goodness sake, where was she when you finally did kiss her? On an operating table, under ether?

BOB. No, as it happens she was in a cab on Forty-fourth Street. Somehow or other she got her fingers slammed in the door. She pretended it was nothing, and we were chatting along. Then suddenly—this was blocks later—she started to cry. I looked at her fingers. (*Taking* TIFFANY's *hand*) Two of the nails were really smashed. And it started out I was just trying to comfort her, and—

TIFFANY. That is the most *un*romantic story I ever heard!

BOB. They certainly won't get a movie out of it. (*Urging her toward door*) I told you it wasn't worth discussing.

TIFFANY (*picks up her handbag*). I know, I kept fishing. Did she cry a lot in taxicabs?

BOB. She never cried again. Not any-place—ever—not once.

(OSCAR *appears from inner office, frowning over a sheaf of papers.*)

OSCAR. These figures for the year—can they represent the *total* profit?

BOB. I'm afraid so. (*Doorbell.* BOB *thinks quickly.*) Oscar, will you get that?

TIFFANY. Just let me *meet* her. Two minutes and I promise I'll go!

BOB (*pulling her toward the kitchen*). We'll go out the back door and I'll get you a cab.

TIFFANY. I feel like I was caught in a raid!

(OSCAR *has been looking on as* BOB *gets* TIFFANY *into the kitchen.*)

BOB. I'm *not* adult and Noel Coward would wash his hands of me. (*He slips into the kitchen, too, and closes the door as* OSCAR *crosses to the main door and opens it not to* MARY *but to* DIRK WINSTON, *who has a large, partially wrapped piece of wood carving in his arms.*)

OSCAR. Hello. Come in.

DIRK. I'm—

OSCAR. Yes, I know. You're Dirk Winston. Bob will be right back. My name is Oscar Nelson. (*We hear* TIFFANY *giggling and protesting "Please, Bob—please!" off in the kitchen area.* OSCAR *and* DIRK *hear it, too.*) Her name is Tiffany Richards.

(*Squeals from* TIFFANY, *off.*)

DIRK. It kind of makes me homesick for the back lot at Paramount. I thought I was late, but . . . (OSCAR, *puzzled, is looking at the package in* DIRK's *arms.*) Suppose I take this thing downstairs and I'll be back in ten minutes.

OSCAR. I think recess should be over by that time.

DIRK (*feeling he should explain the package*). I saw this in an antique shop. (*Undoing the wrapping a bit.*) It's supposed to be Geronimo, but it looks so much like Jack Warner I couldn't resist.

(*He goes, closing the door.* OSCAR *notices the drink* TIFFANY *has left for him. He tastes it, then crosses to the liquor table and pours a generous slug into the drink. He takes a sip. It's better. He looks*

at his fingernails, then goes to the mantel, puts down his drink, picks up a mirror, and examines his tongue. While he is doing so, MARY *enters by the main door. She puts down her overnight bag and then sees* OSCAR.)

MARY. Oscar!

OSCAR. Mary, darling.

MARY. Are you sick?

OSCAR. Of course not. I'm out of my mind. (*Going to her and embracing her*) Hey! I want you to concentrate and give me a better hug than that!

(*We are aware that* MARY *is somewhat abstracted and apprehensive. Also that she is getting her feel of the room again, after all this time.*)

MARY. Oscar—dear Oscar—it's lovely to see you. (*Hesitantly*) Where's—?

OSCAR. He'll be right back. He just— (*Interrupting himself, staring at her*) Wait a minute. What's happened to you? You look absolutely marvelous.

MARY. Did you say that right?

OSCAR. Apparently not, because I didn't get an answer.

MARY (*adopting a television commercial tone, mechanically*). Well, you see, I *had* been using an ordinary shampoo, which left a dull, unattractive film on my hair . . .

OSCAR. Come on, I'm interested. The hair is different—the clothes—the make-up. Clearly loving hands have been at work.

MARY (*putting her coat and handbag aside and sitting down, tentatively*). Yes, but you're not supposed to notice. I mean you're supposed to have an appreciative gleam in your eye, but you don't have to remind me of the dreary hours at Elizabeth Arden's—

OSCAR. Appreciative gleam? I've been casting you lustful glances. You're just too pure to notice. What caused the transformation?

MARY (*still not located in space*). Well, being divorced is like being hit by a Mack truck. If you live through it, you start looking very carefully to the right and to the left. While I was looking I noticed that I was the only twenty-eight-year-old girl wearing a polo coat and no lipstick.

OSCAR. You were? I never noticed. (*Starting toward kitchen*) But let me see if I can locate our—

MARY (*quickly taking a cigarette from*

a box on the table). No, no—please—
wait. Let me have a cigarette first.

OSCAR (*lighting it for her*). You nervous?

MARY. Certainly not. But I haven't seen
Bob in nine months. I guess I can last
another five minutes. Besides, you and
I have a lot to talk about. How's Jennifer?

OSCAR (*quiet and offhand tone*). Well,
she had this illegitimate baby after she
met that man from Gristede's, but it's all
right now. . . .

MARY (*nodding, looking about the
room*). Oh? Good! And how's everything at the office?

OSCAR. You haven't heard one word I
said.

MARY (*caught*). You're right. I'm not
listening. And I *am* nervous. I shouldn't
have come.

OSCAR (*puts his hands on the arm of
her chair. Sympathetically*). Mary, do you
still—

MARY (*quickly*). I don't still—anything.

OSCAR. I'm sorry. I should have realized
that—

MARY. Stop it. Don't give me that sad
spaniel expression, as though you'd just
looked at the X rays. I'm all right, Doctor. Just fine.

(BOB *appears from kitchen, stops short.
His words are awkwardly spaced.*)

BOB. Well. Hello. You did get here.

OSCAR. Of course, she knew the address.
(OSCAR *starts toward the office.*)

BOB (*not wanting to be left alone*).
Oscar!

(MARY *gets to her feet, ill at ease.*)

OSCAR. Be right back.

(OSCAR *goes into office, leaving the door
open.* MARY *turns toward* BOB *and her
nerves now vanish. But* BOB's *are quickly
in bad shape.*)

MARY. Hello.

BOB (*a step to her*). You look very different. You've changed. I was going to
ask you how you've been. But I can see.
You've been fine.

MARY. How about you? Did you ever
clear up that case of athlete's foot?

BOB (*almost under his breath*). No—
you haven't changed.

MARY (*this flusters her briefly. She
crosses to the desk, dips a hand into the
bowl of dried apricots*). Well, you know
what they say—the more we change, the
more we stay the same. Good Lord!

These are dried apricots.

BOB. What did you think they were?

MARY. Ears.

BOB (*ignoring it*). I want to say that I
appreciate your coming. I'm sure you
didn't *want* to.

MARY (*circling below the desk toward
a plant on a low bookcase*). Nonsense. It
put my mind at ease. You can't think
how often I've worried about the philo-
dendron.

BOB (*picking up tax papers*). I'm sure.
Now, Oscar has explained to you that
my—our—1962 income tax returns are
being—

MARY. I advise you to make a clean
breast of it. Admit everything.

BOB. This does not happen to be a subject for comedy. I've got to get this
straightened out. I'm getting married in
two weeks.

MARY (*really stunned*). Oh?

BOB. I thought you knew. Surely Oscar
must have—

MARY. Of course! And it went right
out of my head. (*Sitting near the desk*)
But how nice! Do I know her?

BOB. No, you don't.

MARY. Do you?

BOB (*chooses to ignore this*). Her name
is Tiffany Richards.

MARY. Tiffany. I'll bet she uses brown
ink. And when she writes she draws
little circles over the *i*'s.

BOB. She is a beautiful, lovely girl with
a head on her shoulders.

MARY. How useful!

BOB (*spluttering with irritation*). You
really do have a talent for—you've been
here five minutes, and already I'm—

MARY (*with maddening calm*). Have a
dried apricot.

BOB (*striding to office door*). Oscar,
have you fallen asleep in there?

OSCAR. (*off*). Coming!

BOB (*moving away from* MARY *as* OSCAR
appears from office). Shall we get on with
this? (*To* MARY) I know you have to
get back to Philadelphia—

MARY. I'm staying in town tonight, so
you may consider that my time is your
time.

OSCAR (*sits at the desk, handing* MARY
a batch of canceled checks). Okay, Mary,
will you look through these checks? Most
of them you've signed.

MARY. Oh, dear—I'm not going to remember *any* of these, Oscar—

OSCAR. It'll come. Just give yourself time. You understand that we're particularly looking for items that might be deductible. Business entertaining, professional gifts, and so forth.

MARY (*working her way through the checks*). L. Bernstein—seventy-eight dollars. That's impossible. The only L. Bernstein I know is Leonard Bernstein and I don't know Leonard Bernstein.

OSCAR (*pointing it out*). This is L. Bernstein, D.D.S. A dentist.

BOB (*shaking his head*). I told you— Sidney Bauer is my dentist.

MARY. Dentist, dentist, dentist. (*Snapping her fingers*) Listen—it's that man in Boston!

BOB. What man in Boston?

MARY. Don't you remember that crazy restaurant where you go down all the stairs? And you thought you got a stone in the curry—but it was your inlay?

BOB. Oh.

MARY. And we drove all the way out to Framingham because he was the only dentist who'd take you on Sunday?

BOB. Yeah, yeah, yeah.

MARY. By the way, how is that inlay?

BOB. Just grand. How are your crowns? (*They turn from each other.*)

OSCAR (*stopping this*). *And* we have Mrs. Robert Connors—three hundred dollars.

BOB. Mrs. Connors?

MARY. I thought so long as you walked this earth you'd remember Mrs. Connors. Bootsie Connors and her fish?

BOB. Oh, God. That ghastly weekend in Greenwich.

OSCAR. Okay, tell Daddy.

BOB. Do you remember that young English critic, Irving Mannix?

OSCAR. The angry young man?

BOB. This was two years ago, when he was just a cross young man. At that time he was writing long scholarly articles proving that Shakespeare was a homosexual.

MARY. Sort of the intellectual's answer to *Photoplay*.

BOB. Anyway, he was staying here. And we'd been invited to a party at the Connors'.

MARY. So we brought along dear old Irving.

BOB. Do you know the Connors' place in Greenwich?

OSCAR. No.

BOB. Well, the living room is about the size of the ball room at the St. Regis. You feel it would be just the place to sign a treaty. (*As they become interested in the details of the story* BOB *and* MARY *gradually forget their present situation and relax.*) Anyway, it was all too rich for Irving and he started to lap up martinis. In fifteen minutes he was asking our hostess if it was true that the Venetian paneling had been brought over piece by piece from Third Avenue.

OSCAR. Why didn't you take this charmer home?

BOB. Because he passed out. In the library.

MARY (*it comes back*). On that damn velvet sofa.

BOB. But he came to just long enough to light a cigarette. Presently the sofa was on fire—really on fire. Our hero jumped up and, with stunning presence of mind, put out the blaze with a tank of tropical fish.

MARY. And these were no run-of-the-bowl goldfish. They came from Haiti and were friends of the family. I mean, they had *names*.

OSCAR. Well, he was a writer. I think we can call that professional entertainment. Okay—we have twenty-five dollars to the Beach Haven Inn.

MARY. That must be yours.

BOB. Nonsense! I was never in . . . (*And then he remembers.*) The Booksellers—

MARY AND BOB (*together*). Convention.

BOB. That awful hotel with the iron deer in front.

MARY (*nodding, her eyes lighting up*). With the night clerk who looked like Norman Vincent Peale and was so suspicious.

BOB. No wonder he was suspicious! (*To* OSCAR, *indicating* MARY) He turns around to get the key and this one says just loud enough for him to hear, "Darling, are we doing the right thing? Maybe we ought to *wait*."

MARY. He was *delighted* to come face to face with sin.

BOB. That's probably why he charged us four bucks to bring up three bottles of beer.

MARY (*to* OSCAR). He forgot the bottle opener, and we had to pry them open on the handle of the radiator.

BOB. And one of them was warm or something, so it shot up to the ceiling and all over one of the beds. So we both had to sleep in the other twin bed. . . . (*His voice has slowed down on this last thought. The remembering is suddenly a bit painful. There is a short, awkward silence before* MARY *gets to her feet, deliberately breaking the mood.*)

MARY. Oscar, we're being inefficient. We don't need total recall—just the facts. I'll take these checks into the office and make notes on the ones I can remember.

(*Almost before they realize it, she has left them.* OSCAR *and* BOB *look at one another, then* BOB *looks away.*)

OSCAR. Mary looks wonderful, don't you think?

BOB. Great.

OSCAR. Like a million bucks.

BOB (*nettled*). I'm afraid the figure that comes into my mind is five thousand bucks in alimony.

OSCAR (*notices* DIRK, *who has just stuck his head in at the main door*). Your friend from California.

BOB (*relieved at the interruption; his exuberance is a bit excessive after the strain with* MARY). Dirk! It's good to see you! How long has it been?

DIRK. I don't know. We were still in sailor suits.

BOB (*indicating* OSCAR). By the way, do you know—

OSCAR. We've met.

BOB. You know, Dirk is the expert we *should* consult! (*To* DIRK) You've been married four or five times. How the hell did you manage it?

DIRK (*relaxing into a chair*). I feel like a failure to admit that I was only married three times. Actually, I married my first wife twice—so while there were three marriages, there were just two wives involved.

BOB. Now what? Do you pay both of them alimony?

DIRK. No, my second wife just married a very nice plastic surgeon. He fell in love with her while removing a wart from her shoulder blade. I always thought there was a popular song in that.

BOB. What about your first wife?

DIRK. She died.

BOB. See? Them that has gets!

OSCAR (*rises, picks up manuscript from desk, and gives it to* BOB). I know you two have business to talk about— (BOB *glances at* DIRK's *manuscript, and his face shows his dismay at having to deal with it.*) —so I'll get back to my arithmetic. (*He joins* MARY *in the small office, closing the door.*)

DIRK. Yes! Down to business.

BOB (*avoiding the subject and trying to hold onto his own momentary better spirits*). Dirk, you look great. Younger than ever. How do you do it?

DIRK. I'll tell you this—it gets harder and harder. If I don't get ten full hours' sleep, they can't do a close-up. If I eat a ham sandwich after four o'clock, it shows on the scale. Ham sandwich, hell. I can gain weight from two Bayer aspirins.

BOB. You sound like the curator of your own museum. Come on, now. It's been worth it, hasn't it?

DIRK. Sure. Except that you develop such nutty habits. Do you know what all middle-aged actors do when they're alone in taxicabs?

BOB. What do they do? (DIRK *now demonstrates the business of biting, open-mouthed, from left to right, to strengthen the jaw muscles.*) What's that for?

DIRK. It firms up the jawline, old boy. I'll tell you what I dream of doing. My dearest ambition in life is to let my damn jawline go. In fact, that's why I wrote this book.

BOB (*brought back to the subject, embarrassed*). I see. But—uh—

DIRK. Have you read it?

BOB. Certainly I've read it. Now—the question is, shall I be perfectly frank? (DIRK *immediately rises and picks up the manuscript as if to go.*) You bruise easily. Have you shown this to anybody else?

DIRK. My agent, who thought it was brave, haunting, and hilarious. I brought it to you first because I knew you.

BOB. I'm sorry, Dirk—but the truth is it's not a book at all. For the moment we'll rule out the quality of the writing.

DIRK. Let's not rule out anything. What about the quality of the writing?

BOB. Well, it's—it's—

DIRK. Is "lousy" the word you're groping for?

BOB. Well, let's say it's not prose. Actually, it's not even punctuated. I get the feeling that you waited until you were out of breath and then threw in a semicolon.

DIRK. Hm.

BOB. However, that could be fixed. What can't be fixed is the content. It's nothing but anecdotes, really. It's as though you were just taking up where Louella left off.

DIRK. I gather you do not wish to publish this book. Do you think someone else would take it?

BOB. There are a couple of fringe outfits that I imagine would—

DIRK. I don't want a fringe outfit. Tell me this. How much does it cost to publish a book? Any book?

BOB. It depends on the size of the first printing, the length of the book, the kind of promotion—

DIRK. Let's get down to cases. How much would it cost to bring out my book with a first printing of, say, twelve thousand copies?

BOB. Oh—eight, nine thousand dollars.

DIRK. Let's say I made a check out to you for eighteen thousand dollars. Would you do the book?

BOB. If you proposition women with this same kind of finesse you must get your face slapped a lot.

DIRK. I thought it was worth a try, but don't get mad.

BOB. I'm not mad. I'm surprised. Why does that book mean so much to you? Obviously it isn't the money.

DIRK. It may sound naïve to say it— but being a star has never killed my urge to become an actor. Ten years ago I started to campaign for real parts. But the formula was still making money. So I went right on—passionate kisses and then I'd build the Suez Canal—passionate kisses and then I'd open the golden West.

BOB. What do you figure—you're all through in Hollywood?

DIRK. Technically, no. I have two more pictures to go on my present contract. But when I left, they knew and I knew that I was the sinking ship leaving the rats.

BOB. But why this jump into literature?

DIRK. Well, my press agent thought . . . what the hell, why blame him? *I* thought it might stir up a little interest in me as a man instead of a windup toy. In my fantasies I imagined it would be serialized in *The Saturday Evening Post* with pictures of me looking very seedy. And all

of a sudden producers would be saying, "Don't laugh, but do you know who'd be perfect for the degenerate father— Dirk Winston!"

(MARY *enters from the office, leaving the door open.*)

MARY. Bob, I've done my half. Oscar would like to see you. (*Seeing* DIRK) Oh, excuse me.

DIRK (*rising, pleasantly*). Hello, there.

BOB. This is my—former wife, Mary McKellaway.

MARY. You're Dirk Winston. And your real name is Winston Krib. Dirk is Krib spelled backwards.

DIRK. Good Lord, how did you remember that?

MARY. Oh, I have a head full of the most useless information. I still remember the names of each of the Dionne quintuplets, and the width of the Amazon River.

DIRK. Oh?

MARY. You have no idea how few people care about the width of the Amazon River. I understand you've written a book.

DIRK. That's what I understood, until I talked to Bob here.

MARY. Bob's a special case. He was frightened at an early age by a best seller. (*She is picking up her coat and handbag.*)

DIRK. He was?

BOB. I was not. Why do you say that? It's simply not true. I happen to believe that there's great wisdom in Emerson's remark that you should never read any book until it's a year old. And I'd like to think I'm publishing the kind of books that will be around next year. I'm fed up with novels about tangled lives in Scarsdale—or Old Salem for that matter: (*Quoting, in a mock literary rhythm*) "All he knew was that he was a man and she was a woman or had he made some dreadful mistake."

OSCAR (*off*). Bob! Are you coming?

BOB (*on his way to office*). Be right back, Dirk.

DIRK. Don't think about me. We're all through. I wouldn't want you to be any clearer.

MARY. Bob, I suppose I might as well go too.

BOB (*turns back to* MARY, *something new on his mind*). Right now?

MARY. Well, don't you have a date?

BOB. I am meeting Tiffany—but couldn't you spare just five minutes? There's something I'd like to ask you.

(*Assuming her consent,* BOB *goes into the office.* MARY *stares after him a moment, absently reaching for a cigarette. Then she becomes aware of* DIRK *again, who has started for the main door but is now hesitating, watching her.*)

MARY. I used to love your movies. Of course, I didn't see all of them. My mother wouldn't let me.

DIRK. That's all right. I didn't see all of them, either. My agent wouldn't let me. Are you a writer?

MARY. No, I work for the *Ladies' Home Journal.* I edit the letters to the editor.

DIRK. You mean they have to be edited?

MARY (*nodding*). It does seem a little like incest, doesn't it?

DIRK. Bob did say you were his *former* wife, didn't he?

MARY. That's right.

DIRK. I'm so glad.

MARY. Why?

DIRK. Because I can ask you to dinner. Will you have dinner with me?

MARY. Tonight?

DIRK. You have a date?

MARY. No—no.

DIRK. Then what's wrong with tonight?

MARY. I guess I think we should have known each other longer—like, say, another five minutes.

DIRK. You think you're letting yourself in for an orgy. You think I will ply you with liquor, lure you to my sinful bachelor lodgings, and chase you around the king-size bed.

MARY (*with a look toward the office*). Well, I've never been plied with liquor. Maybe I'd like it, but—

DIRK. Come on, we'll have dinner. And *Duck Soup* is playing at the Museum of Modern Art. I promise you I'll be so respectable you'll find me quite tiresome.

MARY (*on an impulse*). I have a new dress that would look pretty silly all by itself in Schrafft's. Why not? I'd love to. Do you want to pick me up here? What time?

DIRK. Half an hour? (*It occurs to him he'd better check.*) By the way, you don't —live here, do you?

MARY. Oh, no. We're not as civilized as all that. This is business.

DIRK. Fine. (*Passing office door.*) See you, Bob. I've got a call in to the Coast. (*On his way to the main door, turning back to* MARY.) Half an hour?

(MARY *nods, smiling.* DIRK *goes, closing the door.* MARY *turns, a little unsure of herself, sees the galleys on the sofa table, abstractedly picks them up, and puts her cigarette on an ash tray on the table. At almost the same time,* BOB *appears from the office, as though in response to* DIRK'S *farewell, then realizes he is alone with* MARY.)

BOB. Oh. Mary—thanks for waiting— I—

MARY (*she has been aware of his return, but has not looked at him. Now she deliberately reads from the galleys, in a somewhat questioning voice*). "He was alone in the middle of the field. He was grateful once again to be in possession of his own body. The Queen Anne's lace waved in the breeze like a thousand tiny handkerchiefs . . ." (*Looks up.*) This sounds suspiciously like our friend O'Brynner. (*Glancing at the first page of the galleys.*) And no wonder! I thought you weren't going to do this one.

BOB. Why?

MARY. Because this man writes like a sick elf.

BOB (*wanting to brush the matter aside before he is irritated again*). Let's skip that. (*In a hesitant, slightly strained voice*) Mary—

MARY (*adopting his tone*). Bob—

BOB. I've been thinking. (*Starts to sit on the ottoman.*)

MARY. I thought you had an odd expression.

BOB (*jumping up again, a sudden, desperate explosion*). Could you—would it be absolutely impossible for you to listen to me for three minutes without making one single wisecrack?

MARY (*stung—but concealing it*). I could try.

BOB (*earnestly*). I wish you would. I really wish you would. There is something I want to ask you and I can't do it through a barrage of flippantries.

MARY. You'd be surprised. I don't feel flippant at all. What is it you want to ask me?

BOB (*sitting*). You—know I'm getting married again.

MARY. Yes, I know that.

BOB. Well, I find myself stewing over a

very curious thing Tiffany said today.

MARY. Oh?

BOB. Her idea was that people go right on making the same mistakes. I had an eerie feeling that there was something true about that. (*Realizing that he is groping*) What I'm trying to say is that I have by God got to make a better job of it this time. (MARY *turns her head away.* BOB *leans toward her.*) Yes?

MARY. I didn't say anything.

BOB. But you were thinking—

MARY (*turns back to him sharply*). Look, you say your lines, I'll say my lines. You're hoping for better luck this time. *I* hope you'll have better luck this time. Beyond that, I don't see—

BOB. You could tell me what *I* did wrong. When we broke up, I spent many drunken hours thinking how it was all your fault. (MARY *starts to speak.*) Yes, I know I'm painting a charming portrait of myself—Bob McKellaway as a slob and sorehead. But that's how I felt.

MARY. And that's how you still feel.

BOB. No, by the time I calmed down and cleared the last of your bobby pins out of the bathroom, I realized that half the trouble had to be me.

MARY. You think it can be divided into two equal parts—like a sandwich?

BOB. I think success has no rules, but you can learn a great deal from failure.

MARY. I see. And what you're really looking for is the formula for instant marriage.

BOB. No, I'm not as sappy as that. I'm prepared to make a number of different mistakes this time. I would like not to make the same ones. And I would like some advice.

MARY. Had you thought of writing to Dear Abby? (*He rises and moves away. She is immediately penitent.*) Bob, I'm sorry for that. That's the kind of thing I promised not to say. (BOB *returns to her, hopefully.*) But what you're asking is impossible. I can't give you a report card. Is he punctual? Does he complete the task assigned? But you know what? This is so like you. This determination to be sensible in a situation where it isn't sensible to be sensible. You want to analyze, analyze. Like those people who take an overdose of sleeping pills, and sit there making notes while they're dying. "Four A.M. Vision beginning to blur." You'd

do that. You would.

BOB. Maybe.

MARY. What shall I say? That you used to leave your ties on the coffee table? And you always grabbed *The New Yorker* first and took it to the bathroom? And you never talked to me in cars?

BOB. Of course I talked in cars.

MARY. Yes, to the traffic signals. "Come on, dammit, turn green."

BOB. I concentrate when I drive.

MARY. And you were always asking solemn, editorial-type questions beginning Don't You Ever. Don't You Ever order lunch meat? Don't You Ever put the lid back on the mayonnaise? Don't You Ever put your cigarettes out?

BOB (*brandishing* MARY's *still-smoking cigarette and putting it out with great vigor*). Because you never in your life put a cigarette out!

MARY. And you always, always put the ice-cube trays back without filling them.

BOB (*gesturing toward the kitchen*). Ice-cube trays? Is that all you remember?

MARY. Aren't you forgetting one small detail? You're the one who walked out.

BOB. Technically, I suppose that's true.

MARY. Technically? There was nothing technical about it. You got up in the middle of the night and slammed out of here. And you know what? I never knew why.

BOB. Like hell you didn't.

MARY. All I knew was, one moment you were in bed, and the next minute you were banging drawers and dumping shirts into a suitcase.

BOB. And that's *all* you remember? (*Coming nearer*) Let me reconstruct the scene for you. You were in bed reading *McCall's.* I was in the bathroom brushing my teeth. Then I put the lights out, came to bed, put my arms around you, and you said, "Okay, let's get those colored lights going."

MARY. I said that?

BOB. I wouldn't be capable of inventing it.

MARY. And was that so terrible?

BOB. Maybe not. But let us say that it had the effect of a cold shower when I wasn't in the mood for a cold shower.

MARY. I see.

BOB. I grant you it was a very small straw to be the last straw. Another time it would have bounced off me. But it had been such a stinker of a day. We got bad notices on the Caine book. The deal for the serial rights fell through. Oh, the usual. Except that I felt a peculiar need for some warmth. I guess I felt I needed a wife.

MARY (*hotly*). I think I was wifely—a lot.

BOB. Sure. On and off. Between jokes.

(MARY *grabs a sofa pillow as though she were going to hit him with it, but is deflected by* OSCAR's *return from the office. He sees what she is doing.*)

OSCAR. Please don't be embarrassed on my account. I'm delighted. I hate a friendly divorce. A lawyer is never entirely comfortable with a friendly divorce, any more than a good mortician wants to finish his job and then have the patient sit up on the table. (MARY, *without saying a word, picks up her coat, her suitcase, gloves, and handbag and leaves by the main door.* OSCAR *looks at* BOB.) Did you read Walter Lippmann today? I thought it was an awfully good piece.

BOB. Oscar, don't be urbane all the time. I can't stand it. (*Fuming*) You see why I didn't want to see her again? When you said she was coming, I should have walked out that front door! I don't understand it. I thought she had lost the power to enrage me. Maybe I took the bandages off too soon. Maybe I— (*Stops as he sees* MARY *returning with her suitcase.*) Did you forget something?

MARY. No, dammit, I *remembered* something. Having made my dramatic exit, I realized that this is where I'm being picked up. I *have* to stay here for another ten minutes.

BOB. I see.

MARY. And furthermore, I will have to use your room to change in. (*To* OSCAR) Oscar, if the phone rings, it may be for me. Will *you* take it? The Algonquin is supposed to call and confirm my room for tonight.

BOB. There's a new telephone in the . . . (MARY *goes off to the bedroom, not exactly slamming the door but letting it close pretty arrogantly behind her.* BOB *starts to follow but is stopped by* OSCAR.)

OSCAR. Never mind her. We have something more important to talk about. (*Sitting at the desk*) I have been over all the figures and am now ready to give my state of the Union address.

BOB (*trying to tear his mind away from* MARY, *but still edgy and upset*). First, tell me about that tax thing.

OSCAR. Oh, my guess is that we'll get it down somewhere in the neighborhood of eighteen hundred, two thousand dollars.

BOB. That would be more like it.

OSCAR. You said you wanted my advice on the over-all picture. Let me ask you a couple of questions. Tiffany comes from a wealthy family, doesn't she?

BOB. What has that got to do with anything?

OSCAR. A lot. She has to be supported. You can't support her. I have now been through what we shall laughingly call your books, and you're not supporting yourself.

BOB. You're joking.

OSCAR. Then why aren't you laughing?

BOB. Look. If you're trying in some left-handed way to tell me I can't get married, you're wasting your breath. I'm thirty-six years old, and this is a—

OSCAR. Free country? Don't you believe it. People pick up the most erroneous ideas from popular songs. Let me tell you something. If all you've got is the sun in the morning and the moon at night, you're in trouble.

BOB. What are you talking about? I take eighteen thousand a year out of the company—plus bonuses.

OSCAR. That's right.

BOB. That may be cigarette money to the Rockefellers, but it still feels like a lot to me. Hell, my father never made more than five thousand a year in his life and he put four boys through college.

OSCAR. Let's not dwell on the glories of the past. *I* have the figures for *this* year. Do you want to hear them?

BOB. No. (*Starts for bedroom and stops.*) Oh, yes, I suppose so.

OSCAR (*referring to a work sheet*). We start with your base salary—eighteen thousand—plus one thousand dollars sales bonus. By the way, that was down from preceding years.

BOB. Sales were down.

OSCAR. So that's nineteen thousand dollars. Against that, we have: thirty-two hundred, rent; two thousand, eighty, maid service; four thousand, nine hundred, food and liquor; five thousand, alimony to Mary—

BOB. And that's ridiculous. (*Shouting at the bedroom door*) She's working.

OSCAR. That was the decision of the court. You can't do anything about it. (*Picking up where he left off*) Five thousand to Mary. Six hundred and eighty, club dues and entertainment. Six hundred, clothes. Nine hundred, books, furnishings, dry cleaning. Eleven hundred, insurance and medical. Twenty-seven hundred, taxes. We now have a total of twenty-one thousand, one hundred and sixty dollars. You do have three thousand in available savings, but most of that will go for that old tax bill.

BOB. Here, let me see that thing. (*Takes work sheet from Oscar.*)

OSCAR. You can juggle those figures any way you want to. But you're not going to change the fact that you are already spending twenty-one thousand on an income of nineteen. It's not just that you can't support another wife. You'd be ill-advised to buy a canary.

BOB. It can't be as complicated as you're pretending—

OSCAR. Actually, it's even more complicated. You must keep in mind that if you ever wanted to divorce Tiffany, you'd be in a hopeless position, financially.

BOB (*outburst*). I'm not going to divorce Tiffany! Why would I divorce Tiffany?

OSCAR. Your attitude does you credit.

BOB. Here. Some of these expenses I can cut.

OSCAR. Yes, you could move to a cheaper apartment. You don't have to belong to the New York Athletic Club. You might save seven or eight hundred dollars. However, I have met Tiffany. I doubt that you could keep her in cashmere sweaters for that. She doesn't work, does she?

BOB. Oh, she does volunteer things.

OSCAR. Maybe her father would give her an allowance.

BOB. Maybe we could take in boarders. Any more bright ideas? What the hell am I supposed to do? Stay single for the rest of my life and sleep around? Or do I remain celibate and take cold showers and get plenty of exercise?

OSCAR. Fortunately, you belong to the Athletic Club. (*Telephone rings.* OSCAR *answers it.*) Hello. That's right. Can I take the message? (MARY, *in dressing gown, pokes her head out of the bed-room door.*) I see. Will you wait one minute? (*To* MARY) They haven't got a single but they can give you a suite!

MARY. Tell them never mind. I'm not paying twenty-four dollars for one night. I'll go to the Biltmore.

BOB (*not graciously, just realistically*). If you want to, you can stay here. I'm going to be in Goshen for the weekend.

MARY. Stay here?

BOB. I won't be here. You'll be perfectly safe.

MARY. I'm not worried. I was perfectly safe when you *were* here. (MARY *disappears, shutting the door again.*)

BOB. I shouldn't have divorced her. I should have shot her.

OSCAR (*into phone*). Thank you, she'll make other arrangements.

(*Doorbell, as* OSCAR *hangs up.*)

BOB (*going to the front door*). With my luck, this'll be a telegram saying that my rich old uncle died and left his money to a kindly waitress. (BOB *opens the door to* DIRK, *and is surprised to see him.*) Oh. Hello again.

DIRK. Hello. Is she ready?

BOB. Who?

DIRK. Do I get a choice? I'm calling for Mary.

BOB. For Mary? For what?

DIRK. For dinner. Isn't that all right? Should my mother have called your mother?

BOB. Don't be ridiculous. I just didn't know, that's all.

OSCAR. You see, Bob thinks when he brings a book back to the library, it'll never go out again.

BOB. Bob doesn't think anything. I had always supposed that Mr. Winston only went out with women whose names ended in *a*. Like Lana. Or Ava. And I'm a little puzzled as to why he wants to take my ex-wife to dinner.

DIRK. Because she looked hungry. You damn fool! Because she strikes me as an exceptionally attractive girl.

BOB. And you would know.

DIRK. That's right. I don't want to pull rank or anything—but I think it might be fair to assume I know at least as much about women as you do about books. Perhaps more.

BOB. Look, you misunderstand me. I am delighted that you find my former wife attractive. I'm charmed that you are taking her out. If you decide to marry her, I'll send up rockets. In fact, you can count on me as your best man.

OSCAR. Marry her and you count on him as your publisher.

BOB (*overheated*). Absolutely! Now, there's a brilliant idea! Why didn't I think of it? Oscar's got a head on both his shoulders. I could solve your problems, you could solve my problems.

DIRK. You've got to be joking.

BOB (*lying back on the sofa and kicking off his loafers*). Why? This is the age of the deal! You scratch me and I'll scratch you! Don't you read the papers? Why should I be out of touch?

OSCAR. Bob—

DIRK. No, let's listen to him. I couldn't be more impressed. It stirs memories of the past—I keep thinking, "Louis B. Mayer, thou shouldst be living at this hour!"

BOB (*to* OSCAR). See? You're shocked. But he's been around!

DIRK. And back. It couldn't be more reasonable. He has an unmarketable wife and I have an unmarketable book. He thinks we should pool our lack of resources. I haven't had such a fascinating offer in years.

(*The bedroom door opens and* MARY *appears, beautiful in a low-cut dress.*)

MARY. Hello! I think I'm all collected. (*All rise. She senses the tension in the air.*) What are you all staring at? Is something showing?

DIRK. Yes, and it looks delicious. Are we ready? (*He gets* MARY's *coat as* MARY *goes to* OSCAR *and kisses him.*)

MARY (*to* BOB). I suppose it's all right if I pick up that bag later tonight?

BOB. Certainly. But how will you get in?

MARY (*waving a bunch of keys from out of her handbag*). I still have my keys. Have you been missing things?

DIRK. Shall we run along? I double-parked down there.

MARY (*breezing through doorway, calling back to* OSCAR *and* BOB). Good night!

BOB *and* OSCAR (*she's already gone*). Good night.

DIRK (*ready to go, turning back to* BOB *from the doorway, grinning*). I think you've got yourself a deal. (DIRK *goes, closing door behind him.* BOB *heaves a great sigh of exasperation and snatches*

up the galleys.)

OSCAR (*after watching* BOB *for a moment*). I've known you for twenty years and I never realized you had this flair for comedy. (*No answer from* BOB, *trying to concentrate on galleys.*) You *were* joking?

BOB (*crossly*). Of course I was joking. (*Looking up as the thought crosses his mind*) But wouldn't I like to see him try! It'd be an education for him. (OSCAR *pokes the work sheet under his nose.*) Don't, don't, don't. I don't want to hear another word about my untidy affairs. (*Turns his attention to galleys again.*)

OSCAR (*following* BOB *to the desk*). What's the matter with you?

BOB (*sharply, not lyrically, and without looking up*). Say I'm weary, say I'm sad, say that health and wealth have missed me, and you've said it. (BOB *is now rapidly crossing out great sections of the galleys.*)

OSCAR. Why are you *slashing* at those galleys?

BOB. Because this man writes like a sick elf! (*And* BOB *is going at it with renewed vigor as the* CURTAIN *falls.*)

END OF ACT ONE

ACT TWO

The moment the curtain is up, DIRK *and* MARY *enter by the main door, stomping their feet and brushing snow from their clothes. It is shortly after midnight and the room is dark except for the glow from the window.* MARY *turns on the hall light just inside the front door.*

———

DIRK. Did you get wet?

MARY. No, except for my hair.

DIRK. It doesn't look wet.

MARY. No, but you watch. In five minutes it'll be so fuzzy I'll be able to cut a piece off and clean my suede shoes.

DIRK. Would you feel safer if I left the door open?

MARY. Oh dear! I felt perfectly safe until you asked that question.

DIRK. The question is withdrawn.

MARY. Isn't this the silliest snowstorm? (*Going to the window, looking out.*)

DIRK (*closing the door and following her*). I come from California. I think it's a lovely snowstorm.

MARY. But those great big flakes swirling around! It looks so phoney. Like—do you remember those big glass paperweights and you turned them upside down and it snowed? That's how it looks. (*Turns and is surprised to find him right behind her. Unsettled, she points to her bag near the bedroom door.*) Here's that damn bag. Remember—you're not coming back out with me. I'll get a cab.

DIRK. In *this*? You'd never. And here I am—ready—willing—cheaper.

MARY. If I had a brain in my head, I'd have taken it with me and we could have dropped it off at the Biltmore. (MARY *is holding the suitcase in her hand. As* DIRK *goes to take it from her, his hand rests on hers a moment.*)

DIRK. Does everybody tell you how pretty you are?

MARY (*takes her hand away—flustered*). Oh, you *are* a good actor! You could play anything. (*Changing the subject*) You know what? It's really idiotic, our going back out in that blizzard. We're not delivering the serum. (*She comes into the room and turns on a lamp.*) Why don't I just *stay* here? (DIRK *puts the bag down and looks toward the bedroom. In answer to his unspoken question*) Oh, he's safely in Goshen with a beautiful, lovely girl with a head on her shoulders. (*She has remembered* BOB's *description word for word.* DIRK *stares at her a second, then heads for the bar table.*)

DIRK. Do you suppose we can have a drink, or did Bob get the custody of the liquor?

MARY (*she is already a couple of cocktails in, and is beginning to like it*). Sure, let's have a drink. But make mine light. I'm beginning to feel that champagne. (*She turns on another lamp.*) Do you realize we were three hours in that restaurant? That's the nice thing about having dinner with somebody you're not married to. (*She starts to sit on the sofa, then after a glance at* DIRK, *who is making the drinks, discreetly chooses a chair.*) You have so much more to talk about.

DIRK. All I found out about you is that you're allergic to penicillin and you love *The Catcher in the Rye*.

MARY. That's all? That's a lot. I want to hear about you. Are you going to get your book published?

DIRK. I am going to make every possible effort. (*Hands her a drink.*) That's mostly water. (*He moves a chair close to her and sits.*) You and Bob must have spent a lot of time with authors. What do *they* talk about?

MARY. You don't think they talk about *books*? They talk about first serial rights, second serial rights, movie rights, and how they're going to form a corporation to publish their next one so they can call it a capital gain and move to Jamaica.

DIRK. They sound just like actors.

MARY. It's terrible when you feel a writer is trying out his material on you. You never know exactly what reaction they expect, but you have to keep looking so *interested* your eyebrows get tired. (*She has made a concentrated face to show what she means.* DIRK *grins.*)

DIRK. I know a guy who used to work with Disney. He'd actually tell you the whole plot of an animated cartoon—frame by frame. But he was a classic case. He could bore the birds back onto the trees. He never stopped talking—never. If he took a drink, he'd hold his hand up— (*He demonstrates this.*) —so you couldn't put a word in until he was back with you. (MARY *laughs at the demonstration, then calms down into a small silence, which* DIRK *fills.*) Your eyes are so blue —and so liquid. I feel they might spill right down your cheeks.

MARY (*quick with the answer, moving away to get a cigarette, leaving her drink behind*). That's because I need glasses and won't wear them.

DIRK (*curious and interested*). Why do you do that?

MARY. Do what?

DIRK. You jump when you get a compliment.

MARY (*too quickly*). No, I don't.

DIRK. You're actually embarrassed.

MARY (*a shade defensively, lighting her cigarette*). Why should I be embarrassed?

DIRK. I don't know. But you are. You come bustling in to change the subject, like a nervous hostess who's discovered that two of the guests are quarreling. (*Imitating the hostess*) "Now, come along, Harry—there's somebody very nice I want you to meet."

MARY (*sits at one end of sofa*). All right. Pay me pretty compliments and I won't change the subject.

DIRK. And you won't make jokes?

(MARY *is stunned by the echo of* BOB's *remark.*)

MARY. What? What?

DIRK. Shouldn't I have said that?

MARY. No, that's all right. It's been said before. Just recently, in fact. I suppose I should take a course and find out what a girl should answer when a gentleman says "Tell me, pretty maiden, are there any more at home like you?" Though it would hardly pay. It doesn't come up that often.

DIRK. I thought little girls learned things like that when they were three years old. (*He moves nearer to her, bringing her drink.*)

MARY. Oh, but I'm a very retarded case. It's only just this year I learned how to put my hair up in rollers.

DIRK. What did you do before that?

MARY. I wore it pinned back in a bun. And when it had to be cut, *I* cut it, or I went somewhere and *they* cut it. Lately I've been going to Elizabeth Arden, and I want you to know that it's a whole new way of life.

DIRK. So I'm told.

MARY. At Arden's they don't just cut your hair—never. They *shape* it. And they honestly think a good shaping is as important as a cure for cancer. The hairdresser really blanched when he saw my bun. I could hear him thinking, "Thank God she came to me—another month and it might have been too late."

DIRK. Well, I think your hair looks lovely. Now say thank you.

MARY. Thank you.

DIRK. See how easy it is?

MARY (*jumping up, self-conscious*). I— Oh—Tell me about your book. (*Picks up the manuscript.*)

DIRK (*taking the manuscript from* MARY). What can I tell you? It weighs three quarters of a pound. It takes eighty-four cents in stamps to mail it. (*Tosses it on sofa table and goes to the bar for another drink.*)

MARY. Don't talk like that. You mustn't lose faith in it just because Bob didn't like it. Bob's a good publisher but he makes mistakes. Did you have any help with this book?

DIRK. You mean, did I *tell* it to somebody? No.

MARY. I'm glad. All these "as told to" books have such a spooky flavor about them. First the personality is all drained off. Then, to compensate, something else is pumped in—sex or religion or Scott Fitzgerald. I fully expect that any day now we're going to have The Confessions of Saint Augustine—as told to Gerold Frank.

DIRK (*returning to her*). Mary—

MARY. What?

DIRK. You just said Bob makes mistakes. But how did he ever let you slip through his fingers?

MARY. Just lucky, I guess.

DIRK. I think I am beginning to see the clue to this little puzzle.

MARY. What puzzle?

DIRK. You.

MARY. I'd love to think I was a puzzle. A woman of mystery. Smiling and enigmatic on the surface—but underneath, a tigress. (*Change of mood, straightforward*) I hate to admit it, but what you see is all there is. Underneath this plain, girlish exterior, there's a very plain girl.

DIRK. Ah, but what happened to make you *decide* it was such a plain exterior? It was the divorce, wasn't it? It was Bob.

MARY. Bob? I decided *that* when I was thirteen years old. We can't blame Bob for everything.

DIRK. At thirteen, all by yourself, you decided that?

MARY (*sitting on the ottoman*). Oh, there were people around, but I can't say they gave me any argument. Do you ever look at little girls?

DIRK. How little?

MARY (*rather intensely, as she remembers and thinks about it. The intensity is perhaps increased by the amount she's had to drink*). You take two little girls. One of them is pink and round, with curly hair and yards of eyelashes. The other one is pale and bony, with thin, wispy hair and two little ears poking through—like the handles on a sugar bowl. Okay, which one of these little girls is going to have to wear braces on her teeth?

DIRK. The wispy one.

MARY (*as though awarding him a prize*). You've got it. (*Seeing herself again, taking a sip of her drink*) That was me. Braces on my teeth, Band-Aids on my knees, freckles on my nose. All elbows and shoulder blades. For two years running I got picked to play the consumptive orphan in *Michael O'Halloran.*

DIRK. That was talent.

MARY. That was typecasting.

DIRK. All adolescents go through something. I had the worst case of acne in the history of the world. For three years I was a Technicolor marvel. You wouldn't remember when Fleischmann's Yeast was the big thing. I used to eat Fleischmann's Yeast and drink water until I couldn't move without gurgling. I imagine I was actually fermenting.

MARY. I never ate yeast, but once I sent away secretly for Stillman's freckle cream. I guess I used too much, because I just peeled and peeled. I had to pretend it was a sunburn.

DIRK. I used to pretend I hated everybody. Especially girls, because I was too self-conscious to talk to them.

MARY. You made a spectacular recovery.

DIRK. I may even have overdone it. But why didn't you—

MARY. Make a recovery? Well, it was sort of different with me. When I was a kid, I mean really a kid, I never worried about the way I looked, because I thought —I *knew*—I'd grow up to be beautiful just like my sister Clara.

DIRK. Was she so beautiful?

MARY. Clara? She had bright red hair and brown eyes and she always had a faintly startled look, as if she'd just come out of a dark theater into the sunlight. People who met her would be so busy staring they'd forget to finish their sentences.

DIRK. I can see that would have been something of a cross for you.

MARY. No, I thought it was insurance. Clara was six years older than I was, and I thought "I'll grow up to look just like that." One day I was measuring myself— I was about fourteen—and I realized I hadn't grown at all, not an inch, in a whole year. And then it came to me. I wasn't going to grow any more. I was *up*. And I didn't look anything at all like Clara.

DIRK. And you weren't satisfied to look like Mary?

MARY. I certainly was not. I went rushing to my father, and I asked him when I was going to look like Clara. Poor man. He didn't know what to say.

DIRK. What did he say?

MARY. He said "Darling, we wouldn't want two Claras. You're the bright one." That did it. I could have faced being plain, but to be plain *and* bright! In the high school I went to, that was a beatable combination.

DIRK. So you decided to get on the debating team.

MARY. How did you know?

DIRK. Girls who feel they are not going to be invited to dances always get on the debating team.

MARY. And I worked on the school newspaper. And I imagined all the time that I was really Catherine Earnshaw.

DIRK. Catherine who?

MARY. The girl in *Wuthering Heights.* Cathy.

DIRK. Oh, Merle Oberon.

MARY. That's right. I used to dream that somewhere there was a strange, dark man whose heart was quietly breaking for me. On rainy nights I'd open the window and imagine I could hear him calling—"Oh, my wild, sweet Cathy!" The colds I got! And of course the only dark man I ever saw was the middle-aged dentist who used to adjust the braces on my teeth.

DIRK. And you're still cross about it.

MARY. Is that how I sound? I don't feel that way. I feel wistful. I think of that sappy little girl and I wonder what happened to her.

DIRK. Nothing happened. She hasn't changed at all.

MARY. You mean I haven't changed at all? That's a hell of a thing to say.

KIRK. Oh, I'm certain you've changed in appearance. That's clear enough. But you yourself haven't changed. Somewhere inside you, you're *still* wearing braces on your teeth.

MARY. Oh, come, come. I came to the big city. I learned to tip waiters. I read *The New Yorker.* I got married.

DIRK. And nothing took. Do you know what's strange?

MARY. What?

DIRK. Here you are—so lovely. And nobody falls in love with you.

MARY. Oh, is that so? And where did you get that idea?

DIRK. From you.

MARY. You're crazy. I never said—listen, lots of people—well, Bob certainly was in love with me—

DIRK. You really thought so?

MARY. Of course! Why else would he marry me? There was no dowry, or anything.

DIRK. I don't know. Why did he?

MARY (*seriously unsettled beneath her insistent assurance*). Because he felt that —because we both—listen, what is this? (*Rises.*) I haven't answered so many idiotic questions since I tried to open a charge account at Saks! (*Moves away to the fireplace.*) There must be a genteel, ladylike way of telling you that it's none of your damn business!

DIRK. I knew I'd get a rise out of you when I said that about Bob.

MARY. Then why did you say it?

DIRK. Of course Bob was in love with you. But you don't believe it. You never believed it.

MARY (*turns to him, alert*). What did he tell you?

DIRK. Nothing. You're the evidence. Women who believe they're attractive have a certain air about them. You don't. Your reflexes are off.

MARY (*now furious*). I will match my reflexes with your manners any old day! And now, unless you have some other little speech all rehearsed, I suggest you go upstairs or downstairs or wherever it is you call home!

DIRK. Now you're mad.

MARY. Oh, you *are* the quick one! Nothing is wasted on you. Of course I'm mad! What did you expect I'd be?

DIRK. I didn't know. I never met anybody quite like you before.

MARY. We're even. I never met anybody like you, either. (*Sitting at one end of the sofa*) Which doesn't explain why I let myself be taken in by that richer, milder, longer-lasting M-G-M charm.

DIRK. Oh, *were* you—taken in?

MARY. I must have been. Why else would I sit here—babbling like an idiot, pouring out my little girlish secrets! That's not part of my regular act. I don't learn. (DIRK *sits near* MARY *on sofa.*) I guess I never will learn.

DIRK (*putting his hands on her shoulders and speaking earnestly and directly*). Mary, do you know what I feel? I feel—

MARY (*coolly, sarcastically*). You feel as though you were seeing me—for the first time.

DIRK. I'll tell you something you ought to learn. You really ought to learn when to shut up. (*With real dispatch, he takes her into his arms and kisses her firmly.* MARY *is too startled at first to protest, and later she is maybe too interested. When they break off,* DIRK *puts one finger gently to her lips.*) Shh! Now once more— quickly, before you lose your nerve. (*He kisses her again.*)

MARY (*finally*). I feel dizzy.

DIRK. That's suitable.

MARY. It's just that I haven't kissed anybody, lately. But it's like riding a bicycle. It does come back to you.

DIRK. And you don't even have to worry about the calories.

MARY. You know—you're very nice. And about ninety-five per cent correct.

DIRK. About what?

MARY. About a lot of things. But why are you bothering with me?

DIRK. I'm being bribed.

MARY (*taking it as a joke, of course*). I *knew* that. But there must be other reasons. I like *you* because you hurt my feelings and made me lose my temper.

DIRK. And that's a reason?

MARY. To me it is. I've gone so long not reacting to anything, it seems somehow reassuring. It's like—well—if you were absolutely convinced that you had no feeling in your hand, you'd be relieved to burn your fingers.

DIRK (*picking up her hand and kissing it*). What can we do for those fingers? I like you because I think that, with any encouragement, I might fall in love with you. (*She is silent.*) If you're going to say anything, say what you're thinking. Don't invent something.

MARY (*facing up to this*). I'm thinking I'd really like to believe that. So I will.

DIRK. That's my girl. (*And he is kissing her again as* BOB *enters.* BOB, *too, is snowy as he comes in the main door. He stops dead at what he sees.*)

BOB. Mary. What are *you* doing here?

DIRK. Don't ask rhetorical questions. Surely you can see what she's doing.

BOB (*embarrassed, bothered by some instinctive reaction he doesn't understand, and trying to be cordial. After all, it's what he hoped for. His reactions are actually disturbingly mixed*). All I meant, really, was to indicate my surprise that Mary was *here.* I thought we left it that she was going to the Biltmore. I mean—

What *is* the situation now? (*To* MARY, *and still floundering*) I mean, are you just coming or going?

MARY (*sweetly. She's a little bit high*). I'm staying. What about you?

DIRK. We thought you were on your way to Goshen.

BOB (*taking off his coat*). I *was* on my way to Goshen, but there's a blizzard out there. We couldn't even get on the thru-way.

MARY. And I wasn't privy to your change of plans. (*Turns to* DIRK.) Do you know I never in my whole life used the word privy before?

DIRK. Not even for—

MARY (*shaking her head rapidly*). Nope, never. Don't you hate places where they have cute names for the men's room?

DIRK. I hate places where they have cute names for the places. Did you ever hear of a nightclub called the Chez When?

(BOB *moves toward the desk aimlessly. They are continuing their conversation as though he hadn't come in.*)

MARY (*eyes widening*). No.

DIRK. What do you call it when the words are accidentally twisted? Where the minister says the Lord is a shoving leopard—?

MARY. I think that's a spoonerism. I'm always getting words twisted like that. I was buying a hammock for the porch at home. And in a crowded elevator I said, "Miss, where do you have perch forniture?"

DIRK. Perch forniture?

MARY. Don't you just know the un-suitable things that would go on in perch forniture? (*As they laugh, they become more aware of* BOB, *who is feeling very much like a fifth wheel and not liking it.*)

DIRK. Bob, why don't you get yourself a drink?

BOB. Thank you. You're the soul of hos-pitality. (*He does go to get himself a drink.*)

DIRK. Well . . .

MARY. Pay no attention to Bob. It's just that he's systematic. He has his day all planned out. He makes a list. And the snow wasn't on his list and you weren't on his list.

DIRK (*a sly look at* BOB). But we had such an interesting chat at six o'clock. I thought I was definitely in his plans—on his list.

BOB. I'm sorry if I sounded rude. But it happens to be one-thirty, and any hour now I'd like to know where I'm going to lay my head. (*To* MARY) Did I under-stand you to say you were staying here?

MARY (*giddily*). Yes. I'm sleepy. I do not wish to go out into the night that covers me black as the pit from pole to pole. Remember, women and children first. That's the law of the sea. And I'm sure it goes for snowstorms.

BOB. Naturally I don't expect you to go out in this. (*Unable to restrain a note of irony*) Would it be all right if I slept here on the couch?

MARY. Certainly. Be your guest.

DIRK (*to* MARY). Our host is beginning to look glassy-eyed. And since we seem to be sitting on his final resting place, I'd better leave. (*Rising*) But it was a lovely evening. (*Takes* MARY's *hand.*)

MARY (*rising with* DIRK). I thought so. I really thought so.

(*They go hand in hand toward the door.* DIRK *gets his coat.*)

DIRK. I'll call you first thing in the morning. Is ten o'clock too early?

MARY. Ten o'clock is fine.

(DIRK *kisses her lightly but definitely.*)

DIRK (*to* MARY). Good night— (*To* BOB, *cheerily*) Good night!

BOB. Night. (DIRK *goes, closing the main door behind him. There is a slight moment of awkwardness, then* BOB *goes toward the closet.*) Well, I'll get myself a blanket and some sheets. I imagine that extra blanket is still in the storage closet.

MARY (*hasn't stirred*). I imagine.

BOB (*having got out a sheet and blan-ket*). Too bad we can't open the window. This place is full of smoke. (*Waving his arms about to dispel imaginary smoke.*)

MARY. Uh-hm.

BOB (*picks up a large ash tray from the coffee table and dumps the contents of the sofa table ash tray and the mantel ash tray into it. Then empties the large one into the fireplace. Finally, he speaks his mind*). I must say that I'm rather sur-prised at you.

MARY (*bright, cheery*). Yes. I'm a little surprised at me, too.

BOB. You've been drinking.

MARY (*airily*). Yep, that's exactly what I've been doing. It's taught me a valuable lesson. You know what's the matter with this country? Too much sobriety. Too many sober persons.

BOB. May I suggest that you get yourself to bed before you pass right out?

MARY. No, you may not suggest one thing. I do not require your solasitude.

BOB. Solasitude? Solicitude!

MARY (*pleasantly stretching out on the sofa*). All right, that's what I do not require. I feel fine, splendid, top of the morning.

BOB (*cleaning desk ash tray*). I don't get it. I thought you were the conservative, slow-to-warm-up type. Miss Birds Eye Frozen.

MARY. There *was* a rumor like that going round. Isn't it nice to know there's nothing in it.

(BOB *empties the contents of the bookcase and desk ash trays into a wastebasket.*)

BOB. Mary, look. What you do is none of my business. I know that.

MARY. I'm glad you know that.

BOB (*edging toward her, worried*). I never wanted to see you retire to a convent. You *ought* to go out with men. You should get married again. To some man who's in love with you.

MARY (*listening*). What other kind of man would marry me?

BOB. There are men and men. And—well, you don't know what you're getting into here. The idea of you sitting around necking with that bum! What the hell do you know about him?

MARY. Well, let's see. He had a very bad case of acne when he was fourteen years old.

BOB. That clarifies everything. I'm telling you this league is too fast for you, dearie. These glamour boys collect women like stamps—if you want to be added to the collection.

MARY (*sits up on sofa, finally speaking up for herself*). All right. I'll tell you something. He thinks he's falling in love with me.

BOB (*alarmed; feeling responsible*). He said that? Oh, that bastard! But you *couldn't* have believed him?

MARY. Why not?

BOB. Now, honestly. Does it seem very likely that that big, caramel-covered movie idol would come along and just one, two, three, bang, fall in love with a girl like you?

MARY (*sharply hurt, and now fighting tears*). I guess I thought it was possible—even with a girl like me. Isn't that the height of something or other?

BOB (*distressed at what he has said*). Wait, I didn't mean a girl like *you*—I meant any ordinary—

MARY. I *know* what you meant. How could you be clearer? I'm the drab, colorless type and I should know better than to believe it when somebody tells me I'm —pretty. . . . (*She can't help the catch in her voice, try as she may.*)

BOB (*completely unsettled*). Are you going to cry about it?

MARY. Maybe. Maybe. Why not?

BOB. Because you never cry.

MARY. How do you know I never? How do you know? I'll cry if I please! And I please! (*And she lets herself go, having a real, satisfactory cry.*)

BOB. Mary—

MARY (*flinging herself face down on sofa*). Don't you Mary me!

BOB (*out of his depth and railing against it*). It must have something to do with the position of the moon—I don't get it. Some joker tells you you're beautiful and you go all to pieces. I used to tell you you were beautiful and your detachment was marvelous to behold! (*Leans over her.*)

MARY (*sits up—flaring*). You never, never, never told me I was beautiful!

BOB. Of course I did!

MARY. No, you didn't. You said you liked the way I looked.

BOB. That's the same thing.

MARY. It most certainly is not the same thing! The world is full of people that you like the way they look, but you wouldn't say they were beautiful!

BOB. Like who, for instance?

MARY. Like Mrs. Roosevelt!

BOB (*incredulous, entirely serious, and wonderfully maddening*). You didn't think Mrs. Roosevelt was beautiful? My God—the character in that face . . . !

MARY. See? Now I'm a Communist. I'm picking on Mrs. Roosevelt! I *loved* Mrs. Roosevelt. And I'm not talking about character. If there is one thing I'm not interested in having any more of—if there's one thing I'm lousy with—it's character! Oh, why did you come back here tonight? I felt so good. Now I'm cold sober and everything is spoiled!

BOB (*backtracking*). I see that you're

upset. I'm sorry if I—

MARY. You're not sorry. You're merely embarrassed.

BOB. What I *am* is surprised. I never thought I'd find you sobbing on the sofa. For all the world like any other woman. Actually, it's quite becoming. (*Sits near* MARY *and offers his handkerchief.*)

MARY (*taking it and wiping her eyes*). Thank you. I'm so relieved to know that.

BOB. Funny you never cried in the whole five years we were married.

MARY. I figured you were sensitive enough for both of us. You decided right at the beginning that I was the airy type —impervious to wind and weather and small disappointments.

BOB. You make it sound as though I invented your character. For that matter, what's wrong with being the airy type?

MARY (*getting up*). It got to be a bit of a strain. I felt like I was on some damn panel show, twenty-four hours a day. Smiling, affable, humming little snatches of song. Laughing when I didn't know the answers. But affable, affable, affable! You don't know how I longed to get up some morning and feel free for once to be depressed, to be constipated, to be boring. (*Pause*) All right. I was boring.

BOB. No, you were not boring. It's strange we talked so much without communicating. (*The fact has hit him, and he's considering it.*)

MARY. It was hard to communicate with you. You were always communicating with yourself. The line was busy.

BOB (*surprised*). Is that the way it seemed to you?

MARY. It seemed to me that you were taking your emotional temperature six times a day. I could almost hear you asking yourself: "Am I nervous? Am I tense? Did that upset me?" How are you feeling right now?

(BOB *almost doesn't hear this last thrust. He is seriously and soberly thinking back.* MARY *picks up the sheet and blanket.*)

BOB. You're right, of course. I do have a bad habit of asking myself questions— silly questions. But—am I nervous, am I tense? That's more or less reasonable. (*Looking at her*) It was really more foolish than that. I used to ask myself— why doesn't she love me?

MARY (*shocked, unbelieving*). You asked yourself—that?

BOB. All the time.

MARY (*throws bedclothes on sofa, exploding*). That's why I hate intellectuals! They're all so dumb!

BOB. What kind of a statement is that?

MARY. An idiotic statement. I should save my breath and remember that I'm talking to the most sensible man in the western hemisphere.

BOB. Why do you harp on that? I'm not all that sensible.

MARY. But you are! You lead a sensible life. You eat a sensible breakfast. You limit yourself to one pack of cigarettes a day—no more than two cocktails before dinner. You're even sensible about sex.

BOB. Would you like to explain that crack?

MARY. Any man that would tap his wife on the shoulder at eleven o'clock and say "Are you in the mood tonight— because if you're not, I'm going to take a sleeping pill" is just about as sensible as you can get!

BOB (*blanching*). Of course, I don't have Mr. Dirk Winston's technique in these matters.

MARY. No, you don't, more's the pity.

BOB. Look, I didn't mean to bring out your heavy artillery. I merely wanted to save you—

MARY. From what? From Dirk? But I don't want to be saved.

BOB. Just a minute. Surely you—

MARY. If he's just toying with my affections, okay. Maybe I'm in the mood to have my affections toyed with.

BOB. Mary, I promise you—you don't have the whole picture—

MARY. But I've seen the previews. And there's not one thing in this whole world you can do about it. (*Going toward the bedroom.*)

BOB (*starts to follow her, but stops to steel himself*). Mary, I'm ashamed to tell you this, but I think I just *have* to—

MARY (*fiercely*). No, you don't have to, and you're not going to! I won't listen. I had a lovely time—a lovely time, do you hear? And you're not going to spoil it for me! Good night! (*She stomps off into the bedroom, letting the door bang behind her firmly.*)

(BOB *sees* DIRK's *manuscript on sofa table, seizes it, and starts to throw it into the fireplace, then thinks better of it. He goes to his desk and picks up the telephone.*)

BOB. Mr. Winston's apartment, please. (*He fidgets, but the wait is not long. Into phone*) Dirk? You asleep? No, I didn't call to ask if you were asleep. I'm coming down there. I've got to talk to you. (*Pause to listen*) Who's there with you—your agent? Is she pretty? Oh, all right, all right. I believe you. Then you've got to come up here. . . . You make it sound like I was asking you to drive to New Rochelle. It's only one flight up. No, it won't keep until Monday. Listen, it'll only take five minutes—okay, okay. (*Hangs up.*)

(MARY *appears from the bedroom with an alarm clock.* BOB *crosses quickly away from the phone.*)

MARY (*coolly*). Do you want the alarm or shall I keep it?

BOB. You can keep it. I'm hardly likely to *over*sleep on that damn sofa. I'm lucky if I get to sleep. (*Turning off one of the lights.*)

MARY. All right. I'll take the sofa. It doesn't bother me.

BOB (*quickly, alarmed that she'll still be on hand when* DIRK *arrives*). No, no, absolutely not. That's out of the question. Now if you're going to bed, would you go to bed? (*He starts pacing to the window and back to the bar table.*)

MARY (*crossing casually to the alcove bookcase*). What's the matter with you? What are you pacing up and down like that for?

BOB (*stops pacing*). I'm waiting for you to go, instead of which—what are you doing?

MARY. Looking for something to read.

BOB. The place is full of books. What do you want?

MARY. I want something guaranteed not to improve my mind. (*Glancing at books.*) The Gathering Storm . . . The Riddle of Rilke . . . (*Spies* DIRK's *manuscript on the desk.*) Oh. Dirk's book. The very thing. (*She starts for the bedroom, slowing down as her interest is caught by something in the manuscript.*)

BOB. Okay, now. Will you go to bed?

MARY (*slightly puzzled by his urgency*). I'm going. I'm going. (*Taking her suitcase with her, she goes into the bedroom and closes the door.*)

(BOB *breathes a sigh of relief, goes to the main door, opens it slightly so that* DIRK *will not have to ring, then returns to finish making himself a drink. At just this moment* DIRK *can be seen arriving in the corridor. As he is about to put his finger to the bell,* BOB *notices and dives for the door.*)

BOB. *Don't* push that damn buzzer!

DIRK. What's the problem?

BOB. I simply don't want Mary to hear that bell.

DIRK. Shall I come in?

BOB. Yes, of course. (*Drawing him into the room, slightly away from bedroom door. Suddenly he is awkward and nervous in this new situation.*) Listen, can I make you a drink?

DIRK. No, I don't want a drink. I merely want to know why you hauled me up here in the middle of the night.

BOB. Actually, it's only two o'clock. The thing is, I thought that we should—really, what I mean is that I should—(*Doesn't know how to begin.*) You're sure you don't want a drink?

DIRK. Positive.

BOB (*after staring at him helplessly for a second*). Well, I want a drink. (*Goes and gets the one he was making.*)

DIRK. All right. Let's have it.

BOB (*gulping a shot, and taking the plunge*). Look here, Winston . . . you know damn well that all this talk about you and Mary—and my publishing your book—was supposed to be a joke.

DIRK. I thought it was funny.

BOB. Okay, you knew I wasn't serious. Then why—why—?

DIRK. Ah, but you *were* serious! You had the wild-eyed look of a man who knows he has just spoken a true word in jest.

BOB. Look, I shot off my face. A bad habit I must nip in the full bloom. However, I wish to make it absolutely clear that I never intended at any time to make a deal with you involving Mary.

DIRK. And I thought it was an admirable plan! You wouldn't have been losing a wife, you'd have been gaining an author.

BOB. But you've got the whole thing straight now?

DIRK. Certainly.

BOB (*relieved*). I never dreamt that you were *this* anxious to get into print. And

I certainly never thought that Mary—of all people—would sink into girlish incoherence at her first exposure to an actor.

DIRK. Why do you say "of all people—Mary"?

BOB. Because she's got some sense. That she could swallow that corny line!

DIRK. Do you describe everything you don't understand as corny?

BOB. What do you mean?

DIRK. Nothing. I suppose it's all right for me to go now—or did you have some other little confidence to tell me?

BOB. No, that's all. And thank you for coming. You can see I had to clear this up. I'll make your excuses to Mary in the morning.

DIRK. You will what?

BOB. I'll tell her you had to go back to Hollywood—for retakes, or whatever people go back to Hollywood for.

DIRK. And why will you tell her that?

BOB. Well, you don't think you'd be doing her a kindness to continue this little farce?

DIRK. I'm not interested in doing her a kindness. And I *am* going to see her.

BOB (*not understanding at all*). But why? I thought we understood each other. I thought we talked things out!

DIRK. Yes, and you listened very carefully to every word you had to say.

BOB. What do you mean by that?

DIRK. I mean you should take that paper bag off your head. You notice everything but the obvious. What kind of a jerk are you? How dare you suppose that Mary is some kind of a charity case? Where do you get off to suggest that any man who's interested in her has to have three ulterior motives?

BOB (*at a real loss now*). I don't think *that*. I never thought—

DIRK. Well, you gave a very good imitation of somebody who thought that. What I told Mary may well have sounded corny. It seems that I lack literary qualities everywhere. (*Levelly*) But it wasn't a line. (BOB *sinks into the chair at his desk, confused.*) You know, talking to you, I begin to see why Mary is so shy.

BOB (*aghast*). Mary? *Shy?*

DIRK. That's right. Shy *and* insecure. You probably don't believe that, either, even though you're at least two-thirds responsible.

BOB (*he can't be hearing anything*

right). How could I be responsible?

DIRK. I don't know. My guess is that you treated her as though she were intelligent.

BOB. She *is* intelligent.

DIRK (*waving it aside*). Shhh! She'll hear you! (*Going toward door, pausing to size him up.*) Where did you get the habit of making assumptions based only on assumptions? Was your father a lawyer?

BOB (*staring at him*). I'll put it all in a letter.

DIRK. All right. Before I go, I want to say only one thing. Leave her alone. Just leave her alone. Okay? (BOB *isn't grasping.*) I mean—tonight. (*With a gesture to the sofa.*)

BOB (*rising as this penetrates, dumfounded*). Are you nuts? I'm getting married in two weeks!

DIRK. Dandy. I'll send you a pair of book ends. (*He leaves.* BOB *follows him to the door and angrily shoots the bolt. He turns out the hall light, takes off his jacket, picks up the sheet, then throws it down and starts for the bedroom door. He starts to knock on it, but doesn't. Biting his lip, he looks around the room, sees the telephone. With an inspiration, he hurries to it.*)

BOB. Operator? Would you ring this number for me? *My* number. Thank you. (*He hangs up until the phone rings. Then he waits until it stops ringing after three rings. Picks it up.*) Mary? This is Bob. I'm in the living room. (*Pause, while he listens for her to speak. Then the bedroom door whips open and* MARY *appears in the doorway, in pajamas, with the bedroom receiver in her hand.*)

MARY. My God, you *are* in the living room! (*Stares at receiver in her hand, then at him.*) What do you want? (*Holds up one finger, getting into the spirit of the thing, and is repeating her question into receiver as she returns to the bedroom.*) What do you want?

BOB (*exasperated now, into phone*). Oh, stop it! Hang up! You're just trying to make me feel foolish!

MARY (*appearing in bedroom doorway again, with receiver*). *I'm* trying to make *you* look foolish! Who called who from the living room?

BOB. Well, I wasn't going to go barging into your bedroom! (*He hangs up his phone.*) I had something to say to you and there seemed to be no reason why I couldn't say it on the telephone.

MARY (*turning to go*). I'll go back in. You call me again.

BOB. Stay right there! (MARY *merely reaches into the bedroom to hang up her receiver.*) This won't take one minute. I just feel—in all fairness—that I have an obligation to tell you—(*It's a struggle for him, but he's game.*)—that I was wrong, apparently, about Mr. Winston.

MARY. And by what curious process did you arrive at this conclusion?

BOB. I talked to him. He was just up here.

MARY (*her eyes popping*). He *wasn't*— you *didn't*—!

BOB. It was all right. Don't worry. (*Facing her*) He merely told me that I was an insensitive clunk who never appreciated you.

MARY. And what did you say?

BOB. Oh, a number of stupid things. It was not my finest hour. Of course, when he says I didn't appreciate you, that's hogwash. I appreciated you, all right. (*Sits on the sofa.*) I just wasn't able to handle you.

MARY (*softened by* BOB's *direct attitude and drifting into the room*). Don't reproach yourself. I didn't win any prizes for the way I handled you. It takes at least one to make a marriage.

BOB. Do you know how helpless you feel if you have a full cup of coffee in your hand and you start to sneeze? There's nothing to do but just let it splash. That's how I feel in all my relationships any more. Helpless—unable to co-ordinate—splashing everybody.

MARY. You're just tired.

(*Without thinking about it, they seem to have drifted into a perfectly familiar domestic situation.*)

BOB. Listen, you should have heard my various exchanges with Winston today! And thank God you didn't! Talk about a comedy of errors! I try to grasp all sides of the picture. Nobody believes that—but I try.

MARY. Bob, honey—I mean, Bob—I believe it. I certainly believe it. I honestly think you're so busy grasping all sides of the picture that you never stand back and see it.

BOB (*willing to consider this*). Okay.

Give me an example.

MARY. All right. I've been reading Dirk's book. I haven't got very far, but I think it's good.

BOB. Come on now—

MARY. No, you're going to let me finish. It may not win a Pulitzer prize, but it's readable. It's so nice and gossipy. I think it would sell.

BOB. I never said it wouldn't sell. I said I didn't want to do it.

MARY. But why not?

BOB. Oh, we've had this out a hundred times.

MARY. Bob, you won't believe this but I'm glad you have standards. I wouldn't want you to settle for trash. But it's no crime to stay in business. You've got to keep the shop open or you won't be there when a masterpiece comes along. (*Quickly*) Let me get it. (*She dodges briefly into the bedroom for the manuscript, talking as she does, while* BOB *sits and stares at her.*) I'm willing to make you a small bet that you can open it at any page at all and find something that's —nice, interesting. (*Coming back and sitting at one end of the sofa. The atmosphere is casual and they are, for all intents and purposes, man and wife at home alone.*) Maybe it goes to pieces at the end, but I wouldn't know about that. Okay, we'll just open it anywhere. (*Reading from manuscript.*) ". . . Starlets have a reputation for being dumb only because they have such blank expressions. And the smarter they are, the blanker they look, because they've learned that it's impossible to register any emotion without using some muscle which, in time, will produce a wrinkle. Even to look a tiny bit puzzled causes twin lines over the bridge of the nose. (*Glancing at* BOB *to do the expression for him; it strikes her as amusing.* BOB *is simply looking at her. She goes on.*) By the time she is thirty, a starlet has been carefully taught to smile like a dead halibut. The eyes widen, the mouth drops open, but the eye muscles are never involved." (*Turning to* BOB *to explain*) They don't smile like this— (*She smiles as most people do.*) See? You get all these wrinkles. (*Touching her forehead with her fingers to show him.*) They go like this. (*She lets her mouth drop open in a mechanized, slack smile that doesn't involve the eyes.* BOB *is not really hearing her as he looks at her. She becomes aware he isn't responding.*) You don't think that's funny.

BOB (*forced to say something, unable to identify what he's really feeling, the wrong thing pops out*). Haven't you got a robe? (*He rises and crosses away.*)

MARY (*blank*). What do you mean, haven't I got a robe?

BOB (*awkward*). Well—do *you* think it's right for you to be sitting here in your night clothes?

MARY (*blowing*). My night clothes! Good Lord, you'd think it was a black lace bikini! Eight million times you've seen me in pajamas!

BOB. We were married then.

MARY (*staring after him*). Well, look at it this way. The divorce won't be final for two weeks.

BOB (*turns on a lamp*). That may be precisely the point.

MARY. Oh, my, we are so proper! Do you feel yourself in danger of being compromised? Don't worry so much. If I should suddenly throw myself upon you, you could always scream.

BOB. Oh, shut up.

MARY (*continuing blithely*). However, as it happens, I don't have a robe but there must be something around here. (*Sees his overcoat on the window seat.*) Yes, here we are. (*Puts it on; it is, of course, too big for her.*) I trust this will show my good faith and restore your sense of fitness.

BOB. And how do you think you look in that?

MARY (*sweetly*). I don't know. Kind of cute, maybe?

BOB. Boy! All of a sudden you're cocky as hell, aren't you?

MARY. All of a sudden? It took months. It was work, work, work every minute!

BOB. But it's been worth it. Think of having Dirk Winston making passes at you! It must be like getting the Good Housekeeping Seal of Approval.

MARY. Um—sort of.

BOB. When you kissed him, I just hope you didn't damage his porcelain crowns.

MARY (*giggling*). Well, we can't worry about everything. But never mind his crowns, let's talk about his book. (*Reaching for the manuscript on the sofa, secretly pleased at* BOB's *attitude.*)

BOB. I refuse to talk about anything with you in that damn coat. You look like Jackie Coogan in *The Kid*. Here— take it off! (*Reaches for the coat.*)

MARY (*pretending to be shocked, as though fighting for her virtue*). Oh, no— no—please!

BOB (*starting to unbutton it*). Take it off. You only put it on to make me feel like an idiot.

MARY (*struggling*). You're going to break the buttons.

BOB. To hell with the buttons. (*He finally gets the coat off—and they stand facing each other in a moment of nervous intimacy. Instinctively,* MARY *puts her hand to the top of her pajamas.* BOB *backs away slightly.*) No, that's as far as I mean to go. (*Angrily*) Now would you do me a favor, please? Will you please go to bed?

MARY (*below sofa, unsettled herself, now*). Certainly. But what are you so intense about?

BOB. I'm the intense type. Surely you've remarked on that before. I'm asking myself how I feel. And I feel wretched.

MARY. What's the matter?

BOB. You know damn well what's the matter! I feel all involved again. And I won't have it! I will not have it! I was getting over you so nicely. I was cured. My God, I feel like somebody who was getting out of the hospital after nine long months and fell down in the lobby and broke a leg. (*Because he is furious with himself*) And you did it deliberately!

MARY. Did it—did what?

BOB. If you want to pretend that your only purpose in the last half hour was to change my opinion of that book—all right!

MARY (*turns away, more quietly*). But I gather I'm not fooling you—great student of character that you are.

BOB. Okay, what *did* you have in mind —curling up on the sofa, cute as all get-out in your little blue pajamas? No, I'll tell you. You were conducting a little experiment.

MARY. I was?

BOB. You wanted to see—just for the record—if Old Bob wouldn't leap to the bait like our friend Mr. Winston. You just wanted to check and see if I had any little twinges left. (*She says nothing.*) Well?

MARY (*very quietly*). I'm just wondering if that could possibly be true.

BOB. There's no reason for you to be kept in suspense. Yes, if you want to know, I do still feel twinges. God help me. Every now and then a sharp one. Now what do you say?

MARY (*thoughtful for a split second, then, in her perplexity, reverting to type*). Well, I don't know—it *sounds* like a gall bladder attack. (BOB *stares a second, then turns on his heel and grabs his jacket.* MARY *impulsively, and now all regret*) Bob, where are you going?

BOB (*putting on his jacket wildly*). Where am I going? Out! What am I going to do? Nothing! (*He struggles to get quickly into his overcoat, making a mess of the procedure.*)

MARY. Bob, don't be silly! It's still snowing! You'll get pneumonia.

BOB (*hurls his overcoat to the floor and storms out*). Don't you worry your little head. (*Leaving the door open.*)

MARY (*shouting after him*). But where can you possibly go at this hour in the morning? They'll think you're crazy—! (MARY *stands there a moment, her back to us. Then she slowly turns and picks up* BOB's *coat. She comes down to a chair, the coat clutched in her arms. After a second or so, she begins to recite mechanically, like a child writing "lines" as a punishment.*) I must keep my big mouth shut. . . . I must keep my big mouth shut. . . . I must keep my big mouth shut. . . . (*As the* CURTAIN *falls.*)

END OF ACT TWO

ACT THREE

Next morning, rather early.

AT RISE: *The stage is empty but the doorbell is ringing. The sofa is made up with sheet and blanket, but these are obviously unrumpled. In a moment* MARY *comes from the bedroom, still half-asleep. She is in her pajamas.*

———

MARY. Bob . . . (*Staring at the sofa*) Oh. He didn't come back at all. (*She stumbles to the phone.*) Hello. (*Doorbell*) Hello. For heaven's sakes, hello. (*Doorbell again.* MARY *now realizes it isn't the phone.*) Oh. Excuse me. (*Hangs up.*) I'm coming. (*Before she can get to the door, it opens. It is* TIFFANY.) Oh,

hello. Good morning. Oh—you're—I mean, you must be—

TIFFANY (*after a moment of staring at* MARY, *without showing her surprise, she closes the door and speaks cheerily*). I'm Tiffany Richards. And you're Mary, aren't you? Well, I'm delighted to meet you. May I come in?

MARY. Certainly. By all means. I don't know *where* Bob is . . .

TIFFANY (*taking off her coat*). He's probably taking a walk. Lately I've been getting him to take a walk before breakfast. It's the very best thing for a sluggish colon.

MARY (*vaguely, still sleepy and not knowing where to settle or what to do next*). Yes, I can imagine it would be.

TIFFANY (*opening the curtains*). I never dreamt I'd find you here. But I'm so pleased it worked out this way. I've been dying to meet you. And it's a good thing Bob isn't here.

MARY. Why?

TIFFANY. Oh, he'd be bustling me right out the front door. For some reason, he was determined I wasn't going to meet you. You know, you're much shorter than I expected.

MARY (*not bitchy*). Of course I don't have any shoes on.

TIFFANY. It's just that Bob always makes you sound so overpowering. I expected somebody with a husky voice who said "darling" a lot. Harlequin glasses, big jangling bracelets, black velvet toreador pants.

MARY. But I do have a bracelet that jangles. I just don't wear it to bed.

TIFFANY. No, I can tell what you're like just by looking at you. I think you're nice.

MARY. Oh, dear.

TIFFANY. What's the matter?

MARY. It's so early. And you want to be frank and disarming.

TIFFANY. But what's wrong with that?

MARY (*going toward the bedroom, quickly and apologetically*). Oh, nothing, nothing at all. It's just my low metabolism. I don't grasp things this early in the day. I mean, I hear voices, all right, but I can't pick out the verbs. (*Goes into the bedroom.*)

TIFFANY (*taking a dried apricot from the bowl*). You probably don't eat right. My grandmother is like that.

MARY (*returning, rummaging through her purse*). Oh, no. It's not possible! The way I feel and I don't even have a cigarette.

TIFFANY. Look, I wouldn't bother you, but Bob will be back and then I'll *never* get a chance to ask you.

MARY (*looks in the cigarette box on the sofa table*). Ask me? Ask me what? (*From now on* MARY *is making an abstracted effort to listen to* TIFFANY *but what she is really doing is making a methodical and increasingly desperate effort to find a cigarette somewhere around the apartment.*)

TIFFANY. I guess I should warn you that I'm a very practical kind of person. People tease me about it all the time. Last Christmas, when I went to Palm Beach, everybody thought I was crazy because I took along my sun lamp, except it rained every day and I was the only one who came back with a tan.

MARY. Yes, but what did you want to ask me?

TIFFANY. I'm getting to that. Daddy always said that before you move into a house, you should consult the former tenant.

MARY. Oh. (*Checking the bookshelves and* BOB's *desk for a cigarette.*)

TIFFANY. The person who's been living there will know where the storm windows are and whether there's a leak in the basement. Why should you spend six months finding out for yourself?

MARY (*at the desk, too foggy to understand*). They don't have storm windows in this building.

TIFFANY. I'm not talking about the apartment. I'm talking about Bob.

MARY. You want to know if Bob has a leak in the basement? (*Her last resort*) Excuse me—you don't have a cigarette on you, do you?

TIFFANY. I'm sorry. I don't smoke. It's not that I worry about lung cancer, but it does stain your teeth.

MARY. Well, I worry terribly about lung cancer. I also worry about shortness of breath and heart disease. But what really worries me right this minute is that I'm not going to find a cigarette. (*Begins looking through the desk drawers.*)

TIFFANY. Oh, I guess you never do find out. My cousin Harriet knew this boy for seven years. I mean she *thought* she knew him. But on the day they were married they took an overnight train to Chicago. And when they shut the door of their roomette, do you know the first thing he did?

MARY. No, and don't tell me.

TIFFANY. Well, he picked up a book of matches, opened the cover, and started picking his teeth. Like this. (*Demonstrates "picking his teeth" with a lid of book matches. The key turns in the front door and* BOB *enters, the Sunday papers under his arm. He stops, startled and then embarrassed to find the two girls together.*) Hi.

BOB (*pulling himself together with an effort*). Well. This is cozy. (*Then rattled again, quick to overexplain*) Tiffany, I should have explained to you last night that you'd find Mary here. (*Stopping to listen to himself*) Of course, I didn't know last night. (*Now really confused, looking at* MARY) I suppose you've introduced yourselves.

TIFFANY (*rising and kissing* BOB *on the cheek*). Oh yes, of course! (*She goes into the kitchen.*)

BOB. Good morning, Mary.

MARY. Good morning, Bob. Did you have to go without your overcoat?

BOB. At the time I thought so.

MARY. I made up your bed because I expected— (BOB *takes off his jacket.*) What did you do?

BOB. Walked, mostly. (*Looking for a cigarette on the low bookcase.*)

MARY. Don't tell me you're out of cigarettes, too?

BOB (*patting his pockets. But they're empty*). Yes, but you'll find some in the desk drawer.

MARY. No, I looked.

BOB. Well, did you try behind the—

MARY. Yes, and I tried the liquor cabinet and the stamp drawer. (TIFFANY *returns with wheat germ for the fish.*) And the last refuge of all—the Chinese vase—

BOB (*starting his own search*). Don't tell me I'm going to have to go trudging back out in that snow!

TIFFANY. Just for a cigarette? Would you like some breakfast? There's some orange-flavored yogurt.

BOB. Oh, no, no. Lord, no! Tiffany, be a lamb and fold up these sheets. There may be some under the—

MARY. See! If you hadn't dumped every

single ash tray last night I could have found some medium-sized butts.

(TIFFANY *folds up the blanket, watching* MARY *and* BOB *feverishly search every conceivable nook.*)

BOB. We must remain calm. It is statistically impossible that in this whole big apartment there isn't one single—just ask yourself: Where would you go if you were a cigarette? (*From beneath the cushion of a chair he brings up a battered half package.*) Look! Success! (MARY *runs to him.*)

MARY (*as though cooing over a new baby*). There! Did you ever see anything so pretty in your life?

(BOB *is digging for matches to light* MARY's *cigarette.*)

TIFFANY. But they're all squashed!

(MARY *and* BOB *simply turn to stare at* TIFFANY, *simultaneously and incredulously. Then they turn their attention to the serious business of getting the cigarettes lighted, after which they exhale. Forgetting themselves, they speak in unison.*)

MARY *and* BOB. Mmmm—that's *real* coffee! (*Becoming aware of what they have just done, they are a little embarrassed and pause awkwardly.*)

TIFFANY (*looking up as she puts blanket away*). Coffee? What's that about coffee?

BOB (*firmer*). Nothing. Absolutely nothing.

TIFFANY. It must be something.

BOB (TIFFANY *is obviously waiting for an explanation.* BOB *launches into it lamely*). We once heard this announcer on television. It was late at night and I suppose the poor joker was confused from having to talk about so many products all day. Anyway, he started to do a cigarette commercial. He sucked in and smiled and said "Mmmm—that's *real* coffee." (TIFFANY *does not react.*) You see, it *wasn't* worth going into. (*Determined to be brisk and cheerful*) All of which reminds me that I haven't had any coffee. I think I'd better start some up. (BOB *goes into the kitchen almost too quickly, closing the door. There is a slight pause as* TIFFANY *looks at* MARY.)

TIFFANY. How long does it take to have little private jokes?

MARY. What?

TIFFANY. Never mind. (*She begins to*

fold the sheet on the sofa.) I must stop asking questions for which there are no answers. (*Stops folding and looks reflectively at the sheet.*) This sheet isn't even mussed. (*Looks at sofa.*) Nobody slept on this sofa last night.

MARY. No. Bob was going to, but—

TIFFANY. He changed his mind.

MARY. (*not wanting to go into what really happened*). That couch is a little short for him. Anyway, he decided that—

TIFFANY. —he'd rather sleep with you. (*She finishes folding the sheet, matter-of-factly.* MARY's *mouth drops open, but not for long.*)

MARY. You mean—for old times' sake? No, indeed. Bob went—well, as a matter of fact, I don't *know* where he went. But he certainly wasn't here. As you will discover when you ask him.

TIFFANY. I won't ask him.

MARY. (*looking at her*). Because you don't believe me.

TIFFANY. No, I don't.

MARY. Tiffany, when you get a little older, you'll learn not to *invent* problems. All you have to do is wait, and real ones turn up.

TIFFANY. In a way—I think I'm just as glad it happened.

MARY. You are.

TIFFANY. Bob's attitude toward you has always been a little mysterious. I'm hoping this may clear the air.

MARY. Your theory is that he's a little bit homesick and a trip back to the old place may cure him?

TIFFANY. All right, yes. That's what I think. (BOB *returns briskly from the kitchen, carrying a tray with coffee cups and an electric coffee maker on it.*)

MARY. Bob. I'm afraid our little secret is out.

BOB (*casually, unraveling electric cord*). What little secret?

MARY. No, Bob, please, Tiffany *knows*. And she's being very understanding.

BOB (*glancing at* MARY *but kneeling to put the cord into the light socket*). Would you care to be plainer? I'm simply not up to riddles this morning.

MARY. Certainly. I'm trying to tell you that Tiffany is glad we slept together last night. She thinks it will clear the air.

BOB (*hearing it, and instantly up*). What did you say? What?

MARY (*blithely*). I really must get

dressed. (MARY *goes off to the bedroom, closing the door behind her.*)

BOB (*turning to* TIFFANY). Did I hear her correctly?

TIFFANY (*offering him the bowl of apricots*). Bob, whatever you do—please don't apologize.

BOB (*waving the bowl away and circling her*). You're damn right I won't apologize!

TIFFANY. All right, but are you going to snap at *me*?

BOB. Wait a minute. You accept this as a *fact*—and you're not even disturbed?

TIFFANY. Should I be?

BOB. Well, I can think of six reasons why you ought to be. And you can't even think of one?

TIFFANY. It isn't like it was somebody new. It isn't even like you planned it. You're put back into an old situation, and you fall into an old pattern.

BOB. I see.

TIFFANY. Anybody will tell you that the force of habit is stronger than—than love, even.

BOB. And in spite of the fact that I shack up with my ex-wife, you're willing to marry me?

TIFFANY. Certainly.

BOB. My God, haven't you got any principles, any ethics?

TIFFANY (*aroused, finally*). How did my principles ever get into this? What have *I* done?

BOB (*turning away and rubbing his forehead violently. Then he collapses into the chair behind the desk and begins rummaging through the desk drawers*). I've got to take some aspirin. I've got to clear my head.

TIFFANY. What's the matter?

BOB. You've heard of a lost weekend. Well, this has been a found weekend and it's worse.

TIFFANY. I'll get some water. (*She goes into the kitchen, leaving the door ajar.*)

(BOB *now brings out, one by one, about a dozen bottles of pills of varying sizes, including aspirin.*)

BOB. I feel in my bones that this is going to be one little peach of a day. I've got to take something to clear my head or I'm going to goof. I'm going to make some crucial mistake. (TIFFANY *returns with a glass of water.*) And where the hell is Oscar?

TIFFANY. On Sunday, what do you want with Oscar?

BOB (*taking the glass and two aspirins*). There!

TIFFANY. Also take two of those large vitamins. (*With a glance at the bedroom door;* MARY *is on her mind.*)

BOB. Why? (*He opens a bottle and takes out three capsules.*)

TIFFANY. Alcohol works directly on the blood stream. (*He swallows one.*) If you drink too much it lowers the white count, which is one reason why—

BOB (*with another one in his mouth*). No, no—don't give me the details. (*Downs a third.*) Now I've taken three. There. I can feel my white blood count going up already.

TIFFANY (*suddenly noticing the bottle and picking it up*). Bob. You didn't take these?

BOB. You told me to.

TIFFANY. You idiot! These aren't vitamins.

BOB. What are they?

TIFFANY. Sleeping pills.

(BOB *snatches the bottle from her and looks at it.*)

BOB (*to heaven in despair*). Oh, great. Great!

TIFFANY. Do you feel peculiar?

BOB. Not yet.

TIFFANY. Well, you will. We'd better get something.

BOB. It's not going to kill me. You have to take a whole bottle—a hundred and twenty, or something. (*Doorbell.* TIFFANY *starts to answer it.*) That'll be Oscar.

TIFFANY (*on her way to door*). Don't sit down. (BOB *jumps up.*) I think you're supposed to keep walking around.

BOB. You're thinking of concussion. (*He drops into a chair again.*)

TIFFANY (*opening the door.* DIRK *appears*). Oh—come in! You're Dirk Winston, aren't you?

DIRK. Yes. And you're—?

TIFFANY. I'm Tiffany Richards. (*Pulling* DIRK *into the room*) And we've got a problem. Bob has taken some sleeping pills.

DIRK. Bob has!

BOB. Tiffany, please! Don't turn this into a melodrama. (*To* DIRK) I just—

TIFFANY (*To* DIRK, *pointing to the coffee maker*). Do you think you could get him some coffee? I'll go to the drugstore and

see if I can get some benzedrine or
Dexamil—

BOB. They won't give you that without
a prescription.

TIFFANY (*slipping on her coat*). They'll
give me something, don't you worry. I'd
call a doctor, but they want to ask you a
lot of crazy questions, like are you depressed. (*To* DIRK) You'll watch out for
him, won't you?

DIRK. Like a mother. Now, don't worry.
(TIFFANY *rushes out the front door.* DIRK
wanders casually down to BOB.) Why did
you do it?

BOB. Because my life has suddenly become ashes. I didn't know which way to
turn.

DIRK. Come off it. How many did you
take?

BOB. Three. Look, I got the bottles
mixed up. I thought I was taking vitamins. Any more questions?

DIRK. Yeah. Where's Mary?

BOB (*crossly*). Well, the last time I saw
her, she was in pajamas, so I think we
may safely suppose she's dressing.

DIRK. What the hell are you so irritable
about?

BOB. Because I had a rotten night! I
drank too much, slept too little—

DIRK. You're not fooling anybody.
You're mad as a hornet because I'm here
to get Mary.

BOB. Why should I be mad? I'm delighted!

DIRK. You *sound* delighted.

BOB. Never mind my inflections. I just
haven't had your training.

DIRK. You know, there's something very
mysterious about your feeling for Mary.
It's like gas. You can't get it up and you
can't get it down.

BOB (*the thought registers with* BOB *but
he doesn't blanch*). There's a touch of the
poet in you.

(MARY *enters from the bedroom,
dressed, and looking just splendid.*)

MARY (*very cheery, seeing* DIRK). Good
morning!

DIRK. Good morning. You just getting
up?

MARY. Oh, I've been up for an hour. In
fact, I've already had a heart-to-heart talk
with Miss Richards.

BOB (*going to the bar table*). I've got
to have some coffee.

MARY (*sweetly*). And would you bring

me some, please? And a Danish that's—

BOB (*mechanically, swerving from the
coffee maker toward the kitchen*). —cut
down the middle, and no butter. I'll get
it. (*Goes into the kitchen, closing the
door.*)

DIRK. I woke up this morning thinking:
What nice thing just happened to me?
And it was you.

MARY. You're very sweet. And not like
a movie actor at all.

DIRK (*pouring her a cup of coffee*).
Sure I am. Movie actors are just ordinary,
mixed-up people—with agents.

MARY. I should think it would be fun
to be Dirk Winston.

DIRK. It is. There are all kinds of advantages. I can go into any restaurant
at all and the headwaiter will automatically bring me a large pepper mill. Doctors don't get pepper mills—or lawyers.
Not only that, but the headwaiter stands
right there until I use it. I don't want
him to feel a failure, so I grind away.
With the result that I've had too much
pepper on everything for twenty years.
I love the way you smile.

MARY (*nervous, but meaning every
word of it*). Dirk, I want you to know
that I will never forget last evening. You
couldn't possibly know what you did for
me.

DIRK. Yes, but what have I done for
you lately?

MARY. I'm not joking. I'm terribly
pleased—and gratified.

DIRK (*urgently*). Gratified, hell! I don't
want you to be gratified. I want you to be
interested. I want you to say it would
cause you a real pang if you thought you
weren't going to see me again.

MARY. Oh, Dirk, it would—it does.

DIRK. I got a call from the studio at
eight o'clock. They insist that I fly to New
Orleans this morning for some personal
appearance stuff. That picture of mine
is opening there Thursday.

MARY. In New Orleans?

DIRK (*nodding*). The picture is called
King of the Mardi Gras. That's how the
great minds in publicity operate—the
mayor meets me at the airport and hands
me a praline or some damn thing. There's
nothing I can do about it. It's in my contract. Anyway, here's the point. Why
don't you come along?

MARY. But Dirk! I'm a working girl.

DIRK. Surely they could carry on without you for one week. Never underestimate the power of the *Ladies' Home Journal*.

MARY. But you just don't *do* that . . . !

DIRK. Sure you do. You call up and say that you've just had a recurrence of an old football injury. We could have a lot of fun. We could get to know each other.

MARY. But Dirk, I don't go off on trips with movie stars—I read about people like that in the *Journal-American* and I'm scandalized!

DIRK. Come on. Be rash. Fly now, pay later.

(BOB *returns with an empty paper carton.*)

BOB. Dirk, we seem to be all out of everything. Could I ask you to go down to the bakery and get a half-dozen Danish? It's for Mary.

MARY. Oh, let's have toast—anything.

BOB. No, there's nothing out there. I'd go myself, but I'm feeling so groggy.

DIRK (*rising and looking at his watch*). I don't *have* all that time . . . (*And looking at* MARY.)

BOB. It's right in the building. Go left after you get out of the elevator.

DIRK. Well, I started life as a messenger boy.

MARY. Oh, don't bother.

DIRK. That's all right. I have to see if they've got my luggage in the lobby anyway. (*With a curious glance at* BOB, *then at* MARY) Mary—think about it. . . . (*He goes.*)

MARY. I don't know who ate them, but there was a whole bagful last night.

BOB. I stuffed them in the wastebasket.

MARY. You what?

BOB. I wanted to get him out of here so I could talk to you.

MARY (*starting for door as though to stop* DIRK). If that isn't the dumbest thing! Why should he have to—?

BOB (*grabbing her and spinning her around*). It won't hurt him a bit. You know—I'd like to shake you until your teeth rattled.

MARY. Oh, come on! In your whole life you never even shook a bottle of magnesia.

BOB. Why, why, *why* would you tell Tiffany that we slept together last night?

MARY (*honestly*). Look, Bob, whether you believe it or not, I said nothing to

give Tiffany that impression.

BOB (*this rocks him a little*). Then why did she—?

MARY. I don't know. Some people have such a talent for making the best of a bad situation that they go around creating bad situations so they can make the best of them.

BOB. (*trying to think*). She didn't seem upset at all.

MARY. Upset? I got the impression she was delighted.

BOB. I know. I don't understand it. I don't understand anything. (*He sinks into a chair.*) Mary, I'm so miserable.

MARY. Why?

BOB. You should know why. Look, in all the months we've been separated, have you been happier?

MARY (*reflectively*). No.

BOB. Have you—ever thought we might get back together again?

MARY (*trying to hide the emotion she feels*). It crossed my mind. (*She sits near him, tentatively.*)

BOB (*after a breath*). Would you consider it?

MARY (*struggling to control the relief and joy that want to come into her voice*). Bob, do you know what you're saying? Do you *mean* it?

BOB (*surprisingly making no move toward her*). I do mean it. (*Thinking, and even turning away*) I've been behaving like a damn adolescent—refusing to face the simple facts.

MARY (*a little taken aback*). What simple facts?

BOB. Look at the whole thing in sequence. (*Counting the items on his fingers, logically*) A—I wanted a divorce from you because—well, it boils down to something as simple as I didn't think you understood me. Okay. (*Next finger*) B— the minute we got divorced, I discovered what I should have known in the first place—that I'm the kind of man who has to be married.

MARY (*hurt now, but keeping a level tone*). Is that what you discovered?

BOB (*going on with his explanation as though he were addressing a committee, completely unaware of the effect on* MARY). Absolutely. This business of going from flower to flower never did appeal to me. I hate to live alone. I hate to sleep alone. I keep finding myself, at four o'clock in the morning, sitting in the bathroom reading old magazines. So—I decided to get married again. That's C. In the circumstances, it seemed the logical thing to do.

MARY (*taking his tone*). I'd say so—yes.

BOB. But wait a minute. Now I discover that Tiffany really believes that I would actually sleep with one woman on the very eve of marrying another. By this time she should know me better than that. It isn't in my character. I'm really too square. But the point remains. *She* doesn't understand me, either.

MARY (BOB *doesn't notice the acid that begins to creep into her voice*). Okay, we've had A, B, and C. What about D?

BOB (*innocent, and eager to go on explaining*). Well, I ask myself—am I walking with my eyes wide open into another case of incompatibility? In five years will there be another divorce? I don't think I could face it. (*He sinks onto the sofa, yawning.*)

MARY (*casually, still playing along, though we can hear what's going on inside her*). No, and there would be more alimony, too.

BOB. Oh! More alimony, more scenes, more confusion! The thing is, you and I may be incompatible, but we know all about it now. I think we should get married again. It would be the sensible, reasonable thing to do. Don't you? (*He doesn't have to wait too long for his answer.* MARY *rises.*)

MARY. You clunk. You block of wood. You're dumb—you're obtuse—you're—do you know something? I was so much in love with you that when you left I thought I'd die. That's right—big, healthy, well-adjusted Mary—I thought I might just possibly die! I used to sleep with the light on because in the beginning I'd wake up in the dark and forget where I was—and I'd reach out for you. Do you know if I saw a man ahead of me in the subway who walked like you or had shoulders like you, I used to feel faint, really faint. And you have the gall to stand there and talk to me about the sensible reasons why I should come back to you. You and your damn, stinking ABC's! (*She starts for the bedroom.*)

BOB (*with his head blown off*). Wait a minute—just because I try to be rational doesn't mean I don't *feel* anything—

MARY. Well, we won't really know until after the autopsy. Let me give you a little piece of advice. I think you should go right ahead and marry Tiffany. It would be more than a marriage. It would be a merger. You should be as happy as two IBM machines clicking away together!

BOB (*trying to salvage his dignity*). So you're not coming back.

MARY. That's right. *A*—I don't want to, *B*—I don't want to, *C*—I don't want to! (*She starts into the bedroom.*)

(OSCAR *has let himself in,* DIRK *having left the door part-way open.*)

OSCAR. What don't you want to do?

MARY. Oh, hello, Oscar— (*She stops in the bedroom doorway, all passion spent.*)

OSCAR (*closing the door—to* BOB). I got your message. I'm shocked to see you looking so well.

BOB. What do you mean?

OSCAR (*getting out of his coat*). The answering service said it was absolutely urgent that I get over here this morning. *Urgent* was underlined three times.

BOB. Oh. (*An embarrassed glance in* MARY's *direction.*)

OSCAR. I presumed that you were at death's door—waiting for me to draw up your will.

BOB. Of course not. It was really nothing that important. Actually it was really something minor. I mean, it could have—

MARY (*whirling on* BOB, *exasperated*). Oh, stop it! Why don't you tell him why you called him up this morning and asked him to come over? (*To* OSCAR) He thought he'd come back and find nobody here but *me*—and he'd be left alone with me. But think of it—you're too late! The damage has been done.

BOB (*outraged, blowing*). That's right! Listen to *her!* She knows my mind so much better than I do.

MARY. Oscar, when you go back over his accounts, you may deduct the amount he pays me in alimony. I don't want it. I never wanted it. I'm working now, and I don't need it.

BOB (*angrily*). Oh, don't be noble, there's no necessity!

MARY. Oh, but there is! (*To* OSCAR) Do you realize that if this poor soul had to go on paying alimony to me, he could never divorce Tiffany? Oscar, I sat at home and waited nine long months for him to call. Well, I'm not sitting home any longer. (*Heading for the bedroom*) Now I'm going to pack. (MARY goes, *slamming door behind her.*)

OSCAR. Congratulations You seem to have solved everything.

BOB. Oh, Oscar, you don't know what you're talking about! Even my problems have problems! (*Uncontrollably, he yawns right in* OSCAR's *face, then plunges on without pausing, in the same overwrought way.*) What am I going to do? I can't marry Tiffany. She pushes in the bottoms of chocolates!

OSCAR. I never thought you would marry Tiffany.

BOB. Stop sounding like an owl and tell me what to do!

OSCAR. Get Mary back.

BOB. That's the conclusion I came to. But how?

OSCAR. Ask her.

BOB. Ask her? Last night I pleaded with her. Today I tried to be reasonable!

OSCAR (*quietly*). So that's what she's so mad about?

BOB. Yeah! And can you explain to me why *that* should make a woman mad?

OSCAR. Not in the time we have at our disposal. But I can tell you you'd be better off giving her one idiotic reason.

BOB. What do you mean?

OSCAR. Tell her you want her back so you can bite her shoulders.

BOB. You try and tell her something! Do you know that she's actually convinced I never noticed she was pretty? What does she think—I just arrived in from Mars? (*Yawn*) I've got two eyes. Hell, she always was pretty. When I first saw her with that pale hair and that pale face I thought she looked like a lovely piece of white porcelain.

OSCAR. Did you tell her?

BOB. Are you crazy? She would have said "White porcelain—you mean like the kitchen sink?"

OSCAR. Come on, now, you exaggerate.

BOB. Exaggerate? You don't know the half of it. She thinks I'm made of cast iron. She thinks I've never felt even a pang. Like I was some sort of vegetable. Do you know why I put that stinking phone in the bedroom? Because after we broke up I thought she might call me in the middle of the night some night and I

wanted to be sure that I'd hear it. And before she gets out of here this afternoon I'm going to tell her about that phone. She's going to hear a few plain truths. She's not going to call me a block of wood. (*He starts toward the bedroom.*) She's not going to— (*He is stopped by the return of* TIFFANY, *who hurries in by the main door with a small package.*)

TIFFANY. Darling, how do you feel now? Are you all right? Hello, Mr. Nelson. I don't know what this is but he said it would help. (*Gives him a small box wrapped in blue paper.*)

BOB. Thank you, darling. It was sweet of you to dash out and get things. (*But he is plainly befuddled by his own mixed emotions.*)

TIFFANY (*sensing the problem*). Bob— you have something to tell me. You've had something to tell me ever since you came in this morning.

BOB (*evasive*). What? No, I didn't—I don't.

(OSCAR *is trying to make himself invisible by examining the fish tank.*)

TIFFANY. You think you're inscrutable. You're the most scrutable man I ever met. Now, *tell* me—sleepy or no. You know, if you repress things, eventually you become devious—tell me!

BOB. Tiffany! Oscar is going to think *you've* taken an overdose of something.

TIFFANY. Don't worry about Oscar. He hasn't been surprised by anything since Truman was elected president. Tell me!

BOB (*trying to avoid a showdown, scarcely knowing his own mind and not up to a decision anyway*). Tiffany— honey—please—

TIFFANY. (*crisply*). All right, I'll tell you. You've discovered that you're still in love with Mary.

(OSCAR *perks up an ear.*)

BOB (*shocked*). Did I say anything whatsoever to lead you to think that?

TIFFANY. Of course not. And you never would. You'd be much too embarrassed. You'd think it was adolescent and in rather bad taste. Instead, you were going to tell me all the reasons why it would be a mistake for me to marry you. (BOB *is trying to shake his head "no," but she goes confidently on. To* OSCAR) I figured it all out while I was going to the drugstore.

BOB (*groaning and blinking his eyes*).

No, no—not today!

OSCAR. What *are* the reasons? I'm interested even if Bob isn't.

TIFFANY (*systematically and incontrovertibly*). Well, one, he's thirteen years older than I am. That may not seem important now, but in ten years the gap will seem even wider. Then, two— (*She is just as thorough and efficient in her reasoning as* BOB *was with* MARY.) —he's a divorced man, which makes him a bad risk to start with. A girl of my age really deserves better than that. Finally, he's not a rich man, never will be a rich man, and he could never provide the Dior originals and the sable stoles that a girl of my upbringing would naturally expect. (*She has given a good imitation of* BOB, *without sounding unlike herself.*)

BOB. Nonsense! I never would have brought up that part about the money. It never occurred to me.

TIFFANY (*slowly, pointedly, only a shade regretfully*). But all the rest of it— *did* occur to you?

BOB (*terribly embarrassed, and really fighting off sleep now*). Oh, Lord, I don't mind that I'm a bastard. What hurts is that I seem to be such an *inept* bastard. (*Yawning in spite of himself*) Tiffany, what can I say that—

(*At this moment* DIRK *returns by the main door, a bag of buns in his hand.*)

DIRK. I've got the buns.

OSCAR. Congratulations!

DIRK (*noticing that although* BOB *is standing up, supporting himself with the back of a chair, his eyes are closed*). I thought only horses could sleep standing up.

OSCAR. Bob is exceptional. We shall not see his like again.

(MARY *enters from the bedroom with her suitcase and coat.*)

OSCAR (*To* BOB). What is the matter with you?

(BOB *shakes his head to wake himself.*)

BOB. I should have cards printed; I took three sleeping pills by accident. (*He lets himself into a chair, puts his feet on another, and instantly drowses off.*)

TIFFANY. Freud says there are no accidents. I think he wanted to pass out.

MARY. He was anticipating the popular demand. Dirk, I'll bet if I said I was coming to New Orleans with you—you'd go right into shock.

DIRK. What do you want to bet? Mary, are you . . . coming?

MARY (*struggling toward a decision*). I have half a mind to. I used to be superior to this kind of thing. But any minute now I'll be too old.

DIRK. That's right, you'll be seventy and you'll have nothing to repent.

OSCAR. May I come too? She might need a lawyer.

TIFFANY. But you wouldn't go and leave Bob like that!

MARY. We could cover him with a sheet. (*She starts to eat a bun, reflectively.*)

TIFFANY. How can you be so unfeeling?

MARY. My dear he has you. And when he wakes up he has all those dried apricots.

TIFFANY. But he doesn't have me. Not any more. We had an intelligent talk and I'm leaving.

MARY. That's my boy.

OSCAR. I wish he could hear this. I suggest you toss a coin. The loser takes Bob. (*He gives* BOB *an urgent, if surreptitious, poke in the ribs.*)

BOB. What, what? (*Jumping up, grabbing more coffee*) There's something important going on. I've got to stay awake.

DIRK (*quickly, to* MARY). Honey, you know this plane is being met by a gaggle of city officials. That means you have to decide right now. We have to leave in ten minutes.

MARY. Yes, I realize that . . . !

OSCAR (*crossing to* MARY). You understand that once you get on that plane you can't change your mind and get off at 125th Street. Now I think we should thrash this out.

TIFFANY (*composing herself formally on the ottoman*). Yes, that's what I think.

MARY. Sure, why don't we call in David Susskind and have a panel discussion. (BOB *falls asleep again.*) Oh, Oscar, I don't mean to be short with you but if I want to go with Dirk why shouldn't I?

TIFFANY. Well, for one thing, when a conservative person like you decides to embark on an indiscretion, you should practice up on little things before you fly off with a movie actor. You don't start at the top.

OSCAR. You see what she means. There's a hierarchy of skills.

DIRK. Just a minute. What makes you

all so certain that I'm just a movie star on the make and that Mary is another pickup?

TIFFANY. Well, you use a cigarette holder . . . and her very own husband wants her back.

MARY. He is no longer my very own husband.

TIFFANY. But he was and . . .

OSCAR. May I take this one? Remember you and Bob chose each other. Now you'd tell me that you chose Bob in spite of his faults. I'd tell you that you chose him because of his faults. What is missing in him is probably necessary for what is missing in you. Let us not to the marriage of true impediments admit minds.

DIRK. Am I hearing right? Are you suggesting that these two people stay together for mutual therapy? I haven't heard anything so dumb since my press agent told me he was getting married because it made it easier to register at the Plaza.

TIFFANY. Under what circumstances are you in favor of marriage?

DIRK. What do you mean, in favor? Marriage isn't something that has to be supported like low-cost housing or the bill of rights. It's something that happens like a sneeze . . . like lightning. Mary, I'll ask you once more. Will you take a chance? Will you come?

OSCAR. Why should she take a chance? (*To* MARY, *forcibly*) You still yearn after *Bob.* I know you do.

(OSCAR's *stress on the word "Bob" has penetrated the fog, like an alarm bell.* BOB *comes to slightly and looks around.*)

MARY. Are we going to be naïve about this? Asking me whether I yearn after Bob is about as sensible as asking a reformed alcoholic whether he ever thinks about bourbon! What difference does it make? I'm on the wagon for good and sufficient reasons. And I feel a lot better. Dirk, I *am* going with you.

BOB. Where are you going? (*To* OSCAR) Where is she going?

DIRK. She is going to New Orleans with me.

BOB (*coming between* MARY *and* DIRK). Nonsense. I wouldn't let her go as far as the mailbox with you.

DIRK. Look, van Winkle, you have nothing whatever to say about it.

BOB. That's what you think. (*Fighting*

hard for consciousness) I have something very important to say—and—I've been trying to say it since six o'clock this morning. (*He teeters a bit, tries to get a grip on himself.*) Now *everybody* listen— (*With them all attentive, his mind starts to go blank again. He leans against the frame of the closet door and slowly slides to the floor. He is asleep again.*)

MARY (*worried now*). Maybe we should call a doctor. I don't like his color.

DIRK. I don't like his color. I didn't like it yesterday. Come on Mary, let's leave Wynken, Blynken and Nod. (*He picks up* MARY's *suitcase and his coat.*)

MARY. But what if he's really—?

BOB (*with a supreme effort he rises*). Wait a minute, now. It's coming to me. (*Crossing blindly to* TIFFANY) Mary . . . (*Sees his mistake and turns blinking to find* MARY.)

MARY (*going to* BOB *and extending her hand*). I don't know whether you can hear me, but—good-by, Bob.

BOB (*focusing on* DIRK). You are one of the chief causes of why I am so confused. (*Puts his arm around* MARY.) Don't you ever kiss my wife again.

MARY. Bob—you're making a fool of yourself—

BOB (*turning on* MARY *and pushing her toward the window seat*). You shut up. (*Back to* DIRK) You leave her alone. She can't cope with a lounge lizard like you. She's got more goodness in her whole body than you've got in your little finger! (*He looks dazedly at* OSCAR.)

(OSCAR *shakes his head as if to say "No, you didn't get that right."*)

MARY (*moving toward the door*). All right, Dirk—the poor soul doesn't know what he's talking about—

(DIRK *exits with her suitcase and* MARY *is following him when* BOB *summons a last burst of energy and lunges after her.*)

BOB. Oh, don't I? I'm talking about you —you dumb little idiot—and you're not going anywhere with anybody! (*He grabs* MARY *around the waist and propels her into the storage closet. The others exclaim almost simultaneously.*)

MARY. Bob!

DIRK (*re-entering. He has dropped the suitcase in the hall*). Are you out of your . . . ?

(*But* BOB *has quicky shut the door, and locked it with a key. He turns to the others fiercely.*)

BOB. I haven't slept in nine months and I'm sick of it!

DIRK. Hand me that key. If you were in good condition, I could take it from you.

BOB. That is an absolutely true statement. (*He walks to the window and calmly tosses the key through it.*)

DIRK. What did you do that for?

BOB. I was going to swallow it, but it was too big. (*He collapses on the window seat, leans out for some air, and almost overbalances.* OSCAR *grabs his feet to keep* BOB *from falling out.* TIFFANY *screams.*)

MARY (*off*). Let me out of here this minute!

DIRK (*going to the closet door, calling through*). Mary, can you hear? That lunatic has thrown the key out into the snow! (*A big groan from* MARY, *off.*) What are we going to do?

OSCAR. Oh, the snow will melt in a day or two.

TIFFANY. In the movies, they just break the door down.

DIRK. In the movies the door is pieced together by the prop men so all you have to do is blow on it!

MARY (*off*). Dirk! Dirk! Are you still there?

DIRK (*exasperated*). Sure, I'm still here!

MARY (*off*). Well, you shouldn't be! Go this minute!

DIRK. No!

MARY (*off*). Please, Dirk! Those people will be waiting. The studio will be furious!

DIRK. Let them be furious! (*Starting for the desk.*) I'll call them up. (*Remembers*) Oh, Lord, I can't even *get* them now! And if I don't show up all the columns will say I was drunk or being held somewhere on a morals charge. (*Turning on* BOB *as if he'd like to wring his neck.*)

MARY (*off, urgently*). Dirk!

DIRK (*going to the closet door*). I *am* going, honey. I don't see what else to do. I'll call you tonight and we'll set up something. (*To* OSCAR) I depend on you as the only sane member of the group to get her out of there.

BOB. Well, it's been grand seeing you. Do come again.

DIRK (*to* TIFFANY *and* OSCAR, *ignoring* BOB). Good-by. Where's my damn book?

(*He sees it and starts for it.*)

BOB (*snatching up the manuscript*). What are you talking about? You offered this book to me. You can't take it back.

DIRK. You said it stank.

BOB. I did not. I said it wasn't punctuated. I'll punctuate it. (*Weaving toward the window seat.*)

OSCAR (*to* DIRK). You'd better let him keep it or he'll throw it out in the snow.

DIRK. And I left Hollywood and came to New York because I wanted to be among intelligent people! (*Getting into his coat with a sigh*) You know I made three pictures for Cecil B. De Mille and he once said to me: "If you want to get hold of a woman, don't talk to her—get hold of her—pick her up and carry her away." I thought to myself: "This man is a jerk." (*With a glance toward heaven.*) Cecil, forgive me. (DIRK *exits.* OSCAR *picks up a telephone book.*)

BOB (*forcing himself to snap to, and going to the closet door*). Mary! Mary! (*Knocks.*)

TIFFANY. You don't suppose *she's* fallen asleep?

BOB. No, I suppose she's too mad to talk.

OSCAR (*at the desk, opening the classified section of the phone book*). Why don't you try calling a locksmith? Just start with the A's. . . . (TIFFANY *is picking up her coat.*)

TIFFANY. I'd stay if there was anything I could do.

BOB (*blinking*). Oh—Tiffany.

TIFFANY (*holds out her hand*). Good-by.

BOB. Good-by. (*They shake hands. He helps her on with her coat.*) Tiffany, you really are a very sweet girl.

TIFFANY. Yes, I am. (*Turning to* OSCAR) Good-by, Mr. Nelson.

OSCAR. Good-by, my dear. If you're ever looking for a job, I have a large law office and could always use a girl like you.

TIFFANY. Thank you.

(BOB *is now dialing a number from the phone book.*)

OSCAR (*following* TIFFANY *toward the door*). You're not too upset, are you?

TIFFANY. Oh, I'll be upset tomorrow, when the novocain wears off. But even tomorrow I think I'm going to feel it's just as well.

OSCAR. Why?

TIFFANY. I was attracted to Bob in the

first place because he wasn't attracted to me. That intrigued me. I don't want to sound conceited but when you're twenty-one and you're sort of pretty and very rich, you get used to men falling in love with you. But now I ask myself—is it enough that a man is *not* attracted to you? Good-by. (*She goes.*)

BOB (*on the telephone*). Is this the locksmith? I've got a woman locked in here. Certainly I know the woman. Could you come right over? I know it's Sunday. Okay, so it's extra. Ninety-one East Seventy-first Street. (*To* OSCAR, *who is getting into his coat*) He'll be right over.

OSCAR. Good. Then I may safely take my departure.

BOB (*rising, in terror*). Oscar—you wouldn't leave me alone with her?

OSCAR. You'll have the locksmith.

BOB. What will I say?

OSCAR. As little as possible. (*He starts out.*)

BOB (*clutching* OSCAR *by the arms*). Please stay.

OSCAR. No, my dear boy. This dismal scene you needs must act alone.

BOB. Do you think she'll take the next plane after him?

OSCAR. Well, there are other rooms, other keys.

BOB (*. .ling a little, but steadying himself*). You're a big help.

OSCAR. All my clients tell me that. I'll call you tomorrow. (OSCAR *goes.*)

(BOB, *left alone, goes nervously to the closet door.*)

BOB. Mary? Mary, please answer me. (*He kneels down and calls through the keyhole.*) The locksmith is coming— (*The closet door opens unexpectedly and* MARY *appears. She walks past him into the room. He blinks.*) How did you get the door open?

MARY. My keys. (*Shows them.*)

BOB (*rising*). You mean you could have . . . ?

MARY. Yes. I could have.

BOB (*shaking himself, then nodding vaguely*). I know I behaved like a slob . . . doing this.

MARY. Like a slob.

BOB. I made a spectacle of myself.

MARY. You certainly did. It was the silliest thing I ever saw. And do you know what? I was so proud.

BOB (*it's all getting through to him*). Mary! My sweet, beautiful darling. I always thought you were beautiful. I thought you were beautiful as—a piece of white porcelain.

MARY. White porcelain? You mean like— (*She catches herself.*) Oh, that's very sweet. (*He goes to her and takes her in his arms, her head on his shoulder.*) I missed your shoulder more than anything.

BOB. A hundred times I would have crawled on my hands and knees to Philadelphia, but I was afraid—Mary, come home.

MARY. I'm home. (*They kiss. As they do,* BOB *begins to go slack again, sinking slowly onto the sofa.*)

BOB. Oh, Mary, what am I going to do?

MARY (*sitting next to him as he stretches out helplessly*). Why, what's the matter, darling?

BOB. I'm falling asleep again.

MARY (*she lifts his legs onto her lap*). That's all right.

BOB. Yeah. But how will we get those colored lights going?

MARY. We'll manage. (*She starts to take off his shoes and, smiling,* BOB *falls asleep as the* CURTAIN *falls.*)

END OF PLAY

A THOUSAND CLOWNS

Herb Gardner

Presented by Fred Coe and Arthur Cantor
at the Eugene O'Neill Theatre, New York, On April 5, 1962,
with the following cast:

NICK BURNS Barry Gordon

MURRAY BURNS Jason Robards, Jr.

ALBERT AMUNDSON William Daniels

SANDRA MARKOWITZ Sandy Dennis

ARNOLD BURNS A. Larry Haines

LEO HERMAN Gene Saks

Directed by Fred Coe
Scenery designed and lighted by George Jenkins
Costumes by Ruth Morley

It is probably rarer for Broadway to acquire a new expert in the business of entertainment than for the off-Broadway theatre to acquire a new specialist in funerary Absurdity. Herb Gardner, who was born in Brooklyn in 1934, is one of those rare acquisitions. In his twenty-eighth year, he made himself at home on Broadway with *A Thousand Clowns,* his first full-length play. It was while attending the High School of Performing Arts that Mr. Gardner wrote his play in one act, *The Elevator.* From his high school in New York City, he went on to the Carnegie Institute of Technology to study sculpture and to write plays, and from Carnegie Tech to Antioch College. He gave up sculpture in order to study commercial art while working in television, and his judgment was vindicated when the "Nebbish" cartoon characters, created by him, caught the public fancy. The success of the "Nebbish" brought him enough liberty to return to playwriting, and he devoted himself to the writing and rewriting of *A Thousand Clowns*—some details of which presumably reflect his own life. After much rewriting during rehearsals and the out-of-town tryout, the play opened in New York, and the very friendly reception it got for its amusing characterizations and clever lines must have been ample compensation for the preparatory period of anxiety probably known only to inmates of the death cell and playwrights.

Not the least of the assets of this unpretentious comedy is the author's feeling in the play for characters so obviously ill-assorted that they must attract each other. Especially successful is the portrait of the young welfare-society employee who arrives at the home of a noncomformist with one clear and firm purpose, only to find that her feminine impulses and her dreary profession are at odds with each other. One would hardly recommend the play as a case-study, and one may question what a little boy is doing in the unconventional hero's household in the first place. But leaving the premises of the play strictly unexamined is a sensible way of deriving amusement from one of the freshest of recent Broadway entertainments and enjoying among other things the illusion that individuality pays off even in a humdrum society—at least in so far as we are concerned with winning young girls, defeating stodgy bureaucrats, and keeping youthful charges happy. Since the salt of satire is sprinkled liberally throughout the play but without touching particularly serious lesions, Broadway playgoing was well served by this efficient job of insouciant playmaking.

ACT ONE

In complete darkness, before the curtain goes up, we hear the voice of Chuckles the Chipmunk.

———

CHUCKLES' VOICE (*intimately, softly*). Goshes and gollygoods, kidderoonies; now what're all us Chippermunkies gonna play first this fine mornin'?

CHORUS OF KIDS. Gonna play Chuckle-Chip Dancing.

CHUCKLES' VOICE. And with who?

CHORUS OF KIDS. With you!

CHUCKLES' VOICE (*louder*). And who is me?

CHORUS OF KIDS (*screaming*). Chuckles the Chippermunkie! Rayyyyyyyyyyyyyy.

The curtain goes up on this last screaming syllable, revealing MURRAY BURNS' *one-room apartment. The voices of Chuckles and the kids continue but are now coming from an ancient table-model T.V. set at the left. The set is facing away from the audience and is being watched by* NICHOLAS BURNS, *a twelve-year-old. The apartment is on the second floor of a brownstone on the lower West Side of Manhattan. It consists of one large, high-ceilinged room in which borrowed furniture rambles in no meaningful arrangement—some gaudy, some impractical, no matching pieces. It is obvious from* MURRAY BURNS' *apartment that he is a collector, though it is not entirely clear just what he is a collector of. All about the room, on the floor, on the coffee table, on dresser tops, is* MURRAY'S *collection: eighteen broken radios, some with interesting cathedral-style cabinets; over two dozen elaborately disabled clocks of different sizes, some of them on the wall; parts of eight Victrolas, mostly cabinets; a variety of hats, including a Prussian helmet and a deerstalker; a pirate pistol; a bugle; a megaphone; and stacks of magazines and books. It is somehow, though, a very comfortable-looking apartment. There is an alcove at the left, with a small bed, a child's desk and some bookshelves. This is* NICK'S *part of the place and it is very neat, ordered, organized, seeming almost to have nothing to do with the main room. There is a bathroom door at left below the small alcove. Right of the alcove are three large windows and a built-in window seat. A closed venetian blind covers all three windows. At center is a large, comfortable rumpled bed with an elaborate wooden headboard running up the wall almost to the ceiling. The headboard is loaded with clocks, radios, and two lamps. At right is the entrance door to the apartment. To the left of the door are two large office-style filing cabinets in which* MURRAY *keeps some of his clothes, and to the right is a bureau covered with knick-knacks on which* MURRAY'S *hats are hung. Downstage right is the kitchen door; to the left of it is a desk buried under papers, and built-in bookshelves stuffed with a jumble of books and nonsense. There is a closet to the left of the desk. A Morris chair and an armless swivel chair are on either side of a small table at right and there is a brightly colored beach chair at left in front of the windows.*

AT RISE: *It is eight-thirty on a Monday morning; it is rather dark, the only real light is a scattered haze from the television set. The chorus of kids is now singing the "Chuckles Song."* NICK *watches expressionlessly.*

———

CHORUS OF KIDS (*singing*). Who's whitcha at—eight-thirty?
Whose face is so—so dirty?
Who's sparky—who's spunky?
Chip, Chip, Chip, Chip—Chippermunkie!

NICK (*quietly*). Oh, this is terrible. This is rotten.

CHORUS OF KIDS. Who's always good—for funnin'? Whose scooter-bike—keeps runnin'?

(MURRAY *enters from the kitchen carrying a cup of coffee; he is in his mid-thirties. He is wearing shorts and an undershirt and is not quite awake yet.*)

MURRAY (*walking across to the bed*). Get those kids outa here. (*Sits on the bed.*) Nick, what'd I tell you about bringing your friends in here this early in the morning?

NICK. It's not my friends; it's the T.V.

MURRAY. Play with your friends outside. Get those kids out of here. (NICK *turns the set off.* MURRAY *looks over at the front door, waves at it and shouts.*) Good. And none of you kids come back here till this afternoon.

NICK. It wasn't my friends. It was Chuckles the Chipmunk.

MURRAY (*sleepily*). That's very comforting.

NICK (*brings a pack of cigarettes to* MURRAY). Boy, it's a terrible program now. It was a much better show when you were writing it.

MURRAY. When Sandburg and Faulkner quit, I quit. What kind of a day is it outside?

NICK (*going to the kitchen*). It's a Monday.

MURRAY. I mean warm or cold or sunny is what I mean.

NICK. I haven't been outside yet.

MURRAY (*he pulls the blind up revealing the windows; there is no change whatever in the lighting, the room remains dark. The windows have no view other than the gray blank wall of the building a few feet opposite*). Ah, light. (*He leans out of the window, cranes his head around to look up at the sky.*) Can't see a thing. Not a thing. (*Pulls his head back in.*) No matter what time of day or what season, we got a permanent fixture out there; twilight in February.

NICK (*bringing the coffee pot out of the kitchen and filling* MURRAY's *cup*). You better call the weather record like always.

MURRAY. One morning I'll wake up and that damn building'll have fallen down into Seventh Avenue so I can see the weather. (*Picks up the phone; dialing.*) Using a machine to call up another machine. I do not enjoy the company of ghosts. (*Into the phone*) Hello, Weather Lady! Well, I'm just fine, and how is your nasal little self this morning? What's the weather? Uh-huh. That high? And the wind, which way does the wind blow this morning? Ah, good. Uh-huh, all the way to East Point and Block Island. Humidity? Very decent. Whoops, oh, there you go again. You simply *must* learn not to repeat yourself. I keep telling you every morning that once is enough. You'll never learn. (*Hangs up.*) Women seldom sense when they have become boring. (*Goes to the window again, leans out, raises his voice, shouting out of the window.*) Neighbors, I have an announcement for you. I have *never seen* such a collection of dirty windows. Now I want to see you all out there on the fire escape with your Mr. Clean bottles, and let's snap it up . . .

NICK. Gee, Murray, you gotta shout like that every morning?

MURRAY. It clears my head. (*After glancing around clock-filled apartment*) What time is it?

NICK. It's eight-forty.

MURRAY. Well, what're you doing here? Why aren't you·in school?

NICK. It's a holiday. It's Irving R. Feldman's birthday, like you said.

MURRAY. Irving R. Feldman's birthday is my own personal national holiday. I did not open it up for the public. He is proprietor of perhaps the most distinguished kosher delicatessen in this neighborhood and as such I hold the day of his birth in reverence.

NICK. You said you weren't going to look for work today because it was Irving R. Feldman's birthday, so I figured I would celebrate too, a little.

MURRAY. Don't kid *me,* Nick, you know you're supposed to be in school. I thought you *liked* that damn genius' school— why the hell—

NICK. Well, I figured I'd better stay home today till you got up. (*Hesitantly*) There's something I gotta discuss with you. See, because it's this special school for big brains they watch you and take notes and make reports and smile at you a lot. And there's this psychologist who talks to you every week, each kid separately. He's the biggest smiler they got up there.

MURRAY. Because you got brains they figure you're nuts.

NICK. Anyway, we had Show and Tell time in Mrs. Zimmerman's class on Monday; and each kid in the class is supposed to tell about some trip he took and show pictures. Well, y'remember when I made you take me with you to the El Bambino Club over on Fifty-second?

MURRAY. Nick . . . you showed and you told.

NICK. Well, it turned out they're very square up at the Revere School, And sometimes in class, when we have our Wednesday Free-Association-Talk Period, I sometimes quote you on different opinions . . .

MURRAY. That wasn't a good idea.

NICK. Well, I didn't know they were such nervous people there. Murray, they're very nervous there. And then there was this composition I wrote in Creative Writing about the advantages of Unemployment Insurance.

MURRAY. Why did you write about that?

NICK. It was just on my mind. Then once they got my record out they started to notice what they call "significant data." Turns out they've been keeping this file on me for a long time, and checking with that Child Welfare place; same place you got those letters from.

MURRAY. I never answer letters from large organizations.

NICK. So, Murray . . . when they come over here, I figure we'd better . . .

MURRAY. When they come over here?

NICK. Yeah, this Child Welfare crowd, they want to take a look at our environment here.

MURRAY. Oh, that's charming. Why didn't you tell me about this before, Nick?

NICK. Well, y'know, the past coupla nights we couldn't get together.

MURRAY. That was unavoidable. You know when I have a lot of work you stay up at Mrs. Myers'.

NICK (*pointing at the dresser*). Murray; your work forgot her gloves last night.

MURRAY. That's very bright.

NICK. Anyway, for this Child Welfare crowd, I figure we better set up some kind of story before they get here.

MURRAY. You make it sound like a vice raid.

NICK. I mean, for one thing, you don't even have a job right now.

MURRAY. Look, you want me to put up some kind of front when they get here? O.K., I will. Don't worry, kid. I'll snow 'em good.

NICK. I thought maybe you could at least look in the papers for a job, this morning before they get here. So we could tell them about your possibilities.

MURRAY (*without much conviction*). I look every day.

NICK. Couldn't I just read you from the *Times* again like last week? While you get dressed?

MURRAY. O.K., read me from the paper. (*He starts to get dressed.*)

NICK. And then, maybe, you'll take a shave?

MURRAY. All right, all right.

NICK (*picking up the* Times *from the swivel chair*). This paper is three days old.

MURRAY. So what do you want me to do, bury it? Is it starting to rot or something? Read me from the paper.

NICK. But most of these jobs, somebody must have taken them. Look, I'll go down and get a newer—

MURRAY. We do *not* need a newer paper. All the really important jobs stay forever. Now start on the first page of Help-Wanted-Male and read me from the paper.

NICK. O.K. (*Puts on his glasses; reads aloud.*) "Administ, Exoppty. To ninety dollars." What's that?

MURRAY. Administrative Assistant, excellent opportunity. Nothing. Keep reading.

NICK. But ninety dollars would be ninety dollars more than nothing. Nothing is what you make now.

MURRAY. Have you ever considered being the first twelve-year-old boy in space?

NICK. But, ninety dollars . . .

MURRAY. *You* go be an Administ, Exoppty. They *need* men like you. Read further.

NICK (*reading from the paper*). "Versatile Junior, traffic manager, industrial representative organization. One hundred to one hundred twenty-five dollars. Call Mr. Shiffman."

MURRAY (*picks up the cardboard from his shirt collar and talks into it*). Hello, Mr. Shiffman? I read your name in the New York *Times,* so I know you must be real. My name is Mandrake the Magician. I am a versatile Junior and I would like to manage your traffic for you. You see, sir, it has long been my ambition to work in a pointless job, with no future and a cretin like you as my boss . . .

NICK. But, Murray, it says "one hundred twenty-five dollars," that's a lot of . . .

MURRAY. Just read the ads. No editorial comment or personal recommendations. When I need your advice, I'll ask for it. Out of the mouths of babes comes drooling.

NICK. You said that last week. Murray, you don't want a job is the whole thing.

MURRAY. Would you just concentrate on being a child? Because I find your imitation of an adult hopelessly inadequate.

NICK. You want to be your own boss, but the trouble with that is you don't pay yourself anything. (NICK *decides that what he has just said is very funny. He laughs.*) Hey—you don't pay yourself anything—that's a good line—I gotta remember that.

MURRAY. That's what *you* said last week.

NICK. Look, Murray. (*He puts the paper down and stands up.*) Can I speak to you man to man?

MURRAY. That was cute about a year ago, buddy, but that line has got to go.

NICK (*takes off his glasses*). Murray, I am upset. For me as an actual child the way you live in this house and we live is a dangerous thing for my later life when I become an actual person. An unemployed person like you are for so many months is bad for you as the person involved and is definitely bad for me who he lives with in the same house where the rent isn't paid for months sometimes. And I wish you would get a job, Murray. Please.

(MURRAY *tries to control himself but cannot hide his laughter; he sees that* NICK *is offended by this and tries to stop.* NICK *walks away from him, goes to his alcove.*)

MURRAY (*goes to* NICK *in the alcove*). Kid, I know. I'm sorry. You're right. You are. This *is* terrible.

NICK. You're not kidding.

MURRAY. Nick.

NICK. Yeah?

MURRAY. Nick, y'know when I said I was looking for work last week? (*Somewhat ashamed*) Well, I went to the movies. Every day. In the afternoon.

NICK. *Murray,* you mean you really . . .

MURRAY. Now don't give me any of that indignant crap. I happen to be admitting something to you, and it is bad enough I should have to discuss my adult problems with a grotesque cherub, without you giving me dirty looks on top of it. Swell crowd in the movies on a weekday working afternoon. Nobody sits next to anybody, everybody there figures that everybody else is a creep; and *all* of them are right. (*Suddenly smiling, taking* NICK's *arm, trying to change the subject*) Have you ever been to the top of the Empire State Building?

NICK. Yes. Six times. With you. In November.

MURRAY. Oh, really? Have you ever been to the Statue of Liberty?

NICK. No.

MURRAY. Today is Irving R. Feldman's birthday. We will go to the top of the Statue of Liberty and watch the *Queen Elizabeth* come in, full of those tired, poor, huddled masses yearning to breath free.

NICK. Murray, why did you go to the movies in the middle of the afternoon when you said you were looking for work?

MURRAY. There's a window right in her navel, we will look out and see . . .

NICK. What is it? Were you very tired, or what?

MURRAY (*sits down in his chair*). See, last week I was going to check with Uncle Arnie and some of the other agents about writing for some of the new T.V. shows. I was on the subway, on my way there, and I got off at Forty-second Street and went to the movies. (*He leans back in his chair, lights a cigarette;* NICK *sits opposite him on the bed.*) There are eleven movie houses on that street, Nick. It is Movieland. It breathes that seductive, carpety, minty air of the inside of movie houses. Almost as irresistible for me as pastrami. Now, there is the big question as you approach the box office, with the sun shining right down the middle of a working day, whether everybody going in is as embarrassed as you are. But once you are past the awkward stage, and have gotten your ticket torn by the old man inside, all doubts just go away. Because it is dark. And inside it is such a scene as to fracture the imagination of even a nut like yourself, Nick, because inside it is lovely and a little damp and nobody can see you, and the dialogue is falling like rain on a roof and you are sitting deep in front of a roaring, color, Cinemascope, stereophonic, nerve-cooling, heart-warming, spine-softening, perfect-happy-ending picture show and it is Peacefulville, U.S.A. There are men there with neat mustaches who have shaved, and shined their shoes and put on a tie even, to come and sit alone in the movies. And there are near-sighted cute pink ladies who eat secret caramels; and very old men who sleep; and the *ushers;* buddy, you are not kidding *these* boys. They know you are not there because you are waiting for a train, or you are on a vacation, or you work a night job. They know you are there to *see* the *movie.* It is the business and the purpose of your day, and these boys give you their sneaky smile to show you that they know. (*Depressed by his own words; quietly, almost to himself)* Now the moral question for me here, is this: When one is faced with life in the bare-assed, job-hunting raw on the one hand, and eleven fifty-cent double features on the other, what is the mature, sensible, and mentally healthy step to take? *(He is slumped in his chair now.)*

NICK *(seeing* MURRAY's *depression; softly, with concern).* What's wrong, Murray?

MURRAY *(walks slowly to the window, leans against the wall, looks sadly out of the window; speaks quietly).* I don't know. I'm not sure.

NICK. Hey, Murray, you all right . . . ? *(He goes to* MURRAY, *touches his arm. Then smiling suddenly in an attempt to cheer him)* Murray, let's go to the Statue of Liberty.

*(*MURRAY *turns, laughs in agreement, and* NICK *starts for his jacket while* MURRAY *puts his binoculars around his neck and begins putting on his jacket. The doorbell rings.* NICK *looks at* MURRAY, *then goes to answer it.* NICK *is holding the front door only part-way open, hesitating to let in two people we now see standing outside in the hall. They are* ALBERT AMUNDSON *and* SANDRA MARKOWITZ. ALBERT, *graduate of N.Y.U.'s School of Social Work, is a middle-aged man of twenty-eight,* SANDRA, *though a pretty girl of twenty-five, wears clothes obviously more suited to a much older woman.* ALBERT *carries a small briefcase and* SANDRA *carries two manila file envelopes and a gigantic handbag.)*

ALBERT. Hello, young man, I am Mr. Amundson, this is Miss Markowitz. We would like to speak to your uncle.

NICK *(still not opening the door all the way).* Well, I don't know if . . .

ALBERT. Isn't he in?

MURRAY. Hello.

ALBERT. How do you do, Mr. Burns. Miss Markowitz and I are a Social Service unit assigned to the New York Bureau of Child Welfare. We have been asked by the Bureau to— May we come in?

MURRAY. Certainly.

*(*NICK *opens the door all the way, letting them both into the main room.)*

ALBERT. We, Miss Markowitz and I, have been asked by the B.C.W. to investigate and examine certain pupils of the Revere School. There is certain information which the school and the city would like to have, regarding young Nicholas.

MURRAY. Sit down, Miss Markowitz, please. Mr. Amundson. I'll just get rid of these things.

*(*MURRAY *takes pants, shirts, a bugle, a clock, a yoyo, a half-empty bag of peanuts and an ashtray off the chairs, and with one sweeping movement puts all of them on the bed. The three of them take seats around the coffee table,* NICK *standing nervously off to one side.)*

ALBERT. I'd like to explain just why we are here, Mr. Burns . . .

NICK. Would anybody like some coffee?

ALBERT. Why, thank you, Nicholas. Miss Markowitz?

SANDRA. Yes, thank you.

NICK *(whispering to* MURRAY *on his way to the kitchen).* Watch it.

ALBERT *(smiling politely).* It might be best, Mr. Burns, for the child if perhaps you sent him downstairs to play or something, while we have our discussion. Your case is . . .

MURRAY. Our "case." I had no idea we were a "case."

ALBERT. We do have a file on certain students at Revere.

MURRAY. So we're on file somewhere. Are we a great big, fat file, or a li'l teeny file?

ALBERT. Due to the fact that you have chosen not to answer our letters and several of our phone calls, there are many areas in which the file is incomplete, several questions— Mr. Burns, it might be better if the child went outside . . .

MURRAY. You gonna talk dirty?

ALBERT. It would be more advisable for the child not to be present, since Miss Markowitz, who will be discussing the psychological area . . . that is, we will be discussing certain matters which . . .

NICK *(from the kitchen).* Cream and sugar for everybody?

ALBERT *(to the kitchen).* Yes, Nicholas. *(To* MURRAY *again.)* Mr. Burns, it's going to be awkward, with the child present, to . . .

MURRAY *(to* SANDRA*).* Miss Markowitz, may I know your first name?

SANDRA. Sandra.

MURRAY. And you are the psychologist part of this team, Sandy?

SANDRA. That's right, Mr. Burns.

MURRAY *(to* ALBERT*).* And you, I take it, are the brawn of the outfit?

ALBERT. Perhaps I should explain. Mr. Burns, that the Social Service teams which serve Revere School are a carefully planned balance of Social Case Worker, such as myself, and Psychological Social Worker, such as Miss Markowitz, or, actually, *Dr.* Markowitz. (NICK *enters from the kitchen with four cups, gives one each to* ALBERT, SANDRA, MURRAY; *keeps one for himself.*) Mr. Burns, it is not easy to define those elements, those influences and problems which go into the make-up of a young boy.

MURRAY. I thought it was just frogs and snails and puppy dogs' tails.

ALBERT (*using once again his polite smile*). I appreciate the informality with which you approach this meeting, Mr. Burns, but on the more serious side, if I may, Miss Markowitz and I have a few matters . . .

NICK. Is the coffee any good?

ALBERT. Yes, very good. Thank you, Nicholas.

SANDRA. Very nice, Nicholas. (*She sees the cup in* NICK's *hand, speaks with professional interest.*) Are you drinking coffee, Nicholas? Don't you think it would be better if . . .

NICK. No. Milk. I like to drink it from a cup.

MURRAY (*to* SANDRA, *smiling*). Now aren't you ashamed of yourself?

ALBERT (*taking a rather large file out of his briefcase*). Now, to plunge right in here . . .

MURRAY. Sometimes I put his milk in a shot glass. Better for getting him to drink it than adding chocolate syrup.

SANDRA (*firmly*). Mr. Burns, Mr. Amundson and I have several cases to examine today, and we would appreciate a certain amount of cooperation . . .

MURRAY (*to* NICK). East Bronx, Mosholu Parkway.

NICK (*looks at* SANDRA, *then to* MURRAY). With a couple of years in maybe Massachusetts.

MURRAY. No Massachusetts at all. Complete Bronx.

SANDRA. I don't understand what . . .

MURRAY (*sitting on the beach chair*). Oh, excuse me. Nick and I are merely testing our sense of voice and accent. Nick insists he's better at it than I am.

SANDRA (*smiling*). As a matter of fact, the Bronx is right, but it's Grand Con-course.

MURRAY. The Massachusetts thing, way off, right?

SANDRA. Actually I took my graduate work with a professor, a man with a very strong New England accent, who could very well've influenced my speech. Nick is quite right.

NICK (*proudly*). Thank you, lady.

SANDRA. You certainly have a fine ear for sound, Nick. Do you and your uncle play many of these sorts of games together?

NICK. Oh, yes. We play many wholesome and constructive-type games together.

MURRAY. You're a big phony, Nick. Miss Markowitz has beautiful hazel eyes that have read many case histories and are ever watchful, and even clever little boys are not going to snow her. The lady is here for the facts.

ALBERT. Quite so, Mr. Burns. But facts alone cannot complete our examination. (*He takes out a pen, opens to a blank page in the file.*) We wish to understand . . .

NICK (*to* SANDRA, *showing off for her*). Jersey City, maybe Newark. And . . . a little bit of Chicago.

MURRAY. Uh-huh. Think you've hit it, Nick

SANDRA. That's really quite remarkable. Albert—Mr. Amundson *is* from New Jersey, and he went to Chicago University for several . . .

ALBERT (*firmly*). This is really quite beside the point, Sandra . . .

SANDRA. I just think it's quite remarkable, Albert, the boy's ability to . . .

ALBERT (*purposely interrupting her*). Suppose I just plunge right in here, before Dr. Markowitz begins her part of the interview . . .

(*There is a noise at the front door and* ARNOLD BURNS *enters. He is carrying a medium-sized grocery delivery carton filled with a variety of fruit. He makes a rather incongruous delivery boy in that he is in his early forties and dressed in expensive, distinguished clothes, top coat, and hat. He is* MURRAY's *older brother, and his agent. It is obvious in the way he enters and automatically sets the delivery carton down on the desk that this is a daily ritual enacted at this same time every day and in this same manner.* MURRAY *does not even look up to greet him and* NICK *makes some casually mumbled greeting in his direction.*)

ARNOLD. The honeydew melon's in season again but not really ripe yet so . . . (*He turns, sees that there are strangers there.*) Oh, sorry. Didn't know you had company . . . (*Turns, goes to the door.*) See you, Nick. ·

NICK. Yeah, see you, Uncle Arnie. (ARNOLD *exits.*)

ALBERT (*looking at the door*). There is somebody else living here with you?

MURRAY. No. That's just my brother Arnold. He brings fruit every morning on his way to the office. He's a fruit nut.

ALBERT. I see here in the file that our research team spoke to your brother; your agent, I believe. We also called the people at your last business address, N.B.C. . . .

MURRAY (*rising*). You really do a lot of that stuff, calling people, going into my personal . . .

ALBERT. You've refused for quite some time, Mr. Burns, to answer any of our regular inquiries. We understand that you have been unemployed at this point for nearly five months.

NICK (*to* ALBERT). He has an excellent opportunity to be an administrative assistant . . .

ALBERT (*pressing forward*). Other than your activities as free-lance script writer, I understand that you wrote regularly for an N.B.C. program for several years.

MURRAY. I was chief writer for Leo Herman, better known as Chuckles the Chipmunk, friend of the young'uns, and seller of Chuckle-Chips, the potato chips your friend Chuckles the Chipmunk eats and chuckles over.

ALBERT. And the circumstances under which you left the employ of . . .

MURRAY. I quit.

ALBERT. You felt that this was not the work you . . .

MURRAY. I felt that I was not reaching all the boys and girls out there in Televisionland. Actually it was not so much that I wasn't reaching the boys and girls, but the boys and girls were starting to reach *me*. Six months ago, a perfectly adult bartender asked me if I wanted an onion in my martini, and I said, "Gosh n' gollies, you betcha." I knew it was time to quit.

ALBERT. May I ask if this is a pattern; that is, in the past, has there been much shifting of position?

MURRAY. I *always* take an onion in my martini. This is a constant and unswerving . . .

(NICK, *concerned with* MURRAY's *behavior, goes toward him in an attempt to quiet him down.*)

SANDRA (*firmly, standing*). Mr. Burns. Perhaps you are not aware of just how serious your situation is. This entire matter is a subject of intense interest to the B.C.W. The circumstances of this child's environment, the danger of . . .

ALBERT. Our investigation, Mr. Burns, is the result of what the Bureau considers to be almost an emergency case.

NICK. He just likes to kid around, lady. But, see, we really got a great environment here . . .

MURRAY (*to* NICK). Relax, kid. (*To* ALBERT *and* SANDRA) Look, people, I'm sorry. Let's get back to the questions.

SANDRA. Fine. Nick, suppose you and I have a little chat right here.

NICK (*as he sits down next to her*). Fine. I was gonna suggest that myself.

SANDRA. Nick, I bet you love to come home when you've been out playing and you get tired. You say to yourself, "Gee, I'd like to go home now."

NICK. Sure, Right. And I'm happy here. Boy, if you think I'm happy now, you should see me when I'm *really* happy.

MURRAY (*to* SANDRA, *sympathetically*). He's on to you, honey. You're gonna have to be a lot foxier than that . . .

SANDRA. And I'm sure that you and your uncle have a great deal of fun together.

NICK. It's not *all* laughs.

SANDRA. Oh, I'm sure there are times when the fun stops and you have nice talks and your uncle teaches you things, helps you to . . .

NICK. I can do a great Peter Lorre imitation. Murray taught me.

ALBERT. Nicky, what Miss Markowitz means, is that you and your uncle must sometimes . . .

NICK (*in the voice of Peter Lorre, a rather good imitation*). You can't hang me . . . I didn't do it, I tell you . . . that's not my knife . . . I am innocent . . . it's all a mistake . . .

(MURRAY *beams, smiles proudly during*

imitation.)

ALBERT. Nicky, that's not what we meant, we . . .

MURRAY. What's the trouble? That happens to be a very good imitation.

ALBERT. Perhaps; but we are trying to . . .

MURRAY. Can *you* imitate Peter Lorre?

NICK (*confidentially, to* SANDRA). I can do a pretty good James Cagney; I mean it's not fantastic like my Peter Lorre, but it . . .

ALBERT (*raising his voice a bit, somewhat commanding*). Nicholas, please. Try to pay attention. Now if I may proceed to . . .

SANDRA (*aside, to* ALBERT, *somewhat annoyed with him*). Albert, if you'll just let me handle this area. (*Then, to* NICK) Nick, let's talk about games. O.K.?

NICK. O.K.

SANDRA. Now, what kind of games do you like the best?

NICK. Mostly I like educational games and things like that. Murray gets me to develop my natural inquiring mind.

SANDRA. I wonder, do you have any favorite games or toys you'd like to show me? Some plaything that is just the most favorite one of all?

NICK. I just now threw away my collection of *National Geographics* and other educational-type magazines I had a whole collection of . . .

ALBERT. Nicky, Miss Markowitz is very interested in you and cares about you and everything. And if you brought out some of your favorite toys and playthings for her to see, I'm sure that she'd love them just as much as you do.

NICK. Well, there's Bubbles . . . (*He gets up to get it for them.*)

MURRAY. I don't think you'd be interested in seeing Bubbles . . .

(NICK *goes to a cardboard cartoon at the bureau, opens it, and takes out a twenty-four-inch-high plastic statue of a bare-chested hula girl. The statue is in bright colors and has an electric switch as its pedestal.* NICK *places the statue on the table between* ALBERT *and* SANDRA *and turns it on.*)

NICK. Bubbles is what you'd call an electric statue. (*The breasts of the statue light up and continue to blink on and off in spectacular fashion for the next part of the scene.* ALBERT *looks at the*

statue, *begins busily going through the file on his lap.* SANDRA *regards the statue scientifically, professionally.* NICK *smiles proudly over his possession.*) It's got an electric battery timer in there that makes it go on and off like that.

SANDRA. Nick, is this your favorite toy?

NICK. Well, after a while it gets pretty boring. But it's a swell gimmick. There was another one in the store that was even better . . .

MURRAY. Anybody want orange juice or toast or anything?

SANDRA. Nick, tell me . . . do you like best the fact that the chest of the lady lights up?

NICK. Well, you got to admit, you don't see boobies like that every day. You want to see the effect when the lights are out? When the room is dark?

SANDRA. Tell me, Nick, is *that* what you like best about it, that you can be alone in the dark with it.

NICK. Well, I don't know. But in the dark they really knock your eye out.

(ALBERT *is blinking nervously at the blinking lights of the statue.*)

ALBERT (*with strenuous calm*). Perhaps, don't you think we ought to switch it off, turn off the . . .

SANDRA. Nick, does Bubbles, does she in any way, does her face remind you at all of, oh, let me see, your mother, for example?

NICK (*he looks at the face of the statue*). No. I mean, it's just a doll, it's not a statue of anybody I know. I got it in this store downtown.

SANDRA. Her chest, is that something which . . .

NICK (*smiling broadly*). It's *something* all right, isn't it?

SANDRA. When you think of your mother, do you . . .

NICK. I don't think about her much.

SANDRA. But when you *do* think of her, do you remember her face best, or her *hands,* or . . .

NICK. I remember she has this terrific laugh. The kind of laugh that when she laughs it makes you laugh too. Of course, she overdoes that a lot.

SANDRA. I mean, physically, when you think of her, do you, well, when you see Bubbles, and Bubbles goes on and off like that . . .

MURRAY. Sandra, his mother's chest did

not light up. Let's get that settled right now; mark it down in the file.

ALBERT (*nervously; pointing at the blinking statue*). Nicky, I wonder if you would turn those off . . . I mean, turn *it* off, turn her off, unplug it . . .

(MURRAY *turns the statue off, puts it back into the box.*)

SANDRA. Nicky, when you bought this doll . . .

MURRAY. Sandy, why don't I save you a lot of time. Nick is a fairly bright kid and he knows that girls are *not* boys. Other than that his interest in ladies is confined right now to ones that light up or don't light up.

NICK. I mostly like to read books that are healthy, constructive, and extremely educational for a person.

MURRAY. Don't push it, Nick. He does not have any unusual fixations, Sandy. He is no more abnormally interested in your bust than Mr. Amundson is.

ALBERT. Mr. Burns, it is not necessary to . . .

MURRAY. Of course, I might be wrong about that.

ALBERT. Our interest in that doll . . .

MURRAY. You really *are* interested in that doll, Albert.

ALBERT. Our interest . . .

NICK (*to* ALBERT). I'll sell it to you for two dollars. That's fifty cents less than I paid for it.

(SANDRA *is unable to suppress her amusement and laughs happily.*)

ALBERT (*quite annoyed with her*). Sandra, I fail to see . . .

SANDRA (*controlling herself again, but still smiling*). It's just that it was funny, Albert.

ALBERT (*taking command*). Suppose *I* pursue, then, the psychological part of . . .

SANDRA (*bristling at him*). Excuse me, Albert, I really do feel it would be better if *I* were to . . .

MURRAY. Albert, the lady was just laughing because something funny happened. That's actually the best thing to do under the circumstances.

ALBERT. Mr. Burns . . .

MURRAY. How would you all like to go to the Statue of Liberty? I have it on good authority from the Weather Lady that today is a beautiful day.

ALBERT. Is it at all possible, Mr. Burns, for you to stick to the point?

MURRAY. Albert, I bet you'd make Sandy a lot happier if you took her off somewhere once in a while. Doesn't have to be the Statue of Liberty; actually any . . .

ALBERT. My relationship with Dr. Markowitz is of no . . .

MURRAY. Well, there's obviously some relationship. When Nick asked you if you'd have sugar in your coffee before, Albert, you answered for Sandy.

ALBERT. Mr. Burns, this entire interview has reached a point . . .

NICK. I'm going to get my educational books. I left them out on the street.

(*He leaves the apartment, his exit unnoticed by the others.*)

ALBERT. This entire interview, Mr. Burns, has . . .

SANDRA. Mr. Burns, I . . .

ALBERT. Damn it, Sandra, don't interrupt me!

SANDRA. Albert, for goodness sakes, you . . .

ALBERT (*stands up*). Sandra, perhaps we . . . (*To* MURRAY) Would you excuse us for just a moment, Mr. Burns? I'd like to have a short conference with Sandra . . . Miss . . . Dr. Markowitz for a moment. (*She gets up.* ALBERT *and* SANDRA *walk over to the alcove, where* MURRAY *cannot hear them.* MURRAY *starts to peer at them through his binoculars until* ALBERT *turns and looks at him; he then goes to desk and tinkers with clock. Now alone with* SANDRA, ALBERT'S *manner changes somewhat. He speaks more softly and with more warmth, a departure from the stiff, professional manner he uses in dealing with* MURRAY.*) Sandra, what are you *doing,* have we lost all control?

SANDRA. Are you seriously talking to *me* about control?

ALBERT. Dear, I told *you* and I told Dr. Malko. It's much too soon for you to go out on cases. You need another year in the office, behind the lines, I told both of you. You're simply *not* ready.

SANDRA. Really, Albert, you hardly let me get started. I was attempting to deal with the whole child.

ALBERT. Three months out of grad school and you want to go right into the front lines. Not advisable.

SANDRA (*whispering angrily*). Don't you think that this is rather stupid and unprofessional? Right here in front of him you decide to have a conference.

ALBERT. A necessity. I am supposedly the leader of our examining team . . .

SANDRA. Oh, *really* . . .

ALBERT. You get too *involved,* Sandra. Each case, you get much too emotionally involved. This is an exploratory visit, we are *scientists,* dear, you lose sight of the . . .

SANDRA. You make me sick today, Albert. This is no way to approach this man's problem. We . . .

ALBERT (*sighing*). Oh, fine. That's fine. Well . . . fine . . .

(MURRAY, *at the other side of the room, picks up a megaphone.*)

MURRAY (*through the megaphone*). How are we doing? (*Puts the megaphone down, comes over to them in the alcove, sits between them; speaks sympathetically.*) I personally don't feel that you're gonna work out your problems with each other. But I'm glad you came to me because I think I can help you. Al, Sandy is not going to respect you because you threaten her. Respect will have to come gradually, naturally, a maturing process . . .

ALBERT. Mr. Burns . . .

MURRAY. Sandy, I bet he's got a file on you.

ALBERT. Mr. Burns, according to the B.C.W., the child's continuance in your home is in serious and immediate doubt. I am trying to encourage your cooperation . . . (*He is making a genuine attempt to speak warmly, understandingly.*) Aren't you at all willing to answer some questions, to give some evidence in your favor for our report, some evidence to support your competency as a guardian? The Board is thoroughly aware that Nicholas is not legally adopted.

MURRAY. He's my nephew. He's staying with me for a while. He's visiting.

ALBERT. How long has he been here?

MURRAY. Seven years.

ALBERT. So you see, the Child Welfare Board has, I assure you, the right to question . . .

MURRAY (*rises, faces* ALBERT *angrily*). You don't assure me of *anything,* buddy, you make me damn nervous. Do you mean to tell me that four years at N.Y.U. has made you my judge? (ALBERT *shrugs, defeated; crosses to Morris chair for his coat, signals* SANDRA *that they are leaving.*

MURRAY *goes toward them; speaks quietly, apologetically.*) O.K., all right. What do you want to know? I'll be cooperative.

(SANDRA *and* ALBERT *sit down again.*)

ALBERT. Nicholas' father, where is he?

MURRAY. That's not a *where* question. That's a *who* question.

ALBERT. I don't quite . . .

MURRAY. Nick's mother, she didn't quite either.

SANDRA. She is still living . . .

MURRAY. My sister is unquestionably alive.

SANDRA. But her responsibility to the child.

MURRAY. For five years she did everything she could for Nick . . . but get married. Now that's not easy to understand since she used to get married to *everybody*. But, somehow, having Nick matured her, she felt a responsibility not to get married to just *anybody* any more, so she didn't marry Nick's father, nor was she married at the time he was born. You might call Nick a bastard, or "little bastard," depending on how whimsical you feel at the time. Is that the sort of information you wanted? . . . Ah, this situation is the social workers' paradise. What a case history, huh? . . . My sister Elaine showed up here one day with two suitcases, a hatbox, a blue parakeet, a dead gold fish, and a five-year-old child. Three days later she went downstairs to buy a pack of filter-tip cigarettes . . . (MURRAY *shrugs.*) Six years later she returned for the suitcases and the hatbox . . . the parakeet I had given away, the gold fish I had long since flushed down the toilet, and the five-year-old child had, with very little effort, become six years older. When Elaine returned for her luggage I reminded her of the child and the pack of filter-tip cigarettes and suggested that this was perhaps the longest running practical joke in recent history. She was accompanied by a tall chap with sunglasses who was born to be her fifth divorce and who tried to start a small conversation with me. At this point I slapped my sister, Fifth Divorce slugged me, Sister cried, stopped quite suddenly, and then proceeded to explain to me, briefly, her well-practiced theory on the meaning of life, a philosophy falling somewhere to the left of Whoopie. At which point, I remember, I started laughing and then we all laughed and said "good-bye" like people at the end of a long party. That was almost a year ago. And I've still got Nick.

(SANDRA *is obviously sympathetic to this situation, emotionally involved in the story;* ALBERT *continues his cool professionalism, here and there jotting notes in the file.*)

SANDRA. But . . . but I'm sure she must have had *some* concern about Nicholas . . . about the child . . .

MURRAY. His name is not Nicholas. I will admit that he has stayed with that name much longer than the others . . . no, actually he was "Bill" for almost eight months . . .

SANDRA. I'm sure, on his birth certificate . . .

MURRAY. Certainly an elusive document. Not having given him a last name, Elaine felt reticent about assigning him a first one. When Nick first came here this presented a real difficulty. Nick answered to nothing whatsoever. Even the parakeet recognized its own name. Nick only knew I was calling him when he was positive there was no one else in the room.

SANDRA (*very much emotionally involved in this now*). Well, how did you communicate with . . .

MURRAY. I made a deal with him when he was six, up to which time he was known rather casually as Chubby, that he could try out any name he wished, for however long he wished, until his thirteenth birthday, at which point he'd have to decide on a name he liked permanently. He went through a long period of dogs' names when he was still little, Rover and King having a real vogue there for a while. For three months he referred to himself as Big Sam, then there was Little Max, Snoopy, Chip, Rock, Rex, Mike, Marty, Lamont, Chevrolet, Wyatt, Yancy, Fred, Phil, Woodrow, Lefty, The Phantom . . . He received his library card last year in the name of Raphael Sabatini, his Cub Scout membership lists him as Barry Fitzgerald, and only last week a friend of his called asking if Toulouse could come over to his house for dinner. Nick seems to be the one that'll stick, though.

SANDRA. His mother . . . ?

MURRAY. His mother, when last heard, was studying mime in Paris, having been given a sort of scholarship by a twenty-two-year-old handbag heir named Myron, who seems to believe strongly in the development of talent and student exchange. Well, I don't believe I've left anything out.

ALBERT. I was not aware that Nick was an O.W. child.

MURRAY. O.W.?

ALBERT. Out of wedlock.

MURRAY. For a moment I thought you meant Prisoner of War. I think it's that natural warmth of yours that leads me to misunderstand.

ALBERT. But as concerns the child . . . (*Looks around the room*) Where *is* the child?

SANDRA. You preferred not having him here anyway, Albert.

ALBERT (*sharply*). I am perfectly aware, Sandra, of what I *prefer,* and what I do *not* prefer.

SANDRA (*sharply*). I don't care for that tone of voice at *all,* Albert.

ALBERT (*rises, begins to put on his coat; calmly*). Sandra, I understand perfectly what has happened. We have allowed this man to disturb us and we have *both* gotten a bit upset. Now, I really do feel that it's time we got over to that family problem in Queens. It's there in your file, the Ledbetters, the introverted child. We've really given an unreasonable amount of time to this case. This interview, I'm afraid, Mr. Burns, has reached a point . . .

SANDRA (*attempting to sound authoritative*). Albert, I personally feel that it would not be advisable to leave this particular case, at this point.

ALBERT. Sandra, we have done here this morning all we . . .

SANDRA. I feel that we have not really given Mr. Burns a chance to . . .

ALBERT. Sandra, it's really time we left for Queens . . .

SANDRA (*hands* ALBERT *one of her two file envelopes*). Here's the Ledbetter file, I'm staying here.

ALBERT (*raising his voice a little*). Sandra.

SANDRA. I have decided to pursue this case.

ALBERT (*almost shouting*). Sandra, have we lost all professional control?

SANDRA (*angry, flustered*). You just . . . you just go yourself to the Leadbellies . . . you go on to Queens.

ALBERT (*takes her by the arm, gently,*

but firmly). May I just talk to you for a moment?

(ALBERT *leads* SANDRA *over to the alcove.*)

MURRAY. Time out for signals again?

ALBERT (*away from* MURRAY, *now he speaks, softly, less stiffly, though still angry*). What *is* this, dear? What has happened to you today? What are you doing?

SANDRA. I'm doing what I think is right.

ALBERT. I know how you feel, Sandra, but there is no more we can do here.

SANDRA (*emotionally*). I just . . . I just don't understand your behavior when you're on a case. We're supposed to be of some help, he . . .

ALBERT. Of course I want to help. But don't forget that the child is the one who needs protection, who needs . . .

SANDRA. Are you really going to leave that man here like that? You're not going to even try to help him or tell him what to do about the Board separating him from the child . . . I mean . . . just so cold.

ALBERT (*takes her hand*). Dear, you spent much too much time at that graduate school and not enough time in the field. That's your whole trouble. You've got to learn your job, Sandra . . .

SANDRA (*angry, frustrated*). Oh *really*, is that so? Albert Amundson, don't give me any of that nonsense.

ALBERT (*glancing over at* MURRAY). Please, Sandra . . . dear, this is not the time or the place for . . .

SANDRA (*shouting*). Graduate school wouldn't have done *you* any harm, Albert, believe *me!* Oh, this is the most terrible thing . . . (*Very close to tears*) You mean . . . you're just going to leave . . . ? Do you know what you are . . . ? you're a . . . I don't know; . . . but I'll think of something . . .

(ALBERT *walks away, leaving her in the alcove, goes into the main room, calmly picks up his briefcase.*)

ALBERT (*retaining his control, but just a little shaken. To* MURRAY). Mr. Burns . . . You can assume at this point that Miss Markowitz is no longer involved with your case. The Board will be informed that she is no longer involved with this particular case. Her continuing here, to discuss your case . . . at this point . . . is entirely unofficial. You can dismiss

any conference . . . that may resume after I leave . . . when I leave here, from your mind. And, regardless of what you think of me . . .

MURRAY. I think you're a dirty O.W.

(*Some of* SANDRA's *file papers slip from her hand and fall to the floor.*)

ALBERT. And . . . and do you know what *you* are? (*Readying himself to deliver a crushing insult to* MURRAY) Maladjusted! (*Goes to the door, opens it.*) Good afternoon, Mr. Burns. Good afternoon, Sandra.

MURRAY. Good afternoon, Mr. Amundson. Watch out crossing the street.

(ALBERT *exits, closing door sharply behind him.* SANDRA *stands for a moment in the alcove, then begins to pick up the papers she had dropped on the floor.*)

SANDRA. Mr. Burns . . . (*She is making a very strong attempt to control herself, but she is obviously on the verge of tears. She goes into the main room, begins to collect her things to leave.*) Mr. Burns, I must apologize to you. We . . . we have put you . . . you have been put at a disadvantage this morning. You have been involved in a personal problem that has nothing to do whatsoever with your particular case. It is entirely wrong for me to give you this impression of our . . . of our profession. (*She can no longer control herself and becomes, suddenly, a sort of child. She stands quite still, with her hands at her sides, and cries. It is not loud, hysterical crying, but intermittent and disorganized sobs, squeaks, whines, sniffles and assorted feminine noises which punctuate her speech.*) Do you know what? I just lost my job. This is awful. He's right, you know. I'm not suited to my work. I get too involved. That's what he said and he's right. (*Rummaging through her purse for Kleenex*) Please don't look at me. Do you *have* to stand there? Please go away. Still, he didn't have to talk to me like that. This is the first *week* we've ever gone on cases together. I didn't think he'd behave that way. That was no way. Why don't I ever have any Kleenex? (*He gives her the closest thing at hand to blow her nose in, his undershirt from the bed.*) Thank you. (*She sits down on the bed.*) Do you know that even with two fellowships it still cost me, I mean my parents mostly, it cost them seven thousand two hundred and forty-five dollars for me to go through school. I was the eighth youngest person to graduate in New York State last year and I can't stop crying. Maybe if I hurry, if I took a cab, I could still meet him in Queens.

MURRAY. You can't. Queens is closed. It's closed for the season.

SANDRA. Do you know what? (*Her crying lets up a bit.*)

MURRAY. What?

SANDRA (*with a new burst of sobs*). I hate the Ledbetters.

MURRAY. Then I'm sure once I got to know them I'd hate them too.

SANDRA. Mr. Burns, you don't understand. Some of the cases I love and some of them I hate, and that's all wrong for my work, but I can't help it. I hate Raymond Ledbetter and he's only nine years old and he makes me sick and I don't give a damn about him.

MURRAY (*pointing to the file on her lap*). You can't like everybody in your portfolio.

SANDRA. But some of them I like too much and worry about them all day . . . (*She is making an attempt to control her tears.*) It is an obvious conflict against all professional standards. I didn't like Raymond Ledbetter so I tried to understand him, and now that I understand him I hate him.

MURRAY. I think that's wonderful. Can I get you a cup of coffee?

SANDRA (*she turns to* MURRAY *as if to answer him, but instead bursts into fresh tears*). He's gone to Queens and I'll never hear from him again. I wrote out what my married name would be after dinner last night on a paper napkin, Mrs. Albert Amundson, to see how it would look. You know what I think I am, I think I'm crazy.

MURRAY. Well, then, I can talk to you.

SANDRA. We were going to get married. It was all planned, Mrs. Albert Amundson on a napkin. You have to understand Albert. He's really a very nice person when he's not on cases. He's a very intelligent man but last month I fell asleep twice while he was talking. I know him for so long. (*She tries once again to stop crying but the effort only increases her sobs.*) Mr. Burns, don't look at me. Why don't you go away?

MURRAY. But I live here.

SANDRA. I would like everybody to go away.

MURRAY (*attempting to comfort her*). Can I get you a pastrami sandwich?

SANDRA. Oh, I don't know you and I'm crying right in front of you. Go away.

MURRAY. Couldn't you just think of this as Show-and-Tell time?

SANDRA (*turning away again, still seated on the bed*). The minute I got out of school I wanted to go right back inside. (*With a great sob.*) Albert is gone and I just lost my job.

MURRAY (*he walks over to her*). Now, you're really going to have to stop crying, because I am going out of my mind.

SANDRA. I cry all the time and I laugh in the wrong places in the movies. I am unsuited to my profession and I can't do anything right. Last night I burned an entire chicken and after seven years of school I can't work and I've got no place to go. An entire chicken.

MURRAY. If I do my Peter Lorre imitation, will you stop crying?

SANDRA (*she pokes the file-envelope in her lap*). Look what I've done, I've cried on one of my files. The ink is running all over the Grumbacher twins . . .

MURRAY (*in the voice of Peter Lorre, a decent imitation*). It was all a mistake, I didn't stab Mrs. Marmalade . . . it was my knife, but someone else did it, I tell you . . .

SANDRA. That's an awful imitation, Mr. Burns . . .

(*She turns away from him and sobs into the bedclothes. He takes the Bubbles statue out of the box, switches it on, places it on the floor near the bed; it starts to blink on and off. Her face peeks out, she sees the blinking statue and puts her face back into the bedclothes, but we hear some giggles mixing with her sobs now, and then overtaking them, until she finally lifts her face and we see that she is laughing.*)

MURRAY (*smiling*). There. Progress. (*He turns off the statue.*) Would you like a cup of coffee, or a pastrami sandwich or something?

SANDRA. No, thank you. (SANDRA *begins to compose herself, she has stopped crying completely and is wiping her eyes with the undershirt he gave her. Then she begins to fold the undershirt neatly, smoothing it out into a nice little square on her lap.*) This is absolutely the most unprofessional experience I have ever had.

MURRAY. People fall into two distinct categories, Miss Markowitz; people who like delicatessen, and people who don't like delicatessen. A man who is not touched by the earthy lyricism of hot pastrami, the pungent fantasy of corned beef, pickles, frankfurters, the great lusty impertinence of good mustard . . . is a man of stone and without heart. Now, Albert is obviously not a lover of delicatessen and you are well rid of him.

(SANDRA *is still sitting on the bed, her hands folded neatly in her lap on top of her files and his undershirt.*)

SANDRA. What am I going to do? This is an awful day.

MURRAY (*he sits on the swivel chair next to the bed*). Miss Markowitz, this is a beautiful day and I'll tell you why. My dear, you are really a jolly old girl and you are well rid of Albert. You have been given a rare opportunity to return the unused portion and have your money refunded.

SANDRA. But . . . my work . . . what am I going to . . .

MURRAY. You are a lover, Dr. Markowitz, you are a lover of things and people so you took up work where you could get at as many of them as possible; and it just turned out that there were too many of them and too much that moves you. Damn it, please be glad that it turned out you are not reasonable and sensible. Have all the gratitude you can, that you are capable of embarrassment and joy and are a marathon crier.

SANDRA (*looking directly at him*). There is a kind of relief that it's gone . . . the job, and even Albert. But I know what it is, it's just irresponsible. . . . I don't have the vaguest idea who I am. . . .

MURRAY (*he takes her hand*). It's just there's all these Sandras running around who you never met before, and it's confusing at first, fantastic, like a Chinese fire drill. But god *damn,* isn't it great to find out how many Sandras there are? Like those little cars in the circus, this tiny red car comes out and putters around, suddenly its doors open and out come a thousand clowns, whooping and hollering and raising hell.

SANDRA (*she lets go of his hand in order to pick up the undershirt in her lap*).

What's this?

MURRAY. That's my undershirt. How's about going to the Empire State Building with me?

SANDRA. I'll have that coffee now.

MURRAY. You didn't answer my question. Would you like to visit the Empire State Building?

SANDRA. No, not really.

MURRAY. Well, then how about the zoo?

SANDRA. Not just now.

MURRAY. Well, then will you marry me?

SANDRA. What?

MURRAY. Just a bit of shock treatment there. I have found after long experience that it's the quickest way to get a woman's attention when her mind wanders. Always works.

SANDRA. Mr. Burns . . .

MURRAY. Now that you've cried you can't call me Mr. Burns. Same rule applies to laughing. My name is Murray.

SANDRA. Well, Murray, to sort of return to reality for a minute . . .

MURRAY. I will only go as a tourist.

SANDRA. Murray, you know, you're in trouble with the Child Welfare Board. They could really take Nick away. Murray, there's some things you could try to do . . . to make your case a little stronger . . .

MURRAY. Sandra, do you realize that you are not wearing your shoes?

SANDRA (*she looks down at her bare feet*). Oh.

(*The front door opens and* NICK *bursts into the room, laden with books.*)

NICK. Well, here I am with all my favorite books, *Fun in the Rain, The Young Railroader, Great Philosophers, Science for Youth,* a Spanish dictionary. What I did was I left them out in the street when I was playing, and I went down to . . .

MURRAY. Nick, you just killed a month's allowance for nothing. Miss Markowitz isn't even on our case any more.

NICK. I shouldn't have left. You got angry and insulted everybody.

MURRAY. Don't worry about it, Nick, we'll work it out. (*He goes over to the closet for something.*)

NICK (*dropping his books regretfully on the chair*). Four dollars right out the window. (*To* SANDRA) Y'know, I really do read educational books and am encouraged in my home to think.

SANDRA. I'm sure that's true, Nicholas, but I'm not in a position to do you much official good any more.

NICK. We're in real trouble now, right? (*He turns to* MURRAY *who has taken two ukuleles from the closet and is coming toward* NICK.) I figured it would happen; you got angry and hollered at everybody.

MURRAY. Nick, we have a guest, a music lover. . . . (*He hands the smaller of the two ukuleles to* NICK.) We've got to do our song. I am sure it will be requested.

NICK (*protesting, gesturing with his ukulele*). Murray, stop it . . . we—this is no time to sing songs, Murray. . . .

MURRAY (*striking a downbeat on his ukulele*). Come on, where's your professional attitude?

(MURRAY *starts playing* "Yes, Sir, That's My Baby" *on the ukulele, then sings the first line.* NICK *turns away at first, shaking his head solemnly at* MURRAY'S *behavior.* MURRAY *goes on with the second line of the song. Reluctantly,* NICK *begins to pick out the melody on his ukulele, then he smiles in spite of himself and sings the third line along with* MURRAY.

They really go into the song now, singing and playing "Yes, Sir, That's My Baby," *doing their routine for* SANDRA. *She sits in front of them on the bed, smiling, enjoying their act.* NICK *is in the spirit of it now and having a good time. In the middle of the song* NICK *and* MURRAY *do some elaborate soft-shoe dance steps for a few lines, ukuleles held aloft. This is followed by some very fast and intricate two-part ukulele harmony on the last few lines of the song for a big finish.*

SANDRA *applauds.*

MURRAY *and* NICK, *singing and strumming ukes, go into a reprise of the song,* MURRAY *moving forward and sitting down on the bed next to* SANDRA. NICK, *left apart from them now, does a line or two more of the song along with* MURRAY, *then gradually stops.* NICK *considers them both for a moment as* MURRAY *goes on doing the song alone now for* SANDRA. NICK *nods to himself, circles around in front of them and, unnoticed by them, puts his uke down on the window seat,*

goes to his alcove, gets school briefcase and pajamas from his bed. MURRAY *is still playing the uke and singing the song to* SANDRA *as* NICK *goes past them on his way to the front door, carrying his stuff.*)

NICK (*pleasantly, to* SANDRA). Nice to meet you, lady. I'll see you around.

MURRAY (*stops singing, turns to* NICK). Where you off to, Nick?

NICK. Gonna leave my stuff up at Mrs. Myers'. (*Opens the door.*) I figure I'll be staying over there tonight.

(NICK *exits, waving a pleasant goodbye to* SANDRA. SANDRA *looks at the front door, puzzled; then she looks at* MURRAY, *who resumes the song, singing and strumming the uke.*)

CURTAIN

ACT TWO

Scene: MURRAY'S *apartment, eight* A.M. *the following morning.*

At rise: The phone is ringing loudly on the window seat. MURRAY *enters from the bathroom with his toothbrush in his mouth, grabs the phone. The room is as it was at the end of Act One except that there is a six-foot-high folding screen placed around the bed, hiding it from view, and the shades are drawn again on the windows.*

———

MURRAY (*speaks immediately into the phone*). Is this somebody with good news or money? No? Good-bye. (*He hangs up.*) It's always voices like that you hear at eight A.M. Maniacs. (*He pulls up the shade to see what kind of a day it is outside. As usual the lighting of the room changes not at all with the shade up, as before he sees nothing but the blank, grayish wall opposite.*) Crap. (*With a sigh of resignation, he picks up the phone, dials, listens.*) Hello, Weather Lady. I am fine, how are you? What is the weather? Uh-huh . . . uh-huh . . . uh-huh . . . very nice. Only a *chance* of showers? Well, what exactly does that . . . Aw, there she goes again . . . (*He hangs up.*) Chance of showers. (*The phone rings. He picks it up, speaks immediately into it.*) United States Weather Bureau forecast for New York City and vicinity: eight A.M. temperature, sixty-

five degrees, somewhat cooler in the suburbs, cloudy later today with a chance of
. . . (*Looks incredulously at the phone.*)
He hung up. Fool. Probably the most
informative phone call he'll make all day.
(*He stands, opens the window, leans out,
raising his voice, shouting out the window.*) This is your neighbor speaking!
Something must be done about your garbage cans in the alley here. It is definitely
second-rate garbage! By next week I want
to see a better class of garbage, more
empty champagne bottles and caviar cans!
So let's *snap* it up and get on the *ball!*

(SANDRA's *head appears at the top of
the screen, like a puppet's head. She is
staring blankly at* MURRAY, MURRAY *steps
toward her, she continues to stare blankly
at him. Her head suddenly disappears
again behind the screen. The screen
masks the entire bed and* SANDRA *from his
view, and the view of audience. We hear
a rustle of sheets and blankets, silence for
a couple of seconds, and then* SANDRA's
*voice; she speaks in a cold, dignified,
ladylike voice, only slightly tinged with
sleep, impersonal, polite, and distant, like
one unintroduced party guest to another.*)

SANDRA. Good morning.

MURRAY. Good morning.

SANDRA. How are you this morning?

MURRAY. I am fine this morning. How
are you?

SANDRA. I am fine also. Do you have a
bathrobe?

MURRAY. Yes, I have a bathrobe.

SANDRA. May I have your bathrobe,
please?

MURRAY. I'll give you Nick's. It'll fit
you better.

SANDRA. That seems like a good idea.

(*He takes* NICK's *bathrobe from the
hook in the alcove, tosses it over the top
of the screen.*)

MURRAY. There you go.

SANDRA (*her voice from behind the
screen is getting even colder*). Thank you.
What time is it?

MURRAY. It is eight-fifteen and there is
a chance of showers. Did you sleep well?

SANDRA. Yes. How long have you been
up?

MURRAY. Little while.

SANDRA. Why didn't you wake me?

MURRAY. Because you were smiling.
(*Silence for a moment*) How does the
bathrobe fit?

SANDRA. This bathrobe fits fine. (*After
a moment.*) Did you happen to see my
clothes?

MURRAY (*starts for the bathroom*).
They're in the bathroom. Shall I get
them?

SANDRA. No, thank you. (*She suddenly
pops out from behind the screen and
races across the room into the kitchen at
right, slamming the kitchen door behind
her. We hear her voice from behind the
door.*) This isn't the bathroom. This is
the kitchen.

MURRAY. If it *was* the bathroom then
this would be a very extreme version of
an efficiency apartment. (*He goes to the
bathroom to get her clothes, brings them
with him to the kitchen door. He knocks
on the door.*) Here are your clothes. Also
toothpaste and toothbrush.

(*The kitchen door opens slightly, her
hand comes out. He puts the stuff in it,
her hand goes back, the door closes
again.*)

SANDRA. Thank you.

MURRAY. Sandy, is everything all right?

SANDRA. What?

MURRAY. I said, is everything all right?

SANDRA. Yes. I'm using the last of your
toothpaste.

MURRAY. That's all right. There's soap
by the sink.

SANDRA. I know. I found it.

MURRAY. That's good.

SANDRA. It was right by the sink.

MURRAY. Suppose we broaden this discussion to other matters . . .

SANDRA. I saw the soap when I came in.

(*The front door opens and* ARNOLD
BURNS *enters as he did before, carrying a
grocery carton filled with varieties of
fruit. He sets it down on the desk.*)

ARNOLD. Morning, Murray.

MURRAY (*without turning to look at
him*). Morning, Arnold.

ARNOLD. Murray, Chuckles called again
yesterday. I told him I'd talk to you. And
Jimmy Sloan is in from the coast; he's
putting a new panel-show package together . . .

MURRAY. Arnold, you have many successful clients . . .

ARNOLD. Murray . . .

MURRAY. With all these successful people around, where are all of our new
young failures going to come from?

ARNOLD. Murray, those people I saw

here yesterday; they were from the Welfare Board, right? I tried to warn you . . .

MURRAY. Nothing to worry about.

ARNOLD. These Welfare people don't kid around.

MURRAY. Arnold, I don't mind you coming with fruit if you keep quiet, but you bring a word with every apple . . . Everything's fine. You'll be late for the office.

ARNOLD. Is Nick all right?

MURRAY. Fine.

ARNOLD. O.K., good-bye, Murray.

MURRAY. Good-bye, Arnold. (ARNOLD *exits.* MURRAY *talks to the closed kitchen door again.*) There's coffee still in the pot from last night, if you want to heat it up.

SANDRA. I already lit the flame.

MURRAY. Good. The cups are right over the sink. Will you be coming out soon?

SANDRA. I found the cups.

MURRAY. Do you think you will be coming out soon?

SANDRA. Yes, I think so. Cream and sugar in your coffee?

MURRAY. Yes, thank you.

SANDRA. Murray.

MURRAY. Yes.

SANDRA. I'm coming out now.

MURRAY. That's good.

SANDRA. I'm all finished in here so I'm coming out now.

MURRAY. That's very good.

(*The kitchen door opens.* SANDRA, *dressed neatly, comes out of the kitchen, carrying two cups of coffee and* NICK'S *bathrobe.*)

SANDRA (*pausing at kitchen doorway, smiles politely*). Well, here I am. (*She goes to* MURRAY, *gives him a cup, sits on swivel chair. He sits next to her, on the stool. She takes a sip of coffee, straightens her hair. She is quite reserved, though pleasant; she behaves as though at a tea social.*) You know, yesterday was the first time I've ever been to the Statue of Liberty. It's funny how you can live in a city for so long and not visit one of its most fascinating sights.

MURRAY. That is funny. (*He sips his coffee.*) This coffee isn't bad, for yesterday's coffee.

SANDRA. I think it's very good, for yesterday's coffee. (*Takes another sip.*) What kind of coffee is it?

MURRAY. I believe it's Chase and San-

born coffee.

SANDRA. "Good to the last drop," isn't that what they say?

MURRAY. I think that's Maxwell House.

SANDRA. Oh yes. Maxwell House coffee. "Good to the last drop."

MURRAY. It's Chase and Sanborn that used to have the ad about the ingredients: "Monizalles for mellowness" was one.

SANDRA. They used to sponsor Edgar Bergen and Charlie McCarthy on the radio.

MURRAY. Yes. You're right.

SANDRA. "Monizalles for mellowness." I remember. That's right. (*She finishes her coffee, puts her cup down on the table. Then, after a moment*) I have to leave now.

MURRAY. Oh?

SANDRA. Yes. I'll have to be on my way. (*She stands, takes her pocketbook, puts on her shoes and starts to exit.*)

MURRAY (*takes her files from the floor, hands them to her*). Don't forget your files.

SANDRA. Oh yes. My files. (*She takes them from him, stands looking at him.*) Well, good-bye.

MURRAY. Good-bye, Sandra.

SANDRA. Good-bye. (*She walks out of the apartment, and closes the door behind her. Alone in the apartment now,* MURRAY *stands for a moment looking at the door. He then runs to open the door; she has had her hand on the outside knob and is dragged into the room as he does so.*)

MURRAY (*laughing, relieved*). You nut. I was ready to kill you.

SANDRA (*throws her arms around him, drops her bag and files on floor*). What happened? You didn't say anything. I was waiting for you to say something. Why didn't you say something or kiss me or . . .

MURRAY. I was waiting for *you*, for God's sake. (*He kisses her.*)

SANDRA. I didn't know *what* was going on. (*She kisses him, their arms around each other; he leans away from her for a moment to put his coffee cup on the table.*) Don't let me go . . .

MURRAY. I was just putting my coffee cup down . . .

SANDRA. Don't let me go. (*He holds her tightly again.*) Murray, I thought about it, and I probably love you.

MURRAY. That's very romantic. I probably love you too. You have very small feet. For a minute yesterday, it looked like you only had four toes, and I thought you were a freak. I woke up in the middle of the night and counted them. There are five.

SANDRA. I could have told you that.

MURRAY (*he sits in the swivel chair; she is on his lap*). You knocked down maybe seven boxes of Crackerjacks yesterday. You are twelve years old. You sleep with the blanket under your chin like a napkin. When you started to talk about the coffee before, I was going to throw you out the window except there'd be no place for you to land but the trash can from the Chinese restaurant.

SANDRA. You mean that you live above a Chinese restaurant?

MURRAY. Yes. It's been closed for months, though.

SANDRA. Do you mean that you live above an abandoned Chinese restaurant?

MURRAY. Yes, I do.

SANDRA. That's wonderful. (*She kisses him; jumps up from his lap happily excited about what she has to say. Takes off her jacket and hangs it on the back of the Morris chair.*) I didn't go to work this morning and I simply can't tell you how fantastic that makes me feel. I'm not going to do a *lot* of things any more. (*Picks at the material of her blouse.*) This blouse I'm wearing, my mother picked it out, everybody picks out things for me. She gets all her clothes directly from Louisa May Alcott. (*Picks up the stool, changes its position in the room.*) Well, we've all seen the last of this blouse anyway. Do you realize that I feel more at home here after twenty-four hours than I do in my parents' house after twenty-five years? Of course, we'll have to do something about curtains . . . and I hope you didn't mind about the screen around the bed, I just think it gives such a nice, separate bedroomy effect to that part of the room . . . (*Picks up her bag and files from the floor where she dropped them, puts them in the closet. She is moving in.*) Oh, there are so many wonderful tricks you can try with a one-room apartment, really, if you're willing to use your imagination . . . (*He watches helplessly as she moves happily about the apartment judging it with a decorator's eye.*)

I don't care if it sounds silly, Murray, but I was projecting a personality identification with the Statue of Liberty yesterday . . . courageous and free and solid metal . . . (*She kisses him, then continues pacing happily.*) I was here with you last night and I don't give a damn who knows it or what anybody thinks, and that goes for Dr. Malko, Albert, my mother, Aunt Blanche . . . Oh, I'm going to do so many things I've always wanted to do.

MURRAY. For example.

SANDRA. Well . . . I'm not sure right now. And that's marvelous too, I am thoroughly enjoying the idea that I don't know what I'm going to do next. (*Stops pacing.*) Do you have an extra key?

MURRAY. What?

SANDRA. An extra key. Altman's has this terrific curtain sale, thought I'd go and . . .

MURRAY. Well, then I'd better give you some money . . .

SANDRA. No, that's all right. (*Holds out her hand.*) Just the key.

MURRAY. Oh. (*He looks at her blankly for a moment, then reaches into his pocket slowly, finds the key, slowly hands it to her.*)

SANDRA (*snatches up the key, goes on delightedly pacing up and down*). Murray, did we bring back any Crackerjacks?

MURRAY (*pointing to some packages on the desk*). Only stuff we brought back was that cleaning equipment. I'll admit this place is a little dirty, but all that stuff just for . . .

(*The doorbell rings.* SANDRA *flinches for a moment, but then smiles and stands firmly.*)

SANDRA. You'd better answer it, Murray.

MURRAY. Sandra, would you prefer to . . .

(*He indicates the kitchen as a hiding place, but she stands right where she is, refusing to move.*)

SANDRA. I've got no reason to hide from anybody.

(MURRAY *goes to the front door and opens it halfway, but enough for us to see the visitor,* ALBERT AMUNDSON. ALBERT *cannot see beyond the door to where* SANDRA *is standing.*)

ALBERT. Good morning, Mr. Burns.

MURRAY. Albert, how are you?

(SANDRA, *hearing* ALBERT'S *voice, and realizing who it is, goes immediately into the closet, closing the door behind her*.)

ALBERT. May I come in?

MURRAY. Sure.

(MURRAY *opens the front door all the way, allowing* ALBERT *into the main room.* MURRAY *closes the door, then follows* ALBERT *into the room.* MURRAY *smiles to himself when he sees that* SANDRA *is not there and then glances at the closet door.*)

ALBERT. I called you twice this morning, Mr. Burns.

MURRAY. That was you.

ALBERT. That was me. Miss Markowitz did not show up in Queens yesterday.

MURRAY. So?

ALBERT. Her parents are quite upset. I am quite upset. Where is she?

MURRAY. She's hiding in the closet.

ALBERT. We're really all quite anxious to know where she is.

MURRAY. I'm not kidding. She's in the closet.

(ALBERT *goes to the closet, opens the door, sees* SANDRA, *then closes the door.* ALBERT *comes back to* MURRAY.)

ALBERT. She *is* in the closet.

MURRAY. I wouldn't lie to you, Albert.

ALBERT. Why is she in the closet?

MURRAY. I don't know. She's got this thing about closets.

ALBERT. That's a very silly thing for her to be in that closet.

MURRAY. Don't knock it till you've tried it. Now, what else can I do for you?

ALBERT. That's a difficult thing for me to believe. I mean, that she's right there in the closet. You are not a person, Mr. Burns, you are an experience.

MURRAY (*goes into the kitchen*). That's very nice, Albert, I'll have to remember that.

ALBERT. Actually, Dr. Markowitz is not the reason for my visit today. I came here in an official capacity.

MURRAY (*from the kitchen*). You don't wear an official capacity well, Albert. Coffee?

ALBERT. No, thank you.

(MURRAY *brings the pot out, fills the two cups on the table; brings one of the cups of coffee to the closet and hands it through the partly open door.*)

MURRAY (*returns to the table, sits opposite* ALBERT). What have you got on your mind, Albert?

ALBERT (*sits; begins hesitantly*). Burns,

late yesterday afternoon the Child Welfare Board made a decision on your case. Their decision is based on three months of a thorough study; our interview yesterday is only a small part of the . . . I want you to understand that I am not responsible, personally, for the decision they've reached, I . . .

MURRAY. Relax, Albert, I won't even hold you responsible for the shadow you're throwing on my rug.

ALBERT. For eleven months you have avoided contact with the Board, made a farce of their inquiries. You are not employed, show no inclination to gain employment, have absolutely no financial stability . . .

MURRAY. Look, Albert, I . . .

ALBERT. Months of research by the Board and reports by the Revere School show a severe domestic instability, a libertine self-indulgence, a whole range of circumstances severely detrimental to the child's welfare . . .

MURRAY. Look, stop the tap-dancing for a second, Albert; what's going on, what . . .

ALBERT. It is the Board's decision that you are unfit to be the guardian of your nephew, and that action be taken this Friday to remove the child from this home and the deprivation you cause him.

MURRAY. You mean they can really . . . (*Sips his coffee, putting on an elaborate display of calm, showing no emotion.*) Where'd they get this routine from, Charles Dickens?

ALBERT. The Board is prepared to find a more stable, permanent home for your nephew, a family with whom he will live a more wholesome, normal . . .

MURRAY. Look, Albert, there must be some kind of a hearing or something, where I'll have a chance to . . .

ALBERT. You will have the opportunity Thursday to state your case to the Board. If there is some substantial change in your circumstances, some evidence they're not aware of; if you can demonstrate that you are a responsible member of society . . .

MURRAY. It's Tuesday; what the hell am I supposed to do in two days, win the Nobel Peace Prize? They sent you here to tell me this?

ALBERT. No, you were to be informed by the court. But in view of the confusion which took place here yesterday, for which I consider myself responsible, I felt it my duty to come here and explain . . .

MURRAY. Buddy, you speak like you write everything down before you say it.

ALBERT. Yes, I do speak that way, Mr. Burns. I wish that I spoke more spontaneously. I realize that I lack warmth. I will always appear foolish in a conversation with a person of your imagination. Please understand, there is no vengeance in my activities here. I love my work, Mr. Burns. I believe that you are a danger to this child. I wish this were not true, because it is obvious that you have considerable affection for your nephew. It is in your face, this feeling. I admire you for your warmth, Mr. Burns, and for the affection the child feels for you. I admire this because I am one for whom children do not easily feel affection. I am not one of the warm people. But your feeling for the child does not mollify the genuinely dangerous emotional climate you have made for him. (*He moves toward* MURRAY.) I wish you could understand this, I would so much rather you understood, could really hear what I have to say. For yours is, I believe, a distorted picture of this world.

MURRAY. Then why don't you send *me* to a foster home?

ALBERT. I was right. You really can't listen to me. You are so sure of your sight. Your villains and heroes are all so terribly clear to you, and I am obviously one of the villains. (*Picks up his briefcase.*) God save you from your vision, Mr. Burns. (*Goes to the front door, opens it.*) Good-bye. (ALBERT *exits.*)

MURRAY (*stands at the window with his coffee cup in his hand, looking out at gray, blank wall of the building opposite*). Hey, courageous, free one, you can come out now.

(SANDRA *comes out of closet carrying her coffee cup;* MURRAY *does not look at her.*)

SANDRA. I'm sorry, Murray. I'm really very embarrassed. I don't know what happened. I just ran into the closet. And . . . and once I was in there, I just didn't want to come out. I'm sorry, Murray . . .

MURRAY. Don't be nervous, lady, you're just going through an awkward stage. You're between closets. (*Quietly, calmly*) Look, if Nick has to leave, if he goes, he

goes, and my life stays about the same. But it's no good for *him*, see, not for a couple of years, anyway. Right now he's still ashamed of being sharper than everybody else, he could easily turn into another peeled and boiled potato. Are you listening to me?

SANDRA. Yes, of course . . .

MURRAY. Well, make some kind of listening noise then, will you? Wink or nod your head or something.

SANDRA. But, I'm . . .

MURRAY (*casually; gesturing with his coffee cup*). Tell you the truth, it's even a little better for me if he goes. I mean, he's a middle-aged kid. When I signed with the network he sat up all night figuring out the fringe benefits and the pension plan. And he started to make *lists* this year. Lists of everything; subway stops, underwear, what he's gonna do next week. If somebody doesn't watch out he'll start making lists of what he's gonna do next year and the next ten years. Hey, suppose they put him in with a whole family of listmakers? (*Angrily*) I didn't spend six years with him so he should turn into a listmaker. He'll learn to know everything before it happens, he'll learn to plan, he'll learn how to be one of the nice dead people. Are you listening?

SANDRA. Of course, I told you, Murray, I . . .

MURRAY. Then stamp your feet or mutter so I'll know you're there, huh? (*Still speaking quite calmly*) I just want him to stay with me till I can be sure he won't turn into Norman Nothing. I want to be sure he'll know when he's chickening out on himself. I want him to get to know exactly the special thing he is or else he won't notice it when it starts to go. I want him to stay awake and know who the phonies are, I want him to know how to holler and put up an argument, I want a little guts to show before I can let him go. I want to be sure he sees all the wild possibilities. I want him to know it's worth all the trouble just to give the world a little goosing when you get the chance. And I want him to know the subtle, sneaky, important reason why he was born a human being and not a chair. (*Pause*) I will be very sorry to see him go. That kid was the best straight man I ever had. He is a laugher, and laughers are rare. I mean, you tell that kid something funny . . . not just any piece of corn, but something funny, and he'll give you your money's worth. It's not just funny jokes he reads, or I tell him, that he laughs at. Not just set-up funny stuff. He sees street jokes, he has the good eye, he sees subway farce and crosstown-bus humor and all 'the cartoons that people make by being alive. He has a good eye. And I don't want him to leave until I'm certain he'll never be ashamed of it. (*Still quite calmly, unemotionally*) And in addition to that . . . besides that . . . see (*Suddenly; loudly*) Sandy, I don't want him to go. I like having him around here. What should I do, Sandy? Help me out. (*Suddenly slumps forward in his chair, covers his face with his hands; very quietly*) I like when he reads me from the want ads.

SANDRA (*takes his hands*). Murray, don't worry, we'll do something. I know the Board, their procedure, there's things you can do . . .

MURRAY (*quiety, thoughtfully*). What I'll do is I'll buy a new suit. The first thing is to get a dignified suit.

SANDRA. If you could get some kind of a job, get your brother to help you.

MURRAY. Right. Right.

SANDRA. Is there something you can get in a hurry?

MURRAY. Sure, one of those suits with the ready-made cuffs . . .

SANDRA. No, I mean a job. If we could just bring some proof of employment to the hearing, Murray, show them how anxious you are to change. We'll show them you want to be reliable.

MURRAY (*brightening*). Yeah, reliable . . . (*Rises; going toward the phone*) Sandy, we will put on a God-damned show for them. Spectacular reliability; a reliability parade; bands, floats, everything. (*Starts to dial.*) Sandy, go to the files and pick me out a tie that is quiet but at the same time projects a mood of inner strength. (*Into the phone*) Arnold Burns' office, please.

SANDRA (*on her way to the file cabinet*). One quiet tie with a mood of inner strength.

MURRAY (*into the phone*). Hello, Margot? It's Murray. Oh, well, when Arnie comes in here's what you do. First you tell him to sit down. Then you tell him

I want to get a job. When he has recovered sufficiently from that shock, tell him . . . (SANDRA *comes to him with a tie.*) Excuse me a second, Margot . . . (*To* SANDRA, *indicating the tie*) Yes, quiet but with strength. (SANDRA *laughs.*) Sandy, that is the greatest happy laugh I ever heard on a lady. Do that again. (*She laughs again.*) Great. Keep that laugh. I'll need it later. (*Into the phone*) Margot, tell him I'm going downtown to pick up a new suit for myself and a beautiful pineapple for him, call him back in about an hour, O.K.? Thanks, Margot. (*Puts the phone down, goes to get his jacket.*)

SANDRA. Can I come with you? I'd love to buy a suit with you.

MURRAY (*putting on his jacket*). Better not, Sandy. Gotta move fast. These shoes look O.K.? (*She nods, he takes her hand.*) Look, don't go away.

SANDRA. I won't. (*She kisses him.*)

MURRAY (*goes to the front door; turns to her, smiles*). Say "Good luck."

SANDRA. Good luck.

MURRAY (*opening the door*). Now say "You are a magnificent human being."

SANDRA. You are a magnificent human being.

MURRAY (*as he exits*). I *thought* you'd notice.

She stands in door and watches him go as the lights fade out quickly. Immediately, as the lights fade, we hear the voice of Chuckles the Chipmunk (LEO HERMAN).

LEO'S VOICE. Hi there, kidderoonies; there's nothin' more lonelier than a lonely, little looney Chippermunk. So won't ya please come on along with me fer a fun hour, 'cuz that loneliest, littlest, looniest Chippermunk, is *me* . . . Chuckles. (*Lights come up now in* ARNOLD BURNS' *office, later that afternoon. The office is part of a large theatrical agency of which* ARNOLD *is a rather successful member; modern, wood paneling, nonobjective paintings and framed photographs of his clients on the wall, a spectacularly large window behind the desk with a twenty-second-floor skyline view. A large bowl of fruit is on an end table near the door. One of the two phones on* ARNOLD'S *desk is a special speaker-phone, consisting of a small loudspeaker box on the desk which amplifies clearly the voice of who-*

ever is calling. It can also be spoken into from almost any point in the room if one is facing it. As the following scene progresses the speaker-phone is treated by those present as if it were a person in the room, they gesture to it, smile at it. ARNOLD *is alone in his office, leaning against his desk, listening to the speaker-phone, from which we continue to hear the voice of* LEO HERMAN.) God damn it, Arn; that's the intro Murray wrote for me two *years* ago, and it's still lovely, still warm. It's the way the kids know me, the way I say "Hello, kids"; he's a sweetie of a writer.

ARNOLD. That was *last* year he won the sweetie award, Leo.

LEO'S VOICE (*laughs good-naturedly*). Please excuse my little words. They slip out of my face once in a while. Arn, you got my voice comin' out of that speaker-phone in your office, huh? Comes out like the biggest phony you ever met, right? That's how I sound, don't I? Big phony.

ARNOLD. No, Leo.

LEO'S VOICE. I'm getting sick of myself. Hey, Arn, you figure there's a good chance of Murray comin' back with me on the show?

ARNOLD. Can't guarantee it, Leo; I've sent him to one other appointment today, fairly good offer . . .

LEO'S VOICE. Well, I'm hopin' he comes back with *me*, Arn. Funny bit you being the agent for your own brother—what d'ya call that?

ARNOLD. It's called incest. (*The intercom buzzes;* ARNOLD *picks it up.*) O.K., send him in. (*Into the speaker-phone*) Got a call, fellah; check back with you when Murray shows.

LEO'S VOICE. Right, 'bye now.

(MURRAY *enters wearing a new suit and carrying a beautiful pineapple.*)

MURRAY. Good afternoon, Mr. Burns.

ARNOLD. Good afternoon, Mr. Burns. Hey, you really did get a new suit, didn't you? How'd the appointment go with . . .

MURRAY (*putting the pineapple on the desk, gestures around at the office*). Arnold, every time I see you, the agency's put you on a higher floor. I swear, next time I come you'll be up in a balloon.

ARNOLD. Murray, the appointment . . .

MURRAY. Can't get over this office, Arnie. (*Goes to the window, looks out.*) Twenty-second floor. You can see everything. (*Shocked by something he sees out of the window.*) My God, I don't believe it: it's King Kong. He's sitting on top of the Time-Life Building. He . . . he seems to be crying. Poor gorilla bastard, they shoulda told him they don't make those buildings the way they used to . . .

ARNOLD (*raising his hand in the air*). *Hello,* Murray, hello there . . . here we are in my office. Welcome to Tuesday. Now, come *on,* how'd it go with Jimmy Sloan?

MURRAY. He took me to lunch at Stefanos, East Fifty-third. Christ, it's been a coupla years since I hustled around lunchland. There is this crazy hum that I haven't heard for so long, Arnie; eight square yards of idea men, busily having ideas, eating away at their chef's salad like it's Crackerjacks and there's a prize at the bottom.

ARNOLD. And Sloan . . . ?

MURRAY (*sitting on the sofa*). Sloan lunches beautifully, can out-lunch anybody. He used to be a Yes-man but he got himself some guts and now he goes around bravely saying "maybe" to everybody. And a killer, this one, Arnie; notches on his attaché case. Told me this idea he had where I'd be a lovable eccentric on his panel show. This somehow led him very logically to his conception of God, who he says is "probably a really fun guy."

ARNOLD. What'd you tell him about the offer?

MURRAY. I told him good-bye. I don't think he noticed when I left; he focuses slightly to the right of you when he talks, just over your shoulder, so if you stay out of range he can't tell that you're gone. Probaby thinks I'm still there.

ARNOLD. Murray, you told me this morning to get any job I could; Sloan's offer wasn't so bad . . .

MURRAY. Sloan is an idoit.

ARNOLD (*sitting next to him on the sofa; angrily, firmly*). Listen, cookie, I got *news* for you, right now you *need* idiots. You got a bad reputation for quitting jobs; I even had trouble grabbing Sloan for you. Why did you have to go and build your own personal blacklist; why couldn't you just be blacklisted as a Communist like everybody else?

MURRAY. Don't worry, Arnie; I figured

I'd go back with Chuckles. He's ready to take me back, isn't he?

ARNOLD. Yeah, he's ready. I just spoke to him. (*Solemnly*) Hey, Murray, Leo says he came up to your place last January, a week after you quit him, to talk you into coming back with the show. And right in the middle you went into the kitchen and started singing "Yes, Sir, That's My Baby." Just left him standing there. Your way of saying "good-bye."

MURRAY. Well, that was five months ago, Arnie . . .

ARNOLD (*attempts to conceal his amusement, then turns to* MURRAY, *smiling*). So, what'd you do with him, just left him standing there? (*He laughs.*) Like to have been there, seen that, must have been great.

MURRAY. Arnie, it was beautiful.

ARNOLD (*still laughing*). It's about time somebody left Leo Herman standing around talking to himself. (*Rubbing his head*) I wish to God I didn't enjoy you so much. Crap, I don't do you any good at all. (*Then, solemnly again.*) Murray, no fun and games with Leo today, understand? He is absolutely *all* we got left before the hearing Thursday.

MURRAY. Yes, I understand.

ARNOLD (*goes to pick up the phone on the desk*). I wish we coulda got something better for you, kid, but there just wasn't any time.

MURRAY. Well, Chuckles won't be so bad for a while . . .

ARNOLD. No, Murray. (*Puts phone down firmly.*) Not just for a while. You'll really have to stick with Chuckles. I had our agency lawyer check the facts for me. Most the Board'll give you is a probationary year with Nick; a trial period. The Board's investigators will be checking on you every week . . .

MURRAY. That's charming.

ARNOLD. . . . checking to see if you've still got the job, checking with Leo on your stability, checking up on the change in your home environment.

MURRAY. Sounds like a parole board.

ARNOLD (*into the intercom phone*). Margot; get me Leo Herman on the speaker-phone here, his home number. Thanks. (*Puts the phone down.*) He's waiting for our call. Look, Murray, maybe he's not the greatest guy in the world; but y'know, he really *likes* you,

Murray, he . . .

MURRAY. Yeah. I have a way with animals.

ARNOLD (*pointing at* MURRAY). That was your last joke for today. (*A click is heard from speaker-phone;* ARNOLD *turns it on.*) You there, Leo?

LEO'S VOICE. Right, Arn. I'm down here in the basement, in my gymnasium; lot of echoing. Am I coming through, am I coming through O.K.?

ARNOLD. Clearly, Leo. Murray's here.

LEO'S VOICE. Murray! Murray the wonderful wild man; fellah, how are ya?

MURRAY (*takes his hat off, waves hello to the speaker-phone*). O.K., Leo, how're you doing?

LEO'S VOICE. Oh, you crazy bastard, it's damn good to hear that voice again. You're an old monkey, aren't ya?

MURRAY. You sound about the same too, Leo.

LEO'S VOICE. Not the same. I'm *more impossible* than I used to be. Can you imagine that?

MURRAY. Not easily, Leo; no.

LEO'S VOICE. Murray, I need you, fellah; I need you back with the show. Murr', we'll talk a while now, and then I'll come over to your place tonight, go over some ideas for next week's shows. It'll be great, sweetie . . . Oh, there's that word again. "Sweetie," I said that word again. Oh, am I getting *sick* of myself. Big phony. The truth, fellah, I'm the biggest phony you ever met, right?

MURRAY. Probably, Leo.

LEO'S VOICE (*after a pause; coldly*). Probably, he says. There he goes, there goes Murray the old joker, right? You're a jester, right? Some fooler. You can't fool with a scheduled show, Murray; a scheduled show with a tight budget. (*Softly, whispering*) Murray, come closer, tell you a secret . . . (MURRAY *comes closer to the box.*) You're gonna hate me, Murray; I gotta tell you something and I know you're gonna hate me for it, but we can't have the same Murray we used to have on the show. Who appreciates a good joke more than anybody? *Me.* But who jokes too much? (*Suddenly louder*) You!

MURRAY. Leo, couldn't we talk about this tonight when we get together . . .

LEO'S VOICE (*softly again*). It hurt me, Murr', it hurt me what you used to do.

When all those thousands of kids wrote in asking for the definition of a chipmunk and you sent back that form letter sayin' a chipmunk was a . . . was a what?

MURRAY. A cute rat.

LEO'S VOICE (*still soft*). A cute rat; yeah. I remember my skin broke out somethin' terrible. Some jester you are, foolin' around at the script conferences, foolin' around at the studio. Now, we're not gonna have any more of that, are we?

MURRAY (*subservient, apologetic*). No, we won't, I'm sorry, Leo.

LEO'S VOICE. Because we can't fool with the innocence of children, can we? My God, they believe in the little Chipmunk, don't ask me why; I'm nothing; God, I know that. I've been damned lucky. A person like me should get a grand and a half a week for doin' nothin'. I mean, I'm one of the big no-talents of all time, right?

MURRAY. Right . . . I mean, no, Leo, no.

LEO'S VOICE. Oh, I know it's the truth and I don't kid myself about it. But there'll be no more jokin'; right, Murr'? Because I'll tell you the truth, I can't stand it.

MURRAY. Right, Leo.

LEO'S VOICE (*softly*). Good. Glad we cleared that up. Because my skin breaks out somethin' terrible. (*Up again*) You're the best, Murray, such talent, you know I love ya, don't ya? You old monkey.

MURRAY (*to* ARNOLD). Please, tell him we'll talk further tonight, too much of him all at once . . .

ARNOLD. Say, Leo, suppose we . . .

LEO'S VOICE. Murray, I want you to put some fifteen-minute fairy tales into the show. You've got your Hans Christian Andersens there, your Grimm Brothers, your Goldilocks, your Sleepin' Beauties, your Gingerbread Men, your Foxy-Loxies, your legends, your folk tales . . . do I reach ya, Murr'?

MURRAY (*quietly*). Yeah, Leo . . .

LEO'S VOICE. Now, what I want in those scripts is this, Murray, I want you to give 'em five minutes a action, five minutes a poignancy and then five minutes of the moral message; race-relations thing; world-peace thing; understanding-brings-love thing. I don't know. Shake 'em up a little. Controversy. Angry letters from parents. Kid's show with something to say, get some excitement in the industry, wild . . .

MURRAY (*he leans over very close to speaker-phone; whispers into it*). Hey, Leo, I might show up one day with eleven minutes of poignancy, no action and a twelve-second moral message . . .

ARNOLD. Murray, stop it . . .

MURRAY (*shouting into the speaker-phone*). And then where would we be?

(*There is a pause. No sound comes from the speaker-phone. Then:*)

LEO'S VOICE. See how he mocks me? Well, I guess there's plenty to mock. Plenty mocking. Sometimes I try to take a cold look at what I am. (*Very soft*) Sweaty Leo jumping around in a funny costume trying to make a buck out of being a chipmunk. The Abominable Snowman in a cute suit. But I'll tell you something, Murray . . . sit down for a minute. (MURRAY *is standing;* LEO'S VOICE *is still fairly pleasant.*) Are ya sitting down, Murray? (MURRAY *remains standing;* LEO'S VOICE *is suddenly loud, sharp, commanding.*) Murray, sit down! (MURRAY *sits down.*) Good. Now I'm gonna tell you a story . . .

MURRAY (*softly, painfully*). Arnold, he's gonna do it again . . . the story . . .

LEO'S VOICE. Murray . . .

MURRAY (*softly, miserably*). The story I got tattooed to my skull . . .

LEO'S VOICE. On June the third . . .

MURRAY (*hunching over in his chair, looking down at the floor*). Story number twelve . . . the "Laughter of Children" story . . . again . . .

LEO'S VOICE. I will be forty-two years old . . .

MURRAY (*to* ARNOLD; *painfully, pleading*). Arnie . . .

LEO'S VOICE. And maybe it's the silliest, phoniest, cop-out thing . . .

LEO'S VOICE and MURRAY (*in unison*). . . . you ever heard, but the Chipmunk, Chuckles, the little guy I pretend to be, is real to me . . .

LEO'S VOICE. . . . as real to me as . . . as this phone in my hand; those children, don't ask me why, God I don't know, but they believe in that little fellah . . . (MURRAY *looks up from the floor now and over at the speaker-phone, which is on the other side of the room; his eyes are fixed on it.*) Look, Murr', I do what I can for the cash-monies; but also, and I say it without embarrassment, I just love kids, the laughter of children, and we can't have you foolin' with that, Murr', can't have you jokin' . . . (MURRAY *stands up, still looking at the speaker-phone.*) because it's this whole, bright, wild sorta child kinda thing . . . (MURRAY *is walking slowly toward the speaker-phone now;* ARNOLD, *watching* MURRAY, *starts to rise from his chair.*) it's this very up feeling, it's all young, and you can't joke with it; the laughter of children; those warm waves, that fresh, open, spontaneous laughter, you can feel it on your face . . .

MURRAY (*picking the speaker-phone up off the desk*). Like a sunburn . . .

LEO's VOICE. Like a sunburn . . .

ARNOLD (*coming toward* MURRAY *as if to stop him*). Murray . . . wait . . .

LEO's VOICE. And it's a pride thing . . . (MURRAY *turns with the speaker-phone held in his hands and drops it into the wastepaper basket next to the desk. He does this calmly.* ARNOLD, *too late to stop him, stands watching, dumbly paralyzed.* LEO, *unaware, goes right on talking, his voice somewhat garbled and echoing from the bottom of the wastepaper basket.*) . . . so then how lovely, how enchanting it is, that I should be paid so well for something I love so much . . . (*Pause*) Say, there's this noise . . . there's this . . . I'm getting this crackling noise on my end here. . . . What's happened to the phone?

ARNOLD (*sadly, solemnly; looking down into the basket*). Leo, you're in a wastepaper basket.

LEO's VOICE. That you, Murray? . . . There's this crackling noise. . . . I can't hear you. . . . Hello? . . . What's going on? . . .

ARNOLD. Leo, hold it just a minute, I'll get you.

LEO's VOICE. There's this funny noise. . . . Where'd everybody go? Where is everybody? . . . Hello, Murray . . . hello . . . come back . . . come back . . .

ARNOLD (*fishing amongst the papers in basket for the speaker-phone*). I'll find you, Leo, I'll find you. . . . (*Finally lifts the speaker out of the basket, holds it gently, tenderly in his hands like a child, speaks soothingly to it.*) Look, Leo . . . Leo, we had a little . . . some trouble with

the phone, we . . . (*Realizes that he is getting no reaction from the box.*) Leo? . . . Leo? . . . (*As though the box were a friend whom he thinks might have died, shaking the box tenderly to revive it*) Leo . . . Leo, are you there? . . . Are you there? . . . It's dead. (*Turning to look at* MURRAY, *as though announcing the demise of a dear one.*) He's gone.

MURRAY. Well, don't look at me like that, Arnie; I didn't *kill* him. He doesn't *live* in that box. . . . Or maybe he does.

ARNOLD. A man has a job for you so you drop him in a basket.

MURRAY. Arnie, I quit that nonsense five months ago . . .

ARNOLD. Murray, you're a *nut,* a man has a job for you, there's a hearing on Thursday . . .

MURRAY. A fool in a box telling me what's funny, a Welfare Board checking my underwear every week because I don't look good in their files . . . and *I'm* the nut, right? *I'm* the crazy one.

ARNOLD. Murray, you float like a balloon and everybody's waitin' for ya with a pin. I'm trying to put you in *touch,* Murray . . . with *real things;* with . . .

MURRAY (*angrily, taking in the office with a sweep of his hand*). You mean like this office, *real* things, like this office? The world could come to an end and you'd find out about it on the phone. (*Pointing at two framed photographs on* ARNOLD's *desk*) Pictures of your wife six years ago when she was still a piece, and your kids at their cutest four years ago when they looked best for the office. . . . Oh, you're in *touch* all right, Arnie.

ARNOLD (*softly, soothing*). Murray, you're just a little excited, that's all, just relax, everything's gonna be fine . . .

MURRAY (*shouting*). Damn it . . . get angry; I just insulted you, personally, about your wife, your kids; I just said lousy things to you. Raise your voice, at least your eyebrows . . . (*Pleading painfully*) Please, have an argument with me . . .

ARNOLD (*coaxing*). We'll call Leo back, we'll apologize to him . . . (MURRAY *goes to the end table, picks up an apple from the bowl of fruit.*) Everything's gonna be just fine, Murray, you'll see . . . just fine.

MURRAY. Arnie?

ARNOLD. Huh?

MURRAY. Catch. (*Tosses the apple un-*

derhand across the room. ARNOLD *catches it.* MURRAY *exits.*)

ARNOLD (*his hand out from catching the apple*). Aw, Murray . . . (*Lowers his hand to his side; speaks quietly, alone now in the office.*) Murray, I swear to you, King Kong is *not* on top of the Time-Life Building . . .

(ARNOLD *discovers the apple in his hand; bites into it. The lights fade quickly. As they dim, we hear* NICK *humming and whistling "Yes, Sir, That's My Baby." The lights go up on* MURRAY'S *apartment.* NICK'S *humming and whistling fades back so that it is coming from outside the window; the humming grows louder again after a second or two as, it would seem, he descends the fire-escape ladder from Mrs. Myers' apartment. It is early evening. No one is onstage. The apartment has been rather spectacularly rehabilitated by* SANDRA *since we saw it last. The great clutter of* MURRAY'S *nonsense collection, clocks, radios, knickknacks, has been cleared away, the books have been neatly arranged in the bookcases, a hat rack has been placed above the bureau and* MURRAY'S *hats are placed neatly on it. There are bright new bedspreads on the two beds and brightly colored throw pillows, one new curtain is already up at the windows and a piece of matching material is over the Morris chair. The beach chair and swivel chair are gone and the wicker chair has been painted gold, the table has a bright new cloth over it. Pots of flowers are on the table, the bookshelves, the file cabinets, headboard and desk; and geraniums are in a holder hanging from the window molding. The whole place has been dusted and polished and gives off a bright glow. After two lines or so of the song,* NICK *enters through the window from the fire escape, carrying his pajamas and school books.* NICK *sees the new curtain first, and then, from his position on the window seat, sees the other changes in the apartment and smiles appreciatively.* SANDRA *enters from the kitchen, carrying a mixing bowl and a spoon. She smiles, glad to see* NICK.)

SANDRA. Hello, Nick . . .

NICK. Hello, lady. I came in from the fire escape. Mrs. Myers lives right upstairs. I went there after school, I . . . (*Indicating her work on the apartment*) Did . . . did you do all this?

SANDRA. Yes, Nick; do you like it?

NICK (*goes to her, smiling*). I think it's superb. I mean, imagine my surprise when I saw it. (*Pause*) Where's Murray?

SANDRA (*happily telling him the good news*). Nick . . . Murray went downtown to see your Uncle Arnold. He's going to get a job.

NICK. That's terrific. Hey, that's just terrific. (SANDRA *goes to the folded new curtains on the bed, sits down on the bed, unfolds one of the curtains, begins attaching curtain hooks and rings to it;* NICK *sits next to her, helping her as they talk together.*) See, lady, he was developing into a bum. You don't want to see somebody you like developing into a bum, and doing nutty things, right? You know what he does? He hollers. Like we were on Park Avenue last Sunday, it's early in the morning and nobody is in the street, see, there's just all those big quiet apartment houses; and he hollers "Rich people, I want to see you all out on the street for volley ball! Let's snap it up!" And sometimes, if we're in a crowded elevator some place, he turns to me and yells "Max, there'll be no *more* of this self-pity! You're forty, it's time you got *used* to being a midget!" And everybody stares. And he has a wonderful time. What do you do with somebody who hollers like that? Last week in Macy's he did that. (*He laughs.*) If you want to know the truth, it was pretty funny. (SANDRA *smiles.*) I think you're a very nice lady.

SANDRA. Thank you, Nick.

NICK. What do you think of me?

SANDRA. I think you're very nice also.

NICK. A very nice quality you have is that you are a good listener, which is important to me because of how much I talk. (*She laughs, enjoying him.*) Hey, you're some laugher, aren't you, lady?

SANDRA. I guess so, Nick.

NICK (*trying to make her feel at home*). Would you like some fruit? An orange maybe?

SANDRA. No thank you, Nick.

NICK. If you want to call your mother or something, I mean, feel free to use the telephone . . . or my desk if you want to read a book or something . . . or *any* of the chairs . . .

SANDRA. I will, Nick, thank you.

NICK. O.K. (*Pause*) Are you going to

be staying around here for a while?

SANDRA. I might, yes.

NICK (*he rises, picks up the pajamas and books he brought in with him; indicates apartment*). Has . . . has Murray seen . . . all this?

SANDRA. No, not yet.

NICK (*nods*). Not yet. Well . . . (*Goes to the window, steps up on window seat.*) Good luck, lady. (*He exits through the window, carrying his pajamas and school books, goes back up the fire escape.* SANDRA *crosses to window seat, smiling to herself.* MURRAY *enters, unnoticed by her.*)

MURRAY (*standing still at the front door, glancing around at the apartment; to himself*). Oh God, I've been attacked by the *Ladies Home Journal.*

(SANDRA *hears him, goes to him happily.*)

SANDRA. Murray, what a nice suit you bought. How is everything, which job did . . .

MURRAY (*looking around at her work on the apartment*). Hey look at this. You've started to get rid of the Edgar Allan Poe atmosphere.

SANDRA. Don't you like it?

MURRAY (*looking around, noticing his knickknacks are missing*). Sure. Sure. Lotta work. Place has an unusual quality now. Kind of Fun Gothic.

SANDRA. Well, of course I'm really not done yet, the curtains aren't all up, and this chair won't look so bad if we re-upholster . . . Come on, Murray, don't keep me in suspense, which one of the jobs did you . . .

MURRAY (*takes her arm, smiles, seats her on the chair in front of him*). I shall now leave you breathless with the strange and wondrous tale of this sturdy lad's adventures today in downtown Oz. (*She is cheered by his manner and ready to listen.*) Picture, if you will, me. I am walking on East Fifty-first Street an hour ago and I decided to construct and develop a really decorative, general-all-purpose apology. Not complicated, just the words "I am sorry," said with a little style.

SANDRA. Sorry for what?

MURRAY. Anything. For being late, early, stupid, asleep, silly, alive . . . (*He moves about now, acting out the scene on the street for her.*) Well, y'know when you're walking down the street talking to yourself how sometimes you suddenly say a coupla words out loud? So I said, "I'm sorry," and this fella, complete stranger, he looks up a second and says, "That's all right, Mac," and goes right on. (MURRAY *and* SANDRA *laugh.*) He automatically forgave me. I communicated. Five-o'clock rush-hour in midtown you could say, "Sir, I believe your hair is on fire," and they wouldn't hear you. So I decided to test the whole thing out scientifically, I stayed right there on the corner of Fifty-first and Lex for a while, just saying "I'm sorry" to everybody that went by. (*Abjectly*) "Oh, I'm so sorry, sir . . ." (*Slowly, quaveringly*) "I'm terribly sorry, madam . . ." (*Warmly*) "Say there, miss, I'm sorry." Of course, some people just gave me a funny look, but Sandy, I swear, seventy-five percent of them *forgave* me. (*Acting out the people for her*) "Forget it, buddy" . . . "That's O.K., really." Two ladies forgave me in unison, one fella forgave me from a passing car, and one guy forgave me for his dog. "Poofer forgives the nice man, don't you, Poofer?" Oh, Sandy, it was fabulous. I had tapped some vast reservoir. Something had happened to all of them for which they felt *some*body should apologize. If you went up to people on the street and offered them money, they'd refuse it. But everybody accepts apology immediately. It is the most negotiable currency. I said to them, "I am sorry." And they were all so generous, so kind. You could give 'em love and it wouldn't be accepted half as graciously, as unquestioningly . . .

SANDRA (*suspiciously, her amusement fading*). That's certainly . . . that's very interesting, Murray.

MURRAY. Sandy, I could run up on the roof right now and holler, "I am sorry," and half a million people would holler right back, "That's O.K., just see that you don't do it again!"

SANDRA (*after a pause*). Murray, you didn't take any of the jobs.

MURRAY (*quietly*). Sandy, I took whatever I am and put a suit on it and gave it a haircut and took it outside and that's what happened. I know what I said this morning, what I promised, and Sandra, I'm sorry, I'm very sorry. (*She just sits there before him and stares at him expressionlessly.*) Damn it, lady, that was a beautiful apology. You gotta love a guy who can apologize so nice. I rehearsed for over an hour. (*She just looks at him.*) That's the most you should expect from life, Sandy, a really good apology for all the things you won't get.

SANDRA. Murray, I don't understand. What happens to Nick? What about the Welfare Board?

MURRAY (*he takes her hand*). Sandra . . .

SANDRA. I mean, if you don't like the jobs your brother found for you, then take *any* job . . .

MURRAY (*he takes both of her hands and kneels next to her chair*). Oh, Sandy . . . (*Softly, pleading for her to understand*) Nick, he's a wonderful kid, but he's brought the God-damned world in on me. Don't you understand, Sandy, they'd be checking up on me every week; being judged by people I don't know and who don't know me, a committee of ghosts; gimme a month of that and I'd turn into an ashtray, a bowl of corn flakes, I wouldn't know me on the street. . . . (*Looks under chair.*) Have you seen Murray? He was here just a minute ago. . . . (*Looks at her, smiles.*) Hey, have you see Murray? (*Pleading for her to understand*) I wouldn't be of any use to Nick or you or anybody . . .

(SANDRA *moves away from him, goes to the window seat, leaves him kneeling at the chair. She is still holding the curtain she had been working on.*)

SANDRA (*quietly*). I've had no effect on you at all. I've made no difference. You have no idea what it feels like to have no effect on people. I am not a leader. I scored very low in leadership in three different vocational aptitude tests. When I point my finger, people go the other way . . . (*Absently, she begins to fold the curtain neatly in her lap.*)

MURRAY. Sandra . . .

SANDRA. In grad school they put me in charge of the Structured-Childs-Play-Analysis session one day . . . (*She shrugs.*) and all the children fell asleep. I am not a leader.

MURRAY (*going to her at the window seat; warmly, with love*). Oh, Sandy, you are a cute, jolly lady . . . please understand.

SANDRA. When you left this morning, I was so sure . . .

MURRAY. This morning . . . (*He sits next to her on the window seat, his arm around her, his free hand gesturing expansively, romantically.*) Oh, Sandy, I saw the most beautiful sailing this morning . . . The *Sklardahl*, Swedish liner, bound for Europe. It's a great thing to do when you're about to start something new; you see a boat off. It's always wonderful; there's a sailing practically every day this time of year. Sandy, you go down and stand at the dock with all the well-wishers and throw confetti and make a racket with them. . . . Hey, bon voyage, Charley, have a wonderful time. . . . It gives you a genuine feeling of the beginning of things. . . . There's another one Friday, big French ship, two stacker . . .

(SANDRA *has been watching him coldly during this speech; she speaks quietly; catching him in mid-air.*)

SANDRA. Nick will have to go away now, Murray. (*She looks away from him.*) I bought new bedspreads at Altman's, I haven't spoken to my mother in two days, and you went to see a boat off. (*She pauses; then smiles to herself for a moment.*) My goodness; I'm a listmaker. (*She leaves him alone in the window seat.*) I have to have enough sense to leave you, Murray. I can see why Nick liked it here. I would like it here too if I was twelve years old. (*She puts the folded curtain down on a chair, picks up her jacket.*)

MURRAY (*coming toward her, warmly*). Come on, stick with me, Dr. Markowitz, anything can happen above an abandoned Chinese restaurant. . . .

SANDRA (*looking directly at him; quietly*). Maybe you're wonderfully independent, Murray, or maybe, maybe you're the most extraordinarily selfish person I've ever met. (*She picks up her hand bag and starts toward the door.*)

MURRAY (*tired of begging; angrily, as she walks toward the door*). What're you gonna do now, go back and live in a closet? It's really gonna be quite thrilling, you and Albert, guarding the Lincoln Tunnel together.

SANDRA (*turning at the door to look at him*). I think, Murray, that you live in a much, much larger closet than I do.

MURRAY (*painfully*). Lady, lady, please don't look at me like that . . .

SANDRA (*looking about the apartment;*

very quietly). Oh, there are so many really attractive things you can do with a one-room apartment if you're willing to use your imagination. (*Opens the door.*) Good-bye, Murray. (*She exits.* MURRAY *stands still for a moment; then rushes forward to the closed door, angrily.*)

MURRAY (*shouting*). Hey, damn it, you forgot your files! (*Picks up her files from the bureau, opens the door; but she is gone.*) The management is not responsible for personal property! (*Closes the door, puts the files back on the bureau; stands at the door, looking around at the apartment.*) And what the hell did you do to my apartment? Where are my clocks? What'd you do with my stuff? Where's my radios? (*His back to the audience, shouting*) What've we got here; God damn Sunnybrook Farm! What happened to my place? (*Suddenly realizing he is still wearing a new suit, he pulls off his suit jacket, rolls it up into a tight ball, and throws it violently across the room. A moment; then he relaxes, walks casually to the window, puts his favorite hat on, sits, leans back comfortably in the window seat and smiles. He talks out of the window in a loud mock-serious voice.*) Campers . . . the entertainment committee was quite disappointed by the really poor turn-out at this morning's community sing. I mean, where's all that old Camp Chickawattamee spirit? Now, I'd like to say that I . . . (*He hesitates; he can't think of anything to say. A pause; then he haltingly tries again.*) I'd like to say right now that I . . . that . . . that I . . . (*His voice is soft, vague; he pulls his knees up, folds his arms around them, his head bent on his knees; quietly*) Campers, I can't think of anything to say . . .

(*A moment; then*)

CURTAIN

ACT THREE

In the darkness, before the curtain goes up, we hear an old recording of a marching band playing "Stars and Strips Forever." This goes on rather loudly for a few moments. The music diminishes somewhat as the curtain goes up; and we see that the music is coming from an old phonograph on the wicker chair

near the bed. It's about thirty minutes later and, though much of SANDRA's work on the apartment is still apparent, it is obvious that MURRAY has been busy putting his place back into its old shape. The curtains are gone, as is the tablecloth and the material on the Morris chair. All the flower pots have been put on top of the file cabinet. The swivel chair and the beach chair are back in view. Cluttered about the room again is much of MURRAY's nonsense collection, clocks, radios, knickknacks and stacks of magazines.

As the curtain goes up, MURRAY *has just retrieved a stack of magazines, the megaphone and the pirate pistol from the closet where* SANDRA *had put them; and we see him now placing them back around the room carefully, as though they were part of some strict design.* ARNOLD *enters, carrying his attaché case; walks to the beach chair, sits, takes his hat off. The two men do not look at each other. The music continues to play.*

———

ARNOLD (*after a moment*). I didn't even bring a tangerine with me. That's very courageous if you think about it for a minute. (*Looks over at* MURRAY, *who is not facing him, points at record player.*) You wanna turn that music off, please? (*No reply from* MURRAY.) Murray, the music; I'm trying to . . . (*No reply from* MURRAY, *so* ARNOLD *puts his attaché case and hat on table, goes quickly to the record player and turns the music off;* MURRAY *turns to look at* ARNOLD.) O.K., I'm a little slow. It takes me an hour to get insulted. Now I'm insulted. You walked out of my office. That wasn't a nice thing to do to me, Murray . . . (MURRAY *does not reply.*) You came into my office like George God; everybody's supposed to come up and audition for Human Being in front of you. (*Comes over closer to him, takes his arm.*) Aw, Murray, today, one day, leave the dragons alone, will ya? And look at the dragons you pick on; Sloan, Leo, me; silly old arthritic dragons, step on a toe and we'll start to cry. Murray, I called Leo back, I apologized, told him my phone broke down; I got him to come over here tonight. He's anxious to see you, everything's O.K. . . .

MURRAY. Hey, you just never give up,

do you, Arnie?

ARNOLD. Listen to me, Murray, do I ever tell you what to do . . .

MURRAY. Yes, all the time.

ARNOLD. If you love this kid, then you gotta take any kinda stupid job to keep him . . .

MURRAY. Now you're an expert on love.

ARNOLD. Not an expert, but I sure as hell value my amateur standing. Murray, about him leaving, have you told him yet?

MURRAY (softly; realizing ARNOLD's genuine concern). Arnie, don't worry, I know how to handle it. I've got a coupla days to tell him. And don't underrate Nick, he's gonna understand this a lot better than you think.

ARNOLD. Murray, I finally figured out your problem. There's only one thing that really bothers you . . . (With a sweep of his hand) Other people. (With a mock-secretive tone) If it wasn't for them other people, everything would be great, huh, Murray? I mean, you think everything's fine, and then you go out into the street . . . and there they all are again, right? The Other People; taking up space, bumping into you, asking for things, making lines to wait on, taking cabs away from ya . . . The Enemy . . . Well, watch out, Murray, they're everywhere . . .

MURRAY. Go ahead, Arnie, give me advice, at thirty thousand a year you can afford it.

ARNOLD. Oh, I get it, if I'm so smart why ain't I poor? You better get a damn good act of your own before you start giving mine the razzberry. What's this game you play gonna be like ten years from now, without youth? Murray, Murray, I can't watch this, you gotta shape up . . .

MURRAY (turning quickly to face ARNOLD; in a surprised tone). Shape up? (Looks directly at ARNOLD; speaks slowly.) Arnie, what the hell happened to you? You got so old. I don't know you any more. When you quit "Harry the Fur King" on Thirty-eighth Street, remember?

ARNOLD. That's twenty years ago, Murray.

MURRAY. You told me you were going to be in twenty businesses in twenty years if you had to, till you found out what you wanted. Things were always going to change. Harry said you were not behaving maturely enough for a salesman; your clothes didn't match or something . . . (Laughs in affectionate memory of the event.) So the next day, you dressed perfectly, homburg, gray suit, cuff links, carrying a briefcase and a rolled umbrella . . . and you came into Harry's office on roller skates. You weren't going to take crap from anybody. So that's the business you finally picked . . . taking crap from everybody.

ARNOLD. I don't do practical jokes any more, if that's what you mean . . .

MURRAY (grabs both of ARNOLD's arms tensely). Practical, that's right; a way to stay alive. If most things aren't funny, Arn, then they're only exactly what they are; then it's one long dental appointment interrupted occasionally by something exciting, like waiting or falling asleep. What's the point if I leave everything exactly the way I find it? Then I'm just adding to the noise, then I'm just taking up some more room on the subway.

ARNOLD. Murray, the Welfare Board has these specifications; all you have to do is meet a couple specifications . . .

(MURRAY releases his grip on ARNOLD's arms; MURRAY's hands drop to his sides.)

MURRAY. Oh, Arnie, you don't understand any more. You got that wide stare that people stick in their eyes so nobody'll know their head's asleep. You got to be a shuffler, a moaner. You want me to come sit and eat fruit with you and watch the clock run out. You start to drag and stumble with the rotten weight of all the people who should have been told off, all the things you should have said, all the specifications that aren't yours. The only thing you got left to reject is your food in a restaurant if they do it wrong and you can send it back and make a big fuss with the waiter. . . . (MURRAY turns away from ARNOLD, goes to the window seat, sits down.) Arnold, five months ago I forgot what day it was. I'm on the subway on my way to work and I didn't know what day it was and it scared the hell out of me. . . . (Quietly) I was sitting in the express looking out the window same as every morning watching the local stops go by in the dark with an empty head and my arms folded, not feeling great and not feeling rotten, just not feeling, and for a minute I couldn't remember, I didn't know, unless I really concentrated, whether it was a Tuesday or a Thursday . . . or a . . . for a minute it could have been *any* day, Arnie . . . sitting in the train going through any day . . . in the dark through any year. . . . Arnie, it scared the hell out of me. (*Stands up.*) You got to know what day it is. You got to know what's the name of the game and what the rules are with nobody else telling you. You have to own your days and name them, each one of them, every one of them, or else the years go right by and none of them belong to you. (*Turns to look at* ARNOLD.) And that ain't just for weekends, kiddo . . . (*Looks at* ARNOLD *a moment longer, then speaks in a pleasant tone.*) Here it is, the day after Irving R. Feldman's birthday, for God's sake . . . (*Takes a hat, puts it on.*) And I never even congratulated him . . . (*Starts to walk briskly toward the front door.* ARNOLD *shouts in a voice stronger than we have ever heard from him.*)

ABNOLD. Murray! (MURRAY *stops, turns, startled to hear this loud a voice from* ARNOLD. ARNOLD *looks fiercely at* MURRAY *for a moment, then* ARNOLD *looks surprised, starts to laugh.*)

MURRAY. What's so funny?

ARNOLD. Wow, I scared myself. You hear that voice? Look at that, I got you to stop, I got your complete, full attention, the floor is mine now . . . (*Chuckles awkwardly.*) And I can't think of a God-damned thing to say . . . (*Shrugs his shoulders; picks up his hat from the table.*) I have long been aware, Murray . . . I have long been aware that you don't respect me much. . . . I suppose there are a lot of brothers who don't get along. . . . But in reference . . . to us, considering the factors . . . (*Smiles, embarrassed.*) Sounds like a contract, doesn't it? (*Picks up his briefcase, comes over to* MURRAY.) Unfortunately for you, Murray, you want to be a hero. Maybe, if a fella falls into a lake, you can jump in and save him; there's still that kind of stuff. But who gets opportunities like that in midtown Manhattan, with all that traffic. (*Puts on his hat.*) I am willing to deal with the available world and I do not choose to shake it up but to live with it. There's the people who spill things, and the peo-

ple who get spilled on; I do not choose to notice the stains, Murray. I have a wife and I have children, and business, like they say, is business. I am not an exceptional man, so it is possible for me to stay with things the way they are. I'm lucky. I'm gifted. I have a talent for surrender. I'm at peace. But you are cursed; and I like you so it makes me sad, you don't have the gift; and I see the torture of it. All I can do is worry for you. But I will not worry for myself; you cannot convince me that I am one of the Bad Guys. I get up, I go, I lie a little, I peddle a little, I watch the rules, I talk the talk. We fellas have those offices high up there so we can catch the wind and go with it, however it blows. But, and I will not apologize for it, I take pride; I am the best possible Arnold Burns. (*Pause*) Well . . . give my regards to Irving R. Feldman, will ya? (*He starts to leave.*)

MURRAY (*going toward him*). Arnold . . .

ARNOLD. Please, Murray . . . (*Puts his hand up.*) Allow me once to leave a room before you do.

(ARNOLD *snaps on record player as he walks past it to the front door; he exits.* MURRAY *goes toward the closed door, the record player has warmed up and we suddenly hear "Stars and Stripes Forever" blaring loudly from the machine again;* MURRAY *turns at this sound and stands for a long moment looking at the record player as the music comes from it.* NICK *enters through the window from the fire escape, unnoticed by* MURRAY. NICK *looks about, sees that the apartment is not quite what it was an hour before.*)

NICK. Hey, Murray . . .

MURRAY (*turns, sees* NICK). Nick . . . (*Turns the record player off; puts the record on the bed.*)

NICK. Hey, where's the lady?

MURRAY. Well, she's not here right now . . .

NICK (*stepping forward to make an announcement*). Murray, I have decided that since *you* are getting a job today then I made up my mind it is time for *me* also to finish a certain matter which I have been putting off.

MURRAY. Nick, listen, turned out the only job I could get in a hurry was with Chuckles . . .

NICK (*nodding in approval*). Chuckles,

huh? Well, fine. (*Then, grimly*) Just as long as I don't have to watch that terrible program every morning. (*Returning to his announcement*) For many months now I have been concerned with a decision, Murray . . . Murray, you're not listening.

MURRAY (*distracted*). Sure I'm listening, yeah . . .

NICK. The past couple months I have been thinking about different names and considering different names because in four weeks I'm gonna be thirteen and I gotta pick my permanent name, like we said.

MURRAY. Why don't you just go on calling yourself Nick? You've been using it the longest.

NICK. Nick is a name for a short person. And since I am a short person I do not believe I should put a lot of attention on it.

MURRAY. Whaddya mean, where'd you get the idea you were short?

NICK. From people who are taller than I am.

MURRAY. That's ridiculous.

NICK. Sure, standing up there it's ridiculous, but from down here where I am it's not so ridiculous. And half the girls in my class are taller than me. Especially Susan Bookwalter. (NICK *sits dejectedly in the swivel chair.*)

MURRAY (*crouching over next to him*). Nick, you happen to be a nice medium height for your age.

NICK (*pointing at* MURRAY). Yeah, so how is it everybody crouches over a little when I'm around? ·

MURRAY (*straightening up*). Because you're a kid. (*Sits next to him.*) Listen, you come from a fairly tall family. Next couple years you're gonna grow like crazy. Really, Nick, every day you're getting bigger.

NICK. So is Susan Bookwalter. (*Stands.*) So for a couple of months I considered various tall names. Last month I considered, for a while, Zachery, but I figured there was a chance Zachery could turn into a short, fat, bald name. Then I thought about Richard, which is not really tall, just very thin with glasses. Then last week I finally, really, decided and I took out a new library card to see how it looks and today I figured I would make it definite and official. (*He takes*

a library card out of his pocket, hands it to MURRAY.)

MURRAY (*looks at the card, confused*). This is *my* library card.

NICK. No, that's the whole thing; it's mine.

MURRAY. But it says "*Murray* Burns" on it . . .

NICK. Right, that's the name I picked. So I took out a new card to see how it looks and make it official.

MURRAY (*looks at the card, is moved and upset by it, but covers with cool dignity; stands, speaks very formally*). Well, Nick, I'm flattered . . . I want you to know that I'm . . . very flattered by this. (NICK *goes to the alcove to put his school books and pajamas away.*) Well, why the hell did you . . . I mean, damn it, Nick, that's too many Murrays, very confusing . . . (MURRAY *begins to shift the card awkwardly from one hand to the other, speaks haltingly.*) Look, why don't you call yourself George, huh? Very strong name there, George . . .

NICK (*shaking his head firmly*). No. We made a deal it was up to me to pick which name and that's the name I decided on; "Murray."

MURRAY. Well, what about Jack? What the hell's wrong with Jack? Jack Burns . . . sounds like a promising heavyweight.

NICK. I like the name I picked better.

MURRAY (*very quietly*). Or Martin . . . or Robert . . .

NICK. Those names are all square.

LEO'S VOICE (*from behind the door, shouting*). Is this it? Is this the Lion's Den, here? Hey, Murr'!

MURRAY (*softly*). Ah, I heard the voice of a chipmunk.

NICK (*going into the bathroom*). I better go put on a tie.

MURRAY (*goes to the door; stands there a moment, looks over to the other side of the room at* NICK, *who is offstage in the bathroom; smiles, speaks half to himself, very softly*). You coulda called yourself Charlie. Charlie is a very musical name.

(*Then, he opens the door.* LEO HERMAN *enters. He wears a camel's-hair coat and hat. The coat, like his suit, is a little too big for him. He is carrying a paper bag and a large Chuckles statue—a life-size cardboard cutout of himself in his character of Chuckles the Chipmunk; the statue wears a blindingly ingratiating smile.*)

LEO (*with great enthusiasm*). Murray, there he is! There's the old monkey! There's the old joker, right?

MURRAY (*quietly, smiling politely*). Yeah, Leo, here he is. (*Shakes* LEO's *hand.*) It's . . . it's very nice to see you again, Leo, after all this time.

LEO (*turning to see* NICK, *who has come out of the bathroom wearing his tie*). There he is! There's the little guy! (*Goes to* NICK *carrying the statue and the paper bag.*) Looka here, little guy . . . (*Setting the statue up against the wall next to the window.*) I gotta Chuckles statue for you.

NICK (*with his best company manners*). Thank you, Mr. Herman; imagine how pleased I am to receive it. It's a very artistic statue and very good cardboard too.

LEO (*taking a Chuckles hat from the paper bag; a replica of the furry, big-eared hat worn by the statue*). And I gotta Chuckles hat for you too, just like the old Chipmunk wears. (*He puts the hat on* NICK's *head.*)

NICK. Thank you.

LEO (*crouching over to* NICK's *height*). Now that you've got the Chuckles hat, you've got to say the Chuckles-hello.

NICK (*confused, but anxious to please*). The what?

LEO (*prompting him*). "Chip-chip, Chip-permunkie!" (*He salutes.*)

NICK. Oh, yeah . . . "Chip-chip, Chip-permunkie!" (*He salutes too.*)

LEO. May I know your name?

NICK. It's Nick, most of the time.

LEO. Most of the . . . (*Pulling two bags of potato chips from his overcoat pockets*) Say, look what I've got, two big bags of Chuckle-Chip potato chips! How'd ya like to put these crispy chips in some bowls or somethin' for us, huh? (NICK *takes the two bags, goes to the kitchen.*) And take your time, Nick, your uncle 'n' me have some grown-up talkin' to do. (*After* NICK *exits into the kitchen*) The kid hates me. I can tell. Didn't go over very well with him, pushed a little too hard. He's a nice kid, Murray.

MURRAY. How are *your* kids, Leo?

LEO. Fine, fine. But, Murray, I swear, even *they* don't like my show since you stopped writing it. My youngest one . . . my six-year-old . . . (*He can't quite remember.*)

MURRAY. Ralphie.

LEO. Ralphie; he's been watching the Funny Bunny Show now every morning instead of me. (*Begins pacing up and down.*) Oh *boy*, have I been bombing out on the show. Murray, do you know what it *feels* like to bomb out in front of children? You flop out in front of kids and, Murray, I swear to God, they're ready to *kill* you (*Stops pacing.*) Or else, they just stare at you, that's the worst, that hurt, innocent stare like you just killed their pup or raped their turtle or something. (*Goes over to* MURRAY.) Murray, to have you back with me on the show, to see you at the studio again tomorrow, it's gonna be *beautiful*. You're the *best*.

MURRAY. I appreciate your feeling that way, Leo.

LEO. This afternoon, Murray, on the phone, you hung up on me, didn't you?

MURRAY. I'm sorry Leo, I was just kidding . . . I hope you . . .

LEO (*sadly*). Murray, why do you do that to me? Aw, don't tell me, I know, I make people nervous. Who can listen to me for ten minutes? (*Begins pacing up and down again, strokes his tie.*) See *that*? See how I keep touching my suit and my tie? I keep touching myself to make sure I'm still there. Murray, I get this feeling, maybe I vanished when I wasn't looking.

MURRAY. Oh, I'm sure that you're here, Leo.

LEO (*pointing at* MURRAY). See how he talks to me? A little nasty. (*Smiles suddenly.*) Well, I like it. It's straight and it's real and I like it. You know what I got around me on the show? Finks, dwarfs, phonies and frogs. No Murrays. The show: boring, boredom, bore . . . (*Cups his hands around his mouth and shouts.*) boring, boring . . .

(*During these last few words,* SANDRA *has entered through the partly open door.* MURRAY *turns, sees her.*)

SANDRA (*staying near the doorway; reserved, official*). Murray, I believe that I left my files here; I came to get my files; may I have my files, please. I . . . (*She sees* LEO, *comes a few feet into the room.*) Oh, excuse me . . .

MURRAY (*cordially, introducing them*). Chuckles the Chipmunk . . . this is Minnie Mouse.

LEO (*absently*). Hi, Minnie . . .

SANDRA (*looking from one to the other, taking in the situation, smiles; to* LEO). You must be . . . you must be Mr. Herman.

LEO (*mumbling to himself*). Yeah, I must be. I must be him; I'd rather not be, but what the hell . . .

SANDRA (*smiling, as she turns right around and goes to the door*). Well, I'll be on my way . . . (*She exits.* MURRAY *picks up her files from the bureau, goes to the door with them.*)

LEO (*interrupting* MURRAY *on his way to the door*). Very attractive girl, that Minnie; what does she do?

MURRAY. She's my decorator.

LEO (*looking around the apartment*). Well, she's done a *wonderful* job! (*Indicating the apartment with a sweep of his hand*) This place is great. It's loose, it's open, it's free. Love it. Wonderful, crazy place. My God . . . you must make out like mad in this place, huh? (MURRAY *closes door, puts the files back on the bureau;* LEO *is walking around the apartment.*) How come I never came here before?

MURRAY. You were here last January, Leo.

LEO. Funny thing, work with me for three years and I never saw your apartment.

MURRAY. You were here last January, Leo.

LEO (*stops pacing, turns to* MURRAY). Wait a minute, wait a minute, wasn't I here recently, in the winter? Last January, I think . . . (*Goes over to* MURRAY.) Oh, I came here to get you back on the show and you wouldn't listen, you went into the kitchen, sang "Yes, Sir, That's My Baby." I left feeling very foolish, like I had footprints on my face. . . . You old monkey. (*Smiles, musses up* MURRAY's *hair.*) You're an old monkey, aren't ya? (*Starts pacing again.*) You know what I got from that experience? A rash. I broke out something terrible. . . . Minnie Mouse! (*Stops pacing.*) Minnie *Mouse!* (*Laughs loudly, points at the door.*) You told me her name was Minnie Mouse! I swear to God, Murray, I think my mission in life is to feed you straight-lines . . . (*Taking in the apartment with a sweep of his hand.*) It's kind of a fall-out shelter, that's what you got here, Murr', protection against the idiots in the atmos-

phere. Free, freer, freest . . . (*Cups his hands around his mouth, shouts.*) Free! Free! (*Takes off his coat.*) Another year and I'm gonna cut loose from the Goddamn Chipmunk show. Binds me up, hugs me. Finks, dwarfs, phonies and frogs . . . (*Following* MURRAY *to the window seat*) Two of us should do something new, something wild; new kind of kid's show, for adults maybe . . .

MURRAY (*sitting on the window seat*). You told me the same thing three years ago, Leo.

LEO (*sits next to* MURRAY). Well, whaddya want from me? I'm a coward; everybody knows that. (*Suddenly seeing the Chuckles statue against the wall next to him.*) Oh God! (*Points at the statue; in anguish*) Did you ever see anything so *immodest?* I bring a big statue of myself as a gift for a child! I mean, the *pure ego* of it . . . (*Covers his face with his hands.*) I am ashamed. Murray, could you throw a sheet over it or something . . . (*Sees* NICK, *who has just come out of the kitchen with two bowls of potato chips.*) Mmmm, good! Here they are. (*Grabs one bowl from* NICK's *hand, gives it to* MURRAY. *Then* LEO *turns to* NICK, *assumes the character and the voice of Chuckles the Chipmunk; a great mock-frown on his face, he goes into a routine for* NICK.) Oh, goshes, kidderoonies, look at your poor Chippermunk friend; he got his mouff stuck. No matter how hard I try I can't get my mouth unstuck. But maybe—if you Chippermunks yell, "Be happy, Chuckles," maybe then it'll get unstuck . . . (LEO *waits.* NICK *does not react.* LEO *prompts* NICK *in a whisper.*) You're supposed to yell, "Be happy, Chuckles."

NICK. Oh, yeah . . . sure . . . (*Glances quickly at* MURRAY; *then, a little embarrassed, he yells.*) Be happy, Chuckles!

LEO. Oh boy! (*His frown changes to a giant smile.*) You *fixed* me! Looka my mouff! (*He jumps up in the air.*) Now I'm all fixed! (*Gets no reaction from* NICK. NICK *stands patiently in front of* LEO.)

NICK (*offering the other bowl of potato chips to* LEO, *trying to be polite*). Mr. Herman, don't you want your . . .

LEO (*not accepting the potato chips, speaking in his own voice again, stroking his tie nervously*). That was a bit from tomorrow morning's show. You'll know it ahead of all the kids in the neighborhood.

NICK. Thank you.

LEO. That . . . that was one of the funny parts there, when I couldn't move my mouth.

NICK. Yeah?

LEO. Didn't you think it was funny?

NICK. Yeah, that was pretty funny.

LEO (*smiling nervously*). Well, don't you laugh or something when you see something funny?

NICK. It just took me by surprise is all. So I didn't get a chance. (*Offering him the potato chips, politely*) Here's your . . .

LEO. Another funny part was when I jumped up with the smile there, at the end there. That was another one.

NICK. Uh-huh.

LEO (*pressing on, beginning to get tense*). And the finish on the bit, see, I've got the smile . . . (NICK, *looking trapped, stands there as* LEO *switches back to his Chipmunk voice and puts a giant smile on his face.*) Now I'm aaaall fixed, Chippermunks! (*Suddenly mock-pathos in his eyes.*) Oooops! *Now* I got stuck the *other* way! Oh, *oh,* now my face is stuck the *other* way! (*Throws up his arms, does a loose-legged slapstick fall back onto the floor. Remains prone, waiting for* NICK's *reaction.* NICK *stands there looking at* LEO *quite solemnly.*)

NICK (*nods his head up and down approvingly*). That's terrific, Mr. Herman. (*With admiration*) That's all you have to do, you just get up and do that and they pay you and everything.

LEO. You didn't laugh.

NICK. I was waiting for the funny part.

LEO (*sits up*). That was the funny part.

NICK. Oh, when you fell down on the . . .

LEO. When I fell down on the floor here.

NICK. See, the thing is, I was . . .

LEO (*gets up from the floor, paces up and down tensely*). I know, waiting for the funny part. Well, you missed another funny part.

NICK. Another one. Hey, I'm really sorry, Mr. Herman, I . . .

LEO. Forget it . . . I just happen to know that that bit is very *funny.* I can prove it to you. (*Takes small booklet from pocket, opens it, shows it to* NICK.) Now, what does that say there, second line there?

NICK (*reading from the booklet*). "Frown bit; eighty-five percent of audience; outright prolonged laughter on frown bit."

LEO. That's the analysis report the agency did for me on Monday's preview audience. The routine I just did for you, got outright prolonged laughter; eighty-five percent.

MURRAY. You could try him on sad parts, Leo; he's very good on sad parts.

LEO (*goes to* MURRAY *at the window seat, shows him another page in the booklet*). Matter fact, there's this poignant-type bit I did at the Preview Theatre: "Sixty percent of audience; noticeably moved."

MURRAY. They left the theatre?

LEO (*tensely, angrily*). There he is; there's the old joker; Murray the joker, right?

NICK. I do some routines. I can imitate the voice of Alexander Hamilton.

LEO. That's lovely, but I . . .

NICK. I do Alexander Hamilton and Murray does this terrific Thomas Jefferson; we got the voices just right.

MURRAY (*in a dignified voice; to* NICK). Hello there, Alex, how are you?

NICK (*in a dignified voice; to* MURRAY). Hello there, Tom; say, you should have been in Congress this morning. My goodness, there was quite a discussion on . . .

LEO. Now, that's *ridiculous.* You . . . you can't *do* an imitation of Alexander Hamilton; nobody knows what he *sounds* like . . .

NICK (*pointing triumphantly at* LEO). *That's* the *funny* part.

MURRAY (*shaking his head regretfully*). You missed the funny part, Leo.

LEO (*walking away from them*). I'm getting a terrible rash on my neck. (*Turns to them, growing louder and more tense with each word.*) The routine I did for him was *funny.* I was workin' good in front of the kid, I know how to use my God-damn *warmth,* I don't go over with these odd kids; I mean, here I am right in *front* of him, in *person* for God's sake, and he's *staring* at me . . . (*Moves toward them, on the attack.*) It's oddness here, Murray, *oddness.* Alexander *Hamil*ton imitations! Jaded jokes for old men.

Murray, what you've done to this kid. It's a damn shame, a child can't enjoy little animals, a damn shame . . . (*Really on the attack now; waving at the apartment, shouting*) The way you brought this kid up, Murray, grotesque atmosphere, *unhealthy,* and you're not even guilty about it, women in and out, *decorators;* had he been brought up by a *normal* person and not in this *mad*house . . .

NICK (*quietly, going toward* LEO). Hey, don't say that . . .

LEO. A certain kind of freakish way of growing up . . .

NICK (*quietly*). Hey, are you calling me a freak? You called me a freak. Take back what you said.

LEO (*walks away from them, mumbling to himself*). On June third I will be forty-two years old and I'm standing here arguing with a twelve-year-old kid . . . (LEO *quiets down, turns, comes toward* NICK, *sits on bed,* NICK *standing next to him; speaks calmly to* NICK.) See, Nicky, humor is a cloudy, wonderland thing, but simple and clear like the blue, blue sky. All I want is your simple, honest, child's opinion of my routine; for children are too honest to be wise . . .

NICK (*looking directly at* LEO, *calmly, quietly, slowly*). My simple, child's reaction to what you did is that you are not funny. Funnier than you is even Stuart Slossman my friend who is eleven and puts walnuts in his mouth and makes noises. What is not funny is to call us names and what is mostly not funny is how sad you are that I would feel sorry for you if it wasn't for how dull you are and those are the worst-tasting potato chips I ever tasted. And that is my opinion from the blue, blue sky.

(NICK *and* LEO *stay in their positions, looking at each other. A moment; then* MURRAY *throws his head back and laughs uproariously.* LEO *stands; the bowl of potato chips tips over in his hand, the chips spilling onto the floor.*)

LEO (*seeing* MURRAY's *laughter, goes to him at the Morris chair; angrily*). Murray the joker, right? You didn't want to come back to work for me, you just got me up here to step on my face again! (NICK, *unnoticed by* LEO, *has gone quickly into his alcove and comes out now with his ukulele, playing and singing "Yes,*

Sir, That's My Baby" with great spirit. LEO, *hearing this, turns to look at* NICK.) It's the *song.* It's the good-*bye* song. (LEO *grabs his hat and coat quickly, as* NICK *goes on playing, starts for front door, shouting.*) Getting *out,* bunch of *nuts* here, *crazy* people . . .

MURRAY. Leo, wait . . . (*Goes to the door to stop* LEO.) Leo, wait . . . I'm sorry . . . wait . . . (LEO *stops at the door;* MURRAY *goes down toward* NICK, *who is near the alcove, still playing the song.*) Nick, you better stop now . . .

NICK. Come on, Murray, get your uke, we'll sing to him and he'll go away . . .

MURRAY (*quietly*). Nick, we can't . . . (*Gently taking the uke from* NICK, *puts it on the window seat.*) Just put this down, huh?

NICK (*confused by this; urgently*). Come on, Murray, let him go away, he called us names, we gotta get rid of him . . .

MURRAY. Quiet now, Nick . . . just be quiet for a minute . . . (*Starts to go back toward* LEO.)

NICK (*shouting*). Murray, please let him go away . . . (NICK, *seeing the Chuckles statue next to him against the wall, grabs it angrily, throws it down on the floor.*) It's a crummy statue . . . that crummy statue . . . (*Begins to kick the statue fiercely, jumping up and down on it, shouting.*) It's a terrible statue, rotten cardboard . . .

(MURRAY *comes quickly back to* NICK, *holds both of his arms, trying to control him.*)

MURRAY. Aw, Nick, please, no more now, stop it . . .

(*There is a great struggle between them;* NICK *is fighting wildly to free himself from* MURRAY's *arms.*)

NICK (*near tears, shouting*). We don't want jerks like that around here, Murray, let him go away, we gotta get rid of him, Murray, we gotta get rid of him . . .

MURRAY (*lifts the struggling* NICK *up into his arms, hugging him to stop him.*) No, Nick . . . I'm sorry, Nick . . . we can't . . . (NICK *gives up, hangs limply in* MURRAY's *arms.* MURRAY *speaks quietly, with love.*) I'm sorry . . . I'm sorry, kid . . . I'm sorry . . . (*He puts* NICK *down, still holding him.*)

NICK (*after a pause; quietly, in disbe-*

lief). Murray . . .

MURRAY. You better go to your room.

NICK. This is a one-room apartment.

MURRAY. Oh. Then go to your alcove. (NICK *waits a moment, then turns, betrayed, walks over to his alcove, lies down on the bed.* MURRAY *looks over at* LEO, *who is standing at the front door. He walks slowly over to* LEO, *looking down at the floor; humbly*) Leo . . . hope you didn't misunderstand . . . we were just kidding you . . . we . . .

LEO (*coming toward* MURRAY, *apologetically*). I, myself, I got carried away there myself.

MURRAY. We all got a little excited, I guess. (*Reaches out to shake* LEO's *hand.*) So, I'll see you at work in the morning, Leo.

LEO (*smiling, shaking* MURRAY's *hand*). Great to have you back, fellah. (*Pause*) You both hate me.

MURRAY. Nobody hates you, Leo.

LEO. I hollered at the kid, I'm sorry. I didn't mean to cause any upset. I don't get along too good with kids . . .

MURRAY. Don't worry about it.

LEO. Wanna come have a drink with me, Murray? We could . . .

MURRAY. No thanks; maybe another night, Leo.

LEO. Look, after I leave, you horse around a little with the kid, he'll feel better.

MURRAY. Right, Leo.

LEO (*pauses; then comes closer to* MURRAY). Murray . . . that bit I did was funny, wasn't it?

MURRAY (*after a moment*). Yeah, Leo . . . I guess it was just a bad day for you.

LEO (*pointing at the Chuckles statue on the floor; quietly, but giving a command*). You don't want to leave that statue lying around like that, huh, Murray?

MURRAY. Oh, no. (*Goes to statue obediently, lifts it up off the floor, leans it upright against the wall.*) There.

LEO. Fine.

MURRAY. See you tomorrow, Leo.

LEO (*smiles*). Yeah, see ya tomorrow at the studio . . . (*Ruffles up* MURRAY's *hair.*) You old monkey. (*Goes to the door.*) Hey, you're an old monkey, aren't you?

(LEO *exits.* MURRAY *stays at the door for a moment.* NICK *is sitting on the alcove step, his back to* MURRAY.)

MURRAY (*walking over to* NICK, *trying to make peace with him*). Say, I could use a roast-turkey sandwich right now, couldn't you, Nick? On rye, with cole slaw and Russian dressing. . . .

(NICK *does not reply.* MURRAY *sits down next to him on the alcove step.* NICK *refuses to look at* MURRAY. *They are both silent for a moment.*)

NICK. Guy calls us names. Guy talks to us like that. Shoulda got rid of that moron. Coulda fooled the Welfare people or something . . . (SANDRA *enters through the partly open door, unnoticed by them; she stays up in the doorway, watching them.*) We coulda gone to Mexico or New Jersey or someplace.

MURRAY. I hear the delicatessen in Mexico is terrible.

NICK (*after a moment*). I'm gonna call myself *Theodore*.

MURRAY. As long as you don't call yourself Beatrice.

NICK. O.K., fool around. Wait'll you see a Theodore running around here. (*Silent for a moment, his back still to* MURRAY; *then, quietly*) Another coupla seconds he woulda been out the door . . . (*Turns to look at* MURRAY.) Why'd you go chicken on me, Murray? What'd you stop me for?

MURRAY. Because your routines give me outright prolonged laughter, Theodore.

SANDRA (*after a pause*). Four ninety-five for this tablecloth and you leave it around like this . . . (*Picks up the discarded tablecloth from the chair.*) A perfectly new tablecloth and already there are stains on it . . . (*Sits on the Morris chair, starts to dab at the tablecloth with her handkerchief.*) You know, it's very interesting that I left my files here. That I forgot them. I mean, psychologically, if you want to analyze that. Of course, last month I left my handbag in the Automat, and I have no idea what that means at all. (MURRAY *leaves alcove, starts toward her.*) I think that the pattern of our relationship, if we examine it, is very intricate, the different areas of it, especially the whole "good-bye" area of it, and also the "hello" and "how-are-you" area . . . of it.

MURRAY (*standing next to her chair now, smiles warmly*). Hello, Sandy, and how are you?

SANDRA (*looks up at him, smiles po-*

litely). Hello, Murray. (*Goes right back to her work, rubbing the tablecloth with her handkerchief.*) You're standing in my light.

MURRAY. Oh. (*He retreats a step.*)

NICK (*walking over to her*). Hello, lady.

SANDRA. Hello, Nick.

NICK (*indicating her work on the tablecloth*). Lady, can I help you with any of that?

SANDRA. Matter of fact, Nick . . . (*She stands; her arm around* NICK, *she goes to center with him.*) Nick, I don't think the effect, I mean, the overall design of this room, is really helped by all these . . . (*Gesturing to* MURRAY's *stuff around the bed*) these knickknacks.

NICK. You mean the junk?

SANDRA. Yes.

NICK. Yeah, not too good for the overall design.

SANDRA. If you'd just put them away in that carton there. (*She indicates a carton near the bed.*)

NICK. Sure, lady . . .

(NICK *goes quickly to the carton, begins to put* MURRAY's *junk into it—some radios, a megaphone, some clocks.* SANDRA *starts putting the tablecloth on the table.*)

MURRAY (*realizes that they are taking over, moves forward, trying to halt the proceedings*). Hey, Sandy, now wait a minute . . . (*She goes on with her work, putting a piece of material over the Morris chair. He turns at the sound of one of his radio cabinets being dropped into the carton by* NICK.) Listen, Nick, I didn't tell you to . . . Nick . . .

NICK (*looking up from his work*). Wilbur . . . (*Drops a clock into the carton.*) Wilbur Malcolm Burns.

(SANDRA *is putting the flowers back around the room, picking up the magazines.*)

MURRAY (*protesting*). Hey, now, both of you, will ya wait a minute here, will ya just wait . . . (*They ignore him, going on with their work. He shrugs, defeated; gives up, goes over to the windows, away from them, sits down sadly in the window seat.*) Wonder what kind of weather we got out there tonight. (*Looks out of window; as usual, he can see nothing but the gray, blank wall of the building a few feet opposite; sadly, to himself*) Never can see the God-damned weather. We got a permanent fixture out there: twilight in February. Some day that damn building'll fall down into Seventh Avenue so I can see the weather. (*Leans over, begins to talk out of the window.*) Everybody onstage for the Hawaiian number, please . . . (SANDRA, *during these last few lines, has gone to the phone, dialed, listened a few moments and hung up.* MURRAY *hears her hang up, turns to her.*) What're you doing?

SANDRA. I just spoke to the Weather Lady. She says it's a beautiful day. (*She goes back to her work on the apartment.*)

MURRAY (*he continues to talk out the window, softly at first*). Well, then, if you're not ready, we better work on the Military March number. Now the last time we ran this, let's admit it was pretty ragged. I mean, the whole "Spirit of '76" float was in dis*grace*ful shape yesterday . . . O.K. now, let's go, everybody ready . . . (*As* MURRAY *continues to talk out the window,* NICK *looks up from his work, smiles, picks up a record from the bed, puts it on the record player, turns it on.*) Grenadiers ready, Cavalry ready, Cossacks ready, Rough Riders ready, Minute Men ready . . . (*The record player has warmed up now and we hear "Stars and Stripes Forever."* MURRAY *hears the music, turns from the window, smiling, acknowledges* NICK's *assistance; turns to the window again, his voice gradually growing in volume.*) O.K. now, let's go . . . ready on the cannons, ready on the floats, ready on the banners, ready on the flags . . . (*The music builds up with* MURRAY's *voice,* NICK *humming along with the band and* SANDRA *laughing as* MURRAY *shouts.*) Let's go . . . let's go . . . let's go . . . (*His arms are outstretched.*)

CURTAIN

THE CAVE DWELLERS

William Saroyan

Presented by Carmen Capalbo and Stanley Chase
at the Bijou Theater in New York, on October 19, 1957,
with the following cast:

THE DUKE	Wayne Morris	THE YOUNG QUEEN	Francine Admur
THE GIRL	Susan Harrison	THE FATHER	Gerald Hiken
THE QUEEN	Eugenie Leontovich	GORKY	Ronald Weyand
THE KING	Barry Jones	THE MOTHER	Vergel Cook
THE YOUNG OPPONENT	Ivan Dixon	THE SILENT BOY	John Alderman
A WOMAN WITH A DOG	Vergel Cook	THE WRECKING CREW BOSS	Clifton James
A YOUNG MAN	John Alderman	JAMIE	Ivan Dixon

Directed by Carmen Capalbo
Settings by William Pitkin
Costumes by Ruth Morley
Lighting by Lee Watson

THE return of William Saroyan to Broadway was a startling piece of news, and also a welcome one for those who had been refreshed after the usual amount of routine playgoing toward the end of the nineteen-thirties (1939-1940) by his first two plays, *My Heart's in the Highlands* and *The Time of Your Life*, the first beautifully staged by the imaginative actor-director Robert Lewis for the Group Theatre and the second produced by the Theatre Guild in association with Eddie Dowling. His star, which had risen considerably earlier in the sparse medium of the short story with *The Young Man on a Flying Trapeze* and other pieces, began to twinkle out after *The Time of Your Life* won both the New York Drama Circle Award and the Pulitzer Prize in 1940, although there were gratifications enough in several plays (*Love's Old Sweet Song, The Beautiful People,* and *Get Away, Old Man* in 1943) for his partisans, led by George Jean Nathan and John Mason Brown.

Jim Dandy, a surrealistic play, toured widely under academic auspices. In 1942 favorable responses mixed with unfavorable ones also greeted the twin bill of *Talking to You* and *Across the Board on Tomorrow Morning,* revived in October, 1961, with some updating of topical details. It was still possible for a critic, Ted Krause of *Critical Digest,* to write warmly that "The author's positive point of view, his sure ear, and his continuing faith in his 'beautiful people' add up to a charming, meaningful off-Broadway evening." And there was one brief sparkle that even his detractors could not miss without deliberately blinking, the one-act realistic masterpiece about a frame-up and lynching in a small town, *Hello, Out There.*

Resistance to the author's raffish charm mounted and his critics took an increasingly dim view of his optimism in a time of troubles as World War II spread and Nazi barbarities and triumphs multiplied. His friends then and later on, probably to the present day, found it difficult to refute the opposition or to define the nature of their own attraction without resorting to cliché. A Glasgow *Herald* reviewer came about as close as possible to describing a favorable impression when he wrote that Saroyan's plays "give impressionistic pictures of people and their thoughts, and move on a dialogue as crisp and colourful as that of the author's short stories."

William Saroyan was never a man to be daunted by adverse criticism or particularly concerned with defining his objectives to the satisfaction of a "new critic" or, for that matter, an "old" one. He continued to write fiction (and, after 1947, plays as well) spontaneously, if not in fact with recklessness, and with little heed for what is pedantically known as "dramatic structure." In the plays he turned out (and the present editor often found loveliness even in the most inchoate of those he read), Saroyan continued to operate by impulse, by emotional pressure, and perhaps chiefly by trial and error. That is how he happened to write himself back with seeming effortlessness, after more than a decade's absence, into the theatre of his early triumphs, and that is how the New York production of *The Cave Dwellers* by the venturesome firm of Carmen Capalbo and Stanley Chase impressed the correspondent for the London *Times,* who wrote that the play at its best became "luminously moving, gentle, touching, poignant, and sometimes altogether hilarious." Saroyan, who could not be counted upon to "point a moral" but could always "adorn a tale," whatever his own intentions or his critics' desires, returned to Broadway unchanged and "unimproved," but theatrically still more alive than most well-regulated playwrights. His old supporters took heart from this return. And the new generation of playwrights and critics with "Absurdist" tendencies could also have received him as a distant relative to whom kindness should be shown, if they had not been annoyed by the expansiveness of his feelings and his conspicuously sanguine temperament.*

In 1960 Saroyan presented a later play, *Sam the Highest Jumper of Them All,* which he also staged himself at the Theatre Royal (Stratford, London) for a short run; and, according to report, Mr. Saroyan also won the favor of the Vienna public with a new play, *Lily Dafon, or a Paris Comedy,* also slated for staging in West Germany but at this writing unproduced in the American theatre. He remained prolific and he remained undisillusioned.

* A critical treatment of *The Cave Dwellers* by the present editor appears on pages 151-153 in John Gassner's *Theatre at the Crossroads* (Holt, Rinehart and Winston, 1960).

Perhaps the best vindication of himself Saroyan has ever written (and he has not usually written a convincing apologia in prefacing his plays) appears on a Penn State Plays program for a production of *The Cave Dwellers* by Mr. Kelly Yeaton: "Every playwright," Saroyan wrote, "creates a human race. If he writes about mice, machines, angels, monsters, or men and women, they can only be in his own image. . . . Thus I cannot mind that I am accused of not hating the human race. As long as I am willing to go on being a member of that race, it goes against both nature and truth for me to hate it."

ACT ONE

SCENE ONE

The play happens on the stage of an abandoned theatre on the lower East Side of New York, in the midst of a slum-clearing project.

There are three makeshift bunks on the stage. On one of them lies a woman called the QUEEN, *who coughs now and then in her sleep.*

A man called the DUKE *comes in quietly, studies the face of the* QUEEN, *picks up a pile of manuscripts of old plays, dumps them in a corner, opens the top one and stands, looking at it.*

A series of explosions begin, one after another, to which he half-listens.

A GIRL *comes running down the stage alley to the stage door. She makes several unsuccessful attempts to open it, finally pushes it open, comes in, and runs to the farthest bunk, gets in, and pulls the covers over her head.*

The DUKE *goes to the bunk in which the* GIRL *is hiding. After a moment, she puts her head out, looks around, notices the* DUKE, *looks at him out of terror-stricken eyes.*

———

GIRL. For the love of God, what *was* that?

DUKE. All right, now. It's only the wreckers. They're knocking down the rotten old buildings around here.

GIRL (*gets on her feet*). Oh. I didn't know where to run. (*Looks around.*) Where am I?

DUKE. This is an old theatre. Here, I'll show you. This is the stage. There's the orchestra pit, out there's the auditorium, up there's the balcony. Can you see?

GIRL. Yes, now I can see all right. I've never seen a theatre from the *stage* before. It makes me feel—well, kind of proud, I guess. I don't know *why,* but it does. (*She stops suddenly and then speaks softly.*) Well, I guess I'd better go now. Thanks very much.

DUKE. That's all right.

GIRL (*begins to go, stops, turns*). Of course, I'd much rather stay. Can I?

DUKE. *Here?* No, this place is for us. The Queen over there, sick. The King. He'll be back pretty soon. And me. I'm

the Duke. Just names, of course. The Queen used to be on the stage. The King used to be a clown—he was in vaudeville and he did Shakespeare, too—and I used to be in the ring. We've been like a family almost a month now, and this is our home.

GIRL. Could it be my home, too?

DUKE. No, no, we've got rules and regulations. There are other places for other people.

GIRL. Where are the other places?

DUKE. All over. This is *our* place. We found it, and it's a theatre. They're going to knock it down pretty soon, but until they do we've got our— (*Softly*) rules and regulations.

GIRL. What *are* the rules and regulations?

DUKE. *People of the theatre only.* Being in the ring is being in the theatre, too, because—well, the King says so. Besides, after I lost my title, I went on tour. This isn't the first time I've been on the stage. It's just the first time that I've *lived* on one.

GIRL. Couldn't I, too?

DUKE. Are you an actress?

GIRL. Oh, no. But I *am* tired and I've got to find *some* place to stay.

DUKE (*looks over at the* QUEEN, *speaks softer*). Well, what *have* you done?

GIRL. Well, I was at a place where they put guns together.

DUKE. What did you do there?

GIRL. I was on hammers. I never saw the *whole* gun.

DUKE. Real guns?

GIRL. I don't think so. The name of the place was U. S. Toy.

DUKE. Did the company ever put on *entertainments?*

GIRL. Not while I was there.

DUKE. At *school* did you do anything?

GIRL (*shakes head*). Oh, no, I was too shy. Too shy at U. S. Toy, too.

DUKE. *Why?*

GIRL. I've *always* been shy. And afraid, too.

DUKE. Afraid of *what?*

GIRL. I don't know. Everything, I guess, and—every*body.*

DUKE. Are you afraid of *me?*

GIRL. Well, no, but I *am* afraid I won't find a place to stay.

DUKE. Why don't you go home?

GIRL. I haven't *got* a home. (*Pause*)

Can I? Stay?

DUKE. You're young. This is no place for you.

GIRL. Please don't make me go away. I don't know why, but I don't feel so scared here. I kind of feel at home here.

DUKE. You've got to be in the theatre. The King says so, and we all agreed. He believes in the theatre. It's like a religion with him. So what am I going to tell him? Here's a scared girl? No place to go?

GIRL. Could you *teach* me to be in the theatre, maybe?

DUKE. No, that's not the same thing at all. But haven't you *ever* done anything in front of people to make them feel happy, or sad, or proud of themselves?

GIRL. I remember a sidewalk *game* that used to make *me* happy. (*Pause.*)
One potato, two potato, three potato, four!
Five potato, six potato, seven potato more!

DUKE. Anything else?

GIRL (*stands stiffly, salutes*). I pledge allegiance to the Flag, and to the Republic for which it stands. One nation, indivisible, with liberty and justice for all.

DUKE (*considers what he has heard*). Well, you've *been* to the theatre. You've *seen* what they do. Can you do anything like *that*?

GIRL. I never went to the theatre very much—too expensive. At U. S. Toy, though, I used to *dream* a lot, and it was kind of like stuff I'd *seen* in the movies. One whole afternoon I put the hammers in upside down. Well, of course, they fired me. They almost fired another girl first, but it wasn't her. It was me.

DUKE. What were you dreaming *about*?

GIRL. Oh. (*Pause, shyly*) I don't know.

DUKE. Was it like a show on a stage?

GIRL. I don't think so, because it was only me. But I was different. I was beautiful.

DUKE (*after thinking*). Well, I'll *tell* the King you're in the theatre. No harm in telling him, I guess.

GIRL. Will you?

DUKE. Yes. In a way you *are*. At any rate, you're *here*. And who knows? Maybe he'll believe us.

GIRL. Thank you. (*She seems anxious and afraid, as well as relieved.*)

DUKE. When I was afraid just before a fight I used to jump up and down, like this. (*He demonstrates.*) I always *wanted* to holler, too, but of course I couldn't. They'd think I was crazy. A fighter's got to be sure they don't think he's crazy. But if I'd been able to holler just before my big fight, I'd never have lost the crown. (*He looks up, whispers.*) Help me. (*He shouts.*) Help me? (*The* QUEEN *sits up, shakes her head as if to see more clearly, watches.*) It's what I *wanted* to do. It's what I *should* have done. It's what I *never* did. What a fool I was. (*He sits down. The* GIRL *goes to him, reaches a hand out timidly, places it on his head, as a small hand on the head of a big sad dog. After a moment he looks up at her, stands.*) About being in the theatre. Can you *sing*, for instance?

GIRL (*half sings*). How do you do, my partner. How do you do today?

DUKE. Not bad.

GIRL. Will you dance in a circle, if I show you the way?

QUEEN. Welcome to the theatre, Girl, whoever you are!

SCENE TWO

A little later. The GIRL *has tidied up the place. Both unoccupied bunks are made, the tatters and rags straightened and folded neatly. She is now sweeping the floor. The* QUEEN *watches, sits up, rests her head on her elbow.*

QUEEN. Well, now, where *is* the King?

DUKE. He'll be here pretty soon. Just rest now, Queen. Sleep.

QUEEN. *More* sleep? Sleep and sleep? (*Shakes her head.*) Remember this, Duke. And you, Girl. If I sleep and it's time to *eat*, wake me. However deep my sleep may be. *Lift* me *up* out of my bed if need be. Stand beside me, one to the right and one to the left, and if I *still* sleep, walk with me, until I am awake again. Understand?

DUKE. All right, now, don't worry. We'll wake you up.

QUEEN. You, Girl, if I sleep when it's time, you'll get me up?

GIRL. Yes, Queen.

QUEEN. A moment ago I spoke of something. What was it I spoke of a moment ago?

DUKE. No need to remember what you

spoke of.

QUEEN. I said something. What did I say? I remembered something and then I said something. (*Sleepily*) But now I can't remember any more. (*She falls back. The* DUKE *stands over her. Turns away, to the* GIRL.)

DUKE. She's asleep again.

GIRL. Shouldn't she have a doctor?

DUKE. She's old, that's all. She's been this way the whole month I've been here. And then all of a sudden she's up, and alive, and young and *beautiful,* too. There just isn't enough food that's all. She ought to have more food. *Better* food.

GIRL. I won't eat.

DUKE. You've *got* to eat.

GIRL. I'll go away, if you want me to.

DUKE. That's up to the King, now. (*The* DUKE *brings the manuscript out of his back pocket, begins to read it again. The* GIRL *continues to sweep.*)

(*The* KING *comes in, an old, hard, lean man with a long lined face. He is in rags, and yet he moves in a kind of human grandeur. He carries a paper sack with a round loaf of bread in it. As he moves he seems to be deep in thought. The* DUKE *and the* GIRL *wait for him to notice them, but he isn't looking.*)

KING. Enough of violence. Enough, I say. Be done with it. Have done with it.

DUKE (*clears his throat to attract his attention*). King?

KING (*turns, almost unseeing*). Yes? What is it?

DUKE. I looked for work all day. *Any kind.* They seem to be afraid of me, or something, that's all. I looked for money in the streets, too. I got home a little while ago to find the Queen delirious again.

KING. Enough of violence.

DUKE. What violence? Where?

KING. *In*—in—in each of us—crouched, waiting. In everything we do—and *think,* even. Enough of it. (*Softly*) Christ, how the people hate one another to pass the beggar as if he weren't there. To be deaf to his shameful words. A small coin for a great need. (*Soberly*) I've begged all day, begged of my inferiors.

DUKE. I hope *you've* had a little luck.

KING. This loaf of bread, old and hard, but *bread,* at any rate. (*Fishes into his pocket, comes up with a few coins, jingles them, opens his fist, looks at them.*)

These few sad coins. I've begged before. Bad luck in the coins, but worse in the violence—theirs and my own. I've already called them my inferiors. Perhaps they aren't. But if they are, there's no need for *me* to say so. Enough, I'm sick of it. (*Notices the* GIRL.) Who's that standing there?

DUKE. She's in the theatre, too, like ourselves. She speaks well, and has a pleasant singing voice. (*Gestures at the beds.*) She's a helpful girl. But she's ready to go, if we don't want her.

KING. Why should the girl go? There's a whole loaf of bread. (*Goes to the* GIRL.) Welcome, Girl. And don't be afraid of me. I saw no eyes all day that were *not* afraid, and the violence of it has hurt me again, deeper than ever. In the days gone I covered this face with white grease, and red—the clown's mask. But *this* face is the mask, and the other is my true face. Welcome, and do not be afraid. (*The* GIRL *nods. He places the coins in her hand.*) Here is the whole day's gain. Buy something for the Queen. Milk, or medicine, or whatever.

GIRL. Yes, sir.

KING (*to the* DUKE). There were other gains. I saw a dog on a leash, held by a woman in furs. I swear that dog spoke to me with its eyes as clearly as if it had spoken with its breath and tongue and teeth and palate. *Hey, beggar! I'd give my soul to change places with you for only one turn of the world!* The woman in furs gave me nothing, not even the dirty look I've come to count on, and even to cherish a little, since I am of the theatre, and live on being seen, even if hatefully. Any kind of a look is better than none at all. The words of the eyes of the small dog were a great gain, and another was a thought that came to me soon afterwards. A bitter thought, but a true one, and so I must pass it along. When I was rich— Girl, I *have* been rich —when I was abroad in the world, away from the stage, and came upon a beggar —old, twisted, deformed, ugly, dirty, better than half dead—(*Stretches out his arms slowly*)—while I was a wit in the world, a maker of wild laughter and joyous sorrow among the multitudes, did I notice the beggar? Did I *see* him, truly? Did I understand him? Did I love him? Did I give him money? (*Softly*) No, I did not. In my soul I said, *Let him be dead and out of my way. That* was a gain. *Bitter,* but a gain. Violence! My own violence, come home!

QUEEN. Oh, stop your shouting. (*She sits on the bunk, as the* GIRL *watches.*)

KING. Oh, you *are* awake, then?

QUEEN. Wide awake.

KING. And there's *my* bed. That makes a day. Up in the morning. Out to beg. Back in the evening. The table. The food. The company. The talk. And then to bed. (*Softly*) I love it too much.

QUEEN. Well, you're home again, at any rate, and as you see, I'm *up* again. There's one good hour in every day, still. One good *queenly* hour. (*To the* GIRL) I did them all, you know—Catharine, Mary, Ann, Bess, and all the others. A young girl from the most common of families, if in fact you could call it a family at all. A poor weary mother, a poor drunken father, a dirty houseful of dirty brothers and sisters. I sometimes marvel at the way I turned out.

KING. Turned out or turned in, the table's ready, if you are.

QUEEN. I have never been readier, sir.

KING. Your arm then, Woman. (*He takes her by the arm, the* DUKE *and the* GIRL *watch, and then do the same.*)

SCENE THREE

After supper, they are all at the table. The KING *and the* QUEEN *are chewing the last of the bread.*

KING. Well, that's the end of the bread.

QUEEN (*brightly, almost gaily*). Yes, we've eaten it all.

KING. Uptown the lights are on. The theatres are ready. The tickets are sold. The players are putting on their make-up and getting into their costumes. In a moment the curtains will go up, and one by one the plays will begin and The Great Good Friend out there—(*He gestures toward the auditorium.*)—will look and listen. And little by little something will stir in his soul and come to life—a smile, a memory, a reminder of an old forgotten truth, tender regret, kindness. In short, the secret of the theatre.

GIRL (*childlike*). What *is* the secret of the theatre?

QUEEN. Love, of course. Without love,

pain and failure are pain and failure, nothing else. But *with* love they are beauty and meaning themselves.

GIRL. Oh.

QUEEN (*acts*). Entreat me not to leave thee: for whither thou goest, I will go; and where thou lodgest, I will lodge: thy people shall be my people, and where thou diest, will I die.

KING. Bravo, you did that very well.

QUEEN. Oh, King, do a clown's bit. A *kingly* clown's bit.

KING. I belong uptown. I *still* do. I was born there, and then I was put out.

QUEEN. Are you an actor, or a sad old man like all the other sad old men? I thought it was agreed. We are of the theatre. You are to perform, not to be performed *upon.*

KING (*puts a crumb in his mouth*). I'm still eating. Would you have eating a performance, too?

QUEEN. Would you have it something else? Could it possibly *be* something else? Do a bit about *eating!*

KING. We just did that bit, didn't we? (*He puts a crumb between his upper and lower teeth and crushes it with one deliberately large chomp.*)

QUEEN. This time *without* bread. For its own dear sake.

KING. I *am* challenged, Woman. You know I would kill myself for art.

QUEEN. Or *us*—from the wonder of it.

KING (*he gets up quickly*). The great man comes to the famous restaurant, hungry and hushed, and thoughtful, because he remembers when he was nobody and the world was still far away. Now, he wears the unmistakable *scowl* of superiority, and so the *arrogant* headwaiter bows humbly, and conducts him quickly and silently to the best table in the place. However, before accepting the headwaiter's offer to sit—(*He indicates the drawing-out of a chair.*)—he stands a moment to notice who else has come to the holy joint, and to *be* noticed by them. (*The* QUEEN *leans forward, delighted both with his work and her success in having provoked him into it.*) But who is he? (*Pause, extra clearly, now loud, now soft, inventing wildly*) Is he perhaps the new Secretary of State, before his first flight to—— (*Searches for an inept destination.*) Dubrovnik? The Spanish pianist from Palma of the Canary Islands? The man who discovered the *flaw* in the theory of cycles? He who invented the law of loss, or was it only the lollipop? Or is he perhaps the man who learned the language of the Arab tribes, brought the warring chiefs together, engineered the business of the oil? (*Slight pause*) Let them try to guess, it's good for them. In any case, it's time to sit and eat. He eats, and eats, one rare dish after another. (*Comically astonished*) But what's this with the crepe suzettes? A *fly,* isn't it? A *common* fly? (*He stops. The* QUEEN *waits expectantly. He does not go on.*)

QUEEN (*softly*). Well, why do you stop?

KING (*earnestly*). It's part of the bit. A man stops, doesn't he? Suddenly? Unaccountably? He remembers, and he thinks, doesn't he? Is it worth it? All the *trying,* and all the eating? (*Slowly, very clearly*) Joe's dead. Mary's divorced. Johnny's boy is stealing automobiles. Pat's girl is breaking up the home of a dentist.

QUEEN. Bravo!

KING. Thank you for stopping me. I might have gone on forever, from loneliness and despair. (*Pause*) Girl, it's your turn. Do a bit, please.

GIRL. A bit?

DUKE (*whispering*). The Pledge!

GIRL (*salutes*). I pledge allegiance to the Flag, and to the Republic for which it stands. One nation, indivisible, with liberty and justice for all.

KING. What bit is *that?*

DUKE. The National Pledge, King!

KING. I *know* it's the National Pledge. But who the devil put it in a play?

DUKE. One of the new playwrights.

KING. Yes. They're doing that sort of thing these days, aren't they? (*Leaps to his feet, and speaks with a joyous lilt to his voice, almost singing.*) Ah, Lord, what a lark it is to live! Just to live—like a mouse, even. (*He does a light skipping step and breaks into song.*)

Jimmy Jellico, down the road,
Come out of your house and dance with Daisy.
Come out, my foolish, laughing, silly Jimmy.
Your Ma is mad, your Pa is crazy,
Come out, come out, and dance with Daisy.

DUKE. King, I didn't know you could sing, *too!*

KING (*softly*). Your ma is mad, your pa is crazy. (*Pause*) And over there's the bed. I sometimes think I'm dead and have just remembered. It's most strange. And then suddenly there I am—*not* dead. And that's more strange than the other. Your turn then, Duke. A scene from a play, please.

DUKE (*opens the manuscript*). The first act of a play about some people who have come to a little hotel on a side street in a great city.

KING. Yes, yes, in search of— What *are* they in search of, Girl?

DUKE (*whispers, as* GIRL *turns to him for help*). Now, just don't be *afraid,* that's all. *Tell* him.

GIRL. Well, one's looking for his father, another's looking for his mother. Another's looking for a home, another for a place to hide—

QUEEN. There *is* no hiding. None whatsoever. It can't be done.

KING. Ah, let her go on, will you? One seeks a home, another a hiding place. Go on, Girl.

GIRL. One's looking for a husband, another for a wife.

DUKE (*turning a page of the manuscript*). Ah, here we are. The lobby of the hotel. (*To the* GIRL) The moment I *saw* you I was sure I knew you.

GIRL. I was sure I knew *you,* too.

KING. Is that from the play?

DUKE. Yes, King. The moment I saw you I was sure I knew you.

GIRL. I was sure I knew you, too.

QUEEN. No, no, don't go back. *Never* go back.

DUKE. But the line's repeated, Queen.

QUEEN. Ah, well, then.

DUKE (*acts*). I said to myself, I know her. I've seen her before.

GIRL. I said to myself, I know him. I've seen him before.

KING (*after a pause*). Go on, please.

DUKE (*swiftly*). That's all there is. He tries to smile and be polite, and so does she, but it doesn't help, so she goes up to her room, and he goes out into the street.

KING. Another new playwright, I presume.

DUKE. Yes, sir.

KING. Very strange, I must say.

QUEEN. It's not strange at all.

KING. Nothing *happens.*

QUEEN. Nothing happens! It's the story of our lives.

KING. Yes, it is actually, isn't it? (*Pause*) Girl?

GIRL. Yes, King.

KING. Stand before me, please.

GIRL (*stands there*). Yes, King.

KING. Do not be afraid. (*Pause*) You have a bed?

DUKE. I'd like her to have my bed.

QUEEN. *Your* bed? You'd be dead by morning without your bed.

DUKE. My clothes are warm.

QUEEN. You must be very strong and handsome inside to be able to love with so much *courtesy.*

DUKE. No, Queen. I am a slob, inside and out, and all because fifteen years ago in my last fight, I was afraid I might kill my opponent with one blow. And so, down *I* went, killed with one blow by my opponent. (*Pause*) Whether I'm dead or alive by morning, the Girl will be safe in my bed. Courtesy, or whatever you want to call it, Queen, is like training for a big fight, anyway, except that now I can look up and holler all I like.

KING. Holler *what?*

DUKE (*softly but clearly*). Help me to win without killing my opponent!

SCENE FOUR

Later. Storm. Wind. The sounds of human sleeping—breathing, murmuring, a hum.

———

The GIRL *is asleep in the* DUKE'S *bed. The* QUEEN *in her bed, and the* KING *in his.*

The DUKE *is walking up and down, to keep warm. Every now and then he shadow-boxes in silence. Stops, bundles himself in his rags, walks again. He is remembering his big fight. He walks the boundary of the fight ring, takes his corner, and waits, looking up now and then. The gong is heard, but differently—like a chime—almost an invitation to sleep. And out of nowhere comes the charging young* OPPONENT *in trunks and boxing gloves. The* DUKE *puts up his arms and works fearfully, trying to keep away, but suddenly the* OPPONENT *tags him. He wobbles, tries to clinch, but is caught again, and his knees buckle. The* OPPO-*NENT tags him quickly, and steps back to watch the* DUKE *collapse. A voice is heard far away whispering one, two, three, four, five, six, seven, eight. . . . The* DUKE *gets to his feet, but the* OPPONENT *is on him again. He tries to clinch, but fails. Again the* OPPONENT *steps back to watch the* DUKE *collapse. The* DUKE *is counted out, as he gets to one knee. The* OPPONENT *helps him up, embraces him quickly, pats him on the back, and goes. The* DUKE *stands, dazed, unbelieving, and then sinks to one knee again.*

The GIRL *sits up suddenly, notices him. Gets out of the bunk, fully clothed. Goes to him, shyly.*

She takes him by the arm, as if from the ring of failure and disgrace of long ago, and helps him into the bunk.

The GIRL *listens to the* DUKE *as he breathes heavily and then slowly quiets down and falls asleep. She then wanders around in the dim light to see if there is anything she might do, but there isn't. She is cold, she shivers, her teeth chatter.*

She sits on a box and begins to work in the gun factory, doing the same thing over and over. A handsome YOUNG MAN *comes, dancing a tango, bows to her, they dance, and then the* YOUNG MAN *goes.*

The KING *sits up, notices the* GIRL, *gets off his bunk, and goes to her. Takes her by the arm to his bunk, and helps her to lie down. When she is asleep, the* KING *begins to walk around to keep warm, too. He then lies down and curls up like an animal, in the hope of finding warmth, but there is no warmth in him or in his rags or in curling up.*

A WOMAN *with a small dog on a leash appears. The* KING *gets up quickly, becomes abject, holds out his hat. The* WOMAN *stops, looks away. The dog looks up at the* KING. *The* KING'S *voice is heard whispering for the dog: Hey, beggar! beggar! I'd give my soul to change places with you for only one turn of the world. The* WOMAN *and the dog go.*

The QUEEN *sits up, goes to him, takes him to her bed, helps him to lie upon it, and waits until he has fallen asleep.*

The QUEEN *begins to cough, and then she sees herself as a beautiful young girl in rags, who comes and stares up at her a moment and then goes.*

The KING, *the* DUKE, *and the* GIRL *sit up at the same time, look at the* QUEEN, *and then at one another. They listen to the raging storm. The* GIRL *goes to the* QUEEN. *The* KING *goes to the Stage Door, bolts it, places his ear to the door, and listens. The* DUKE *stands beside him.*

DUKE. We all woke up at the same time, King.

KING. Yes, I know we did.

GIRL. I dreamed a dream of love—again.

QUEEN. And I a dream of life—my own, almost gone now, swift and silent, and speechless.

KING. I saw the little dog.

DUKE. And I lost the fight. King, what's going on?

KING. We've come to a time.

DUKE. What *kind* of a time?

KING. Cold. I'm cold. (*His very voice seems frozen. He puts an arm around the* QUEEN, *another around the* GIRL. *The* DUKE *does the same. They stamp their feet to keep warm, and move slowly in a small circle.*)

QUEEN. Why do you gather us into a circle?

KING. Because we can get a little warmth from one another in a circle, that's why.

QUEEN (*steps out of the circle, annoyed*). No, I refuse to join that church.

KING. It's no church. It's *us*—sleepless and cold.

QUEEN. No, I refuse.

KING. We're cold, Woman, in a cold night, in a cold building, in a cold city.

QUEEN. King, you're scared. Of dying, I suppose. But for God's sake, Man, please do not let a little cold and a little fear make a fool of you. I'm cold, too, and so is she, and so is he, and for all I know this is my last night, or yours, or theirs, or anybody's, but until my mind is gone entirely, I intend to stay alive as if this were the morning of the first day, and I, a young girl with the world to seek. (King, I say there is no death, even though I know I shall soon be no longer among the living.)

KING. What the devil are you talking about, Woman? Or have you gone mad?

GIRL. Is that from a play?

DUKE. Oh, no.

GIRL. Can I say something, then?

DUKE. Of course you can.

GIRL. Queen, it *was* warmer when you were in the circle.

QUEEN. We need a fire, then, not a philosophy. (*She coughs.*)

GIRL. You didn't cough while you were in the circle.

QUEEN. I don't want the circle to cure my cough. My cough is not an illness. It's a language I haven't learned to understand yet.

GIRL (*to the* DUKE). I said something. Now, you say something.

DUKE. O.K. (*To the* QUEEN) It is better to stand together than to stand alone.

QUEEN. Duke, believe me, were you one of my own three sons, I couldn't cherish you more, but I am afraid that what you have just said can do my pride as a mother very little good.

KING. Moses Himself almost said the same thing.

QUEEN. Go ahead, then. Hang together. Circle around like animals. Kneel and pray. Weep and moan. I'd rather freeze to death alone.

KING. Will there *never* be a woman a man can be *glad* he met?

GIRL (*to the* DUKE, *quickly*). I'm going to say something more. Oh, Queen, stay with us.

QUEEN. Listen, Girl. You and I invent no philosophies and no religions. We go along with the boys—until we get fed-up to here. (*She indicates her nose.*) And then we say, Boys, go on alone now, please. Kill yourselves in the name of God, or truth, or justice, or the moon, or water, or ice cream, or anything else you can think of. Kill yourselves, and then explain it to us. We'll be here waiting, and once again we'll listen to the pitiful and preposterous explanation—how you were wrong but right but wrong but right.

KING. I give up. If Christ Himself had had you around He would have sold oranges for a living.

QUEEN. I wish He *had*. Oranges are nice. I remember especially their lovely smell in the wintertime.

KING. All of the great thinkers and prophets would have forgotten their noble visions and pure dreams.

QUEEN. They *should* have. Their noble dreams and their pure visions didn't help—didn't help, Man. And *did* hinder.

KING. Hinder *what*?

QUEEN. The *real* challenge. The *only* challenge, as you know. The challenge that is in each of us. If we are nothing involved in nothing and wish to be something involved in something, let us discover how we may achieve this transformation without fear, without lies, without humiliation, without belittlement of ourselves and others, without violence. You came in from the streets not many hours ago and spoke against violence, didn't you?

KING. Oh, I am the villain of the world, and all because I am a man. Woman, I'm *cold*. I believed that with our arms about one another we might be a little warmer in our poor bodies. Now, (why do you make of this simple act a crime against reason and right,) thought and—theology, for instance?

GIRL. Are they acting?

DUKE. Oh, no, they're living.

QUEEN. That little circle is the mother —and the father—of violence.

KING. Gathering together is an act of love.

QUEEN. Not at all. It's an act of fear. Fear of others unknown to us. But who *are* they, excepting ourselves again? They aren't people from another planet. They haven't two heads to our one, four arms to our two, or another way to start and stop life. If you can't think, Man, at least try to remember. You're not cold, you're frightened. There is no danger, you're old.

KING. A whole month she lies on that bed hanging onto life by the barest thread, but tonight when I must protect my family, she becomes Joan of Arc herself, grown old.

QUEEN. Protect? There is no protection.

KING. No illness, no death, no danger, no defense, no protection. Girl, speak to your mother, please. Comfort her. She's mad, she speaks in tongues, nobody can follow her.

GIRL. It *is* cold.

QUEEN. We're agreed on that.

DUKE. We all woke up at the same time.

QUEEN. We're agreed on that, too.

GIRL. We all feel—*strange*. As if something were happening *everywhere,* not here alone.

QUEEN. The *weather* is happening everywhere.

DUKE. No, something else, Queen. I've dreamed of losing the fight before. I *lost* the fight. Why wouldn't I dream of losing it? So it can't be that. I've been in bad weather before, too, and not inside, either. Outside. So it can't be that, either. It's something else, and I'm scared to death.

GIRL. I'm not. Of anything.

DUKE. No? When you first came here you were afraid of everything, and now you say you're not afraid of anything. How did *that* happen?

GIRL (*earnestly, trying to guess*). I don't know. Nothing's changed, except that I *am* here. (*Softly*) And thankful to each of you. (*To the* QUEEN) It isn't that you're *like* my mother, as my poor mother never was, you *are* my mother. (*To the* KING) And you my father. (*To the* DUKE) And you—well, not my brother, and not my lover, or my husband, either, but something like *all* of them put together. (*To the* QUEEN) He's a man. A very *kind* man. And now that I know he's scared, I love him more than ever.

DUKE. You love me?

GIRL. Yes.

DUKE. Since when?

GIRL. Since the minute I saw you, when I came out of hiding, expecting to see a whole world in ruins, and life itself breathing its last breath, and saw you instead, on this stage. Since *then*. A hundred years ago.

DUKE (*to the* QUEEN). Don't tell *me* something isn't happening. When I was young and strong, I was not loved. Oh, there were many, one after another, but I wasn't *loved*. I knew it, and they knew it. It was a game, nothing more, and fun while it lasted. I was false, and they were false, and there was money to spend —and pride, and power, and arrogance, and youth, and laughter. And lies to use up. I didn't care. I wore the Crown, didn't I? I'd won the title, hadn't I? (*Almost amused but also amazed*) And then I lost the title, and they were all gone. And I was stupid. I'd *always* been stupid—just strong and swift and lucky. Don't love me, Girl. I'm used to it.

GIRL. I love you.

DUKE. Don't pity me, either. Pity hurts worse than hatred, worse than ridicule. I'm *not* kind. When I was young and *truly* myself, and there was one like you among the others, I never so much as *saw* her. There is no kindness in me.

GIRL (*to the* QUEEN). I love him. (*To the* KING) Why? Am I too good for him? Am I radiant suddenly in the middle of the night? I can't sleep. I can't rest. I can't forget. I'm cold and alone, and I don't *want* to be any more.

(*Sounds of slow footsteps, of shuffling, stumbling, and falling are heard in the alley. Everybody hears the sounds, but as the sounds are faint, they do not pay very much attention to them.*)

DUKE. Thank you for your love, Girl. Thank you very much, but in the morning— (*In the alley a* WOMAN's *moan is heard, long and drawn out.*) In the morning, Girl— (*A* MAN's *voice is heard mumbling:* "Soon, soon now, soon.")— when this strange night is over.

(*There is a slow rattling of the bolted door, and then three knocks, not very loud, and slowly. The* DUKE *whispers.*)

DUKE. King, there's somebody out there.

(*An animal moan is heard.*)

GIRL. Who is it?

QUEEN. Open the door, King. It's somebody in need of help.

DUKE. No, let me open it. I'm scared to death, but—well, I'm the strongest here. (*He moves, the* KING *stops him.*)

KING. How can *we* help? We have nothing here. Three beds for four people. Rags for clothes. No food. No fire. How can *we* help?

QUEEN. By not being afraid, of course.

KING. But I *am* afraid, and so are you. I don't know what's out there. I'm not even sure it's human. Sometimes it sounds human, sometimes it doesn't. But even if we weren't afraid, why should *we* open the door? There's a whole world out there, full of fortunate people in their own homes, not in a hulk of a haunted theatre. Let *them* help, whoever or whatever it is. (*He listens.*) Perhaps they've gone, in any case. (*A* WOMAN's *soft moan is heard again.*) Ah, I don't know what to make of it. Why should they come here? We're better than half-dead ourselves. How can we help? Help with *what*?

(*Sounds*)

QUEEN. You made a human circle a moment ago. Bring *them* into that circle, as an act of love.

(*Sounds*)

KING. I don't know who they are.

QUEEN. It doesn't matter who they are. They are in need. This is a theatre, Man, not a cave. We are people of the theatre, not animals.

(*Sounds*)

KING. I can't argue with a woman. Let's ask one another, then, if this is what we must do. Girl, shall we open the door?

(*Sounds*)

GIRL. Yes, King.

KING. That's *already* two against two. How about you, Duke?

DUKE. I don't know. I don't seem to be able to think any more, but if the girl *does* love me, as she says she does, and says open the door, what can I, twice her size, ten times her strength, say? I'll open the door, King.

(*Sounds*)

KING. Well, now, it's three to one, and the last is myself, six charlatans, and half a dozen lunatics. I'll open the door.

DUKE. No, let me, King.

KING. Stand together at the edge of the stage there. It's a large theatre, and there are other places in which to hide, if need be.

(*They stand together at the edge of the stage. The* KING *stands up straight, ready to go.*)

QUEEN. King?

KING. Yes, Woman?

QUEEN. I love you, sir.

KING. You talk too much. (*The* KING *walks swiftly to the door, opens it, and a* MAN *leaning upon it almost falls into his arms.*)

MAN (*whispers*). Thank you, thank you, thank you. (*The* KING *supports him, helps him in. A huge black* BEAR, *walking upright, follows the* MAN. *The* QUEEN, *the* GIRL, *and the* DUKE *gasp, the* KING *turns, sees the* BEAR, *tries to hide behind the* MAN.) Don't be afraid of him. But for God's sake, somebody please help my wife.

(*A* WOMAN's *long moan is heard, then a cry of a newborn baby. The* MAN *begins to walk toward the sound, falls upon the* BEAR, *who holds him up. The* GIRL *runs out, followed by the* QUEEN.)

ACT TWO

SCENE ONE

Several hours later.

The BEAR *stands to one side, chained to the floor. It still moans, but softer, and sways.*

On one cot lies the MAN *asleep.*

On another lies a WOMAN, *also asleep.*

The GIRL *and the* QUEEN *are busy around the third cot, on which an* INFANT *sleeps.*

The DUKE *is gone. The* KING *is at the open Stage Door, waiting apprehensively. The* QUEEN *looks over at him now and then. The* KING *turns from the door, goes to the* BEAR, *looks at it.*

———

KING (*almost to himself*). A moaning bear in the middle of the night? In New York City? How should I have known? Is a bear human? (*To the* BEAR) You scared me, sir. (*The* BEAR *replies with a soft moan.*) Yes, things are much improved now. (*To the* GIRL) And how is the child?

GIRL. Suppose we *hadn't* opened the door?

KING. God help me, I was against it. I'll never deny *that*. I thought it was—anything but a trained bear, and a human family. A trained bear has saved the life of a new man, his mother, and his father. (*The* BEAR *moans.*) You moan most fearfully, sir. (*The* BEAR *moans sweetly.*) It wasn't like that a little while ago, but then there was reason enough for it not to be.

QUEEN. You talk good sense to the bear, King. Better sense than to the rest of us.

KING. I've always loved them. I associate them with my father. You understand, Woman, I'm uneasy about how long the Duke's been gone. And I'm worried about the few coins he had with which to buy a little milk for the boy.

QUEEN. Was there enough?

KING. Enough perhaps for one bottle. A *small* bottle, most likely. I tell you, there's no money in begging any more. (*Suddenly*) What the devil's happened to him? (*He thinks a moment.*) Oh, no!

QUEEN. What are you thinking?

KING. A foul and base thought, Woman. I refuse to name it. (*Ashamed*) Could it be—oh, no—I refuse.

QUEEN. Could it be *what*?

KING. The Duke has run off with the money?

QUEEN. Foul and base indeed. Of course not. But could he have fallen somewhere?

He's not strong at all, you know. (*To the* GIRL, *who has joined them*) A whole month, and he's had no real food—and he needs food more than we do. Could he have fallen somewhere?

GIRL (*wraps a shawl around her*). I'll go look for him.

QUEEN. Well, now, let's not *all* disappear, one by one. No! He's not fallen. I'm sure of it. It was daybreak when he went out. There are few places where milk may be bought at that hour. He'll certainly be back soon, but when the milk is here, remember this—I shall be in charge. For us, *water*—all of us, including *you*, sir. (*The* BEAR *nods, moans.*) The milk's for the mother only.

KING. What about the child?

QUEEN. The mother will take care of the child, as she already has.

KING. Oh.

QUEEN. We have no bottles and no formulas, and the mother has everything.

GIRL. I have this ring. Perhaps I can sell it, and buy some—bread. (*She hands the ring to the* QUEEN, *who examines it.*)

QUEEN. It's a beautiful ring, Girl.

GIRL. It *looks* real, doesn't it?

QUEEN. Terribly. And it *is*, too, but it isn't worth money. Now, there is water in the jug. We can each drink *water,* at any rate. When the mother and father are restored a little—well, who knows? Perhaps the father has money.

KING. He has a bear, no money. If he'd had money, would he have come to this door, in that storm?

QUEEN. Very well, then, a bear. Now our acting company has been enlarged by one trained bear, and—

KING. Just a minute. You're not thinking they're to stay for some time?

QUEEN. They're *here*, sir. And, as you know, they barely made it. (*Very clearly*) These people—and I include the bear—are *here*. Beyond that door, beyond this theatre, is a whole world of wealth, in which no door opened for them. Why, I don't know, and I don't care. They're here. For how long is none of my business, but while they *are* here, they *are* here, and friends, and members of the family.

(*Running is heard. They all turn toward the door. The* DUKE, *breathless, comes in, carrying a whole wire crate containing six quart-bottles of milk. The*

KING *closes the door and puts the metal bolt in place.*)

QUEEN. Bravo!

DUKE. I'm a *poor* thief!

QUEEN. Under that bed, Duke.

(*The* DUKE *hurries to the* MOTHER's *bed with the crate, slides it under, and out of sight.*)

DUKE. I'll go to jail if I *must*, but they can't have back the milk. They can't have *both*.

KING. You were seen?

DUKE. I was *chased*. (*He brings out the coins.*) There were no stores open. (*He hands the money to the* KING.) A mile away, or more, I found a restaurant, but what they wanted for *one* quart was more than I had. I wanted a cup of coffee more than anything I've ever wanted in my whole life— (*He looks over at the* MOTHER *asleep, and at the* CHILD.) —but I went out and started walking again, and there all of a sudden right in front of me was the milk wagon. (*Pause*) The whole place is covered with snow. All of the ruins around us are covered. I mean, I cut *through* the ruins when they chased me.

KING. *Who* chased you?

DUKE. The milkman, and a boy. His son, I guess. (*Softly*) One thing I don't understand. They ran in silence. They didn't shout *stop thief!* The father was swiftest at first, and then the son left him far behind. I'll tell you this. When I was in training for the big fight I never ran the way I did just now. I don't get it. I'll go to jail, but nobody but the mother can have that milk.

KING. You'd better have a little yourself.

DUKE. No. It's not for me. If I had stolen it for *myself*, I could never have run that well.

KING. And the boy and his father? You lost them?

DUKE. How could I lose them? We ran in snow.

KING. Hide, then. Over there.

DUKE. *Hide*, King? After I ran *that* way? No, thank you. I don't want to hide. (*Footsteps are heard, quick and light.*) Well, here he is. (*They all look at one another. There is a gentle, almost polite, knock on the door. The* DUKE *goes to open it. The* KING *stops him.*)

KING. Wait. Wait.

DUKE. No, we waited last time. It's all

right. I don't mind. (*The* DUKE *opens the door, and there in the doorway is a* BOY *of eighteen or nineteen, dark and grave of face. He looks at the* DUKE, *recognizes him, says nothing, and as the* DUKE *steps back, somewhat asking him in by that movement, the* BOY *comes in. He takes his time looking around—at everybody and everything. His eyes go back again and again to the* GIRL, *but his face remains grave. Nobody says anything. The* BOY *passes beside each bed, looking at each occupant, and then back at the group watching him. He looks up to the top of the theatre, and far out into the auditorium. He goes to the* MOTHER's *bed, squats, draws out the crate, looks around at everybody, shoves the crate back. He gets up, and walks back to the Stage Door.*)

DUKE (*softly*). I'll go with you to the police, if you like.

(*The* BOY *looks at him, looks at the* GIRL, *shakes his head, turns and goes. Everybody looks at one another.*)

DUKE. Well, why didn't he speak? Why didn't he say *something*?

GIRL. He *can't* speak.

DUKE. How do you know?

GIRL. He told me so.

DUKE. How could he tell you so? He didn't say one word!

GIRL. He told me a lot of things.

(*An explosion is heard, falling debris, and the voices of the* WORKERS.)

KING (*straightens up, hands coins to* QUEEN). Off to work, then. In the snow perhaps the people will be more generous. (*Goes to the door, stops, turns.*) I hate to beg. (*He goes, followed by the* DUKE.)

SCENE TWO

Early that afternoon. The MOTHER *of the infant has the* CHILD *beside her in bed, the bed partly screened off. The* CHILD *cries. Stops.*

———

QUEEN. Oh, what a lovely voice, what a lovely *anger* in that voice!

MOTHER. Oh, Mother, your love for my child makes me proud.

(*The* FATHER, *working over an open straw suitcase, brings out cymbals for the* BEAR, *turns, looks, listens.*)

FATHER. Well, feed the boy, will you, Wife? It's a miracle the poor fellow's alive, so feed him, feed him.

MOTHER (*to the* QUEEN). I *love* to feed him. I never knew.

FATHER. So now you know.

MOTHER (*to the* GIRL). Get with a man, to get your own man, like this fellow.

QUEEN. Soon, now, but it is still a secret.

GIRL. What is?

QUEEN. The *Silent* Boy, of course.

GIRL. No, Queen. I love the other. DUKE

QUEEN. The other is a boy, too, or *was*, but it is *not* him you love.

GIRL. Him alone. No other.

QUEEN. To argue love is lovely, but the Silent Boy *is* love.

GIRL. No, Queen.

QUEEN. Ah, then, love them both.

GIRL. No, just the one, my husband.

FATHER. Women! It's all women here! And the secrets of them. (*To the* BEAR) All right, Gorky, to work! One, two, three—*now*! (*The* BEAR *strikes the cymbals together in a rhythm, as the* FATHER *sings:*) Walking on my own two feet, walking, walking down the street. The street was fair, the street was sweet, walking on my own two feet. (*He stops.*) Good, Gorky. (*He gives* GORKY *a cube of sugar.*) Now, rest a moment, while I get my coat and cap. (*He fishes into the open suitcase on the floor, brings out a coat which he puts on, and a cap, both bright and covered with buttons and bells. Another cap he puts on the* BEAR. *He goes to the women.*) Well, now, Gorky's ready again, and so am I, Wife. We'll go out and work. With luck, who knows? Perhaps a little money for a big family.

QUEEN. You've had no food. There's milk in the jug. For you and for the bear.

FATHER. After work, perhaps, if we've had luck. (*The* BEAR *moans.*) Well, perhaps a little for Gorky, then.

QUEEN. A little for yourself, too.

FATHER. I work best hungry. It's been the way of my life. (*Points.*) That child began in hunger. *She* was my bread and wine, and now she's his, too, and the both of them to me, a miracle. Great good God, I thought the door would never open. I knew you were in here, because Gorky would not leave the door. Would you, Man? (*The* BEAR *moans as the* FATHER *receives a bowl of milk from the* QUEEN *and places it on the floor before* GORKY. *The* QUEEN *pours milk into another bowl, holds it out to the* MAN. *He*

shakes *his head.*) FATHER. Ready, then, Gorky! One, two, three, now: (*The* BEAR *clangs the cymbals together, as the* FATHER *and the* BEAR *walk to the far end of the stage, turn, and go straight to the Stage Door, and out.*) Oh, I was walking down the street, walking, walking down the street. Walking on my own two feet, walking on my own two feet. The street was fair, the street was sweet, walking on my own two feet. . . .

SCENE THREE

A little later. The three women, alone. The QUEEN *is at the table. The* GIRL *is seated on a small box beside the sleeping* MOTHER *and* CHILD, *humming softly. After a moment, she sings softly in a kind of lullaby: Rock, rock, rock to sleep. A mother and a man. Rock in the dark, rock in the light. Rock in the heart the whole long night. Rock, rock, rock to sleep. A woman and a man.*

———

GIRL. Oh, if only I were beautiful, as she is.

QUEEN. Oh, you *will* be, don't you worry about *that*. It's the *birth* that's made her beautiful. Here. Drink this. To his good health. (*She thrusts bowl at the* GIRL.)

GIRL (*takes the bowl*). His?

QUEEN. Yes, Girl. The Silent Boy.

GIRL. How, Queen? Do I wait all my life for love, and then when it comes, do I say suddenly, Ah, no, *that* was not love, *this* is love?

QUEEN. Yes, Girl.

GIRL. No, Queen. No.

QUEEN. The Boy loves you, and you love him. He told you so better than if he had speech. And you told *him* so.

GIRL. I didn't.

QUEEN. You didn't *want* to, because you thought it was wrong. But you did. Be *glad* you did.

GIRL. How can I be glad? The Man loves me, and needs me, and only last night I *begged* him not to deny his love. How can I be glad?

QUEEN. Be glad, and never mind how.

GIRL. I'm not that kind of a woman.

QUEEN. You're the only kind. It's just that you're only beginning to learn what kind it is. To be kind to the Man is to be unkind to the Boy. Unkind to him is unkind to life, and to yourself.

GIRL. If that's true, I don't want to be kind to myself. Or to life. (*Suddenly*) I wish the Man had never stolen, and the Boy had never followed him here.

QUEEN. Why don't you thank God you love him?

GIRL. I'll never see him again, that's why. Everyone I ever loved I never saw again. And I ached and *rotted*. (*With decision*) I love the Man. No other. I'll see *him* again.

QUEEN. You'll see the Boy again, too.

GIRL (*stands, looks at the* QUEEN *with terrible earnestness*). I will, won't I? (*The* QUEEN *smiles. The* GIRL *seems shocked at herself*.) No, Queen. It's not true. I love only the Man, not the Boy. Let me have my poor Man, and let someone else have the fair Boy. He's not for me. He never was. Besides, my Man outran him. Oh, I was proud—until—

QUEEN. Until you saw the Boy!

GIRL. Why is that so? *How* is it so? It *is* so, but why? The way he stood there, and walked, and looked, and *understood*. Oh, thank God I'll never see *him* again. My love is too good for me. But why?

QUEEN. In the theatre, long ago, I had a part once—a girl in love as you are. And I was torn, and angry, and ashamed, and frightened, and insecure. Did I love him? Did he love me? And if I did, and if he did, would we *both* know? Or wouldn't we, and then would I lose the other, too? Or the *little* love I had for the other? Would that little be gone, too? And then nothing at all? (*Stops*.) I was very good in that part.

GIRL. And how did it turn out?

QUEEN. It was a bad play.

GIRL. Oh, no, please. How did it turn out? The Boy, of course. You loved the Boy, of course. And he loved you.

QUEEN (*obviously not telling the truth*). I never found out. It was the fault of the *play*. Plays are *written*. They can go *any* way.

GIRL. And which way did *that* play go?

QUEEN. The bad way. The man who wrote the play—ah, what a sad man, and yet how he could write. He came to the rehearsals, and now and then explained why this and why that, but it was all to the end that he was sad, and very troubled, and deathly sick. He drank all the time and tried to pretend he knew why the play was bad.

GIRL. Why *was* it bad?

QUEEN. He *said* it was because it was true, but that's the lie that's always told by the writers of bad plays, as if anything *weren't* true. As if one of the true may not be chosen over another. Poor man, poor lying wonderful man. He was joyous in my girl's failure. True, he said. It's true to lose, he said. He rejoiced in my wretchedness.

GIRL. Oh, no, no.

QUEEN. Oh, it was a good part, and believe me I made the most of it. I lost the Boy. I lost the Man, but the play ran and ran. Ah, you see, the playwright said, how right I was to choose the true. The people know. And all the time it wasn't so at all, it was the art of *us*, the players, that the people cherished. The play was bad, but do you know, it is still considered a *good* play? Unbelievable, and yet there it is. Why, the man who wrote it drank himself to death before the play closed. Oh, he chose the true all right. He chose hate, or hate chose him. It was his business to choose love, to write a better play, and to live to write another.

GIRL. But what happened, what happened to *you* in the play?

QUEEN. It wasn't to me, it was to *him*, the playwright. I played my part. That's my work, *our* work. We don't write them, we perform them.

GIRL. In the play what happened to you? He *said* it was true. Is the same thing going to happen to me?

QUEEN. What happened to me in the play *is* going to happen to you, too, or not, as you choose, as if *you* were writing the play, choosing from among the true, the true for you, which is the Silent Boy, who was not chosen for me by the playwright.

GIRL. How do I choose? Is it as simple as that? I love him. I'm *ashamed* that I do, but I do. So how do I choose? What have I got to do with it? Who chose him to be the milkman's son? Who chose the Duke to go out and steal the milk? Who chose the Silent Boy to follow him here? Who chose him to come in and to look and to understand? I didn't.

QUEEN. Ah, but when he looked at you, and looked again, you, and nobody else, chose him to love you.

GIRL. And what did *he* choose?

QUEEN. And he chose to love you, as you know.

GIRL. And he went, as silently as he came, and there we are—nowhere again, nothing again.

QUEEN. He'll be back.

GIRL. Do you think so? Do you really think so? I've waited all day. Why hasn't he come back? I love him, but if he doesn't come back, *who* do I love? Do I wait, and then go looking for him?

QUEEN. He'll come looking for *you.*

GIRL. He will, won't he? That *is* the truth, isn't it? No matter what happened in the play, he will come looking for me, won't he?

QUEEN. Yes, he will. But if he doesn't—

GIRL. No, he *must.* Please don't even *think* he may not. I'm thinking *that,* and I need you to stop me.

QUEEN. Ah, well, we shall see, we shall see. (*Points.*) Rest there on the King's bed. You've had no sleep. And I shall lie here, on the lonely bed of the poor brave Duke, God help him.

SCENE FOUR

A little later. The QUEEN *is making the bed she has slept on. The* GIRL *is making the one she has slept on. The* KING *comes in. He has lost one of his shoes, and he is angry at himself.*

———

KING. Ah, damn me, I went out with two shoes, and I came back with one.

QUEEN. Where is the other?

KING. Just let me damn me first, please —damn me, damn me, damn me. Now what the devil am I going to do with only one shoe? How am I to get about? (*Rubbing his foot, after removing the rag of a sock*) There ought to be a pair of shoes somewhere in this theatre. Girl, see if you can find me a pair of shoes, will you please?

GIRL. Lost your shoe? How can a man lose his shoe? His head, perhaps, his heart, his mind—how can he lose a shoe?

KING. Look for a pair of shoes, please— damn me, damn me, damn me. Where's the bear? Where's the man of the bear?

QUEEN. They're out to work. The bear crashes cymbals together, and the man sings. He wears a colored coat and cap.

KING. And the bear?

QUEEN. A colored cap.

KING. Damn me, damn me, damn me— what's the name of that bear? Don't tell me, I'll guess. Is it Lear, the great Father? Lear was once *my* name—damn me.

QUEEN. What happened to your shoe?

KING. Hatchet, rue; latchet, rue; patchet, rue; rickey—rue—wash!

QUEEN. Oh, speak, Clown!

KING. Damn me, damn me, damn me— I *am* speaking. Hatchet, latchet, patchet! Did you find me a pair of shoes, Girl?

GIRL. No, King.

KING. Damn me.

QUEEN. Will you please talk sense?

KING. The infant? The mother?

QUEEN. They're both well.

KING. The Silent Boy? Did he come back?

(*The* GIRL *turns, and looks at the* KING.)

QUEEN. No, but he will.

KING. Damn me, damn me. What name have they given the boy?

QUEEN. He's a boy, and they know it, and the boy knows it, and knows *how* a boy's a boy, and so all day he's gotten along *without* a name.

KING. Call him George. It's a nice name. Henry. That's a nice name, too. I once knew a Polish clown named Stanislaus. He never *looked* the part. Stan, that's all—Stan. Damn me, damn me, damn me. (*Suddenly*) I gambled my shoe, and lost it. Call him Frederic. There's a nice *sound* to Frederic.

QUEEN. *Gambled your shoe?*

KING. Yes, gambled my shoe, gambled my shoe. The Wreckers, knocking down the rotten old buildings, just a little off from here. I thought I'd get a coin or two, after a whole day of failure—not one coin—not one, but a small boy gave me this. I'll never see that Boy again, most likely, but one day when *he's* an old man, a small boy will give him something. (*He shows a yo-yo.*) The Boss of the wrecking crew out there, and ten or eleven others, white and black, at coffee time, standing around a little fire in the ruins. Call the man Patrick. It's a nice name. Ah, you all need a laugh, I said, and I need a little of that coffee, so the Boss fills a mug for me, and another worker lights me one of his own cigarettes. The snow is coming down soft, soft. I'll give you a laugh, I said. Ah, we've had our laughs all day, they said.

The falling walls make us laugh. Ah, then, I said, I'll give you a tear. (*He looks over at the* MOTHER *and the sleeping* INFANT.) Call him Robert. It's a fine name. *You?* Give us a tear? they said. How? I'm a clown, I said. Very well, they said, give one of us a tear, just *one* of us, and *each* of us will give you a coin. But fail, Clown, and what will you give *us?* I wasn't thinking. My shoe, I said. The shoe of my right foot. Call the boy John. John's one of the nicest names of all.

QUEEN. You lost *that* bet?

KING. Ah, the world's laughing. The workers laugh. In the snow, even. I did my captured-thief bit that brought tears to the eyes of the world only a few years ago. I did the hungry man who stole the apple pie. Call the boy Richard. Ah, Richard's a fine name. He'll do well called Richard. Had I been called Richard I might have been a *chef!* I did my rejected lover bit, and all they did was laugh —but not hard enough to bring a tear to *one* eye, and every one of them has *two.* I cheated a little because I knew I was losing, and I did a little of my ridiculed-orator bit, where the man speaks most nobly and all they do is throw vegetables at him. And then a little of my bashful boy bit. Was it twenty years ago that it made everybody weep? And blow their noses? The workers only laughed. They drank coffee and smoked cigarettes and laughed. I bent down to take off my shoe, but the Boss said, Ah, keep the shoe, Clown, keep it. But I refused. I may be a shameless beggar but I am a proud clown. Damn me, damn me, damn me.

QUEEN. It was only a game They didn't mean it.

KING. Woman, for the love of God, I *did* mean it. What the devil's happened to the world? To the workers? Not one tear in one eye. If I've lost my art what good is my shoe? (*Explosion, debris, voices*) That's them. Damn me, damn me, damn me! (*Suddenly*) Ah, they even *offered* me coins, but I refused them.

QUEEN. You had no right to refuse coins.

KING. Did I have a right to fail? No, but I failed. (*He looks at his bed.*) And there's my bed.

QUEEN. Lie down, then. You've had no sleep or rest. That's why you failed.

KING. Is it, Woman? Is that it?

QUEEN. Go, lie down.

KING. Oh, I long to. I *long* to, Woman. Forever, if you ask me. (*He stretches out.*) Damn me, damn me, damn me for my failure. Call the boy—Clown. (*He falls asleep.*)

SCENE FIVE

An hour or two later. The KING *is still stretched out on his bed. The* BEAR *is chained to the floor. The* FATHER *is working with the* DUKE, *and the* BEAR, *in a new act. The* QUEEN *and the* GIRL *are setting the table—bread, mainly.*

FATHER. All right now, Gorky. Watch carefully. (*Puts his arms around the* DUKE.) This man is my friend. He's *your* friend. He saved our lives. Now, with the woman with a child to look after, we need this man's help. Instead of marching, music, songs and dances—*wrestling!* A man and a bear. The Duke, and you, Gorky. (*Embraces the* DUKE.) See? I embrace him—but gently, gently. Understand? He is a friend, a dear friend. We need him. In three hours of work without the woman, you and I, Gorky, earned nothing, not one coin. Oh, the weather was against us, but even in the worst weather, *with* the woman, we have always managed to earn *something.* (*To the* DUKE) All right, now, don't be afraid, Duke. Gorky understands. You understand, don't you, Gorky? A friend? A very dear friend? You are to *play* at wrestling with him. You are not to wrestle in earnest. He is a man, and you are a bear, another thing. (*The* BEAR *listens, turning its head this way and that, as if to get the meaning of what the* FATHER *is saying.*) Are you ready, Duke? (*The* QUEEN *and the* GIRL *stop to watch.*)

DUKE. Well, wrestling's not my line, you know. I'm ready, but I've never wrestled. A man, *or* a bear. (*Looks around.*) I wish the King were awake.

FATHER. Gorky's an intelligent man— well, I *think* of him as a man. He's stronger than ten strong men, but he's gentle, too. A father and a brother to those he loves.

DUKE. I love Gorky, but does Gorky love me?

FATHER. Well, he's beginning to, he's

beginning to. He senses that everybody here is a friend, but he's not sure yet. I'm teaching him now, and he learns quickly. (*Gives* GORKY *a cube of sugar. Hands one to the* DUKE. *The* DUKE *starts to eat it.*) No. No. Give the sugar to Gorky.

(*The* DUKE *steps up to* GORKY, *holds the cube of sugar out to him, but the* BEAR *doesn't take it.*)

DUKE. You see? He doesn't love me at all.

FATHER. Gorky? My boy? This is my friend. *Your* friend. Take the sugar from him. (GORKY *is undecided.*) Take it, Gorky. (GORKY *does not take it.*)

DUKE. I *want* to help. We've got a child to take care of now. All day I saw all kinds of things that I wanted to *take*—for the Boy. But I lost my nerve. I took nothing.

GIRL. I'm glad. I worried that you *might* take something and that I might never see you again.

DUKE. I begged, too, but I'm a poor beggar. Prizefighters always are. I've got to help, that's all. I'm not afraid of the bear. It's just that I'm not a wrestler. Couldn't we box?

FATHER. Oh, no. That is an American sport. The bear is a European. If you were to strike him one blow that hurt him a little, just a *little*, perhaps no more than an irritation, he would go mad, and he would kill. Boxing is swift and violent. He could never understand it. But wrestling is another thing. He will soon associate it with friendship and love and simple animal play. Don't be afraid.

GIRL. No, please. *I am afraid.* I love the bear, as we all do. But the wrestling of a man and a bear—it will never seem true to the people, in any case.

(DUKE *eats the sugar cube, noisily and slowly.*)

FATHER. True or not, they love it, and it brings in money. Streets, fairs, carnivals, perhaps even the circus, at last. My problem is that I am small, no match at all for the bear, but the Duke is a big man, almost as big as a bear, and their wrestling together would make our fortune. When I wrestle, it's a joke. (*Quickly*) All right, Gorky. (*He seizes* GORKY, *tries to throw him. The* BEAR *picks him up in his arms, rocks him, kisses him, murmurs to him, puts him down gently.*) You see? It would never

do. I've tried and tried. If I were to strike him, which I have done only once, when he began to walk after a man who had kicked him, a man he would have crushed to death, Gorky *still* loved me. If I were to strike him, it wouldn't help matters any. He's never understood why I struck him, how I could do a thing like that to him—*him*—and even now, after three long years, he still broods about it. Some things he understands, and some he doesn't. He has never been able to associate that sudden violence in me with love, and yet he has gone along on faith, waiting, waiting for understanding. (*To the* DUKE) If we work slowly and patiently tonight, tomorrow we will have the beginning of a great new act. We will all be working again. Now Gorky, my father, my brother, my son, listen to me. This man is our friend. (*He embraces the* DUKE. *The* KING *sits up, half-asleep, watches and listens.*)

GIRL. No. No. Something else. He is a kind man, and he will *try*, he will try *anything* that may help, but no. I'm afraid.

DUKE. Do you love me, Girl? Is that it? (*The* QUEEN *holds out her arm toward the* GIRL, *as if to urge her to speak truthfully.*) Because if you *do* love me, then by God the bear must love me, too.

QUEEN. Of course she loves you, Duke. We all love you. You *are* kind.

DUKE. I mean *love*, Queen. Does she love *me*, or was that last night? Another time, another story?

GIRL. I love you.

QUEEN. Wait a moment, child.

DUKE. We are all hungry and cold and lonely, but if you do not love me entirely, as foolishly as you did last night, there is no need to pretend.

GIRL. I love you.

QUEEN. Oh, wait, wait. Love speaks a strange language. Man, she *does* love you. Of course she loves you. Besides kindness, there is great handsomeness in you, which no woman could not love in men in general, and in the one man of her heart. (*She stops.*)

DUKE. Go on, Queen.

QUEEN. She is ashamed that *while* she loves you, she also loves—

GIRL. No. No.

QUEEN. —the Silent Boy. In your youth, in the days of your fame, it was so with

you, too, Man. You remember. Of course
you do.

DUKE. I remember, Queen. (*To the*
GIRL.) Thank you for pretending, Girl,
and please be glad. *Be glad.* I am your
friend.

(*The* GIRL *throws herself into his arms,
sobbing. The* DUKE *smiles, as he comforts
her, whispering.*) I *am* your friend. (*The*
GIRL *draws away, then goes to the* QUEEN.
The DUKE *looks around, and then goes
to the* KING. *He begins to walk toward
the door suddenly.*)

QUEEN. Duke? (*The* DUKE *stops. She
goes to him. Turns him around.*) What
is it, Man?

DUKE (*as if he were saying, "I want to
beg God for Grace"*). I want to beg. (*He
gestures.*)

QUEEN. You've had no food. Take this
bread.

DUKE. Bread, Queen? (*He struggles
with his emotions, looks up, speaks bitterly, powerfully.*) Give the bread to the
well-fed Boy! (*Earnestly*) Oh, I'm sorry.
Please forgive me. (*He hurries out.*)

FATHER. He's too old for you, Girl.

GIRL (*angry*). He's *not* too old. My love
is too little. No man loves as *he* loves,
and yet I do *not* love him, and the Silent
Boy doesn't know I'm alive. Oh, I hate
love.

FATHER. Ah, you may lose them both,
and find another, or two others, and lose
them, too, from loving them too much or
too little or something else. And still the
world is there, and you're on the stage,
right in the middle of everything. Love
has no reason, or rightness, or way. (*He
waves at his wife.*) The *Bear* loved her.
I didn't, at first. The bear *hummed* when
he saw her. His soul turned sweet and
gentle. For me it might have been her, it
might have been somebody else. The Bear
decided for me, and there she is, the
mother of my son, my firstborn. Of all
the women in the world was *she* the only
one to be the mother of my son? No,
Girl. It happened. It happened, and now
it's the law, and history. It's a long world,
Girl. It's a big time, and love is a *word,*
if you're not busy with a bear, or a boy
to put on his feet.

GIRL. I want to believe in love, Queen,
whether it's a word or something else.

FATHER. It's a word all right, *and*
something else, too. And that's the part

that's hard to follow. What else is it?
(*Almost jabbering*) Well, get up, get up
now, get along into another day. Love is
getting along into another day, getting
to work, whatever your work is. The
rest of love is—who knows? I love her.
And I love the boy beside her. What
does that mean? What does it *mean?* It
means I've got to teach the Bear to wrestle
a big man without hurting him. And *our*
big man has gone. Now, he'll come back,
won't he?

QUEEN. I wonder. There were tears in
the poor man's eyes.

GIRL. Tears in *his* eyes? *He* belongs
here. And now he's gone, and I'm here,
and I *don't* belong here. He lied for me,
Queen, out of kindness and pity. What
theatre have I known? One potato, two
potato? Is that being in the theatre? I
pledge allegiance to the Flag. Is that acting? How do you do, my partner. Is that
something in an opera? I came here lost,
and he found me, and helped me, and
protected me. He saved my life. I've
learned more since I've been here than in
all the rest of the time of my life. He
lied to let me stay, and I told the truth
to drive him out. Queen, I'll go find him
now, and just say I'm sorry for being
such a truthful *dirty* liar, and then I'll go
my way.

KING (*gets up, speaks softly*). Well, if
anyone here should be angry, it should
be *me.* Angry only that we know nothing, and that we can't learn. But I am
not even angry about that, Girl, and there
is no need for you to be, either. This is
how it is. If we were in a palace, instead
of in this cave, this would be how it is.
If we had everything, and *more* than
everything, this would be how it is. If
we loved God and God loved us, this
would be how it is. And I am not angry.
I cannot be angry. This is the world, this
is us, this is all there is, and we do not
understand.

GIRL. Then, what's it for, Father?
What's it for?

KING. For *this, precisely* this.

GIRL. The lies, too?

KING. There are no lies. What's it *for?*
It's for putting up with—with humor, if
possible. Without excuses, without astonishment, without regret, without
shame, without any system and order
more elaborate than courtesy and love. Do

not be angry at yourself for being who you are. If you *think* you are *not* truth and beauty, perhaps you are mistaken.

GIRL. Thank you, Father. I don't belong here.

KING. Nobody *belongs* here, but here we are. My father and my mother didn't *think!* No, they didn't. But even if they had, as so many have, I still wouldn't belong here, and nobody else would, either. The Bear belongs here, and all his kind. We're another creature. We know enough to know we know nothing, and it is terrible and wonderful. They know nothing but do not know that they know nothing, and it is neither terrible nor wonderful—it just is. His name is Gorky. But his mother never gave him the name. She looked at him and there he was. A bear, and not a tiger, or a rabbit, or a hawk. We think, and remember, and speak, and laugh, and sing, and dance, and *make things* of all kinds, on purpose. We do all these things because we *don't* belong here. It's not our place. It's a cave. What are we doing in a cave? We're angels. What are we doing in bodies? (*Pause*) For some reason, we're trying our best, helplessly, to pretend that we *are* in them, that we *belong* in them, and that we *are* here, and that we belong here. (*He goes to the door.*) I'll go fetch my shoe, now. I failed, and I know I failed. (*He goes.*)

GIRL. I'll go now, too.

FATHER (*shouts*). Ah, stay, Girl! You've been a great help to my wife and son.

GIRL. He didn't come back. I thought he would. I thought he loved me.

FATHER. How do you know he doesn't?

QUEEN. He did this morning.

GIRL. This morning. How far away this morning is. And so he loved me this morning, and this is tonight, and he didn't come back. There's no reason for me to stay any longer. Goodbye.

FATHER (*shouts*). Goodbye! Everybody's always saying goodbye. You've got no place to go. Before you've even left, it's already as good as another year gone by anyway, and you've come back—so stay, stay!

(*There is a loud and merry knock at the door. The* QUEEN *and the* GIRL *look at one another, desperately, hopefully. The* FATHER *goes to the door, opens it. It is the* WRECKING CREW BOSS, *and a* NEGRO HELPER.)

BOSS (*comes in, looks at everybody, then speaks softly*). What's this? We knocked as a joke. People? Here? What's that over there?

FATHER. That's Gorky, my bear. And who are you, sir?

BOSS. The foreman of the wrecking crew. And the women, what are *they* doing here?

FATHER. *A moment ago* they were arguing about love. How it works and what it means. Maybe you can tell 'em. What's it mean?

BOSS. I don't know, but I know that this beautiful old building is next for the dynamite. (*He glances up, and around.*)

FATHER. The dynamite? This is a theatre, man.

BOSS. So it is, so it is, but down it comes just the same first thing tomorrow morning, along with all the other buildings in this area. Rooming houses, offices, stores, churches—all old, all rotted, all finished—to make way for the new. But I've loved every poor old wreck of a place that my men and I have brought down. Look up there, Jamie—it's a *high* and handsome place, now, isn't it?

FATHER. Yes, while you're at it, Jamie, look over there. That's my wife. She became a mother early this morning. Beside her is my son. They can't be moved now. They need time.

BOSS (*near a box*). May I sit down? I have a longing to sit down in here.

QUEEN. Welcome, sir.

BOSS (*looking at her strangely*). Thank you. (*Looks at the* GIRL, *as he sits.*) And the girl there? She's your daughter?

QUEEN. In a manner of speaking.

BOSS. What manner is that?

QUEEN. For three months short of a year an old man of the theatre and I have lived here. He found this theatre in the morning, and I found it in the afternoon. He called me the Queen, and I called him the King. Then, a month ago, an old prizefighter found this place, and yesterday this girl found it. All in all, a family—a great Clown begging as a free man in the human streets rather than leave the theatre, and me and the prizefighter, and this Girl, who *is* my daughter.

BOSS. A great *Clown?* (*Looks at* JAMIE.) How many shoes does he wear?

QUEEN. Two when he has two, but now he has one.

BOSS. We know the man. This afternoon he made us roar with laughter. Madam, what is your problem?

QUEEN. *Mine, sir?* I have no problem.

BOSS. The problem of your family, then?

QUEEN. Love, of course. Survival, and love. And what is *your* problem, sir?

BOSS. How best, swiftest, most safely, and least expensively to bring this—mansion—down into ruins, and then to clear away the debris.

QUEEN. Simple.

BOSS (*holding a crust of bread*). May I?

QUEEN. Please, sir. And something to drink?

BOSS. No, thanks, just this bread. I am confused, and my teeth need something to work upon. I'm poor at words, and at *thinking,* too, if you ask me. (*He chews.*) Jamie, boy?

JAMIE. Yes, sir?

BOSS. What can we do, Jamie?

JAMIE. I could go find the Old Man and give him back his shoe. I've kept it in a safe place, but he could never find it. I just thought it ought to be kept in a safe place.

BOSS. The mother and the child can't be moved, Jamie.

JAMIE. No, sir, they can't.

BOSS. Tomorrow's Friday, and the day after is Saturday, and then Sunday. (*He thinks a moment, and then speaks suddenly.*) Jamie, tell my boys, tell my crew, tell them all at once and one by one, do you hear, Jamie?

JAMIE. Yes, sir.

BOSS. All at once and one by one, Boys, he says we're all to be sick tomorrow, and the day after. Use the name you have for me among you, I don't mind— I've only pretended to mind. Tell them the Madman says we're all to be sick tomorrow, and the day after. That's all. Just sick. Every one of us. At home. In bed. Coughing, and sweating. I want to study this problem *carefully.* It may take me a little time.

JAMIE. Yes, sir.

BOSS. And Jamie?

JAMIE. Yes, sir.

BOSS (*brings money from his pocket*). Find the Great Man, and give him back his shoe, and then step into that little store we all go to at lunchtime. Buy us —well, you know, Jamie, the things we like—but a lot of it. I'm very hungry.

JAMIE. Yes, sir. Everybody sick until Monday morning.

BOSS. Jamie?

JAMIE. Yes, sir.

BOSS. If anybody asks why— (*He waits a long time, shakes his head quickly.*) There is no why.

JAMIE. Yes, sir. (*JAMIE turns and goes quickly, as the BOSS keeps chewing bread.*)

QUEEN. *I'd* like to ask why?

BOSS. (*looking around from one to the other*). The truth?

QUEEN. If you know the truth, sir.

BOSS. I know, Queen. The King came by as we stopped for coffee and cigarettes this afternoon. He said he would make us laugh—for a coin. And my men said, Why, we're laughing all the time, make us weep, and you'll have a *lot* of coins. And he worked, and worked well, and all we did was laugh—all except one, Queen, that I know of—myself! One who wept bitterly from the beginning of the great Clown's work to the end of it, and fell to the bottom of his soul with grief and admiration at the Clown's refusal of our coins, and the forefeiture of his shoe. Myself, and more than likely Jamie, too. (*Pause*) And more than likely each of the others, too, each of us unwilling, Queen, *unwilling* to let the other know of his pity and love for his Father. *That* is why.

QUEEN. I thought it was for the child.

BOSS. No. I have my own, know them and love them and understand them, and don't understand them, and probably never will. It is for the Father. The King. The Madman. The Clown. The *Father* of the Child. (*He gets up suddenly, speaks softly.*) I must go along here now and study the problem. (*He goes. The GIRL looks around at everybody, goes to the BEAR, rests her head on his shoulder, then turns and runs out.*)

FATHER (*shouts*). Gorky, I wish you'd stop liking only pretty girls!

SCENE SIX

Early Monday morning. The FATHER *is up. The* MOTHER *is up. The* CHILD *is in her arms. The* BEAR *is waiting. The family suitcase is packed. The* QUEEN *is up. The* KING *is up. Everybody is doing little things in silence. Making bundles, folding things, tying shoelaces and packages.*

———

KING. Well, Queen.

QUEEN. Yes, King.

KING. Monday.

QUEEN. Yes, Monday. The first day of the week.

KING. And the last day of the World.

QUEEN. Oh, stop.

KING. Do you know it's the name of the theatre, *actually?* I found out only yesterday, out front.

QUEEN. I had no idea. In any case, you've got both your shoes, and I've got all my things.

KING. And we've eaten well these past few days.

QUEEN. Yes, we have.

KING. There's another theatre that's been dark for years. (*Points.*) A little up, and east.

QUEEN. Oh, no, no.

KING. Where, then?

QUEEN. Where all the others are. I don't mind.

KING. Alone?

QUEEN. What a strange question, King. What a strange word. Who can be alone?

KING. You can. I've seen you alone when I've been right beside you. Alone?

QUEEN. Yes, I think so.

KING. Well, let me carry your bundle until you're there, at any rate. I've nothing of my own to carry.

QUEEN (*sweetly*). Would you? Just until I'm there? (KING *smiles.*) I've never understood such places too well. Where they are, and how one obtains entrance.

KING. It's the same with me, of course, but I'll ask, and we'll find out.

FATHER. You're both welcome to come with us.

QUEEN. You're very kind. Oh, no, thank you.

MOTHER. We'll do very well. I know we will. There will be plenty for all of us, and we *need* your help.

KING. The Duke *might* have learned to wrestle the Bear, or the other way around.

FATHER. Yes, yes, that would have helped a lot.

KING (*looks up and all around*). Well . . .

(*Footsteps are heard, and then a knock at the door. The* KING *opens the door, and there in the doorway is the* DUKE, *and behind him the* SILENT BOY. *They come in.*)

DUKE (*looks around, nodding to each*). Well, here he is. Where's the Girl?

QUEEN. She left soon after you did. She went out to find *you.*

DUKE. I've been looking for this Boy. He can't speak, but he *can* understand, and I've told him the Girl loves him.

QUEEN. Boy? Do you love the Girl? (*The* BOY *looks at the* DUKE, *then back at the* QUEEN, *then nods one nod.*) Well, she's been gone for several days now. But she's somewhere about. Look for her. You'll find her. Because she'll be looking for *you.*

(*The* CREW BOSS *comes in, walking slowly and thoughtfully, followed by* JAMIE, *with papers in his hands: charts, floor plans, and so on. The* BOSS *nods at everybody, looks up at the problem. He looks at his watch.*)

KING. We're ready. We're on our way, and thank you very much.

BOSS (*goes to the* KING, *looks at him intently*). Good luck, Father. Good luck, all. (*He and* JAMIE *go.*)

FATHER (*to the* DUKE). Join us. We need you. We'll be working the streets at first, but soon we'll get to the circus, I'm sure.

(*The* DUKE *thinks about this, but does not reply. The* FATHER *and* MOTHER *smile at the others awkwardly, and nod, and the* FATHER *unloosens the* BEAR's *chain. They begin to go.*)

QUEEN. Oh . . . (*The* MOTHER *stops.*) May I have one last look at the child, please? (*The* MOTHER *hurries to the* QUEEN, *who looks intently at the* CHILD, *then nods, and the* FATHER *and the* BEAR *and the* MOTHER *go, all of them waving, including the* BEAR.)

(*The* DUKE *looks around, bewildered because the* GIRL *is gone. He looks up. The* SILENT BOY *nods, and turns to go. The* DUKE *stops him, shakes his head, looks up. They all wait in silence. The* GIRL *comes in through the open door.*)

GIRL. I've come back for my man, if he'll have me. (*The* DUKE *turns and looks at her. The* GIRL *runs to his arms. The* DUKE *puts one hand at the back of her neck and the other at the back of the* BOY's *neck and holds them in place, staring at one another, speechless. Slowly, little by little, the* DUKE *draws them together, and they embrace. He looks up.*)

DUKE. Thank you, sir. (*He turns and hurries out. After a moment the* KING *and* QUEEN *embrace the embracing* BOY *and* GIRL, *and then gesture at them to get along. They go, with their arms around one another.*)

QUEEN. All right, King. (*She looks around and up, smiling.*)

KING. I'll be along in a moment. (*The* QUEEN *smiles at him, turns and, walking like a Queen, goes out. The* KING *looks around, too, and then out into the auditorium.*)

KING. Farewell, then—womb, cave, hiding place, home, church, world, theatre— a fond and loving farewell. (*He works the yo-yo.*) Farewell, and welcome! (*He waves to the theatre, and goes walking swiftly.*)

OH DAD, POOR DAD, MAMMA'S HUNG YOU IN THE CLOSET AND I'M FEELIN' SO SAD

A Pseudoclassical Tragifarce in a Bastard French Tradition

Arthur L. Kopit

Presented at the Phoenix Theatre, New York, by arrangement with Roger L. Stevens, on February 26, 1962, with the following cast:

MADAME ROSEPETTLE	Jo Van Fleet	BELLBOYS	Jaime Sanchez
JONATHAN	Austin Pendleton		Anthony Ponzini
ROSALIE	Barbara Harris		Ernesto Gonzalez
COMMODORE. ROSEABOVE	Sandor Szabo		Louis Waldon
HEAD BELLBOY	Tony Lo Bianco		David Faulkner
			Barry Primus

Directed by Jerome Robbins
Scenery by William and Jean Eckart
Costumes by Patricia Zipprodt
Lighting by Thomas Skelton
Music by Robert Prince

SCENE. The action takes place in Port Royale, a city somewhere in the Caribbean. The play is in three scenes without intermission.

Broadway production:

Presented by Roger L. Stevens and T. Edward Hambleton, by arrangement with the Phoenix Theatre, at the Morosco Theatre in New York on August 27, 1963, with the following cast:

MADAME ROSEPETTLE	Hermione Gingold	BELLBOYS	Jaime Sanchez
JONATHAN	Sam Waterston		Thom Koutsoukos
ROSALIE	Alix Elias		Gary Garth
COMMODORE ROSEABOVE	Sandor Szabo		Ernesto Aponte
HEAD BELLBOY	John Hallow		Peter Lenahan
			Carl Guttenberger

(Other production credits same as for original production.)

For some time before the production of *Oh Dad, Poor Dad, Mamma's Hung You in the Closet and I'm Feelin' So Sad,* the reputation of the play was being dubiously established by persistent reports about a Harvard prodigy who was heading for New York with a play bearing the longest title in the theatre. That the respected Phoenix Theatre, one of New York's experimental—you might call it "off-Broadway" —groups had put it on its production schedule made the reputation less dubious, as did the fact that the firm of Hill and Wang had listed it for publication. The Phoenix Theatre, headed by T. Edward Hambleton and Norris Houghton, we knew, was not an irresponsible group of dilettantes, and Arthur Wang and Larry Hill had one of the youngest but also one of the most reputable companies in the publishing business. The play opened in New York about a year after the advance publicity reached its peak, and a strange thing happened—the play looked as good as it was supposed to be (and perhaps even better) in the Phoenix production staged by the choreographer Jerome Robbins. There were indeed skeptics who insisted on regarding it as a piece of juvenile self-indulgence, but playgoers kept on filling the pleasant little theatre in the Seventies that had become the new home of the Phoenix. And more than that, opinions of the play kept on improving. It was no longer about a stunt but about an engrossing entertainment that people spoke.

People even got used to the title; it had ceased to be fashionable to quip about it, as had a New York wit who declared that he had already read Kopit's play but hadn't yet gone through the title. It was even possible that playgoers who paid the work its proper tribute of laughter were laughing with considerable uncertainty. The play projected youthful anxiety—call it "castration anxiety" if you are not averse to employing psychoanalytical jargon. Mr. Kopit expressed in jocular and fantastic terms a widespread fear of the voracious woman or even nymphet who figuratively devours the male—an observation not exclusively Strindbergian or altogether subjective. The form and style of the work agreed, in fact, with the ambivalence present in this confection of the bizarre and the romantic on which serious studies may yet be written. The work was fantastic and clinical, entertaining and disconcerting, and technically both a comedy and a grotesque melodrama. And its ultra-skeptical view of love, romance, domesticity, and mother-son relationships, all in one respect or another associated with the "norms" of life, enrolled the play in the recently fashionable "Theatre of the Absurd" imported from the Left Bank theatre of Ionesco and Genet.

Arthur L. Kopit, the author of the so-called Absurdist play that was so very funny yet so disturbing below the surface, was born in New York City on May 10, 1937.

After attending the Lawrence High School on Long Island, he went to Harvard and started writing plays, nine of which were produced by academic theatrical groups. *Oh Dad* . . . was one of these, and was first performed by Harvard undergraduates in January, 1960. The play had its professional premiere during the summer of 1961 in England. It was hardly a success there, but the New York production half a year later (February 26, 1962), presented by the Phoenix Theatre in association with Roger L. Stevens, established itself quickly as something no true-blue follower of the arts could afford to miss. Even a reserved critic of the work such as Alan Downer, to whom it was essentially an expanded revue skit, was willing to admit that it had a "vitality" or "an enthusiasm for audacious play that the contemporary theatre can ill spare" (*Quarterly Journal of Speech,* October, 1962, p. 269).

Meanwhile, Kopit had graduated from Harvard in 1959 and won a Shaw Travelling Fellowship for a year's sojourn in Europe. His further and reputable career was yet to be determined. *Oh Dad* . . . , translated into French by Marcel Aymé, was scheduled to open early in the fall of 1963 in Paris; it would be interesting and it might be instructive to know what the Left Bank of Ionesco, Adamov, and Genet would think of the play. Mr. Kopit was, however, bent upon other business; he was working on a new comedy bearing the extravagant title *Asylum or What the Gentlemen Are Up To Not To Mention the Ladies,* withdrawn by him after a brief initial presentation at the Theatre de Lys in Greenwich Village in 1963.

Kopit's rich farcicality may not be sufficiently apparent in the text of *Oh Dad* . . . , which is a thoroughly theatrical one, depending upon dexterity by the director and his cast, rather than a literary piece; and this is quite remarkable in the work of a young Phi Beta Kappa from Harvard, as well as fortunate since the theme of Momism would have otherwise been tiresomely overfamiliar. The bizarreness of the work, a quality that cannot be insisted on too much (and the author agrees), must become evident as a subject for laughter rather than of morbid interest, regardless of what psychological interpretation is put upon it by those who are undaunted by the author's statement (to his interviewer, Frances Herridge of the New York *Post,* March 9, 1962), that his own family is "quite the opposite" of the voraciously over-protective mother of the play.

It does appear, however, that an attitude toward women not without the ambivalence of a youthful artist was an undercurrent in the writing. It clearly affects the treatment of the boy-girl affair in the play and gives depth and macabre humor to the work while disturbing its unity. Kopit gave vent to this feeling himself in declaring in his *Post* interview that he did think "it's difficult to have any free relationship with a woman," since "a woman's social needs are different from a man's" and "the more feminine she is the more permanently she wants him"—which "makes tension between them." At the same time it must be noted that the difficult marriage of overt farce and inner anxiety in the play results in an imperfect blending of moods in *Oh Dad.* . . . Unkind critics may blame this defect, which stage production cannot be expected to eradicate, on a young writer's inexperience and penchant for improvisation and attribute to him a self-conscious effort to imitate fashionable Absurdist drama in the free-wheeling manner of Ionesco's extravaganzas. The present editor believes there is more to the play than undergraduate recklessness and imitativeness.

As restaged by Jerome Robbins, the director of the original "off-Broadway" Phoenix Theatre production, *Oh Dad, Poor Dad* . . . reopened on Broadway at the Morosco Theatre on August 27, 1963, for a limited run prior to a national tour under the auspices of Roger L. Stevens and T. Edward Hambleton. The new production, which featured Hermione Gingold as Madame Rosepettle, was broader than the original one. The new staging, combined with Miss Gingold's stylization of her role as the mother and the swivel-hipped caricature of a nymphet by Alix Elias, whose voice became as imperious as the virago-mother's, pointed up the cartoon-like qualities of the play. One reviewer, Mr. Richard Watts, Jr., of the New York *Post,* actually enjoyed it most this time as a travesty of Tennessee Williams, while regretting that the obviousness of the new production deprived the play of some of its odd fascination. Those who found the play alternately weird and funny or ghoulish and loony did not have to reach for definitions of the style, but for those who prefer an exact label the term "surrealistic farce" was readily available.

SCENE ONE

SCENE: *A lavish hotel suite somewhere in the Caribbean.*

AT RISE: *As the curtain goes up a platoon of* BELLBOYS *is seen hurrying about. Some are opening the shades on the windows, others are dusting. A group of* BELLBOYS *enter with extravagant luggage. They march to the master bedroom. Another group enters with duplicate luggage, only smaller. They march to the other bedroom in the suite. Enter* BELLBOYS ONE *and* TWO, *carrying a coffin. They look about the room nervously.*

WOMAN'S VOICE (*offstage*). Put it in the bedroom!

BELLBOYS ONE AND TWO. The bedroom. (BELLBOY ONE *goes toward the bedroom at stage left.* BELLBOY TWO *starts toward the bedroom at stage right. The handles come off the coffin. It falls to the floor as* MADAME ROSEPETTLE *enters, dressed in black, a veil covering her face, with* JONATHAN *trailing behind her. The* BELLBOYS *are frozen with terror.*)

MADAME ROSEPETTLE. *Fools!*

HEAD BELLBOY. Uh—*which* bedroom, madame?

MADAME ROSEPETTLE. *Which* bedroom? Why the *master* bedroom, of course. Which bedroom did you think? (*The* BELLBOYS *smile ashamedly, bow, pick up the coffin and carry it toward the master bedroom.*) Gently! (*They open the bedroom doors.* MADAME ROSEPETTLE *lowers her eyes as the blinding rays of sunlight stream from the room.*) People have no respect for coffins nowadays. They think nothing of the dead. (*Short pause*) I wonder what the dead think of them? (*Short pause*) Agh! The world is growing dismal.

(*The door to the master bedroom opens and* BELLBOYS ONE *and* TWO *reappear, coffin still in hand.*)

BELLBOY ONE. Uh—begging madame's pardon.

BELLBOY TWO. Sorry to interrupt.

MADAME ROSEPETTLE. Speak up! Speak up!

BELLBOY ONE. Well—you see—

BELLBOY TWO. Yes, you see—

BELLBOY ONE. We were curious.

BELLBOY TWO. Yes. Curious.

BELLBOY ONE. Uh—just *where* in ma-

dame's bedroom would she like it to be put?

MADAME ROSEPETTLE. Next to the *bed,* of course!

BELLBOYS ONE AND TWO. Of course. (*Exit,* BELLBOYS ONE *and* TWO.)

MADAME ROSEPETTLE. Morons!—Imbeciles. (*Enter two* BELLBOYS *carrying two large black-draped plants before them. They look about the room, then nod and walk out to the porch.*) Ah, my plants! (*They set the plants down.*) Uh—not so close together. They fight. (*The* BELLBOYS *move the plants apart.*)

(BELLBOY THREE *enters carrying a dictaphone on a silver tray and black drapes under his arm.* BELLBOYS ONE *and* TWO *exit fearfully from the master bedroom.*)

HEAD BELLBOY. The dictaphone, madame.

MADAME ROSEPETTLE. Ah, splendid.

HEAD BELLBOY. Where would madame like it to be put?

MADAME ROSEPETTLE. Oh, great gods, are you all the same? The center table, naturally. One never dictates one's memoirs from *anywhere* but the center of a room. Any nincompoop knows that.

HEAD BELLBOY. It must have slipped my mind.

MADAME ROSEPETTLE. You flatter yourself.

HEAD BELLBOY. Will there be something else?

MADAME ROSEPETTLE. Will there be something else, he asks? *Will there be something else? Of course* there'll be something ese. There's *always* something else. That's one of the troubles with Life.

HEAD BELLBOY. Sorry, madame.

MADAME ROSEPETTLE. Yes, so am I. (*Pause*) Oh, this talk is getting us nowhere. Words are precious. On bellboys they're a waste. And so far you have thoroughly wasted my time. Now to begin:—

HEAD BELLBOY. Madame, I'm afraid this must end.

MADAME ROSEPETTLE (*incredulously*). I —beg your pardon?

HEAD BELLBOY. I said this must end! I and *not* a *common* bellboy, madame—I'm a lieutenant. (Notice the stripes if you will.) I am a lieutenant, madame. And being a lieutenant am in charge of other bellboys and therefore entitled, I think, to a little more respect from you.

MADAME ROSEPETTLE. Well—*you* may consider yourself a lieutenant, lieutenant, but *I* consider you a *bore!* If you're going to insist upon pulling rank, however, I'll have you know that I am a Tourist. (Notice the money if you will.) I am a Tourist, my boy.—And being a Tourist am in charge of you. Remember that and I'll mail you another stripe when I leave. As for "respect," we'll have no time for *that* around here. We've got too many important things to do. Right, Albert?

JONATHAN. Ra-ra-ra-rrrright.

MADAME ROSEPETTLE. Now, to begin: you may pick up the drapes which were so ingeniously dropped in a lump on my table, carry them into the master bedroom and tack them over my window panes. I don't wear black in the tropics for my health, my boy. I'm in mourning. And while I'm here in Port Royale, no single speck of sunlight shall enter and brighten the mournful gloom of my heart —at least, not while I'm in my bedroom. Well, go on, lieutenant, go on. Forward to the field of battle, head high. Tack the drapes across my windows and when my room is black, call me in.

HEAD BELLBOY (*weakly*). Yes, madame. (*He picks up the drapes and leaves.*)

MADAME ROSEPETTLE. In Buenos Aires the lieutenant clicked his heels when leaving. That's the trouble with these revolutionaries. No regard for the duties of rank. Remind me, Edward, to have this man fired, first thing in the morning. He'll never do.

(JONATHAN *takes a pad of paper out of his pocket and writes with a pencil he has tied on a chain about his neck. Enter* BELLBOYS ONE *and* FIVE *carrying miniature treasure chests.*)

BELLBOY FIVE. The stamp collection, madame.

MADAME ROSEPETTLE. Ah, Robinson! Your fantastic stamp collection. Look! It's arrived.

BELLBOY ONE. Where would madame like it put?

MADAME ROSEPETTLE. Where would you like it put, my love?

JONATHAN. Uh—uh—uh—

MADAME ROSEPETTLE. Now—now, let's not start stammering again. You know what I think of it.

JONATHAN. Ummmm—

MADAME ROSEPETTLE. My dear, what is wrong with your tongue?

JONATHAN. Uhhhh—

MADAME ROSEPETTLE. But they're *only* bellboys.

JONATHAN. Ummmm—

(*Enter* BELLBOYS TWO *and* THREE, *also with miniature treasure chests.*)

BELLBOY TWO. The coin collection, madame. Where would you like it put?

MADAME ROSEPETTLE. Edward, your fabulous collection of coins has just arrived as well. *Now*—where would you like it put?

JONATHAN. Ummmm—

MADAME ROSEPETTLE. Oh, great gods! Can't you for once talk like a normal human being without showering the room with your inarticulate spit!?

JONATHAN. I-I-I-I—I—da—da—

MADAME ROSEPETTLE. Oh, very well. Very well— If you can't muster the nerve to answer—stick out your paw and point.

(*He thrusts out his trembling hand and points to a large set of transparent drawers held by an elegant gold frame.*)

JONATHAN. If—if—they would—be so kind.

MADAME ROSEPETTLE. Of course they would! They're *bellboys*. Remember that. It's your first Lesson in Life for the day. (*To the* BELLBOYS.) No! Don't get the stamps in with the coins. They stick!

HEAD BELLBOY (*he returns from the master bedroom*). I'm terribly sorry to disturb you, madame, but I find that— that I don't seem to have a—uh—

MADAME ROSEPETTLE. I wondered when you'd ask. (*She takes a huge hammer out of her purse and hands it to him.*)

HEAD BELLBOY (*ashamedly*). Thank you —madame. (*He turns nervously and starts to leave.*)

MADAME ROSEPETTLE (*cuttingly*). Bellboy? (*He stops.*) The nails.

HEAD BELLBOY. Yes, of course. How foolish of me.

MADAME ROSEPETTLE (*she reaches into her purse again and takes out a fistful of nails which she promptly dumps in his hands*). Keep the extras. (*He exits, once more, into the master bedroom.*) In Buenos Aires the lieutenant came equipped with a pneumatic drill. *That's* what I call service. Remind me, Robinson darling, to have this man barred from all hotels, everywhere. *Everywhere.* (JONATHAN *scratches a large "X" on his pad.*

The other BELLBOYS *have now finished putting the stamps and coins away.* MADAME ROSEPETTLE *goes over and dips her hand in the box. To* BELLBOY TWO) Here, for your trouble: a little something. It's a Turkish piaster—1876. Good year for piasters. (*To* BELLBOY FIVE) And for you a—a 1739 Danzig gulden. Worth a fortune, my boy. A *small* fortune, I will admit, but nevertheless a fortune. (*To* BELLBOY THREE) And for you we have a—a—1962 DIME!! *Edward*—what is a dime doing in here? Fegh! (*She flings the dime to the ground as if it had been handled by lepers. The* BELLBOYS *leap to get it.*)

JONATHAN (*sadly*). Some—some—some day—it will be—as rare as the others.

MADAME ROSEPETTLE. Some day! *Some day!* That's the trouble with you, Robinson. Always an optimist. I trust you have no more such currency contaminating your fabulous collection. H'm, Albert? Do I assume correctly? H'm? Do I? H'm? Do I? H'm? Do I?

JONATHAN. Ya—yes.

MADAME ROSEPETTLE. Splendid. Then I'll give you your surprise for the day.

JONATHAN. Na—now?

MADAME ROSEPETTLE. Yes, now.

JONATHAN. In—in—front of—*them?*

MADAME ROSEPETTLE. Turn your backs, bellboys. (*She digs into her handbag and picks out a coin in a velvet box.*) Here, Edward, my sweet. The rarest of all coins for your rarest of all collections. A 1572 Javanese Yen-Sen.

JONATHAN (*excitedly*). How—how many—were—were minted?

MADAME ROSEPETTLE. None.

JONATHAN. Na—none?

MADAME ROSEPETTLE. I made it myself. (*She squeezes his hand.*) ·So glad you like it. (*To the* BELLBOYS.) You may turn around now. (*The sound of a hammer is heard offstage.*) If you must bang like that, my boy, then please bang with some sort of rhythm. Oh, the lieutenant in Buenos Aires, remember him, Robinson? How he shook when he drilled. I fairly danced that day. (*She begins to dance, the other* BELLBOYS *clapping in rhythm.*) That's enough. That's enough. (*She stops.*)

BELLBOY FOUR (*he enters pushing a huge treasure chest, on rollers*). The, uh —book collection, madame.

(JONATHAN *leaps up in glee.*)

MADAME ROSEPETTLE. Albert, *look.* Albert! *Look!* Your unbelievable collection of books. *It's arrived.*

JONATHAN. Ca—ca—could they—open it—I—I-I wonder?

MADAME ROSEPETTLE. You want to see them, eh Albert? You really want to see them again? That badly? You really want to see them again, that badly?

JONATHAN Yyyyyyessssss.

MADAME ROSEPETTLE. Then let the trunk be opened.

(*They open the trunk. Hundreds of books fall onto the floor.* JONATHAN *falls on top of them like a starved man upon food.*)

JONATHAN (*emotionally*). Tra-Tra-Trollope — Ha-Haggard — Daudet — Ga-Ga-Gautier—ma-mmmmy old—fffriends. La—lllook at them all. Sh-Sh-Sholokhov—Alain-Fournier — Alighieri — Turturturgenev. My—old friends. (*He burrows into them, reading to himself in wild abandon.*)

MADAME ROSEPETTLE (*coldly*). All right, Albert, that's enough.

(*He looks up bewildered. She stares at him disapprovingly.*)

JONATHAN. But—

MADAME ROSEPETTLE. That's enough— Get up, get up— Come, off your knees. Rise from your books and sing of love.

JONATHAN. But I—I can't sing.

MADAME ROSEPETTLE. Well, stand up anyway. (*He rises sadly. Short pause*) All right! Now where's Rosalinda.

THE NEAREST BELLBOY. Who?

MADAME ROSEPETTLE. My fish. I want my fish. Who has my fish?

A VOICE (*from outside the door*). I have it, madame.

(*Enter* BELLBOY TWO *carrying, at arms' length, an object covered by a black cloth. He wears large, thick, well-padded gloves —the sort a snake trainer might wear when handling a newly caught cobra.*)

MADAME ROSEPETTLE. Ah, splendid. Bring it here. Put it here, by the dictaphone. Near my memoirs. Bring it here, bellboy. But set it gently, if you will. (*He sets it down.*) Now. The black shawl of mourning, bellboy. Remove it, if you will. But gently. Gently. Gently as she goes. (*The* BELLBOY *lifts off the shawl. Revealed is a fish bowl with a fish and a cat's skeleton inside.*) Ah, I see you fed it today. (*She reaches into her handbag and extracts a pair of long tongs. She plucks the skeleton from the fish bowl.*) Siamese, I presume.

BELLBOY TWO. No, madame. Alley.

MADAME ROSEPETTLE. *WHAT!?* A common alley cat? Just who do you think I am? What kind of fish do you think I have? *Alley cat? Alley cat? Indeed.* In Buenos Aires, I'll have you know, Rosalinda was fed nothing but Siamese *kittens,* which are even more tender than Siamese cats. *That's* what I call consideration! Edward, make note: we will dismiss this creature from the bellboy squad *first thing in the morning!*

(JONATHAN *scribbles on his pad.*)

BELLBOY TWO. Madame, please, there were no Siamese cats.

MADAME ROSEPETTLE. There are *always* Siamese cats!

BELLBOY TWO. Not in Port Royale.

MADAME ROSEPETTLE. Then you should have flown to Buenos Aires. I would have paid the way. Give me back your Turkish piaster. (*He hands back the coin.*) No. Never mind. Keep it. It's not worth a thing except in Istanbul, and hardly a soul uses anything but traveler's checks there anyhow! Shows you should never trust me.

BELLBOY TWO. Madame, *please.* I have a wife.

MADAME ROSEPETTLE. And *I* have a fish. I dare say there are half a million men in Port Royale with wives. But show me one person with a silver piranha fish and then you'll be showing me something. Your marital status does not impress me, sir. You are common, do you hear? Common! While my piranha fish is *rare.*

ROSALINDA THE FISH (*sadly*). Glump.

MADAME ROSEPETTLE. Oh, dear thing. You can just tell she's not feeling up to snuff. *Someone will pay for this!*

HEAD BELLBOY (*enters from the bedroom*). Well, I'm finished.

MADAME ROSEPETTLE. You certainly are.

HEAD BELLBOY. I beg your pardon?

MADAME ROSEPETTLE. Edward, make note. First thing in the morning we speak to the chef. Subject: Siamese cats—kittens if possible, though I seriously doubt it here. And make a further note, Albert my darling. Let's see if we can't get our cats on the American plan, while we're at it.

(JONATHAN *scribbles on his pad of paper.*)

HEAD BELLBOY. Madame, is there something I can—

MADAME ROSEPETTLE. QUIET! And put that hammer down. (*He puts it down. She puts it back in her purse.*) You have all behaved rudely. If the sunset over Guanabacoa Bay were not so full of magenta and wisteria blue I'd leave this place tonight. But the sunset *is* full of magenta and wisteria blue, and so I think I'll stay. Therefore, beware. Madame Rosepettle will have much to do. She won't have time for hiring and firing people like you. Right, Robinson? (JONATHAN *opens his mouth to speak but no words come out.*) I said, *right, Robinson?* (*Again he tries to speak, and again no words come out.*) RIGHT, ROBINSON!? (*He nods.*) There's your answer. Now get out and leave us alone. (*They start to exit.*) No. Wait. (*They stop.*) A question before you go. That yacht in the harbor.

HEAD BELLBOY. *Which* yacht in the harbor?

MADAME ROSEPETTLE The pink one, of course—187 feet long, I'd judge. Who owns it?

HEAD BELLBOY. Why, Commodore Roseabove, madame. It's a pretty sloop.

MADAME ROSEPETTLE (*distantly.*) Roseabove. *Roseabove*—I like that name.

HEAD BELLBOY. Madame realizes, of course, it's the largest yacht at the island.

MADAME ROSEPETTLE. It's also the largest yacht in Haiti, Puerto Rico, Bermuda, the Dominican Republic and West Palm Beach. I haven't checked the Virgin Islands yet. I thought I'd leave them till last. But I doubt if I'll find a larger one there. I take great pleasure, you see, in measuring yachts. My hobby, you might say. (*The* BELLBOYS *exit.*) Edward, make note. First thing in the morning we re-staff this hotel. (JONATHAN *scribbles on his pad of paper.* MADAME ROSEPETTLE *walks over to the French windows and stares wistfully out. There is a short silence before she speaks. Dreamily, with a slight smile*) Roseabove. I like that name.

ROSALINDA THE FISH (*gleefully*). Gleep.

MADAME ROSEPETTLE (*fondly*). Ah, listen. My lovely little fish. She, too, is feeling better already. She, too. You can tell—you can tell. (MADAME ROSEPETTLE

*who is now standing beside her fish,
picks up the mouthpiece of her dictaphone.) My Memoirs.* Port Royale—Part
One—The Arrival. (*Pause, while she
thinks of what to say*) Sorry to say, once
again, nothing unusual to report.

(*The lights now begin to fade on* MA-
DAME ROSEPETTLE *as* JONATHAN, *standing
alone by the porch, sneaks out a little
ways and peeks down at the streets below.
As carnival music is heard, the lights
fade.*)

SCENE TWO

*The place is the same. The time, two
weeks later.* JONATHAN *is in the room with*
ROSALIE, *a girl some two years older than
he and dressed in sweet girlish pink.*

———

ROSALIE. But if you've been here two
weeks, why haven't I seen you?

JONATHAN. I've—I've been in my room.

ROSALIE. All the time?

JONATHAN. Yes—all the time.

ROSALIE. Well, you must get out sometimes. I mean, sometimes you simply
must get out. You just couldn't stay inside all the time—could you?

JONATHAN. Yyyyyes.

ROSALIE. You never get out at all? I
mean, never at all?

JONATHAN. Some-sometimes, I do go
out on the porch. M-Ma-Mother has some
—Venus'-flytraps which she bra-brought
back from the rain forests of Va-Va-Va-
Venezuela. They're va-very rrrrare and
need a—a lot of sunshine. Well, sir, she
ka-keeps them on the porch and I—I
feed them. Twice a day, too.

ROSALIE. Oh.

JONATHAN. Ma-Ma-Mother says everyone
must have a vocation in life. (*With a
slight nervous laugh*) I ga-guess that's—
my job.

ROSALIE. I don't think I've ever met
anyone before who's fed—uh—Venus'-
flytraps.

JONATHAN. Ma-Ma-Mother says I'm va-
very good at it. I—don't know—if—I
am, but—that's—what she says so I—
guess I am.

ROSALIE. Well, uh, what do you—feed
them? You see, I've never met anyone
before who's fed Venus'-flytraps so—that's
why I don't know what—you're supposed
to feed them.

JONATHAN (*happy that she asked*). Oh,
I fa-feed them—l-l-lots of things. Ga-ga-
green peas, chicken feathers, rubber bands.
They're—not very fussy. They're—nice,
that way. Ma-Ma-Mother says it it it ga-
gives me a feeling of a-co-co-complish-
ment. Iffff you would—like to to see
them I—could show them to you. It's—
almost fa-feeding time. It is, and—and I
could show them to you.

ROSALIE. No. That's all right. (JONATHAN
looks away, hurt.) Well, how about later?

JONATHAN. Do-do-do you ra-really ww-
wwwwant to see them?

ROSALIE. Yes. Yes, I really think I would
like to see them—later. If you'll show
them to me then, I'd really like that.
(JONATHAN *looks at her and smiles. There
is an awkward silence while he stares at
her thankfully.*) I still don't understand
why you never go out. How can you just
sit in—?

JONATHAN.   SometimeswhenI'monthe-
porchIdootherthings.

ROSALIE. *What?*

JONATHAN. Sa-sa-sometimes, when I'm
—on the porch, you know, when I'm on
the porch? Sssssssome-times I—do *other
things,* too.

ROSALIE. What sort of things? (JONA-
THAN *giggles.*) What sort of things do
you do?

JONATHAN. Other things.

ROSALIE (*coyly.*) What do you mean,
"Other things?"

JONATHAN. Other things besides feeding my mother's plants. Other things besides that. That's what I mean. Other
things besides that.

ROSALIE. What kind of things—*in particular?*

JONATHAN. Oh, watching.

ROSALIE. Watching?

JONATHAN. Yes. Like—watching.

ROSALIE. Watching what? (*He giggles.*)
Watching what?

JONATHAN. You.

(*Short pause. She inches closer to him
on the couch.*)

ROSALIE. What do you mean—watching
me?

JONATHAN. I—watch you from the
porch. That's what I mean. I watch you
from the porch. I watch you a lot, too.
Every day. It's—it's the truth. I—I swear
it—is. I watch you ev'ry day. Do you
believe me?

ROSALIE. Of course I believe you, Albert. Why—

JONATHAN. Jonathan!

ROSALIE. What?

JONATHAN. Jonathan. Ca-ca-call me Ja-Jonathan. That's my name.

ROSALIE. But your mother said your name was—

JONATHAN. Nooooo! Call—me Jonathan. Pa-pa-please?

ROSALIE. All right—Jonathan.

JONATHAN (*excitedly*). You *do* believe me! You rrrreally do believe me. I-I can tell!

ROSALIE. Of course I believe you. Why shouldn't—?

JONATHAN. You want me to tell you how I watch you? You want me to tell you? I'll bet you'll na-never guess.

ROSALIE. How?

JONATHAN. *Guess.*

ROSALIE. (*ponders*). Through a telescope?

JONATHAN. How did you guess?

ROSALIE. I—I don't know. I was just joking. I didn't really think that was—

JONATHAN. I'll bet everyone watches you through a telescope. I'll bet everyone you go out with watches you through a telescope. That's what I'll bet.

ROSALIE. No. Not at all.

JONATHAN. Well, that's how I watch you. Through a telescope.

ROSALIE. I never would have guessed that.

JONATHAN. I thought you were—ga-going to say I—I watch you with—with love in my eyes or some—thing like that. I didn't think you were going to guess that I—watch you through a telescope. I didn't think you were going to guess that I wa-watch you through a telescope on the fa-first guess, anyway. Not on the *first guess.*

ROSALIE. Well, it was just a guess.

JONATHAN (*hopefully*). Do you watch *me* through a telescope?

ROSALIE. I never knew where your room was.

JONATHAN. Now you know. Now will you watch me?

ROSALIE. Well, I—don't have a telescope.

JONATHAN (*getting more elated and excited*). You can make one. That's how I got mine. I made it. Out of lenses and tubing. That's all you need. Lenses and tubing. Do you have any lenses?

ROSALIE. No.

JONATHAN. Do you have any tubing?

ROSALIE. No.

JONATHAN. Oh. (*Pause*) Well, would you like me to tell you how I made mine in case you find some lenses and tubing? Would you like that?

ROSALIE (*disinterestedly*). Sure, Jonathan. I think that would be nice.

JONATHAN. Well, I made it out of lenses and tubing. The lenses I had because Ma-Ma-Mother gave me a set of lenses so I could see my stamps better. I have a fabulous collection of stamps, as well as a fantastic collection of coins and a simply unbelievable collection of books. Well, sir, Ma-Ma-Mother gave me these lenses so I could see my stamps better. She suspected that some were fake so she gave me the lenses so I might be—able to see. You see? Well, sir, I happen to have nearly a billion sta-stamps. So far I've looked closely at 1,352,769. I've discovered three actual fakes! Number 1,352,767 was a fake. Number 1,352,768 was a fake, and number 1,352,769 was a fake. They were stuck together. Ma-Mother made me feed them immediately to her flytraps. Well— (*He whispers.*) one day, when Mother wasn't looking—that is, when she was out, I heard an airplane flying. An airplane—somewhere—far away. It wasn't very loud, but still I heard it. An airplane. Flying—somewhere, far away. And I ran outside to the porch so that I might see what it looked like. The airplane. With hundreds of people inside it. Hundreds and hundreds and hundreds of people. And I thought to myself, if I could just see—if I could just see what they looked like, the people, sitting at their windows, looking out—and flying. If I could see— *just once*—if I could see *just once* what they looked like—then I might—know what I—what I . . . (*Slight pause*) So I —built a telescope in case the plane ever— came back again. The tubing came from an old blowgun. (*He reaches behind the bureau and produces a huge blowgun, easily a foot larger than he.*) Mother brought it back from her last hunting trip to Zanzibar. The lenses were the lenses she had given me for my stamps. So I built it. My telescope. A telescope so I might be able to see. And— (*He walks out to the porch.*) and—and I *could* see!

I could! I COULD! I really could. For miles and miles I could see. For miles and miles and *miles! (He begins to lift it up to look through but stops, for some reason, before he's brought it up to his eye.)* Only . . . *(He hands it to* ROSALIE. *She takes it eagerly and scans the horizon and the sky. She hands it back to him.)*

ROSALIE *(with annoyance).* There's nothing out there to see.

JONATHAN *(sadly).* I know. That's the trouble. You take the time to build a telescope that can sa-see for miles, then there's nothing out there to see. Ma-Mother says it's a Lesson in Life. *(Pause)* But I'm not sorry I built my telescope. And you know why? Because I saw you. Even if I didn't see anything else, I did see you. And—and I'm—very glad. *(*ROSALIE *moves slightly closer to him on the couch. She moistens her lips.)* I—I remember, you were standing across the way in your penthouse garden playing blind man's buff with ten little children. *(After a short pause, fearfully)* Are—are they by any chance—*yours?*

ROSALIE *(sweetly).* Oh, I'm not married.

JONATHAN. Oh!

ROSALIE. I'm a baby sitter.

JONATHAN *(with obvious relief).* Oh.

ROSALIE. I work for the people who own the penthouse.

JONATHAN. I've never seen them around.

ROSALIE. I've never seen them, either. They're never home. They just mail me a check every week and tell me to make sure I keep the children's names straight.

JONATHAN. If you could tell me which way they went I could find them with my telescope. It can see for miles.

ROSALIE. They must love children very much, to have so many, I mean. What a remarkable woman she must be. *(Pause)* There's going to be another one, too! Another child is coming! I got a night letter last night.

JONATHAN. By airplane?

ROSALIE. I don't know.

JONATHAN. I bet it was. I can't see at night. Ma-Mother can but I can't. I'll bet that's when the planes fly.

ROSALIE *(coyly).* If you like, I'll read you the letter. I have it with me. *(She unbuttons the top of her blouse and turns around in a coquettish manner to take the letter from her brassiere. Reading)* "Have had another child. Sent it yester-

day. Will arrive tomorrow. Call it Cynthia."

JONATHAN. That will make eleven. That's an awful lot of children to take care of. I'll bet it must be wonderful.

ROSALIE. Well, they do pay very well.

JONATHAN. They pay you?

ROSALIE. Of course— What did you think? *(Pause. Softly, seductively)* Jonathan? *(He does not answer but seems lost in thought. With a feline purr)* Jonathan?

JONATHAN. Yyyyyes?

ROSALIE. It gets very lonesome over there. The children go to sleep early and the parents are never home so I'm always alone. Perhaps—well, Jonathan, I thought that perhaps you might—visit me.

JONATHAN. Well—well—well, you—you see—I—I——

ROSALIE. We could spend the evenings together—at my place. It gets so lonesome there, you know what I mean? I mean, I don't know what to do. I get so lonesome there.

JONATHAN. Ma-ma-ma-maybe you—you can—come over—here? Maybe you you can do—that.

ROSALIE. Why are you trembling so?

JONATHAN. I'm—I'm—I'm—I'm—

ROSALIE. Are you afraid?

JONATHAN. Nnnnnnnnnnnnnnnnnnnno. Whaaaaaaaaaa—why—should I—be—afraid?

ROSALIE. Then why won't you come visit me?

JONATHAN. I—I—I—I—

ROSALIE. I don't think you're allowed to go out. That's what I think.

JONATHAN. Nnnn-o. I—I can—can—can—

ROSALIE. Why can't you go out, Jonathan? I want to know.

JONATHAN. Nnnnnnnnn—

ROSALIE. Tell me, Jonathan!

JONATHAN. I—I—

ROSALIE. I said I want to know! *Tell me.*

JONATHAN. I—I don't know. I don't know why. I mean. I've—nnnnnnnnever really thought—about going out. I—guess it's—just natural for me to—stay inside. *(He laughs nervously as if that explained everything.)* You see—I've got so much to do. I mean, all my sssssstamps and—ca-coins and books. The pa-pa-plane might fffffffly overhead while I was was going downstairs. And then thhhhere are —the plants ta-to feeeeeeed. And I enjoy vvvery much wa—watching you and all yyyyyyour chil-dren. I've—really got so ma-many things—to—do. Like—like my future, for instance. Ma-Mother says I'm going to be great. That's—that's—that's what she—says. I'm going to be great. I sssswear. Of course, she doesn't know ex-actly what I'm—going to be great in— so she sits every afternoon for—for two hours and thinks about it. Na-na-natu-rally I've—got to be here when she's thinking in case she—thinks of the an-swer. Otherwise she might forget and I'd never know—what I'm ga-going to be great in. You—see what I mean? I mean, I've—I've ggggggot so many things to do I—just couldn't possibly get *anything* done if I ever—went—outside. (*There is a silence.* JONATHAN *stares at* ROSALIE *as if he were hoping that might answer her question sufficiently. She stares back at him as if she knows there is more.*) Be-sides, Mother locks the front door.

ROSALIE. I thought so.

JONATHAN. No! You-you don't under-stand. It's not what you think. She doesn't lock the door to ka-ka-keep me in, which would be malicious. She—locks the door so I can't get out, which is for my own good and therefore—beneficent.

CUCKOO CLOCK (*from the master bed-room*). Cuckoo! Cuckoo! Cuckoo!

ROSALIE. What's that?

JONATHAN (*fearfully*). A warning.

ROSALIE. What do you mean, a warn-ing?

JONATHAN. A warning that you have to go. Your time is up.

ROSALIE. My time is what?

JONATHAN. Your time is up. You have to go. Now. At once. Right away. You can't stay any longer. You've got to go!

ROSALIE. Why?

JONATHAN (*puzzled; as if this were the first time the question had ever occurred to him*). I don't really know.

CUCKOO CLOCK (*louder*). Cuckoo! Cuckoo! Cuckoo!

(JONATHAN *freezes in terror.* ROSALIE *looks at him calmly.*)

ROSALIE. Why did your mother ask me to come up here?

JONATHAN. What?

ROSALIE. Why did your mother ask me—?

JONATHAN. So I—I could meet you.

ROSALIE. Then why didn't you ask me yourself? Something's wrong around here, Jonathan. I don't understand why you didn't ask me yourself.

JONATHAN. Ma-Mother's so much bet-ter at those things.

CUCKOO CLOCK (*very loudly*). CUCK-OO! CUCKOO! CUCKOO!

JONATHAN. You've got to get out of here! That's the third warning. (*He starts to push her toward the door.*)

ROSALIE. Will you call me on the phone?

JONATHAN. Please, you've got to go!

ROSALIE. Instead of your mother telling me to come, will you come and get me yourself? Will you at least call me? Wave to me?

JONATHAN. Yes-yes—I'll do that. Now get out of here!

ROSALIE. I want you to promise to come and see me again.

JONATHAN. Get out!

ROSALIE (*coyly*). Promise me.

JONATHAN. GET OUT! (*He pushes her toward the door.*)

ROSALIE. Why do you keep looking at that door?

JONATHAN (*almost in tears*). *Please.*

ROSALIE. Why do you keep looking at that door?

JONATHAN. *Please!* You've got to go be-fore it's too late!

ROSALIE. There's something very wrong here. I want to see what's behind that door. (*She starts toward the master bed-room.* JONATHAN *throws his arms about her legs and collapses at her feet, his face buried against her thighs.*)

JONATHAN (*sobbing uncontrollably*). I love you.

(ROSALIE *stops dead in her tracks and stares down at* JONATHAN.)

ROSALIE. What did you say?

JONATHAN. I-I-I llllllllove you. I love you, I love you, I love you, I— (*The* CUCKOO CLOCK *screams, cackles, and goes out of its mind, its call ending in a crazed, strident rasp as if it had broken all its springs, screws and innards. The door to the master bedroom opens.* MADAME ROSEPETTLE *appears. Weakly*) Too late.

MADAME ROSEPETTLE. Two warnings are enough for any man. Three are enough for any woman. The cuckoo struck three times and then a fourth and still she's here. May I ask why?

ROSALIE. You've been listening at the keyhole, haven't you!

MADAME ROSEPETTLE. I'm talking to my son, harlot!

ROSALIE. What did you say!

MADAME ROSEPETTLE. Harlot, I called you! Slut, scum, sleazy prostitute catching and caressing children and men. Stroking their hearts. I've seen you.

ROSALIE. What are you talking about?

MADAME ROSEPETTLE. Blind man's buff with the children in the garden. The red-headed one—fifteen, I think. Behind the bush while the others cover their eyes. Up with the skirt, one-two-three and it's done. Don't try to deny it. I've seen you in action. I know your kind.

ROSALIE. That's a lie!

MADAME ROSEPETTLE. Life is a lie, my sweet. Not words but Life itself. Life in all its ugliness. It builds green trees that tease your eyes and draw you under them. Then when you're there in the shade and you breathe in and say, "Oh God, how beautiful," that's when the bird on the branch lets go his droppings and hits you on the head. Life, my sweet, beware. It isn't what it seems. I've seen what it can do. I've watched you dance.

ROSALIE. What do you mean by that?

MADAME ROSEPETTLE. Last night in the ballroom. I've watched you closely and I know what I see. You danced too near those men and you let them do too much. Don't try to deny it. Words will only make it worse. It would be best for all concerned if you left at once and never came again. Good day. (MADAME ROSE-PETTLE turns to leave. ROSALIE does not move.)

ROSALIE. Why don't you let Jonathan out of his room?

MADAME ROSEPETTLE. Who?

ROSALIE. Jonathan.

MADAME ROSEPETTLE. Who?

ROSALIE. Your son.

MADAME ROSEPETTLE. You mean Albert? Is that who you mean? Albert?

JONATHAN. Pa-pa-please do-don't.

MADAME ROSEPETTLE. Is that who you mean, slut? H'm? Speak up? Is that who you mean?

ROSALIE. I mean your son.

MADAME ROSEPETTLE. *I don't let him out because he is my son.* I don't let him

out because his skin is as white as fresh snow and he would burn if the sun struck him. I don't let him out because outside there are trees with birds sitting on their branches waiting for him to walk beneath. I don't let him out because you're there, waiting behind the bushes with your skirt up. I don't let him out because he is *susceptible.* That's why. Because he is *susceptible.* Susceptible to trees and to sluts and to sunstroke.

ROSALIE. Then why did you come and get me?

MADAME ROSEPETTLE. Because, my dear, my stupid son has been watching you through that stupid telescope he made. Because, in short, he wanted to meet you and I, in short, wanted him to know what you were really like. Now that he's seen, you may go.

ROSALIE. And if I choose to stay? (*Pause.*)

MADAME ROSEPETTLE (*softly; slyly*). Can you cook?

ROSALIE. Yes.

MADAME ROSEPETTLE. How well?

ROSALIE. Fairly well.

MADAME ROSEPETTLE. Not good enough! My son is a connoisseur. A connoisseur, do you hear? I cook him the finest foods in the world. Recipes no one knows exist. Food, my sweet, is the finest of arts. And since you can't cook you are artless. You nauseate my son's aesthetic taste. Do you like cats?

ROSALIE. Yes.

MADAME ROSEPETTLE. What kind of cats?

ROSALIE. Any kind of cats.

MADAME ROSEPETTLE. Alley cats?

ROSALIE. Especially alley cats.

MADAME ROSEPETTLE. I thought so. Go, my dear. Find yourself some weeping willow and set yourself beneath it. Cry of your lust for my son and wait, for a mocking bird waits above to deposit his verdict on your whorish head. My son is as white as fresh snow and you are tainted with sin. You are garnished with garlic and turn our tender stomachs in disgust.

ROSALIE. Why did you come to Port Royale?

MADAME ROSEPETTLE. To find *you!*

ROSALIE. And now that you've found me—?

MADAME ROSEPETTLE. I throw you out!

I toss you into the garbage can! I heard everything, you know. So don't try to call. The phone is in my room—*and no one goes into my room but me.* (*She stares at* ROSALIE *for a moment, then exits with a flourish.* ROSALIE *and* JONATHAN *move slowly toward each other. When they are almost together,* MADAME ROSE-PETTLE *reappears.*) One more thing. If, by some chance, the eleventh child named Cynthia turns out to be a Siamese cat, give it to me. I, too, pay well.

(MADAME ROSEPETTLE *turns toward her room.* ROSALIE *starts toward the door.* JONATHAN *grabs her hand in desperation.*)

JONATHAN (*in a whisper*). Come back again. Pa-please—come back again.

(*For a moment* ROSALIE *stops and looks at* JONATHAN. *But* MADAME ROSEPETTLE *stops too, and turning, looks back at both of them, a slight smile on her lips.* ROSA-LIE, *sensing her glance, walks toward the door, slipping from* JONATHAN'S *out-stretched hands as she does. The lights fade about* JONATHAN, *alone in the center of the room.*)

CURTAIN

SCENE THREE

The hotel room at night, one week later. JONATHAN *is alone in the living room. He is sitting in a chair near the fish bowl, staring at nothing in particular with a particularly blank expression on his face. A clock is heard ticking softly in the distance. For an interminably long time it continues to tick while* JONATHAN *sits in his chair, motionless. After a while the ticking speeds up almost impercepti-bly and soon after, laughter is heard. At first it is a giggle from the rear of the theatre, then a cough from the side, then a self-conscious laugh from the other side, then a full, gusty belly-roar from all cor-ners of the theatre. Soon the entire world is hysterical. Cuban drums begin to beat. Fireworks explode. Orgiastic music is heard.* JONATHAN *continues to sit, mo-tionless. Only his eyes have begun to move. The clock continues to tick. The laughter grows louder: the laughter of the insane. Suddenly* JONATHAN *leaps up and rushes to the French windows, his*

fingers pressed against his ears. He slams the French windows shut. The noises stop. JONATHAN *closes his eyes and sighs with relief. The French windows sway unsteadily on their hinges. They tip for-ward. They fall to the floor. They shatter. The laughter returns.* JONATHAN *stares down at them in horror. The* VENUS'-FLY-TRAPS *grow larger and growl.*

VENUS'-FLYTRAPS (*viciously*). Grrrrrrrr.

(*The piranha fish stares hungrily from its bowl.*)

ROSALINDA THE FISH (*more viciously*). Grarrgh!

(*The* FLYTRAPS *lunge at* JONATHAN *but he walks dazedly past, unaware of their snapping petals, and goes out to the edge of the balcony. He stares out in complete bewilderment. The laughter and music of a carnival, the sounds of* PEOPLE *danc-ing in the streets fill the air. He looks down at them sadly. Meekly he waves. The sounds immediately grow softer and the* PEOPLE *begin to drift away. He watches as they leave. Behind him the* FLYTRAPS *keep growing and reaching out for him, but of this he is unaware. He only stands at the railing, looking down. A last lingering laugh is heard somewhere in the distance, echoing. The door to the suite opens. The* BELLBOYS *enter and set a small table, two small chairs, a cham-pagne bottle and ice bucket, and a small vase with one wilting rose. They spray the room with an atomizer. They exit, except for a* VIOLINIST. *The lights fade in the room and only the table is lit. The music grows in brilliance. The* COMMODORE *and* MADAME ROSEPETTLE *waltz into the room. A spot of light follows them about the floor.*)

THE COMMODORE. How lovely it was this evening, madame, don't you think? (*She laughs softly and demurely and discreetly lowers her eyes. They waltz about the floor.*) How gentle the wind was, ma-dame. And the stars, how clear and bright they were, don't you think? (*She turns her face away and smiles softly. They begin to whirl about the floor.*) Ah, the waltz. How exquisite it is, madame, don't you think? *One*-two-three, *one*-two-three, *one*-two-three. Ahhhhh, madame, how classically simple. How stark; how strong —how romantic—how sublime. (*She gig-gles girlishly. They whirl madly about the floor.*) Oh, if only **madame** knew how I've waited for this moment. If only madame knew how long. How this week, these nights, the nights we shared together on my yacht; the warm, wonderful nights, the almost-perfect nights, the would-have-been-perfect nights had it not been for the crew peeking through the portholes. Ah, those nights, madame, those nights; almost alone but never quite; but now, tonight, at last, we *are* alone. And now, madame, now we are ready for romance. For the night was made for love. And tonight, madame— we will love.

MADAME ROSEPETTLE (*with the blush of innocence*). Oh, Commodore, how you do talk.

(*They whirl about the room as the lilting rhythm of the waltz grows and sweeps on and on.*)

THE COMMODORE (*suavely*). Madame, may I kiss you?

MADAME ROSEPETTLE. Why?

THE COMMODORE (*after recovering from the abruptness of the question*). Your lips . . . are a thing of beauty.

MADAME ROSEPETTLE. My lips, Commodore, are the color of blood. (*She smiles at him. He stares blankly ahead. They dance on.*) I must say, you dance exceptionally well, Commodore—for a man your age.

THE COMMODORE (*bristling*). I dance with *you,* madame. That is why I dance well. For to dance with you, madame— is to hold you.

MADAME ROSEPETTLE. Well, I don't mind your holding me, Commodore, but at the moment you happen to be holding me too tight.

THE COMMODORE. I hold you too dear to hold you too tight, madame. I hold you close, that is all. And I hold you close in the hope that my heart may feel your heart beating.

MADAME ROSEPETTLE. *One*-two-three, *one*-two-three. You're not paying enough attention to the music, Commodore. I'm afraid you've fallen out of step.

THE COMMODORE. Then lead me, madame. Take my hand and lead me wherever you wish. For I would much rather think of my words than my feet.

MADAME ROSEPETTLE (*with great sweetness*). Why certainly, Commodore. Certainly. If that is what you want—it will be my pleasure to oblige. (*They switch

hands and she begins to lead him about the floor. They whirl wildly about, spinning faster than they had when the* COMMODORE *led*.) Beautiful, isn't it, Commodore? The waltz. The Dance of Lovers. I'm so glad you enjoy it so much. (*With a gay laugh she whirls him around the floor. Suddenly he puts his arms about her shoulders and leans close to kiss her. She pulls back.*) Commodore! You were supposed to spin just then. When I squeeze you in the side it means *spin!*

THE COMMODORE (*flustered*). I—I thought it was a sign of affection.

(*She laughs.*)

MADAME ROSEPETTLE. You'll learn. (*She squeezes him in the side. He spins about under her arm.*) Ah, you're learning.

(*He continues to spin, around and around, faster and faster like a runaway top while* MADAME ROSEPETTLE, *not spinning at all, leads him about the floor, a wild smile of ecstasy spreading over her face.*)

THE COMMODORE. Ho-ho, ho-ho. Stop. I'm dizzy. Dizzy. Stop, please. Stop. Ho-ho. Stop. Dizzy. Ho-ho. Stop. Too fast. Slow. Slower. Stop. Ho-ho. Dizzy. Too dizzy. Weeeeeee! (*And then, without any warning at all, she grabs him in the middle of a spin, and kisses him. Her back is to the audience, so the* COMMODORE'S *face is visible. At first he is too dizzy to realize that his motion has been stopped. But shortly he does, and his first expression is that of shock. But the kiss is long and the shock turns into perplexity and then, finally, into panic; into fear. He struggles desperately and breaks free from her arms, gasping wildly for air. He points weakly to his chest, gasping.*) Asthma. (*His chest heaves as he gulps in air.*) Couldn't breathe. Asthmatic. Couldn't get any air. (*He gasps for air. She starts to walk toward him, slowly.*) Couldn't get any . . . air. (*She nears him. Instinctively he backs away.*) You—you surprised me—you know. Out —of breath. Wasn't—ready for that. Didn't—expect you to kiss me.

MADAME ROSEPETTLE. I know. That's why I did it. (*She laughs and puts her arm tenderly about his waist.*) Perhaps you'd prefer to sit down for a while, Commodore? Catch your breath, so to speak. Dancing can be so terribly tiring—

when you're growing old. Well, if you like, Commodore, we could just sit and talk. And perhaps—sip some pink champagne, eh? Champagne?

THE COMMODORE. Ah, champagne.

MADAME ROSEPETTLE (*she begins to walk with him toward the table*). And just for the two of us.

THE COMMODORE. Yes. The two of us. Alone.

MADAME ROSEPETTLE (*with a laugh*). Yes. All alone.

(*Exit, the* VIOLINIST.)

THE COMMODORE. At last.

MADAME ROSEPETTLE. With music in the distance.

THE COMMODORE. A waltz.

MADAME ROSEPETTLE. A *Viennese* waltz.

THE COMMODORE. The Dance of Lovers.

MADAME ROSEPETTLE (*she takes his hand, tenderly*). Yes, Commodore. The Dance of Lovers. (*They look at each other in silence.*)

THE COMMODORE. Madame, you have won my heart. And easily.

MADAME ROSEPETTLE. No, Commodore. You have lost it. *Easily.* (*She smiles seductively. The room darkens till only a single spot of light falls upon the table set in the middle of the room. The waltz plays on.* MADAME ROSEPETTLE *nods to the* COMMODORE *and he goes to sit. But before he can pull his chair out, it slides out under its own power. He places himself and the chair slides back in, as if some invisible waiter had been holding it in his invisible hands.* MADAME ROSEPETTLE *smiles sweetly and, pulling out her chair herself, sits. They stare at each other in silence. The waltz plays softly. The* COMMODORE *reaches across the table and touches her hand. A thin smile spreads across her lips. When finally they speak, their words are soft; the whispered thoughts of lovers.*) Champagne?

THE COMMODORE. Champagne.

MADAME ROSEPETTLE. Pour?

THE COMMODORE. Please.

(*She lifts the bottle out of the ice bucket and pours with her right hand, her left being clasped firmly in the* COMMODORE'S *passionate hands. They smile serenely at each other. She lifts her glass. He lifts his. The music swells.*)

MADAME ROSEPETTLE. A toast?

THE COMMODORE. To you.

MADAME ROSEPETTLE. No, Commodore, to you.

THE COMMODORE. No, madame. To us.

MADAME ROSEPETTLE *and* THE COMMODORE (*together*). To us. (*They raise their glasses. They gaze wistfully into each other's eyes. The music builds to brilliance. The* COMMODORE *clicks his glass against* MADAME ROSEPETTLE'S *glass. The glasses break.*)

THE COMMODORE (*furiously mopping up the mess*). Pardon, madame! Pardon!

MADAME ROSEPETTLE (*flicking some glass off her bodice*). Pas de quoi, monsieur.

THE COMMODORE. *J'étais emporté par l'enthousiasme du moment.*

MADAME ROSEPETTLE (*extracting pieces of glass from her lap*). Pas de quoi. (*She snaps her fingers gaily. Immediately a* WAITER *appears from the shadows with a table in his hands. It is already covered with a table cloth, two champagne glasses, two candelabras [the candles already flickering in them], and a vase with one wilting rose protruding. Another* WAITER *whisks the wet table away. The new table is placed. The* WAITERS *disappear into the shadows.* MADAME ROSEPETTLE *lifts the bottle of champagne out of the ice bucket.*) Encore?

THE COMMODORE. *S'il vous plait.* (*She pours. They lift their glasses in toast. The music swells again.*) To us.

MADAME ROSEPETTLE. To us, Monsieur —Commodore. (*They clink their glasses lightly. The* COMMODORE *closes his eyes and sips.* MADAME ROSEPETTLE *holds her glass before her lips, poised but not touching; waiting. She watches him. Softly*) Tell me about yourself.

THE COMMODORE. My heart is speaking, madame. Doesn't it tell you enough?

MADAME ROSEPETTLE. Your heart, monsieur, is growing old. It speaks with a murmur. Its words are too weak to understand.

THE COMMODORE. But the feeling, madame, is still strong.

MADAME ROSEPETTLE. Feelings are for animals, monsieur. Words are the specialty of Man. Tell me what your heart has to say.

THE COMMODORE. My heart says it loves you.

MADAME ROSEPETTLE. And how many others, monsieur, has your heart said this to?

THE COMMODORE. None but you, madame. None but you.

MADAME ROSEPETTLE. And pray, monsieur, just what is it that I've done to make you love me so?

THE COMMODORE. Nothing, madame. And that is why. You are a strange woman, you see. You go out with me and you know how I feel. Yet, I know nothing of you. You disregard me, madame, but never discourage. You treat my love with indifference—but never disdain. You've led me on, madame. That is what I mean to say.

MADAME ROSEPETTLE. I've led you to my room, monsieur. That is all.

THE COMMODORE. To me, that is enough.

MADAME ROSEPETTLE. I know. That's why I did it.

(*The music swells. She smiles distantly. There is a momentary silence.*)

THE COMMODORE (*with desperation*). Madame, I must ask you something. Why are you here? (*Short pause.*)

MADAME ROSEPETTLE. Well, I have to be somewhere, don't I?

THE COMMODORE. But why here, where I am? Why in Port Royale?

MADAME ROSEPETTLE. You flatter yourself, monsieur. I am in Port Royale only because Port Royale was in my way. . . . I think I'll move on tomorrow.

THE COMMODORE. For—home?

MADAME ROSEPETTLE (*laughing slightly*). Only the very young and the very old have homes. I am neither. So I have none.

THE COMMODORE. But—surely you must come from somewhere.

MADAME ROSEPETTLE. Nowhere you've ever been.

THE COMMODORE. I've been many places.

MADAME ROSEPETTLE (*softly*). But not many enough. (*She picks up her glass of champagne and sips, a distant smile on her lips.*)

THE COMMODORE (*with sudden, overwhelming and soul-rending passion*). Madame, don't go tomorrow. Stay. My heart is yours.

MADAME ROSEPETTLE. How much is it worth?

THE COMMODORE. A fortune, madame.

MADAME ROSEPETTLE. Good. I'll take it in cash.

THE COMMODORE. But the heart goes with it, madame.

MADAME ROSEPETTLE. And you with the heart, I suppose?

THE COMMODORE. Forever.

MADAME ROSEPETTLE. Sorry, monsieur. The money's enticing and the heart would have been nice, but you, I'm afraid, are a bit too bulky to make it all worth while.

THE COMMODORE. You jest, madame.

MADAME ROSEPETTLE. I never jest, monsieur. There isn't enough time.

THE COMMODORE. Then you make fun of my passion, madame, which is just as bad.

MADAME ROSEPETTLE. But, monsieur, I've never taken your passion seriously enough to make fun of it.

THE COMMODORE (*there is a short pause. The* COMMODORE *sinks slowly back in his seat. Weakly, sadly*). Then why have you gone out with me?

MADAME ROSEPETTLE. So that I might drink champagne with you tonight.

THE COMMODORE. That makes no sense.

MADAME ROSEPETTLE. It makes *perfect* sense.

THE COMMODORE. Not to me.

MADAME ROSEPETTLE. It does to me.

THE COMMODORE. But *I* don't understand. And I *want* to understand.

MADAME ROSEPETTLE. Don't worry, Commodore. You will.

THE COMMODORE. When?

MADAME ROSEPETTLE. Soon.

THE COMMODORE. How soon?

MADAME ROSEPETTLE. Very soon. (*He stares at her in submissive confusion. Suddenly, with final desperation, he grabs her hands in his and, leaning across the table, kisses them passionately, sobbingly. In a scarcely audible whisper*) Now.

THE COMMODORE. Madame—I love you. Forever. Don't you understand? (*He kisses her hands again. A smile of triumph spreads across her face.*) Oh, your husband— He must have been—a wonderful man—to have deserved a woman such as you. (*He sobs and kisses her hands again.*)

MADAME ROSEPETTLE (*nonchalantly*). Would you like to see him?

THE COMMODORE. A snapshot?

MADAME ROSEPETTLE. No. My husband. He's inside in the closet. I had him stuffed. Wonderful taxidermist I know. H'm? What do you say, Commodore?

Wanna peek? He's my very favorite trophy. I take him with me wherever I go.

THE COMMODORE (*shaken. Not knowing what to make of it*). Hah-hah, hah-hah. Yes. Very good. Very funny. Sort of a—um—*white elephant,* you might say.

MADAME ROSEPETTLE. *You* might say.

THE COMMODORE. Well, it's—certainly very—courageous of you, a—a woman still in mourning, to—to be able to laugh at what most other women wouldn't find —well, shall we say—funny.

MADAME ROSEPETTLE. Life, my dear Commodore, is never funny. It's grim! It's there every morning breathing in your face the moment you open your red baggy eyes. Life, Mr. Roseabove, is a husband hanging from a hook in the closet. Open the door too quickly and your whole day's shot to hell. But open the door just a little ways, sneak your hand in, pull out your dress and your day is made. Yet he's still there, and waiting—and sooner or later the moth balls are gone and you have to clean house. Oh, it's a bad day, Commodore, when you have to stare Life in the face, and you will find he doesn't smile at all; just hangs there—with his tongue sticking out.

THE COMMODORE. I—don't find this—very funny.

MADAME ROSEPETTLE. Sorry. I was hoping it would give you a laugh.

THE COMMODORE. I don't think it's funny at all. And the reason that I don't think it's funny at all is that it's not my kind of joke. One must respect the dead.

MADAME ROSEPETTLE. Then tell me, Commodore—why not the living, too? (*Pause. She lifts out the bottle of champagne and pours herself some more.*)

THE COMMODORE (*weakly, with a trace of fear*). How—how did he die?

MADAME ROSEPETTLE. Why, I killed him, of course. Champagne? (*She smiles sweetly and fills his glass. She raises hers in toast.*) To your continued good health. (*He stares at her blankly. The music swells in the background.*) Ah, the waltz, monsieur. Listen. The waltz. The Dance of Lovers. Beautiful—*don't you think?*

(*She laughs and sips some more champagne. The music grows to brilliance. The* COMMODORE *starts to rise from his chair.*)

THE COMMODORE. Forgive me, madame. But—I find I must leave. Urgent busi-

ness calls. Good evening. (*He tries to push his chair back, but for some reason it will not move. He looks about in panic. He pushes frantically. It does not move. It is as if the invisible waiter who had come and slid the chair out when he went to sit down, now stood behind the chair and held it in so he could not get up. And as there are arms on the chair, the* COMMODORE *cannot slide out at the sides.* MADAME ROSEPETTLE *smiles.*)

MADAME ROSEPETTLE. Now you don't *really* want to leave—do you, Commodore? After all, the night is still so young—and you haven't even seen my husband yet. Besides, there's a little story I still must tell you. A bedtime story. A fairy tale full of handsome princes and enchanted maidens; full of love and joy and music; tenderness and charm. It's my very favorite story, you see. And I never leave a place without telling it to at least one person. So please, Commodore, won't you stay? . . . *Just for a little while?* (*He stares at her in horror. He tries once more to push his chair back. But the chair does not move. He sinks down into it weakly. She leans across the table and tenderly touches his hand.*) Good. I knew you'd see it my way. It would have been such a shame if you'd had to leave. For you see, Commodore, we are, in a way, united. We share something in common—you and I. We share desire. For you desire me, with love in your heart. While I, my dear Commodore—desire your heart. (*She smiles sweetly and sips some more champagne.*) How simple it all is, in the end. (*She rises slowly from her chair and walks over to him. She runs her hands lovingly through his hair and down the back of his neck. The light on the table dims slightly.* MADAME ROSEPETTLE *walks slowly away. A spot of light follows her as she goes. Light on the table fades more. The* COMMODORE *sits, motionless.*) His name was Albert Edward Robinson Rosepettle III. How strange and sad he was. All the others who had come to see me had been tall, but he was short. They had been rich, while he was poor. The others had been handsome, but Albert, poor Albert, he was as ugly as a humid day . . . (*She laughs sadly, distantly.*) and just about as wet, too. Oh, he was a fat bundle of sweat, Mr. Roseabove. He was nothing but one great torrent of perspiration. Winter and summer, spring and fall, Albert was dripping wet. Yes, he was round and wet and hideous and I never could figure out how he ever got such a name as Albert Edward Robinson Rosepettle III.

Oh, I must have been very susceptible indeed to have married Albert. I *was* twenty-eight and that *is* a susceptible year in a woman's life. And of course I *was* a virgin, but still I— Oh, stop blushing, Mr. Roseabove. I'm not lying. It's all true. Part of the cause of my condition, I will admit, was due to the fact that I still hadn't gone out with a man. But I am certain, Mr. Roseabove, I am certain that despite your naughty glances my virtue would have remained unsoiled, no matter what. You see, I had spoken to men. (Their voices are gruff.) And in crowded streets I had often brushed against them. (Their bodies, I found, are tough and bony.) I had observed their ways and habits, Mr. Roseabove. Even at that tender age I had the foresight to realize I must know what I was up against. So I watched them huddled in hallways, talking in nervous whispers and laughing when little girls passed by. I watched their hands in crowded buses and even felt their feeling elbows on crowded streets. And then, one night, when I was walking home I saw a man standing in a window. I saw him take his contact lenses out and his hearing aid out of his ear. I saw him take his teeth out of his thin-lipped mouth and drop them into a smiling glass of water. I saw him lift his snow-white hair off of his wrinkled white head and place it on a gnarled wooden hat tree. And then I saw him take his clothes off. And when he was done and didn't move but stood and stared at a full-length mirror whose glass he had covered with towels, then I went home and wept.

And so one day I bolted the door to my room. I locked myself inside, bought a small revolver just in case, then sat at my window and watched what went on below. It was not a pretty sight. Some men came up to see me. I did not let them in.
"Hello in there," they said.
"Hello in there,
My name is Steven.
Steven S. (for Steven) Steven.

One is odd
But two is even.
I know you're hot
So I'm not leavin'."
. . . or something like that.
(*Short pause*) But they all soon left anyway. I think they caught the scent of a younger woman down the hall. And so I listened to the constant sound of feet disappearing down the stairs. I watched a world walk by my window; a world of lechery and lies and greed. I watched a world walk by and I decided not to leave my room until this world came to me, *exactly* as I wanted it.

One day Albert came toddling up the stairs. He waddled over to my room, scratched on the door and said, in a frail and very frightened voice, "Will you please marry me?" And so I did. It was as simple as that. (*Pause. Then distantly*) I still wonder why I did it though. I still wonder why. (*Short pause. Then with a laugh of resignation*) I don't know. . . . Yes, maybe it's because one look at Albert's round, sad face and I knew he could be mine . . . that no matter where he went, or whom he saw, or what he did, Albert could be mine, my husband, my lover, my own—mine to love, mine to live with, mine to kill. . . .

And so we were wed. That night I went to bed with a man for the first time in my life. The next morning I picked up my mattress and moved myself into another room. Oh, how easily is Man satisfied. How easily is his porous body saturated with "fun." All he asks is a little sex and a little food and there he is, asleep with a smile and snoring. Never the slightest regard for you, lying in bed next to him, your eyes open wide. No, he stretches his legs and kicks you in the shins; stretches his arms and smacks you in the eye. Oh, how noble, how magical, how marvelous is Love.

So you see, Mr. Roseabove, I *had* to leave his room. For as long as I stayed there I was not safe. After all, we'd only met the day before and I knew far too little about him. But now that we were married I had time to find out more. A few of the things I thought I should know were: what had he done before we'd met, what had he wanted to do, what did he *still* want to do, what was he doing about it? What did he dream about while he slept? What did he think about when he stared out the window? What did he think about when I wasn't near?

These were the things that concerned me most. And so I began to watch him closely.

My plan worked best at night, for that was when he slept. . . . I would listen at my door until I heard his door close. Then I'd tiptoe out and watch him through his keyhole. When his lights went out I'd open up his door and creep across the floor to his bed, and then I'd listen more. My ear became a stethoscope that recorded the fluctuations of his dream life. For I was waiting for him to speak, waiting for the slightest word that might betray his sleeping, secret thoughts. . . . But no, Albert only snored, and smiled, and slept on and on. And that, Mr. Roseabove, is how I spent my nights! —next to him, my husband, my "Love." I never left his side, never took my eyes from his sleeping face. I dare you to find me a wife who's as devoted as that. (*She laughs. Short pause.*)

A month later I found that I was pregnant. It had happened that first horrible night. How like Albert to do something like that. I fancy he knew it was going to happen all the time, too. I do believe he planned it that way. One night, one shot, one chance in a lifetime and bham! you've had it. It takes an imaginative man to miss. It takes someone like Albert to do something like that. But yet, I never let on. Oh, no. Let him think I'm simply getting fat, I said. And that's the way I did it, too. I, nonchalantly putting on weight; Albert nonchalantly watching my belly grow. If he knew what was happening to me he never let me know it. He was as silent as before. (*Pause.*)

Twelve months later my son was born. He was so overdue that when he came out he was already teething. He bit the index finger off the poor doctor's hand and snapped at the nurse till she fainted. I took him home and put him in a cage in the darkest corner of my room. But still I—

THE COMMODORE. Was it a large cage?

MADAME ROSEPETTLE. What?

THE COMMODORE. Was his cage large? I hope it was. Otherwise it wouldn't be very comfortable.

MADAME ROSEPETTLE. I'm sorry. Did I say cage? I meant crib. I put him in a crib and set the crib in a corner of my room where my husband would not see him. For until I found out exactly why he'd married me, I would not tell him that a son had been born. (*Pause.*)

Shortly after that, Rosalinda came. She was one of Albert's many secretaries. You know, I've always felt there was something star-crossed about those two, for she was the only person I ever met who was equally as ugly as he.

Well, naturally I never let on that I knew she had come. I simply set an extra place at the table and cooked a little bit more. And at night, instead of preparing one, I prepared two beds. Instead of fluffing one pillow I fluffed up two and straightened an extra pair of sheets. I said good night as politely as I could and left them alone—the monster and my husband, two soulmates expressing their souls through sin. And while they lay in bed I listened at the keyhole. And when they slept I crept in and listened more. Albert had begun to speak!

After months of listening for some meager clue he suddenly began to talk in torrents. Words poured forth and I, like some listening sponge, soaked them up and stayed for more. At last he was talking in his sleep! He told her things he never told to me. Words of passion and love. He told her how he worshiped the way she cooked; how he worshiped the way she talked; how he'd worshiped the way she'd looked when he'd first met her; even the way she looked now. And this to a hideous, twisted slut of a woman sleeping in sin with him! Words he never told to me. I ask you, Mr. Roseabove, I ask you, how much is a woman supposed to take?

Ah, but the signs of regret were beginning to show. And oh, how I laughed when I found out: when I saw how tired he'd begun to look, when I noticed how little he ate; how little he spoke; how slowly he seemed to move. It's funny, but he never slept any more. I could tell by his breathing. And through the keyhole at night I could see his large, round, empty eyes shining sadly in the dark. (*Pause.*)

Then one night he died. One year

after she had come he passed on. The doctors don't know why. His heart, they said, seemed fine. It was as large a heart as they'd ever seen. And yet he died. At one o'clock in the morning his heart stopped beating. (*She laughs softly.*) But it wasn't till dawn that she discovered he was dead. (*She starts to laugh louder.*)

Well, don't you get it? Don't you catch the irony, the joke? What's wrong with you!? He died at one. At ONE O'CLOCK IN THE MORNING!! Dead!! Yet she didn't know he was dead till dawn. (*She laughs again, loudly.*)

Well don't you get the point? The point of this whole story? What is wrong with you? He was lying with her in bed for nearly six hours, *dead,* and she never knew it. What a lover he must have been! WHAT A LOVER! (*She laughs uproariously but stops when she realizes he's not laughing with her.*)

Well don't you see? Their affair, their sinfulness—it never even existed! He tried to make me jealous but there was nothing to be jealous of. He was *mine!* Mine all the time, even when he was in bed with another, even in death . . . *he was mine!* (THE COMMODORE *climbs up in his chair and crawls over his arm rest. He begins to walk weakly toward the door.*) Don't tell me you're leaving, Commodore. Is there something wrong? (THE COMMODORE *walks weakly toward the door, then runs the last part of the way. In panic he twists the doorknob. The doorknob comes off. He falls to the ground.*) Why Commodore, you're on your knees! *How romantic.* Don't tell me you're going to ask me to marry you again? Commodore, you're trembling. What's wrong? Don't tell me you're afraid that I'll accept?

THE COMMODORE (*weakly*). I . . . I-I . . . feel . . . sa-sorry for your . . . ssssson . . . that's . . . all I can . . . sssssay.

MADAME ROSEPETTLE. And I feel sorrier for you! For you are *nothing!* While my son is mine. His skin is the color of fresh snow, his voice is like the music of angels, and his mind is pure. For he is safe, Mr. Roseabove, and it is *I* who have saved him. Saved him from the world beyond that door. The world of you. The world of his father. A world waiting to devour those who trust in it; those who love. A world vicious under

the hypocrisy of kindness, ruthless under the falseness of a smile. Well, go on, Mr. Roseabove. Leave my room and enter your world again—your sex-driven, dirt-washed waste of cannibals eating each other up while they pretend they're kissing. Go, Mr. Roseabove, enter your blind world of darkness. My son shall have only light!

(*She turns with a flourish and enters her bedroom.* THE COMMODORE *stares helplessly at the door knob in his hand. Suddenly the door swings open, under its own power.* THE COMMODORE *crawls out. The door closes behind him, under its own power. From outside can be heard the sound of a church bell chiming. The bedroom door reopens and* MADAME ROSE-PETTLE *emerges wearing an immense straw hat, sun glasses, tight toreador pants and a short beach robe. She carries a huge flashlight. She is barefoot. She tiptoes across the floor and exits through the main door. The church bell chimes thirteen times.* JONATHAN *emerges from behind the* VENUS'-FLYTRAPS. *He runs to the door, puts his ear to it then races back to the balcony and stares down at the street below. Carnival lights flash weirdly against the night sky and laughter drifts up. The* VENUS'-FLYTRAPS *reach out to grab him but somehow he senses their presence and leaps away in time.*)

VENUS'-FLYTRAPS (*gruffly*). Grrrrrrrr!

(JONATHAN *backs up, staring in horror at the now huge leaves which snap at him hungrily, reaching for him. He backs, accidentally, into the table on which the fish and the dictaphone lie. He jars the table in doing so. The dictaphone makes a strange noise and begins to speak.*)

THE DICTAPHONE (MADAME ROSEPETTLE'S *voice*). ". . . And of course, could one ever forget those lovely seaside shops—"

(JONATHAN *slams the buttons on the machine. The tape stops and starts to play backwards. The* PLANTS *grow.* JONATHAN, *in horror, slams the buttons again. The tape whirls at the wrong speed. The voice shrieks wildly.* JONATHAN *stares at it in horror as the tape runs out and turns, clicking on its spool. He hits the right button and the machine stops. The* FISH *giggles.* JONATHAN *stares at it in horror. The* PLANTS *snarl.* JONATHAN *runs to the wall and smashes the glass case that* covers the fire axe. He takes out the axe. He advances cautiously toward the FLY-TRAPS. He feints and attacks; they follow his movements. He bobs, they weave. It is a cat-and-mouse game of death. Suddenly JONATHAN leaps upon them and hacks them apart till they fall to the floor, writhing, then dead. JONATHAN stands above them, victorious, panting, but somehow seeming to breathe easier. Slowly he turns and looks at the fish bowl. His eyes seem glazed, his expression insanely determined. He walks slowly toward the bowl. There are three knocks on the door to the suite. He does not hear them. He raises his axe. The door opens. ROSALIE enters, pursued by a group of gayly drunken BELLBOYS. She laughs and closes the door on them. She herself is dressed in an absurdly childish pink party dress, complete with crinolines and frills—the portrait of a girl ten years old at her first "staying-up-late party." Her shoes are black leather pumps and she wears short pink socks. Her cheeks have round circles of rouge on them—like a young girl might have who had never put on make-up before. She carries masks and party favors.)

ROSALIE. Jonathan! Jonathan! What have you done? (JONATHAN stops. He does not look at her but continues to stare at the fish bowl.) Jonathan! Put down that silly old axe. You might hurt yourself. (He still does not answer but only stares at the bowl. He does not lower the axe.) Jonathan! (Slowly he turns and faces her.)

JONATHAN. I killed it.

ROSALIE. Ssh. Not so loudly. Where'd you put her body?

JONATHAN (pointing to the plants). There.

ROSALIE. Where? I don't see a body. Where is she?

JONATHAN. Who?

ROSALIE. Your mother.

JONATHAN. I haven't killed my mother. I've killed her plants. The ones I used to feed. I've chopped their hearts out.

ROSALIE (with an apologetic laugh). I thought you'd—killed your mother. (The PIRANHA FISH giggles. JONATHAN turns and stares at it again. He starts to move towards it, slowly.) Jonathan, stop. (He hesitates, as if he were uncertain about what to do. Slowly he raises the axe.) Jonathan! (He smashes the axe against the fish bowl. It breaks. The fish screams.)

ROSALINDA THE FISH (fearfully). AAIE-EEEEEEEEEEEEEE!!!

ROSALIE. Now look at the mess you've made.

JONATHAN. Do you think it can live without water?

ROSALIE. What will your mother say when she gets back?

JONATHAN. Maybe I should hit it again. Just in case. (He strikes it again.)

ROSALINDA THE FISH (mournfully). UGHHHHHHHH!

(JONATHAN stares in horror at the dead fish. He drops the axe and turns away, sickened and weak. ROSALIE walks over and touches him gently, consolingly on the arm.)

ROSALIE. There's something bothering you, isn't there?

(Pause. JONATHAN does not answer at first, but stares off into space frightened, bewildered.)

JONATHAN (weakly). I never thought I'd see you again. I never thought I'd talk to you again. I never thought you'd come.

ROSALIE. Did you really think that?

JONATHAN. She told me she'd never let you visit me again. She said no one would ever visit me again. She told me I had seen enough.

ROSALIE. But I had a key made.

JONATHAN. She—she hates me.

ROSALIE. What?

JONATHAN. She doesn't let me do anything. She doesn't let me listen to the radio. She took the tube out of the television set. She doesn't let me use her phone. She makes me show her all my letters before I seal them. She doesn't—

ROSALIE. Letters? What letters are you talking about?

JONATHAN. Just—letters I write.

ROSALIE. To whom?

JONATHAN. To people.

ROSALIE. Other girls? Could they be to other girls by any chance?

JONATHAN. No. They're just to people. No people in particular. Just people in the phone book. Just names. So far I've covered all the "A's" and "B's" up to Barrera.

ROSALIE. What is it you say to them? Can you tell me what you say to them—or is it private? Jonathan, just what do you say to them!?

JONATHAN. Mostly I just ask them what they look like. (*Pause. Suddenly he starts to sob in a curious combination of laughter and tears.*) But I don't think she ever mails them. She reads them, then takes them out to mail. But I don't think she ever does. I'll bet she just throws them away. Well, if she's not going to mail them, why does she say she will? I—I could save the stamps.

ROSALIE. Guess why I had this key made.

JONATHAN. I'll bet she's never even mailed one. From Abandono to Barrera, not one.

ROSALIE. Do you know why I had this key made? Do you know why I'm wearing this new dress?

JONATHAN. She tells me I'm brilliant. She makes me read and re-read books no one's ever read. She smothers me with blankets at night in case of a storm. She tucks me in so tight I can't even get out till she comes and takes my blankets off.

ROSALIE. Try and guess why I'm all dressed up.

JONATHAN. She says she loves me. Every morning, before I even have a chance to open my eyes, there she is, leaning over my bed, breathing in my face and saying, "I love you, I love you."

ROSALIE. Jonathan, isn't my dress pretty?

JONATHAN. But I heard everything to-night. I heard it all when she didn't know I was here. (*He stares off into space, bewildered.*)

ROSALIE. What's the matter? (*He does not answer.*) Jonathan, what's the matter?

JONATHAN. But she must have known I was here. She *must* have known! I mean —where could I have gone? (*Pause*) But—if that's the case—*why did she let me hear?*

ROSALIE. Jonathan, I do wish you'd pay more attention to me. Here, look at my dress. You can even touch it if you like. Guess how many crinolines I have on. Guess why I'm wearing such a pretty, new dress. *Jonathan!*

JONATHAN (*distantly*). Maybe—it didn't make any difference to her—whether I heard or not. (*He turns suddenly to her and hugs her closely. She lets him hold her, then she steps back and away from him. Her face looks strangely old and determined under her girlish powder and pinkness.*)

ROSALIE. Come with me.

JONATHAN. What?

ROSALIE. Leave and come with me.

JONATHAN (*fearfully*). Where?

ROSALIE. Anywhere.

JONATHAN. Wha'—wha'—what do you mean?

ROSALIE. I mean, let's leave. Let's run away. Far away. Tonight. Both of us, together. Let's run and run. Far, far away.

JONATHAN. You—mean, leave?

ROSALIE. Yes. Leave.

JONATHAN. Just like that?

ROSALIE. Just like that.

JONATHAN. But—but—but—

ROSALIE. You want to leave, don't you?

JONATHAN. I—I don't—don't know. I—I—

ROSALIE. What about the time you told me how much you'd like to go outside, how you'd love to walk by yourself, any-where you wanted?

JONATHAN. I—I don't—know.

ROSALIE. Yes, you do. Come. Give me your hand. Stop trembling so. Everything will be all right. Give me your hand and come with me. Just through the door. Then we're safe. Then we can run far away, somewhere where she'll never find us. Come, Jonathan. It's time to go.

JONATHAN. There are others you could take.

ROSALIE. But I don't love them.

(*Pause.*)

JONATHAN. You—you *love* me?

ROSALIE. Yes, Jonathan. I love you.

JONATHAN. Wha-wha-why?

ROSALIE. Because you watch me every night.

JONATHAN. Well—can't we stay here?

ROSALIE. No!

JONATHAN. Wha-wha-whhhhy?

ROSALIE. *Because I want you alone.* (JONATHAN *turns from her and begins to walk about the room in confusion.*) I want you, Jonathan. Do you understand what I said? *I want you for my husband.*

JONATHAN. I—I—can't, I mean, I—I want to go—go with you very much but I—I don't think—I can. I'm—sorry. (*He sits down and holds his head in his hands, sobbing quietly.*)

ROSALIE. What time will your mother be back?

JONATHAN. Na—not for a while.

ROSALIE. Are you sure?

JONATHAN. Ya-yes.

ROSALIE. Where is she?

JONATHAN. The usual place.

ROSALIE. What do you mean, "the usual place"?

JONATHAN (*with a sad laugh*). The beach. (ROSALIE *looks at* JONATHAN *quizzically*.) She likes to look for people making love. Every night at midnight she walks down to the beach searching for people lying on blankets and making love. When she finds them she kicks sand in their faces and walks on. Sometimes it takes her as much as three hours to chase everyone away. (ROSALIE *smiles slightly and walks toward the master bedroom.* JONATHAN *freezes in fear. She puts her hand on the door knob.*) WHAT ARE YOU DOING!? (*She smiles at him over her shoulder. She opens the door.*) STOP!! You can't go in there!!! STOP!!

ROSALIE (*she opens the door completely and beckons him to come*). Come.

JONATHAN. Close it. Quickly!

ROSALIE. Come, Jonathan. Let's go inside.

JONATHAN. Close the door!

ROSALIE (*with a laugh*). You've never been in here, have you?

JONATHAN. No. And you can't go in, either. No one can go in there but Mother. It's her room. Now close the door!

ROSALIE (*she flicks on the light switch. No lights go on*). What's wrong with the lights?

JONATHAN. There are none. Mother's in mourning. (ROSALIE *walks into the room and pulls the drapes from off the windows. Weird colored lights stream in and illuminate the bedroom in wild, distorted, nightmarish shadows and lights. They blink on and off, on and off. It's all like some strange, macabre fun house in an insane amusement park. Even the furniture in the room seems grotesque and distorted. The closet next to the bed seems peculiarly prominent. It almost seems to tilt over the bed. Still in the main room*) What have you done!? (ROSALIE *walks back to the door and smiles to him from within the master bedroom.*) What have you done?

ROSALIE. Come in, Jonathan.

JONATHAN. GET OUT OF THERE!

ROSALIE. Will you leave with me?

JONATHAN. I can't!

ROSALIE. But you want to, don't you?

JONATHAN. Yes, yes, I want to, but I told you—I—I—I can't. I can't! Do you understand? I can't! Now come out of there.

ROSALIE. Come in and get me.

JONATHAN. Rosalie, *please.*

ROSALIE (*bouncing on the bed*). My, what a comfortable bed.

JONATHAN. GET OFF THE BED!!!

ROSALIE. What soft, fluffy pillows. I think I'll take a nap.

JONATHAN. Rosalie, *please listen to me.* Come out of there. You're not supposed to be in that room. Please come out. Rosalie, *please.*

ROSALIE. Will you leave with me if I do?

JONATHAN. Rosalie—? I'll—I'll show you my stamp collection if you'll promise to come out.

ROSALIE. Bring it in here.

JONATHAN. Will you come out then?

ROSALIE. Only if you bring it in here.

JONATHAN. But I'm not allowed to go in there.

ROSALIE (*poutingly*). Then I shan't come out!

JONATHAN. You've got to!

ROSALIE. Why?

JONATHAN. Mother will be back.

ROSALIE. She can sleep out there. (ROSALIE *yawns.*) I think I'll take a little nap. This bed is so comfortable. Really, Jonathan, you should come in and try it.

JONATHAN. MOTHER WILL BE BACK SOON!!

ROSALIE. Give her your room then if you don't want her to sleep on the couch. I find it very nice in here. Good night. (*Pause.*)

JONATHAN. If I come in, will you come out?

ROSALIE. If you don't come in I'll never come out.

JONATHAN. And if I do?

ROSALIE. Then I may.

JONATHAN. What if I bring my stamps in?

ROSALIE. Bring them and find out.

JONATHAN (*he goes to the dresser and takes out the drawer of stamps. Then he takes out the drawer of coins*). I'm bringing the coins, too.

ROSALIE. How good you are, Jonathan.

JONATHAN (*he takes a shelf full of books*). My books, too. How's that? I'll show you my books and my coins and my stamps. I'll show you them all. Then will you leave?

ROSALIE. Perhaps. (*He carries them all into the bedroom and sets them down next to the bed. He looks about fearfully.*) What's wrong?

JONATHAN. I've never been in here before.

ROSALIE. It's nothing but a room. There's nothing to be afraid of.

JONATHAN (*he looks about doubtfully.*) Well, let me show you my stamps. I have one billion, five—

ROSALIE. Later, Jonathan. We'll have time. Let me show you something first.

JONATHAN. What's that?

ROSALIE. You're trembling.

JONATHAN. What do you want to show me?

ROSALIE. There's nothing to be nervous about. Come. Sit down.

JONATHAN. What do you want to show me?

ROSALIE. I can't show you if you won't sit down.

JONATHAN. I don't want to sit down!

(*She takes hold of his hand. He pulls it away.*)

ROSALIE. Jonathan!

JONATHAN. You're sitting on Mother's bed.

ROSALIE. Then let's pretend it's my bed.

JONATHAN. It's not your bed!

ROSALIE. Come, Jonathan. Sit down here next to me.

JONATHAN. We've got to get out of here. Mother might come.

ROSALIE. Don't worry. We've got plenty of time. The beach is full of lovers.

JONATHAN. How do you know?

ROSALIE. I checked before I came.

(*Pause.*)

JONATHAN. Let—let me show you my coins.

ROSALIE. Why are you trembling so?

JONATHAN. Look, we've got to get out! Something terrible will happen if we don't.

ROSALIE. Then leave with me.

JONATHAN. The bedroom?

ROSALIE. The hotel. The island. Your mother. Leave with me, Jonathan. Leave with me now, before it's too late.

JONATHAN. I—I—I—

ROSALIE. I love you, Jonathan, and I won't give you up. I want you . . . all for myself. Not to share with your mother,

but for me, alone—to love, to live with, to have children by. I want you, Jonathan. You, whose skin is softer and whiter than anyone's I've ever known. Whose voice is quiet and whose love is in every look of his eye. I want you, Jonathan, and I won't give you up.

(*Short pause.*)

JONATHAN (*softly, weakly*). What do you want me to do?

ROSALIE. Forget about your mother. Pretend she never existed and look at me. Look at my eyes, Jonathan; my mouth, my hands, my skirt, my legs. Look at me, Jonathan. Are you still afraid?

JONATHAN. I'm not afraid. (*She smiles and starts to unbutton her dress.*) What are you doing!? No!

ROSALIE (*she continues to unbutton her dress*). Your mother is strong, but I am stronger. (*She rises and her skirt falls about her feet. She stands in a slip and crinolines.*) I don't look so pink and girlish any more, do I? (*She laughs.*) But you want me anyhow. You're ashamed but you want me anyhow. It's written on your face. And I'm very glad. Because I want you. (*She takes off a crinoline.*)

JONATHAN. PUT IT ON! *Please,* put it back on!

ROSALIE. Come, Jonathan. (*She takes off another crinoline.*) Lie down. Let me loosen your shirt.

JONATHAN. No . . . NO . . . NO! STOP! *Please,* stop!

(*She takes her last crinoline off and reaches down to take off her socks. The lights outside blink weirdly. Wild, jagged music with a drum beating in the background is heard.*)

ROSALIE. Don't be afraid, Jonathan. Come. Lie down. Everything will be wonderful. (*She takes her socks off and lies down in her slip. She drops a strap over one shoulder and smiles.*)

JONATHAN. Get off my mother's bed!

ROSALIE. I want you, Jonathan, all for my own. Come. The bed is soft. Lie here by my side. (*She reaches up and takes his hand. Meekly he sits down on the edge of the bed. The closet door swings open suddenly and the corpse of Albert Edward Robinson Rosepettle III tumbles forward stiffly and onto the bed, his stone-stiff arms falling across* ROSALIE'S *legs, his head against her side.* JONATHAN, *too terrified to scream, puts his hand across his mouth and sinks down onto the bed, almost in a state of collapse. Outside the music screams.*) Who the hell is this!

JONATHAN. It-it-it-it—it—it's—

ROSALIE. What a stupid place to keep a corpse. (*She pushes him back in the closet and shuts the door.*) Forget it, Jonathan. I put him back in the closet. Everything's fine again.

JONATHAN. It's—it's—it's my—my—my—

ROSALIE (*kneeling next to him on the bed and starting to unbutton his shirt*). It's all right, Jonathan. It's all right. Sshh. Come. Let me take off your clothes.

JONATHAN (*still staring dumbly into space*). It's—it's my—ffffather.

(*The closet door swings open again and the* CORPSE *falls out, this time his arms falling about* ROSALIE's *neck.* JONATHAN *almost swoons.*)

ROSALIE. Oh, for God's sake. (*She pushes him off the bed and onto the floor.*) Jonathan . . . ? LISTEN TO ME, JONATHAN! STOP LOOKING AT HIM AND LOOK AT ME! (*He looks away from his father, fearfully, his mouth open in terror.*) I love you, Jonathan, and I want you *now*. Not later and not as partner with your mother but now and by myself. I want you, Jonathan, as my husband. I want you to lie with me, to sleep with me, to be with me, to kiss me and touch me, to live with me, *forever*. Stop looking at him! He's dead! Listen to me. I'm alive. I want you for my husband! Now help me take my slip off. Then you can look at my body and touch me. Come, Jonathan. Lie down. I want you forever.

JONATHAN. Ma-Mother was right! You *do* let men do anything they want to you.

ROSALIE. Of course she was right! Did you really think I was that sweet and pure? Everything she said was right. (*She laughs.*) Behind the bushes and it's done. One-two-three and it's done. Here's the money. Thanks. Come again. Hah-hah! Come again! (*Short pause*) So what!? It's only you I love. They make no difference.

JONATHAN. You're dirty! (*He tries to get up but can't, for his father is lying in front of his feet.*)

ROSALIE. No, I'm not dirty. I'm full of love and womanly feelings. I want chil-dren. Tons of them. I want a husband. Is that dirty? Take off your clothes.

JONATHAN. NO!!

ROSALIE. Forget about your father. Drop your pants on top of him, then you won't see his face. Forget about your mother. She's gone. Forget them both and look at me. Love is so beautiful, Jonathan. Come and let me love you; tonight and forever. Come and let me keep you mine. Mine to love when I want, mine to kiss when I want, mine to have when I want. Mine. All mine. So come, Jonathan. Come and close your eyes. It's better that way. Close your eyes so you can't see. Close your eyes and let me lie with you. Let me show you how beautiful it is . . . love.

(*She lies back in bed and slowly starts to raise her slip.* JONATHAN *stares at her legs in horror. Then, suddenly, he seizes her crumpled skirt and throws it over her face, and smothers her to death. At last he rises and, picking up his box of stamps, dumps the stamps over her limp body. He does the same with his coins and finally, his books, until at last she is buried. Then, done, he throws his hands over his eyes and and turns to run. But as he staggers past the corpse of his father, his father's lifeless arms somehow come to life for an instant and, reaching out, grab* JONATHAN *by the feet.* JONATHAN *falls to the floor. For a moment he lies there, stretched across his father's body, too terrified to move. But a soft, ethereal-green light begins to suffuse the room and heavenly harp music is heard in the air. As if his body had suddenly become immortal and weightless* JONATHAN *rises up from the floor and with long, slow, dream-like steps [like someone walking under water], he floats through the bedroom door and drifts across the living room, picking up his telescope on the way. He floats out to the balcony and begins to scan the sky. The harp music grows louder and more paradisiacal: Debussy in Heaven. While under the harp music, soft, muffled laughter can be heard; within the bedroom, within the living room, from the rear of the theatre, laughter all about. His* MOTHER *tiptoes into the living room. Her hair is awry, her hat is on crooked, her blouse hangs wrinkled and out of her pants. Her legs are covered with sand.*)

MADAME ROSEPETTLE. Twenty-three couples. I annoyed twenty-three couples, all of them coupled in various positions, all equally distasteful. It's a record, that's what it is. It's a record! (*Breathing heavily from excitement she begins to tuck in her blouse and straighten her hair. She notices the chaotic state of the room. She shrieks slightly.*) What has happened!? (*She notices the plants.*) My plants! (*She notices the fish.*) Rosalinda! Great gods, my fish has lost her water! ALBERT! ALBERT! (*She searches about the room for her son. She sees him standing on the porch.*) Ah, there you are, Edward; what has been going on during my brief absence? What are you doing out here when Roslinda is lying in there dead? DEAD!? Oh, God, dead. (*She gives her fish artificial respiration, but alas, it does not work.*) Robinson, answer me. What are you looking for? I've told you there's nothing out there. This place is a mad-house. That's what it is. A madhouse. (*She turns and walks into her bedroom. An airplane is heard flying in the distance.* JONATHAN *scans the horizon frantically. The plane grows nearer.* JONATHAN *follows it with his telescope. It flies overhead. It begins to circle about. Wildly, desperately,* JONATHAN *waves his arms to the plane. It flies away.* MADAME ROSE-PETTLE *re-enters the room.*) ROBINSON! I went to lie down and I stepped on your father! I lay down and I lay on some girl. Robinson, there is a woman on my bed and I do believe she's stopped breathing. What is more, you've buried her under your fabulous collection of stamps, coins and books. I ask you, Robinson. As a mother to a son I ask you. *What is the meaning of this?*

BLACKOUT

CURTAIN

ORPHEUS DESCENDING

Tennessee Williams

Presented by the Producers Theatre
at the Martin Beck Theatre in New York on March 21, 1957,
with the following cast:

DOLLY HAMMA Elizabeth Eustis

BEULAH BINNINGS Jane Rose

PEE WEE BINNINGS Warren Kemmerling

DOG HAMMA David Clarke

CAROL CUTRERE Lois Smith

EVA TEMPLE Nell Harrison

SISTER TEMPLE Mary Farrell

UNCLE PLEASANT John Marriott

VAL XAVIER Cliff Robertson

VEE TALBOTT Joanna Roos

LADY TORRANCE Maureen Stapleton

JABE TORRANCE Crahan Denton

SHERIFF TALBOTT R. G. Armstrong

MR. DUBINSKY Beau Tilden

WOMAN Janice Mars

DAVID CUTRERE Robert Webber

NURSE PORTER Virgilia Chew

FIRST MAN Albert Henderson

SECOND MAN Charles Tyner

Directed by Harold Clurman
Setting by Boris Aronson
Costumes by Lucinda Ballard
Lighting by Feder

Orpheus Descending, staged by Harold Clurman, had but 64 performances on Broadway under the excellent auspices of the Producers Theatre—that is, Robert Whitehead. It was plain to adverse critics that the control needed when a playwright lashes out at the world was absent; the author lashed out too much at too many evils and their representatives all at the same time. The author added the provocation of his extraordinary talent for the theatre, which here became too theatrical and too wearing on the nerves and on the playgoer's credulity. Louis Kronenberger, with every desire to do justice to the play, complained that "the overwrought social critic in Williams helps to lead the craftsman astray" here—and that "it is hard, finally, to separate the world's violence from his own." But with *Orpheus Descending,* Tennessee Williams was one of the period's few playwrights who took note of "the world's violence" and wrung anguish and pity from the inferno-world. In addition, he composed the play as a poet as well as a melodramatist, using dark pigments irradiated with lyricism, especially in scenes dealing with the Eurydice character of the play. It is not necessary to like Tennessee Williams' protest against the world, the flesh, and the devil as well as against a particular region and state of mind. But it is difficult not to consider a theatre poet's privately symbolic yet also socially suggestive jeremiad without some regard. Among the very many plays which season after season crumble publicly and shower the playgoer with fragments from an exploding fantasy and conscience, *Orpheus Descending* is a failed work to which, as Williams' colleague Arthur Miller would have put it, "attention must be paid." *

Orpheus Descending is a revised, or rather amplified and re-created, version of Tennessee Williams' *Battle of Angels,* which the Theatre Guild produced in 1940 and did not bring to New York after an unsuccessful tryout in Boston. It was the author's first professional production, and the present version therefore conveys a sense of continuity to those who have followed this remarkable playwright's career with admiration and concern. Nowhere else in Mr. Williams' dramatic work, except possibly in the more inchoate and transparent *Camino Real,* may one find fuller representation of the romantic side of his talent. If the present editor found *Battle of Angels* the fresher work, which is not surprising in so early a play, *Orpheus Descending* exemplifies a tenacity and tension that should not be overlooked. It exemplifies a drive for expression that was with this playwright from the start of his career and has become indurated with the advance of years.

Mr. Williams has been much obsessed by death—with the artist's fate, which is to be destroyed; with love as a form of death or shabby *Liebestod;* with society, especially small-town and Southern, as an inferno for persons unfortunate enough to be imbued with an artist's sensibility. The author is also apt to indulge in the diabolism of early *Sturm und Drang* romanticism that accords well with his view of the malign propensities of men and society. And for all his talent for tight dramatic structure, he is apt to turn to "open structure" and give his plot free passageway in several directions.

This structural expansiveness reappeared in *Sweet Bird of Youth,* produced with popular success in 1959 as both a sex drama and a social drama of sorts; the hero who once infected the heroine with venereal disease is emasculated by her vengeful, fascistic father and brother. And idealization of the artist as life's lovely and delicate victim and of death as the mystic Comforter appeared in the latest Williams drama, *The Milk Train Doesn't Stop Here Anymore,* produced in the 1962-63 season. In this work a sponging poet was at once a Christ and a Death symbol; and the object of the author's misplaced (it seems to me) compassion was a frowsy, ludicrously aggressive virago who is ripe for the Reaper.

But whereas *Sweet Bird of Youth,* which was commercially successful, and *The Milk Train . . . ,* which was not, were, regardless of scattered merits, largely fabrications, *Orpheus Descending* originated in the very depths of the author's feelings. It may be a calculated drama in the analogies between the Orpheus myth and the fate of the main characters, but the author's underlying reactions to their situation and their victimization by environment are genuine. (It would be a sorry world indeed if one

---

* For the present editor's closer observations and strictures on *Orpheus Descending,* the reader may turn to John Gassner's *Theatre at the Crossroads,* pp. 223-226. Essays on several other Williams plays of the period will be found in the same volume on pages 226-231; a general essay on the author's earlier plays and work as a whole, on pages 77-91.

couldn't be romantic and honestly stirred at the same time.) And genuine too in *Orpheus Descending* is Mr. Williams' sense of alienation, which he summarized just before this period in a book of verse, *In the Winter of Cities* (New Directions, 1956), in the line "the freaks of the cosmic circus are men." Criticism of this and other latter-day Williams productions came with special force from the distinguished critic Louis Kronenberger. Reviewing *Sweet Bird of Youth* in the introduction to the *Best Plays of 1958-1959,* Mr. Kronenberger wrote: "It is not that Mr. Williams takes so grisly a view of life, it is that he also takes so lurid a one; not that he sings such frenzied arias, but that he sings them two octaves higher than they are written. . . . There is an art to cursing life no less than to conveying it."

In mitigation of this general reproof, I can only cite and (having had him in a seminar in New York when the first version of the play was completed) confirm Mr. Williams' introductory paragraph in the book that contains the play:

"Why have I stuck so stubbornly to this play: For seventeen years, in fact? Well, nothing is more precious to anybody than the emotional record of his youth, and you will find the trail of my sleeve-worn heart in this completed play that I now call *Orpheus Descending*. On its surface it was and still is the tale of a wild-spirited boy who wanders into a conventional community of the South and creates the commotion of a fox in a chicken coop." *

In truth, *Orpheus Descending* was a youthful play in its first incarnation as *Battle of Angels,* and remains one in its present one.

* Introduction—"The Past, the Present, and the Perhaps"—to *"Orpheus Descending"* with *"Battle of Angels,"* New Directions, 1955, 1958.

ACT ONE

Prologue

scene: *The set represents in nonrealistic fashion a general drygoods store and part of a connecting "confectionery" in a small Southern town. The ceiling is high and the upper walls are dark, as if streaked with moisture and cobwebbed. A great dusty window upstage offers a view of disturbing emptiness that fades into late dusk. The action of the play occurs during a rainy season, late winter and early spring, and sometimes the window turns opaque but glistening silver with sheets of rain. "TORRANCE MERCANTILE STORE" is lettered on the window in gilt of old-fashioned design.*

Merchandise is represented very sparsely and it is not realistic. Bolts of pepperel and percale stand upright on large spools, the black skeleton of a dressmaker's dummy stands meaninglessly against a thin white column, and there is a motionless ceiling fan with strips of flypaper hanging from it.

There are stairs that lead to a landing and disappear above it, and on the landing there is a sinister-looking artificial palm tree in a greenish-brown jardiniere.

But the confectionery, which is seen partly through a wide arched door, is shadowy and poetic as some inner dimension of the play.

Another, much smaller, playing area is a tiny bedroom alcove which is usually masked by an Oriental drapery which is worn dim but bears the formal design of a gold tree with scarlet fruit and fantastic birds.

At the rise of the curtain two youngish middle-aged women, DOLLY *and* BEULAH, *are laying out a buffet supper on a pair of pink-and-gray-veined marble-topped tables with gracefully curved black-iron legs, brought into the main area from the confectionery. They are wives of small planters and tastelessly overdressed in a somewhat bizarre fashion.*

A train whistles in the distance and dogs bark in response from various points and distances. The women pause in their occupations at the tables and rush to the archway, crying out harshly.

———

DOLLY. Pee Wee!
BEULAH. Dawg!

DOLLY. Cannonball is comin' into th' depot!

BEULAH. You all git down to th' depot an' meet that train!

(*Their husbands slouch through, heavy, red-faced men in clothes that are too tight for them or too loose, and mudstained boots.*)

PEE WEE. I fed that one-armed bandit a hunnerd nickels an' it coughed up five.

DOG. Must have hed indigestion.

PEE WEE. I'm gonna speak to Jabe about them slots. (*They go out and a motor starts and pauses.*)

DOLLY. I guess Jabe Torrance has got more to worry about than the slot machines and pinball games in that confectionery.

BEULAH. You're not tellin' a lie. I wint to see Dr. Johnny about Dawg's condition. Dawg's got sugar in his urine again, an as I was leavin' I ast him what was the facks about Jabe Torrance's operation in Mimphis. Well—

DOLLY. What'd he tell you, Beulah?

BEULAH. He said the worse thing a doctor ever can say.

DOLLY. What's that, Beulah?

BEULAH. Nothin' a-tall, not a spoken word did he utter! He just looked at me with those big dark eyes of his and shook his haid like this!

DOLLY (*with doleful satisfaction*). I guess he signed Jabe Torrance's death warrant with just that single silent motion of his haid.

BEULAH. That's exactly what passed through my mind. I understand that they cut him open—(*Pauses to taste something on the table.*)

DOLLY. —An' sewed him right back up! —that's what I heard . . .

BEULAH. I didn't know these olives had seeds in them!

DOLLY. You thought they was stuffed?

BEULAH. Uh-huh. Where's the Temple sisters?

DOLLY. Where d'you think?

BEULAH. Snoopin' aroun' upstairs. If Lady catches 'em at it she'll give those two old maids a touch of her tongue! She's not a Dago for nothin'!

DOLLY. Ha, ha, no! You spoke a true word, honey . . . (*Looks out door as car passes.*) Well, I was surprised when I wint up myself!

BEULAH. You wint up you'self?

DOLLY. I did and so did you because I seen you, Beulah.

BEULAH. I never said that I didn't. Curiosity is a human instinct.

DOLLY. They got two separate bedrooms which are not even connectin'. At opposite ends of the hall, and everything is so dingy an' dark up there. Y'know what it seemed like to me? A county jail! I swear to goodness it didn't seem to me like a place for white people to live in!—that's the truth . . .

BEULAH (*darkly*). Well, I wasn't surprised. Jabe Torrance bought that woman.

DOLLY. Bought her?

BEULAH. Yais, he bought her, when she was a girl of eighteen! He bought her and bought her cheap because she'd been thrown over and her heart was broken by that—(*Jerks head toward a passing car, then continues:*)—that Cutrere boy. . . . *Oh*, what a—*Mmmm*, what a— *beautiful* thing he was. . . . And those two met like you struck two stones together and made a fire!—yes—fire . . .

DOLLY. What?

BEULAH. *Fire!*—Ha . . . (*Strikes another match and lights one of the candelabra. Mandolin begins to fade in. The following monologue should be treated frankly as exposition, spoken to audience, almost directly, with a force that commands attention.* DOLLY *does not remain in the playing area, and after the first few sentences, there is no longer any pretense of a duologue.*)—Well, that was a long time ago, before you and Dog moved into Two River County. Although you must have heard of it. Lady's father was a Wop from the old country and when he first come here with a mandolin and a monkey that wore a little green velvet suit, ha ha.—He picked up dimes and quarters in the saloons—this was before Prohibition. . . . —People just called him The Wop, nobody knew his name, just called him 'The Wop,' ha ha ha. . . .

DOLLY (*off, vaguely*). Anh-hannnh. . . .

(BEULAH *switches in the chair and fixes the audience with her eyes, leaning slightly forward to compel their attention. Her voice is rich with nostalgia, and at a sign of restlessness, she rises and comes straight out to the proscenium, like a pitchman. This monologue should set the nonrealistic key for the whole production.*)

BEULAH. Oh, my law, well, that was Lady's daddy! Then come Prohibition an' first thing ennyone knew, The Wop had took to bootleggin' like a duck to water! He picked up a piece of land cheap, it was on the no'th shore of Moon Lake which used to be the old channel of the river and people thought some day the river might swing back that way, and so he got it cheap. . . . (*Moves her chair up closer to proscenium.*) He planted an orchard on it; he covered the whole no'th shore of the lake with grapevines and fruit trees, and then he built little arbors, little white wooden arbors with tables and benches to drink in and carry on in, ha ha! And in the spring and the summer, young couples would come out there, like me and Pee Wee, we used to go out there, an' court up a storm, ha ha, just court up a—storm! Ha ha!—The county was dry in those days, I don't mean dry like now, why, now you just walk a couple of feet off the highway and whistle three times like a jaybird and a nigger pops out of a bush with a bottle of corn!

DOLLY. Ain't that the truth? Ha ha.

BEULAH. But in those days the county was dry for true, I mean bone dry except for The Wop's wine garden. So we'd go out to The Wop's an' drink that Dago red wine an' cut up an' carry on an' raise such cane in those arbors! Why, I remember one Sunday old Doctor Tooker, Methodist minister then, he bust a blood vessel denouncing The Wop in the pulpit!

DOLLY. Lawd have mercy!

BEULAH. Yes, ma'am!—Each of those white wooden arbors had a lamp in it, and one by one, here and there, the lamps would go out as the couples begun to make love . . .

DOLLY. *Oh*—oh . . .

BEULAH. What strange noises you could hear if you listened, calls, cries, whispers, moans—giggles. . . . (*Her voice is soft with recollection.*)—And then, one by one, the lamps would be lighted again, and The Wop and his daughter would sing and play Dago songs. . . . (*Bring up mandolin: voice under* 'Dicitencello Vuoi.') But sometimes The Wop would look around for his daughter, and all of a sudden Lady wouldn't be there!

DOLLY. Where would she be?

BEULAH. She'd be with David Cutrere.

DOLLY. Awwwwww—ha ha . . .

BEULAH. —Carol Cutrere's big brother, Lady and him would disappear in the orchard and old Papa Romano, The Wop, would holler, "Lady, Lady!"—no answer whatsoever, no matter how long he called and no matter how loud. . . .

DOLLY. Well, I guess it's hard to shout back, "Here I am, Papa," when where you are is in the arms of your lover!

BEULAH. Well, that spring, no, it was late that summer . . . (DOLLY *retires again from the playing area.*)—Papa Romano made a bad mistake. He sold liquor to niggers. The Mystic Crew took action. —They rode out there, one night, with gallons of coal oil—it was a real dry summer—and set that place on fire!— They burned the whole thing up, vines, arbors, fruit trees. —Pee Wee and me, we stood on the dance pavilion across the lake and watched that fire spring up. Inside of tin minutes the whole nawth shore of the lake was a mass of flames, a regular sea of flames, and all the way over the lake we could hear Lady's papa shouting, "Fire, fire, fire!"—as if it was necessary to let people know, and the whole sky lit up with it, as red as Guinea red wine! —Ha ha ha ha. . . . Not a fire engine, not a single engine pulled out of a station that night in Two River County! —The poor old fellow, The Wop, he took a blanket and run up into the orchard to fight the fire singlehanded— *and* burned *alive.* . . . Uh-huh! *burned alive.* . . . (*Mandolin stops short.* DOLLY *has returned to the table to have her coffee.*) You know what I sometimes wonder?

DOLLY. No. What do you wonder?

BEULAH. I wonder sometimes if Lady has any suspicion that her husband, Jabe Torrance, was the leader of the Mystic Crew the night they burned up her father in his wine garden on Moon Lake?

DOLLY. Beulah Binnings, you make my blood run cold with such a thought! How could she live in marriage twenty years with a man if she knew he'd burned her father up in his wine garden?

(*Dog bays in distance.*)

BEULAH. She could live with him in hate. People can live together in hate for a long time, Dolly. Notice their passion for money. I've always noticed when couples don't love each other they

develop a passion for money. Haven't you seen that happen? Of course you have. Now there's not many couples that stay devoted forever. Why, some git so they just barely tolerate each other's existence. Isn't that true?

DOLLY. You couldn't of spoken a truer word if you read it out loud from the Bible!

BEULAH. Barely tolerate each other's existence, and some don't even do that. You know, Dolly Hamma, I don't think half as many married min have committed suicide in this county as the Coroner says has done so!

DOLLY (*with voluptuous appreciation of* BEULAH's *wit*). You think it's their wives that give them the deep six, honey?

BEULAH. I don't think so, I know so. Why there's couples that loathe and despise the sight, smell and sound of each other before that round-trip honeymoon ticket is punched at both ends, Dolly.

DOLLY. I hate to admit it but I can't deny it.

BEULAH. But they hang on together.

DOLLY. Yes, they hang on together.

BEULAH. Year after year after year, accumulating property and money, building up wealth and respect and position in the towns they live in and the counties and cities and the churches they go to, belonging to the clubs and so on and so forth and not a soul but them knowin' they have to go wash their hands after touching something the other one just put down! ha ha ha ha ha!—

DOLLY. Beulah, that's an evil laugh of yours, that laugh of yours is evil!

BEULAH (*louder*). Ha ha ha ha ha!— But you know it's the truth.

DOLLY. Yes, she's tellin' the truth! (*Nods to audience.*)

BEULAH. Then one of them—gits— *cincer* or has a—*stroke* or somethin'?— The other one—

DOLLY. —Hauls in the loot?

BEULAH. That's right, hauls in the loot! Oh, my, then you should see how him or her blossoms out. New house, new car, new clothes. Some of 'em even change to a different church!—If it's a widow, she goes with a younger man, and if it's a widower, he starts courtin' some chick, ha ha ha ha ha!

And so I said, I said to Lady this morning before she left for Mamphis to bring Jabe home, I said, "Lady, I don't suppose you're going to reopen the confectionery till Jabe is completely recovered from his operation." She said, "It can't wait for anything that might take that much time." Those are her exact words. It can't wait for anything that might take that much time. Too much is invested in it. It's going to be done over, redecorated, and opened on schedule the Saturday before Easter this spring!—Why?—Because—she knows Jabe is dying and she wants to clean up quick!

DOLLY. An awful thought. But a true one. Most awful thoughts are.

(*They are startled by sudden light laughter from the dim upstage area. The light changes on the stage to mark a division.*)

Scene One

The women turn to see CAROL CUTRERE *in the archway between the store and the confectionery. She is past thirty and, lacking prettiness, she has an odd, fugitive beauty which is stressed, almost to the point of fantasy, by a style of makeup with which a dancer named Valli has lately made such an impression in the bohemian centers of France and Italy, the face and lips powdered white and the eyes outlined and exaggerated with black pencil and the lids tinted blue. Her family name is the oldest and most distinguished in the country.*

BEULAH. Somebody don't seem to know that the store is closed.

DOLLY. Beulah?

BEULAH. What?

DOLLY. Can you understand how anybody would deliberately make themselves look fantastic as that?

BEULAH. Some people have to show off, it's a passion with them, anything on earth to get attention.

DOLLY. I sure wouldn't care for that kind of attention. Not me. I wouldn't desire it. . . .

(*During these lines, just loud enough for her to hear them,* CAROL *has crossed to the pay-phone and deposited a coin.*)

CAROL. I want Tulane 0370 in New Orleans. What? Oh. Hold on a minute.

(EVA TEMPLE *is descending the stairs, slowly, as if awed by* CAROL's *appearance.* CAROL *rings open the cashbox and removes some coins; returns to deposit coins in phone.*)

BEULAH. She helped herself to money out of the cashbox.

(EVA *passes* CAROL *like a timid child skirting a lion cage.*)

CAROL. Hello, Sister.

EVA. I'm Eva.

CAROL. Hello, Eva.

EVA. Hello . . . (*Then in a loud whisper to* BEULAH *and* DOLLY) She took money out of the cashbox.

DOLLY. Oh, she can do as she pleases, she's a Cutrere!

BEULAH. Shoot . . .

EVA. What is she doin' barefooted?

BEULAH. The last time she was arrested on the highway, they say that she was naked under her coat.

CAROL (*to operator*). I'm waiting. (*Then to women*)—I caught the heel of my slipper in that rotten boardwalk out there and it broke right off. (*Raises slippers in hand.*) They say if you break the heel of your slipper in the morning it means you'll meet the love of your life before dark. But it was already dark when I broke the heel of my slipper. Maybe that means I'll meet the love of my life before daybreak. (*The quality of her voice is curiously clear and childlike.* SISTER TEMPLE *appears on stair landing bearing an old waffle iron.*)

SISTER. Wasn't that them?

EVA. No, it was Carol Cutrere!

CAROL (*at phone*). Just keep on ringing, please, he's probably drunk. (SISTER *crosses by her as* EVA *did.*) Sometimes it takes quite a while to get through the living-room furniture. . . .

SISTER.—She a *sight?*

EVA. Uh-huh!

CAROL. Bertie?—Carol!—Hi, doll! Did you trip over something? I heard a crash. Well, I'm leaving right now, I'm already on the highway and everything's fixed, I've got my allowance back on condition that I remain forever away from Two River County! I had to blackmail them a little. I came to dinner with my eyes made up and my little black sequin jacket and Betsy Boo, my brother's wife, said, "Carol, you going out to a fancy dress ball?" I said, "Oh, no, I'm just going jooking tonight up and down the Dixie Highway between here and Memphis like I used to when I lived here." Why, honey, she flew so fast you couldn't see her passing and came back in with the ink still wet on the check! And this will be done once a month as long as I stay away from Two River County. . . . (*Laughs gaily.*)—How's Jackie? Bless his heart, give him a sweet kiss for me! Oh, honey, I'm driving straight through, not even stopping for pickups unless you need one! I'll meet you in the Starlite Lounge before it closes, or if I'm irresistibly delayed, I'll certainly join you for coffee at the Morning Call before the all-night places have closed for the day . . . —I—Bertie? Bertie? (*Laughs uncertainly and hangs up.*)—let's see, now. . . . (*Removes a revolver from her trench-coat pocket and crosses to fill it with cartridges back of counter.*)

EVA. What she looking for?

SISTER. Ask her.

EVA (*advancing*). What're you looking for, Carol?

CAROL. Cartridges for my revolver.

DOLLY. She don't have a license to carry a pistol.

BEULAH. She don't have a license to drive a car.

CAROL. When I stop for someone I want to be sure it's someone I want to stop for.

DOLLY. Sheriff Talbot ought to know about this when he gits back from the depot.

CAROL. Tell him, ladies. I've already given him notice that if he ever attempts to stop me again on the highway, I'll shoot it out with him. . . .

BEULAH. When anybody has trouble with the law—

(*Her sentence is interrupted by a panicky scream from* EVA, *immediately repeated by* SISTER. *The* TEMPLE SISTERS *scramble upstairs to the landing.* DOLLY *also cries out and turns, covering her face. A Negro* CONJURE MAN *has entered the store. His tattered garments are fantastically bedizened with many talismans and good-luck charms of shell and bone and feather. His blue-black skin is daubed with cryptic signs in white paint.*)

DOLLY. Git him out, git him out, he's going to mark my baby!

BEULAH. Oh, shoot, Dolly. . . . (DOLLY

has now fled after the TEMPLE SISTERS, *to the landing of the stairs. The* CONJURE MAN *advances with a soft, rapid, toothless mumble of words that sound like wind in dry grass. He is holding out something in his shaking hand.*) It's just that old crazy conjure man from Blue Mountain. He cain't mark your baby.

(*Phrase of primitive music or percussion as* NEGRO *moves into light.* BEULAH *follows* DOLLY *to landing.*)

CAROL (*very high and clear voice*). Come here, Uncle, and let me see what you've got there. Oh, it's a bone of some kind. No, I don't want to touch it, it isn't clean yet, there's still some flesh clinging to it. (*Women make sounds of revulsion.*) Yes, I know it's the breastbone of a bird but it's still tainted with corruption. Leave it a long time on a bare rock in the rain and the sun till every sign of corruption is burned and washed away from it, and then it will be a good charm, a white charm, but now it's a black charm, Uncle. So take it away and do what I told you with it. . . . (*The* NEGRO *makes a ducking obeisance and shuffles slowly back to the door.*) Hey, Uncle Pleasant, give us the Choctaw cry. (NEGRO *stops in confectionery.*) He's part Choctaw, he knows the Choctaw cry.

SISTER TEMPLE. Don't let him holler in *here!*

CAROL. Come on, Uncle Pleasant, *you* know it!

(*She takes off her coat and sits on the R. window sill. She starts the cry herself. The* NEGRO *throws back his head and completes it: a series of barking sounds that rise to a high sustained note of wild intensity. The women on the landing retreat further upstairs. Just then, as though the cry had brought him,* VAL *enters the store. He is a young man, about 30, who has a kind of wild beauty about him that the cry would suggest. He does not wear Levi's or a T-shirt, he has on a pair of dark serge pants, glazed from long wear and not excessively tight-fitting. His remarkable garment is a snakeskin jacket, mottled white, black and gray. He carries a guitar which is covered with inscriptions.*)

CAROL (*looking at the young man*). Thanks, Uncle . . .

BEULAH. Hey, old man, you! Choctaw! Conjure man! Nigguh! Will you go out-a *this sto'? So we can come back down stairs?*

(CAROL *hands* NEGRO *a dollar; he goes out right cackling.* VAL *holds the door open for* VEE TALBOTT, *a heavy, vague woman in her forties. She does primitive oil paintings and carries one into the store, saying*)

VEE. I got m'skirt caught in th' door of the Chevrolet an' I'm afraid I tore it. (*The women descend into store: laconic greetings, interest focused on* VAL.) Is it dark in here or am I losin' my eyesight? I been painting all day, finished a picture in a ten-hour stretch, just stopped a few minutes fo' coffee and went back to it again while I had a clear vision. I think I got it this time. But I'm so exhausted I could drop in my tracks. There's nothing more exhausting than that kind of work on earth, it's not so much that it tires your body out, but it leaves you drained inside. Y'know what I mean? Inside? Like you was burned out by something? Well! Still! —You feel you've accomplished something when you're through with it, sometimes you feel— *elevated!* How are you, Dolly?

DOLLY. All right, Mrs. Talbott.

VEE. That's good. How are *you*, Beulah?

BEULAH. Oh, I'm all right, I reckon.

VEE. Still can't make out much. Who is that there? (*Indicates* CAROL's *figure by the window. A significant silence greets this question.* VEE, *suddenly*) *Oh!* I thought her folks had got her out of the county . . . (CAROL *utters a very light, slightly rueful laugh, her eyes drifting back to* VAL *as she moves back into confectionery.*) Jabe and Lady back yet?

DOLLY. Pee Wee an' Dawg have gone to the depot to meet 'em.

VEE. Aw. Well, I'm just in time. I brought my new picture with me, the paint isn't dry on it yet. I thought that Lady might want to hang it up in Jabe's room while he's convalescin' from the operation, cause after a close shave with death, people like to be reminded of spiritual things. Huh? Yes! This is the Holy Ghost ascending. . . .

DOLLY (*looking at canvas*). You didn't put a head on it.

VEE. The head was a blaze of light, that's all I saw in my vision.

DOLLY. Who's the young man with

yuh?

VEE. Aw, excuse me, I'm too worn out to have manners. This is Mr. Valentine Xavier, Mrs. Hamma and Mrs.—I'm sorry, Beulah. I never *can* get y' last name!

BEULAH. I fo'give you. My name is Beulah Binnings.

VAL. What shall I do with this here?

VEE. Oh, that bowl of sherbet. I thought that Jabe might need something light an' digestible so I brought a bowl of sherbet.

DOLLY. What flavor is it?

VEE. Pineapple.

DOLLY. Oh, goody, I love pineapple. Better put it in the icebox before it starts to melt.

BEULAH (*looking under napkin that covers bowl*). I'm afraid you're lockin' th' stable after the horse is gone.

DOLLY. Aw, is it melted already?

BEULAH. Reduced to juice.

VEE. Aw, shoot. Well, put it on ice anyhow, it might thicken up. (*Women are still watching* VAL.) Where's the icebox?

BEULAH. In the confectionery.

VEE. I thought that Lady had closed the confectionery.

BEULAH. Yes, but the Frigidaire's still there.

(VAL *goes out R. through confectionery.*)

VEE. Mr. Xavier is a stranger in our midst. His car broke down in that storm last night and I let him sleep in the lockup. He's lookin' for work and I thought I'd introduce him to Lady an' Jabe because if Jabe can't work they're going to need somebody to help out in th' store.

BEULAH. That's a good idea.

DOLLY. Uh-huh.

BEULAH. Well, come on in, you all, it don't look like they're comin' straight home from the depot anyhow.

DOLLY. Maybe that wasn't the Cannonball Express.

BEULAH. Or maybe they stopped off fo' Pee Wee to buy some liquor.

DOLLY. Yeah . . . at Ruby Lightfoot's.

(*They move past* CAROL *and out of sight.* CAROL *has risen. Now she crosses into the main store area, watching* VAL *with the candid curiosity of one child observing another. He pays no attention but concentrates on his belt buckle which he is repairing with a pocketknife.)*

CAROL. What're you fixing?

VAL. Belt buckle.

CAROL. Boys like you are always fixing something. Could you fix my slipper?

VAL. What's wrong with your slipper?

CAROL. Why are you pretending not to remember me?

VAL. It's hard to remember someone you never met.

CAROL. Then why'd you look so startled when you saw me?

VAL. Did I?

CAROL. I thought for a moment you'd run back out the door.

VAL. The sight of a woman can make me walk in a hurry but I don't think it's ever made me run.—You're standing in my light.

CAROL (*moving aside slightly*). Oh, excuse me. Better?

VAL. Thanks. . . .

CAROL. Are you afraid I'll snitch?

VAL. Do what?

CAROL. Snitch? I wouldn't; I'm not a snitch. But I can prove that I know you if I have to. It was New Year's Eve in New Orleans.

VAL. I need a small pair of pliers. . . .

CAROL. You had on that jacket and a snake ring with a ruby eye.

VAL. I never had a snake ring with a ruby eye.

CAROL. A snake ring with an emerald eye?

VAL. I never had a snake ring with any kind of an eye. . . . (*Begins to whistle softly, his face averted.*)

CAROL (*smiling gently*). Then maybe it was a dragon ring with an emerald eye or a diamond or a ruby eye. You told us that it was a gift from a lady osteopath that you'd met somewhere in your travels and that any time you were broke you'd wire this lady osteopath collect, and no matter how far you were or how long it was since you'd seen her, she'd send you a money order for twenty-five dollars with the same sweet message each time. "I love you. When will you come back?" And to prove the story, not that it was difficult to believe it, you took the latest of these sweet messages from your wallet for us to see. . . . (*She throws back her head with soft laughter. He looks away still further and busies him-self with the belt buckle.*)—We followed you through five places before we made contact with you and I was the one that made contact. I went up to the bar where you were standing and touched your jacket and said, "What stuff is this made of?" and when you said it was snakeskin, I said, "I wish you'd told me before I touched it." And you said something not nice. You said, "Maybe that will learn you to hold back your hands." I was drunk by that time which was after midnight. Do you remember what I said to you? I said, "What on earth can you do on this earth but catch at whatever comes near you, with both your hands, until your fingers are broken?" I'd never said that before, or even consciously thought it, but afterwards it seemed like the truest thing that my lips had ever spoken, what on earth can you do but catch at whatever comes near you with both your hands until your fingers are broken. . . . You gave me a quick, sober look. I think you nodded slightly, and then you picked up your guitar and began to sing. After singing you passed the kitty. Whenever paper money was dropped in the kitty you blew a whistle. My cousin Bertie and I dropped in five dollars, you blew the whistle five times and then sat down at our table for a drink, Schenley's with Seven Up. You showed us all those signatures on your guitar. . . . Any correction so far?

VAL. Why are you so anxious to prove I know you?

CAROL. Because I want to know you better and better! I'd like to go out jooking with you tonight.

VAL. What's jooking?

CAROL. Oh, don't you know what that is? That's where you get in a car and drink a little and drive a little and stop and dance a little to a juke box and then you drink a little more and drive a little more and stop and dance a little more to a juke box and then you stop dancing and you just drink and drive and then you stop driving and just drink, and then, finally, you stop drinking. . . .

VAL. —What do you do, then?

CAROL. That depends on the weather and who you're jooking with. If it's a clear night you spread a blanket among the memorial stones on Cypress Hill, which is the local bone orchard, but if it's not a fair night, and this one certainly isn't, why, usually then you go to the Idlewild cabins between here and Sunset on the Dixie Highway. . . .

VAL. —That's about what I figured. But I don't go that route. Heavy drinking and smoking the weed and shacking with strangers is okay for kids in their twenties but this is my thirtieth birthday and I'm all through with that route. (*Looks up with dark eyes.*) I'm not young any more.

CAROL. You're young at thirty—I hope so! I'm twenty-nine!

VAL. Naw, you're not young at thirty if you've been on a Goddam party since you were fifteen! (*Picks up his guitar and sings and plays "Heavenly Grass." CAROL has taken a pint of bourbon from her trench-coat pocket and she passes it to him.*)

CAROL. Thanks. That's lovely. Many happy returns of your birthday, Snakeskin. (*She is very close to him.* VEE *enters and says sharply*)

VEE. Mr. Xavier don't drink.

CAROL. Oh, ex-cuse *me!*

VEE. And if you behaved yourself better your father would not be paralyzed in bed!

(*Sound of car out front. Women come running with various cries.* LADY *enters, nodding to the women, and holding the door open for her husband and the men following him. She greets the women in almost toneless murmurs, as if too tired to speak. She could be any age between thirty-five and forty-five, in appearance, but her figure is youthful. Her face taut. She is a woman who met with emotional disaster in her girlhood; verges on hysteria under strain. Her voice is often shrill and her body tense. But when in repose, a girlish softness emerges again and she looks ten years younger.*)

LADY. Come in, Jabe. We've got a reception committee here to meet us. They've set up a buffet supper.

(JABE *enters. A gaunt, wolfish man, gray and yellow. The women chatter idiotically.*)

BEULAH. Well, look who's here!

DOLLY. Well, *Jabe!*

BEULAH. I don't think he's been sick. I think he's been to Miami. Look at that wonderful color in his face!

DOLLY. I never seen him look better in my life!

BEULAH. Who does he think he's foolin'? Ha ha ha!—not *me!*

JABE. Whew, Jesus—I'm mighty—tired. . . .

(*An uncomfortable silence, everyone staring greedily at the dying man with his tense, wolfish smile and nervous cough.*) .

PEE WEE. Well, Jabe, we been feedin' lots of nickels to those one-arm bandits in there.

DOG. An' that pinball machine is hotter'n a pistol.

PEE WEE. Ha ha.

(EVA TEMPLE *appears on stairs and screams for her sister.*)

EVA. Sistuh! Sistuh! Sistuh! Cousin Jabe's here!

(*A loud clatter upstairs and shrieks.*)

JABE. Jesus. . . .

(EVA *rushing at him—stops short and bursts into tears.*)

LADY. Oh, cut that out, Eva Temple!—What were you doin' upstairs?

EVA. I can't help it, it's so good to see him, it's so wonderful to see our cousin again, oh, Jabe, *blessed!*

SISTER. Where's Jabe, where's precious Jabe? Where's our precious cousin?

EVA. Right here, Sister!

SISTER. Well, bless your old sweet life, and lookit the color he's got in his face, will you?

BEULAH. I just told him he looks like he's been to Miami and got a Florida suntan, haha ha!

(*The preceding speeches are very rapid, all overlapping.*)

JABE. I ain't been out in no sun an' if you all will excuse me I'm gonna do my celebratin' upstairs in bed because I'm kind of—worn out. (*Goes creakily to foot of steps while* EVA *and* SISTER *sob into their handkerchiefs behind him.*)—I see they's been some changes made here. Uh-huh. Uh-huh. How come the shoe department's back here now? (*Instant hostility as if habitual between them.*)

LADY. We always had a problem with light in this store.

JABE. So you put the shoe department further away from the window? That's sensible. A very intelligent solution to the problem, Lady.

LADY. Jabe, you know I told you we got a fluorescent tube coming to put back here.

JABE. Uh-huh. Uh-huh. Well. Tomorrow I'll get me some niggers to help me move the shoe department back front.

LADY. You do whatever you want to, it's your store.

JABE. Uh-huh. Uh-huh. I'm glad you reminded me of it.

(LADY *turns sharply away. He starts up stairs.* PEE WEE *and* DOG *follow him up. The women huddle and whisper in the store.* LADY *sinks wearily into chair at table.*)

BEULAH. That man will never come down those stairs again!

DOLLY. Never in this world, honey.

BEULAH. He has th' death sweat on him! Did you notice that death sweat on him?

DOLLY. An' yellow as butter, just as yellow as—

(SISTER *sobs.*)

EVA. Sister, Sister!

BEULAH (*crossing to* LADY). Lady, I don't suppose you feel much like talking about it right now but Dog and me are so worried.

DOLLY. Pee Wee and me are worried sick about it.

LADY. —About what?

BEULAH. Jabe's operation in Memphis. Was it successful?

DOLLY. Wasn't it successful?

(LADY *stares at them blindly. The women, except* CAROL, *close avidly about her, tense with morbid interest.*)

SISTER. Was it too late for surgical interference?

EVA. Wasn't it successful?

(*A loud, measured knock begins on the floor above.*)

BEULAH. Somebody told us it had gone past the knife.

DOLLY. We do hope it ain't hopeless.

EVA. We hope and pray it ain't hopeless.

(*All their faces wear faint, unconscious smiles.* LADY *looks from face to face; then utters a slight, startled laugh and springs up from the table and crosses to the stairs.*)

LADY (*as if in flight*). Excuse me, I have to go up, Jabe's knocking for me. (LADY *goes upstairs. The women gaze after her.*)

CAROL (*suddenly and clearly, in the silence*). Speaking of knocks, I have a knock in my engine. It goes knock, knock, and I say who's there. I don't know whether I'm in communication with some dead ancestor or the motor's about to drop out and leave me stranded in the dead of night on the Dixie Highway. Do you have any knowledge of mechanics? I'm sure you do. Would you be sweet and take a short drive with me? So you could hear that knock?

VAL. I don't have time.

CAROL. What have you got to do?

VAL. I'm waiting to see about a job in this store.

CAROL. I'm offering you a job.

VAL. I want a job that pays.

CAROL. I expect to pay you.

(*Women whisper loudly in the background.*)

VAL. Maybe sometime tomorrow.

CAROL. I can't stay here overnight; I'm not allowed to stay overnight in this county. (*Whispers rise. The word "corrupt" is distinguished. Without turning, smiling very brightly*) What are they saying about me? Can you hear what those women are saying about me?

VAL. —Play it cool. . . .

CAROL. I don't like playing it cool! What are they saying about me? That I'm corrupt?

VAL. If you don't want to be talked about, why do you make up like that, why do you—

CAROL. To show off!

VAL. What?

CAROL. *I'm an exhibitionist!* I want to be noticed, seen, heard, felt! I want them to know I'm alive! Don't you want them to know you're alive?

VAL. I want to live and I don't care if they know I'm alive or not.

CAROL. Then why do you play a guitar?

VAL. Why do you make a Goddam show of yourself?

CAROL. That's right, for the same reason.

VAL. We don't go the same route. . . . (*He keeps moving away from her; she continually follows him. Her speech is compulsive.*)

CAROL. I used to be what they call a Christ-bitten reformer. You know what that is?—A kind of benign exhibitionist. . . . I delivered stump speeches, wrote letters of protest about the gradual massacre of the colored majority in the county. I thought it was wrong for pellagra and slow starvation to cut them down when the cotton crop failed from army worm or boll weevil or too much rain in summer. I wanted to, tried to, put up free clinics, I squandered the money my mother left me on it. And when that Willie McGee thing came along—he was sent to the chair for having improper relations with a white whore—(*Her voice is like a passionate incantation.*) I made a fuss about it. I put on a potato sack and set out for the capitol on foot. This was in winter. I walked barefoot in this burlap sack to deliver a personal protest to the Governor of the State. Oh, I suppose it was partly exhibitionism on my part, but it wasn't completely exhibitionism; there was something else in it, too. You know how far I got? Six miles out of town—hooted, jeered at, even spit on!—every step of the way—and then arrested! Guess what for? Lewd vagrancy! Uh-huh, that was the charge, "lewd vagrancy," because they said that potato sack I had on was not a respectable garment. . . . Well, all that was a pretty long time ago, and now I'm not a reformer any more. I'm just a "lewd vagrant." And I'm showing the "S.O.B.S." how lewd a "lewd vagrant" can be if she puts her whole heart in it like I do mine! All right. I've told you my story, the story of an exhibitionist. Now I want you to do something for me. Take me out to Cypress Hill in my car. And we'll hear the dead people talk. They do talk there. They chatter together like birds on Cypress Hill, but all they say is one word and that one word is "live," they say "Live, live, live, live, live!" It's all they've learned, it's the only advice they can give.—Just live. . . . (*She opens the door.*) Simple!—a very simple instruction. . . . (*Goes out. Women's voices rise from the steady, indistinct murmur, like hissing geese.*)

WOMEN'S VOICES. —No, not liquor! Dope!

—Something not normal all right!

—Her father and brother were warned by the Vigilantes to keep her out of this county.

—She's absolutely degraded!

—Yes, corrupt!

—Corrupt! (*Etc., etc.*)

(*As if repelled by their hissing voices,*

VAL *suddenly picks up his guitar and goes out of the store as—*VEE TALBOTT *appears on the landing and calls down to him.*)

VEE. Mr. Xavier! Where is Mr. Xavier?

BEULAH. Gone, honey.

DOLLY. You might as well face it, Vee. This is one candidate for salvation that you have lost to the opposition.

BEULAH. He's gone off to Cypress Hill with the Cutrere girl.

VEE (*descending*). —If some of you older women in Two River County would set a better example there'd be more decent young people!

BEULAH. What was that remark?

VEE. I mean that people who give drinkin' parties an' get so drunk they don't know which is their husband and which is somebody else's and people who serve on the altar guild and still play cards on Sundays—

BEULAH. Just stop right there! Now I've discovered the source of that dirty gossip!

VEE. I'm only repeating what I've been told by others. I never been to these parties!

BEULAH. No, and you never will! You're a public kill-joy, a professional hypocrite!

VEE. I try to build up characters! You and your drinkin' parties are only concerned with tearin' characters down! I'm goin' upstairs, I'm goin' back upstairs! (*Rushes upstairs.*)

BEULAH. Well, I'm glad I said what I said to that woman. I've got no earthly patience with that sort of hypocriticism. Dolly, let's put this perishable stuff in the Frigidaire and leave here. I've never been so thoroughly disgusted!

DOLLY. Oh, my Lawd. (*Pauses at stairs and shouts*) PEE WEE! (*Goes off with the dishes.*)

SISTER. Both of those wimmen are as common as dirt.

EVA. Dolly's folks in Blue Mountain are nothin' at all but the poorest kind of white trash. Why, Lollie Tucker told me the old man sits on the porch with his shoes off drinkin' beer out of a bucket!—Let's take these flowers with us to put on the altar.

SISTER. Yes, we can give Jabe credit in the parish notes.

EVA. I'm going to take these olive-nut

sandwiches, too. They'll come in handy for the Bishop Adjutant's tea.

(DOLLY and BEULAH *cross through*.)

DOLLY. We still have time to make the second show.

BEULAH (*shouting*). Dog!

DOLLY. Pee Wee! (*They rush out of store.*)

EVA. Sits on the porch with his shoes off?

SISTER. Drinkin' beer out of a bucket! (*They go out with umbrellas, etc. Men descend stairs.*)

SHERIFF TALBOTT. Well, it looks to me like Jabe will more than likely go under before the cotton comes up.

PEE WEE. He never looked good.

DOG. Naw, but now he looks worse. (*They cross to door.*)

SHERIFF. Vee!

VEE (*from landing*). Hush that bawling. I had to speak to Lady about that boy and I couldn't speak to her in front of Jabe because he thinks he's gonna be able to go back to work himself.

SHERIFF. Well, move along, quit foolin'.

VEE. I think I ought to wait till that boy gits back.

SHERIFF. I'm sick of you making a goddam fool of yourself over every stray bastard that wanders into this county.

(*Car horn honks loudly.* VEE *follows her husband out. Sound of cars driving off. Dogs bay in distance as lights dim to indicate short passage of time.*)

SCENE TWO

A couple of hours later that night. Through the great window the landscape is faintly luminous under a scudding moonlit sky. Outside a girl's laughter, CAROL'S, *rings out high and clear and is followed by the sound of a motor, rapidly going off.*

VAL *enters the store before the car sound quite fades out and while a dog is still barking at it somewhere along the highway. He says "Christ" under his breath, goes to the buffet table and scrubs lipstick stain off his mouth and face with a paper napkin, picks up his guitar which he had left on a counter.*

Footsteps descending: LADY *appears on the landing in a flannel robe, shivering in the cold air; she snaps her fingers im-patiently for the old dog, Bella, who comes limping down beside her. She doesn't see* VAL, *seated on the shadowy counter, and she goes directly to the phone near the stairs. Her manner is desperate, her voice harsh and shrill.*

LADY. Ge' me the drugstore, will you? I know the drugstore's closed, this is Mrs. Torrance, my store's closed, too, but I got a sick man here, just back from the hospital, yeah, yeah, an emergency, wake up Mr. Dubinsky, keep ringing till he answers, it's an emergency! (*Pause: she mutters under her breath:*) —Porca la miseria!—I wish I was dead, dead, dead. . . .

VAL (*quietly*). No, you don't, lady.

She gasps, turning and seeing him, without leaving the phone, she rings the cashbox open and snatches out something.)

LADY. What're you doin' here? You know this store is closed!

VAL. I seen a light was still on and the door was open so I come back to—

LADY. You see what I got in my hand? (*Raises revolver above level of counter.*)

VAL. You going to shoot me?

LADY. You better believe it if you don't get out of here, mister!

VAL. That's all right, Lady, I just come back to pick up my guitar.

LADY. To pick up your guitar? (*He lifts it gravely.*)—Huh. . . .

VAL. Miss Talbott brought me here. I was here when you got back from Memphis, don't you remember?

LADY. —Aw. Aw, yeah. . . . You been here all this time?

VAL. No. I went out and come back.

LADY (*into the phone*). I told you to keep ringing till he answers! Go on, keep ringing, keep ringing! (*Then to* VAL:) You went out and come back?

VAL. Yeah.

LADY. What for?

VAL. You know that girl that was here?

LADY. Carol Cutrere?

VAL. She said she had car trouble and could I fix it.

LADY. —Did you fix it?

VAL. She didn't have no car trouble, that wasn't her trouble, oh, she had trouble, all right, but *that* wasn't it. . . .

LADY. What was her trouble?

VAL. She made a mistake about me.

LADY. What mistake?

VAL. She thought I had a sign "Male at Stud" hung on me.

LADY. She thought you—? (*Into phone suddenly*) Oh, Mr. Dubinsky, I'm sorry to wake you up but I just brought my husband back from the Memphis hospital and I felt my box of luminal tablets in the—I got to have some! I ain't slep' for three nights, I'm going to pieces, you hear me, I'm going to pieces, I ain't slept in three nights, I got to have some to-night. Now you look here, if you want to keep my trade, you send me over some tablets. Then bring them yourself, God damn it, excuse my French! Because I'm going to pieces right this minute! (*Hangs up violently.*)—*Mannage la miseria!*—Christ. . . . I'm shivering!—It's cold as a Goddam ice-plant in this store, I don't know why, it never seems to hold heat, the ceiling's too high or something, it don't hold heat at all.—Now what do you want? I got to go upstairs.

VAL. Here. Put this on you. (*He removes his jacket and hands it to her. She doesn't take it at once, stares at him questioningly and then slowly takes the jacket in her hands and examines it, running her fingers curiously over the snakeskin.*)

LADY. What is this stuff this thing's made of? It looks like it was snakeskin.

VAL. Yeah, well, that's what it is.

LADY. What're you doing with a snakeskin jacket?

VAL. It's a sort of a trademark; people call me Snakeskin.

LADY. Who calls you Snakeskin?

VAL. Oh, in the bars, the sort of places I work in—but I've quit that. I'm through with that stuff now. . . .

LADY. You're a—entertainer?

VAL. I sing and play the guitar.

LADY. —Aw? (*She puts the jacket on as if to explore it.*) It feels warm all right.

VAL. It's warm from my body, I guess. . . .

LADY. You must be a warm-blooded boy. . . .

VAL. That's right. . . .

LADY. Well, what in God's name are you lookin' for around here?

VAL. —Work.

LADY. Boys like you don't work.

VAL. What d'you mean by boys like me?

LADY. Ones that play th' guitar and go around talkin' about how warm they are. . . .

VAL. That happens t' be the truth. My temperature's always a couple degrees above normal the same as a dog's, it's normal for me the same as it is for a dog, that's the truth. . . .

LADY. —Huh!

VAL. You don't believe me?

LADY. I have no reason to doubt you, but what about it?

VAL. —Why—nothing. . . .

(*LADY laughs softly and suddenly; VAL smiles slowly and warmly.*)

LADY. You're a peculiar somebody all right, you sure are! How did you get around here?

VAL. I was driving through here last night and an axle broke on my car, that stopped me here, and I went to the county jail for a place to sleep out of the rain. Mizz Talbott took me in and give me a cot in the lockup and said if I hung around till you got back that you might give me a job in the store to help out since your husband was tooken sick.

LADY. —Uh-huh. Well—she was wrong about that. . . . If I took on help here it would have to be local help, I couldn't hire no stranger with a—snakeskin jacket and a guitar . . . and that runs a temperature as high as a dog's! (*Throws back her head in another soft, sudden laugh and starts to take off the jacket.*)

VAL. Keep it on.

LADY. No, I got to go up now and you had better be going . . .

VAL. I got nowhere to go.

LADY. Well, everyone's got a problem and that's yours.

VAL. —What nationality are you?

LADY. Why do you ask me that?

VAL. You seem to be like a foreigner.

LADY. I'm the daughter of a Wop bootlegger burned to death in his orchard!—Take your jacket. . . .

VAL. What was that you said about your father?

LADY. Why?

VAL. —A "Wop bootlegger"?

LADY. —They burned him to death in his orchard! What about it? The story's well known around here. (*JABE knocks on ceiling.*) I got to go up, I'm being called for. (*She turns out light over counter and at the same moment he begins to sing softly with his guitar: "Heavenly*

Grass." *He suddenly stops short and says abruptly:)*

VAL. I do electric repairs. (LADY *stares at him softly.*) I can do all kinds of odd jobs. Lady, I'm thirty today and I'm through with the life that I've been leading. (*Pause. Dog bays in distance.*) I lived in corruption but I'm not corrupted. Here is why. (*Picks up his guitar.*) My life's companion! It washes me clean like water when anything unclean has touched me. . . . (*Plays softly, with a slow smile.*)

LADY. What's all that writing on it?

VAL. Autographs of musicians I run into here and there.

LADY. Can I see it?

VAL. Turn on that light above you. (*She switches on green-shaded bulb over counter.* VAL *holds the instrument tenderly between them as if it were a child; his voice is soft, intimate, tender.*) See this name? Leadbelly?

LADY. Leadbelly?

VAL. Greatest man ever lived on the twelve-string guitar! Played it so good he broke the stone heart of a Texas governor with it and won himself a pardon out of jail. . . . And see this name Oliver? King Oliver? That name is immortal, Lady. Greatest man since Gabriel on a horn. . . .

LADY. What's this name?

VAL. Oh. That name? That name is also immortal. The name Bessie Smith is written in the stars!—Jim Crow killed her, John Barleycorn and Jim Crow killed Bessie Smith but that's another story. . . . See this name here? That's another immortal!

LADY. Fats Waller? Is his name written in the stars, too?

VAL. Yes, his name is written in the stars, too. . . .

(*Her voice is also intimate and soft: a spell of softness between them, their bodies almost touching, only divided by the guitar.*)

LADY. You had any sales experience?

VAL. All my life I been selling something to someone.

LADY. So's everybody. You got any character reference on you?

VAL. I have this—letter. (*Removes a worn, folded letter from a wallet, dropping a lot of snapshots and cards of various kinds on the floor. He passes the letter to her gravely and crouches to collect the dropped articles while she peruses the character reference.*)

LADY (*reading slowly aloud*). "This boy worked for me three months in my auto repair shop and is a real hard worker and is good and honest but is a peculiar talker and that is the reason I got to let him go but would like to—(*Holds letter closer to light.*)—would like to—keep him. Yours truly." (VAL *stares at her gravely, blinking a little.*) Huh—Some reference!

VAL. —Is that what it says?

LADY. Didn't you know what it said?

VAL. No.—The man sealed the envelope on it.

LADY. Well, that's not the sort of character reference that will do you much good, boy.

VAL. Naw. I guess it ain't.

LADY. —However. . . .

VAL. —What?

LADY. What people say about you don't mean much. Can you read shoe sizes?

VAL. I guess so.

LADY. What does 75 David mean? (VAL *stares at her, shakes head slowly.*) 75 means seven and one half long and David means "D" wide. You know how to make change?

VAL. Yeah, I could make change in a store.

LADY. Change for better or worse? Ha ha!—Well—(*Pause*) Well—you see that other room there, through that arch there? That's the confectionery; it's closed now but it's going to be reopened in a short while and I'm going to compete for the night life in this county, the after-the-movies trade. I'm going to serve setups in there and I'm going to redecorate. I got it all planned. (*She is talking eagerly now, as if to herself.*) Artificial branches of fruit trees in flower on the walls and ceilings!—It's going to be like an orchard in the spring!—My father, he had an orchard on Moon Lake. He made a wine garden of it. We had fifteen little white arbors with tables in them and they were covered with—grapevines and—we sold Dago red wine an' bootleg whiskey and beer.—They burned it up! My father was burned up in it. . . . (JABE *knocks above more loudly and a hoarse voice shouts* "Lady!" *Figure appears at the door and calls:* "Mrs. Torrance?") Oh, that's the sandman with my sleeping tablets.

(*Crosses to door.*) Thanks, Mr. Dubinsky, sorry I had to disturb you, sorry I— (*Man mutters something and goes. She closes the door.*) Well, go to hell, then, old bastard. . . . (*Returns with package.*) —You ever have trouble sleeping?

VAL. I can sleep or not sleep as long or short as I want to.

LADY. Is that right?

VAL. I can sleep on a concrete floor or go without sleeping, without even feeling sleepy, for forty-eight hours. And I can hold my breath three minutes without blacking out; I made ten dollars betting I could do it and I did it! And I can go a whole day without passing water.

LADY (*startled*). Is *that* a fact?

VAL (*very simply as if he'd made an ordinary remark*). That's a fact. I served time on a chain gang for vagrancy once and they tied me to a post all day and I stood there all day without passing water to show the sons of bitches that I could do it.

LADY. —I see what that auto repair man was talking about when he said this boy is a peculiar talker! Well—what else can you do? Tell me some more about your self-control!

VAL (*grinning*). Well, they say that a woman can burn a man down. But I can burn down a woman.

LADY. Which woman?

VAL. Any two-footed woman.

LADY (*throws back her head in sudden friendly laughter as he grins at her with the simple candor of a child*). —Well, there's lots of two-footed women round here that might be willin' to test the truth of that statement.

VAL. I'm saying I could. I'm not saying I would.

LADY. Don't worry, boy. I'm one two-footed woman that you don't have to convince of your perfect controls.

VAL. No, I'm done with all that.

LADY. What's the matter? Have they tired you out?

VAL. I'm not tired. I'm disgusted.

LADY. Aw, you're disgusted, huh?

VAL. I'm telling you, Lady, there's people bought and sold in this world like carcasses of hogs in butcher shops!

LADY. You ain't tellin' me nothin' I don't know.

VAL. You might think there's many and many kinds of people in this world but,

Lady, there's just two kinds of people, the ones that are bought and the buyers! No!—there's one other kind . . .

LADY. What kind's that?

VAL. The kind that's never been branded.

LADY. You will be, man.

VAL. They got to catch me first.

LADY. Well, then, you better not settle down in this county.

VAL. You know they's a kind of bird that don't have legs so it can't light on nothing but has to stay all its life on its wings in the sky? That's true. I seen one once, it had died and fallen to earth and it was light-blue colored and its body was tiny as your little finger, that's the truth, it had a body as tiny as your little finger and so light on the palm of your hand it didn't weigh more than a feather, but its wings spread out this wide but they was transparent, the color of the sky and you could see through them. That's what they call protection coloring. Camouflage, they call it. You can't tell those birds from the sky and that's why the hawks don't catch them, don't see them up there in the high blue sky near the sun!

LADY. How about in gray weather?

VAL. They fly so high in gray weather the Goddam hawks would get dizzy. But those little birds, they don't have no legs at all and they live their whole lives on the wing, and they sleep on the wind, that's how they sleep at night, they just spread their wings and go to sleep on the wind like other birds fold their wings and go to sleep on a tree. . . . (*Music fades in.*)—They sleep on the wind and . . . (*His eyes grow soft and vague and he lifts his guitar and accompanies the very faint music.*)—never light on this earth but one time when they die!

LADY. —I'd like to be one of those birds.

VAL. So'd I like to be one of those birds; they's lots of people would like to be one of those birds and never be—corrupted!

LADY. If one of those birds ever dies and falls on the ground and you happen to find it, I wish you would show it to me because I think maybe you just imagine there is a bird of that kind in existence. Because I don't think nothing living has ever been that free, not even nearly. Show me one of them birds and I'll say, Yes,

God's made one perfect creature!—I sure would give this mercantile store and every bit of stock in it to be that tiny bird the color of the sky . . . for one night to sleep on the wind and—float!—around under th'—stars . . . (JABE *knocks on floor.* LADY's *eyes return to* VAL.) —Because I sleep with a son of a bitch who bought me at a fire sale, and not in fifteen years have I had a single good dream not one—oh!—*Shit . . .* I don't know why I'm—telling a stranger—this. . . . (*She rings the cashbox open.*) Take this dollar and go eat at the Al-Nite on the highway and come back here in the morning and I'll put you to work. I'll break you in clerking here and when the new confectionery opens, well, maybe I can use you in there.—That door locks when you close it!—But let's get one thing straight.

VAL. What thing?

LADY. I'm not interested in your perfect functions, in fact you don't interest me no more than the air that you stand in. If that's understood we'll have a good working relation, but otherwise trouble! —Of course I know you're crazy, but they's lots of crazier people than you are still running loose and some of them in high positions, too. Just remember. No monkey business with me. Now go. Go eat, you're hungry.

VAL. Mind if I leave this here? My life's companion? (*He means his guitar.*)

LADY. Leave it here if you want to.

VAL. Thanks, Lady.

LADY. Don't mention it.

(*He crosses toward the door as a dog barks with passionate clarity in the distance. He turns to smile back at her and says*)

VAL. I don't know nothing about you except you're nice but you are just about the nicest person that I have ever run into! And I'm going to be steady and honest and hard-working to please you and any time you have any more trouble sleeping, I know how to fix that for you. A lady osteopath taught me how to make little adjustments in the neck and spine that give you sound, natural sleep. Well, g'night, now.

(*He goes out. Count five. Then she throws back her head and laughs as lightly and gaily as a young girl. Then she turns and wonderingly picks up and*

runs *her hands tenderly over his guitar as the curtain falls.*)

ACT TWO

Scene One

The store, afternoon, a few weeks later. The table and chair are back in the confectionery. LADY *is hanging up the phone.* VAL *is standing just outside the door. He turns and enters. Outside on the highway a mule team is laboring to pull a big truck back on the icy pavement. A Negro's voice shouts: "Hyyyyyyyyy-up."*

VAL (*moving to R. window*). One a them big Diamond T trucks an' trailors gone off the highway last night and a six mule team is tryin' t' pull it back on. . . . (*He looks out window.*)

LADY (*coming from behind to R. of counter*). Mister, we just now gotten a big fat complaint about you from a woman that says if she wasn't a widow her husband would come in here and beat the tar out of you.

VAL (*taking a step toward her*). Yeah? —Is this a small pink-headed woman?

LADY. *Pin*-headed woman did you say?

VAL. Naw, I said, "Pink!"—A little pink-haired woman, in a checkered coat with pearl buttons this big on it.

LADY. I talked to her on the phone. She didn't go into such details about her appearance but she did say you got familiar. I said, "How? by his talk or behavior?" And she said, "Both!"—Now I was afraid of this when I warned you last week, "No monkey business here, boy!"

VAL. This little pink-headed woman bought a valentine from me and all I said is my *name* is Valentine to her. Few minutes later a small colored boy come in and delivered the valentine to me with something wrote on it an' I believe I still got it. . . . (*Finds and shows it to* LADY *who goes to him.* LADY *reads it, and tears it fiercely to pieces. He lights a cigarette.*)

LADY. Signed it with a lipstick kiss? You didn't show up for this date?

VAL. No, ma'am. That's why she complained. (*Throws match on floor.*)

LADY. Pick that match up off the floor.

VAL. Are you bucking for sergeant, or something? (*He throws match out the door with elaborate care. Her eyes follow his back.* VAL *returns lazily toward her.*)

LADY. Did you walk around in front of her that way?

VAL (*at counter*). What way?

LADY. Slew-foot, slew-foot! (*He regards her closely with good-humored perplexity.*) Did you stand in front of her like that? That close? In that, that— *position?*

VAL. What position?

LADY. Ev'rything you do is suggestive!

VAL. Suggestive of what?

LADY. Of what you said you was through with—somethin'—*Oh, shoot, you know what I mean.*—Why'd 'ya think I give you a plain, dark business suit to work in?

VAL (*sadly*). Un-hun. . . . (*Sighs and removes his blue jacket.*)

LADY. Now what're you takin' that off for?

VAL. I'm giving the suit back to you. I'll change my pants in the closet. (*Gives her the jacket and crosses into alcove.*)

LADY. Hey! I'm sorry! You hear me? I didn't sleep well last night. Hey! I said I'm sorry! You hear me? (*She enters alcove and returns immediately with* VAL's *guitar and crosses to D.R. He follows.*)

VAL. Le' me have my guitar, Lady. You find too many faults with me and I tried to do good.

LADY. I told you I'm sorry. You want me to get down and lick the dust off your shoes?

VAL. Just give me back my guitar.

LADY. I ain't dissatisfied with you. I'm pleased with you, sincerely!

VAL. You sure don't show it.

LADY. My nerves are all shot to pieces. (*Extends hand to him.*) Shake.

VAL. You mean I ain't fired, so I don't have to quit? (*They shake hands like two men. She hands him guitar—then silence falls between them.*)

LADY. You see, we don't know each other, we're, we're—just gettin'—acquainted.

VAL. That's right, like a couple of animals sniffin' around each other. . . .

(*The image embarrasses her. He crosses to counter, leans over and puts guitar behind it.*)

LADY. Well, not exactly like that, but—!

VAL. We don't know each other. How do people get to know each other? I used to think they did it by touch.

LADY. By what?

VAL. By touch, by touchin' each other.

LADY (*moving up and sitting on shoe-fitting chair which has been moved to R. window*). Oh, you mean by close—contact!

VAL. But later it seemed like that made them more strangers than ever, uhh, huh, more strangers than ever. . . .

LADY. Then how d'you think they get to know each other?

VAL (*sitting on counter*). Well, in answer to your last question, I would say this: Nobody ever gets to know *no body*! We're all of us sentenced to solitary confinement inside our own skins, for life! You understand me, Lady?—I'm tellin' you it's the truth, we got to face it, we're under a lifelong sentence to solitary confinement inside our own lonely skins for as long as we live on this earth!

LADY (*rising and crossing to him*). Oh, no, I'm not a big optimist but I cannot agree with something as sad as that statement!

(*They are sweetly grave as two children; the store is somewhat dusky. She sits in chair R. of counter.*)

VAL. Listen!—When I was a kid on Witches Bayou? After my folks all scattered away like loose chicken's feathers blown around by the wind?—I stayed there alone on the bayou, hunted and trapped out of season and hid from the law!—Listen!—All that time, all that lonely time, I felt I was—waiting for something!

LADY. What for?

VAL. What does anyone wait for? For something to happen, for anything to happen, to make things make more sense. . . . It's hard to remember what that feeling was like because I've lost it now, but I was waiting for something like if you ask a question you wait for someone to answer, but you ask the wrong question or you ask the wrong person and the answer don't come.

Does everything stop because you don't get the answer? No, it goes right on as if the answer was given, day comes after day and night comes after night, and you're still waiting for someone to answer the question and going right on as if the question was answered. And then—well

—then. . . .

LADY. Then what?

VAL. You get the make-believe answer.

LADY. What answer is that?

VAL. Don't pretend you don't know because you do!

LADY. —Love?

VAL (*placing hand on her shoulder*). That's the make-believe answer. It's fooled many a fool besides you an' me, that's the God's truth, Lady, and you had better believe it. (LADY *looks reflectively at* VAL *and he goes on speaking and sits on stool below counter.*)—I met a girl on the bayou when I was fourteen. I'd had a feeling that day that if I just kept poling the boat down the bayou a little bit further I would come bang into whatever it was I'd been so long expecting!

LADY. Was she the answer, this girl that you met on the bayou?

VAL. She made me think that she was.

LADY. How did she do that?

VAL. By coming out on the dogtrot of a cabin as naked as I was in that flat-bottom boat? She stood there a while with the daylight burning around her as bright as heaven as far as I could see. You seen the inside of a shell, how white that is, pearly white? Her naked skin was like that.— Oh, God, I remember a bird flown out of the moss and its wings made a shadow on her, and then it sung a single, high clear note, and as if she was waiting for that as a kind of a signal to catch me, she turned and smiled, and walked on back in the cabin. . . .

LADY. You followed?

VAL. Yes, I followed. I followed, like a bird's tail follows a bird, I followed!

I thought that she give me the answer to the question, I'd been waiting for, but afterwards I wasn't sure that was it, but from that time the question wasn't much plainer than the answer and—

LADY. —What?

VAL. At fifteen I left Witches Bayou. When the dog died I sold my boat and the gun. . . . I went to New Orleans in this snakeskin jacket. . . . It didn't take long for me to learn the score.

LADY. What did you learn?

VAL. I learned that I had something to sell besides snakeskins and other wild things' skins I caught on the bayou. I was corrupted! That's the answer. . . .

LADY. Naw, that ain't the answer!

VAL. Okay, *you* tell me the answer!

LADY. I don't know the answer, I just know corruption ain't the answer. I know that much. If I thought that was the answer I'd take Jabe's pistol or his morphine tablets and—

(*A woman bursts into store.*)

WOMAN. I got to use your pay-phone!

LADY. Go ahead. Help yourself. (*Woman crosses to phone, deposits coin.* LADY *crosses to confectionery. To* VAL) Get me a coke from the cooler.

(VAL *crosses and goes out R. During the intense activity among the choral women,* LADY *and* VAL *seem bemused as if they were thinking back over their talk before. For the past minute or two a car horn has been heard blowing repeatedly in the near distance.*)

WOMAN (*at phone*). Cutrere place, get me the Cutrere place, will yuh? David Cutrere or his wife, whichever comes to the phone!

(BEULAH *rushes in from the street to R.C.*)

BEULAH. Lady, Lady, where's Lady! Carol Cutrere is—!

WOMAN. Quiet, please! I am calling her brother about her! (LADY *sits at table in confectionery. At phone*) Who's this I'm talking to? Good! I'm calling about your sister, Carol Cutrere. She is blowing her car horn at the Red Crown station, she is blowing and blowing her car horn at the Red Crown station because my husband give the station attendants instructions not to service her car, and she is blowing and blowing and blowing on her horn, drawing a big crowd there and, Mr. Cutrere, I thought that you and your father had agreed to keep that girl out of Two River County for good, that's what we all understood around here.

(*Car horn.*)

BEULAH (*listening with excited approval*). Good! Good! Tell him that if—

(DOLLY *enters.*)

DOLLY. She's gotten out of the car and—

BEULAH. *Shhh!*

WOMAN. Well, I just wanted to let you know she's back here in town makin' another disturbance and my husband's on the phone now at the Red Crown station— (DOLLY *goes outside and looks off.*) trying to get the Sheriff, so if she gits picked up again by th' law, you can't say I didn't warn you, Mr. Cutrere. (*Car horn.*)

DOLLY (*coming back in*). Oh, good! Good!

BEULAH. Where is she, where's she gone now?

WOMAN. You better be quick about it. Yes, I do. I sympathize with you and your father and with Mrs. Cutrere, but Carol cannot demand service at our station, we just refuse to wait on her, she's not—Hello? Hello? (*She jiggles phone violently.*)

BEULAH. What's he doin'? Comin' to pick her up?

DOLLY. Call the Sheriff's office! (BEULAH *goes outside again.* VAL *comes back with a bottle of Coca-Cola—hands it to* LADY *and leans on juke box. Going out to* BEULAH.) What's goin' on now?

BEULAH (*outside*). Look, look, they're pushing her out of the station driveway. (*They forget* LADY *in this new excitement. Ad libs continual. The short woman from the station charges back out of the store.*)

DOLLY. Where is Carol?

BEULAH. Going into the White Star Pharmacy!

(DOLLY *rushes back in to the phone.*)

BEULAH (*crossing to* LADY). Lady, I want you to give me your word that if that Cutrere girl comes in here, you won't wait on her! You hear me?

LADY. No.

BEULAH. —What? Will you refuse to wait on her?

LADY. I can't refuse to wait on anyone in this store.

BEULAH. Well, I'd like to know why you can't.

DOLLY. Shhh! I'm on the phone!

BEULAH. Who you phonin' Dolly?

DOLLY. That White Star Pharmacy! I want to make sure that Mr. Dubinsky refuses to wait on that girl! (*Having found and deposited coin*) I want the White Far Starmacy. I mean the— (*Stamps foot.*)—White Star Pharmacy!—I'm so upset my tongue's twisted! (LADY *hands coke to* VAL. BEULAH *is at the window.*) I'm getting a busy signal. Has she come out yet?

BEULAH. No, she's still in the White Star!

DOLLY. Maybe they're not waiting on her.

BEULAH. Dubinsky'd wait on a purple-bottom baboon if it put a dime on th' counter an' pointed at something!

DOLLY. I know she sat at a table in the Blue Bird Café half'n hour last time she was here and the waitresses never came near her!

BEULAH. That's different. They're not foreigners there! (DOLLY *crosses to counter.*) You can't ostracize a person out of this county unless everybody cooperates. Lady just told me that she was going to wait on her if she comes here.

DOLLY. Lady wouldn't do that.

BEULAH. *Ask* her! She told *me* she would!

LADY (*rising and turning at once to the women and shouting at them*). Oh, for God's sake, no! I'm not going to refuse to wait on her because you all don't like her! Besides I'm delighted that wild girl is givin' her brother so much trouble! (*After this outburst she goes back of the counter.*)

DOLLY (*at phone*). Hush! Mr. Dubinsky! This is Dolly Hamma, Mr. "Dog" Hamma's wife! (CAROL *quietly enters the front door.*) I want to ask you, is Carol Cutrere in your drugstore?

BEULAH (*warningly*). Dolly!

CAROL. No. She isn't.

DOLLY. —What?

CAROL. She's here.

(BEULAH *goes into confectionery.* CAROL *moves toward* VAL *to D.R.C.*)

DOLLY. —Aw!—Never mind, Mr. Dubinsky, I—(*Hangs up furiously and crosses to door.*)

(*A silence in which they all stare at the girl from various positions about the store. She has been on the road all night in an open car: her hair is blown wild, her face flushed and eyes bright with fever. Her manner in the scene is that of a wild animal at bay, desperate but fearless.*)

LADY (*finally and quietly*). Hello, Carol.

CAROL. Hello, Lady.

LADY (*defiantly cordial*). I thought that you were in New Orleans, Carol.

CAROL. Yes, I was. Last night.

LADY. Well, you got back fast.

CAROL. I drove all night.

LADY. In that storm?

CAROL. The wind took the top off my car but I didn't stop. (*She watches* VAL *steadily; he steadily ignores her; turns aways and puts bottles of Coca-Cola on a table.*)

LADY (*with growing impatience*). Is something wrong at home, is someone sick?

CAROL (*absently*). No. No, not that I know of, I wouldn't know if there was, they—may I sit down?

LADY. Why, sure.

CAROL (*crossing to chair at counter and sitting*). —They pay me to stay away so I wouldn't know. . . . (*Silence.* VAL *walks deliberately past her and goes into alcove.*)—I think I have a fever, I feel like I'm catching pneumonia, everything's so far away. . . .

(*Silence again except for the faint, hissing whispers of* BEULAH *and* DOLLY *at the back of the store.*)

LADY (*with a touch of exasperation*). Is there something you want?

CAROL. Everything seems miles away. . . .

LADY. Carol, I said is there anything you want here?

CAROL. Excuse me!—yes. . . .

LADY. Yes, what?

CAROL. Don't bother now. I'll wait.

(VAL *comes out of alcove with the blue jacket on.*)

LADY. Wait for what, what are you waiting for! You don't have to wait for nothing, just say what you want and if I got it in stock I'll give it to you!

(*Phone rings once.*)

CAROL (*vaguely*). —Thank you—no. . . .

LADY (*to* VAL). Get that phone, Val.

(DOLLY *crosses and hisses something inaudible to* BEULAH.)

BEULAH (*rising*). I just want to wait here to see if she does or she don't.

DOLLY. She just said she would!

BEULAH. Just the same, I'm gonna wait!!

VAL (*at phone*). Yes, sir, she is.—I'll tell her. (*Hangs up and speaks to* LADY.) Her brother's heard she's here and he's coming to pick her up.

LADY. *David Cutrere is not coming in this store!*

DOLLY. Aw-aw!

BEULAH. David Cutrere used to be her lover.

DOLLY. I remember you told me.

LADY (*wheels about suddenly toward the women*). Beulah! Dolly! Why're you back there hissing together like geese? (*Coming from behind counter to R.C.*) Why don't you go to th'—Blue Bird and —have some hot coffee—talk there!

BEULAH. It looks like we're getting what they call the bum's rush.

DOLLY. I never stay where I'm not wanted and when I'm not wanted somewhere I never come back! (*They cross out and slam door.*)

LADY (*after a pause*). What did you come here for?

CAROL. To deliver a message.

LADY. To me?

CAROL. No.

LADY. Then who? (CAROL *stares at* LADY *gravely a moment, then turns slowly to look at* VAL.)—Him?—Him? (CAROL *nods slowly and slightly.*) OK, then, give him the message, deliver the message to him.

CAROL. It's a private message. Could I speak to him alone, please?

(LADY *gets a shawl from a hook.*)

LADY. Oh, for God's sake! Your brother's plantation is ten minutes from here in that sky-blue Cadillac his rich wife give him. Now look, he's on his way here but I won't let him come in, I don't even want his hand to touch the door-handle. I know your message, this boy knows your message, there's nothing private about it. But I tell you, that this boy's not for sale in my store!—Now—I'm going out to watch for the sky-blue Cadillac on the highway. When I see it, I'm going to throw this door open and holler and when I holler, I want you out of this door like a shot from a pistol!—that fast! Understand?

(NOTE: *Above scene is overextended. This can be remedied by a very lively performance. It might also help to indicate a division between the Lady-Val scene and the group scene that follows.*)

(LADY *slams door behind her. The loud noise of the door slam increases the silence that follows.* VAL's *oblivious attitude is not exactly hostile, but deliberate. There's a kind of purity in it; also a kind of refusal to concern himself with a problem that isn't his own. He holds his guitar with a specially tender concentration, and strikes a soft chord on it. The girl stares at* VAL: *he whistles a note and tightens a guitar string to the pitch of the whistle, not looking at the girl. Since this scene is followed by the emotional scene between* LADY *and* DAVID, *it should be keyed somewhat lower than written; it's important that* VAL *should not seem brutal in his attitude toward* CAROL; *there should be an air between them of two lonely children.*)

VAL (*in a soft, preoccupied tone*). You told the lady I work for that you had a message for me. Is that right, Miss? Have you got a message for me?

CAROL (*she rises, moves a few steps toward him, hesitantly.* VAL *whistles, plucks guitar string, changes pitch*). You've spilt some ashes on your new blue suit.

VAL. Is that the message?

CAROL (*moves away a step*). No. No, that was just an excuse to touch you. The message is—

VAL. What?

(*Music fades in—guitar.*)

CAROL. —I'd love to hold something the way you hold your guitar, that's how I'd love to hold something, with such— *tender protection!* I'd love to hold *you* that way, with that same—*tender protection!* (*Her hand has fallen onto his knee, which he has drawn up to rest a foot on the counter stool.*)—Because you hang the moon for me!

VAL (*he speaks to her, not roughly but in a tone that holds a long history that began with a romantic acceptance of such declarations as she has just made to him, and that turned gradually to his present distrust. He puts guitar down and goes to her*). Who're you tryin' t' fool beside you'self? You couldn't stand the weight of a man's body on you. (*He casually picks up her wrist and pushes the sleeve back from it.*) What's this here? A human wrist with a bone? It feels like a twig I could snap with two fingers. . . . (*Gently, negligently, pushes collar of her trench coat back from her bare throat and shoulders. Runs a finger along her neck tracing a vein.*) Little girl, you're transparent, I can see the veins in you. A man's weight on you would break you like a bundle of sticks. . . .

(*Music fades out.*)

CAROL (*gazes at him, startled by his perception*). Isn't it funny! You've hit on the truth about me. The act of love-making is almost unbearably painful, and yet, of course, I do bear it, because to be not alone, even for a few moments, is worth the pain and the danger. It's dangerous for me because I'm not built for childbearing.

VAL. Well, then, fly away, little bird, fly away before you—get broke. (*He turns back to his guitar.*)

CAROL. Why do you dislike me?

VAL (*turning back*). I never dislike nobody till they interfere with me.

CAROL. How have I interfered with you? Did I snitch when I saw my cousin's watch on you?

VAL (*beginning to remove his watch*). —You won't take my word for a true thing I told you. I'm thirty years old and I'm done with the crowd you run with and the places you run to. The Club Rendezvous, the Starlite Lounge, the Music Bar, and all the night places. Here —(*Offers watch.*)—take this Rolex Chronometer that tells the time of the day and the day of the week and the month and all the crazy moon's phases. I never stole nothing before. When I stole that I known it was time for me to get off the party, so take it back, now, to Bertie. . . . (*He takes her hand and tries to force the watch into her fist. There is a little struggle, he can't open her fist. She is crying, but staring fiercely into his eyes. He draws a hissing breath and hurls watch violently across the floor.*)—That's my message to you and the pack you run with!

CAROL (*flinging coat away*). I RUN WITH NOBODY!—I hoped I could run with you. . . . (*Music stops short.*) You're in danger here, Snakeskin. You've taken off the jacket that said: "I'm wild, I'm alone!" and put on the nice blue uniform of a convict! . . . Last night I woke up thinking about you again. I drove all night to bring you this warning of danger. . . . (*Her trembling hand covers her lips.*)— The message I came here to give you was a warning of danger! I hoped you'd hear me and let me take you away before it's —too late.

(*Door bursts open.* LADY *rushes inside, crying out*)

LADY. *Your brother's coming, go out! He can't come in!* (CAROL *picks up coat and goes into confectionery, sobbing.* VAL *crosses toward door.*) *Lock that door! Don't let him come in my store!*

(CAROL *sinks sobbing at table.* LADY *runs up to the landing of the stairs as* DAVID CUTRERE *enters the store. He is a tall man in hunter's clothes. He is hardly less handsome now than he was in his youth but something has gone: his power is that of a captive who rules over other captives. His face, his eyes, have something of the same desperate, unnatural hardness that* LADY *meets the world with*.)

DAVID. Carol?

VAL. She's in there. (*He nods toward the dim confectionery into which the girl has retreated.*)

DAVID (*crossing*). Carol! (*She rises and advances a few steps into the lighted area of the stage.*) You broke the agreement. (CAROL *nods slightly, staring at* VAL. *Harshly*) All right. I'll drive you back. Where's your coat? (CAROL *murmurs something inaudible, staring at* VAL.) Where is her coat, where is my sister's coat?

(VAL *crosses below and picks up the coat that* CAROL *has dropped on the floor and hands it to* DAVID. *He throws it roughly about* CAROL's *shoulders and propels her forcefully toward the store entrance.* VAL *moves away to D.R.*)

LADY (*suddenly and sharply*). Wait, please!

(DAVID *looks up at the landing; stands frozen as* LADY *rushes down the stairs.*)

DAVID (*softly, hoarsely*). How—are you, Lady?

LADY (*turning to* VAL). Val, go out.

DAVID (*to* CAROL). Carol, will you wait for me in my car?

(*He opens the door for his sister; she glances back at* VAL *with desolation in her eyes.* VAL *crosses quickly through the confectionery. Sound of door closing in there.* CAROL *nods slightly as if in sad response to some painful question and goes out of the store. Pause.*)

LADY. I told you once to never come in this store.

DAVID. I came for my sister. . . . (*He turns as if to go.*)

LADY. No, wait!

DAVID. I don't dare leave my sister alone on the road.

LADY. I have something to tell you I never told you before. (*She crosses to him.* DAVID *turns back to her, then moves away to D.R.C.*)—I—carried your child in my body the summer you quit me. (*Silence.*)

DAVID. —I didn't know.

LADY. No, no. I didn't write you no letter about it; I was proud then; I had pride. But I had your child in my body the summer you quit me, that summer

they burned my father in his wine garden, and you, you washed your hands clean of any connection with a Dago bootlegger's daughter and—(*Her breathless voice momentarily falters and she makes a fierce gesture as she struggles to speak.*)—took that—society girl that—restored your homeplace and give you such—(*Catches breath.*)—wellborn children. . . .

DAVID. —I—didn't know.

LADY. Well, now you do know, you know now. I carried your child in my body the summer you quit me but I had it cut out of my body, and they cut my heart out with it!

DAVID. —I—didn't know.

LADY. I wanted death after that, but death don't come when you *want* it, it comes when you don't want it! I wanted death, then, but I took the next best thing. *You* sold *yourself. I* sold *my* self. *You* was bought. *I* was bought. You made whores of us both!

DAVID. —I—didn't know. . . .

(*Mandolin, barely audible,* "Dicitincello Vuoi.")

LADY. But that's all a long time ago. Some reason I drove by there a few nights ago; the shore of the lake where my father had his wine garden? You remember? You remember the wine garden of my father? (DAVID *stares at her. She turns away.*) No, you don't? You don't remember it even?

DAVID. —Lady, I don't—remember—anything else. . . .

LADY. The mandolin of my father, the songs that I sang with my father in my father's wine garden?

DAVID. Yes, I don't remember anything else. . . .

LADY. *Core Ingrata! Come Le Rose!* And we disappeared and he would call, *"Lady? Lady?"* (*Turns to him.*) How could I answer him with two tongues in my mouth! (*A sharp hissing intake of breath, eyes opened wide, hand clapped over her mouth as if what she said was unendurable to her. He turns instantly, sharply away.—Music stops short.* JABE *begins to knock for her on the floor above. She crosses to stairs, stops, turns.*) I hold hard feelings!—Don't ever come here again. If your wild sister comes here, send somebody else for her, not you, not you. Because I hope never to feel this knife again in me. (*Her hand is on her chest; she breathes with difficulty. He turns away from her; starts toward the door. She takes a step toward him.*) And don't pity me neither. I haven't gone down so terribly far in the world. I got a going concern in this mercantile store, in there's the confectionery which'll reopen this spring, it's being done over to make it the place that all the young people will come to, it's going to be like—(*He touches the door, pauses with his back to her.*)—the wine garden of my father, those wine-drinking nights when you had something better than anything you've had since!

DAVID. Lady—*That's*—

LADY. —*What*?

DAVID. —*True!* (*Opens door.*)

LADY. Go now. I just wanted to tell you my life ain't over. (*He goes out as* JABE *continues knocking. She stands, stunned, motionless till* VAL *quietly re-enters the store. She becomes aware of his return rather slowly; then she murmurs*) I made a fool of myself. . . .

VAL. What?

(*She crosses to stairs.*)

LADY. *I made a fool of myself!* (*She goes up the stairs with effort as the lights change slowly to mark a division of scenes.*)

SCENE TWO

Sunset of that day. VAL *is alone in the store, as if preparing to go. The sunset is fiery. A large woman opens the door and stands there looking dazed. It is* VEE TALBOTT.

VAL (*turning*). Hello, Mrs. Talbott.

VEE. Something's gone wrong with my eyes. I can't see nothing.

VAL (*going to her*). Here, let me help you. You probably drove up here with that setting sun in your face. (*Leading her to shoe-fitting chair at R. window*) There now. Set down right here.

VEE. Thank you—so—much. . . .

VAL. I haven't seen you since that night you brought me here to ask for this job.

VEE. Has the minister called on you yet? Reverend Tooker? I made him promise he would. I told him you were new around here and weren't affiliated to any church yet. I want you to go to ours.

VAL. —That's—mighty kind of you.

VEE. The Church of the Resurrection, it's Episcopal.

VAL. Uh, huh.

VEE. Unwrap that picture, please.

VAL. Sure. (*He tears paper off canvas.*)

VEE. It's the Church of the Resurrection. I give it a sort of imaginative treatment. You know, Jabe and Lady have never darkened a church door. I thought it ought to be hung where Jabe could look at it, it might help to bring that poor dying man to Jesus. . . .

(VAL *places it against chair R. of counter and crouches before the canvas, studying it long and seriously.* VEE *coughs nervously, gets up, bends to look at the canvas, sits uncertainly back down.* VAL *smiles at her warmly, then back to the canvas.*)

VAL (*at last*). What's this here in the picture?

VEE. The steeple.

VAL. Aw.—Is the church steeple red?

VEE. Why—no, but—

VAL. Why'd you paint it red, then?

VEE. Oh, well, you see, I—(*Laughs nervously, childlike in her growing excitement.*)—I just, just *felt* it that way! I paint a thing how I feel it instead of always the way it actually is. Appearances are misleading, nothing is what it looks like to the eyes. You got to have—*vision—to see!*

VAL. —Yes. Vision. Vision!—to see. . . . (*Rises, nodding gravely, emphatically.*)

VEE. I paint from vision. They call me a visionary.

VAL. Oh.

VEE (*with shy pride*). That's what the New Orleans and Memphis newspaper people admire so much in my work. They call it a primitive style, the work of a visionary. One of my pictures is hung on the exhibition in Audubon Park museum and they have asked for others. I can't turn them out fast enough!—I have to wait for—visions, no, I—I can't paint without—visions . . . I couldn't *live* without visions!

VAL. Have you always had visions?

VEE. No, just since I was born, I—(*Stops short, startled by the absurdity of her answer. Both laugh suddenly, then she rushes on, her great bosom heaving with curious excitement, twisting in her chair, gesturing with clenched hands.*) I was born, I was born with a caul! A sort of thing like a veil, a thin, thin sort of a web was over my eyes. They call that a caul. It's a sign that you're going to have visions, and I did, I had them! (*Pauses for breath; light fades.*)—When I was little my baby sister died. Just one day old, she died. They had to baptize her at midnight to save her soul.

VAL. Uh-huh. (*He sits opposite her, smiling, attentive.*)

VEE. The minister came at midnight, and after the baptism service, he handed the bowl of holy water to me and told me, "Be sure to empty this out on the ground!"—I didn't. I was scared to go out at midnight, with, with—death! in the —house and—I sneaked into the kitchen; I emptied the holy water into the kitchen sink—thunder struck!—the kitchen sink turned black, the kitchen sink turned absolutely black!

(SHERIFF TALBOTT *enters the front door.*)

TALBOTT. Mama! What're you doin'?

VEE. Talkin'.

TALBOTT. I'm gonna see Jabe a minute, you go out and wait in th' car. (*He goes up. She rises slowly, picks up canvas and moves to counter.*)

VEE. —Oh, I—tell you!—since I got into this painting, my whole outlook is different. I can't explain how it is, the difference to me.

VAL. You don't have to explain. I know what you mean. Before you started to paint, it didn't make sense.

VEE. —What—what didn't?

VAL. Existence!

VEE (*slowly and softly*). No—no, it didn't . . . existence didn't make sense. . . . (*She places canvas on guitar on counter and sits in chair.*)

VAL (*rising and crossing to her*). You lived in Two River County, the wife of the county Sheriff. You saw awful things take place.

VEE. Awful! Things!

VAL. Beatings!

VEE. Yes!

VAL. Lynchings!

VEE. Yes!

VAL. Runaway convicts torn to pieces by hounds!

(*This is the first time she could express this horror.*)

VEE. *Chain-gang dogs!*

VAL. Yeah?

VEE. Tear fugitives!

VAL. Yeah?

VEE. —to *pieces.* . . . (*She had half risen: now sinks back faintly.* VAL *looks beyond her in the dim store, his light eyes have a dark gaze. It may be that his speech is too articulate: counteract this effect by groping, hesitations.*)

VAL (*moving away a step*). But violence ain't quick always. Sometimes it's slow. Some tornadoes are slow. Corruption—rots men's hearts and—rot is slow. . . .

VEE. —How do you—?

VAL. Know? I been a witness, I know!

VEE. *I* been a witness! *I* know!

VAL. We seen these things from seats down front at the show. (*He crouches before her and touches her hands in her lap. Her breath shudders.*) And so you begun to paint your visions. Without no plan, no training, you started to paint as if God touched your fingers. (*He lifts her hands slowly, gently from her soft lap.*) You made some beauty out of this dark country with these two, soft, woman hands. . . . (TALBOTT *appears on the stair landing, looks down, silent.*) Yeah, you made some beauty! (*Strangely, gently, he lifts her hands to his mouth. She gasps.* TALBOTT *calls out*)

TALBOTT. Hey! (VEE *springs up, gasping. Descending*) *Cut this crap!* (VAL *moves away to R.C. To* VEE) Go out. Wait in the car. (*He stares at* VAL *till* VEE *lumbers out as if dazed. After a while*) Jabe Torrance told me to take a good look at you. (*Crosses to* VAL.) Well, now, I've taken that look. (*Nods shortly. Goes out of store. The store is now very dim. As door closes on* TALBOTT, VAL *picks up painting; he goes behind counter and places it on a shelf, then picks up his guitar and sits on counter. Lights go down to mark a division as he sings and plays "Heavenly Grass."*)

SCENE THREE

As VAL *finishes the song,* LADY *descends the stair. He rises and turns on a green-shaded light bulb.*

VAL (*to* LADY). You been up there a long time.

LADY. —I gave him morphine. He must be out of his mind. He says such awful things to me. He says I want him to die.

VAL. You sure you don't?

LADY. I don't want no one to die. Death's terrible, Val. (*Pause. She wanders to the front window R. He takes his guitar and crosses to the door.*) You gotta go now?

VAL. I'm late.

LADY. Late for what? You got a date with somebody?

VAL. —No. . . .

LADY. Then stay a while. Play something. I'm all unstrung. . . . (*He crosses back and leans against counter; the guitar is barely audible, under the speeches.*) I made a terrible fool of myself down here today with—

VAL. —That girl's brother?

LADY. Yes, I—threw away—pride. . . .

VAL. His sister said she'd come here to give me a warning. I wonder what of?

LADY (*sitting in shoe-fitting chair*).— I said things to him I should of been too proud to say. . . .

(*Both are pursuing their own reflections; guitar continues softly.*)

VAL. Once or twice lately I've woke up with a fast heart, shouting something, and had to pick up my guitar to calm myself down. . . . Somehow or other I can't get used to this place, I don't feel safe in this place, but I—want to stay. . . . (*Stops short; sound of wild baying.*)

LADY. The chain-gang dogs are chasing some runaway convict. . . .

VAL. *Run boy! Run fast, brother! If they catch you, you never will run again! That's*—(*He has thrust his guitar under his arm on this line and crossed to the door.*)—*for sure. . . . (The baying of the dogs changes, becomes almost a single savage note.)*—Uh-huh—*the dogs've got him. . . .* (*Pause*) They're tearing him to pieces! (*Pause. Baying continues. A shot is fired. The baying dies out. He stops with his hand on the door; glances back at her; nods; draws the door open. The wind sings loud in the dusk.*)

LADY. *Wait!*

VAL. —Huh?

LADY. —Where do you stay?

VAL. —When?

LADY. Nights.

VAL. I stay at the Wildwood cabins on the highway.

LADY. You like it there?

VAL. Uh-huh.

LADY. —Why?

VAL. I got a comfortable bed, a two-burner stove, a shower and icebox there.

LADY. You want to save money?

VAL. I never could in my life.

LADY. You could if you stayed on the place.

VAL. What place?

LADY. This place.

VAL. Whereabouts on this place?

LADY (*pointing to alcove*). Back of that curtain.

VAL. —Where they try on clothes?

LADY. There's a cot there. A nurse slept on it when Jabe had his first operation, and there's a washroom down here and I'll get a plumber to put in a hot an' cold shower! I'll—fix it up nice for you. . . . (*She rises, crosses to foot of stairs. Pause. He lets the door shut, staring at her.*)

VAL (*moving D.C.*). —I—don't like to be—obligated.

LADY. There wouldn't be no obligation, you'd do me a favor. I'd feel safer at night with somebody on the place. I would; it would cost you nothing! And you could save up that money you spend on the cabin. How much? Ten a week? Why, two or three months from now you'd—save enough money to—(*Makes a wide gesture with a short laugh as if startled.*) Go on! Take a look at it! See if it don't suit you!—All right. . . .

(*But he doesn't move; he appears reflective.*)

LADY (*shivering, hugging herself*). Where does heat go in this building?

VAL (*reflectively*). —Heat rises. . . .

LADY. You with your dog's temperature, don't feel cold, do you? I do! I turn blue with it!

VAL. —Yeah. . . .

(*The wait is unendurable to* LADY.)

LADY. *Well, aren't you going to look at it, the room back there, and see if it suits you or not?!*

VAL. —I'll go and take a look at it. . . .

(*He crosses to the alcove and disappears behind the curtain. A light goes on behind it, making its bizarre pattern translucent: a gold tree with scarlet fruit and white birds in it, formally designed. Truck roars; lights sweep the frosted window.* LADY *gasps aloud; takes out a pint bottle and a glass from under the counter, setting them down with a crash that makes her utter a startled exclama-*

tion: then a startled laugh. She pours a drink and sits in chair R. of counter. The lights turn off behind the alcove curtain and VAL *comes back out. She sits stiffly without looking at him as he crosses back lazily, goes behind counter, puts guitar down. His manner is gently sad as if he had met with a familiar, expected disappointment. He sits down quietly on edge of counter and takes the pint bottle and pours himself a shot of the liquor with a reflective sigh. Boards creak loudly, contracting with the cold.* LADY's *voice is harsh and sudden, demanding)*

LADY. *Well, is it okay or—what?*

VAL. I never been in a position where I could turn down something I got for nothing in my life. I like that picture in there. That's a famous picture, that "September Morn" picture you got on the wall in there. Ha ha! I might have trouble sleeping in a room with that picture. I might keep turning the light on to take another look at it! The way she's cold in that water and sort of crouched over in it, holding her body like that, that— might—ha ha!—sort of keep me awake . . .

LADY. Aw, you with your dog's temperature and your control of all functions, it would take more than a picture to keep you awake!

VAL. I was just kidding.

LADY. I was just kidding too.

VAL. But you know how a single man is. He don't come home every night with just his shadow.

(*Pause. She takes a drink.*)

LADY. You bring girls home nights to the Wildwood cabins, do you?

VAL. I ain't so far. But I would like to feel free to. That old life is what I'm used to. I always worked nights in cities and if you work nights in cities you live in a different city from those that work days.

LADY. Yes. I know, I—imagine. . . .

VAL. The ones that work days in cities and the ones that work nights in cities, they live in different cities. The cities have the same name but they are different cities. As different as night and day. There's something wild in the country that only the night people know. . . .

LADY. Yeah, I know!

VAL. I'm thirty years old!—but sudden changes don't work, it takes—

LADY. —Time—yes. . . .

(*Slight pause which she finds disconcerting. He slides off counter and moves around below it.*)

VAL. You been good to me, Lady.— Why d'you want me to stay here?

LADY (*defensively*). I told you why.

VAL. For company nights?

LADY. Yeah, to, to!—guard the store, nights!

VAL. To be a night watchman?

LADY. Yeah, to be a night *watchman.*

VAL. You feel nervous alone here?

LADY. Naturally now! Jabe sleeps with a pistol next to him but if somebody broke in the store, he couldn't git up and all I could do is holler!—Who'd *hear* me? They got a telephone girl on the night shift with—sleepin' sickness, I think! Anyhow, why're you so suspicious? You look at me like you thought I was *plottin'.* —Kind people *exist:* Even me! (*She sits up rigid in chair, lips and eyes tight closed, drawing in a loud breath which comes from a tension both personal and vicarious.*)

VAL. I understand, Lady, but. . . . Why're you sitting up so stiff in that chair?

LADY. Ha! (*Sharp laugh; she leans back in chair.*)

VAL. You're still unrelaxed.

LADY. I know.

VAL. Relax. (*Moving around close to her.*) I'm going to show you some tricks I learned from a lady osteopath that took me in, too.

LADY. What tricks?

VAL. How to manipulate joints and bones in a way that makes you feel like a loose piece of string. (*Moves behind her chair. She watches him.*) Do you trust me or don't you?

LADY. Yeah, I trust you completely, but—

VAL. Well then, lean forward a little and raise your arms up and turn sideways in the chair. (*She follows these instructions.*) Drop your head. (*He manipulates her head and neck.*) Now the spine, Lady. (*He places his knee against the small of her backbone and she utters a sharp, startled laugh as he draws her backbone hard against his kneecap.*)

LADY. Ha, ha!—That makes a sound like, like, like!—boards contracting with cold in the building, ha, ha!

(*He relaxes.*)

VAL. Better?

LADY. Oh, yes!—much . . . thanks. . . .

VAL (*stroking her neck*). Your skin is like silk. You're light skinned to be Italian.

LADY. Most people in this country think Italian people are dark. Some are but not all are! Some of them are fair . . . very fair. . . . My father's people were dark but my mother's people were fair. Ha ha! (*The laughter is senseless. He smiles understandingly at her as she chatters to cover confusion. He turns away, then goes above and sits on counter close to her.*) My mother's mother's sister—come here from Monte Cassino, to die, with relations!—but I think people always die alone . . . with or without relations. I was a little girl then and I remember it took her such a long, long time to die we almost forgot her.—And she was so quiet . . . in a corner. . . . And I remember asking her one time, Zia Teresa, how does it feel to die?—Only a little girl would ask such a question, ha ha! Oh, and I remember her answer. She said— "It's a lonely feeling."

I think she wished she had stayed in Italy and died in a place that she knew. . . . (*Looks at him directly for the first time since mentioning the alcove.*) Well, there is a washroom, and I'll get the plumber to put in a hot and cold shower! Well—(*Rises, retreats awkwardly from the chair. His interest seems to have wandered from her.*) I'll go up and get some clean linen and make up that bed in there. (*She turns and walks rapidly, almost running, to stairs. He appears lost in some private reflection but as soon as she has disappeared above the landing, he says something under his breath and crosses directly to the cashbox. He coughs loudly to cover the sound of ringing it open; scoops out a fistful of bills and coughs again to cover the sound of slamming drawer shut. Picks up his guitar and goes out the front door of store.* LADY *returns downstairs, laden with linen. The outer darkness moans through the door left open. She crosses to the door and a little outside it, peering both ways down the dark road. Then she comes in furiously, with an Italian curse, shutting the door with her foot or shoulder, and throws the linen down on counter. She crosses abruptly to cashbox, rings it open*

and discovers theft. Slams drawer violently shut.) Thief! Thief! (*Turns to phone, lifts receiver. Holds it a moment, then slams it back into place. Wanders desolately back to the door, opens it and stands staring out into the starless night as the scene dims out. Music: blues— guitar.*)

SCENE FOUR

Late that night. VAL *enters the store, a little unsteadily, with his guitar; goes to the cashbox and rings it open. He counts some bills off a big wad and returns them to the cashbox and the larger wad to the pocket of his snakeskin jacket. Sudden footsteps above; light spills onto stair landing. He quickly moves away from the cashbox as* LADY *appears on the landing in a white sateen robe; she carries a flashlight.*

LADY. Who's that?

(*Music fades out.*)

VAL. —Me.

(*She turns the flashlight on his figure.*)

LADY. Oh, my God, how you scared me!

VAL. You didn't expect me?

LADY. How'd I know it was you I heard come in?

VAL. I thought you give me a room here.

LADY. You left without letting me know if you took it or not. (*She is descending the stairs into store, flashlight still on him.*)

VAL. Catch me turning down something I get for nothing.

LADY. Well, you might have said something so I'd expect you or not.

VAL. I thought you took it for granted.

LADY. I don't take nothing for granted. (*He starts back to the alcove.*) Wait!— I'm coming downstairs. . . . (*She descends with the flashlight beam on his face.*)

VAL. You're blinding me with that flashlight. (*He laughs. She keeps the flashlight on him. He starts back again toward the alcove.*)

LADY. The bed's not made because I didn't expect you.

VAL. That's all right.

LADY. I brought the linen downstairs and you'd cut out.

VAL. Yeah, well—(*She picks up linen*

on counter.) Give me that stuff. I can make up my own rack. Tomorrow you'll have to get yourself a new clerk. (*Takes it from her and goes again toward alcove.*) I had a lucky night. (*Exhibits a wad of bills.*)

LADY. Hey! (*He stops near the curtain. She goes and turns on green-shaded bulb over cashbox.*)—Did you just open this cashbox?

VAL. —Why you ask that?

LADY. I thought I heard it ring open a minute ago, that's why I come down here.

VAL. —In your—white satin kimona?

LADY. *Did you just open the cashbox?!*

VAL. —I wonder who did if I didn't. . . .

LADY. Nobody did if you didn't, but somebody did! (*Opens cashbox and hurriedly counts money. She is trembling violently.*)

VAL. How come you didn't lock the cash up in the safe this evening, Lady?

LADY. Sometimes I forget to.

VAL. That's careless.

LADY. —Why'd you open the cashbox when you come in?

VAL. I opened it twice this evening, once before I went out and again when I come back. I borrowed some money and put it back in the box an' got all this left over! (*Shows her the wad of bills.*) I beat a blackjack dealer five times straight. With this much loot I can retire for the season. . . . (*He returns money to pocket.*)

LADY. *Chicken-feed!*—I'm sorry for you.

VAL. You're sorry for me?

LADY. I'm sorry for you because nobody can help you. I was touched by your—strangeness, your strange talk.— That thing about birds with no feet so they have to sleep on the wind?—I said to myself, "This boy is a bird with no feet so he has to sleep on the wind," and that softened my fool Dago heart and I wanted to help you. . . . Fool, me! —I got what I should of expected. You robbed me while I was upstairs to get sheets to make up your bed! (*He starts out toward the door.*) I guess I'm a fool to even feel disappointed.

VAL (*stopping C. and dropping linen on counter*). You're disappointed in me. I was disappointed in you.

LADY (*coming from behind counter*). —How did I disappoint you?

VAL. There wasn't no cot behind that

curtain before. You put it back there for a purpose.

LADY. It was back there!—folded behind the mirror.

VAL. It wasn't back of no mirror when you told me three times to go and—

LADY (*cutting in*). I left that money in the cashbox on purpose, to find out if I could trust you.

VAL. You got back th' . . .

LADY: No, no, no, I can't trust you, now I know I can't trust you, I got to trust anybody or I don't want him.

VAL. That's OK, I don't expect no character reference from you.

LADY. I'll give you a character reference. I'd say this boy's a peculiar talker! But I wouldn't say a real hard worker or honest. I'd say a peculiar slew-footer that sweet talks you while he's got his hand in the cashbox.

VAL. I took out less than you owed me.

LADY. Don't mix up the issue. I see through you, mister!

VAL. I see through you, Lady.

LADY. What d'you see through me?

VAL. You sure you want me to tell?

LADY. I'd love for you to.

VAL. —A not so young and not so satisfied woman, that hired a man off the highway to do double duty without paying overtime for it. . . . I mean a store clerk days and a stud nights, and—

LADY. God, no! You—! (*She raises her hand as if to strike at him.*) Oh, God no . . . you cheap little—(*Invectives fail her so she uses her fists, hammering at him with them. He seizes her wrists. She struggles a few moments more, then collapses, in chair, sobbing. He lets go of her gently.*)

VAL. It's natural. You felt—lonely. . . .

(*She sobs brokenly against the counter.*)

LADY. Why did you come back here?

VAL. To put back the money I took so you wouldn't remember me as not honest or grateful—(*He picks up his guitar and starts to the door nodding gravely. She catches her breath; rushes to intercept him, spreading her arms like a crossbar over the door.*)

LADY. NO, NO, DON'T GO . . . I NEED YOU!!! (*He faces her for five beats. The true passion of her outcry touches him then, and he turns about and crosses to the alcove. . . . As he draws the curtain across it he looks back at her.)* TO LIVE. . . . TO GO ON LIVING!!!

(Music fades in—"Lady's Love Song"— guitar. He closes the curtain and turns on the light behind it, making it translucent. Through an opening in the alcove entrance, we see him sitting down with his guitar. LADY *picks up the linen and crosses to the alcove like a spellbound child. Just outside it she stops, frozen with uncertainty, a conflict of feelings, but then he begins to whisper the words of a song so tenderly that she is able to draw the curtain open and enter the alcove. He looks up gravely at her from his guitar. She closes the curtain behind her. Its bizarre design, a gold tree with white birds and scarlet fruit in it, is softly translucent with the bulb lighted behind it. The guitar continues softly for a few moments; stops; the stage darkens till only the curtain of the alcove is clearly visible.)*

CURTAIN

ACT THREE

SCENE ONE

An early morning. The Saturday before Easter. The sleeping alcove is lighted. VAL *is smoking, half dressed, on the edge of the cot.* LADY *comes running, panting downstairs, her hair loose, in dressing robe and slippers and calls out in a panicky, shrill whisper.*

LADY. Val! Val, he's comin' downstairs!
VAL *(hoarse with sleep)*. Who's—what?
LADY. Jabe!
VAL. Jabe?
LADY. I swear he is, he's coming down stairs!
VAL. What of it?
LADY. Jesus, will you get up and put some clothes on? The damned nurse told him that he could come down in the store to check over the stock! You want him to catch you half dressed on that bed there?
VAL. Don't he know I sleep here?
LADY. Nobody knows you sleep here but you and me. *(Voices above.)* Oh, God!—they've started.

NURSE. Don't hurry now. Take one step at a time.

(Footsteps on stairs, slow, shuffling. The professional, nasal cheer of a nurse's voice.)

LADY *(panicky)*. Get your shirt on! Come out!
NURSE. That's right. One step at a time, one step at a time, lean on my shoulder and take one step at a time.

(VAL rises, still dazed from sleep. LADY gasps and sweeps the curtain across the alcove just a moment before the descending figures enter the sight-lines on the landing. LADY breathes like an exhausted runner as she backs away from the alcove and assumes a forced smile. JABE *and the nurse,* MISS PORTER, *appear on the landing of the stairs and at the same moment scudding clouds expose the sun. A narrow window on the landing admits a brilliant shaft of light upon the pair. They have a bizarre and awful appearance, the tall man, his rusty black suit hanging on him like an empty sack, his eyes burning malignantly from his yellow face, leaning on a stumpy little woman with bright pink or orange hair, clad all in starched white, with a voice that purrs with the faintly contemptuous cheer and sweetness of those hired to care for the dying.)*

NURSE. Aw, now, just look at that, that nice bright sun comin' out.
LADY. Miss Porter? It's—it's cold down here!
JABE. What's she say?
NURSE. She says it's cold down here.
LADY. The—the—the air's not warm enough yet, the air's not heated!
NURSE. He's determined to come right down, Mrs. Torrance.
LADY. I know but—
NURSE. Wild horses couldn't hold him a minute longer.
JABE *(exhausted)*. —Let's—rest here a minute. . . .
LADY *(eagerly)*. Yes! Rest there a minute!
NURSE. Okay. We'll rest here a minute. . . .

(They sit down side by side on a bench under the artificial palm tree in the shaft of light. JABE *glares into the light like a fierce dying old beast. There are sounds from the alcove. To cover them up,* LADY *keeps making startled, laughing sounds in her throat, half laughing, half panting,*

chafing her hands together at the foot of the stairs, and coughing falsely.) ...

JABE. Lady, what's wrong? Why are you so excited?

LADY. It seems like a miracle to me.

JABE. What seems like a miracle to you?

LADY. You coming downstairs.

JABE. You never thought I would come downstairs again?

LADY. Not this quick! Not as quick as this, Jabe! Did you think he would pick up as quick as this, Miss Porter?

(JABE *rises.*)

NURSE. Ready?

JABE. Ready.

NURSE. He's doing fine, knock wood.

LADY. Yes, knock wood, knock wood! (*Drums counter loudly with her knuckles.* VAL *steps silently from behind the alcove curtain as the* NURSE *and* JABE *resume their slow, shuffling descent of the stairs. Moving back to D.R.C.*) You got to be careful not to overdo. You don't want another setback. Ain't that right, Miss Porter?

NURSE. Well, it's my policy to mobilize the patient.

LADY (*to* VAL *in a shrill whisper*). Coffee's boiling, take the Goddamn coffee pot off the burner! (*She gives* VAL *a panicky signal to go in the alcove.*)

JABE. Who're you talking to, Lady?

LADY. To—to—to Val, the clerk! I told him to—get you a—chair!

JABE. Who's that?

LADY. Val, Val, the clerk, you know Val!

JABE. Not yet. I'm anxious to meet him. Where is he?

LADY. Right here, right here, here's Val! (VAL *returns from the alcove.*)

JABE. He's here bright and early.

LADY. The early bird catches the worm!

JABE. That's right. Where is the worm?

LADY (*loudly*). Ha ha!

NURSE. Careful! One step at a time, Mr. Torrance.

LADY. Saturday before Easter's our biggest sales-day of the year, I mean second biggest, but sometimes it's even bigger than Christmas Eve! So I told Val to get here a half hour early.

(JABE *misses his step and stumbles to foot of stairs.* LADY *screams.* NURSE *rushes down to him.* VAL *advances and raises the man to his feet.*)

VAL. Here. Here.

LADY. Oh, my God.

NURSE. Oh, oh!

JABE. I'm all right.

NURSE. Are you sure?

LADY. Are you sure?

JABE. Let me go! (*He staggers to lean against counter, panting, glaring, with a malignant smile.*)

LADY. Oh, my God. Oh, my—God. . . .

JABE. This is the boy that works here?

LADY. Yes, this is the clerk I hired to help us out, Jabe.

JABE. How is he doing?

LADY. Fine, fine.

JABE. He's mighty good-looking. Do women give him much trouble?

LADY. When school lets out the high-school girls are thick as flies in this store!

JABE. How about older women? Don't he attract older women? The older ones are the buyers, they got the money. They sweat it out of their husbands and throw it away! What's your salary, boy, how much do I pay you?

LADY. Twenty-two fifty a week.

JABE. You're getting him cheap.

VAL. I get—commissions.

JABE. Commissions?

VAL. Yes. One percent of all sales.

JABE. Oh? Oh? I didn't know about that.

LADY. I knew he would bring in trade and he brings it in.

JABE. I bet.

LADY. Val, get Jabe a chair, he ought to sit down.

JABE. No, I don't want to sit down. I want to take a look at the new confectionery.

LADY. Oh, yes, yes! Take a look at it! Val, Val, turn on the lights in the confectionery! I want Jabe to see the way I done it over! I'm—real—proud! (VAL *crosses and switches on light in confectionery. The bulbs in the arches and the juke box light up.*) Go in and look at it, Jabe. I am real proud of it!

(*He stares at* LADY *a moment; then shuffles slowly into the spectral radiance of the confectionery.* LADY *moves D.C. At the same time a calliope becomes faintly audible and slowly but steadily builds.* MISS PORTER *goes with the patient, holding his elbow.*)

VAL (*returning to* LADY). He looks like death.

LADY (*moving away from him*). Hush!

(VAL *goes up above counter and stands in the shadows.*)

NURSE. Well, isn't this artistic.

JABE. Yeh. Artistic as hell.

NURSE. I never seen anything like it before.

JABE. Nobody else did either.

NURSE (*coming back to U.R.C.*). Who done these decorations?

LADY (*defiantly*). I did them, all by myself!

NURSE. What do you know. It sure is something artistic.

(*Calliope is now up loud.*)

JABE (*coming back to D.R.*). Is there a circus or carnival in the county?

LADY. What?

JABE. That sounds like a circus calliope on the highway.

LADY. That's no circus calliope. It's advertising the gala opening of the Torrance Confectionery tonight!

JABE. Doing what did you say?

LADY. It's announcing the opening of our confectionery, it's going all over Glorious Hill this morning and all over Sunset and Lyon this afternoon. Hurry on here so you can see it go by the store. (*She rushes excitedly to open the front door as the ragtime music of the calliope approaches.*)

JABE. I married a live one, Miss Porter. How much does that damn thing cost me?

LADY. You'll be surprised how little. (*She is talking with an hysterical vivacity now.*) I hired it for a song!

JABE. How much of a song did you hire it for?

LADY (*closing door*). Next to nothing, seven-fifty an hour! And it covers three towns in Two River County!

(*Calliope fades out.*)

JABE (*with a muted ferocity*). Miss Porter, I married a live one! Didn't I marry a live one? (*Switches off lights in confectionery.*) Her daddy "The Wop" was just as much of a live one till he burned up. (LADY *gasps as if struck. With a slow, ugly grin*) He had a wine garden on the north shore of Moon Lake. The new confectionery sort of reminds me of it. But he made a mistake, he made a bad mistake, one time, selling liquor to niggers. We burned him out. We burned him out, house and orchard and vines and "The Wop" was burned

up trying to fight the fire. (*He turns.*) I think I better go up.

LADY. —Did you say "WE"?

JABE. —I have a kind of a cramp. . . .

NURSE (*taking his arm*). Well, let's go up.

JABE. —Yes, I better go up. . . . (*They cross to stairs. Calliope fades in.*)

LADY (*almost shouting as she moves D.C.*). Jabe, did you say "WE" did it, did you say "WE" did it?

JABE (*at foot of stairs, stops, turns*). Yes, I said "WE" did it. You heard me, Lady.

NURSE. One step at a time, one step at a time, take it easy.

(*They ascend gradually to the landing and above. The calliope passes directly before the store and a clown is seen, or heard, shouting through megaphone.*)

CLOWN. Don't forget tonight, folks, the gala opening of the Torrance Confectionery, free drinks and free favors, don't forget it, the gala opening of the confectionery.

(*Fade.* JABE *and the* NURSE *disappear above the landing. Calliope gradually fades. A hoarse cry above. The* NURSE *runs back downstairs, exclaiming*)

NURSE. He's bleeding, he's having a hemm'rhage! (*Runs to phone.*) Dr. Buchanan's office! (*Turns again to* LADY.) Your husband is having a hemm'rhage!

(*Calliope is loud still.* LADY *appears not to hear. She speaks to* VAL.)

LADY. Did you hear what he said? He said "We" did it, "WE" burned—house —vines—orchard—"The Wop" burned fighting the fire. . . .

(*The scene dims out; calliope fades out.*)

Scene Two

Sunset of the same day. At rise VAL *is alone. He is standing stock-still down center stage, almost beneath the proscenium, in the tense, frozen attitude of a wild animal listening to something that warns it of danger, his head turned as if he were looking off stage left, out over the house, frowning slightly, attentively. After a moment he mutters something sharply, and his body relaxes; he takes out a cigarette and crosses to the store entrance, opens the door and stands looking out. It has been raining steadily and will rain again in a while, but right now it is clearing: the sun breaks through, suddenly, with great brilliance; and almost at the same instant, at some distance, a woman cries out a great hoarse cry of terror and exaltation; the cry is repeated as she comes running nearer.*

VEE TALBOTT *appears through the window as if blind and demented, stiff, groping gestures, shielding her eyes with one arm as she feels along the store window for the entrance, gasping for breath.* VAL *steps aside, taking hold of her arm to guide her into the store. For a few moments she leans weakly, blindly panting for breath against the oval glass of the door, then calls out.*

VEE. I'm—*struck blind!*

VAL. You can't see?

VEE. —No! Nothing. . . .

VAL (*assisting her to stool below counter*). Set down here, Mrs. Talbott.

VEE. —Where?

VAL (*pushing her gently*). Here. (VEE *sinks moaning onto stool.*) What hurt your eyes, Mrs. Talbott, what happened to your eyes?

VEE (*drawing a long, deep breath*). The vision I waited and prayed for all my life long!

VAL. You had a vision?

VEE. I saw the eyes of my Saviour!—They struck me blind. (*Leans forward, clasping her eyes in anguish.*) Ohhhh, they burned out my eyes!

VAL. Lean back.

VEE. Eyeballs burn like fire. . . .

VAL (*going off R.*). I'll get you something cold to put on your eyes.

VEE. I knew a vision was coming, oh, I had many signs!

VAL (*in confectionery*). It must be a terrible shock to have a vision. . . . (*He speaks gravely, gently, scooping chipped ice from the soft-drink cooler and wrapping it in his handkerchief.*)

VEE (*with the naïveté of a child, as* VAL *comes back to her*). I *thought* I would see my Saviour on the day of His passion, which was yesterday, Good Friday, that's when I expected to see Him. But I was mistaken, I was—disappointed. Yesterday passed and nothing, nothing much happened but—today—(VAL *places handkerchief over her eyes.*)—this afternoon, somehow I pulled myself together

and walked outdoors and started to go to pray in the empty church and meditate on the Rising of Christ tomorrow. Along the road as I walked, thinking about the mysteries of Easter, veils!—(*She makes a long shuddering word out of "veils."*)—seemed to drop off my eyes! Light, oh, light! I never have seen such brilliance! it PRICKED my eyeballs like NEEDLES!

VAL. —Light?

VEE. Yes, yes, light. YOU know, you know we live in light and shadow, that's, that's what we *live* in, a world of—*light* and—*shadow.* . . .

VAL. Yes. In light and shadow. (*He nods with complete understanding and agreement. They are like two children who have found life's meaning, simply and quietly, along a country road.*)

VEE. A world of light and shadow is what we live in, and—it's—confusing. . . .

(*A man is peering in at store window.*)

VAL. Yeah, they—*do get*—*mixed.* . . .

VEE. Well, and then—(*Hesitates to recapture her vision.*)—I heard this clap of thunder! Sky!—Split open!—And there in the split-open sky, I saw, I tell you, I *saw* the TWO HUGE BLAZING EYES OF JESUS CHRIST RISEN!— Not crucified but Risen! I mean Crucified and *then* RISEN!—The blazing eyes of Christ Risen! And then a great—(*Raises both arms and makes a great sweeping motion to describe an apocalyptic disturbance of the atmosphere.*)—His hand! —*Invisible!*—I didn't *see* his hand!—But it *touched* me—*here!* (*She seizes* VAL's *hand and presses it to her great heaving bosom.*)

TALBOTT (*appearing R. in confectionery, furiously*). VEE!

(*She starts up, throwing the compress from her eyes. Utters a sharp gasp and staggers backward with terror and blasted ecstasy and dismay and belief, all confused in her look.*)

VEE. You!

TALBOTT. VEE!

VEE. *You!*

TALBOTT (*advancing*). VEE!

VEE (*making two syllables of the word "eyes"*). —The Ey—es! (*She collapses, forward, falls to her knees, her arms thrown about* VAL. *He seizes her to lift her. Two or three men are peering in at the store window.*)

TALBOTT (*pushing* VAL *away*). Let go of her, don't put your hands on my wife! (*He seizes her roughly and hauls her to the door.* VAL *moves up to help* VEE.) Don't move. (*At door, to* VAL) I'm coming back.

VAL. I'm not goin' nowhere.

TALBOTT (*to* DOG, *as he goes off L. with* VEE). Dog, go in there with that boy.

VOICE (*outside*). Sheriff caught him messin' with his wife.

(*Repeat:* ANOTHER VOICE *at a distance.* "DOG" HAMMA *enters and stands silently beside the door while there is a continued murmur of excited voices on the street. The following scene should be underplayed, played almost casually, like the performance of some familiar ritual.*)

VAL. What do you want?

(DOG *says nothing but removes from his pocket and opens a spring-blade knife and moves to D.R.* PEE WEE *enters. Through the open door—voices.*)

VOICES (*outside*). —Son of a low-down bitch foolin' with—
—That's right, ought to be—
—Cut the son of a—

VAL. What do you—?(PEE WEE *closes the door and silently stands beside it, opening a spring-blade knife.* VAL *looks from one to the other.*)—It's six o'clock. Store's closed.

(*Men chuckle like dry leaves rattling.* VAL *crosses toward the door; is confronted by* TALBOTT; *stops short.*)

TALBOTT. Boy, I said stay here.

VAL. I'm not—goin' nowhere. . . .

TALBOTT. Stand back under that light.

VAL. Which light?

TALBOTT. That light. (*Points.* VAL *goes behind counter.*) I want to look at you while I run through some photos of men wanted.

VAL. I'm not wanted.

TALBOTT. A good-looking boy like you is always wanted. (*Men chuckle.* VAL *stands in hot light under green-shaded bulb.* TALBOTT *shuffles through photos he has removed from his pocket.*)—How tall are you, boy?

VAL. Never measured.

TALBOTT. How much do you weigh?

VAL. Never weighed.

TALBOTT. Got any scars or marks of identification on your face or body?

VAL. No, sir.

TALBOTT. Open your shirt.

VAL. What for? (*He doesn't.*)

TALBOTT. Open his shirt for him, Dog. (DOG *steps quickly forward and rips shirt open to waist.* VAL *starts forward; men point knives; he draws back.*) That's right, stay there, boy. What did you do before?

(PEE WEE *sits on stairs.*)

VAL. Before—what?

TALBOTT. Before you come here?

VAL. —Traveled and—played. . . .

TALBOTT. Played?

DOG (*advancing to C.*). What?

PEE WEE. With wimmen?

(DOG *laughs.*)

VAL. No. Played guitar—and sang. . . . (VAL *touches guitar on counter.*)

TALBOTT. Let me see that guitar.

VAL. Look at it. But don't touch it. I don't let nobody but musicians touch it. (*Men come close.*)

DOG. What're you smiling for, boy?

PEE WEE. He ain't smiling, his mouth's just twitching like a dead chicken's foot. (*They laugh.*)

TALBOTT. What is all that writing on the guitar?

VAL. —Names. . . .

TALBOTT. What of?

VAL. Autographs of musicians dead and living.

(*Men read aloud the names printed on the guitar: Bessie Smith, Leadbelly, Woody Guthrie, Jelly Roll Morton, etc. They bend close to it, keeping the open knife blades pointed at* VAL's *body;* DOG *touches neck of the guitar, draws it toward him.* VAL *suddenly springs, with catlike agility, onto the counter. He runs along it, kicking at their hands as they catch at his legs. The* NURSE *runs down to the landing.*)

MISS PORTER. *What's going on?*

TALBOTT (*at the same time*). Stop that! (JABE *calls hoarsely above.*)

MISS PORTER (*excitedly, all in one breath, as* JABE *calls*). Where's Mrs. Torrance? I got a very sick man up there and his wife's disappeared. (JABE *calls out again.*) I been on a whole lot of cases but never seen one where a wife showed no concern for a—(JABE *cries out again. Her voice fades out as she returns above.*)

TALBOT (*overlapping* NURSE's *speech*). Dog! Pee Wee! You all stand back from that counter. Dog, why don't you an'

Pee Wee go up an' see Jabe. Leave me straighten this boy out, go on, go on up.

PEE WEE. C'mon, Dawg. . . .

(*They go up.* VAL *remains panting on counter.*)

TALBOTT (*sits in shoe chair at R. window. In* TALBOTT'S *manner there is a curious, half-abashed gentleness, when alone with the boy, as if he recognized the purity in him and was, truly, for the moment, ashamed of the sadism implicit in the occurrence*). Awright, boy. Git on down off th' counter, I ain't gonna touch y'r guitar. (VAL *jumps off counter.*) But I'm gonna tell you something. They's a certain county I know of which has a big sign at the county line that says, "Nigger, don't let the sun go down on you in this county." That's all it says, it don't threaten nothing, it just says, "Nigger, don't let the sun go down on you in this county!" (*Chuckles hoarsely. Rises and takes a step toward* VAL.) Well, son! You ain't a nigger and this is not that county, but, son, I want you to just imagine that you seen a sign that said to you: "Boy, don't let the sun rise on you in this county." I said "rise," not "go down" because it's too close to sunset for you to git packed an' move on before that. But I think if you value that instrument in your hands as much as you seem to, you'll simplify my job by not allowing the sun tomorrow to rise on you in this county. 'S that understood, now, boy? (VAL *stares at him, expressionless, panting. Crossing to door*) I hope so. I don't like *violence.* (*He looks back and nods at* VAL *from the door. Then goes outside in the fiery afterglow of the sunset.* Dogs bark in the distance. Music fades in: "Dog Howl Blues"—minor—guitar. Pause in which VAL remains motionless, cradling guitar in his arms. Then VAL's faraway troubled look is resolved in a slight abrupt nod of his head. He sweeps back the alcove curtain and enters the alcove and closes the curtain behind him. Lights dim down to indicate a division of scenes.*)

SCENE THREE

Half an hour later. The lighting is less realistic than in the previous scenes of the play. The interior of the store is so dim that only the vertical lines of the pillars *and such selected items as the palm tree on the stair landing and the ghostly paper vineyard of the confectionery are plainly visible. The view through the great front window has virtually become the background of the action: A singing wind sweeps clouds before the moon so that the witchlike country brightens and dims and brightens again. The Marshal's hounds are restless: their baying is heard now and then. A lamp outside the door sometimes catches a figure that moves past with mysterious urgency, calling out softly and raising an arm to beckon, like a shade in the under kingdom.*

At rise, or when the stage is lighted again, it is empty but footsteps are descending the stairs as DOLLY *and* BEULAH *rush into the store and call out, in soft shouts:*

———

DOLLY. Dawg?

BEULAH. Pee Wee?

EVA TEMPLE (*appearing on landing and calling down softly in the superior tone of a privileged attendant in a sick-chamber*). Please don't shout!—Mr. Binnings and Mr. Hamma (*Names of the two husbands*) are upstairs sitting with Jabe. . . . (*She continues her descent. Then* SISTER TEMPLE *appears, sobbing, on landing.*) —Come down carefully, Sister.

SISTER. Help me, I'm all to pieces. . . .

(EVA *ignores this request and faces the two women.*)

BEULAH. Has the bleedin' quit yit?

EVA. The hemorrhage seems to have stopped. Sister, Sister, pull yourself together, we all have to face these things sometime in life.

DOLLY. Has he sunk into a coma?

EVA. No. Cousin Jabe is conscious. Nurse Porter says his pulse is remarkably strong for a man that lost so much blood. Of course he's had a transfusion.

SISTER. Two of 'em.

EVA (*crossing to* DOLLY). Yais, an' they put him on glucose. His strength came back like magic.

BEULAH. She up there?

EVA. *Who?*

BEULAH. Lady!

EVA. No! When last reported she had just stepped into the Glorious Hill Beauty Parlor.

BEULAH. You don't mean it.

EVA. Ask Sister!

SISTER. She's planning to go ahead with—!

EVA. —The gala opening of the confectionery. Switch on the lights in there, Sister. (SISTER *crosses and switches on lights and moves off R. The decorated confectionery is lighted.* DOLLY *and* BEULAH *exclaim in awed voices.*)—Of course it's not normal behavior; it's downright lunacy, but still that's no excuse for it! And when she called up at five, about one hour ago, it wasn't to ask about Jabe, oh, no, she didn't mention his name. She asked if Ruby Lightfoot had delivered a case of Seagram's. Yais, she just shouted that question and hung up the phone, before I could—(*She crosses and goes off R.*)

BEULAH (*going into confectionery*). Oh, I understand, now! Now I see what she's up to! Electric moon, cut-out silver-paper stars and artificial vines? Why, it's her father's wine garden on Moon Lake she's turned this room into!

DOLLY (*suddenly as she sits in shoe chair*). Here she comes, here she comes!

(*The* TEMPLE SISTERS *retreat from view in confectionery as* LADY *enters the store. She wears a hooded rain-cape and carries a large paper shopping bag and paper carton box.*)

LADY. Go on, ladies, don't stop, my ears are burning!

BEULAH (*coming in to U.R.C.*). —Lady, oh, Lady, Lady. . . .

LADY. Why d'you speak my name in that pitiful voice? Hanh? (*Throws back hood of cape, her eyes blazing, and places bag and box on counter.*) Val? Val! Where is that boy that works here? (DOLLY *shakes her head.*) I guess he's havin' a T-bone steak with French fries and coleslaw fo' ninety-five cents at the Blue Bird. . . . (*Sounds in confectionery.*) Who's in the confectionery, is that you, Val? (TEMPLE SISTERS *emerge and stalk past her.*) Going, girls? (*They go out of store.*) Yes, gone! (*She laughs and throws off rain-cape, onto counter, revealing a low-cut gown, triple strand of pearls and a purple satin-ribboned corsage.*)

BEULAH (*sadly*). How long have I known you, Lady?

LADY (*going behind counter, unpacks paper hats and whistles*). A long time, Beulah. I think you remember when my people come here on a banana boat from Palermo, Sicily, by way of Caracas, Venezuela, yes, with a grind-organ and a monkey my papa had bought in Venezuela. I was not much bigger than the monkey, ha ha! You remember the monkey? The man that sold Papa the monkey said it was a very young monkey, but he was a liar, it was a very old monkey, it was on its last legs, ha ha ha! But it was a well-dressed monkey. (*Coming around to R. of counter.*) It had a green velvet suit and a little red cap that it tipped and a tambourine that it passed around for money, ha ha ha. . . . The grind-organ played and the monkey danced in the sun, ha ha! —"O Sole Mio, Da Da Da daaa . . . !" (*Sits in chair at counter.*)—One day, the monkey danced too much in the sun and it was a very old monkey and it dropped dead. . . . My papa, he turned to the people, he made them a bow and he said, "The show is over, the monkey is dead." Ha ha! (*Slight pause. Then* DOLLY *pipes up venomously*)

DOLLY. Ain't it wonderful Lady can be so brave?

BEULAH. Yaiss, wonderful! Hanh. . . .

LADY. For me the show is not over, the monkey is not dead yet! (*Then suddenly*) Val, is that you, Val? (*Someone has entered the confectionery door, out of sight, and the draught of air has set the wind-chimes tinkling wildly.* LADY *rushes forward but stops short as* CAROL *appears. She wears a trench coat and a white sailor's cap with a turned-down brim, inscribed with the name of a vessel and a date, past or future, memory or anticipation.*)

DOLLY. Well, here's your first customer, Lady.

LADY (*going behind counter*). —Carol, that room ain't open.

CAROL. There's a big sign outside that says "Open Tonite!"

LADY. It ain't open to you.

CAROL. I have to stay here a while. They stopped my car, you see, I don't have a license; my license has been revoked and I have to find someone to drive me across the river.

LADY. You can call a taxi.

CAROL. I heard that the boy that works for you is leaving tonight and I—

LADY. *Who said he's leaving?*

CAROL (*crossing to counter*). Sheriff Talbott. The County Marshal suggested I get him to drive me over the river since he'd be crossing it too.

LADY. You got some mighty wrong information!

CAROL. Where is he? I don't see him?

LADY. Why d'you keep coming back here bothering that boy? He's not interested in you! Why would he be leaving here tonight? (*Door opens off as she comes from behind counter.*) Val, is that you, Val? (CONJURE MAN *enters through confectionery, mumbling rapidly, holding out something.* BEULAH *and* DOLLY *take flight out the door with cries of revulsion.*) No conjure stuff, go away!

(*He starts to withdraw.*)

CAROL (*crossing to U.R.C.*). Uncle! The Choctaw cry! I'll give you a dollar for it.

(LADY *turns away with a gasp, with a gesture of refusal. The* NEGRO *nods, then throws back his turkey neck and utters a series of sharp barking sounds that rise to a sustained cry of great intensity and wildness. The cry produces a violent reaction in the building.* BEULAH *and* DOLLY *run out of the store.* LADY *does not move but she catches her breath.* DOG *and* PEE WEE *run down the stairs with ad libs and hustle the* NEGRO *out of the store, ignoring* LADY, *as their wives call:* "PEE WEE!" *and* "DAWG!" *outside on the walk.* VAL *sweeps back the alcove curtain and appears as if the cry were his cue. Above, in the sick room, hoarse, outraged shouts that subside with exhaustion.* CAROL *crosses downstage and speaks to the audience and to herself.*)

CAROL. Something is still wild in the country! This country used to be wild, the men and women were wild and there was a wild sort of sweetness in their hearts, for each other, but now it's sick with neon, it's broken out sick, with neon, like most other places. . . . I'll wait outside in my car. It's the fastest thing on wheels in Two River County! (*She goes out of the store R.* LADY *stares at* VAL *with great asking eyes, a hand to her throat.*)

LADY (*with false boldness*). Well, ain't you going with her?

VAL. I'm going with no one I didn't come here with. And I come here with no one.

LADY. Then get into your white jacket.

I need your services in that room there tonight. (VAL *regards her steadily for several beats. Clapping her hands together twice*) Move, move, stop goofing! The Delta Brilliant lets out in half'n hour and they'll be driving up here. You got to shave ice for the setups!

VAL (*as if he thought she'd gone crazy*). "Shave ice for the setups"? (*He moves up to counter.*)

LADY. Yes, an' call Ruby Lightfoot, tell her I need me a dozen more half-pints of Seagram's. They all call for Seven-and-Sevens. You know how t' sell bottle goods under a counter? It's OK. We're gonna git paid for protection. (*Gasps, touching her diaphragm.*) But one thing you gotta watch out for is sellin' to minors. Don't serve liquor to minors. Ask for his driver's license if they's any doubt. Anybody born earlier than—let's see, twenty-one from—oh, I'll figure it later. Hey? Move! Move! Stop goofing!

VAL (*placing guitar on counter*). —You're the one that's goofing, not me, Lady.

LADY. Move, I said, *move!*

VAL. What kick are you on, are you on a benny kick, Lady? 'Ve you washed down a couple of bennies with a pot of black coffee t' make you come on strong for th' three o'clock show? (*His mockery is gentle, almost tender, but he has already made a departure; he is back in the all-night bars with the B-girls and raffish entertainers. He stands at counter as she rushes about. As she crosses between the two rooms, he reaches out to catch hold of her bare arm and he pulls her to him and grips her arms.*)

LADY. Hey!

VAL. Will you quit thrashin' around like a hooked catfish?

LADY. Go git in y'r white jacket an'—

VAL. Sit down. I want to talk to you.

LADY. I don't have time.

VAL. I got to reason with you.

LADY. It's not possible to.

VAL. You can't open a night-place here this night.

LADY. You bet your sweet life I'm *going* to!

VAL. Not *me*, not *my* sweet life!

LADY. I'm betting *my* life on it! Sweet or *not* sweet, I'm—

VAL. Yours is yours, mine is mine. . . . (*He releases her with a sad shrug.*)

LADY. You don't get the point, huh? There's a man up there that set fire to my father's wine garden and I lost my life in it, yeah, I lost my life in it, *three* lives was lost in it, two *born* lives and one—not. . . . I was made to commit a *murder* by him up there! (*Has frozen momentarily.*)—I want that man to see the wine garden come open again when he's dying! I want him to hear it coming open again here tonight! While he's dying. It's necessary, no power on earth can stop it. Hell, I don't even want it, it's just necessary, it's just something's got to be done to square things away, to, to, to—be *not defeated! You get me? Just to be not defeated!* Ah, oh, I won't be defeated, not again, in my life! (*Embraces him.*) Thank you for staying here with me!—God bless you for it. . . . Now please go and get in your white jacket . . .

(VAL *looks at her as if he were trying to decide between a natural sensibility of heart and what his life's taught him since he left Witches' Bayou. Then he sighs again, with the same slight, sad shrug, and crosses into alcove to put on a jacket and remove from under his cot a canvas-wrapped package of his belongings.* LADY *takes paper hats and carnival stuff from counter, crosses into confectionery and puts them on the tables, then starts back but stops short as she sees* VAL *come out of alcove with his snakeskin jacket and luggage.*)

LADY. That's not your white jacket, that's that snakeskin jacket you had on when you come here.

VAL. I come and I go in this jacket.

LADY. *Go,* did you say?

VAL. Yes, ma'am, I did, I said go. All that stays to be settled is a little matter of wages.

(*The dreaded thing's happened to her. This is what they call "the moment of truth" in the bull ring, when the matador goes in over the horns of the bull to plant the mortal sword-thrust.*)

LADY. —So you're—cutting out, are you?

VAL. My gear's all packed. I'm catchin' the southbound bus.

LADY. Uh-huh, in a pig's eye. You're not conning me, mister. She's waiting for you outside in her high-powered car and you're—

(*Sudden footsteps on stairs. They break apart,* VAL *puts suitcase down, drawing back into shadow, as* NURSE PORTER *appears on the stair landing.*)

NURSE PORTER. Miss Torrance, are you down there?

LADY (*crossing to foot of stairs*). Yeah. I'm here. I'm back.

NURSE PORTER. Can I talk to you up here about Mr. Torrance?

LADY (*shouting to* NURSE). I'll be up in a minute. (*Door closes above.* LADY *turns to* VAL.) OK, now, mister. You're scared about something, ain't you?

VAL. I been threatened with violence if I stay here.

LADY. I got paid for protection in this county, plenty paid for it, and it covers you too.

VAL. No, ma'am. My time is up here.

LADY. Y' say that like you'd served a sentence in jail.

VAL. I got in deeper than I meant to, Lady.

LADY. Yeah, and how about me?

VAL (*going to her*). I would of cut out before you got back to the store, but I wanted to tell you something I never told no one before. (*Places hand on her shoulder.*) I feel a true love for you, Lady! (*He kisses her.*) I'll wait for you out of this county, just name the time and the . . .

LADY (*moving back*). Oh, don't talk about love, not to me. It's easy to say "Love, Love!" with fast and free transportation waiting right out the door for you!

VAL. D'you remember some things I told you about me the night we met here?

LADY (*crossing to R.C.*). Yeah, many things. Yeah, temperature of a dog. And some bird, oh, yeah, without legs so it had to sleep on the wind!

VAL (*through her speech*). Naw, not that; not that.

LADY. And how you could burn down a woman? I said "Bull!" I take that back. You can! You can burn down a woman and stamp on her ashes to make sure the fire is put out!

VAL. I mean what I said about gettin' away from . . .

LADY. How long've you held this first steady job in your life?

VAL. Too long, too long!

LADY. Four months and five days, mister. All right! How much pay have you took?

VAL. I told you to keep out all but—

LADY. Y'r living expenses. I can give you the figures to a dime. Eighty-five bucks, no, ninety! Chicken-feed, mister! Y'know how much you got coming? IF you get it? I don't need paper to figure, I got it all in my head. You got five hundred and eighty-six bucks coming to you, not, not chicken-feed, that. But, mister. (*Gasps for breath.*)—If you try to walk out on me, now, tonight, without notice!—You're going to get just nothing! A great big zero. . . . (*Somebody hollers at door off R.: "Hey! You open?" She rushes toward it shouting, "CLOSED! CLOSED! GO AWAY!"—VAL crosses to the cashbox. She turns back toward him, gasps*) Now you watch your next move and I'll watch mine. You open that cashbox and I swear I'll throw open that door and holler, clerk's robbing the store!

VAL. —Lady?

LADY (*fiercely*). Hanh?

VAL. —Nothing, you've—

LADY. —Hanh?

VAL. Blown your stack. I will go without pay.

LADY (*coming to C.*). Then you ain't understood me! With or without pay, you're staying!

VAL. I've got my gear. (*Picks up suitcase. She rushes to seize his guitar.*)

LADY. Then I'll go up and git mine! And take this with me, just t'make sure you wait till I'm—(*She moves back to R.C. He puts suitcase down.*)

VAL (*advancing toward her*). Lady, what're you—

LADY (*entreating with guitar raised*). Don't—!

VAL. —Doing with—

LADY. —Don't!

VAL. —my guitar!

LADY. *Holding it for security while I*—

VAL. Lady, you been a lunatic since this morning!

LADY. Longer, longer than morning! I'm going to keep hold of your "life companion" while I pack! I am! I am goin' to pack an' go, if you go, where you go! (*He makes a move toward her. She crosses below and around to counter.*) You didn't think so, you actually didn't think so? What was I going to do, in your opinion? What, in your opinion, would I be doing? Stay on here in a store full of bottles and boxes while you go

far, while you go fast and far, without me having your—forwarding address!—even?

VAL. I'll—give you a forwarding address. . . .

LADY. Thanks, oh, thanks! Would I take your forwarding address back of that curtain? "Oh, dear forwarding address, hold me, kiss me, be faithful!" (*Utters grotesque, stifled cry; presses fist to mouth. He advances cautiously, hand stretched toward the guitar. She retreats above to U.R.C., biting lip, eyes flaring. JABE knocks above.*) Stay back! You want me to smash it!

VAL (*D.C.*). He's—knocking for you. . . .

LADY. I know! Death's knocking for me! Don't you think I hear him, knock, knock, knock? It sounds like what it is! Bones knocking bones. . . . Ask me how it felt to be coupled with death up there, and I can tell you. My skin crawled when he touched me. But I endured it. I guess my heart knew that somebody must be coming to take me out of this hell! You did. You came. Now look at me! I'm alive once more! (*Convulsive sobbing controlled: continues more calmly and harshly.*)—I won't wither in dark! Got that through your skull? Now. Listen! Everything in this rotten store is yours, not just your pay, but everything Death's scraped together down here!—but Death has got to die before we can go. . . . You got that memorized, now?—Then get into your white jacket!—*Tonight is the gala opening*—(*Rushes through confectionery.*)—of the confectionery—(VAL *runs and seizes her arm holding guitar. She breaks violently free.*) Smash me against a rock and I'll smash your guitar! I will, if you—(*Rapid footsteps on stairs.*) Oh, Miss Porter! (*She motions VAL back. He retreats into alcove.* LADY *puts guitar down beside juke box.* MISS PORTER *is descending the stairs.*)

NURSE PORTER (*descending watchfully*). You been out a long time.

LADY (*moving U.R.C.*). Yeah, well, I had lots of—(*Her voice expires breathlessly. She stares fiercely, blindly, into the other's hard face.*)

NURSE PORTER. —Of what?

LADY. Things to—things to—take care of. . . . (*Draws a deep, shuddering breath, clenched fist to her bosom.*)

NURSE PORTER. Didn't I hear you shouting to someone just now?

LADY. —Uh-huh. Some drunk tourist made a fuss because I wouldn't sell him no—liquor. . . .

NURSE (*crossing to the door*). Oh. Mr. Torrance is sleeping under medication.

LADY. That's good. (*She sits in shoe-fitting chair.*)

NURSE. I gave him a hypo at five.

LADY. —Don't all that morphine weaken the heart, Miss Porter?

NURSE. Gradually, yes.

LADY. How long does it usually take for them to let go?

NURSE. It varies according to the age of the patient and the condition his heart's in. Why?

LADY. Miss Porter, don't people sort of help them let go?

NURSE. How do you mean, Mrs. Torrance?

LADY. Shorten their suffering for them?

NURSE. Oh, I see what you mean. (*Snaps her purse shut.*)—I see what you mean, Mrs. Torrance. But killing is killing, regardless of circumstances.

LADY. Nobody said killing.

NURSE. You said "shorten their suffering."

LADY. Yes, like merciful people shorten an animal's suffering when he's. . . .

NURSE. A human being is not the same as an animal, Mrs. Torrance. And I don't hold with what they call—

LADY (*overlapping*). *Don't give me a sermon*, Miss Porter. I just wanted to know if—

NURSE (*overlapping*). I'm not giving a sermon. I just answered your question. If you want to get somebody to shorten your husband's life—

LADY (*jumping up; overlapping*). Why, how dare you say that I—

NURSE. I'll be back at ten-thirty.

LADY. Don't!

NURSE. What?

LADY (*crossing behind counter*). Don't come back at ten-thirty, don't come back.

NURSE. I'm always discharged by the doctors on my cases.

LADY. This time you're being discharged by the patient's wife.

NURSE. That's something we'll have to discuss with Dr. Buchanan.

LADY. I'll call him myself about it. I don't like you. I don't think you belong in the nursing profession, you have cold eyes; I think you like to watch pain!

NURSE. I know why you don't like my eyes. (*Snaps purse shut.*) You don't like my eyes because you know they see clear.

LADY. Why are you staring at *me*?

NURSE. I'm not staring at you, I'm staring at the curtain. There's something burning in there, smoke's coming out! (*Starts toward alcove.*) Oh.

LADY. Oh, no, you don't. (*Seizes her arm.*)

NURSE (*pushes her roughly aside and crosses to the curtain.* VAL *rises from cot, opens the curtain and faces her coolly*). Oh, excuse me! (*She turns to* LADY.)—The moment I looked at you when I was called on this case last Friday morning I knew that you were pregnant. (LADY *gasps.*) I also knew the moment I looked at your husband it wasn't by him. (*She stalks to the door.* LADY *suddenly cries out.*)

LADY. Thank you for telling me what I hoped for is true.

MISS PORTER. You don't seem to have any shame.

LADY (*exalted*). No. I don't have shame. I have—great—joy!

MISS PORTER (*venomously*). Then why don't you get the calliope and the clown to make the announcement?

LADY. You do it for me, save me the money! Make the announcement, all over!

(NURSE *goes out.* VAL *crosses swiftly to the door and locks it. Then he advances toward her, saying*)

VAL. Is it true what she said?

(LADY *moves as if stunned to the counter; the stunned look gradually turns to a look of wonder. On the counter is a heap of silver and gold paper hats and trumpets for the gala opening of the confectionery.*)

VAL (*in a hoarse whisper*). Is it true or not true, what that woman told you?

LADY. You sound like a scared little boy.

VAL. She's gone out to tell.

(*Pause.*)

LADY. You gotta go now—it's dangerous for you to stay here. . . . Take your pay out of the cashbox, you can go. Go, go, take the keys to my car, cross the river into some other county. You've done what you came here to do. . . .

VAL. —It's true then, it's—?

LADY (*sitting in chair of counter*). True as God's word! I have life in my body, this dead tree, my body, has burst in flower. You've given me life, you can go!

(*He crouches down gravely opposite her, gently takes hold of her knotted fingers and draws them to his lips, breathing on them as if to warm them. She sits bolt upright, tense, blind as a clairvoyant.*)

VAL. —Why didn't you tell me before?

LADY. —When a woman's been childless as long as I've been childless, it's hard to believe that you're still able to bear!—We used to have a little fig tree between the house and the orchard. It never bore any fruit, they said it was barren. Time went by it, spring after useless spring, and it almost started to—die. . . . Then one day I discovered a small green fig on the tree they said wouldn't bear! (*She is clasping a gilt paper horn.*) I ran through the orchard. I ran through the wine garden shouting, "Oh, Father, it's going to bear, the fig tree is going to bear!"—It seemed such a wonderful thing, after those ten barren springs, for the little fig tree to bear, it called for a celebration—I ran to a closet, I opened a box that we kept Christmas ornaments in!—I took them out, glass bells, glass birds, tinsel, icicles, stars. . . . And I hung the little tree with them, I decorated the fig tree with glass bells and glass birds, and silver icicles and stars, because it won the battle and it would bear! (*Rises, ecstatic.*) Unpack the box! Unpack the box with the Christmas ornaments in it, put them on me, glass bells and glass birds and stars and tinsel and snow! (*In a sort of delirium she thrusts the conical gilt paper hat on her head and runs to the foot of the stairs with the paper horn. She blows the horn over and over, grotesquely mounting the stairs, as VAL tries to stop her. She breaks away from him and runs up to the landing, blowing the paper horn and crying out*) I've won, I've won, Mr. Death, I'm going to bear! (*Then suddenly she falters, catches her breath in a shocked gasp and awkwardly retreats to the stairs. Then turns screaming and runs back down them, her cries dying out as she arrives at the floor level. She retreats haltingly as a blind person, a hand stretched out to* VAL, *as slow, clumping footsteps and*

hoarse breathing are heard on the stairs. She moans.*)—Oh, God, oh—God. . . .

(*JABE appears on the landing, by the artificial palm tree in its dully lustrous green jardiniere, a stained purple robe hangs loosely about his wasted yellowed frame. He is death's self, and malignancy, as he peers, crouching, down into the store's dimness to discover his quarry.*)

JABE. Buzzards! Buzzards! (*Clutching the trunk of the false palm tree, he raises the other hand holding a revolver and fires down into the store.* LADY *screams and rushes to cover* VAL's *motionless figure with hers.* JABE *scrambles down a few steps and fires again and the bullet strikes her, expelling her breath in a great* "*Hah!*" *He fires again; the great* "*Hah!*" *is repeated. She turns to face him, still covering* VAL *with her body, her face with all the passions and secrets of life and death in it now, her fierce eyes blazing, knowing, defying and accepting. But the revolver is empty; it clicks impotently and* JABE *hurls it toward them; he descends and passes them, shouting out hoarsely*) I'll have you burned! I burned her father and I'll have you burned! (*He opens the door and rushes out onto the road, shouting hoarsely*) The clerk is robbing the store, he shot my wife, the clerk is robbing the store, he killed my wife!

VAL. —Did it—?

LADY. —Yes!—it did. . . . (*A curious, almost formal, dignity appears in them both. She turns to him with the sort of smile that people offer in apology for an awkward speech, and he looks back at her gravely, raising one hand as if to stay her. But she shakes her head slightly and points to the ghostly radiance of her make-believe orchard and she begins to move a little unsteadily toward it. Music.* LADY *enters the confectionery and looks about it as people look for the last time at a loved place they are deserting.*) The show is over. The monkey is dead . . .

(*Music rises to cover whatever sound Death makes in the confectionery. It halts abruptly. Figures appear through the great front window of the store, pocket-lamps stare through the glass and someone begins to force the front door open.* VAL *cries out.*)

VAL. Which way! (*He turns and runs through the dim radiance of the con-*

fectionery, out of our sight. Something slams. Something cracks open. Men are in the store and the dark is full of hoarse, shouting voices.)

VOICES OF MEN (*shouting*). —Keep to the walls! He's armed!

—Upstairs, Dog!

—Jack, the confectionery!

(*Wild cry back of store*) Got him. GOT HIM!

—They got him!

—Rope, git rope!

—Git rope from th' hardware section!

—I got something better than rope!

—What've you got?

—What's that, what's he got?

—A BLOWTORCH!

—Christ. . . .

(*A momentary hush.*)

—Come on, what in hell are we waiting for?

—Hold on a minute, I wanta see if it works!

—Wait, Wait!

—LOOK here!

(*A jet of blue flame stabs the dark. It flickers on* CAROL's *figure in the confectionery. The men cry out together in hoarse passion crouching toward the fierce blue jet of fire, their faces lit by it like the faces of demons.*)

—Christ!

—It works!

(*They rush out. Confused shouting behind. Motors start. Fade quickly. There is almost silence, a dog bays in the distance. Then—the* CONJURE MAN *appears with a bundle of garments which he examines, dropping them all except the snakeskin jacket, which he holds up with a toothless mumble of excitement.*)

CAROL (*quietly, gently*). What have you got there, Uncle? Come here and let me see. (*He crosses to her.*) Oh yes, his snakeskin jacket. I'll give you a gold ring for it. (*She slowly twists ring off her finger. Somewhere there is a cry of anguish. She listens attentively till it fades out, then nods with understanding.*)— Wild things leave skins behind them, they leave clean skins and teeth and white bones behind them, and these are tokens passed from one to another, so that the "fugitive kind" can always follow their kind. . . .

(*The cry is repeated more terribly than before. It expires again. She draws the jacket about her as if she were cold, nods to the old* NEGRO, *handing him the ring. Then she crosses toward the door, pausing halfway as* SHERIFF TALBOTT *enters with his pocket-lamp.*)

SHERIFF. Don't no one move, don't move! (*She crosses directly past him as if she no longer saw him, and out the door. He shouts furiously.*) Stay here! (*Her laughter rings outside. He follows the girl, shouting*) Stop! Stop! (*Silence. The* NEGRO *looks up with a secret smile as the curtain falls slowly.*)

GIDEON

Paddy Chayefsky

Presented by Fred Coe and Arthur Cantor
at The Plymouth Theatre, New York, on November 9, 1961,
with the following cast:

THE ANGEL	Fredric March	ZALMUNNA	Paul Marin
JOASH	Mitchell Jason	SOLDIERS	Bernard Chessler
ABIMELECH	Victor Kilian		Tom Klunis
HELEK	Martin Garner		Amnon Meskin
JETHER	Robert Weiss		Meir Ovadia
GIDEON	Douglas Campbell	ONZI	David Hooks
TIRZAH	Florence Anglin	SECOND ELDER	Martin Garner
HAGLAH	Anna Berger	THIRD ELDER	Victor Kilian
WOMEN OF MANASSEH	Bathsheba Garnett	WOMEN OF SUCCOTH	Florence Anglin
	Gubi Mann		Anna Berger
	Ilene Tema		Bathsheba Garnett
SHILLEM	Eric Berry		Gubi Mann
JAHLEEL	David Hooks		Ilene Tema
HEZEKIAH	Alan Manson	ORPAH	Lorraine Egypt
MALCHIEL	Mark Lenard	MAHLAH	Bathsheba Garnett
PURAH	George Segal	MILCAH	Ilene Tema
ZEBAH	Alan Bergmann	ADINOAB	Gubi Mann

Directed by Tyrone Guthrie
Sets and lighting by David Hays
Costumes by Domingo A. Rodriguez
Produced in association with Carnegie Productions, Inc.

TIME: 1100 B.C.
ACT ONE. SCENE 1: The tent of Joash. SCENE 2: A hill at Harod.
    SCENE 3: Near the ford at Beth-barah.
ACT TWO. SCENE 1: Near the city of Succoth. SCENE 2: The tent of Joash.

THE author of *Gideon,* Paddy Chayefsky, first became known to the public as a meticulous realist wedded to the commonplace life. The impression was first created by an original script, *Marty,* for television, and in this mass medium it was almost a miracle to encounter (except in the case of documentaries) a veracious account of life as it is lived rather than as it is fancied by routinized imaginations. *Marty,* both as a television play and later as a motion picture, created an impression that was subsequently strengthened by the advent of Chayefsky's first Broadway play, *The Middle of the Night,* which dealt with the unlikely romance of a middle-aged widower and an unhappily married young woman. Mr. Chayefsky made this romance altogether believable, and then some. The production, in which Edward G. Robinson played the starring role with perfect conviction, got a mixed press but won a large public. As a result, New York critics, who sensed a resemblance to "soap opera" of the palmy days of the radio serial, were alarmed. Their reservations may have influenced the author, who next turned to imaginative drama in the folk-comedy of *The Tenth Man* and in the Biblical drama *Gideon,* strenuously blending the common with the uncommon in the same work and making the blend uniquely his own.

But if this readjustment of his sights surprised some reviewers it would not have astonished his most confident sponsor, the late Phyllis Anderson of the Theatre Guild, who found remarkable potentialities in his writing and communicated her confidence to the present editor on many an occasion. She saw a thread of vivid color in the weave of his drab fabric which could be easily overlooked in a writer who seemed attached only to the commonplaces of little people. He seemed, in fact, cast exactly for this occupation and no other. Born on January 29, 1923 as the son of an orthodox Jewish dairy manager in the Bronx, Paddy Chayefsky acquired a routine high-school education, and then attended the City College of New York and Fordham University. World War II, in which he served as a private, was not the occasion for a brilliant career for him, although it was not altogether uneventful when he was in France and stepped on a land mine. Television jobs followed while two of his full-length plays were awaiting productions that failed to materialize. Then came the success of the naturalistic plays *Marty* and *Middle of the Night.* But the new slanting of his talents toward imaginative theatre was not far off; and it is an index of his success in the new style that both *The Tenth Man* and *Gideon* should have won the directorial supervision of Tyrone Guthrie, one of England's most imaginative contemporary directors.

It is not easy to define the attitude of those to whom *Gideon* is antipathetic because they cannot accept the play as either Biblical or philosophical drama. It is perhaps no easier to explain the reaction of those who, like the present editor, derived gratification from the play without quite knowing what they made of it, and, indeed, what the author, whose own intentions were clear enough, had made of it. They were attracted by Mr. Chayefsky's separate treatments of Gideon as history's common man and of "The Angel" as theology's Yahweh, the Deity of the Old Testament whose behavior is also ultra-human—that is, egocentric, jealous, and as capricious as Gideon's is unsteady. One could be amused and here and there even touched by Gideon's ambivalent relations with The Lord and by the latter's troubles with Gideon, his only half willing instrument. In the somewhat heavy last scene one could find a profundity of sorts and more than a little relevance to the present precarious age of runaway knowledge and mechanics. One could find amidst lines perhaps too self-conscious (such as Gideon's saying to his God, "I asked you that I might delude myself with some spurious grandeur"), The Angel's sound warning against making a cult of man even in fancy, and Gideon's admission to the Lord ("The Angel"), who wants him to love him, "I fear you, God. Perhaps that's the only love a man can give his god." But the prime experience for those who did not reject the play must surely have been a rueful sense of the attraction-repulsion relationship of God and Man in history, as well as of course in that immensely human document the Old Testament, which no modern dramatist except a rhapsodist like Paul Claudel can successfully approach without a considerable quality of irony. The irony is there in Chayefsky's play, which could have used even more of it. Toward the end of the play Gideon declares, "You seem blurred, my Lord!" One could say the same thing to Mr. Chayefsky and yet maintain, much as Gideon does with his Lord, a rather fascinated relationship with the play.

For the most part the reception accorded to *Gideon* on Broadway was favorable except for qualifications (not exactly severe) to the effect that the conclusion is fuzzy. A minority report rendered with some vehemence in *The New Republic* (Nov. 23, 1959) by Robert Brustein, considered the play a concession to "the growing religiosity in the suburbs" by a prophet of "Middle Seriousness." Perhaps a lighter and more ironic performance might have drawn a milder dissent. And perhaps Mr. Chayefsky deserved rebuke for not having stuck to his original intent to treat the Biblical story more economically as a one-act play and "a quick, ironic joke" after having been inspired to reread the Bible by a visit to Israel and a journey to Beersheba and the desert in 1960. But the attributes of *Gideon* his admirers enjoyed and detractors loathed were an imaginative outcropping of the chief element that made him a successful playwright in the first place—namely, the concern with the common man and the latter's human reluctance to accept his insignificance. Man's entire ambivalent relationship with Deity is involved in this urge to set himself up as an independent individual and master of his destiny. But the difficulty of fully dramatizing this subject is not, of course, an exclusively American, middle-class, or middle-brow problem.*

---

* The reader interested in the problem of making modern adaptations of Biblical material could arrive at some basis for comparison by turning to Odets' *The Flowering Peach*, Obey's *Noah*, Giraudoux's *Judith*, Bridie's *Tobias and the Angel*, and other modern plays.

ACT ONE

SCENE ONE

"Now the angel of the Lord came and sat under the oak at Ophrah, which belonged to Joash, the Abiezrite, as his son Gideon was beating out wheat in the wine press to hide it from the Midianites."

The time is June, 1100 B.C.

The scene is the hill country of Manasseh, west of the Jordan River in Biblical Palestine.

Stage right is a wine press. Upstage of the wine press is a terebinth tree. Upstage center is a crude, stone sacrificial altar. Stage left is a black Bedouin-like tent.

At rise, a man with a black beard, almost entirely enshrouded in long black Mosiac robes, is leaning against the terebinth tree. He is an ANGEL.

Enter the elders, JOASH, ABIMELECH, *and* HELEK, *followed by a frightened boy of twelve, whose name is* JETHER. *The elders are all in their sixties. They wear variously colored robes. They hurry to the stone altar upstage center, lift their faces and begin to wail softly. They beat their breasts, pour ashes from the altar's hearth over their heads.*

JOASH (*crying out*). O Mighty Ba-al! Progenitor of Oxen! Rider of the Clouds and the Bringer of Rain! Hear the entreaty of your servant Joash . . .

ABIMELECH. . . . and of Abimelech his kinsman.

JOASH. Hear the entreaty of Joash of the house of Abiezer of the tribe of Manasseh.

HELEK. O Puissant Ba-al!

JOASH. O Mighty Ba-al! Hear the voice of your servant Joash!

ABIMELECH. Do not ignore Abimelech his kinsman.

HELEK. Nor Helek son of Zoar.

JOASH. All-potent Father! O Mighty Ba-al! The Midianites are upon us again! (*The four men burst into fresh wailing. They beat their breasts. They pour ashes on their heads. They rend their garments.*) We have seen their tents in Gilead on the other side of the Jordan River. Every year, for eight years, they have thundered up from the desert of Havilah, one hundred

thousand swarming nomads, their camels and their flocks. Like locusts, they devour everything before them, the harvests of Reuben, the barley of Gad. And now they are here again, this vast savage multitude. From our hills, we have seen the glint of their earrings and the golden crescents that hang from their camels. As far as the eye can see, their black tents darken the land of Gilead. Soon they will cross the Jordan and devour us here.

HELEK. Woe is Manasseh! Woe unto us here in Manasseh!

JOASH. They will take our daughters to be their servants.

ABIMELECH.
O Divine Ba-al! Save us! Redeem us!
Smite them with plagues, smite them with lightning.
Strike with your cudgels.

JOASH.
Give us a hero,
A redeemer, a savior.
Raise up a prince who will lead us in battle!
Raise up a hero!
You donkey! What have you brought here? (*This last, needless to say, was hardly addressed to Ba-al, but rather to a strapping, good-natured, bearded fellow in his late thirties named* GIDEON, *who has just entered carrying the carcass of a newly slaughtered young goat. He pauses at this greeting.*)

GIDEON. Father, I am bringing the sacrifice, as you asked me.

JOASH. A bullock! A bullock! I said to slaughter a bullock, Gideon, not a kid!

GIDEON. Oh, I heard you to say a kid.

ABIMELECH. Oh, let's get on with this sacrifice.

JOASH. My son Gideon has brought in a kid instead of a bullock.

ABIMELECH. Well, offer the kid then. We all want to get back to our tents and hide whatever we can before the Midianites come.

JOASH (*taking the kid from* GIDEON *and putting it on the altar, muttering*). Five sons I had; four were killed by the Midianites, and this is the one who was spared. (*Pulling his knife from its scabbard*) Now, does anyone remember the ritual we followed last year?

HELEK. It didn't help much last year so I shouldn't worry too much about repeating it exactly.

ABIMELECH. You dip your hand in the blood of the sacrifice and sprinkle it on the horns of the altar and . . .

JOASH. Yes, yes, I remember all that. It's the portion I'm asking about. How much of the animal do we actually offer? Does the right shoulder and upper right joint sound familiar to anyone?

HELEK. No, no, the proper portion for a sacrifice to My Lord Ba-al is the two cheeks, the stomach, the shoulders and all the fat thereof.

JOASH. Oh, I know that's not right.

ABIMELECH (*reaching impatiently for the knife in* JOASH's *hand*). Oh, let me do it.

JOASH. No, I'm chief of the clan.

ABIMELECH. Well, finish up with it then.

JOASH (*dipping his hand into the blood of the sacrificial kid and sprinkling some on the ground*). It's a mangy little animal. Why don't we just offer up the whole kid and be done with it?

ABIMELECH. Good.

JOASH (*now rubbing the blood on the tips of the horns of the altar*). Gideon, while I'm doing this—there are some sheaves of wheat that I brought into the tent. Beat them out and put the threshed wheat in a sack and hide the sack in that cave we used last year.

GIDEON. Yes, Father.

JOASH (*now applying some blood to his forehead, the thumb of his right hand, and to the toe of his right foot. He nudges* ABIMELECH). You see the point? We shall have to thresh the wheat harvest by hand and in secret. If the Midianites see us threshing the wheat on the hilltop, they will know we have had a good harvest and it shall go all the worse with us.

ABIMELECH. Oh, that is true. And I have just sent our cousin Lamech up to the threshing floor on the hill. Gideon, you had better send someone up to the threshing floor straightaway to tell Lamech to come down before the Midianites see him.

GIDEON. Yes, Uncle. (*He turns to the boy* JETHER.) Jether, my son, go to the threshing floor and tell Lamech to come down straightaway.

(JETHER, *far more interested in the ritual at the altar, pays his father no attention*.)

HELEK (*to* JOASH). You forgot to sprin-

kle the blood seven times around the altar.

JOASH. No, no, I've already done that.

GIDEON (*annoyed at his son's indifference, he appeals to his father*). Father, he never does what I ask him.

JOASH (*peremptorily to the boy*). Go to Lamech and bring him down from the threshing floor.

(*The boy leaps to his charge, exiting upstage and around the tent*.)

ABIMELECH. What shall we do with the herds this year?

HELEK. Well, let us finish with the prayers, and then we can decide what to do with the women and the cattle.

ABIMELECH. I hear wailing. The women have heard the news.

(*Indeed, far offstage left, we can hear the keening of* WOMEN. JOASH *turns back to the altar*.)

JOASH. O My Lord Ba-al, you are god over all other gods. And let the people say . . .

THE OTHER ELDERS. Amen.

(GIDEON *goes into the tent, and hoists several large sheaves of wheat effortlessly onto his shoulders*.)

JOASH.
You have banished Yam to the waters.
You seize the womb of Anath and you are sire to eagles,
And you are father to the grape.
And let the . . .
(*He pauses to watch his son* GIDEON *carrying the sheaves of wheat upstage and around the tent*.) Where are you going now?

GIDEON (*turning*). Do you speak to me, Father?

JOASH. I said where are you going?

GIDEON. I am taking these sheaves of wheat, as you asked me to, up to the threshing floor on the hill and . . .

ABIMELECH. Up to the threshing floor! You witless ass! You have just sent your son to tell Lamech to come down from the threshing floor!

GIDEON. But, Uncle, my father has asked me to thresh these sheaves of wheat . . .

JOASH. I said to beat them out! Beat them out in the wine press!

GIDEON (*utterly confused*). Beat the wheat out in the wine press?

HELEK. What a donkey!

JOASH. Gideon, if you go up to the

threshing floor, the Midianites will see you. They are only across the river. Do you want them to know we are reaping a good harvest? Go to the wine press, you goat, and beat out the sheaves with a stick.

(*Enter two women,* TIRZAH *and* HAGLAH, *in a state of panic. They wear blue and purple robes.*)

THE WOMEN. Oh, my lord Joash, the Midianites are upon us!

JOASH. Yes, yes, we know about that. We are offering prayers to Ba-al now. (ABIMELECH *suddenly bolts for the wings.*) Where are you going?

ABIMELECH. I have my own fields to reap! (*He exits.*)

JOASH (*to* THE WOMEN). Foolish ladies, you must get back to your gleaning. (*To* HELEK, *who is also bolting away*) We haven't finished the prayers!

HELEK (*exiting*). Bother the prayers!

THE WOMEN. See how Israel is brought low, how the elders scurry. As lions shall they devour the daughters of Israel.

JOASH (*wearily*). Oh, it is all too much for me. (*He enters the tent and squats gloomily down on his haunches.*)

GIDEON (*calling from the wine press*). Shall I continue beating out the wheat, Father?

JOASH. Yes! (*Mutters.*) Donkey.

(HAGLAH, GIDEON's *mother, goes off.* TIRZAH, GIDEON's *wife, remains, moving in and out of view in the tent as she gathers the stores of the household and puts them in baskets. There is a moment of silence, interrupted only by the pounding of* GIDEON's *stick as he beats at the kernels of wheat in the wine press. The black-bearded* ANGEL, *who has been watching it all from the shade of the terebinth tree, now steps forward to* GIDEON *and regards the big fellow, whacking away at the wheat.*)

THE ANGEL. The Lord is with you, O mighty man of valor. (GIDEON, *who had not noticed the* ANGEL *till now, looks up, a little startled.*) I said, the Lord is with you, O mighty man of valor.

(*This greeting, needless to say, disconcerts* GIDEON. *He darts a quick look back to the tent to see if anyone is around to take the fellow off his hands. He pounds a few more whacks, then smiles sheepishly at the stranger, raises his hand in a gesture of "Be right back," and*

shuffles quickly into the tent. His father is squatting unhappily on his haunches in the middle of the tent.)

GIDEON. Father, there is a very strange fellow by our terebinth tree.

JOASH. Well, give him what cakes we have on the hearth and show him the road to Schechem.

GIDEON (*hurriedly gathering cakes*). I was beating the wheat, you see, and this fellow suddenly came up, saying . . . (*He hurries out of the tent, across to the stranger now perched on the edge of the wine press. He offers the cakes and a skin of water.*) We have only these. We are very oppressed here. But you must hurry south before the Midianites come. I will show you the road. One makes for Schechem and then into Ephraim, and then others will show you the roads to Judah. I must get to my work. I have this wheat to beat here. It is a slow business. (GIDEON *picks up his beating stick and gets back to his work. But the calm stranger unnerves him.* THE ANGEL *sits perched on the edge of the wine press amiably munching the flat cakes he has been given.*) Sir, it is hard for me to do my work if you sit there like that.

THE ANGEL (*affably*). I am the Lord your God, Gideon, who brought you out of the iron furnace of Egypt and delivered you from bondage.

(GIDEON *considers this announcement for a moment.*)

GIDEON. Well, as you say, sir. Now, let me be about my work.

THE ANGEL. I am the Lord your God, Gideon. I have heard your groans under the Midianite yoke. You have cried out to Ba-al, but it is my ears that heard. My wrath was hot against you, for you have bowed down and served the Amorite gods and the Ba-als of the Canaanites. My name is Jealous, Gideon, for I am a Jealous God; and I have delivered you into the hands of the Midianites. But I have remembered the covenant I made with Jacob and the bargain I struck with Moses, and I will redeem you from the Midianite oppression. For My Name is the Loving God, the Gracious God, the Merciful God, and I have hearkened to your groans.

(*This is all a little too much for poor* GIDEON. *He makes a few half-hearted whacks at the wheat in the wine press, nods his head nervously a few times.*)

GIDEON (*mutters*). Excuse me. (*He turns and shuffles back across the stage to his father's tent and goes in again.*) It is a very strange stranger, indeed, Father. He seems a Hebrew from the cut of his beard, but I—it would be better if you came forth and dealt with him.

JOASH (*in despair*). Leave me be, Gideon.

(GIDEON *nods nervously and takes a few tentative steps out of the tent, and would perhaps have made his way back to the wine press, but he is petrified into a halt by the sudden booming of the stranger's voice.* THE ANGEL *is now standing in all his black majestic height, and he roars out in volcanic tones.*)

THE ANGEL. I am the Lord your God who brought you out of the house of Egypt! With signs and wonders I delivered you from bondage! Ten plagues I hurled at Pharaoh to awe you with my might. I drove back the sea with a strong east wind, and Israel walked through the waters! The horse and the rider I cast into the sea, but you walked through water! Would that not be a sign enough? Would that not be wonder enough? But you are a stubborn people! From that day to this have you rebelled against the Lord! Did I not rain bread from the heavens! Did I not strike water from the rock at Horeb? How long will you murmur against me? I shattered the walls of Jericho with trumpets. Thirty-one kings with their cities and walls did I give into your hand! But this mighty God was not enough for you! A cult of whores did you require! Mincing priests with crushed testicles! You have made cuttings in your skin and tattoos upon your brows! You have reveled before eyeless gods! You have debauched before stumps of trees! You are a stiff-necked people! You have done evil in mine eyes!

(GIDEON, *now thoroughly unnerved by what seems a raging lunatic, looks back to the tent to see why his father and wife haven't come running out at this outburst. But the two people in the tent do not seem to have heard.*)

GIDEON (*nervously*). Sir, I do not know why you are so enraged.

THE ANGEL. Gideon, do you not know me? It is hardly four generations since Moses. Do not the young men know my name any more? I am your Lord Yahweh, the Kinsman of Jacob, who was the father of all the houses in Israel.

GIDEON. I have heard the old men talk of My Lord Yahweh.

THE ANGEL. Well, I am he.

GIDEON. I shall not say you are not.

THE ANGEL. I tell you I, even I, am he!

GIDEON. Pray, sir, do not shout.

THE ANGEL. What a stiff-necked fellow you are!

GIDEON (*thoroughly distressed*). What would you have me say? I am a poor farmer, beating out wheat in his wine press. Suddenly, a black-bearded stranger appears at my elbow and shouts at me: "I am your God!" Well, I find this all an unusual business. I do not hold everyday traffic with gods. I said: "Very well." What else should I have said? And you have abused me roundly and hold me back from my pressing work.

THE ANGEL. I did not mean to discomfort you.

GIDEON. And now that I am put to it, I will tell you plainly—I do not believe in gods. I am not all as witless as my fellows sometimes think me. I have thought about these matters lately, and I do not believe in gods. You say that you are the god, Yahweh. The fact is, sir, in these parts, you are but a minor divinity. When I was a boy, you were more highly thought of, I think. But we Abiezrites are poor men, hill farmers. Our soil is hard, and we must pray for fertility, so we adopted a goddess with breasts and a womb, Ishtar—a sportive lady, I must say; her festivals are lively times. A farmer, you see, needs a romping god. And Yahweh, as I recall, was grim. Oh, sir, we have had all manner of gods here— the Bull-El, Yam, Mot, pin-breasted Ashtartes, Anu, Anath, the Mother Goddess of the wonderful womb, and now we have added the rain Ba-al of Beth-shean! And to all these gods I gave my full and primitive awe. I truly, truly served them. For I am a child in many ways and truly thought the wind did love me, and that the thunder was angry at something I did, and that I sliced our poor Lord Ba-al in half as I sickled my wheat, for such is the story, you know, that Ba-al dies each year at harvest. How I wailed as I reaped! I truly, truly thought the air was cluttered with fierce powers. But lately I have come to wondering.

THE ANGEL. Gideon . . .

GIDEON (*indicating the sacrificial kid*). What god will eat this sacrifice? Only that black bird. You say god to me, but I am a farmer, sir; I know a crow for a crow. A carrion crow is not much of a god really; I can chase him away with a stick.

THE ANGEL. Dear Gideon . . .

GIDEON. I have never asked of any god more than my own, that my trees bear olives, that my ewes bear lambs, the natural increase of things, no special favor. I did ask for seven sons; I have but one.

THE ANGEL. You shall have seventy sons, I promise you. And I shall redeem you from the Midianites.

GIDEON. Perhaps so. But lately, as I say, I have come to wondering.

THE ANGEL. Let us be friends, Gideon. For I am, in truth, the Lord your God, and I would have you believe in me. (*There is something so gentle about the black-bearded stranger that* GIDEON *must look at him.*) The Lord is with you, O mighty man of valor.

(GIDEON *looks quickly away, then squats on his haunches in the manner of the East.*)

GIDEON. If the Lord is with us, sir, then why are we as we are? In my time, it has always been hard for a Hebrew.

(THE ANGEL *now squats beside* GIDEON, *as two Oriental farmers might sit for a chat.*)

THE ANGEL. Come, we will talk as kinsmen, for I am the first of your tribe. I like you, Gideon; you are a straightforward man.

GIDEON. Well, you are quick to temper, I see, but there is a sweetness in you.

THE ANGEL. Then, we are friends.

GIDEON. Brothers, since you say so.

THE ANGEL. My brother then, you are a farmer. You know the ways of covenants. When you sell your cow to the caravan and the merchant gives you nothing in exchange, you will rise in anger, I should think.

GIDEON. Aye.

THE ANGEL. It is a breach, is it not?

GIDEON. It is a breach.

THE ANGEL. Well, so it is with me. I have made covenant with the people of Israel, and they have defaulted. I have filled my part of the contract. I promised Jacob I would make of him a great people, and indeed I did. Jacob was but a wandering Aramaean with a household of seventy people when I sent him down into Egypt. And when I led them out of the land of Egypt, the house of Jacob had become six hundred families, rich with flocks and servants. And I gathered the whole full twelve tribes of them at Mount Nebo by the Jordan River. And I put the matter to them plainly there. "Look here," spoke I, "let us renew this covenant of ours, so that things are clear between us. I shall give this land across the Jordan to you, and you shall prosper there. Your part of the bargain is simple enough. You shall not bow down to any other god. I am the Lord your God, and there is no other god. You shall not serve any other god." Could it have been more plainly stated?

GIDEON. No, it was plainly said.

THE ANGEL. Well, after Moses came Joshua, and after Joshua, there rose a new generation in Israel who knew not the Lord, and they played the harlot after the Amorite gods. And such gods, really! A stone lady with a bulbous belly! As you say, with more colorful rites than mine perhaps, but I really did think you Hebrews were a cleverer breed than that. Do you really think if you lay with a priestess, your seed will fecundate barley? Come, Gideon, this is merely magic and not fitting for a noble house. It is beyond my understanding—really it is!—what you see in these other gods. The men of Sumer pray to the moon, but your god made the moon and many moons like it. The Philistines bow down to a flea, and the Egyptians—oh, well, the Egyptians will pray to anything. Cats, fish, vermin, frogs, rams, bulls, asps and adders, anything really. But your god is no cat. Nor can his likeness be chipped from stone. Not by gold nor red carbuncle can your god be wrought. Your god is beyond dimension. Your god, Hebrew, is beyond all other gods. Your god is all. Your god is everything. I am what is. I am the Lord! What was it we were talking of?

GIDEON. You were saying our fathers bowed down to other gods.

THE ANGEL. Your fathers indeed! Have *you* not bowed down to Marduk? And now it is Ishtar and the rain Ba-al of Beth-shean. And so I have given you into the hands of the Midianites. (*He has risen now to his full godlike majesty. His voice booms out.*) This one last time shall I redeem you! This one last time, ye Hebrews! (GIDEON *looks nervously around, surprised that nobody seems to hear* THE ANGEL.) But if you break faith with me one more time, then cursed shall you be in the city and cursed shall you be in the field! You shall serve your enemies in nakedness! I shall make brutes of you! Your women shall eat their own afterbirth! Your men shall eat their sons in hunger. Among all nations, you shall find no rest! For I am the Lord! I am the Lord! I am the Lord! (*He is abruptly affable again.*) I shall raise up from among you a redeemer, and he shall deliver you from the Midianites.

GIDEON (*terrified now*). How shall we know this redeemer?

THE ANGEL. I shall come to him in the guise of a stranger, and I shall say unto him: "The Lord is with you, O mighty man of valor."

(GIDEON *nods his head slowly. Then he scowls as he begins to understand.*)

GIDEON. I?

THE ANGEL. You shall be the redeemer. Gideon the son of Joash, the son of Abiezer, the son of Gilead, the son of Machir, the son of Manasseh.

GIDEON. You cannot be serious.

THE ANGEL. You shall be the redeemer.

GIDEON. Sir, I am Gideon, the donkey of the clan. Ask anyone in Ophrah or on the hills. They shall tell you Gideon is a good enough fellow but an ass. Will you gird a donkey and make him your general? Of course, it is a prank. I am often the butt of such pranks. It is a prank, is it not? Of course. Ho! Gideon the general! What an idea! (*He looks anxiously at* THE ANGEL *who seems quite serious about the whole matter.*) Sir, I am not a soldier. I wouldn't know which end of the sword is haft.

THE ANGEL. You are a mighty man of valor.

GIDEON. I will not hear any more of this. Really, I . . . the very idea of it has put me at my wit's end. Who will join Gideon's army?

THE ANGEL. The spirit of the Lord shall come upon you, and all Israel shall heed your words.

GIDEON. No, no, sir, I will have no part of this.

(*Enter* HELEK, *running from stage right. He is aghast with panic and quite out of breath.*)

HELEK (*shouting*). They come! They come! The Midianites come!

ABIMELECH'S VOICE (*offstage left*). They come! They come! Midian comes!

HELEK (*hurrying across to the tent*). Joash! They come! The shepherds have seen them. They are crossing the river.

JOASH (*at his tent flap*). Oh, dear me!

(ABIMELECH *comes hurtling in from stage left.*)

ABIMELECH. They have entered the river! Lamech has seen them from the threshing floor! (*He flings himself down before the altar.*) O Mighty Ba-al! Let it be quick and done with this year!

JOASH (*walking about at a loss.*) Is there time to gather the elders and hold council?

(*Far offstage,* THE WOMEN *begin a long, ululating wail.*)

THE ANGEL (*to* GIDEON). Sound the trumpet, man of valor, and gather your army.

(GIDEON, *who has quite forgotten the stranger in this flurry of panic, turns and regards him blankly.*)

JOASH (*shaking with fear and indecision*). Each man must do what is right in his own eyes. Take what you can and run for the caves.

GIDEON (*crosses to* JOASH). Father, I pray you, talk with this stranger, for he frightens me.

JOASH. What stranger?

GIDEON. The man by the terebinth tree.

JOASH. The terebinth tree?

GIDEON. The black-bearded man in the heavy black robes. His hand is outstretched towards us.

JOASH. There is no man by the terebinth tree. Have you lost your wits entirely?

(GIDEON *turns slowly and stares at* THE ANGEL *as* THE WOMEN OF MANASSEH *enter, lamenting.* JETHER, *the boy, is with them, terrified and clutching at his mother's robe.*)

THE WOMEN.
The Kings of Midian ford the Jordan.
The blood of Gilead drips from their swords.

THE ELDERS. O! We are oppressed!

THE WOMEN.
The quiet Jordan heaves with waves.
Thousand on thousand push into the

water.

They come! They come! Midian comes!

THE ELDERS. O! We are wounded and suffer!

THE ANGEL (*to* GIDEON, *who is staring with wide-eyed interest at him*). The spirit of the Lord is upon you, Gideon, and the people shall do as you tell them.

(GIDEON *turns slowly to the elders.*)

GIDEON (*in a state of possession*).

Rise up, ye elders!

Hear the oracle of Gideon, the son of Joash,

The oracle of the man whose eye is opened!

The Lord of Jacob will redeem you.

The God of Moses is here,

And the Midianites will flee before you seven ways!

(*The elders look up from their postures of prostration.*)

HELEK. On my head, is this Gideon who prophesies? (*He stands slowly.*)

GIDEON. Sound the trumpet, Father! Gather the Abiezrites upon this hill. We shall make war with Midian. (*He seizes his fathers' sacrificial knife from the altar and, with a quick, violent stroke slashes off a section of* HELEK's *robe.*) Send messengers throughout Manasseh. This is what they shall say to the chiefs of Manasseh: "Whosoever does not come out after Gideon, thus shall my sword be brought down upon him." Let them come to me at Harod. There shall we gather an army. The battle shall be met in three days' time. It is the word of the Lord! The trumpet, Father! Go fetch the horn and sound it! (JOASH *shuffles dumbly into his tent.*) It is the word of the lord, Helek. (HELEK *turns blankly and exits slowly off stage right. To* ABIMELECH.) Send men servants to Asher, to Naphtali and to Zebulun. Take a yoke of oxen and chop them into pieces, and let your men servants say this to the chiefs: "Whoever does not come out after Gideon, thus shall it be done to his herds." The Lord is with you.

A WOMAN. We have raised up a savior!

(ABIMELECH *nods his head numbly and moves slowly off stage left.*)

GIDEON. Rise, ye women, and take the aged and children to the stronghold at Schechem. If you come into your monthly weakness in these three days, hide ye from the others, for it is an unclean thing

and a bad omen for the battle.

THE WOMEN (*rising and intoning*).

We have raised up a savior.

As a lion does he rise up.

As the wild ox who gores the foe.

(THE WOMEN *exeunt stage left. The boy,* JETHER, *pauses a moment to regard his father with new interest.* GIDEON *beams at him and the boy exits.* JOASH *comes out of the tent, carrying a large silver trumpet.* GIDEON *stares at him blankly. Now,* JOASH *lets loose a mighty blast.* GIDEON *winces against the loud clarion.*)

JOASH. Shall we sound the horn again, my lord Gideon?

(GIDEON *turns, startled at this appellation. It pleases him. He looks at* THE ANGEL *who nods approval. He smiles.*)

GIDEON. Yes, I suppose we had better.

(*The fact is that* GIDEON *is very pleased by his new prominence; he is not quite sure of what has happened but is quite pleased nevertheless.* JOASH *sounds the trumpet again, its blast reverberates throughout the theatre.* GIDEON *tugs at his beard as he considers the whole remarkable incident favorably. The* CURTAIN *comes down quickly.*)

SCENE TWO

"Then Jerubaal (that is, Gideon) and all the people who were with him, rose early and encamped beside the spring of Harod; and the camp of Midian was north of them by the hill of Moreh in the valley."

———

The hill at Harod. It is late afternoon, three days later.

Upstage is a small spur of a hill. On the spur is GIDEON's *tent. Downstage of this spur is a second smaller spur. Both spurs drop away to stage level some feet from the right wing. They are separated by a small defile.*

At rise, GIDEON *is seated downstage against the lower spur. His chin rests gloomily on the palm of his right hand. He is accoutered for war: he wears a leather corselet which chafes him and a leather baldric studded with iron pieces.*

In the tent are SHILLEM *the Naphtalite and* JAHLEEL *the Zebulunite.* SHILLEM *is a grizzled old warrior in his late sixties. He wears a brass cuirass, a woolen helmet with lappets, a leather belt and greaves.*

He holds a mighty warbow over which he fusses throughout the scene. JAHLEEL *is a man in his fifties, robed and turbaned. He squats on the carpets.* PURAH, *the manservant of* GIDEON, *stands guard stage left of the tent. He is armed with a mattock. One or two* SOLDIERS *are occasionally visible upstage of the tent.*

Enter two warriors in their late forties. They are HEZEKIAH *and* MALCHIEL. HEZE-KIAH *is stripped to the waist and wears a short skirtlike garment that comes to the knees. A pouch of stones, slung over his shoulder, dangles at his hip. He carries a sling.* MALCHIEL *wears a knee-length tunic, girdled by a leather belt, and holds a spear. They poke their heads into the tent.*

———

HEZEKIAH. Peace be with you, is this the tent of Gideon?

SHILLEM. Aye.

HEZEKIAH. We are the captains from Asher. I am Hezekiah of the house of Immah.

MALCHIEL. I am his brother Malchiel of the house of Immah.

SHILLEM. Peace be unto you. I am Shillem, captain of Naphtali, and there sits Jahleel the Zebulunite.

(PURAH, *at last aware that someone is going into the tent, wheels and brandishes his mattock.*)

PURAH. Who enters the tent of Gideon?

SHILLEM. Rest, rest, sentry, it is only the captains from Asher. (*At* PURAH's *challenge,* GIDEON *stood and peeked over his spur to see the new arrivals. Now he squats again.*) The sentry is an imbecile. I can't step out of this tent to yawn that he doesn't challenge me with his plowshare. Well, how many have you brought with you?

HEZEKIAH. Eight thousand. We are pitched at the southern foot of the hill.

SHILLEM. Eight thousand fishermen from Asher. Well, that brings us now to thirty-two thousand. Well, we are fully met, the hosts of Israel. Thirty-two thousand fishers and husbandmen, armed with mattocks and trammels, a few dirks and darts, harpoons, and some old battle-axes, and flint axes at that. Ha! Not ten archers in the lot. I captained fifty men for Barak when we drove Sisera down the slopes of Tabor into the Kishon River. I mention it, not to bore you with an old warrior's

tales, but to say merely that I know the shape of an army, and in truth, captains of Zebulun and Asher, this is an undistinguished garrison we have gathered here. We had expected the men of Asher yesterday.

HEZEKIAH. Yes, well, it wasn't easy to gather eight thousand men to make war simply because a zealot named Gideon suggested it. I mean, a messenger from Manasseh, brandishing a chopped-up cow, came racing up to the gates of my city, shouting: "Whosoever does not come out after Gideon," and so forth and so forth— well, it's hard to take that sort of thing seriously. I didn't want to come at all, but my brother Malchiel here is a more enthusiastic follower of prophets.

MALCHIEL (*a fanatic sort*). We have been told this Gideon is a charismatic man and that he walks in a blinding circle of light.

SHILLEM. Well, not too blinding. I wouldn't put him down as completely feckless, but he does seem to lack a forceful grip on things.

JAHLEEL. Aye.

SHILLEM. I took our general, Gideon, up to the crest of this hill this morning. We lay on our bellies and looked down on the Midianite camp in the valley. Their tents stretch ten miles from Shunem to the foothills of Gilboa. If I had to hazard a number, I would count them at a hundred thousand.

JAHLEEL. And there are another twenty thousand Amalekites who ride with them.

SHILLEM. And Gideon prophesied we should smite the Midianites on the third day, and this is the third day.

JAHLEEL. And late in the afternoon of the third day.

SHILLEM. Well, as I say, we looked down upon this awesome multitude, and I said to Gideon: "My General, what plan of battle have you for this?" "I haven't the beginnings of an idea," he said, "have you?" And that was this morning.

HEZEKIAH. You mean we have no plan of battle?

SHILLEM. Absolutely none at all. So I have been conceiving a clever shift or two. Still, we are badly favored in this battle, badly favored. (*He takes a small branch and begins marking the ground at their feet.*) Well, attend. Here we sit on the hill of Harod. Here lay the

Midianites in the Valley of Jezreel below.

(*The others gather around him. Down-stage,* THE ANGEL, *in excellent spirits, enters.* GIDEON *offers him a quick, sulky look.*)

GIDEON. Where have you been?

THE ANGEL (*a little surprised at this sulkiness*). Why are you suddenly so cross? When I left you this morning, you flung yourself at my feet, kissed the hem of my robe and vowed eternal love to me. Now, what occasions this new petulance? Oh, come, Gideon, I have grown so fond of you these past three days. And it is lovely here at Harod at this hour. See all this arbutus; it is a sweet night.

GIDEON. This corselet my uncle gave me chafes.

THE ANGEL (*squatting down beside* GIDEON). Oh, take it off. I told you yesterday to take it off. It is much too hot for leather. But you will posture as a general and swagger among the troops. You have your baldric on backwards, I might add.

GIDEON. My manservant Purah said this was the way.

THE ANGEL. And put away that poniard. You will not need it. A handsome one though. Here, let me look at it. Made of an antelope's horn. Is it also your uncle's?

GIDEON. Yes.

THE ANGEL. Very handsome.

GIDEON. The old man Shillem of Naphtali is driving me out of my wits.

THE ANGEL. A vain old man, why do you listen to him?

GIDEON. He keeps clutching my arm and saying: "What have you in the way of a battle plan?" Well, what am I to say? The men of Asher have finally come. Their captains sit in my tent now. "What is the plan of battle?" they shall say. And what am I to answer? The people shout at me as I walk among the tents: "We've left half a harvest in the field. The first grapes will be ripening in a week! We want to be home!" "The Lord of Moses is with you," I answer, "and you shall not fear." Well, I shall have to have something cleverer to say than that, for they grumble a great deal. I said we would engage the Midianites in three days' time, and it is the third day now. And you went off this morning, and here it is dusk. I've been looking for you all through the hills. And you say wherefore do I sulk?

THE ANGEL. You shall have your battle plan. Have no fear.

GIDEON. Why have you kept it secret?

THE ANGEL. You never asked me for it. You have been sporting among the people, playing the prince. I watched you shout orders from your tent and gravely scratch maps on the ground. This rodomontade was your diversion; I would not spoil it for you. And I meant you also to know your own incompetence. It shall not be said, when this victory over Midian is won, that it was won by Gideon or any other general. This victory shall be mine. It shall be a miracle. It shall be clear to all Israel that only the hand of God delivered them.

GIDEON. Pray, sir, what is the plan?

THE ANGEL. You shall require three hundred lamps, each filled with an hour's oil.

GIDEON. Three hundred lamps?

THE ANGEL. And three hundred horns.

GIDEON. What manner of horns?

THE ANGEL. Any manner so long as each can blow a loud blast. Go see to these requisitions quickly. It is dusk now, and night falls abruptly in June.

GIDEON. Pray, sir, these three hundred lamps—what is the reason for these three hundred lamps and three hundred horns?

THE ANGEL. Yes, another thing. The Midianites will flee seven ways before you this night.

GIDEON. This night? Is it tonight then, the battle?

THE ANGEL. In panic shall they flee down the Jordan valley. They will try to escape across the Jordan at Beth-barah which is in Ephraim. Therefore, send messengers into Ephraim, and let them say to the chiefs of Ephraim: "Set men at Beth-barah and smite the Midianites as they flee to the fords." Quickly, Gideon, for these are matters of the moment.

GIDEON. Sir, these lamps—I cannot flatly march into that tent, saying "Get three hundred lamps and three hundred horns," turn on my heel and flatly walk out again. My captains shall, with some justification, think it a strange instruction.

THE ANGEL (*ending all argument*). I am the Lord.

(GIDEON *scowls, darts a probing look or two at* THE ANGEL, *then turns and starts climbing up the defile between the spurs.*)

JAHLEEL (*at the tent flap*). Attend! He comes!

SHILLEM (*coming to the tent flap*). Ho, Gideon! The captains of Asher are here with eight thousand men!

PURAH (*whirling and challenging* GIDEON). Who approaches the tent of Gideon?

GIDEON (*wearily*). It is only I, Purah, it is only I.

SHILLEM (*as* GIDEON *clambers up to the upper spur*). We have contrived a plan of assault, O General, suggested by Joshua's tactics when he captured the City of Ai. It is our plan to entice the Amalekites off the slopes of Gilboa by sending . . .

HEZEKIAH. Peace be with you, Gideon.

GIDEON. Peace be with you, men of Asher.

SHILLEM. . . . by sending a small band of decoys to the east to—

GIDEON. Captains of Asher, gather from your men three hundred lamps, each filled with an hour of oil, and three hundred horns for blowing.

(*This gives everybody something to think about for a moment.*)

SHILLEM. Three hundred lamps and three hundred horns. What is the purpose of three hundred lamps and three hundred horns?

GIDEON. You know as much as I. So spoke the Lord to me, and so I speak it to you. (*To* JAHLEEL) Captain of Zebulun, send three messengers to the proud prince of Ephraim at Shiloh. Let them say this: "Guard the fords at Beth-barah. This very night, the Midianites, fleeing in panic, will try to cross the Jordan there. Let them smite the Midianites, preserve not one that breathes." Straightaway now, all of you.

MALCHIEL. It is tonight then, that the battle is met?

GIDEON. So spoke the Lord to me.

SHILLEM. Three hundred lamps, each with an hour's oil in it. What are we to do with three hundred lamps?

JAHLEEL. Pray, Gideon, a sensible forethought this guarding the fords at Beth-barah where the Midianites shall flee in panic. What still bears consideration—to me at least—is how does one get the Midianites to flee there in panic?

GIDEON. I am as curious as you. (*He turns on his heel and starts down the defile again.*)

SHILLEM. As gods go, this Lord Yahweh has a whimsical turn of mind, don't you think? Three hundred trumpets. Ha!

MALCHIEL. It is said that with the blowing of trumpets, Joshua took Jericho.

SHILLEM. Well, there was more to it than that, I'm sure. Joshua had a sizable command of a thousand families.

HEZEKIAH (*dubiously*). I shall go gather the requisitions. (*He exits.*)

SHILLEM. My plan, I thought, had considerable merit. You see, having drawn off the Amalekites . . .

PURAH (*whirling to challenge* GIDEON *en route back*). Who passes there?

GIDEON. Oh, in the name of heaven, you donkey, it is only I!

SHILLEM. Having drawn off the Amalekites, we retire quickly to the east of the Jordan in Gad, where we would reassemble the hosts . . .

JAHLEEL. I had better go send messengers to the proud prince of Ephraim. (*He exits.*)

MALCHIEL. He did not seem especially compelling, this Gideon. We have diviners in Dor whose eyes flash with actual flame. How is this Gideon when prophecy comes upon him? The priests of Cybele leap into the air, slash themselves with knives, spinning and shrieking in Corybantic frenzy till they sink to the ground, self-bloodied eunuchs. The signs have not been good for this battle, Captain of Naphtali. Our men of Acco say a shark washed ashore the day before with a fish in its teeth still wriggling. It is a bad foreboding.

(GIDEON *has rejoined* THE ANGEL *downstage. He is waiting a little anxiously for* THE ANGEL, *who is deep in thought, to speak.*)

THE ANGEL. How many men have you in your camp?

(GIDEON *calculates for a moment.*)

GIDEON. Thirty-two thousand with the eight thousand from Asher.

THE ANGEL. Too many. We shall have to cut your forces down.

GIDEON (*unashamedly alarmed*). Cut them down?

THE ANGEL. If Midian is defeated by thirty-two thousand, then will Israel vaunt itself, saying: "It was by our own hand that we were delivered." And, yea, they shall know it was by the hand of

God alone. Now, therefore, go to your chiefs and say: "Proclaim in the ears of the people, saying: 'Whoever is fearful and trembling, let him return home.' "

GIDEON. Oh, dear me!

THE ANGEL. Quickly, Gideon.

GIDEON. Pray, sir, you have charged me to go to my chiefs and say: "Proclaim in the ears of the people, saying: 'All those who are fearful and trembling, they may return to their farms.' "

THE ANGEL. Aye.

GIDEON. Pray, sir, if we were to proclaim in the ears of the people, saying: "All those who are fearful and trembling, you may return to your farms," then, sir, would you see such a sweeping exodus as would make you pale. These hills would be desolate in an hour. And I, in all probability, will be leading the pack.

THE ANGEL. Quickly, Gideon, for we mean to make battle tonight.

GIDEON. This cuirass is unendurable! Why didn't you tell me one wears an undergarment with these things? I had to learn it from Shillem this morning. "Do you not have a sagum underneath?" he said. I didn't even know what a sagum was. He studied me for a moment, unfavorably, to say the least. Oh, sir, surely you must see the consequences—even I who do not know what a sagum is can see that if we tell the fearful of heart to go home we shall be left with a shocking small army, a few reluctant husbands and some larking boys who think this whole matter a frolic. Oh, no, sir, I pray you! Shall I say to my chiefs: "We are outnumbered four to one. Therefore we are too many"? They think me a howling jackal as it is. And they shall think you the same. If you had only seen their faces when I passed on that matter of the oil lamps. They looked, to put the kindest word on it, they looked askance at me. Oh, this cuirass!

THE ANGEL (rising into his lordly fury and roaring out). I am the Lord! I have said I shall redeem the house of Israel! With one man, if I choose it so, shall I redeem you! (GIDEON looks nervously back to see if they are being overheard.) Gideon, take heed! My anger waxes hot against you! I shall consume you with my wrath! I shall open the earth, and I shall swallow you up into the earth!

GIDEON (rather cowed). All right, pray, do not shout, sir. All right, it shall be done. (He turns and with a show of petulance, starts back up the defile. PURAH, ever-alert fellow, wheels again to challenge him, but GIDEON wearily waves him back. GIDEON calls as he clambers up to the upper spur) Chiefs of Zebulun, Asher, and Naphtali . . . (JAHLEEL, who is back by now, MALCHIEL, and SHILLEM rise as GIDEON enters the tent.) Well, harken to this. It is the word of the Lord, spoken in a voice of thunder. You are each to go to your separate camps and proclaim in the ears of your people, saying: "Whoever is fearful and trembling, let him return home."

SHILLEM. Are you insane?

GIDEON (his own temper exploding). Well, what am I to do? It is the word of the Lord! He spoke it to me; I speak it to you! I too am ill-disposed to this idea! If we are to talk of those who tremble and fear, well, sir, I am surely captain of that army! This dreadful cuirass, may it be cursed, and all who put it on them! (He wrenches at the bindings of the cuirass as he storms about.) If you think you can manage matters better, Naphtalite, well, then, you are general now; I am done with being general! I have been hearing nothing these past two days but what a wily warrior you are. You can parley with the Lord. I don't know why he picked on me in the first place!

SHILLEM. Peace, peace, Gideon.

GIDEON. Go and parley with him yourself if you think you can reap a better crop from him than I! He stands at the foot of that second spur, a large man with a black beard, robed in black linen of such richness as you have never seen. Murmur to him, if you will! Show the stiffness of your neck to him, not to me.

JAHLEEL. But the Lord keeps himself invisible to all but you.

GIDEON. Well, perhaps, I am insane. Have you ever considered that? Not every man who sees a vision is a prophet! You may all be gathered here at the fancy of a maniac! At any moment, I may drop down to all fours and howl like a laboring heifer! (He wrenches the cuirass off and throws it down angrily.) Ah! That's better! Look at me, welted and raw. And my baldric was on backwards. My manservant shall feel my stick soon enough for that. Well, I shall say once more what was enjoined me by this angel whom only I can see. The Lord Yahweh feels that an army of thirty-two thousand Israelites will detract from the miraculous nature of his deliverance. He wants a smaller army. So go forth to your separate peoples and proclaim in their ears, saying: "Whoever is fearful and trembling, let him return home." (*The chiefs look questioningly at one another, shrug, and troop out of the tent.* GIDEON *stands wearily for a moment; then goes out of the tent and calls to* PURAH.) Purah, go and charge my captains of Manasseh: "Go among the tents of Manasseh and proclaim in the ears of the men, saying: 'All those who fear the battle tonight may go home.'" (*A delighted smile breaks across* PURAH's *face and he leaps to his charge.*) And return here to me. I shall need you. (*Some of his joy abated,* PURAH *exits. It is noticeably darker on stage now. Evening is come. After a moment,* THE ANGEL *strolls up the defile and goes into the tent.*)

THE ANGEL. Well, they have gone to do as you bid them. You were truly lordly in your wrath.

GIDEON. Thank you.

THE ANGEL. Now then—by sending the fearful home, you will be left with an army of ten thousand men. And this will still be too many.

GIDEON. I had expected as much.

THE ANGEL. Of these ten thousand who shall be left, three hundred are such great cowards they are even too frightened to escape. You shall know them by the following test: you shall take the ten thousand down to the springs of Harod and let them drink of the water. And those that kneel down to drink, cupping their hands, these shall you send home to their farms. And those that lap the water, as a dog laps, these shall number three hundred. These three hundred, Gideon, shall be your band of deliverers.

GIDEON. For my curiosity alone, why those who lap the water as a dog laps?

THE ANGEL. These three hundred are such frightened men they shall lie upon their bellies and lap furtively for fear the Midianites might hear even their drinking.

GIDEON. Well, then, an army of three hundred uncompromising cowards, armed, I assume, with the three hundred oil lamps and the three hundred horns.

THE ANGEL. Ah! You see the battle plan then!

GIDEON. What battle plan?

THE ANGEL. It is an artful ruse. Place one hundred men at Shunem, one hundred more to the north at Endor, and a third company you shall keep right here with you. Then, upon a signal, all three companies shall light their lanterns, wave them in the air, all the while blowing loud blasts on their trumpets. The Midianites will then flee in panic down the valley to Beth-barah where you have already planned a savage greeting for them.

(GIDEON *regards* THE ANGEL *for a long moment in a manner that can only be called quizzical.*)

GIDEON. This is the plan for which you had me assemble four tribes of Israel to make war?

THE ANGEL. Aye.

GIDEON. One company of cowards in Shunem, another in Endor, and the third here, waving lanterns and blowing trumpets—that is the substance of it?

THE ANGEL. Aye.

GIDEON. Sir, I have heard at least five plans from that old fraud Shillem that I would deem more probable.

THE ANGEL. Well, it is intended to be a miracle, Gideon.

GIDEON. Oh, that is clear enough. (*He strides out of the tent, throwing up his arms in a gesture of deep annoyance.*) It is a silly plan, sir! A blithe and silly plan! Three hundred tootling cowards will not send a hundred thousand and more men of Midian ranting down the Jordan Valley. The Midianites will simply look up and say: "What is that tootling?" Then they will unsheathe their scimitars, root us out and slash us up. It is a preposterous plan! And see how clear this night! A full moon, not a cloud! No night for hidden warfare, this! That olive bush one mile hence is visible. See! See! The chiefs have told the fearful they can go home. See how they race for their tents. Whisk! That one was folded quickly. And there!, that man is already scuttling down the slope to the caravan road to Bezek. How they scramble! Come and see! (THE ANGEL *ambles out of the tent to join* GIDEON *on the spur.*) How many did you compute would be left? Ten thousand? A rash estimate, my Lord.

There will not even be three hundred from which to cull your cowards.

THE ANGEL. Whatever has come over you?

GIDEON. I'm finished with being a soldier.

THE ANGEL. You believed in me this morning.

GIDEON. Yes, then I did, but now I don't.

THE ANGEL. I have given you proofs of my godhood. I have performed wonders at your whim. Yesterday, at this very hour, you tested me. "See," you said, "I place this fleece of wool upon this hill. Now, prove to me you are truly the Lord. In the morning, let me see a heavy dew upon this fleece; but let there be no dew at all on the hill. The hill shall be dry, the fleece alone wet." And I performed this prodigy for you.

GIDEON. Yes, you did.

THE ANGEL. In the morning, it was as you asked. The hill was dry; the fleece was conclusively wet. You seemed convinced. You were effusive in your faith this morning.

GIDEON. Yes, I know. I fell to the ground, didn't I? And shouted: "Turn away from me! Show me not your face! For I have seen the face of the Lord, and I will surely die!" I hope nobody saw us. But then you went off. The sun rose fully up, and the tents around me came awake with the shouts of mortal men. I looked down at the sopping piece of wool in my hand; it seemed a soggy thing to have served a miracle. The fact is, all this dew on the fleece is really not much more than any conjurer's artifice. The diviners of Phrygia are said to change sticks into snakes—I should like to see that. And then I thought: Well, it's one thing to do sleight of hand with pieces of wool but quite another to smite one hundred and twenty thousand Midianites. Oh, well, you know how doubts will gallop. Within an hour, I had arrived at full despair.

THE ANGEL (*snorts*). I too can make sticks into snakes. What manner of snake will you have? An asp? A python? A horned viper? Oh, Gideon, would you have your God a wandering magician, slapping a timbrel and kicking his heels?

GIDEON. Do not rise in wrath against me, sir.

THE ANGEL. I am not in wrath. I am plainly confused. And sore at heart. I have loved you, and you have turned your back.

GIDEON. I do find you personable, sir.

THE ANGEL. Personable! Gideon, one does not merely fancy God. I demand a splendid love from you, abandoned adoration, a torrent, a storm of love.

GIDEON. I'm afraid I'm not the splendid sort, my Lord.

THE ANGEL. I shall make you love me. I'll do another miracle for you, if that will bolster you. The moon is too manifest for you, is it? Shall I eclipse it? Come, tell me what manner of miracle would please you.

GIDEON. No miracles at all. I have no faith in miracles; they are too easily denied. (*He scowls unhappily down at his feet. Then, his face slowly brightens, and he turns to* THE ANGEL, *bursting with an idea.*) If you could send me a dream, my Lord . . .

THE ANGEL. A dream?

GIDEON. Yes, a dream. I put great stock in dreams.

THE ANGEL. A dream? You will not honor my miracles performed openhandedly before your eyes, but you put great stock in dreams.

GIDEON. Oh, sir, it is a well-known fact that dreams portend the future. If I could but have a dream, or, better yet, some other man's. The dreams of other men are frequently more significant.

THE ANGEL. What a devious mind man has developed. Well, then, what would you say to a royal dream? The dream, let us say, dreamed last night by Zalmunna or Zebah, the kings of Midian?

GIDEON. Oh, well, sir, such a dream, of course, would be most portentous. But surely I would not . . .

THE ANGEL. See then, there in that defile, two men, crowned by rubied aigrettes. I really think this must be Zebah and Zalmunna, kings of Midian. Yes, one sees the vivid colors of their tunics now. Royally caparisoned. Oh, that *is* good linen.

(*At this point, enter* ZEBAH *and* ZALMUNNA. *They are indeed richly caparisoned. Their jeweled crowns, girdles, sheaths, earrings and pendants glisten and gleam in the moonlight. They are both deeply involved with troubled thoughts.*)

ZEBAH. And that is not all. Let us pause here in this quiet spot, for I must tell you of this dream.

(*They pause at the foot of the spur.*)

THE ANGEL (*sotto voce to* GIDEON). What luck! We are going to hear his dream.

(GIDEON *doesn't answer. He has been staring at the kings of Midian in utter amazement, mouth agape and eyes bulging, ever since they were first pointed out to him.*)

ZEBAH (*to* ZALMUNNA). Hear, then, this dream of Zebah, king of Midian. Behold, I dreamed a dream; and lo, a cake of barley bread tumbled into the camp of Midian and came to my tent, and struck it so that it fell, and turned it upside down, so that the tent lay flat. What meaning do you put on this, Zalmunna?

ZALMUNNA. It is an evil dream, Zebah. This is no other than the sword of Gideon the son of Joash, a man of Israel; into his hand God has given Midian and all the host. (ZEBAH *clutches his head with both hands and moans softly.* ZALMUNNA *looks nervously around.*) Come, let us hurry from this spot. It is frightening here. I hear flappings and flutterings. What are you staring at?

ZEBAH (*so frightened he can hardly talk. He points upward*). The moon! The moon!

(ZALMUNNA *looks up, and terror sweeps across his face.*)

ZALMUNNA. Eclipsed! It is eclipsed!

ZEBAH. Ay!

ZALMUNNA (*tugging at his fellow king*). Oh! Come! Come!

(*He finally tugs* ZEBAH *from his petrified fright, and they rush off. On the upper spur,* GIDEON, *now spotted by the only light on the black stage, stares after the fleeing kings. The expression of astonishment he wore all through this last sudden incident now slowly changes to aghast awe. He stares up at the darkened moon, and then slowly turns to* THE ANGEL.)

GIDEON (*backing slowly away in awe; whispering*). Holy! Holy! Holy! Thou art the Lord! Thou art truly the Lord! (*He suddenly cringes, hides his face in his hands.*) O! Turn away from me. I have seen the face of the Lord, and I will die!

THE ANGEL (*moves slowly to* GIDEON; *gently*). Do not fear, you will not die. I am but a personation of the Lord.

(GIDEON *sinks to his knees and embraces the knees of* THE ANGEL. *He slowly lifts his face. His countenance gleams; his lips are parted in a smile of inspirited exaltation. He begins to chant in the fashion of Oriental psalmody.*)

GIDEON.

Give ear, O Heavens! God our Lord is One!

Hear, O Kings; give ear, O princes! Glory!

Proclaim the Name of God, to Him I sing!

A psalm of love to God, the Lord of Israel!

I love Thee, Lord.

Holy! Holy! Holy!

(*The lights dim out slowly.*)

CURTAIN

SCENE THREE

"So Gideon and the three companies blew the trumpets and broke the jars, holding in their left hands the torches, and in their right hands the trumpets to blow and they cried . . . 'For the Lord and for Gideon!'"

———

A ridge overlooking the fords at Bethbarah, some hours later that night.

At rise, THE ANGEL *is standing patiently stage right, regarding the battlefield about him. Two Hebrew* SOLDIERS *hurtle in from downstage right.*

———

FIRST SOLDIER. For the Lord and for Gideon!

(*He sounds a blast on his trumpet and disappears over the ridge. The* SECOND SOLDIER *pauses to briefly loot one of the bodies on the ground.*)

SECOND SOLDIER. For the Lord and for Gideon!

(*He exits over the ridge. Enter* GIDEON, *running in from downstage left, panoplied for war again, sweated and exultant, and waving his flambeau.*)

GIDEON (*shouting*). For the Lord and for Gideon! (*He rushes to the crest of the ridge where he stands and blows a triumphant blast on his trumpet.*)

THE ANGEL. Gideon . . .

GIDEON (*shouting down into the val-*

ley). You men of Ephraim, there by the river! Can you hear me? What is the outcome here? Have you the kings of Midian, Zebah and Zalmunna, in your hand?

THE ANGEL. Gideon . . .

(*A* THIRD SOLDIER *dashes in from the wings.*)

THIRD SOLDIER (*shouting*). For the Lord and for Gideon! (*He exits over the ridge.*)

GIDEON (*shouting after him*). Naphtalite! Go to the river bank! Send me a captain of Ephraim to report the events that have happened here at Beth-barah!

THE ANGEL. Gideon . . .

(GIDEON, *at last aware of* THE ANGEL, *turns and regards him with shocked and unbelieving eyes, then bursts into exultant laughter.*)

GIDEON. My Lord, we have won the battle! Were you there at the beginning? Did you see the slaughter that took place in Jezreel? At least thirty thousand Midianites dead in Jezreel alone. Carpeted! I say Jezreel is carpeted with Midian's dead! You cannot put your foot down but there is a body underneath it. I say thirty thousand—perhaps more— countless! countless!—and another forty or fifty thousand, trampled, slashed, drowned in their flight down the Jordan Valley to here. It was hideous! Oh, look on this, a child! And that absurd camel there, it makes me cry. (*Indeed he has suddenly begun to cry.* THE ANGEL *proffers him a leather skin of water.*) Thank you. Oh, I am weary. Picture, if you can, the sleeping camp of Midian at ten o'clock last night. Their tents lay darkly east and west across the Jezreel valley. Some oxen lowed, a clink here and there as the Midianite sentries took up the middle watch. I lit my lamp and shouted: "For the Lord and for Gideon!" On this signal, my three hundred men, now widely spaced in three troops, as you directed, shouted: "For the Lord and for Gideon!", blew trumpets, smashed pottery, stamped their feet and made as much noise as they could. Down below us, the men of Midian came yawning from their tents to see what all the clamor was. Then, suddenly, the cattle in the western camp were in stampede. They came crashing eastward through the tents, raising up a storm of dust so that no man knew his

brother. The Midianites in the east, thinking themselves besieged, leaped into the dust with their swords, and the Midianites of the west, fleeing before their cattle, found themselves engaged in war with their own brothers until, my Lord, the whole vast multitude, one hundred thousand men and women, their young and old and all their animals, fled in shrieking frenzy to the Jordan River. I stood upon the hill at Harod, transfixed by the sight of it!

(*A* FOURTH SOLDIER *enters, shouting.*)

FOURTH SOLDIER. For the Lord and for Gideon! (*He exits.*)

GIDEON. Then, at the Jordan, down from the hills came the men of Naphtali and Asher and the houses of Manasseh with their sickles and plowshares, and reaped the Midianites as so much wheat. At last, the shreds and tatters of this mighty host came splashing into the shoals here at Beth-barah, where the men of Ephraim sprang from their ambush and smote the survivors until surely there is not one left that breathes. The vultures will be flapping thick tomorrow. I see the soldiers have begun to gather the stray cows and sheep. There is much looting going on. Indeed, I stripped a corpse myself just before. (*He indicates a jeweled sheath on his baldric, and tries to pull out the falcate sword from the sheath; he can't get it out.*) They have a strange curved sword, these Midianites, with the honed edge outward. One slashes away. It seems awkward. Oh, my Lord, it came to pass, as you said. One hundred and twenty thousand Midianites lie slain this night. How great you are, my Lord, and how impermanent is man. (*He begins to snicker and giggle.*) Forgive me, my Lord, forgive me . . . (*In a moment, he has yielded to a spasm of uncontrollable laughter. He stands, clutching his sides, shouting and wheezing, lurching about, stumbling over bodies. He manages to squeeze out bursts of sentences.*) Oh, my Lord! You will not believe this! Oh! It is so comical, let me gather my wits! Oh, I am a foolish ass indeed! Oh! Oh! Oh! My Lord, one hundred twenty thousand Midianites were slain this night, the entire host of them, or so it seems! Oh! Oh! One hundred twenty thousand of them slain, and I, the captain of the hosts of Israel . . . Oh!

Oh! Oh! . . . and I, my Lord, I, the captain of the hosts, did not so much as unsheathe my dagger! I took no part at all in the whole bloody battle! Do you understand, my Lord? Oh! I never got within a mile of a Midianite! I watched the whole night from the hills! (*It is too much for him.* GIDEON *has to lie down flat on his back. Tears of laughter stream from his eyes. After a moment, he sits up, spent and sighing.*) Forgive me, my Lord. I have been shaken badly this night. I am not my own master.

THE ANGEL. It is not yet finished, Gideon. The kings of Midian with fifteen thousand of their men have escaped across the river.

GIDEON. Oh? I shall have to gather my three hundred men. (*Wearily he starts to rise.*)

THE ANGEL. No, no, rest, Gideon. There are some moments yet till dawn. You shall pursue after Zebah and Zalmunna then.

GIDEON (*lying back exhausted on the ground*). The kings of Midian . . .

THE ANGEL. The kings of Midian are halfway to the walled city of Karkor. You will have them in your hand tomorrow night. Now rest and spend this interlude with me.

GIDEON (*closing his eyes*). Have I found favor in your eyes tonight, my Lord?

THE ANGEL (*gently*). Indeed you have. (THE ANGEL *now sits cross-legged besides* GIDEON's *resting body. A silence falls between the two.*)

GIDEON (*after a moment*). Have you loved many men, my Lord?

THE ANGEL. I loved all men. It is my essence.

GIDEON. I mean, men with whom you have truly commerced face-to-face as you have with me.

THE ANGEL. Five or six, perhaps.

GIDEON. Were they as pleasing to you as I am, my Lord?

THE ANGEL (*smiling*). What a vain fellow you are.

GIDEON. Understand, my Lord, I do not hold these other loves to your discredit.

THE ANGEL. Are you being kind to me, Gideon? Now you must own that is vain of you. And you are something of a prig too, taking this high moral tone, even if I were no more than the dissolute lady you seem to think me.

GIDEON. Oh, my Lord, you are God, and your name is One!

THE ANGEL. I am just teasing you, Gideon.

GIDEON. I love you more than I have ever loved anyone.

THE ANGEL. I know you do.

GIDEON. I thought of nothing but you the whole night. I am possessed by all the lunacy of love. If I could, I would cover you with veils, God, and keep you hidden behind the curtains in my tent. Oh! Just say again you love me, God.

THE ANGEL. I do, Gideon.

GIDEON. I do not know why. I must say, I do not know why.

THE ANGEL. I hardly know why myself, but then passion is an unreasonable thing. (*He leans back against a rock, rather pensive.*) Let me consider. I have loved five men, or six if I add in Phinehas, but I could not say I truly loved Phinehas. Phinehas was high priest in the years that followed Joshua, and we spoke ten times or so of sacerdotal things, the setting of the year's calendar, such matters as that. A nice man, Phinehas, good family, son of Eleazar the son of Aaron—you cannot be better bred than that; but, still, not my sort. Too pinchpenny with his passions. The costive soul makes priests; it does not make lovers. Abraham, Isaac, Jacob of course . . . Joshua. But the man I most loved was Moses.

GIDEON. Yes?

THE ANGEL. I loved him very much. I do not think I shall love any man so much again. And he was scarcely Hebrew. He was bred as an Egyptian and married a gentile woman. Yes, I think the man was still uncircumcised the day I first beheld him herding sheep at Horeb, a hulking, harelipped, solitary man, quite unattractive really, stammered, dour—nay, say sullen—lacking wit, one of those ever-earnest fellows. Yet I fancied Moses from the very first. Gaunt he stood against the crags of Horeb, a monumentally impassioned man. It is passion, Gideon, that carries man to God. And passion is a balky beast. Few men ever let it out the stable. It brooks no bridle; indeed, it bridles you; it rides the rider. Yet, it inspirits man's sessile soul above his own inadequate world and makes real such things as beauty, fancy, love, and God and all those other things that are not quite molecular but are. Passion is the very fact of God in man that makes him other than a brute. I must own, Gideon, yours was an old and cold and settled soul, and I huffed and puffed quite a bit before I found the least flame of passion in you.

GIDEON. What is it that you love in me, my Lord? These other men were saints or prophets, but I am an ordinary sort. I am as all men are.

THE ANGEL. Well, perhaps *that* is your special attraction, your ordinariness. I would have plain men love me, not just saints.

GIDEON. Well, that isn't very nice.

THE ANGEL. Oh, Gideon, you are difficult.

GIDEON. Well, I do not think it gratifying to be loved for one's lack of distinction. (*He stands, ruffled.*) I thought I managed my duties well tonight.

THE ANGEL. Indeed, you did.

GIDEON. To speak plainly, I think I make a good show of being a general. I have a commanding voice and am not unhandsome in my armor.

THE ANGEL. You make a splendid figure.

GIDEON. You find me amusing.

THE ANGEL. Well, you are a pompous ass.

GIDEON. Yes, so I am. (*His natural good humor returns, and he laughs agreeably at himself.*) Oh, it is indeed the truth, God. Like all modest men, I am impossibly vain. I amuse even myself, strutting about, shouting—well, not really shouting; I'm cleverer than that at the charade. I put myself forth more as the calm but resolute general, imperative but not forbidding. What a peacock I am! It is amusing, isn't it?

THE ANGEL. It is. (GIDEON *sits down beside* THE ANGEL, *a little sad now.*)

GIDEON. I have had very little esteem in my life, my Lord, and I do not think there is much harm in my relishing this one moment of honor. I have this one son, Jether, who is twelve years old, the son of my first wife, and even he uses me lightly. I am not esteemed, my Lord, even in my own tent, and this has given me great pain.

(THE ANGEL *regards* GIDEON *compassionately.*)

THE ANGEL. I shall give you seventy sons, Gideon; they shall praise your name. You shall know the ardor of many wives.

GIDEON. I should like that.

THE ANGEL. Oh, Gideon, I shall bless you. I shall make your fields to prosper. I shall make your cattle fat. Your father shall kneel before you and embrace your knees. All Israel shall say: "Regard Gideon; he is the most blessed of men, for he is beloved of God." You seem displeased by all this good fortune. (*This last in reference to a scowl deepening on* GIDEON's *brow.*)

GIDEON. Yes, well, all this greatness, all this good fortune which you will make mine, will not really be mine. It is all but a gift from God. There is no honor that reflects to me in it at all, merely that I am beloved of God.

THE ANGEL. Well, that is a somewhat less than gracious thing to say. The love of God will not suffice for you indeed.

GIDEON (*ashamed*). I spoke coarsely, Lord. Forgive me.

THE ANGEL. I wonder if this vanity of yours is as ingenuous as it seemed, and if it is not a sinister thing rather. What is vanity in man really, but the illusion that he has a purpose? Do not presume to matter, Gideon, for in the house of God you matter not. My universe is large beyond your knowing; there is no beginning, there is no end to it. You are a meaningless thing and live only in my eye. I shall make you great, Gideon, because I love you; but it is merely my caprice. If you displease me, I shall destroy you in a whim of temper. To love me, Gideon, you must abandon all your vanities. They are presumptuous and will come between us.

GIDEON (*truly penitent*). Oh, my Lord, that could never be.

THE ANGEL. Consider how you have already reduced me to some kind of clever if wanton lady who finds you handsome and sends you into battle with her handkerchief.

GIDEON. My Lord, I . . .

THE ANGEL. Surely, I shall see you tomorrow vaunting yourself before the armies, saying it was by your hand, and not mine, that Israel was redeemed from the Midianites.

GIDEON. Oh, my Lord, I would sooner cut my throat with this—(*He wrenches as his Midianite sword again, and again it sticks to its scabbard.*)—with this—Oh! How do they manage with these things? At any rate, if I could get it out of its scabbard, I would slit my throat with it before I derogated you, my Lord.

THE ANGEL (*laughing*). Oh, Gideon. I love you, and I will exalt you over all men. But I fear you will betray me.

(GIDEON *gives up on the sword, turns to* THE ANGEL *and regards him with manifest devotion. He kneels before* THE ANGEL, *takes the latter's hand and presses it to his lips.*)

GIDEON (*fervently*). The Lord is my God, the Lord is One. He is vast, ineffable, the maker and the mover of all things, and He has paused to love me; shall I ask for other blessings? God, do not fear my vanity. I will never betray you.

(THE ANGEL, *touched, gently strokes the bowed head before him. Enter tired* SOLDIERS, *straggling slowly across the stage.*)

SOLDIER (*wearily*). For the Lord and for Gideon.

(*They disappear over the ridge. The first streaks of dawn are now lightening the sky.* THE ANGEL *marks the coming of day.*)

THE ANGEL. It's morning now, Gideon. (*He is interrupted by the entrance of* SHILLEM. *That is, two* SOLDIERS *enter, bracing a rubber-legged and wheezing* SHILLEM *between them. Despite his dreadful condition, the old man holds fast to his warbow.* THE ANGEL *notes* SHILLEM's *entrance with a smile.*) The troops of Shillem have come.

SHILLEM (*gasping; to the two* SOLDIERS). Here—set me here. (*The two* SOLDIERS *sit him gently down, propped up against a large rock, where he slumps, all but dead of exhaustion.*)

GIDEON. Oh, Shillem! I told you to stay behind. You will exhaust yourself with all this racing up and down these hills. (*To* THE ANGEL) The old popinjay fell in a faint five minutes after the slaughter in Jezreel began. It seems the sight of blood sickens him.

THE ANGEL (*laughing*). Go then, Gideon, and find Shethulah, the prince of Ephraim. He's very arrogant and will

not like a man from Manasseh such as you ordering him about.

GIDEON. Oh, dear. (*To the two* SOLDIERS.) Go and join your fellows on the river bank. I will be shortly there.

(*The two* SOLDIERS *exit.*)

THE ANGEL (*to* GIDEON). The spirit of the Lord shall be with you. (*He exits with a casual wave of his hand.*)

GIDEON (*giving* SHILLEM *his skin of water*). Here, drink this and rest.

(*It is more than* SHILLEM *can manage to even raise the skin of water to his lips. It dangles slackly from his fingers.*)

SHILLEM. Oh, Gideon, tell no one, I beg you, that I swooned at the sight of battle.

GIDEON. Shillem, my old captain, we are all wretched cowards, the full three hundred of us.

SHILLEM. I spent the night, hiding in a cave, clutching my warbow.

GIDEON. Yes, I know. Now, rest here. I must go find the proud prince of Ephraim and learn the state of things here at Beth-barah. (*He exits over the ridge.* SHILLEM, *alone now, allows himself a sob or two.*)

SHILLEM. Oh, how despicable I am. Let all men know that Shillem is a coward, a rabbit, a . . .

(*He breaks off as* HEZEKIAH *and* MALCHIEL *and two* SOLDIERS *enter from stage right, waving their lamps and shouting.*)

HEZEKIAH, MALCHIEL, SOLDIERS. For the Lord and for Gideon! (*They are about to clamber across the ridge when* HEZEKIAH *sees* SHILLEM *sprawled downstage.* HEZEKIAH *comes puffing down to the old man, sits beside him, crosses his legs.*)

HEZEKIAH (*sighing*). Well, we seem to have won the war and decimated the entire host of Midian—how did we ever manage to do that? Well, I daresay we shall find sensible explanations for everything. You were with Gideon, were you not? That put you in the thick of it. Did you kill many of the enemy?

(*A brief struggle for virtue ensues in* SHILLEM.)

SHILLEM (*mumbling*). Two or three.

HEZEKIAH. Two or three, did you say?

SHILLEM. Dozen.

HEZEKIAH. Two or three dozen!

SHILLEM. Yes, I was with Gideon, as you say, when the Midianite herds broke into stampede. Seeing the Midianites disconcerted, I led a charge down from my hill, panicking the foe into headlong flight to the Jordan valley. This, I would have to say, was the pivotal point of the battle.

(MALCHIEL, *who has been walking slowly about the stage examining the battlefield, now looks up, his bold, fanatic eyes blazing in his dark, sweated face.*)

MALCHIEL. We have heard fantastic stories of Gideon's deeds. A woman of Manasseh told us she saw Gideon leap from a tree into a pack of ten Midianites and smite them all with ten strokes of his spear.

SHILLEM. She told you all wrong. His weapon was an ox-goad, and there were twenty of the foe, not ten.

HEZEKIAH. Twenty?

MALCHIEL. Twenty men did Gideon smite with an ox-goad! Here, look on this! A serpent has coiled itself upon this fallen Midianite. This augurs significantly.

HEZEKIAH (*nudging* SHILLEM). My brother is adroit at divination.

MALCHIEL (*with fanatic fervor*). What manner of god is this Yahweh of Gideon's? His incarnation is the bull; his ideogram is the coiled serpent. (*He scoops up a handful of dirt and lets it fall back to the ground. He kneels and studies the patterns it makes.*)

HEZEKIAH (*winking at* SHILLEM). My brother divines from the configurations of the ground and sees great significance in pebbles.

MALCHIEL (*studying the geomantic pattern*). Regard. A crescent moon and, here again, a coiled viper upon a cloven heart. Oh, dazzling among gods is this Yahweh; he is both sun and moon; and Gideon is his only son. Behold! The morning star! Gideon is single among men as the morning star is single in the heavens! Sing praise! Cry out for Gideon! The son of Yahweh, the bull-god! 'Ay! (*He stands stiffly upright and promptly falls into a dead faint.* SHILLEM, *rather taken aback by this, sits up with a start.*)

HEZEKIAH. He'll be all right. He is given to these ecstatic moments.

SHILLEM. Is he really?

HEZEKIAH. He spends much time with Phoenician priests who are emotional. But I prefer to find more reasonable explanations for things than gods. I am not a little known in my own city of Kanah as a scholar and have predicted several eclipses. I read and write a competent Egyptian hand and have some knowledge of medicinal herbs. Actually, I attracted some attention in learned circles a few years ago with my theory of the ecliptic of the sun; you may have heard something of that.

SHILLEM. Look here, are we to leave your brother lying around like that?

HEZEKIAH. I think that when all the facts are known, this improbable battle will seem more probable. It was a clever stratagem of Gideon's, stampeding the cattle; and, of course, your opportune assault on the Midianite flank explains much of the enemy's panic. Piece by piece, the events of the night become less mystical.

SHILLEM. On my soul!

(*This last refers to the entrance of* SHETHULAH, *a prince of Ephraim, followed by several* SOLDIERS, *who loom up from the upstage side of the ridge.* SHETHULAH *is holding aloft two grisly decapitated heads.*)

SHETHULAH. Behold the heads of Oreb and Zeeb, princes of Midian, the sons of the kings of Midian. (MALCHIEL *remains in his trance.* HEZEKIAH *rises.*) Which of you three is Gideon the son of Joash the Abiezrite?

SHILLEM. He has gone to the river to find the prince of Ephraim.

SHETHULAH. I am the prince of princes of Ephraim. I am Shethulah the son of Elishama, the son of Ammihud, the son of Ephraim, the son of Joseph. Bring forth this Gideon, send men after him so that he may account to me for what he did, that he has made war on Midian but he did not ask my counsel. Is not Ephraim the prince among all the tribes of Israel, the most populous in number, the richest in wealth? Who shall lead the tribes of Israel in war? Shall it not be Ephraim?

(HEZEKIAH *considers this statement with scholarly detachment.*)

HEZEKIAH (*to* SHILLEM). These Ephraimites are so superior really. There's no historical basis for it at all, you know.

SHETHULAH. Captain of Asher, go with your men down to the valley and chop off the hands of all the dead that we may make a count of how many slain.

HEZEKIAH. Sir, it's all very well to play the proud prince with the chief of Naphtali here and me, but I suggest you be more humble when Gideon comes. Know the manner of man this Gideon is. Know that Gideon leaped from a tree and smote —(*Turns to* SHILLEM.)How many did you say, twenty?

SHILLEM. Did I say twenty? Oh, well, in that case, it was nearer forty.

(*For a long moment,* HEZEKIAH *studies* SHILLEM *with the scientist's skeptical eye. Then, he turns back to* SHETHULAH.)

HEZEKIAH. Eighty men did Gideon smite with an ox-goad.

SHETHULAH (*very impressed*). Eighty men!

(*At this moment,* MALCHIEL *springs up to his feet with a shrill cry.*)

MALCHIEL. Ay! The vision of Malchiel! The oracle of a man whose eye is opened! Hear the history of Gideon.

SHILLEM (*crying out*). Tell us your vision, oh, holy man!

HEZEKIAH (*seizing the elbow of the startled* SHETHULAH). My brother, sir, is adroit at divination and not to be taken lightly.

(GIDEON *appears, coming up from the far side of the ridge. He pauses on the crest to hear* MALCHIEL's *testimony. At the same time,* THE ANGEL *enters and stands downstage right, watching.*)

MALCHIEL (*in a trance*). The great god, Yahweh, the god of Moses, who is the bull, who is the lion; in his left hand is a crescent sword, in his right hand is a ball of fire; he saw a woman of Manasseh. He leaned over her lips. He raised his voice and said: "Behold her lips are as sweet as a bunch of grapes." In the perfume of the cedars did they lay. When dawn broke, a cloud black as night rose from heaven's foundations. The great god Yahweh rose into the sky in a chariot of lapis lazuli and gold. In the arms of the Manassehite woman he placed an infant. On its brow was coiled the sacred asp. Behold! It was Gideon, the man-god, the son of Yahweh, the redeemer of Israel, the man of valor, the god Gideon!

(*A silence follows this enthusiastic statement.*)

GIDEON (*from the crest of the ridge*). Oh, Malchiel, you cannot be serious.

(*All whirl at the sound of* GIDEON's *voice.* MALCHIEL *falls to his knees and prostrates himself.*)

SHILLEM. There, ye Ephraimites, stands Gideon, who with an ox-goad smote one hundred men!

(GIDEON *bursts into laughter.*)

GIDEON. A hundred men! Oh, Shillem, what a fearful fiction! What have you been telling this noble man? For you, sir, must surely be Shethulah, the prince of princes in Ephraim. (*He descends in obsequious haste from the ridge. For a moment he and* SHETHULAH, *who is now in abject awe of* GIDEON, *vie with each other in the gestures of deference.*)

SHETHULAH (*humbly proffering the decapitated heads of the Midianite princes to* GIDEON). Behold the heads of Oreb and Zeeb, the princes of Midian.

GIDEON. Don't give them to me. I wouldn't know what to do with them. Hang them on the walls of your city. I think that is the practice. (*Winking at* THE ANGEL) How many did he have me killing with an ox-goad, one hundred? (*He bursts into laughter; to* SHETHULAH) The truth is, great lord, I killed no Midianites at all.

(SHETHULAH *looks up startled.*)

SHETHULAH. You killed no Midianites at all?

GIDEON (*beaming*). Not a one.

(*Rage sweeps across the Ephraimite prince's face. He is furious at being gulled and regards* SHILLEM *and* HEZEKIAH *with a fierce eye.*)

SHETHULAH. Then, Gideon, you shall account to me for what you have done, that you made war against Midian and did not seek my counsel. Shall Manasseh lead the hosts and Ephraim be the scavengers? Did not Jacob bless Ephraim before his brother, saying: "Ephraim shall be greater than his brother Manasseh"? I shall take command of the hosts of Israel now, Gideon! (*He seizes a whip from one of the soldiers and would lash* GIDEON *but is intercepted by* GIDEON.)

GIDEON. Hear, O Ephraimite! Do not contend with me for glory, for it is neither yours nor is it mine! This glory is the Lord's! Give praise to the Lord for he has triumphed gloriously. Bow down! (*All sink to their knees and bow their heads down to the ground.* GIDEON *surveys the supplicating backs for a moment, then turns and slowly walks to where* THE ANGEL *stands stage right, regarding*

GIDEON *with effulgent love.* GIDEON *prostrates himself before* THE ANGEL.) Did you truly fear my vanity? Oh, timeless and immane God, I yearn after you and seek only to be pleasing in your eye.

THE ANGEL. Rise up, good Gideon, and pursue after the kings of the enemy.

(GIDEON *stands.*)

GIDEON. Rise up! We have more war to make! These are my charges to you all. Let the Ephraimites count the dead and bury them that the land may be clean of carrion and that the jackals may not overrun us. Captains of Asher and Naphtali, come with me. We shall pursue after the kings of Midian. (*The others all stand. Again,* GIDEON *tries to wrench his Midianite sword from its scabbard to flourish it, but again it sticks. Flourishing his empty hand instead, he shouts.*) For Gideon and for the Lord! (*He leaps out of view over the ridge.* SHILLEM, HEZEKIAH, MALCHIEL *and* SOLDIERS, *brandishing their weapons, exit quickly after him.*)

SHILLEM, HEZEKIAH, MALCHIEL *and* SOLDIERS. For Gideon and for the Lord!

(SHETHULAH *and his Ephraimite* SOLDIERS *follow after them, shouting.*)

EPHRAIMITES. For Gideon and for the Lord!

(*They exit over the ridge.* THE ANGEL *is now left alone onstage, frowning thoughtfully. He detaches himself from the arch and shuffles to center stage where he tugs at his beard pensively.*)

THE ANGEL (*muttering*). "For Gideon and for the Lord," indeed. It used to be: "For the Lord and for Gideon." (*He shrugs in the ageless Hebrew fashion and strides offstage left. The* CURTAIN *comes down quickly.*)

ACT TWO

SCENE ONE

"*And the elders of Succoth said, Are Zebah and Zalmunna in your hand, that we should give bread to your army? And Gideon said, Therefore when the Lord has delivered Zebah and Zalmunna into my hand, then I will tear your flesh.*"

—

A threshing floor on a hill by the city of Succoth.

The time is two days later in the afternoon.

At rise, there are three senior gentlemen, obviously prisoners, standing disconsolately at stage left. A rope joins their necks, and their hands are tied in front of them. These are the elders of Succoth. There are supposed to be seventy-four more of them offstage. We can perhaps see one or two. A guard stands in attendance on them. A second soldier stares off upstage over a parapet. He is apparently a LOOKOUT.

THE ANGEL *now appears, climbing up to the top of the threshing floor. He stands a moment, amiably looking around. Suddenly* THE LOOKOUT *straightens to attention and shouts:*

—

THE LOOKOUT. Gideon is here! He is at the gates!

VOICE (*off*). He comes! Gideon comes!

(*Shouts and alarum are heard offstage;* SHILLEM *suddenly looms up out of the pit, clambering up to the threshing floor.*)

SHILLEM. Prepare the feast! Soldiers, clear the space before the gates! Maidens, bring fruit here, bring wine! Bring skewers of meat for Gideon! (*More shouts and alarum off down in the pit.* WOMEN OF SUCCOTH *come scurrying up bearing bowls of pomegranates, grapes, figs, slabs of steaming mutton, and skins of wine.* SHETHULAH, *the Ephraimite prince, also enters, champing away on a leg of lamb as he does. Both he and* SHILLEM *are nicely drunk.* SHILLEM *regards the elders standing stage right.*) The elders of Succoth, are they all here? Seven and seventy of them? Oh, you wretched chiefs of Succoth! You will surely die today. This is what Gideon charged me this morning: "Go in advance, Shillem," said he, "my mighty captain, and capture the seven and seventy elders of Succoth, for they are Hebrews; yet, they jeered at the word of the Lord. The wrath of God is hot against them and they shall die." (*A ram's horn is heard far offstage. Shouting down into the pit*) Bugler, sound your trumpet!

(*The ram's horn sounds offstage, closer than before, and a bugler onstage responds. The stage crowds up with people.*)

ALL (*singing*).
Hosanna! Hosanna!
Make melody to Gideon!
Barak has slain his thousands!

But Gideon tens of thousands!
He is as the wild ox who gores the foe!
Barak has slain his thousands!
But Gideon tens of thousands!
O Israel! O Israel!
Israel! Israel!

VOICES. They are here! They are here!
Gideon is here!

(*Indeed,* MALCHIEL *comes bouncing up to the top of the threshing floor, where he stands addressing the multitude in the pit.*)

MALCHIEL. We have won the battle of Karkor! With twenty thousand men of Reuben and Gad, we smote the last of Midian! There is not one left that breathes! Great was the glory of Barak, of Ehud and Othniel, but sovereign is the glory of Gideon. Bow down!

(*Everyone on the threshing floor and presumably everyone in the pit bends low in homage. A hush falls on the stage. In the midst of it,* GIDEON *enters climbing up from the pit, followed by* HEZEKIAH *and two* WOMEN *who thrust baskets of grapes and pomegranates at the conquering hero.*)

FIRST WOMAN. The first grapes of the year, my lord Gideon.

SECOND WOMAN. The first of the summer fruits, my lord Gideon.

(GIDEON *seems pleased by all this homage. He surveys the pit below him rather grandly.* THE ANGEL *now crosses to* GIDEON *and claps him heartily on the back.* GIDEON *turns startled. A quick look of apprehension sweeps over his face. He wheels on the obeisant people around him and below him and thunders out.*)

GIDEON. Be still, you foolish people! Am I the Lord that you bring me first fruits? Make no god of me! It was the Lord that redeemed you from Midian! Rise up, then, rise up! (*He looks for approval from* THE ANGEL *and almost stumbles over a maiden at his feet. She is a darkly savage and sinuous thing of fourteen, a marriageable age in those days.*) Rise up, you silly woman. Whose maiden is this?

SHILLEM. She is Orpah the daughter of the elder Ozni, standing there.

GIDEON. The daughter of Ozni? He was most guilty of all the elders. Poor maiden, her father shall die first. (*Turns to the elders, raising a foreboding finger at them.*) Regard the elders of Succoth!

OZNI (*an elder, flinging himself at* GIDEON's *feet*). O, Puissant Gideon, hear our suffrage.

A SECOND ELDER. Pity us, my lord.

A THIRD ELDER. O, pity us, sire.

GIDEON. One day ago, you elders, my three hundred men and I, hot in pursuit of Zebah and Zalmunna, came to these gates. And you seven and seventy elders of Succoth with Ozni the son of Deuel at your head came forth to meet us. "Pray," I said, "give loaves of bread to the people who follow me; for they are faint, and I am pursuing after Zebah and Zalmunna, the kings of Midian." And you all did taunt me. "Are Zebah and Zalmunna already in your hand," you said to me, "that we should give bread to your army?" "These are the soldiers of the Lord!" I said. "Give them food, or will you mock the Lord?" And you, Ozni, son of Deuel, then said: "Show us Zebah and Zalmunna in your hand, and we shall give you loaves of bread." Well, then, bring forth Zebah and Zalmunna! (*Enter* ZEBAH *and* ZALMUNNA, *their hands tied in front of them, their necks joined by a rope. They are guarded by two* SOLDIERS.) Behold! Zebah and Zalmunna, the kings of Midian, are in my hand! (*The two kings drop to their knees, place their faces at* GIDEON's *feet.* GIDEON *puts a foot on the neck of* ZEBAH.) We do not practice mutilation in Israel. I shall kill you plainly, Zebah and Zalmunna. (*With a quick, strong, downward thrust,* GIDEON *plunges his spear into* ZEBAH's *ribs. The Medianite king emits a short, strangled gasp and topples over dead. The spear remains in* GIDEON's *hand, now dripping red with blood. With a second quick thrust, he dispatches* ZALMUNNA, *who screams out shrilly and falls, the spear protruding slantwise from under his arm. A frightened silence fills the stage.*) This was Midian; a violent tribe. They lived ten generations. They are no more. As it was with the kings of Midian, O elders, so shall it be with you. (GIDEON *wrenches the spear loose from* ZALMUNNA's *body, turns, strides to the elders on the tower, raising his spear above his head.*) The Voice of the Lord came to me, thundering: "Smite the elders of Succoth, preserve not one, so that all Israel may know the fear of God!" (*But the sheer piteousness of the three old men before him stays his hand. Mutely, they stare up at him, tears streaming down their cheeks. One of the* WOMEN *breaks into a high-pitched wail.* GIDEON *lowers his spear, darts a nervous look at* THE ANGEL.) Well, I'm faint; I marched all day. Set food and wine before me that I may eat and drink. I shall kill these old men after that. (*The* WOMEN *scurry off.* GIDEON *addresses the host of people on-stage.*) Give praise to the Lord, for he is the kinsman, he is the rock, he is a man of war. Bow down! (*The people all go down upon their knees and bow their heads forward so that their brows touch the floor between their hands—the full salaam.* GIDEON *regards the stage of bowed backs, then turns and looks for* THE ANGEL, *now downstage right again.* GIDEON *ambles over, rubbing his neck and sighing wearily.*) I slept two hours last night, if that much, and ache in every bone. We left Karkor at break of day. It is almost thirty miles and a mountainous route. I had not thought to see you here, my Lord.

THE ANGEL. Will you not embrace me?

GIDEON. Oh, indeed, yes of course. (*He kneels quickly, kisses the hem of* THE ANGEL's *robe, and stands.*)

THE ANGEL. That was perfunctory, Gideon.

GIDEON. Well, I made battle all last night, God, and marched all day and ate nothing but some figs and cake. I do not feel affectionate at the moment.

THE ANGEL. You are not pleased that I am here.

GIDEON. Well, I have many things to do, my Lord. It would be better if you waited for me at my tent at Ophrah.

THE ANGEL. Like your other wives.

GIDEON. You are being quarrelsome. You know you are more than wife to me. I am on edge and close to temper, and I pray you, leave me to myself for the moment.

THE ANGEL. As you say. I shall wait beside your tent at Ophrah for you.

GIDEON. I should be home within a day or two.

THE ANGEL. Will you not embrace me before I go?

(GIDEON *sighs a brief sigh of exasperation, goes to his knees again, and brushes the hem of* THE ANGEL's *robe with his lips.* THE ANGEL *starts off, but* GIDEON, *still on his knees, calls him.*)

GIDEON. Oh, my Lord.

THE ANGEL (*turning*). Yes?

GIDEON (*standing*). My Lord, about these elders of Succoth here. You came to me in a dream last night and said: "Smite them all, preserve not one that breathes." Yet, I wonder, is that not perhaps too harsh a penalty? They seem so piteous a lot of senior gentlemen. And they are Hebrews, my Lord. They are our people.

THE ANGEL. They made light of the Lord. Will you pass by while men make light of me?

GIDEON. I thought perhaps to scourge them with whips, forty lashes less one for each. That would surely instruct them in the fear of God.

THE ANGEL. These men are utter wretches, Gideon. Of all the clans of Gad, these men of Succoth have done most evilly in mine eyes. I have had it in mind several times to strike them down.

GIDEON. I pity them, my Lord.

THE ANGEL. It is not just this matter of their taunting you. The men of Succoth have married their sons to the daughters of Moab and practice the ways of Moab. They lie with men as with a woman and uncover the nakedness of their own daughters. They eat unslaughtered meat with its carrion blood still in it, oppress the stranger and revile the widow and the orphan. They are a miscreant folk. Smite these elders, every one, Gideon, preserve not one, so that all Israel may hear and fear, so that the name of the Lord shall be a name of terror in their hearts, and they shall walk in my ways again.

GIDEON. Well, I shall kill them then since you wish it.

THE ANGEL. Oh, Gideon, you make so much of death. You must not be so temporal. It is all right for the bulk of men to fear death, for in death they fear me. But, in truth, there isn't anything to it at all. Nothing happens, nothing changes; the essence of things goes on. You see, you measure things in time, but there is no time in truth. You live now ten million years ago and are at this moment ten million years hence, or more; for there are no years. The slaying of seventy-seven elders happens but it does not happen, for they live even so and have died before, and all is now, which was and is forever.

Oh, dear, I see this is heavy going for you.

GIDEON. Well, I follow you here and there a bit; not everything of course.

THE ANGEL. Well, you shouldn't bother your head with all these speculations anyway. I am the final truth of all things, Gideon, so you need only love me and live your life as I will it for you, and it shall be a seemly thing.

GIDEON. My point, you see, is that I pity these old men.

THE ANGEL. Of course you do. But you are being vain again, for to pity a man's death is to say his life was significant, which it isn't. Now, let us have an end to this. Go and smite the elders. I am the Lord.

GIDEON. As you say.

THE ANGEL (*turning to go*). Then, peace be with you, Gideon. I shall wait for you beside your tent.

GIDEON (*nervously shuffling his feet*). My Lord—

THE ANGEL. Yes?

GIDEON. My Lord—oh, how shall I say it? My Lord, the people have made much of me these past few days. Well, as you see, even here in Succoth. But what an ovation was accorded to me at Mahanaim! Great crowds gathered along the highway and shouted my name. Maidens came forth with dancing and with timbrels. I fancy that sort of thing, as, of course, you know. And twice today, Malchiel there, who is an enthusiastic man, stood up before thousands—at Mahaniam and at Jogbehah too—and called me king, and the people shouted as with one voice: "Amen!" I would like to be king, my Lord.

THE ANGEL. But Gideon—

GIDEON. I could hardly sleep last night for thinking of myself as king. That demon vanity crept into my tent like a succubus and had me trying on different crowns, diadems from Babylon and pschents from Egypt. I finally dropped off, having decided I looked best with no crown at all, a modest king, receiving the ambassadors from Armenia while plowing his own fields, distinguishable from his servants only by his noble bearing. Well, you know what a vain ass I am. Oh, Lord, could I not be king of Israel?

THE ANGEL. Gideon, I am king of Israel. To say Israel needs another king suggests I am inadequate.

GIDEON (*in a burst of temper*). I do not think I ask so very much! I do not say I will usurp your throne. I only ask for a nominal crown and a few trappings. Some purfled robes, perhaps a modest palace. You are ever accusing me of wishing to cheat you! Indeed, I meant to make your name greater. I would build altars for you and enforce your laws. All I ask was a bit of pomp because I am a vain fellow and like to preen before the people. Well, then I am vain! That is my manner! You could indulge me in this minor frailty. Just this one time!

THE ANGEL (*furiously*). Do you shout at the Lord?

GIDEON (*striding angrily about*). I have served you well, have I not? You vowed you would exalt me above my fellows. And do not say you did not, because you did. You said you would bless me and that you would do such and such, and, in particular, you said you would exalt me above my fellows.

THE ANGEL. Gideon, beware!

GIDEON (*turning sulkily away*). I warned you I was in a temper.

THE ANGEL. You are a presumptuous man!

GIDEON. Nor is it an easy thing to love you, God.

THE ANGEL. I struck Korah down, and all his household, for less cause than this. I opened the ground and swallowed them, he and his household, and Dathan and Abiram, and all their households. I made Miriam a leper white as snow for less insurbordinate ways, and she was a prophetess of the Lord and a sister to Moses. I burnt to death the sons of Aaron, who were priests, enveloped them in flame for a mere breach of hieratic conduct. Then what shall I do with you, Gideon, who shout at the Lord?

(GIDEON, *squatting down on his haunches at the opposite end of the stage, is still sullen.*)

GIDEON. I did not mean to shout.

THE ANGEL. I will not make you king over these people, for they shall see a king and forget about the Lord. They shall bow down to the king, and they shall not bow down to me. They will seek blessings from this king who cannot bless and fear this king who cannot frighten. Therefore I am the king over Israel, and the people shall bow down to me and fear me and seek my blessings. Surely, this is clear to you.

GIDEON (*mutters, sulking*). Yes, yes, yes.

THE ANGEL. Oh, Gideon, let us not quarrel, for I love you.

GIDEON. I am in this sullen temper. I cannot seem to master it.

THE ANGEL (*crossing to* GIDEON *and squatting beside him*). You are worn with battle and marching. Then rest and let me see your true and amiable self next time we meet.

GIDEON. Do not be kind to me, my Lord. I shall only cry.

THE ANGEL. I said I shall exalt you above your fellows, and I shall. I vowed seventy sons to you; well, then, know that both your wives at home are now with child. Indeed, from this moment, all women shall plead to be your wives. Now that should please you. (GIDEON *works up a shallow smile.*) Come, give me your hand. If I have given you some hurt, then take my hand and show me it is over with. (GIDEON, *keeping his eyes petulantly down, lets* THE ANGEL *take his hand and clasp it.*) No, eat and rest; then go and smite the elders of this city as I have instructed you, preserve not one.

(GIDEON *nods bleakly.*)

GIDEON. I would be left to myself now, my Lord.

THE ANGEL. Of course. (*He stands.*) I shall wait for you beside your tent at Ophrah. Before I go, will you not say you love me?   ·

GIDEON (*mutters*). I love you, God.

THE ANGEL (*sighs*). Peace be with you, Gideon.

GIDEON. Peace be with you, my Lord. (THE ANGEL *turns and exits down the ladder.* GIDEON *bows his head and murmurs.*) Hallowed, sanctified, glorious, magnified, holy is the Lord. The Lord is perfect, he shall reign for ever and ever. (*He looks up, notes* THE ANGEL *is gone. He stands, regards the stage of bowed backs. He is still in a black temper.*) Rise up! Rise up! I asked for food. Bring me water to bathe my feet. (*He indicates the bodies of* ZEBAH *and* ZALMUNNA.) And get rid of that carrion there. (*The people rise quickly. The* WOMEN *scurry up from the pit, bringing steaming meat, bowls of* *fruit and skins of wine to where the various captains are gathered.* GIDEON *crosses to them.*) Here, give me that skin of wine before you've drunk it all.

SHILLEM (*giving a skin of wine to* GIDEON). I was telling these Ephraimites, O Gideon, how last night at Karkor four Midianites descended on me in a bunch . . .

(*He sees* GIDEON *is in no mood for campfire stories and breaks off.* ORPAH *has made herself* GIDEON'S *handmaiden. As he stands, scowling and swilling the wine, she unwraps his girdle and unwinds his ankle-length outer garment.*)

GIDEON (*muttering*). It is not easy to be loved by God, I tell you that.

SHILLEM. What did you say, my lord Gideon?

GIDEON. Perhaps you chiefs and princes think it is a splendid state to be loved by God; well, it is not. Do this, do that, such-and-such, so-and-so, constant demands, and what does one get for a thank you? Ah, well, let us not speak of it any more. It only puts me in a fury.

(GIDEON *wrenches a chunk of meat from the bowl beside him and champs angrily at it. His ugly mood has cast rather a pall over all the others onstage. During the above speech, the maiden* ORPAH *is called to one side by her father,* OZNI, *the elder. By dumb show, they make clear a plot is hatching. She suddenly whirls away from her father, her eyes flashing. She gives her tabret a good whack and stamps her foot. Then she turns her full voluptuous attention on* GIDEON, *who has looked briefly up at her.* ORPAH *lifts her face high and chants out in the high-pitched manner of Oriental song.*)

ORPAH.

Wherefore do they lament, the virgins of Succoth?

Let them weep for their fathers to-morrow.

Rejoice, ye maidens of Israel!

Rejoice and dance at the gates!

See the blood of Midian!

See how it gels in the dust!

Rejoice, ye virgins of Israel!

It is not thy blood in the dust!

Recall how they ripped thee, Virgins.

They defiled thee on the highways.

Then rejoice, O Virgin of Israel!

Thy blood remains clean for thy marriage.

On the night of thy wedding, O Virgin,
Shall thy blood for the first time be seen.
Thy husband shall flourish thy night-
dress
And shout: "See the stains of innocence!"
Sing praise, O maidens, to Gideon!
Let thy husbands cry out: "Amen!"
Hosanna!

(*She smashes her tabret and leaps into savage dance. The* SOLDIERS *and captains, needless to say, find her dance diverting.*)

SHILLEM. The hot sun and the wine and the dancing rouse the blood, do they not?

SHETHULAH. Aye.

GIDEON. Aye.

(GIDEON *watches the voluptuous dance with evident interest. Suddenly, with a swoop,* ORPAH *sinks to the ground at* GIDEON's *feet and remains huddled, trembling, prostrate. The elder,* OZNI, *cannily noting the appreciation* GIDEON *entertains for his daughter, scrambles closer to* GIDEON, *pulling along with him the other two elders whose necks are joined to his by a rope.*)

OZNI. Oh, my lord Gideon, I see my maiden daughter Orpah here is pleasing in your eye. Could you think of her—well, in a manner of speaking—as a sacrifice of atonement that we wretched men of Succoth offer up to you? Take my daughter here as wife, great Gideon, and be merciful with us and spare our lives.

SECOND ELDER. Spare us, my lord.

(GIDEON *sullenly regards the piteous old faces staring at him, takes a good look at the girl again, considers the suggestion for a moment.*)

GIDEON. Well, it is an interesting idea. But it can't be done. It was the word of the Lord that you must die; I cannot gainsay God. (*Fairly drunk now, he turns, glowering, to his captains.*) I spoke to the Lord about this, you know. I said: "They are such piteous old wretches, and they are our own brothers. Must I kill them?" "Oh," spoke the Lord, "indeed you must!" And he told me some wild farrago of things concerning the temporal inadequacies of man, now, was and is and all manner of things like that. Oh, let me say again, it is not an easy thing to love God. One must transcend all the frailties of man. Do you not think I would

like this juicy doxy here for a wife? But even that is denied me. (*He seizes another skin of wine, takes a long swallow, and squats down on his haunches, belligerently drunk.*) I would ask of you, have I done well by the Lord?

SHETHULAH. Indeed you have.

GIDEON. Is there anyone here—I protest, is there anyone here who has ever heard me reprehend the Lord in any way?

SHILLEM. You have praised his name with every breath.

GIDEON. Well, then, what comes of this? I spoke with the Lord and said: "The people think of me as their king, and I think it sensible that I should be king over these people. All other peoples have kings. There are kings in Tyre, Byblos, Boetia, in every Phoenician city, and the Egyptians indeed have had a full pedigree of pharaohs. They are well into their twenty-third dynasty by now."

HEZEKIAH. Twentieth.

GIDEON. Twentieth? Well, twentieth then. It does not belittle the argument. The point is, great empires are in the making in Ashur and in Babylon. Shall we always be the subject people?

MALCHIEL (*showing interest for the first time*). And let the people say:

THE CAPTAINS. Amen.

GIDEON. In these words did I speak to the Lord: "Shall we not be a mighty nation too? May I not sit upon a throne as well as Tiglath-Pileser? Let Syria raise bowls of silver tribute above their heads to me! We are the crossroads of Asia here! Let the caravans from Aram pay duty on Gideon's highways!"

MALCHIEL. And let the people say:

THE CAPTAINS. Amen!

GIDEON. I would make a good king, I think.

SHILLEM. Oh, and I might be your vizier.

GIDEON. Well, you shall have to do without your vizierate and I without my crown. For these ambitions are vanity and show a lack of faith in God. The Lord brushed the whole idea aside and terrified me with horrible deaths for just the mentioning of it.

(MALCHIEL *drops suddenly to one knee before* GIDEON, *his zealot's eyes glowing.*)

MALCHIEL. Be our king, Gideon, and rule over us. This is the moment now to take the crown. The victory over Midian does make the other kings of Canaan tremble at your name. You have but to show your might of twenty thousand men before the gates of Megiddo or of Dor, and the Girgashite kings will fall in the dust before you and pay you tribute.

SHETHULAH. The Jebusites rule Jerusalem and the Amorites Beth-Shean. But stretch forth your palm, and these kings will put their cities in it.

GIDEON. Nay, nay, my captains, do not press me.

MALCHIEL. Does not all Israel cry out for a king? We shall be as a nation among nations. What say you, captain of Ephraim?

SHETHULAH. Let him be our king and rule over us.

MALCHIEL. What say you, chief of Naphtali?

SHILLEM. Let him be our king.

MALCHIEL (*standing*). And my brother here and I are Asher. Reuben and Gad sit twenty thousand strong at the foot of the hill. Will Judah say nay to his redeemer? Will not Benjamin cry out: "Amen." You will give the Sea back to Zebulun and return Dan's inheritance wrenched from him by the Philistines. There will be peace again in Israel, and travelers will not fear the highways. For you will be "the Good King Gideon," and the land shall prosper. And let the people say:

ALL. Amen!

(GIDEON *sits cross-legged on the skins, his head bowed, the cynosure of all eyes. He looks up, deeply moved.*)

GIDEON (*gently*). Nay, I will not rule over you, and my son will not rule over you; the Lord will rule over you. (*He rises and regards the assembled host around and below him.*) You shall love the Lord your God with all your soul and with all your heart and with all your might, for he is in truth our king, and we need no other. (*To his captains*) I have been insolent and have made the Lord unattractive in your eyes with my grumbling. (*He turns back to all the people, raises his hands high.*) Come, let us give offering up to God. We have taken much spoil; this is the portion I ask for myself: give me all the golden rings Midian wore in his ears and all the golden crescents Midian hung about the

necks of his camels. I shall melt these golden things and make a sacred golden garment as a gift to the Lord. I shall set it on a high place by my tent, and in the sun it shall be seen for many miles. All who see it shall think of the Lord and remember his great victory. And let the people say:

ALL. Amen!

GIDEON. Give me my spear! The spirit of the Lord is upon me, and I shall kill these elders! (MALCHIEL *puts* GIDEON's *spear into his hand.* GIDEON *turns sharply, face set, and strides to where* OZNI *and the two other prostrate* ELDERS *are still hunched over on their knees, backs bowed in abject fear.* GIDEON *raises the spear above his head and cries out in a mighty voice.*) The Lord our God is a wrathful God! His name is the Great and the Mighty and the Terrible God, the Devouring God! Let not his wrath be raised against you as with these taunting men! (*He stands a moment, spear upraised, and then a look of horror crosses his face. Slowly he brings the spear down and lets it dangle from his hand. He stands a moment, trembling with a kind of dread.*) I cannot do it. Let them live, Shillem, scourge them, if you will, with whips, with briars of the wilderness and thorns. For surely man must have more meaning than this. (*He shuffles disconsolately, even guiltily, a few steps away, casting a nervous look up to heaven.*)

SHILLEM. Well then, soldiers, go gather me briars from the wilderness and thorns and make a scourge for me. (*He nudges* OZNI *gently.*) Well, it is better than being killed, isn't it?

OZNI (*delight slowly spreading across his face*). Yes, I suppose it is.

SHILLEM (*to* GIDEON). The girl, Gideon, is yours, you know.

(GIDEON, *who had quite forgotten about* ORPAH, *is delighted at being reminded. He sweeps her over his shoulder and carries her off. The people of Succoth, needless to say, spring up into great rejoicing. The* WOMEN *smash tabrets and cymbals and dance enthusiastically. The* ELDERS *gaily sing out.*)

ELDERS. Hosanna! Hosanna! Sing glory to Gideon! His name is Merciful. He has redeemed us from Midian! The land is free, O Israel!

Thy sons stand up, O Israel!
Thy daughters dance, O Israel!
Hosanna! Hosanna!

(*The* ELDERS, *escorted by* SOLDIERS, *start offstage; the* WOMEN *dance; the stage is a scene of tumultuous revelry as the* CURTAIN *comes quickly down.*)

SCENE TWO

"*And Gideon made an ephod of it and put it in his city, in Ophrah; and all Israel played the harlot after it there, and it became a snare to Gideon and to his family.*"

———

The same as Act 1, Scene 1; by the tents of JOASH.

It is two days later.

At rise, THE ANGEL *is striding about the stage, glowering and furious. He looks down the road to Schechem.*

———

THE ANGEL. Ah, here he comes, hugging to his chest the sacred golden garment he has made for me. Oh, he shall know my wrath, indeed he shall. (*Enter* GIDEON, *huffing and puffing, holding the golden ephod to his chest with both hands. It is crudely made but recognizable as a simple waist-length garment with shoulder-straps, and it glitters and glistens handsomely.* ORPAH *follows a few wifely paces behind, robed and veiled, and carrying a large bundle of her belongings on her head.* THE ANGEL *regards* GIDEON's *entrance with a cold eye and says in an icy tone*) The Lord is with you, O mighty man of valor.

GIDEON (*startled*). Oh! Peace be with you, my Lord. (*He sets the golden ephod down atop the altar upstage.*) This is for you, my Lord. I fashioned it myself. My Lord, I must have some few words with you, but first let me make my presence known to my father and my wives. Oh, here stands my new wife, Orpah the daughter of Ozni. Uncover your face, my wife, so that the Lord may look upon you. Here, here, he stands by the tree here.

(ORPAH *lowers her veil and turns blankly to the tree.*)

THE ANGEL (*coldly*). Very handsome.

GIDEON. Yes. Well, let me go embrace my father and make my presence known. I hope my gifts find favor in your eye.

THE ANGEL. Go and seek your father.

GIDEON. Yes, well, in a moment then. (*He takes* ORPAH's *arm and starts for the tent.*) He is invisible to you then, too. (ORPAH *nods, looks nervously back to the terebinth tree.*) He is in a black temper.

(JOASH *comes bursting out of the tent.*)

JOASH. He is here! He is here among us! Come forth to greet him! Oh, my son, come let me embrace you. (*From out of the tent now pour* TIRZAH, MAHLAH, HOGLAH, MILCAH, ADINOAB, *and* JETHER, GIDEON's *son. They all stand at the tent flap staring in mute adoration at the returning hero.* JOASH *embraces* GIDEON.) Oh, my son, what honor you have brought to this house! The people of Abiezer are waiting for us now up on the threshing hill. Now, that you have come, we shall start the festival of summer fruits. Oh, Gideon, I am most blessed of fathers. Let water be brought that he may bathe his feet.

GIDEON. My father, this is a Gadite woman who is my wife. Her name is Orpah daughter of Ozni of the house of Eliasaph, a princely house. Give her your blessing and make her welcome in your tent.

JOASH (*to* ORPAH, *bowing low at his feet*). Rise up, my daughter, take off your veil. You are in your own home.

GIDEON (*embracing* HOGLAH). My mother, let me embrace you. (*To* TIRZAH *and* MAHLAH.) My wives, this is the Gadite Orpah. Bring water that she may bathe her feet and drink. She is dear to me; honor her.

JOASH. Sit, my son, and let us attend you.

(*Skins have been spread on the ground.* GIDEON *and* ORPAH *sit on them and have their feet bathed and are served cakes and water.* GIDEON *looks anxiously back to* THE ANGEL; *then tries to give his attention to his family.*)

GIDEON. These other ladies here are the widows of my brothers. This is my son, Jether, a pensive boy. His uncles call him donkey as they once called me. Well, you shall have sweeter names now. You are the only son of Gideon.

MAHLAH. Nay, nay, my lord. Oh, let my lord be told.

JOASH. Your wife Mahlah is with child again.

TIRZAH. And I do think the same, my

lord. I too have passed my time.

GIDEON (*scowls, darts a nervous look at* THE ANGEL). Yea, God did promise me seventy sons. (*Turns back to* JETHER *with a gentle smile and takes the boy's hand.*) But this is Jether, my first-born, who shall be a prince in Manasseh after me and whose opinion I hold dear.

(*The boy stares up at him in open-mouthed adulation.*)

JOASH. Oh, my son, we have heard such stories of your gallantry in war. Every passing soldier adds fifty to the host of Midianites you have slain.

GIDEON. Oh, I slew a few perhaps.

(THE ANGEL *snorts and throws up his hands.*)

THE ANGEL. Oh!

(GIDEON *turns to* THE ANGEL, *his face appealing for indulgence, but he receives only a baleful glare.*)

GIDEON (*turning sadly back to his son*). In truth, I killed no Midianites at all. These stories you have heard are but the usual legends of the battlefield.

JOASH. Your father was the general, boy. He stands behind and regards the course of things so that he may direct the over-all tactic and maneuver.

GIDEON. Yes, yes, that is true, of course.

JOASH. It was your father who conceived the plan to stampede the Midianite cattle with lamps and trumpets.

GIDEON. Ah, there, of course, I must take the credit, and—(*He looks back to* THE ANGEL, *who glowers at him again.*) Well, even this was not my doing. The Lord our God instructed me what to do; I merely did it.

(*The boy,* JETHER, *is obviously disappointed by this, and* GIDEON *is pained by his disappointment.*)

JOASH. But there passed through here just yesterday a prince of Asher whose name was Hezekiah the son of Immah, who expounded to us for many hours on the war and said that Gideon was among the great generals.

GIDEON. Did he say that indeed?

JOASH. Aye, and this Hezekiah is well known as a scholar and knows many things.

GIDEON. Oh, indeed, he predicts the eclipses of the moon and has measured the ecliptic of the sun as it revolves around the earth.

JOASH. And this Hezekiah described

the history of the war, and indeed God did not enter into it at all. "We are all men of reason here," he said, "and need not explain all things in supernatural ways. The savage will say God gave us into the hand of the Midianites," said Hezekiah, "but was it not in fact the economic conditions of drought in the desert that drove the Midianites upon us." And then he said: "Was it the spirit of God that aroused the tribes of Israel to rebel, or was it not rather the need to protect our growing cities, our increase in caravan trade, and the beginnings of our mercantile interests? Is the panic of the one hundred and twenty thousand Midianites so hard to understand when one realizes the superstitious spirit of the men of Midian? For these were a primitive people with a crumbling social fabric. All that was needed was a bold and ingenious general who could exploit these weaknesses of Midian." And, indeed, Gideon, that was you.

(GIDEON *considers this explanation a moment.*)

GIDEON. Well, it is not altogether illogical, is it?

JOASH. "Indeed," said this Hezekiah, "who is this Yahweh of Gideon's? Has anyone seen him or heard his words? Only Gideon." It was Hezekiah's contention, Gideon, that Yahweh was a masterful fiction you created to inspirit the troops.

GIDEON (*eagerly*). Now, how did his reasoning go again? It was the economic conditions prevailing in the desert of Havilah that . . .

THE ANGEL (*roaring*). Gideon! Will you countenance this pomander of utter nonsense?

(*The smile disappears from* GIDEON's *face, and he sighs unhappily.*)

GIDEON. Ah. (*He regards his son anxiously.*) It is none of it true, my son. It was the Lord our God who gave us into the hand of Midian, for we had bowed down to false gods, and it was the Lord our God who redeemed us by the strength of his hand alone. Yea, though none of you may see nor hear him, he is here among us now, and I see and hear him. There is no honor due me at all, but that I am the device of God.

(JETHER, *embarrassed by his father's humility, lowers his eyes and shuffles away upstage.* GIDEON *watches him go anxiously.*)

JOASH (*now suddenly terrified*). He is here among us, did you say, the Lord our God?

GIDEON (*watching his son*). Aye.

(JOASH *immediately prostrates himself to the ground as do all the others onstage, excepting* JETHER—*who has suddenly noticed the glistening ephod on the upstage altar*—*and* GIDEON, *who is watching him. The boy approaches the ephod to examine it.*)

THE ANGEL. Do not let him touch it, Gideon. It is a thing of God, and he will die.

(*The boy reaches out to touch the ephod.*)

GIDEON (*crying out*). Do not touch it! It is holy! You will die!

JOASH (*looking up*). My son, you have carried it in your hands for twenty miles.

GIDEON. I have given it to God, and it is holy now. Not you nor I nor the Levite priests of God may touch it, for it is a holy thing.

JOASH. Behold the sacred golden garment Gideon has made for God!

GIDEON (*stands and faces* THE ANGEL). There is no putting it off, my Lord, but I must have a word with you.

THE ANGEL. And I with you, Gideon.

GIDEON (*to his father*). My father, go and make ready for the festival on the hill. Let my new wife be taken to my tent. Leave me here alone. I must speak with the Lord. (*The others rise quickly and exit off into the tent. For a moment, the stage is silent,* GIDEON *downstage in frowning concentration and* THE ANGEL *upstage waiting in cold anger. Then* GIDEON *turns to* THE ANGEL.) My Lord, we have always spoken plainly with each other.

THE ANGEL. I am not pleased with this golden ephod you have made. It is a pagan thought to think your God wears golden undercoats.

GIDEON. I fashioned it for love of you, my Lord.

THE ANGEL. Indeed, you did not, but as a wily gift to turn aside my wrath. You betrayed me at Succoth, Gideon. I charged you to slay the elders, and you did not. Shall you say who shall die and who shall live? I am the Lord. I kill, and I make alive. Shall you gainsay me? Have you

seen the end of time? Do you know the beginning and what came before that? Do you know whence you rose? Do you know where you go? Are you God now that you give life where I have taken it away?

GIDEON. I pitied the old men, my Lord.

THE ANGEL. And I watched you sit there now, greedily believing all of Hezekiah's chimera and claptrap about the socio-economic conditions in the desert of Havilah—you, who have seen the Lord face to face and beheld his wonders.

GIDEON. Well, Hezekiah is well spoken of as a scholar. He knows all about the ecliptic of the sun as it revolves around the earth.

THE ANGEL. The sun does not revolve around the earth, you imbecile; the earth revolves about the sun.

GIDEON. Oh, that is patent nonsense, my Lord. The sun obviously revolves around the earth.

THE ANGEL. Oh! I do not know how I bear with you!

GIDEON (*crying out*). Oh, my Lord, let me go!

THE ANGEL. Let you go?

GIDEON. We have made a covenant of love between us, you and I. Release me from that covenant.

THE ANGEL. Are you suggesting some sort of divorce between your God and you?

GIDEON. We make an ill-matched pair, my Lord. You surely see we never meet but tempers rise between us. It is too much for me, this loving God. I cannot manage it. I am a plain man and subject to imperfect feelings. I shall betray you many times, and you shall rise in wrath against me and shall punish me with mighty penalties, and I cannot continue in this way, my Lord. Oh, let me say it plainly. I do not love you, Lord, and it is unreasonable to persist with each other when there is no love.

THE ANGEL (*startled*). You do not love me?

GIDEON. I tried to love you, but it is too much for me. You are too vast a concept for me. To love you, God, one must be a god himself. I did not kill the elders of Succoth, and I shall tell you why. I raised my spear above their heads, but in that moment I felt a shaft of terror that chills me even now. It was as if the nakedness of all things was exposed to me, and I saw myself and all men for what we truly are, suspensions of matter, flailing about for footholds in the void, all the while slipping back screaming into endless suffocations. That is the truth of things, I know, but I cannot call it truth. It is too hideous, an intolerable state of affairs. I cannot love you, God, for it makes me a meaningless thing.

THE ANGEL (*thoroughly exasperated*). Oh!

GIDEON. My Lord, it is elemental in me to aspire to be greater than myself. This is your own doing, for you gave me passion that I might raise myself to you. You have uncovered your nakedness before me. How shall I think myself an aimless brute now?

THE ANGEL. I meant you to love me, but you are merely curious. You have no feeling for me then at all?

GIDEON. I fear you, God. I am in mortal dread of you. Perhaps, that is the only love a man can give his god.

THE ANGEL (*deeply hurt*). What shall we do then, Gideon?

GIDEON. Let me go, God.

THE ANGEL. Let you go—whatever does that mean? Gideon, there is no divorce from God. I am truth and exist. You cannot deny that I am. I stand palpably here before you, as real as rock, a very actual thing with whom you have commerced face-to-face.

GIDEON. Aye, my Lord. I see you and hear you. So I beg of you, my Lord—go from my sight. Make not your presence known to me again that I might say: "God is a dream, a name, a thought, but not a real thing."

THE ANGEL. But I am a real thing.

GIDEON. I would pretend that you were not.

(THE ANGEL *is a little startled at this.*)

THE ANGEL. Let me review this. You would pretend God is not, although you know that he is, so that you might be a significant creature which you know you are not. Oh! This is beyond even God's understanding! And you do not love me! I found you a mournful farmer, and I have loved you and raised you up and uncovered your soul, and gave you many satisfactions. And now you turn on me like a disgruntled husband and would send me packing back to my father's tent. This was not the case when you needed me, was it? Oh! What protestations of ardor you made then! And I was susceptible enough to think the man did love me. I have been too kind with you, indeed I have! If fear is all the love you have for me, then you shall fear me, Gideon. You betrayed me at Succoth. You have given the life of men greater value than the word of God. Behold then, Gideon! Know that there is a God, and that his will is all there is. As I blessed you for your love, so shall I punish you for your infidelity. You did not slay the seven and seventy elders of Succoth. Then, the seventy sons I promised you shall die in their stead.

GIDEON (*sinks to the ground, stricken*). Oh!

THE ANGEL. They shall die in bitterness by each other's hands. As you contend with me, so shall they contend among themselves.

GIDEON. Oh, God, this is most cruel!

THE ANGEL. It seems just weight to me. Behold then, Gideon. I give life and I take it away. I bless, and I punish. I am pleased, and I rise in wrath. This is the law of the universe; there is no other.

GIDEON (*shriveled now into a terrified ball on the ground*). Oh, my Lord, I cannot continue in this way! (GIDEON, *frozen in terror, huddles hunched against further lashes of punishment. After a moment, he looks slowly up, his face drawn into an expression of intense anguish. His eye is caught by the appearance of* JETHER, *who has shuffled out of the tent and would come to his father but sees that the latter is on his knees in profound prayer.*) Spare me at least my one only son, my Lord. I have never known his love. His mother taught him her contempt, but now, I think, he might love me, and I would like that, God. (JOASH, ORPAH *and the other* WOMEN *now come out of the tent, stop at the sight of* GIDEON, *on his knees in prayer, and stand silently and a little frightened.*) Behold mine own small world of people there. Could I not pretend there is some reason for their being here? Pretend, my Lord, no more than that. Let me have at least some bogus value.

THE ANGEL (*gently*). I am truth, Gideon. I cannot vary.

(GIDEON *bows his head, utterly crushed.*

Then he slowly looks up again, but apparently does not see THE ANGEL *immediately.*)

GIDEON. My Lord?

THE ANGEL. Yes?

(GIDEON *looks around the stage.*)

GIDEON. God?

THE ANGEL. I am by the wine press now.

GIDEON. God?

THE ANGEL. Here, Gideon, by the press.

GIDEON. Are you still here?

THE ANGEL. Here, over here.

GIDEON (*standing*). Ah, yes, you do seem blurred. My Lord, I asked you one small thing, that I might delude myself with some spurious grandeur.

THE ANGEL. And I answered: "No, it will not do." You want the universe to please your eye, Gideon, and not mine. You would be God yourself. Hear me well, O Hebrew. I am a jealous God and brook no other gods, not even you. Why have I come here at all but to put an end to false idols? You have done well in pulling down the effigies of Ba-al, but do not think to set yourself up on their empty altars. Do not make a cult of man, not even in fancy.

GIDEON (*looking around*). My Lord? My Lord?

THE ANGEL. Attend me, Gideon, and mark my words.

GIDEON. My Lord?

THE ANGEL. Where are you looking, Gideon? I am here.

GIDEON. My Lord, where are you gone?

THE ANGEL. Here! I stand here! By the wine press here! I have not moved!

GIDEON. My Lord, please speak to me. We are not finished.

THE ANGEL. What is this game?

GIDEON. My Lord!

THE ANGEL. I stand right here!

GIDEON. Where are you, Lord? The matter is not finished!

THE ANGEL (*crying out*). O Gideon, do not forsake me!

GIDEON. God! Where are you, God? I cannot see you, God! You have not answered what I asked you!

(*At this point,* ABIMELECH *and* HELEK *come hurrying in from upstage left behind the tent.*)

ABIMELECH. Ah! There he is! They said they saw him on the road!

HELEK. Oh, Gideon, how good to have you back.

(JOASH *peremptorily admonishes the new arrivals to silence. Indeed,* GIDEON's *scene with* THE ANGEL *has been watched with mingled dread and confusion by his family. Now,* GIDEON *stands center stage, as if transfixed, staring up to the heavens.* THE ANGEL, *who had turned exasperatedly away at the interruption, now moves intently to* GIDEON, *as angry as only a scorned god can be.*)

THE ANGEL. Gideon, I pray you, do not scorn me! I will not be so cast off out of hand. You leave this house, return not to it ever. For I have had my fill of your betrayals, your sordid harlotries with other gods. And now there are new strumpets on the highway. Well, go then to those painted dialectics and libertine philosophies and logics that wait along the road for gulls like you, and, for a shekel, shrilly promise you the secret sensuality of time and space. You will be ravished, fleeced, and soon abandoned in some red-threaded hovel of despair. Then do not hope that God awaits at home when with ragged beard the penitent returns. Turn not your face from me! Beware my wrath! There is no divorce from God! Hear that! God gives no divorce, but just his curse!

(GIDEON, *to all effects and purposes, has not heard a word.*)

GIDEON. I do not see you, God, nor hear you now. What was between us now is done. And let the people say: "Amen."

(*A long silence fills the stage. After a moment,* JOASH *calls tentatively to his son.*)

JOASH. My son, the house of Abiezer waits to honor you on the threshing hill.

(*By the wine press,* THE ANGEL *looks sadly at his hands.*)

THE ANGEL. Gideon, I am the Lord your God who brought you out of the land of Egypt. I broke the bars of your yoke and made you stand erect. Will you spurn my statutes? Will you break my covenant?

GIDEON (*his eyes closed against* THE ANGEL's *words*). I must aspire, God.

THE ANGEL (*thundering*). Then I shall do this to you and to all of Israel! I will make your heavens like iron and your earth like brass! I will scatter you among the nations!

(*With great effort,* GIDEON *forces his attention back to the others onstage.*)

GIDEON (*to his family*). Well, come, then, let us go to the festival.

THE ANGEL. I will unsheathe the sword after you! Your land shall be a desolation, and your cities shall be a waste!

GIDEON (*forcing his attention on the ephod*). I shall put on this golden garment and wear it to the festival. (GIDEON, *with set jaw, starts upstage to the ephod.* THE ANGEL *raises his arm in lordly threat.*)

THE ANGEL (*thundering*). Gideon! Do not touch it! This thing is mine!

GIDEON (*whirls and cries out*). O God! I cannot believe in you! If you love me, let me believe at least in mine own self! If you love me, God!

(THE ANGEL *stares at* GIDEON *with a face strained by deep emotion. Then his upraised arm falls to his side.*)

THE ANGEL. I love you, Gideon!

(GIDEON *promptly turns and takes hold of the ephod.*)

GIDEON. Father, help me to put it on.

(*With the apprehensive help of* JOASH *and of his son,* JETHER, GIDEON *contrives to get the weighty ephod over his head and down onto his body.*)

GIDEON. What a heavy thing it is.

(THE ANGEL, *still deeply moved, looks up, smiles.*)

THE ANGEL. Oh, indeed it is.

ABIMELECH (*staring in awe at the gold-clad* GIDEON). We all wait to hear you tell the miracle of God's victory over Midian.

(GIDEON *turns slowly to the elders.*)

GIDEON. A miracle? Why do you call it that? (*Wrapping his arms around his uncles, he leads the small procession of his family off stage right.*) Nay, my uncles, the war with Midian was not mysterious, but only the inevitable outgrowth of historico-economic, socio-psychological and cultural forces prevailing in these regions.

(*They all exit off stage right to attend the festival of summer fruits on the hill.* THE ANGEL *has watched them go with amusement. Now, he cannot resist bursting into laughter.*)

THE ANGEL. Oh, it is amusing. (*He moves downstage, quite cheerful now, and regards the audience. Behind him, the stage is empty. After a moment he recites:*)

God no more believes it odd
That man cannot believe in God.
Man believes the best he can,
Which means, it seems, belief in man.
Then let him don my gold ephod
And let him be a proper god.
Well, let him try it anyway.
With this conceit, we end the play.

(THE ANGEL *bows. The lights black out.*)

CURTAIN

J.B.

Archibald MacLeish

Presented by Alfred De Liagre, Jr., at the Anta Theatre, New York, on December 11, 1958, with the following cast:

FIRST ROUSTABOUT Clifton James
SECOND ROUSTABOUT James Olson
NICKLES Christopher Plummer
MR. ZUSS Raymond Massey
PROMPTER Ford Rainey
J.B. Pat Hingle
SARAH Nan Martin
DAVID Arnold Merritt
MARY Ciri Jacobsen
JONATHAN Jeffrey Rowland
RUTH Candy Moore

REBECCA Merry Martin
THE GIRL Janet Ward
MRS. BOTTICELLI Helen Waters
MRS. LESURE Fay Sappington
MRS. ADAMS Judith Lowry
MRS. MURPHY Laura Pierpont
JOLLY Lane Bradbury
BILDAD Bery Conway
ZOPHAR Ivor Francis
ELIPHAZ Andreas Voutsinas

Associate producer: Joseph I. Levine
Directed by Elia Kazan
Designed by Boris Aronson
Costumes by Lucinda Ballard
Lighting by Tharon Musser
Music by David Amram

In this production the setting is arranged on stage in full sight of the audience by Roustabouts of the circus.

It may be difficult to believe that a verse drama, a retelling of the Job story in modern terms, and a morality and discussion play at that, could have scored a run of 364 performances on Broadway before the curtain fell on the production of *J.B.* on October 24, 1959. But this is what happened and we are free to draw one of two conclusions. A prevalent one was that *J.B.* was a good play and an honorable a work by one of America's prominent poets and public figures, Mr. Archibald MacLeish; and a dissident one was that success was earned less by the interest of the play than by the staging of *J.B.* by the gifted director Elia Kazan, whatever one may think of his judgment in guiding the revision of the play for Broadway after its highly regarded production at Yale by the School of Drama.

Born on May 7, 1892, in a suburb of Chicago into a Scotch Presbyterian family of early settlers of the city and, on his mother's side, a seafaring New England family, MacLeish was well prepared for his career or rather for the several careers in which he has distinguished himself. From Hotchkiss preparatoy school he went to Yale, where he excelled both as a student and an athlete and became editor of the literary magazine. From Yale he went to the Harvard Law School, where he led his class in his last year. After teaching at Harvard for a year, he took employment in a highly respectable Boston law firm, where he could probably have thrived in the profession for which he had prepared himself. But he yielded to the seductions of a literary career, having had the tangible encouragement of getting his first volume of verse, *Tower of Ivory,* published in 1917 while serving in France as a captain of artillery in the First World War. Taking up residence abroad, he became a member of the avant-garde led by Pound and Eliot, and published *The Happy Marriage and Other Poems* in 1924. He did not return to the states until 1928. His literary life was subsequently interrupted by editorial duties on *Fortune* magazine and by association with liberal causes and support of President Franklin Delano Roosevelt during the difficult years of the New Deal and World War II. He excelled in journalism and was entrusted with the supervision of the Federal government's information agency. In later years, after leaving the government, he became a professor of English at Harvard and took charge of the university's creative writing program.

In 1935, Mr. MacLeish entered the theatre with an experimental production of *Panic,* a formal verse play about the Wall Street panic which initiated the great economic depression and challenged economic and social thinking in the United States. Strongly anti-fascist, he wrote the powerful radio drama *The Fall of the City* in 1937; and aroused by the Spanish Civil War bombing of civilian centers by the Italian air force supporting General Franco's effort to overthrow the Spanish republic, he composed a second impressive radio play, *Air Raid,* a year or so later. These short dramatic pieces in verse set high literary standards in radio drama and were of a quality never excelled and but rarely equaled by himself and others.

These works were all products of a world-crisis that culminated in the holocaust of World War II. In the years of the postwar crisis, Mr. MacLeish moved nearer to the question of evil itself. That his answer to the problem, put in such general terms, would be at best tentative was as foregone a conclusion as that it would give rise to conflicting opinion. Popular support went to the work as a piece of theatre; argument over the moral and theological validity of the work was expectedly strong (even the Book of Job upon which Mr. MacLeish based *J.B.* has aroused argument); and some trenchant dramatic criticism (by Kenneth Tynan and others) has been expended upon the work. But the work has been strongly championed, too, and *J.B.* was one of the few plays of the recent period in American drama which deserved serious consideration.*

The reader of *J.B.* will have many a question to raise. One complaint is that J.B. is so commonplace and that the majestic Job theme has been reduced to ordinary sentiments. Another criticism was especially well put by John Ciardi in the *Saturday Review* concerning J.B.'s God: "Just as I am convinced that I should take *Him* as the blank stone face of the naturalistic universe, I find him speaking Old Testament, and somehow I have trouble taking that as the idiom of star-blinded nothingness." Another problem is the relation of Mr. Zuss and Mr. Nickles, the "Godmask" and

* Readers interested in further discussion of *J.B.* may be referred to an essay in John Gassner's *Theatre at the Crossroads,* pages 298-304 (Holt, Rinehart & Winston, 1960).

"Satanmask" framing characters of the plays, to the central section of the Job story —to which the best answer is that the play is "theatrical" in orientation; the author simply uses the play as a springboard for reflection on "the human condition" and a framework for a demonstration of values. A perceptive appreciation of the theatrical fascination of the work came from Walter Kerr (New York *Herald Tribune* review of December 30, 1958). He observed, for example, how the moment the circus hawker who plays Satan puts on his Satanmask to play his role, "he discovers that the mask has its own life, that it speaks for him, that, in fact, he cannot silence it."

Still another criticism, concerning the character of J.B., the modern Job who is a wealthy American businessman, is that his personality makes his misfortunes inadequate as an analogue, which the author apparently hoped they would be, to the misery of the millions of victims of totalitarianism. The pretension of J.B.'s would-be comforters, however, successfully project the delusions of modern society into the Job story, as do also the cartoon figures of cheap journalism in the play. It was inevitable that the language, the very attempt to write a modern American verse drama, should disturb some watchful observers. The drama critic for *Encounter* magazine of London, Nigel Dennis, spoke for them in remarking that "the poet's place in contemporary drama is still the uneasy one of a man in evening dress trying to look natural in a transport café." Yet it would be hard to find another American writer of verse drama who has mediated so well between the claims of prose and of verse in a work intended for the non-coterie stage; and the one prospect Mr. MacLeish could not entertain, of course, in writing a morality play for the times was that of achieving a merely esoteric *succès d'estime*.

THE SCENE *throughout is a corner inside an enormous circus tent where a side show of some kind has been set up. There is a rough stage across the corner, on the left of which a wooden platform has been built at a height of six or seven feet. A wooden ladder leans against it. To the right is a deal table with seven straight chairs. There is a door-shaped opening in the canvas to the right rear. Above, a huge, slanted pole thrusts the canvas out and up to make the peak of the corner. Clothes that have the look of vestments of many churches and times have been left about at one side and the other of the stage and the light at the beginning —such light as there is—is provided by bulbs dangling from hanks of wire. The feel is of a public place at late night, the audience gone, no one about but maybe a stagehand somewhere cleaning up, fooling with the lights.*

THE PROLOGUE

MR. ZUSS, *followed by* NICKLES, *enters from the dimness off to the left. They stop at the edge of the side-show stage. Both wear the white caps and jackets of circus vendors. Both are old.* MR. ZUSS, *who has a bunch of balloons hitched to his belt, is large, florid, deep-voiced, dignified, imposing.* NICKLES *is gaunt and sardonic; he has a popcorn tray slung from straps across his shoulders. Both betray in carriage and speech the broken-down actor fallen on evil days but nevertheless and always actor. Throughout the Prologue, from the moment when they mount the side-show stage, they jockey for position, gesture, work themselves up into theatrical flights and rhetorical emotions, play to each other as though they had an actual audience before them in the empty dark.*

MR. ZUSS. This is it.
NICKLES.   This is what?
MR. ZUSS.   Where they play the play,
                      Horatio!
NICKLES. Bare stage?
MR. ZUSS.   Not in the least.
Heaven and earth. That platform's
                      Heaven.
(*They step up onto the stage together.*)
NICKLES. Looks like Heaven!
MR. ZUSS.   As you remember it?

NICKLES. Somebody's got to. You weren't
                      there.
They never sold balloons in Heaven—
Not in my time.
MR. ZUSS.   Only popcorn.
(NICKLES *shrugs a shudder of disgust, heaving his tray.*)
NICKLES. The two best actors in America
Selling breath in bags . . .
MR. ZUSS.   and bags
To butter breath with . . .
NICKLES.   when they sell.
MR. ZUSS. Merchandise not moving,
                     Nickles?
NICKLES. Moves wherever I do—all of it.
No rush to buy your worlds, I notice.
MR. ZUSS. I could sell one to a . . .
NICKLES.   . . . child!
You told me. Where's the earth?
MR. ZUSS.   Earth?
Earth is where that table is:
That's where Job sits—at the table.
God and Satan lean above.
(MR. ZUSS *peers anxiously up into the canvas sky.*)
I wonder if we'd better?
NICKLES.   What?
MR. ZUSS. Play it.
NICKLES.   Why not? Who cares? *They*
                     don't.
MR. ZUSS. At least we're actors. They're
                    not actors.
Never acted anything.
NICKLES.   That's right.
They only own the show.
MR. ZUSS.   I wonder . . .
NICKLES. They won't care and they won't
                    know.
(*His eyes follow* MR. ZUSS's *up to the dangling bulbs.*)
Those stars that stare their stares at me—
Are those the staring stars I see
Or only lights . . .
           not meant for me?
MR. ZUSS. What's that got to do with
                   anything?
NICKLES. Very little. Shall we start?
MR. ZUSS. You think we ought to?
NICKLES   They won't care.
MR. ZUSS. Let's start . . .
What staring stars?
NICKLES.   They aren't.
They're only lights. Not meant.
MR. ZUSS.   Why don't we
Start?
NICKLES. You'll play the part of . . .
MR. ZUSS.   Naturally!

NICKLES. Naturally! And your mask?

MR. ZUSS. Mask!

NICKLES. Mask. Naturally. You wouldn't play God in your
Face would you?

MR. ZUSS. What's the matter with it?

NICKLES. God the Creator of the Universe?
God who hung the world in time?
You wouldn't hang the world in time
With a two-days' beard on your chin or a pinky!
Lay its measure! Stretch the line on it!
(MR. ZUSS *stares coldly at* NICKLES, *unhitches his balloon belt with magnificent deliberation, drops it, steps forward to the front of the wooden stage, strikes an attitude.*)

MR. ZUSS. *Whatsoever is under the whole Heaven is mine!*

NICKLES. That's what I mean.
You need a mask.

MR. ZUSS (*heavy irony*). Perhaps a more
Accomplished actor . . .

NICKLES. Kiss your accomplishments!
Nobody doubts your accomplishments—none of them—
The one man for God in the theater!
They'd all say that. Our ablest actor.
Nobody else for the part, they'd say.

MR. ZUSS. You make me humble.

NICKLES. No! I'm serious.
The part was written for you.

MR. ZUSS (*gesture of protest*). Oh!

NICKLES. But this is God in *Job* you're playing:
God the Maker: God Himself!
Remember what He says?—the hawk
Flies by His wisdom! And the goats—
Remember the goats? He challenges Job with them:
Dost thou know the time of the wild goats?
What human face knows time like that time?
You'd need a face of fur to know it.
Human faces know too much too little.

MR. ZUSS (*suspiciously*).
What kind of mask?

NICKLES. You'll find one somewhere.
They never play without the masks.

MR. ZUSS. It's God the Father I play—not
God the boiling point of water!

NICKLES. Nevertheless the mask is imperative.
If God should laugh
The mare would calf
The cow would foal:

Diddle my soul . . .

MR. ZUSS (*shocked*).
God never laughs! In the whole Bible!

NICKLES. That's why I say. *We* do.

MR. ZUSS. *I* don't.

NICKLES. *Job* does. He covers his mouth with his hand.

MR. ZUSS. Job is abashed.

NICKLES. He says he's abashed.

MR. ZUSS. He should be abashed: it's rank irreverence—
Job there on the earth . . .

NICKLES. On his dung heap . . .

MR. ZUSS. Challenging God!

NICKLES. Crying to God.

MR. ZUSS. Demanding *justice* of *God!*

NICKLES. Justice!
No wonder he laughs. It's ridiculous. All of it.
God has killed his sons, his daughters,
Stolen his camels, oxen, sheep,
Everything he has and left him
Sick and stricken on a dung heap—
Not even the consciousness of crime to comfort him—
The rags of reasons.

MR. ZUSS. God is reasons.

NICKLES. For the hawks, yes. For the goats. They're grateful.
Take their young away they'll sing
Or purr or moo or splash—whatever.
Not for Job though.

MR. ZUSS. And that's why.

NICKLES. Why what?

MR. ZUSS. He suffers.

NICKLES. Ah? Because he's . . .
Not a bird you mean?

MR. ZUSS. You're frivolous . . .

NICKLES. That's precisely what you do mean!
The one thing God can't stomach is a man,
That scratcher at the cracked creation!
That eyeball squinting through into His Eye,
Blind with the sight of Sight!
(NICKLES *tugs himself free of his tray.*)
Blast this . . .

MR. ZUSS. God created the whole world.
Who is Job to . . .

NICKLES. Agh! the world!
The dirty whirler! The toy top!

MR. ZUSS (*kicking savagely at the popcorn tray and the balloon belt to shove them under the platform*).
What's so wrong with the world?

NICKLES. Wrong with it!

Try to spin one on a dung heap!
(MR. ZUSS *does not answer. He goes on
kicking at the tray.* NICKLES *sits on a
rung of the ladder. After a time he be-
gins to sing to himself in a kind of tune-
less tune.*)
NICKLES. I heard upon his dry dung heap
That man cry out who cannot sleep:
"If God is God He is not good,
If God is good He is not God;
Take the even, take the odd,
I would not sleep here if I could
Except for the little green leaves in the
                                        wood
And the wind on the water."
(*There is a long silence.*)
MR. ZUSS. You are a bitter man.
NICKLES (*pompously*).   I taste of the
                                        world!
I've licked the stick that beat my brains
                                        out:
Stock that broke my father's bones!
MR. ZUSS. Our modern hero! Our Odysseus
Sailing sidewalks toward the turd
Of truth and touching it at last in tri-
                                        umph!
The honest, disillusioned man!
You sicken me.
NICKLES (*hurt*).   All right, I sicken you.
No need to be offensive, is there?
If you would rather someone else . . .
MR. ZUSS. Did what?
NICKLES.   Played Job.
MR. ZUSS.   What's Job to do with it?
NICKLES. Job was honest. He saw God—
Saw him by that icy moonlight,
By that cold disclosing eye
That stares the color out and strews
Our lives . . . with light . . . for nothing.
MR. ZUSS.   Job!
I never thought of you for Job.
NICKLES. You never thought of me for
                                        Job!
What did you think of?
MR. ZUSS.   Oh, there's always
Someone playing Job.
NICKLES.   There must be
Thousands! What's that got to do with it?
Thousands—not with camels either:
Millions and millions of mankind
Burned, crushed, broken, mutilated,
Slaughtered, and for what? For thinking!
For walking round the world in the
                                        wrong
Skin, the wrong-shaped noses, eyelids:
Sleeping the wrong night wrong city—
London, Dresden, Hiroshima.

There never could have been so many
Suffered more for less. But where do
I come in?
(MR. ZUSS *shuffles uncomfortably.*)
                Play the dung heap?
MR. ZUSS. All we have to do is start.
Job will join us. Job will be there.
NICKLES. I know. I know. I know. I've
                                        seen him.
Job is everywhere we go,
His children dead, his work for nothing,
Counting his losses, scraping his boils,
Discussing himself with his friends and
                                        physicians,
Questioning everything—the times, the
                                        stars,
His own soul, God's providence.
What do *I* do?
MR. ZUSS.   What do *you* do?
NICKLES. What do I do? You play God.
MR. ZUSS. I play God. I think I mentioned
                                        it.
NICKLES. You play God and I play . . .
(*He lets himself down heavily on the
rung of the ladder.*)
                                        Ah!
MR. ZUSS (*embarrassed*).
I had assumed you knew.
(NICKLES *looks up at him, looks away.*)
MR. ZUSS.   You see,
I think of you and me as . . . opposites.
NICKLES. Nice of you.
MR. ZUSS.   I didn't mean to be nasty.
NICKLES. Your opposite! A demanding
                                        role!
MR. ZUSS.   I know.
NICKLES. But worthy of me? Worthy of
                                        me!
MR. ZUSS. I have offended you. I didn't
                                        mean to.
NICKLES. Did I say I was offended?
(*There is an awkward silence.* NICKLES,
*his face in his hands, begins to hum the
tune to his little song.* MR. ZUSS *looks up
and around into the corners of the sky,
his head moving cautiously. At length*
NICKLES *begins to sing the words.*)
I heard upon his dry dung heap
That man cry out who cannot sleep:
"If God is God He is not good,
If God is good He is not God;
Take the even, take the odd,
I would not sleep here if I could . . ."
(*Silence.*)
So I play opposite to God!
(*Silence.*)
Father of Lies they call me, don't they?

(MR. ZUSS *does not answer. He is still searching the dark above. Silence.* NICKLES *goes back to the song.*)
"I would not sleep here if I could
Except for the little green leaves in the
wood
And the wind on the water."
(*Silence. Then suddenly, theatrically,* NICKLES *is on his feet.*)
Who knows enough to know they're lies?
Show me the mask!
MR. ZUSS.   What mask?
NICKLES (*attitude*).   My mask!
MR. ZUSS. Are you sure you wear a mask?
NICKLES. Meaning only God should wear
one?
MR. ZUSS. Meaning are you sure it's there.
NICKLES. *They* never play without them.
MR. ZUSS.   Yes but
Where?
NICKLES. Where? In Heaven probably:
Up on the platform there in Heaven!
MR. ZUSS. Yes . . . You wouldn't care
to . . .
NICKLES.   What?
MR. ZUSS. Find it for yourself?
NICKLES.   In Heaven?
Heaven is your department, Garrick.
MR. ZUSS. My department! I suppose it is.
Here! Hold this! Hold it! Steady . . .
(NICKLES *steadies the ladder.* MR. ZUSS *climbs warily, keeping his eye on the canvas darkness; heaves himself over the rail; rummages around on the platform; turns, holding out a huge white, blank, beautiful, expressionless mask with eyes lidded like the eyes of the mask in Michelangelo's* Night.)
NICKLES. That's not mine—not *his.* It's
His.
I've known that face before. I've seen it.
They find it under bark of marble
Deep within the rinds of stone:
God the Creator . . . (*nastily*) of the
animals!
MR. ZUSS (*outraged*).   God of
Everything that is or can!
NICKLES. Is or can—but cannot know.
MR. ZUSS. There is nothing those closed
eyes
Have not known and seen.
NICKLES.   Except
To know they see: to know they've seen
it.
Lions and dolphins have such eyes.
They know the way the wild geese
know—

Those pin-point travelers who go home
To Labradors they never meant to,
Unwinding the will of the world like
string.
What would they make of a man, those
eyelids?
MR. ZUSS. Make of him! They *made* him.
NICKLES.   Made him
Animal like any other
Calculated for the boughs of
Trees and meant to chatter and be grate-
ful!
But womb-worm wonders and grows
wings—
(NICKLES *breaks off, struck by his own words, goes on:*)
It actually does! The cock-eyed things
Dream themselves into a buzz
And drown on windowpanes. He made
them
Wingless but they learn to wish.
That's why He fumbles Job. Job wishes!—
Thinks there should be justice some-
where—
Beats his bones against the glass.
Justice! In this cesspool! Think of it!
Job knows better when it's over.
MR. ZUSS. Job knows justice when it's over.
Justice has a face like this.
NICKLES. Like blinded eyes?
MR. ZUSS.   Like skies.
NICKLES.   Of stone.
Show me the other.
(MR. ZUSS *ducks away, rummaging in the clutter on the platform; turns again.*)
MR. ZUSS.   You won't find it
Beautiful, you understand.
NICKLES.   I know that.
Beauty's the Creator's bait.
Not the Uncreator's: his
Is Nothing, the no-face of Nothing
Grinning with its not-there eyes.
Nothing at all! Nothing ever! . . .
Never to have been at all!
(MR. ZUSS *turns, lifts the second mask above* NICKLES' *gesturing. This is large as the first but dark to the other's white, and open-eyed where the other was lidded. The eyes, though wrinkled with laughter, seem to stare and the mouth is drawn down in agonized disgust.*)
MR. ZUSS. Well?
(NICKLES *is silent.*)
MR. ZUSS (*cheerfully*).
That's it.
(*Silence.*)
          You don't care for it?

It's not precisely the expression
Anyone would choose. I know that.
Evil is never very pretty:
Spitefulness either. Nevertheless it's
His—you'll grant that, won't you?—the
                                    traditional
Face we've always found for him anyway.
God knows where we go to find it:
Some subterranean memory probably.
(NICKLES *has approached the ladder, star-*
ing. He does not reply.)
Well, if you won't you won't. It's your
Option. I can't say I blame you.
I wouldn't do it. Fit my face to
That! I'd scrub the skin off afterward!
Eyes to those eyes!
NICKLES (*harshly*).   You needn't worry.
Your beaux yeux would never bear that
Look of . . .
MR. ZUSS (*smugly*). No. I know.
NICKLES.   . . . of pity!
Let me have it.
(NICKLES *starts up the ladder, the mask in*
MR. ZUSS's *hands above him.*)
                    Evil you call it!
Look at those lips: they've tasted some-
                                    thing
Bitter as a broth of blood
And spat the sup out. Was that evil?
(*He climbs another rung.*)
Was it?
(*Another rung.*)
            Spitefulness you say:
You call that grin of anguish spite?
(*He pulls himself over the rail, takes the*
mask in his hands.)
I'd rather wear this look of loathing
Night after night than wear that other
Once—that cold complacence . . .
(MR. ZUSS *has picked up the first mask*
again, lifts it.)
NICKLES.   Horrible!
Horrible as a star above
A burning, murdered, broken city!
I'll play the part! . . .
                    Put your mask on! . . .
Give me the lines! . . .   .
MR. ZUSS.   What lines?
NICKLES   His!
Satan's!
MR. ZUSS. They're in the Bible aren't
                                    they?
NICKLES. We're supposed to speak the
                                    Bible?
MR. ZUSS. *They* do . . .
(*The light bulbs fade out, yellow to red*
to gone. A slow, strong glow spots the

platform throwing gigantic shadows up
across the canvas. Back to back the shad-
ows of MR. ZUSS *and* NICKLES *adjust their*
masks. The masked shadows turn to each
other and gravely bow. Their gestures
are the stiff formal gestures of panto-
mime. Their voices, when they speak,
are so magnified and hollowed by the
masks that they scarcely seem their own.)
GODMASK. *Whence comest thou?*
SATANMASK. *From going to and fro in*
                            the earth
(*There is a snicker of suppressed laugh-*
ter.)
And from walking up and down in it . . .
(*A great guffaw.* MR. ZUSS *tears off his*
mask.)
MR. ZUSS (*shouting*).   Lights!
(*The spotlight fades out. The dangling*
bulbs come feebly on.)
Nobody told you to laugh like that.
What's so funny? It's irreverent. It's im-
                                    pudent.
After all, you are talking to God.
That doesn't happen every Saturday
Even to kitchen kin like you.
Take that face off! It's indecent!
Makes me feel like scratching somewhere!
(NICKLES *painfully removes his mask.*)
NICKLES. Do I look as though I'd laughed?
If you had seen what I have seen
You'd never laugh again! . . .
(*He stares at his mask.*)
                    Weep either . . .
MR. ZUSS. You roared. I heard you.
NICKLES.   Those eyes *see.*
MR. ZUSS. Of course they see—beneath the
                                    trousers
Stalking up the pulpit stair:
Under the skirts at tea—wherever
Decent eyes would be ashamed to.
Why should you laugh at that?
NICKLES.   It isn't
That! It isn't that at all!
They see the *world.* They do. They see it.
From going to and fro in the earth,
From walking up and down, they see it.
I know what Hell is now—to *see.*
Consciousness of consciousness . . .
MR. ZUSS.   Now
Listen! This is a simple scene.
I play God. You play Satan.
God is asking where you've been.
All you have to do is tell him:
Simple as that. "In the earth," you an-
                                    swer.

NICKLES. *Satan* answers.

MR. ZUSS.　　　All right—Satan.
What's the difference?

NICKLES.　　　　Satan *sees.*
He sees the parked car by the plane tree.
He sees behind the fusty door,
Beneath the rug, those almost children
Struggling on the awkward seat—
Every impossible delighted dream
She's ever had of loveliness, of wonder,
Spilled with her garters to the filthy floor.
Absurd despair! Ridiculous agony!
(*He looks at the mask in his hands.*)
What has any man to laugh at!
The panting crow by the dry tree
Drags dusty wings. God's mercy brings
The rains—but not to such as he.

MR. ZUSS. You play your part, I'll say
　　　　　　　　　that for you.
In it or out of it, you play.

NICKLES. You really think I'm playing?

MR. ZUSS.　　　　　　Aren't you?
Somebody is. Satan maybe.
Maybe Satan's playing *you.*
Let's begin from the beginning.
Ready!
(*They take their places back to back.*)
Masks!
(*They raise their masks to their faces.*)
Lights!
(*The bulbs go out. Darkness. Silence. In
the silence:*)

A DISTANT VOICE.　　*Whence comest thou?*

MR. ZUSS. That's my line.

NICKLES.　　　I didn't speak it.

MR. ZUSS. You did. Stop your mischief,
　　　　　　　　　won't you?

NICKLES. Stop your own! Laughing.
　　　　　　　　　Shouting.

MR. ZUSS. Lights, I said!
(*The spotlight throws the enormous
shadows on the canvas sky.*)

GODMASK.　　　Whence comest thou?

SATANMASK. *From going to and fro in
　　　　　　　　the earth* . . .
(*A choked silence.*)
And from walking up and down in it.

GODMASK. *Hast thou considered my serv-
　　　　　　　　ant Job
That there is none like him on the earth
A perfect and an upright man, one
That feareth God and escheweth evil?*
(*The platform lights sink, the masked
shadows fading with them, as a strong
light comes on below isolating the table
where* J.B. *stands with his wife and children.*)

SCENE ONE

*The Platform is in darkness, the Table
in light.* J.B., *a big, vigorous man in his
middle or late thirties, stands at one end.
At the other stands his wife,* SARAH, *a
few years younger than her husband, a
fine woman with a laughing, pretty face
but a firm mouth and careful eyes, all
New England. She is looking reprovingly
but proudly at her five blond sons and
daughters, who shift from foot to foot behind their chairs, laughing and nudging
each other:* DAVID, *13;* MARY, *12;* JONA-
THAN, *10;* RUTH, *8;* REBECCA, *6. Two
buxom, middle-aged maids in frilly aprons
stand behind with their hands folded.
The children subside under their mother's
eyes.*

SARAH. J.B. . . .
(*The heads bow.*)

J.B.　　Our Father which art in Heaven
Give us this day our daily bread.

REBECCA *and* RUTH (*pulling their chairs
out, clattering into them*). Amenamen.

THE OLDER CHILDREN (*less haste but no
　　　　　　　　less eagerness*). Amen!

THE MAIDS (*wheeling majestically but ur-
　　　　　　　　gently to go out*). Amen!

SARAH (*to* J.B. *over the rattle of dishes
and the clatter of talk as she sits down*).
That was short and sweet, my darling.

J.B. (*sitting down*). What was?

SARAH.　　　　　Grace was.

J.B. (*cheerfully*).　　All the essentials.

SARAH. Give? Eat?

J.B.　　　Besides they're hungry.

SARAH. That's what grace is for—the
　　　　　　　　hunger.
Mouth and meat by grace amazed,
God upon my lips is praised.

J.B. You think they stand in need of it
　　　　　　　　　—grace?
Look at them!

SARAH (*beaming*).　Yes! Look! Oh look!
(*The maids parade in with a huge turkey
on a silver platter, china serving dishes
with domed, blue covers, a gravy boat, a
bottle of wine in a napkin.*)

MARY. Papá! Papá! He heard! He heard!

DAVID. Who did?

RUTH.　　Ourfatherwhichartinheaven.

J.B. (*nudging the bird gently with his
finger*). He did indeed. What a bird He
　　　　　　　　　sent us!
Cooked to a turn!

RUTH.　　　　He heard! He heard!

JONATHAN. He heard! He heard! He sent
a bird!

SARAH. That's enough now, children.
Quiet!
Your father's counting.

J.B.   Not today.
Not this gobbler. Feed a regiment.
Know what I was thinking, Sally?

SARAH. What?

J.B.   How beautiful you are.

SARAH. With your eye on a turkey? I like
that!

J.B. Why not? It's an eye-filling bird.
Just look at it.

SARAH. Someday you might look at *me*.

J.B. I'm always looking at you, Sarah.
(*He rises, knife and steel in hand, clash-
ing them against each other in a noble
rhythm.*)
Everywhere I look I see you.

SARAH (*scornfully*).
You never even see my clothes.

J.B. (*a shout of laughter*). It's true. I
don't. But I see *you*.

SARAH (*mock indignation*). J! B!

J.B. And what's wrong with the turkey?
What's wrong with that bottle of wine,
either—
Montrachet or I'll drink the whole of it!
What's wrong with the bird or the wine
or with anything—
The day either—what's wrong with the
day?
(*He begins carving expertly and rapidly.*)
Tell me what day it is.

JONATHAN.   Turkey Day.

MARY. Cranberry Day.

RUTH.   Succotash Day.

DAVID. When we all can have white

JONATHAN.   And giblets to bite.

RUTH. And two kinds of pie.

JONATHAN.   And squash in your eye.

MARY. And mashed potatoes with puddles
of butter.

JONATHAN. And gravy and such.

REBECCA.   . . . and . . . and . . .
(*The children are screaming with laughter.*)

SARAH. Children!

JONATHAN (*gasping*).   And all eat too
much.

SARAH.   Children!
Quiet! Quiet every one of you or
Kate will take it all—everything—
Knives, forks, turkey, glasses . . .

J.B. Not the wine though.

SARAH.   Job, I'm serious.

Answer your father's question, Jonathan.
Tell him what day it is.

JONATHAN (*hushed*).   Thanksgiving.

SARAH. What day is that?

JONATHAN.   Thanksgiving Day.

DAVID. The Day we give thanks to God.

MARY.   For His goodness.

SARAH. And did you, David? Did you,
Mary?
Has any one of you thanked God?
Really thanked Him?
(*There is an awkward silence.*)
Thanked Him for everything?
(*The children's heads are down.* J.B.
busies himself with his carving.)

SARAH (*gently*). God doesn't give all this
for nothing:
A good home, good food,
Father, mother, brothers, sisters.
We too have our part to play.
If we do our part He does His,
He always has. If we forget Him
He will forget. Forever. In everything.
David!
(*DAVID raises his head reluctantly.*)
Did you think of God?
(*DAVID does not reply.*)
Did you think, when you woke in your
beds this morning,
Any one of you, of Him?
(*Silence.*)

J.B. (*uncomfortable*). Of course they did.
They couldn't have helped it . . .
Bit of the breast for you, Rebecca?

SARAH. Please, Job. I want them to answer
me.

J.B. How can they answer things like
that?
Gravy? That's the girl . . .
They know though.
Gift of waking, grace of light,
You and the world brought back to-
gether,
You from sleep, the world from night,
By God's great goodness and mercy . . .
Wing for Mary? Wing for Mary! . . .
They know all that. It's hard to talk
about.

SARAH (*flushed, an edge to her voice*).
Even if it's hard we have to.
We can't just take, just eat, just—relish!
Children aren't animals.

J.B. (*he goes on with his serving*).
Sweet Sal! Sweet Sal!
Children know the grace of God
Better than most of us. They see the
world

The way the morning brings it back to
them,
New and born and fresh and wonder-
ful . . .
Ruth? She's always ravenous . . .
                          I remember . . .
Jonathan? He never is . . .
                          . . . when I was
Ten I used to stand behind
The window watching when the light
                                began,
Hidden and watching.
                      That's for David—
Dark and thin.
MARY.   Why? Why hidden?
J.B. Hidden from the trees of course.
I must have thought the trees would see
                                        me
Peeking at them and turn back.
REBECCA. Back where?
J.B. Back where they came from, baby.
That's for your mother: crisp and gold.
RUTH. Father, you'd be cold. You didn't.
SARAH (*the edge still there*).
He still does. He lies there watching
Long before I see the light—
Can't bear to miss a minute of it:
Sun at morning, moon at night,
The last red apple, the first peas!
I've never seen the dish he wouldn't
Taste and relish and want more of:
People either!
J.B. (*serving himself with heaping
             spoons*). Come on, Sal!
Plenty of people I don't like.
(*He sits down. Pours himself a glass of
wine.*)
I like their being people though . . .
(*Sips his wine.*)
Trying to be.
SARAH.   You're hungry for them—
Any kind. People and vegetables:
Any vegetables so long as
Leaves come out on them. He loves
                                leaves!
J.B. You love them too. You love them
                                better.
Just because you know their names
You think you choose among your flowers:
Well, you don't. You love the lot of
                                them.
SARAH. I can't take them as a gift though:
I owe for them. We do. We *owe*.
J.B. Owe for the greening of the leaves?
SARAH.   Please!
Please, Job. I want the children
Somehow to understand this day, this . . .

Feast . . .
(*Her voice breaks.*)
J.B. Forgive me, Sal. I'm sorry—but they
Do. They understand. A little.
Look at me, all of you.
                  Ruth, you answer:
Why do we eat all this, these dishes,
All this food?
(RUTH *twists her napkin.*)
                  You say, Rebecca.
You're the littlest of us all.
Why?
REBECCA.   Because it's good?
SARAH.   Baby!
Ah, my poor baby!
J.B.   Why your poor baby?
She's right, isn't she? It is. It's good.
SARAH. Good—and God has sent it to us!
J.B. She knows that.
SARAH.   Does she?
(*She raises her head sharply.*)
                          Job! . . .
                                  do *you*?
(*Their eyes meet; hers drop.*)
Oh, I think you do . . .
                      but sometimes—
Times like this when we're together—
I get frightened, Job . . .
                        we have so
Much!
J.B. (*dead serious*). You ought to think
                                  I do.
Even if no one else should, you should.
Never since I learned to tell
My shadow from my shirt, not once,
Not for a watch-tick, have I doubted
God was on my side, was good to me.
Even young and poor I knew it.
People called it luck: it wasn't.
I never thought so from the first
Fine silver dollar to the last
Controlling interest in some company
I couldn't get—and got. It isn't
Luck.
MARY.   That's in the story.
JONATHAN.   Tell the
Story.
RUTH.   Tell the lucky story.
REBECCA. Lucky, lucky, tell the lucky.
J.B. (*getting to his feet again to carve*).
Tell the story?
                  Drumstick, David?
Man enough to eat a drumstick?
You too, Jonathan?
REBECCA.   Story, story.
J.B. Fellow came up to me once in a
                                restaurant:

"J.B.," he says—I knew him . . .
Mary, want the other wing?
"Why do you get the best of the rest of
us?"
Fellow named Foley, I think, or Sullivan:
New-come man he was in town.
MARY. Your turn, Mother.
SARAH.   Patrick Sullivan.
J.B. AND THE CHILDREN (*together in a
shouted chant*).
Patrick Sullivan, that's the man!
J.B. "Why do you get the best of the rest
of us?
I've got as many brains as you.
I work as hard. I keep the lamp lit.
Luck! That's what it is," says Sullivan.
"Look!" I said. "Look out the window!"
"What do you see?" "The street," he tells
me.
J.B. AND THE CHILDREN (*as before*).
"The street?" says I. "The street," says he.
J.B. "What do you want me to call it?"
he asks me.
"What do I want you to call it?" says I.
"A road," says I. "It's going somewhere."
"Where?" says he. "You say," I said to
him.
J.B. AND THE CHILDREN.
"God knows!" says Mr. Sullivan.
J.B. "He does," says I. "That's where it's
going.
That's where I go too. That's why."
"Why what?" says he. "I get the best of
you:
It's God's country, Mr. Sullivan."
J.B. AND THE CHILDREN.
"God forbid!" says Mr. Sullivan.
J.B. I laughed till I choked. He only
looked at me.
"Lucky so-and-so," he yells.
SARAH. Poor Mr. Sullivan.
J.B. (*soberly*).   He was wrong.
It isn't luck when God is good to you.
It's something more. It's like those dizzy
Daft old lads who dowse for water.
They feel the alder twig twist down
And know they've got it and they have:
They've got it. Blast the ledge and water
Gushes at you. And they knew.
It wasn't luck. They knew. They felt the
Gush go shuddering through their shoul-
ders, huge
As some mysterious certainty of opulence.
They couldn't hold it. I can't hold it.
(*He looks at* SARAH.)
I've always known that God was with
me.

I've tried to show I knew it—not
Only in words.
SARAH (*touched*).   Oh, you have,
I know you have. And it's ridiculous,
Childish, and I shouldn't be afraid . . .
Not even now when suddenly everything
Fills to overflowing in me
Brimming the fulness till I feel
My happiness impending like a danger.
If ever anyone deserved it, you do.
J.B. That's not true. I don't deserve it.
It's not a question of deserving.
SARAH. Oh, it is. That's all the question.
However could we sleep at night . . .
J.B. Nobody *deserves* it, Sarah:
Not the world that God has given us.
(*There is a moment's strained silence,
then* J.B. *is laughing.*)
J.B. But I believe in it, Sal. I trust in it.
I trust my luck—my life—our life—
God's goodness to me.
SARAH (*trying to control her voice*). Yes!
you do!
I know you do! And that's what frightens
me!
It's not so simple as all that. It's not.
They mustn't think it is. God punishes.
God rewards and God can punish.
God is just.
J.B. (*easy again*). Of course He's just.
He'll never change. A man can count on
Him.
Look at the world, the order of it,
The certainty of day's return
And spring's and summer's: the leaves'
green—
That never cheated expectation.
SARAH (*vehemently*). God can reward
and God can punish.
Us He has rewarded. Wonderfully.
Given us everything. Preserved us.
Kept us from harm, each one—each one.
And why? Because of you . . .
(J.B. *raises his head sharply.*)
SARAH.   No!
Let me say it! Let me say it!
I need to speak the words that say it—
I need to hear them spoken. Nobody,
Nobody knows of it but me.
You never let them know: not anyone—
Even your children. They don't know.
(J.B. *heaves himself out of his chair,
swings round the table, leans over* SARAH,
his arms around her.)
J.B. Eat your dinner, Sal my darling.
We love our life because it's good:
It isn't good because we love it—

Pay for it—in thanks or prayers. The
thanks are
Part of love and paid like love:
Free gift or not worth having.
You know that, Sal . . .
(*He kisses her.*)
better than anyone.
Eat your dinner, girl! There's not a
Harpy on the roof for miles.
(*She reaches up to touch his cheek with
her hand.*)
SARAH. Nevertheless it's true, Job. You
Can trust your luck because you've earned
the
Right to trust it: earned the right
For all of us to trust it.
J.B. (*back at his own place, filling his
glass again*). Nonsense!
We get the earth for nothing, don't we?
It's given to us, gift on gift:
Sun on the floor, airs in the curtain.
We lie a whole day long and look at it
Crowing or crying in our cribs:
It doesn't matter—crow or cry
The sun shines, the wind blows . . .
Rebecca! Back for more already?
REBECCA. I want the wishbone please.
J.B. Whatever
For?
REBECCA. To wish.
SARAH. For what, my baby?
REBECCA. For the wishbone.
SARAH (*pulling REBECCA into her lap*).
Little pig!
Wishing for wishes!
J.B. (*forking the wishbone onto Rebec-
ca's plate*). That's my girl!
SARAH. She is! The spit and image of you!
Thinking she can eat the world
With luck and wishes and no thanks!
J.B. That isn't fair. We're thankful, both
of us.
SARAH (*cuddling REBECCA*).
Both! And both the same! Just look at
you!
A child shows gratitude the way a woman
Shows she likes a pretty dress—
Puts it on and takes it off again—
That's the way a child gives thanks:
She tries the world on. So do you.
J.B. God understands that language,
doesn't He?
He should. He made the colts.
SARAH. But you're not
Colts! You talk. With tongues. Or ought
to.
J.B. And we use them, don't we, baby?

We love Monday, Tuesday, Wednesday.
SARAH (*rocking REBECCA on her knees*).
We love Monday, Tuesday, Wednesday.
Where have Monday, Tuesday, gone?
Under the grass tree,
Under the green tree,
One by one.
JONATHAN. Say it again, Mother . . .
Mother!
SARAH. I never said it before. I don't
Know . . .
How would you think it would go?
How does it go, Job? You said it.
J.B. I didn't. I said we loved the world:
Monday, Tuesday, Wednesday, all of it.
SARAH. How would you think it would
go, Jonathan?
(*The words fall into a little tune as she
repeats them.*)
I love Monday, Tuesday, Wednesday.
Where have Monday, Tuesday, gone?
Under the grass tree,
Under the green tree,
One by one.
Caught as we are in Heaven's quandary,
Is it they or we are gone
Under the grass tree,
Under the green tree?
I love Monday, Tuesday, Wednesday.
One by one.
REBECCA (*drowsily*). Say it again.
SARAH. Say it again?
JONATHAN. You say it, Father.
J.B. To be, become, and end are beauti-
ful.
REBECCA. That's not what she said at all.
J.B. Isn't it? Isn't it?
SARAH (*kissing her*). Not at all.
(*The light fades, leaving the two shadows
on the canvas sky.*)

SCENE TWO

*The Platform. As the platform light
comes on, the figures fade from the canvas sky and* MR. ZUSS *and* NICKLES
*straighten up, lifting their masks off,
stretching, yawning.*

———

MR. ZUSS. Well, that's our pigeon.
NICKLES. Lousy actor.
MR. ZUSS. Doesn't really act at all.
NICKLES. Just eats.
MR. ZUSS. And talks.
NICKLES. The love of life!
Poisoning their little minds
With love of life! At that age!

MR. ZUSS.   No!
Some of that, I thought, was beautiful.
NICKLES. Best thing you can teach your
                                    children
Next to never drawing breath
Is choking on it.
MR. ZUSS   Who said that?
Someone's spoiled philosophy, it sounds
                                    like:
Intellectual butter a long war
And too much talking have turned rancid.
I thought he made that small familiar
Feast a true thanksgiving . . . only . . .
NICKLES. Only what?
MR. ZUSS.   Something went wrong.
NICKLES. That's what I've been telling
                                    you.
MR. ZUSS.   He didn't
Act.
NICKLES.   He can't. He's not an actor.
MR. ZUSS. I wonder if he knows?
NICKLES.   Knows what?
MR. ZUSS. Knows that he's in it?
NICKLES.   Is he?
MR. ZUSS.   Certainly.
NICKLES. How can you tell?
MR. ZUSS.   That's him. That's Job.
He has the wealth, the wife, the children,
Position in the world.
NICKLES.   The piety!
MR. ZUSS. He loves God, if that's what
                            you're saying.
A perfect and an upright man.
NICKLES. Piety's hard enough to take
Among the poor who *have* to practice it.
A rich man's piety stinks. It's insuffer-
                                    able.
MR. ZUSS. You're full of fatuous aphorisms,
                            aren't you!
A poor man's piety is hope of having:
A rich man *has* his—and he's grateful.
NICKLES. Bought and paid for like a
                            waiter's smirk!
You know what talks when that man's
                            talking?
All that gravy on his plate—
His cash—his pretty wife—his children!
Lift the lot of them, he'd sing
Another canticle to different music.
MR. ZUSS. That's what Satan says—but
                                    better.
NICKLES. It's obvious. No one needs to
                                    say it.
MR. ZUSS. You don't like him.
NICKLES.   I don't have to.
You're the one who has to like him.
MR. ZUSS. I thought you spoke of Job

with sympathy.
NICKLES. Job on his dung hill, yes. That's
                                    human.
That makes sense. But this world-master,
This pious, flatulent, successful man
Who feasts on turkey and thanks God!—
He sickens me!
MR. ZUSS.   Of course he sickens you,
He trusts the will of God and loves—
(MR. ZUSS *is swollen with indignation and
rhetoric. He swoops his mask up from
the rail with a magnificent gesture, holds
it.*)
Loves a woman who must sometime,
                                somewhere,
Later, sooner, leave him; fixes
All his hopes on little children
One night's fever or a running dog
Could kill between the dark and day;
Plants his work, his enterprise, his labor,
Here where every planted thing
Fails in its time but still he plants it . . .
NICKLES (*nastily*). God will teach him
                            better won't He?
God will show him what the world is
                                    like—
What man's like—the ignoble creature,
Victim of the spinning joke!
MR. ZUSS. Teach him better than he knows!
God will show him God!
NICKLES (*shrugging*).   It's the same
Thing. It hurts.
MR. ZUSS (*gathering momentum*). God
                            will teach him!
God will show him what God *is*—
Enormous pattern of the steep of stars,
Minute perfection of the frozen crystal,
Inimitable architecture of the slow,
Cold, silent, ignorant sea-snail:
The unimaginable will of stone:
Infinite mind in midge of matter!
NICKLES. Infinite mush! Wait till your
                                    pigeon
Pecks at the world the way the rest do—
Eager beak to naked bum!
MR. ZUSS. You ought to have your tongue
                            torn out!
NICKLES. All men should: to suffer si-
                            lently.
MR. ZUSS. Get your mask back on! I tell
                                    you
Nothing this good man might suffer,
Nothing at all, would make him yelp
As you do. He'd praise God no matter.
NICKLES (*whispering*).
Why must he suffer then?
(*The question catches* MR. ZUSS *with his*

mask halfway to his face. He lowers it
slowly, staring into it as though the
answer might be written inside.)
MR. ZUSS (*too loud*).   To praise!
NICKLES (*softly*). He praises now. Like
a canary.
(MR. ZUSS *lifts his mask again.*)
MR. ZUSS. Well, will you put it on or
won't you?
NICKLES. Shall I tell you why?
(*violently*)   To learn!
Every human creature born
Is born into the bright delusion
Beauty and loving-kindness care for him.
Suffering teaches! Suffering's good for
us!
Imagine men and women dying
Still believing that the cuddling arms
Enclosed them! They would find the
worms
Peculiar nurses, wouldn't they? Wouldn't
they?
(*He breaks off; picks his mask up; goes
on in a kind of jigging chant half to
himself.*)
What once was cuddled must learn to kiss
The cold worm's mouth. That's all the
mystery.
That's the whole muddle. Well, we learn
it.
God is merciful and we learn it . . .
We learn to wish we'd never lived!
MR. ZUSS. This man will not.
NICKLES.   Won't he? Won't he?
Shall I tell you how it ends?
Shall I prophesy? I see our
Smug world-master on his dung heap,
Naked, miserable, and alone,
Pissing the stars. Ridiculous gesture!—
Nevertheless a gesture—meaning
All there is on earth to mean:
Man's last word . . . and worthy of him!
MR. ZUSS. This man will not. He trusts
God.
No matter how it ends, he trusts Him.
NICKLES. Even when God tests him?—
tortures him?
MR. ZUSS. Would God permit the test
unless
He knew the outcome of the testing?
NICKLES. Then why test him if God
knows?
MR. ZUSS. So Job can see.
NICKLES.   See what?
MR. ZUSS.   See God.
NICKLES. A fine sight from an ash heap,
certainly!

MR. ZUSS. Isn't there anything you under-
stand?
It's from the ash heap God is seen
Always! Always from the ashes.
Every saint and martyr knew that.
NICKLES. And so he suffers to see God:
Sees God because he suffers. Beautiful!
MR. ZUSS. Put on your mask. I'd rather
look at . . .
NICKLES. I should think you would! A
human
Face would shame the mouth that said
that!
(*They put their masks on fiercely, stand-
ing face to face. The platform light fades
out. The spotlight catches them, throwing
the two masked shadows out and up.
The voices are magnified and hollow,
the gestures formal, as at the end of the
Prologue.*)
GODMASK. *Hast thou considered my serv-
ant Job*
*That there is none like him on the earth,
A perfect and an upright man, one
That feareth God and escheweth evil?*
SATANMASK (*sardonic*).
Doth Job fear God for naught?
(*The* GOD-SHADOW *turns away in a ges-
ture of anger.*)
SATANMASK (*deprecatingly*).
*Hast thou not made an hedge about him
And about his house
And about all that he hath on every side?
Thou hast blessed the work of his hands
And his substance is increased.*
(*The voice drops.*)
*But put forth thine hand now and touch
All that he hath . . .*
(*The voice becomes a hissing whisper.*)
and he will
Curse thee to thy face!
GODMASK (*in a furious, great voice, arm
thrown out in a gesture of contemptuous
commitment*).
Behold!
All that he hath is in thy power!
(*The* SATAN-SHADOW *bows mockingly;
raises its two arms, advancing until the
shadows become one shadow. The light
fades. Suddenly, out of the darkness the*
DISTANT VOICE *of the Prologue.*)
THE DISTANT VOICE.   *Only . . .*
(*Silence.*)
GODMASK. *Only*
Upon himself
Put not forth thy hand!
(*Darkness. The crash of a drum; a single*

stroke. Silence.)

NOTE: *The play is conceived and written without breaks, but if recesses in the action are desired one might well be made at this point.*

SCENE THREE

The Table. As the lights come on the two leaning shadows, one thrown upon the other, are visible on the canvas sky. They fade as the scene brightens. The table has been pushed to one side as though against a window in a living room. SARAH *stands before it arranging flowers in a bowl.* J.B. *is straddling a chair, watching.*

SARAH. Look, Job! Look! Across the street. Two soldiers.

J.B.   What about them?

SARAH.   Only they
Stare so.

J.B.   Stare at what?

SARAH.   The house.
I think they're drunk . . . A little.

(J.B. *rises, stands beside her, his arm around her waist.*)

J.B.   Plastered!

SARAH. One of them anyway. He wobbles.

J.B. That's no wobble. That's a waltz step.

SARAH. They're crossing over.

J.B.   They sure are.

SARAH. What do you think they . . .

J.B.   Listen!

SARAH.   Yes . . .
What do you think they want, two soldiers?

J.B. No idea. Johnson will tend to them.

SARAH. I've never seen such staring eyes.

J.B. Glazed. Just glazed.

SARAH.   They keep on ringing.
I know what it is, J.B.,
They have some kind of message for us.
David has sent them with a message—
Something about his regiment. They're coming
Every day now, ship by ship.
I hear them in the harbor coming.
He couldn't write and so he sent them.

J.B. Pretty drunk for messengers, those soldiers.

SARAH. What does it matter. They're just boys.

They've just got home. It doesn't matter.

J.B. Johnson's a judge of drunks. He'll handle them.

SARAH. He mustn't send them off. Don't let him!

(*There is a commotion outside the canvas door. A voice, off.*)

VOICE. Two young . . . gentlemen to see you.
Friends, they say, of Mr. David.

SARAH. Oh, I knew! I knew! I knew!

VOICE (*off*). That's telling him, Puss-foot!

VOICE (*off*).   Puss-face!

(*The two* MESSENGERS *enter, dressed as soldiers. The* FIRST *is flushed and loud; the* SECOND, *very drunk, pale as bone.*)

J.B. Come in, gentlemen. Come in. Come in.
David's friends are always welcome.
This is David's mother.

SARAH.   Won't you sit
Down?

FIRST MESSENGER. What did I tell you, Punk!
Any friends of David's.

SECOND MESSENGER.   Any at
All . . .

FIRST M.   I told you that boy meant it.
What did I say when I see the joint?
That's the number, Punk, I told you.
Old Ten Twenty: that's the number.

(*He turns to* SARAH.)
Twenty if you're men, he told us—
Ten for horses' whatses. What the
Hell, he always said: we're friends.

SECOND M. Any at all he always . . .

FIRST M.   Pardon the
Language, lady.

SECOND M.   Any a' . . .

SARAH.   There!
Sit down.

FIRST M. It's just, we saw the number.

SARAH. And David asked you to drop in.

FIRST M.   Any friend of his, he told us.
Any time.

SECOND M.   And we were cold:
A cold, hard march . . .

FIRST M.   What the
Hell's the matter with *you!* You drunk?

SARAH. Sit by the fire, both of you. Where was he?

FIRST M. Where was who?

SARAH.   David.

FIRST M.   When?

J.B. When he told you.

FIRST M.   In the mess.
Any friend of his, he told us.

Any time at all. Why?
You think we're lying to you?
J.B.   Certainly
Not.
FIRST M. You think we never knew him?
SARAH. Of course. Of course you do.
FIRST M.   We knew him.
SECOND M. Fumbling among the faces . . .
                              knew him . . .
Night . . . our fingers numb . . .
FIRST M.   Will you shut
Up or will I clout you, Big Mouth!
(*To* SARAH.)
That's why we come: because we knew
                                  him.
To tell you how we knew him.
SARAH.   Thank you.
(*Silence.*)
SECOND M. How it was with him . . .
FIRST M.   Listen, Punk!
SECOND M. How, by night, by chance,
                              darkling . . .
By the dark of chance . . .
FIRST M.   He's drunk.
SECOND M. How, the war done, the guns
                              silent . . .
No one knows who gave the order.
FIRST M. (*raising his voice*).
Like I say, because he said to.
Any friend of his he said to.
Just to tell you we knew David:
Maybe drink to David maybe . . .
SARAH. Yes! Oh yes! Let's drink to David!
J.B.!
J.B.   Bourbon? Scotch?
FIRST M.   Now you're
Cooking! Take your pants off, Punk:
We're in.
SARAH.   That's right. Put your feet up.
Oh, they're not too dirty. David's are
Dirtier. I'm sure of that.
FIRST M. David's feet! I'll say they are.
Look! What's going on here! David's
Feet!
SARAH. I meant—with all that marching.
FIRST M. I don't get it. Look, it's true
They didn't have the right length lumber:
We did the best we could . . .
(J.B. *starts to his feet.*)
J.B.   What in
God's name are you saying, soldier?
SARAH (*rising*).
What does he mean, the lumber?
(*Silence.*)
FIRST M.   You don't
Know? Ain't that the army for you!
(*To the* SECOND MESSENGER.)

They don't know. They never told them.
SARAH. Told us what?
FIRST M.   We better go.
SARAH. No! Please! Please! No!
FIRST M. Come on, we're getting out, you
                              lunkhead.
J.B. Not until you've told me. Sarah!
Perhaps you'd better, Sarah . . .
SARAH.   Please,
I want to hear it.
FIRST M.   Jesus! . . . Jesus! . . .
(*There is a long silence. The* SECOND
MESSENGER *turns slowly to* J.B., *his face
drunken white, his eyes blank.*)
SECOND M. *I only am escaped alone to tell
                              thee . . .*
(*The focus of light opens to include the
Platform where* MR. ZUSS *and* NICKLES
*stand staring down, their masks in their
hands.* MR. ZUSS's *face is expressionless.*
NICKLES *wears a twisted grin. The* SEC-
OND MESSENGER's *head falls forward onto
his knees.*)
SECOND M. . . . My tongue loosened by
                              drink . . .
                              my thought
Darkened as by wind the water . . .
That day is lost where it befell . . .
SARAH (*she is holding herself by the
          straining of her clenched hands*).
What is it we were never told?
J.B.   It isn't
True you little drunken liar!
It can't be true! It isn't possible!
(*Silence. The passion ebbs from* J.B.'s
voice.)
We had a letter from him.
(*Silence. Then, uncertainly*)
                              After the
End of it we had a letter. . . .
(NICKLES *jerks a crooked leg over the rail,
starts awkwardly down the ladder, watch-
ing intently, peering back up at* MR. ZUSS,
watching.)
SECOND M. What shall I say to you . . . ?
                    What I saw . . . ?
What I believe I saw . . . ?
                              Or what
I must have seen . . .
                    and have forgotten?
SARAH (*a cry*). David is our son, our son,
                              our son.
NICKLES (*prompting her from his ladder
          in a harsh half-whisper*).
That's the tune. He's ours. Go on with it:
Can't be happening to *us!* Can't be!
God won't let it happen, not to

Our kind, God won't!

(*He leers up at* MR. ZUSS.)

J.B. (*turning* SARAH *away from the* SEC-
OND MESSENGER *into his arms*). Sarah!

                        Sarah!

David's all right. He has to be. He is.
I know he is. The war is over.
It never could have happened—never—
Never in this world.

NICKLES (*the whisper harsher*). Couldn't
                            it?

Ask him! Couldn't it? Suppose it did
                         though:
What would the world be made of then?

SECOND M. I only am escaped alone, com-
                         panions
Fallen, fallen, fallen . . .

                 the earth
Smell remembers that there was a man.

SARAH. Job! He's dead! God has taken
                          him!

(*The focus of light narrows, is extinguished.*)

SCENE FOUR

   *Darkness. Silence. Then the crash of a
drum. Silence again. Then two cigarettes
are lighted, one high above the stage, one
lower. Then gradually the lights come on,
making four circles across the front of
the stage like the circles of sidewalk
brightness under street lamps. Where the
cigarettes were lighted* MR. ZUSS *and*
NICKLES *are now visible on the platform
rail and the ladder, squatting there like
two tramps on the stairs of a stoop, turning their heads together one way and
then the other, watching, not speaking.
After a time the* FIRST MESSENGER *comes
strolling in from their right, a news
camera slung from his neck. The* SECOND
*follows with a notebook. They wear bat-
tered felt hats with their khaki shirts and
trousers. They are followed at a little distance by a stylishly dressed girl.*

———

GIRL. I don't like it.

FIRST MESSENGER.   You'll do fine.

GIRL. I wish I was home in bed with a
                         good
Boy or something. I don't like it.

FIRST M. You'll do fine.

GIRL.   I won't do fine:
I'm frightened.

FIRST M. All you do, you go up to them,
Get them talking, keep them looking.

GIRL. Go up to them yourselves, why
                         don't you?

FIRST M. Sure, and get the brush-off. Girl
                         like
You can keep them talking; keep them
Looking, that is. Pretty girl.

GIRL. I don't like it.

SECOND M.   You'll get used to it.

GIRL. Not where I work. Not Society.
Society page they never die.
Girl gets asked. Girl gets married.
Girl gets photographed in night club.
Girl gets older. Girl gets off.
Never catch them dead on Society.

SECOND M. Like the robins.

FIRST M.   Yeah, like robins.

GIRL. Why the robins?

SECOND M.   Never see one
Dead.

FIRST M.   Nor sparrows neither.

SECOND M.   Either.

FIRST M. Never hardly. Must be millions.

SECOND M. Hardly ever see one dead.

GIRL. What happens to them?

SECOND M.   They get over it.

GIRL. Over what?

SECOND M.   Over being there.

GIRL. All I know is I don't like it.
Keep them talking till a flash bulb
Smacks them naked in the face—
It's horrible!

FIRST M.   It's genius! Listen, lady!
How do I get the photograph without?
Answer me that. How do I get the
Look a mother's face has maybe
Once in a lifetime: just before
Her mouth knows, when her eyes are
                       knowing?

GIRL. I can't do it.

FIRST M.   *She* can't do it!
All you got to do is walk.
Wiggle your can. Keep them looking.
Then he tells them. Then I take them.
Then you beat it. Then that's that.
Except the drink we're going to buy you
Payday evening if you're good—
And if you're not there's lots of liars.

SECOND M. You don't have to tell them: I
                         do.

GIRL. Why do *you*?

SECOND M.   Because I have to.
I'm the one that has to tell them.

GIRL. Why?

SECOND M. (*shrugging*).
       Oh . . .

GIRL.   Why?

SECOND M.   There's always

Someone has to tell them, isn't there?

GIRL.   Someone else can.

SECOND M.   No. There's always . . .

(*He is groping from word to word.*)

Someone chosen by the chance of seeing,
By the accident of sight,
By stumbling on the moment of it,
Unprepared, unwarned, unready,
Thinking of nothing, of his drink, his
                                              bed,
His belly, and it happens, and he sees
                                              it . . .

(*He winces his eyes shut.*)

Caught in that inextricable net
Of having witnessed, having seen . . .
He alone!

GIRL (*gently*).   But you don't have to.

(*To the* FIRST MESSENGER.)

Why does he have to?

SECOND M.   It was I.
I only. I alone. The moment
Closed us together in its gaping grin
Of horrible incredulity. I saw their
Eyes see mine! We *saw* each other!

FIRST M. He has to. He was there. He
                                           saw it.

Route Two. Under the viaduct.
Traveling seventy—seventy-five—
Kid was driving them was drunk,
Had to be drunk, just drove into it.
He was walking home. He saw it.
Saw it start to, saw it had to,
Saw it. J.B.'s son. His daughter.
Four in all and all just kids.
They shrieked like kids he said.

SECOND M.   Then silent.
Blond in all that blood that daughter.

GIRL (*her voice rising*).
He can't tell them *that!*

FIRST M.   He has to.
Someone has to. They don't know.
They been out all evening somewhere.

GIRL (*hysterically*).
They don't have to know!

FIRST M.   They have to.

(NICKLES *and* MR. ZUSS *on their perches
have seen something off to their right.
They turn their heads together.*)

GIRL. No!

FIRST M. (*looking right, pulling his camera
                                           around*).
That's them. They're coming. Quiet!

GIRL. I can't do it.

FIRST M. (*brutally*).   You can do it.

(J.B. *and* SARAH, *arm in arm, walk slowly
into the first circle of light.* NICKLES *and*
MR. ZUSS *lean forward, their masks dan-*

gling from their hands.)

SECOND M. (*under his breath, staring at
                              them as they come*).
I only, I alone, to tell thee . . .
I who have understood nothing, have
                                           known
Nothing, have been answered nothing . . .

GIRL (*crossing to meet them with an af-
fected walk, the* FIRST MESSENGER *screen-
ing himself behind her, the* SECOND *fol-
lowing*).   Good
Evening! What a pleasant evening!
Back from the theatre so soon?
We're neighbors, don't you know? You've
                                           met my
Miffkin walking me each morning:
You know Muff, my purple poodle . . .
Isn't it a pleasant evening!

SECOND M. I'm from the press. There's
                              been an accident . . .

(*He falters.*)

FIRST M. Four kids in a car. They're dead.
Two were yours. Your son. Your daugh-
                                           ter.
Cops have got them in a cab.
Any minute now they'll be here.

(*He raises his camera over the girl's
shoulder.*)

GIRL (*in her own voice, screaming*).
Don't look! Cover your face!

SARAH (*with scarcely the breath to say it*).
Mary . . . Jonathan . . .

(*The flash.* J.B. *throws his elbows up as
if to ward off a blow.* SARAH *does not
move.*)

J.B.   You bastards!
I'll beat your god damned brains out . . .

(*He lunges after them blinded by the
flash as they scatter.*)
                                           Where have you
Gone?

(SARAH *moves like a sleepwalker through
the circles of light, one after the other,
touches a chair, goes down on her knees
beside it, clinging to it.*)

J.B.   Answer me!

(*Silence.*)

J.B.   Answer me!

(*Silence.*)

SARAH (*her voice dead*).   It wasn't
They that did it . . .

(J.B. *comes slowly back out of the darkness, sees her, crosses to her. There is a
long silence,* J.B. *looking right and left
along the street.*)

SARAH.   Why did He do it to them?
What had they done to Him—those chil-

dren . . .
What had they done to Him . . .
         and we—
What had *we* done? . . .
         What had *we* done?
J.B. Don't, Sarah. Don't!
(NICKLES *lights a cigarette, grins back over his shoulder to* MR. ZUSS *in the handful of yellow glare.*)
J.B.   It doesn't
Help to think that.
SARAH.   Nothing helps! . . .
Nothing can help them now.
J.B. (*a clumsy gesture*).   It . . . happened . . .
SARAH (*fiercely*).
Yes, and Who let it happen?
J.B. (*awkwardly*).   Shall we . . .
Take the good and not the evil?
We have to take the chances, Sarah:
Evil with good.
(*Then, in a desperate candor*)
        It doesn't mean there
Is no good!
NICKLES (*in his cracked whisper*).
Doesn't it? Doesn't it?
MR. ZUSS (*silencing* NICKLES *with his hand, his whisper hardly heard*).
Go on! Go on! That path will lead you.
SARAH (*bitterly*). When you were lucky it was God!
J.B. Sticks and stones and steel are chances.
There's no will in stone and steel . . .
(*His voice breaks.*)
It happens to us . . .
(*He drops on his knees beside her.*)
SARAH.   No! . . .
        Don't touch me!
(*She clings to the chair, motionless, not weeping.*)
(*The circles of light fade out.*)

SCENE FIVE

The dark diminishes until the white coats of MR. ZUSS *and* NICKLES *are visible on the platform.* MR. ZUSS *lifts a padded drumstick.* NICKLES *balances on the rail and starts cautiously down the ladder.*

MR. ZUSS. Ready?
NICKLES (*cheerfully*). Got to be, don't they?
MR. ZUSS.   I meant
You.
NICKLES. They've got no choice. Disaster—

Death—mankind are always ready—
Ready for anything that hurts.
MR. ZUSS. And you?
NICKLES.   I too! I too!
MR. ZUSS.   Provided
Someone else will bleed the blood
And wipe the blinded eye?
NICKLES.   I watch
Your world go round!
MR. ZUSS.   It must be wearing.
NICKLES. Oh, it has its compensations.
Even a perfect and an upright man
Learns if you keep turning long enough.
First he thought it wasn't happening—
Couldn't be happening—not to him—
Not with you in the stratosphere tooting the
Blue trombone for the moon to dance.
Then he thought it chanced by chance!
(*a dry hiccup of laughter*)
Childish hypothesis of course
But still hypothesis—a start—
A pair of tongs to take the toad by—
Recognition that it *is* a toad:
Not quite comfort but still comfortable,
Eases the hook in the gills a little:
He'll learn.
MR. ZUSS (*preoccupied*). Learn what?
NICKLES.   Your—purpose for him?
MR. ZUSS. Keep your tongue in your teeth, will you?
(*He notices* NICKLES' *descent on the ladder for the first time.*)
Here! Wait a minute! Wait a
Minute! Where are you off to?
NICKLES.   Bit of a
Walk in the earth for my health—or somebody's.
(*bitterly*)
Up and down in the earth, you know—
Back and forth in it . . .
MR. ZUSS.   Leave him alone!
NICKLES. He needs a helping hand: you've seen that—
A nudge from an old professional.
MR. ZUSS.   Leave him a
Lone! He can't act and you know it.
NICKLES. He doesn't have to act. He suffers.
It's an old role—played like a mouthorgan.
Any idiot on earth
Given breath enough can breathe it—
Given tears enough can weep.
All he needs is help to see.
MR. ZUSS. See what?
NICKLES.   That bloody drum-stick

striking;
See Who lets it strike the drum!
(MR. ZUSS, *whose lifted arm has been
slowly falling, raises it abruptly.*)
MR. ZUSS. Wait!
(*He starts to strike the drum, stops the
stroke in mid-air.*)
    Wait for me. I'm coming.
Down!
    Wait!
        Wait I tell you!
(*The stroke of the drum. The light fades
out.*)

(*Out of the dark two circles of light, one
on the platform, one on the table. Behind
the table are the two* MESSENGERS. *The*
FIRST, *wearing a police sergeant's cap,
sits on a chair. The* SECOND, *wearing a
patrolman's cap, stands beside him.* J.B.,
*a raincoat over rumpled clothes, stands
facing them. Above, on the platform, as
on the landing of a stair,* SARAH *stands
pulling a dressing gown around her
shoulders.* NICKLES *and* MR. ZUSS, *their
masks in their hands, straddle a couple
of chairs beyond the circle of light which
centers on the table.*
FIRST M. Sorry to question you like this.
We got to get the story.
J.B. (*impatiently*).   Go on.
FIRST M. Turning your house into a . . .
J.B.   No. Go on.
It doesn't matter.
SARAH (*toneless*). Nothing matters but to
Know.
FIRST M.   How many children?
(*Silence.*)
J.B.   Two.
FIRST M. (*writing*). Girls?
SARAH.   We had two boys.
FIRST M. (*writing*).   Girls.
Names?
J.B.   Ruth. Rebecca.
SARAH.   Ruth is the
Oldest . . . now.
FIRST M.   And you last saw her?
J.B. Ruth?
SARAH (*her voice rising*).
It's Rebecca is missing!
J.B. (*silencing her*).   He
Knows!
SARAH (*harshly*). No, it's God that knows!
(*There is an awkward silence. When*
SARAH *speaks again her voice is dead.*)
She's the littlest one. She's gone.
FIRST M. How long ago?

SARAH.   Oh . . . hours!
FIRST M. It's three in the morning now.
J.B.   Since seven.
FIRST M. (*writing*).
And you reported it?
J.B.   Yes.
FIRST M.   When?
J.B. One o'clock. A quarter after.
We looked for her everywhere, of course.
Then we thought—I thought—if some-
                body . . .
Maybe the telephone would ring.
FIRST M. And you'd do better on your
                own?
J.B. (*reluctantly*). Yes.
SARAH (*with rising violence*).
            Yes! Yes! Yes!
We believe in our luck in this house!
We've earned the right to! We believe
                in it . . .
(*bitterly*)
All but the bad!
NICKLES (*rocking back on his chair*).
            That's playing it!
That's playing it!
(*He begins to sing in his cracked whis-
per, beating a jazzed rhythm on the back
of his mask as though it were a banjo.*)
If God is Will
And Will is well
Then what is ill?
God still?
Dew tell!
(MR. ZUSS *does not seem to hear. He is
listening intently to the scene at the
table.*)
FIRST M.   And nobody telephoned?
J.B. Nobody telephoned.
FIRST M. (*writing*). Dressed? How was
                she
Dressed?
J.B. (*turning for the first time to look up
                at* SARAH).
        White?
SARAH.   White! You saw her
Glimmering in the twilight.
FIRST M. (*writing*).   White.
SARAH.   All but her
Shoes.
(*The* FIRST MESSENGER *looks up at the*
SECOND.)
FIRST M.   Her shoes were what?
SARAH.   Red.
(*The* FIRST MESSENGER *looks up again.
The* SECOND *turns his face away.*)
FIRST M. Rebecca have a red umbrella?
SARAH. Parasol.

FIRST M. Little toy umbrella.

SARAH (*startled*). Parasol. Yes, she might have had one.

FIRST M. You mean she owned one?

SARAH. Yes. It belonged to a Big doll we bought her once.
Scarlet silk. It opens and closes.
She kept it when the doll gave out.
She used to take it to bed with her even—
Open and close it.

(*The* FIRST MESSENGER *looks up for the third time at the* SECOND, *whose face, still turned away, is like stone.*)

J.B. (*a step forward*). You've found the parasol!

SECOND M. (*not looking at him; a voice without expression or tone*).
What will it tell you? Will it tell you why?

J.B. (*to* FIRST M.). I asked you: have you found the parasol?

FIRST M. He's the one. Ask him. He'll tell you.

SECOND M. (*with difficulty, like a man speaking out of physical pain*).
Can the tooth among the stones make answer? . . .

Can the seven bones reply? . . .

Out in the desert in the tombs
Are potter's figures: two of warriors,
Two of worthies, two of camels,
Two of monsters, two of horses.
Ask them why. They will not answer you . . .

(*He brushes his hand heavily across his face.*)

Death is a bone that stammers . . .

a tooth

Among the flints that has forgotten.

J.B. (*violently*).
Ask him! Has he found the parasol!

FIRST M. We don't know. He found an umbrella—
Doll's umbrella—red.

SARAH. Oh, where?

J.B. Nothing else? Just the umbrella?

FIRST M. (*to* SECOND).
Tell them, will you!

(*The* SECOND MESSENGER *does not move or speak. The* FIRST *shrugs, looks down at his pencil, rattles it off in a matter-of-fact monotone.*)

Just past midnight

Pounding his beat by the back of the lumberyard
Somebody runs and he yells and they stumble—
Big kid—nineteen maybe—
Hopped to the eyes and scared—scared
Bloodless he could barely breathe.
Constable yanks him up by the britches:
"All right! Take me to it!"
Just a shot in the dark, he was so
Goddam scared there had to be something . . .
Well . . .
He took him to it . . .
back of the
Lumber trucks beside the track.

J.B. Go on.

FIRST M. She had a toy umbrella.
That was all she had—but shoes:
Red shoes and a toy umbrella.
It was tight in her fist when he found her —still.

J.B. Let me see it! The umbrella!

FIRST M. Constable will show it to you.

(*The* SECOND MESSENGER *takes something wound in newspaper out of his pocket. He does not look at it or them. The* FIRST MESSENGER *half opens it, lays it on the table.*)

SARAH. Oh, my baby! Oh, my baby!

(*The* FIRST MESSENGER *gets out of his chair, stands a moment awkwardly, goes out. The* SECOND *follows.* J.B. *stands motionless over the table.* SARAH *hugs her dressing gown around her, rocking herself slowly, her head bowed.*)

NICKLES (*leaning forward toward* J.B., *a wheedling whisper*).
Now's the time to say it, mister.

MR. ZUSS. Leave him alone!

J.B. (*touching the parasol*). The Lord giveth . . .

(*His voice breaks.*)

the
Lord taketh away!

MR. ZUSS (*rising, whispering*). Go on!
Go on! Finish it! Finish it!

NICKLES. What should he
Finish when he's said it all?

MR. ZUSS. Go on!

NICKLES. To what? To where? He's got there, hasn't he?
Now he's said it, now he knows.
He knows Who gives, he knows Who takes now.

(J.B. *stands silent over the parasol.*)

MR. ZUSS. Why won't he play the part he's

NICKLES. Because he isn't.

MR. ZUSS. Isn't what?

NICKLES. Isn't playing. He's not playing.
He isn't in the play at all.
He's where we all are—in our suffering.
Only . . .

(NICKLES *turns savagely on* MR. ZUSS.)

. . . Now he knows its Name!

(NICKLES *points dramatically toward the
canvas sky.* MR. ZUSS's *head tilts back
following the gesture. He freezes into
immobility.*)

MR. ZUSS. Look! Look up!

NICKLES. That's your direction.

MR. ZUSS. Look, I say! The staring stars!

NICKLES. Or only lights not meant . . .

(NICKLES *twists his crooked neck, looks
sidewise upward. The canvas sky has disappeared into a profound darkness. There
seem to be stars beyond it.*)

NICKLES. You're mad.
You've lost your mind. You're maundering . . .

(*They rise together, their heads back,
peering into the darkness overhead.*)

NICKLES. . . . maundering.

MR. ZUSS. Let's get back where we belong.

NICKLES. Go on!

MR. ZUSS. No; you.

NICKLES. All right . . . together.

(*They take each other's arm as the light
fades.*)

SCENE SIX

*Darkness and silence as before. The
drum—a great crash and a long roll fading out. A gray light which has no visible source drifts across the stage where
tables and chairs are scattered and over-
turned.* MR. ZUSS *and* NICKLES *are huddled together on their platform peering
down.* J.B., *his clothes torn and white
with dust, faces what was once the door.
The two* MESSENGERS, *wearing steel hel-
mets and brassards, stand there, carrying*
SARAH *between them.*

FIRST MESSENGER. She said she lived
around here somewhere.
This is all there is.

J.B. Sarah!

FIRST M. Where do you want her?

J.B. Sarah! Sarah!

FIRST M. On the floor? You got a floor.

You're lucky if you got a floor.

(*They lay her carefully down.* J.B. *takes
his torn coat off, rolls it into a pillow,
kneels to put it under her head.*

J.B. Where was she?

FIRST M. Underneath a wall.

(*indicating* SECOND MESSENGER)
He heard her underneath a wall
Calling.

(*to* SECOND MESSENGER)
Tell him what you heard her . . .

SECOND M. (*imitating*).
Ruth! . . . Ruth!

FIRST M. Nobody answered:
Nobody could have.

(J.B. *does not look up or speak. The* FIRST
MESSENGER *starts toward the door, kicking a fallen chair out of his way.*)

You been down there?
Whole block's gone. Bank block. All of it.
J.B.'s bank. You know. Just gone.
Nothing left to show it ever.
Just the hole.

(SARAH *stirs, opens her eyes.* J.B. *leans
over her. She turns away.*)

J.B.'s millions!
That's a laugh now—J.B.'s millions!
All he's got is just the hole.
Plant went too—all of it—everything.
Ask him! Just the hole. He'll tell you.

SARAH (*faintly, her voice following the
rhythm of the* SECOND MESSENGER).
Ruth! . . . Ruth!

FIRST M. He can tell you.
He can tell you what he saw.

SARAH (*tonelessly like a voice counting*).
David . . . Jonathan . . . Mary . . .
Ruth . . .
I cannot say the last.

J.B. (*his hands on hers*). Rebecca.

SARAH. David . . . Jonathan . . . Mary
. . . Ruth . . .

J.B. (*looking up over his shoulder, to the*
SECOND MESSENGER).
You didn't find . . . there wasn't . . .

FIRST M. Tell him.
Tell him what you heard.

SECOND M. I heard
Two words. I don't know what they
mean.
I have brought them to you like a pair of
pebbles
Picked up in a path or a pair of
Beads that might belong to somebody.

J.B. There wasn't . . . anyone beside?

SECOND M. (*almost a whisper*).
I only am escaped alone to tell thee.

SARAH. David . . . Jonathan . . . Mary . . .
                                    Ruth . . .
J.B. Sarah!
(*Silence.*)
            Listen to me!
(*Silence.*)
                        Sarah!
Even desperate we can't despair—
Let go each other's fingers—sink
Numb in that dumb silence—drown there
Sole in our cold selves . . .

                        We cannot! . . .

God is there too, in the desperation.
I do not know why God should strike
But God is what is stricken also:
Life is what despairs in death
And, desperate, is life still . . .

                                    Sarah!
Do not let my hand go, Sarah!
Say it after me:

                    The Lord
Giveth . . . Say it.
SARAH (*mechanically*). The Lord giveth.
J.B.   The Lord taketh away . . .
SARAH (*flinging his hand from hers,
                shrieking*).   Takes!
Kills! Kills! Kills! Kills!
(*Silence.*)
J.B.   Blessed be the name of the Lord.
(*The light fades.*)

SCENE SEVEN

*Darkness. Silence. Then, out of the
dark,* MR. ZUSS's *voice. It has recovered its
confidence and timbre.*

———

MR. ZUSS.   Well, my friend . . .
(*The platform comes into light,* MR.
ZUSS *and* NICKLES *are still where they
were, leaning over, elbows on the rail.
They straighten up, stretching.*)
            . . . you see the position.
You see how it all comes out in the end.
Your fears were quite unfounded, weren't
                                    they?
NICKLES (*sourly*).
My fears for you?
MR. ZUSS.   For me? . . . For me!
Why should you fear for me?
NICKLES.   I can't
Think!
MR. ZUSS.   No, for him.

NICKLES.   That ham!
MR. ZUSS. Ham?
NICKLES.   Ham!
MR. ZUSS (*pleasantly*).   And you've been
                                telling me
Over and over that he isn't in it—
Isn't acting even: only
Living—breathing . . .
NICKLES.   Man can muff his
Life as badly as his lines and louder.
In it or out of it he's ham.
He wouldn't understand if twenty
Thousand suffocating creatures
Shrieked and tore their tongues out at
                                    him
Choking in a bombed-out town. He'd be
Thankful!
MR. ZUSS. (*stiffly*).   I think he under-
                                stands it
Perfectly! I think that great
Yea-saying to the world was wonderful—
That wounded and deliberate Amen—
That—affirmation!
NICKLES.   Affirmation!
Ever watch the worms affirming?
Ever hear a hog's Amen
Just when the knife first hurt? Death is
Good for you! It makes you glisten!
Get the large economy container,
Five for the price of one!

                        You think it's
Wonderful . . .
(*He wheels on* MR. ZUSS *in a sudden
fury.*)
                    I think it stinks!
One daughter raped and murdered by an
                                    idiot,
Another crushed by stones, a son
Destroyed by some fool officer's stupidity,
Two children smeared across a road
At midnight by a drunken child—
And all with God's consent!—foreknowl-
                                    edge!—
And he blesses God!
(*NICKLES points dramatically at the white,
calm, unconcerned mask in* MR. ZUSS's
hands.)
                        It isn't decent!
It isn't moral even! It's disgusting!
His weeping wife in her despair
And he beside her on his trembling
                                    ham-bones
Praising God! . . . It's nauseating!
MR. ZUSS. You don't lose gracefully, do
                                    you?
NICKLES (*snarling*).   I don't

Lose.

MR. ZUSS.   You have.

NICKLES.   That's not the end of it.

MR. ZUSS. No, but that's the *way* it ends.

NICKLES. Could have ended.

MR. ZUSS.   What do you mean?

NICKLES. Would have, if God had been
                                    content
With this poor crawling victory. He isn't.
Still He must pursue, still follow—
Hunt His creature through his branching
                                        veins
With agony until no peace is left him—
All one blazing day of pain:
Corner him, compel the answer.
He cannot rest until He wrings
The proof of pain, the ultimate certainty.
God always asks the proof of pain.

MR. ZUSS. And Job, in his affliction, gives
                                        it.

NICKLES. No! God overreaches at the
                                    end—
Pursues too far—follows too fearfully.
He seals him in his sack of skin
And scalds his skin to crust to squeeze
The answer out, but Job evades Him.

MR. ZUSS. Who can evade the will of God!
It waits at every door we open.
What does Dante say? His will . . .

NICKLES. Don't chant that chill equation
                                    at me!

MR. ZUSS. His will: our peace.

NICKLES. Will was never peace, no matter
Whose will, whose peace.
Will is rule: surrender is surrender.
You *make* your peace: you don't give in
                                    to it.
Job will make his own cold peace
When God pursues him in the web too
                                    far—
Implacable, eternal Spider.
A man can always cease: it's something—
A judgment anyway: reject
The whole creation with a stale pink pill.

MR. ZUSS. World is Will. Job can't reject
                                    it.

NICKLES. God has forgotten what a man
                                    can do
Once his body hurts him—once
Pain has penned him in where only
Pain has room to breathe. He learns!
He learns to spit his broken teeth out—
Spit the dirty world out—spit!

MR. ZUSS. And that's the end of every-
                                thing—to *spit*?

NICKLES. Better than that other end
Of pain, of physical agony, of suffering

God prepares for all His creatures.

MR. ZUSS. *Is* it better? *Is* it better?
Job has suffered and praised God.
Would Job be better off asleep
Among the clods of earth in ignorance?

NICKLES. Yes, when he suffers in his body:
Yes, when his suffering is *him*.

MR. ZUSS. His suffering will praise.

NICKLES.   It will not.

MR. ZUSS.   Well,
We still have time to see.

NICKLES. Better than that other end

NICKLES.   Put on your
Mask! You'll see!

(*The light has faded but the faces of the
actors are still visible.*)

MR. ZUSS (*raising his mask*).   Put on
                                your own!

(NICKLES *leans over to find it, searching
the floor of the platform with his hands.
A long silence. From the silence at
length:*)

THE DISTANT VOICE. *Has thou considered
                        my servant Job
That there is none like him on the earth,
A perfect and an upright man, one
That feareth God and escheweth evil?*

NICKLES. Wait a minute! I can't find . . .

THE DISTANT VOICE (*louder*). *And still he
                    holdeth fast his integrity . . .*

NICKLES. Wait a minute, can't you? What
                                    the . . .

THE DISTANT VOICE (*almost a whisper*).
*Although thou movedst me against him
To destroy him . . .*

(NICKLES *rises, his mask in his two hands.
He wheels on* MR. ZUSS *only to see that*
MR. ZUSS *also has his mask in his hands
and stands staring up into the canvas sky.*)

(THE DISTANT VOICE *is barely audible.*)
                        without cause . . .

(*Silence. The two old actors stand side by
side, holding their masks, their heads
moving slowly together as they search the
dark.*)

NICKLES.   Who said that?

(*Silence.*)

MR. ZUSS. They want us to go on.

NICKLES.   Why don't you?

MR. ZUSS. He was asking *you*.

NICKLES.   Who was?

MR. ZUSS.   He was.

NICKLES. Prompter probably. Prompter
                                somewhere.
Your lines he was reading weren't they?

MR. ZUSS. Yes but . . .

NICKLES (*shouting*).   Anybody there?

(*Silence*).

MR. ZUSS. They want us to go on. I told you.

NICKLES. Yes. They want us to go on . . . I don't like it.

MR. ZUSS.   We began it.

(*They put their masks on slowly. The lights fade out. The huge shadows appear on the canvas sky, facing each other.*)

GODMASK. . . . *And still he holdeth fast his integrity*
Although thou movedst me against him
To destroy him . . .
(*His voice breaks.*)
                                without cause.

SATANMASK. *Skin for skin, yea, all that a man*
Hath will he give for his life.
But put forth thine hand now and touch
His bone and his flesh
And he will curse thee to thy face.

(*The* GOD-SHADOW *raises its arm again in the formal gesture of contemptuous commitment.*)

GODMASK. *Behold he is in thine hand* . . .

(*The* GOD-SHADOW *turns away. Silence.*)
                                        but . . .
Save his life!

(*The two shadows lean together over the earth.*)

NOTE: *A second break in the action may be made here if it is thought desirable.*

SCENE EIGHT

(*There is no light but the glow on the canvas sky, which holds the looming, leaning shadows. They fade as a match is struck. It flares in* SARAH'S *hand, showing her face, and glimmers out against the wick of a dirty lantern. As the light of the lantern rises,* J.B. *is seen lying on the broken propped-up table, naked but for a few rags of clothing.* SARAH *looks at him in the new light, shudders, lets her head drop into her hands. There is a long silence and then a movement in the darkness of the open door where four women and a young girl stand, their arms filled with blankets and newspapers. They come forward slowly into the light.*)

NICKLES (*unseen, his cracked, cackling voice drifting down from the darkness of the platform overhead*).

Nevers fails! Never fails!
Count on you to make a mess of it!
Every blessed blundering time
You hit at one man you blast thousands.
Think of that Flood of yours—a massacre!
Now you've fumbled it again:
Tumbled a whole city down
To blister one man's skin with agony.

(NICKLES' *white coat appears at the foot of the ladder. The women, in the circle of the lantern, are walking slowly around* J.B. *and* SARAH, *staring at them as though they were figures in a show window.*)

NICKLES. Look at your works! Those shivering women
Sheltering under any crumbling
Heap to keep the sky out! Weeping!

MRS. ADAMS. That's him.

JOLLY ADAMS.   Who's him?

MRS. ADAMS.   Grammar, Jolly.

MRS. LESURE. Who did she say it was?

MRS. MURPHY.   Him she said it was.
Poor soul!

MRS. LESURE. Look at them sores on him!

MRS. ADAMS. Don't look, child. You'll remember them.

JOLLY ADAMS (*proudly*). Every sore I seen
I remember.

MRS. BOTTICELLI. Who did she say she said it was?

MRS. MURPHY.   Him.

MRS. ADAMS. That's his wife.

MRS. LESURE.   She's pretty.

MRS. BOTTICELLI.   Ain't she.
Looks like somebody we've seen.

MRS. ADAMS (*snooting her*). I don't believe you would have seen her:
Picture possibly—her picture
Posed in the penthouse.

MRS. BOTTICELLI.   Puce with pants?

MRS. ADAMS. No, the negligee.

MRS. BOTTICELLI.   The net?

MRS. ADAMS. The simple silk.

MRS. BOTTICELLI.   Oh la! With sequins?

MRS. MURPHY. Here's a place to park your poodle—
Nice cool floor.

MRS. LESURE.   Shove over, dearie.

(*The women settle themselves on their newspapers off at the edge of the circle of light.* NICKLES *has perched himself on a chair at the side. Silence.*)

J.B. (*a whisper*). God, let me die!

(NICKLES *leers up into the dark toward the unseen platform.*)

SARAH (*her voice dead*). You think He'd

Even to that?

(Silence. SARAH *looks up, turning her face away from* J.B. *She speaks without passion, almost mechanically.)*

SARAH.   God is our enemy

J.B. No . . . No . . . No . . . Don't
Say that Sarah!

*(*SARAH'S *head turns toward him slowly as though dragged against her will. She stares and cannot look away.)*

                 God has something.
Hidden from our hearts to show.

NICKLES. She knows! She's looking at it!

J.B.   Try to
Sleep.

SARAH *(bitterly).* He should have kept it
                                    hidden.

J.B. Sleep now.

SARAH.   You don't have to see it:
I do.

J.B.   Yes, I know.

NICKLES *(a cackle).* He knows!
He's back behind it and he knows!
If he could see what she can see
There's something else he might be
                                    knowing.

J.B. Once I knew a charm for sleeping—
Not as forgetfulness but gift,
Not as sleep but second sight,
Come and from my eyelids lift
The dead of night.

SARAH.   The dead . . .
                      of night . . .

(She drops her head to her knees, whispering.)

Come and from my eyelids lift
The dead of night.

(Silence.)

J.B.   Out of sleep
Something of our own comes back to us:
A drowned man's garment from the sea.

*(*SARAH *turns the lantern down. Silence. Then the voices of the women, low.)*

MRS. BOTTICELLI. Poor thing!

MRS. MURPHY.   Poor thing!
Not a chick nor a child between them.

MRS. ADAMS. First their daughters. Then
                              their sons.

MRS. MURPHY. First son first. Blew him
                              to pieces.
More mischance it was than war.
Asleep on their feet in the frost they
                         walked into it.

MRS. ADAMS. Two at the viaduct: that
                         makes three.

JOLLY ADAMS *(a child's chant).* Jolly saw

the picture! the picture!

MRS. ADAMS. Jolly Adams, you keep quiet.

JOLLY ADAMS. Wanna know? The whole
                         of the viaduct . . .

MRS. ADAMS. Never again will you look
                         at them! Never!

MRS. LESURE. Them magazines! They're
                         awful! Which?

MRS. MURPHY. And after that the little
                              one.

MRS. BOTTICELLI.   Who in the
World are they talking about, the little
                              one?
What are they talking?

MRS. LESURE.   I don't know.
Somebody dogged by death it must be.

MRS. BOTTICELLI. Him it must be.

MRS. LESURE.   Who's him?

MRS. ADAMS. You know who.

MRS. MURPHY.   You remember the . . .

MRS. ADAMS. Hush! The child!

MRS. MURPHY. Back of the lumberyard.

MRS. LESURE. Oh! Him!

MRS. MURPHY. Who did you think it
                              was—
Penthouse and negligees, daughters and
                              dying?

MRS. BOTTICELLI. Him? That's him? That
                         millionaire?

MRS. LESURE. Millionaires he buys like
                         cabbages.

MRS. MURPHY. He couldn't buy cabbages
                         now by the look of him:
The rags he's got on.

MRS. BOTTICELLI. Look at them sores!

MRS. MURPHY. All that's left him now is
                              her.

MRS. BOTTICELLI. Still that's something—
                         a good woman.

MRS. MURPHY. What good is a woman to
                         him with that hide on him?—
Or he to her if you think of it.

MRS. ADAMS.   Don't!

MRS. LESURE. Can you blame her?

MRS. MURPHY.   I don't blame her.
All I say is she's no comfort.
She won't cuddle.

MRS. ADAMS.   Really, Mrs. . . .

MRS. MURPHY. Murphy call me. What's
                         got into you? . . .
Nothing recently I'd hazard.

MRS. ADAMS. You're not so young your-
                         self, my woman.

MRS. MURPHY. Who's your woman? I was
                         Murphy's.

MRS. LESURE. None of us are maids en-
                              tirely.

MRS. MURPHY. Maids in mothballs some might be.

MRS. ADAMS. Who might?

MRS. MURPHY.   You might.

MRS. ADAMS.   You! you're . . . historical!

MRS. MURPHY. I never slept a night in history!

MRS. BOTTICELLI. *I* have. Oh, my mind goes back.

MRS. ADAMS. None of that! We have a child here!

(*Silence.*)

How far back?

MRS. BOTTICELLI.   I often wonder.
Farther than the first but . . . where?

MRS. MURPHY. What do you care? It's lovely country.

(*Silence.*)

Roll a little nearer, dearie,
Me back side's froze.

MRS. LESURE.   You smell of roses.

MRS. MURPHY. Neither do you but you're warm.

MRS. BOTTICELLI.   Well,
Good night, ladies. Good night, ladies . . .

(*Silence. Out of the silence, felt rather than heard at first, a sound of sobbing, a muffled, monotonous sound like the heavy beat of a heart.*)

J.B. If you could only sleep a little
Now they're quiet, now they're still.

SARAH (*her voice broken*).

I try. But oh I close my eyes and . . .
Eyes are open there to meet me!

(*Silence. Then* SARAH's *voice in an agony of bitterness.*)

My poor babies! Oh, my babies!

(J.B. *pulls himself painfully up, sits huddled on his table in the feeble light of the lamp, his rags about him.*)

J.B. (*gently*). Go to sleep.

SARAH.   *Go!* Go where?
If there were darkness I'd go there.
If there were night I'd lay me down in it.
God has shut the night against me.
God has set the dark alight
With horror blazing blind as day
When I go toward it . . .
                        close my eyes.

J.B. I know. I know those waking eyes.
His will is everywhere against us—
Even in our sleep, our dreams . . .

NICKLES (*a snort of laughter up toward the dark of the platform*).

Your will, *his* peace!
Doesn't seem to grasp that, does he?

Give him another needling twinge
Between the withers and the works—
He'll understand you better.

J.B.   If I
Knew . . . If I knew why!

NICKLES.   If he knew
Why he wouldn't be there. He'd be
Strangling, drowning, suffocating,
Diving for a sidewalk somewhere . . .

J.B. What I *can't* bear is the blindness—
Meaninglessness—the numb blow
Fallen in the stumbling night.

SARAH (*starting violently to her feet*).
Has death no meaning? Pain no meaning?

(*She points at his body.*)

Even these suppurating sores—
Have they no meaning for you?

NICKLES.   Ah!

J.B. (*from his heart's pain*).
God will not punish without cause.

(NICKLES *doubles up in a spasm of soundless laughter.*)

J.B. God is just.

SARAH (*hysterically*).   God is just!
If God is just our slaughtered children
Stank with sin, were rotten with it!

(*She controls herself with difficulty, turns toward him, reaches her arms out, lets them fall.*)

Oh, my dear! my dear! my dear!
Does God demand deception of us?—
Purchase His innocence by ours?
Must we be guilty for Him?—bear
The burden of the world's malevolence
For Him who made the world?

J.B.   He
Knows the guilt is mine. He must know:
Has He not punished it? He knows its
Name, its time, its face, its circumstance,
The figure of its day, the door,
The opening of the door, the room, the
                        moment . . .

SARAH (*fiercely*). And you? Do you? You
                        do not know it.
Your punishment is all you know.

(*She moves toward the door, stops, turns.*)

I will not stay here if you lie—
Connive in your destruction, cringe to it:
Not if you betray my children . . .

I will not stay to listen . . .

                        They are
Dead and they were innocent: I will not
Let you sacrifice their deaths
To make injustice justice and God good!

J.B. (*covering his face with his hands*).

My heart beats. I cannot answer it.

SARAH. If you buy quiet with their innocence—

Theirs or yours . . .

(*softly*) I will not love you.

J.B. I have no choice but to be guilty.

SARAH (*her voice rising*). We have the
choice to live or die,

All of us . . .

curse God and die . . .

(*Silence.*)

J.B. God is God or we are nothing—
Mayflies that leave their husks behind—
Our tiny lives ridiculous—a suffering
Not even sad that Someone Somewhere
Laughs at as we laugh at apes.
We have no choice but to be guilty.
God is unthinkable if we are innocent.

(SARAH *turns, runs soundlessly out of the
circle of light, out of the door. The
women stir.* MRS. MURPHY *comes up on
her elbow.*)

MRS. MURPHY. What did I say? I said
she'd walk out on him.

MRS. LESURE. She did.

MRS. BOTTICELLI. Did she?

MRS. MURPHY. His hide was
too much for her.

MRS. BOTTICELLI.
His hide or his heart.

MRS. MURPHY. The hide comes between.

MRS. BOTTICELLI.
The heart is the stranger.

MRS. MURPHY. Oh, strange!
It's always strange the heart is: only
It's the skin we ever know.

J.B. (*raising his head*).
Sarah, why do you not speak to me? . . .
Sarah!

(*Silence.*)

MRS. ADAMS. Now he knows.

MRS. MURPHY. And he's alone now.

(J.B.'s *head falls forward onto his knees.
Silence. Out of the silence his voice in
an agony of prayer.*)

J.B. *Show me my guilt, O God!*

NICKLES. His
Guilt! His! You heard that didn't you?
He wants to feel the feel of guilt—
That putrid poultice of the soul
That draws the poison in, not out—
Inverted catheter! You going to show
him?

(*Silence.* NICKLES *rises, moves toward
the ladder.*)

Well? You going to show him . . .

Jahveh?

(*Silence. He crosses to the ladder's foot.*)

Where are those cold comforters of yours
Who justify the ways of God to
Job by making Job responsible?—
Those three upholders of the world—
Defenders of the universe—where are
they?

(*Silence. He starts up the ladder. Stops.
The jeering tone is gone. His voice is
bitter.*)

Must be almost time for comfort! . . .

(NICKLES *vanishes into the darkness above.
The light fades.*)

SCENE NINE

Darkness.

J.B.'s VOICE. *If I had perished from the
womb, not having
Been . . .*

(*A light without source rises slowly like
the light at evening which enlarges everything. The canvas walls dissolve into distance, the canvas sky into endlessness. The
platform has been pushed away to the
side until only the ladder is visible. The
women and the child are huddled together like sleeping figures on a vast
plain.* J.B. *is alone in an enormous loneliness. Out of that seeming distance the*
THREE COMFORTERS *come shuffling forward dressed in worn-out clothing.*
ZOPHAR, *a fat, red-faced man, wears the
wreck of a clerical collar.* ELIPHAZ, *lean
and dark, wears an intern's jacket which
once was white.* BILDAD *is a squat, thick
man in a ragged wind-breaker. The
women do not see them, but* JOLLY
ADAMS *sits suddenly up clapping her
hands to her mouth.* J.B., *his head on his
arms, sees nothing.*)

J.B. Death cannot heal me . . .
Death
Will leave my having been behind it
Like a bear's foot festering in a trap . . .

JOLLY ADAMS (*her voice rising word by
word to a scream*).
Look! Look! Look! Look!
Mother! Mother!

(*The women pull themselves up. The*
THREE COMFORTERS *shuffle on, squat in
the rubbish around* J.B.: ZOPHAR *lighting
the stub of a fat, ragged cigar;* ELIPHAZ
lighting a broken pipe; BILDAD *lighting a
crumpled cigarette.*)

MRS. MURPHY. Agh, the scavengers!

MRS. BOTTICELLI. Three old pokey crows
　　　　　　　　　they look like.
MRS. MURPHY. They are, too. It's the smell
　　　　　　　　　　of the suffering.
See that leather-backed old bucket?—
Kind of character you hear from
Sundays in a public park
Pounding the hell out of everything . . .
　　　　　　　　　　you know.
MRS. BOTTICELLI. *I* know. Wall Street.
　　　　　　　　　Bakers. Bankers.
MRS. LESURE. All the answers in a book.
MRS. BOTTICELLI. Russkys got them all—
　　　　　　　　　the answers.
MRS. MURPHY. Characters like that, they
　　　　　　　　　　smell the
Human smell of heartsick misery
Farther than a kite smells carrion.
MRS. LESURE. Who's the collar?
MRS. MURPHY. 　　Some spoiled priest.
MRS. BOTTICELLI. They can smell it farther
　　　　　　　　　　even.
MRS. LESURE. Not as far as dead-beat doc-
　　　　　　　　　　tors:
They're the nosies.
MRS. MURPHY. 　　　Let them nose!
(*A tremendous yawn.*)
Ohhh, I'm halfway over . . .
　　　　　　　　　　drownding
Down and down . . .
　　　　　　I hear the seagulls
Singing soundings in the sea . . .
(*She lets herself fall back on her news-*
papers. The others follow one by one.)
JOLLY ADAMS. I don't hear them.
MRS. BOTTICELLI. 　　Pound your ears.
MRS. LESURE. Slip your moorings . . . Oh,
　　　　　　　　　I'm numb.
MRS. MURPHY. Come alongside, dear.
MRS. LESURE. 　　　　　I'm coming.
MRS. BOTTICELLI. That doctor one, he
　　　　　　　　　makes me creep.
MRS. MURPHY. Keep your thumb on your
　　　　　　　thoughts or he'll diddle them.
MRS. BOTTICELLI. Let him pry: he'll lose
　　　　　　　　　an eyeball.
MRS. LESURE. He's a peeper. Watch your
　　　　　　　　　sleep.
MRS. MURPHY. Who was she, all gore, all
　　　　　　　　　story,
Dabbled in a deep blood sea,
And what she washed in, that was she?
MRS. LESURE (*from her dream*).
Some queen of Scotland . . .
MRS. MURPHY. 　　Queen of Scones . . .
(*A long silence. The* THREE COMFORTERS
squat smoking and waiting. At length

J.B. *pulls himself painfully up to kneel*
on his table, his face raised.)
J.B. (*a whisper*). God! My God! My God!
　　　　　　　　　What have I
Done?
(*Silence.*)
BILDAD (*removing his cigarette*). Fair
　　　　　　　　　question, Big Boy.
Anyone answer you yet? No answer?
ZOPHAR (*removing his cigar*). That was
　　　　　　　answered long ago—
Long ago.
ELIPHAZ (*knocking out his pipe*). In
　　　　　　　　dreams are answers.
How do your dreams go, Big Boy? Tell!
J.B. (*peering*). Is someone there? Where?
　　　　　　　　　I cannot
See you in this little light
My eyes too fail me . . .
(*Silence.*)
　　　　　　　　　Who is there?
(*Silence.*)
I know how ludicrous I must look,
Covered with rags, my skin pustulant . . .
(*Silence.*)
I know . . .
(*Silence.*)
　　　　　I know how others see me.
(*A long silence.*)
Why have you come?
BILDAD (*a coarse laugh*). 　For comfort,
　　　　　　　　　Big Boy.
Didn't you ring?
ZOPHAR (*a fat laugh*). 　　That's it: for
　　　　　　　　　comfort!
ELIPHAZ (*a thin laugh*). All the comfort
　　　　　　　you can find.
BILDAD. All the kinds of.
ELIPHAZ. 　　　　*All* the comforts.
ZOPHAR. You called us and we came.
J.B. 　　　　　　　　　I called
God.
BILDAD. 　Didn't you!
ELIPHAZ. 　　　　　Didn't you just!
ZOPHAR. Why should God reply to *you*
From the blue depths of His Eternity?
ELIPHAZ. Blind depths of His Unconcon-
　　　　　　　　　sciousness?
BILDAD. Blank depths of His Necessity?
ZOPHAR. God is far above in Mystery.
ELIPHAZ. God is far below in Mindless-
　　　　　　　　　ness.
BILDAD. God is far within in History—
Why should God have time for you?
J.B. The hand of God has touched me.
　　　　　　　　　Look at me!
Every hope I ever had,

Every task I put my mind to,
Every work I've ever done
Annulled as though I had not done it.
My trace extinguished in the land,
My children dead, my father's name
Obliterated in the sunlight everywhere . . .
Love too has left me.
BILDAD   Love!
(*A great guffaw.*)
What's love to Him? One man's misery!
J.B. (*hardly daring*). If I am innocent . . . ?
BILDAD (*snort of jeering laughter*).
Innocent! Innocent!
Nations shall perish in their innocence.
Classes shall perish in their innocence.
Young men in slaughtered cities
Offering their silly throats
Against the tanks in innocence shall
                                    perish.
What's your innocence to theirs?
God is History. If you offend Him
Will not History dispense with you?
History has no time for innocence.
J.B. God is just. We are not squeezed
Naked through a ridiculous orifice
Like bulls into a blazing ring
To blunder there by blindfold laws
We never learn or can, deceived by
Stratagems and fooled by feints,
For sport, for nothing, till we fall
We're pricked so badly.
BILDAD (*all park-bench orator*).
Screw your justice!
History is justice!—time
Inexorably turned to truth!—
Not for one man. For humanity.
One man's life won't measure on it.
One man's suffering won't count, no
                                    matter
What his suffering; but All will.
At the end there will be justice!—
Justice for All! Justice for everyone!
(*Subsiding*)
On the way—it doesn't matter.
J.B. Guilt matters. Guilt must always
                                    matter.
Unless guilt matters the whole world is
Meaningless. God too is nothing.
BILDAD (*losing interest*).
You may be guiltier than Hell
As History counts guilt and not
One smudging thumbprint on your con-
                                    science.
Guilt is a sociological accident:
Wrong class—wrong century—
You pay for your luck with your licks,
                                    that's all.

(ELIPHAZ *has been fidgeting. Now he
breaks in like a professor in a seminar,
poking a forefinger at the air.*)
ELIPHAZ. Come! Come! Come! Guilt is a
Psychophenomenal situation—
An illusion, a disease, a sickness:
That filthy feeling at the fingers,
Scent of dung beneath the nails . . .
ZOPHAR (*outraged, flushed, head thrown
                                    back*).
Guilt is illusion? Guilt is reality!—
The one reality there is!
All mankind are guilty always!
BILDAD (*jeering*). The Fall of Man it
                                    felled us all!
(J.B.'s *voice breaks through the squab-
bling with something of its old authority.*)
J.B. *No doubt ye are the people
And wisdom shall die with you!* I am
Bereaved, in pain, desperate, and you
                                    mock me!
There was a time when men found pity
Finding each other in the night:
Misery to walk with misery—
Brother in whose brother-guilt
Guilt could be conceived and recognized.
We have forgotten pity.
ELIPHAZ.   No.
We have surmounted guilt. It's quite,
Quite different, isn't it? You see the dif-
                                    ference.
Science knows now that the sentient spirit
Floats like the chambered nautilus on a
                                    sea
That drifts it under skies that drive:
Beneath, the sea of the subconscious;
Above, the winds that wind the world.
Caught between that sky, that sea,
Self has no will, cannot be guilty.
The sea drifts. The sky drives.
The tiny, shining bladder of the soul
Washes with wind and wave or shudders
Shattered between them.
ZOPHAR.   Blasphemy!
BILDAD.   Bullshit!
ELIPHAZ (*oblivious*). There is no guilt,
                                    my man. We all are
Victims of our guilt, not guilty.
We kill the king in ignorance: the voice
Reveals: we blind ourselves. At our
Beginning, in the inmost room,
Each one of us, disgusting monster
Changed by the chilling moon to child,
Violates his mother. Are we guilty?
Our guilt is underneath the Sybil's
Stone: not known.
J.B. (*violently*).   I'd rather suffer

Every unspeakable suffering God sends,
Knowing it was I that suffered,
I that earned the need to suffer,
I that acted, I that chose,
Than wash my hands with yours in that
Defiling innocence. Can we be men
And make an irresponsible ignorance
Responsible for everything? I will not
Listen to you!
(J.B. *pulls his rags over his head.*)
ELIPHAZ (*shrugging*).   But you will.
                                          You will.
ZOPHAR. Ah, my son, how well you said
                                             that!
How well you said it! Without guilt
What is a man? An animal, isn't he?
A wolf forgiven at his meat,
A beetle innocent in his copulation.
What divides us from the universe
Of blood and seed, conceives the soul in
                                                 us,
Brings us to God, but guilt? The lion
Dies of death: we die of suffering.
The lion vanishes: our souls accept
Eternities of reparation.
But for our guilt we too would vanish,
Bundles of corrupting bones
Bagged in a hairless hide and rotting.
Happy the man whom God correcteth!
He tastes his guilt. His hope begins.
He is in league with the stones in cer-
                                             tainty.
(J.B. *pulls his rags from his head, drags
himself around toward the voice.*)
J.B. *Teach me and I will hold my tongue.
Show me my transgression.*
ZOPHAR (*gently*).   No.
No, my son. You show *me*.
(*He hunches forward dropping his voice.*)
Search your inmost heart! Question it!
Guilt is a deceptive secret,
The labor often of years, a work
Conceived in infancy, brought to birth
In unpredictable forms years after:
At twelve the palpable elder brother;
At seventeen, perhaps, the servant
Seen by the lamp by accident . . .
J.B. (*urgently, the words forced from
                                       him*). My
Sin! Teach me my sin! My wickedness!
Surely iniquity that suffers
Judgment like mine cannot be secret.
Mine is no childish fault, no nastiness
Concealed behind a bathroom door,
No sin a prurient virtue practices
Licking the silence from its lips
Like sugar afterwards. Mine is flagrant,

Worthy of death, of many deaths,
Of shame, loss, hurt, indignities
Such as these! Such as these!
Speak of the sin I must have sinned
To suffer what you see me suffer.
ZOPHAR. Do we need to name our sins
To know the need to be forgiven?
Repent, my son! Repent!
J.B. (*an agony of earnestness*). I sit here
Such as you see me. In my soul
I suffer what you guess I suffer.
Tell me the wickedness that justifies it.
Shall I repent of sins I have not
Sinned to understand it? Till I
Die I will not violate my integrity.
ZOPHAR (*a fat chuckle*). Your integrity!
                                          Your integrity!
What integrity have you?—
A man, a miserable, mortal, sinful,
Venal man like any other.
You squat there challenging the universe
To tell you what your crime is called,
Thinking, because your life was virtuous,
It can't be called. It can. Your sin is
Simple. You were born a man!
J.B. What is my fault? What have I
                                            done?
ZOPHAR (*thundering*). What is your fault?
                                     Man's heart is evil!
What have you done? Man's will is evil.
Your fault, your sin, are heart and will:
The worm at heart, the wilful will
Corrupted with its foul imagining.
(J.B. *crouches lower in his rags. Silence.*)
J.B. Yours is the cruelest comfort of them
                                                   all,
Making the Creator of the Universe
The miscreator of mankind—
A party to the crimes He punishes . . .

Making my sin . . .
                    a horror . . .
                              a deformity . . .
ZOPHAR (*collapsing into his own voice*).
If it were otherwise we could not bear
                                              it . . .
Without the fault, without the Fall,
We're madmen: all of us are madmen . . .
(*He sits staring at his hands, then re-
peats the phrase:*)
Without the Fall
   We're madmen all.
We watch the stars
   That creep and crawl . . .
BILDAD. Like dying flies
   Across the wall
Of night . . .

ELIPHAZ. and shriek . . .
And that is all.
ZOPHAR. Without the Fall . . .
(*A long silence. Out of the silence at
last* J.B.*'s voice, barely audible.*)
J.B. *God, my God, my God, answer me!*
(*Silence.*)
(*His voice rises.*)
*I cry out of wrong but I am not heard . . .
I cry aloud but there is no judgment.*
(*Silence.*)
(*Violently*)
*Though He slay me, yet will I trust in
Him . . .*
(*Silence.*)
(*His voice drops.*)
*But I will maintain my own ways before
Him . . .*
(*Silence.*)
(*The ancient human cry.*)
*Oh, that I knew where I might find
Him!—
That I might come even to His seat!
I would order my cause before Him
And fill my mouth with arguments.*
(*There is a rushing sound in the air.*)
*Behold,
I go forward but He is not there,
Backward, but I cannot perceive Him . . .*
(*Out of the rushing sound, the* DISTANT
VOICE; J.B. *cowers as he hears it, his rags
over his head.*)
THE DISTANT VOICE. *Who is this that dark-
eneth counsel
By words without knowledge? . . .*

*Where wast thou
When I laid the foundations of the
earth . . .*

*When the morning stars sang together
And all the sons of God shouted for
Joy?*

Hast thou commanded the morning?

*Hast thou entered into the springs of the
sea
Or hast thou walked in the search of the
depth?*

*Have the gates of death been opened
unto thee?*

*Where is the way where light dwelleth?
And as for darkness, where is the place
thereof?*

*Hast thou entered into the treasures of
the snow?*

*By what way is the light parted
Which scattereth the east wind upon the
earth?*

*Can'st thou bind the sweet influences of
the Pleiades?*

*Hast thou given the horse strength?
Hast thou clothed his neck with thunder?*

*He saith among the trumpets, Ha, ha;
He smelleth the battle afar off,
The thunder of the captains and the
shouting.*

*Doth the eagle mount up at thy com-
mand?*

*Her eyes behold afar off.
Her young ones also suck up blood:
And where the slain are, there is she . . .*
(*The rushing sound dies away. The* THREE
COMFORTERS *stir uneasily, peering up into
the darkness. One by one they rise.*)
BILDAD. The wind's gone round.
ZOPHAR. It's cold.
BILDAD. I told you.
ELIPHAZ. I hear the silence like a sound.
ZOPHAR. Wait for me!
BILDAD. The wind's gone round.
(*They go out as they came. Silence.* J.B.
*sits motionless, his head covered. The
rushing sound returns like the second,
stronger gust of a great storm.* THE VOICE
rises above it.)
THE DISTANT VOICE. *Shall he that con-
tendeth with the Almighty instruct
Him? . . .*
(*The rushing sound dies away again.
The women sit up, huddle together.*)
JOLLY ADAMS (*screaming*).
Mother! Mother! what was
That?
MRS. ADAMS. The wind, child. Only the
wind.
Only the wind.
JOLLY ADAMS. I heard a word.
MRS. ADAMS. You heard the thunder in the
wind.
JOLLY ADAMS (*drowsy*).
Under the wind there was a word . . .
(MRS. ADAMS *picks her up. The women
gather their newspapers and blankets and
stumble out into the darkness through*

the door. For the third time the rushing
sound returns.)
THE DISTANT VOICE. *He that reproveth God,*
                              let him answer it!
J.B. *Behold, I am vile; what shall I an-*
                              swer thee?
I will lay mine hand upon my mouth.
THE DISTANT VOICE. *Gird up thy loins like*
                              a man:
I will demand of thee, and declare thou
                              unto me.
(J.B. *pulls himself painfully to his knees.)*
Wilt thou disannul my judgment?
(J.B. *does not answer.)*
Wilt thou condemn
Me that thou mayest be righteous?

Hast thou an arm like God? Or canst thou
Thunder with a voice like Him?

Deck thyself now with majesty and excel-
                              lency
And array thyself with glory and beauty
                              . . .

Then will I also confess unto thee
That thine own right hand can save thee.

(J.B. *raises his bowed head.)*
J.B. (*gently*). *I know that thou canst do*
                              everything . . .
(*The rushing sound dies away.*)
And that no thought can be withholden
                              from thee.
Who is he that hideth counsel without
                              knowledge?
Therefore have I uttered that I under-
                              stood not:
Things too wonderful for me, which I
                              knew not.

Hear, I beseech thee, and I will speak:
                              . . .
(*Silence.*)
I have heard of thee by the hearing of
                              the ear . . .
But now . . .
(*His face is drawn in agony.*)
                    mine eye seeth thee!
(*He bows his head. His hands wring each*
other.)
                              Wherefore
I abhor myself . . . and repent . . .
(*The light fades.*)

SCENE TEN

The Platform. As the lights come on
the two actors turn violently away from

each other, tearing their masks off.
NICKLES, *with a gesture of disgust, skims*
his into a corner.

———

NICKLES. Well, that's that!
MR. ZUSS.   That's . . . that!
(*Silence. After a time* NICKLES *looks cau-*
tiously around at MR. ZUSS.)
NICKLES. What's the matter with you?
MR. ZUSS.   Nothing.
NICKLES. You don't look pleased.
MR. ZUSS.   Should I?
NICKLES.   Well,
You were right weren't you?
MR. ZUSS (*too loud*). Of course I was right.
NICKLES (*too soft*). Anyway, you were
                              magnificent.
MR. ZUSS.   Thank you.
(*He looks at the mask in his hands: puts*
it down as though it had stung him. Si-
lence. MR. ZUSS *pretends to be busy with*
a shoelace.)
MR. ZUSS. Why did you say that?
NICKLES.   What did I say?
MR. ZUSS. Why did you say it like that?
NICKLES.   Like what?
MR. ZUSS (*imitating*).
"Anyway!" . . .
              "*Anyway*, you were magnificent!"
NICKLES. You know. "Anyway." Regard-
                              less.
MR. ZUSS.   Regardless of
What?
NICKLES. Now, wait a minute! Wait a
Minute! You were magnificent. I said so.
MR. ZUSS. Go on. Finish it.
NICKLES.   Finish what?
MR. ZUSS. Regardless of . . . ?
NICKLES.   . . . being right, of course.
What's got into you, my friend? What's
                              eating you?
Being magnificent and being right
Don't go together in this universe.
It's being wrong—a desperate stubborn-
                              ness
Fighting the inextinguishable stars—
Excites imagination. You were
Right. And knew it. And were admirable.
Notwithstanding!
(*Snickering*)   anyway!
(*A snarl*)   regardless!
MR. ZUSS. I knew you noticed.
NICKLES.   Of course I noticed.
What lover of the art could fail to!
(*Something in* MR. ZUSS's *expression stops*
him.)
                              Noticed

What?

MR. ZUSS. That tone! That look he gave me!

NICKLES. He misconceived the part entirely.

MR. ZUSS. Misconceived the world! Buggered it!

NICKLES. Giving in like that! Whimpering!

MR. ZUSS. Giving in! You call that arrogant,

Smiling, supercilious humility
Giving in to God?

NICKLES.   Arrogant!
His suppurating flesh—his children—
Let's not talk about those children—
Everything he ever had!
And all he asks is answers of the universe:
All he asks is reasons why—
Why? Why? And God replies to him:
God comes whirling in the wind replying—
What? That God knows more than he does.
That God's more powerful than he!—
Throwing the whole creation at him!
Throwing the Glory and the Power!
What's the Power to a broken man
Trampled beneath it like a toad already?
What's the Glory to a skin that stinks!
And this ham actor!—what does *he* do?
How does he play Job to that?
(*Attitude*)
"Thank you!" "I'm a worm!" "Take two!"
Plays the way a sheep would play it—
Pious, contemptible, goddam sheep
Without the spunk to spit on Christmas!
(MR. ZUSS *has watched* NICKLES' *mounting rage in silence, staring at him.* NICKLES *breaks off, shuffles, looks at* MR. ZUSS, *crosses to the ladder, swings a leg across the rail.*)
Well . . .
(*He swings the other over.*)
          you said he would . . .
(*He starts down.*)
                    you're right.
(*Another rung.*)
I'm wrong.
(*Another.*)
          You win.
(*Another.*)
                    God always wins.
(*He peers down into the dark under the platform.*)
Where did I put that . . . popcorn?

MR. ZUSS.   Win!
Planets and Pleiades and eagles—
Screaming horses—scales of light—
The wonder and the mystery of the universe—
The unimaginable might of things—
Immeasurable knowledge in the waters
          somewhere
Wandering their ways—the searchless
          power
Burning on the hearth of stars—
Beauty beyond the feel of fingers—
Marvel beyond the maze of mind—
The whole creation! And God showed
          him!
God stood stooping there to show him!
Last Orion! Least sea shell! . . .
And what did Job do?
(MR. ZUSS *has worked himself up into a dramatic fury equaling* NICKLES'.)
          Job . . . just . . . sat!
(*Silence.*)
Sat there!
(*Silence.*)
          Dumb!
(*Silence.*)
                    Until it ended!
Then! . . . you heard him!
(MR. ZUSS *chokes.*)
                    Then, he *calmed* me!
Gentled me the way a farmhand
Gentles a bulging, bugling bull!
Forgave me! . . .
          for the world! . . .
                    for everything!

NICKLES (*poking around in the shadow under the platform*).
Nonsense! He repented, didn't he—
The perfect and the upright man!
He repented!

MR. ZUSS.   That's just it!
He repented. It was *him*—
Not the fear of God but *him*!

NICKLES. Fear? Of course he feared. Why wouldn't he?
God with all those stars and stallions!
He with little children's bones!

MR. ZUSS (*pursuing his mounting indignation*).
. . . As though Job's suffering were justified
Not by the Will of God but Job's
Acceptance of God's Will . . .

NICKLES.   Well,
What did you hope for? Hallelujahs?

MR. ZUSS (*not hearing*). . . . In spite of everything he'd suffered!

In spite of all he'd lost and loved
He understood and he forgave it! . . .
NICKLES (*a contemptuous snort as he
straightens to face* MR. ZUSS *on the plat-
form*).
What other victory could God win?
The choice is swallowing this swill of
world
Or vomiting in the trough. Job swallowed
it,
That's your triumph!—that he swallowed
it.
MR. ZUSS. . . . He'd heard of God and
now he saw Him!
Who's the judge in judgment there?
Who plays the hero, God or him?
Is God to be *forgiven?*
NICKLES.   Isn't He?
Job was innocent, you may remember . . .
(*Silence.*)
(*A nasty singsong*)
The perfect and the upright man!
MR. ZUSS (*deflated*). Don't start that
again! I'm sick of it.
NICKLES. *You* are!
MR. ZUSS.   *I* am. Sick to death.
(*Swinging his leg over the rail and start-
ing down the ladder*)
I'd rather sell balloons to children . . .
Lights! . . .
(*He shouts.*)
          Turn those lights on, can't you?
Want to see me break my neck?
(*The platform lights go out. Total dark-
ness. Louder*)
Lights! Lights! That's not the end of it.
NICKLES (*in the darkness*). Why isn't that
the end? It's over.
Job has chosen how to choose.
You've made your bow? You want an-
other?
(*The dangling light bulbs come feebly
on. By their light* J.B. *can still be seen
kneeling on his broken table.* MR. ZUSS
and NICKLES *crawl under the platform
after their traps. Their voices come from
the shadow, punctuated by grunts and
wheezes.*)
MR. ZUSS. You know as well as I there's
more . . .
There's always one more scene no matter
Who plays Job or how he plays it . . .
God restores him at the end.
NICKLES (*a snort*). God restores us all.
          That's normal.
That's God's mercy to mankind . . .
We never asked Him to be born . . .

We never chose the lives we die of . . .
They beat our rumps to make us breathe
          . . .
But God, if we have suffered patiently,
Borne it in silence, stood the stench,
Rewards us . . .

          gives our dirty selves back.
(MR. ZUSS *emerges in his white jacket,
adjusting his cap.*)
MR. ZUSS. Souls back!
NICKLES.   Selves back! Dirty selves
We've known too well and never wanted.
MR. ZUSS. That's not this play.
(NICKLES *backs out with his jacket and
cap and tray; puts them on.*)
NICKLES.   Hell it isn't.
(MR. ZUSS *tightens his balloon belt.*)
MR. ZUSS. God restores him *here.* On
          earth.
NICKLES (*balancing his tray*). So Job gets
          his in cash. That's generous.
What percentage off for cash?
MR. ZUSS. Gets all he ever had and more—
Much more.
NICKLES (*cheerfully ironic*). Sure. His
          wife. His children!
MR. ZUSS (*embarrassed*).
He gets his wife back, and the chil-
          dren . . .
Follow in nature's course.
(NICKLES, *who has stooped to pick up a
bag of popcorn, straightens slowly, stares
at* MR. ZUSS.)
NICKLES (*harshly*).   You're lying.
MR. ZUSS. I'm not lying.
NICKLES.   I say you're lying.
MR. ZUSS. Why should I lie. It's in the
          Book.
NICKLES (*jeering*). Wife back! Balls! He
          wouldn't touch her.
He wouldn't take her with a glove!
After all that filth and blood and
Fury to begin again! . . .
This fetid earth! That frightened Heaven
Terrified to trust the soul
It made with Its own hands, but testing
          it,
Tasting it, by trial, by torture,
Over and over till the last, least town
On all this reeling, reeking earth
Stinks with a spiritual agony
That stains the stones with excrement
          and shows
In shadow on each greasy curtain!
After life like his to take
The seed up of the sad creation

Planting the hopeful world again—
He can't! . . . he won't! . . . he wouldn't
touch her!
MR. ZUSS. He does though.
NICKLES (*raging*). Live his life again?—
Not even the most ignorant, obstinate,
Stupid or degraded man
This filthy planet ever farrowed,
Offered the opportunity to live
His bodily life twice over, would accept
it—
Least of all Job, poor, trampled bastard!
(MR. ZUSS *has finished fooling with his
balloons. He straightens up and marches
off without a glance at* NICKLES.)
It can't be borne twice over! Can't be!
MR. ZUSS. It is though. Time and again it
is—
Every blessed generation . . .
(*His voice drifts back as he disappears.*)
Time and again . . .
Time and again . . .
(NICKLES *starts to follow, looks back, sees
J.B. kneeling in his rubble, hesitates,
crosses, squats behind him, his vendor's
cap pushed back on his head, his tray on
his knees.*)
NICKLES. J.B.!
J.B. Let me alone.
NICKLES. It's me.
(J.B. *shrugs.*)
I'm not the Father. I'm the—Friend.
J.B. I have no friend.
NICKLES. Oh, come off it.
You don't have to act with me.
(J.B. *is silent.*)
O.K. Carry on.
All I wanted was to help.
Professional counsel you might call it . . .
(J.B. *is silent.*)
Of course you know how all this ends?
. . .
(J.B. *is silent.*)
I wondered how you'd play the end.
J.B. Who knows what the end is, ever?
NICKLES. I do. You do.
J.B. Then don't tell me.
NICKLES. What's the worst thing you can
think of?
J.B. I have asked for death. Begged for
it. Prayed for it.
NICKLES. Then the worst thing can't be
death.
J.B. Ah!
NICKLES. You know now.
J.B. No. You tell me.
NICKLES. Why should I tell you when you

know?
J.B. Then don't. I'm sick of mysteries.
Sick of them.
NICKLES. He gives it back to you.
J.B. What back?
NICKLES. All of it.
Everything He ever took:
Wife, health, children, everything.
J.B. I have no wife.
NICKLES. She comes back to you.
J.B. I have no children.
NICKLES (*a nasty laugh*). You'll have
better ones.
J.B. My skin is . . .
(*He breaks off, staring at the skin of his
naked arms.*)
NICKLES. Oh come on! I know the
Look of grease paint!
J.B. . . . whole! It's healed!
NICKLES (*heavily ironic*).
You see? You see what I mean? What
He plans for you?
(J.B., *staring at his arms, is silent.*)
NICKLES (*leaning forward, urgently*).
Tell me how you play the end.
Any man was screwed as Job was! . . .
(J.B. *does not answer.*)
I'll tell you how you play it. Listen!
Think if all the mucked-up millions
Since this bugged world began
Said, No!, said, Thank you!, took a rope's
end,
Took a window for a door,
Swallowed something, gagged on some-
thing . . .
(J.B. *lifts his head: he is listening but not
to* NICKLES.)
None of them knew the truth as Job does.
None of them had his cause to know.
J.B. Listen! Do you hear? There's some-
one . . .
NICKLES (*violently*). Job won't take it! Job
won't touch it!
Job will fling it in God's face
With half his guts to make it spatter!
He'd rather suffocate in dung—
Choke in ordure—
J.B. (*rising*). There is someone—
Someone waiting at the door.
NICKLES (*pulling his cap down, rising
slowly*). I know.
(*The dangling lights dim out.*)

SCENE ELEVEN

*A light comes from the canvas door.
It increases as though day were beginning*

somewhere. NICKLES *has gone.*

———

J.B. Who is it?
(*He crosses toward the door walking
with his old ease. Stops.*)
                    Is there someone there?
(*There is no answer. He goes on. Reaches
the door.*)
Sarah!
(*The light increases. She is sitting on the
sill, a broken twig in her hand.*)
SARAH. Look, Job: the forsythia,
The first few leaves . . .
                    not leaves though . . .
                              petals . . .
J.B. (*roughly*). Get up!
SARAH.   Where shall I go?
J.B.   Where you went!
Wherever!
(*She does not answer. More gently.*)
                    Where?
SARAH.   Among the ashes.
All there is now of the town is ashes.
Mountains of ashes. Shattered glass.
Glittering cliffs of glass all shattered
Steeper than a cat could climb
If there were cats still . . .
                    And the pigeons—
They wheel and settle and whirl off
Wheeling and almost settling . . .
                    And the silence—
There is no sound there now—no wind
                              sound—
Nothing that could sound the wind—
Could make it sing—no door—no door-
                              way . . .
Only this.
(*She looks at the twig in her hands.*)
                    Among the ashes!
I found it growing in the ashes,
Gold as though it did not know . . .
(*Her voice rises hysterically.*)
I broke the branch to strip the leaves off—
Petals again! . . .
(*She cradles it in her arms.*)
                    But they so clung to it!
J.B. Curse God and die, you said to me.
SARAH. Yes.
(*She looks up at him for the first time,
then down again.*)
                    You wanted justice, didn't you?
There isn't any. There's the world . . .
(*She begins to rock on the doorsill, the
little branch in her arms.*)
Cry for justice and the stars
Will stare until your eyes sting. Weep,
Enormous winds will thrash the water.

Cry in sleep for your lost children,
Snow will fall . . .
                    snow will fall . . .
J.B. Why did you leave me alone?
SARAH.   I loved you.
I couldn't help you any more.
You wanted justice and there was none—
Only love.
J.B.   He does not love. He
Is.
SARAH. But we do. That's the wonder.
J.B. Yet you left me.
SARAH.   Yes, I left you.
I thought there was a way away . . .

Water under bridges opens
Closing and the companion stars
Still float there afterwards. I thought the
                              door
Opened into closing water.
J.B. Sarah!
(*He drops on his knees beside her in the
doorway, his arms around her.*)
SARAH.   Oh, I never could!
I never could! Even the forsythia . . .
(*She is half laughing, half crying.*)
Even the forsythia beside the
Stair could stop me.
(*They cling to each other. Then she rises,
drawing him up, peering at the darkness
inside the door.*)
J.B.   It's too dark to see.
(*She turns, pulls his head down between
her hands and kisses him.*)
SARAH. Then blow on the coal of the heart,
                              my darling.
J.B. The coal of the heart . . .
SARAH.   It's all the light now.
(SARAH *comes forward into the dim room,*
J.B. *behind her. She lifts a fallen chair,
sets it straight.*)
Blow on the coal of the heart.
The candles in churches are out.
The lights have gone out in the sky.
Blow on the coal of the heart
And we'll see by and by . . .
(J.B. *has joined her, lifting and straight-
ening the chairs.*)
                    We'll see where we are
The wit won't burn and the wet soul
                              smoulders
Blow on the coal of the heart and we'll
                              know . . .
We'll know . . .
(*The light increases, plain white daylight
from the door, as they work.*)
                              CURTAIN

ALTERATIONS IN THE BROADWAY VERSION OF J.B.

The text of *J.B.* given above is the original version published by Houghton Mifflin in 1958. This is also the version produced at the Yale University School of Drama on April 2, 1958, under the direction of F. Curtis Canfield with settings by Donald Oenslager, costumes and masks by Richard Casler, lighting by Joan Larkey, and incidental music by Samuel Pottle. The cast of that production follows:

MR. ZUSS	*circus vendors*	Ray Sader
MR. NICKLES		Bernard Engel
THE DISTANT VOICE		Russ Moro
SARAH, J.B.'S WIFE		Margaret Andrews
J.B.		James Shepherd
REBECCA		Ann Satterthwait
RUTH		Suzanne Hull
MARY	*J.B.'s children*	Janie Herndon
DAVID		James Inman
JONATHAN		Brandon Stoddard
FIRST MAID		Judith Williams
SECOND MAID		Linda Robinson
FIRST MESSENGER		Ian Cadenhead
SECOND MESSENGER		William O'Brien
GIRL		Edith Lebok
BILDAD		Richard Forsyth
ZOPHAR	*J.B.'s comforters*	Joseph Hardy
ELIPHAZ		Fletcher Coleman
MRS. ADAMS		Bette Engel
JOLLY ADAMS		Janie Herndon
MRS. LESURE		Judith Williams
MRS. MURPHY		Edith Lebok
MRS. BOTTICELLI		Linda Robinson

Numerous alterations were made in the version finally brought to Broadway under the direction of Mr. Elia Kazan. (His correspondence with the author was published in the May 1959 issue of *Esquire* magazine, pages 144-58, under the title of "The Staging of a Play: the Notebooks and Letters behind Elia Kazan's Staging of Archibald MacLeish's *J.B.*")

The alterations and additions that possess some importance occur in the second of the two acts of the Broadway version, which starts with Scene 9 of our reprinted Houghton Mifflin text.

After the conversation between Mrs. Murphy and the other women (abbreviated and altered) comes the following passage:

J.B. (*on his knees at last*). Show me my guilt, O God!

(*Silence.*)

MR. ZUSS (*to* NICKLES). The time has come, Nickles! The time has come! Remember those proud prophecies of yours? Take everything he had and he'd curse God? Touch him in the flesh and he'd curse God? Well, have you heard him cursing God? God has done everything you asked for: God has destroyed him without cause.
. . .
NICKLES. God has destroyed his *wealth*, his *children*, Stripped raw tatters from his *skin*, Touched his *flesh*, but him himself God has not touched. Teach his soul! Show him that there are no reasons! Show him neither God nor man Has reasons adequate to his catastrophes! Do you think he'll call God *then*? Not in that voice, anyway!

MR. ZUSS. Teach him what you please!

You've lost him.
Touch him in the soul! You've lost.
J.B. Show me my guilt, O God.
NICKLES (a leer up at MR. ZUSS). Silence!
The still silence of the stars!
J.B. Is there not anyone to answer me?
Where is the wisdom of this world
That once knew answers where there
                      were no answers?
(Silence.)
Where are the answerers to answer it?
NICKLES (contemptuously). Silence!
The slow silence of the soul!

The next important insertion comes with the arrival of the Comforters:

NICKLES. Mr. Zuss! Who *are* they?
MR. ZUSS (perfect assurance: he knows
            The Book). Comforters.
NICKLES. What comforters?
MR. ZUSS. Job's comforters.
Every time they play this play
Job's comforters come by. To comfort
                  him.
NICKLES. I know! To justify the ways of
                  God to
God by making Job responsible—
Making him . . . worthy of his . . .
                  wretchedness—
Giving him that dear gift of guilt,
That putrid poultice of the soul that pulls
The poison in not out! That dirty
Thumb our generation sucks at.
MR. ZUSS. What are you afraid of, Nickles?
Afraid he'll join the rest and take
Their answers? . . . and be comforted?
                  . . .

After Zophar's line "If it were otherwise we could not bear it . . ." J.B. is given the following speech:

J.B. I can bear anything a man can bear
If I can *be* one—if my life
Somehow can justify my living—
If my own self can answer. You
Refuse me even that. You tell me
One man's guilt is meaningless:
History has no time for guilt—
Science has no sign for guilt—
God created all men guilty.
Comforters you call yourselves!
I tell you those old women by the wall
Who sleep there shivering have given
                  comfort
Greater than all of yours together.
They gave their misery to keep me warm.
(He huddles in his rags, his head down.)

Thereupon Zophar with "all the fervor of his conviction" gives his speech on the "Fall"—i.e., "Adam's fall."

Then, after the lyrical passage on the "Fall," Nickles is given the following speech while the Comforters are shown departing:

NICKLES (gesturing contemptuously at
their departing backs, his voice rising in
                  bitter triumph).
You think he'll squat there in his anguish
                  now
Begging the universe to love him?
He knows now that no reasoning on earth
Can justify the suffering he suffers.
He knows the good is not rewarded,
He knows the evil is not punished,
He knows his life is meaningless. It's
                  done.
It's done with—over! He'll curse God!
He'll never lift his voice again
To that deaf, unintelligible Heaven!

The most radical alteration came after J.B., having heard the "Distant Voice," declares "I abhor myself and repent . . ." From this point on, the Broadway version is given below in full:

(Silence. MR. ZUSS and NICKLES stare at
J.B. from the steps and the platform;
NICKLES with an expression of incredulous
disgust, MR. ZUSS beaming.)
NICKLES. Well, that's that!
MR. ZUSS. (his head raised in gratitude to
the darkness overhead). That's . . . that.
NICKLES. You win.
MR. ZUSS. Of course I win. I told you.
NICKLES. Pious, contemptible, goddam
                  sheep!
(He throws his rag of costume on the
floor.)
Repenting! And for what? For asking
Reasons of the universe! For asking why!
MR. ZUSS (exalted). He'd heard of God
              and now he saw Him.
Planets and Pleiades and eagles,

Screaming horses, scales of light—
Last Orion, least sea shell,
The wonder and the mystery of the uni-
verse,

Beauty beyond the feel of fingers,
Marvel beyond the maze of mind,
The whole creation: searchless power
Burning upon the hearth of stars—
NICKLES. Where did I put that *popcorn*
. . .

(*He fumbles around under the platform
while* MR. ZUSS *stands above, lost in the
ecstasy of his triumph. Below them in the
ring, unseen by both,* J.B. *has lifted his
face, straightened his body, and kneels
staring out into the darkness before him,
his mouth working, his eyes alive. The
magnificent great words he has heard return to his mouth in broken phrases and
in his own voice—the sour of mortality
on them.*)

J.B. Hast thou an arm like God . . . like
God . . .
MR. ZUSS. His was the true repentance,
wasn't it?
J.B. Deck thyself now in majesty and ex-
cellency . . .
(*He looks down at his filthy blanket.*)
MR. ZUSS. True repentance is the *fear* of
God!
J.B. Then will I also confess unto thee
That thine own right hand . . .
(*He lifts his trembling hand before his
eyes.*)
can save thee. . . .
MR. ZUSS. God's Will never changes,
never
Can change, never will change—
Never!
Comfort, you see, is not a changing fash-
ion,
Comfort is one and always and the
Same for every human heart.
We have no comfort but the fear of God.
NICKLES (*who has been hitching his tray
on*).
He feared, my friend. Why not? Why
wouldn't he?
J.B. Wherefore . . . I abhor myself . . .
and repent . . .
NICKLES. God with all those stars and
stallions . . .
Throwing the whole creation at him!
He with little children's bones . . .
J.B. Wherefore I abhor myself and *repent!*
NICKLES. Let's not talk about those chil-
dren!

MR. ZUSS. He's made his choice.
NICKLES. Made *his choice?*
The choice is swallowing this swill of
world
Or vomiting in the trough. Job swallowed
it.
That's God's triumph—that he swallowed
it.
MR. ZUSS (*thundering*). Is God to be for-
given?
NICKLES (*the supreme insolence*). Isn't
He?
(*He turns his back on* J.B. *and crosses
towards the aisle by which he entered.*)
MR. ZUSS (*choking with anger*). That's
not the end!
NICKLES Why not? You win.
You've made your bow. You want an-
other?
MR. ZUSS (*shouting angrily after him*).
You know as well as I there's more.
There's always one more scene no matter
Who plays Job or how. You're running
Out! You haven't got the guts to
Play your part through. You're no actor!
You're a popcorn peddler to the heart!
NICKLES (*stung in his professional pride*).
What other scene?
MR. ZUSS. The scene that ends it.
God restores him at the end.
NICKLES. God restores us all. That's nor-
mal.
That's God's mercy to mankind.
We never asked Him to be born.
We never chose the lives we die of.
They beat our rumps to make us breathe.
But, God, if we have suffered patiently,
Borne it in silence, stood the stench,
Rewards us!
Gives our dirty souls back.
MR. ZUSS. God restores him *here.*
On *earth.*
Gives him all he ever had and
More!
NICKLES (*starting out*). Sure! His wife.
His children.
MR. ZUSS. He gets his wife back and the
children
Follow in nature's course.
NICKLES (*turning*). You're lying.
MR. ZUSS. I'm not lying.
NICKLES (*passionately*). I say you're lying.
MR. ZUSS. Why should I lie? It's in the
Book.
NICKLES (*racing back down the aisle,
vaulting onto the stage*).
Wife back! Wife! He wouldn't touch her.

He wouldn't take her with a glove!
After all that filth and blood and
Fury to begin again!
After life like his to take
The seed up of the sad creation
Planting the hopeful world again . . .
He can't. He won't. He wouldn't touch
                                        her.
MR. ZUSS. He does though.
NICKLES. Live his life again?
Not even the most ignorant, obstinate,
Stupid or degraded man
This filthy planet ever farrowed
Offered the opportunity to live
His bodily life twice over, would accept
                                        it . . .
Least of all Job; poor, trampled bastard!
It can't be borne twice over! Can't be!
MR. ZUSS (*complete assurance, master of
                    the situation*).
It is though. Time and again it is . . .
Every blessed generation . . .
Time and
Again. Time and again.
J.B. (*bringing himself to his feet, stand-
ing there, swaying, his voice no longer
inward, but strong, and firm and simple
            —his own voice*). Must I be
Dumb because my mouth is mortal?—
Blind because my eyes will one day
Close forever? Is that my wickedness—
That I am weak?
(*Silence.* MR. ZUSS *and* NICKLES *stare at
him.*)
NICKLES. Did you hear that?
MR. ZUSS (*a long pause*). I did.
NICKLES. What does it mean?
MR. ZUSS. I don't
Know.
J.B. Must my breath, my breathing, be
                                forgiven me?
NICKLES (*dropping his tray, grinning back
up over his shoulder at* MR. ZUSS *dumb
            and incredulous on his platform*).
Time and again, eh? Time and again?
(*He tiptoes into the ring towards* J.B.)
Not this generation, Mister.
(*He stands behind* J.B.)
J.B.!
J.B. (*a new strength and assurance*).
Let me alone.
NICKLES. It's me.
I'm not the Father. I'm the . . .
Friend.
J.B. I have no friend.
NICKLES. O come off it.
You don't have to act with me.

(J.B. *is silent.*)
O.K. Carry on.
All I wanted was to help.
Professional counsel you might call it . . .
(J.B. *is silent.*)
Of course you know how all this ends?
(J.B. *is silent.*)
I wondered how you'd play the end.
J.B. What other is there?
NICKLES. You don't know?
(*Silence.*)
Why should I tell you when you know?
J.B. I have asked for death.
Begged for it. Prayed for it.
NICKLES. Then the worst thing can't be
death.
(J.B. *stares at him.*)
He gives it back to you.
J.B. What back?
NICKLES. Everything.
Everything He ever took—
Wife, health, children . . . everything.
J.B. I have no wife.
NICKLES. He gives her back to you.
J.B. I have no children.
NICKLES. You'll have better ones.
J.B. My skin is . . .
(*He breaks off, staring at his naked
arms.*)
NICKLES. O come on! I know the
Look of grease paint!
J.B. Whole! It's healed!
NICKLES (*heavily ironic*). You see? You
                        see what I mean?—
What He plans for you?
Tell me how you play the end!
Tell me how you play it. Listen!
Any man was screwed as Job was . . .
(J.B. *is silent, staring at his arms, his
hands.* NICKLES' *voice rises urgently. As
he speaks,* SARAH *appears at the edge of
the circle of light. She is draggled, dis-
arrayed, moves vaguely.* NICKLES *see her.*)
I'll tell you how you play it! Listen!
Think if all the mucked-up millions
Since this buggered world began
Said No!—said Thank you! took a rope's
                                        end—
Took a window for a door—
Swallowed something—gagged on some-
                                thing . . .
(J.B. *lifts his head listening but not to*
NICKLES.)
Not one of them had known what you
                                        know.
Not one was taught *Job's* truth!
J.B. There's someone . . .

NICKLES. Job won't take it! Job won't
touch it!
J.B. There's someone standing at the door.
NICKLES. Job won't take it! Job won't
touch it!
(*He dashes up the stair of the platform.*)
Job will fling it in God's face
With half his guts to make it spatter!
He'd rather suffocate in dung,
Drown in ordure—
(*He attempts to scale the stairs to the
high perch.*)
Suffocate in dung,
Drown in ordure!
(NICKLES *collapses on the stair.* MR. ZUSS
*flings off his robe in a gesture of triumph
and strides down the stair, his face shin-
ing. He enters the ring where* J.B. *and*
SARAH *stand opposite each other, she look-
ing up at him, half tender, half afraid;
he, his mouth grim, turned away.*)
MR. ZUSS. Job! Job! Job! You've answered
him!
J.B. Let me alone. I am alone.
I'll sweat it out alone.
MR. ZUSS. You've found
The answer at the end! You've answered
him!
We take what God has sent—the God-
send.
(*A gesture toward* SARAH. J.B. *is silent.*)
There is no resolution of the mystery
Of unintelligible suffering but the dumb
Bowed head that makes injustice just
By yielding to the Will that willed it—
Yielding to the Will that willed
A world where there can be injustice.
You've learned that now. You've bowed
your head.
(J.B. *is silent.* SARAH *takes a tentative
step toward him.*)
The end is the acceptance of the end.
We take what God has willed.
J.B. (*to* MR. ZUSS. *Savagely*). I will not
Duck my head again to thunder—
that bullwhip crackling at my ears!
Although
He kill me with it—I must know.
(NICKLES *has risen and is making his
way slowly down the stair.*)
MR. ZUSS (*astonished. He could not have
heard what he has heard*).
We have no peace but in obedience.
Our peace is acquiescence in the Will of
God.
His Will our Peace!
J.B. I'll find a foothold

(NICKLES *crosses down platform and down
steps.*)
Somewhere *knowing.*
Life is a filthy farce, you say,
And nothing but a bloody stage
Can bring the curtain down and men
Must have ironic hearts and perish
Laughing . . .
Well, *I* will not laugh!
(*He swings on* MR. ZUSS.)
And neither will I weep among
The silent who lie down to die
In meek relinquishment protesting
Nothing, questioning nothing, asking
Nothing but to rise again and bow!
Neither the bowing nor the blood
Will make an end for me now!
Neither the
Yes in ignorance . . . the No in spite . . .
Neither of them!
(MR. ZUSS *exits to ramp at left.*)
Neither of them!
(NICKLES *crosses down to right ramp.*)
Sarah!
Why have you come back again?
SARAH (*confused, holding out the small
green branch like a child.*) Look Job.
The first few leaves . . .
Not leaves though—
Petals. I found it in the ashes growing
Green as though it did not know . . .
All that's left there now is ashes . . .
Mountains of ashes, shattered glass,
Glittering cliffs of glass all shattered
Steeper than a cat could climb
If there were cats still . . .
J.B. Why?
SARAH. I broke the
Branch to strip the leaves off.
Petals
(*Fastens branch to pole.*)
Again!
But they so clung to it!
J.B. Curse
God and die! You said that to me.
SARAH. Yes. You wanted justice didn't
you?
J.B. Cry for justice and the stars
Will stare until your eyes sting!
Weep,
Enormous winds will thrash the water!
SARAH. Cry in sleep for your lost children,
Snow will fall. . . . Snow will fall.
J.B. You left me, Sarah.
SARAH. Yes, I left you.
I thought there was a way away.
Out of the world. Out of the world.

Water under bridges opens
Out of the world. Out of the world.
Closing and the companion stars
Still float there afterwards. I thought the
                                        door
Opened into closing water.
J.B. Sarah!
SARAH. Oh, I never could.
I never could. Even this.
Even the green leaf on the branch could
                                        stop me.
J.B. Why have you come back again?
SARAH. Because I love you.
J.B. Because you love me!
The one thing certain in the hurtful
                                        world
Is love's inevitable heartbreak.
What's the future but the past to come
Over and over, love and loss,
What's loved most lost most.
(SARAH *has moved into the rubble of the
ring, setting things to right. She picks up
the broken stub of a candle, looks here
and there for something to set it on. Her
mind is on her task, not on* J.B.'s *words.*)
SARAH. I know that, Job.
J.B. Nothing is certain but the loss of
                                        love.
And yet . . . you say you love me!
SARAH. Yes.
J.B. The stones in those dead streets would
                                        crack
With terrible indecent laughter
Hearing *you* and *me* say love!
SARAH. I have no light to light the candle.

J.B. (*violently*). You have *our* love to light
                                        it with!
Blow on the coal of the heart, poor
                                        Sarah.
SARAH. Blow on the coal of the heart . . . ?
J.B. The candles in churches are out.
The lights have gone out in the sky!
SARAH. The candles in churches are out.
The lights have gone out in the sky.
Blow on the coal of the heart
And we'll see by and by . . . we'll see
                                        where we are.
We'll know. We'll know.
J.B. (*slowly, with difficulty, the hard
words said at last*).
We can never know.
He answered me like the stillness of a
                                        star
That silences us asking.
No, Sarah, no:
We *are* and that is all our answer.
We are and what we are can suffer.
But . . . what suffers loves.
And love
Will live its suffering again,
Risk its own defeat again,
Endure the loss of everything again
And yet again and yet again
In doubt, in dread, in ignorance, unan-
                                        swered,
Over and over, with the dark before,
The dark behind it . . . and still live . . .
                                        still love.

(THE PLAY IS ENDED)

The reader, producer, director, and public relations officer would be well advised to read the "Foreword by the Author," reprinted in the Samuel French volume from *The New York Times*. Significant passages from this Foreword follow:

"My play is put in motion by two broken-down actors who believe, themselves, that the play *is* the Book of Job and that one of them is acting God, and the other Satan. When J.B. and his family appear, however, it is not out of the Bible that they come. . . .

"I badly needed an ancient structure in which to build the contemporary play which has haunted me for five years past and the structure of the poem of Job is the only one I know into which our modern history will fit. . . .

"As for ourselves there can be very few of us who are perfect, but the enormous, nameless disasters which have befallen whole cities, entire peoples, in two great wars and many small ones, have destroyed the innocent together with the guilty—and with no 'cause' our minds can grasp. . . .

"Where Job's Comforters undertook to persuade him against the evidence of his own inner conviction, that he *was* guilty, ours attempt to persuade us that we are *not*—that we cannot be—that, for psychological reasons, or because everything is determined in advance by economic necessity anyway, or because we are damned before we are started, guilt is impossible. Our Comforters are, if anything, less comfortable than Job's for . . . if we cannot even be guilty then there are no reasons."

And in the following passage the author endeavors to justify the conclusion to which objections have been raised by some of the play's critics.

". . . man can *live* his truth, his deepest truth, but cannot speak it. It is for this reason that love becomes the ultimate human answer to the ultimate human question. Love, in reason's terms, answers nothing. . . . What love does is to affirm. It affirms the worth of life in spite of life. It affirms the wonder and the beauty of the human creature, mortal and insignificant and ignorant though he be. . . . It answers life with life and so justifies that bravely tolling line of Shakespeare's which declares that love 'bears it out even to the edge of doom.' . . . J.B., like Job, . . . acquiesces in the vast indifference of the Universe as all men must who truly face it; takes back his life again. In love. To live."

THE BEST MAN

Gore Vidal

Presented by The Playwrights' Company
at the Morosco Theatre, New York, on March 31, 1960,
with the following cast:

WILLIAM RUSSELL	Melvyn Douglas	DR. ARTINIAN	Hugh Franklin
ART HOCKSTADER	Lee Tracy	REPORTER 1	Howard Fischer
SENATOR JOE CANTWELL	Frank Lovejoy	REPORTER 2	Tony Bickley
ALICE RUSSELL	Leora Dana	REPORTER 3	Barbara Berjer
MABEL CANTWELL	Kathleen Maguire	REPORTER 4	Tom McDermott
MRS. GAMADGE	Ruth McDevitt	DELEGATES, OTHER REPORTERS	
DON BLADES	Joseph Sullivan		John Dorrin
DICK JENSEN	Karl Weber		Mitchell Erickson
SHELDON MARCUS	Graham Jarvis		Ruth Tobin
SENATOR CARLIN	Gordon B. Clarke		

Directed by Joseph Anthony
Sets and lighting by Jo Mielziner
Costumes by Theonie V. Aldredge

Born at West Point in 1925, Gore Vidal enlisted in the United States Army shortly after graduating from Phillips Exeter Academy. A precocious as well as prolific writer of fiction, he produced his first novel, *Williwaw,* at the age of nineteen. The novels that followed in fairly rapid order confirmed him in the writing profession, which also brought him into motion pictures and television. He entered the theatre with an airy but here and there invigorating as well as consistently funny farce, *Visit to a Small Planet,* which opened in New York at the Booth Theatre on February 7, 1957. The outstanding piece of science fiction in our theatre because spiced with satire, it was treated to a lively production staged by Cyril Ritchard (who also performed in it) and it scored a run of 338 performances before closing in January, 1958.

After such success Mr. Vidal simply had to come back for a second fling on Broadway, which he did with *The Best Man* on March 31, 1960, at a larger theatre, the Morosco. The production, which closed in New York in July, 1961, had 520 performances. He reappeared as a playwright in January, 1962, as the adapter of the Swiss playwright Duerrenmatt's *Romulus,* a mordant quasi-historical comedy about the fall of Roman civilization. This time Mr. Vidal's luck changed. Despite this minor fiasco, and even though he has had many irons in the fire, one of them being practical politics, he is unlikely to overlook the Broadway stage after the friendly reception of his first two plays.

The Best Man happens to be a rarely cultivated type of political comedy nowadays, but political satire is of course a perfectly legitimate art that playwrights have practiced since the time of Aristophanes. Mr. Vidal's play did not constitute any great challenge, but it scored many a small point with considerable liveliness. It is hardly surprising that the New York press should have welcomed *The Best Man* and that there should have been a large cosmopolitan audience for it. It is possible for ardent critics to become exercised over the surface lightness and facile earnestness of the author and for complaisant older reviewers to be totally indifferent to the issue that agitated the author—namely, the nature of Presidential politics. Somewhere between the two extremes will be found the proper boundaries of *The Best Man.* That it was considered the most successful political comedy of the period (although some claims could be urged in behalf of a somewhat earlier piece, *The Gang's All Here,* by Jerome Lawrence and Robert E. Lee) was, moreover, a large compliment to the author in a period when political theatre was at a low ebb.

ACT ONE

SCENE ONE

A hotel suite in Philadelphia . . . perhaps July 1960. From stage right to left: a bedroom with twin beds, a connecting hall, and a living room. There is a door from living room to hall and one from bedroom to hall. At stage right, a door to the bathroom. At stage left, a door to the office part of the suite, from which can be heard telephones ringing and the buzz of talk.

Dominating the living room, stage left, is a television set. There is also a bar upstage and of course the usual number of chairs and sofas. The décor is early Conrad Hilton. On the wall, a poster proclaims WILLIAM RUSSELL FOR PRESIDENT. *The candidate, according to his portrait, is a strong, youthful-looking man of fifty. There are also various placards around the room, propped against walls and furniture:* HUSTLE WITH RUSSELL . . . , A GREAT GOVERNOR, A GREAT SECRETARY OF STATE, AND THE NEXT PRESIDENT OF THE U.S., *and similar political sentiments.*

Since one hotel suite is apt to look very like another, this same set could be used for the opposition's suite downstairs, so that when the narrative shifts to the other suite all that would need changing would be specific props: for instance, the placards there would itemize the virtues of Senator Joe Cantwell for President: YOU'LL DO WELL WITH CANTWELL, GO WITH JOE, *etc. Fortunately,* The Best Man's *New York production was designed by Jo Mielziner, a crafty user of twin turntables which made it possible to have two sets which were shifted with great speed. The Cantwell suite resembled the Russell suite in layout, except that everything was reversed: the Cantwell living room was at right and the bedroom at left. The director made an amiable point in furnishing the Russell bedroom with twin beds and the Cantwell bedroom with a double bed.*

As the curtain rises, photographers and newsmen set off a great flash of camera bulbs, aimed at WILLIAM *and* ALICE RUSSELL, *who enter from the hall, followed by* REPORTERS, PHOTOGRAPHERS, *a* BELLBOY *and* DICK JENSEN, Bill Russell's *campaign manager.*

JENSEN *is in his late forties: intense, devoted, apprehensive by nature. There is a babble of sound: strident questions—* "Any statement?" "What about California?" "The labor bill?" "Just one more, Mr. Secretary," "Red China?" "How many delegates you got?" *During this* RUSSELL *tries to be heard; his wife stands rigidly beside him.* ALICE RUSSELL *is in her early forties. She is a handsome, slender, gray-haired lady of the Old American Establishment, not quite as diffident and shy as she appears.*

———

JENSEN. O.K., boys! O.K. Give him air! One question at a time . . .

REPORTER 1. Mr. Secretary, as of today how many delegates do you have sewed up?

RUSSELL (*lightly*). When it comes to delegates, we neither sow nor do we reap.

REPORTER 1 (*puzzled*). What was that again, Mr. Secretary?

RUSSELL. I said . . .

JENSEN. Mr. Russell was making a joke, he means we . . .

REPORTER 2 (*helpfully*). He said neither do they sow . . .

REPORTER 3. But what about Ex-President Hockstader? Have you got his endorsement yet?

RUSSELL. In a word . . . no.

REPORTER 3. Do you think you'll get it?

RUSSELL. Ask him. There's a rumor he's in Philadelphia.

REPORTER 4. Yes. He's upstairs. He's going to make a statement tonight. He says it's between you and Senator Cantwell . . .

RUSSELL. So we'll just have to wait until tonight.

REPORTER 1. Mrs. Russell, what do *you* think your husband's chances are?

ALICE (*uncertainly*). Well, I . . . I don't really know. I mean, we have to wait for the convention, don't we?

REPORTER 2. Mr. Secretary, if there's a deadlock between you and Senator Cantwell, whom do you think will be the dark horse candidate?

RUSSELL. Jack Paar. (*Smiles.*) I'm sorry, but I'm not about to build up a dark horse when I am doing my best to look like the light horse.

REPORTER 2. Sir, what do you think of Governor Merwin's chances?

RUSSELL. John Merwin is a very talented young man. We don't know much about him, of course, but . . .

REPORTER 4 (*quickly*). Would you consider Governor Merwin as a running mate?

REPORTER 3. Yes.

RUSSELL. I might. He's one of a number of capable men.

REPORTER 3. Mr. Secretary, how did you interpret the Gallup poll this morning?

RUSSELL. I didn't interpret it because I didn't see it.

REPORTER 4. Senator Cantwell's picked up two per cent from you since last week . . .

JENSEN (*overlapping*). But we're still leading by nine per cent in the country with . . .

RUSSELL. But you *can* say I don't believe in polls . . .

JENSEN (*nervously*). What the Secretary means is . . .

RUSSELL (*firmly*). I don't believe in polls. Accurate or not. And if I may bore you with one of my little sermons: life is not a popularity contest; neither is politics. The important thing for any government is educating the people about issues, *not* following the ups and downs of popular opinion.

REPORTER 3 (*in for the kill*). Does that mean you don't respect popular opinion? Do you think a President ought to ignore what the people want?

RUSSELL (*serenely*). If the people want the wrong thing, if the people don't understand an issue, if they've been misled by the press (*Politely*)—by *some* of the press—then I think a President should ignore their opinion and try to convince them that his way is the right way.

REPORTER 2. Do you think the people mistrust intellectuals in politics?

RUSSELL (*smiles*). I'm glad you asked that question. Bertrand Russell seems to think so. He once wrote that the people in a democracy tend to think they have less to fear from a stupid man than from an intelligent one.

REPORTER 1 (*lost*). Bertrand . . . ?

RUSSELL. Bertrand Russell.

REPORTER 1 (*slow, false dawning*). Oh, the same name . . .

RUSSELL (*amused*). Yes. But no relative, unfortunately.

REPORTER 3 (*the taste of blood*). Wasn't Bertrand Russell *fired* from City College of New York?

RUSSELL (*sadly*). Yes, he was fired. But only for moral turpitude . . . *not* for incompetence as a philosopher.

REPORTER 4. What image do you feel Senator Cantwell is projecting at the moment?

RUSSELL. Image? He's behaving himself, if that's what you mean.

REPORTER 4 (*solemnly*). But hasn't his *basic* image changed in the last year?

RUSSELL. I'm afraid I don't know much about images. That's a word from advertising where you don't sell the product, you sell the image of the product. And sometimes the image is a fake.

REPORTER 3 (*slyly*). But after all, your own image . . .

RUSSELL. Is a poor thing but mine own. Paint me as I am, warts and all!

REPORTER 1. What?

RUSSELL. Oliver Cromwell.

(JENSEN *starts rounding up the press.*)

JENSEN. O.K., fellows, we'll have a statement for you in about an hour. Headquarters are through there. The mimeograph machine has been repaired and . . .

RUSSELL. And wisdom flows by the yard.

(JENSEN *herds the* REPORTERS *off stage left. All except* REPORTER 3. *She has followed* ALICE *into the bedroom.* RUSSELL *says good-by to the* REPORTERS *at the door.*)

REPORTER 1 (*urgently*). Mr. Secretary . . .

(*A flood of last-minute questions and photographers shouting: "Just one more."*)

RUSSELL (*apologetically*). I have a feeling Dick Jensen would like the candidate to stop talking. I'll see you all later, after the delegations. Until then, as Senator Cantwell would say, may the best man win!

(*The* REPORTERS *and* JENSEN *are gone.* RUSSELL *is relieved until he hears the cold-edged voice of* REPORTER 3 *in the bedroom.*)

REPORTER 3. How do you like Philadelphia, Mrs. Russell?

ALICE. Well, I just got here . . . I used to visit here as a girl.

(RUSSELL *comes to the rescue. He propels* REPORTER 3 *to the door at stage left.*)

RUSSELL. Please, *please*. Wait till we

unpack.

REPORTER 3. Do you drink the tap water?

RUSSELL. I have no intention of losing Pennsylvania by admitting that I boil the local water.

(REPORTER 3 *departs with an unamused grimace.* RUSSELL *shudders.* JENSEN *returns.*)

JENSEN (*groans*). Bertrand Russell at a press conference.

RUSSELL (*placating*). All right, Dick, all right, no more jokes. From now on we project blandness. A candidate should not mean but be. And no matter *what* happens, I shall smile: serenely, fatuously, ineluctably. (RUSSELL, *smiling, hat in hand, marches, waving and beaming, to the bedroom. Intoning*) Floods destroy the Middle West, and the candidate smiles. Half the world is starving, and the candidate smiles. War is declared, and the candidate smiles. Is there anything more indecent than the human face when it smiles? (ALICE *takes the hat. He returns to the connecting hall and looks into the mirror.*) All these predatory teeth, reminding us of our animal descent.

JENSEN. Steady. No mention of Darwin. Evolution is out of bounds. Before the Garden of Eden was the Word. And *stop* looking in the mirror.

RUSSELL. I never pass a mirror I don't look in it. I wonder why?

(ALICE *has gone to hang a coat in the wall closet. En route, she answers him.*)

ALICE (*briskly*). Vanity. (ALICE *returns to her unpacking in the bedroom.*)

RUSSELL (*thoughtfully*). I look to remind myself I really exist. One needs constant proofs.

ALICE. I better use the bathroom while I've got a chance.

RUSSELL (*genuine concern*). Alice, *don't* drink the *water!*

(*The telephone in the living room rings.*)

JENSEN (*answers it*). Who? Oh, Mrs. Gamadge, good to hear your voice . . . ! Yes, ma'am. Well, he's got the Texas delegation coming in about twenty minutes, but (*Looks to* RUSSELL *for guidance.* RUSSELL *nods.*) if you come over right now . . . Oh, good, you're in the hotel . . . fine. We'll see you then. (*Puts down receiver.*) Our national committee woman.

RUSSELL. The only known link between the N.A.A.C.P. and the Ku Klux Klan. How does she do it? How? How? (RUSSELL *is studying the carpet as he paces oddly downstage.*)

JENSEN (*curiously*). Bill . . . may I ask a very personal question?

RUSSELL. Personal? There is no other kind between us . . .

JENSEN. What the hell are you doing when you start that hopscotch thing up and down the floor?

RUSSELL. As we say at press conferences, I'm glad you asked that question. I am . . . oh, damn! (*He steps back suddenly.*) The ancient Romans used to examine the entrails of animals in order to learn the future. I am told on very good authority that my rival, Senator Cantwell, goes to an astrologist in Kalorama Road, Washington, for guidance. I, lacking all superstition, study the future in multiples of threes. Put simply—and we are nothing if not experts at putting things simply, are we?—I find a carpet with workable pattern. This one's perfect. Now if I step on a leaf—see?—before I have completed three full steps *between* leaves, I will *not* get what I want. If, however, I can take three paces *without* touching that leaf, I will get what I want. I may say, I never cheat. (*Scowls.*) Hell! However, I can on occasion go for the best two out of three. I also make bets with myself. For instance, if the man I'm talking to does not answer me within the count of three, I get what I want. (*He finishes his walk just short of where* JENSEN *is seated at stage left.*) Ah, victory! I hope I've answered your question lucidly?

JENSEN. Yes, you have. But let's keep it *our* secret. (*A* WOMAN AID *enters with a stack of newspapers from left.*) My own vice is the daily horoscope. (AID *goes.*) So what did you win?

RUSSELL. The nomination. And on the first ballot, too! (*He sits on downstage sofa.*) My God, I'm keyed up! I feel like I'm going to jump out of my skin. I can't sit still . . . (JENSEN *crosses to him.*)

JENSEN. Well, you won't do much sitting still between now and Wednesday. Here's today's schedule. Most of the delegations will come to us. (*Shows* RUSSELL *paper.*) See? It's a tight schedule, starting with Texas at 11:15, then . . .

RUSSELL (*unable to attend*). We're getting so close . . . so close! And what's going to happen?

JENSEN. You! We've got the delegates. It's yours on the first ballot. If you get Ex-President Hockstader's endorsement . . .

(*The door buzzer in the connecting hall sounds. There is a noise of voices from the outside corridor.*)

RUSSELL AND JENSEN (*in unison*). Mrs. Gamadge!

(*They both cross to the hall door. JENSEN opens it. MRS. GAMADGE, small, plump, elderly, sails into view, surrounded by NEWSMEN and PHOTOGRAPHERS. She is serene in the knowledge that she is the Voice of the American Woman, by default. Her manner is an odd mixture of coziness and steeliness.*)

MRS. GAMADGE (*beams*). Mr. Secretary . . . (MRS. GAMADGE *seizes* RUSSELL *for a picture. They pose, her left arm around him, her right arm raised in salute. Then* JENSEN *ushers out the press.*)

RUSSELL (*sudden energy*). Mrs. Gamadge, it's wonderful to see you! Come on in. Sit down. Have a drink. You know Dick Jensen, don't you? My campaign manager.

(MRS. GAMADGE *shakes* JENSEN's *hand as she crosses to a sofa.*)

MRS. GAMADGE. Such a lovely hotel for a convention. I always say the hotel you're at makes all the difference at a convention. Does Mrs. Russell like your suite?

RUSSELL. Practically a home away from home.

MRS. GAMADGE (*narrowly*). She *is* here with you, isn't she?

(RUSSELL *pulls out a chair for her.*)

RUSSELL. Yes. This is the good chair.

MRS. GAMADGE. I'll sit *here,* thank you. (MRS. GAMADGE *unfurls on the sofa.*)

JENSEN. I must say, I'm glad to meet you at last, Mrs. Gamadge.

MRS. GAMADGE. And I'm glad to get a chance to see you, Mr. Jensen. I love egg-heads in politics.

JENSEN (*taken aback*). Oh, well . . .

RUSSELL (*quickly*). What can I get you to drink?

MRS. GAMADGE. I don't drink, Mr. Secretary. A Coke or a glass of soda, maybe. Anything. (*Turns to* JENSEN, *sweetly.*) Professors like you give such a tone to these conventions. No, I really mean it.

Of course a lot of the women don't like them but I do. Though of course I didn't like the New Deal.

(RUSSELL *gives her a glass.*)

RUSSELL. Here's your soda . . .

(*She takes it with a nice smile.*)

MRS. GAMADGE. A great many of the women are suspicious of you professors, Mr. Jensen. . . . You don't mind my speaking like this?

JENSEN. Certainly not, Mrs. Gamadge. After all, talking to you is like . . . well, like talking to the average American housewife. (JENSEN *is aware* MRS. GAMADGE *has frozen on "average." He stammers.*) I mean *you're* not average but you speak for them . . .

MRS. GAMADGE. Very nicely put, Mr. Jensen. (*To* RUSSELL.) I don't know why everyone says he's so conceited.

RUSSELL. Dick? Stuck up? Why, he's the spirit of humility . . . an old shoe, in fact! As for being intellectual, he can hardly get through the Greek Anthology without a trot.

MRS. GAMADGE (*nods*). Yes. (*To business*) You see, the women like a regular kind of man, like General Eisenhower. Now he really appeals to the women. That nice smile. He has such a way with him . . . he inspires confidence because he doesn't seem like anything but *just folks.* You could imagine him washing up after dinner, listening to his wife's view on important matters.

RUSSELL (*quietly*). Yes, indeed you can.

MRS. GAMADGE. Nothing pushy or aggressive or all those things we women don't like in our men. He's just grand! Now, Mr. Secretary, there is no doubt in anybody's mind you are going to get the nomination on the first ballot . . .

RUSSELL. There is doubt in *my* mind . . .

MRS. GAMADGE (*no time for diversion*). Yes . . . yes . . . yes . . . now let's face facts a minute. You don't mind if I talk turkey?

RUSSELL. No. By all means . . . turkey.

MRS. GAMADGE. You are not the ideal candidate for the women. You know that, I suppose.

RUSSELL. Well, what . . . what women do you have in mind?

MRS. GAMADGE (*coldly*). The women don't like your trying to be funny all the time.

RUSSELL. No, no. It is a flaw, I agree.

MRS. GAMADGE. The women are *very* suspicious of a man who doesn't take things seriously. So just don't try to be smart-aleck and talk over their heads. I hope you don't mind my talking like this but there isn't much time.

RUSSELL. I am certainly grateful for your . . . candor.

(MRS. GAMADGE *rises and circles with empty glass toward the bar.*)

MRS. GAMADGE. Now we want to see more of your wife. A lot more.

RUSSELL (*sits stage left*). She was sick, you know, during the primaries . . .

MRS. GAMADGE. And your two fine sons. They're very attractive and that was a nice spread of them in *Life,* at the barbecue. Very, very nice. We'll want more of that. But most important, your wife should be at your side at all times. She must *seem* to be advising you. The women must feel that there is a woman behind you (MRS. GAMADGE *has maneuvered herself into position behind* RUSSELL'S *chair*), as there has been a woman behind every great man since the world began!

(RUSSELL, *aware of* MRS. GAMADGE'S *presence, rises and crosses to* JENSEN *at right.*)

RUSSELL. Alice plans to campaign with me, if . . .

MRS. GAMADGE. She's a tremendous asset. I don't need to tell you. The women like the way she doesn't wear make-up and looks like a lady, and seems shy . . .

RUSSELL. She is shy.

MRS. GAMADGE. She doesn't make the women feel jealous. And that's good. Keep her with you, Mr. Secretary, at all times. It did Adlai Stevenson great harm, not having a wife, and trying to be funny all the time, too. Great harm. (MRS. GAMADGE *returns to sofa and sits down.*) Now I want to ask you a blunt question: what truth is there in the rumor that there has been . . . marital discord between you and Mrs. Russell?

RUSSELL (*evenly*). Mrs. Gamadge, my wife is here in Philadelphia. If I am nominated, she will do everything possible to be a helpful candidate's wife . . .

MRS. GAMADGE. Could I see her?

RUSSELL. Of course. (*Crosses to bedroom door.*) Alice . . . come on out and meet Mrs. Gamadge.

(ALICE *signals* RUSSELL *to wait while she arranges her blouse.*)

MRS. GAMADGE (*to* JENSEN). Now Mabel Cantwell is *such* a nice woman. Really one of the girls. You feel like you've known her all your life. Last time I was in Washington, Mabel gave this lovely dessert luncheon for me with four tables of canasta . . .

(*Somewhat nervously,* ALICE *enters and starts to cross to* MRS. GAMADGE, *who has risen and, to her alarm, started backing away with a speculative look, taking in everything.*)

ALICE. How very nice to see you . . .

MRS. GAMADGE (*slowly, deliberately*). You . . . couldn't . . . look . . . better! I mean it! I like the whole thing . . . especially the naturally gray hair, that is *such* an important point with the women. Of course Mabel Cantwell dyes her hair, but she gets away with it because she does such a bad job the women feel sorry for her.

(*A* WOMAN AID *enters from left. She gives* JENSEN *a note and goes.* JENSEN *shows the note to* RUSSELL. MRS. GAMADGE *observes this byplay.*)

MRS. GAMADGE. Oh, I know you have a million things to do! Anyway, I just want you to know that I'm for you, Mr. Secretary, and I'm sure you and Mrs. Russell are a winning team. (*To* ALICE, *cozily*) When you're the First Lady just remember this: don't do too much . . . like Mrs. Roosevelt. The women didn't like that. On the other hand, don't do too little . . . like Mrs. Eisenhower. The women don't like that either. All in all, Grace Coolidge was really the best, bless her heart. My husband had such a crush on her . . .

JENSEN. How *is* Mr. Gamadge?

(RUSSELL *signals belatedly but the gaffe is made.*)

MRS. GAMADGE (*quietly*). Mr. Gamadge passed on in 1956. He was stricken during the New Hampshire primaries.

JENSEN. Oh, I didn't know that. I'm sorry . . .

MRS. GAMADGE. So am I. He was a fine man, though he didn't like politics. He suffered his terminal thrombosis while I was in Wisconsin, that same year. (*Hearty handclasp*) Bill, *go to it!* The women are in your corner!

RUSSELL. You don't know how much that means to me . . . Sue-Ellen.

MRS. GAMADGE (*to* ALICE, *warmly*). Us girls will have a get-together real soon. And that's a promise.

ALICE. I do hope so, Mrs. Gamadge.

MRS. GAMADGE (*at the door, the knife*). Oh, by the way! A little bird tells me Joe Cantwell has a surprise for you.

RUSSELL. A surprise?

MRS. GAMADGE. Uh-huh. He's going to smear you with something . . . so they say.

RUSSELL (*startled*). Smear me?

MRS. GAMADGE (*gaily*). But here I am telling you what you already know. I'm sure you can handle it. 'By, Bill. 'By, Dick!

(*In a burst of sound from the newsmen in the corridor,* MRS. GAMADGE *goes.*)

ALICE. Smear you, Bill? With what?

RUSSELL (*frowns*). I don't know.

(JENSEN *waves note.*)

JENSEN. Well, Alice, word has come from on high. We're about to have a visit from our distinguished Ex-President.

ALICE. I must say he's one of the ones I like . . . except when he tells those long stories.

RUSSELL. Which will it be? The kiss . . . or the knife.

JENSEN. How can you miss? Like the rest of us he loves a winner.

ALICE. And he does like *you*, Bill.

RUSSELL. I don't know. He's a funny old bird.

(WOMAN AID *appears in doorway left.*)

JENSEN. Yes?

AID. The "Volunteer Women for Russell" are on the mezzanine. They want to know if they can see Mrs. Russell.

RUSSELL. Are you up to it?

ALICE. Of course I am. Tell them I'll join them in a few minutes. (ALICE *goes into bedroom to get ready.* WOMAN *gives several sheets to* JENSEN.)

AID. Copies of the Secretary's speech for tonight.

JENSEN. I'll check them now.

(AID *goes, left.*)

RUSSELL (*indicates speech*). You might let me look at it, too. I'd like to know what I'm saying.

JENSEN. Come off it, your speech writers . . .

(RUSSELL *takes the speech and glances through it.*)

RUSSELL. . . . are the best money can buy. They have written speeches for Eisenhower, Truman, Dewey, Hockstader, Roosevelt, Hoover and Harold Stassen. Which proves they are men of overpowering conviction.

JENSEN. Do you want to write four speeches a day on top of everything else?

RUSSELL. Of course I want to. But I can't. There isn't time. But it's a shameful business, speech by committee . . .

JENSEN. Not to mention *President* by committee.

(RUSSELL *hands back the speech.*)

RUSSELL. Please tell the writers *again* that the word "alternative" is always singular. There is only *one* alternative per situation.

JENSEN. I will denounce them as anti-semanticists . . .

(JENSEN *goes off left.* RUSSELL, *thoughtfully, goes into bedroom.*)

RUSSELL. Only one alternative per situation . . . unfortunately. That's grammar.

ALICE (*dryly*). And marriage. . . . Oh, I left my handbag . . . (ALICE *goes into bathroom.* RUSSELL *starts to unpack a suitcase. She returns.*)

RUSSELL. I'm sorry we're . . . in such close quarters.

ALICE. I don't mind. If you don't.

RUSSELL. Odd, after all these years apart. Separate rooms, separate lives.

ALICE (*smiles*). As someone sooner or later says: politics make strange bedfellows.

RUSSELL. Yes.

ALICE. Certainly there's nothing stranger than the two of us in the same room.

RUSSELL. I don't suppose I'm the first candidate to be in this situation.

ALICE. Bill . . . don't apologize. I said I'd do what I could to help. And I will. Besides, I really want you to be President.

RUSSELL. Why?

ALICE. I don't know. Perhaps I'm unexpectedly ambitious. Perhaps I want to be First Lady. Or perhaps I look forward to seeing you occasionally. (*Quickly*) Don't look alarmed! Only in line of duty. You know, an unexpected meeting in the East Room, an ambiguous encounter in the Lincoln Bedroom . . .

RUSSELL (*amused*). Alice . . .

ALICE. Yesterday, a woman from the press wanted to know what changes I would make when we moved into the White House. I said nothing of a *structural* nature would be changed . . . Will it?

RUSSELL (*awkwardly*). You know . . . I *do* like the idea of the two of us back together again.

ALICE (*suddenly sharp*). Bill, I am not a delegation from the Legion of Decency. You don't have to charm me. (ALICE *goes to hall, hangs up a blouse.*)

RUSSELL. I wasn't trying to. I mean it. I know it's tough . . .

ALICE. Tough? (*Returns to bedroom.*) Only for you. You're the one who has a problem. How to get girls into the White House. Or will you have a special place on K Street where the President, in disguise of course, can meet new . . . people. (RUSSELL *scowls and goes into bathroom with his shaving gear.*)

RUSSELL (*from the bathroom*). Why do you say things like that?

ALICE. Obviously because I'm frustrated. Isn't that the usual excuse women give? And isn't that the usual reason?

(RUSSELL *returns to the bedroom, and his unpacking.*)

RUSSELL. When the desire to make love to someone goes, it goes and nothing on earth can bring it back. Between us, it went.

ALICE. For you.

RUSSELL. I suppose what I wanted in marriage was a friend.

ALICE. And instead you got a very conventional girl who wanted a husband, who wanted . . . No. I will *not* put on that record again. I don't know why but we never manage to say anything new when we get onto the subject of my inadequacy and your . . . what shall we call it this time? Athleticism? Since according to the ground rules of our marriage we may call it anything except plain old-fashioned promiscuity.

RUSSELL. Look, if you'd rather not be with me, and have to go through with this . . . this gloomy farce, then don't. Quit! Right now.

ALICE. Quit? Certainly not. I like circuses. Besides, I'm good for you, isn't that what Dr. Artinian said? After your breakdown? You are the link, he said, between father and sons, between William Russell and the world.

RUSSELL. Dr. Artinian was right.

ALICE. But I wonder what I would have done that summer at Watch Hill, when we first met at the club, if someone had

said: "The handsome young man you've just fallen in love with will always need you . . . *as a link.*" I think if I had known then what I know now I would have slashed my wrists in front of the buffet table and beautifully bled to death between the chicken salad and the lobster Newburgh.

RUSSELL (*smiles*). Luckily, you are not given to melodrama. (*Both go into living room.*)

ALICE. Not yet anyway. But you are very nearly a great man and I suppose I can endure anything because of that. . . . So here we are.

RUSSELL. Somewhat past our youth . . . and friends?

ALICE. It would be nice if we were, wouldn't it? Do I look all right for the "Volunteer Women for Russell"?

RUSSELL. You do.

ALICE (*dryly*). I ought to. I am a founding member of that considerable body.

(ART HOCKSTADER, *a former President, in his late seventies but alert despite his years, enters from the bathroom door at right. He crosses warily to the connecting hall, where he sees* ALICE, *who is about to go.*)

HOCKSTADER. Hi, honey . . .

(ALICE *is startled.*)

ALICE. Oh! Mr. President!

HOCKSTADER. You look mighty pretty, Miss Alice . . . as usual! (HOCKSTADER'S *accent is rural American.*)

RUSSELL (*joining them*). Mr. President!

HOCKSTADER. Just plain Art Hockstader to you . . .

ALICE. Where did you come from?

HOCKSTADER (*indicates right*). Through the privy. There's a door into the next suite. I sneaked through.

ALICE. You look wonderful, after your operation!

HOCKSTADER. Ought to. Nothin but a hernia from bouncin my grandson too hard.

RUSSELL. What can I get you to drink? No, no, don't tell me . . . bourbon and branch water. (RUSSELL *goes to the living-room bar.*)

HOCKSTADER. With which I shall strike a blow for liberty. (*To the departing* ALICE) Don't let anyone know I'm here. (ALICE *nods and goes.*) Well, son, how do you like politics?

RUSSELL. I like it so much I'm beginning to worry.

HOCKSTADER. Awful, ain't it? Worse than gamblin, I sometimes think. Me, I was hooked when I was no more than this high (*Indicates a child*), and a certain fourflusher named William Jennings Bryan came to town. His last campaign, I guess. . . . Well, they shot the works: torchlight parade, picnic, the works! Then finally up there on the back of an old dray, out in a field, this fellow gets up and you never heard such hollerin from a crowd. Big man he was or so he looked to me, about nine foot tall with hair sweeping over his collar and that square red face of his, and when he spoke I tell you it was like thunder on a summer evenin and everythin was still, listenin. I used to know that speech by heart, it was the famous one. (*Imitates a fustian political voice.*) "You shall not press down upon the brow of labor this crown of thorns. You shall not crucify mankind upon a cross of gold!"

RUSSELL. Hurray! (RUSSELL *gives* HOCKSTADER *his drink.*)

HOCKSTADER. You betcha! Anyway, it was then and there that a certain farm boy named Art Hockstader said: I am goin to be a politician and get the folks riled up and eat plenty of barbecue and fried chicken at picnics and have all the pretty girls a-hangin on my every word.

RUSSELL (*carefully*). Your endorsement, Art, is a very important thing for anybody who wants to be nominated.

HOCKSTADER. I know it is. (*Smiles.*) So, indulge an old duffer! After all, gettin you fellows to listen to my stories and squirm a bit, waitin to see who I'm goin to put my money on, I tell you it's about the only pleasure I got left.

RUSSELL. I'm squirming.

HOCKSTADER (*gentle sadism*). Bill, I have a fatherly feeling about you . . .

RUSSELL. And I have . . .

HOCKSTADER (*continues through him*). Even though I have certain doubts about you.

RUSSELL. Doubts?

HOCKSTADER (*nods*). I'm kind of responsible for your career. You were *my* Secretary of State, and you were a swell one . . . but as you know the people don't give a damn about Secretaries of State. They think the whole foreign thing's a mess anyway and the man who's got to deal with it . . . well, I'm afraid the plain folks think the Secretary of State by definition is a foreigner.

RUSSELL (*ruefully*). I know. And if he doesn't like it here he better go back where he came from.

HOCKSTADER. Exactly. Of course you were a fine governor before that. Though Rhode Island is hardly what we call a king-makin state. . . . Anyway, it isn't your ability I doubt. Hell, you're ten times as well qualified as I was, and look at me! Possibly one of the greatest statesmen of all time!

RUSSELL. You were pretty good.

HOCKSTADER. I certainly was. (*Dryly.*) Though it's practically our secret right now, as there has been no overpowering popular movement to add me to that rock garden at Mt. Rushmore. But that's not for me to worry about. No, my objection to you, I guess, was prejudice. For one thing you're a Fancy Dan from the East. But I am nothin if not a realist. The Age of the Great Hicks to which I belong is over. The people trust you rich boys, figurin since you got a lot of money of your own you won't go stealin theirs. I'm sure those people who like this Rockefeller are really thinkin in the back of their minds if they make him President he might decide to pay off the national debt out of his own pocket! If he would, *I'd* vote for him.

RUSSELL. What do you think of Joe Cantwell?

HOCKSTADER (*smiles*). That's a leading question.

RUSSELL. Well, I *am* proposing myself as a leader.

HOCKSTADER. O.K., I'll follow. Joe Cantwell is nothin but ambition. Just plain naked ambition.

RUSSELL. And to get himself elected he will lie . . .

HOCKSTADER (*nods*). Yep.

RUSSELL. He will cheat . . .

HOCKSTADER. Yep.

RUSSELL. He will destroy the reputations of others . . .

HOCKSTADER. Yep.

RUSSELL. Good. So I assume you are endorsing me for the nomination.

HOCKSTADER. Hell, no! Because he's a bastard don't mean he wouldn't be a good candidate. Or even a good President . . .

RUSSELL. Joe Cantwell a good . . . ! You're not serious.

HOCKSTADER. Well, he's got a real sense of how to operate.

RUSSELL. To operate? No. To accommodate! If the people are conservative . . .

HOCKSTADER. He'll be conservative.

RUSSELL. And if they're radical . . .

HOCKSTADER. He'll be radical. Oh, I tell you, son, he is a kind of ring-tailed wonder and don't you underestimate him.

RUSSELL. I don't.

HOCKSTADER. Of course he hasn't got your brains, but then very few of us are as bright as you.

RUSSELL. Now, Art . . .

HOCKSTADER. No, I mean it. You are a superior man of the sort we don't get very often in politics. While Joe's just another of the mediocre boys, like me . . . only smoother of course. A newer model.

RUSSELL. No, he is *not* like you. He'll do anything to win. And that makes him dangerous.

HOCKSTADER. Now I wouldn't go that far. (*The first turn to the screw.*) At least he knows his own mind.

RUSSELL. And you think I don't know my own mind?

HOCKSTADER (*equably*). Well, son, you got such a good mind that sometimes you're so busy thinkin how complex everything is important problems don't get solved.

RUSSELL (*smiles*). No, I am not that subtle. I am not that undecided. I am not Prince Hamlet.

HOCKSTADER (*a diversion*). Hamlet! Lot of fine speeches in that play. Lot of fine speeches in *you,* Bill.

RUSSELL (*urgently*). Art, *don't* support Cantwell!

HOCKSTADER. Now, what makes you think I'm goin to?

RUSSELL. I mean it. And I am not thinking about myself. I'm thinking about the country.

HOCKSTADER. You got to admit, Joe Cantwell ain't afraid to act.

RUSSELL. Neither am I afraid to act.

HOCKSTADER (*dreamily*). Oh? Well, now, I seem to recall how once when you were at a conference with the Russians you were all set to agree to continue nuclear tests, but then when the roof fell in on my administration, I found

you had gone and talked yourself up the other side of the street.

RUSSELL. I hesitated only because . . .

HOCKSTADER. I'll say you hesitated. Now you don't catch Joe Cantwell hesitatin. No, sir. He's sharp. He's tough.

RUSSELL. He is not tough. He is expedient and that's a very different thing, and I promise you if Joe were President he'd be the greatest appeaser in history.

HOCKSTADER. I would hardly call him an appeaser . . .

RUSSELL. Suppose the Chinese were to threaten to occupy India and we were faced with the possibility of a world war, the *last* world war. Now that is the kind of thing you and I understand and I think we could handle it without going to war and without losing India. But what would Joe do? He would look at the Gallup poll. And what would the Gallup poll tell him? Well, ask the average American, do you want to run the risk of being blown up to save India? And he'll say, hell, no! Joe would do the popular thing: to hell with India, and we would be the weaker for it, and that day we're all afraid of would be closer.

(HOCKSTADER *finishes his drink and rises.*)

HOCKSTADER. Son, you've been reading too much of that Joe Alsop fellow. Things are never *that* bad! (*Thoughtfully.*) Bill, you know it gets mighty lonely in the White House. Worse for me, I guess, than for you. I'd never lived in a big house with a lot of servants, the way you were brought up. But the worst part is, there's nobody you can believe . . . that's the awful thing: everybody's lying to you all day long. . . . Then my wife died . . . (*Sighs.*) The wonder is that most of us aren't worse than we are. (*Suddenly*) Bill, do you believe in God?

RUSSELL (*startled*). Do I . . . ? Well, I was confirmed in the Episcopal Church.

HOCKSTADER. Hell, that wasn't what I asked. I'm a Methodist and I'm still askin: do you believe there's a God and a Day of Judgment and a Hereafter?

RUSSELL. No. I believe in us. In man.

HOCKSTADER (*nods*). I've often pretended I thought there was a God, for political purposes.

RUSSELL (*smiles*). So far I haven't told a lie in this campaign. I've never used the word "God" in a speech.

HOCKSTADER. Well, the world's changed since I was politickin. In those days you had to pour God over everything, like ketchup. (*He sits on the bench downstage.*) No, I don't believe there's a Hereafter. We pass this way just once. And then . . . nothing. Bill, I am dying.

RUSSELL (*stunned*). What?

HOCKSTADER. That thing about the hernia was just another lie, I'm afraid. (*Dryly*) I hope you don't disapprove. . . . I got the doctors to say the operation was a great success, but it wasn't. I got cancer of the innerds and they tell me I may last just long enough to attend the next Inaugural.

(RUSSELL *rises, crosses to him.*)

RUSSELL. Art, I'm . . . ! Look, isn't there . . .

HOCKSTADER. There is nothin they can do, except give me these pills to cut the pain. I tell you, son, I am scared to death. (*Laughs.*) That's a phase for you: "Scared to death" is exactly right. I don't fancy being nothin, just a pinch of dust. No, sir, I don't like that at all.

(RUSSELL *puts his hand on* HOCKSTADER's *shoulder.*)

RUSSELL. I wish I could say something reassuring, but you wouldn't fall for it anyway.

(HOCKSTADER *shrugs away* RUSSELL's *hand.*)

HOCKSTADER. The only good thing I find is that the rest of you sons of bitches are going to join me. There's some consolation I reckon in that. (*Sighs.*) Oh, I tell you if there is any point to this universe it sure as hell evades me.

RUSSELL. The whole thing's a tragedy. For all of us. (*Crosses to the sofa.*) But there's hope in this: Every act we make sets off a chain of reaction which never ends. And if we are reasonably . . . good, well, there *is* some consolation in that, a kind of immortality.

HOCKSTADER (*dryly*). I suggest you tell yourself that when *you* finally have to face a whole pile of nothin up ahead. (*Rises briskly.*) But at the moment I'm alive. And we go into the convention hall day after tomorrow and act like life is all there is . . . which, come to think of it, is true.

(JENSEN *looks in from the office at left.*)

JENSEN. The Texas Delegation is here.

(*Sees* HOCKSTADER.) Oh, hello, Mr. . . .

(HOCKSTADER *motions to* JENSEN *to say nothing.* JENSEN *nods and shuts the door.*)

HOCKSTADER. Bill, don't tell anybody what I told you.

RUSSELL. Of course not.

HOCKSTADER. Meanwhile, I am going to keep you in suspense, until tonight at dinner.

RUSSELL. And then?

HOCKSTADER. I will throw my support like a bridal bouquet to the lucky man. (HOCKSTADER *beams; he starts to cross to hall; he pauses.*) Oh, these rumors about you and your lady friends . . . won't do you a bit of harm. *But* keep out of trouble. You haven't gone and written any letters like some fellows do?

RUSSELL (*smiles*). No. No letters.

HOCKSTADER. Good boy. She's a nice girl, Alice.

RUSSELL. I think so.

HOCKSTADER (*slyly*). And you never tell a lie, do you? Well, good! Glad to hear it! (*Grimaces with pain.*) Christ, that upper plate of mine pinches! I was going to get a new one but they said it would take a couple of months to make. So I figured I could hold out with what I got.

(*Both men are now at the hall.*)

RUSSELL. Art . . .

(*There are several whoops and rebel yells from stage left.*)

HOCKSTADER. You go on in there with those crazy Texans. (*Chuckles.*) I sure wish I was a fly on that wall, listening to you tell the whole *truth* about what you really think of the depletion of oil resources allowance!

RUSSELL (*laughs*). Get out of here, you old bum . . .

(*Both men are now in the bedroom.* HOCKSTADER *smiles, as he crosses to the bathroom door at right.*)

HOCKSTADER. Now is that a respectful way to talk to the end of an era? The last of the Great Hicks as he shuffles off the stage? By way of the privy.

(HOCKSTADER *waves as he exits.* RUSSELL *goes back into the living room.* JENSEN *enters.*)

JENSEN (*eagerly*). Well? What did he say?

RUSSELL. He won't let us know till tonight.

JENSEN. He's going to come out for you. I know it!

RUSSELL (*slowly*). No, he's going to support Joe Cantwell.

JENSEN (*startled*). What! Oh, you're out of your mind. Come on, hurry up, the natives of Texas are getting restless. Now remember on the oil issue . . .

RUSSELL. I know. I know. Double talk! (*As he follows* JENSEN *off right*) For those whom we are about to deceive, oh Lord, make us truly compassionate!

CURTAIN

SCENE TWO

The Cantwell suite. A few minutes later. MABEL CANTWELL, *a blonde, pretty woman of forty in a dressing gown, lies on a sofa, watching television and drinking a martini. Around the room, placards and posters implore us to vote for Senator Joe Cantwell.*

COMMENTATOR'S VOICE. This is John Fox with the news. Well, I guess you all know this has been some day for Philadelphia, a real old-fashioned convention day, first since 1940. We got some pictures here of the candidates arriving at the Thirtieth Street station. There's the front-runner, William Russell, with Mrs. Russell . . .

MABEL (*perfunctorily*). Boo!

COMMENTATOR'S VOICE. Then, just before noon, Senator Joe Cantwell arrived.

MABEL. Yea, team! (MABEL's *accent is Southern.*)

COMMENTATOR'S VOICE. There he is getting off the train. And there's His Honor again, meeting him. The Senator's with Don Blades, his campaign manager. Oh, and there's *Mrs.* Cantwell. (MABEL *is suddenly alert. She studies herself carefully on the screen.*)

MABEL (*alarm*). Oh, my Lord, that hat! (MABEL *goes into the bedroom, picks up the offending hat and goes into bathroom to try it on. The television set continues to sound.*)

REPORTER'S VOICE. Senator, do you have a statement . . . ? We're here to . . .

CANTWELL'S VOICE. All I can say is that come Wednesday I only hope that the best man wins . . .

MABEL (*mechanically from bathroom*). . . . the best man wins.

(*There is a noise of* REPORTERS *as the hall door opens.* DON BLADES, *a lean gray man, ushers the smiling* JOE CANTWELL *into the living room.* CANTWELL *is in his forties. His manner is warm, plausible. Though under great tension, he suggests ease. He has a tendency not to listen when preoccupied. He poses for one more photograph, arms victoriously raised. Then* BLADES *gets the* REPORTERS *out.* CANTWELL *relaxes full-length on the sofa.*)

BLADES. That went well, Joe (*Turns off set.*) You better rest before dinner.

CANTWELL. About Hockstader, what did he say when you saw him? What *exactly* did he say?

BLADES (*for the hundredth time*). He said he hadn't made up his mind, but he would by tonight.

CANTWELL (*calls*). Mabel, honey! Come on out. It's just Don Blades and me.

(MABEL *appears. She throws herself on him. They embrace warmly.*)

CANTWELL (*laughing*). Hey, come on! You better get dressed. We got to go down to dinner in (*Looks at watch.*) thirty minutes.

MABEL. I'll be ready . . . don't you worry, baby. Fix yourself a drink, Don.

(BLADES *is at the bar upstage.*)

BLADES. Can I get you anything, Mabel?

MABEL. Oh, no, I don't think so. I don't . . . well, maybe just the teeniest martini, to settle my stomach. (*Concern*) Oh, Joe, you look so tired.

CANTWELL (*automatically*). Never felt better. (CANTWELL *picks up a newspaper and reads, frowning.*)

MABEL. Well, I finally got through that women's tea and I've been here watching the TV. We got awful nice coverage, Joe . . . though that new hat of mine is clearly a mistake. It looks like I have no chin, but even with no chin I certainly look better than Alice Russell. My God, she is a chilly-looking woman, just like an English teacher I had back at State College, the spittin image . . . from Boston she was and always wore her hair in this bun with no make-up and of course thought she was the cat's meow . . .

(BLADES *gives her a drink.*)

BLADES. Here you go, Mabel.

MABEL. Thank you, Don.

CANTWELL. Hey, Don, that joke of

yours looks pretty good.

BLADES. Oh? Which one was that?

CANTWELL (*reads*). "At his press conference yesterday, Senator Cantwell quipped: 'Bill Russell has more solutions than there are problems.'"

(MABEL *tastes the martini. She sighs.*)

MABEL. Don, the best martinis are made five to one, not five to four.

BLADES. I never could make a mixed drink.

MABEL (*to* CANTWELL). All the papers say Hockstader's going to come out for Bill Russell, heaven knows why, with your record in the Senate . . .

CANTWELL (*shuts his eyes*). I am tired. (*Then he sits up, abruptly. He turns to* BLADES.) I got to see Hockstader. Right now. Before that dinner.

BLADES. What are you going to tell him?

CANTWELL. Everything. The works. Maybe he won't come out for me afterwards but he'll sure drop Bill Russell.

BLADES (*rises*). O.K. You're the boss.

CANTWELL. Go on up there. He's on the seventh floor. Tell him I've *got* to see him before dinner which is in (*Looks at watch.*) twenty-seven minutes.

BLADES. Aye, aye, my captain.

(CANTWELL *is on his feet. He turns irritably to* MABEL.)

CANTWELL. Mabel, come on, get dressed!

MABEL. I'll be ready, Joe, stop worryin' . . . don't get all het up. (*She embraces him.*) Why is big Poppa Bear so mean to poor little Momma Bear?

CANTWELL. Baby, I'm sorry. (*He goes into their private baby talk.*) Poppa Bear is never mean to his Momma Bear, never ever. (*His own voice*) But, honey, you've *got* to get dressed!

MABEL. O.K., I will . . . I will. Joe, when are you going to spring that . . . that stuff about Bill Russell?

CANTWELL. Tomorrow.

MABEL. The *whole* thing?

CANTWELL. Pow! (CANTWELL *goes into bedroom, searching for his electric razor.*)

MABEL (*rapturously*). And then we are on our way to 1600 Pennsylvania Avenue! Oh, my, it's thrilling, isn't it? Seems just like yesterday we were skimpin along hardly able to pay the bills to have Gladys's teeth straightened, ad now just look at us! Poppa Bear and Momma Bear and the baby bears all in the White House!

CANTWELL (*from bedroom*). Where's my electric razor?

MABEL. I'll get it! (*She goes quickly into bedroom.*) I'll just start putting on my clothes and . . . (*She finds the razor and gives it to him.*)

CANTWELL. Where's that last Gallup poll?

MABEL. I think Don Blades got it. Anyway, you're two per cent higher than last week with twelve per cent undecided. Merwin gained one per cent and Russell's lost two per cent.

CANTWELL. And Red China?

MABEL (*promptly*). Forty-seven per cent against recognition. Twenty-three per cent in favor. Thirty per cent don't know. I'm wearing the green organza tonight, the one from Neiman Marcus, Allan Bates sent me. I think it looks real summery and nice . . .

CANTWELL (*frowns*). That's not enough in favor. Russell's a fool making an issue out of China this soon . . .

(MABEL *removes her dressing gown and starts to get into her dress.*)

MABEL. I had my hair done this morning by the man in the hotel; he's very nice but terribly swishy. Anyway he didn't get the curls too tight. . . . At least I don't think so. He said Alice Russell had her hair done, too. (*Unnoticed by* MABEL, CANTWELL *goes into living room, sits at desk, turns on electric razor and reads a newspaper.*) He said she refuses to entertain the thought of using so much as a rinse. Well, bully for her! She looks easily ten years older than she is. (*Frowns.*) Joe, do you think I've gained weight? Around the hips? Honey, you listenin to me? (*Realizing he is in the other room,* MABEL, *pouting, crosses to living-room door, the back of her dress unzipped.*) No, I guess you're not . . . You never listen to poor Mama Bear any more. (*Pause*) Joe? Have you ever been unfaithful to me?

CANTWELL (*turns off razor*). No. Did you see Walter Lippmann this morning? Listen to what that guy says: "The country's affairs will be in good hands should William Russell be our next President." (*Slaps the paper down.*) I don't know why I don't appeal to those would-be intellectuals. My image just doesn't project to them like his does. (*Notices* MABEL *at last.*) Well, look at you! Just good enough to eat . . . (*He starts to*

nuzzle her in a bearish way.) Mmmm—
mm—

MABEL (*happily nuzzled*). Now what
are you doing to me? Don't muss my hair!
Now come on! Stop it! And zip me up!
(*She turns around. As* JOE *zips her dress,
she returns to her theme.*) Joe, are you
sure you haven't been unfaithful to me
maybe just one little time? On one of
those junkets? Like that awful one to
Paris you took, where the Senators got
drunk and Clarence Wetlaw contracted a
social disease and Helen Wetlaw was fit
to be tied?

CANTWELL. Mabel, honey, there's nobody else. And even if there was, how
would I have the time? I operate on a
tight schedule. (*Kisses her briefly.*) You
know that.

(BLADES *enters from corridor door.*)

BLADES. Joe, I talked to Hockstader.

CANTWELL. Well?

BLADES. He'll be right down.

CANTWELL. And?

BLADES. Not a clue.

CANTWELL. O.K. Get me that file on
Russell. (*To* MABEL, *indicating bedroom*)
Honey, you go in there . . . fix your face
or something. The President's on his way
down.

(MABEL *nods and crosses to hall.*)

MABEL. Joe . . . play it cool, like the kids
say now.

CANTWELL. I will.

(BLADES *gives him a manila folder.*)

BLADES. This ought to do the trick.

CANTWELL. I'll say it will. (*Turns the
pages.*) Oh, cute. Very cute. How's the
New York delegation?

BLADES. Still split down the middle.

CANTWELL. Well, they won't be split
after this.

(*A sound of excited voices from corridor.*)

BLADES. Here he comes. Are you ready?

(CANTWELL *nods; he takes a position at
stage right.*)

CANTWELL. All set. (*Warningly*) Don:
remember . . . flatter him!

(BLADES *nods, opens the door.* HOCK-
STADER *in evening dress pushes his way
through a mob of newsmen.*)

CANTWELL. Mr. President!

(CANTWELL *beams and crosses to* HOCK-
STADER *as* BLADES *shuts out the press.*)

HOCKSTADER. Hello, Blades . . . Hi, Joe!

(HOCKSTADER *indicates the corridor door.*)

Well, this ought to start some rumors.

(CANTWELL *is now shaking his hand
warmly.*)

CANTWELL. Gosh, I'm sorry, sir. We
should've arranged for you to come in the
back way.

HOCKSTADER. Oh, that's all right. We're
gettin near that time anyway. (*Taps coat
pocket.*) Got my speech right here. My
teeth are in and I'm rarin to go. (*Indicates* CANTWELL.) What about you?
Where's your party suit?

CANTWELL (*seriously*). I have it all
timed. It takes me exactly three minutes
to get into a tux. Two minutes for an
ordinary business suit, and that's including vest.

HOCKSTADER (*smiles*). Well, ain't you a
ring-tailed wonder? (*Crosses to bar.*)
You don't mind if I strike myself a blow
for liberty?

CANTWELL. Let me . . . please . . .
(*Gestures to* BLADES *to help.*) Don!

HOCKSTADER (*fixes his own drink*).
That's all right. I know Joe doesn't have
the habit. People who don't drink never
realize how thirsty we old bucks get long
round sundown. (*Turns thoughtfully to*
CANTWELL.) No, sir, you don't drink, you
don't smoke, you don't philander; fact,
you are about the purest young man I
have ever known in public life.

CANTWELL. I try to be.

(HOCKSTADER *crosses to sofa downstage.*)

HOCKSTADER. Well, I am a great admirer of virtue, though a somewhat
flawed vessel of grace myself. (HOCK-
STADER *sits.*)

CANTWELL. Now, Mr. President . . .
you're an ideal to us in the party. (CANT-
WELL *sits opposite him stage left.* BLADES
is seated stage right.)

HOCKSTADER (*dryly*). Sure, Joe, sure
. . . Young man, you've done a remarkable job in the Senate. Most of the time.

CANTWELL (*quickly*). *Most* of the time?

HOCKSTADER (*nods*). There *have* been
moments when I have questioned your
methods.

CANTWELL. Well, you have to fight fire
with fire, Mr. President.

HOCKSTADER. And the end justifies the
means?

CANTWELL. Well, yes, sir. Yes. That is
what I believe.

HOCKSTADER. Well, son, I have news for

you about both politics and life . . . and may I say the two are *exactly* the same thing? There are no ends, Joe, only means.

CANTWELL. Well, I don't like to disagree with you, sir, but that's just sophistry. I mean . . .

HOCKSTADER (*amused*). Now! None of them two-bit words on poor old Art Hockstader. I'm just an ignorant country boy. All I'm saying is that what matters in our profession . . . which is really life . . . is *how* you do things and *how* you treat people and what you really feel about 'em, *not* some ideal goal for society, or for yourself.

CANTWELL (*his District-Attorney voice*). Then am I to assume, Mr. President, from the statement you have just made, that you are against planning anything?

HOCKSTADER (*laughs*). Oh, here it comes! I know that voice! Senator Cantwell, boy crusader, up there on the TV with these small-time hoodlums cringing before his righteousness.

BLADES (*to the rescue*). Now, Mr. President, Joe was *assigned* that Subcommittee. He didn't ask for it . . . and that's a fact.

HOCKSTADER. Sure. Sure. And he just fell into that big issue: how the United States is secretly governed by the Mafia.

CANTWELL. It happened to be true. Any time you want to look at my files, Mr. President . . .

HOCKSTADER. Last time somebody asked me to look at his files, it was Senator McCarthy.

CANTWELL (*grimly*). I hope, sir, you're not comparing me to him.

HOCKSTADER. No . . . no, Joe. You're a much smoother article. After all, you've got an end to which you can justify your means, getting to be President. Poor old McCarthy was just wallowing in headlines . . . sufficient to the day were the headlines thereof. No, you're much brighter, much more ruthless.

CANTWELL. I realize some of my methods upset a lot of people . . .

BLADES (*righteously*). But, Mr. President, if we hadn't been tough we would never have cracked the Mafia the way we did.

(HOCKSTADER *smiles during this.*)

CANTWELL. What's so funny about that, sir?

HOCKSTADER. Nothing, only you know and I know and everybody knows . . . except I'm afraid the TV audience . . . that there never was a Mafia like you said. There was no such thing. You just cooked it up.

CANTWELL (*dangerously*). So we're going to get that number, are we? Well, my figures prove . . .

HOCKSTADER (*sharply*). You went after a bunch of poor Sicilian bandits on the lower East Side of New York and pretended they were running all the crime in America. Well, they're not. Of course we have a pretty fair idea who is, but you didn't go after any of them, did you? No, sir, because those big rascals are heavy contributors to political campaigns.

BLADES (*beginning*). Maybe Joe didn't go after all of them, sir . . .

HOCKSTADER. Just barely scratched the surface . . .

CANTWELL. But *you* should talk. J. Edgar Hoover considered you the most morally lax President in his entire career . . .

HOCKSTADER (*serenely*). I reserve my opinion of J. Edgar Hoover for a posthumous memoir or maybe a time capsule to be dug up when he has finally cleansed the republic of undesirables.

CANTWELL. Hoover is a great American!

HOCKSTADER (*amused*). But we're all "great Americans," Joe. (*More seriously*) No, I don't object to your headline-grabbing and crying "Wolf" all the time, that's standard stuff in politics, but it disturbs me you take yourself so seriously. It's par for the course trying to fool the people but it's downright dangerous when you start fooling yourself.

(MABEL CANTWELL, *in the bedroom, has heard voices grow angry. She crosses to the hall and listens at the living-room door.*)

CANTWELL (*carefully*). Mr. President, I take myself seriously. Because I am serious. This is important to me. To all of us. Which is why I don't want any little lectures from you on how to be a statesman. And if you really want to know, I think the record of your administration is one of the heaviest loads our party has to carry.

(HOCKSTADER *is on his feet, suddenly furious.* MABEL *enters.*)

MABEL. Why, Mr. President! What a

nice surprise, your dropping in on us like this!

(HOCKSTADER *regains his composure.*)

HOCKSTADER. Well, I was invited down here by this young man for a little conference, and here he is, turning my head with flattery.

MABEL (*rapturously*). Joe admires you, I guess, more than any man in public life.

CANTWELL (*to* MABEL). Honey, leave us alone. (*Indicates to* BLADES *that he leave, too.*) Don.

(BLADES *exits right.*)

MABEL. All right, but Joe, you have to get dressed soon.

CANTWELL. O.K.

MABEL. You certainly look fine, Mr. President, after your little vacation in the hospital . . .

HOCKSTADER. Fit as a fiddle. Never felt better.

(MABEL *goes into connecting hall. She shuts the door. She listens.*)

CANTWELL. I'm sorry, sir, flying off the handle like that.

HOCKSTADER (*smiles*). That's O.K. You just got a case of the old pre-convention jitters . . . Now I assume you didn't ask me down here to discuss the virtues of J. Edgar Hoover.

CANTWELL. No, I didn't. (*Awkwardly*) I know you don't like me . . .

HOCKSTADER. Now that you mention it, I don't. I never have.

CANTWELL. And I've never liked your kind of politician. But that's neither here nor there. I don't expect you to come out for me tonight . . .

(HOCKSTADER *crosses to the bar upstage. He fixes himself another drink.*)

HOCKSTADER. I should warn you I have often endorsed men I disliked, even mistrusted, because I thought they'd do the job.

(CANTWELL *has gone to the desk. He picks up the file.* HOCKSTADER *suffers a spasm of pain at the bar. He clutches his stomach.* CANTWELL *does not notice this.*)

CANTWELL. So I have something to show you about your friend William Russell. It's all here in this file. I want you to look at it and . . . (CANTWELL *looks at* HOCKSTADER; *he realizes something is wrong.*) What's the matter with you?

HOCKSTADER (*with difficulty*). Just . . .

had to take one of my pills. (*Takes a pill.*) Pep me up. (CANTWELL *nods, goes downstage to sofa. He sits.* HOCKSTADER *looks at him thoughtfully.*) Joe, you believe in God, don't you?

CANTWELL (*promptly*). Yes, I do.

HOCKSTADER. And you believe there's a Hereafter? And a Day of Judgment?

CANTWELL (*sincerely*). I do. If I didn't think there was some meaning to all of this I wouldn't be able to go on. I'm a very religious guy, in a funny way. (CANTWELL *spreads the contents of the folder on the coffee table.*)

HOCKSTADER. I'm sure you are. (*Sighs.*) Times like this I wish I was. Dying is no fun, let me tell you. And that's what I'm doing. (CANTWELL *has not been listening.*)

CANTWELL (*briskly*). Now it's all here. Psychiatrist reports . . . everything. And don't ask *how* I got it. My means might've been ruthless but for once I think you'll agree the end was worth it.

(HOCKSTADER *is taken aback at being ignored. He comes downstage. He indicates the papers contemptuously.*)

HOCKSTADER. What is all this . . . crap?

CANTWELL. Several years ago *your* candidate, William Russell, had what is known as a nervous breakdown.

HOCKSTADER. I know that.

CANTWELL. He was raving mad for almost a year.

HOCKSTADER. He was not raving mad. It was exhaustion from overwork . . .

CANTWELL. That was the press release. The real story's right here . . .

HOCKSTADER. I know the real story.

CANTWELL. Then you know it's political dynamite. A full report on his mental state. How he deserted his wife, how their marriage has always been a phony, a political front . . .

HOCKSTADER. I won't begin to speculate on how you got hold of this . . .

CANTWELL. And all the big words are there, manic depressive, paranoid pattern, attempted suicide . . .

HOCKSTADER. He never attempted suicide.

CANTWELL. I'm sorry. It says right here that he did. See? (*Points to page.*) There. Suicidal tendencies . . .

HOCKSTADER. We've all got suicidal *tendencies.* But he never tried to kill himself.

CANTWELL. But the point is he *could*.

HOCKSTADER. I thought you said he *did* try.

CANTWELL. I did not say he did. I said he could. And then all that combined with playing around with women . . .

HOCKSTADER. So what?

CANTWELL. I suppose you find promiscuity admirable?

HOCKSTADER. I couldn't care less. I was brought up on a farm and the lesson of the rooster was not entirely lost on me. A lot of men need a lot of women and there are worse faults, let me tell you.

CANTWELL (*suspiciously*). What do you mean by that?

HOCKSTADER. Just that there are rumors about every public man. Why, when I was in the White House they used to say I had paresis, and how I was supposed to be keepin this colored girl over in Alexandria, silliest damn stories you ever heard but it gave a lot of people a lot of pleasure talkin about it. You know, when that Kinsey fellow wrote that book about how many men were doin this and how many men were doin that, I couldn't help but think how right along with all this peculiar activity there was a hell of a lot of *nothin* goin on!

CANTWELL. All right, leaving the moral issue out, do you think it a good idea to elect a man President who is mentally unstable?

HOCKSTADER. He is not mentally unstable and you know it.

CANTWELL (*inexorably*). A manic depressive? Apt to crack up under stress? (HOCKSTADER *gets the point.*)

HOCKSTADER. So that's your little number, is it?

CANTWELL (*evenly*). If Russell doesn't withdraw before Wednesday, I am going to see that every delegate gets a copy of this psychiatric report and I am going to challenge Russell openly. I'm going to ask him if he really feels that a man with his mental record should be President of the United States. Frankly, if I were he, I'd pull out before this (*Indicates papers.*) hits the fan.

HOCKSTADER. Well, you are *not* Russell . . . to state the obvious. And he might say in rebuttal that after his breakdown he served a right rough period as Secretary of State and did not show the strain in any way.

CANTWELL. One of the psychiatrists reports that this pattern of his is bound to repeat itself. He is bound to have another breakdown.

HOCKSTADER. You and your experts! You know as well as I do those head-doctors will give you about as many different opinions as you want on any subject.

CANTWELL (*reasonably*). I realize that, which is why I am going to propose that he be examined, before Wednesday, by a nonpartisan group of psychiatrists to determine if he is sane.

HOCKSTADER. You know he won't submit to that.

CANTWELL. If he doesn't, that means he has something to hide.

HOCKSTADER. Wow! You sure play rough, don't you?

CANTWELL. I regard this as a public service. (*Urgently*) Look, I'm not asking you to support me. I don't even *want* your support. But I do want you to think twice before endorsing a man who is known to be psychopathic.

HOCKSTADER. You got it figured, of course, that even to hint that a man's not right in his head will be enough to knock him off? When do you plan to throw this at him?

CANTWELL. Tomorrow.

HOCKSTADER. And of course you've waited for the last minute so he won't have a chance to clear himself before the convention starts. That's right smart.

CANTWELL (*not listening*). We'll have to work out some way for him to get out of the race gracefully. I thought maybe he could say . . . well, nervous exhaustion . . . doesn't feel up to the rigors of a campaign, something like that.

HOCKSTADER. And if he doesn't withdraw "gracefully"?

CANTWELL (*taps folder*). This will be circulated. And I will demand he be examined by psychiatrists.

HOCKSTADER. I suppose you realize you are now open to the same kind of treatment.

CANTWELL. I have nothing to hide in my private or public life.

HOCKSTADER. Are you absolutely certain?

CANTWELL (*carefully*). Just . . . try . . . anything.

HOCKSTADER. Well, looks like we're goin to have an ugly fight on our hands.

Yes, sir, a real ugly fight. (*Crosses to up-stage door. He turns.*) So now I am going to let you have it. And when I finish with you, my boy, you will know what it is like to get in the ring with an old-time killer. I am going to have your political scalp and hang it on my belt, along with a lot of others.

CANTWELL (*dangerously*). Don't mix with me, Hockstader.

HOCKSTADER. You can't touch me. But I can send you back to the insurance business. (*He removes his speech from his pocket, almost sadly.*) And just think! I was going to endorse *you* for President.

CANTWELL. I don't believe you.

HOCKSTADER. It's not that I mind your bein a bastard, don't get me wrong there . . . It's your bein such a *stupid* bastard I object to. (*Contemptuously,* HOCKSTADER *tosses the speech at* CANTWELL's *feet. Then he turns and exits to the corridor, fling-ing the door open. Flash-bulbs go off. As* HOCKSTADER *disappears into the crowd of newsmen,* CANTWELL *picks up the speech and starts to read.*)

CURTAIN

ACT TWO

SCENE ONE

The Russell suite. The next afternoon. A delegation is being shown out by RUS-SELL *and* JENSEN. *They pump hands. Rus-sell placards are waved At the bar stands* SENATOR CARLIN, *a ponderous politician of the prairies.*

JENSEN. O.K., gentlemen . . . we'll see you tomorrow, in the convention hall.

DELEGATE (*to* RUSSELL, *warmly*). Bill, we'll nominate you on the first ballot to-morrow . . . and that's a promise . . .

RUSSELL (*smiles*). If nominated, I will run. If elected, I will serve. Thanks.

JENSEN (*to the last* DELEGATE). We'll be in touch with you . . . (*To* RUSSELL) Well, what do you think?

RUSSELL. Looks all right. Nobody's mentioned mental health yet.

CARLIN. What *did* you fellows think of Hockstader's speech last night?

(BOTH RUSSELL *and* JENSEN *turn, startled.*)

RUSSELL. Senator Carlin! I thought you'd left . . .

CARLIN. No. Just stayed to fix myself a snort, if you don't mind. Now about Hockstader's speech last night . . .

RUSSELL. Well, I was as surprised as anybody.

CARLIN. You thought he was going to endorse you?

JENSEN (*quickly*). We certainly did.

CARLIN. And then the old man just got up and talked plain double talk . . .

JENSEN. At least he didn't endorse Cant-well. (JENSEN *goes off left.*)

CARLIN. No. He didn't endorse *nobody.* For a minute I thought he was going to surprise us and come out for John Mer-win, just to be ornery. Now I hear you were with the old man later on last night. What's he up to? My boys think a lot of old Art and they'll go along with him . . .

RUSSELL. We were having a council of war, I guess you'd call it.

CARLIN. They say Joe's got something on you, something pretty bad.

RUSSELL. Something untrue. And frankly I'm not very worried. I'm a lot more worried about the labor plank in the platform . . .

CARLIN (*exasperated*). Oh, Christ, Bill! Lay off labor, will you? You got their vote now, so don't go stirring up a lot of snakes. After all, *you're* the liberal candidate . . .

RUSSELL. What is a liberal, Senator? (RUSSELL *crosses to bedroom, picks up dictionary, returns to living room, thumb-ing pages.*)

CARLIN (*groans*). And I thought Adlai Stevenson was a pain in the neck. A liberal is a . . . well, you, Bill Russell, are a liberal, that's what a liberal is. You.

RUSSELL. According to the dictionary a liberal is one who "favors changes and reforms tending in the direction of further democracy." Well, I am in favor of further democracy for the unions' rank and file . . .

CARLIN. Bill, please . . . I'm just a poor dumb party hack . . .

RUSSELL. I'm sorry, Senator. The terrible thing about running for President is you become a compulsive talker, forever an-swering questions no one has asked you.

CARLIN. Well, let me ask *you* a question. Would you consider offering the Vice-

President nomination to Cantwell?

RUSSELL. No.

CARLIN (*sourly*). For a compulsive talker, you sure don't have much to say on that subject. (*Sighs.*) Jeez, I hate an open convention. You can't ever tell what's going to happen!

RUSSELL (*smiles*). They're never that open.

CARLIN. I suppose we better try for a Catholic . . . that seems to be the big thing this year . . . for *second* place, that is. (JENSEN *returns with papers.*) Bill, *don't* make things tough for yourself! You got the nomination now so leave the controversial things alone.

RUSSELL. I can't help it. I am driven by a mad demon, by some imp of the perverse . . . (CARLIN *looks at him narrowly.* JENSEN *gives him a warning look.*) That is, I am *compelled* to say what I think.

CARLIN. O.K., but try to lay off stuff like Red China, especially when you know Henry Luce is an absolute nut on China and you don't want to lose *Time* and *Life* when they're already behind you in the interests of good government and all that crap. . . . So keep Henry Luce happy, will you? Once you're President, you can eat with chopsticks for all anybody cares.

RUSSELL. I will be diplomatic.

CARLIN. You know, Cantwell's releasing a statement today. To all the delegates. He says it'll knock you off.

RUSSELL. We're ready for him. He may be the master of the half truth and the insinuation, but we've got the facts.

CARLIN. And the *whole* truth?

RUSSELL (*lightly*). No man has the whole truth.

CARLIN. Oh, brother! Good luck, Bill. Let me know if there's anything I can do for you. I'm with you one hundred per cent, in spite of your damned dictionary.

RUSSELL. Thank you, Senator.

(CARLIN *goes.* RUSSELL *goes into the bedroom and sits wearily on the bed.*)

RUSSELL. Dick, where's Dr. Artinian?

JENSEN. On his way from the airport. (JENSEN *enters bedroom, sits on chair opposite the bed.*)

RUSSELL. And Hockstader?

JENSEN. Talking to delegates. . . . Bill, I've finally got a line on Cantwell. I got some real dirt . . .

RUSSELLS Of all the stunts, this is the craziest! If you'll excuse my obsessive use of words like "mad" and "crazy."

JENSEN. You could've cut the air with a knife when you made that crack about being "driven by a mad demon" . . .

(RUSSELL *has started his walk across the carpet.*)

RUSSELL. Well, they re-elected Eisenhower after a heart attack and an ileitis operation . . . didn't seem to hurt him.

JENSEN. But there was never any question about his mind or his judgment being affected. (RUSSELL *has completed his walk.*) Well? What's the score?

RUSSELL (*smiles*). I still get it on the first ballot but it was a near miss: I nearly stepped on that leaf, the one by the table . . . it's a bitch. (*Indicates newspaper.*) What about your daily horoscope?

JENSEN (*from memory*). "A.M. Fine for getting apparel in order. P.M. do not quarrel with loved one." Bill, you may have to pull a Nixon.

RUSSELL. And what does "pull a Nixon" mean?

JENSEN. Go on television. And cry on the nation's shoulder. With *two* cocker spaniels.

RUSSELL. And tell them I'm not crazy? No. I admit it's possible to look directly into a camera and persuade the people I won't steal their money, but I promise you, Dick, you can't look a camera in the face and say, "Honest, I'm not crazy. I just had a nervous breakdown like any regular fellow might." No, it won't work.

JENSEN. Why not?

RUSSELL. Because it won't. And even if it did, I couldn't do it. (*Chuckles.*) I might . . . laugh. It's too idiotic.

(ALICE *enters from corridor door.*)

RUSSELL. How was the meeting?

ALICE. I made a speech. At least I started to read the one Dick gave me. Then halfway through I gave up and made my own speech, and do you know what? It was terrible! (*Suddenly grave*) What's happened?

RUSSELL. Dr. Artinian's on his way to Philadelphia. He's going to tell the press that I am not and never was insane.

ALICE. It gets worse and worse, doesn't it?

RUSSELL. Yes, it does.

(JENSEN *rises, crosses to connecting-*

hall door.)

JENSEN. I've got to get back to work. Here. (*He puts a schedule on the other twin bed.*) We have Ohio in twenty minutes. Then one more go at California.

RUSSELL. Send Dr. Artinian in the second he gets here.

(JENSEN *nods, exits left.*)

ALICE. Does this mean they could publish everything about us? Our marriage and . . . *everything?*

RUSSELL. Yes.

(ALICE *sits on the same twin bed as* RUSSELL; *they are back to back.*)

ALICE. Will they?

RUSSELL. I don't know. I think it's just a bluff right now, to frighten me.

ALICE. It frightens me. I should hate to think of the children reading all that about us. Oh, it is filthy . . . filthy!

RUSSELL. Do you want me to quit?

ALICE (*a pause*). No.

(RUSSELL *puts his hand on* ALICE's; *she smiles.*)

ALICE. How very odd!

RUSSELL. What?

ALICE. Do you realize that this is the first time you've touched me when there wasn't a camera or someone in the room? (*There is a tense moment; then he pats her hand briskly and rises; he picks up the sheet of paper* JENSEN *left on the other bed.*)

RUSSELL. Well, here's your schedule. Your next appointment is . . . Oh, my God, I forgot all about this!

ALICE (*grimly*). I haven't. Mabel Cantwell and I face the press together. Can I get out of it?

RUSSELL. No. Better not.

ALICE. Then I'll get ready. We're meeting in her suite. She made the point very tactfully over the phone that (ALICE *lapses into deep Mabelese.*) accordin to protocol the wife of a reignin Senator outranks the wife of a former Secretary of State.

RUSSELL (*equally Southern*). Well, bless my soul!

(ALICE *goes.* DR. ARTINIAN, *a distinguished-looking psychiatrist . . . the first to be depicted in the American theater without a Mittel-Europa accent . . . enters with* JENSEN *from left.* RUSSELL *crosses living room to greet him, just as the buzzer from the corridor sounds.* JENSEN *hurries to corridor door.*)

RUSSELL. Robert, I'm glad you could get away like this . . .

ARTINIAN. I had to.

(JENSEN *opens corridor door to admit* HOCKSTADER, *who darts in while* JENSEN *pushes back the press.*)

RUSSELL. Dr. Artinian . . . President Hockstader.

(HOCKSTADER *and* ARTINIAN *shake hands.*)

HOCKSTADER. You Bill's head-doctor?

ARTINIAN. That's right. And I'm a very great admirer of yours, Mr. President.

HOCKSTADER. Well, I'm *not* an admirer of yours. Why don't you people keep your damned files where nobody can get at 'em?

ARTINIAN. We do. Or we thought we did. Apparently somebody from Cantwell's office bribed one of our nurses . . . they got the entire case history.

RUSSELL. Robert, in one hour Cantwell's releasing that file on me. Now I know this sounds silly, but when he does, I want you to meet the press and tell them I am *not* mentally unstable.

ARTINIAN. Of course I will. You don't know how guilty I feel about this. (ARTINIAN *turns to exit left with* JENSEN.)

HOCKSTADER (*suddenly*). He *is* all right, isn't he?

ARTINIAN (*smiles*). Mr. Russell is one of the sanest men I ever have known.

HOCKSTADER. Then what's all that stuff about suicide tendencies and manic-mania or whatever you call it?

ARTINIAN. Just technical phrases which may sound sinister to a layman. He is certainly *not* a manic depressive. Anyone's psychological profile could be made to sound . . . damaging.

RUSSELL (*lightly*). In the South a candidate for sheriff once got elected by claiming that his opponent's wife had been a thespian.

JENSEN. We'll find a room for you here, Doctor. And I'll get somebody to help you with your statement.

ARTINIAN. Thank you. I also brought the Institute's lawyer with me. By way of making amends, Bill, we're filing suit against Cantwell for theft . . .

HOCKSTADER (*pleased*). That's the ticket. Go to it, Doc.

ARTINIAN (*to* RUSSELL). I'll be ready when you want me.

RUSSELL (*warmly*). Many thanks, Robert.

(ARTINIAN *and* JENSEN *go off left.* RUS-SELL *is about to follow when* HOCKSTADER *stops him.*)

HOCKSTADER. Bill, I want you to myself a minute. Now what's this I hear about you not going on the TV?

RUSSELL. I can't.

HOCKSTADER. How the hell you goin to fight this thing if you don't?

RUSSELL. Dr. Artinian . . .

HOCKSTADER (*disgust*). Dr. Artinian! That's just *one* doctor. They'll say he's a friend of yours. Cantwell's going to insist they have half the medical profession look you over between now and tomorrow . . . (*Pacing happily*) Oh, I tell you, Bill, I feel wonderful! Up all night . . . on the go all morning, seein delegates . . . I tell you there is *nothin* like a dirty low-down political fight to put the roses in your cheeks.

RUSSELL (*concerned*). How *do* you feel?

HOCKSTADER. Immortal! Now a lot of the delegates know that somethin's up. They don't know what . . .

RUSSELL (*abruptly*). Art, why didn't you endorse me last night?

HOCKSTADER (*awkwardly*). Look, Bill, this isn't easy to say, but you might as well know: I came to Philadelphia to nominate Cantwell.

RUSSELL (*nods*). I knew that.

HOCKSTADER (*taken aback*). You did! How?

RUSSELL (*wryly*). Prince Hamlet has second sight. He sees motives as well as ghosts upon the battlement.

HOCKSTADER. Guess I ain't as sly as I figured I was.

RUSSELL. Did you decide to help me now because of what Joe's doing? Bringing up that breakdown business?

HOCKSTADER. No. No. Matter of fact . . . speaking as a professional politician . . . I kind of admire what he's doing. It's clever as all hell. No, Joe Cantwell lost me because he wasn't smart. He made a mistake. He figured I was goin to back you when I wasn't. You got my message. Joe didn't. Now that's a serious error. Shows he don't understand character and a President if he don't understand anything else has got to understand people. Then he got flustered when I needled him. A President don't get flustered when a man gives him the needle. He keeps a straight face, like poker. (*Smiles.*) Like you're doin right now. But what does Joe do? He don't run scared; he runs terrified. He fires off a cannon to kill a bug. And that is just plain dumb and I mean to knock him off . . . which means that you, I guess, are goin to be our next President.

RUSSELL. President . . . but by default. Because you still have your doubts about me, don't you?

HOCKSTADER. Yes, I still have my doubts. Bill, I want a strong President . . .

RUSSELL. An immoral President?

(HOCKSTADER *turns away disgustedly.*)

HOCKSTADER. They hardly come in any other size.

RUSSELL. You don't believe that . . .

(JENSEN *enters with a plump, bald, nervous man of forty-odd who resembles an unmade studio couch.*)

JENSEN. This is Sheldon Marcus.

HOCKSTADER (*irritably*). Who the hell is Sheldon Marcus? (HOCKSTADER *turns, sees that the man is already in the room; he flashes a Presidential smile and, hand outstretched, crosses to* MARCUS.) If you'll excuse me, sir?

MARCUS. That's all right. I . . . I never thought I'd meet a President. (MARCUS *rubs his shaken hand against his trouser leg.*) My hands sweat. I . . . I'm nervous, I guess. You see, I just now came in from Wilmington, where I live, outside Wil-mington's actually where I live, a suburb you never heard of called . . .

RUSSELL. Dick, what's this all about? I'm Bill Russell.

JENSEN. Mr. Marcus served in the army with Joe Cantwell . . .

HOCKSTADER. In the army? (*Starts to beam with anticipation.*) Ah . . . ah . . . *Now* we're gettin somewhere. Well, what was it? Was he a member of the Ku Klux Klan? The Communist Party? Or did he run away when the guns went off?

MARCUS. Well, sir, Mr. President, sir, uh, we weren't anywheres around where there were guns . . .

JENSEN. They were both in the Aleu-tians. On the island of Adak. The Quar-termaster Corps.

MARCUS (*nods*). We were there for a year, well, maybe more like eighteen months for me and, oh, maybe sixteen, seventeen months for Joe, he came there February '43 and I got there . . .

RUSSELL (*to* JENSEN). Dick, what are you trying to prove?

HOCKSTADER. Now shush, Bill. And let's hear the dirt, whatever it is.

MARCUS. Well . . . Joe . . . (*Pauses in an agony of embarrassment.*) Oh, I sure hate talking about him, telling something so awful . . .

JENSEN. I had a lead on this months ago. I finally tracked it down. . . . Tell them, Mr. Marcus.

MARCUS. Well, Joe Cantwell was a captain and I was a captain and Joe Cantwell was . . . was . . . well, he was . . . you know how it is sometimes when there's all those men together and . . . and . . .

JENSEN. And no female companionship . . .

MARCUS. That's right, though we had some nurses later on, but not enough to make much difference. I mean there were all those men . . .

JENSEN (*helpfully*). And no women.

RUSSELL (*irritated*). Oh, for Christ's sake, Dick, stop it, will you?

HOCKSTADER (*soothingly*). Now . . . now, let's not get ahead of ourselves.

RUSSELL. You know Joe isn't that, and if he was, so what?

HOCKSTADER. I find this very interesting. Mr. Marcus . . . Captain Marcus, I should say . . .

MARCUS (*gabbling*). I was a major, actually, promoted just before my discharge in '46. I'm in the reserve . . . the *inactive* reserve . . . but if there was another war I would be . . .

HOCKSTADER (*through him*). Major Marcus, am I to understand by the way you are beating slowly around the bush that Joe Cantwell is what . . . when I was a boy . . . we called a de-generate?

MARCUS (*relieved to have the word said*). Yes, sir, Mr. President, sir, that's just what I mean . . .

RUSSELL (*amused in spite of himself*). I don't believe it! Nobody with that awful wife and those ugly children could be anything but normal!

HOCKSTADER. Bill! Patience. Whether *you* believe it or not is beside the point.

RUSSELL. And even if it were true I'm damned if I'd smear him with something like that . . .

HOCKSTADER (*patiently and slowly*). Bill, I, like you, am a tolerant man. I *personally* do not care if Joe Cantwell enjoys deflowering sheep by the light of a full moon. But I *am* interested in finding a way to stop him cold.

RUSSELL. Damn it, Art, this is exactly the kind of thing I went into politics to stop! The business of gossip instead of issues, personalities instead of policies. . . . We've got enough on Cantwell's *public* life to defeat him without going into his private life which is nobody's business!

HOCKSTADER (*sharply*). Any more than yours is?

RUSSELL. Any more than mine is.

HOCKSTADER. But Cantwell *is* using your private life . . .

RUSSELL. All the more reason for my *not* using his. I'm not Cantwell.

HOCKSTADER (*reasonably*). But nobody's used anything *yet*.

RUSSELL. Look here, Art, you are *not* my campaign manager. I am the one running for President, not you. (*To* JENSEN, *grimly*.) And as for you, Dick . . .

JENSEN (*growing desperate*). Bill, at least *listen* to the man.

RUSSELL. No!

HOCKSTADER. I'm beginnin to wonder if maybe I'm tryin to help the wrong team.

RUSSELL (*losing control*). Perhaps you are. Perhaps you'd be happier with Cantwell, helping him throw his mud! (*A tense silence.* HOCKSTADER *remains impassive.* RUSSELL *recovers himself quickly. He is contrite.*) Art, I'm sorry. I didn't mean that.

HOCKSTADER (*amused*). Observe how I kept a straight face while being insulted?

RUSSELL. You know that I only meant . . .

HOCKSTADER (*through him*). Yes, I know. (*Wheedling*) Now, Bill, as a favor to an old man in his . . . sunset years, will you just listen to Major Marcus? That's all. Just listen.

RUSSELL. All right, Art. I'll listen. But only as a favor to . . . to a friend.

HOCKSTADER. That's fine, Bill. You just relax now and let events take their course. (HOCKSTADER *crosses to the dazed* MARCUS.) After all, how often does a million dollars (*Pats* MARCUS.) drop in your lap? Not to mention the Presidency. (*Propels* MARCUS *to a chair downstage.*) Sit down, Major Marcus, sit down. Please. Make yourself comfortable. Fact, I will mix you a drink myself with these old skilled fingers, and while I do you will tell us your story. (*Crosses to bar.*) Omitting no details, no matter how sordid.

(RUSSELL *turns upstage, revolted.*)

MARCUS. Well, Mr. President, there was this guy up on Adak, and his name was Fenn, Bob Fenn. That is, *Robert* Fenn. (*Light starts to fade.*) I don't know his middle initial but I guess it's all there in the record, how this Lieutenant Fenn . . .

CURTAIN

Scene Two

The Cantwell suite. A few minutes later. MABEL, ALICE *and* MRS. GAMADGE *sit in a row on the sofa in the living room.* MRS. GAMADGE *is in a long evening dress with a vast corsage.* REPORTERS *and* CAMERAMEN *are winding up a press conference.* BLADES *hovers, directs.*

BLADES. All right, boys . . . come on . . . that's enough . . . our girls have got a lot to do . . .

REPORTER 1. Mrs. Russell, where are your sons now?

ALICE. They . . . well, one's in Watch Hill and the other's traveling . . . he's in Europe. I wish now we had them here, for the experience.

(*A flash-bulb goes off.*)

MABEL. Oh, I blinked my eyes! (*To* REPORTER 1 *gaily*) Joe and I were going to bring our girls to Philadelphia but then we decided, no, this sort of thing is just too hectic for children . . .

REPORTER 2. Mrs. Russell . . . how's *Mr.* Russell today?

ALICE. He's just fine . . .

REPORTER 3. There has been a rumor that he is not in the very best of health.

ALICE (*growing steely*). I have never seen him in better health.

MABEL. My Joe just blossoms during a campaign! On the go all the time! I don't know *where* he gets the energy.

ALICE. In fact, my husband . . .

MRS. GAMADGE (*through her*). Joe Cantwell is a real dynamo!

ALICE (*a second try*). In fact, my husband . . .

MABEL. I sometimes think Joe has got nerves of iron. Nothing ever seems to upset him.

MRS. GAMADGE (*nods*). He has a great inner calm, which is almost spiritual.

ALICE (*gamely*). My husband . . .

BLADES. O.K. That's it, fellows . . .

(*The* REPORTERS *start to go.*)

REPORTER 3 (*to* ALICE). What do you think's going to happen tomorrow? Do you think Mr. Russell's got it on the first ballot?

ALICE. I certainly hope so!

MABEL (*butter would not melt, etc.*). Well, as for me, I just hope the best man wins! I mean for the country and everything.

MRS. GAMADGE. Amen to that!

(BLADES *follows* REPORTERS *out into corridor.*)

BLADES. Good day, ladies!

(*The three women are alone.* MRS. GAMADGE *sighs gustily.*)

MABEL. Well, *that* was an ordeal, wasn't it, Mrs. Russell?

ALICE. I'm sure it wasn't for you. (*Afraid this sounded too sharp, amends.*) I mean you've done so much of this . . . kind of thing. (*Rises.*) I have to go.

(MABEL *gets to her feet quickly.*)

MABEL. Oh, stay and have a drink . . . just for a minute. I don't have anything to do till (*Looks at schedule.*) . . . till four-fifteen. So let's play hooky!

ALICE. I'm afraid I have an appointment in fifteen minutes.

MRS. GAMADGE. They have us girls on timetables just like trains. Will you look at me? (*She rises.*) All ready to moderate the fashion show at five o'clock. (MRS. GAMADGE *crosses to bar for a Coca Cola, which she drinks with a straw.*)

MABEL (*cozily*). It's a shame we couldn't do everything together, instead of first you meetin one group and then me meetin the same group . . . What can I fix you? (MABEL *makes herself a drink.*)

ALICE. Nothing, thanks. It's too early for me.

(MRS. GAMADGE *is back on the sofa, reading a newspaper.*)

MRS. GAMADGE. Well, didn't Art Hockstader surprise everybody last night?

MABEL. Personally, I think he's an old meanie the way he's holding out. And you know why? (*Indicates newspaper.*) Publicity! He absolutely revels in the limelight. . . . Oh, Mrs. Russell, I don't believe you've seen my children.

ALICE. I've seen pictures of them.

They're very . . . pretty.

(MABEL *holds up a photograph.*)

MABEL. That's Gladys there, the oldest . . . with the braces on her teeth. I'm afraid they're all going to have to have braces and Lord knows *where* they got those teeth from. Both Joe and I have perfect teeth, and oh! what a fortune it is having children's teeth straightened! Do you have a picture of your boys?

ALICE. No. Not with me . . .

MRS. GAMADGE. So good-looking . . .

MABEL. Yes! That was a nice spread on them in *Life*. Such *warm* pictures! You and Mr. Russell certainly get a lot of coverage from *Life*, much more than we do.

ALICE. Oh? I thought we were neck and neck.

MABEL. No. I'm afraid Joe and I must simply forget Mr. Luce. You're *his* candidate. For the time being. Oh, come on, sit down. (*Affectionately.*) I do like the way you do your hair.

ALICE. Oh? Well . . .

MABEL. You look so like this English teacher I had at State College. A wonderful woman in every way . . .

ALICE. Thank you. But I'm afraid I'm not wonderful . . .

MABEL. Now . . . no false modesty! You are wonderful *and* courageous. I always say Alice Russell is the most courageous woman in public life, don't I, Sue-Ellen?

(MRS. GAMADGE, *immersed in her paper, nods.*)

ALICE (*curiously*). In what way, courageous?

MABEL. Why, that committee you were on!

MRS. GAMADGE (*suddenly alert*). Committee? *What* committee?

MABEL (*ready for the kill*). You know —in New York City, the one where you did all that work for *birth control*.

MRS. GAMADGE (*horror*). Birth control! I didn't know that.

ALICE. Well, it *was* twenty years ago. And of course I'm not supposed to mention it now . . . (*To* MABEL) as *you* know.

MRS. GAMADGE. I should hope not! You'll have the Catholics down on us like a ton of bricks. The rhythm cycle, yes (*Makes a vague circular motion with her hand*), but anything else . . . is out.

MABEL. Of course I'm against any kind of artificial means of birth control except where it's a matter of health maybe, but believe me I think it took the courage of a lion to be in favor of people using these contraceptive things when you're in public life. Of course I guess you didn't know then your husband would be running for President one day and when you do that you just can't afford to offend a lot of nice people who vote.

ALICE. I realize that. We must offend no one. Of course, if you offend no one, you don't please anyone very much, either, do you? But I suppose that is an occupational hazard in politics. We are all interchangeably inoffensive.

(*There is a pause.*)

MRS. GAMADGE. Well, now!

MABEL (*overlapping*). Well, hooray for Mrs. Russell! Do you know, you sounded just like your husband then? Didn't she, Sue-Ellen? Didn't she sound just like Bill Russell when he's being witty and profound and way over our poor heads!

ALICE (*rising*). I'd like to think intelligence was contagious. But I'm afraid it isn't, at least in my case. Bill has the brains. I'm not awfully quick.

MABEL. Oh, yes, you are, honey!

ALICE. I've really got to go. (ALICE *turns upstage.* MRS. GAMADGE *and* MABEL *follow her.*)

MRS. GAMADGE. You girls are an absolute inspiration to the American woman, *and I mean it* . . . each in your different way.

ALICE. Thank you very much . . . for that.

MABEL (*one last shot*). Oh, by the way, how *is* Mr. Russell's health? I mean *really*? I thought he looked so peaked last night at the dinner and someone did say . . .

ALICE (*grimly*). The reporters are gone, Mrs. Cantwell. You know as well as I do he's perfectly all right. Good-by.

MRS. GAMADGE. 'By.

(ALICE *goes.*)

MABEL. Well . . . listen to her! "The reporters are gone, Mrs. Cantwell!" If she wasn't so high and mighty she'd take the hint and start saying right now he isn't feeling good so that when he has to pull out there'd be some preparation . . . (MABEL *goes into bedroom and flops onto the rumpled bed.*)

MRS. GAMADGE (*following her*). Mabel,

I don't like anything about what Joe's doing. It's plain dirty and I should warn you: I'm a loyal party worker and I'll see that the women are all behind Bill Russell.

MABEL. *Under* him is more their usual position. It's just sex, sex, sex, morning, noon and night with that Bill Russell.

MRS. GAMADGE. Now, Mabel, unless you were in the room, how would you know?

MABEL. I read that report. Bill Russell is a neurotic who has had a breakdown and his sex life is certainly not normal. Sleeping around with all those women is just plain immature. And we don't want an immature President, do we?

MRS. GAMADGE. We've had some very good Presidents who have slept around a lot more than Bill Russell ever did. And in the White House, too.

(BLADES, CANTWELL *and* CARLIN *enter living room from corridor.*)

MABEL (*hears them*). Here come the men!

MRS. GAMADGE. And I must get back to the women. (*She is about to leave through the corridor door when she is surprised to see* CARLIN. *She comes into the living room.*) Hello, Senator Carlin. Didn't expect to see you *here*.

CARLIN. Just happened to be in the neighborhood.

(CANTWELL *comes up behind* MRS. GAMADGE *and kisses the back of her neck. She squeals.*)

CANTWELL. Hi, Sue-Ellen!

MRS. GAMADGE (*quickly recovered*). Joe, I hope you don't mind if I take the bull by the horns and tell you right now that anything to do with *private* lives is out in politics.

CANTWELL. I couldn't agree more.

MRS. GAMADGE. That's an unwritten law and it's a good one. Once you throw at a man that he has a mistress or an illegitimate child or something like that you get sympathy for him. (*Sadly*) I don't know why but you do. You also make yourself vulnerable because nobody's a saint. Not even you, Joe. So keep what you men do *in* bed *out* of politics. (*She goes, waving gaily.*) 'By, Joe. 'By, Bill. 'By, Mabel.

CANTWELL (*to* BLADES). Photostats ready?

BLADES. All neatly bound. Six hundred copies to be released to the delegates at

three-thirty P.M. Russell's doctor is in town. That means there's going to be some kind of a statement.

CANTWELL (*nods*). He's going to fight.

CARLIN. Aren't you fellows afraid of getting into trouble? Stealing medical records?

BLADES (*quickly*). We didn't steal them.

CANTWELL. They were given to us. *Pro bono publico.* Now just look at this . . . (CANTWELL *shows* CARLIN *the file. The phone rings in living room.* MABEL *answers it.*)

MABEL. Yes? Who? Oh, Dick Jensen! Yes, Joe's here. Just a sec. You hold on now. (*To* CANTWELL, *excited*) This is it, honey! They're giving up!

CANTWELL (*takes phone*). Hi, Dick. Howsa boy? Fine . . . Well, gosh, I don't see how I can delay much longer. I've told everybody three-thirty. Of course I'd sort of hoped Bill would be helpful. You know, for the Party's sake. He could back out so easily now, on this health issue . . . Yeah? Well, frankly, I don't see any point to postponing . . . Do I know who? Shel-don Mar-cus? No, I don't think so . . . *Where?* (*Harshly*) I want to see Russell. Right now . . . Well, try and fix it; I'll be right here. (*He hangs up, frowning.*)

MABEL. Well, honey, what did he say? Come on now . . . give with the T.L.!

BLADES (*concerned*). You aren't going to meet with Russell, are you? I thought we'd decided . . .

CANTWELL. Hold that stuff on Russell.

BLADES. Hold it? But we can't. We promised the delegates, three-thirty, we said . . .

CANTWELL. I said hold it.

MABEL (*alarm*). Joe, what's happening?

(CANTWELL *takes the file from* CARLIN.)

CANTWELL. Senator, if you'll excuse me . . .

CARLIN. Oh, sure . . . sure . . . Well, good-by, Mrs. Cantwell. (*At the door, he turns to* CANTWELL.) You know where to find me . . . *after* three-thirty. (CARLIN *goes.*)

CANTWELL (*to* BLADES). Go on. Stop that release.

BLADES (*bewildered*). O.K. . . . . you're the boss.

(BLADES *goes off right.* CANTWELL *goes into bedroom. He sits down on the bed, thinking hard.* MABEL *follows, panic beginning.*)

MABEL. Joe, what did Russell say to you? What's he doing to you?

(CANTWELL *looks at her blankly.* MABEL *begins to understand.*)

MABEL. It's not . . . it's not . . . (MABEL *stops. Slowly,* CANTWELL *nods.* MABEL, *horrified, sits beside him on the bed, her arm around him.*)

MABEL (*softly*). Oh, my God!

CURTAIN

SCENE THREE

The Russell suite. A few minutes later. MARCUS *has just finished his story.* RUSSELL *stands upstage, back to audience.* HOCKSTADER *starts to rise from sofa to give* MARCUS *some papers he's been studying. He sits back suddenly.* MARCUS *takes the papers from him, as* JENSEN *enters from left.*

————

JENSEN (*excitedly*). You should've heard Cantwell's voice! First time I've ever heard him stuck! (*To* RUSSELL) He wants to see you. So I said three-thirty and he agreed without a peep. That means *no* announcement to the delegates.

(RUSSELL *turns and crosses to* MARCUS, *who rises.*)

RUSSELL. Mr. Marcus, I want to thank you. I know that all this must be as . . . distasteful to you as it is to us. (RUSSELL *shakes* MARCUS' *hand.*)

MARCUS. Well, yes, it is . . . Peggy, my wife, oh, she was fit to be tied when I said I'd talked to Mr. Jensen and was going to come here and see you. She knew the whole story of course. I tell her everything, we have no secrets, Mrs. Marcus and me . . .

(RUSSELL *talks through him as he tries to get him off stage left.*)

RUSSELL. Yes . . . yes . . . well, many thanks.

JENSEN (*to* MARCUS). Would you wait . . . please? In my office? That's the second room, across the hall.

MARCUS. Yes, sir, Mr. Jensen. (*To* HOCKSTADER.) I guess this is the biggest moment of my life, meeting you, Mr. President, sir.

(HOCKSTADER, *seated, shakes his hand.*)

HOCKSTADER. I expect this *is* the biggest moment of your life, Major. You may have changed history. Excuse me for not getting up.

(MARCUS *is now beginning to enjoy the situation.*)

MARCUS. I'll say one thing, I certainly never thought back in '44 when Joe Cantwell and I were on Adak that sixteen years later we'd be here in this hotel with him running for President and me talking to you, sir, who I always admired (*Confidentially*), though I didn't vote for you the second time. You see, Mrs. Marcus felt that . . .

HOCKSTADER (*dulcet tones*). Let your vote, Major Marcus, remain between you and your God.

MARCUS (*overcome by this wisdom*). I guess that's right. Yes. Yes! I'll remember that, sir, I really will . . . (*To* JENSEN, *at door*) I won't have to see Joe, will I?

JENSEN. We hope not.

MARCUS. He's just awful when he's mad . . . he's got this temper. It's like stepping on a snake, stepping on Joe. He can be real scary.

(JENSEN *gets him through the door at last.*)

JENSEN. We'll remember that. Thanks a lot. See you in a few minutes. . . . (*To* RUSSELL.) Bill, we've done it! We've stopped Joe Cantwell!

RUSSELL (*indicates a folder on the coffee table in front of* HOCKSTADER). I'm not going to use this.

JENSEN (*quickly*). Of course you're not. Except privately. We just take this to Joe and say: "If you make an issue out of this breakdown, *we* make an issue out of a certain bit of court-martial testimony . . ."

(ALICE *enters from corridor.*)

RUSSELL. Alice, how did it go?

ALICE. My cheeks are tired from smiling for the camera. (*To* HOCKSTADER) But I must say I'm beginning to like politics, Mr. President, especially when Mrs. Gamadge tells me that I'm an inspiration to American women . . . in my way.

HOCKSTADER. You're an inspiration to me, Miss Alice. Excuse me for not getting up, but would you fetch me some branch water, some just *plain* branch water?

ALICE. Of course. (ALICE *goes to bar*.) Well, first we talked about Mabel's children. Then we talked about *my* children. Then we discussed the role of women in politics. We both agreed that woman's true place was in the home.

RUSSELL. I'm sure Mrs. Gamadge was eloquent on that subject.

ALICE. Eloquent to the point of obsession. We also agreed that women should be informed about issues.

HOCKSTADER. Worst damn thing ever happened to this country, giving the women the vote. Trouble, trouble, trouble. They got no more sense than a bunch of geese. Give 'em a big smile and a pinch on the . . . anatomy and you got ten votes.

ALICE (*smiles*). May I quote you, Mr. President?

HOCKSTADER. I will deny ever having made such a vile and un-American statement. (*Takes glass.*) Thank you, ma'am.

ALICE (*to* RUSSELL). And, finally, there were some pointed references to your health . . .

RUSSELL. Which means they've started. Mentally unstable. Apt to crack up . . . already showing signs of the strain. (*Sighs.*) As a matter of fact, I *am* showing signs of strain.

(JENSEN *holds up folder*.)

JENSEN. Bill, you can stop them. Right now. We've got the ultimate weapon, massive retaliation as Foster Dulles used to say. (WOMAN AID *opens door at left; she whispers something to* JENSEN, *who nods. She goes.* JENSEN *beams*.) We have a visitor.

(BLADES *enters, simulating jauntiness*.)

BLADES. Gentlemen . . . Mr. President! (HOCKSTADER *ignores him*.)

RUSSELL. Mr. Blades, contrary to what you may have been told, I'm *not* seeing Joe Cantwell.

BLADES. Oh? But I thought you were. I thought Joe said you'd meet in his room because there aren't so many reporters down there . . .

JENSEN (*to* RUSSELL). That's right, Bill. I said we'd be right down . . .

RUSSELL. You did!

(BLADES *studies every nuance, trying to get a sense of what is happening*.)

BLADES. So I came up to work out some way of getting the Secretary downstairs without anybody seeing him. I

checked the service elevator and . . .

HOCKSTADER. Dick, you and that hatchet man there go try out the bathroom route. Through the bedroom. Into the next suite and on down.

BLADES (*probing*). O.K., Mr. President, but if the Secretary *isn't* going downstairs . . .

HOCKSTADER (*cold command*). Get moving, boys.

(JENSEN *indicates for* BLADES *to go with him*.)

JENSEN. Come on, Don. This is the dry run. (*Reluctantly,* BLADES *follows* JENSEN *into the bathroom by way of the bedroom*.)

RUSSELL (*to* HOCKSTADER). I'm not going to do this.

HOCKSTADER. You have to.

ALICE. Do what?

HOCKSTADER. He's got the stuff to knock off Cantwell. Only your lily-livered husband won't go through with it.

ALICE (*to* RUSSELL). You can keep them from bringing up all that . . . mental business?

RUSSELL. Maybe . . .

HOCKSTADER. Definitely.

ALICE. Then do it!

RUSSELL. But you don't know what it is I have to do.

ALICE (*fiercely*). I don't care! If you took a gun and shot him I'd help you if I thought that was the only way of keeping our lives . . . private.

HOCKSTADER. Atta girl! Listen to her, Bill. *She* don't run from a fight.

RUSSELL. You know I'm not afraid.

HOCKSTADER (*exasperation*). Then what is wrong with you? Why are you hesitatin *this* time?

RUSSELL. Look, I'm not being righteous and I'm not being fastidious and I do want to win. But how can I, in all conscience, use . . . *this,* even against Cantwell!

HOCKSTADER (*furiously*). I should've stuck with Cantwell! Because listenin to you hem and haw and talk about your conscience is turnin me against you fast. My God, what would happen if you had to make a quick decision in the White House when maybe all our lives depended on whether you could act fast . . . and you just sat there, the way you're doin now, having a high old time with your divided conscience.

RUSSELL (*hotly*). I am *not* divided! I know what I should do and this is *not* it.

HOCKSTADER. Then you don't want to be king of the castle. So stay away from us. Be a saint on your own time. Because you aren't fit to lead anybody.

RUSSELL (*stung*). Why? Because I don't "fire off a cannon to kill a bug"? Because I don't have that quick mindless reaction you seem to confuse with strength? Well, I promise you, there is more danger in a President who acts on animal reflex than in one who is willing to reflect before he acts, who has some vestigial moral sense that goes beyond himself. Don't you see? If I start to fight like Cantwell I lose all meaning . . .

HOCKSTADER (*evenly*). If you don't start to fight, you are finished. Now I am here to tell you this: power is not a toy we give to good children; it is a weapon and the strong man takes it and he uses it and I can assure you he don't turn it on himself nor let another man come at him with a knife that he don't fight back. Well, that knife is at your throat and if you don't go down there and beat Cantwell to the floor with this very dirty stick, then you got no business in this big league, and bastard or not I'll help Joe Cantwell take the whole damned world if he wants it, because it's not for you and never will be!

(*A long moment, broken by the return of* JENSEN *and* BLADES *from the bathroom stage right.*)

JENSEN. Well, the coast is clear. We're all set.

BLADES. First, we pass through a suite containing a hosiery salesman and a woman . . . perhaps not his wife.

JENSEN. Definitely not his wife. (*To* RUSSELL.) He looks forward to meeting you even though he hopes Cantwell gets the nomination. His companion betrayed no intimacy with the names of either candidate.

BLADES. Then we go down the back stairs and through a room occupied by a widow from Bangor, Maine, who is for Russell . . .

JENSEN. And from there we go to the Cantwell bathroom and then . . . they meet and make history!

BLADES. That's right! Though what's going on beats me.

(HOCKSTADER *has been eying* RUSSELL *coldly during this.*)

HOCKSTADER (*to* RUSSELL, *softly*). Here's your chance. Your *last* chance. Take it. Go down there. I want a strong President to keep us alive a while longer.

(RUSSELL *makes his decision. He turns to* BLADES *and* JENSEN. *He motions toward the bedroom.*)

RUSSELL. Wait for me in there.

BLADES (*as he goes*). How are you feeling, Mr. President?

HOCKSTADER (*grimly*). Just fine, considering the alternative.

(*Chuckling,* BLADES *joins* JENSEN *at the bathroom door.* RUSSELL *picks up the documents.*)

RUSSELL (*half to himself*). And so, one by one, these compromises, these small corruptions destroy character.

HOCKSTADER. To want power is corruption already. Dear God, you hate yourself for being human.

RUSSELL. No. I only want to *be* human . . . and it is not easy. Once this sort of thing starts, there is no end to it which is why it should never begin. And if *I* start . . . well, Art, how does it end, this sort of thing? *Where* does it end?

HOCKSTADER. In the grave, son, where the dust is neither good nor bad, but just nothing.

(RUSSELL *looks first at* HOCKSTADER; *then at* ALICE. *He goes into the bedroom.* ALICE *follows him; she pauses at the door and watches as* RUSSELL *exits to the bathroom, where* JENSEN *and* BLADES *are waiting.*)

ALICE (*slowly*). You are a good man, Mr. President.

HOCKSTADER. I reckon I am, when all's said and done. (HOCKSTADER, *in pain, tries to take one of his pills; he cannot get his hand to his mouth.*)

ALICE. But I don't know if this is the right thing for Bill to do. (ALICE *continues to look after* RUSSELL, *unaware of* HOCKSTADER's *pain.*)

HOCKSTADER. At least I put a fire under the candidate. I just hope it don't go out . . . Now don't you get alarmed (ALICE *turns on this, startled.*) but I want you to go over and pick up that phone and ask for Dr. Latham, he's in the hotel. Tell him I'm in here . . . tell him to come quick, through the back way. Tell him to bring a stretcher because I can't move. (ALICE, *horrified, goes quickly to the telephone.*) I'm afraid the old man is just about dead.

CURTAIN

ACT THREE

SCENE ONE

The Cantwell suite. A moment later. CANTWELL *is on the telephone in the living room.* MABEL *is beside him. Both wait, nervously.*

CANTWELL (*at last*). Yes, that's right. The name is Conyers, General Conyers . . . C-o-n-y-e-r-s . . . Yes, this is Senator Cantwell. Yes, it's an emergency. You . . . What? Oh, no! (*To* MABEL) They can't find him!

MABEL. But he *has* to be there!

CANTWELL (*into telephone*). Try his quarters, then. (*Softly, to himself*) Dammit, dammit, dammit.

MABEL. Are you sure General Conyers will back you up?

CANTWELL. He better. (*Into telephone*) Well, isn't there a phone anywhere near there? (*To* MABEL) He's playing golf! (*Into telephone*) O.K. Tell him as soon as you find him to call Senator Cantwell, in Philadelphia. The number is Walnut 8-7593 . . . Got it? Thank you. (CANTWELL *puts receiver down; he rises, starts to pace, thinking hard.*)

MABEL. But you've *got* to talk to him before they come down here.

CANTWELL. It's too late now. (*Thoughtfully*) Maybe it's just as well . . . (*Starts to plan.*) Now, let's see: Conyers . . . the delegates . . . Sheldon Marcus. (*Slowly*) Yes, Sheldon Marcus . . .

MABEL. Joe, I am scared to death . . .

CANTWELL. Well, don't be. (*Soothingly*) Come here, poor Momma Bear. (*He embraces her.*) And don't worry. Poppa Bear isn't going to get shot down this close to the honey-tree.

MABEL. I just don't know how they can use something like that which is so untrue, which is a dirty lie and everybody knew it was a lie even at the time . . . Oh, how I hate politics!

(*The telephone rings.* CANTWELL *breaks away to answer it.*)

CANTWELL. Conyers! (*Into telephone*) Yes? Who? (*Startled*) Oh, Mrs. Russell . . . Yes, this is Joe Cantwell . . . No, Bill isn't here yet. I guess he's still on his way down . . . *What?* Oh, that's awful! And you say he's . . . Yes, of course. Of course I'll tell Bill. The second he gets here. Yes. . . . He's a great guy. Yes, thank you. Good-by, Mrs. Russell. (*Puts down receiver.*) Art Hockstader just collapsed. They've taken him to the hospital. He's dying.

MABEL. Dying? I thought he . . .

CANTWELL. That hernia stuff was a lot of bull.

MABEL. But what's this going to do to us, his dying now?

CANTWELL. Find out what hospital he's at.

(RUSSELL, BLADES *and* JENSEN *emerge from the bathroom into the bedroom.* CANTWELL *hears them. He gestures warningly to* MABEL, *who is about to exit right.*)

CANTWELL. Not a word about Hockstader. I don't want anything to upset this meeting.

(MABEL *nods and goes.* CANTWELL *gets himself into position as the three men enter the living room.*)

BLADES. Well, here we are!

JENSEN. Touch and go for a while there but we made it. Nobody saw us.

(RUSSELL *and* CANTWELL *stare at one another curiously. A long silence, interrupted by* MABEL's *return.*)

MABEL (*gaily*). Well, now, will you look at that! I tell you they look just like two wild animals in the zoo! (*Pause*) Well, come on now . . . somebody *say* something! It's just politics, that's all, isn't like the end of the world or anything . . .

JENSEN (*flatly*). Yet.

MABEL. I had such a nice visit with your wife, Mr. Russell . . . and she is getting to be a real campaigner, isn't she? (*Starts to cross to bar.*) Could I fix you a drink or something? We have just about everything. Let me see, there's gin and there's Scotch and there's bourbon with branch water like President Hockstader always used to . . . (*She stops of her own accord, remembering.*)

CANTWELL. I don't think we want a drink, Mabel.

RUSSELL. No, thank you.

MABEL (*to* BLADES). Well, in that case I believe we must make ourselves scarce,

Don.

BLADES (*to* RUSSELL). Let me know when you're ready to go back upstairs. (BLADES *exits right.*)

CANTWELL (*to* RUSSELL). Is Sheldon Marcus in the hotel?

JENSEN. Yes.

CANTWELL. Could I see him? (*To* RUSSELL) I'd like to ask him some questions . . . front of you, if it's all right.

(RUSSELL *nods.*)

JENSEN. I'll bring him down.

CANTWELL (*indicates office to right*). Have him wait in there.

(JENSEN *goes off stage, left.*)

MABEL. Well, I guess you two boys want to be alone. (*To* RUSSELL) Now you go easy on my Joe . . . who is the best husband that ever was, ever! Well, good-by, now . . . (*To* CANTWELL, *nervously*) Joe honey, if you want me I'll be over in Sue-Ellen Gamadge's room, we're having a real old-time henfest this afternoon, with all the governors' wives.

(CANTWELL *nods to her, encouragingly.* MABEL *crosses through bedroom and exits left.*)

CANTWELL. Well, Bill, here we are . . . the main event like they say.

RUSSELL. The main event. And here we stand, as Martin Luther said . . .

CANTWELL (*misunderstanding*). Oh, I'm sorry . . . sit down, please . . .

RUSSELL. And it is not safe to move.

CANTWELL. Who said what?

RUSSELL. Martin Luther said: it is not safe to move. (*Explaining*) Luther was . . .

CANTWELL (*irritably*). You don't need to tell me who Martin Luther was. I happen to be a Protestant. I'm a very religious kind of guy . . . Bill.

RUSSELL (*ironically*). You don't need to tell *me* that . . . Joe. (RUSSELL *sits on the sofa downstage.* CANTWELL *remains standing.*)

CANTWELL (*stung*). You really do think you're better than all of us, with your bad jokes, and the admiration of a lot of bleeding-heart fellow travelers and would-be intellectuals who don't mean a thing in this country!

RUSSELL (*appreciatively*). That was very good, Joe. Pure Cantwell. Known as the multiple lie. Or in this case the multiple-lie-plus-confused-statement. For instance, you say that I think I'm better than the rest of you . . .

CANTWELL (*quickly*). You don't deny . . .

RUSSELL (*chuckling*). Excellent. Interrupt before the answer begins. That's vintage Cantwell . . .

CANTWELL (*District Attorney's voice*). I'm not interested in your sophistry. Your contempt. Your deliberate refusal to answer . . .

RUSSELL (*bangs ashtray on coffee table*). Mr. Chairman! Mr. Chairman! Point of order! (*Laughs.*) Oh, how're you going to keep them down in the Senate once they've been on TV?

CANTWELL (*smiles*). Very funny. Very cute. I like that. You should have your own TV show.

RUSSELL. Thank you. I'm sure you meant that as a compliment. . . . Joe, I came down here to convince you that there are some things a man cannot do even in politics . . .

(CANTWELL *sits opposite him downstage.*)

CANTWELL (*not listening*). Now I have given you every hint, every opportunity in the past two days to pull out of the race. Considering your medical history, it could be done so easily . . . so logically. All you'd have to do is claim exhaustion, fatigue . . . like the last time . . . and then this ugly business would never come up and the Party could then unite behind its candidate . . .

RUSSELL. You?

CANTWELL (*nods*). And we take the election in November.

RUSSELL. You make it sound so simple, but it isn't. For one thing, you'll be sued for the theft of my case history.

CANTWELL (*tries to interrupt*). Bill . . .

RUSSELL. But that's not the point.

CANTWELL (*again*). Bill . . .

RUSSELL. What I want you to realize . . .

CANTWELL (*voice of reason*). Bill! I didn't steal it. The thing was *given* to me, unsolicited. Anyway, I'm sure your doctor won't file suit if you ask him not to.

RUSSELL (*taken aback*). Why should I ask him not to?

CANTWELL (*promptly*). Party unity. What's the point of smearing me when I'm the one who's got to get us into the White House?

RUSSELL. What makes you so certain

you're going to be nominated?

CANTWELL (*as to a child*). Because I expect you to withdraw . . . because you've got no choice. Then who else is there? Except me.

RUSSELL (*stunned*). You are . . . amazing! I came down here with enough political nitroglycerine not only to knock you out of the race but out of politics altogether, and there you sit and blandly tell me *I'm* the one to withdraw.

CANTWELL (*through him*). I also promise to use you, once I'm elected. And that's a solemn promise, Bill. You can have any post in the cabinet you want, excepting Secretary of State, where I'm all hung up with somebody else. Or you can go as our first Ambassador to Red China . . . (RUSSELL *looks at him, amazed.*) That's right. You'll be happy to know I intend to recognize Red China, though I won't make an issue of it until public opinion is more . . .

RUSSELL (*thoughtfully*). Never defend, always attack. You're very good at this, Joe. I mean that.

CANTWELL. Another thing you ought to know since you've made such a point about it in your attacks on me: politically we are almost the same on every important issue. *Only* I am less reckless than you. I believe in timing. I don't see anything to be gained by launching a policy just to have it shot down maybe for good because the climate wasn't right.

RUSSELL. And you call that leadership?

CANTWELL. There are many ways of leading; the worst one is making brilliant speeches on the right side at the wrong time. I know how to wait . . .

RUSSELL. You are candid.

(CANTWELL, *bursting with energy and self-righteousness, starts to pace.*)

CANTWELL (*passionately*). And I'm right! Because I was born to this. You weren't. I know in my bones how to do this thing. I understand the people of this country. Because I'm one of them. I know how to maneuver. How to win. I knew from the time I won my first election I was going to be President and nobody was going to stop me. Not even the brilliant, witty, aristocratic, intellectual William Russell, who has no more to do with the people of this country than I have to do with the Groton Harvard Wall Street set.

RUSSELL. Well, there is no immediate need to start a class war. I am not better qualified to be President because I went to Harvard than you are because you worked your way through a state college. But as you probably know there is a certain suspicion of the self-made man these days. People aren't as naïve as you think. Any man who fights his way to the top is certainly to be admired, but the people sometimes wonder: how exactly did he do it? And whom did he hurt along the way? The self-made man often makes himself out of pieces of his victims. (RUSSELL *rises and crosses to* CANTWELL *as his own rage begins.*) You are something of a Frankenstein monster, Joe, made out of the bits and pieces of Sicilian bandits . . . and your political opponents . . . all assembled before our eyes on television.

CANTWELL (*coldly*). *How* I was made is not the question. What matters is, I am here.

RUSSELL. And you think that your basic public *image* has changed?

CANTWELL. It has. According to the Gallup poll only twelve per cent of the people even remember that there was a Mafia hearing.

RUSSELL. I remember.

CANTWELL. The image that they have of Cantwell is the way I am now . . .

RUSSELL. Smooth, cautious, beyond reproach . . .

CANTWELL. That is right. People forget. Nobody's going to get any mileage out of my past so let's get this Aleutian business over with. I'm going to question Sheldon Marcus now and you're going to get the surprise of your life.

(RUSSELL *turns away from him; he sits again on the sofa.*)

RUSSELL. Nothing *you* do ever surprises me, Joe. What *I* do, however, is beginning to surprise me. (*He touches the folder in his jacket pocket.*) I never thought I could bring up something like this against any man. It revolts me . . .

CANTWELL (*generously*). Oh, come on! Don't give it a second thought. Look, I don't blame you. I'd certainly use it against you if it was there . . .

RUSSELL. That's the point; *you* would. I wouldn't. Or never thought I would.

(CANTWELL *sees a possible break in the enemy line.*)

CANTWELL. Then what are you doing down here? What have you got this joker Marcus standing by for except to smear me as a homosexual which I'm not.

RUSSELL. *I* never said you were . . .

CANTWELL (*relentlessly*). Then what are you doing here if you don't think I am?

RUSSELL. Had you paused at any point in your offensive, I would have told you *why* I came here and *what* I mean to do.

CANTWELL (*triumphantly*). I hope you realize you have just admitted that you don't believe this accusation against me. That you are openly confessing collusion . . .

RUSSELL (*abruptly*). Joe, shut up! (*Rises.*) Art Hockstader was right when he said you're not very sensitive to people. You're so busy trying to win you never stop to figure out *what* it is you're winning.

CANTWELL (*simulated weariness*). I am only trying to stick to the issue at hand. I don't believe in indulging in personalities.

RUSSELL. Come off it, Joe! I came here to try and convince you to drop that nonsense against me just as I mean to drop this nonsense against you. These things are irrelevant and dishonest, not to mention untrue. They cancel each other out. So I wish you would please join me by *not* indulging in personalities. (*Holds up folder.*) I'll tear this up and send Sheldon Marcus back where he came from, if you drop that business against me.

CANTWELL (*nods*). I see. You came here to make a deal with me.

RUSSELL (*a sigh of exasperation*). No! I came here to . . .

(CANTWELL *is growing confident.*)

CANTWELL (*warmly*). Look, Bill, it makes perfect sense, what you're doing. And I have no hard feelings. Really, I mean it. (CANTWELL *pats* RUSSELL *on the back.*) So don't be apologetic.

RUSSELL. You have *no* feelings, I would say.

CANTWELL. And perhaps you have too many. Perhaps you *are* too emotional. The report on your breakdown said you might have thought of committing suicide . . .

RUSSELL. Who hasn't thought of it?

CANTWELL. I never have. And I don't think a President should. No matter how tough the going is.

RUSSELL (*amused*). Am I to understand you want to save the country from me? That you are genuinely afraid I'm unstable?

CANTWELL. Yes, I am. You just admitted you thought of suicide . . .

RUSSELL. Then, Joe, if I'm so unstable, why did you offer me the ambassadorship to Red China?

CANTWELL (*promptly*). The President can keep tabs on an ambassador. Nobody can keep tabs on a President.

RUSSELL (*nods*). Never pause for an answer, in the best tradition of a television performer. . . . Well, let's get this dirty business over with. I won't throw my mud if you won't throw your mud.

CANTWELL. And we go into convention tomorrow and you get nominated on the first ballot? No.

RUSSELL. Well, then . . . good luck. And may "the best man" win, assuming we don't knock each other off *and* the Party. (RUSSELL *turns to go.* CANTWELL *signals frantically.*)

CANTWELL. Now wait a minute . . . Wait a minute! Bill! I realize we've got to work something out. And I'm willing to be reasonable, only you have *got* to . . .

RUSSELL (*exploding*). Stop it! Either we declare a moratorium on mud or we both let fly.

(*Swiftly* CANTWELL *shifts his tack. He goes to door at right.*)

CANTWELL. O.K. (*Opens door, looks through into office.*) Don, send Mr. Marcus in. (*To* RUSSELL) Can I see that court-martial testimony? (RUSSELL *gives him testimony. He studies it, as* MARCUS *enters, nervously. A long moment. Then* CANTWELL *speaks, still studying documents.*) Hi, Shelly, how's the boy? Long time no see.

MARCUS. Yeah . . . Joe . . . long time. . . . Hello again, Mr. Russell.

RUSSELL. Joe wants to ask you some questions . . .

MARCUS. Well, I really ought to be getting back to Wilmington, you see, my wife . . .

CANTWELL. You live in Wilmington, eh? Great town . . . used to have some cousins there named Everly, Jack and Helen Everly, maybe you know them, in real estate . . .

MARCUS. Well, it's not Wilmington proper, actually, where I live, it's a suburb where Peggy and I live. I don't think I know anybody named (*For the first time* CANTWELL *looks at* MARCUS, *who steps back in alarm.*) Everly . . .

CANTWELL (*smiles*). Shelly, you put on a lot of weight.

MARCUS. Well, it's Peggy . . . it's my wife Peggy's cooking, she's a wonderful cook . . . (*Close to tears*) I thought, Mr. Russell, I wouldn't have to . . . to . . .

CANTWELL. To see your old buddy? Now you know I would've been fit to be tied if I had known Shelly Marcus from Adak was in town and hadn't come to see me.

MARCUS. Well, I . . . I know how busy you are . . . *both* you men are . . . running for this President thing, and I was just . . . well, passing by.

CANTWELL (*pleasantly*). And you thought you would pause just long enough to smear your old buddy?

MARCUS. Now, Joe, don't get mad at me . . . it was . . . it was my duty!

CANTWELL. To get even with me for seeing you were passed over for promotion because of incompetence. (*To* RUSSELL) Always a good idea to start with the motive.

RUSSELL (*to* MARCUS). Is this true?

MARCUS (*taken aback*). Well, no, not really . . . I mean my efficiency report was . . .

CANTWELL (*in for the death*). Can be found in army records! Unsatisfactory! I was adjutant and I personally stopped his promotion *and* his transfer *and* he knew it. (*Picks up documents.*) Now, on 6 April 1944 into my quonset hut at the army base on Adak there moved a Lieutenant Fenn . . .

MARCUS. That was the one, like I told you . . . that was the one . . . we all knew . . .

CANTWELL. We shared the same hut for three months.

MARCUS. Just the two of them. Like I told you. It's all in the record there . . . they were, you know . . . they were . . .

CANTWELL (*inexorably*). Fenn was caught with an enlisted man *in flagrante delicto* on the afternoon of 14 June 1944 in the back of the post church. The M.P.s caught him . . .

MARCUS (*rapidly*). That's right. And that's when he broke down and told about everything and everybody . . . the M.P.s laid this trap for him . . . they'd been tipped off . . .

CANTWELL. By the Advocate General . . .

MARCUS. That's right. By Colonel Conyers, he was the one finally broke up this whole ring of degenerates . . . And Fenn when he was caught gave, oh, maybe twenty, thirty names and one of those names was Joe Cantwell, his roommate . . .

CANTWELL. Correct. Now: what happened to those twenty-eight officers and men who were named at the courtmartial?

MARCUS. They were all separated from the service . . . Section 8 we called it . . . for the good of the service, they were all kicked out . . .

CANTWELL. All except one.

MARCUS. That's right . . . all except you.

CANTWELL (*smiles at* RUSSELL). And why wasn't I?

MARCUS. I . . . well . . . I don't know. I suppose it's in the records or something. But I know I thought then what a lot of people thought: how Joe must've pulled some pretty fancy wires to save his neck. Yes, sir, he was a real operator, he could get out of *anything,* and that's the truth . . . Anyways, it's all there in the courtmartial; how he was one of them, named under oath by Lieutenant Fenn.

RUSSELL (*to* MARCUS). Where is Lieutenant Fenn now?

CANTWELL. He's dead.

MARCUS. That's right, he died after the war in that plane crash, you remember the one? Out in Detroit, that freak one where the lightning hit the engine and . . .

RUSSELL (*to* CANTWELL). If you were innocent, why did Fenn name you?

CANTWELL (*coldly, carefully*). Because I was the one who turned him in.

MARCUS (*stunned*). You were!

CANTWELL. This clown wouldn't know but I'm ashamed of *you,* Bill, for not doing your homework, for not checking with a certain Colonel, now Major General, Conyers who was the Advocate General up there. (*Turns on* MARCUS, *who retreats before him.*) You see, Shelly, when I found out what was going on I went to Conyers and told him what I had discovered about my roommate. We laid a trap for Fenn and he fell into it. At the trial I gave secret evidence against him and that's why he named me: *in revenge,* and that's why no action was ever or could ever be taken against me. (*To* RUSSELL) I even got promoted on the strength of having helped clear those types out of our command.

MARCUS. Oh, I bet that isn't so . . . I bet you'll find he sneaked out of it like he did everything else . . . I know Joe Cantwell . . .

RUSSELL (*to* CANTWELL). Can you prove this?)

(CANTWELL *nods. He is now upstage at desk.*)

CANTWELL. A few minutes ago I talked with the Advocate General. His name is Conyers. He's in Colorado now. He told me he would back me up. In every way. (CANTWELL *gives* RUSSELL *the telephone number.*) Here's his name and phone number. He's expecting a call from you, Bill. (*Like a carnivore,* CANTWELL *stalks the terrified* MARCUS *to the door.*) And now, Shelly Marcus, if you ever say one word about this to anybody, I will have you up for libel, *criminal* libel . . .

MARCUS. Now, look here, Joe, don't you threaten me . . . (MARCUS *grabs his briefcase and raincoat and tries to get to the corridor door before* CANTWELL *reaches him.*)

CANTWELL. In fact, I will involve you personally in that whole mess at Adak and by the time I finish with you . . .

MARCUS. Don't you bully me, Joe, don't you try to intimidate me . . .

CANTWELL. I'll make you wish you'd never been born!

(*Just as* CANTWELL *seems about to seize him,* MARCUS *bolts into the connecting hall. He opens the corridor door. But to his horror,* NEWSMEN *and* PHOTOGRAPHERS *burst in. He is borne straight back to* CANTWELL, *who smiles and straightens* MARCUS'S *jacket. Then he turns him about for the* PHOTOGRAPHERS, *who want a picture.*)

CANTWELL. Just one second . . . (*Puts arms about* MARCUS'S *shoulders.*) Sure was swell to see you, Shelly. Next time when you drop by, bring the wife, bring . . . uh, Peggy. Mabel and I'd love to meet her. Love to see you both. You come see us now in Washington. (*Poses again with* MARCUS.) How's that?

PHOTOGRAPHER. Hold it!

(MARCUS *goes, surrounded by* NEWSMEN. CANTWELL *shuts the corridor door after them. He pauses a moment in the connecting hall, unobserved by* RUSSELL. *He passes his hand wearily across his face. Then he pulls himself together and returns to the living room.*)

CANTWELL. I'm sorry to disappoint you, Bill, but this won't work. I'm covered on every side. You won't be able to make this thing stick for two minutes. And I should also warn you: this is the kind of desperate last-minute smear that always backfires on the guy who makes it. Ask Art Hockstader. He'll tell you. (RUSSELL *stares at him with a fascinated revulsion.*) Well, go on. If you don't believe me, you got General Conyers' number in your hand. Call him.

RUSSELL. True? False? We've both gone beyond the "truth" now. We're in dangerous country. (RUSSELL *drops the paper with the telephone number on the sofa.*)

CANTWELL (*begins*). Every word I said was true . . .

RUSSELL. You are worse than a liar. You have no sense of right or wrong. Only what will work. (RUSSELL *picks up court-martial testimony.*) Well, *this* is going to work.

CANTWELL. But you're not going to use that now!

RUSSELL. Oh, yes! Yes! I'll use *anything* against you. I can't let you be President. (RUSSELL *crosses to bedroom.* CANTWELL *tries to block his way.* RUSSELL *pushes him aside. Both men go into bedroom.*)

CANTWELL. Hey! What are you going to do? Bill, you're not really going to use that stuff. You can't. Look, it's . . . it's too dirty! Honest to God, nobody will believe it! (RUSSELL *pauses at the bathroom door. He looks at* CANTWELL; *then he turns and goes into the bathroom.* CANTWELL, *near breaking, shouts after him.*) O.K. Russell, go ahead, it's your funeral. Against me, you haven't got a chance. (CANTWELL *sits down on the bed, his back to the audience. For the first time he seems exhausted, played out. Then he picks up the bedside telephone.*) Send Don Blades in . . . and keep trying on that Colorado call.

(BLADES *enters living room from right.*
He hurries into bedroom. CANTWELL *does
not acknowledge him.*)

BLADES. Well, what happened? (BLADES
peers into bathroom.) Where's Russell?
Joe? (*Sudden alarm*) Hey, Joe!

(CANTWELL *is recalled from some
private reverie. He looks at* BLADES; *he
smiles suddenly; his tone is casual.*)

CANTWELL. Oh, Don, hi. (CANTWELL
rises and crosses to living room. BLADES
follows.)

BLADES. What's Russell up to? What's
this all about? What's he got on you?

CANTWELL (*thoughtfully*). You know
what that guy said just now? He said I
wasn't very sensitive about other people.
He said I didn't understand character . . .

BLADES. Is that what he came down
here for? To give you a lecture?

CANTWELL (*nods*). Yeah. Pretty much.
(CANTWELL *sees the paper with* GENERAL
CONYERS' *telephone number on it; he picks
it up; he smiles.*) Well, I have news for
him. I am a very good judge of character. (*Abruptly*) You can release that
stuff on Russell now. One copy to every
delegate. (*Excitement*) Don, we're home
free. (*He rolls the paper into a tight
wad.*) And I'll make you a bet: Russell
quits before the first ballot. (CANTWELL
*flicks the wad across the room. The room
goes dark.*)

CURTAIN

SCENE TWO

*Russell suite. The next afternoon. The
television set is on.* JENSEN *watches it
while going through papers at the desk.
There is band music from the convention
hall. In the bedroom,* ALICE *finishes packing. The telephone rings.*

JENSEN (*answers it*). Who? Oh, Senator Joseph. No, he's not back yet. No, I
don't know what to do. He's still over
at the hospital. He's with President Hockstader and there's no way to phone . . . I
guess we just stand by. How's the ballot-
ing? (*Frowns.*) Oh, no!

(RUSSELL *enters from corridor, murmuring "No comment" to the press.*)

JENSEN. Wait a minute, Senator. He's
here. (*To* RUSSELL) Bill, it's Senator
Joseph. He's in the convention hall.

They're into the sixth ballot. It's still a
deadlock. Cantwell's leading but nobody's
got a majority. Merwin's sitting tight.
Joseph says if you let him blast Cantwell
now, we're in on the next ballot.

RUSSELL. What was the voting on the
fifth ballot?

JENSEN (*looks at paper*). Cantwell 474,
Russell 386, Merwin 214 . . . all the
favorite sons are gone. And nobody's
budging yet.

RUSSELL. What about Merwin? If I
were to get his 214 votes . . .

JENSEN. You'd win. But he's hanging
on. Senator Joseph's trying to reach him
now, to see if he'll take on second spot
with you . . .

RUSSELL. Cantwell must be trying the
same thing . . .

JENSEN. Merwin's holding out for the
best possible terms.

RUSSELL (*smiles*). He's showing unexpected character, isn't he?

JENSEN (*urgently*). You've *got* to make
up your mind! You've got to let our boys
get that stuff on Cantwell to the delegates. We can ask for a recess before
the seventh ballot. Then . . .

RUSSELL. Tell the Senator to wait.

JENSEN. But we *can't* wait . . .

RUSSELL (*firmly*). I said, wait, Dick.

JENSEN (*into telephone*). Not yet . . .
(*He hangs up.*) Bill, what's wrong with
you? We've lost a night and a day, but
one word from you and we can still
wreck Joe Cantwell.

RUSSELL. I know.

JENSEN. Then why are you holding
back? What have you got to lose? Joe's
done his worst. Every delegation's got a
copy of your case history and believe it or
not we're still in business. I don't know
why, but we are.

RUSSELL. Which means perhaps that
dirt does not always stick . . .

JENSEN. Enough did. You lost three
hundred votes because of it.

RUSSELL. But not all to Cantwell. Merwin picked up over a hundred of my
votes. And that is a sign of something . . .

JENSEN. Disgust.

RUSSELL. Or human decency.

JENSEN. Decency? At a *convention*?

RUSSELL (*smiles*). I am an optimist.
(RUSSELL *goes into the bedroom.*)

ALICE. I packed. I thought no matter
what happens, we'll be leaving tonight.

RUSSELL. Yes, we'll be leaving.

ALICE. How was Art?

RUSSELL. They wouldn't let me see him today. He's still unconscious.

(JENSEN, *who has been watching the television set, leaps to his feet and goes to the bedroom.*)

JENSEN (*desperately*). Bill, I don't want to press you, but will you please make up your mind. The sixth ballot's almost over and . . . (*Telephone in bedroom rings;* JENSEN *answers it.*) Who? Oh, it's you . . . He does? Now? (*To* RUSSELL) It's Don Blades. Cantwell wants to see you.

RUSSELL. I'm sure he does. (*Smiles.*) All right. Tell him to come up. I'd like to see Joe again. (RUSSELL *goes into living room;* ALICE *follows.*)

JENSEN (*into telephone*). O.K. He'll see you. (*Puts receiver down.*)

ALICE (*to* RUSSELL). What do you think Cantwell wants?

RUSSELL. A deal. What else does Joe Cantwell ever want. (*Picks up newspaper.*) Oh, have you seen his latest statement? "The rumors about William Russell's health have been maliciously exaggerated." He's wonderful.

JENSEN. Look, before he gets here, let me call Senator Joseph . . .

RUSSELL. No, Dick.

JENSEN. But yesterday you were willing to do anything!

RUSSELL. That was yesterday. I lost my temper. And did rather a poor imitation of Joe Cantwell. I was remarkably melodramatic. I even turned my own stomach. But today I'm myself again!

JENSEN. Bill . . .

ALICE. Leave him alone, Dick.

RUSSELL. There is a certain relief to knowing that the worst has happened to you and you're still alive . . . and kicking. (*Looks at television set.*) Ah . . . there's my old friend Senator Carlin. True to the end. (RUSSELL *turns up volume.*)

CARLIN'S VOICE (*booming*). . . . . This Sovereign State casts forty-four votes for the next Preznighstays Joe Cantwell!

(RUSSELL *turns the volume off.*)

RUSSELL (*thoughtfully*). Senator Carlin has every characteristic of a dog, except loyalty.

(BLADES *and* CANTWELL *enter. The press is violent in its attentions. With some difficulty, they are got out of the room.*)

BLADES. Gentlemen . . .

CANTWELL. Hello, Bill . . .

RUSSELL (*gaily*). Hi, Joe! What a nice surprise, your coming here like this!

CANTWELL. Yes. . . . Mrs. Russell, I'm Joe Cantwell . . . I don't think we've met. (CANTWELL *shakes* ALICE'S *hand.*)

ALICE. How do you do.

CANTWELL (*mechanically*). We talked on the phone, I guess.

RUSSELL. Sit down, Joe. (CANTWELL *sits.*) I thought you would be busy working on your acceptance speech. Or is it already written?

CANTWELL (*begins*). Now, Bill, as I see the picture . . .

RUSSELL. I've been working for months on *my* acceptance speech, trying to strike that delicate balance between humility and confidence.

CANTWELL. Yes. Now as I see this convention . . .

RUSSELL. *You* of course have a gift for hitting the right note.

CANTWELL. Yes . . .

RUSSELL. I like the way you always manage to state the obvious with a sense of real discovery.

CANTWELL. Yes, Now, Bill . . .

RUSSELL. And that wonderful trick you have for . . .

CANTWELL (*exploding*). Bill, at least let me get one word in edgewise!

RUSSELL (*laughs*). I'm sorry, Joe. I couldn't resist it. (*To the others*) I was using Joe's technique: never let the other man get started. Talk right through him. Also, whenever Joe starts a sentence with "Now, Bill" . . . you know he's up to no good.

CANTWELL (*quickly*). Now, Bill . . .

RUSSELL. See?

(CANTWELL *controls himself with some difficulty.*)

CANTWELL. Very cute. Bill, this convention is really hung up and the way things are going we may never nominate anybody.

BLADES. And who wants to spend the next four years in Philadelphia?

CANTWELL. Believe me when I say I have given the whole thing a lot of thought: and I want you to be on my ticket.

RUSSELL. Well, that's very generous, Joe. But tell me, how can I possibly run for Vice-President when I am at this very moment suffering from one of my frequent nervous breakdowns?

CANTWELL. There was no way of keeping a report like that secret. Anyway, you've got to admit we handled the whole thing darned well. I mean look at the papers: practically no mention . . .

RUSSELL. Just as there was no mention of the fact that Art Hockstader is dying?

CANTWELL. Art didn't want anybody to know how sick he was. Did he, Mrs. Russell? He was a great old guy. You know he's dead, don't you? (RUSSELL *rises, shaken*. CANTWELL *does not notice the other man's response*.) Now, as I see the picture, delegate-wise . . .

RUSSELL. I didn't know . . . Art was dead.

CANTWELL. Oh? Yeah, he died about half an hour ago. He knew it was all over last night when I saw him.

RUSSELL (*startled*). You saw him?

CANTWELL. That's right. Just for a few minutes, while he was still conscious . . .

RUSSELL. Oh, no, no! Don't tell us that Art Hockstader with his dying breath said, "Bless you, Joe, go to it!" And handed on the torch.

(CANTWELL *gets to his feet, angrily*.)

CANTWELL. You certainly like to jump to conclusions, don't you? If you really want to know what Art said, I'll tell you: he said, "To hell with both of you," meaning you as well as me.

BLADES. He sure was a funny old bird. Full of hell right to the end. But his day was done . . . just as well he conked out when he did.

(ALICE *goes into the bedroom*.)

RUSSELL. Will you two please get out?

JENSEN. Bill!

(RUSSELL *turns to follow* ALICE.)

CANTWELL. Look, Russell, for a lot of reasons we want you on the ticket and, frankly, if I were you, I'd show a little . . . well, gratitude.

(RUSSELL *wheels about, fiercely*.)

RUSSELL. Gratitude! Do you realize all I have to do is call Senator Joseph . . .

BLADES (*quickly*). But you know that story about Joe was a bum rap, so how could you use it?

RUSSELL. Since when has the truth been a deterrent at this convention? It is also not true that I am mentally unstable . . .

BLADES (*quickly*). But it *is* true that

you had a mental breakdown, and that is a fact the voters should know.

(CANTWELL *stops* BLADES *with a gesture*.)

CANTWELL. Bill, I solemnly promise before these witnesses that I will give you anything you want . . . the Vice-Presidency, Secretary of State . . . commitment or no commitment . . . It's yours if you throw me your votes on the next ballot.

JENSEN (*delighted*). Bill, come on, they're scared!

BLADES. Oh, no, we're not!

JENSEN. They're sweating ice!

CANTWELL. I want a united front, for the sake of the Party.

JENSEN. Look at them squirm!

BLADES. Who's squirming? Anyway, we got all the votes we need right now.

JENSEN. Where?

BLADES. Governor Merwin.

JENSEN. He won't play with you.

BLADES. He's offered to. But Joe doesn't want Merwin on the ticket. He'd rather have the Secretary here . . .

JENSEN. Merwin refused to be on the ticket with Joe and you know it . . . if he'd agreed, you wouldn't be up here, sweating!

BLADES (*angrily*). I am not sweating!

JENSEN. Bill, we've got them. We've really got them. Let me call Senator Joseph?

CANTWELL. I wish you would. And tell him you'll support me, in the interest of Party unity, and that you'll accept the second spot on the ticket . . .

JENSEN (*overlaps*). And tell him you're ready to lower the boom on Cantwell?

(RUSSELL *at bedroom door. He looks at* ALICE. *He decides*.)

RUSSELL. All right, call him.

(ALICE *returns to the living room. She sits on the downstage sofa*.)

JENSEN. Put me through to Senator Joseph. Extension 12, convention hall . . . Hello . . . that you, Senator? Well, brace yourself. This is it. Our man is about to fight . . .

(RUSSELL *comes to telephone*.)

BLADES (*pleads*). Russell, don't. You *can't* use that stuff. Joe's our only hope. He's the Party's only hope.

CANTWELL. Shut up, Don. We don't have to worry about Mr. Russell. He always does the right thing.

RUSSELL (*to* CANTWELL). Thank you. (*Into telephone*) Senator? This is William Russell. I'm coming down to the convention hall in a few minutes to make a statement. Before I do, I want you to get to the chairman of the next delegation pledged to me . . . Utah? All right. Tell the chairman to announce to the convention that I have withdrawn from the race.

JENSEN (*aghast*). Bill!

BLADES (*ecstatic*). Mr. Secretary, I swear you won't regret . . .

RUSSELL. And that I am releasing my 384 delegates with instructions to support Governor John Merwin.

JENSEN. Merwin!

BLADES. But . . . but you can't . . .

(RUSSELL *puts the receiver down.*)

RUSSELL. I can. And I have.

JENSEN. Merwin's nobody!

RUSSELL. Well, he is now somebody . . . (*Turns to* CANTWELL, *who has sunk to a bench, his hand over his face.*) Neither the angel of darkness nor the angel of light . . . if I may exaggerate my goodness . . . has carried the day. We canceled each other out.

(JENSEN *indicates the television set.*)

JENSEN (*bitterly*). Allowing the angel of grayness to win, as usual.

RUSSELL. The light blinds us . . . and we're all afraid of the dark. (*To* CANTWELL) I meant it, Joe, when I said I could never let you be President.

BLADES (*viciously*). Well, you just cut your own throat. You are through in politics.

RUSSELL. Joe Cantwell is through in politics.

(BLADES *crosses to upstage door.*)

BLADES. He had a deal! I bet he had a deal with Merwin all along, the tricky son of a . . . (BLADES *slams the door after him.* CANTWELL *looks at* RUSSELL *for the first time; he is genuinely puzzled.*)

CANTWELL (*slowly*). I don't understand you.

RUSSELL. I know you don't. Because you have no sense of responsibility toward anybody or anything and that is a tragedy in a man and it is a disaster in a President! You said you were religious. Well, I'm not. But I believe profoundly in *this* life and what we do to one another and how this monstrous "I," the self, must become "we" and draw the line at murder in the games we play with one another, and try to be good even when there is no one to force us to be good.

(CANTWELL *rises. He speaks carefully, without rancor.*)

CANTWELL. You don't understand me. You don't understand politics. You don't understand this country and the way it is and the way we are. You are a fool. (CANTWELL *goes, shutting the corridor door after him.* RUSSELL *shakes his head.*)

RUSSELL. We're not the way Joe thinks we are. At least not yet.

JENSEN. You don't even know Merwin. Nobody knows him. He's a man without a face.

RUSSELL. Don't underestimate him. Men without faces tend to get elected President, and power or responsibility or honor fill in the features, usually pretty well.

JENSEN. I'm afraid, Bill, your conscience is my enemy. (JENSEN *goes off stage right.* RUSSELL *looks after him a moment, then he notices the "Hustle with Russell" placard.*)

RUSSELL (*smiles*). Well, everyone hustled except Russell. (*Notices television set.*) Here comes Utah. (RUSSELL *turns up volume.*)

DELEGATE'S VOICE. State of Utah at the instruction of that great American and Secretary of State William Russell (*Cheering*) casts its fourteen pledged votes to the next Preznighstays that great Governor John Merwin!

COMMENTATOR'S VOICE. This is the break in the deadlock! An unexpected development! There's real excitement down on the floor . . .

(RUSSELL *turns off set.*)

RUSSELL. There it is! (*To* ALICE) Well, we've got work to do. Do you want to come down to the convention? Or wait here till I get back?

ALICE. I'll go with you.

RUSSELL. What . . . do you think?

ALICE. I wish you'd been nominated.

RUSSELL. So do I.

ALICE. But I like the way you . . . really won.

RUSSELL. Thank you. Life is a choice, they say. I've made mine.

ALICE (*smiles*). And without doing your one-two-three walk.

RUSSELL. You know, Alice, you don't have to stay with me, if you don't want to.

ALICE. I know I don't have to.

RUSSELL (*tentatively*). But . . . *would* you like to? Even though you'll never have the chance to be another Grace Coolidge?

ALICE. Now it's *my* turn to choose? (RUSSELL *nods*.) Of course I'll stay. (ALICE *rises*.)

RUSSELL. I'm glad. But I warn you: the fires of autumn burn notoriously low.

ALICE (*smiles*). Well, I've been cold such a long time.

(RUSSELL *takes her arm. They start to go upstage to the corridor door when* REPORTERS *burst in from stage right. Ad-libbed cries of "Statement!" Flash-bulbs go off.* RUSSELL *finally quiets them.*)

RUSSELL. You may say that I think Governor Merwin will make a fine candidate, and I shall do everything I can to help him and the Party. (*Starts to go, pauses.*) Oh. (*Smiles.*) And I am of course happy: the best man won! (RUSSELL *and* ALICE *followed by* REPORTERS *cross upstage, as the* CURTAIN FALLS.)

OTHER AMERICAN PLAYS OF INTEREST
PRODUCED ON BROADWAY *
January, 1957–June, 1963
(in chronological order)

A CLEARING IN THE WOODS. By Arthur Laurents. January 10, 1957.

VISIT TO A SMALL PLANET. By Gore Vidal. February 7, 1957.

THE TUNNEL OF LOVE. By Joseph Fields and Peter De Vries. February 13, 1957.

A HOLE IN THE HEAD. By Arnold Schulman. February 28, 1957.

A MOON FOR THE MISBEGOTTEN. By Eugene O'Neill. May 2, 1957. (For text, see *Best American Plays: Fourth Series, 1951-1957.*)

NEW GIRL IN TOWN. A musical based on Eugene O'Neill's play *Anna Christie,* with book by George Abbott, music and lyrics by Bob Merrill. May 14, 1957.

WEST SIDE STORY. A musical based on a conception by Jerome Robbins, with book by Arthur Laurents, music by Leonard Bernstein, lyrics by Stephen Sondheim. September 26, 1957.

MISS LONELYHEARTS. By Howard Teichmann, based on the novel by Nathaniel West. October 3, 1957.

COMPULSION. By Meyer Levin, based on his novel bearing the same title. October 24, 1957.

THE SQUARE ROOT OF WONDERFUL. By Carson McCullers. October 30, 1957.

JAMAICA. A musical with book by E. Y. Harburg and Fred Saidy, lyrics by E. Y. Harburg, music by Harold Arlen. October 31, 1957.

FAIR GAME. By Sam Locke. November 2, 1957.

THE MUSIC MAN. A musical comedy with book, music, and lyrics by Meredith Willson; story by Meredith Willson and Franklin Lacey. December 19, 1957.

SUNRISE AT CAMPOBELLO. By Dore Schary. January 30, 1958.

BLUE DENIM. By James Leo Herlihy and William Noble. February 27, 1958.

WHO WAS THAT LADY I SAW YOU WITH? By Norman Krasna. March 3, 1958.

SAY, DARLING. By Richard Bissell, Abe Burrows, and Marian Bissell, based on the novel by Richard Bissell, with songs by Betty Comden, Adolph Green and Jule Styne. April 3, 1958.

THE GIRLS IN 509. By Howard Teichmann. October 15, 1958.

ONCE MORE WITH FEELING. By Harry Kurnitz. October 21, 1958.

THE PLEASURE OF HIS COMPANY. By Samuel Taylor, with Cornelia Otis Skinner. October 22, 1958.

THE MARRIAGE-GO-ROUND. By Leslie Stevens. October 29, 1958.

FLOWER DRUM SONG. A musical based on the novel by C. Y. Lee; book by Oscar Hammerstein II and Joseph Fields, lyrics by Oscar Hammerstein II, music by Richard Rodgers. December 1, 1958.

THE DISENCHANTED. By Budd Schulberg and Harvey Breit, based on the novel by Budd Schulberg. December 3, 1958.

* The dates refer to the opening of the play in New York, which often took place *after* an out-of-town "tryout" run of at least several weeks. The plays listed are of interest for a variety of reasons not necessarily connected with any particular merit in the stage production or any distinction in the writing. The listing is intended to provide a general view of the period and to supplement the Introduction.

THE COLD WIND AND THE WARM. By S. N. Behrman, suggested by his *New Yorker* series of essays and his book *The Worcester Account*. December 8, 1958.

THIRD BEST SPORT. By Eleanor and Leo Bayer. December 30, 1958.

RASHOMON. By Fay and Michael Kanin, based on stories by Ryunosuke Akutagawa. January 27, 1959.

TALL STORY. By Howard Lindsay and Russel Crouse, suggested by the Howard Nemerov novel *The Homecoming Game*. January 29, 1959.

REQUIEM FOR A NUN. By Ruth Ford and William Faulkner, adapted from the Faulkner novel. January 30, 1959.

THE RIVALRY. By Norman Corwin. February 7, 1959.

A MAJORITY OF ONE. By Leonard Spigelgass. February 16, 1959.

A RAISIN IN THE SUN. By Lorraine Hansberry. March 11, 1959.

KATAKI. By Shimon Wincelberg. April 9, 1959.

ONCE UPON A MATTRESS. A musical with book by Jay Thompson, Marshall Barer, and Dean Fuller, music by Mary Rodgers, lyrics by Marshall Barer. May 11, 1959.

THE GANG'S ALL HERE. By Jerome Lawrence and Robert E. Lee. October 1, 1959.

THE MIRACLE WORKER. By William Gibson. October 19, 1959.

TAKE ME ALONG. A musical based on Eugene O'Neill's play *Ah, Wilderness!* with book by Joseph Stein and Robert Russell, music and lyrics by Robert Merrill. October 22, 1959.

THE TENTH MAN. By Paddy Chayefsky. November 5, 1959.

THE SOUND OF MUSIC. A musical suggested by *The Trapp Family Singers* by Maria Augusta Trapp; with book by Howard Lindsay and Russel Crouse, lyrics by Oscar Hammerstein II, music by Richard Rodgers. November 16, 1959.

ONLY IN AMERICA. By Jerome Lawrence and Robert E. Lee, based on the book by Harry Golden. November 19, 1959.

FIORELLO! A musical with book by Jerome Weidman and George Abbot, music by Jerry Bock, lyrics by Sheldon Harnick. November 23, 1959.

A LOSS OF ROSES. By William Inge. November 28, 1959. (Motion picture title: *The Stripper*, June 20, 1963.)

THE ANDERSONVILLE TRIAL. By Saul Levitt. December 29, 1959.

THE DEADLY GAME. By James Yaffe, based on a novel by Friedrich Duerrenmatt. February 2, 1960.

LOVELY LIGHT. A dramatization of the poems and letters of Edna St. Vincent Millay, arranged and presented by Dorothy Stickney. February 8, 1960.

TOYS IN THE ATTIC. By Lillian Hellman. February 25, 1960.

GREENWILLOW. A musical, based on the novel by B. J. Chute, with book by Lesser Samuels and Frank Loesser, music and lyrics by Frank Loesser. March 8, 1960.

DEAR LIAR. Adapted for the stage from the correspondence of Mrs. Patrick Campbell and Bernard Shaw by Jerome Kilty. March 17, 1960.

BYE BYE BIRDIE. A musical, with book by Michael Stewart, music by Charles Strouse, lyrics by Lee Adams. April 14, 1960.

THE WORLD OF CARL SANDBURG. Adapted by Norman Corwin from the works of Carl Sandburg. September 14, 1960.

THE WALL. By Millard Lampell, based on the novel by John Hersey. October 11, 1960.

INVITATION TO A MARCH. By Arthur Laurents. October 29, 1960.

PERIOD OF ADJUSTMENT. By Tennessee Williams. November 10, 1960.

UNDER THE YUM-YUM TREE. By Lawrence Roman. November 16, 1960.

ADVISE AND CONSENT. By Loring Mandel, based on the novel by Allen Drury. November 17, 1960.

CRITIC'S CHOICE. By Ira Levin. December 14, 1960.

DO RE MI. A musical with book by Garson Kanin, music by Jule Styne, lyrics by

Betty Comden and Adolph Green. December 26, 1960.

COME BLOW YOUR HORN. By Neil Simon. February 22, 1961.

THE DEVIL'S ADVOCATE. By Dore Schary, based on the novel by Morris L. West. March 9, 1961.

BIG FISH, LITTLE FISH. By Hugh Wheeler. March 15, 1961.

A FAR COUNTRY. By Henry Denker. April 4, 1961.

CARNIVAL. A musical based on material by Helen Deutsch, with book by Michael Stewart, music and lyrics by Bob Merrill. April 13, 1961.

PURLIE VICTORIOUS. By Ossie Davis. September 28, 1961.

BLOOD, SWEAT AND STANLEY POOLE. By James and William Goldman. October 5, 1961.

MILK AND HONEY. A musical by Don Appel, music and lyrics by Jerry Herman. October 10, 1961.

HOW TO SUCCEED IN BUSINESS WITHOUT REALLY TRYING. A musical based on the novel by Shepherd Mead, with book by Abe Burrows, Jack Weinstock and Willie Gilbert, music and lyrics by Frank Loesser. October 14, 1961.

KWAMINA. A musical with book by Robert Alan Aurthur, music and lyrics by Richard Adler. October 23, 1961.

SUNDAY IN NEW YORK. By Norman Krasna. November 29, 1961.

DAUGHTER OF SILENCE. By Morris L. West, adapted from his novel. November 30, 1961.

TAKE HER, SHE'S MINE. By Phoebe and Henry Ephron. December 21, 1961.

A GIFT OF TIME. By Garson Kanin, based on Lael Tucker Wertenbaker's *Death of a Man*. February 22, 1962.

NO STRINGS. A musical with book by Samuel Taylor, music and lyrics by Richard Rodgers. March 15, 1962.

I CAN GET IT FOR YOU WHOLESALE. A musical based on the novel by Jerome Weidman, with book by Weidman, music and lyrics by Harold Rome. March 22, 1962.

A FUNNY THING HAPPENED ON THE WAY TO THE FORUM. A musical based on the plays of Plautus and Terence, book by Burt Shevelove and Larry Gelbart, music and lyrics by Stephen Sondheim. May 8, 1962.

SEIDMAN AND SONS. By Elick Moll, based on his novel. October 15, 1962.

TCHIN-TCHIN. By Sidney Michaels, based on a French play by François Billetdoux. October 25, 1962.

LITTLE ME. By Neil Simon, based on a book by Patrick Dennis. November 17, 1962.

LORD PENGO. By S. N. Behrman, suggested by the author's book on Joseph Duveen. November 19, 1962.

THE MILK TRAIN DOESN'T STOP HERE ANYMORE. By Tennessee Williams. January 16, 1963.

NATURAL AFFECTION. By William Inge. January 31, 1963.

DEAR ME, THE SKY IS FALLING. By Leonard Spigelgass. March 2, 1963.

CHILDREN FROM THEIR GAMES. By Irwin Shaw. April 11, 1963.

OTHER AMERICAN PLAYS OF INTEREST, PRODUCED IN THE OFF-BROADWAY THEATRE *

ME, CANDIDO. By Walt Anderson. Season of 1956-57.

CAREER. By James Lee. April 30, 1957.

A LAND BEYOND THE RIVER. By Loften Mitchell. Season of 1956-57.

THE BROTHERS KARAMAZOV. Adapted from the Dostoevsky novel, by Boris Tumarin and Jack Sydow. December 9, 1957.

GARDEN DISTRICT (SOMETHING UNSPOKEN and SUDDENLY LAST SUMMER). By Tennessee Williams. January 7, 1958.

* Dates of premieres are supplied only when important or readily available.

WINKELBERG. By Ben Hecht. Season of 1957-58.

SIGN OF WINTER. By Ettore Rella. Season of 1957-58.

MAIDENS AND MISTRESSES AT THE ZOO. By Meade Roberts. Season of 1958-59.

I RISE IN FLAME CRIED THE PHOENIX. By Tennessee Williams. Season of 1958-59.

THE MAN WHO NEVER DIED. By Barrie Stavis. Season of 1958-59.

ULYSSES IN NIGHTTOWN. Stage treatment of a sequence from Joyce's novel *Ulysses,* by Oliver Saylor and Marjorie Barkenstein. Season of 1958-59.

COMIC STRIP. By George Panetta. May, 1958.

MANY LOVES. By William Carlos Williams. January 13, 1959.

THE CONNECTION. By Jack Gelber. July 15, 1959.

U.S.A. By John Dos Passos and Paul Shyre, based on the Dos Passos novel. October 28, 1959.

LITTLE MARY SUNSHINE. A musical comedy with book, lyrics and music by Rick Besoyan. November 18, 1959.

THE PRODIGAL. By Jack Richardson. February 11, 1960.

THE FANTASTICKS. A musical suggested by Rostand's *Les Romanesques,* with book and lyrics by Tom Jones and music by Harvey Schmidt. May 3, 1960.

EARNEST IN LOVE. A musical comedy based on Oscar Wilde's *The Importance of Being Earnest,* with book and lyrics by Anne Croswell, music by Lee Pockriss. May, 1960.

A COUNTRY SCANDAL. Adapted by Alex Szogyi from Chekhov's *That Worthless Fellow Platonov.* May 5, 1960.

THE ZOO STORY. By Edward Albee. January 14, 1960.

THE IDIOT. By Boris Tumarin and Jack Sydow, based on the novel by Dostoevsky. September 25, 1960.

BORAK. By Robert D. Hock. December 13, 1960.

THE AMERICAN DREAM. By Edward Albee. January 24, 1961.

CALL ME BY MY RIGHTFUL NAME. By Michael Shurtleff. January 31, 1961.

THE DEATH OF BESSIE SMITH. By Edward Albee. March 1, 1961.

GALLOWS HUMOR. By Jack Richardson. April 18, 1931.

COCKEYED KITE. By Joseph Caldwell. September 13, 1961.

THE THRACIAN HORSES. By Maurice Valency. September 27, 1961.

CLANDESTINE ON THE MORNING LINE. By Josh Greenfeld. October 30, 1961.

SHADOWS OF HEROES. By Robert Ardrey. December 5, 1961. Presented in London in 1958 under the title of *Stone and Star.* (See Henry Hewes' *The Best Plays of 1961-62,* pp. 150-169, for abbreviated text.)

BLACK NATIVITY. By Langston Hughes. December 11, 1961.

WHO'LL SAVE THE PLOWBOY? By Frank D. Gilroy. January 9, 1962.

PLAYS FOR BLEECKER STREET. By Thornton Wilder. January 11, 1962.

THE DAYS AND NIGHTS OF BEEBEE FENSTERMAKER. By William Snyder. September 17, 1962.

WHISPER INTO MY GOOD EAR and MRS. DALY HAS A LOVER. By William Hanley. October 1, 1962.

HEY YOU, LIGHT MAN! By Oliver Hailey. March 1, 1963.

SAVE ME A PLACE AT FOREST LAWN. By Lorees Yerby. May 8, 1963.

THE TIGER and THE TYPISTS. By Murray Schisgal. February 4, 1963.

THE BRIG. By Kenneth H. Brown. May 15, 1963.

CAGES. By John Carlino. June 10, 1963.